COMPUTER CRIME LAW

Fifth Edition

■ ■ ■

Orin S. Kerr
Professor of Law
University of California, Berkeley

AMERICAN CASEBOOK SERIES®

American Casebook Series is a trademark registered in the U.S. Patent and Trademark Office.

© West, a Thomson business, 2006
© 2009, 2013 Thomson Reuters
© 2018 LEG, Inc. d/b/a West Academic
© 2022 LEG, Inc. d/b/a West Academic
      444 Cedar Street, Suite 700
      St. Paul, MN 55101
      1-877-888-1330

West, West Academic Publishing, and West Academic are trademarks of West Publishing Corporation, used under license.

Printed in the United States of America

ISBN: 978-1-64708-479-0

In memory of my father, the original Professor Kerr

PREFACE

This casebook presents an overview of the legal issues raised by computer-related crimes. The materials are organized around three questions. First, what conduct involving a computer is prohibited by criminal law? Second, what legal rules govern the collection of digital evidence in criminal investigations? Third, what powers do state, national, and foreign governments have to investigate and prosecute computer crimes? The first question looks at the substantive law of computer crimes, and is addressed in Chapters 2, 3, and 4. The second question examines the law of criminal procedure for digital evidence, and is covered in Chapters 5 and 6. The third question considers the role of jurisdiction and sovereignty in a world of global online crime, and is addressed in Chapters 7 and 8.

Although the materials are intended primarily for classroom use, my hope is that they will reach a broader audience. First, the materials should be helpful to criminal law practitioners. Computer crime law lacks a treatise that summarizes the field and explains how the pieces fit together. In light of that, I have made special efforts to explain basic doctrine in a way that practitioners should find useful. The law remains complex and sometimes uncertain, and this book makes no effort to pretend otherwise. At the same time, I hope these materials will serve as a reference work for prosecutors and defense attorneys in need of a primer on existing law.

The book also should be a useful resource for scholars. Computer crime law is fairly new, and many issues remain open. Surprisingly little has been written about the major issues in the field. My hope is that the framework introduced in this book will help encourage and direct future scholarly efforts. To that end, the extensive commentary in these materials attempts both to review existing scholarship and to ask important questions for scholars to answer.

In assembling these materials, I have assumed that readers have some experience with the study of criminal law, such as a first-year law school survey course. At the same time, I have not assumed that readers are familiar with the law of criminal procedure or have any special technical background with computers. Students with advanced knowledge of computers or criminal procedure will have a slight advantage understanding a few concepts. But the advantages on the whole are modest. In any event, no such background is assumed or required.

This project began with materials assembled for a seminar in the Fall 2000 semester. The first edition of this casebook appeared in 2006, followed by the second edition in 2009, the third edition in 2013, and the fourth edition in 2018. I am pleased that readers have found the materials sufficiently useful to justify a fifth edition.

To improve the readability of the materials, I have taken the liberty of removing citations, deleting unrelated portions of opinions, and otherwise streamlining the cases without indicating that the original material has been altered. Readers in need of greater precision should always consult the original sources.

ORIN S. KERR

September 2021
Berkeley, California

ACKNOWLEDGMENTS

Excerpts from the following books and articles appear with the kind of permission of the copyright holders.

Bellia, Patricia L., Defending Cyberproperty, 79 N.Y.U. L. Rev. 2164 (2004). Copyright © 2004 by New York University Law Review. Reprinted by permission.

Berg, Terrence, WWW.WILDWEST.GOV: The Impact of the Internet on State Power to Enforce the Law, B.Y.U. L. Rev. 1305 (2000). Copyright © 2000 Brigham Young University Law Review. Reprinted by permission.

Brenner, Susan W., Need for Reciprocal Enforcement of Warrants and Subpoenas in Cybercrime Cases, 37 Prosecutor 29 (2003). Copyright © 2003 by the author. Reprinted by permission.

Citron, Danielle Keats; Franks, Mary Anne; Criminalizing Revenge Porn, 49 Wake Forest Law Review 345 (2014). Copyright © 2014 by the authors. Reprinted by permission.

Demetriou, Christina; Silke, Andrew; A Criminological Internet "Sting": Experimental Evidence of Illegal and Deviant Visits to a Website Trap, 43 Brit. J. Criminology 213 (2003). Copyright © 2003 by Oxford University Press. Reprinted by permission.

Howell, Beryl A., Real World Problems of Virtual Crime, 7 Yale J. L. & Tech. 103 (2004–2005). Copyright © 2005 by the author. Reprinted by permission.

Ingraham, Donald G., On Charging Computer Crime, 2 Computer/L.J. 429 (1980). Copyright © 1980 by John Marshall Journal of Computer & Information Law. Reprinted by permission.

Katyal, Neal Kumar, Criminal Law In Cyberspace, 149 U. Penn. L. Rev. 1003 (2001). Copyright © 2001 by University of Pennsylvania Law Review. Reprinted by permission.

Kerr, Orin, Cybercrime's Scope: Interpreting "Access" and "Authorization" in Computer Misuse Statutes, 79 N.Y.U. L. Rev. 1596 (2003). Copyright © 2003 by New York University Law Review.

Olivenbaum, Joseph M., Ctrl-Alt-Delete: Rethinking Federal Computer Crime Legislation, 27 Seton Hall L. Rev. 574 (1997).

Rasch, Mark, Ashcroft's Global Internet Power-Grab, available at http://www.securityfocus.com/columnists/39 (Nov. 25, 2001). Copyright © 2001 by the author. Reprinted by permission.

Rychlak, Ronald J., Legal Problems with On-Line Gambling, Engage: The Journal of the Federalist Society's Practice Groups Volume 6, Issue 1 (2005). Copyright © 2005 by the Federalist Society. Reprinted by permission from The Federalist Society.

Solove, Daniel J., Reconstructing Electronic Surveillance Law, 72 Geo. Wash. L. Rev. 1264 (2004). Copyright © 2004 by The George Washington Law Review. Reprinted by permission.

Stevenson, Dru, Entrapment by Numbers, 16 U. Fla. J. L. & Pub. Pol'y 1 (2005). Copyright © 2005 by University of Florida Journal of Law and Public Policy. Reprinted by permission.

SUMMARY OF CONTENTS

TABLE OF CONTENTS

TABLE OF CASES

The principal cases are in bold type.

TABLE OF STATUTES

TABLE OF AUTHORITIES

COMPUTER CRIME LAW

Fifth Edition

CHAPTER 1

INTRODUCTION

■ ■ ■

What is a computer crime? What topics are covered in a course on computer crime law? And what makes computer crimes different from other types of crimes?

These are three good questions, and this short introductory chapter will provide a few answers. The chapter begins with a brief overview of the field of computer crime law, as well as the coverage of this book. It then offers a hypothetical that introduces the basic differences between the law of traditional physical crimes and the law of computer crimes.

A. OVERVIEW OF COMPUTER CRIME LAW

There are two reasons to label criminal conduct a computer crime. First, an individual might use a computer to engage in criminal activity. Second, the evidence needed to prove a criminal case might be stored in computerized form. The law governing use of a computer to commit a crime is *substantive* computer crime law, because it concerns the scope of substantive conduct that has been criminalized. The law governing the collection of computerized evidence is *procedural* computer crime law, because it concerns the legal procedures investigators can use to collect digital evidence in criminal investigations.

Substantive computer crime law divides into two basic categories: computer misuse crimes and traditional crimes. Computer misuse crimes are a new type of criminal offense involving intentional interference with the proper functioning of computers. Examples include hacking offenses, virus crimes, and denial-of-service attacks. These offenses punish interference with the intended operation of computers, either by exceeding a user's privileges (as in the case of a hacking crime) or by denying privileges to others (as in the case of a denial-of-service attack).

As the label implies, traditional crimes are traditional criminal offenses facilitated by computers. These are information crimes with obvious physical-world counterparts. Examples include Internet fraud schemes, online threats, distributing digital images of child pornography, and theft of trade secrets over the Internet.

Procedural computer crime law consists of two relatively discrete topics. The first topic is the Fourth Amendment, which prohibits unreasonable searches and seizures. In the physical world, the Fourth Amendment creates constitutional limits on where the police can go and what evidence the police can collect in criminal investigations. Procedural computer crime law considers how the Fourth Amendment applies in the case of digital evidence collection. When is retrieving evidence from a computer a "search"? When is it a "seizure"? When is the search or seizure "reasonable"?

The second area of procedural computer crime law is statutory privacy law. Traditional criminal procedure is primarily constitutional law, but much of the law regulating digital evidence collection derives from three privacy statutes: the Wiretap Act, the Pen Register statute, and the Stored Communications Act. As a practical matter, the divide between statutory and constitutional law often tracks the divide between evidence collection from stand-alone computers and computer networks. The law regulating retrieval of evidence from stand-alone computers is predominantly constitutional, and the law governing computer network surveillance is a mix of constitutional and statutory law.

Jurisdictional disputes provide the third area of inquiry in computer crime law. Traditional crimes usually are local. The defendant, the victim, and the evidence often are in the same place, and the charges tend to be brought under state criminal codes wherever the offense occurred. Computer crimes present a very different dynamic. A defendant in one place may connect to a computer in a second place and launch an attack against a computer located in a third place. The victim, the defendant, and the evidence are located in different places—maybe different states, or even different countries. As a result, the law must define for each sovereign what kinds of conduct outside its borders can and should be criminalized, as well as what procedures regulate extraterritorial evidence collection. The global nature of Internet surveillance and terrorism investigations also creates jurisdictional friction between two competing legal regimes, the law of criminal investigations and the law of national security investigations.

The organization of this book tracks these three basic questions. Chapters 2, 3, and 4 address the substantive law of computer crimes; Chapters 5 and 6 cover procedural law; and Chapters 7 and 8 explore jurisdictional issues. In an investigation, the three questions typically present themselves in the reverse order from their order in the book. After a crime has occurred, the first issues are jurisdictional: What agency has jurisdiction over the offense, as well as the ability to collect evidence to prove it in court? The next issues are procedural: What rules must law enforcement officials follow to collect evidence and identify the suspect? The final questions are substantive: What crimes have been committed that the government can charge in court and try to prove beyond a reasonable doubt?

The three questions of computer crime law are really variations on a single theme, and that theme explains why it makes sense to study computer crime law in a separate course. The facts of computer crimes tend to be different from the facts of equivalent physical crimes. The shift from physical crimes to digital crimes changes the facts of how and where crimes are committed as well as how and where evidence is collected. When the facts change, the law must change with it. Old laws must adapt and new laws must emerge to restore the function of preexisting law.

Of course, the broad policy goals of criminal law and procedure are timeless. Criminal law identifies public conduct that is harmful and culpable, and criminal procedure articulates reasonable limits on police powers. In a broad sense, nothing is new. But implementing those policy goals with legal rules depends on the facts, and the facts of digital crimes consistently challenge the assumptions of existing substantive, procedural, and jurisdictional laws. We can begin with the old legal rules, but after a while it becomes clear that some of the old rules need to bend and others need replacement. Computer crime law is the search for and study of new answers to timeless questions of criminal law when the facts switch from a physical environment to a digital environment.

B. COMPARING PHYSICAL CRIMES AND COMPUTER CRIMES

Consider the following two hypotheticals. The first is a traditional physical crime; the second is a roughly analogous computer crime. What if anything changes when we switch from the first example to the second example?

Physical Crime

Fred Felony is a resident of Phoenix, Arizona. Fred finds himself low on cash one day, and he decides to rob a jewelry store in downtown Phoenix. Fred drives to the store and parks his car on the street in front of the store. He walks into the store and browses for a few minutes until the other customers depart.

After the customers leave, Fred pulls out a gun and runs over to the clerk working at the store that day. "This is a stick-up!" he yells to the clerk. "Give me some gold and no one will get hurt!" The clerk is frightened, and she nervously opens one of the cabinets and hands Fred a collection of gold jewelry. Fred grabs the jewelry and stuffs it into a bag he is carrying. He runs out of the store, jumps into his getaway car, and speeds away.

After Fred leaves, the clerk immediately calls the store manager. She reports that the robber took jewelry with a retail value of about $5,000. Fred returns home with the loot and hides the jewelry in a closet for safekeeping. After a week, he visits a local Phoenix pawn shop and sells the jewelry for $800 in cash.

Computer Crime

This time, Fred Felony decides to commit his crime using a computer. Fred decides that he will steal credit cards remotely instead of stealing gold jewelry in person. His new target: An e-commerce company located in Los Angeles, California.

Fred connects to the Internet from his home in Phoenix using his home Internet service, provided by a national company located in Pennsylvania. Although Fred's ultimate goal is to hack into the e-commerce site in Los Angeles, he first loops his attack through an intermediary computer to disguise his tracks. Starting from his Pennsylvania-based provider, Fred hacks into a computer in Ottawa, Canada, run by the Canadian tourism bureau. With access to the Canadian computer established, Fred targets the server of the e-commerce site in Los Angeles.

After several tries, Fred eventually guesses the master password correctly and logs in to the server hosted by the Los Angeles e-commerce site. He locates a file containing five hundred credit card numbers and downloads it to his computer at home. Later that day, Fred visits an Internet relay chat room occasionally used to arrange the sale of stolen credit card numbers. He sells the numbers for $800 to a user who goes by the handle "Boris11." Boris11 wires the $800 directly to an online bank account Fred controls. Fred does not know where Boris11 is located, but Boris11's English is quite poor. Fred suspects that Boris11 lives somewhere in Eastern Europe.

The next morning, an employee at the e-commerce site in Los Angeles realizes that the company has been victimized and that the credit card file has been accessed. The company spends $50,000 upgrading its computer security to ensure that no such attacks are successful again. It then notifies its customers and their banks that the breach occurred. Although the banks put a hold on all five hundred accounts, they are too late. By the time the accounts are frozen, an unknown individual in Moscow runs up a tab of $40,000 on several of the stolen accounts.

NOTES AND QUESTIONS

1. *Substantive law.* Compare the physical crime and the computer crime from the standpoint of substantive law. What crimes did Fred commit when he entered the jewelry store with a gun and ordered the store clerk to hand over the jewelry? How serious are those crimes? What harms did Fred cause? Why should the law deter such activity, and why was it morally culpable?

Now turn to the computer crime. How was Fred's conduct different in the second hypothetical? What harms did Fred cause when he committed the computer crime? Why should the law deter such activity, and why was it morally culpable? Did Fred actually "steal" anything, and does it matter? Is the computer crime fundamentally the same as the physical crime, or is it different?

Does punishing the computer crime require new laws, or are the traditional laws applicable in the case of the physical crime also sufficient to punish the computer crime? Which offense should be punished more severely: the physical crime or the computer crime? What punishment is appropriate for each?

2.   *Procedural law.* Now compare the two crimes from the perspective of investigatory procedure. Imagine that you are a police officer in Phoenix, Arizona, and you are called to the jewelry store to investigate the crime just hours after it occurred. You want to collect evidence, identify a suspect, and prove your case beyond a reasonable doubt in court. What evidence can you collect, and how do you collect it? Who do you interview? What questions do you ask? What kind of evidence are you likely to find? How would you plan to investigate the case and prove it beyond a reasonable doubt in court?

Again, switch to the computer crime. Now imagine that you are a Los Angeles police officer called by the e-commerce company after they discover that they have been hacked and the file accessed without permission. What evidence do you collect, and how do you collect it? Who do you interview? What questions do you ask? What kind of evidence are you likely to find? How might you plan to investigate the case and trace the crime back to the wrongdoer?

What legal rules should regulate the steps you would take to investigate the physical crime? What rules should regulate the steps needed to investigate the computer crime? Are they the same or are they different?

3.   *Tracing connections back to their source.* As you ponder these questions, it may help to know a little bit about how computer intrusion investigations generally work. Most investigations follow two basic steps: tracing communications over the Internet back to their source, and then recovering and analyzing the computer used in the offense.

Investigators attempt to track communications to their source by collecting network logs. Computer networks normally are run by a system administrator, or "sysadmin" for short, who is responsible for keeping the computer running and for troubleshooting difficulties. System administrators ordinarily set their computers to generate records known as logs that record how the network was used. For example, a server might be configured to record the incoming Internet Protocol (IP) addresses and times of every attempt to log in to an account on the server. (IP addresses are numerical addresses that are akin to Internet phone numbers. Every user connected to the Internet is assigned an IP address, and the address is used to send information to the user.) In the case of an e-commerce site, it's a good bet that the network system administrator will have configured the network to generate access logs that recorded the time, IP address, and any other relevant information about each login into the network.

To trace back the crime, the investigators normally must go step by step, hop by hop, tracing the chain of communications from server to server. This is true because the IP addresses stored in a log only record the most immediate hop back in the chain of communications. If the e-commerce site in Los Angeles kept logs of the intrusion, those logs will show the attack coming from the Canadian tourism bureau in Ottawa, not Fred in Phoenix. At each stage investigators must try to collect evidence of the prior hop until they trace the attack back to the wrongdoer.

Most computer hacking investigations end with the seizure and subsequent search of the suspect's personal computer. The reason is simple: Because there are no eyewitnesses to most computer crimes, proving a case beyond a reasonable doubt usually requires direct evidence. The discovery of stolen files or other evidence on a suspect's personal computer can provide powerful evidence that the computer owner was responsible for the offense (and if no such evidence exists, can help exonerate the suspect). Personal computers often keep very detailed records of how and when they have been used, and those records can provide very powerful evidence in court.

What legal rules should regulate these steps of computer crime investigations? Should investigators need a search warrant or other authorization to collect logs from system administrators? Should they need a warrant or other authorization to search the suspect's computer for evidence? What rules should govern the search of the computer?

4. *Jurisdictional issues.* Finally, compare the physical crime and the computer crime from the standpoint of jurisdiction. What agency should investigate the jewelry store robbery? Where is the evidence of the crime located? If Fred is caught and prosecuted, what court will bring charges? Is the physical crime a case for state or federal investigators?

Now consider the computer crime. You are a Los Angeles police officer called to investigate the crime, and the system administrator tells you that his logs indicate the attack came from Ottawa, Canada. Does the Los Angeles Police Department have any powers to collect evidence in Canada? For that matter, if you can trace the attack back to the service provider based in Pennsylvania, do you have authority to collect evidence in Pennsylvania? Imagine you decide to pass up the case to the Federal Bureau of Investigation field office in Los Angeles. Can they collect evidence in Canada? How can they obtain the records needed to trace the crime?

Imagine the FBI successfully traces the attack through the Canadian site and the Pennsylvania service provider back to Fred Felony's home in Arizona. Can Fred Felony be charged with a violation of California law? Arizona law? Federal law? Should he be prosecuted in Phoenix? Los Angeles? What if the Canadian authorities want to bring Fred Felony to Ottawa to face charges for hacking into the Canadian tourism bureau site. Can Fred be extradited to

Canada? If the Canadian authorities request the FBI's assistance in gathering evidence to charge Fred Felony in Canada, does the FBI have an obligation to provide that assistance?

5.   *The road ahead.* Keep these questions in mind as you study the chapters ahead. The materials will start with substantive law, turn next to procedural law, and finish with jurisdictional issues. By the end of the book, you will be able to answer all of these questions for any computer-related crime.

CHAPTER 2

COMPUTER MISUSE CRIMES

■ ■ ■

Computer misuse crimes are offenses involving interference with the proper functioning of computers. Every computer is programmed to perform a particular set of functions for a particular set of users. Interfering with those functions can be a culpable act that causes significant harm.

Computer misuse can occur in two distinct ways. First, a user might exceed his privileges on a computer. For example, a person might hack into a remote network and view confidential files he is not supposed to see. Second, a person might deny others their privileges to use a computer. For example, a person might launch a denial-of-service attack that incapacitates a target network. Legitimate users will try to use the network but find that they cannot. These two types of computer misuse are distinct, but represent two sides of the same coin. In the first, the user exceeds his own privileges; in the second, the user denies privileges to others.

This chapter explores the law of computer misuse. It begins with a policy question: Should computer misuse be a crime, and if so, when? The materials then consider whether traditional criminal laws can address computer misuse, or whether new statutes are needed. The remaining parts of the chapter study the three most common types of computer misuse statutes: unauthorized access statutes, computer fraud statutes, and computer damage statutes.

A. WHY PUNISH COMPUTER MISUSE?

Every first-year law student learns that there are two major reasons why wrongful acts are punished. The first reason is utilitarian. Utilitarians believe that punishment should be imposed because it can decrease the amount of crime in the future. For example, criminal punishment can deter harmful conduct: the prospect of punishment can encourage a person not to commit a criminal act. Punishment also can prevent crime by incapacitating or rehabilitating a defendant. *See generally* Herbert L. Packer, The Limits of the Criminal Sanction 39–61 (1968).

The second goal of criminal punishment is retribution. Retributivists believe that punishment should be imposed to ensure that individuals receive their just deserts. Some retributivists believe that punishment reflects society's revenge against the wrongdoer; from this perspective, punishment is an "eye for an eye." Others contend that punishment restores the moral order by denying the wrongdoer's claim to superiority. The common theme of retributive approaches to punishment is that they look back at the wrongfulness of the defendant's act rather than look forward at the effect punishment will have on future criminal activity.

Do these theories justify punishment for computer misuse? Consider the following problem.

UNITED STATES V. SWARTZ

In 2011 and 2012, the United States Department of Justice prosecuted an Internet activist named Aaron Swartz for alleged computer-related crimes. Tragically, Swartz committed suicide before his case went to trial. As a result, no legal decision was handed down. But consider the alleged facts of the government's case against Swartz, and ask whether what Swartz did should be deemed a crime if the facts are true—and if so, what punishment would have been appropriate.

JSTOR, short for *Journal Storage*, sells universities, libraries, and publishers online access to a database of over 1,000 academic journals. JSTOR charges as much as $50,000 a year for an annual university subscription fee, at least parts of which go to pay copyright fees to the owners of the articles in the database. A username and password are ordinarily needed to access the JSTOR website. However, access can be had without a username and password from a computer network owned by a university that has purchased a subscription. Users that visit JSTOR must agree to use JSTOR in a particular way. They generally can download only one article at a time, and the JSTOR software is configured to block efforts to download large numbers of articles.

Aaron Swartz objected to the idea that scientific knowledge in academic papers available through JSTOR was not available to the public for free. In a writing he titled the Guerilla Open Access Manifesto, Swartz argued that there was an obligation to make academic papers available to all. He wrote: "There is no justice in following unjust laws. It's time to come into the light and, in the grand tradition of civil disobedience, declare our opposition to this private theft of public culture. We need to take information, wherever it is stored, make our copies and share them with the world."

Swartz devised a plan to copy JSTOR's entire database and then make it publicly available via filesharing networks. Although Swartz had legitimate access to JSTOR at Harvard University, where he was a fellow at an academic center on ethics, he decided to access JSTOR from the Massachusetts Institute of Technology (MIT). Swartz did not have an account or a formal relationship with MIT, but MIT is known for having relatively open account practices.

Swartz purchased a laptop and went into a building at MIT. He used the MIT wireless network to create a guest account on MIT's network. Swartz then accessed JSTOR and executed a program called "keepgrabbing" that circumvented JSTOR's limits on how many articles a person could download. Using the "keepgrabbing" program, Swartz began to download a massive number of articles. MIT and JSTOR eventually realized what was happening, and they blocked Swartz's computer from being able to access the MIT network by banning the IP address that he was using on MIT's network.

To circumvent the IP address ban, Swartz changed his IP address and continued to download the articles in bulk. JSTOR then blocked Swartz's new IP address. To stop Swartz from just changing IP addresses and continuing to copy more articles, JSTOR next blocked a range of IP addresses from MIT and contacted MIT for more help. MIT responded by canceling the new account and blocking Swartz's computer from accessing the MIT address by banning his media access control (MAC) address, a unique identifier associated with his laptop.

Swartz next bought a new laptop, and he also used a program that faked a new MAC address on his old laptop to circumvent MIT's ban. Using the two laptops and the program designed to circumvent JSTOR's limits on downloading articles, Swartz started to download a significant chunk of JSTOR's database. A day or two later, JSTOR responded by blocking all of MIT's access for a few days.

Swartz's next strategy was to connect directly to MIT's network. Swartz entered a basement closet in a building at MIT that contained a server. Swartz connected his computer directly to the server and hid his computer under a box so no one would see it. The closet was normally locked and Swartz did not have the key, although the lock to the door apparently was broken and the door could be pushed open without the key. Over several weeks, Swartz succeeded in downloading a major portion of JSTOR's database.

Investigators were on to Swartz at this point, however. Investigators installed a video camera in the closet to catch Swartz when he accessed the closet to swap out storage devices or retrieve his computer. Swartz was caught on camera, and he even seems to have realized that he was being watched: At one point he was filmed entering the closet using his bicycle helmet as a mask over his face to avoid being identified. Swartz was spotted on MIT's campus soon after by the police. He tried to run away, but he was chased and caught. Criminal charges followed.

NOTES AND QUESTIONS

1.   *The policy question.* Should Aaron Swartz's alleged conduct be a crime? If the conduct should be a crime, what punishment is appropriate? If you think Swartz should receive a lesser punishment because he was caught before his plan was completed, what punishment would be appropriate if Swartz had completed his alleged plan and released the entire JSTOR database to the public?

2.   *United States v. Evens.* In 2015, a judge sentenced Charles Evens to 25 months in federal prison for an e-mail hacking scheme. Evens hacked into

the personal e-mail accounts of hundreds of young women looking for nude pictures they had taken of themselves. When he found such pictures, Evens would sell them to a website that posted them for public viewing. *See* Matt Hamilton, *Judge Sentences 'Revenge Porn' Hacker To 2 Years In Federal Prison*, Los Angeles Times, November 16, 2015.

In your view, is a 25-month sentence appropriate for this crime? What is the appropriate punishment for a single act of hacking into an e-mail account? How about hacking into hundreds of e-mail accounts? And how much should the punishment depend on what Evens was looking for when he hacked into the accounts and what he did with the personal information he collected?

3. *The Hacker Ethic.* In the early days of computers in the late 1950s and early 1960s, a culture developed among some users that encouraged creative experimentation. In his book *Hackers*, Steven Levy focuses on the members of a student club at the Massachusetts Institute of Technology called the Tech Model Railroad Club. Members spent a great deal of time working on an early computer called the TX-0, and developed a number of principles that later coalesced into the "Hacker Ethic."

The Hacker Ethic reflects an open and free approach to using and exploring computers. One principle is that "access to computers—and anything which might teach you something about the way the world works—should be unlimited and total." Another related principle teaches that "all information should be free." The basic idea is that any computer user should have a right to tinker with and improve any computer, and that rules governing access should not be followed. *See* Steven Levy, Hackers 24–28 (1984). The term "hackers" was originally used in this sense to refer to skilled and enthusiastic computer programmers with a deep understanding of how computers work. Over time, however, the term has become synonymous with those who commit acts of unauthorized access to computers. *See* Pekka Himanen, The Hacker Ethic, at vii–ix (2001).

Does the hacker ethic help answer when computer misuse should be criminalized? Consider the argument that misuse consistent with the hacker ethic can help improve security. Hackers can identify security flaws and create patches, or inform others that the flaws exist. In addition, a teenager who becomes skilled at exploiting today's computers may become tomorrow's computer security professional tasked with protecting important networks. If hackers need to explore computers to improve them, should the law ensure that such exploration is possible? Is the notion that hacking is a form of "misuse" itself misguided?

Alternatively, is the hacker ethic a juvenile mythology that simply attempts to excuse harmful activity? Consider the teaching that "information should be free." Do you think that a person's private medical records should be free? Can the hacker ethic coexist with widely-held beliefs in the value of privacy?

4. *Responsibility for the consequences of poor computer security.* Every computer network is run by a system administrator who is tasked with keeping the network operating smoothly, responding to problems, setting up new accounts, and performing other routine network maintenance tasks. System administrators are usually the first to notice and respond to network intrusions. Consider this imaginary (but representative) exchange of views between a hacker and a system administrator:

> Hacker: System administrators should blame themselves if their networks are vulnerable. Many system administrators pay little or no attention to security, and their negligence is the true cause of most of the financial losses that result from so-called "computer crime." Hackers raise the level of network security by testing networks, offering solutions to existing vulnerabilities, and making sure that security remains a priority. Taking steps to understand a network shouldn't be a crime. Instead, it should be recognized as a public service.

> System Administrator: Your argument blames the victim for being victimized. We don't blame homeowners when their houses are burglarized just because they left weak locks on their front doors; instead, we blame the burglars. Also, it's hard to see why we should thank hackers for forcing us to spend money on network security, given that it is the hackers themselves we are trying to keep out. Here's an analogy: people who live in high-crime neighborhoods may have several locks on their doors and steel bars on their windows, but they don't thank the local burglars for encouraging them to raise the level of security in their homes. All hacking without the target's consent should be criminalized.

> Hacker: You're missing the point. Unlike homes, computers are inherently open. Any computer attached to the Internet can be accessed by millions of people around the world at any moment. The question is not *whether* a computer will be compromised, but rather *when* and *how*. In this environment, network operators should be responsible for network security, and should recognize that hackers play a vital role in helping system administrators secure their networks against the *real* criminals.

> System Administrator: No, you're the one who is missing the point. This is my network, and you don't have a right to break in to it. If you want to help me by exposing my network's vulnerabilities, you can just ask me for permission. If I think you can help me, I will let you try to hack in. But that's for me to decide, not you.

> Hacker: You are mired in the old way of thinking. Computers are different, and the law needs to recognize that.

Who has the stronger argument? If you think the hacker's argument is stronger, does it follow that "state and federal governments should immediately decriminalize all forms of non-malicious hacking?" Michael Lee, et al., Comment, *Electronic Commerce, Hackers, and the Search for Legitimacy: A Regulatory Proposal*, 14 Berkeley Tech. L.J. 839, 882 (1999). If so, how would you articulate the difference between malicious hacking and non-malicious hacking?

5. *Culpability and intent to profit.* Some hackers abide by the hacker ethic, and hack for the intellectual excitement or the thrill. Others hack for profit. Some attempt to hack into e-commerce sites to collect credit card numbers that can be sold later in anonymous Internet chat rooms. Others gain unauthorized access to distribute spam anonymously for a fee, or to look for an advantage over business competitors. Organized crime groups are actively involved in computer hacking. The groups hire hackers both to steal credit card numbers and to break into victim sites and demand expensive "consulting fees" in exchange for not doing significant damage. Others are hired to break into computers and find trade secrets that can be sold to competitors or outsiders.

Does computer misuse deserve greater punishment when undertaken for profit? On one hand, perhaps computer misuse combined with a profit motive is likely to be more harmful because intent to profit generally suggests a lack of concern for other possible harms or the likelihood the conduct will be repeated. On the other hand, some of the harms caused by computer misuse are unintentional byproducts of otherwise intentional activity. The harm may have no direct link to the intent to profit. For example, imagine a person hacks into a computer for profit, and accidentally causes a great deal of damage to the server. Is that hacking really more culpable by virtue of the intent to profit?

6. *Alternative of civil remedies?* Civil damages can provide an alternative to criminal punishment when conduct is not particularly culpable and can be deterred through payment of money damages. This raises two issues. First, at what point does computer misuse become sufficiently culpable that some kind of criminal punishment is more appropriate than a civil judgment? And second, how effective is the threat of a civil suit if it is easy to escape detection and many people lack the ability to pay damages?

B. PROPERTY CRIMES AS A RESPONSE TO COMPUTER MISUSE

Assuming computer misuse should be criminalized, at least in some circumstances, the next question becomes *how* to criminalize it. Does the problem of computer misuse require new criminal laws? Or can traditional criminal laws handle these new crimes? This section considers whether traditional property crime laws can address the problem of computer misuse, or, alternatively, whether computer misuse requires the passage of new laws.

The enormous potential harms of computer misuse first became apparent in the early 1970s.[1] At that time, no legislature had enacted a computer crime statute. When prosecutors considered bringing criminal charges for computer misuse, they naturally turned to existing property crime laws, such as laws prohibiting trespass, burglary, and theft. The fit proved a poor one, however. In the case of trespass and burglary, the scope of existing laws plainly did not extend to computer misuse. In the case of theft, the law could be stretched to apply, but required judicial sleight of hand and resort to an unpredictable legal fiction.

Consider the crimes of trespass and burglary, both predominantly state offenses. Trespass crimes generally punish knowing entrance or presence on another person's property despite notice that the property owner forbids it. At common law, burglary prohibited "breaking and entering" into a building without authorization and with the intent to commit a crime therein. Modern statutes tend to focus more on entering a building or occupied structure without license or privilege, combined with intent to commit a crime inside. Like trespass crimes, burglary focuses on the entry onto property without permission. Unlike trespass, however, burglary requires the intent to commit a crime, and usually carries relatively stiff criminal penalties.

At first blush, trespass and burglary law may appear to provide a logical starting point for applying property crimes to punish and deter computer misuse. It has been noted widely that many acts of computer misuse resemble trespasses. A user can exceed her privileges on a computer much like a trespasser can exceed her privileges on physical land. Computer hacking, for example, is akin to a trespass in cyberspace. Similarly, a hacker may break into a computer with intent to do mischief much like a burglar might break into a house with the same intent.

Despite the common principles, it seems that criminal trespass and burglary statutes have never been used to prosecute computer misuse. The primary reason is that both trespass and burglary statutes remain closely tied to the physical world rather than a virtual one. For example, trespass statutes generally require that part of the defendant's person pass the line of the threshold of the property trespassed. The same goes for burglary offenses. Criminal trespass and burglary statutes focus narrowly on presence of a human body on physical land, not interference with property rights more generally. This limited scope makes it difficult to apply trespass or burglary statutes to computer misuse; because the user does not physically enter the target computer, the existing statutes do not apply. Indeed, it appears that no criminal prosecution has ever used burglary or general criminal trespass statutes to prosecute computer misuse.

---

[1]   This material is adapted from Orin S. Kerr, *Cybercrime's Scope: Interpreting "Access" and "Authorization" in Computer Misuse Statutes*, 78 N.Y.U. L. Rev. 1596, 1605–10 (2003).

In contrast with burglary and trespass, the crime of theft has been used often to prosecute computer misuse. Theft crimes consist of a family of related offenses, including larceny, embezzlement, conversion, fraud, and false pretenses. Today, most states have consolidated these various crimes into a single theft statute, which prohibits larceny, embezzlement, and false pretenses together. Federal theft crimes are more limited in scope, reflecting the constitutional limits of federal criminal law. The mail fraud and wire fraud statutes are the broadest federal theft offenses; they prohibit many interstate fraudulent schemes to obtain property. These statutes make it illegal to send an interstate wire, radio, or television communication, or to place a stolen item in the U.S. mail or with an interstate mail carrier, to help further a fraudulent scheme designed to obtain money or property.

Efforts to prosecute computer misuse as theft crimes generally follow a fairly simple rationale. By upsetting intended privileges relating to a computer, the thinking goes, the defendant committed a theft—the taking of property belonging to another. This rationale may seem plausible at first blush, but it creates serious difficulties defining a property interest and then identifying when that property has been taken. Theft statutes presume the existence of an identifiable piece of property, some clearly-defined "thing," that when taken deprives the owner of its bounty. We can understand this easily in the case of tangible property. For example, if someone steals my bicycle, it is easy to identify the property stolen (the bicycle) and to tell whether or not I have been deprived of it (either I have the bicycle or I don't).

In the case of computer misuse, however, identifying a property interest and then concluding that it was taken can require considerable creativity.

UNITED STATES V. SEIDLITZ

United States Court of Appeals for the Fourth Circuit, 1978.
589 F.2d 152.

FIELD, SENIOR CIRCUIT JUDGE.

Bertram Seidlitz appeals from his conviction on two counts of fraud by wire in violation of 18 U.S.C. § 1343.[1] As grounds for reversal, he urges that the prosecution failed to establish certain material elements of the crime.

---

[1] The federal wire fraud statute, 18 U.S.C. § 1343, provides:

Whoever, having devised or intending to devise any scheme or artifice to defraud, or for obtaining money or property by means of false or fraudulent pretenses, representations, or promises, transmits or causes to be transmitted by means of wire, radio, or television communication in interstate or foreign commerce, any writings, signs, signals, pictures, or sounds for the purpose of executing such scheme or artifice, shall be fined not more than $1,000 or imprisoned not more than five years, or both.

Although advanced in a somewhat novel factual context, we find appellant's contentions to be without merit.

On January 1, 1975, defendant Seidlitz assumed the position of Deputy Project Director for Optimum Systems, Inc. (OSI), a computer service company which was under contract to install, maintain, and operate a computer facility at Rockville, Maryland, for use by the Federal Energy Administration (FEA). Under the arrangement between OSI and FEA, persons working for FEA in various parts of the country could use key boards at communications terminals in their offices to send instructions over telephone circuits to the large computers in Rockville, and the computers' responses would be returned and reflected on a CRT (cathode ray tube) terminal which is a typewriter-like device with a keyboard and display screen similar to a television screen upon which the information is displayed as it is sent and received.[2] Mr. Seidlitz helped to prepare the software which was installed at the Rockville facility as part of the project, and he was also responsible for the security of the central computer system. During his tenure, he had full access to the computers and to a software system known as "WYLBUR" which resided within them. In June, 1975, Seidlitz resigned this job and returned to work at his own computer firm in Alexandria, Virginia.

William Coakley, a computer specialist employed by FEA, was assigned temporarily to the OSI facility. On December 30, 1975, in an attempt to locate a friend who might be using the OSI system, he had the computer display the initials of everyone who was then using the WYLBUR software. Among the initials displayed by the computer were those of his supervisor, who was standing nearby and who was not using the computer. Suspicious that an unauthorized "intruder" might be using these initials in order to gain access to the system, Coakley asked Mr. Ewing, an OSI employee, if Ewing could determine what was happening. He also asked Mr. Wack, an OSI supervisor, if he (Wack) could determine whether the mysterious user was at a remote terminal or at one of the terminals within the OSI complex which were directly wired to the computer and did not employ telephone circuits. Ewing instructed the computer to display for him the data it was about to transmit to the possible intruder, and it proved to be a portion of the "source code" of the WYLBUR software system. Using other data provided by the computer, Wack concluded that the connection

---

2 A remote user would dial on an ordinary telephone one of the several unpublished telephone numbers to which OSI subscribed and which were assigned to the computers. He would then connect the telephone to his terminal so that messages could be relayed between the terminal and the computers in the form of signals traveling over the telephone line. Because any of a number of commercially available terminal units could accomplish such a link to the computers, the user, as a security precaution, had to enter on his terminal keyboard a special access code before he would be permitted full use of the system. The code contained, among other things, the user's personal initials, which were to be invalidated when he left OSI or FEA. This "access code" would be communicated to the central computers which, if they recognized the code as belonging to an authorized user, would proceed to perform the work the individual sent along.

was by telephone from outside the complex. At his request, the telephone company manually traced the call to the Alexandria office of the defendant.[7] Wack was told that the trace was successful, but the telephone company informed him that it could not divulge the results of the trace except in response to a legal subpoena.

The following day, OSI activated a special feature of the WYLBUR system known as the "Milten Spy Function," which automatically recorded, after they had been received by the machinery at Rockville, any requests made of the computer by the intruder. The "spy" also recorded, before they were sent out to the intruder over the telephone lines, the computer's responses to such requests. Mr. Wack again asked the telephone company to trace the line when it was suspected that the unauthorized person, employing the same initials, was using the computer to receive portions of the WYLBUR source code. This manual trace on December 31 led once more to the defendant's office in Virginia, although OSI was not so informed.

Advised by OSI of the events of December 30 and 31, the FBI on January 3, 1976, secured, but did not then execute, a warrant to search the defendant's Alexandria office. At the FBI's suggestion, the telephone company conducted two additional manual traces when alerted to incoming calls by OSI, but in each instance the calls were terminated before the traces had progressed beyond the telephone company's office in Lanham, Maryland, which served 10,000 subscribers. The phone company then installed "originating accounting identification equipment" in the Lanham office, the function of which was to automatically and quickly ascertain, without intercepting the contents of any communication, the telephone number of any of the 10,000 area telephones from which any subsequent calls to the OSI computers originated. Two such calls were made on the morning of January 9, and the equipment attributed both of them to a phone at the defendant's Lanham residence. That afternoon, the FBI executed the warrant to search Seidlitz' Alexandria office, seizing, among other items, a copy of the user's guide to the OSI system and some 40 rolls of computer paper upon which were printed the WYLBUR source code. A warrant was then issued to search the Seidlitz residence in Lanham, where officers found a portable communications terminal which contained a teleprinter for receiving written messages from the computer, as well as a notebook containing information relating to access codes previously assigned to authorized users of the OSI computers.

The indictment handed down on February 3, 1976, charged that the defendant had, on December 30 and 31, transmitted telephone calls in interstate commerce as part of a scheme to defraud OSI of property

---

[7] A manual trace is accomplished without listening in on the line or breaking into the conversation. It entails a physical tracing of the telephone circuitry backward through the various switching points from the equipment which receives the call.

consisting of information from the computer system. A motion to suppress the evidence seized from the office and the residence was considered at a hearing on April 30, after which the district judge rendered an oral opinion rejecting the defendant's argument that the searches were invalidated by the use of illegal electronic surveillance to obtain the information contained in the affidavits supporting the warrants.

Over defense objection, much of the challenged evidence was admitted at trial, and the telephone traces, as well as the operation of the "Milten Spy," were described to the jury. In the face of this evidence, the defendant conceded that he had retrieved the information from the computers, but claimed to have acted only out of concern for the security of the OSI system. In negation of fraudulent intent, Seidlitz testified that he acquired the data with the sole intention of presenting the printouts to OSI officials to prove to them that the steps taken to prevent unauthorized use of the computers were inadequate. Additionally, it was his position at trial that the WYLBUR software was not a trade secret or other property interest of OSI sufficient to qualify as "property" within the meaning of the wire fraud statute. On appeal he argues that the evidence before the jury was insufficient to establish either his fraudulent intent or that WYLBUR constituted "property."

Viewed in the light most favorable to the government, there was sufficient evidence from which the jury could find that the WYLBUR system was "property" as defined in the instruction given by the trial judge which is not contested on appeal. Even though software systems similar to OSI's WYLBUR were in use at non-OSI facilities, the evidence that OSI invested substantial sums to modify the system to suit its peculiar needs, that OSI enjoyed a multi-million dollar competitive advantage because of WYLBUR, and that OSI took steps to prevent persons other than clients and employees from using the system permitted a finding that the pilfered data was the property of OSI and not, as the defendant contends, property in the public domain subject to appropriation by persons such as himself. In a similar vein, the defendant disputes the sufficiency of the evidence to establish fraudulent intent, but in essence his argument is only that he feels the jury should not have discredited his own explanation of the purpose for which he acquired the WYLBUR data. It is of no consequence that Seidlitz was not shown by the government to have used the data retrieved from the OSI computers in his own business or to have attempted to sell it to others, and the circumstantial evidence in this case is ample to support a finding of the requisite intent.

NOTES AND QUESTIONS

1.   *What is property?* WYLBUR was a text-editing program that allowed users to direct computers to perform particular tasks. In what sense was the

WYLBUR software "property?" Scholars and judges have struggled to agree upon a simple definition of property. Consider the following definitions:

A.   "That is property to which the following label can be attached. To the world: Keep off X unless you have my permission, which I may grant or withhold. Signed: private citizen. Endorsed: the state." Felix S. Cohen, *Dialogue on Private Property*, 9 Rutgers L. Rev. 357, 374 (1954).

B.   "Give someone the right to exclude others from a valued resource, i.e., a resource that is scarce relative to the human demand for it, and you give them property. Deny someone the exclusion right and they do not have property." Thomas W. Merrill, Essay, *Property and the Right to Exclude*, 77 Neb. L. Rev. 730, 730 (1998).

C.   Property "consists in the free use, enjoyment, and disposal of all his acquisitions, without any control or diminution, save only by the laws of the land." 1 William Blackstone, Commentaries on the Laws of England *138.

D.   Property is "a euphonious collection of letters which serves as a general term for the miscellany of equities that persons hold in the commonwealth." Walter Hamilton, 11 Encyclopedia of the Social Sciences 528 (1937).

Under which of these definitions is the WYLBUR software property?

2.   *Computer use and data as property.* Whatever conceptual problems may be raised by labeling information as property for the purpose of property crime statutes, courts have done so in a wide range of cases involving computers. Courts have concluded that computer usage was property, *see* United States v. Collins, 56 F.3d 1416, 1420 (D.C. Cir. 1995), that the data stored in a computer counted as property, *see* United States v. Girard, 601 F.2d 69, 71 (2d Cir. 1979), and even that the password that controlled access to a computer account was property, *see* People v. Johnson, 560 N.Y.S.2d 238, 241, 243–44 (Crim. Ct. 1990).

3.   *The deception requirement.* Conviction under the federal wire fraud statute requires intent to defraud, which requires knowing conduct together with intent to deceive. *See* United States v. Keller, 14 F.3d 1051, 1056 (5th Cir. 1994). Who did Seidlitz deceive when he logged on to the OSI computer and instructed the computer to send him data? One answer might be the OSI computer itself: Seidlitz identified himself to the computer as William Coakley's supervisor, tricking the computer into giving him access. But is it possible to deceive a machine? Imagine that a car thief picks the lock on a car door, and then steals the car. Would the thief be guilty of fraud, on the theory that he tricked the car lock into opening by convincing the lock that he was the car's rightful owner?

4.   *Is hacking into a computer to change college grades a scheme to obtain "money or property"?* In United States v. Barrington, 648 F.3d 1178 (11th Cir.

2011), an undergraduate at Florida A&M University ("FAMU") obtained the username and passwords of employees at the university registrar's office. The defendant used the usernames and passwords to access FAMU's grading system over the Internet. For a fee, the defendant changed grades, added credits, and altered the residencies of several non-resident students so they would qualify for in-state tuition. The Eleventh Circuit concluded that the defendant violated the federal Wire Fraud statute because he had engaged in a scheme to obtain money or property:

> Count One expressly alleged that the changing of student grades from failing to passing "had the effect of awarding the students who had received the 'F' grades thousands of dollars in credit hours to which they were not entitled" and that the change in residency of out-of-state students reduced "the total tuition owed by these students to FAMU by thousands of dollars."
>
> Barrington's focus on whether a student's grade constitutes a property interest is far too narrow. Although changing grades was the manner in which the scheme was carried out, the "money or property" of which FAMU was deprived was the lost tuition resulting from the unearned hours credited to the students, rather than the actual grades. Moreover, Barrington ignores the demonstrated financial loss FAMU suffered as a result of the companion aspect of the scheme, the reimbursement of tuition to the out-of-state students whose residencies had been changed.
>
> FAMU undeniably has a property right in tuition generated by class hours a student registers for, as well as the higher tuition paid by non-resident students. By changing failing grades to passing grades, the conspirators endeavored to obtain unearned credit hours for students who were not entitled to them. Had their grades not been changed, those students would have had to repeat the failed classes or take equivalent hours, either of which would have generated additional tuition for FAMU. By changing the residencies of out-of-state students, the conspirators sought to obtain tuition reimbursement for those students, who otherwise would have been required to pay higher, non-resident tuition. The unearned credit hours and reimbursed tuition constitute "money or property" obtained by wire fraud.

Id. at 1191–92. In a footnote, the court considered whether the value of higher grades would have triggered a violation of the Wire Fraud statute even without a showing that the university might suffer a financial loss:

> The Government makes a compelling argument that the students' willingness to pay to have their grades changed from, for example, a "D" to a "B," indicates that they placed value in higher grades. Although a higher grade may not be quantifiable in financial terms, the University certainly has an intangible property interest in the integrity of its grading system. Moreover, as alleged in the

indictment, increased grade point averages resulting from the grade changes made students eligible for financial aid such as scholarships, loans and grants. Others were able to maintain their scholarships because of their improved GPAs. In sum, there is ample evidence that the scheme alleged in Count One deprived FAMU of property or money and "things of value," independent of an improved grade in and of itself.

Id. at 1192 n.11.

STATE V. MCGRAW

Supreme Court of Indiana, 1985.
480 N.E.2d 552.

PRENTICE, JUSTICE.

Defendant was charged with nine counts of theft under Ind. Code § 35–43–4–2, by information alleging that he knowingly exerted "unauthorized control over the property of the City of Indianapolis, Indiana, to-wit: the use of computers and computer services with intent to deprive the City of Indianapolis." He was convicted upon two counts, following a trial by jury. The trial court, thereafter, granted his renewed motion to dismiss, citing, among other grounds, the insufficiency of the evidence. The Court of Appeals reversed the trial court and ordered the verdicts reinstated.

Defendant was employed by the City of Indianapolis, as a computer operator. The City leased computer services on a fixed charge or flat rate basis, hence the expense to it was not varied by the extent to which it was used. Defendant was provided with a terminal at his desk and was assigned a portion of the computer's information storage capacity, called a "private library," for his utilization in performing his duties. No other employees were authorized to use his terminal or his library.

Defendant became involved in a private sales venture and began soliciting his co-workers and using a small portion of his assigned library to maintain records associated with the venture. He was reprimanded several times for selling his products in the office and on "office time," and he was eventually discharged for unsatisfactory job performance and for continuing his personal business activities during office hours.

Defendant, at the time of his being hired by the City, received a handbook, as do all new employees, which discloses the general prohibition against the unauthorized use of city property. Other city employees sometimes used the computer for personal convenience or entertainment; and although Defendant's supervisor knew or suspected that Defendant was using the computer for his business records, he never investigated the matter or reprimanded Defendant in this regard, and such use of the computer was not cited as a basis for his discharge.

Defendant, following his discharge, applied for and received unemployment compensation benefits, over the protest of the City. He requested a former fellow employee to obtain a "print-out" of his business data and then to erase it from what had been his library. Instead, the "print-out" was turned over to Defendant's former supervisor and became the basis for the criminal charges.

Assuming that Defendant's use of the computer was unauthorized and that such use is a "property" under the theft statute, there remains an element of the offense missing under the evidence. The act provides: "A person who knowingly or intentionally exerts unauthorized control over property of another person with *intent* to deprive the other of any part of its value or use, commits theft, a class D felony." Ind. Code § 35–43–4–2. It is immediately apparent that the *res* of the statute, the harm sought to be prevented, is a deprivation to one of his property or its use—not a benefit to one which, although a windfall to him, harmed nobody.

The Court of Appeals focused upon Defendant's unauthorized use of the computer for monetary gain and upon the definition of "property" as used in the statute and as defined by Ind. Code § 35–41–1–2, which we may assume, arguendo, includes the "use" of a computer, although we think that it would be more accurate to say that the *information* derived by use of a computer is *property*. Having determined that Defendant's use was property, was unauthorized and was for his monetary benefit, it concluded that he committed a theft. Our question is, "Who was deprived of what?"

Not only was there no evidence that the City was ever deprived of any part of the value or the use of the computer by reason of Defendant's conduct, the uncontradicted evidence was to the contrary. The computer was utilized for City business by means of terminals assigned to various employee-operators, including Defendant. The computer processed the data from the various terminals simultaneously, and the limit of its capacity was never reached or likely to have been. The computer service was leased to the City at a fixed charge, and the tapes or discs upon which the imparted data was stored were erasable and reusable. Defendant's unauthorized use cost the City nothing and did not interfere with its use by others. He extracted from the system only such information as he had previously put into it. He did not, for his own benefit, withdraw City data intended for its exclusive use or for sale.

Thus, Defendant did not deprive the City of the "use of computers and computer services" as the information alleged that he intended to do. We find no distinction between Defendant's use of the City's computer and the use, by a mechanic, of the employer's hammer or a stenographer's use of the employer's typewriter, for other than the employer's purposes. Under traditional concepts, the transgression is in the nature of a trespass, a civil matter—and a de minimis one, at that. Defendant has likened his conduct to the use of an employer's vacant bookshelf, for the temporary storage of one's personal items, and to the use of an employer's telephone facilities for toll-free calls. The analogies appear to us to be appropriate.

We have written innumerable times, that intent is a mental function and, absent an admission, it must be determined by courts and juries from a consideration of the conduct and natural and usual consequences of such conduct. It follows that when the natural and usual consequences of the conduct charged and proved are not such as would effect the wrong which the statute seeks to prevent, the intent to effect that wrong is not so inferable. No deprivation to the City resulted from Defendant's use of the computer, and a deprivation to it was not a result to be expected from such use, hence not a natural and usual consequence. There was no evidence presented from which the intent to deprive, an essential element of the crime, could be inferred.

PIVARNIK, JUSTICE, dissenting.

I must dissent from the majority opinion wherein the majority finds that Defendant did not take property of the City "with intent to deprive the owner of said property." In the first place, intent is clearly shown in that Defendant used the City computer system for his personal business, well knowing that he was doing so and well knowing that it was unauthorized. I think the Court of Appeals properly focused upon Defendant's unauthorized use of the computer for monetary gain and upon the definition of property as used in the statute and as defined by Ind. Code § 35–41–1–2. Time and use are at the very core of the value of a computer system. To say that only the information stored in the computer plus the tapes and discs and perhaps the machinery involved in the computer system, are the only elements that can be measured as the value or property feature of that system, is incorrect.

I think it is irrelevant that the computer processed the data from various terminals simultaneously and the limit of its capacity was never reached by any or all of the stations, including the defendant's. It is also irrelevant that the computer service was leased to the City at a fixed charge and that the tapes or discs upon which the imparted data was stored were erasable and reusable. The fact is the City owned the computer system of all the stations including the defendant's. The time and use of that equipment at that station belonged to the City. Thus, when the defendant used the computer system, putting on data from his private business and taking it out on printouts, he was taking that which was property of the City and converting it to his own use, thereby depriving the City of its use and value. The majority says: "Thus, Defendant did not deprive the City of the 'use of computers and computer services' as the information alleged that he intended to do." I disagree. I feel that is exactly what he did and I think the Court of Appeals properly found so.

NOTES AND QUESTIONS

1. *Deprivation, or right to exclude?* The majority argues that McGraw's conduct did not deprive the City of its property. But did McGraw infringe upon the City's right to exclude others from using its valuable resources? If the City's computer resembles a limitless fountain of property, as the majority's opinion suggests, doesn't the City have a right to control who should receive its bounty?

On the other hand, do you think an employee should be prosecuted criminally for using his employer's computer for personal reasons when that use does not interfere with the employer's interests? Do you think this question influenced the court in *McGraw*?

2. *Who gained and who lost.* In the case of physical property, depriving the owner of property transfers that property from its owner to the defendant. The victim's loss is the same as the defendant's gain, namely the property taken. In *McGraw*, by contrast, the defendant received a benefit but the victim did not suffer a loss. The owner retained the property allegedly "taken."

This also occurred in the *Seidlitz* case. Seidlitz obtained a copy of the WYLBUR software, which potentially harmed OSI by allowing Seidlitz or others to compete against OSI on a more equal footing. But OSI's loss did not equal Seidlitz's gain: OSI was not deprived of WYLBUR, but rather of the economic benefits flowing from the exclusive use of WYLBUR. *Seidlitz* held that the WYLBUR program was property, which seems plausible. But did Seidlitz have intent to deprive OSI of that property? Should it matter?

3. *Does conversion offer a better alternative?* The doctrine of conversion might be used to prosecute an employee's computer misuse when the employee does not intend to deprive others of the use of the computer. Unlike theft, conversion does not generally require an intent to deprive the owner of the property.

This approach was tried in United States v. Collins, 56 F.3d 1416 (D.C. Cir. 1995). Collins, an employee of the Defense Intelligence Agency, used a highly classified government computer network to store hundreds of personal documents relating to his interest in ballroom dancing. He was charged with converting government property in violation of 18 U.S.C. § 641. The D.C. Circuit rejected the government's theory that Collins had converted government property by using the classified computer network for personal purposes:

> The cornerstone of conversion is the unauthorized exercise of control over property in such a manner that *serious interference* with ownership rights occurs. Section 228 of the Restatement (Second) of Torts states "one who is authorized to make a particular use of a chattel, and uses it in a manner exceeding the authorization, is subject to liability for conversion to another whose right to control the use of the chattel is thereby *seriously violated*." (emphasis added). The interference is of such a magnitude that the converter must pay

the rightful owner the full value of the property converted. Restatement (Second) of Torts § 222A.

The court's decision in *United States v. Wilson*, 636 F.2d 225 (8th Cir. 1980), is illuminating on this point. Appellant was found guilty by a jury of converting government property in violation of section 641. Specifically, appellant was charged with converting secretarial time by using a government secretary to type documents for his personal business. No evidence existed, however, that the work interfered with the secretary's official duties. The district court granted a motion for judgment of acquittal, and the appellate court affirmed this judgment. The court held there was no evidence that appellant's conduct seriously interfered with the rights of the government. The court focused on the fact that appellant and his secretary had little or no assigned work during the period in question. Consequently, appellant could not have seriously interfered with the government's ownership rights because the government was never deprived of the use or possession of its property. Thus, while appellant may have engaged in a breach of fiduciary duty, his conduct was not criminal.

Similarly, the government did not provide a shred of evidence in the case at bar that appellant seriously interfered with the government's ownership rights in its computer system. While appellant concedes he typed in data and stored information on the computer regarding his personal activities, no evidence exists that such conduct prevented him or others from performing their official duties on the computer. The government did not even attempt to show that appellant's use of the computer prevented agency personnel from accessing the computer or storing information. Thus, appellant's use of the government computer in no way seriously interfered with the government's ownership rights.

Id. at 1420–21.

Compare *Collins* with United States v. Girard, 601 F.2d 69 (2d Cir. 1979). In *Girard,* a corrupt Drug Enforcement Administration (DEA) agent used the DEA's computer to access and download files identifying undercover DEA agents that he then planned to sell to drug dealers. The defendant was charged with converting government property in violation of 18 U.S.C. § 641. The Second Circuit affirmed the conviction, announcing in a conclusory fashion that the defendant had converted the government's property.

How do you reconcile *Collins* and *Girard*? Is the difference that *Girard* had at best thwarted DEA investigations and at worst risked the lives of DEA undercover agents, but *Collins* had not caused any harm to his government employer?

Imagine that you are a defense attorney in a future § 641 case that involves less harm than the facts of *Girard* but more harm than the facts of

Collins. How can you persuade the court that your case is more like *Collins* than *Girard*?

4.   *A critical perspective on using theft law to punish computer misuse.* Does the law of theft provide a useful way of prohibiting computer misuse? Consider:

> When computer misuse caused harm to a victim in some way, courts [applying theft law to computer misuse] generally concluded that property had in fact been taken and held the defendants liable. When no appreciable harm resulted, courts tended to find that no property was taken and hold that the defendants had committed no crime. To the extent that it was made explicit, the reasoning seemed to go something like this: When a person is harmed, the person loses something of value; when a person loses something of value, they are deprived of property. Therefore the infliction of harm triggers a theft. This reasoning allowed courts to reach reasonable results in particular cases, but followed no deeper principle than the courts' ex post assessments of whether particular instances of computer misuse had caused substantial harm.

Orin S. Kerr, *Cybercrime's Scope: Interpreting "Access" and "Authorization" in Computer Misuse Statutes,* 78 N.Y.U. L. Rev. 1596, 1611 (2003). If the use of theft law to punish computer misuse was result-oriented, is that a good thing or a bad thing?

5.   *Arguments for and against computer crime statutes.* Starting in the late 1970s, dissatisfaction with the cases applying theft law to computer misuse led to a movement to adopt new computer misuse statutes. State computer crime prosecutor Donald Ingraham offered one rationale for such statutes in an early article. *See* Donald G. Ingraham, *On Charging Computer Crime,* 2 Computer/L.J. 429 (1980). Ingraham reasoned that computer crime statutes were needed for the same reason criminal codes prohibit burglary and trespass. It would be possible to repeal burglary and trespass laws and simply prosecute every property crime as a theft, Ingraham noted. But such an approach would be quite awkward:

> For example, attempted commercial burglary could be regarded as a usurpation of store floor space, and treated as a theft of the property interest in occupancy. Under such a statute, the victim would necessarily be compelled to calculate the value of the property invaded and the duration of the invasion. The prosecution would be for the theft of those values, and not for the intrusion as a crime complete in itself. It is precisely that absurdity—the requirement that the victim prepare evidence of an injury other than that with which he is really concerned—which the so-called computer crime bills have recognized and sought to redress.

Id. at 429–30.

More recently, some commentators have questioned whether the specific computer crime statutes are necessary. Joseph Olivenbaum has argued that traditional property laws are sufficient to deter and punish computer misuse:

> Legislators and others apprehensive about the misuse of technology too often have perceived a need to enact statutes to counteract "computer crimes" that are in fact already existing crimes accomplished with new techniques. To the extent that such statutes merely prohibit conduct that is already criminal, they are simply redundant. To the extent that they are drafted in "technology-specific" language, the pace of technological change and the ingenuity of computer-literate criminals guarantee that those statutes will be obsolete almost as soon as they are enacted. To the extent that they focus on technological means, rather than on the harm caused by a defendant's conduct, those statutes tend towards overbreadth by sweeping within their ambit anyone who uses the means regardless of result. To the extent that computer-specific statutes are enacted by legislators unfamiliar or uncomfortable with technology, such statutes tend to reflect a lack of clarity or understanding or, sometimes, simply fear. Thus, a "computer-specific" approach results, too often, in criminal statutes that are unnecessary, imprecise, clumsy, over-inclusive, or ineffective.

Joseph M. Olivenbaum, *Ctrl-Alt-Delete: Rethinking Federal Computer Crime Legislation*, 27 Seton Hall L. Rev. 574, 575–76 (1997).

In an article on the differences between physical crime and virtual crime, Susan Brenner has also expressed some skepticism about the need for new laws. "[T]he principles we have traditionally used to impose liability for crimes," Brenner argues, "can be extrapolated to encompass many, if not all, of the activities characterized as cybercrimes." Brenner contends that this approach is preferable to "trying to devise new principles of criminal liability, a new law of cybercrimes, to address anti-social behavior occurring within or committed via cyberspace." Brenner acknowledges that "there may be reasons for devising a new law of cybercrimes, such as the greater harms that can be inflicted by cybercriminals and the advantages they enjoy in avoiding detection and prosecution." However, she cautions against taking "hasty action" because we should "wait to see how crime in cyberspace evolves before committing ourselves to the adoption of cybercrime laws." Susan W. Brenner, *Is There Such a Thing as "Virtual Crime?"* 4 Cal. Crim. L. Rev. 1, ¶ 129 (2001).

In contrast, Beryl Howell, formerly the Chief Counsel to the Senate Judiciary Committee and now a federal judge, has defended the computer-specific approach to prohibiting computer misuse against such criticisms:

> Specific laws directed to specific problems are important for two main reasons. First, they serve to guide law enforcement as to how investigations may be conducted with appropriate respect for civil liberties and privacy. Second, specific laws make clear to people the boundary of legally permissible conduct.

Does this require endless effort to update the laws to keep pace with technology? Yes, but Congress returns every year with the job of making new laws. Will the pace of legal changes always be behind technological developments? Yes, but in my view the correct pace is a slow one. By the time a proposal has gone through the legislative process, the problem it seeks to address will have become more defined. Policy-makers are better able to craft a narrow and circumscribed law to address a clearly defined problem, and thus, minimize the risk of an overly expansive law that could chill innovation and technological development.

Beryl A. Howell, *Real World Problems of Virtual Crime*, 7 Yale J. L. & Tech. 103, 104–105 (2004–2005).

When evaluating the need for computer crime statutes, it is worth noting that criminal codes contain many technology-specific statutes. For example, the United States Code includes statutes criminalizing the destruction of aircraft (18 U.S.C. § 32), use of aircraft or motor vehicles to hunt protected wild horses (18 U.S.C. § 47), sending a threatening communication through the postal mail (18 U.S.C. § 876), using a radio or television station to broadcast information about an unauthorized lottery (18 U.S.C. § 1304), broadcasting obscene language by radio (18 U.S.C. § 1464), carjacking (18 U.S.C. § 2119), transporting stolen vehicles (18 U.S.C. § 2312), selling or receiving stolen vehicles (18 U.S.C. § 2313), and engaging in telemarketing fraud (18 U.S.C. § 2326). In light of this list, do you think that a statute prohibiting computer misuse is really out of place? Are technology-specific criminal statutes the exception or the rule?

C. UNAUTHORIZED ACCESS STATUTES

1. INTRODUCTION TO UNAUTHORIZED ACCESS STATUTES

The perceived deficiencies of prosecuting computer misuse using theft laws led the federal government and all fifty states to enact statutes specifically prohibiting computer misuse. Florida passed the first state statute in 1978; the final state to enact a statute was Vermont in 1999. Congress enacted the first federal computer crime law in 1984, broadened it considerably in 1986, and then updated it in various ways after that. No two of these statutory schemes are exactly alike, and many of the laws enumerate several distinct crimes in response to different types of misuse. *See generally* Susan W. Brenner, *State Cybercrime Legislation in the United States of America: A Survey*, 7 Rich. J.L. & Tech. 28 (2001).

Despite the differences among the federal and state statutes, the statutory schemes share a number of basic features. The most important is the common building block of unauthorized access to a computer. Every state and the federal government has an unauthorized access statute. This basic offense is usually supplemented by other elements to create additional criminal prohibitions, such as statutes prohibiting computer fraud and computer damage.

To understand modern computer crime law, it is essential to understand the meaning of the basic prohibition on unauthorized access to a computer. The most helpful way to learn about unauthorized access statutes is to focus primarily on the influential federal statute, 18 U.S.C. § 1030. 18 U.S.C. § 1030 is the federal computer misuse statute, sometimes referred to as the Computer Fraud and Abuse Act or CFAA. Section 1030(a) lists seven distinct crimes, most of which are keyed to the basic unauthorized access prohibition.

Oddly, the first of the seven crimes is the least important in practice: § 1030(a)(1) is an extremely narrow statute that prohibits accessing a computer without authorization or exceeding authorized access to obtain classified information to injure the United States or aid a foreign power. Although it is the first in the list of § 1030(a) crimes, it is rarely used.

In contrast, § 1030(a)(2) is one of the most frequently charged sections of § 1030. Section 1030(a)(2) prohibits accessing a computer without authorization or exceeding authorized access and obtaining information. Section 1030(a)(3) is only rarely used, and it applies specifically to United States government computers. The statute prohibits accessing a United States government computer without authorization.

Section 1030(a)(4) is the federal computer fraud statute: it combines the unauthorized access prohibition of § 1030(a)(2) with the basic workings of the wire fraud statute.

Section 1030(a)(5) is the federal computer damage statute. It prohibits both unauthorized damage to a computer and also unauthorized access that results in damage.

Section 1030(a)(6) prohibits computer password trafficking, and is based heavily on the federal credit card fraud statute, 18 U.S.C. § 1029.

Finally, § 1030(a)(7) is an extortion statute, based largely on the federal interstate threat statute, 18 U.S.C. § 875. Section 1030(a)(7) prohibits extorting money or other property using threats to cause damage to computers.

The remaining sections of 18 U.S.C. § 1030 supplement the basic seven crimes in 18 U.S.C. § 1030(a). Section 1030(b) makes clear that attempts are covered by the statute; any attempt to engage in conduct that would be a violation of § 1030(a) if successful is considered a violation of § 1030(b). Section 1030(c) contains the statutory maximum punishments for all of the different §§ 1030(a) and (b) offenses. Section 1030(c) is quite detailed, as Congress chose to treat some § 1030 offenses as misdemeanors, others as felonies with 5-year maximum punishments, and others as more serious felonies. This subsection effectively adds elements to the different § 1030 crimes to trigger felony liability in some circumstances.

Sections 1030(d), 1030(f), and 1030(h) are mostly unimportant for our purposes. They concern jurisdiction, oversight, and create an exception for government investigations in some cases. In contrast, § 1030(e) and § 1030(g) are noteworthy. Section 1030(e) is critical from a doctrinal perspective because it contains statutory definitions of all of the key terms used elsewhere.

Section 1030(g) is important at a conceptual level because it explains much of the shape of existing law. Section 1030(g) provides a civil remedy for some kinds of violations, permitting victims of computer misuse to sue in federal court. Thanks to § 1030(g), most of the published cases interpreting § 1030 arise in the civil context rather than the criminal context.

2. WHAT IS ACCESS?

Now that we have seen the basic framework of two unauthorized access statutes, let's look in depth at the meaning of "access." The prohibition on unauthorized access can be understood at a very general level as a sort of computer trespass crime. The statute focuses on the defendant's rights at the time he accesses the computer. Liability does not hinge on whether we can artificially define some kind of property interest, or whether the computer owner was deprived of some kind of right. Instead, the law monitors the defendant's "access" to the victim computer and then asks whether that access was authorized. But what is "access" to a computer? Consider the following discussion:

> Obviously a computer user does not access a computer by physically getting inside the computer. Some other principle must govern. But what principle should that be? One approach would look at computers from the standpoint of virtual reality, and try to draw analogies between using a computer and entering real property. We could say that access hinges on whether the user has made a virtual entrance into the computer. For example, imagine a user tries to use a password-protected computer network and is confronted by a screen that requires a valid username and password to proceed. We might say that this screen is akin to a lock on a front door, and that entering a username and password is like using a key to open the lock. This approach suggests that a user who enters a valid username and password has accessed the computer, but a user who inputs an incorrect name or password has been denied access.
>
> Similarly, we could say that visiting a publicly accessible website is something like visiting an open store in the physical world.

Determining whether access has occurred then depends on whether visiting an open store can be deemed "entering" in the physical world. The correct answer is not obvious: Visiting a website could be seen as equivalent to viewing a shop window from a public street rather than actually entering the store. But at a conceptual level, the analogy to virtual space provides one heuristic to understand what it means to "access" a computer.

The virtual analogy does not provide the only tool, however. We can also look at the question of access from the standpoint of physical reality, in which we recognize that computers are simply machines that communicate with each other by sending and receiving information. For example, when a user visits a website, the user's computer sends requests to the computer that hosts the website asking the computer to send back computer files; when the files are returned to the user, the user's computer reassembles the files and presents them in the form of a website. If we focus on how computers operate, we can interpret access by looking to whether a user has sent communications that have physically entered the computer. For example, one standard could be that a user accesses a computer when she sends a command to that computer instructing the computer to perform a task, and the computer performs the request as instructed. Another standard could be that a user accesses a computer when the user sends a command requesting information in return and the computer responds by sending back information to the user. In this sense, accessing a computer is no different from simply using a computer.

Notably, physical-world standards and virtual-world standards can produce different outcomes. Imagine a user wishes to log on to a password-protected computer, and sends a request to the computer asking it to send back the page that prompts the user to enter a username and password. The computer complies, sending the page back to the user. This would not access the computer from a virtual perspective, as it would be something like walking up to a locked door but not yet trying the key. From a physical-world perspective, however, the request would be an access; the user sent a command to the computer and received the desired response. Similarly, consider whether sending an e-mail accesses the computers of the recipient's Internet service provider. From a virtual perspective, the answer would seem to be no; a user who sends an e-mail to the ISP does not understand herself to have "entered" the ISP. From a physical perspective, however, the answer seems to be yes; the user has in fact sent a communication to the ISP that its servers received and processed.

Which standard governs? The statutes themselves offer little guidance. Most computer crime statutes (including the federal statute) do not define access, and most statutes that do include a definition shed little light on these questions.

Orin S. Kerr, *Cybercrime's Scope: Interpreting "Access" and "Authorization" in Computer Misuse Statutes,* 78 N.Y.U. L. Rev. 1596, 1619–21 (2003). Consider these questions as you read the following case construing "access" in the context of a state unauthorized access statute.

STATE V. RILEY

Supreme Court of Washington, 1993.
846 P.2d 1365.

GUY, JUSTICE.

Northwest Telco Corporation is a company that provides long distance telephone service. Telco's customers dial a publicly available general access number, then enter an individualized 6-digit access code and the long distance number they wish to call. A computer at Telco's central location then places the call and charges it to the account corresponding to the entered 6-digit code.

On January 9, 1990, Cal Edwards, Director of Engineering at Telco, observed that Telco's general access number was being dialed at regular intervals of approximately 40 seconds. After each dialing, a different 6-digit number was entered, followed by a certain long distance number. Edwards observed similar activity on January 10, between 10 p.m. and 6 a.m. From his past experience, Edwards recognized this activity as characteristic of that of a "computer hacker" attempting to obtain the individualized 6-digit access codes of Telco's customers. Edwards surmised that the hacker was using a computer and modem to dial Telco's general access number, a randomly selected 6-digit number, and a long distance number. Then, by recording which 6-digit numbers enabled the long distance call to be put through successfully, the hacker was able to obtain the valid individual access codes of Telco's customers. The hacker could then use those codes fraudulently to make long distance calls that would be charged improperly to Telco's paying customers.

On January 11, Edwards contacted Toni Ames, a U.S. West security investigator, and requested her assistance in exposing the hacker. In response, Ames established a line trap, which is a device that traces telephone calls to their source. By 3 p.m., Ames had traced the repeated dialing to the home of Joseph Riley in Silverdale, Washington. The dialing continued until 6 a.m. on January 12.

Ames contacted the Kitsap County Prosecutor's Office on January 12, 1990, and was directed to Investigator Richard Kitchen. Kitchen filed an affidavit for a search warrant after interviewing both Ames and Edwards.

On January 16, Kitchen arrived at Riley's house with the search warrant. Prior to executing the search, Kitchen informed Riley of his rights, although Riley was not arrested. Kitchen then questioned Riley about the occupancy of the house to ascertain which occupant was responsible for the hacking. Riley then admitted having attempted to obtain Telco customer access codes. Riley told Kitchen that he had tried to obtain the access codes for 3 days in the past week, but that he was not certain of the specific dates.

Evidence discovered during the subsequent search included four stolen access codes, a computer program that conducted the rapid repeated dialing and entry of random 6-digit numbers, handwritten notes detailing Riley's hacking activity, and a how-to-hack manual.

Riley was later charged with and convicted of two counts of computer trespass against Telco.

Riley contends that his convictions of computer trespass against Telco must be reversed because his conduct—repeatedly dialing Telco's general access number and entering random 6-digit numbers in an attempt to discover access codes belonging to others—does not satisfy the statutory definition of computer trespass. We disagree.

RCW 9A.52.110 provides in relevant part that "a person is guilty of computer trespass in the first degree if the person, without authorization, intentionally gains access to a computer system or electronic data base of another."

Riley contends the telephone company's long distance switch is not a "computer" under RCW 9A.52.110. We reject this contention. The trial court explicitly found that the switch is a computer. This finding was based on unrebutted expert testimony. A trial court's findings of fact will not be disturbed on appeal when they are supported by undisputed evidence.

Riley also argues that acts accomplished by simply dialing the telephone are not encompassed within the statutorily defined crime of computer trespass, and are merely the equivalent of placing a telephone call. He contends he is not guilty of computer trespass because he did not enter, read, insert, or copy data from the telephone system's computer switch.

Riley's acts were not equivalent to placing a telephone call. He used his home computer to dial Telco's general access number and enter random 6-digit numbers representing customer access codes every 40 seconds for several hours at a time. Moreover, RCW 9A.52.110 criminalizes the unauthorized, intentional "access" of a computer system. The term "access" is defined under RCW 9A.52.010(6) as "to approach or otherwise make use of any resources of a computer, directly or by electronic means." Riley's repeated attempts to discover access codes by sequentially entering random 6-digit numbers constitute "approaching" or "otherwise making use of any resources of a computer". The switch is a computer. Long distance calls are processed through the switch. Riley was approaching the switch each time he entered the general access number, followed by a random 6-digit number representing a customer access code, and a destination number. Therefore, Riley's conduct satisfied the statutory definition of "access" and so was properly treated as computer trespass.[5]

NOTES AND QUESTIONS

1. *State v. Allen.* Compare *Riley* to State v. Allen, 917 P.2d 848 (Kan. 1996), which had facts similar to those of *Riley.* Allen used his computer to dial up access numbers of Southwestern Bell, and he then faced the prompts that asked him for a password that would enable him to make free long-distance telephone calls. The access numbers were only supposed to be known to Southwestern Bell employees. There was no direct evidence that Allen had responded to the password prompt. The Kansas Supreme Court held that Allen had not accessed Southwestern Bell's computers:

> Webster's defines "access" as "freedom or ability to obtain or make use of." Webster's New Collegiate Dictionary, p. 7 (1977). This is similar to the construction used by the trial court to find that no evidence showed that Allen had gained access to Southwestern Bell's computers. Until Allen proceeded beyond the initial banner and entered appropriate passwords, he could not be said to have had the ability to make use of Southwestern Bell's computers or obtain anything. Therefore, he cannot be said to have gained access to Southwestern Bell's computer systems as gaining access is commonly understood.

Id. at 114. *Allen* suggests that a person accesses a computer only when she goes beyond the initial prompt and gains the ability to make use of the computer. Put another way, *Allen* requires actually getting "inside" the computer. Merely "knocking on the door" is not enough. This appears to be a virtual reality approach to access, in which access requires a kind of virtual entrance to the machine. Are *Riley* and *Allen* consistent?

2. *Should "access" be defined, and if so, how?* The statutory definition of "access" used by the Washington statute at issue in *Riley* was influenced by an early bill introduced in Congress in 1977, the Federal Computer Systems Protection Act introduced by Senator Ribicoff. S. 1766, 95th Cong. (1977). *See generally* Michael M. Krieger, *Current and Proposed Computer Crime*

---

[5] This interpretation of the statute does not criminalize repeated dialing of a busy telephone number because a computer trespass conviction requires an "intent to commit another crime". RCW 9A.52.110(1)(a). It is not disputed that Riley had such an intent.

Legislation, 2 Computer/L.J. 721, 723 (1980) (compiling legislation). Senator Ribicoff's bill was never enacted by Congress, but it did influence a number of state computer crime statutes. Notably, Congress opted not to define "access" when it enacted 18 U.S.C. § 1030. Do you think it is wise for legislatures to try to define access, or should they leave it up to the courts to decide on a case-by-case basis?

3. *The Supreme Court's guidance on interpreting "access" in 18 U.S.C. § 1030.* The United States Supreme Court recently handed down its first decision interpreting 18 U.S.C. § 1030. *See* Van Buren v. United States, 141 S.Ct. 1648 (2021) (discussed at page 50). Although *Van Buren* was about the meaning of "exceeds authorized access," not the meaning of "access" itself, the Supreme Court offered the following guidance on how to interpret "access":

> When interpreting statutes, courts take note of terms that carry technical meanings. "Access" is one such term, long carrying a "well established" meaning in the "computational sense"—a meaning that matters when interpreting a statute about computers. American Heritage Dictionary 10 (3d ed. 1992). In the computing context, "access" references the act of entering a computer "system itself" or a particular "part of a computer system," such as files, folders, or databases. 1 Oxford English Dictionary 72 (2d ed. 1989) ("to gain access to data, etc., held in a computer or computer-based system, or the system itself"); Random House Dictionary of the English Language 11 (2d ed. 1987) ("Computers. to locate (data) for transfer from one part of a computer system to another."); see also C. Sippl & R. Sippl, Computer Dictionary and Handbook 2 (3d ed. 1980) ("concerns the process of obtaining data from or placing data in storage"); Barnhart Dictionary of New English 2 (3d ed. 1990) ("to retrieve (data) from a computer storage unit or device"); Microsoft Computer Dictionary 12 (4th ed. 1999) ("to gain entry to memory in order to read or write data"); A Dictionary of Computing 5 (6th ed. 2008) ("to gain entry to data, a computer system, etc.").

The Supreme Court's interpretive approach seems to be a sort of 'techie textualism.' When interpreting a term in a statute about computers, you should consider the meaning of the term within the technical community.

How much do these dictionary definitions help define the meaning of access in the CFAA today? The meaning of access may not have seemed a difficult issue in the 1980s when the CFAA was first enacted. Given that computer technologies are different today than they were in the 1980s, how much can these definitions provide answers?

4. *Access in a networked world.* In a world of computer networks, concepts of access have to consider not just one computer, but many. For example, imagine you are at home and you access the Internet from your home computer via your Internet provider. You spend a few minutes surfing the web, and then you intentionally distribute a computer virus as an attachment to an e-mail. Did you "access" your home computer? Your provider's server? Routers

and mailservers that may have transferred your communications in the course of delivery? The webserver that stored the files you retrieved when you were surfing the web? The provider of the person who received your e-mail? The providers of other people who eventually received the virus? *See, e.g.,* Online v. National Health Care Discount, Inc., 121 F. Supp.2d 1255 (N.D. Iowa 2000) ("For purposes of the CFAA, when someone sends an e-mail message from his or her own computer, and the message then is transmitted through a number of other computers until it reaches its destination, the sender is making use of all of those computers, and is therefore "accessing" them."); Moulton v. VC3, No. 1:00CV434-TWT, 2000 WL 33310901, at *7 (N.D. Ga. 2000) (holding that a "port scan," checking to see if a networked computer is responsive at a particular port, does not access the computer scanned).

5.   *Which is better, a virtual approach to access or a physical approach to access?* Should whether a computer is deemed "accessed" depend on whether the virtual equivalent of an entry occurred? Or should the key question be whether communications physically entered the computer to interact with it even if there was no virtual entrance? Scholars have disagreed on the question. The author of these materials has argued in favor of a broad physical approach that would find an access even without a virtual entrance:

> The problem with a narrow construction of access is that individual users interact with computers in countless ways for countless reasons, and it is difficult to carve out a type of interaction that should be exempted entirely from computer misuse laws. A typical computer user might log on to a network using a password, open files stored on a server, surf the web, and send e-mail. If any one of these activities does not constitute an access, then that entire category of activity may be exempted from laws that are designed broadly to prohibit exceeding privileges on a computer.

> Further, the distinctions between different types of use are sufficiently fluid, and the technology of the Internet changes so rapidly, that such distinctions would prove highly unstable and ultimately arbitrary. While a narrow meaning for access may have made sense in the 1970s, today's technologies cannot support it.

> In light of the difficulty of drawing robust and sensible lines between different types of interactions with computers and limiting access to just some of them, the better approach is to allow access to refer broadly to any successful interaction with a computer, no matter how minor.

Orin S. Kerr, *Cybercrime's Scope: Interpreting "Access" and "Authorization" in Computer Misuse Statutes,* 78 N.Y.U. L. Rev. 1596, 1647–48 (2003). In contrast, Professor Bellia has argued in favor of a narrower virtual reality approach to access that would require a virtual entry:

> The narrower reading of "access" is in fact the more natural one. The provisions [of 18 U.S.C. § 1030] clearly contemplate conduct that

involves obtaining information not generally available to the public, including national security information and financial and other records, or conduct that involves access to computers that are nonpublic. Since the information is not available to the public, it is necessarily segregated by code—whether by a password or other technical measure, or by being placed on a system not generally accessible to the public.

Patricia L. Bellia, *Defending Cyberproperty*, 79 N.Y.U. L. Rev. 2164, 2254 (2004). Does the passage from *Van Buren* in Note 3, which came long after this scholarly debate, resolve which interpretation is correct?

6.   *How much does the meaning of access matter if access must also be unauthorized?* Liability under an unauthorized access statute requires more than just access: that access must also be "without authorization" or must "exceed authorized access." The fact that the prohibition on access never stands alone raises the question of how much the definition of access actually matters in practice.

In particular, consider those cases in which a broad physical interpretation of access leads to the conclusion that the computer was accessed, but a narrow virtual interpretation leads to the conclusion that it was not. From a virtual perspective, the computer will not have been accessed because the virtual user was not let "inside." That is, there was no password gate or other barrier that demarcated the entry into the computer. But this same concept can be restated from a physical perspective using concepts of authorization. From a physical perspective, the computer will have been accessed, but there will be no liability because any such access will have been authorized. Any access that is not blocked by a password gate or other barrier is authorized access.

If this is correct, then the definition of access may not be very important. The real work in interpreting the scope of computer misuse statutes may come instead from the meaning of authorization.

3. WHAT IS AUTHORIZATION? THE CASE OF CODE-BASED RESTRICTIONS

Perhaps the most complex issues raised by computer misuse statutes concern authorization. Most computer misuse statutes criminalize unauthorized access to a computer, and some prohibit exceeding authorized access. In contrast, authorized access remains legal. This raises obvious questions. When is access unauthorized? Who can grant the authority to access a computer, and in what circumstances? Given that millions of computer users access millions of computers every day, finding the line between authorized and unauthorized access obviously is quite important.

To understand authorization, it may be useful to identify three basic ways in which access might be unauthorized. Every computer is configured to permit its users to enjoy a set of privileges, and there are three basic ways to set those privileges: by code, by contract, or by social norms. This means that a computer user can engage in computer misuse in three possible ways: by circumventing code-based restrictions, by breaching contract-based restrictions, or by breaching social norms on computer access.

When an owner regulates privileges by code, the owner or her agent designs and programs the computer's hardware and software so that the code limits each user's privileges. Perhaps every user must have an account, and access to that account is protected by a password. This regulates privileges by code because it limits the ability of others to access a particular person's account. For a user to exceed privileges imposed by code, the user must somehow "trick" the computer into giving the user greater privileges. The code creates a barrier designed to limit privileges.

Alternatively, a computer owner or operator may regulate computer privileges by contract. Access to the computer can be conditioned on the user's promise to abide by a set of terms such as Terms of Service for an e-mail account or Terms of Use for a website. Regulation by contract offers a significantly weaker form of regulation than regulation by code. Regulation by code enforces limits on privileges by actually blocking the user from performing the proscribed act, at least absent circumvention.

In contrast, regulation by contract works by conditioning access based on a promise. To borrow a physical-world analogy, the difference between regulation by code and regulation by contract resembles the difference between trying to keep a stranger out by locking the front door, on one hand, and trying to keep a stranger out by putting a sign in front of the open door announcing that strangers may not enter.

Both types of regulatory approaches are familiar to every computer user. For example, imagine that you sign up for Internet service with a local Internet service provider and that the service comes with an e-mail account. Signing up for the service requires you to agree to the ISP's Terms of Service, and also requires you to select a username and password. If you use the account in a way that violates the Terms of Service, you will be breaching a contract-based restriction. You agreed to comply with the ISP's Terms of Service, but you accessed the ISP while violating that agreement. Now imagine that your friend Fred wants to read your e-mail, and successfully guesses your username and password and accesses your account without your permission. In that case, Fred has circumvented a code-based restriction. He has bypassed the password gate that was created to limit access to your account.

Third, computer use might be unauthorized if it violates a social norm on computer use. Social norms are widely shared attitudes that specify what behaviors an actor ought to exhibit. In the context of computer misuse, access might violate a social norm if most computer users would understand that you're not supposed to access the computer in that particular way even if it does not circumvent a code-based restriction or breach an explicit contract-based restriction.

For example, perhaps it is understood that a user is not supposed to use an automated software program to send thousands of web queries in a short period of time to a particular web server, causing the server to slow down considerably. In such a case, social norms may set up an implicit contractual restriction; by accessing the computer in a way contrary to the expectations of most users, the access may be implicitly unauthorized. (This is arguably just a version of regulation by contract, but for our purposes it helps to treat it separately.)

Should circumvention of a code-based restriction make an access "without authorization" or in excess of authorization? How about breach of a contract-based restriction? How about breach of a social norm? The following materials consider these questions, beginning with the relatively straightforward case of code-based restrictions.

UNITED STATES v. MORRIS
United States Court of Appeals for the Second Circuit, 1991.
928 F.2d 504.

JON O. NEWMAN, CIRCUIT JUDGE.

Section 2(d) of the Computer Fraud and Abuse Act of 1986, 18 U.S.C. § 1030(a)(5)(A) (1988), punishes anyone who intentionally accesses without authorization a category of computers known as "federal interest computers" and damages or prevents authorized use of information in such computers, causing loss of $1,000 or more. The issues raised are what satisfies the statutory requirement of "access without authorization."

These questions are raised on an appeal by Robert Tappan Morris from the May 16, 1990, judgment of the District Court for the Northern District of New York convicting him, after a jury trial, of violating 18 U.S.C. § 1030(a)(5)(A). Morris released into INTERNET, a national computer network, a computer program known as a "worm"[2] that spread and multiplied, eventually causing computers at various educational institutions and military sites to "crash" or cease functioning.

---

[2]   In the colorful argot of computers, a "worm" is a program that travels from one computer to another but does not attach itself to the operating system of the computer it "infects." It differs from a "virus," which is also a migrating program, but one that attaches itself to the operating system of any computer it enters and can infect any other computer that uses files from the infected computer.

We conclude that there was sufficient evidence for the jury to conclude that Morris acted "without authorization" within the meaning of section 1030(a)(5)(A). We therefore affirm.

Facts

In the fall of 1988, Morris was a first-year graduate student in Cornell University's computer science Ph.D. program. Through undergraduate work at Harvard and in various jobs he had acquired significant computer experience and expertise. When Morris entered Cornell, he was given an account on the computer at the Computer Science Division. This account gave him explicit authorization to use computers at Cornell. Morris engaged in various discussions with fellow graduate students about the security of computer networks and his ability to penetrate it.

In October 1988, Morris began work on a computer program, later known as the INTERNET "worm" or "virus." The goal of this program was to demonstrate the inadequacies of current security measures on computer networks by exploiting the security defects that Morris had discovered. The tactic he selected was release of a worm into network computers. Morris designed the program to spread across a national network of computers after being inserted at one computer location connected to the network. Morris released the worm into INTERNET, which is a group of national networks that connect university, governmental, and military computers around the country. The network permits communication and transfer of information between computers on the network.

Morris sought to program the INTERNET worm to spread widely without drawing attention to itself. The worm was supposed to occupy little computer operation time, and thus not interfere with normal use of the computers. Morris programmed the worm to make it difficult to detect and read, so that other programmers would not be able to "kill" the worm easily.

Morris also wanted to ensure that the worm did not copy itself onto a computer that already had a copy. Multiple copies of the worm on a computer would make the worm easier to detect and would bog down the system and ultimately cause the computer to crash. Therefore, Morris designed the worm to "ask" each computer whether it already had a copy of the worm. If it responded "no," then the worm would copy onto the computer; if it responded "yes," the worm would not duplicate. However, Morris was concerned that other programmers could kill the worm by programming their own computers to falsely respond "yes" to the question. To circumvent this protection, Morris programmed the worm to duplicate itself every seventh time it received a "yes" response. As it turned out, Morris underestimated the number of times a computer would be asked the question, and his one-out-of-seven ratio resulted in far more copying than he had anticipated. The worm was also designed so that it would be killed when a computer was shut down, an event that typically occurs once every week or two. This would have prevented the worm from accumulating on one computer, had Morris correctly estimated the likely rate of reinfection.

Morris identified four ways in which the worm could break into computers on the network:

(1) through a "hole" or "bug" (an error) in SEND MAIL, a computer program that transfers and receives electronic mail on a computer;

(2) through a bug in the "finger demon" program, a program that permits a person to obtain limited information about the users of another computer;

(3) through the "trusted hosts" feature, which permits a user with certain privileges on one computer to have equivalent privileges on another computer without using a password; and

(4) through a program of password guessing, whereby various combinations of letters are tried out in rapid sequence in the hope that one will be an authorized user's password, which is entered to permit whatever level of activity that user is authorized to perform.

On November 2, 1988, Morris released the worm from a computer at the Massachusetts Institute of Technology. MIT was selected to disguise the fact that the worm came from Morris at Cornell. Morris soon discovered that the worm was replicating and reinfecting machines at a much faster rate than he had anticipated. Ultimately, many machines at locations around the country either crashed or became "catatonic."

When Morris realized what was happening, he contacted a friend at Harvard to discuss a solution. Eventually, they sent an anonymous message from Harvard over the network, instructing programmers how to kill the worm and prevent reinfection. However, because the network route was clogged, this message did not get through until it was too late. Computers were affected at numerous installations, including leading universities, military sites, and medical research facilities. The estimated cost of dealing with the worm at each installation ranged from $200 to more than $53,000.

Morris was found guilty, following a jury trial, of violating 18 U.S.C. § 1030(a)(5)(A). He was sentenced to three years of probation, 400 hours of community service, a fine of $10,050, and the costs of his supervision.

Discussion

Morris argues that there was insufficient evidence to convict him of unauthorized access. Morris was authorized to use computers at Cornell, Harvard, and Berkeley, all of which were on INTERNET. As a result, Morris was authorized to communicate with other computers on the network to send electronic mail (SEND MAIL), and to find out certain information about the users of other computers (finger demon).

[However,] the evidence permitted the jury to conclude that Morris's use of the SEND MAIL and finger demon features constituted access without authorization. Morris's conduct here falls well within the area of unauthorized access. Morris did not use either of those features in any way related to their intended function. He did not send or read mail nor discover information about other users; instead he found holes in both programs that permitted him a special and unauthorized access route into other computers.

Moreover, the jury verdict need not be upheld solely on Morris's use of SEND MAIL and finger demon. As the District Court noted, in denying Morris' motion for acquittal, "the evidence also demonstrated that the worm was designed to spread to other computers at which he had no account and no authority, express or implied, to unleash the worm program. Moreover, there was also evidence that the worm was designed to gain access to computers at which he had no account by guessing their passwords. Accordingly, the evidence did support the jury's conclusion that defendant accessed without authority as opposed to merely exceeding the scope of his authority."

In light of the reasonable conclusions that the jury could draw from Morris's use of SEND MAIL and finger demon, and from his use of the trusted hosts feature and password guessing, his challenge to the sufficiency of the evidence fails.

The District Court decided that it was unnecessary to provide the jury with a definition of "authorization." We agree. Since the word is of common usage, without any technical or ambiguous meaning, the Court was not obliged to instruct the jury on its meaning.

NOTES AND QUESTIONS

1.　*The intended function test.* The *Morris* opinion suggests two ways in which access to a computer can be "without authorization." The first is the intended function test. According to the court, Morris accessed federal interest computers without authorization because he did not use SENDMAIL and finger demon "in any way related to their intended function."

Although the *Morris* court does not provide an elaborate explanation of the intended function test, it appears to derive largely from a sense of social norms in the community of computer users. Under these norms, software designers design programs to perform certain tasks, and network providers enable the programs to allow users to perform those tasks. Providers implicitly authorize users to use their computers to perform the intended functions, but implicitly do not authorize users to exploit weaknesses in the programs that allow them to perform unintended functions. When a user exploits weaknesses in a program and uses a function in an unintended way to access a computer, that access is "without authorization."

How can a court determine the "intended function" of a computer program or command? Should the court seek out its primary author and ask him what function he had in mind when he created it? How should a court determine the purpose of a computer command that is an open source project, such as the finger demon command at issue in *Morris*, and that has no one author?

What level of generality should a court apply to determine the intended function of a computer command? The meaning of the intended function test hinges on this question. For example, is the intended function of e-mail software to send communications generally? Or is its intended function to send communications in the form of e-mail messages, or to send communications in a way that complies with the network provider's Terms of Service? As the intended function of a command or program is described in increasingly specific ways, the scope of criminality that the intended function test creates will expand. Conversely, the more general the function, the narrower the scope of conduct that the intended function test prohibits.

2. *Password guessing.* The *Morris* opinion suggests that gaining access to a computer by correctly guessing or using a stolen password also can constitute access "without authorization." This makes sense: Guessing a password is something like picking a physical lock, and using a stolen password is something like making a copy of the key and using it without the owner's permission. Indeed, bypassing password gates using stolen or guessed passwords is a common way to "hack" into a computer.

3. *The Pulte Homes case. Morris* indicates that circumvention of code-based restrictions to a computer constitutes "access without authorization." But consider the converse question: Does establishing "access without authorization" require circumvention of code-based restrictions?

In Pulte Homes, Inc. v. Laborers' International Union of North America, 648 F.3d 295 (6th Cir. 2011), a union launched a campaign to bombard the telephone and Internet systems of a company that was involved in a labor dispute. According to the complaint, the union, known as the Laborers' International Union of North America (LIUNA), hired an auto-dialing service to place thousands of calls to clog access to the phone system of the company, Pulte Homes. LIUNA also urged its members to send thousands of e-mails that overloaded Pulte Homes' system. Pulte Homes filed a civil suit under 18 U.S.C. § 1030(a)(5)(B)–(C), which prohibits intentionally accessing a computer "without authorization" but does not prohibit merely exceeding authorized access.

The Sixth Circuit concluded that the access to Pulte Homes's computer systems could not be "without authorization" because the Internet and telephone systems were open to be used by the public:

> Because Congress left the interpretation of "without authorization"
> to the courts, we again start with ordinary usage. The plain meaning

of "authorization" is "the conferment of legality; sanction." Commonly understood, then, a defendant who accesses a computer "without authorization" does so without sanction or permission.

In addition, comparing the phrase "without authorization" to another, somewhat similar phrase in the CFAA further informs the proper interpretation. The CFAA criminalizes both accessing a computer "without authorization" and "exceeding authorized access" to a computer. Despite some similarities in phrasing, we must, if possible, give meaning to both prohibitions. We can.

Unlike the phrase "without authorization," the CFAA helpfully defines "exceeds authorized access" as accessing a computer with authorization and using such access to obtain or alter information in the computer that the accesser is not entitled so to obtain or alter." 18 U.S.C. § 1030(e)(6). Under this definition, an individual who is authorized to use a computer for certain purposes but goes beyond those limitations has exceeded authorized access. In contrast, a person who uses a computer without authorization *has no rights, limited or otherwise,* to access the computer in question.

We ask, then, whether LIUNA had *any* right to call Pulte's offices and e-mail its executives. It did—and LIUNA's methods of communication demonstrate why.

LIUNA used unprotected public communications systems, which defeats Pulte's allegation that LIUNA accessed its computers "without authorization." Pulte allows all members of the public to contact its offices and executives: it does not allege, for example, that LIUNA, or anyone else, needs a password or code to call or e-mail its business. Rather, like an unprotected website, Pulte's phone and e-mail systems were open to the public, so LIUNA was authorized to use them. And though Pulte complains of the number, frequency, and content of the communications, it does not even allege that one or several calls or e-mails would have been unauthorized. Its complaint thus amounts—at most—to an allegation that LIUNA exceeded its authorized access.

Because Pulte does not allege that LIUNA possessed *no* right to contact Pulte's offices and its executives, it fails to satisfy one of the elements—access "without authorization"—of its claim.

Id. at 303–04.

4.   *Ending employment as a withdrawal of authorization.* A person who has been given permission to set up and access a computer account has authorization to access the account. The flip side of this principle is that a computer owner can withdraw permission to use the account and render subsequent access without authorization. This doctrine comes up most often in the context of former employees using company accounts. "When the employer has rescinded permission to access the computer and the defendant uses the

computer anyway," that use is an access "without authorization." LVRC Holdings LLC v. Brekka, 581 F.3d 1127 (9th Cir. 2009). Put another way, an employee ordinarily cannot use a company account after being fired from the company.

For example, in United States v. Shahulhameed, 629 Fed.Appx. 685 (6th Cir. 2015), the defendant was an IT contractor for Toyota Motors who was accused of harassment. When managers at Toyota learned of the allegation, they ordered employee Andrew Sell to fire Shahulhameed immediately. Sell called and e-mailed Shahulhameed at around midnight and told him that he was fired and should not report to work the next day or have any future contact with anyone at Toyota. Overnight, Shahulhameed accessed his Toyota Motors account and altered some files in ways that rendered several Toyota servers inoperable. Shahulhameed's account was not disabled until the next morning.

The Sixth Circuit held that Shahulhameed's overnight access to his account was unauthorized:

> Shahulhameed argues that his access was authorized because Toyota did not disable his user account until at least eight hours after his conversation with Andrew Sell. But Toyota's failure to disable his account does not mean that his access was authorized; the phone call and email from Sell are sufficient to establish a lack of authorization. Given the late hour—Sell e-mailed Shahulhameed around midnight—it is not surprising that Toyota waited until the next business day to disable his account. A reasonable jury could have found that Shahulhameed was not authorized to access Toyota's computer systems.

Id. at 688.

5.   *Shared passwords.* It is common for people to share passwords to certain kinds of computer accounts. Abby might buy a Netflix account and share her password with her roommates Barbara and Cathy. If Barbara and Cathy use Abby's username and password to access Abby's Netflix account, is their access authorized because it was with Abby's permission? Or is the access unauthorized because Abby's account was only for Abby's use?

In United States v. Nosal ("Nosal II"), 844 F.3d 1024 (9th Cir. 2016), former employees of a company asked a friend who was a current employee to tell them her username and password so they could use the company's computer network. The current employee did so. The former employees then used the current employee's username and password to access the network and obtain valuable company trade secrets. The Ninth Circuit divided on whether the former employees had authorization to access the company network.

The Ninth Circuit majority ruled that the former employees did not have authorization to access the company network because their authorization rights had been withdrawn when they left the company. The majority ruled that when the former employees left, their access rights to the company's network were cut off. Obtaining the current employee's credentials "blatantly circumvented the affirmative revocation of [the former employees'] computer system access" and amounted to gaining access "through the back door when the front door had been firmly closed." *Id.* at 1029.

Judge Reinhardt dissented. According to Judge Reinhardt, the current employee's permission rendered the access authorized and therefore legal:

> Take the case of an office worker asking a friend to log onto his email in order to print a boarding pass, in violation of the system owner's access policy; or the case of one spouse asking the other to log into a bank website to pay a bill, in violation of the bank's password sharing prohibition. There are other examples that readily come to mind, such as logging onto a computer on behalf of a colleague who is out of the office, in violation of a corporate computer access policy, to send him a document he needs right away.
>
> Was access in these examples authorized? Most people would say "yes." Although the system owners' policies prohibit password sharing, a legitimate account holder "authorized" the access. Thus, the best reading of "without authorization" in the CFAA is a narrow one: a person accesses an account "without authorization" if he does so without having the permission of *either* the system owner *or* a legitimate account holder.

Id. at 1051 (Reinhardt, J., dissenting). In response to the dissent, the majority fired back:

> The dissent frames the question upside down in assuming that permission from [the current employee] is at issue. Under this approach, ignoring reality and practice, an employee could undermine the company's ability to control access to its own computers by willy nilly giving out passwords to anyone outside the company—former employees whose access had been revoked, competitors, industrious hackers or bank robbers who find it less risky and more convenient to access accounts via the Internet rather than through armed robbery.

Id. at 1037.

After *Nosal II*, the legal status of password sharing remains murky. *See generally* Daniel Victor, *As 'Game of Thrones' Returns, Is Sharing Your HBO Password O.K.?* New York Times, July 13, 2017. According to one study, companies that provide streaming video online lost $500 million of revenue to password sharing in 2015. *See id.* At the same time, video streaming companies appear to be in no hurry to pursue civil suits or criminal prosecutions. In 2016, the CEO of Netflix, Reed Hastings, described password sharing as "something [companies] have to learn to live with, because there's so much legitimate password sharing, like you sharing with your spouse, with your kids." The CEO of HBO, Richard Plepler, expressed the view in 2015 that the losses to password sharing were not yet a big enough number to trigger strong action: "Should it become a big number, we will deal with it." *Id.*

Enforcement strategy aside, do the companies have a good case that use of a shared password without the company's permission is an access without authorization?

6.   *Circumventing IP address blocks.* Even if circumventing a code-based restriction ordinarily makes an access unauthorized, that does not answer what counts as circumventing a code-based restriction. In Craigslist v. 3Taps, 964 F. Supp.2d 1178 (N.D. Cal. 2013), the court considered whether circumventing an IP address block makes access to a website unauthorized.

A company named 3Taps aggregated and republished ads from the popular Craigslist website by scraping data from Craigslist. Craigslist responded by sending 3Taps a cease-and-desist letter and by blocking the IP addresses associated with 3Taps' computers. 3Taps continued to access Craigslist by changing the IP addresses by which its computers accessed Craigslist's servers. Craigslist sued 3Taps under the CFAA. In light of "the use of a technological barrier to ban all access," the court ruled, "3Taps' deliberate decision to bypass that barrier and continue accessing the website constituted access 'without authorization' under the CFAA." *Id.* at 1186. The court added:

> IP blocking may be an imperfect barrier to screening out a human being who can change his IP address, but it is a real barrier, and a clear signal from the computer owner to the person using the IP address that he is no longer authorized to access the website.

Id. at n.7. Is this argument persuasive? It is trivially easy for a computer user to circumvent a block of the user's IP address. For example, a person could simply use a virtual private network to come in with a different IP address. Is the right question whether the computer owner sent a signal that access is unwanted or whether the computer owner has imposed a substantial barrier to access?

7.   *Why isn't all access authorized?* Consider the following hypothetical criticism:

> The concept of unauthorized access to a computer is nonsensical. Access to a computer is always authorized. A user can access a computer only if the computer authorizes the user to access it. In fact, what we call computer hacking is really the art of convincing a computer to authorize you to access the computer. When you hack in to a computer, you gain the computer's authorization to access it. Accordingly, all access is authorized.

What does this assume about how authorization to access a computer is granted or denied? What does it assume about *who* has the authority to grant authorized access to a computer?

The High Court of Australia's opinion in Kennison v. Daire, 160 C.L.R. 129 (1986), may help you answer these questions. In *Daire*, a man withdrew $200 from an offline automatic teller machine (ATM) using an expired card from a closed account. Bank employees had programmed their computers to dispense money whenever a person used an ATM card from that bank using a proper password. When the ATMs were offline, however, the machines were programmed to dispense money without checking whether there was money in the relevant account, or even if the account was still open. The defendant in *Daire* intentionally exploited this defect, took $200, and was charged and convicted of larceny. On appeal, he argued that he had not committed larceny because the bank, through the ATM, had consented to him taking the money. The High Court of Australia rejected the argument:

> The fact that the bank programmed the machine in a way that facilitated the commission of a fraud by a person holding a card did not mean that the bank consented to the withdrawal of money by a person who had no account with the bank. It is not suggested that any person, having the authority of the bank to consent to the particular transaction, did so. The machine could not give the bank's consent in fact and there is no principle of law that requires it to be treated as though it were a person with authority to decide and consent. The proper inference to be drawn from the facts is that the bank consented to the withdrawal of up to $200 by a card holder who presented his card and supplied his personal identification number, only if the card holder had an account which was current. It would be quite unreal to infer that the bank consented to the withdrawal by a card holder whose account had been closed.

Id. at 130. Do you agree? How do you know what "the bank" wanted? Who is "the bank," anyway? The person who programmed the bank's computer? The local branch manager? The bank's CEO?

4. WHAT IS AUTHORIZATION? THE CASE OF CONTRACT-BASED RESTRICTIONS

The most controversial applications of the Computer Fraud and Abuse Act involve claims of liability for conduct that does not breach code-based restrictions. In some cases, the conduct only violates a written restriction on access imposed by the owner or operator of the computer. Such restrictions can be called violations of contract-based restrictions, as the written restrictions amount to a kind of contract: The computer owner conditions authorized access on compliance with the written terms.

Should violations of written restrictions on computer access violate the Computer Fraud and Abuse Act? For the most part, the key legal question is whether violating a contract-based restriction "exceeds authorized access." Importantly, this is a defined term under the statute: 18 U.S.C. § 1030(e)(6) defines "exceeds authorized access" as "to access a computer with authorization and to use such access to obtain or alter information in the computer that the accesser is not entitled so to obtain or alter."

VAN BUREN V. UNITED STATES

United States Supreme Court, 2021.
141 S.Ct. 1648.

JUSTICE BARRETT delivered the opinion of the Court.

Nathan Van Buren, a former police sergeant, ran a license-plate search in a law enforcement computer database in exchange for money. Van Buren's conduct plainly flouted his department's policy, which authorized him to obtain database information only for law enforcement purposes. We must decide whether Van Buren also violated the Computer Fraud and Abuse Act of 1986 (CFAA), which makes it illegal "to access a computer with authorization and to use such access to obtain or alter information in the computer that the accesser is not entitled so to obtain or alter."

He did not. This provision covers those who obtain information from particular areas in the computer—such as files, folders, or databases—to which their computer access does not extend. It does not cover those who, like Van Buren, have improper motives for obtaining information that is otherwise available to them.

I

This case stems from Van Buren's time as a police sergeant in Georgia. In the course of his duties, Van Buren crossed paths with a man named Andrew Albo. The deputy chief of Van Buren's department considered Albo to be very volatile and warned officers in the department to deal with him carefully. Notwithstanding that warning, Van Buren developed a friendly relationship with Albo. Or so Van Buren thought when he went to Albo to ask for a personal loan. Unbeknownst to Van Buren, Albo secretly recorded that request and took it to the local sheriff's office, where he complained that Van Buren had sought to shake him down for cash.

The taped conversation made its way to the Federal Bureau of Investigation (FBI), which devised an operation to see how far Van Buren would go for money. The steps were straightforward: Albo would ask Van Buren to search the state law enforcement computer database for a license plate purportedly belonging to a woman whom Albo had met at a local strip club. Albo, no stranger to legal troubles, would tell Van Buren that he wanted to ensure that the woman was not in fact an undercover officer. In return for the search, Albo would pay Van Buren around $5,000.

Things went according to plan. Van Buren used his patrol-car computer to access the law enforcement database with his valid credentials. He searched the database for the license plate that Albo had provided. After obtaining the FBI-created license-plate entry, Van Buren told Albo that he had information to share.

The Federal Government then charged Van Buren with a felony violation of the CFAA on the ground that running the license plate for Albo violated the "exceeds authorized access" clause of 18 U.S.C. § 1030(a)(2).[1] The trial evidence showed that Van Buren had been trained not to use the law enforcement database for an improper purpose, defined as any personal use. Van Buren therefore knew that the search breached department policy. And according to the Government, that violation of department policy also violated the CFAA. Consistent with that position, the Government told the jury that Van Buren's access of the database for a non-law-enforcement purpose violated the CFAA concept against using a computer network in a way contrary to "what your job or policy prohibits." The jury convicted Van Buren, and the District Court sentenced him to 18 months in prison.

Van Buren appealed to the Eleventh Circuit, arguing that the "exceeds authorized access" clause applies only to those who obtain information to which their computer access does not extend, not to those who misuse access that they otherwise have. While several Circuits see the clause Van Buren's way, the Eleventh Circuit is among those that have taken a broader view. Consistent with its Circuit precedent, the panel held that Van Buren had violated the CFAA by accessing the law enforcement database for an inappropriate reason. We granted certiorari to resolve the split in authority regarding the scope of liability under the CFAA's "exceeds authorized access" clause.

II

A. 1

Both Van Buren and the Government raise a host of policy arguments to support their respective interpretations. But we start where we always do: with the text of the statute. Here, the most relevant text is the phrase "exceeds authorized access," which means "to access a computer with authorization and to use such access to obtain . . . information in the computer that the accesser is not entitled so to obtain." § 1030(e)(6).

The parties agree that Van Buren accessed a computer with authorization when he used his patrol-car computer and valid credentials to log into the law enforcement database. They also agree that Van Buren obtained information in the computer when he acquired the license-plate record for Albo. The dispute is whether Van Buren was "entitled so to obtain" the record.

"Entitle" means "to give a title, right, or claim to something." Random House Dictionary of the English Language 649 (2d ed. 1987). See also

---

[1]   Van Buren also was charged with and convicted of honest-services wire fraud. In a separate holding not at issue here, the United States Court of Appeals for the Eleventh Circuit vacated Van Buren's honest-services fraud conviction as contrary to this Court's decision in McDonnell v. United States, 579 U.S. 550 (2016).

Black's Law Dictionary 477 (5th ed. 1979) ("to give a right or legal title to"). The parties agree that Van Buren had been given the right to acquire license-plate information—that is, he was "entitled to obtain" it—from the law enforcement computer database. But was Van Buren "entitled *so* to obtain" the license-plate information, as the statute requires?

Van Buren says yes. He notes that "so," as used in this statute, serves as a term of reference that recalls "the same manner as has been stated" or "the way or manner described." Black's Law Dictionary, at 1246. The disputed phrase "entitled so to obtain" thus asks whether one has the right, in "the same manner as has been stated," to obtain the relevant information. And the only manner of obtaining information already stated in the definitional provision is via a computer one is otherwise authorized to access. Putting that together, Van Buren contends that the disputed phrase—"is not entitled *so* to obtain"—plainly refers to information one is not allowed to obtain *by using a computer that he is authorized to access.* On this reading, if a person has access to information stored in a computer—*e.g.,* in "Folder Y," from which the person could permissibly pull information—then he does not violate the CFAA by obtaining such information, regardless of whether he pulled the information for a prohibited purpose. But if the information is instead located in prohibited "Folder X," to which the person lacks access, he violates the CFAA by obtaining such information.

The Government agrees that the statute uses "so" in the word's term-of-reference sense, but it argues that "so" sweeps more broadly. It reads the phrase "is not entitled *so* to obtain" to refer to information one was not allowed to obtain *in the particular manner or circumstances in which he obtained it.* The manner or circumstances in which one has a right to obtain information, the Government says, are defined by any specifically and explicitly communicated limits on one's right to access information. As the Government sees it, an employee might lawfully pull information from Folder Y in the morning for a permissible purpose—say, to prepare for a business meeting—but unlawfully pull the same information from Folder Y in the afternoon for a prohibited purpose—say, to help draft a resume to submit to a competitor employer.

The Government's interpretation has surface appeal but proves to be a sleight of hand. While highlighting that "so" refers to a "manner or circumstance," the Government simultaneously ignores the definition's further instruction that such manner or circumstance already will "have been stated, asserted, or described." Brief of United States at 18 (quoting Black's Law Dictionary, at 1246; 15 Oxford English Dictionary, at 887). Under the Government's approach, the relevant circumstance—the one rendering a person's conduct illegal—is not identified earlier in the statute. Instead, "so" captures *any* circumstance-based limit appearing *anywhere*— in the United States Code, a state statute, a private agreement, or anywhere else. And while the Government tries to cabin its interpretation by suggesting that any such limit must be specifically and explicitly stated, express, and inherent in the authorization itself, the Government does not identify any textual basis for these guardrails.

Van Buren's account of "so"—namely, that "so" references the previously stated manner or circumstance in the text of § 1030(e)(6) itself—is more plausible than the Government's. "So" is not a free-floating term that provides a hook for any limitation stated anywhere. It refers to a stated, identifiable proposition from the preceding text; indeed, "so" typically represents a word or phrase already employed, thereby avoiding the need for repetition. Myriad federal statutes illustrate this ordinary usage. We agree with Van Buren: The phrase "is not entitled so to obtain" is best read to refer to information that a person is not entitled to obtain by using a computer that he is authorized to access.

2

The Government's primary counterargument is that Van Buren's reading renders the word "so" superfluous. Recall the definition: "to access a computer with authorization and to use such access to obtain . . . information in the computer that the accesser is not entitled *so* to obtain." § 1030(e)(6) (emphasis added). According to the Government, "so" adds nothing to the sentence if it refers solely to the earlier stated manner of obtaining the information through use of a computer one has accessed with authorization. What matters on Van Buren's reading, as the Government sees it, is simply that the person obtain information that he is not entitled to obtain—and that point could be made even if "so" were deleted. By contrast, the Government insists, "so" makes a valuable contribution if it incorporates all of the circumstances that might qualify a person's right to obtain information. Because only its interpretation gives "so" work to do, the Government contends, the rule against superfluity means that its interpretation wins.

But the canon does not help the Government because Van Buren's reading does not render "so" superfluous. As Van Buren points out, without "so," the statute would allow individuals to use their right to obtain information in nondigital form as a defense to CFAA liability. Consider, for example, a person who downloads restricted personnel files he is not entitled to obtain by using his computer. Such a person could argue that he was "entitled to obtain" the information if he had the right to access personnel files through another method (*e.g.,* by requesting hard copies of the files from human resources). With "so," the CFAA forecloses that theory of defense. The statute is concerned with what a person does on a computer; it does not excuse hacking into an electronic personnel file if the hacker could have walked down the hall to pick up a physical copy.

This clarification is significant because it underscores that one kind of entitlement to information counts: the right to access the information by using a computer. That can expand liability, as the above example shows. But it narrows liability too. Without the word "so," the statute could be read to incorporate all kinds of limitations on one's entitlement to information. The dissent's take on the statute illustrates why.

3

While the dissent accepts Van Buren's definition of "so," it would arrive at the Government's result by way of the word "entitled." One is "entitled" to do something, the dissent contends, only when proper grounds are in place. Deciding whether a person was "entitled" to obtain information, the dissent continues, therefore demands a "circumstance dependent" analysis of whether access was proper. This reading, like the Government's, would extend the statute's reach to any circumstance-based limit appearing anywhere.

The dissent's approach to the word "entitled" fares fine in the abstract but poorly in context. The statute does not refer to "information that the accesser is not entitled to obtain." It refers to "information that the accesser is not entitled *so to obtain*." 18 U.S.C. § 1030(e)(6) (emphasis added). The word "entitled," then, does not stand alone, inviting the reader to consider the full scope of the accesser's entitlement to information. The modifying phrase "so to obtain" directs the reader to consider a specific limitation on the accesser's entitlement: his entitlement to obtain the information "in the manner previously stated." And as already explained, the manner previously stated is using a computer one is authorized to access. Thus, while giving lipservice to Van Buren's reading of "so," the dissent, like the Government, declines to give "so" any limiting function.[5]

4

The Government falls back on what it describes as the "common parlance" meaning of the phrase "exceeds authorized access." According to the Government, any ordinary speaker of the English language would think that Van Buren "exceeded his authorized access" to the law enforcement database when he obtained license-plate information for personal purposes. The dissent, for its part, asserts that this point "settles" the case.

If the phrase "exceeds authorized access" were all we had to go on, the Government and the dissent might have a point. But both breeze by the CFAA's explicit definition of the phrase "exceeds authorized access." When "a statute includes an explicit definition" of a term, we must follow that

---

[5] For the same reason, the dissent is incorrect when it contends that our interpretation reads the additional words "under any possible circumstance" into the statute. Our reading instead interprets the phrase "so to obtain" to incorporate the single "circumstance" of permissible information access identified by the statute: obtaining the information by using one's computer.

definition, even if it varies from a term's ordinary meaning. So the relevant question is not whether Van Buren exceeded his authorized access but whether he exceeded his authorized access *as the CFAA defines that phrase*. And as we have already explained, the statutory definition favors Van Buren's reading.

B

While the statute's language spells trouble for the Government's position, a wider look at the statute's structure gives us even more reason for pause.

The interplay between the "without authorization" and "exceeds authorized access" clauses of subsection (a)(2) is particularly probative. Those clauses specify two distinct ways of obtaining information unlawfully. *First*, an individual violates the provision when he "accesses a computer without authorization." *Second*, an individual violates the provision when he "exceeds authorized access" by accessing a computer "with authorization" and then obtaining information he is "not entitled so to obtain." Van Buren's reading places the provision's parts into an harmonious whole. The Government's does not.

Start with Van Buren's view. The "without authorization" clause, Van Buren contends, protects computers themselves by targeting so-called outside hackers—those who "access a computer without any permission at all." LVRC Holdings LLC v. Brekka, 581 F.3d 1127, 1133 (C.A.9 2009). Van Buren reads the "exceeds authorized access" clause to provide complementary protection for certain information within computers. It does so, Van Buren asserts, by targeting so-called inside hackers—those who access a computer with permission, but then exceed the parameters of authorized access by entering an area of the computer to which that authorization does not extend.

Van Buren's account of subsection (a)(2) makes sense of the statutory structure because it treats the "without authorization" and "exceeds authorized access" clauses consistently. Under Van Buren's reading, liability under both clauses stems from a gates-up-or-down inquiry—one either can or cannot access a computer system, and one either can or cannot access certain areas within the system.[8] And reading both clauses to adopt a gates-up-or-down approach aligns with the computer-context understanding of access as entry.[9]

---

[8] For present purposes, we need not address whether this inquiry turns only on technological (or "code-based") limitations on access, or instead also looks to limits contained in contracts or policies.

[9] Van Buren's gates-up-or-down reading also aligns with the CFAA's prohibition on password trafficking. Enacted alongside the "exceeds authorized access" definition in 1986, the password-trafficking provision bars the sale of "any password or similar information through which a computer may be accessed without authorization." § 1030(a)(6). The provision thus contemplates a "specific type of authorization—that is, authentication," which turns on whether a

By contrast, the Government's reading of the "exceeds authorized access" clause creates inconsistencies with the design and structure of subsection (a)(2). As discussed, the Government reads the "exceeds authorized access" clause to incorporate purpose-based limits contained in contracts and workplace policies. Yet the Government does not read such limits into the threshold question whether someone uses a computer "without authorization"—even though similar purpose restrictions, like a rule against personal use, often govern one's right to access a computer in the first place. Thus, the Government proposes to read the first phrase "without authorization" as a gates-up-or-down inquiry and the second phrase "exceeds authorized access" as one that depends on the circumstances. The Government does not explain why the statute would prohibit accessing computer information, but not the computer itself, for an improper purpose.[10]

The Government's position has another structural problem. Recall that violating § 1030(a)(2), the provision under which Van Buren was charged, also gives rise to civil liability. See § 1030(g). Provisions defining "damage" and "loss" specify what a plaintiff in a civil suit can recover. "Damage," the statute provides, means "any impairment to the integrity or availability of data, a program, a system, or information." § 1030(e)(8). The term "loss" likewise relates to costs caused by harm to computer data, programs, systems, or information services. § 1030(e)(11). The statutory definitions of "damage" and "loss" thus focus on technological harms—such as the corruption of files—of the type unauthorized users cause to computer systems and data. Limiting "damage" and "loss" in this way makes sense in a scheme aimed at preventing the typical consequences of hacking. The term's definitions are ill fitted, however, to remediating "misuse" of sensitive information that employees may permissibly access using their computers. Van Buren's situation is illustrative: His run of the license plate did not impair the integrity or availability of data, nor did it otherwise harm the database system itself.

---

user's credentials allow him to proceed past a computer's access gate, rather than on other, scope-based restrictions. Bellia, A Code-Based Approach to Unauthorized Access Under the Computer Fraud and Abuse Act, 84 Geo. Wash. L. Rev. 1442, 1470 (2016); cf. A Dictionary of Computing, at 30 (defining "authorization" as a "process by which users, having completed an authentication stage, gain or are denied access to particular resources based on their entitlement").

[10] Unlike the Government, the dissent would read both clauses of subsection (a)(2) to require a circumstance-specific analysis. Doing so, the dissent contends, would reflect that property law generally protects against both unlawful entry *and* unlawful use. This interpretation suffers from structural problems of its own. Consider the standard rule prohibiting the use of one's work computer for personal purposes. Under the dissent's approach, an employee's computer access would be *without* authorization if he logged on to the computer with the purpose of obtaining a file for personal reasons. In that event, obtaining the file would not violate the "exceeds authorized access" clause, which applies only when one accesses a computer "*with* authorization." § 1030(e)(6). The dissent's reading would therefore leave the "exceeds authorized access" clause with no work to do much of the time—an outcome that Van Buren's interpretation (and, for that matter, the Government's) avoids.

III

To top it all off, the Government's interpretation of the statute would attach criminal penalties to a breathtaking amount of commonplace computer activity. Van Buren frames the far-reaching consequences of the Government's reading as triggering the rule of lenity or constitutional avoidance. That is not how we see it: Because the text, context, and structure support Van Buren's reading, neither of these canons is in play. Still, the fallout underscores the implausibility of the Government's interpretation. It is extra icing on a cake already frosted.

If the "exceeds authorized access" clause criminalizes every violation of a computer-use policy, then millions of otherwise law-abiding citizens are criminals. Take the workplace. Employers commonly state that computers and electronic devices can be used only for business purposes. So on the Government's reading of the statute, an employee who sends a personal e-mail or reads the news using her work computer has violated the CFAA. Or consider the Internet. Many websites, services, and databases authorize a user's access only upon his agreement to follow specified terms of service. If the "exceeds authorized access" clause encompasses violations of circumstance-based access restrictions on employers' computers, it is difficult to see why it would not also encompass violations of such restrictions on website providers' computers. And indeed, numerous *amici* explain why the Government's reading of subsection (a)(2) would do just that—criminalize everything from embellishing an online-dating profile to using a pseudonym on Facebook.

In response to these points, the Government posits that other terms in the statute—specifically "authorization" and "use"—may well serve to cabin its prosecutorial power. Yet the Government stops far short of endorsing such limitations. Nor does it cite any prior instance in which it has read the statute to contain such limitations—to the contrary, Van Buren cites instances where it hasn't. If anything, the Government's current CFAA charging policy shows why Van Buren's concerns are far from hypothetical. The policy instructs that federal prosecution "*may not be warranted*"—not that it would be prohibited—"if the defendant exceeds authorized access solely by violating an access restriction contained in a contractual agreement or term of service with an Internet service provider or website."[12] And while the Government insists that the intent requirement serves as yet another safety valve, that requirement would do nothing for those who intentionally use their computers in a way their job

---

[12] Memorandum from U. S. Atty. Gen. to U. S. Attys. & Assistant Attys. Gen. for the Crim. & Nat. Security Divs., Intake and Charging Policy for Computer Crime Matters 5 (Sept. 11, 2014), https://www.justice.gov/criminal-ccips/file/904941/download. Although the Government asserts that it has historically prosecuted only core conduct like Van Buren's and not the commonplace violations that Van Buren fears, the contrary examples Van Buren and his *amici* cite give reason to balk at that assurance.

or policy prohibits—for example, by checking sports scores or paying bills at work.

One final observation: The Government's approach would inject arbitrariness into the assessment of criminal liability. The Government concedes, as it must, that the "exceeds authorized access" clause prohibits only unlawful information access, not downstream information misuse. But the line between the two can be thin on the Government's reading. Because purpose-based limits on access are often designed with an eye toward information misuse, they can be expressed as either access or use restrictions. For example, one police department might prohibit *using a confidential database* for a non-law-enforcement purpose (an access restriction), while another might prohibit *using information from the database* for a non-law-enforcement purpose (a use restriction). Conduct like Van Buren's can be characterized either way, and an employer might not see much difference between the two. On the Government's reading, however, the conduct would violate the CFAA only if the employer phrased the policy as an access restriction. An interpretation that stakes so much on a fine distinction controlled by the drafting practices of private parties is hard to sell as the most plausible.

IV

In sum, an individual "exceeds authorized access" when he accesses a computer with authorization but then obtains information located in particular areas of the computer—such as files, folders, or databases—that are off limits to him. The parties agree that Van Buren accessed the law enforcement database system with authorization. The only question is whether Van Buren could use the system to retrieve license-plate information. Both sides agree that he could. Van Buren accordingly did not exceed authorized access to the database, as the CFAA defines that phrase, even though he obtained information from the database for an improper purpose. We therefore reverse the contrary judgment of the Eleventh Circuit and remand the case for further proceedings consistent with this opinion.

JUSTICE THOMAS, with whom THE CHIEF JUSTICE and JUSTICE ALITO join, dissenting.

Both the common law and statutory law have long punished those who exceed the scope of consent when using property that belongs to others. A valet, for example, may take possession of a person's car to park it, but he cannot take it for a joyride. The Computer Fraud and Abuse Act extends that principle to computers and information. The Act prohibits exceeding the scope of consent when using a computer that belongs to another person. Specifically, it punishes anyone who "intentionally accesses a computer without authorization or exceeds authorized access, and thereby obtains" information from that computer. 18 U.S.C. § 1030(a)(2).

The question here is straightforward: Would an ordinary reader of the English language understand Van Buren to have "exceeded authorized access" to the database when he used it under circumstances that were expressly forbidden? In my view, the answer is yes. The necessary precondition that permitted him to obtain that data was absent.

For purposes of this appeal, it is agreed that Van Buren was authorized to log into a government database and that he used his entry to obtain fake license-plate information from that database. I thus agree with the majority that this case turns on whether Van Buren was "entitled so to obtain" the fake license-plate information. I also agree that "so" asks whether Van Buren had a right to obtain that information through the means identified earlier in the definition: (1) accessing a computer with authorization and (2) using that access to obtain information in the computer. In other words, Van Buren's conduct was legal only if he was entitled to obtain that specific license-plate information by using his admittedly authorized access to the database.

He was not. A person is entitled to do something only if he has a right to do it. Black's Law Dictionary 477 (5th ed. 1979). Van Buren never had a right to use the computer to obtain the specific license-plate information. Everyone agrees that he obtained it for personal gain, not for a valid law enforcement purpose. And without a valid law enforcement purpose, he was *forbidden* to use the computer to obtain that information.

Entitlements are necessarily circumstance dependent; a person is entitled to do something only when "proper grounds" or facts are in place. Black's Law Dictionary, at 477. Focusing on the word "so," the majority largely avoids analyzing the term "entitled," concluding at the outset in a single sentence that Van Buren *was* entitled to obtain this license-plate information. But the plain meaning of "entitled" compels the opposite conclusion. Because Van Buren lacked a law enforcement purpose, the proper grounds did not exist. He was not entitled to obtain the data when he did so.

A few real-world scenarios illustrate the point. An employee who is entitled to pull the alarm in the event of a fire is not entitled to pull it for some other purpose, such as to delay a meeting for which he is unprepared. A valet who obtains a car from a restaurant patron is—to borrow the language from § 1030(e)(6)—entitled to access the car and entitled to use such access to park and retrieve it. But he is not entitled to use such access to joyride. And, to take an example closer to this statute, an employee of a car rental company may be entitled to access a computer showing the GPS location history of a rental car and use such access to locate the car if it is reported stolen. But it would be unnatural to say he is entitled to use such access to stalk his ex-girlfriend.

The majority offers no real response. It notes that "entitled" is modified by "so" and that courts must therefore consider whether a person is entitled to use a computer to obtain information. But if a person is not entitled to obtain information *at all*, it necessarily follows that he has no right to access the information by using a computer. Van Buren was not entitled to obtain this information at all because the condition precedent needed to trigger an entitlement—a law enforcement purpose—was absent.

Next, the majority's reading is at odds with basic principles of property law. By now, it is well established that information contained in a computer is property. Nobody doubts, for example, that a movie stored on a computer is intellectual property. Federal and state law routinely define property to include computer data. And even the majority acknowledges that this statute is designed to protect property. Yet it fails to square its interpretation with the familiar rule that an entitlement to use another person's property is circumstance specific.

Consider trespass. When a person is authorized to enter land and entitled to use that entry for one purpose but does so for another, he trespasses. What is true for land is also true in the computer context; if a company grants permission to an employee to use a computer for a specific purpose, the employee has no authority to use it for other purposes.

Consider, too, the common understanding of theft. A person who is authorized to possess property for a limited purpose commits theft the moment he exercises unlawful control over it, which occurs whenever consent or authority is exceeded. ALI, Model Penal Code § 223.2(1) (1980). To again borrow the language from § 1030(e)(6), a police officer may have authority to access the department's bank account and use such access to cover law enforcement expenses, but he is nonetheless guilty of embezzlement if he uses such access to line his pockets. He would not be exonerated simply because he would be entitled so to obtain funds from the account under other circumstances.

Unable to square its interpretation with established principles of property law, the majority contends that its interpretation is more harmonious with a separate clause in the statute that forbids accessing a computer without authorization. In the majority's telling, this clause requires "a gates-up-or-down inquiry—one either can or cannot access a computer system," so it makes sense to read the "exceeds authorized access" clause in the same sentence to include the same approach.

I agree that the two clauses should be read harmoniously, but there is no reason to believe that if the gates are up in a single instance, then they must remain up indefinitely. An employee who works with sensitive defense information may generally have authority to log into his employer-issued laptop while away from the office. But if his employer instructs him not to log in while on a trip to a country where network connections cannot be trusted, he accesses the computer without authorization if he logs in anyway. For both clauses, discerning whether the gates are up or down requires considering the circumstances that cause the gates to move.

The majority ends with policy arguments. Concerned about criminalizing a "breathtaking amount of commonplace computer activity," the majority says that the way people use computers today "underscores the implausibility of the Government's interpretation." But statutes are read according to their ordinary meaning at the time Congress enacted the statute. The majority's reliance on modern-day uses of computers to determine what was plausible in the 1980s wrongly assumes that Congress in 1984 was aware of how computers would be used in 2021.

I also would not so readily assume that my interpretation would automatically cover so much conduct. Many provisions plausibly narrow the statute's reach. For example, the statute includes the strict *mens rea* requirement that a person must intentionally exceed authorized access. The statute thus might not apply if a person *believes* he is allowed to use the computer a certain way because, for example, that kind of behavior is common and tolerated. The Act also concerns only obtaining or altering information *in* the computer, not using the Internet to check sports scores stored in some distant server (*i.e.*, a different computer). The majority does not deny that many provisions plausibly narrow the focus of this statute. It simply faults the government for not arguing the point more forcefully. I would not give so much weight to the hypothetical concern that the Government *might* start charging innocuous conduct and that courts *might* interpret the statute to cover that conduct.

The majority's argument also proves too much. Much of the Federal Code criminalizes common activity. Absent aggravating factors, the penalty for violating this Act is a misdemeanor. This Act thus penalizes mine-run offenders about as harshly as federal law punishes a person who removes a single grain of sand from the National Mall; breaks a lamp in a Government building; or permits a horse to eat grass on federal land. The number of federal laws and regulations that trigger criminal penalties may be as high as several hundred thousand. It is understandable to be uncomfortable with so much conduct being criminalized, but that discomfort does not give us authority to alter statutes.

In the end, the Act may or may not cover a wide array of conduct because of changes in technology that have occurred since 1984. But the text makes one thing clear: Using a police database to obtain information in circumstances where that use is expressly forbidden is a crime. I respectfully dissent.

NOTES AND QUESTIONS

1. *What counts as a closed "gate" that makes an area "off limits"?* The majority opinion in *Van Buren* states that liability under the CFAA hinges on a "gates-up-or-down inquiry." A person accesses a computer without authorization when he enters a computer that is "off limits to him," and he exceeds authorized access when he enters "particular areas of the computer— such as files, folders, or databases—that are off limits to him." But what counts as a "gate" that is "down" under this inquiry? How do you know what makes access to a particular computer or area of the computer "off limits"?

On one hand, some language in *Van Buren* suggests liability normally will require breaching some sort of code-based restriction. The majority refers to the statute as "a scheme aimed at preventing the typical consequences of hacking," and agrees that access without authorization targets "outside hackers" while exceeding authorized access targets "inside hackers." Further, Footnote 9 suggests that liability might hinge on authentication, "which turns on whether a user's credentials allow him to proceed."

On the other hand, some language in *Van Buren* suggests that CFAA liability might extend beyond breaching code-based restrictions to some kind of contractual or policy restrictions. In particular, Footnote 8 leaves the point unresolved: It states that "for present purposes, we need not address whether this inquiry turns only on technological (or 'code-based') limitations on access, or instead also looks to limits contained in contracts or policies."

2. *The case of the curious law firm associate.* Chris Curious is a law firm associate. One of the firm's clients is a famous actor named Hom Tanks. As a firm employee, Chris has technological access to confidential client information on the law firm's server. But Chris has been told, in no uncertain terms, that he is only permitted to access client information on cases and matters for which he has been formally assigned. Any access to folders from other matters is strictly prohibited. Chris has not been assigned to any matter for Hom Tanks, but Chris loves every Hom Tanks movie and wants to know more about him. In a moment of weakness, Chris looks through the Tanks client files stored on the firm server. Under *Van Buren*, has Chris violated the CFAA?

3. *The policy question.* As a matter of policy, should it be a crime to intentionally violate express conditions of access to a computer? Consider the following scenarios:

A. A government employee who has access to a sensitive national security database that he is expressly permitted to use only for official government business instead uses the database in order to collect private data and sell it to the Chinese government.

B. A Social Security Administration employee who has access to a Social Security database that he is only permitted to use for official reasons instead uses the database just to check out private information on friends and others for purely personal reasons.

C.   An associate of a consulting company who is told that he can only access his employer's computer files for work-related reasons instead looks through the employer's files because he is thinking of leaving to start a competitor business and is looking for ideas of future clients and services.

D.   A city employee who is told that he can only access the city's computer for work-related reasons instead spends five minutes a day surfing the Internet for pornography.

E.   A mother who signs up for a MySpace account that the Terms of Service condition on being entirely truthful in setting up a profile instead lies on the profile and uses the MySpace account anyway.

F.   A law student who is forbidden by law school policy to access the law school network during class intentionally violates the rule by checking his e-mail during a particularly boring lecture.

G.   You receive an e-mail from a friend that a new website, www.dontvisitme.com, has some incredible pictures posted that you must see. But there's a catch: The Terms of Service of the website clearly and unambiguously say that no one is allowed to visit the website. You want to see the pictures anyway and visit the website from your home Internet connection.

H.   A political blog announces a new rule that readers only are allowed to visit the blog if they plan to vote Republican in the next Presidential election. A reader who plans to vote for the Democratic nominee visits the blog in violation of the rule.

As a matter of policy, which of these eight scenarios describe conduct that should be a crime? Based on your answer, what is the most desirable interpretation of "exceeds authorized access"? Is criminal liability for breaching contract-based restrictions consistent with the theories of punishment? Is breaching a contractual restriction on access always or often a morally culpable act that demands punishment from a retributive perspective? Is it always or often a harmful act that the law should attempt to deter? Or does that depend on the nature of the restriction?

4.   *The MySpace Suicide Case: United States v. Drew.* Footnote 12 of *Van Buren* refers to examples of criminal prosecutions brought under the government's broad interpretation of the CFAA. The best-known such case is United States v. Drew, 259 F.R.D. 449 (C.D. Cal. 2009), sometimes known as the 'MySpace Suicide Case.'

The Drew prosecution started with a terrible tragedy in a suburb of St. Louis, Missouri. In October 2006, a 13-year-old girl named Megan Meier committed suicide. Meier had regularly used the social media networking site MySpace, a then-popular forerunner to today's Facebook. In the weeks before her death, Meier had communicated with a MySpace profile of what appeared to be a handsome 16-year-old boy named Josh Evans. The Evans account had befriended Meier, and Evans expressed his admiration and affection for Meier.

But the online friendship soured. In messages sent soon before Meier committed suicide, Evans had abruptly ended the relationship. According to one witness, the last message Evans had sent to Meier had said, "You're a shitty person, and the world would be a better place without you in it." Lauren Collins, *Friend Game*, The New Yorker, Jan. 13, 2008.

An investigation into Meier's suicide revealed that Josh Evans did not exist. The account was fake. It had been created by a group that knew Meier and used it to learn what Meier was saying about her friend Sarah Drew. The senior member of the group was Sarah's mother, Lori Drew. Other participants included Ashley Grills, an 18-year-old employee of Mrs. Drew who actually devised the idea and used the account, and Sarah Drew herself. See Kim Zetter, *Government's Star Witness Stumbles: MySpace Hoax Was Her Idea, Not Drew's*, Wired, Nov. 20, 2008.

The Evans hoax became a national news story. Media coverage focused on Lori Drew's role. Many were outraged that Drew had not been charged with causing Meier's death. *See, e.g.,* Christopher Maag, *A Hoax Turned Fatal Draws Anger But No Charges*, N.Y. Times, Nov. 28, 2007. Despite intense public demand to punish Drew, Missouri state prosecutors declined to file charges after concluding that Drew had not committed any crime.

Federal prosecutors in Los Angeles were more creative. They realized that MySpace had expansive terms of service. By using MySpace, the terms stated, "you represent and warrant that . . . all registration information you submit is truthful and accurate" and that "you will maintain the accuracy of such information." *Drew*, 259 F.R.D. at 454. Using an account with a fake name and picture account violated MySpace's terms of service. According to the prosecution, this rendered every use of the Evans account an unauthorized access in violation of 18 U.S.C. § 1030(a)(2). And the case could be brought in Los Angeles because MySpace's computer servers were in Los Angeles County even though all of the people involved were in Missouri.

A federal grand jury in the Central District of California returned a four-count felony indictment against Drew. The indictment charged her with conspiring to violate MySpace's terms of service as well as aiding and abetting terms-of-service violations on three specific dates when the Evans account was used. Each terms-of-service violation was a felony, the indictment charged, because it furthered a tortious act under 18 U.S.C. § 1030(c)(2)(B)—specifically, intentional infliction of emotional distress.

The trial of Lori Drew lasted five days in federal court in Los Angeles. In an unusual move, the United States Attorney himself personally led the prosecution. Ashley Grills testified for the government under an immunity agreement. The jury deadlocked on the conspiracy count, and it acquitted on the felony counts based on intentional infliction of emotional distress. However, the jury convicted Drew of three misdemeanor counts of § 1030(a)(2) for aiding and abetting the violation of MySpace's terms of service. The jury foreperson later explained in a media interview that the jury had acquitted on the felony counts because it lacked evidence of Drew's intent to inflict emotional distress. At the same time, the foreperson viewed the terms-of-service violations alone as serious wrongs, at least in the "gross circumstances of someone killing themselves." Kim Zetter, *Jurors Wanted to Convict Lori Drew of Felonies, But Lacked Evidence*, Wired, Dec. 1, 2008.

The government's sentencing memorandum asked the court to impose the statutory maximum prison sentence: 36 months, consisting of one year for each use of the Evans account that Drew aided and abetted. *See* Sentencing Memorandum of the United States, United States v. Drew, 2009 WL 1269549 (C.D. Cal.). The District Court never sentenced Drew, however, because the court granted the defendant's motion to dismiss on the ground that construing the CFAA to cover MySpace's terms of service would render the statute void for vagueness. *See Drew*, 259 F.R.D. at 464. The prosecution filed a notice of appeal but later withdrew it, ending the case in the district court.

5.   *Access after receiving a cease-and-desist letter, Part 1: The Power Ventures case.* Under *Van Buren*, access that violates computer use policies does not violate the CFAA. But does the same principle apply when written notice is provided in the form of a cease-and-desist letter? A cease-and-desist letter is a formal letter, usually drafted by an attorney, requesting that the recipient stop doing something that the sender believes is unlawful. If a website owner's lawyer drafts such a letter and tells the recipient to stop visiting the website, is subsequent access without authorization?

Put another way, is there a legal difference between visiting a computer despite posted website terms of use that tell a visitor that he lacks permission to access the computer and visiting a computer despite a cease-and-desist letter that communicates that same message? In the language of *Van Buren*, does a cease-and-desist letter put "down" the "gate," rendering access "off limits"?

In Facebook v. Power Ventures, 844 F.3d 1058 (9th Cir. 2016), Power Ventures ("Power") had created a service that aggregated social media information for Internet users. Users who subscribed to the service authorized Power to access their social media accounts and to make their social media accounts all available and accessible at Power.com. Facebook objected to the use of Power's service by Facebook account holders. Facebook sent a cease-and-desist letter to Power explaining that Power's access to Facebook's website violated Facebook's terms of service. Facebook eventually sued Power under the CFAA for continuing to access its users' Facebook accounts after receiving Facebook's cease-and-desist letter.

The Ninth Circuit held that accessing Facebook after receiving the cease-and-desist letter was unauthorized and therefore violated the CFAA:

> Here, initially, Power users arguably gave Power permission to use Facebook's computers to disseminate messages. Power reasonably

could have thought that consent from Facebook users to share the promotion was permission for Power to access Facebook's computers. In clicking the "Yes, I do!" button, Power users took action akin to allowing a friend to use a computer or to log on to an e-mail account. Because Power had at least arguable permission to access Facebook's computers, it did not initially access Facebook's computers "without authorization" within the meaning of the CFAA.

But Facebook expressly rescinded that permission when Facebook issued its written cease and desist letter to Power. Facebook's cease and desist letter informed Power that it had violated Facebook's terms of use and demanded that Power stop soliciting Facebook users' information, using Facebook content, or otherwise interacting with Facebook through automated scripts.

Id. at 1067.

Is that approach consistent with *Van Buren*? *Power Ventures* preceded *Van Buren* by five years, so the *Power Ventures* court did not directly address that question. However, in a precedent already on the books at the time, United States v. Nosal, 676 F.3d 854 (9th Cir. 2012) ("*Nosal I*"), the Ninth Circuit had adopted the view later adopted by the Supreme Court in *Van Buren* that violating terms of use does not violate the CFAA. *Power Ventures* distinguished *Nosal I* in the following way:

First, *Nosal I* involved employees of a company who arguably exceeded the limits of their authorization. Here, by contrast, Facebook explicitly revoked authorization for any access, and this case does not present the more nuanced question of exceeding authorization. *Nosal I* involved a defendant who "exceeded authorization," while this case involves a defendant who accessed a computer "without authorization."

Second, although *Nosal I* makes clear that violation of the terms of use of a website cannot itself constitute access without authorization, this case does not involve non-compliance with terms and conditions of service. Facebook and Power had no direct relationship, and it does not appear that Power was subject to any contractual terms that it could have breached.

Finally, *Nosal I* was most concerned with transforming otherwise innocuous behavior into federal crimes simply because a computer is involved. It aimed to prevent criminal liability for computer users who might be unaware that they were committing a crime. But, in this case, Facebook clearly notified Power of the revocation of access, and Power intentionally and admittedly refused to comply. *Nosal I*'s concerns about overreaching or an absence of culpable intent simply do not apply here, where an individualized cease-and-desist letter is a far cry from the permission skirmishes that ordinary Internet users may face.

> Accordingly, we hold that, after receiving the cease and desist letter from Facebook, Power intentionally accessed Facebook's computers knowing that it was not authorized to do so, making Power liable under the CFAA.

Id. at 1068–69.

Are you persuaded? Does this reasoning survive *Van Buren*? More broadly, what exactly is the difference between a posted term on a website or an express condition of employment and a written direction in a cease-and-desist letter? *Power Ventures* focused on the difference in intent: Although people might not realize they are violating terms of service, it is much harder to miss a stern warning in a formal cease-and-desist letter. Notably, however, that concern is already addressed by a different element of the CFAA. To violate the CFAA, a person must intentionally access a computer without authorization or intentionally exceed authorized access. Given that the statute expressly requires intent in addition to lack of authorization, why should possible differences in intent determine whether access is unauthorized?

6.   *Creating fictitious user accounts to view nonpublic information in violation of terms of service.* Imagine a website allows anyone to register for an account, and to then view nonpublic information, on the condition, expressed in the terms of service, that they must provide their real names when they register the account. Does an act of creating and then using an account with a fake name in violation of the terms of service violate the CFAA? In the language of *Van Buren*, is the gate "up" because anyone can create an account? Or is the gate "down" because a username and password is needed to view the information and accounts are only supposed to be given to those who register using their real names?

In Sandvig v. Sessions, 315 F. Supp.3d 1 (D.D.C. 2018), a group of researchers created fictitious accounts on public websites in violation of their terms of service. The researchers used the accounts to access information that was only available to those with an account. Judge Bates concluded that creating fictitious user accounts could exceed authorized access:

> Unlike plaintiffs' other conduct, which occurs on portions of websites that any visitor can view, creating false accounts allows [a computer user] to access information on those sites that is both limited to those who meet the owners' chosen authentication requirements and targeted to the particular preferences of the user. Creating false accounts and obtaining information through those accounts would therefore [be a prohibited act of exceeding authorized access.]

Id. at 27.

5.   WHAT IS AUTHORIZATION? THE CASE OF NORMS-BASED RESTRICTIONS

Should misuse of a computer render access to that computer unauthorized even if it neither circumvents a code-based restriction nor breaches an explicit restriction? Are there some types of computer use that are simply understood as sufficiently out of bounds or contrary to the computer owner's interests that such access should be deemed in excess of authorization? If so, it might be considered a norms-based approach to authorization. Access that violates generally understood social norms on normal or reasonable computer access might render that access without authorization or in excess of authorization. Does the CFAA recognize a norms-based theory of liability? Should it?

EF CULTURAL TRAVEL BV v. ZEFER CORP.

United States Court of Appeals for the First Circuit, 2003.
318 F.3d 58.

BOUDIN, CIRCUIT JUDGE.

Defendant Zefer Corporation seeks review of a preliminary injunction prohibiting it from using a "scraper tool" to collect pricing information from the website of plaintiff EF Cultural Travel BV. This court earlier upheld the injunction against co-defendant Explorica, Inc. *EF Cultural Travel BV v. Explorica, Inc.*, 274 F.3d 577 (1st Cir. 2001) ("*EF I*"). The validity of the injunction as applied to Zefer was not addressed because Zefer's appeal was stayed when it filed for bankruptcy, but the stay has now been lifted.

EF and Explorica are competitors in the student travel business. Explorica was started in the spring of 2000 by several former EF employees who aimed to compete in part by copying EF's prices from EF's website and setting Explorica's own prices slightly lower. EF's website permits a visitor to the site to search its tour database and view the prices for tours meeting specified criteria such as gateway (*e.g.*, departure) cities, destination cities, and tour duration. In June 2000, Explorica hired Zefer, which provides computer-related expertise, to build a scraper tool that could "scrape" the prices from EF's website and download them into an Excel spreadsheet.

A scraper, also called a "robot" or "bot," is nothing more than a computer program that accesses information contained in a succession of webpages stored on the accessed computer. Strictly speaking, the accessed information is not the graphical interface seen by the user but rather the HTML source code—available to anyone who views the site—that generates the graphical interface. This information is then downloaded to the user's computer. The scraper program used in this case was not designed to copy all of the information on the accessed pages (*e.g.*, the descriptions of the tours), but rather only the price for each tour through each possible gateway city.

Zefer built a scraper tool that scraped two years of pricing data from EF's website. After receiving the pricing data from Zefer, Explorica set its own prices for the public, undercutting EF's prices an average of five percent. EF discovered Explorica's use of the scraper tool during discovery in an unrelated state-court action brought by Explorica's President against EF for back wages.

EF then sued Zefer, Explorica, and several of Explorica's employees in federal court. Pertinently, EF sought a preliminary injunction on the ground that the copying violated the federal Copyright Act, and various provisions of the Computer Fraud and Abuse Act ("CFAA"). The district court refused to grant EF summary judgment on its copyright claim, but it did issue a preliminary injunction against all defendants based on one provision of the CFAA, ruling that the use of the scraper tool went beyond the "reasonable expectations" of ordinary users. The preliminary injunction states *inter alia*:

> Defendant Explorica, Inc., its officers, agents, servants, employees, successors and assigns, all persons acting in concert or participation with Explorica, Inc., and/or acting on its behalf or direction are preliminarily enjoined to refrain, whether directly or indirectly, from the use of a "scraper" program, or any other similar computer tool, to access any data useable or necessary for the compilation of prices on or from the website of plaintiff EF Cultural Travel and its related entities, and/or the EF Tour Database.

The defendants appealed, but soon after briefing was completed, Zefer filed for bankruptcy and its appeal was automatically stayed. 11 U.S.C. § 362(a)(1). Explorica's appeal went forward and in *EF I* a panel of this court upheld the preliminary injunction against Explorica. The panel held that the use of the scraper tool exceeded the defendants' authorized access to EF's website because (according to the district court's findings for the preliminary injunction) access was facilitated by use of confidential information obtained in violation of the broad confidentiality agreement signed by EF's former employees.

EF argues at the outset that our decision in *EF I* is decisive as to Zefer. But the ground we adopted there in upholding the injunction as to the other defendants was that they had apparently used confidential information to facilitate the obtaining of the EF data. Explorica was created by former EF employees, some of whom were subject to confidentiality agreements. Zefer's position in that respect is quite different than that of Explorica or former EF employees. It signed no such agreement, and its prior knowledge as to the agreement is an open question.

EF suggests that Zefer must have known that information provided to it by Explorica had been improperly obtained. This is possible but not certain, and there are no express district court findings on this issue; indeed, given the district court's much broader basis for its injunction, it had no reason to make any detailed findings as to the role of the confidentiality agreement. What can be gleaned from the record as to

Zefer's knowledge certainly does not permit us to make on appeal the finding urged by EF.

What appears to have happened is that Philip Gormley, Explorica's Chief Information Officer and EF's former Vice President of Information Strategy, e-mailed Zefer a description of how EF's website was structured and identified the information that Explorica wanted to have copied; this may have facilitated Zefer's development of the scraper tool, but there is no indication that the structural information was unavailable from perusal of the website or that Zefer would have known that it was information subject to a confidentiality agreement.

EF also claims that Gormley e-mailed Zefer the "codes" identifying in computer shorthand the names of EF's gateway and destination cities. These codes were used to direct the scraper tool to the specific pages on EF's website that contained EF's pricing information. But, again, it appears that the codes could be extracted more slowly by examining EF's webpages manually, so it is far from clear that Zefer would have had to know that they were confidential. The only information that Zefer received that was described as confidential (passwords for tour-leader access) apparently had no role in the scraper project.

EF's alternative ground for affirmance is the rationale adopted by the district court for the preliminary injunction. That court relied on its "reasonable expectations" test as a gloss on the CFAA and then applied it to the facts of this case. Although we bypassed the issue in *EF I,* the district court's rationale would embrace Zefer as readily as Explorica itself. But the gloss presents a pure question of law to be reviewed *de novo* and, on this issue, we differ with the district court.

The CFAA provision relied upon by the district court states:

> Whoever . . . knowingly and with intent to defraud, accesses a protected computer without authorization, or exceeds authorized access, and by means of such conduct furthers the intended fraud and obtains anything of value, unless the object of the fraud and the thing obtained consists only of the use of the computer and the value of such use is not more than $ 5,000 in any 1-year period . . . shall be punished as provided in subsection (c) of this section.

18 U.S.C. § 1030(a)(4). The statute defines "exceeds authorized access" as "to access a computer with authorization and to use such access to obtain or alter information in the computer that the accesser is not entitled so to obtain or alter." *Id.* § 1030(e)(6). The CFAA furnishes a civil remedy for individuals who suffer damages or loss as a result of a violation of the above section. *Id.* § 1030(g).

At the outset, one might think that EF could have difficulty in showing an intent to defraud. But Zefer did not brief the issue on the original appeal before bankruptcy. In addition, there may be an argument that the fraud requirement should not pertain to injunctive relief. Accordingly, we bypass these matters and assume that the fraud requirement has been satisfied or is not an obstacle to the injunction.

The issue, then, is whether use of the scraper "exceeded authorized access." A lack of authorization could be established by an explicit statement on the website restricting access. (Whether public policy might in turn limit certain restrictions is a separate issue.) Many webpages contain lengthy limiting conditions, including limitations on the use of scrapers.[3] However, at the time of Zefer's use of the scraper, EF had no such explicit prohibition in place, although it may well use one now.

The district court thought that a lack of authorization could also be inferred from the circumstances, using "reasonable expectations" as the test; and it said that three such circumstances comprised such a warning in this case: the copyright notice on EF's homepage with a link directing users to contact the company with questions; EF's provision to Zefer of confidential information obtained in breach of the employee confidentiality agreements; and the fact that the website was configured to allow ordinary visitors to the site to view only one page at a time.

We agree with the district court that lack of authorization may be implicit, rather than explicit. After all, password protection itself normally limits authorization by implication (and technology), even without express terms. But we think that in general a reasonable expectations test is not the proper gloss on subsection (a)(4) and we reject it. However useful a reasonable expectations test might be in other contexts where there may be a common understanding underpinning the notion, its use in this context is neither prescribed by the statute nor prudentially sound.

Our basis for this view is not, as some have urged, that there is a "presumption" of open access to Internet information. The CFAA, after all, is primarily a statute imposing limits on access and enhancing control by information providers. Instead, we think that the public website provider can easily spell out explicitly what is forbidden and, consonantly, that nothing justifies putting users at the mercy of a highly imprecise, litigation-spawning standard like "reasonable expectations." If EF wants to ban scrapers, let it say so on the webpage or a link clearly marked as containing restrictions.

---

[3]   For example, the "legal notices" on one familiar website state that "you may print or download one copy of the materials or content on this site on any single computer for your personal, non-commercial use, provided you keep intact all copyright and other proprietary notices. Systematic retrieval of data or other content from this site to create or compile, directly or indirectly, a collection, compilation, database or directory without written permission from America Online is prohibited." AOL Anywhere Terms and Conditions of Use, *at* http://www.aol.com/copyright.html (last visited Jan. 14, 2003).

This case itself illustrates the flaws in the "reasonable expectations" standard. Why should the copyright symbol, which arguably does not protect the substantive information anyway, or the provision of page-by-page access for that matter, be taken to suggest that downloading information at higher speed is forbidden. EF could easily include—indeed, by now probably has included—a sentence on its home page or in its terms of use stating that "no scrapers may be used," giving fair warning and avoiding time-consuming litigation about its private, albeit "reasonable," intentions.

Needless to say, Zefer can have been in no doubt that EF would dislike the use of the scraper to construct a database for Explorica to undercut EF's prices; but EF would equally have disliked the compilation of such a database manually without the use of a scraper tool. EF did not purport to exclude competitors from looking at its website and any such limitation would raise serious public policy concerns.

NOTES AND QUESTIONS

1. *Reconsidering Zefer Corp. after Van Buren.* The First Circuit's decision in *Zefer Corp.* declines to hinge the legal standard on "highly imprecise, litigation-spawning" norms of computer access because, in its view, a website owner can simply write terms of service that will trigger CFAA liability. Years later in *Van Buren*, however, the Supreme Court rejected *Zefer Corp.*'s premise by concluding that written terms on use cannot control CFAA liability. After *Van Buren*, should the norms-based approach to CFAA liability be resurrected? If so, what kind of website scraping should be deemed unlawful?

2. *Is there a presumption of open access to public websites? The continuing case of hiQ Labs, Inc. v. LinkedIn Corp.* Whether a presumption of open access to public websites exists is the subject of ongoing litigation in hiQ Labs, Inc. v. LinkedIn Corp., 938 F.3d 985 (9th Cir. 2019), which was vacated and remanded in light of *Van Buren* in LinkedIn Corp. v. hiQ Labs, Inc., ___ U.S. ___, 2021 WL 2405144 (2021).

hiQ Labs ("HiQ") is a data analytics company that scrapes the LinkedIn profiles of users who have set their profiles to be available to the public without the need to log in to a LinkedIn account. HiQ then analyzes the data and sells it. In an effort to stop HiQ's accessing LinkedIn's site, LinkedIn sent a cease-and-desist letter to HiQ warning that HiQ was not permitted to access the public profiles on LinkedIn's site and that accessing LinkedIn's website violated the CFAA and other laws.

HiQ then sued LinkedIn, seeking a declaratory judgment that LinkedIn could not stop HiQ from visiting LinkedIn's public profiles. HiQ also sought a preliminary injunction requiring LinkedIn to continue to provide access to LinkedIn's website. The district court granted the preliminary injunction, effectively barring LinkedIn from blocking HiQ's access to its website while the litigation was pending. LinkedIn appealed the district court's preliminary injunction, and the Ninth Circuit affirmed. Ninth Circuit precedent limited the court's review to a narrow question about the CFAA: Whether HiQ's conduct "clearly" violated the CFAA or there was at least a "serious question" about it. The Ninth Circuit held that there was a serious question as to whether HiQ violated the CFAA.

According to the Ninth Circuit, access to "websites that are accessible to the general public" is inherently authorized and cannot violate the CFAA. An unauthorized access can occur only when access occurs to "private computer networks and websites" that are "protected by a password authentication system and not visible to the public." 938 F.3d at 1003. This is the correct interpretation of the CFAA, the Ninth Circuit reasoned, because the CFAA is focused on virtual "breaking and entering." *Id.* at 1001. The concept of "breaking and entering" only makes sense when there is an authentication system such as a password gate that requires bypassing. Accessing information available to the public, like a public LinkedIn page, is therefore authorized:

> The legislative history of section 1030 makes clear that the prohibition on unauthorized access is properly understood to apply only to private information—information delineated as private through use of a permission requirement of some sort. As one prominent commentator has put it, an authentication requirement, such as a password gate, is needed to create the necessary barrier that divides open spaces from closed spaces on the Web. Moreover, elsewhere in the statute, password fraud is cited as a means by which a computer may be accessed without authorization, *see* 18 U.S.C. § 1030(a)(6), bolstering the idea that authorization is only required for password-protected sites or sites that otherwise prevent the general public from viewing the information.
>
> Put differently, the CFAA contemplates the existence of three kinds of computer information: (1) information for which access is open to the general public and permission is not required, (2) information for which authorization is required and has been given, and (3) information for which authorization is required but has not been given (or, in the case of the prohibition on exceeding authorized access, has not been given for the part of the system accessed). Public LinkedIn profiles, available to anyone with an Internet connection, fall into the first category. With regard to such information, the "breaking and entering" analogue invoked so frequently during congressional consideration has no application, and the concept of "without authorization" is inapt.
>
> For all these reasons, it appears that the CFAA's prohibition on accessing a computer "without authorization" is violated when a person circumvents a computer's generally applicable rules regarding access permissions, such as username and password requirements, to gain access to a computer. It is likely that when a computer

network generally permits public access to its data, a user's accessing that publicly available data will not constitute access without authorization under the CFAA.

Id. at 1001–03.

The Ninth Circuit then distinguished *Nosal II* (see page 46) and *Power Ventures* (see page 65) on the ground that both of those precedents involved access limited by a username and password. In *Power Ventures*, Facebook had sent Power Ventures a cease-and-desist letter prohibiting Power Ventures from accessing the Facebook accounts that Facebook users had permitted Power Ventures to access. The Ninth Circuit held that Power Ventures had violated the CFAA by ignoring the cease-and-desist letter. According to the Ninth Circuit in *hiQ Labs v. LinkedIn*, however, a different result was appropriate when the cease-and-desist letter tried to limit access to areas of a public website that were not protected by a username and password:

> Facebook requires its users to register with a unique username and password, and Power Ventures required that Facebook users provide their Facebook username and password to access their Facebook data on Power Ventures' platform. While Power Ventures was gathering user data that was protected by Facebook's username and password authentication system, the data hiQ was scraping was available to anyone with a web browser.

> In sum, *Nosal II* and *Power Ventures* control situations in which authorization generally is required and has either never been given or has been revoked. As *Power Ventures* indicated, the two cases do not control the situation present here, in which information is presumptively open to all comers.

Id. at 1002.

Shortly after deciding *Van Buren*, the Supreme Court vacated the ruling in *LinkedIn v. hiQ Labs* and sent it back to the Ninth Circuit with directions to consider whether its prior decision was consistent with *Van Buren*.

How should the Ninth Circuit rule on remand? Is the Ninth Circuit's "breaking and entering" test different from the Supreme Court's "gates-up-or-down inquiry"?

3. *Authorization to visit a hard-to-guess website address: The case of United States v. Auernheimer.* Is the CFAA violated when a person visits a complex website address that the website owner intended to remain hidden? In United States v. Auernheimer, 748 F.3d 525 (3d Cir. 2014), AT&T had created a website to allow iPad owners with AT&T wireless accounts to access their account information. The AT&T website was available at the Internet address https://dcp2.att.com. The website featured a login prompt asking visitors for their e-mail addresses and passwords. To make it easier for iPad owners to access their accounts, AT&T programmed its website to automatically pre-populate the login prompt with the e-mail address associated with registered iPads according to AT&T's account records.

AT&T knew the correct e-mail address to use because iPads that visited AT&T's website were programmed to automatically visit a specific address unique to that iPad's serial number, a 19 or 20 digit number known as an ICC-ID number. If a user entered in the website address https://dcp2.att.com into the iPad's browser, the iPad would actually visit a specific page with the ICC-ID number in the address.

For example, an iPad with an ICC-ID number of 12345678901234567890 would automatically visit this address:

https://dcp2.att.com/OEPClient/openPage?
ICCID=12345678901234567890&IMEI=0.

From the user's perspective, an iPad that visited the AT&T website found that the "e-mail" part of the login prompt was automatically filled in with the user's e-mail address. This feature was designed to save users time. Because the e-mail address would appear automatically, the user only needed to manually enter in the account password to log in to the user's account.

AT&T's website design had a specific consequence: When any computer using the correct browser setting visited that particular website address, the AT&T website would return the e-mail address associated with that specific ICC-ID number that would in normal circumstances be used to fill in the login prompt. That is, AT&T configured its website so that it would share the account e-mail address with anyone—not just the account holder—who entered the correct website address.

Daniel Spitler and Andrew Auernheimer exploited this feature and created a program called "account slurper" that visited millions of specific addresses on the AT&T website. When the account slurper would hit on an address associated with an active account, it would record the e-mail address that AT&T provided. Spitler and Auernheimer used the program to collect 114,000 e-mail addresses before AT&T discovered the access and disabled the feature that automatically provided the e-mail addresses. Spitler and Auernheimer were charged with conspiracy to violate the felony provisions of the CFAA. According to the indictment, they had conspired to commit an unauthorized access in violation of 18 U.S.C. § 1030(a)(2)(C) in furtherance of New Jersey's state unauthorized access law. Spitler pled guilty and testified against Auernheimer, and a jury convicted Auernheimer of conspiracy to violate the CFAA.

On appeal, Auernheimer argued that there was no unauthorized access as a matter of law because the "account slurper" program merely visited a public website to see information that AT&T had published on the web. According to Auernheimer, a difficult-to-guess address on a public website was still a public webpage: Access was therefore inherently authorized. The government responded that Spitler's program had used computer expertise to breach a code-based barrier and collect information from AT&T's website that AT&T had never intended to be collected. No reasonable computer user would have expected someone to visit an address with a long ICC-ID, the government argued, making the ICC-ID akin to a password that the account slurper program had illegally guessed.

The Third Circuit vacated Auernheimer's conviction without deciding whether the conduct violated the CFAA. As a result, the court did not decide whether the access was unauthorized. However, the court did add a footnote about liability under New Jersey's unauthorized access law that may have hinted at the court's views about CFAA liability:

> No evidence was advanced at trial that the account slurper ever breached any password gate or other code-based barrier. The account slurper simply accessed the publicly facing portion of the login screen and scraped information that AT&T unintentionally published.

United States v. Auernheimer, 748 F.3d 525, 534 n.5 (3d Cir. 2014).

Which side had the better argument? Was using the program to collect 114,000 e-mail addresses unauthorized because AT&T clearly did not want or expect such access by outsiders? Or was it authorized because AT&T posted the information on the web for anyone to collect? If you think the access was unauthorized, what line would you draw between authorized and unauthorized access? For example, if it matters that the ICC-ID is very long, how short would have been short enough to make the address guessing legal? Alternatively, if you think the access was authorized, why should guessing a long ICC-ID be legal while guessing even a short password is illegal?

4. *Viewing data on a misconfigured website that was supposed to be password-protected.* In Vox Marketing Group v. Prodigy Promos, ___ F. Supp.3d ___, 2021 WL 3710130 (D. Utah 2021), Vox used its website to share pricing information about proposed orders and fulfilled orders with its customers. The pages with this information were supposed to be password-protected, with each customer needing a password to see its own orders on Vox's website. Unbeknownst to Vox, however, at some point the password-protection feature became disabled. Employees at a business competitor, Prodigy Promos, realized that Vox's order information was available without a password. By experimenting with different addresses at Vox's website, they were able to learn the details of Vox's orders. They accessed customer order pages on Vox's website over twenty thousand times.

Vox later sued, claiming (among other things) that Prodigy Promos employees violated the CFAA when they accessed the order information that was intended to be password-protected. The defendants moved for summary judgment, arguing that their visits to the publicly-available website were authorized as a matter of law. Judge Nielson denied the motion for summary judgment:

> The court readily agrees that general public access is at least presumptively authorized to computers, websites, or webpages that are accessible through the internet without a password. But the court is not persuaded that this presumption is irrebuttable or that there

is a per se rule that one can never obtain access to a computer "without authorization" except by hacking a password.

To be sure, in Van Buren v. United States, 141 S.Ct. 1648 (2021) the Supreme Court endorsed a "gates-up-or-down" inquiry to determine whether an individual's access to a computer was "without authorization" under the CFAA, explaining that "one either can or cannot access a computer system, and one either can or cannot access certain areas within the system." But the court expressly declined to decide whether "this inquiry turns only on technological (or 'code-based') limitations on access, or instead also looks to limits contained in contracts or policies." *Id.* at n.8.

Password protection, of course, is one example of a technological (or 'code-based') limitation on access. And there can be no doubt that when a computer, website, or webpage is password protected, one who obtains access to information by hacking the password obtains access "without authorization." It does not follow, however, that hacking a password is the only way that one can obtain access "without authorization."

Nor is the court convinced that this categorical proposition is sound. While it certainly may be true in most cases that general public access to computers connected to the internet is authorized when the computer is not password protected, it is easy enough to imagine circumstances in which this general rule seems not to hold true. For example, if an employee at an office left her computer open while stepping out for a few minutes, it would certainly seem that access to that computer and its files by another individual while the employee was gone would be "without authorization"—even if the computer and the files were not password protected.

The court concludes that a reasonable jury could find that Defendants knew that Vox intended the OrderPrint and PrintDelivery pages to be password protected but that the password protection was not completely effective, and that Defendants nevertheless knowingly exploited the defect in the password protection to obtain access to the OrderPrint and PrintDelivery pages.

Viewed in this manner, Defendants' knowledge seems comparable to that of someone who learns that the locking mechanism of a physical door does not securely engage when the door is locked and shut, and that the door can thus be opened by rattling the handle or the door itself until the lock disengages. And just as one who knowingly goes through a locked door in such a manner is no more authorized to enter than someone who picks the lock, the court believes that a reasonable jury could find that Defendant was no more authorized to obtain access to the OrderPrint proposals and PrintDelivery documents by knowingly exploiting a defect in Vox's password protection than it would have been to obtain access to these proposals by hacking a password.

Id. at *3–*5.

Judge Nielson analogizes visiting a URL that its owner wrongly believed was password-protected to rattling a door handle to open a malfunctioning lock on a door. Is the analogy persuasive? Or is it more like walking by a store and seeing inside through a window when the store owner incorrectly thought the drapes were closed?

Judge Nielson also suggests that this result follows from the same principle that governs when a user leaves a computer unattended and an unauthorized person looks through it. Do you agree? Or is there an intuitive difference between physical access to a computer (which presumptively only authorizes specific users) and access through a public website address (which presumptively authorizes everyone)?

5.   *The CFAA and disloyal employees, both current and former.* Before *Van Buren*, some courts had held that a disloyal employee commits an unauthorized access whenever the employee accesses the employer's computer for reasons adverse to the employer's interests even if there no express policy prohibiting that access. For example, Shurgard Storage Centers, Inc. v. Safeguard Self Storage, Inc., 119 F. Supp.2d 1121 (W.D. Wash. 2000), interpreted the phrase "without authorization" as adopting agency principles embodied in the Restatement (Second) of Agency § 112. That section states that "the authority of an agent terminates if, without knowledge of the principal, he acquires adverse interests or if he is otherwise guilty of a serious breach of loyalty to the principal." Applying the Restatement to current employees who accessed their current employer's computer to help a future employer, *Shurgard* held that the purpose to aid the future employer made the employee's access without authorization:

> Under this rule, the authority of the plaintiff's former employees ended when they allegedly became agents of the defendant. Therefore, for the purposes of this 12(b)(6) motion, they lost their authorization and were "without authorization" when they allegedly obtained and sent the proprietary information to the defendant via e-mail.

Id. at 1125. Although some lower courts agreed with *Shurgard* before *Van Buren*, its reasoning seems unlikely to survive *Van Buren*. A current employee's lack of loyalty would not seem to bring "down" a "gate" on access.

But what if the employee is fired and continues to access the account? Recall the pre-*Van-Buren* cases on ending employment as a withdrawal of authorization discussed in Note 5 on pages 37–38. In those cases, the termination of the employment relationship was deemed to eliminate authorization. Are *those* cases consistent with *Van Buren*? Does the end of an employment relationship bring down the gate that permitted the user to access the employee account? *See* United States v. Eddings, 2021 WL 2527966

(E.D.Pa. 2021) (denying a motion to dismiss on similar facts after *Van Buren*, and stating that "the mere fact that [the defendant] retained possession of a password which allowed her to access the server post-employment does not, under *Van Buren*, mean that she necessarily was authorized to access the server").

D. 18 U.S.C. § 1030(a)(2) AND ITS FELONY ENHANCEMENTS

It is now time to study a few provisions of 18 U.S.C. § 1030(a) in depth. We will start with § 1030(a)(2), which is the most commonly charged section of the statute. Section 1030(a)(2) states that it is a crime if a person:

intentionally accesses a computer without authorization or exceeds authorized access, and thereby obtains—

(A) information contained in a financial record of a financial institution, or of a card issuer as defined in section 1602(n) of title 15, or contained in a file of a consumer reporting agency on a consumer, as such terms are defined in the Fair Credit Reporting Act (15 U.S.C. 1681 et seq.);

(B) information from any department or agency of the United States; or

(C) information from any protected computer.

How serious are § 1030(a)(2) violations under federal law? It depends. Federal law classifies crimes into felonies and misdemeanors. Misdemeanors are less serious offenses, and felonies are more serious offenses. Federal law classifies misdemeanors as crimes punishable by one year or less of prison time. Felonies are crimes that allow the possibility of a sentence of more than one year of prison. *See* 18 U.S.C. § 3559(a). As a result, it is possible to classify federal crimes as felonies or misdemeanors based on the maximum statutory punishment the offense allows.

Under this framework, the seriousness of § 1030(a)(2) violations depends on the circumstances. Ordinarily, 18 U.S.C. § 1030(a)(2) are misdemeanors. *See* 18 U.S.C. § 1030(c)(2)(A). However, violations of the statute can become felony crimes if the government proves additional elements of the crime found in 18 U.S.C. § 1030(c)(2)(B):

(i) the offense was committed for purposes of commercial advantage or private financial gain;

(ii) the offense was committed in furtherance of any criminal or tortious act in violation of the Constitution or laws of the United States or of any State; or

(iii) the value of the information obtained exceeds $5,000.

In effect, the three provisions in § 1030(c)(2)(B) can be considered add-ons to 18 U.S.C. § 1030(a)(2) liability. If the government charges a felony violation of § 1030(a)(2) and alleges one of these three provisions, it must prove the existence of the provision as an extra element of the offense beyond a reasonable doubt. If the government cannot prove the felony element, the government can obtain a misdemeanor conviction under § 1030(a)(2), as the misdemeanor violation is a lesser-included offense of the felony charge.

The materials will explore 18 U.S.C. § 1030(a)(2) by beginning with the misdemeanor provisions and then turning to the felony enhancements.

1.   18 U.S.C. § 1030(a)(2) MISDEMEANOR LIABILITY

The starting point of misdemeanor liability under 18 U.S.C. § 1030(a)(2) is an intentional act of access without authorization or exceeding authorized access. The Senate Report that accompanied a change of the mental state from "knowingly" to "intentionally" in 1986 offered the following explanation of the intent requirement:

> Intentional acts of unauthorized access—rather than mistaken, inadvertent, or careless ones—are precisely what the Committee intends to proscribe. The Committee is concerned that the "knowingly" standard in the existing statute might be inappropriate for cases involving computer technology. The Senate's Report on the Criminal Code states that a person is said to act knowingly if he is aware "that the result is practically certain to follow from his conduct, whatever his desire may be as to that result."

> While appropriate to many criminal statutes, this standard might not be sufficient to preclude liability on the part of those who inadvertently "stumble into" someone else's computer file or computer data. This is particularly true in those cases where an individual is authorized to sign onto and use a particular computer, but subsequently exceeds his authorized access by mistakenly entering another computer file or data that happens to be accessible from the same terminal. Because the user had "knowingly" signed onto that terminal in the first place, the danger exists that he might incur liability for his mistaken access to another file. This is so because, while he may not have desired that result, i.e., the access of another file, it is possible that a trier of fact will infer that the user was "practically certain" such mistaken access could result from his initial decision to access the computer.

> The substitution of an "intentional" standard is designed to focus Federal criminal prosecutions on those whose conduct evinces a

clear intent to enter, without proper authorization, computer files or data belonging to another. Again, this will comport with the Senate Report on the Criminal Code, which states that "intentional" means more than that one voluntarily engaged in conduct or caused a result. Such conduct or the causing of the result must have been the person's conscious objective.

S. Rep. No. 99–432, *reprinted in* 1986 U.S.C.C.A.N. 2479, 2483–84.

When you first read § 1030(a)(2), it may seem that the elements of misdemeanor liability contain several important provisions beyond intentional unauthorized access. In truth, however, these requirements provide relatively low thresholds. These low thresholds ensure that § 1030(a)(2) misdemeanor liability is the broadest kind of liability in the CFAA.

Consider the requirement that the defendant must obtain information under (a)(2)(A), (B), or (C). The Senate Report that accompanied the passage of § 1030(a)(2) explains that this is a very low hurdle:

The Department of Justice has expressed concerns that the term "obtains information" in 18 U.S.C. 1030(a)(2) makes that subsection more than an unauthorized access offense, i.e., that it might require the prosecution to prove asportation of the data in question. Because the premise of this subsection is privacy protection, the Committee wishes to make clear that "obtaining information" in this context includes mere observation of the data. Actual asportation, in the sense of physically removing the data from its original location or transcribing the data, need not be proved in order to establish a violation of this subsection.

S. Rep. No. 99–432 (1986), *reprinted in* 1986 U.S.C.C.A.N. 2479, 2484. It is unclear whether § 1030(a)(2) requires actual observation of the data or whether merely coming into possession of the data is sufficient. In any event, the fact that most computer intruders will see information inside the victim network means that most computer hacking will end up violating 18 U.S.C. § 1030(a)(2).

Misdemeanor liability under § 1030(a)(2) also requires the government to show that the computer satisfied one of the categories of computers listed in § 1030(a)(2)(A)–(C). On one hand, sections 1030(a)(2)(A) and (a)(2)(B) are narrow. The former covers financial records as defined in § 1030(e)(4)–(5), and the latter covers only information obtained from United States government computers as defined in § 1030(e)(7). But these provisions generally do not matter because § 1030(a)(2)(C) has vast scope. Section 1030(a)(2)(C) requires that information be obtained from any "protected computer." Section 1030(e)(2) defines a "protected computer" as a computer:

(A) exclusively for the use of a financial institution or the United States Government, or, in the case of a computer not exclusively for such use, used by or for a financial institution or the United States Government and the conduct constituting the offense affects that use by or for the financial institution or the Government;

(B) which is used in or affecting interstate or foreign commerce or communication, including a computer located outside the United States that is used in a manner that affects interstate or foreign commerce or communication of the United States; or

(C) that—(i) is part of a voting system; and (ii)(I) is used for the management, support, or administration of a Federal election; or (II) has moved in or otherwise affects interstate or foreign commerce;

As we will see in Chapter 7, most computers are "protected computers" because computers that affect interstate commerce includes any computers that can be regulated under the scope of the Commerce Clause of the United States Constitution.

Further, the statutory definition of "computer" is very broad. 18 U.S.C. § 1030(e)(1) defines "computer" as:

an electronic, magnetic, optical, electrochemical, or other high speed data processing device performing logical, arithmetic, or storage functions, and includes any data storage facility or communications facility directly related to or operating in conjunction with such device, but such term does not include an automated typewriter or typesetter, a portable hand held calculator, or other similar device.

Courts have interpreted this definition expansively. Consider two cases. First, in United States v. Mitra, 405 F.3d 492 (7th Cir. 2005), a college student commandeered the radio system used by police, fire, ambulance, and other emergency workers in Madison, Wisconsin. The radio system was a Motorola Smartnet II, a sophisticated system that used a computer to host many different communications on a small number of radio frequencies. Mitra had learned how to control the system using a radio transmitter, and he used his transmitter to block the radio system to stop receiving signals. Mitra's conduct effectively blocked Madison emergency workers from being able to use their radio system and to coordinate emergency responses to incidents in the city.

Mitra was charged and convicted of violating 18 U.S.C. § 1030(a)(5), and appealed his conviction on the ground that the Madison radio system was not a "computer" covered by § 1030. In an opinion by Judge Easterbrook, the Seventh Circuit disagreed and affirmed the conviction:

Every cell phone and cell tower is a "computer" under this statute's definition; so is every iPod, every wireless base station in the corner coffee shop, and many another gadget. Reading § 1030 to cover all of these, and police radio too, would give the statute wide coverage, which by Mitra's lights means that Congress cannot have contemplated such breadth.

Well of course Congress did not contemplate or intend this particular application of the statute. But although legislators may not know about [it], they *do* know that complexity is endemic in the modern world and that each passing year sees new developments. That's why they write general statutes rather than enacting a list of particular forbidden acts. And it is the statutes they enacted—not the thoughts they did or didn't have—that courts must apply.

Section 1030 is general. Exclusions show just *how* general. Subsection (e)(1) carves out automatic typewriters, typesetters, and handheld calculators; this shows that other devices with embedded processors and software are covered. As more devices come to have built-in intelligence, the effective scope of the statute grows. This might prompt Congress to amend the statute but does not authorize the judiciary to give the existing version less coverage than its language portends.

Id. at 495.

The Eighth Circuit offered a similarly broad interpretation of "computer" in United States v. Kramer, 631 F.3d 900 (8th Cir. 2011). In *Kramer*, the defendant used a Motorola Motorazr V3 cell phone to make voice calls and send text messages in the course of criminal activity. The defendant argued that his cell phone was not a "computer" for purposes of 18 U.S.C. § 1030(e)(1), but the Eighth Circuit disagreed:

The language of 18 U.S.C. § 1030(e)(1) is exceedingly broad. If a device is "an electronic or other high speed data processing device performing logical, arithmetic, or storage functions," it is a computer. This definition captures any device that makes use of a electronic data processor, examples of which are legion. Additionally, each time an electronic processor performs any task—from powering on, to receiving keypad input, to displaying information—it performs logical, arithmetic, or storage functions. These functions are the essence of its operation. See The New Oxford American Dictionary 277 (2d ed. 2005) (defining "central processing unit" as "the part of a computer in which operations are controlled and executed").

Furthermore, there is nothing in the statutory definition that purports to exclude devices because they lack a connection to the

Internet. To be sure, the term computer "does not include an automated typewriter or typesetter, a portable hand held calculator, or other similar device." 18 U.S.C. § 1030(e)(1). But this hardly excludes all non-Internet-enabled devices from the definition of "computer"—indeed, this phrasing would be an odd way to do it. Whatever makes an automated typewriter "similar" to a hand held calculator—the statute provides no further illumination—we find few similarities between those items and a modern cellular phone containing an electronic processor. Therefore we conclude that cellular phones are not excluded by this language.

Id. at 902–03.

For all of the above reasons, misdemeanor liability under § 1030(a)(2) is the broadest kind of criminal liability in the Computer Fraud and Abuse Act.

2. 18 U.S.C. § 1030(a)(2) FELONY LIABILITY

Although 18 U.S.C. § 1030(a)(2) violations ordinarily are misdemeanors, they can become more serious felony offenses when one of three circumstances exists:

(i) the offense was committed for purposes of commercial advantage or private financial gain;

(ii) the offense was committed in furtherance of any criminal or tortious act in violation of the Constitution or laws of the United States or of any State; or

(iii) the value of the information obtained exceeds $5,000.

18 U.S.C. § 1030(c)(2)(B). The following materials consider the meaning of these three enhancements.

UNITED STATES V. BATTI
United States Court of Appeals for the Sixth Circuit, 2011.
631 F.3d 371.

KAREN NELSON MOORE, CIRCUIT JUDGE.

Luay Batti was convicted of improperly accessing information from a protected computer, in violation of 18 U.S.C. § 1030(a)(2)(C) and (c)(2)(B)(iii). He appeals the district court's finding that the value of the information that he obtained exceeded $5,000.

I.

Luay Batti worked in the IT department of Campbell-Ewald, an advertising company in Michigan, for about six years, until he was fired in

March 2007. The events leading to his termination began about six months earlier when Batti accessed Campbell-Ewald's computer server and copied confidential computer files belonging to Campbell-Ewald's CEO without authorization. Although these files were normally stored on the CEO's desktop computer, they had been moved by the company to the company's server while the CEO's computer was being replaced. Within these files were confidential pieces of information including executive compensation, financial statements of the firm, goals and objectives for senior executives of the company reporting to the chairman, and some strategic plans.

The record does not reveal why Batti retained this information for six months, but, on the evening of February 27, 2007, he went to the office of Campbell-Ewald's Vice Chairman and General Manager, Joseph Naporano, to talk about the information he had obtained. Batti's ostensible purpose in approaching Naporano was merely to inform him of the weaknesses in Campbell-Ewald's computer-security barriers and to complain about the IT department's management. At this meeting, Batti also gave Naporano a letter in which Batti set out his complaints and a computer disk containing some of the CEO's files that Batti had copied. The disk also contained video footage that Campbell-Ewald had purchased for use in television commercials for its largest client, General Motors. Soon afterwards, Naporano began to investigate the security weaknesses mentioned by Batti, and, within a few days, Naporano fired Batti for exercising "bad judgment" in accessing and copying the CEO's files.

About six weeks later, on April 18, 2007, while the security review was still underway, Naporano learned of two websites that contained confidential information regarding Campbell-Ewald and GM, along with emails sent between officials of these two companies. These websites were open to the public for an unknown—yet likely brief—amount of time, but almost immediately after Campbell-Ewald discovered them they became password-protected. Greatly alarmed by what was clearly a breach of the company's computer-security system, and unaware of exactly how broad the breach was, Naporano contacted the police and an IT security firm, who recommended that Naporano contact the FBI.

The FBI determined that Batti had accessed Campbell-Ewald's confidential files no fewer than twenty-one times after his firing, twice through a Campbell-Ewald server and nineteen times through the email account of another Campbell-Ewald employee, Steve Majoros. The FBI conducted a search of Batti's home on April 19, 2007. In an interview with the FBI, Batti admitted that he had accessed Campbell-Ewald's system through its server and Majoros's webmail. On the latter point, Batti admitted that he had learned Majoros's username and password in the course of his employment with Campbell-Ewald; although Majoros had slightly altered his password after Batti was fired, Batti was able to guess the new password through trial and error.

Batti was charged with one count, a violation of 18 U.S.C. § 1030(a)(2)(C) and (c)(2)(B)(iii). In the Indictment, the government sought a felony conviction by alleging, pursuant to subsection (B)(iii), that Batti "obtained information valued in excess of $5,000.00." At a bench trial held on October 28, 2008, the district court heard testimony from FBI Agent Bryan Taube and Naporano regarding Batti's intrusions. Naporano also testified that Campbell-Ewald paid about $305,000 for the television-commercial footage that Batti accessed and put on the disk that he gave Naporano.

The district court found that the $305,000 amount best represented the value of the information that Batti had obtained in his intrusions; it therefore ruled for the government on the issue of whether the value exceeded $5,000. In coming to this conclusion, the district court noted that there was virtually no case law interpreting how to define or measure the "value of the information obtained," but it found persuasive cases regarding the value of stolen goods under 18 U.S.C. § 2314. The courts in these cases held that, where a stolen good does not have any readily ascertainable market value, any reasonable method may be used to calculate its value, including the cost of production, research, or design. Accordingly, the district court looked to Campbell-Ewald's cost of production of the video footage that Batti posted online, which, at approximately $305,000, was well over the $5,000 threshold.

II.

Batti's challenge to the district court's conclusion that the value of the information obtained exceeded $5,000 requires an interpretation of 18 U.S.C. § 1030(c)(2)(B)(iii). Section 1030 of Title 18 contains no definition of the term "value," as used in 18 U.S.C. § 1030(c)(2)(B)(iii), however, and § 1030 does not otherwise indicate how a court should determine whether the "value of the information obtained exceeds $5,000." 18 U.S.C. § 1030(c)(2)(B)(iii).

Batti argues that the district court committed a legal error because he asserts that "there was *no* evidence that his actions had any impact on the company's use of these commercials." Batti Br. at 18. In other words, Batti contends that, because he did not damage the information in any way, the court could not find that the "value of the information obtained" exceeded $5,000. The district court rejected this argument on the ground that the statute does not require that the information obtained lost value as a result of the defendant's illicit actions. As the district court stated:

> There simply is no requirement under the pertinent subsections of § 1030 that Defendant's unauthorized access must have led to any sort of loss, that the value of the information must have been diminished as a result of his conduct, or that he somehow must have profited from his actions. Rather, the trier of fact—in this

case, the Court—is called upon only to determine the value of the information through some appropriate means.

We agree with the district court. The statute here requires only a determination of the "value of the information obtained," not whether that value decreased. Furthermore, the statute contains specific definitions of the terms "loss" and "damage," either of which could be said to include an alleged decrease in the value of the video footage obtained by Batti. These terms—"loss" and "damage"—are used in other provisions within § 1030, but not in subsection (c)(2)(B)(iii). Given that the terms "loss" and "damage" encompass the type of decrease in value described by Batti, the absence of these terms in § 1030(c)(2)(B)(iii) supports the conclusion that the "value of the information obtained" bears no relation to whether that value was diminished by the defendant's actions. We therefore reject Batti's argument that a diminution in value constitutes the statutory measure.

Batti also argues that the district court should have used the market value of the information, and that there was no 'market' available to set a value on the information. We believe there is also no merit in this argument, because, as we explain below, although there may be no readily ascertainable market value for the video footage that Batti obtained, the cost of production of that footage was a permissible basis on which the district court could rely in determining whether the value of the information obtained exceeded $5,000.

Subsection (a)(2)(C) was added to 18 U.S.C. § 1030 in 1996 in order to protect against the interstate or foreign theft of information by computer. In particular, Congress was concerned about the fact that electronically stored information "is intangible, and it has been held that the theft of such information cannot be charged under more traditional criminal statutes such as Interstate Transportation of Stolen Property, 18 U.S.C. § 2314." S. Rep. No. 104–357 at *7 (citing *United States v. Brown*, 925 F.2d 1301, 1308 (10th Cir. 1991)). Subsection (a)(2)(C) ensures that the theft of intangible information by the unauthorized use of a computer is prohibited in the same way theft of physical items are protected.

Regarding the penalties for violations of subsection (a)(2)(C), the Senate Report states that violations involving information of "nominal" or "minimal" value constitute misdemeanors, punishable under § 1030(c)(2)(A). For violations involving "valuable information" and "misusing information in other more serious ways," however, the felony provision of § 1030(c)(2)(B) applies. Furthermore, Congress identified precisely the types of violations worthy of felony punishment by including within § 1030(c)(2)(B) three preconditions to its application. In order to punish a violation of § 1030(a)(2)(C) as a felony, the government must prove one of the following:

    (i)   the offense was committed for purposes of commercial advantage or private financial gain;

    (ii)   the offense was committed in furtherance of any criminal or tortious act in violation of the Constitution or laws of the United States or of any State; or

    (iii) the value of the information obtained exceeds $5,000.

18 U.S.C. § 1030(c)(2)(B)(i)–(iii). The Senate Report notes that the first two of these preconditions derive from the copyright statute, 17 U.S.C. § 506(a), and the wiretap statute, 18 U.S.C. § 2511(1)(d). S. Rep. No. 104–357 at *8. Moreover, these two provisions "are intended to have the same meaning as in those statutes." *Id.*

    Subsection (iii) is similar to the transporting-stolen-goods statute mentioned by the Senate Report as the inspiration for the 1996 amendment, 18 U.S.C. § 2314, in that both require the "value" of the object of the violation to exceed $5,000. Section 2314 prohibits transport[ing], transmitting, or transferring in interstate or foreign commerce any goods, wares, merchandise, securities or money, *of the value of $5,000 or more,* knowing the same to have been stolen, converted or taken by fraud. 18 U.S.C. § 2314 (emphasis added). Consequently, given the absence of case law interpreting the term "value" in § 1030(c)(2)(B)(iii), we may consider parallel interpretations of § 2314. We also recognize a key difference between the two statutes: although § 1030 prohibits obtaining information, § 2314 prohibits transporting, transmitting, or transferring proscribed items. Thus, as the Senate Report notes, the crux of the offense under subsection 1030(a)(2)(C) is the abuse of a computer to obtain the information, and actual asportation need not be proved."

    Examination of the definition of "value" in 18 U.S.C. § 2311 reveals that the market value of the stolen good constitutes the primary relevant benchmark for the determination of the value of stolen "goods, wares, merchandise, securities or money" in § 2314. According to § 2311, " 'Value' means the face, par, or market value, whichever is the greatest, and the aggregate value of all goods, wares, and merchandise, securities, and money referred to in a single indictment shall constitute the value thereof." 18 U.S.C. § 2311. Yet when a particular item does not have a readily ascertainable market value, courts have permitted the use of any reasonable method to calculate value, including the cost of production, research, or design.

    With this approach in mind, we believe that, where information obtained by a violation of § 1030(c)(2)(B)(iii) does not have a readily ascertainable market value, it is reasonable to use the cost of production as a means to determine the value of the information obtained. The district court here believed that the amount Campbell-Ewald paid for the "spots" or video footage that Batti later obtained could be viewed as the footage's market value, but the district court also recognized that footage of this type is not sold on a typical retail market. As a result, the district court believed that the amount that Campbell-Ewald paid for the footage could also be viewed as the cost of production for the development of advertisements or commercials.

We see no error in this approach. Section 1030(a)(2)(C) protects, broadly, "information obtained from any protected computer," and it is often the case, as it was here, that this information is intangible and lacks any easily ascertainable market value. In such circumstances, we approve of the use of "any reasonable method" to determine the value of information obtained by a breach of § 1030(a)(2)(C), whether this determination is being made by the district court in a bench trial or by a jury. We hold that the district court's use of the cost of production here was a reasonable, and therefore permissible, method by which to determine the value of the information obtained by Batti. We recognize, however, that, given the broad nature of the statute, violations of § 1030(a)(2)(C) may arise in many different contexts. We therefore express no opinion regarding either the propriety of other methods by which to calculate the value of information obtained under 18 U.S.C. § 1030(a)(2)(C) and (c)(2)(B)(iii) or the applicability of the method we approve today to dissimilar factual circumstances.

NOTES AND QUESTIONS

1. *The origins of the felony enhancements.* Each of the felony enhancements that apply to § 1030(a)(2) violations derives from similar language in other areas of federal criminal law.

First, the requirement of an offense having been "committed for purposes of commercial advantage or private financial gain" was taken from the copyright statutes. *See* 17 U.S.C. § 506(a)(1)(A) ("Any person who willfully infringes a copyright shall be punished . . . if the infringement was committed . . . for purposes of commercial advantage or private financial gain").

Second, the requirement that an offense be committed "in furtherance of any criminal or tortious act in violation of the Constitution or laws of the United States or of any State" was taken from the wiretap laws. *See* 18 U.S.C. § 2511(2)(d) ("It shall not be unlawful under this chapter for a person not acting under color of law to intercept a wire, oral, or electronic communication where such person is a party to the communication or where one of the parties to the communication has given prior consent to such interception unless such communication is intercepted for the purpose of committing any criminal or tortious act in violation of the Constitution or laws of the United States or of any State.").

Third, as the *Batti* court notes, the requirement that the value of the information obtained must exceed $5,000 resembles the federal statute prohibiting the interstate transportation of stolen property. *See* 18 U.S.C.

§ 2314 (providing for punishment of "whoever transports, transmits, or transfers in interstate or foreign commerce any goods, wares, merchandise, securities or money, of the value of $5,000 or more, knowing the same to have been stolen, converted or taken by fraud").

2. *Double-counting and § 1030(a)(2) felonies.* The second felony enhancement states that a § 1030(a)(2) crime becomes a felony if "the offense was committed in furtherance of any criminal or tortious act in violation of the Constitution or laws of the United States or of any State." 18 U.S.C. § 1030(c)(2)(B)(ii). This provision creates difficult interpretive questions because there are many "criminal or tortious act[s]" prohibited by laws other than the CFAA that nonetheless overlap substantially with the CFAA. The question is, how much overlap is too much overlap, such that it is improper double-counting to treat a § 1030(a)(2) violation as a felony based on the act being committed "in furtherance of" a law that resembles § 1030(a)(2) itself?

This issue first arose in United States v. Cioni, 649 F.3d 276 (4th Cir. 2011), which involved hacking into a personal e-mail account. Federal criminal law contains two misdemeanor offenses that apply to hacking into an e-mail account. The first, 18 U.S.C. § 2701, specifically prohibits hacking into an e-mail account stored on an ISP's server. The second, 18 U.S.C. § 1030(a)(2), generally prohibits hacking into any computer, which will always be implicated when a person hacks into an e-mail account. In *Cioni*, the government tried to harness this overlap to turn a misdemeanor into a felony: It argued that hacking into an e-mail account constitutes a felony on the ground that it is a § 1030(a)(2) violation in furtherance of a § 2701 violation.

The Fourth Circuit rejected this argument in *Cioni*. According to the Fourth Circuit, the enhancement of § 1030(c)(2)(B)(ii) applies only when the crime furthered is distinct from the underlying § 1030 offense. This narrow construction avoids a "merger" problem that implicates double jeopardy principles by punishing a defendant twice for the same conduct. The Fourth Circuit vacated the felony conviction and ordered the district court to reduce the conviction to a misdemeanor § 1030(a)(2) violation:

> If the government had proven that Cioni accessed [the victim's] e-mail inbox and then used the information from that inbox to access another person's electronic communications, no merger problem would have arisen. But the government charged and attempted to prove two crimes using the same conduct of attempting, but failing, to access only [the victim's] e-mail account. This creates a merger problem, implicating double jeopardy principles.

Id. at 283.

Contrast *Cioni* with United States v. Steele, 595 Fed.Appx. 208 (4th Cir. 2014). In *Steele*, the defendant used a backdoor account to access confidential business documents stored on the computers of his former corporate employer. The defendant was convicted of a felony version of § 1030(a)(2)(C) on the ground that his unauthorized access had been in furtherance of theft of the valuable documents in violation of Virginia's grand larceny statute. On appeal, Steele argued that the felony enhancement was improper under *Cioni*. The Fourth Circuit distinguished *Cioni* and affirmed the felony conviction:

> Steele contends that his conduct of accessing protected computers improperly supported both a violation of § 1030(a)(2)(C) and the accompanying felony enhancement under Va. Code Ann. section 18.2–95. We disagree. Primarily, proof of § 1030(a)(2)(C) requires only that the defendant read or observe data; actual asportation need not be proved. The Virginia statute, on the other hand, criminalizes grand larceny, which by definition requires proof of an actual taking.
>
> In this case, Special Agent Etienne, who investigated Steele's conduct, testified that the FBI recovered evidence that Steele not only accessed emails and bid documents but actively downloaded them and saved them to multiple hard drives connected to his personal computer. In addition, the government provided the jury with a summary chart of the charges against Steele, listing specific documents supporting those charges, the value associated with those documents, and the location where they were found on Steele's computer hard drives. Through this evidence, the government was able to show that Steele's conduct included not simply reading or observing protected information but also downloading ("taking") that information.
>
> In sum, because the government used different conduct to prove the two offenses, Steele's felony convictions for violating the CFAA do not raise the double jeopardy concerns implicated by Cioni.

Id. at 214.

Did *Steele* persuasively apply *Cioni*? Recall that § 1030(a)(2)(C) requires obtaining information, which the legislative history says is satisfied by observing it. What is the difference between merely "obtaining" or "observing" information (covered by § 1030(a)(2)(C)) and actually "taking" or "downloading" that information (covered by the Virginia grand larceny statute)? Observing information over a remote network requires transmitting a copy so that it can be observed by the remote viewer. How is that different from "downloading" it? Is information not stolen for purposes of a larceny statute unless it is permanently saved?

United States v. Auernheimer, 2012 WL 5389142 (D.N.J. 2012), *vacated on other grounds*, 748 F.3d 525 (3d Cir. 2014), raised an interesting variation on the problem. Every state has a CFAA-equivalent criminal law that prohibits unauthorized access to a computer at the state level. In *Auernheimer*, the government argued that a misdemeanor violation of § 1030(a)(2) becomes a felony under § 1030(c)(2)(B)(ii) if the act also violates the state unauthorized access law. In that instance, the government argued, the offense becomes a federal unauthorized access crime in furtherance of a state unauthorized access crime. The district court agreed, at least when the state unauthorized access includes an extra element that § 1030(a)(2) does not have:

> Although there is an overlap of facts for the first two elements of each offense, N.J.S.A. 2C:20–31(a) requires the additional component that defendant "knowingly or recklessly discloses or causes to be disclosed any data . . . or personal identifying information." Hence, an essential N.J.S.A. 2C:20–31(a) element requires proof of conduct not required for a CFAA offense.

2012 WL 5389142 at *4.

On appeal, Auernheimer argued that the district court was mistaken because the key question was whether the government had charged two different acts, not two different statutes. Otherwise, mere overlap with analogous state unauthorized access statutes would transform every § 1030(a)(2) misdemeanor into a felony. The Third Circuit vacated the defendant's conviction on venue grounds without reaching the felony enhancement issue. If the Third Circuit had reached the issue, how should it have ruled?

3.   *18 U.S.C. § 1030 and repeat offenders.* The scope of liability under 18 U.S.C. § 1030 sometimes depends on whether a defendant has a prior conviction under the statute. As a practical matter, this issue arises only rarely. But misdemeanor offenses under the various sections of § 1030 can become felonies if a particular defendant has a prior conviction for violating or attempting to violate § 1030. Further, felony violations can become more serious felony offenses when a defendant has a prior § 1030 conviction. *See* 18 U.S.C. § 1030(c)(1)(B), § 1030(c)(2)(B)(iii), § 1030(c)(3)(B), § 1030(c)(4)(C)(i), and § 1030(c)(4)(D)(i).

4.   *The forgotten 18 U.S.C. § 1030(a)(3).* Although § 1030(a)(2) gets a lot of attention, it is worth pausing for a moment to consider its rarely-used neighbor, § 1030(a)(3). This section states that it is a crime if a person:

> intentionally, without authorization to access any nonpublic computer of a department or agency of the United States, accesses such a computer of that department or agency that is exclusively for the use of the Government of the United States or, in the case of a computer not exclusively for such use, is used by or for the Government of the United States and such conduct affects that use by or for the Government of the United States.

Violations of § 1030(a)(3) are misdemeanors unless the defendant has a prior conviction under § 1030. If the defendant has a prior conviction, the crime is a felony punishable by up to ten years in prison. *See* 18 U.S.C. § 1030(c)(2)(C).

Section 1030(a)(3) is different from § 1030(a)(2) in a number of ways. First, § 1030(a)(3) applies only to access into United States government computers. Second, it is a simple trespass statute; there is no requirement that any information be obtained by the defendant. Third, the basic prohibition is limited to "access without authorization," whereas § 1030(a)(2) includes both a defendant who "accessed without authorization" and a defendant who "exceeds authorized access." As we will see, the precise distinction between access without authorization and exceeding authorized access can be difficult to follow. But the limitation of § 1030(a)(3) reflects a design for the statute to reach only a limited class of cases.

The Senate Report that accompanied the enactment of the modern version of 18 U.S.C. § 1030(a)(3) included the following discussion of its scope:

> It applies to acts of simple trespass against computers belonging to, or being used by or for, the Federal Government. The Department of Justice and others have expressed concerns about whether the present subsection covers acts of mere trespass, i.e., unauthorized access, or whether it requires a further showing that the information perused was "used, modified, destroyed, or disclosed." To alleviate those concerns, the Committee wants to make clear that the new subsection will be a simple trespass offense, applicable to persons without authorized access to Federal computers.

S.Rep. 99–432 (1986), reprinted in 1986 U.S.C.C.A.N. 2479, 2484.

18 U.S.C. § 1030(a)(3) is largely forgotten today because it has been eclipsed by 18 U.S.C. § 1030(a)(2). In 1984, when both provisions were first enacted, § 1030(a)(2) was exceedingly narrow: It applied only to financial records held by financial institutions and consumer files held by consumer reporting agencies. See Pub. L. 98–473, § 2102 (1984). Over time, however, § 1030(a)(2) has expanded dramatically. Today, § 1030(a)(2) is so broad that it covers most conduct that could be prosecuted under § 1030(a)(3).

E. 18 U.S.C. § 1030(a)(4) AND COMPUTER FRAUD STATUTES

Computer fraud statutes are hybrids between unauthorized access statutes and fraud statutes. The federal computer fraud statute is 18 U.S.C. § 1030(a)(4). It punishes whoever:

> knowingly and with intent to defraud, accesses a protected computer without authorization, or exceeds authorized access, and by means of such conduct furthers the intended fraud and obtains anything of value, unless the object of the fraud and the thing obtained consists only of the use of the computer and the value of such use is not more than $5,000 in any one-year period.

All § 1030(a)(4) crimes are felonies; the maximum punishment is 5 years for the first offense, and 10 years if the defendant has a prior § 1030 conviction. See 18 U.S.C. § 1030(c)(3).

The hybrid status of § 1030(a)(4) is readily apparent from its text. On one hand, it clearly is closely related to § 1030(a)(2). The basic prohibition on accessing a protected computer without authorization or exceeding authorized access is shared between the two. On the other hand, the prohibition is also similar to the wire fraud statute, 18 U.S.C. § 1343. The wire fraud statute punishes whoever,

> having devised or intending to devise any scheme or artifice to defraud, or for obtaining money or property by means of false or fraudulent pretenses, representations, or promises, transmits or causes to be transmitted by means of wire, radio, or television communication in interstate or foreign commerce, any writings, signs, signals, pictures, or sounds for the purpose of executing such scheme or artifice.

Section 1030(a)(4) puts the two basic concepts together. It combines the intent to defraud and obtaining of anything of value from the wire fraud statute and matches it with the *actus reus* of accessing a protected computer without authorization or exceeding authorized access from § 1030(a)(2). The hybrid status raises interesting questions about why § 1030(a)(4) exists. Just what does it punish that the combination of § 1030(a)(2) and the wire fraud statute does not?

The difference between unauthorized access statutes, wire fraud statutes, and computer fraud statutes was explored in the Senate Report that accompanied the enactment of § 1030(a)(4):

> The new subsection 1030(a)(4) to be created by this bill is designed to penalize thefts of property via computer that occur as part of a scheme to defraud. It will require a showing that the use of the computer or computers in question was integral to the intended fraud and was not merely incidental. It has been suggested that the Committee approach all computer fraud in a manner that directly tracks the existing mail fraud and wire fraud statutes. However, the Committee was concerned that such an approach might permit prosecution under this subsection of acts that do not deserve classification as "computer fraud."

> The Committee was concerned that computer usage that is wholly extraneous to an intended fraud might nevertheless be covered by this subsection if the subsection were patterned directly after the current mail fraud and wire fraud laws. If it were so patterned, the subsection might be construed as covering an individual who had devised a scheme or artifice to defraud solely because he used a computer to keep records or to add up his potential "take" from the crime.

> The Committee does not believe that a scheme or artifice to defraud should fall under the ambit of subsection (a)(4) merely because the offender signed onto a computer at some point near to the commission or execution of the fraud. While such a tenuous

link might be covered under current law where the instrumentality used is the mails or the wires, the Committee does not consider that link sufficient with respect to computers. To be prosecuted under this subsection, the use of the computer must be more directly linked to the intended fraud. That is, it must be used by an offender without authorization or in excess of his authorization to obtain property of another, which property furthers the intended fraud. Likewise, this subsection may be triggered by conduct that can be shown to constitute an attempted offense.

This approach is designed, in part, to help distinguish between acts of theft via computer and acts of computer trespass. In intentionally trespassing into someone else's computer files, the offender obtains at the very least information as to how to break into that computer system. If that is all he obtains, the offense should properly be treated as a simple trespass. But because the offender has obtained the small bit of information needed to get into the computer system, the danger exists that his and every other computer trespass could be treated as a theft, punishable as a felony under this subsection.

The Committee remains convinced that there must be a clear distinction between computer theft, punishable as a felony, and computer trespass, punishable in the first instance as a misdemeanor. The element in the new paragraph (a)(4), requiring a showing of an intent to defraud, is meant to preserve that distinction, as is the requirement that the property wrongfully obtained via computer furthers the intended fraud.

S. Rep. No. 99–432, at 10 (1986), *reprinted in* 1986 U.S.C.C.A.N. 2479, 2488.

UNITED STATES V. CZUBINSKI

United States Court of Appeals for the First Circuit, 1997.
106 F.3d 1069.

TORRUELLA, CHIEF JUDGE.

Defendant-appellant Richard Czubinski appeals his jury conviction on nine counts of wire fraud, and four counts of computer fraud, 18 U.S.C. § 1030(a)(4). The wire fraud and computer fraud prosecution that led to the conviction survived serious challenges put forward by Czubinski in various pre-trial motions. Given the broad scope of the federal fraud statutes, motions charging insufficient pleadings or selective prosecution generally deserve careful consideration. We need not scrutinize the lower court's rejection of the defendant's arguments in favor of dismissing the indictment, however, because we reverse the conviction on the clearer ground that the trial evidence mustered by the government was insufficient to support a guilty verdict, and hold that the defendant's motion for judgment of acquittal should have been granted on all counts. Unauthorized browsing of taxpayer files, although certainly inappropriate conduct, cannot, without more, sustain this federal felony conviction.

Background

For all periods relevant to the acts giving rise to his conviction, the defendant Czubinski was employed as a Contact Representative in the Boston office of the Taxpayer Services Division of the Internal Revenue Service. To perform his official duties, which mainly involved answering questions from taxpayers regarding their returns, Czubinski routinely accessed information from one of the IRS's computer systems known as the Integrated Data Retrieval System ("IDRS"). Using a valid password given to Contact Representatives, certain search codes, and taxpayer social security numbers, Czubinski was able to retrieve, to his terminal screen in Boston, income tax return information regarding virtually any taxpayer—information that is permanently stored in the IDRS "master file" located in Martinsburg, West Virginia. In the period of Czubinski's employ, IRS rules plainly stated that employees with passwords and access codes were not permitted to access files on IDRS outside of the course of their official duties.[1]

In 1992, Czubinski carried out numerous unauthorized searches of IDRS files. He knowingly disregarded IRS rules by looking at confidential information obtained by performing computer searches that were outside of the scope of his duties as a Contact Representative, including, but not limited to, the searches listed in the indictment. Audit trails performed by internal IRS auditors establish that Czubinski frequently made unauthorized accesses on IDRS in 1992. For example, Czubinski accessed information regarding: the tax returns of two individuals involved in the David Duke presidential campaign; the joint tax return of an assistant district attorney (who had been prosecuting Czubinski's father on an unrelated felony offense) and his wife; the tax return of Boston City Counselor Jim Kelly's Campaign Committee (Kelly had defeated Czubinski in the previous election for the Counselor seat for District 2); the tax return of one of his brothers' instructors; the joint tax return of a Boston Housing Authority police officer, who was involved in a community organization with one of Czubinski's brothers, and the officer's wife; and the tax return of a woman Czubinski had dated a few times. Czubinski also accessed the

---

[1]   In 1987 Czubinski signed an acknowledgment of receipt of the IRS Rules of Conduct, which contained the following rule: Employees must make every effort to assure security and prevent unauthorized disclosure of protected information data in the use of Government owned or leased computers. In addition, employees may not use any Service computer system for other than official purposes.

In addition, Czubinski received separate rules regarding use of the IDRS, one of which states: Access only those accounts required to accomplish your official duties.

files of various other social acquaintances by performing unauthorized searches.

Nothing in the record indicates that Czubinski did anything more than knowingly disregard IRS rules by observing the confidential information he accessed. No evidence suggests, nor does the government contend, that Czubinski disclosed the confidential information he accessed to any third parties. The government's only evidence demonstrating any intent to use the confidential information for nefarious ends was the trial testimony of William A. Murray, an acquaintance of Czubinski who briefly participated in Czubinski's local Invisible Knights of the Ku Klux Klan chapter and worked with him on the David Duke campaign. Murray testified that Czubinski had once stated at a social gathering in "early 1992" that "he intended to use some of that information to build dossiers on people" involved in "the white supremacist movement." There is, however, no evidence that Czubinski created dossiers, took steps toward making dossiers (such as by printing out or recording the information he browsed), or shared any of the information he accessed in the years following the single comment to Murray. No other witness testified to having any knowledge of Czubinski's alleged intent to create "dossiers" on KKK members.

The record shows that Czubinski did not perform any unauthorized searches after 1992. He continued to be employed as a Contact Representative until June 1995, when a grand jury returned an indictment against him on ten counts of federal wire fraud under 18 U.S.C. §§ 1343, 1346, and four counts of federal interest computer fraud under 18 U.S.C. § 1030(a)(4).

The portion of the indictment alleging wire fraud states that Czubinski defrauded the IRS of confidential property by using his valid password to acquire confidential taxpayer information as part of a scheme to: 1) build "dossiers" on associates in the KKK; 2) seek information regarding an assistant district attorney who was then prosecuting Czubinski's father on an unrelated criminal charge; and 3) perform opposition research by inspecting the records of a political opponent in the race for a Boston City Councilor seat. The wire fraud indictment, therefore, articulated particular personal ends to which the unauthorized access to confidential information through interstate wires was allegedly a means.

The portion of the indictment setting forth the computer fraud charges stated that Czubinski obtained something of value, beyond the mere unauthorized use of a federal interest computer, by performing certain searches—searches representing a subset of those making up the mail fraud counts.

Discussion

I.   The Wire Fraud Counts

To support a conviction for wire fraud, the government must prove two elements beyond a reasonable doubt: (1) the defendant's knowing and willing participation in a scheme or artifice to defraud with the specific intent to defraud, and (2) the use of interstate wire communications in furtherance of the scheme. Although defendant's motion for judgment of acquittal places emphasis on shortcomings in proof with regard to the second element, by arguing that the wire transmissions at issue were not proved to be interstate, we find the first element dispositive and hold that the government failed to prove beyond a reasonable doubt that the defendant willfully participated in a scheme to defraud within the meaning of the wire fraud statute.

The government correctly notes that confidential information may constitute intangible "property" and that its unauthorized dissemination or other use may deprive the owner of its property rights. *See Carpenter v. United States*, 484 U.S. 19, 26 (1987). Where such deprivation is effected through dishonest or deceitful means, a "scheme to defraud," within the meaning of the wire fraud statute, is shown. Thus, a necessary step toward satisfying the "scheme to defraud" element in this context is showing that the defendant intended to "deprive" another of their protected right.

The government, however, provides no case in support of its contention here that merely accessing confidential information, without doing, or clearly intending to do, more, is tantamount to a deprivation of IRS property under the wire fraud statute. In *Carpenter*, for example, the confidential information regarding the contents of a newspaper column was converted to the defendants's use to their substantial benefit. *See id.* at 27 (defendants participated in "ongoing scheme to share profit from trading in anticipation" of newspaper column). We do not think that Czubinski's unauthorized browsing, even if done with the intent to deceive the IRS into thinking he was performing only authorized searches, constitutes a "deprivation" within the meaning of the federal fraud statutes.

Binding precedents, and good sense, support the conclusion that to "deprive" a person of their intangible property interest in confidential information under section 1343, either some articulable harm must befall the holder of the information as a result of the defendant's activities, or some gainful use must be intended by the person accessing the information, whether or not this use is profitable in the economic sense. Here, neither the taking of the IRS' right to "exclusive use" of the confidential information, nor Czubinski's gain from access to the information, can be shown absent evidence of his "use" of the information. Accordingly, without evidence that Czubinski used or intended to use the taxpayer information (beyond mere browsing), an intent to deprive cannot be proven, and, a fortiori, a scheme to defraud, is not shown.

All of the cases cited by the government in support of their contention that the confidentiality breached by Czubinski's search in itself constitutes a deprivation of property in fact support our holding today, for they all involve, at a minimum, a finding of a further intended use of the confidential information accessed by the defendants. The government's best support comes from *United States v. Seidlitz*, 589 F.2d 152, 160 (4th Cir. 1978), in which a former employee of a computer systems firm secretly accessed its files, but never was shown to have sold or used the data he accessed, and was nevertheless convicted of wire fraud. The affirming Fourth Circuit held, however, that a jury could have reasonably found that, at the time the defendant raided a competitor's computer system, he intended to retrieve information that would be helpful for his own start-up, competing computer firm. In the instant case, Czubinski did indeed access confidential information through fraudulent pretenses—he appeared to be performing his duties when in fact he used IRS passwords to perform unauthorized searches. Nevertheless, it was not proven that he intended to deprive the IRS of their property interest through either disclosure or use of that information.

The resolution of the instant case is complex because it is well-established that to be convicted of mail or wire fraud, the defendant need not successfully carry out an intended scheme to defraud. The government does not contend either that Czubinski actually created dossiers or that he accomplished some other end through use of the information. It need not do so. All that the government was required to prove was the intent to follow through with a deprivation of the IRS's property and the use or foreseeable use of interstate wire transmissions pursuant to the accomplishment of the scheme to defraud. In the case at bar, the government failed to make even this showing.

The fatal flaw in the government's case is that it has not shown beyond a reasonable doubt that Czubinski intended to carry out a scheme to deprive the IRS of its property interest in confidential information. Had there been sufficient proof that Czubinski intended either to create dossiers for the sake of advancing personal causes or to disseminate confidential information to third parties, then his actions in searching files could arguably be said to be a step in furtherance of a scheme to deprive the IRS of its property interest in confidential information.

Mere browsing of the records of people about whom one might have a particular interest, although reprehensible, is not enough to sustain a wire fraud conviction on a "deprivation of intangible property" theory. Curiosity on the part of an IRS officer may lead to dismissal, but curiosity alone will not sustain a finding of participation in a felonious criminal scheme to deprive the IRS of its property.

II.   The Computer Fraud Counts

Czubinski was convicted on all four of the computer fraud counts on which he was indicted; these counts arise out of unauthorized searches that also formed the basis of four of the ten wire fraud counts in the indictment. Specifically, he was convicted of violating 18 U.S.C. § 1030(a)(4), a provision enacted in the Computer Fraud and Abuse Act of 1986. Section 1030(a)(4) applies to:

> whoever ... knowingly and with intent to defraud, accesses a Federal interest computer without authorization, or exceeds authorized access, and by means of such conduct furthers the intended fraud and obtains anything of value, unless the object of the fraud and the thing obtained consists only of the use of the computer.

We have never before addressed section 1030(a)(4). Czubinski unquestionably exceeded authorized access to a Federal interest computer. On appeal he argues that he did not obtain "anything of value." We agree, finding that his searches of taxpayer return information did not satisfy the statutory requirement that he obtain "anything of value." The value of information is relative to one's needs and objectives; here, the government had to show that the information was valuable to Czubinski in light of a fraudulent scheme. The government failed, however, to prove that Czubinski intended anything more than to satisfy idle curiosity.

The plain language of section 1030(a)(4) emphasizes that more than mere unauthorized use is required: the "thing obtained" may not merely be the unauthorized use. It is the showing of some additional end—to which the unauthorized access is a means—that is lacking here. The evidence did not show that Czubinski's end was anything more than to satisfy his curiosity by viewing information about friends, acquaintances, and political rivals. No evidence suggests that he printed out, recorded, or used the information he browsed. No rational jury could conclude beyond a reasonable doubt that Czubinski intended to use or disclose that information, and merely viewing information cannot be deemed the same as obtaining something of value for the purposes of this statute.[15]

The legislative history further supports our reading of the term "anything of value." In the game of statutory interpretation, statutory

---

[15] The district court, in denying a motion to dismiss the computer fraud counts in the indictment, found that the indictment sufficiently alleged that the confidential taxpayer information was itself a "thing of value" to Czubinski, given his ends. The indictment, of course, alleged specific uses for the information, such as creating dossiers on KKK members, that were not proven at trial. In light of the trial evidence—which, as we have said, indicates that there was no recording, disclosure or further use of the confidential information—we find that Czubinski did not obtain "anything of value" through his unauthorized searches.

language is the ultimate trump card, and the remarks of sponsors of legislation are authoritative only to the extent that they are compatible with the plain language of section 1030(a)(4). Here, a Senate co-sponsor's comments suggest that Congress intended section 1030(a)(4) to punish attempts to steal valuable data, and did not wish to punish mere unauthorized access:

> The acts of fraud we are addressing in proposed section 1030(a)(4) are essentially thefts in which someone uses a federal interest computer to wrongly obtain something of value from another. . . Proposed section 1030(a)(4) is intended to reflect the distinction between the theft of information, a felony, and mere unauthorized access, a misdemeanor.

132 Cong. Rec. 7128, 7129, 99th Cong., 2d. Sess. (1986). The Senate Committee Report further underscores the fact that this section should apply to those who steal information through unauthorized access as part of an illegal scheme:

> The Committee remains convinced that there must be a clear distinction between computer theft, punishable as a felony [under section 1030(a)(4)], and computer trespass, punishable in the first instance as a misdemeanor [under a different provision]. The element in the new paragraph (a)(4), requiring a showing of an intent to defraud, is meant to preserve that distinction, as is the requirement that the property wrongfully obtained via computer furthers the intended fraud.

S. Rep. No. 432, 99th Cong., 2d Sess., *reprinted in* 1986 U.S.C.C.A.N. 2479, 2488. For the same reasons we deemed the trial evidence could not support a finding that Czubinski deprived the IRS of its property, *see* discussion of wire fraud under section 1343 *supra,* we find that Czubinski has not obtained valuable information in furtherance of a fraudulent scheme for the purposes of section 1030(a)(4).

Conclusion

We add a cautionary note. The broad language of the mail and wire fraud statutes are both their blessing and their curse. They can address new forms of serious crime that fail to fall within more specific legislation. On the other hand, they might be used to prosecute kinds of behavior that, albeit offensive to the morals or aesthetics of federal prosecutors, cannot reasonably be expected by the instigators to form the basis of a federal felony. The case at bar falls within the latter category. Also discomforting is the prosecution's insistence, before trial, on the admission of inflammatory evidence regarding the defendant's membership in white supremacist groups purportedly as a means to prove a scheme to defraud, when, on appeal, it argues that unauthorized access in itself is a sufficient ground for conviction on all counts. Finally, we caution that the wire fraud statute must not serve as a vehicle for prosecuting only those citizens whose views run against the tide, no matter how incorrect or uncivilized such views are.

NOTES AND QUESTIONS

1. *Comparing § 1030(a)(4) and § 1030(a)(2).* Consider the key differences between computer fraud and basic unauthorized access. *Czubinski* and the legislative history of § 1030 instruct that the most basic difference is that the unauthorized access and retrieval of information in a case of computer fraud is part of a broader scheme that harms the victim in an appreciable way. Absent such a broader scheme to harm the victim, the crime is mere trespass, a misdemeanor unauthorized access violation under § 1030(a)(2). Was Czubinski guilty of violating 18 U.S.C. § 1030(a)(2)(B)? If he was, why did the government charge Czubinski under § 1030(a)(4) instead? (Hint: Think of the penalties.)

With that said, the felony provisions of § 1030(a)(2) create a great deal of overlap with § 1030(a)(4). Felony liability under § 1030(a)(2) is triggered if the offense was committed "for purposes of commercial advantage or private financial gain," the offense was committed "in furtherance of any criminal or tortious act in violation of the Constitution or laws of the United States or of any State," or the value of the information obtained exceeds $5,000. 18 U.S.C. § 1030(c)(2). How different is this from *Czubinski*'s requirement of a broader scheme to harm the victim? To the extent there is a difference, which is a better approach?

2. *Comparing § 1030(a)(4) and § 1343.* Note the basic differences between the computer fraud statute and the wire fraud statute. The actus reus of computer fraud is accessing a computer without authorization or exceeding authorized access, while the actus reus of wire fraud is transmitting a wire, radio, or television communication across state or national boundaries. In effect, the unauthorized access to a computer replaces the interstate requirement. The computer fraud statute also requires that the actus reus must further the fraud, while the wire fraud statute does not. Further, the computer fraud statute specifies that "use of the computer" cannot be the object of value fraudulently obtained if "the value of such use is not more than $5,000 in any one-year period," while the wire fraud statute contains no analogous limitation.

The limitation on use of a computer as an object obtained under the computer fraud statute is largely a leftover from the economics of computer usage in the 1980s. At that time, computers were rare and computer usage often had considerable economic value. Unauthorized access to a computer per se could impose costs on the computer's owner. The legislative history of § 1030(a)(4) suggests that the limitation on computer use as an object of value was designed to distinguish computer fraud from unauthorized access:

> The mere use of a computer or computer service has a value all its own. Mere trespasses onto someone else's computer system can cost

the system provider a "port" or access channel that he might otherwise be making available for a fee to an authorized user. At the same time, the Committee believes it is important to distinguish clearly between acts of fraud under (a)(4), punishable as felonies, and acts of simple trespass, punishable in the first instance as misdemeanors. That distinction would be wiped out were the Committee to treat every trespass as an attempt to defraud a service provider of computer time. One simply cannot trespass into another's computer without occupying a portion of the time that that computer service is available. Thus, that suggested approach would treat every act of unauthorized entry to a Federal interest computer—no matter how brief—as an act of fraud, punishable at the felony level. The Committee does not believe this is a proper approach to this problem. For that reason, the Committee has excluded from coverage under this subsection those instances where "the object of the fraud and the thing obtained consists only of the use of the computer."

S. Rep. No. 99–432, at 10 (1986), *reprinted in* 1986 U.S.C.C.A.N. 2479, 2488. Note that the requirement of $5,000 applies only in the now-extremely rare case that the use of the computer is the property taken. In the general case, § 1030(a)(4) does not impose a requirement that $5,000 of property must be obtained.

F. 18 U.S.C. § 1030(a)(5) AND COMPUTER DAMAGE STATUTES

Computer damage statutes are the third and final type of basic computer misuse statute. Computer damage statutes focus on the harm inflicted on the computer owner and attempt to impose criminal liability for conduct that caused a particular amount of harm. Computer damage statutes can be divided into two types. Some computer damage statutes are focused on conduct that exceeds privileges to use a computer. These statutes typically combine the basic prohibition on unauthorized access with an additional requirement that the conduct caused a particular amount of damage or harm.

Other statutes focus on conduct that denies privileges to other users. Such provisions do not require unauthorized access, but instead look to unauthorized acts of deleting, damaging, altering, or rendering inaccessible a set of files or programs on the victim computer. The line between the two types of computer damage statutes can be slippery in practice, in part because a user may exceed his privileges in the course of engaging in conduct that ultimately denies privileges to others. Indeed, many state statutes combine the two types into a single prohibition.

The federal computer damage statute is found at 18 U.S.C. § 1030(a)(5). Like violations of § 1030(a)(2), violations of § 1030(a)(5) can be misdemeanors or felonies. It helps to consider misdemeanor liability first, and felony liability second.

1.   18 U.S.C. § 1030(a)(5) MISDEMEANOR LIABILITY

In its current form, enacted in 2008, 18 U.S.C. § 1030(a)(5) prohibits three basic misdemeanor offenses. It punishes whoever

(A) knowingly causes the transmission of a program, information, code, or command, and as a result of such conduct, intentionally causes damage without authorization, to a protected computer;

(B) intentionally accesses a protected computer without authorization, and as a result of such conduct, recklessly causes damage; or

(C) intentionally accesses a protected computer without authorization, and as a result of such conduct, causes damage and loss.

There is considerable overlap among the three prohibitions of 18 U.S.C. § 1030(a)(5). The first prohibition targets conduct that denies privileges to other users, such as sending out computer viruses and launching denial-of-service attacks. 18 U.S.C. § 1030(a)(5)(A) prohibits "knowingly caus[ing] the transmission of a program, information, code, or command, and as a result of such conduct, intentionally caus[ing] damage without authorization, to a protected computer." Note that the absence of authorization does not refer to the access, but rather to causing damage. While it may seem odd that the statute would require that the damage be unauthorized, authorized damage is possible. For example, an employee may be authorized to encrypt information belonging to an employer; the act of encrypting data constitutes damage because it impairs the availability of the encrypted information.

The second and third prohibitions in § 1030(a)(5) are variations on unauthorized access statutes. 18 U.S.C. § 1030(a)(5)(B) prohibits "intentionally access[ing] a protected computer without authorization, and as a result of such conduct, recklessly caus[ing] damage." Note that the authorization requirement extends only to access "without authorization," and does not include exceeding authorized access. Here the conduct element is accessing a protected computer without authorization, and the result element that must be caused by the access is "damage."

The third prohibition, 18 U.S.C. § 1030(a)(5)(C), is very similar to the second prohibition, 18 U.S.C. § 1030(a)(5)(B). There are only two differences. The first difference is that a violation of 18 U.S.C. § 1030(a)(5)(C) must cause both damage *and* some amount of loss, while a violation of 18 U.S.C. § 1030(a)(5)(B) need only cause damage. The second difference is the mens rea with respect to causing an impairment to the integrity or availability of data or information. The second prohibition requires that the defendant must be reckless with respect to causing that impairment; the third prohibition imposes strict liability with respect to causing the impairment. The Senate Report that accompanied the enactment of these provisions explained Congress's decision to punish even entirely accidental damage:

> Although those who intentionally damage a system, without authority, should be punished regardless of whether they are authorized users, it is equally clear that anyone who knowingly invades a system without authority and causes significant loss to the victim should be punished as well, even when the damage caused is not intentional. In such cases, it is the intentional act of trespass that makes the conduct criminal. To provide otherwise is to openly invite hackers to break into computer systems, safe in the knowledge that no matter how much damage they cause, it is no crime unless that damage was either intentional or reckless. Rather than send such a dangerous message (and deny victims any relief), it is better to ensure that section 1030(a)(5) criminalizes all computer trespass, as well as intentional damage by insiders, albeit at different levels of severity.

S. Rep. 104–357, at 11 (1996).

18 U.S.C. § 1030(a)(5)(A) is different from other provisions of § 1030 because it prohibits unauthorized damage instead of unauthorized access. This raises obvious questions: When is a person authorized to damage a computer? How clear must authorization be, and how can it be provided? The following recent case sheds light on the answers.

UNITED STATES v. THOMAS
United States Court of Appeals for the Fifth Circuit, 2017.
877 F.3d 591.

GREGG COSTA, CIRCUIT JUDGE.

Michael Thomas worked as the Information Technology Operations Manager for ClickMotive, LP, a software and webpage hosting company. Upset that a coworker had been fired, Thomas embarked on a weekend campaign of electronic sabotage. He deleted over 600 files, disabled backup operations, eliminated employees from a group email a client used to contact the company, diverted executives' emails to his personal account, and set a "time bomb" that would result in employees being unable to remotely access the company's network after Thomas submitted his resignation. Once ClickMotive discovered what Thomas did, it incurred over $130,000 in costs to fix these problems.

A jury found Thomas guilty of knowingly causing the transmission of a program, information, code, or command, and as a result of such conduct, intentionally causing damage without authorization, to a protected computer. 18 U.S.C. § 1030(a)(5)(A). Thomas challenges the "without authorization" requirement of this provision of the Computer Fraud and Abuse Act. He contends that because his IT job gave him full access to the system and required him to "damage" the system—for example, at times his duties included deleting certain files—his conduct did not lack authorization. But we conclude that Thomas's conduct falls squarely within the ordinary meaning of the statute and affirm his conviction.

I.

Thomas's duties at ClickMotive included network administration; maintaining production websites; installing, maintaining, upgrading, and troubleshooting network servers; ensuring system security and data integrity; and performing backups. He was granted full access to the network operating system and had the authority to access any data and change any setting on the system. Thomas was expected to perform his duties using his "best efforts and judgment to produce maximum benefit" to ClickMotive.

Thomas was not happy when his friend in the IT department was fired. It was not just a matter of loyalty to his former colleague; a smaller IT staff meant more work for Thomas. So Thomas, to use his word, "tinkered" with the company's system. The tinkering, which started on a Friday evening and continued through Monday morning, included the following:

- He deleted 625 files of backup history and deleted automated commands set to perform future backups.

- He issued a command to destroy the virtual machine that performed ClickMotive's backups for one of its servers and then Thomas failed to activate its redundant pair, ensuring that the backups would not occur.

- He tampered with ClickMotive's pager notification system by entering false contact information for various company employees, ensuring that they would not receive any automatically-generated alerts indicating system problems.

- He triggered automatic forwarding of executives' emails to an external personal email account he created during the weekend.

- He deleted pages from ClickMotive's internal "wiki," an online system of internal policies and procedures that employees routinely used for troubleshooting computer problems.

- He manually changed the setting for an authentication service that would eventually lead to the inability of employees to work remotely through VPN. Changing the setting of the VPN authentication service set a time bomb that would cause the VPN to become inoperative when someone rebooted the system, a common and foreseeable maintenance function.

- And he removed employees from e-mail distribution groups created for the benefit of customers, leading to customers' requests for support going unnoticed.

Thomas was able to engage in most of this conduct from home, but he did set the VPN time bomb on Sunday evening from ClickMotive's office, which he entered using another employee's credentials. It was during this visit to the office that Thomas left his resignation letter that the company would see the next day. When the dust settled, the company incurred over $130,000 in out-of-pocket expenses and employees' time to undo the harm Thomas caused. In a subsequent interview with the FBI, Thomas stated that he engaged in this conduct because he was frustrated with the company and wanted to make the job harder for the person who would replace him.

A grand jury eventually charged Thomas with the section 1030(a)(5)(A) offense. But two days before the grand jury met, Thomas fled to Brazil. Nearly three years later, Thomas was arrested when he surrendered to FBI agents at Dallas/Fort Worth International Airport.

At trial, company employees and outside IT experts testified that none of the problems ClickMotive experienced as a result of Thomas's actions would be attributable to a normal system malfunction. They further stated that Thomas's actions were not consistent with normal troubleshooting and maintenance or consistent with mistakes made by a novice. ClickMotive employees asserted that it was strange for the wiki pages to be missing and that someone in Thomas's position would know that changing the setting of the VPN authentication service would cause it to become inoperative when someone rebooted the system.

ClickMotive's employee handbook was not offered at trial and there was no specific company policy that governed the deletions of backups, virtual machines, or wiki modifications. Employees explained, however, that there were policies prohibiting interfering with ClickMotive's normal course of business and the destruction of its assets, such as a virtual machine or company data. Thomas's own Employment Agreement specified he was bound by policies that were reasonably necessary to protect ClickMotive's legitimate interests in its clients, customers, accounts, and work product.

The jury instructions included the statutory definition of "damage," which is "any impairment to the integrity or availability of data, a program, a system, or information." 18 U.S.C. § 1030(e)(8). The district court denied Thomas's proposed instruction for "without authorization," which was "without permission or authority." It did not define the phrase.

After the jury returned a guilty verdict, the district court sentenced Thomas to time served (which was the four months since he had been detained after returning to the country), plus three years of supervised release, and ordered restitution of $131,391.21.

II.

A.

Because Thomas's argument that he was authorized to damage a computer seems nonsensical at first glance, it is helpful at the outset to explain the steps he takes to get there. He first points out that his job duties included "routinely deleting data, removing programs, and taking systems offline for diagnosis and maintenance." Thomas says this conduct damaged the computer within the meaning of the Computer Fraud and Abuse Act because damage is defined to just mean "any impairment to the integrity or availability of data, a program, a system, or information," 18 U.S.C. § 1030(e)(8); there is no requirement of harm. And the damage he caused by engaging in these routine tasks was not "without authorization" because it was part of his job. So far, so good.

Next comes the critical leap: Thomas argues that because he was authorized to damage the computer when engaging in these routine tasks, *any* damage he caused while an employee was not "without authorization." Thus he cannot be prosecuted under section 1030(a)(5)(A). This argument is far reaching. If Thomas is correct, then the damage statute would not reach any employee who intentionally damaged a computer system as long as any part of that employee's job included deleting files or taking systems offline.

Thomas's support for reading the statute to cover only individuals who had no rights, limited or otherwise to impair a system comes from cases addressing the separate "access" provisions of section 1030. *See, e.g., LVRC Holdings LLC v. Brekka*, 581 F.3d 1127, 1133 (9th Cir. 2009) ("A person who uses a computer 'without authorization' has no rights, limited or otherwise, to access the computer in question."). But there are important differences between the "access" and "damage" crimes that make it inappropriate to import access caselaw into the damage statute.

Section 1030(a)(5)(A) is the only independent "damage" provision, meaning it does not also require a lack of authorization to access the computer. *Contrast* 18 U.S.C. § 1030(a)(5)(B), (C) (both applying to damage that results from unauthorized access of a computer). It prohibits intentionally causing damage without authorization. As discussed, the statute defines damage. And as numerous courts have recognized in discussing both the damage and access provisions, the ordinary meaning of "without authorization" is "without permission." Indeed, Thomas asked that the jury be told that "without authorization" means "without permission or authority"; he did not seek an instruction that "without authorization" is limited to those who have no rights to ever impair a system.

As the caselaw and Thomas's proposed instruction recognize, the plain meaning of the damage provision is that it makes it a crime to intentionally impair a computer system without permission. And notably, it applies to particular acts causing damage that lacked authorization. *See* 18 U.S.C. § 1030(e)(8) (defining damage to include a single impairment of the system). Nothing in the statutory text says it does not apply to intentional acts of damage that lacked permission if the employee was allowed to engage at other times in other acts that impaired the system.

"Without authorization" modifies damage rather than access. Section 1030(a)(5)(A) makes no distinction between all-or-nothing authorization and degrees of authorization. Its text therefore covers situations when the individual never had permission to damage the system (an outsider) or when someone who might have permission for some damaging acts causes other damage that is not authorized (an insider). Tellingly, other subsections of the same damage statute are limited to those who inflict damage while "intentionally access[ing] a protected computer without authorization." 18 U.S.C. § 1030(a)(5)(B), (C). Because section 1030(a)(5)(A) is the one subsection of the damage statute that also applies to insiders, it would make no sense to import a limitation from the access statutes that is aimed at excluding insider liability.

Nor is there a significant threat that liability under the damage statute would extend to largely innocuous conduct because the requirement of "intentionally causing damage" narrows the statute's reach.

We conclude that Section 1030(a)(5)(A) prohibits intentionally damaging a computer system when there was no permission to engage in that particular act of damage. To the extent more is needed to flesh out the scope of "permission" when a defendant has some general authority to impair a network, there is helpful guidance in one of our cases addressing an access statute, which if anything should define authorization more narrowly for the reasons we have discussed. *United States v. Phillips*, 477 F.3d 215, 219 (5th Cir. 2007), says to look at the expected norms of intended use.

B.

There is overwhelming evidence to support the jury's view that Thomas did not have permission to engage in the weekend damage campaign.

The nature of Thomas's conduct is highly incriminating. No reasonable employee could think he had permission to stop the system from providing backups, or to delete files outside the normal protocols, or to falsify contact information in a notification system, or to set a process in motion that would prevent users from remotely accessing the network. Thomas emphasizes the unlimited access he had to the system that gave him the ability to inflict this damage. But it is not conceivable that any employee, regardless of their level of computer access, would be authorized to cause these problems. The incidents for which Thomas was held liable were nothing like the periodic acts he performed as part of his duties. Those tasks may have impaired the system on a limited basis in order to benefit the computer network in the long run. Routine deletions of old files provide that benefit by increasing storage space. Taking systems offline allows for necessary maintenance.

In contrast, the various types of damage Thomas caused during the last few days before he resigned resulted in over $130,000 in remediation costs. Regardless of whether the definition of "damage" under the statute requires a showing of harm, impairments that harm the system are much less likely to be authorized than those that benefit the system. It would rarely if ever make sense for an employer to authorize an employee to harm its computer system.

The harmful acts themselves would be enough to support the verdict, but Thomas's words and conduct in response to the criminal investigation provide additional support. When questioned by federal agents, he acknowledged the distinction we have just made. He did not say that he caused the damage in order to maintain or improve the system; instead, his motive was to make things more difficult for the person hired to replace him. And his flight to Brazil is not what is expected of someone who had permission to engage in the conduct being investigated.

The circumstances surrounding the damaging acts provide even more support for the finding of guilt. Thomas committed the various acts one after the other in a concentrated time span beginning Friday evening and continuing through the weekend. Thomas did most of this from home, but the one time he had to go the office he did so using another employee's credentials. One of his acts—falsification of contact information in the alert system—prevented Thomas's conduct from being detected during the weekend as employees would not receive notifications about the damage to the system. He submitted his resignation immediately after completing the damage spree and timed the most damaging act—the one that would prevent remote access—so that it would not occur until he was gone. Why this sequence of events if Thomas had permission to cause the damage? All of this provided ample support to conclude that Thomas lacked permission to inflict the damage he caused.

The judgment of the district court is affirmed.

NOTES AND QUESTIONS

1. *General overview of mental states (mens rea).* In criminal law, a mens rea is the mental state required with respect to each element of the offense to establish criminal liability. Although federal law does not follow the Model Penal Code generally, the legislative history of § 1030 suggests that its drafters wished to incorporate the MPC's mens rea provisions. *See, e.g.,* S. Rep. 101–544, at 9 (1990 amendments) ("The standard for recklessness used in the bill is taken from the Model Penal Code."); S. Rep. No. 99–432, *reprinted in* 1986 U.S.C.C.A.N. 2479, 2483–84 (1986 amendments) (discussing intent using the key phrases of the MPC). Under this framework, the primary mental states are intent, knowledge, and recklessness. *See* Model Penal Code § 2.02 (Official Draft 1962). The precise meaning of each mental state can vary depending on whether the element is a conduct element (describing the defendant's actions), a result element (describing a fact caused by the defendant's actions), or an attendant circumstances element (describing the state of the world surrounding the defendant's actions).

Specifically, a person acts intentionally when it is his conscious object to engage in conduct of that nature or to cause such a result; in the case of attendant circumstances, a person acts intentionally with respect to that element if he is aware of the element's existence, or he hopes or believes it will occur. *See* § 2.02(2)(a). A person acts knowingly if he is aware that his conduct is of that nature or that such circumstances exist; in the case of result elements, he acts knowingly if he is practically certain his conduct will cause such a result. *See* M.P.C. § 2.02(2)(b). Finally, a person acts recklessly if he consciously disregards a substantial and unjustifiable risk that the element exists or will result, and the disregard of the risk involves a gross deviation from the standard of a law-abiding person in the actor's situation considering the nature and purpose of the actor's conduct and the circumstances known to him. *See* M.P.C. § 2.02(2)(c).

2. *The mental states of 18 U.S.C. § 1030(a)(5).* Now consider the prohibition of § 1030(a)(5)(A), which punishes "knowingly caus[ing] the transmission of a program, information, code, or command, and as a result of such conduct, intentionally caus[ing] damage without authorization, to a protected computer." Under this provision, the transmission must be knowing, and both the causing of damage and the lack of authorization must be intentional. (Note that this standard does not require knowledge of or intent to satisfy the legal standards of damage or lack of authorization. Rather, it requires intent to impair the integrity or availability of data without authorization.)

In contrast, § 1030(a)(5)(B) prohibits "intentionally access[ing] a protected computer without authorization, and as a result of such conduct, recklessly caus[ing] damage." Here, the access and lack of authorization must be intentional, and the causing of damage must be reckless. The only somewhat ambiguous element in this provision is the attendant circumstance element "protected computer." It is not entirely clear from the text of the statute whether it requires intent that the computer is a protected computer, which in this case would mean awareness that the computer is a government computer or a computer used in or affecting interstate or foreign commerce or communication. The general rule is that there is no mens rea required for jurisdictional elements in federal criminal law, which suggest that in all likelihood this is a strict liability element. Either way, the definition of protected computer is sufficiently broad that this question seems unlikely to arise often.

Finally, § 1030(a)(5)(C) prohibits "intentionally access[ing] a protected computer without authorization, and as a result of such conduct, caus[ing] damage and loss." The access and lack of authorization must be intentional. Further, the unauthorized access must cause both damage and at least some amount of loss. However, the offense is strict liability as to damage and loss: No mental state is required.

3. *The meaning of "damage."* The three provisions of § 1030(a)(5) all require the causing of "damage." Damage is defined in 18 U.S.C. § 1030(e)(8) as "any impairment to the integrity or availability of data, a program, a system, or information." The meaning of the phrase "impairment to the integrity or availability of data, a program, a system, or information" can be found in technical authorities as well as legal ones, as the terms "integrity" and "availability" are well known in the field of computer security. Computer security specialists generally refer to the three foundational goals of computer security as protecting the confidentiality, integrity, and availability of data or information. *See, e.g.,* Matt Bishop, Introduction to Computer Security (2004).

Congress presumably intended availability and integrity to have the same meaning in § 1030 that they have in the computer security field. It seems likely that the third basic concept, confidentiality, was excluded from the damage definition because confidentiality is about exposure of information, a matter dealt with in § 1030(a)(2) rather than § 1030(a)(5).

Of the two concepts Congress did use, the availability of data or information is easier to understand. A denial-of-service attack impairs the availability of data or information, as does encrypting the data or information. Conduct that causes the computer be taken off-line for repairs also impairs its availability. More broadly, conduct that interferes with the proper functioning of computers by denying other users their privileges impairs the availability of data, a program, a system, or information.

Impairing the "integrity" of information is somewhat more difficult to understand. As one treatise on computer security explains:

Integrity refers to the trustworthiness of data or resources, and it is usually phrased in terms of preventing improper or unauthorized change. Integrity includes data integrity (the content of the information) and origin integrity (the source of the data, often called authentication). The source of the information may bear on its accuracy and credibility and on the trust that people place in the information. . .

Example: A newspaper may print information obtained from a leak at the White House but attribute it to the wrong source. The information is printed as received (preserving data integrity), but its source is incorrect (corrupting origin integrity).

Matt Bishop, Introduction to Computer Security 3 (2004).

For an interpretation of "damage," consider Pulte Homes, Inc. v. Laborers' International Union of North America, 648 F.3d 295 (6th Cir. 2011). Pulte Homes Inc. sued a labor union, Laborers' International Union of North America (LIUNA), for orchestrating an effort to disrupt the company's phone and e-mail systems. According to the complaint, the union bombarded the company's sales offices with thousands of phones calls and e-mails:

To generate a high volume of calls, LIUNA both hired an auto-dialing service and requested its members to call Pulte. It also encouraged its members, through postings on its website, to "fight back" by using LIUNA's server to send e-mails to specific Pulte executives. Most of the calls and e-mails concerned Pulte's purported unfair labor practices, though some communications included threats and obscene language. Yet it was the volume of the communications, and not their content, that injured Pulte. The calls clogged access to Pulte's voicemail system, prevented its customers from reaching its sales offices and representatives, and even forced one Pulte employee to turn off her business cell phone. The e-mails wreaked more havoc: they overloaded Pulte's system, which limits the number of e-mails in an inbox; and this, in turn, stalled normal business operations because Pulte's employees could not access business-related e-mails or send e-mails to customers and vendors.

According to the complaint, "the calls impeded access to voicemail, prevented Pulte's customers from reaching its sales offices and representatives, and forced an employee to turn off her cell phone. And LIUNA's e-mails—which overloaded Pulte's system—curtailed normal business operations because Pulte's employees could not access and respond to e-mails." *Id.* at 301. The Sixth Circuit concluded that this result constituted "damage" under § 1030(e)(8):

To understand "damage," we consult both the statutory text and ordinary usage. Under the CFAA, "any impairment to the integrity or availability of data, a program, a system, or information" qualifies as "damage." *Id.* § 1030(e)(8). Because the statute includes no definition for three key terms—"impairment," "integrity," and "availability"—we look to the ordinary meanings of these words. "Impairment" means a "deterioration" or an "injurious lessening or weakening." 7 Oxford English Dictionary 696 (2d ed. 1989) [hereinafter OED]. The definition of "integrity" includes an "uncorrupted condition," an "original perfect state," and "soundness." *Id.* at 1066. And "availability" is the "capability of being employed or made use of." 1 OED, *supra*, at 812. Applying these ordinary usages, we conclude that a transmission that weakens a sound computer system—or, similarly, one that diminishes a plaintiff's ability to use data or a system—causes damage.

LIUNA's barrage of calls and e-mails allegedly did just that. At a minimum, according to the complaint's well-pled allegations, the transmissions diminished Pulte's ability to use its systems and data because they prevented Pulte from receiving at least some calls and accessing or sending at least some e-mails. *Cf. Czech v. Wall St. on Demand, Inc.*, 674 F. Supp.2d 1102, 1117–18 (D.Minn. 2009) (dismissing a CFAA transmission claim because the plaintiff failed to allege that the defendant's text messages stopped her from receiving or sending any calls or text messages).

The diminished-ability concept that we endorse here is not novel: several district courts have already adopted it. *See, e.g., Condux Int'l, Inc. v. Haugum*, 2008 WL 5244818, at *8 (D.Minn. 2008) ("The damage contemplated by subsection (a)(5)(A)(i) requires some diminution in the completeness or useability of data or information on a computer system."); *Becker v. Toca*, 2008 WL 4443050, at *5 (E.D.La. 2008) ("Error messages and slow processing constitute impairments to the integrity or availability of data."); *Am. Online, Inc. v. Nat'l Health Care Disc., Inc.*, 121 F. Supp.2d 1255, 1274 (N.D. Iowa 2000) ("When a large volume of unsolicited bulk e-mail causes slowdowns or diminishes the capacity of AOL to serve its customers, an impairment has occurred to the 'availability' of AOL's system.").

Moreover, our interpretation comports with two decisions from sister circuits. The Third Circuit sustained a transmission conviction where the defendant "admitted that in using the direct e-mailing method and sending thousands of e-mails to one inbox, the targeted inbox would flood with e-mails and thus impair the user's ability to access his other 'good' e-mails." *United States v. Carlson*, 209 Fed.Appx. 181, 185 (3d Cir. 2006). And the Seventh Circuit, in *United States v. Mitra*, 405 F.3d 492, 494 (7th Cir. 2005), upheld the defendant's transmission conviction because he impaired the availability of an emergency communication system when data that he sent interfered with the way the computer allocated communications to the other 19 radio channels and stopped the flow of information among public-safety officers. That these decisions involve criminal prosecutions is irrelevant. In both cases, the government proved beyond a reasonable doubt that the transmissions impaired the availability of the computer equipment; here, Pulte adequately alleges that result.

Because Pulte alleges that the transmissions diminished its ability to send and receive calls and e-mails, it accordingly alleges an impairment to the integrity or availability of its data and systems— i.e., statutory damage.

Id. at 301–02.

4. *How far can "damage" go?* For a case that stretches the meaning of "damage," consider Yoder & Frey Auctioneers, Inc. v. EquipmentFacts, LLC, 774 F.3d 1065 (6th Cir. 2014). Yoder & Frey is an auction company that used to do business with EquipmentFacts ("Efacts"). After the relationship soured, employees at Efacts decided to harm Yoder & Frey by placing fake bids at Yoder & Frey's auction and then not paying for the items they had won. To do this, the Efacts employees correctly guessed the passwords for two existing Yoder & Frey online auction accounts. They used the accounts to place fake bids that won 20 auctions worth over $1 million. When no one paid for the items, Yoder & Frey investigated and realized that employees at Efacts had placed the fake bids.

Yoder & Frey filed a civil suit against Efacts under 18 U.S.C. § 1030(a)(5)(C). The Sixth Circuit ruled that placing the fake bids had "damaged" the Yoder & Frey computers:

> [A Yoder & Frey employee] testified: "If ultimately the winning bid was for $10,000, it would have prevented an auction participant not only from bidding but from actually winning the item. So a false $10,000 winning bid would have precluded a legitimate buyer from actually acquiring that item at $10,000." By placing false bids and occupying bidding slots, Efacts impaired the integrity of the program and/or system because legitimate bidders were unable to bid that same amount. Stated differently, Efacts' conduct interfered with the ability of the auction platform to function as intended—true bidders were unable to acquire the items at issue for their lowest possible price.

Id. at 1073.

Are you persuaded? Imagine you visit eBay and you place a winning bid for a $10 item but you have no intention of paying. Have you "damaged" eBay's computers? What if you place your winning bid in good faith but later you forget to pay? Does your forgetfulness "damage" eBay by interfering with the intended function of the auction platform to match items with the highest paying bidders? Or are you a "true bidder" because you had a good faith intent to pay when you placed your bid?

Alternatively, consider a different rationale for the Sixth Circuit's conclusion that damage occurred. The Efacts employees had guessed passwords to access private Yoder & Frey auction accounts. Why didn't those acts of unauthorized access impair the integrity of the data in the compromised accounts?

5. *The transmission requirement.* 18 U.S.C. § 1030(a)(5)(A) requires "knowingly caus[ing] the transmission of a program, information, code, or command." What exactly does this mean?

In International Airport Centers v. Citrin, 440 F.3d 418 (7th Cir. 2006), an employee of a real estate business decided to leave his company and go into business himself. The employee, Citrin, had been provided a laptop computer by his employer, IAC. To ensure that IAC would be unable to access files on the laptop, Citrin obtained and used a "secure erase" software program that permanently deleted files on the laptop. IAC brought a civil suit against Citrin, claiming that deleting the files had violated 18 U.S.C. § 1030(a)(5)(A)(i). In an opinion by Judge Posner, the Seventh Circuit ruled that these facts established "the transmission of a program, information, code, or command":

> Citrin argues that merely erasing a file from a computer is not a "transmission." Pressing a delete or erase key in fact transmits a command, but it might be stretching the statute too far (especially since it provides criminal as well as civil sanctions for its violation) to consider any typing on a computer keyboard to be a form of "transmission" just because it transmits a command to the computer.

> There is more here, however: the transmission of the secure-erasure program to the computer. We do not know whether the program was downloaded from the Internet or copied from a floppy disk (or the equivalent of a floppy disk, such as a CD) inserted into a disk drive that was either inside the computer or attached to it by a wire. Oddly, the complaint doesn't say; maybe IAC doesn't know—maybe all it knows is that when it got the computer back, the files in it had been erased.

> But we don't see what difference the precise mode of transmission can make. In either the Internet download or the disk insertion, a program intended to cause damage (not to the physical computer, of course, but to its files—but "damage" includes "any impairment to the integrity or availability of data, a program, a system, or information," 18 U.S.C. § 1030(e)(8)) is transmitted to the computer electronically.

> There is the following contextual difference between the two modes of transmission, however: transmission via disk requires that the malefactor have physical access to the computer. By using the Internet, Citrin might have erased the laptop's files from afar by transmitting a virus. Congress was concerned with both types of attack: attacks by virus and worm writers, on the one hand, which come mainly from the outside, and attacks by disgruntled programmers who decide to trash the employer's data system on the way out (or threaten to do so in order to extort payments), on the other.

Id. at 419–20.

2. 18 U.S.C. § 1030(a)(5) FELONY LIABILITY

Although some violations of § 1030(a)(5) are only misdemeanors, violations of § 1030(a)(5)(A) and § 1030(a)(5)(B) can become felonies in some circumstances. For example, they can become felonies in the unlikely event that a defendant has a previous § 1030 conviction. *See* 18 U.S.C. § 1030(c)(4)(C)(i) (imposing a 20 year statutory maximum punishment). Violations of § 1030(a)(5)(A) can be particularly serious felonies if the conduct involves the causation of bodily injury or death. If the defendant "attempts to cause or knowingly or recklessly causes serious bodily injury from conduct in violation of subsection (a)(5)(A)," the offense is a felony with a 20-year maximum punishment. 18 U.S.C. § 1030(c)(4)(E). If the defendant "attempts to cause or knowingly or recklessly causes death from conduct in violation of subsection (a)(5)(A)," the offense is a felony with a maximum punishment of life in prison. 18 U.S.C. § 1030(c)(4)(F).

These circumstances are rare, however. It is much more common for prosecutors to charge felony liability under § 1030(a)(5) based on the felony enhancements provided in 18 U.S.C. § 1030(c)(4)(A)(i). Under this section of the statute, a misdemeanor violation of § 1030(a)(5)(A) or § 1030(a)(5)(B) becomes a felony if any of the following six harms was caused by the defendant's conduct:

(I) loss to 1 or more persons during any 1-year period (and, for purposes of an investigation, prosecution, or other proceeding brought by the United States only, loss resulting from a related course of conduct affecting 1 or more other protected computers) aggregating at least $5,000 in value;

(II) the modification or impairment, or potential modification or impairment, of the medical examination, diagnosis, treatment, or care of 1 or more individuals;

(III) physical injury to any person;

(IV) a threat to public health or safety;

(V) damage affecting a computer used by or for an entity of the United States Government in furtherance of the administration of justice, national defense, or national security; or

(VI) damage affecting 10 or more protected computers during any 1-year period.

See 18 U.S.C. § 1030(c)(4)(A)(i) (imposing a 5-year statutory maximum punishment when such harms result with § 1030(a)(5)(B) offenses); 18 U.S.C. § 1030(c)(4)(B)(i) (imposing a 10-year statutory maximum punishment when such harms result with § 1030(a)(5)(A) offenses). In most cases, the above list effectively draws the line between mere misdemeanor § 1030(a)(5) violations and more serious felony § 1030(a)(5) violations.

Most of the enhancements reflect efforts to identify particularly sensitive types of computers or computer data and their resulting harms. The most important of the six felony enhancements in 18 U.S.C. § 1030(c)(4)(A)(i) is the first one listed:

> loss to 1 or more persons during any 1-year period (and, for purposes of an investigation, prosecution, or other proceeding brought by the United States only, loss resulting from a related course of conduct affecting 1 or more other protected computers) aggregating at least $5,000 in value.

Under this provision, a felony conviction under § 1030(a)(5) can be obtained if there is at least $5,000 in loss. The parenthetical concerning cases brought by the United States is designed to limit § 1030(a)(5) civil claims in class action lawsuits while allowing aggregation of losses from a course of conduct in criminal cases. Thus, in criminal cases, the loss is calculated by adding up the losses from the defendant's "course of conduct" over any 1-year period.

This framework raises two questions. What is the methodology for calculating $5,000 of loss? And second, what mens rea applies with respect to this element? The following cases consider these questions in turn. It is worth noting that both cases interpret earlier generations of § 1030(a)(5), and therefore use slightly different terminology and interpret slightly different text. It turns out that the cases remain highly relevant, however: In both cases, the current text of § 1030(a)(5) was written in part to codify their holdings.

UNITED STATES V. MIDDLETON

United States Court of Appeals for the Ninth Circuit, 2000.
231 F.3d 1207.

GRABER, CIRCUIT JUDGE.

Defendant Nicholas Middleton challenges his conviction for intentionally causing damage to a "protected computer" without authorization, in violation of 18 U.S.C. § 1030(a)(5)(A). Defendant argues that the trial court incorrectly instructed the jury on the "damage" element of the offense and that the government presented insufficient evidence of the requisite amount of damage. We disagree with each of Defendant's contentions and, therefore, affirm the conviction.

Factual and Procedural Background

Defendant worked as the personal computer administrator for Slip.net, an Internet service provider. His responsibilities included installing software and hardware on the company's computers and providing technical support to its employees. He had extensive knowledge of Slip.net's internal systems, including employee and computer program passwords. Dissatisfied with his job, Defendant quit. He then began to write threatening e-mails to his former employer.

Slip.net had allowed Defendant to retain an e-mail account as a paying customer after he left the company's employ. Defendant used this account to commit his first unauthorized act. After logging in to Slip.net's system, Defendant used a computer program called "Switch User" to switch his account to that of a Slip.net receptionist, Valerie Wilson. This subterfuge allowed Defendant to take advantage of the benefits and privileges associated with that employee's account, such as creating and deleting accounts and adding features to existing accounts.

Ted Glenwright, Slip.net's president, discovered this unauthorized action while looking through a "Switch User log," which records all attempts to use the Switch User program. Glenwright cross-checked the information with the company's "Radius Log," which records an outside user's attempt to dial in to the company's modem banks. The information established that Defendant had connected to Slip.net's computers and had then switched to Wilson's account. Glenwright immediately terminated Defendant's e-mail account.

Nevertheless, Defendant was able to continue his activities. Three days later, he obtained access to Slip.net's computers by logging in to a computer that contained a test account and then using that test account to gain access to the company's main computers. Once in Slip.net's main system, Defendant accessed the account of a sales representative and created two new accounts, which he called "TERPID" and "SANTOS." Defendant used TERPID and SANTOS to obtain access to a different computer that the company had named "Lemming." Slip.net used Lemming to perform internal administrative functions and to host customers' websites. Lemming also contained the software for a new billing system. After gaining access to the Lemming computer, Defendant changed all the administrative passwords, altered the computer's registry, deleted the entire billing system (including programs that ran the billing software), and deleted two internal databases.

Glenwright discovered the damage the next morning. He immediately contacted the company's system administrator, Bruno Connelly. Glenwright and Connelly spent an entire weekend repairing the damage that Defendant had caused to Slip.net's computers, including restoring access to the computer system, assigning new passwords, reloading the billing software, and recreating the deleted databases. They also spent many hours investigating the source and the extent of the damage. Glenwright estimated that he spent 93 hours repairing the damage; Connelly estimated that he spent 28 hours; and other employees estimated that they spent a total of 33 hours. Additionally, Slip.net bought new software to replace software that Defendant had deleted, and the company hired an outside consultant for technical support.

Defendant was arrested and charged with a violation of 18 U.S.C. § 1030(a)(5)(A). He moved to dismiss the indictment, arguing that Slip.net was not an "individual" within the meaning of the statute. The district court denied the motion, holding that "the statute encompasses damage sustained by a business entity as well as by a natural person." *United States v. Middleton,* 35 F. Supp.2d 1189, 1192 (N. D. Cal. 1999).

The case was then tried to a jury. Defendant filed motions for acquittal, arguing that the government had failed to prove that Slip.net suffered at least $5,000 in damage. The district court denied the motions. Defendant requested a jury instruction on the meaning of "damage." This request, too, was denied, and the court gave a different instruction.

The jury convicted Defendant. The district court sentenced him to three years' probation, subject to the condition that he serve 180 days in community confinement. The court also ordered Defendant to pay $9,147 in restitution. This timely appeal ensued.

Discussion

Congress originally enacted the Computer Fraud and Abuse Act in 1984. The 1990 version of § 1030(a)(5)(A) prohibited conduct that damages a "Federal interest computer" and "causes loss to one or more others of a value aggregating $1,000 or more." A "Federal interest computer" was defined as a computer owned or used by the United States Government or a financial institution, or "one of two or more computers used in committing the offense, not all of which are located in the same State." 18 U.S.C. § 1030(e)(2)(A) & (B) (1990). In 1994, Congress replaced the term "Federal interest computer" with the phrase "computer used in interstate commerce or communication" and changed the damage provision to read, "causes loss or damage to one or more other persons of value aggregating $1,000 or more." 18 U.S.C. § 1030(a)(5)(A)(ii)(II)(aa) (1995). Before the 1994 amendment, a hacker could escape the statute's prohibitions by containing activities within a single state. Congress' 1994 amendment attempted to broaden the statute's reach. Congress' 1994 amendments also added a private cause of action for victims of computer crime. 18 U.S.C. § 1030(g).

In 1996, Congress amended § 1030(a)(5) to its current form, using the term "protected computer" and concomitantly expanding the number of computers that the statute "protected." 18 U.S.C. § 1030(a)(5) & (e)(2). The 1996 amendments also altered the definition of damage to read, "loss aggregating at least $5,000 in value during any 1-year period to one or more individuals." 18 U.S.C. § 1030(e)(8)(A). We have found no explanation for this change. We do not believe, however, that this change evidences an intent to limit the statute's reach.

To the contrary, Congress has consciously broadened the statute consistently since its original enactment. The Senate Report on the 1996 amendments notes:

> As intended when the law was originally enacted, the Computer Fraud and Abuse statute facilitates addressing in a single statute the problem of computer crime... *As computers continue to proliferate in businesses and homes, and new forms of computer crimes emerge, Congress must remain vigilant to ensure that the Computer Fraud and Abuse statute is up-to-date and provides law enforcement with the necessary legal framework to fight computer crime.*

S.Rep. No. 104–357, pt. II (emphasis added). The report instructs that "the definition of 'damage' is amended to be sufficiently broad to encompass the types of harm against which people should be protected." The report notes that the interaction between § 1030(a)(5)(A) (the provision that prohibits conduct causing damage) and § 1030(e)(8) (the provision that defines damage) will prohibit a hacker from stealing passwords from an existing log-on program, when this conduct requires "all system users to change their passwords, and requires the system administrator to devote resources to resecuring the system. If the loss to the victim meets the required monetary threshold, the conduct should be criminal, and the victim should be entitled to relief."

Defendant argues that the district court instructed the jury improperly on the definition of "damage." Defendant requested this instruction: "Damage does not include expenses relating to creating a better or making a more secure system than the one in existence prior to the impairment." The court refused the request and gave a different instruction. The court explained to the jury that "damage" is an impairment to Slip.net's computer system that caused a loss of at least $5,000. The court continued:

> The term "loss" means any monetary loss that Slip.net sustained as a result of any damage to Slip.net's computer data, program, system or information that you find occurred.

> And in considering whether the damage caused a loss less than or greater than $5,000, you may consider any loss that you find was a natural and foreseeable result of any damage that you find occurred.

> In determining the amount of losses, you may consider what measures were reasonably necessary to restore the data, program, system, or information that you find was damaged or what measures were reasonably necessary to resecure the data, program, system, or information from further damage.

In reviewing jury instructions, the relevant inquiry is whether the instructions as a whole are misleading or inadequate to guide the jury's deliberation. In this case, the district court's instructions on "damage" and "loss" correctly stated the applicable law. Defendant concedes that "damage" includes any loss that was a foreseeable consequence of his criminal conduct, including those costs necessary to "resecure" Slip.net's computers. He does not argue, therefore, that the court misstated the law.

Defendant contends instead that the court's instruction might have led the jury to believe that it could consider the cost of creating a better or more secure system and that his proposed additional instruction was needed to avoid that possibility. The district court's instruction, when read in its entirety, adequately presented Defendant's theory. The court instructed the jury that it could consider only those costs that were a "natural and foreseeable result" of Defendant's conduct, only those costs that were "reasonably necessary," and only those costs that would "resecure" the computer to avoid "further damage." That instruction logically excludes any costs that the jury believed were excessive, as well as any costs that would merely create an improved computer system unrelated to preventing further damage resulting from Defendant's conduct. In particular, the term "resecure" implies making the system as secure as it was before, not making it more secure than it was before. We presume that the jury followed the court's instructions.

Because the district court's instructions fairly and adequately covered the elements of the offense, we review the instruction's 'precise formulation' for an abuse of discretion. The district court in this case did not abuse its discretion in rejecting Defendant's "precise formulation" of the definition of "damage."

Defendant's final argument is that the government presented insufficient evidence of the requisite $5,000 in damage. The government computed the amount of damage that occurred by multiplying the number of hours that each employee spent in fixing the computer problems by their respective hourly rates (calculated using their annual salaries), then adding the cost of the consultant and the new software. The government estimated the total amount of damage to be $10,092. Defendant and the government agree that the cost of Glenwright's time made up the bulk of that total.

Defendant observes that Slip.net paid Glenwright a fixed salary and that Slip.net did not pay Glenwright anything extra to fix the problems caused by Defendant's conduct. There also is no evidence, says Defendant, that Glenwright was diverted from his other responsibilities or that such a diversion caused Slip.net a financial loss. Defendant argues that, unless Slip.net paid its salaried employees an extra $5,000 for the time spent fixing the computer system, or unless the company was prevented from making $5,000 that it otherwise would have made because of the employees' diversion, Slip.net has not suffered "damage" as defined in the statute. We disagree.

In *United States v. Sablan*, 92 F.3d 865, 869 (9th Cir. 1996), this court held that, under the Sentencing Guidelines for computer fraud, it was permissible for the district court to compute "loss" based on the hourly wage of the victim bank's employees. The court reasoned, in part, that the bank would have had to pay a similar amount had it hired an outside contractor to repair the damage. Analogous reasoning applies here. There is no basis to believe that Congress intended the element of "damage" to depend on a victim's choice whether to use hourly employees, outside contractors, or salaried employees to repair the same level of harm to a protected computer. Rather, whether the amount of time spent by the employees and their imputed hourly rates were reasonable for the repair tasks that they performed are questions to be answered by the trier of fact.

Our review of the record identifies sufficient evidence from which a rational trier of fact could have found that Slip.net suffered $5,000 or more in damage. Glenwright testified that he spent approximately 93 hours investigating and repairing the damage caused by Defendant. That total included 24 hours investigating the break-in, determining how to fix it, and taking temporary measures to prevent future break-ins. Glenwright testified that he spent 21 hours recreating deleted databases and 16 hours reloading and configuring the billing software and its related applications. Glenwright estimated that his time was worth $90 per hour, based on his salary of $180,000 per year. He also testified, among other things, that he did not hire an outside contractor to repair the damage because he believed that he, as a computer expert with a pre-existing knowledge of the customized features of his company's computers, could fix the problems more efficiently. It is worth noting that, because the jury had to find only $5,000 worth of damage, it could have discounted Glenwright's number of hours or his hourly rate considerably and still have found the requisite amount of damage.

Other Slip.net employees testified to the hours that they spent fixing the damage caused by Defendant, and to their respective salaries. The government then presented expert testimony from which a jury could determine that the time spent by the employees was reasonable. Defendant cross-examined the government's witnesses on these issues vigorously, and he presented contrary expert testimony. By the verdict, the jury found the government witnesses' testimony to be more credible, a finding that was within its power to make. We hold, on this record, that the conviction was not based on insufficient evidence.

NOTES AND QUESTIONS

1.   *The codification of Middleton.* In 2001, Congress restructured 18 U.S.C. § 1030(a)(5) and codified the holding of *Middleton*. Before 2001, the section prohibited causing damage and defined damage as impairment to the availability or integrity of information that caused at least $5,000 in loss. The 2001 amendment redefined "damage" without the loss requirement and defined "loss" in 18 U.S.C. § 1030(e)(11) as follows:

> the term "loss" means any reasonable cost to any victim, including the cost of responding to an offense, conducting a damage assessment, and restoring the data, program, system, or information to its condition prior to the offense, and any revenue lost, cost incurred, or other consequential damages incurred because of interruption of service.

The Justice Department has explained that this amendment was designed to "codify the appropriately broad definition of loss adopted in Middleton." *See* Computer Crime and Intellectual Property Section (CCIPS), *Field Guidance on New Authorities that Relate to Computer Crime and Electronic Evidence Enacted in the USA Patriot Act of 2001.*

2.   *Types of costs included in the loss definition.* The definition of loss in § 1030(e)(11) is quite broad. It refers to "any" reasonable cost, and includes what appears to be a non-exclusive list of costs taken largely from the *Middleton* case. What categories of costs can you imagine that are not expressly included in the list? A computer intrusion can incur monetary losses for the victim in a number of different ways. Imagine that an intruder gains unauthorized access to the servers of XYZ Corporation, an e-commerce company, and publicizes the intrusion. The following occurs as a consequence of the intrusion:

A.   The company hires a security consultant to assess the damage and patch the vulnerability.

B.   The company calls a meeting of the board of directors to discuss possible responses, and the meeting lasts a full day. An expensive lunch is served.

C.   The company hires a very skillful public relations specialist to deal with press attention relating to the intrusion.

D.   The company loses a stream of future business when the public hears that XYZ has poor computer security.

E.   Rumors that XYZ has poor security pushes its publicly-traded stock down one dollar per share.

F.   The company loses revenue when it has to take its website offline for one day.

     G.   The company loses a stream of future business when a client becomes so frustrated the website is down that he decides he will never work with XYZ again.

All of these events are associated with monetary losses, either directly or by occupying XYZ employees for a number of hours. Which of these losses are covered by 18 U.S.C. § 1030(e)(11)?

    3.   *An example.* In United States v. Millot, 433 F.3d 1057 (8th Cir. 2006), a former employee of Aventis Pharmaceuticals hacked in to the Aventis network and deleted the account belonging to another employee. Aventis had outsourced its security functions to International Business Machines (IBM), and two IBM employees spent a total of 407 hours reconstructing the deleted account, investigating the intrusion, and performing a security audit to verify that all existing access accounts belonged to current employees. The contract between Aventis and IBM required both IBM employees to work full-time on Aventis security matters, although IBM normally billed its staff's services at $50 per hour. The government calculated damages at $20,350 ($50 per hour x 407 hours). The Eighth Circuit affirmed the conviction, rejecting the defendant's argument that the hours spent by the employees did not count because their costs were absorbed by the contract: "This argument neglects the fact that the hours spent . . . addressing the issues caused by Millot's unauthorized intrusion could have been spent on other duties under the contract." *Id.* at 1061.

    4.   *The required nexus between the computer harm and the monetary loss.* In Nexans Wires S.A. v. Sark-USA, Inc., 319 F. Supp.2d 468 (S.D.N.Y. 2004), the plaintiff was a German company that kept the pricing schedules and manufacturing information for its line of advanced copper and optical fiber products in a password-protected area of a client's computer server in New York. According to the complaint, employees of the client company accessed that information and used it to start a competitor company to compete against the plaintiff company. The plaintiff company sued the competitor company, claiming that the defendants' unauthorized access to the plaintiff's data had triggered at least a $5,000 "loss" in two ways. First, the plaintiff had paid for its senior executives to take two trips from Germany to the client's headquarters in New York to discuss "the activities of [their] faithless employees" with the executives of the client. Second, it claimed it had lost two business opportunities taken by the defendant, which was now competing with the plaintiff.

    The district court rejected the plaintiff's arguments that either could be considered losses under § 1030. The international trips could not be counted as losses because they were not related to a technological harm, the court concluded:

        Nothing in either case law or legislative history suggests that something as far removed from a computer as the travel expenses of senior executives constitutes "loss." Therefore, the international travel expenses that plaintiffs' senior executives incurred to attend a meeting with their customer's senior executive, in which no computers are said to have been examined, and no computer consultant [is] said to have been present cannot satisfy the $5,000 "loss" requirement of the statute.

Id. at 477. The court also rejected the plaintiff's argument that they had suffered "loss" when they had lost business to the competitor company given its use of the allegedly stolen data:

> The "revenue lost" which constitutes "loss" under § 1030(e)(11) appears from the plain language of the statute to be revenue lost "because of [an] interruption of service." § 1030(e)(11). Therefore, if [the plaintiffs] had lost revenue because the computer systems of [the client] were down, that would seem to be the type of lost revenue contemplated by the statute. However, plaintiffs are not claiming to have lost money because the computers of [the client] were inoperable, but rather because of the way the information was later used by defendants.

Id. According to the court, this was insufficient: "revenue lost because the information was used by the defendant to unfairly compete after extraction from a computer does not appear to be the type of 'loss' contemplated by the statute." *See also* Int'l Chauffeured Serv. v. Fast Operating Corp., 2012 WL 1279825, at *4 (S.D.N.Y. 2012) (holding that the cost of monitoring for indications of further unauthorized access after an initial intrusion was not "loss"); Shirokov v. Dunlap, Grubb & Weaver, 2012 WL 1065578, at *24 (D. Mass. 2012) (concluding that legal fees cannot constitute "loss" under the CFAA because they "are not directly attributable to the defendants' alleged access of his computer"); Better HoldCo v. Beeline Loans, 2021 WL 3173736 (S.D.N.Y. 2021) ("An investigation—particularly one led by counsel—into the extent of any misappropriation of confidential information is not a cost of responding to an offense because it is not done to identify, investigate, or remedy any covered damage. To hold otherwise would eviscerate the requirement that damage be related to a technological harm.")

     5.   *Considering lost sales.* In B&B Microscopes v. Armogida, 532 F. Supp.2d 744 (W.D. Pa. 2007), an employee named Armogida developed a valuable computer program known as the KPICS System for his employer B&B Microscopes. At some point, Armogida decided that the program belonged to him rather than his employer, and he quit the company and deleted the program from the laptop computer his employer had provided him for his work. When asked, Armogida refused to provide B&B Microscopes with a copy of the KPICS System. Instead, Armogida represented to purchasers that the software belonged to him, and he sold a copy of the software to the State of Utah for a profit of $10,000.

     B&B Microscopes sued Armogida under § 1030 and claimed $51,400 in loss. The alleged loss consisted of $1,400 for a computer forensic analysis to attempt to recover the KPICS software from the laptop, and $50,000 in expected lost profits for the sale of the KPICS program over the course of one year. The District Court recognized $11,400 in loss but rejected the larger claim as too speculative:

> B&B sustained a loss of $1,400 relating to the costs incurred in performing a damage assessment. I find such costs to be reasonable under the circumstances.
>
> Additionally, B&B sustained a loss of $10,000 relating to lost revenue because of an "interruption of service." B&B was deprived of the opportunity to sell the KPICS System when the data related to the KPICS System was deleted from Armogida's laptop. B&B had no other access to the underlying algorithm necessary to reproduce the KPICS System. Accordingly, the loss of the data from Armogida's laptop constituted an interruption of service within the meaning of 18 U.S.C. § 1030(e)(11).
>
> I reject, as too speculative, B&B's contention that it lost $50,000.00 in revenue from the first year of sales of the KPICS System. Instead, I find that B&B lost $10,000 in profit from the sale Armogida made of the KPICS System to the State of Utah.

Id. at 758–59.

6. *Must revenue lost, or even all losses, relate to interruption of service?* Courts have held that "revenue lost" must be limited to those losses that occurred because of interruption of service. *See* Andrews v. Sirius XM Radio Inc., 932 F.3d 1253, 1263 (9th Cir. 2019); Yoder & Frey Auctioneers, Inc. v. EquipmentFacts, LLC, 774 F.3d 1065, 1073–74 (6th Cir. 2014); Nexans Wires S.A. v. Sark-USA, Inc., 166 Fed. App'x 559, 562 (2d Cir. 2006).

On the other hand, district courts have disagreed on whether *all* losses must relate to the interruption of service. Some courts have reasoned that the phrase "incurred because of interruption of service" at the end of the statutory definition modifies all of the different kinds of losses. As a result, all costs must have been incurred because of an interruption of service to count as "losses" under the statute. As one court reasoned:

> This Court concludes that all loss must be as a result of "interruption of service." Otherwise, it would appear that the second half of the "loss" definition is surplusage. If loss could be any reasonable cost without any interruption of service, then why would there even be a second half to the definition that limits some costs to an interruption of service. Rather, the better reading (though reasonable minds surely can differ until the Court of Appeals decides the issue) appears to be that all "loss" must be the result of an interruption of service. This conclusion is supported by the legislative intent in the CFAA, a criminal statute, to address interruption of service and damage to protected computers.

Cont'l Grp., Inc. v. KW Prop. Mgmt., 622 F. Supp.2d 1357, 1371 (S.D. Fla. 2009).

Other district courts have taken a different view. For example, in *Dice Corp. v. Bold Techs.*, 2012 WL 263031 (E.D. Mich. 2012), the court reasoned that the phrase "incurred because of interruption of service" modified only the phrase "any revenue lost, cost incurred, or other consequential damages." On that reading, the definition of loss includes two basic categories:

(1) "the cost of responding to an offense, conducting a damage assessment, and restoring the data, program, system, or information to its condition prior to the offense," and

(2) additional costs caused by "interruption of service," such as "any revenue lost, cost incurred, or other consequential damages" incurred by the interruption of service.

The *Dice* court's reasoning relied heavily on the legislative history of the loss definition. A year before Congress enacted the definition of loss, an earlier bill contained a nearly identical definition that had the various clauses clearly separated out. That bill, known as the Enhancement of Privacy and Public Safety in Cyberspace Act, S. 3083, 106th Cong. (2000), offered the following definition:

the term "loss" includes—(A) the reasonable costs to any victim of—(i) responding to the offense; (ii) conducting a damage assessment; and (iii) restoring the system and data to their condition prior to the offense; and (B) any lost revenue or costs incurred by the victim as a result of interruption of service.

The *Dice* court reasoned that Congress's enactment of similar words a year later had tried to establish the same meaning. As a result, the costs of responding to the offense, conducting a damage assessment, and restoring the system and data do not have to relate to the interruption of service. *See id.* at *2.

Which view do you think is more persuasive as a matter of statutory interpretation? Is the legislative history helpful? And which definition do you think is more faithful to the *Middleton* case that the statutory definition attempted to codify?

7.   *The reasonableness requirement.* The definition of loss that codifies the holding of *Middleton* requires that the relevant costs must be "reasonable." 18 U.S.C. § 1030(e)(11). As a textual matter, the definition does not make clear whether the enumerated examples are categories of loss that Congress deems reasonable per se, or whether costs involving those enumerated examples must be scrutinized for reasonableness. The *Middleton* opinion suggests the latter, as it approvingly noted that the jury instruction used at trial in that case "logically excludes any costs that the jury believed were excessive." Thus it seems likely that all costs must be scrutinized for reasonableness to count as "loss" for the purposes of getting to $5,000.

Does that make sense? The legal question is whether the conduct prohibited in § 1030(a)(5)(A) "caused" the loss. Principles of causation in criminal law ordinarily do not ask whether the victim's suffering was reasonable. The question is only whether the conduct was the 'but for' and 'proximate' cause of the result. Under this approach, the defendant ordinarily must take the victim as he finds him. For example, if a man assaults an elderly lady, and the elderly lady dies from the shock to her frail system, a defendant cannot escape liability for the homicide on the ground that a younger woman would have been able to survive the assault. *See, e.g.*, People v. Brackett, 510 N.E.2d 877 (Ill. 1987). The victim's condition is relevant only if the victim engages in unforeseeable conduct that breaks the chain of causation, severing the link of culpability between the conduct and the result.

Is the reasonableness requirement in § 1030(e)(11) consistent with this principle? Under the existing definition, a hacker can raise the hypothetical question of whether a more careful victim would have suffered the specified harm (that is, the $5,000 loss). Whether the victim reasonably suffered $5,000 in loss becomes a question of fact for the jury, in effect putting the victim on trial.

Is this a sensible approach? The *Middleton* court seemed concerned that a victim should not be able to use a minor event as an excuse to upgrade its computer security, thus triggering $5,000 in loss and suddenly making the minor event a major felony. If a victim uses a minor event as an excuse to spend money on security, however, isn't the problem that the minor event did not actually *cause* the loss, rather than that the loss wasn't *reasonable*? Does the reasonableness requirement in § 1030(e)(11) erroneously incorporate questions of causation into the definition of loss?

8. *The role of expert witnesses.* Does *Middleton* turn 18 U.S.C. § 1030(a)(5) prosecutions into battles between dueling expert witnesses? The defense expert witness will testify that a reasonable victim would have been able to respond to the unauthorized activity by suffering less than $5,000 in loss, and the government expert witness will testify that a reasonable victim would have suffered more than $5,000 in loss. Does it make sense for computer hacking trials to be focused on the loss suffered by this hypothetical reasonable victim? How well do you think jurors can tell which expert witness is correct?

9. *Costs of patching a security flaw as "loss."* When a computer is restored following a hack, it is standard for the restorer to "patch" the security flaw (that is, correct the programming error or bug) that allowed the hacker to gain unauthorized access to the network. Can the costs of patching the system be included in the loss? Doesn't patching the security flaw go beyond restoring the computer to its prior condition, and actually result in a more secure computer than existed previously? Or should a court assume that before the unauthorized activity the computer was secure, and that any costs that go towards bringing the computer back to the level of security that the computer network was believed to have is part of the reasonable loss?

In State v. Allen, 917 P.2d 848 (Kan. 1996), Allen used his modem to dial up the computers of Southwestern Bell in an apparent effort to place unauthorized free long distance phone calls. Although Southwestern Bell could not establish that Allen had "accessed" their computers, Allen's conduct led

Southwestern Bell to decide to invest $23,796 towards enhancing its computer security. The Supreme Court of Kansas rejected the prosecution's argument that Allen had "damaged" Southwestern Bell under the Kansas computer crime statute. According to the Court, "the State is essentially saying that a person looking at a no trespassing sign on a gate causes damage to the owner of the gate if the owner decides as a result to add a new lock." *Id.* at 853.

10. *The one-year rule for calculating $5,000 in loss.* The test for aggregating $5,000 in loss for § 1030(a)(5) felonies comes with a durational limit: The loss must be "during any 1-year period." 18 U.S.C. § 1030(c)(4)(A)(i)(I). This can be important when the loss involves a recurring cost. For example, in United States v. Goodyear, 795 Fed. Appx. 555 (10th Cir. 2019), a company responded to ongoing cyberattacks by hiring CloudFlare, an IT protection service. CloudFlare cost the company $400 a month. In reviewing the jury's conclusion that the company had suffered $5,000 in loss, the Tenth Circuit included $4,800 in CloudFlare expenses: $400 per month for the one-year period. *See id.* at 560.

The mental states that attach to the elements of § 1030(a)(5) are mostly clear from the face of the statute. However, felony violations of § 1030(a)(5) will generally be based on the conduct having caused one of the felony enhancements of 18 U.S.C. § 1030(c)(4)(A)(i). What mental state should apply to these felony enhancements? The following case considers that question, based on an early version of the statute which incorporated the felony enhancement directly into the text of § 1030(a)(5) rather than placing them in § 1030(c)(4)(A)(i).

UNITED STATES V. SABLAN
United States Court of Appeals for the Ninth Circuit, 1996.
92 F.3d 865.

HUG, CHIEF JUDGE.

Bernadette H. Sablan appeals her conviction for computer fraud under 18 U.S.C. § 1030(a)(5) following a conditional guilty plea. Sablan argues that the district court wrongly interpreted the elements of the crime and, alternatively, that the statute is unconstitutional. We affirm Sablan's conviction and her sentence.

Facts

In the early hours of August 15, 1992, Sablan, a former employee of the Bank of Hawaii's Agana, Guam branch, left a bar where she had been drinking with a friend. Sablan had recently been fired from the bank for circumventing security procedures in retrieving files. That morning, Sablan left the bar and entered the closed bank through an unlocked loading dock door. She went to her former work site (using a key she had kept) and used an old password to log into the bank's mainframe. Sablan contends that she then called up several computer files and logged off. The Government asserts that Sablan changed several of the files and deleted others. Under either version, Sablan's conduct severely damaged several bank files.

Sablan was charged with computer fraud in violation of 18 U.S.C. § 1030(a)(5). In a pretrial motion to dismiss, Sablan attacked the statute for its failure to require a *mens rea* for each of the essential elements of the offense. In the alternative, Sablan requested a jury instruction that required the Government to prove intent as to all elements of the crime. In particular, Sablan wanted the jury to be instructed that the Government needed to prove that she had the intent to damage bank files. The district court denied the motion and ruled that, as used in the computer fraud statute, the word "intentionally" applied only to the access element of the crime. Sablan then entered into a conditional plea agreement that preserved her right to appellate review of the issue raised in her motion.

Discussion

Sablan contends on appeal that the computer fraud statute must have a *mens rea* requirement for all elements of the crime. She asserts that the indictment was defective because it did not allege the appropriate *mens rea* required by the statute. In the alternative, Sablan asserts that a jury instruction was required to inform the jurors that the state had to prove intent for every element of the crime.

Sablan was convicted under the version of the computer fraud statute in effect from 1986 to 1994. That statute stated:

> (a) Whoever—(5) intentionally accesses a Federal interest computer without authorization, and by means of one or more instances of such conduct alters, damages, or destroys information in any such Federal interest computer ... and thereby—(A) causes loss to one or more others of a value aggregating $1,000 or more during any one year period; shall be punished as provided.

18 U.S.C. § 1030 (amended by Pub.L. No. 103–354). In order to have violated the statute, a defendant must have (1) accessed (2) a federal interest computer (3) without authorization and (4) have altered, damaged, or destroyed information (5) resulting in the loss to one or more others (6) of at least one thousand dollars. The district court held that the statute's *mens rea* requirement, "intentionally," applied only to the access element of the crime.

A.

We begin our analysis by noting that the statute is ambiguous as to its *mens rea* requirement. Although the statute explains that one must "intentionally access a Federal interest computer without authorization, and destroy information in any such Federal interest computer," punctuation sets the "accesses" phrase off from the subsequent "damages" phrase. With some statutes, punctuation has been used to indicate that a phrase set off by commas is independent of the language that followed. However, punctuation is not always decisive in construing statutes. In *Liparota v. United States*, 471 U.S. 419 (1985), and *United States v. X-Citement Video*, 513 U.S. 64 (1994), for example, the Supreme Court applied the mental state adjacent to initial words to later clauses without regard to intervening punctuation. In both cases, the Supreme Court resorted to legislative history to clarify the ambiguous language.

We conclude that the comma after "authorization" does not resolve the ambiguity. Allowing the *mens rea* requirement to reach subsequent elements of the crime would comport with general linguistic rules. Similarly, it is proper to read the statute without extending "intentionally" to the other clauses of the sentence. Therefore, we look to the statute's legislative history to clear up the textual ambiguity.

In *United States v. Morris*, 928 F.2d 504 (2d Cir. 1991), the Second Circuit examined the legislative history of the computer fraud statute and concluded that the "intentionally" standard applied only to the "accesses" element of the crime. The court focused on the fact that the original version of the statute, passed in 1984, punished anyone who

> *knowingly* accesses a computer without authorization, or having accessed a computer with authorization, uses the opportunity such access provides for purposes to which such authorization does not extend, and by means of such conduct *knowingly* uses, modifies, destroys, or discloses information in, or prevents authorized use of, such computer, if such computer is operated for or on behalf of the Government of United States and such conduct affects such operation.

Pub.L. No. 98–473, subsection (a)(3) (amended latest by Pub.L. No. 103–354) (emphasis added). When the statute was amended in 1986, the scienter requirement was changed from knowingly to intentionally and the second *mens rea* reference was eliminated. By contrast, other subsections of section 1030 retained the "dual-intent" language by placing the *mens rea* requirement at the beginning of both the "accesses" phrase and the "damages" phrase. *See, e.g.*, 18 U.S.C. § 1030(a)(1). The court concluded that the decision of Congress not to repeat the scienter requirement within this statute evidenced an intent not to require the Government to prove a defendant's intent to cause damage.

Sablan urges this court to reject the holding in *Morris*, contending that the 1986 bill was intended only to apply to those who intentionally damage computer data. She points to one line in a Senate report that evidenced a desire to retain the dual intent language: "The new subsection 1030(a)(5) to be created by the bill is designed to penalize those who intentionally alter, damage, or destroy certain computerized data belonging to another." 1986 U.S.C.C.A.N. at 2488. Thus, Sablan argues, the computer fraud statute has a *mens rea* requirement for the damages clause of the bill. We disagree.

As the *Morris* court concluded:

> Despite some isolated language in the legislative history that arguably suggests a scienter component for the "damages" phrase of section 1030(a)(5)(A), the wording, structure, and purpose of the subsection, examined in comparison with its departure from the format of its predecessor provision persuade us that the "intentionally" standard applies only to the "accesses" phrase of section 1030(a)(5)(A), and not to its "damages" phrase.

We adopt the reasoning of the *Morris* court and hold that the computer fraud statute does not require the Government to prove that the defendant intentionally damaged computer files.

B.

Sablan contends that if the computer fraud statute does not have a *mens rea* requirement for the damages element of the offense, the statute is unconstitutional. Relying on the Supreme Court's decision in *X-Citement Video,* Sablan states that a *mens rea* must be applied to all elements of an offense or due process standards are violated. We review *de novo* the district court's determination of federal constitutional law.

The Supreme Court has never ruled that *mens rea* is a constitutional requirement. However, in *X-Citement Video,* the Supreme Court stated that a statute without any scienter requirements "would raise serious constitutional doubts." Sablan contends that lack of a scienter requirement for the damages element of the offense renders the statute constitutionally infirm. In *X-Citement Video,* the Court construed the "knowingly" scienter requirement beyond the most proximate clause of 18 U.S.C. § 2252 to clarify that one charged with trafficking in child pornography must know that the material involves the use of a minor.

After reviewing the cases interpreting criminal statutes to include broadly applicable scienter requirements the Court held that the "presumption in favor of a scienter requirement should apply to each of the statutory elements which criminalize otherwise innocent conduct." However, the computer fraud statute does not criminalize otherwise innocent conduct. Under the statute, the Government must prove that the defendant intentionally accessed a federal interest computer without authorization. Thus, Sablan must have had a wrongful intent in accessing the computer in order to be convicted under the statute. This case does not present the prospect of a defendant being convicted without any wrongful intent as was the situation in *X-Citement Video*. Therefore, we hold that the computer fraud statute's *mens rea* requirement is sufficient to meet constitutional standards.

NOTES AND QUESTIONS

1. *Strict liability felony enhancements.* Although *Sablan* involves an earlier generation of § 1030(a)(5), one critical aspect of it appears to survive into the current version of the statute: The felony enhancements found in § 1030(c)(4)(A)(i) are strict liability. That is, it does not matter whether a defendant intended to cause $5,000 in loss, or intended to cause physical injury, or intended to cause damage affecting 10 or more computers. All that matters is that the defendant *did in fact do so*. The resulting harm can be a freakish accident, and will nonetheless raise the level of liability from a misdemeanor to a felony under § 1030(c)(4)(A)(i).

2. *Mental states and the theories of punishment.* Is strict liability for the felony enhancements found in § 1030(c)(4)(A)(i) consistent with the theories of punishment? Does a defendant whose conduct accidentally or through freakish circumstances leads to greater harm deserve greater punishment? Should the law seek to deter such unlucky defendants? Or is the point that by punishing unlucky defendants, the law can deter other defendants from engaging in inherently risky conduct? To what extent should the difficulty of proving mens rea enter into the equation? How can the government prove intent to damage, or intent to cause a particular amount of damage?

Your answer to these questions may be guided by your sense of whether computer intrusions are inherently risky and harmful or usually innocent and sometimes even helpful. If you believe that hacking is inherently dangerous and likely to cause harm, then you may find it appropriate to punish those whose intrusions lead to additional harm. On the other hand, if you see most intrusions as generally harmless, you may conclude that the mens rea requirements of § 1030(a)(5) are far too broad.

3. *The role of awareness and intent.* Consider the following hypothetical cases. Which of the two defendants deserves a greater punishment? What kinds of criminal liability are they likely to face under 18 U.S.C. § 1030?

A. *Discovered Versus Undiscovered Attacks.* On Monday, Hacker Bob hacks into the servers of the XYZ corporation and snoops around. On Tuesday, Hacker Joe hacks into the servers of the same company and also snoops around. On Wednesday, the system administrator at XYZ corporation finds evidence of Joe's attack and spends 50 hours over the next week (at a rate of $125 per hour) responding to the attack, conducting a damage assessment, and resecuring the server. The system administrator never notices Bob's attack.

B. *Differing Intents.* Two friends, Kate and Jane, don't like a large Internet service provider called Burns Online. Kate decides that she wants to destroy Burns Online by inflicting as much loss as she can upon it. Jane decides that she wants to cause only an infinitesimal amount of harm to Burns Online. Both Kate and Jane download a program that purports to allow the user to launch a denial-of-service attack. Jane configures the program so that it will disable Burns Online for only 1 second; Kate configures the program so that it will disable Burns Online indefinitely. At the second that Jane launches her one-second attack, a doctor who is a subscriber to Burns Online attempts to send an e-mail to one of his patients urging his patient to exercise more and maintain a balanced diet. Due to the one-second attack, he cannot send it, and decides to log off. Kate's attack takes Burns Online offline for ten minutes, until the system administrator at Burns Online comes up with a defense against it.

4. *Due process and the meaning of authorization.* The *Sablan* court concludes that requiring the government to prove intentional access without authorization is sufficient to satisfy any constitutional requirements of mens rea; the remaining elements can be strict liability elements without violating the Due Process clause. Although the Supreme Court has never expressly held that mens rea is a constitutional requirement, it has tended to read a mens rea requirement into criminal statutes when the conduct otherwise prohibited is innocent conduct. *See generally* Staples v. United States, 511 U.S. 600 (1994). The *Sablan* court concludes that no such construction of § 1030(a)(5) is needed because the Section "does not criminalize otherwise innocent conduct." Because the government must prove intentional access without authorization, there must be wrongful intent. *Sablan*, 92 F.3d at 869. Does this analysis hinge on a narrow definition of "without authorization"? If you adopt a broad contract-based or norms-based view of authorization, is § 1030(a)(5) unconstitutional?

5. *Additional means of proving felony violations of § 1030(a)(5).* Establishing $5,000 of loss is the most common way to trigger the felony provisions of § 1030(a)(5). However, 18 U.S.C. § 1030(c)(4)(A)(i) lists six ways of triggering felony liability, and proving $5,000 of loss is only the first of the six ways. Recall the other five harms that, if caused, trigger felony liability:

(II) the modification or impairment, or potential modification or impairment, of the medical examination, diagnosis, treatment, or care of 1 or more individuals;

(III) physical injury to any person;

(IV) a threat to public health or safety;

(V) damage affecting a computer used by or for an entity of the United States Government in furtherance of the administration of justice, national defense, or national security; or

(VI) damage affecting 10 or more protected computers during any 1-year period.

18 U.S.C. § 1030(c)(4)(A)(i). Let's take a look at the other five provisions in the order that they appear, which also happens to be the chronological order in which they were added by Congress.

The provision involving medical diagnosis and treatment traces back to the original version of § 1030(a)(5) enacted in 1986. In the 1986 statute, there were two just types of harms that could establish a § 1030(a)(5) violation: establishing pecuniary loss (then just $1,000, later changed to $5,000), and impairing medical diagnosis or treatment. According to the Senate Report accompanying the 1986 legislation, the concern with medical diagnoses and treatment was largely a response to a 1983 episode that received significant press attention:

> A group of adolescents known as the '414 Gang' broke into the computer system at Memorial Sloan-Kettering Cancer Center in New York. In so doing, they gained access to the radiation treatment records of 6,000 past and present cancer patients and had at their fingertips the ability to alter the radiation treatment levels that each patient received. No financial losses were at stake in this case, but the potentially life-threatening nature of such mischief is a source of serious concern to the Committee.

> The Sloan-Kettering case is but one example of computer crimes directed at altering medical treatment records. Where such conduct impairs or potentially impairs an individual's medical care, the Committee does not believe a showing of financial losses is necessary. Tampering with computerized medical treatment records, especially given the potentially life-threatening nature of such conduct, is serious enough to warrant punishment without a showing of pecuniary loss to the victim or victims. The Committee also wishes to make clear that convictions are attainable under this subsection without a showing that the victim was actually given an incorrect or harmful treatment, or otherwise suffered as a result of the changed medical record. That his examination, diagnosis, treatment, or care was potentially changed or impaired is sufficient to warrant prosecution under this subsection.

S. Rep. 99–432 (1986), at *2–3, 12.

The next two of these provisions, those involving physical injury and threats to public health and safety, were added in 1996 as part of a general expansion of the scope of 18 U.S.C. § 1030. At the time, Congress saw that computer networks and the Internet were beginning to assume a larger role in American life. The Senate Report accompanying the legislation expanded the types of covered harms to recognize the new ways that computers could be used to harm the public:

> As the [National Information Infrastructure] and other network infrastructures continue to grow, computers will increasingly be used for access to critical services such as emergency response systems and

air traffic control, and will be critical to other systems which we cannot yet anticipate. Thus, the definition of "damage" is amended to be sufficiently broad to encompass the types of harm against which people should be protected.

S. Rep. 104–357 (1996), at *11.

The next provision, involving government computers used in furtherance of the administration of justice, national defense, or national security, was added in 2001 as part of the USA Patriot Act. The Justice Department Field Guide to the Patriot Act offered the following argument in its favor:

> Section 1030 previously had no special provision that would enhance punishment for hackers who damage computers used in furtherance of the administration of justice, national defense, or national security. Thus, federal investigators and prosecutors did not have jurisdiction over efforts to damage criminal justice and military computers where the attack did not cause over $5,000 loss (or meet one of the other special requirements). Yet these systems serve critical functions and merit felony prosecutions even where the damage is relatively slight. Indeed, attacks on computers used in the national defense that occur during periods of active military engagement are particularly serious—even if they do not cause extensive damage or disrupt the war-fighting capabilities of the military—because they divert time and attention away from the military's proper objectives. Similarly, disruption of court computer systems and data could seriously impair the integrity of the criminal justice system.

Computer Crime and Intellectual Property Section (CCIPS), *Field Guidance on New Authorities that Relate to Computer Crime and Electronic Evidence Enacted in the USA Patriot Act of 2001*. This provision was addressed in United States v. Mitra, 405 F.3d 492 (7th Cir. 2005), which involved interference with a radio system used by local police, fire, ambulance, and other emergency workers in Madison, Wisconsin. The court noted with apparent approval the government's argument that interfering with messages sent over the system implicated this language because the defendant had "hacked into a governmental safety-related communications system." *Id.* at 495.

The final provision, involving damage that affects 10 or more protected computers during any 1-year period, was added in 2008 in response to the increasingly widespread practice of compromising large numbers of computers and then controlling them remotely. The computers that are compromised are generally known as "zombies," and are then used as "bots" (short for "robots") by the wrongdoer who controls them. The wrongdoer can then use the botnet (that is, the collection of bots) to send out spam, launch a distributed denial-of-service attack, or for other purposes. Under this provision, an individual who compromises ten or more computers as part of the creation of a botnet will trigger felony liability under § 1030(a)(5).

6.   *The big picture on the law of computer misuse.* The scope of criminal liability for computer misuse is very broad. A critic of existing law might say that the legislature's basic approach is to criminalize everything and then rely on prosecutorial discretion to select appropriate cases for criminal punishment.

Is this criticism accurate? And if it is, do you think the legislature has acted wisely? Computer technologies and social practices change rapidly, and it may be difficult for the law to keep up. Is it sensible for legislatures to impose broad criminal liability ex ante, so that prosecutors are rarely or never in a position of being unable to charge a worthy case? Or should the legislature only impose liability narrowly, so that new computer technologies can evolve without the threat of criminal punishment? Do you trust prosecutors to charge only appropriate cases? Does the threat of criminal punishment have a significant chilling effect on legitimate computer use?

G. HACKING BACK

Computer intrusions and denial-of-service attacks can cause a significant amount of economic and other damage to their victims. Should an owner/operator of a victim computer have a right to "hack back" against an intruder? If *A* launches an attack at *B* in violation of 18 U.S.C. § 1030, should *B* be allowed to launch a counterattack at *A* designed to stop *A*'s attack? Should the counterattack violate § 1030 as well, or should it be excused under principles of "cyber-self-defense"?

Although there have been no judicial decisions on the question, the general consensus is that "hacking back" is ordinarily illegal. 18 U.S.C. § 1030 prohibits victims from engaging in unauthorized access or causing unauthorized damage to the computers of their attackers just as it prohibits the original attack.

Some have proposed that there should be a cyber-self-defense doctrine to allow hacking back. Current law, however, does not seem to recognize such a doctrine. Although state courts generally recognize a limited "defense of property" defense to state crimes, it is not clear that federal law recognizes such a defense to federal crimes.

Further, courts that have applied such doctrines in the context of state or local law have generally limited it to using "as much force as is reasonably necessary to eject a trespasser from his property." Shehyn v. United States, 256 A.2d 404, 406 (D.C. 1969). Hacking back usually does not involve "eject[ing] a trespasser." Although hacking back can take different forms, usually it involves going back to the trespasser's computer and either damaging it or disabling it.

State courts have recognized a privilege to retrieve stolen property from the land of someone who has stolen it. *See* Restatement (Second) of Torts § 198(1) (1965) ("One is privileged to enter land in the possession of another, at a reasonable time and in a reasonable manner, for the purpose of removing a chattel to the immediate possession of which the actor is entitled, and which has come upon the land otherwise than with the actor's consent or by his tortious conduct or contributory negligence."). However, this state law privilege has not been adopted in federal criminal law or applied to the Internet context.

Should it? Consider the following bill language amending the CFAA that was proposed as part of a discussion draft by Representative Tom Graves (R-Ga) in May 2017.

ACTIVE CYBER DEFENSE CERTAINTY ACT 2.0, § 3

Section 1030 of title 18, United States Code, is amended by adding at the end the following: "(I) ACTIVE CYBER DEFENSE MEASURES NOT A VIOLATION.—

"(1) GENERALLY.—It is a defense to a prosecution under this section that the conduct constituting the offense was an active cyber defense measure.

"(2) DEFINITIONS.—In this subsection—

"(A) the term 'victim' means an entity that is a victim of a persistent unauthorized intrusion of the individual entity's computer;

"(B) the term 'active cyber defense measure'—(i) means any measure—(I) undertaken by, or at the direction of, a victim; and (II) consisting of accessing without authorization the computer of the attacker to the victim' own network to gather information in order to: 1) establish attribution of criminal activity to share with law enforcement and other United States Government agencies responsible for cybersecurity; 2) disrupt continued unauthorized activity against the victim's own network; or 3) monitor the behavior of an attacker to assist in developing future intrusion prevention or cyber defense techniques,

but;

"(ii) does not include conduct that—(I) destroys or renders inoperable information that does not belong to the victim that is stored on a computers of another; (II) causes physical or financial injury to another person; (III) creates a threat to the public health or safety; or (IV) exceeds the level of activity required to perform reconnaissance on an intermediary computer to allow for attribution of the origin of the persistent cyber intrusion;

"(C) the term 'attacker' means a person or an entity that is the source of the persistent unauthorized intrusion into the victim's computer; and

"(D) the term 'intermediary computer' means a person or entity's computer that is not under the ownership or control of the attacker but has been used to launch or obscure the origin of the persistent cyber-attack."

NOTES AND QUESTIONS

1. Does the proposed bill language explain when hacking back is permitted and how much hacking back is allowed? Does it go too far, or not far enough?

2. *The case for a legal right to hack back.* A number of activists and scholars have argued that victims of computer misuse should have a legal right to hack back and disable attacks against them. Michael O'Neill has argued that "just as settlers in the American West could not reliably count on the local sheriff to protect them, and instead kept a weapon handy to stymie potential aggressors, Internet users may need to protect themselves." Michael E. O'Neill, *Old Crimes in New Bottles: Sanctioning Cybercrime*, 9 Geo. Mason. L. Rev. 237, 277 (2000). According to Professor O'Neill, the threat of a counterstrike will deter attacks. "Just as a homeowner may defend his house, . . . computer companies ought to not only be permitted, but encouraged, to unleash their considerable talents to launch countermeasures against cyber-criminals." *Id.* at 280. *See also* Bruce Smith, *Hacking, Poaching, and Counterattacking: Digital Counterstrikes and the Contours of Self-Help*, 1 J.L. Econ. & Pol'y 171, 191 (2005).

Stewart Baker has argued that victims of persistent attacks should have self-help options because government agencies are poorly equipped to help victims of computer misuse:

> Surely everyone would be happier if businesses could hire their own network defenders to do battle with attackers. This would greatly reinforce the thin ranks of government investigators. It would make wide-ranging government access to private networks less necessary. And busting the government monopoly on active defense would probably increase the diversity, imagination, and effectiveness of the counterhacking community.

Stewart Baker, *The Hackback Debate*, Steptoe Cyberblog, November 2, 2012.

3. *The case against a legal right to hack back.* Opponents of lawful hacking back point out that that it is very easy to disguise your tracks online. Victims often are unable to tell who is attacking them, which means that counterattacks will accidentally be launched against innocent third parties. Those innocent third parties will in turn believe they are under attack, and they will launch counterattacks as well. The result will be vastly more computer misuse, not less, as the legal right to hack back will set off a chain reaction of legal hacking misattributed to and victimizing innocent third parties.

Richard Epstein has noted that the high risk of error in a cyber-counterattack raises a number of difficult legal questions:

> What should be done if the program picks up the wrong target and wrecks the computer of an innocent party? What should be done if the attacked target is a zombie computer that has unwittingly

transferred the offending material across cyberspace? Are there any limits of proportionality that are associated with these attacks? Should the self-help remedy be denied on the grounds that some form of civil liability could be imposed?

Richard Epstein, *The Theory and Practice of Self-Help*, 1 J.L. Econ. & Pol'y 1, 31 (2005).

4.   *Beacons*. A company that fears it might lose valuable data to outside hackers might use a beacon, which can be defined as software hidden in data that sends an alert if it is removed from the company's network. The beacon might be programmed to send a communication back to the company's network revealing the IP address where the beacon (and the stolen data surrounding it) is now located. The beacon could also be programmed to send more information back to the company, including the details of the network where the beacon is located.

If data is stolen, and a beacon placed in the data sends an alert, does usage of the beacon constitute an unauthorized access into the computer where the data now resides in violation of 18 U.S.C. § 1030?

5.   *Alternatives beyond criminal law*. Although criminal laws such as the CFAA are part of the response to computer misuse, surely they are not the only response. This is intuitive in the physical world. If a neighborhood suffers a spate of burglaries, neighborhood residents are not likely to see the details of burglary statutes as the primary problem (or amendments to those statutes as the primary solution). The same is true with computer misuse. This raises the question of what other laws and legal theories, beyond criminal laws, are needed to help address computer misuse.

For example, some scholars have suggested imposing civil liability on ISPs for the criminal acts of their subscribers. The idea is that this will encourage ISPs to monitor and disable wrongdoers before significant harms occur. *See, e.g.*, Doug Lichtman & Eric Posner, *Holding Internet Service Providers Accountable*, in The Law and Economics of Cybersecurity (Mark Grady & Francesco Parisi eds., 2005). Others have suggested that computer owners should be subject to negligence suits if their poor computer security facilitates computer misuse offenses. *See, e.g.*, Stephen E. Henderson & Matthew E. Yarbrough, *Suing the Insecure?: A Duty of Care in Cyberspace*, 32 N.M. L. Rev. 11 (2002).

Do such proposals complement the need for computer misuse laws such as 18 U.S.C. § 1030, or could they replace such statutes? More broadly, what is the purpose of computer misuse laws? Is their purpose to punish culpable individuals? To deter criminal activity? To improve computer security? What kinds of laws beyond unauthorized access, computer fraud, and computer damage statutes are needed to address computer misuse crimes?

CHAPTER 3

TRADITIONAL CRIMES

■ ■ ■

There are many types of computer crimes beyond the computer misuse offenses covered in the previous chapter. Of course, not all crimes are relevant to a course in computer crime law. Computers are tools that transmit and store information, which means that crimes with no necessary link to transmitting information are not likely to arise often in computer-related cases. At the same time, a number of traditional crimes do involve transmitting and storing information. These information-based crimes often find a natural home in the world of computers and the Internet. In some cases, the computer's ability to process and transmit information quickly and with relative anonymity has led entire subcultures of criminal activity to migrate from the physical world to a digital environment.

The purpose of this chapter is to study traditional crimes committed using computers. As with the previous chapter, the materials will focus primarily on federal law with some coverage of state law. The chapter begins with laws concerning economic crimes, such as theft and copyright infringement, that exist primarily to protect economic interests. The materials turn next to crimes against persons, such as threats and harassment. The next subjects are vice crimes, such as Internet gambling and obscenity-related offenses. The chapter concludes with laws regarding child exploitation crimes such as offenses involving images of child pornography.

As you read these materials, consider whether criminal conduct changes when it shifts from the physical world to computer networks. Many of these crimes raise the issue of "old wine in new bottles," and ask us to adjust concepts and statutory language from an old set of facts to a new one. Should it matter whether a crime is committed using computer networks and the Internet? Does anything change when a traditional crime is committed using computers?

A. ECONOMIC CRIMES

Control of information can have considerable economic value. A file stored on a server may contain valuable secrets about a new product to go on the market. Alternatively, the file may be an expensive piece of software or a sought-after movie or sound recording. Whatever the source of the file's value, that value depends on information control. The more widely available information becomes, the less valuable it tends to be. You might pay for a stock tip from a private investment manager, but you won't pay if you can read the same stock tip in the newspaper for free. You might have exclusive rights to control access to a new piece of software, but fewer people are likely to purchase those rights if they can obtain illegal copies easily for free.

How should criminal law regulate control of information to protect these economic interests? Federal criminal law includes four types of information control statutes: general property crimes, such as theft and possession of stolen property; specific information-based crimes such as the Economic Espionage Act of 1996; statutes that govern authentication devices; and intellectual property laws such as the copyright statutes.

1. PROPERTY CRIMES

Property crimes were originally designed to protect interests in physical property. The basic idea is that physical property has an owner who enjoys the right to exclude others from accessing or using that property. Taking property away from the owner without the owner's consent constitutes theft. Retaining the property, knowing it has been taken from its owner, constitutes possession of stolen property.

Can these principles be used to protect rights in information? Does information have an "owner"? What does it mean for information to be "stolen"? What does it mean to "possess" information?

PEOPLE V. JOHNSON
Criminal Court for the City of New York, 1990.
560 N.Y.S.2d 238.

CHARLES J. HEFFERNAN, JR., JUDGE.

This is another in a series of nearly identical fact patterns prosecuted in this jurisdiction with increasing frequency: a charge that use of an illegally possessed AT&T credit card number was unlawfully offered, for a fee, to travelers at the Port Authority terminal in Manhattan. Here, as in other cases, the People assert that the "service" was offered by a form of huckstering—in this case, that defendant's words were "you can call the whole world for $8.00." Such cases have engaged various legal issues, determined by the crimes charged in the respective prosecutions.

This case [considers whether] charging criminal possession of stolen property in the fifth degree (P.L. § 165.40), should be dismissed for facial insufficiency on the ground that a telephone credit card number is not "property" under P.L. § 155.00(1).

The Facts

Deponent [a police officer who saw the alleged crime occur] states that he observed defendant at the above location saying to passersby "you can call the whole world for $8.00" and that deponent approached an unapprehended individual who said he was from Poland, and deponent then observed defendant pull a small scrap of paper from defendant's pocket and start dialing a number from the paper onto a phone.

Deponent further states that when defendant saw deponent approach, deponent observed defendant tear said scrap of paper and throw it to the ground.

Deponent states that he is informed by Tony Largo, of AT&T security that the number on said piece of paper had been used to make approximately 240 calls during the 2 hours before the defendant was arrested, and informant is the custodian of the phone computer code system and the credit card number and states that defendant had no permission or authority to access or attempt to access the phone computer code systems or to possess or use the said credit card number.

Deponent further states that defendant was apprehended in an area which had signs posted that said the area was for "Ticketed Passengers Only" and that deponent observed defendant had no bus ticket.

The Stolen Property Count

Defendant moves to dismiss the third count of the information, charging the crime of criminal possession of stolen property in the fifth degree (P.L. § 165.40), also on the ground of facial insufficiency. Defendant rests his argument on the opinion in *People v. Molina,* 145 Misc.2d 612 (Crim. Ct. Queens Co. 1989), where the court granted an identical motion on essentially identical facts. In both cases the allegation was that defendant possessed telephone credit card numbers belonging to AT&T, such numbers being written on a piece of paper that defendant possessed.

The court noted that:

> the potentially unique 14 digit pattern and sequence of these numbers could support the People's assertion that they are unique AT&T credit card numbers. The identity of the nature of the numbers is not mere speculation. Adequate support for the conclusion that they are AT&T card numbers was provided by a representative of New York Telephone. It is also worth noting that defendant possessed three different patterns of numbers, and all were identified as having the necessary unique AT&T pattern. Any claims by defendant that these numbers had an independent significance goes towards challenging findings made by a trier of fact. This aspect of the complaint is sufficient.

Molina, supra, at 614, 615.

What troubled the *Molina* court, however, was the "property" element of the crime, the court finding that the defendant was not accused of holding the actual AT&T credit cards from which the numbers were presumably obtained. The court noted that the paper on which the numbers were written is the tangible personal property of the defendant, not of the credit card holders—a fact that would seemingly be undisputed. Nor would a reasonable person likely gainsay the *Molina* court's view that the credit card holders have no possessory interest in that paper.

The final step in the *Molina* analysis, however, is the point at which this court takes respectful departure from that holding: *i.e.,* that "the numbers in and of themselves are not tangible property." *Molina, supra,* at 615. It was the belief of that court that a more expansive reading would violate the rule that criminal statutes are to be strictly and narrowly construed.

Strict construction, however, need not ignore the clear import of facts and circumstances attending a criminal allegation implicating a technically-oriented charge. To do so would be unmindful of the ever-changing nature of American technology and its components.

P.L. § 155.00(1) defines "property" as meaning "any money, personal property, real property, computer data, computer program, thing in action, evidence of debt or contract, or any article, substance or thing of value, including any gas, steam, water or electricity, which is provided for a charge or compensation."

To rest the distinction between culpability and inculpability upon the type of physical material on which the credit card number is listed—or upon the absence of such material—would be to defeat the purpose underlying the statute at issue. The generic crime of criminal possession of stolen property is meant to proscribe knowing possession of property wrongfully taken from a lawful holder. On the facts before this court, there is little, if any, relevance to the form in which the telephone credit card number is possessed. Under the *Molina* rationale, a person who steals a telephone credit card would be criminally liable if he or she is found in possession of the card. The thief would escape liability, however, by either recording the card number on a piece of paper owned by the wrongdoer and then destroying the card, or by committing the number to memory after destroying the card.

The lack of logic in that thesis is evidenced by the following question: Is the number with the card of any more value to a person intent on placing phone calls without charge than is the number without the card? The number itself is what is crucial, and not who has the superior possessory interest in the paper on which the number is recorded, or whether the number is written as opposed to being memorized.

Such a number clearly has inherent value, apart from the card onto which the numbers are embossed. Most other credit cards require either that the card be presented for use or, as a pre-condition to its acceptance for use by telephone, that some verifying data as to the card or the party to whom it was issued be tendered. The use of a telephone credit card, on the other hand, is not encumbered by such constraints. Rather, a person in possession of a validly issued telephone credit card number can place a local, national or international call without immediate scrutiny simply by inputting the credit card number by dialing or pushing a button on the telephone instrument. Lawful bearers of that number will incur later cost for that service. Those who come into possession of those numbers without authorization, however, can place calls at no cost; the bill for those calls will, in due course, be sent to the lawful holder of the credit cards. It is, therefore, beyond quarrel that a telephone credit card number qualifies as a "thing of value."

More, however, is required in this analysis. While a telephone credit card number is a "thing of value," care must be taken to be sure that the number in question is indeed such a number. A court must be satisfied that the number possessed is not some innocuous number, innocently had by a defendant. Such a judgment can be made, of course, only in the context of attending circumstances. In the context of a motion to dismiss a count of an information for facial insufficiency, a court must look to the information itself.

The information before the court contains several factual assertions that are helpful in deciding whether the number in question was an AT&T credit card, as opposed to something else: (1) a security representative of AT&T, Tony Largo, states that he is the custodian of the phone computer system and the credit card number; (2) Mr. Largo also states that defendant had no permission to possess that number; (3) Detective Joseph Rullo of the Port Authority Police Department states that he saw defendant saying to passersby "you can call the whole world for $8.00"; (4) Detective Rullo further states that he saw defendant approach a person who said that he was from Poland, that defendant pulled a scrap of paper from defendant's pocket and began to dial a number from that paper onto a telephone; (5) Detective Rullo states that when defendant saw Detective Rullo approaching, defendant tore the scrap of paper and threw it to the ground; (6) Mr. Largo states that the number on the paper had been used to make approximately 240 calls during the 2 hours before defendant's apprehension.

The confluence of those factors persuades this court that the number that defendant is charged with possessing is, indeed, an AT&T credit card number, a "thing of value." That is, however, not the end of the inquiry on the question whether the telephone credit card number is "property" under P.L. § 155.00(1).

The statute couples "thing of value" with the modifying clause "which is provided for a charge or compensation." On the facts pled herein, there is no indication that the card was provided to the lawful owner in exchange for immediate charge or compensation. Nor need there be such an assertion. For the charge attaching to the credit card number is, of course, a subsequent charge, for calls that are placed by using that number. This is sufficient to meet the compensation or charge requirement of P.L. § 155.00(1).

Accordingly, this court does not concur with the sole challenge made by defendant to the facial sufficiency of the pleading of the count charging Criminal Possession of Stolen Property in the Fifth Degree: *i.e.*, that the number on the slip of paper in question is not "property" within the statutory definition. On the facts at bar, the AT&T telephone credit card number qualifies for inclusion within the statutory definition of "property."

NOTES AND QUESTIONS

1. *Is an access code property?* The defendant in *Johnson* wrongfully obtained a calling card number that enabled him to place long-distance phone calls for free. The number was an access code—a password, a sort of intangible key—and its market value derived from the value of the service that could be accessed using the number.

Individuals use access codes every day. E-mail passwords and ATM PINs are common examples. You can probably think of less high-tech examples as well. In high school, you probably had a locker that you protected with a combination lock. In grade school, you may have conditioned access to your neighborhood clubhouse on an entrant's knowledge of the "secret password." The combination for the lock and the secret password are both access codes. In the past, did you think of these access codes as your property? Does the fact that an access code can be used to obtain property mean that the access code is itself property? Why wasn't Johnson charged with fraud for placing the illegal calls, instead of possession of stolen property for knowing the card number?

2. *What does it mean to "possess" a number?* The legal concept of possession generally requires two elements: knowledge of the property and control over it. If you put a piece of paper in your wallet, you possess that paper because you know the paper exists and you control the contents of your pocket. Does it make sense to say that you also possess the intangible writing on the piece of paper, such as a number written on it? Can you control a number in the same way that you can control a physical object?

Arguably, the *Johnson* court evades this difficulty by simply eliminating the control requirement of possession and equating possession with knowledge. The court reasons that Johnson would be liable for possessing stolen property if he had merely seen the calling card numbers and then memorized them. Does that make sense?

Imagine a robber holds up a victim at gun point, demands that the victim tell him something valuable, and that the victim, afraid for his life, tells the robber his credit card number. If the robber memorizes the number, *Johnson* suggests, he would be guilty of possessing stolen property. What if the robber takes out an advertisement in the local newspaper that says, "Memorize this stolen credit card number!" and includes the number? Would anyone who reads the advertisement carefully be guilty of possessing stolen property, even if they have no intent to use the number fraudulently? What if the robber simply forgets the credit card number? Does he no longer possess the stolen property?

3. *The guilty act requirement.* Every Anglo-American crime must include a guilty act (in Latin, an "actus reus"). *See* Wayne R. LaFave, Criminal Law 206 (3d ed. 2000). According to this doctrine, the government cannot punish merely having a state of mind. If possession can be satisfied by knowledge alone, does the crime of possessing stolen property violate this principle? If you were the defense attorney in *Johnson*, what argument would you make on appeal to persuade a higher court that the trial court's construction is inconsistent with the actus reus requirement?

4. *If information can be property, what does it take for information to become "stolen" property?* Physical property becomes stolen when someone intentionally takes it away from its owner. The same concept can apply to data: if Joe steals Jane's iPod, the data files stored in the iPod are stolen in exactly the same way as the physical iPod itself. But what if the information is divorced from physical storage media? If Joe copies Jane's computer data and Jane retains her copy, is that data stolen?

The facts of *Johnson* are instructive. AT&T issued a calling card to a legitimate customer, and Johnson found out the number and used it to place calls billed to that customer's account. Try to identify exactly what (if anything) made that number stolen. Was it stolen simply because Johnson possessed the number and was not an authorized account holder? This seems somewhat unlikely. Was the number stolen because Johnson did not have a legitimate business reason to possess the number? Was it stolen because Johnson had an intent to use the number to place calls but not pay for them?

Another possibility is that the word "stolen" expresses a result, not a legal status. Was the number stolen because Johnson deserves punishment for using AT&T's services without their permission?

5. *The value of information.* Under the New York law at issue in *Johnson*, property includes any "thing of value." Whether data has value is contextual, of course. Go back to the hypothetical in which a robber holds up a victim at gun point and demands that the victim tell him something valuable. The victim, afraid for his life, advises the robber to buy stock in General Motors. Is that advice a "thing of value"? Does it depend on whether General Motors' stock later goes up or down?

As these questions suggest, attempts to value a number generally measure the benefit of the use of that number in a specific context, rather than the value of the number as an abstract matter. Thus in *Johnson*, the court looked to the specific context in which Johnson had the number to determine whether he would use the number to obtain valuable services. The number was a thing of value because Johnson was using the number to obtain valuable services for free; in the court's terms, the number was not merely "some innocuous number, innocently had by a defendant."

Is this a helpful way to determine the value of information? What is the court really measuring?

UNITED STATES V. ALEYNIKOV

United States Court of Appeals for the Second Circuit, 2012.
676 F.3d 71.

DENNIS JACOBS, CHIEF JUDGE.

Sergey Aleynikov was convicted, following a jury trial in the United States District Court for the Southern District of New York (Cote, J.), of stealing and transferring some of the proprietary computer source code used in his employer's high frequency trading system, in violation of the National Stolen Property Act, 18 U.S.C. § 2314 (the "NSPA"), and the Economic Espionage Act of 1996, 18 U.S.C. § 1832 (the "EEA"). On appeal, Aleynikov argues, *inter alia*, that his conduct did not constitute an offense under either statute. We agree, and reverse the judgment of the district court.*

BACKGROUND

Sergey Aleynikov, a computer programmer, was employed by Goldman Sachs & Co. from May 2007 through June 2009, developing computer source code for the company's proprietary high-frequency trading ("HFT") system. An HFT system is a mechanism for making large volumes of trades in securities and commodities based on trading decisions effected in fractions of a second. Trades are executed on the basis of algorithms that incorporate rapid market developments and data from past trades. The computer programs used to operate Goldman's HFT system are of three kinds: [1] market connectivity programs that process real-time market data and execute trades; [2] programs that use algorithms to determine which trades to make; and [3] infrastructure programs that facilitate the flow of information throughout the trading system and monitor the system's performance.

Aleynikov's work focused on developing code for this last category of infrastructure programs in Goldman's HFT system. High frequency trading is a competitive business that depends in large part on the speed with which information can be processed to seize fleeting market

---

* Editor's Note: The discussion of Aleynikov's liability under the EEA is deleted from the opinion here but is discussed in detail in the material on the EEA on pages 166 to 169.

opportunities. Goldman closely guards the secrecy of each component of the system, and does not license the system to anyone. Goldman's confidentiality policies bound Aleynikov to keep in strict confidence all the firm's proprietary information, including any intellectual property created by Aleynikov. He was barred as well from taking it or using it when his employment ended.

By 2009, Aleynikov was earning $400,000, the highest-paid of the twenty-five programmers in his group. In April 2009, he accepted an offer to become an Executive Vice President at Teza Technologies LLC, a Chicago-based startup that was looking to develop its own HFT system. Aleynikov was hired, at over $1 million a year, to develop the market connectivity and infrastructure components of Teza's HFT system. Teza's founder (a former head of HFT at Chicago-based hedge fund Citadel Investment Group) emailed Aleynikov (and several other employees) in late May, conveying his expectation that they would develop a functional trading system within six months. It usually takes years for a team of programmers to develop an HFT system from scratch.

Aleynikov's last day at Goldman was June 5, 2009. At approximately 5:20 p.m., just before his going-away party, Aleynikov encrypted and uploaded to a server in Germany more than 500,000 lines of source code for Goldman's HFT system, including code for a substantial part of the infrastructure, and some of the algorithms and market data connectivity programs. Some of the code pertained to programs that could operate independently of the rest of the Goldman system and could be integrated into a competitor's system. After uploading the source code, Aleynikov deleted the encryption program as well as the history of his computer commands. When he returned to his home in New Jersey, Aleynikov downloaded the source code from the server in Germany to his home computer, and copied some of the files to other computer devices he owned.

On July 2, 2009, Aleynikov flew from New Jersey to Chicago to attend meetings at Teza. He brought with him a flash drive and a laptop containing portions of the Goldman source code. When Aleynikov flew back the following day, he was arrested by the FBI at Newark Liberty International Airport.

The indictment charged him with violating the NSPA, which makes it a crime to transport, transmit, or transfer in interstate or foreign commerce any goods, wares, merchandise, securities or money, of the value of $5,000 or more, knowing the same to have been stolen, converted or taken by fraud, 18 U.S.C. § 2314.

The court held that the source code for Goldman's HFT system constitutes "goods" that were "stolen" within the meaning of the NSPA because, though source code is intangible, it contains highly confidential trade secrets related to the Trading System that would be valuable for any firm seeking to launch, or enhance, a high-frequency trading business.

The jury convicted Aleynikov. He was sentenced to 97 months of imprisonment followed by a three-year term of supervised release, and was ordered to pay a $12,500 fine. Bail pending appeal was denied because Aleynikov, a dual citizen of the United States and Russia, was feared to be a flight risk.

DISCUSSION

Aleynikov argues that the source code—as purely intangible property—is not a "good" that was "stolen" within the meaning of the NSPA. We conclude that Aleynikov's conduct did not constitute an offense under the NSPA.

The NSPA makes it a crime to transport, transmit, or transfer in interstate or foreign commerce any goods, wares, merchandise, securities or money, of the value of $5,000 or more, knowing the same to have been stolen, converted or taken by fraud. 18 U.S.C. § 2314. The statute does not define the terms "goods," "wares," or "merchandise." The decisive question is whether the source code that Aleynikov uploaded to a server in Germany, then downloaded to his computer devices in New Jersey, and later transferred to Illinois, constituted stolen "goods," "wares," or "merchandise" within the meaning of the NSPA. Based on the substantial weight of the case law, as well as the ordinary meaning of the words, we conclude that it did not.

A.

We first considered the applicability of the NSPA to the theft of intellectual property in *United States v. Bottone*, 365 F.2d 389 (2d Cir. 1966) (Friendly, J.), in which photocopied documents outlining manufacturing procedures for certain pharmaceuticals were transported across state lines. Since the actual processes themselves (as opposed to photocopies) were never transported across state lines, the "serious question" (we explained) was whether the papers showing the processes that were transported in interstate or foreign commerce were 'goods' which had been 'stolen, converted or taken by fraud' in view of the lack of proof that any of the physical materials so transported came from the manufacturer's possession. We held that the NSPA was violated there, observing that what was "stolen and transported" was, ultimately, "tangible goods," notwithstanding the clever intermediate transcription and use of a photocopy machine.

However, we suggested that a different result would obtain if there was no physical taking of tangible property whatsoever: "To be sure, where no tangible objects were ever taken or transported, a court would be hard pressed to conclude that 'goods' had been stolen and transported within the meaning of 2314." Hence, we observed, the statute would presumably not extend to the case where a carefully guarded secret formula was memorized, carried away in the recesses of a thievish mind and placed in writing only after a boundary had been crossed. *Bottone* itself thus treats its holding as the furthest limit of a statute that is not endlessly elastic: Some tangible property must be taken from the owner for there to be deemed a "good" that is "stolen" for purposes of the NSPA.

Bottone's reading of the NSPA is confirmed by the Supreme Court's opinion in *Dowling v. United States,* 473 U.S. 207 (1985), which held that the NSPA did not apply to an interstate bootleg record operation. *Dowling* rejected the Government's argument that the unauthorized use of the musical compositions rendered them "stolen, converted or taken by fraud." Cases prosecuted under the NSPA "have always involved physical 'goods, wares, or merchandise' that have themselves been 'stolen, converted or taken by fraud' "—even if the stolen thing does not "remain in entirely unaltered form," and "owes a major portion of its value to an intangible component." *Id.* at 216.

"This basic element"—the taking of a physical thing—"comports with the common-sense meaning of the statutory language: by requiring that the 'goods, wares or merchandise' be 'the same' as those 'stolen, converted or taken by fraud,' the provision seems clearly to contemplate a physical identity between the items unlawfully obtained and those eventually transported, and hence some prior physical taking of the subject goods." *Id.*

We join other circuits in relying on *Dowling* for the proposition that the theft and subsequent interstate transmission of purely intangible property is beyond the scope of the NSPA.

In a close analog to the present case, the Tenth Circuit affirmed the dismissal of an indictment alleging that the defendant transported in interstate commerce a computer program containing source code that was taken from his employer. *United States v. Brown,* 925 F.2d 1301, 1305, 1309 (10th Cir. 1991). Citing *Dowling,* the court held that the NSPA applies only to physical 'goods, wares or merchandise' and that purely intellectual property is not within this category. It can be represented physically, such as through writing on a page, but the underlying, intellectual property itself, remains intangible. The Court concluded that the computer program itself is an intangible intellectual property, and as such, it alone cannot constitute goods, wares, merchandise, securities or moneys which have been stolen, converted or taken for purposes of the NSPA.

The Government argues that a tangibility requirement ignores a 1988 amendment, which added the words "transmit" and "transfer" to the terms: "transport, transmit, or transfer." The Government contends that the added words reflect an intent to cover generally transfers and transmissions of non-physical forms of stolen property. The evident purpose of the amendment, however, was to clarify that the statute applied to non-physical electronic transfers of *money*. Money, though it can be intangible, is specifically enumerated in § 2314 as a thing apart and distinct from "goods," "wares," or "merchandise." The addition to the possible means of transport does not bespeak an intent to alter or expand the ordinary meaning of "goods," "wares," or "merchandise" and therefore does not obviate the Government's need to identify a predicate good, ware, merchandise, security, or money that has been stolen.

B.

By uploading Goldman's proprietary source code to a computer server in Germany, Aleynikov stole purely intangible property embodied in a purely intangible format. There was no allegation that he physically seized anything tangible from Goldman, such as a compact disc or thumb drive containing source code, so we need not decide whether that would suffice as a physical theft. Aleynikov later transported portions of the source code to Chicago, on his laptop and flash drive. However, there is no violation of the statute unless the good is transported with knowledge that "the same" has been stolen; the statute therefore presupposes that the thing stolen was a good or ware, etc., *at the time of the theft.* The wording contemplates a physical identity between the items unlawfully obtained and those eventually transported. The later storage of intangible property on a tangible medium does not transform the intangible property into a stolen good. Because Aleynikov did not "assume physical control" over anything when he took the source code, and because he did not thereby deprive Goldman of its use, Aleynikov did not violate the NSPA.

As the district court observed, Goldman's source code is highly valuable, and there is no doubt that in virtually every case involving proprietary computer code worth stealing, the value of the intangible code will vastly exceed the value of any physical item on which it might be stored. But federal crimes are solely creatures of statute. We decline to stretch or update statutory words of plain and ordinary meaning in order to better accommodate the digital age.

NOTES AND QUESTIONS

1.   *Theft law and technological change.* In *Aleynikov*, the Second Circuit refuses to "stretch or update statutory words of plain and ordinary meaning in order to better accommodate the digital age." But in the prior case, *Johnson*, the court adopted a broad interpretation of the statute so as to not be "unmindful of the ever-changing nature of American technology and its components." Which is the better approach? Can you reconcile *Johnson* and *Aleynikov*?

2.   *The policy question.* As a matter of policy, should Aleynikov be punished? If he should be punished, what crime should he be found guilty of

having violated? Imagine you think that Aleynikov should be punished, and that you have to amend the NSPA to bring his conduct within the language of the statute. How would you amend the statute?

3. *The line-drawing problem.* Imagine John works for a company in New York that sells widgets. As part of his job, John has access to a one-page document belonging to the company that contains its secret method for manufacturing high-quality widgets at low cost. John decides to leave his company and to start a competing widget company in New Jersey. John concludes that he needs to bring a copy of the document to New Jersey to start his business. Consider the following ways that John could take advantage of his access to the document to help start his competing business:

A. John could steal a paper copy of the document in New York and carry it with him to New Jersey.

B. John could make a photocopy of the document, return the original, and carry the photocopy with him to New Jersey.

C. John could save an electronic copy of the document on a thumb drive and bring the thumb drive with him to New Jersey.

D. John could send himself an e-mail from New York to New Jersey and attach a .pdf of the document to the e-mail.

E. John could memorize the document, travel to New Jersey, and then recreate a copy of the document from memory.

Which of these acts should count as the interstate transportation of stolen property?

4. In United States v. Agrawal, 726 F.3d 235 (2d Cir. 2013), a quantitative analyst named Agrawal was working at a high-frequency trading group at a company named SocGen in New York City. Agrawal decided to seek employment opportunities elsewhere. In effort to impress prospective employers, Agrawal came into his regular office one day, printed out more than a thousand pages of SocGen's trading code, and physically transported the papers in his backpack to his apartment in New Jersey. During subsequent interviews, Agrawal promised prospective employers that he could replicate the valuable code for them to use to compete against SocGen. As in *Aleynikov*, Agrawal was charged with violating 18 U.S.C. § 2314.

Under the deferential standard of plain error review (applied because Agrawal did not challenge the issue at trial), the Second Circuit the affirmed the conviction for violating 18 U.S.C. § 2314 because Agrawal stole a physical copy of the code:

> Relying on *Aleynikov,* Agrawal challenges the legal sufficiency of his NSPA charge, complaining that he too is accused of stealing computer code constituting only intangible property. The argument fails because it ignores *Aleynikov's* emphasis on the format in which intellectual property is taken. In *Aleynikov,* the defendant stole computer code in an intangible form, electronically downloading the

code to a server in Germany and then from that server to his own computer. By contrast, Agrawal stole computer code in the tangible form of thousands of sheets of paper, which paper he then transported to his home in New Jersey. This makes all the difference. As *Aleynikov* explained, a defendant who transfers code electronically never assumes "physical control" over anything tangible. *Id.* By contrast, a defendant such as Agrawal, who steals papers on which intangible intellectual property is reproduced, *does* assume physical control over something tangible as is necessary for the item to be a 'good' for purposes of the NSPA.

Here, Agrawal produced paper copies of SocGen's computer code in the company's office, on its paper and with its equipment. The fact that the code had been in an intangible form before Agrawal, a SocGen employee, himself reproduced it on company paper is irrelevant. The papers belonged to SocGen, not Agrawal. When Agrawal removed this tangible property from SocGen's offices without authorization, and transported it to his home in New Jersey, he was engaged in the theft or conversion of a "good" in violation of the NSPA.

Id. at 251–52.

5. *State law versus federal law.* The Second Circuit ruled in *Aleynikov* that Aleynikov could not be convicted of transporting stolen property under the federal NSPA because he didn't obtain anything sufficiently tangible. Notably, however, state statutes can adopt different principles. Following the Second Circuit's decision in *Aleynikov*, New York state prosecutors brought charges against Aleynikov under a New York state law, unlawful use of secret scientific material. That law, Penal Law § 165.07, states:

A person is guilty of unlawful use of secret scientific material when, with intent to appropriate to himself or another the use of secret scientific material, and having no right to do so and no reasonable ground to believe that he has such right, he makes a tangible reproduction or representation of such secret scientific material by means of writing, photographing, drawing, mechanically or electronically reproducing or recording such secret scientific material.

A New York state jury convicted Aleynikov of this offense. The trial judge set aside the jury's verdict on grounds that roughly resembled the Second Circuit's reasoning. According to the trial judge, the evidence was insufficient to show that Aleynikov made a "tangible reproduction or representation" of the source code. *See* People v. Aleynikov, 49 Misc.3d 286 (N.Y. Sup. Ct. 2015).

On appeal, the New York Court of Appeals (the state's highest court) ruled that the conviction was proper because Aleynikov made a "tangible reproduction" when he copied the source code:

Ideas begin in the mind. By its very nature, an idea, be it a symphony or computer source code, begins as intangible property. However, the medium upon which an idea is stored is generally physical, whether it is represented on a computer hard drive, vinyl record, or compact disc. The changes made to a hard drive or disc when information is copied onto it are physical in nature. The representation occupies space. Consequently, a statute that criminalizes the making of a tangible reproduction or representation of secret scientific material by electronically copying or recording applies to the acts of a defendant who uploads proprietary source code to a computer server.

A rational jury could have found that the "reproduction or representation" that defendant made of Goldman's source code, when he uploaded it to the German server, was tangible in the sense of "material" or "having physical form." The jury heard testimony that the representation of source code has physical form. Kumar, the computer engineer, testified that while source code, as abstract intellectual property, does not have physical form, the representation of it is material. He explained that when computer files are stored on a hard drive or CD, they are physically present on that hard drive or disc, and further stated that data is visible in aggregate when stored on such a medium. The jury also heard testimony that source code that is stored on a computer takes up physical space in a computer hard drive. Given that a reproduction of computer code takes up space on a drive, it is clear that it is physical in nature. In short, the changes that are made to the hard drive or disc, when code or other information is stored, are physical.

People v. Aleynikov, 104 N.E.3d 687, 688, 697 (N.Y. 2018). *See also* People v. Aleynikov, 76 A.D.3d 444 (N.Y. App. Div. 2019) (concluding that "there is no inconsistency between the Second Circuit's determination that the codes were intangible when transported and this Court's determination that defendant made a tangible reproduction when he uploaded them to the German server, where they resided within a physical medium.").

6. *Does sending an electronic signal "transport" property?* When property is tangible, it is possible to track its motion to establish that it has been transported across state lines. If property is merely electronic data, however, the only property being transported are the electrons that constitute the bits and bytes of the data. Does setting up a circuit that sends electrons across state lines "transport" property? In United States v. Gilboe, 684 F.2d 235 (2d Cir. 1982), a defendant wired an electronic funds transfer to the Bahamas. The defendant argued that he did not actually "transport" any property to the Bahamas. In an opinion by Judge Feinberg, the Second Circuit disagreed:

Electronic signals in this context are the means by which funds are transported. The beginning of the transaction is money in one account and the ending is money in another. The manner in which the funds were moved does not affect the ability to obtain tangible paper dollars or a bank check from the receiving account. Indeed, we suspect that actual dollars rarely move between banks, particularly in international transactions. If anything, the means of transfer here were essential to the success of the fraudulent scheme. Defendant depended heavily on his ability to move funds rapidly out of reach of disgruntled shipowners who were to receive payment within days of loading the grain. And it was not until the funds, through a series of bank transfers, came to rest in the Bahamas that defendant's scheme was complete.

Id. at 238. Is the court right to focus not on the details of how the technology works, but rather on the net effect of the transaction? And if so, is there a justification for why transfers of money should be covered by the statute but not transfers of other valuable data?

7. *Property crimes and information misuse.* Cases such as *Johnson* and *Aleynikov* consider whether to rework traditional property crimes to address information misuse. The cases assume that information is property that has an owner who sets the rules for its proper usage. When a wrongdoer obtains a copy of that information and misuses it in violation of those rules, the misuse renders that copy stolen property. Retaining the information constitutes possession of stolen property (*Johnson*), and sending that information can be considered transporting it (the government's argument in *Aleynikov*). Taken together, such cases create a theoretical framework for punishing misuse of information using general property crimes.

Should courts adopt this theory? Both *Johnson* and *Aleynikov* involve individuals who deserved punishment for their harmful acts. Both men committed acts that deserve punishment and that the law should try to deter. But how close is the nexus between the defendants' wrongful acts and the theory of criminal liability applied by the courts? Is a general crime of information misuse derived from property law appropriate?

You should note the similarity between a broad crime of information misuse and the broad readings of the Computer Fraud and Abuse Act debated in Chapter Two. Both regimes imagine a proper usage of computers and/or information, and both punish deviations from that proper usage. In the case of computer misuse crimes, access at some point becomes unauthorized; in the case of information misuse crimes, information at some point becomes stolen. The similarity between these two theories explains why Aleynikov was charged with violating the CFAA in addition to the NSPA. The district court dismissed the CFAA charge and the dismissal was not appealed, but it was another theory the prosecution tried to use to punish Aleynikov.

Does either regime feature a clear way to distinguish proper from improper conduct? Is the law here premised mostly on an intuition that at some point conduct becomes harmful enough that it should trigger criminal sanctions? If so, do some principles explain that intuition, or is it simply a moral judgment made on a case-by-case basis? From an ethical perspective, is it appropriate for prosecutors to make aggressive arguments about the scope of traditional criminal laws, or should they focus on prosecuting conduct that is clearly proscribed by existing statutes? Why am I asking so many questions? (Heh, just kidding.)

2. THE ECONOMIC ESPIONAGE ACT

One alternative to charging information misuse under general property crimes is for the legislature to enact new criminal statutes that punish information misuse in specific contexts. An example of this approach is the Economic Espionage Act of 1996 (EEA), Pub. L. No. 104–294, codified at 18 U.S.C. §§ 1831–39. The EEA was designed to punish and deter the theft of a specific type of information, namely trade secrets.

UNITED STATES V. GENOVESE

United States District Court for the Southern District of New York, 2005.
409 F. Supp.2d 253.

PAULEY, J.

By Indictment dated January 3, 2005, the Government charged the defendant, William P. Genovese, Jr., with one count of unlawfully downloading and selling a trade secret in violation of 18 U.S.C. § 1832(a)(2). Genovese moves to dismiss the Indictment pursuant to Rule 12(b)(3)(B) of the Federal Rules of Criminal Procedure. Genovese contends that the statute criminalizing trade secret theft is facially overbroad in violation of the First Amendment and unconstitutionally vague as applied to him. For the reasons set forth below, Genovese's motion to dismiss the Indictment is denied.

Background

In February 2004, portions of Microsoft Corporation's source code for two of its computer operating systems, Windows NT 4.0 and Windows 2000, appeared on the Internet.

The Indictment charges Genovese with downloading, copying, selling and attempting to sell Microsoft source code without authorization. Specifically, the Government contends that on February 12, 2004, Genovese posted a message on his website offering the code for sale: "win2000 source code jacked . . . and illmob.org got a copy of it . . . im sure if you look hard you can find it or if you wanna buy it ill give you a password to my ftp."

According to the Complaint, an investigator retained by Microsoft responded to the message later that month by sending Genovese an email that offered twenty dollars for the code. After Genovese accepted the offer, the investigator transferred twenty dollars to Genovese through an online payment service. Genovese then provided access to the source code through his FTP server. Microsoft alerted the FBI. In July 2004, an undercover Government agent contacted Genovese and purchased the Microsoft source code. Genovese was arrested and charged with violating 18 U.S.C. § 1832(a)(2).

Discussion

Section 1832 was enacted as part of the Economic Espionage Act of 1996. In relevant part, the statute applies to anyone who,

> with intent to convert a trade secret, that is related to or included in a product that is produced for or placed in interstate or foreign commerce, to the economic benefit of anyone other than the owner thereof, and intending or knowing that the offense will, injure any owner of that trade secret, knowingly . . . without authorization copies, duplicates, sketches, draws, photographs, downloads, uploads, alters, destroys, photocopies, replicates, transmits, delivers, sends, mails, communicates, or conveys such information.

18 U.S.C. § 1832(a)(2). "Trade secret," in turn, is defined to encompass

> all forms and types of financial, business, scientific, technical, economic, or engineering information, including patterns, plans, compilations, program devices, formulas, designs, prototypes, methods, techniques, processes, procedures, programs, or codes, whether tangible or intangible, and whether or how stored, compiled, or memorialized physically, electronically, graphically, photographically, or in writing if (A) the owner thereof has taken reasonable measures to keep such information secret; and (B) the information derives independent economic value, actual or potential, from not being generally known to, and not being readily ascertainable through proper means by, the public.

18 U.S.C. § 1839(3). The statute carries a ten-year maximum term of imprisonment. 18 U.S.C. § 1832(a).

Genovese argues that § 1832 violates the First Amendment because it restricts protected speech and sweeps more broadly than necessary. A statute is unconstitutionally overbroad if there exists "a substantial risk that application of the provision will lead to the suppression of speech." *Nat'l Endowment for the Arts v. Finley,* 524 U.S. 569, 580 (1998). When a litigant challenges a statute on its face as overly broad, the prudential limitations against third party standing are relaxed, and the litigant may assert the rights of individuals whose interests might be affected by the statute but who are not before the court.

While the First Amendment protects the formulation of source code and other types of trade secrets encompassed by the EEA, *see Universal City Studios, Inc. v. Corley,* 273 F.3d 429, 445–46 (2d Cir. 2001), the statute criminalizes their unauthorized copying, duplicating, downloading and uploading. 18 U.S.C. § 1832(a)(2). Moreover, the EEA limits its reach to such conduct that is done "with intent to convert a trade secret . . . to the economic benefit of anyone other than the owner thereof." 18 U.S.C. § 1832(a)(2). Such conduct is not protected speech. *See United States v. Thompson*, 76 F.3d 442, 452 (2d Cir. 1996) ("A prohibition against corrupt acts is clearly limited to constitutionally unprotected and purportedly illicit activity."). Because § 1832 is specifically targeted toward illegal activity and does not reach protected speech, the statute is not unconstitutionally overbroad.

The void-for-vagueness doctrine requires that a statute define the criminal offense with sufficient precision "that ordinary people can understand what conduct is prohibited." *Kolender v. Lawson*, 461 U.S. 352, 357 (1983). Courts must also consider whether the law provides explicit standards for those who apply it. Vagueness challenges to statutes which do not involve First Amendment freedoms must be examined in the light of the facts of the case at hand.

Genovese does not contend that § 1832(a)(2) imprecisely describes the prohibited act (*i.e.,* that an individual is guilty if he "copies, duplicates, sketches, draws, photographs, downloads, uploads, alters, destroys, photocopies, replicates, transmits, delivers, sends, mails, communicates, or conveys" a trade secret). Rather, he maintains that Section 1839(3)'s definition of "trade secret" is unconstitutionally vague as applied to the facts of this case and does not afford due process. Specifically, Genovese argues that having found the source code on the Internet after it had been released to the general public by a third-party, he could not have known that it was "not . . . generally known to . . . the public" and that Microsoft had taken "reasonable measures" to safeguard it.

1. "Not . . . generally known to . . . the public"

Genovese maintains that "he had every reason to believe the code had become publicly available" when he found it on the Internet. However, a trade secret does not lose its protection under the EEA if it is temporarily, accidentally or illicitly released to the public, provided it does not become "generally known" or "readily ascertainable through proper means." 18 U.S.C. § 1839(3)(B). Genovese merges these two standards and, in so doing, elevates the standard for trade secret status to one of absolute secrecy. This formulation impermissibly writes the critical modifier "generally" out of the statutory definition and attempts to inject a vagueness otherwise absent from the facts of this case.

Indeed, a reasonable inference from Genovese's website posting is that he knew that the source code derived independent value because it was not "generally known." The Government alleges that he described the code as "jacked" and indicated that others would have to "look hard" to find it elsewhere. As such, Genovese was on notice that Microsoft had not publicly released the code and recognized its public scarcity. Moreover, because Genovese offered the code for sale and successfully sold it, he was on notice that it derived value from its relative obscurity, notwithstanding that it was available from other sources. *See United States v. Hsu,* 40 F. Supp.2d 623, 630–31 (E.D. Pa. 1999) (rejecting a similar challenge to the definition of "trade secret" where the evidence showed that the defendant "knew (or at a minimum believed) that the information he was seeking to acquire was not generally known to or readily ascertainable through proper means by the public").

A statute may also be unconstitutionally vague if it "authorizes and even encourages arbitrary and discriminatory enforcement." *City of Chicago v. Morales,* 527 U.S. 41, 56 (1999). In this regard, Genovese argues that the statute provided no guidance to law enforcement officials to determine whether the source code constituted a trade secret. However, just as Genovese's announcement and conduct reflect his belief that the "jacked" source code was valuable because it was not generally known, it provided the FBI reason to believe that Genovese was trafficking in Microsoft's trade secret.

2.   "Reasonable measures"

With respect to the "reasonable measures" element of the EEA's "trade secret" definition, Genovese contends that he "was in no position to make a determination about whether Microsoft took any measures to protect the secrecy of its source code, let alone whether those measures were 'reasonable.'"

Once again, Genovese's website posting belies any claim that he was a casual Internet browser who happened upon the source code without knowledge of its owner or the manner in which the code entered the public domain. As discussed above, the posting reveals that Genovese knew that a third-party had "jacked" the source code from Microsoft. Having acknowledged both that the source code was proprietary to Microsoft and that someone else penetrated whatever safeguards Microsoft enlisted to protect it, Genovese cannot now argue that the statute was insufficient to put him on notice that the source code constituted a trade secret under the EEA. For Section 1839(3)'s "trade secret" definition to survive a vague-as-applied challenge, a "defendant need not have been aware of the particular security measures taken by" the trade secret's owner, as long as the "defendant knew the information was proprietary." *United States v. Krumrei,* 258 F.3d 535, 539 (6th Cir. 2001) (noting that the defendant "was aware that he was selling confidential information to which he had no claim").

In this case, one can infer that Genovese knew not only that the source code was proprietary, but that any protective measures by Microsoft had been circumvented. At a later stage in this proceeding, Genovese may choose to argue to this Court or to a jury that Microsoft's measures were not "reasonable," or that Genovese could not have known what, if any, measures Microsoft maintained. For purposes of his vagueness challenge, however, Genovese's knowledge that the source code belonged to Microsoft and that others had stolen it was sufficient for him to "reasonably understand" that the conduct alleged in the Indictment was proscribed by Section 1832(a)(2).

As such, Section 1839(3) defines "trade secret" with "sufficient definiteness" so that an ordinary person in Genovese's position could understand that trafficking in the Windows source code was prohibited by law. As applied to the facts of this case, the statute is not so vague that it violates the defendant's due process.

NOTES AND QUESTIONS

1. *The merits question.* Assuming the court is correct that prosecuting Genovese does not raise constitutional difficulties, do you think Genovese violated the Economic Espionage Act? Assume that Genovese found a copy of the source code online, copied it, and uploaded it to his ftp server. Assume from the facts that he knew the source code had been stolen from Microsoft and that Microsoft did not want the code to be available to the public. To be liable, Genovese must have "intent to convert a trade secret," "to the economic benefit of anyone other than the owner thereof," "intending or knowing that the offense will, injure any owner of that trade secret," and must upload, download or copy it "knowingly . . . without authorization."

Has Genovese done so? Does it matter if the source code is widely available online? Did Genovese know that his conduct would injure Microsoft? Given that he found the copy online, is his conduct clearly "without authorization"? The legislative history of the EEA indicates that "authorization is the permission, approval, consent or sanction of the owner" to obtain, destroy or convey the trade secret. 142 Cong. Rec. S12202, S12212 (daily ed. Oct. 2, 1996).

2. How much narrower is the EEA compared to the general property approach seen in *Johnson*? How does it compare to the NSPA as interpreted in *Aleynikov*? Which approach do you prefer?

3. *When does information become stolen, redux.* Consider how the EEA handles the problem of identifying when information such as a trade secret becomes "stolen." The EEA punishes one who:

(1) steals, or without authorization appropriates, takes, carries away, or conceals, or by fraud, artifice, or deception obtains such information;

(2) without authorization copies, duplicates, sketches, draws, photographs, downloads, uploads, alters, destroys, photocopies,

replicates, transmits, delivers, sends, mails, communicates, or conveys such information;

(3) receives, buys, or possesses such information, knowing the same to have been stolen or appropriated, obtained, or converted without authorization[.]

18 U.S.C. §§ 1831(a), 1832(a). Does this answer the question? Note that the definition of a trade secret may make it easier to determine when a trade secret is "stolen" or copied "without authorization." A trade secret exists only if it has an identifiable owner who has exercised his right to exclude others from his property by taking reasonable measures to keep it a secret. Reasonable measures generally include the imposition of clear rules governing when the secret can be copied, transmitted, and conveyed. In that context, then, copying or distributing the trade secret in violation of the rules needed to ensure that the secret remains a secret constitutes a copying or distributing "without authorization."

Does this shed light on the broader problem of identifying when information is "stolen"? Does it provide a reason to limit information misuse crimes to trade secrets?

<h1 style="text-align:center">UNITED STATES V. AGRAWAL</h1>

United States Court of Appeals for the Second Circuit, 2013.
726 F.3d 235.

REENA RAGGI, CIRCUIT JUDGE:

Defendant Samarth Agrawal was entrusted by his former employer, the French bank Société Générale ("SocGen"), with access to confidential computer code that the bank used to conduct high frequency securities trades. Agrawal abused this trust by printing the code onto thousands of sheets of paper, which he then physically removed from the bank's New York office to his New Jersey home, where he could use them to replicate SocGen's trading systems for a competitor who promised to pay him hundreds of thousands of dollars. The question on this appeal is thus not whether Agrawal is a thief. He is. The question is whether Agrawal properly stands convicted for his thievery in the United States District Court for the Southern District of New York under specific federal laws, namely, the Economic Espionage Act ("EEA"), *see* 18 U.S.C. § 1832.

I.   BACKGROUND

The crimes at issue derive from Agrawal's employment between early 2007 and November 2009 at SocGen's New York offices. Agrawal began his career as a "quantitative analyst" in SocGen's High Frequency Trading ("HFT") Group. The HFT Group engaged in "index arbitrage," a process that seeks to profit by quickly exploiting fleeting differences in the prices of securities. Toward this end, the HFT Group used two computer trading systems, "ADP" and "DQS" to determine when to purchase and sell securities. Each system was made up of highly complicated computer code developed over the course of some years at a cost of several million dollars to SocGen. Using the ADP and DQS systems, the HFT Group executed trades that generated more than $10 million in annual revenue for SocGen during 2007, 2008, and 2009.

Unbeknownst to SocGen, Agrawal was then actively pursuing outside job opportunities. Toward that end, on June 8, 2009, he met with representatives of a New York-based hedge fund, Tower Research Capital. Agrawal told Tower that he was running one of SocGen's two index arbitrage strategies, had a "complete understanding" of that strategy, and could help build a "very similar" system for Tower.

On Saturday, June 13—five days after his meeting with Tower and the day after he acquired access to SocGen's DQS code—Agrawal came into SocGen's New York office, printed out more than a thousand pages of the DQS code, put the printed pages into a backpack, and physically transported the papers to his apartment in New Jersey. Three days later, on June 16, Agrawal again met with Tower partners to discuss replicating SocGen's HFT strategies for Tower. On July 10, Tower proposed to hire Agrawal for this purpose, offering him salary and bonuses exceeding $500,000.

Agrawal informally accepted Tower's offer in August 2009, but delayed disclosing this fact to SocGen for some months in order both to gain more experience with its HFT systems and to collect an anticipated bonus in October. Meanwhile, during August and September 2009, Agrawal copied and printed hundreds more pages of SocGen's HFT code and brought them to his home.

On April 19, 2010, the day Agrawal was to begin work at Tower, FBI agents arrested him at his home in New Jersey. Searches of his apartment resulted in the seizure of thousands of pages of carefully indexed and filed computer code pertaining to SocGen's two HFT systems. Agrawal admitted to an arresting agent that he had printed out the code and taken it home without disclosing that fact to his SocGen supervisors or receiving authorization to do so.

II. DISCUSSION

Where, as here, a defendant failed to raise a sufficiency objection in the district court and presents it for the first time on appeal, we review for plain error. Under that standard, an appellate court may, in its discretion, correct an error not raised at trial only where the appellant demonstrates that (1) there is an error; (2) the error is clear or obvious, rather than subject to reasonable dispute; (3) the error affected the appellant's substantial rights, which in the ordinary case means it affected the outcome of the district court proceedings; and (4) the error seriously affect[s] the fairness, integrity or public reputation of judicial proceedings.

The Electronic Espionage Act, as in effect at the time of Agrawal's indictment and conviction, stated in relevant part as follows:

> Whoever, with intent to convert a trade secret, that is *related to or included in* a *product that is produced for or placed in interstate or foreign commerce*, to the economic benefit of anyone other than the owner thereof, and intending or knowing that the offense will injure any owner of that trade secret, knowingly—
>
> (1) steals, or without authorization appropriates, takes, carries away, or conceals, or by fraud, artifice, or deception obtains such information;
>
> (2) without authorization copies, duplicates, sketches, draws, photographs, downloads, uploads, alters, destroys, photocopies, replicates, transmits, delivers, sends, mails, communicates or conveys such information; [or]
>
> (3) receives, buys, or possesses such information, knowing the same to have been stolen or appropriated, obtained, or converted without authorization;
>
> [is guilty of a crime].

18 U.S.C. § 1832 (emphasis added). The highlighted statutory language—the jurisdictional element of the statute—is the focus of Agrawal's sufficiency challenge.

In *United States v. Aleynikov,* 676 F.3d 71 (2d Cir. 2012), this court construed the phrase "a product that is produced for or placed in interstate or foreign commerce" as a limitation on the scope of the EEA, signaling that Congress did not intend to invoke its full Commerce Clause power to criminalize the theft of trade secrets.[7] *Aleynikov* explained that for a product to be "placed in" commerce, it must have already been introduced into the stream of commerce and have reached the marketplace. Products being developed or readied for the marketplace qualified as being 'produced for,' if not yet actually 'placed in,' commerce. But a product could not be deemed "produced for" commerce simply because its purpose is to facilitate

---

[7]   *Aleynikov's* identification of a congressional intent to limit the reach of the EEA has since been disavowed by Congress itself, which quickly amended the EEA to remove the purportedly limiting language and to clarify its intent to reach broadly in protecting against the theft of trade secrets. *See* Theft of Trade Secrets Clarification Act of 2012, Pub.L. No. 112–236, 126 Stat. 1627 (providing for EEA to be amended to strike phrase "or included in a product that is produced for or placed in" and to insert phrase "a product or service used in or intended for use in," so that relevant language now reads: "Whoever, with intent to convert a trade secret, that is related to a product or service used in or intended for use in interstate or foreign commerce. . . ."); 158 Cong. Rec. S6978–03 (daily ed. Nov. 27, 2012) (statement of Sen. Leahy) (observing that *Aleynikov* decision "cast doubt on the reach" of EEA, and that "clarifying legislation that the Senate will pass today *corrects* the court's narrow reading to ensure that our federal criminal laws adequately address the theft of trade secrets" (emphasis added)).

On this appeal, we have no occasion to construe the revised EEA. Rather, we are obliged to apply the EEA as it existed at the time of Agrawal's conviction and as construed in *Aleynikov.*

or engage in such commerce; such a construction of the EEA's product requirement would deprive the statutory language of any limiting effect.

Aleynikov's construction of the phrase "a product that is produced for or placed in interstate commerce" controls on this appeal. We note, however, that the reversal of Aleynikov's EEA conviction was based on the application of that phrase to the particular "product" that was the basis of the jurisdictional allegation in his case. As we explain below, the present case was submitted to the jury on a very different product theory than that relied on in *Aleynikov.* Thus, the same construction that prompted reversal in *Aleynikov* leads to affirmance here.

In *Aleynikov,* the EEA charge was submitted to the jury on the theory that the trade secret converted by the defendant, *i.e.,* the proprietary computer code, was "included in" a single product: Goldman Sachs's confidential trading system. The jury instructions in *Aleynikov* unambiguously stated that "the indictment [in that case] charges that the Goldman Sachs high-frequency *trading platform* is a product," and that the jury's responsibility was to "determine whether the trading platform was produced for or placed in interstate or foreign commerce." (emphasis added).

This had been the court's and the parties' understanding of the *Aleynikov* indictment from the start. In its opinion denying the defendant's motion to dismiss the indictment, the court noted the parties' agreement "that the trade secret at issue in [the EEA Count] is the source code, and that the relevant 'product' is the Trading System." *United States v. Aleynikov,* 737 F. Supp.2d 173, 178 (S.D.N.Y. 2010). It was on this understanding that this court held the *Aleynikov* indictment legally insufficient.

As *Aleynikov* construed the phrase "a product that is produced for or placed in interstate or foreign commerce," Goldman Sachs's trading system could not constitute such a product because Goldman Sachs had no intention of selling its HFT system or licensing it to anyone. To the contrary, the value of the system depended entirely on preserving its secrecy.

Agrawal submits that *Aleynikov* mandates the same conclusion here because the computer code at issue, like the code in *Aleynikov,* was included in a confidential HFT system. But this case differs from *Aleynikov* in an important respect. Here, neither the prosecution nor the district court presented the case to the jury on the theory that SocGen's *trading system* was the "product" placed in interstate commerce. Nor did they suggest that the EEA's jurisdictional nexus was satisfied by computer code (the stolen trade secret) being "included in" that "product."

Rather, the record reveals that EEA jurisdiction was here put to the jury on a more obvious, convincing—and legally sufficient—theory that was not pursued and, therefore, not addressed in *Aleynikov:* that the *securities* traded by SocGen using its HFT systems, rather than the systems themselves, were the "products . . . placed in" interstate commerce. Under that theory, the jurisdictional nexus was satisfied because SocGen's stolen computer code "related to" the securities (the product) it identified for purchase and sale.

While Agrawal's indictment did not state this theory in so many words, it did allege that SocGen engaged in high-frequency trading in securities on national markets such as the New York Stock Exchange and NASDAQ Stock Market. This effectively identified securities as products traded in interstate commerce.

Of course, the EEA further requires a nexus between the converted trade secret and the product produced for or placed in interstate commerce. *See* 18 U.S.C. § 1832(a) (requiring that trade secret "relate to" or be "included in" product). In *Aleynikov,* where the employer's HFT system was the sole product at issue, the prosecution contended that the stolen computer code was included in that product. Where, as here, the relevant product is publicly traded securities, the statute's "related to" provision comes into play: Was the stolen code related to traded securities? We answer that question "yes."

The term "related to" cannot be construed as coextensive with "included in." Rather, the nexus provision must be read to indicate that a trade secret may *relate to* a product placed in or produced for interstate commerce, without being *included in* that product. As the Supreme Court has recognized, the ordinary meaning of "related to" is broad: "to stand in some relation; to have bearing or concern; to pertain; refer; to bring into association with or connection with." *Morales v. Trans World Airlines,* 504 U.S. 374, 383 (1992). For this reason, the Supreme Court has cautioned that the term must be read in context. For example, where "related to" is used in legislation creating a discrete exception to a general rule, it may not be construed so expansively as to swallow the general rule.

No such concern arises here, despite our colleague's conclusory contention otherwise. The EEA's nexus provision creates no exception to an otherwise applicable general rule; rather, it signals Congress's intent to exercise its Commerce Clause authority to address the theft of trade secrets.

To be sure, in *Aleynikov,* the court concluded that Congress did not exercise its full Commerce Clause authority in the EEA because it limited the *products* that could satisfy the statute's jurisdictional requirement to those "produced for or placed in" interstate commerce. The statutory text provides no similar basis for concluding that, once a product so produced or so placed is identified, Congress intended further to limit the EEA's reach through a restrictive nexus provision. The use of so deliberately expansive a term as "related to" hardly signals such intent. Nor can it be inferred from the EEA's legislative history. Accordingly, we conclude that the term "related to," as used in the EEA's nexus provision, is intended to reach broadly rather than narrowly, consistent with its usual meaning.

On this appeal, we need not delineate the outer limits of that reach because we easily conclude that SocGen's HFT code related to publicly traded securities in such a way as to bring the theft of the HFT code within the EEA. The code existed for the sole purpose of trading in securities, and its considerable value derived entirely from the existence of a market for securities. In short, the confidential code was valuable only in relation to the securities whose interstate trades it facilitated.

Because publicly traded securities thus satisfy the product and nexus requirements of the EEA's jurisdictional element, Agrawal cannot satisfy the final two prongs of plain-error review in complaining of legal insufficiency in the pleading or proof of this element.

POOLER, CIRCUIT JUDGE, dissenting:

Agrawal's EEA count should have failed just as it did in *Aleynikov*. Instead, the majority reaches the opposite conclusion, upholding Agrawal's EEA conviction. It adopts the government's new theory—advanced for the first time on appeal—that the securities, not the HFT System were the alleged "product," and that the code was sufficiently "related to" those securities. No doubt the majority's misapprehension of both law and fact is in part driven by its conviction that the defendant is a "thief" and its wish to retroactively apply Congress's amendment to the EEA. However, whether or not Agrawal's EEA count would stand under the new statute, we are bound by precedent and not by the benefits of hindsight.

NOTES AND QUESTIONS

1. *Congress amends the EEA in response to Aleynikov.* As footnote 7 of *Agrawal* notes, Congress amended the EEA in response to *Aleynikov* by passing the Theft of Trade Secrets Clarification Act of 2012, Pub.L. 112–236. The new language was explicitly designed to overturn *Aleynikov*'s EEA ruling. Under the 2012 amendment, the statute punishes (with new language in italics):

> Whoever, with intent to convert a trade secret, that is related to *a product or service used in or intended for use in* interstate or foreign commerce, to the economic benefit of anyone other than the owner thereof, and intending or knowing that the offense will, injure any owner of that trade secret, knowingly—(1) steals, or without authorization appropriates, takes, carries away, or conceals, or by fraud, artifice, or deception obtains such information; (2) without authorization copies, duplicates, sketches, draws, photographs, downloads, uploads, alters, destroys, photocopies, replicates,

transmits, delivers, sends, mails, communicates, or conveys such information.

18 U.S.C. 1832(a). The nexus requirement under the current statute is now relatively straightforward: The trade secret must simply be "related to a product or service used in or intended for use in interstate or foreign commerce." Further, under *Agrawal*, the phrase "related to" is given a broad reading.

2.   *Source lists as trade secrets.* In United States v. Nosal, 828 F.3d 865 (9th Cir. 2016), the defendant was convicted of violating the EEA when he obtained a database called "Searcher" from the Korn/Ferry executive search firm. "Searcher" was described as an "internal database of information on over one million executives, including contact information, employment history, salaries, biographies and resumes, all compiled since 1995." The database "included data from a number of public and quasi-public sources like LinkedIn, corporate filings and Internet searches, and also included internal, non-public sources, such as personal connections, unsolicited resumes sent to Korn/Ferry and data inputted directly by candidates via Korn/Ferry's website."

On appeal following conviction, the defendant argued that the Searcher database was not a trade secret under the EEA. The Ninth Circuit disagreed:

> The notion of a trade secret often conjures up magic formulas, like Coca Cola's proprietary formula, technical drawings or scientific data. So it is no surprise that such technically complex cases have been brought under the EEA. But the scope of the EEA is not limited to these categories and the EEA, by its terms, includes financial and business information.

> The thrust of Nosal's argument is that the source lists are composed largely, if not entirely, of public information and therefore couldn't possibly be trade secrets. But he overlooks the principle that a trade secret may consist of a compilation of data, public sources or a combination of proprietary and public sources. It is well recognized that it is the secrecy of the claimed trade secret as a whole that is determinative. The fact that some or all of the components of the trade secret are well-known does not preclude protection for a secret combination, compilation, or integration of the individual elements. Expressed differently, a compilation that affords a competitive advantage and is not readily ascertainable falls within the definition of a trade secret.

> The source lists in question are classic examples of a trade secret that derives from an amalgam of public and proprietary source data. To be sure, some of the data came from public sources and other data came from internal, confidential sources. But cumulatively, the Searcher database contained a massive confidential compilation of data, the product of years of effort and expense. Each source list was the result of a query run through a propriety algorithm that

generates a custom subset of possible candidates, culled from a database of over one million executives.

The source lists were not unwashed, public-domain lists of all financial executives in the United States, nor otherwise related to a search that could be readily completed using public sources. Had the query been "who is the CFO of General Motors" or "who are all of the CFOs in a particular industry," our analysis might be different. Instead, the nature of the trade secret and its value stemmed from the unique integration, compilation, cultivation, and sorting of, and the aggressive protections applied to, the Searcher database.

Id. at 881–82.

3. *Congress adds a civil remedy for EEA violations.* In 2016, Congress enacted the Defend Trade Secrets Act to add a civil remedy for EEA violations. Under the new statute, codified at 18 U.S.C. § 1836, victims of trade secret theft have a federal civil cause of action based on the criminal law precedents developed under the EEA. Specifically, the statute provides that the "owner of a trade secret that is misappropriated may bring a civil action under this subsection if the trade secret is related to a product or service used in, or intended for use in, interstate or foreign commerce." § 1836(b)(1). The requirement that the trade secret is "related to a product or service used in, or intended for use in, interstate or foreign commerce" is the same language Congress used to define the criminal scope of the EEA in its 2012 amendment designed to overturn *Aleynikov.* For a summary of the Defend Trade Secrets Act, *see* Peter J. Toren, *The Defend Trade Secrets Act,* 28 No. 7 Intell. Prop. & Tech. L.J. 3 (2016).

3. IDENTITY THEFT AND ACCESS DEVICE FRAUD

The federal criminal code contains three information misuse statutes that deal specifically with misuse of authentication and access devices: 18 U.S.C. § 1028, 18 U.S.C. § 1028A, and 18 U.S.C. § 1029.

18 U.S.C. § 1028 is the federal identity theft statute. It prohibits fraud and misuse of identification documents such as driver's licenses and passports. The statute treats fake identification documents as a kind of contraband, and it contains the kinds of prohibitions that you might find in the narcotics laws. For example, the statute prohibits creating such documents, possessing them with intent to use them, and possessing machines for making fake identification documents with the intent to use them to make fake IDs. *See generally* 18 U.S.C. § 1028(a)(1)–(8).

18 U.S.C. § 1028A is the aggravated identity theft statute. It adds a sentencing enhancement of an extra two-year prison sentence when a person commits one of the specifically enumerated offenses, and then, "during and in relation" to that crime, "knowingly transfers, possesses, or uses, without lawful authority, a means of identification of another person." 18 U.S.C. § 1028A(a)(1). The list of enumerated offenses includes

wire fraud, immigration offenses, theft from the United States, and social security fraud. *See* 18 U.S.C. § 1028A(c). The idea behind this statute is that someone who commits a fraud by using someone else's identification has committed an aggravated crime that deserves extra punishment.

18 U.S.C. § 1029 is the federal access device fraud statute. It prohibits fraud and misuse of credit card numbers, computer passwords, and other types of information that control account access. An "access device" is broadly defined as:

> any card, plate, code, account number, electronic serial number, mobile identification number, personal identification number, or other telecommunications service, equipment, or instrument identifier, or other means of account access that can be used, alone or in conjunction with another access device, to obtain money, goods, services, or any other thing of value, or that can be used to initiate a transfer of funds (other than a transfer originated solely by paper instrument).

18 U.S.C. § 1029(e)(1). The statute also defines an "unauthorized access device" as "any access device that is lost, stolen, expired, revoked, canceled, or obtained with intent to defraud." 18 U.S.C. § 1029(e)(3). Among the acts prohibited by this statute are trafficking in and possessing unauthorized access devices with intent to defraud. *See* § 1029(a)(2)–(3).

The basic thinking behind all three statutes is the same: Access to information, property, and other rights may hinge on documents or data that are designed to authenticate individuals. The use of false or fraudulently obtained authentication methods can cause significant harms. The statutes try to deter that use by prohibiting possessing, buying, selling, and making documents or data that provide false authentication. All three statutes attempt to punish and deter the harms associated with false identification by punishing misuse of identification information even if no access rights are fraudulently obtained.

UNITED STATES V. BARRINGTON

United States Court of Appeals for the Eleventh Circuit, 2011.
648 F.3d 1178.

WHITTEMORE, DISTRICT JUDGE.

Marcus Barrington appeals his convictions for three counts of aggravated identity theft.

Barrington's convictions arose from a scheme he and his co-conspirators concocted to access FAMU's internet-based grading system. The scheme was developed after Secrease and Barrington, roommates at the time, began discussing how to change grades for friends who were applying to graduate school. During the summer of 2007, Barrington changed grades for himself, Jacquette and several fraternity brothers using forged University grade change slips. When that method became ineffective in part because they ran out of blank grade change slips, they developed a plan to access the system using keylogger software.

Secrease was with Barrington in the Registrar's Office in August 2007 when they attempted to install the first keylogger. They eventually installed keylogger software on various University computers, including an office computer used by a Registrar employee and four terminals placed in the University's grand ballroom during registration. The keyloggers covertly recorded the keystrokes made by Registrar employees as they signed onto their computers, capturing their usernames and passwords. That data was automatically transmitted to various email accounts, including Barrington's personal email address.

Using the surreptitiously obtained usernames and passwords, the conspirators accessed FAMU's grading system, changed grades, added credits for courses which had been failed or not taken, and changed the residencies of several non-resident students to qualify them for in-state tuition. The changes were made via the Internet from the conspirators' home computers, campus computers at FAMU and Florida State University, and from several wireless laptops.

A joint investigation by FAMU's Police Department and the FBI determined that FAMU's protected grading system had been accessed by unauthorized means. The investigation was triggered after a FAMU professor discovered that one of his students, Barrington's sister, had received two unauthorized grade changes. The University subsequently discovered that between August and October 2007, approximately 30 to 35 unauthorized changes were made to Barrington's grades, all but one from a lower grade to an A. Barrington's sister received 5 grade changes from F or C to A. Jacquette received approximately 43 grade changes and Secrease received approximately 36. Ultimately, the investigation revealed that in excess of 650 unauthorized grade changes had been made, involving at least 90 students. As a result of the grade changes and residency changes, the University incurred a loss of $137,000 in tuition it otherwise would have received.

In September 2007, Barrington and his sister were questioned by FAMU police. Barrington denied any knowledge of the grade changes. Within hours, and after learning that the University had reversed the grade changes, Barrington organized a meeting at his house with Jacquette, Secrease, and some of the students whose grades had been changed. Barrington instructed them to deny all knowledge of the scheme if questioned by police. They agreed to re-install keyloggers on the Registrar's computers so that the grades could be changed a second time. Barrington drew a map and directed students where to go to carry out the plan. Some of them went to the Registrar's Office where they distracted employees so that others could install keyloggers using flash drive devices. Afterwards, the group celebrated at a local Chili's restaurant.

At some point, Secrease was terminated from his job at the University, losing access to the University's computer lab. Barrington provided funds to Jacquette for the purchase of a laptop computer. Notwithstanding that law enforcement had discovered the scheme and the University was reversing the grade changes, the conspirators continued to make grade changes using the laptop.

In an effort to conceal their involvement, the conspirators made random grade changes for students who had not been involved originally. Jacquette explained that this was done to "throw things off by broadening the list of names" of students whose grades had been changed. Barrington told Jacquette that random grade changes would indicate that either there was a "flaw or hiccup" in the computer system, or that another group of students was responsible. According to Jacquette, Barrington's "logic was, if grade changes continue[d], there [was] no way the police would think that [he did it because] he had to be an absolute idiot to continue doing it after they've already contacted him. But if it continued, they would think that it must be someone else."

In November 2007, search warrants were executed at the conspirators' residences, resulting in the seizure of documents containing the usernames and passwords of seven FAMU Registrar employees, handwritten notes outlining classes and grades and directing certain grade changes, FAMU student transcripts, restricted student enrollment documents, and student class information and ID numbers. In Barrington's room, the officers found an index card with usernames and passwords of Registrar employees written on it. They did not find the laptop that had been used to make the grade and residency changes. It was later determined that Barrington had taken it for safekeeping to the home of another student, who ultimately turned it over to the police. An analysis of the laptop confirmed that it had been used to effect grade and residency changes.

Jacquette consented to a search of his cell phone. On his phone were the usernames and passwords of several Registrar employees. Jacquette testified that this information came from an index card written by Barrington.

Barrington testified at trial. He essentially denied any involvement in the scheme, claiming that he was merely present during the installation of the keyloggers, the grade changing and the concealment activities. In rebuttal, an FBI agent who took Barrington's Rule 11 proffer testified that Barrington admitted to having participated in the scheme to obtain the usernames and passwords, acting as a lookout while Secrease and Jacquette installed the keyloggers on Registrar computers, having used the passwords, and having asking to have his sister's and another female student's grades changed. The Government also called Sheerie Edwards, a friend of Barrington's. She testified that after discussing with Barrington that she had not done well in certain classes, he told her that her grades could be "fixed." She gave him a list of the classes. Later, Barrington called her and told her to look at her grades online. When she did, she saw that her grades had been changed.

Barrington was convicted on all counts, [and on appeal he] contends that the evidence was insufficient to support his convictions on Counts Three, Four and Five for aggravated identity theft. He argues that the passwords the conspirators used to access the Registrar's computer system belonged to the university and do not constitute personal identity information of the individual university employees.

Although Barrington moved for judgment of acquittal pursuant to Rule 29, he did not move for judgment of acquittal on the aggravated identity theft counts. Accordingly, we review the sufficiency of the evidence supporting these convictions for plain error.

There is no plain error. To prove a violation of 18 U.S.C. § 1028A, the evidence must establish that the defendant: (1) knowingly transferred, possessed, or used; (2) the means of identification of another person; (3) without lawful authority; (4) during and in relation to a felony enumerated in § 1028A(c).

To gain access to the Registrar's protected grading system, the conspirators targeted specific "higher up" Registrar employees who they knew had access to the system through their individualized usernames and passwords, which the employees changed every thirty days. Secrease identified the targeted employees and explained that the group established "very close relationships" with these individuals so that "they could get access to their computers." The keyloggers were installed on the computers of these targeted employees to obtain their confidential and unique passwords.

Each of the key elements required for a conviction under § 1028A was proven. The Government proved that Barrington, without authority, knowingly used the usernames and passwords of the Registrar employees during and in relation to the wire fraud conspiracy. The conspirators knew that the usernames and passwords were unique to the employees and would enable them to access the protected grading system. Barrington and his co-conspirators targeted them for that very purpose.

The usernames and passwords were sufficient to identify the specific Registrar employees who had authority to access FAMU's protected grading system. By statutory definition, a "means of identification" includes "any name or number" when used in conjunction with any other information "to identify a specific individual." 18 U.S.C. § 1028(d)(7). The overriding requirement of the definition is that the means of identification must be sufficient to identify a specific individual.

Clearly, the usernames and passwords, considered together, constituted a "means of identification" for those specific individuals and Barrington knew that. In sum, the evidence was sufficient to support Barrington's convictions for aggravated identity theft. There is no plain error.

Next, Barrington contends that the district court erred (1) in failing to instruct the jury that the Government must prove that he "knowingly" used a means of identification that he knew "belonged" to another person and (2) failed to instruct the jury on the term "means of identification." We review for plain error because Barrington did not object to the district court's instructions.

The district court instructed the jury that it could find Barrington guilty only if all of the following facts are proved beyond a reasonable doubt:

First: That the defendant knowingly possessed a means of identification of another person; and

Second: That the defendant possessed the means of identification without lawful authority; and

Third: That the defendant possessed the means of identification during and in relation to a violation of Title 18, United States Code, Section 1343, namely wire fraud.

While the district court did instruct the jury that Barrington must "knowingly" possess a means of identification, the court did not instruct the jury that Barrington must know that the identification belonged to another person or define the term "means of identification."

However, even assuming there was arguably plain error in the instructions, Barrington has not carried his burden to show his substantial rights were affected. The evidence was overwhelming that Barrington and his co-conspirators knew that the usernames and passwords they surreptitiously obtained were unique to specific employees of the Registrar's office. Likewise, the evidence demonstrated beyond all reasonable doubt that they knew that the passwords were a means of verifying those employees' identities and their authority to access the grading system and therefore belonged to the specific employee. Considering the strength of the evidence and the instruction which was given, we find that the failure of the district court to define the term "means of identification" did not affect Barrington's substantial rights. Nor, in the context of this case, did the absence of an instruction on the knowing use of a means of identification belonging to another person affect his substantial rights.

In this day and age of protected computer access, jurors are well equipped to apply a common sense definition to the term "means of identification" in the context of this case. No reasonable juror would fail to appreciate that the unique passwords of the targeted Registrar employees belonged to them in the sense that they were "sufficient to identify a specific individual." Any error in the instructions did not adversely affect the outcome of the trial or the substantial rights of Barrington.

NOTES AND QUESTIONS

1. *What is a "means of identification"?* 18 U.S.C. § 1028(d)(7) defines a "means of identification" as:

> any name or number that may be used, alone or in conjunction with any other information, to identify a specific individual, including any—(A) name, social security number, date of birth, official State or government issued driver's license or identification number, alien registration number, government passport number, employer or taxpayer identification number; (B) unique biometric data, such as fingerprint, voice print, retina or iris image, or other unique physical representation; (C) unique electronic identification number, address, or routing code; or (D) telecommunication identifying information or access device (as defined in section 1029(e));

Do you agree with the *Barrington* court that a username and password combination for a computer account is a "means of identification" under this definition? Notably, a username and password normally can't be used to identify a person *to a person*. They can only be used as a way of identifying a person *to a computer*. Does a means of identifying someone to a computer (but not a person) count as a means of identification?

As you learned in Chapter 2, using another person's username and password to access his computer account is a common way to gain unauthorized access to the account and then commit fraud. Does it make sense that such acts are not only wire fraud but also aggravated identity theft? Imagine you steal another person's car keys and you then use the keys to steal his car. Are you committing aggravated identity theft on the ground that you identified yourself to the car as its owner? If not, is a username and password more like car keys or more like a driver's license?

2. *The requirement of another real person.* In Flores-Figueroa v. United States, 556 U.S. 646 (2009), the defendant was a citizen of Mexico who resided in the United States. To secure employment, the defendant gave his employer a fake name and a counterfeit Social Security number and alien registration card. The defendant was charged with committing the crime of aggravated identity theft under 18 U.S.C. § 1028A(a)(1), which prohibits committing a predicate offense while "knowingly" using a means of identification "of another person." The defendant claimed that he did not actually know that the Social Security number he had provided belonged to another person. He knew it was

not his own number, but he did not know if the number had been assigned to someone else.

The Supreme Court held that, as a matter of statutory interpretation, the Government must prove knowledge that the number belonged to another person. The Court rejected the prosecution's argument that this interpretation would create practical problems because the government normally would not know whether an illegal immigrant knew that the number belonged to another:

> In the classic case of identity theft, intent is generally not difficult to prove. For example, where a defendant has used another person's identification information to get access to that person's bank account, the Government can prove knowledge with little difficulty. The same is true when the defendant has gone through someone else's trash to find discarded credit card and bank statements, or pretends to be from the victim's bank and requests personal identifying information. Indeed, the examples of identity theft in the legislative history (dumpster diving, computer hacking, and the like) are all examples of the types of classic identity theft where intent should be relatively easy to prove, and there will be no practical enforcement problem. . . [T]o the extent that Congress may have been concerned about criminalizing the conduct of a broader class of individuals, the concerns about practical enforceability are insufficient to outweigh the clarity of the text.

Id. at 656.

3.   *Revisiting the Johnson case.* Recall the facts of People v. Johnson, 560 N.Y.S.2d 238 (Crim. Ct. N.Y. 1990), from the beginning of this Chapter. Johnson possessed an AT&T credit card number on a slip of paper. The number was stolen and was being used by Johnson without the consent of the account holder. At the federal level, Johnson's criminal liability is clear. 18 U.S.C. § 1029(a)(6) punishes whoever, "without the authorization of the issuer of the access device, knowingly and with intent to defraud solicits a person for the purpose of . . . offering an access device . . . or selling information regarding . . . an access device." Isn't this exactly what Johnson did? Does it make more sense for Johnson to be punished under a specific access device fraud statute or a general property crime statute?

4.   *Does 18 U.S.C. § 1028A add two years of jail time to felony CFAA violations that involve stolen passwords?* 18 U.S.C. § 1028A adds a sentencing enhancement of an extra two years in prison when a person, "during and in relation" to a statutory predicate felony crime, "knowingly transfers, possesses, or uses, without lawful authority, a means of identification of another person." The list of predicate crimes includes "a felony violation of . . . any provision contained in this chapter (relating to fraud and false statements)." 18 U.S.C. § 1028A(c)(4). That chapter refers to Chapter 47, which spans from 18 U.S.C. § 1001 to 18 U.S.C. § 1040 and collects many of the federal fraud crimes.

At first blush, this seems sensible. Congress was worried about using means of identification to further felony fraud schemes. It makes sense that the list of predicate offenses would include felonies listed in the fraud and false statements section of the criminal code.

But consider a possible unintended consequence of this broad statutory language. Congress placed the CFAA in the "Fraud and False Statements" chapter of the criminal code. Again, this seems sensible at first: The statute is the Computer *Fraud* and Abuse Act, after all. But recall that only a small part of the CFAA, 18 U.S.C. § 1030(a)(4), actually involves fraud. Most of the CFAA is about computer trespass—unauthorized access—not fraud. But because the entire CFAA is in the fraud and false statements chapter, it appears that any felony violation of § 1030 can be a predicate offense under § 1028A.

This may lead to bizarre results when paired with the reasoning of *Barrington*. In particular, it raises the possibility that a computer trespass using a stolen password might count as aggravated identity theft. To see this, imagine two hackers: Alan and Barbara. They each hack into Cathy's personal e-mail account with intent to profit in violation of 18 U.S.C. § 1030(a)(2). Alan hacks into the account by simply entering in Cathy's stolen username and password. Barbara hacks into the account by running sophisticated software that exploits a security flaw. Should Alan receive two more years of punishment than Barbara because Alan used "a means of identification of another person" while Barbara did not?

4. COPYRIGHT LAW

Copyright law is designed to provide economic incentives for authors to create new and original works such as stories, books, music, and movies. Digital technologies and the Internet have begun to revolutionize how such original works are made and distributed, raising a number of vital questions about the future of copyright law. At the same time, copyright law is overwhelmingly an area of civil law, not criminal law. The rights granted under the copyright laws generally are enforced by civil lawsuits brought by copyright owners, not criminal indictments obtained by federal prosecutors. The role of criminal law in the enforcement of copyright law traditionally has been much narrower than the role of civil law. As a result, few criminal copyright cases have been brought.

Should computer-facilitated copyright infringement change that traditional role? The Internet facilitates copyright infringement on a grand scale; it is now far easier and cheaper than ever before to copy and distribute copyrighted works in a relatively anonymous environment. Should criminal copyright laws be enforced to deter the digital reproduction and distribution of copyrighted materials? Can criminal prosecutions limit infringement in a way that civil penalties cannot? Or are criminal prosecutions too heavy-handed given that technology and social practice is in considerable flux?

a) Introduction

DAVID GOLDSTONE—PROSECUTING INTELLECTUAL PROPERTY CRIMES

Computer Crime and Intellectual Property Section.
United States Department of Justice (2001).

The central precept of copyright law is:

For a limited time, an original work in fixed form may not be copied (or otherwise infringed) without permission.

Copyright law is intended to protect the creators of original expressive works. Copyright law protects the original expression of an idea or concept in tangible form (be it a novel, a song, a carpet design, or computer source code), but does not extend to protection of the idea or concept itself. Thus, copyright law protects interests distinct from those protected by the patent laws, which provide exclusive rights to inventors of new methods or processes, and the trademark laws, which protect the exclusive use of certain names and slogans in connection with certain goods or services.

A rich body of law has developed to give greater content to this edict, supported by an administrative scheme established and refined by Congress. For federal prosecutors, however, the critical aspects of copyright law can be distilled to a few basic questions: What is the legal basis for creating a property right in original intellectual property, such as a book, a movie, or computer software? What are the major developments in federal copyright protection? How does intellectual property become protected by copyright law? Does it need to be registered? How long does that protection last? What counts as "infringement" of a copy? Is infringement really a crime, and, if so, why? What if the infringer was not making any money?

What is the legal basis for creating a "property right" in original intellectual property, such as a book, a movie, or computer software? Since 1790, Congress has enacted numerous statutes developing and fine-tuning the copyright law, which is now codified primarily in Title 17 of the United States Code. The Constitution grants Congress both general authority to regulate interstate commerce, U.S. Const. art. I, § 8, cl. 3, and specific authority "to Promote the Progress of Science and Useful Arts, by securing for Limited Times to Authors and Inventors the exclusive Right to their respective Writings and Discoveries." U.S. Const. art. I, § 8, cl. 8.

What are the major developments in federal copyright protection? Since 1790, Congress has enacted and repeatedly amended copyright laws, with a trend of continually increased coverage and increased remedies. Beginning in 1909, Congress also imposed criminal penalties for certain types of copyright infringement. The major revision in 1976 was a watershed moment in copyright law; it revolutionized copyright law by establishing federal pre-emption over state law. *See* 17 U.S.C. § 301. Other significant recent legislative developments include: (1) the Computer Software Copyright Act of 1980 (codified at 17 U.S.C. §§ 101, 117), which clarified that computer software is entitled to copyright protection; (2) expansion of criminal penalties for certain works in 1982 and for all works in 1992; *see* 17 U.S.C. § 506 and 18 U.S.C. § 2319; (3) the creation of an exclusive right pertaining to digital audio transmission of sound recordings by the Digital Performance Right in Sound Recordings Act of 1995 (1995); (4) the criminalization of large-scale copying even in the absence of economic motivation by the No Electronic Theft (NET) Act (1997); (5) the 1998 extension of the term of copyrights; *see* Sonny Bono Copyright Term Extension Act (1998); and (6) the Digital Millennium Copyright Act (codified at 17 U.S.C. §§ 1201–1205).

How does intellectual property become protected by copyright law? Does it need to have been registered with the Copyright Office? Congress has provided copyright protection to all "original works of authorship fixed in any tangible medium of expression, now known or later developed, from which they can be perceived, reproduced, or otherwise communicated, either directly or with the aid of a machine or device." 17 U.S.C. § 102(a). This definition has two components, originality and fixation, which set the outer limits of federal copyright protection. While copyright protection exists from the time of the creation of a work, civil infringement actions may be brought only with respect to those works that have been registered with the Register of Copyrights. Similarly, criminal prosecutions should be sought only after the infringed works have been registered.

How long does copyright protection last? The term of copyright protection for works created in 1978 or later is life of the author plus seventy years. Pre-1978 works are protected for ninety-five years from the date of creation. Corporate copyrights are treated similarly.

What constitutes "infringement" of a copyrighted work? Generally, infringement is the violation of one of five exclusive rights granted to a copyright owner by federal law. The five exclusive rights are: (1) reproduction, (2) distribution, (3) public display, or (4) public performance of the copyrighted work, as well as (5) preparation of derivative works based upon the original copyrighted work. *See* 17 U.S.C. § 106(1)–(5). An unlicensed use of the copyright is not an infringement unless it conflicts with one of these specific exclusive rights conferred by the copyright statute.

What makes copyright infringement a crime? Is it a felony? Copyright infringement is a crime where it is done willfully and either: (1) for commercial advantage or private financial gain, 17 U.S.C. § 506(a)(1); or (2) by reproduction or distribution on a large scale (i.e., copying works with a total retail value of over $1,000), 17 U.S.C. § 506(a)(2). Felony punishment is provided only for reproduction or distribution of at least 10 copies during any 180 days of copyrighted works worth more than $2,500. 18 U.S.C. § 2319(b)–(c). The reason that copyright infringement is a crime is to punish and deter the misappropriation of intellectual property that an author—who may have no means to prevent copying—invested time, energy and money to create.

What other criminal laws protect copyrighted material besides 17 U.S.C. § 506(a) and 18 U.S.C. § 2319? A number of other federal laws specifically protect copyrighted works. 18 U.S.C. § 2318 prohibits the counterfeit labeling of copyrighted works. Further, in 1994, Congress created 18 U.S.C. § 2319A, which expressly covers the unauthorized "fixation" of and trafficking in recordings and musical videos of live musical performances. Systems of copyright management are protected by 17 U.S.C. § 1201 and § 1202. 17 U.S.C. § 506 also provides lesser criminal sanctions for conduct which does not constitute copyright infringement but which nonetheless undermines the integrity of the copyright system, such as for false representations in copyright applications.

There are four essential elements to a charge of felony copyright infringement. In order to obtain a felony conviction under 17 U.S.C. § 506(a) and 18 U.S.C. § 2319, the government must demonstrate that:

1.   A copyright exists,

2.   It was infringed by the defendant by reproduction or distribution of the copyrighted work,

3.   The defendant acted willfully, and

4.   The defendant infringed at least 10 copies of one or more copyrighted works with a total retail value of more than $2,500 within a 180-day period.

See 17 U.S.C. § 506(a)(2); 18 U.S.C. § 2319(a), (c)(1). The maximum punishment for this crime is 3 years imprisonment and $250,000.

Another element, if proven, enhances the maximum penalty: That the defendant acted "for purposes of commercial advantage or private financial gain." If it is proven, the statutory maximum prison sentence can rise to 5 years. *See* 17 U.S.C. § 506(a)(1); 18 U.S.C. § 2319(a), (b)(1). Moreover, a commercial motivation case will usually have better jury appeal than a case without commercial motivation. Indeed, if commercial motivation is not alleged, defendants may be more inclined to raise the affirmative defense of fair use, codified at 17 U.S.C. § 107, since fair use defenses are more plausible when defendants do not profit financially by their acts of infringement.

NOTES AND QUESTIONS

1. *What makes criminal copyright different from civil copyright.* Many of the statutory elements of copyright liability are relatively clear-cut. Consider, for example, the requirement that the defendant's conduct infringed an existing copyright via reproduction or distribution. Downloading a copyrighted computer file constitutes reproducing it, and sending it to another counts as distribution. The primary legal issues raised in criminal copyright cases tend to be the willfulness requirement, fair use, and (if needed) the requirement of an intent to profit.

2. *Fair use.* Copying or distributing copyrighted works does not constitute infringement if it falls within the statutory fair use exception:

> The fair use of a copyrighted work . . . for purposes such as criticism, comment, news reporting, teaching (including multiple copies for classroom use), scholarship, or research, is not an infringement of copyright. In determining whether the use made of a work in any particular case is a fair use the factors to be considered shall include—
>
> (1) the purpose and character of the use, including whether such use is of a commercial nature or is for nonprofit educational purposes;
>
> (2) the nature of the copyrighted work;
>
> (3) the amount and substantiality of the portion used in relation to the copyrighted work as a whole; and
>
> (4) the effect of the use upon the potential market for or value of the copyrighted work.

17 U.S.C. § 107. The fair use doctrine requires applying this multi-factor test in light of the specific facts of the case.

The fair use defense arose in a civil case brought for downloading music over a peer-to-peer network in BMG Music v. Gonzalez, 430 F.3d 888 (7th Cir. 2005). The defendant, Cecilia Gonzalez, downloaded copyrighted music using the Kazaa file-sharing network. Judge Easterbrook held that the fair use defense did not apply to her conduct:

> A "fair use" of copyrighted material is not infringement. Gonzalez insists that she was engaged in fair use under the terms of 17 U.S.C. § 107—or at least that a material dispute entitles her to a trial. It is undisputed, however, that she downloaded more than 1,370 copyrighted songs during a few weeks and kept them on her computer until she was caught. Her position is that she was just sampling music to determine what she liked enough to buy at retail. Because this suit was resolved on summary judgment, we must assume that Gonzalez is telling the truth when she says that she owned compact discs containing some of the songs before she downloaded them and that she purchased others later. She concedes, however, that she has

never owned legitimate copies of 30 songs that she downloaded. (How many of the remainder she owned is disputed.)

Instead of erasing songs that she decided not to buy, she retained them. It is these 30 songs about which there is no dispute concerning ownership that formed the basis of the damages award. This is not a form of time-shifting, along the lines of *Sony Corp. of America v. Universal City Studios*, Inc., 464 U.S. 417 (1984) (*Betamax*). A copy downloaded, played, and retained on one's hard drive for future use is a direct substitute for a purchased copy—and without the benefit of the license fee paid to the broadcaster. The premise of *Betamax* is that the broadcast was licensed for one transmission and thus one viewing. *Betamax* held that shifting the time of this single viewing is fair use. The files that Gonzalez obtained, by contrast, were posted in violation of copyright law; there was no license covering a single transmission or hearing—and, to repeat, Gonzalez kept the copies. Time-shifting by an authorized recipient this is not. See William M. Landes & Richard A. Posner, *The Economic Structure of Intellectual Property Law* 117–22 (2003).

Section 107 provides that when considering a defense of fair use the court must take into account "(1) the purpose and character of the use, including whether such use is of a commercial nature or is for nonprofit educational purposes; (2) the nature of the copyrighted work; (3) the amount and substantiality of the portion used in relation to the copyrighted work as a whole; and (4) the effect of the use upon the potential market for or value of the copyrighted work." Gonzalez was not engaged in a nonprofit use; she downloaded (and kept) whole copyrighted songs (for which, as with poetry, copying of more than a couplet or two is deemed excessive); and she did this despite the fact that these works often are sold per song as well as per album. This leads her to concentrate on the fourth consideration: "the effect of the use upon the potential market for or value of the copyrighted work."

As she tells the tale, downloading on a try-before-you-buy basis is good advertising for copyright proprietors, expanding the value of their inventory. The Supreme Court thought otherwise in *MGM Studios v. Grokster,* 545 U.S. 913 (2005), with considerable empirical support. As file sharing has increased over the last four years, the sales of recorded music have dropped by approximately 30%. Perhaps other economic factors contributed, but the events likely are related. Music downloaded for free from the Internet is a close substitute for purchased music; many people are bound to keep the downloaded files without buying originals.

Id. at 889–90.

b)　The Willfulness Requirement

The willfulness requirement provides the most important line distinguishing civil from criminal copyright liability. Under current law, infringement cannot be a crime unless it is "willful." What does it mean to infringe a copyright willfully?

UNITED STATES V. MORAN

United States District Court for the District of Nebraska, 1991.
757 F. Supp. 1046.

RICHARD G. KOPF, UNITED STATES MAGISTRATE JUDGE.

The parties have consented to try this misdemeanor case before me. Trial was held on January 15, 1991, and briefs were received on January 23, 1991. I now find that the defendant is not guilty of the alleged willful infringement of a copyrighted video cassette in violation of 17 U.S.C. § 506(a).

Facts

Dennis Moran, the defendant, is a full-time Omaha, Nebraska, police officer and the owner of a "mom-and-pop" movie rental business which rents video cassettes of copyrighted motion pictures to the public. On April 14, 1989, agents of the Federal Bureau of Investigation executed a court-ordered search warrant on the premises of Moran's business. The FBI seized various video cassettes appearing to be unauthorized copies of copyrighted motion pictures, including "Bat 21," "Big," "Crocodile Dundee II," "The Fourth Protocol," "Hell-Bound: Hellraiser II," and "Mystic Pizza." The parties have stipulated that these six motion pictures are validly copyrighted motion pictures. The parties have further stipulated that each of the six motion pictures was distributed to Moran, with the permission of the copyright holder, between February 1, 1989, and April 14, 1989. The parties have further stipulated that at least one of the movies identified was reproduced by Moran onto a video cassette, without the authorization of the copyright holder, placed into inventory for rental, and subsequently rented.

At the time the FBI executed the search warrant, Moran was fully cooperative. He told the FBI agents he put the "duped" copies out for rental and held the "originals" back because he feared the "original" motion pictures would be stolen or damaged. Moran told the FBI agents at the time they executed the warrant that he believed this practice was legal as long as he had purchased and was in possession of the "original" motion picture. Moran further advised the FBI agents that he would affix to the "duped" copies title labels for the copyrighted motion pictures and a copy of the FBI copyright warning label commonly found on video cassette tapes. Moran advised the FBI agents that he put the title labels and FBI warning on the tapes to stop customers from stealing or duplicating the tapes.

Moran testified at trial. He indicated that he had been employed as an Omaha, Nebraska, police officer for approximately twenty-two-and-a-half years, including service as a narcotics investigator and as a bodyguard to the mayor of the City of Omaha. Moran has a reputation for honesty among his associates.

Moran testified that he began to "insure" copyrighted video cassettes, meaning that he duplicated copyrighted video cassettes which he had validly purchased from distributors, when he realized copyrighted tapes were being vandalized. Moran testified he was under the impression that "insuring" tapes was legal whereas "pirating" tapes was not. For practical purposes, Moran defined "insuring" versus "pirating" as meaning that he could duplicate a copyrighted tape provided he had purchased the copyrighted tape and did not endeavor to rent both the copyrighted tape and the duplicate he had made. Moran testified that he formulated his belief about "insuring" versus "pirating" when talking with various colleagues in the business and from reading trade publications. However, Moran was not able to specifically identify the source of his information.

There was no persuasive evidence that Moran made multiple copies of each authorized version of the copyrighted material. The evidence indicates that Moran purchased more than one copyrighted tape of the same movie, but the persuasive evidence also reveals that Moran made only one copy of each copyrighted tape he purchased. There was no persuasive evidence that Moran endeavored to rent both the copyrighted tape and the duplicate. When Moran made the unauthorized copy, he put the unauthorized copy in a package made to resemble as closely as possible the package containing the original copyrighted motion picture Moran had purchased from an authorized distributor.

Law

Moran makes two arguments. First, Moran argues that the government must prove that he had the specific intent to violate the law, that is, he knew that what he was doing was illegal and he committed the act nevertheless. Secondly, Moran argues that he did not have the specific intent to violate the law and, as a consequence, should be found not guilty.

In pertinent part 17 U.S.C. § 506(a) punishes as a criminal any "person who infringes a copyright willfully and for purposes of commercial advantage or private financial gain." Pursuant to 17 U.S.C. § 106(3), the owner of a copyright has the exclusive right to "distribute copies . . . of the copyrighted work to the public by sale or other transfer of ownership, or by rental, lease, or lending." The "exclusive right" of the owner of a copyright is subject to a variety of exceptions. *See* 17 U.S.C. §§ 107–118.

A.

It must first be determined whether the word "willfully," as used in 17 U.S.C. § 506(a), requires a showing of "bad purpose" or "evil motive" in the sense that there was an "intentional violation of a known legal duty." Adopting the research of the Motion Picture Association of America, the government argues that the term "willful" means only "an intent to copy and not to infringe." On the other hand, Moran argues that the use of the word "willful" implies the kind of specific intent required to be proven in federal tax cases, which is to say, a voluntary, intentional violation of a known legal duty.

The general rule is, of course, that ignorance of the law or mistake of the law is no defense to a criminal prosecution. However, when the term "willfully" is used in complex statutory schemes, such as federal criminal tax statutes, the term "willful" means a "voluntary, intentional violation of a known legal duty." *Cheek v. United States,* 498 U.S. 192 (1991) (holding in a criminal tax prosecution that a good faith misunderstanding of the law or a good faith belief that one is not violating the law negates willfulness, whether or not the claimed belief or misunderstanding is objectively reasonable). As the Court recognized in *Cheek,* in *United States v. Murdock,* 290 U.S. 389, 396 (1933), the Supreme Court said that:

> Congress did not intend that a person, by reason of a bona fide misunderstanding as to his liability for the tax, as to his duty to make a return, or as to the adequacy of the records he maintained, should become a criminal by his mere failure to measure up to the prescribed standard of conduct.

This was evidently so because "the proliferation of statutes and regulations has sometimes made it difficult for the average citizen to know and comprehend the extent of the duties and obligations imposed by the tax law."

Apparently no case has compared and analyzed the competing arguments, i.e., whether the word "willfully" requires either a showing of specific intent, as suggested by Moran, or the more generalized intent suggested by the government. Indeed, a leading text writer acknowledges that there are two divergent lines of cases, one of which requires specific intent and another which does not. 3 M. Nimmer & D. Nimmer, *Nimmer on Copyright,* § 15.01 at 15–5 n. 13 (1990) (hereinafter *Nimmer*). As pointed out by the government, some courts have suggested that "willful" only means an intent to copy, not to infringe. On the other hand, as suggested by Moran, other courts have seemingly required evidence of specific intent. At least two courts have specifically approved jury instructions essentially stating that an act of infringement done "willfully" means an act voluntarily and purposely done with specific intent to do that which the law forbids, that is to say, with bad purpose either to disobey or disregard the law. None of the cases recognize that there are divergent lines of cases on this point, and none of the cases endeavor to explain why one line of cases is more compelling than the other.

I am persuaded that under 17 U.S.C. § 506(a) "willfully" means that in order to be criminal the infringement must have been a "voluntary, intentional violation of a known legal duty." *Cheek,* 111 S.Ct. at 610. I am so persuaded because I believe that in using the word "willful" Congress intended to soften the impact of the common-law presumption that ignorance of the law or mistake of the law is no defense to a criminal prosecution by making specific intent to violate the law an element of federal criminal copyright offenses. I came to this conclusion after examining the use of the word "willful" in the civil copyright infringement context and applying that use to the criminal statute.

In the civil context there is "strict liability" for infringement, even where the infringement was "innocent." In this connection, a plaintiff in a civil case need not prove actual damages, but rather may seek what are called statutory damages. The term "willful" is used in the context of statutory damages, and it is instructive to compare the definition of the term "willful," as used in the civil context regarding statutory damages, with the definition of the term "willful" used in the criminal context.

In the statutory damage context, a civil plaintiff is generally entitled to recover no less than $250.00 nor more than $10,000.00 per act of infringement. 17 U.S.C. § 504(c)(1). But where the infringement is committed "willfully," the court in its discretion may increase the award of statutory damages up to a maximum of $50,000.00 per act of infringement. 17 U.S.C. § 504(c)(2). On the other hand, in the case of "innocent infringement," if the defendant sustains the burden of proving he/she was not aware, and had no reason to believe, that his/her acts constituted an infringement of the copyright, and the court so finds, the court may in its discretion reduce the applicable minimum to $100.00 per act of infringement. 17 U.S.C. § 504(c)(2).

As noted text writers have concluded, the meaning of the term "willful," used in 17 U.S.C. § 504, must mean that the infringement was with knowledge that the defendant's conduct constituted copyright infringement. *Nimmer, supra,* § 14.04[B][3] at 14–40.3–14–40.4 (citations omitted). Otherwise, there would be no point in providing specially for the reduction of awards to the $100.00 level in the case of "innocent" infringement since any infringement which was nonwillful would necessarily be innocent.

The circuit courts of appeal which have considered the issue have all adopted *Nimmer's* formulation with regard to the meaning of the word "willful" for purposes of 17 U.S.C. § 504(c)(2) and statutory civil damages. In other words, the term "willful," when used in the civil statutory damage statute, has consistently been interpreted to mean that the infringement must be "with knowledge that the defendant's conduct constitutes copyright infringement." *Nimmer, supra*, § 14.04[B][3] at 14–40.3–14–40.4.

There is nothing in the text of the criminal copyright statute, the overall scheme of the copyright laws, or the legislative history to suggest that Congress intended the word "willful," when used in the criminal statute, to mean simply, as the government suggests, an intent to copy. Rather, since Congress used "willful" in the civil damage copyright context to mean that the infringement must take place with the defendant being knowledgeable that his/her conduct constituted copyright infringement, there is no compelling reason to adopt a less stringent requirement in the criminal copyright context. Accordingly, I find that "willfully," when used in 17 U.S.C. § 506(a), means a "voluntary, intentional violation of a known legal duty."

B.

Having determined that the standard enunciated by the Supreme Court in *Cheek* applies, it is important to recognize that the rule does not require that a defendant's belief that his conduct is lawful be judged by an objective standard. Rather, the test is whether Moran truly believed that the copyright laws did not prohibit him from making one copy of a video cassette he had purchased in order to "insure" against vandalism. In other words, the test is not whether Moran's view was objectively reasonable, but rather, whether Moran truly believed that the law did not proscribe his conduct. Of course, the more unreasonable the asserted belief or misunderstanding, the more likely it is that the finder of fact will consider the asserted belief or misunderstanding to be nothing more than simple disagreement with known legal duties imposed by the law, and will find that the government has carried its burden of proving knowledge.

Most of the government's argument that it proved beyond a reasonable doubt that Moran violated the criminal copyright statute, even if the word "willfully" is defined as Moran suggests, is based upon the assumption that Moran's beliefs must be "objectively" reasonable. As indicated above, Moran's beliefs need not have been objectively reasonable; rather, if Moran truly believed that he was not subject to the copyright laws, then his subjective belief would defeat a finding that he "willfully" violated the statute.

First, I note that I had an opportunity to observe Moran when he testified. Moran struck me as an honest, albeit naive, person. I was left with the definite impression that Moran was befuddled and bewildered by the criminal prosecution.

Second, although Moran is a local police officer of long standing, there is nothing in his background to suggest any particular sophistication about business matters, and there is no evidence to suggest that he has any particular knowledge about the intricacies of the copyright laws. When confronted by FBI agents upon the execution of the search warrant, Moran was entirely cooperative. On the day the search warrant was executed, he told his story in the same way he now tells his story.

Third, Moran said he had heard from others and read in various publications that it was legally appropriate to engage in the practice he called "insuring." Moran could not cite the specific source of his information. In this regard, I note that the copyright laws permit libraries and archives to replace a copyrighted article that is damaged, deteriorated, lost, or stolen, if the library or archives have, after reasonable effort, determined that an unused replacement cannot be obtained at a fair price. 17 U.S.C. § 108(c). While Moran obviously did not operate his business as a library or archives, the government's assertion that the practice of "insuring" is patently unreasonable is belied by the recognition that under certain circumstances certain users of copyrighted materials may lawfully engage in copying activity which is similar to Moran's conduct.

Fourth, Moran testified that he made only one copy of the original motion picture purchased from the authorized distributor. The government doubts his testimony, but offers no persuasive evidence to contradict it. Moreover, Moran testified that he never rented both the original copyrighted version of the video cassette purchased from the authorized distributor and the copy he made. Instead, he testified that he always held back the original motion picture. Once again, the government doubts this testimony in its brief, but offers no persuasive evidence to the contrary. Furthermore, the evidence indicates that Moran purchased more than one authorized cassette of a particular motion picture, but made only one duplicate for each authorized cassette purchased.

This evidence suggests that Moran was not acting with a willful intention to violate the copyright laws because if he had such an intention it would make absolutely no sense to purchase multiple authorized video cassettes and then make only one duplicate of each authorized cassette. It would have been far simpler, and certainly more lucrative, for Moran to purchase one authorized cassette of a particular motion picture and make multiple copies from the authorized version. In this way Moran would have had to pay only one fee. The fact that Moran seems to have consistently followed the practice of buying an authorized version, but making only one copy of it, suggests that he was acting in accordance with his belief that to duplicate an authorized version in order to "insure it" was lawful so long as only one copy was made and the authorized version and copy were not both rented.

Fifth, the government argues that Moran must have known that what he was doing constituted a copyright infringement because he had before him the FBI warning label and in fact affixed such labels to the unauthorized copies he made. In pertinent part, the FBI warning states, "Federal law provides severe civil and criminal penalties for the *unauthorized* reproduction, distribution or exhibition of copyrighted motion pictures and video tapes" (emphasis added). Moran explained that he thought these warning labels applied to the renting public, not to him. The use of the word "unauthorized" on the warning label suggested to Moran that vendors who had purchased an authorized version were not subject to the legal restrictions expressed in the warning to the extent that the practice of "insuring" was legal. As Moran suggests, the FBI warning label does not specifically address the claim of legality professed by Moran. Accordingly, Moran's failure to heed the warning label is not determinative.

Sixth, the government further argues that Moran's effort to place the unauthorized copy into a video cassette package displaying a label on its spine and an FBI warning label suggests a sinister motivation. I disagree. Moran's testimony, as I understood it, indicated that when he made a copy he endeavored to make the duplicate look like the original in all respects. After all, the whole purpose of the practice of "insuring" was to use the unauthorized copy in lieu of the original when renting to the public. It was perfectly consistent with Moran's view of the law to make the unauthorized copy look as nearly as possible like the authorized version.

In summary, when Moran's actions were viewed from the totality of the circumstances, the government failed to convince me beyond a reasonable doubt that Moran acted willfully. Moran is a long-time street cop who was fully cooperative with law enforcement authorities. He is obviously not sophisticated and, at least from the record, his business operation of renting movies to the public was not large or sophisticated. Rather, Moran's business appears to have been of the "mom-and-pop" variety. Moran's practice of "insuring," while obviously shifting the risk of loss from Moran to the copyright holder, was conducted in such a way as not to maximize profits, which one assumes would have been his purpose if he had acted willfully. For example, Moran purchased multiple authorized copies of the same movie, but he made only one unauthorized copy for each authorized version purchased. This suggests that Moran truly believed that what he was doing was in fact legal. I therefore find Moran not guilty.

NOTES AND QUESTIONS

1. *Identifying willfulness.* Compare *Moran* to United States v. Draper, 2005 WL 2746665 (W.D. Va. 2005). The defendant Don Draper (yes, "Mad Men" fans, this was his given name) sold pirated DVD copies of the movie *Passion of the Christ* at a time when the movie was still showing in theaters. Postal inspectors learned of Draper's conduct when a package directed to him broke open during shipping, revealing 100 pirated DVDs. An investigation revealed

that Draper had previously sold a copy of the DVD to another postal employee. Postal inspectors resealed the package and then delivered it to Draper: When Draper accepted the package, he was arrested and charged with copyright infringement. The District Court held a bench trial, and the central question at trial was whether Draper's copyright violations were "willful." Draper testified in his own defense, and he told the judge that a stranger had sent him the package and that he did not know what the package contained or that the DVD he sold was unauthorized.

The Court ruled that the violations were willful and that Draper was guilty. The judge summarized the evidence supporting his conclusion as follows:

> Before his arrest, Draper told the Postal Inspector that he was aware that others were selling illegal DVDs in the area and that he had seen *Barber Shop II* and *Passion of the Christ* for sale on Fayette Street. Postmaster Corbett testified that he witnessed Draper offering to sell a DVD of the *Passion of the Christ* at the post office, and that in connection with such efforts, Draper said that it was a "good copy" from New York. Corbett testified that he told Draper that the movie was then number one in theater box offices and that he could not sell such contraband on postal service property. Thus, Draper was clearly aware that selling such DVDs was illegal, and his efforts to sell the pirated video were neither mistaken nor inadvertent.
>
> Katherine Baugus, a postal worker, testified that she bought a copy of the *Passion of the Christ,* in March, 2004 from Draper for $15. Baugus stated that shortly thereafter, the Postal Inspector called Corbett about the package containing one hundred (100) pirated copies of the movie. Baugus became concerned that the video was not legitimate and returned it to Draper, telling him that she did not want it if there was something wrong with it. Draper accepted the DVD back, and although he was not asked for a refund, Draper did not give Baugus her money back. Thereafter, the package with the one hundred (100) pirated DVDs was delivered to Draper. Both this incident and his earlier attempt to sell the DVD to postal employees clearly establishes that Draper was put on notice that his conduct was improper.
>
> Furthermore, Draper's testimony was not credible. Draper stated that he had been given one copy of the *Passion of the Christ* DVD by a stranger who also showed Draper a number of other items he was peddling, including designer clothes. Draper stated that he gave this stranger his address and was told to expect a package, but Draper claimed that he had no idea what was going to be in the package. Of course, when the package arrived, it contained one hundred (100) unauthorized copies of the movie. Draper testified that he offered to sell the DVD to Baugus that day because this stranger had given him a copy, he had no way to play the movie, and he happened to have it

in his possession at the post office. Draper said that he knows nothing of movies, release dates of DVDs, or the copyright laws. While Draper testified that he had only a ninth grade education and had some years ago suffered a head injury due to a gunshot wound, his own admissions to the agents indicate that he was aware that the sale of such movies was illegal, and the evidence made plain the willful nature of his actions.

Id. at 2.

2. *Does willfulness draw a proper line between civil and criminal copyright liability?* The willfulness requirement is designed to ensure that defendants are not held criminally liable when the law is murky. It is an exception to the usual rule that "ignorance of the law is no excuse." When Congress uses the willfulness standard, ignorance of the law *is* an excuse. Criminal liability is reserved for cases in which a defendant knew he acted wrongfully.

Does the willfulness requirement create a sensible line between civil and criminal copyright liability? A defendant can have an entirely unreasonable belief that his conduct was lawful. Under the willfulness standard as construed in *Cheek* and applied in *Moran*, however, no crime has occurred so long as the defendant actually believes that he has acted legally. How does a defendant know whether his conduct is illegal if there are so few cases addressing the scope of copyright liability online?

3. *The debate over the willfulness standard.* Despite the clear holding of *Moran*, the meaning of willfulness in criminal copyright law is not necessarily settled. *See* Lydia Pallas Loren, *Digitization, Commodification, Criminalization: The Evolution of Criminal Copyright Infringement and the Importance of the Willfulness Requirement*, 77 Wash. U. L.Q. 835, 872 (1999). A majority of modern courts have adopted the *Cheek* approach applied in *Moran*. Some courts have suggested a different test, however. For example, the Seventh Circuit has stated that a defendant acts willfully when he realizes "a high likelihood of being held by a court of competent jurisdiction to be [in] violation of a criminal statute." United States v. Heilman, 614 F.2d 1133, 1138 (7th Cir. 1980).

The Ninth Circuit has offered the following argument for why the *Cheek* approach applied in *Moran* is correct:

In 1997, Congress updated the statutory provision governing criminal copyright infringement by inserting the language that . . . "evidence of reproduction or distribution of a copyrighted work, by itself, shall not be sufficient to establish willful infringement." No Electronic Theft (NET) Act, Pub.L. 105–147, § 2(b) (1997) (codified as amended at 17 U.S.C. § 506(c)). This language was in response to the "on-going debate about what precisely is the 'willfulness' standard in the Copyright Act." 143 Cong. Rec. S12,689 (daily ed. Nov. 13, 1997) (statement of Sen. Orrin Hatch); see also id. at 12,690 (statement of

Sen. Patrick Leahy) ("This clarification was included to address the concerns expressed because the standard of 'willfulness' for criminal copyright infringement is not statutorily defined and the court's interpretations have varied somewhat among the Federal circuits."); H.R.Rep. No. 105–339, at 9 (1997) (explaining that the Subcommittee on Courts and Intellectual Property amended the bill "to define 'willful' misconduct" in response to "questions concerning the meaning of the word and its application in the electronic environment"). Upon passage of the bill in the Senate, Senator Hatch stated that willful "ought to mean the intent to violate a known legal duty. As Chairman of the Judiciary Committee, that is the interpretation that I give to this term. Otherwise, I would have objected and not allowed this bill to pass by unanimous consent." 143 Cong. Rec. S12, 689.

As a practical matter, requiring only a general intent to copy as a basis for a criminal conviction would not shield any appreciable amount of infringing conduct from the threat of prosecution. Civil liability will not lie if an author fortuitously creates a work that is substantially similar to another author's copyrighted work. To infringe a copyright, one must copy the protected work. Copying is of necessity an intentional act. If we were to read 17 U.S.C. § 506(a)'s willfulness requirement to mean only an intent to copy, there would be no meaningful distinction between civil and criminal liability in the vast majority of cases. That cannot be the result that Congress sought.

United States v. Liu, 731 F.3d 982, 990–91 (9th Cir. 2013). It's worth pondering how different these standards are. What is the difference between knowing that you are violating the law and realizing a high likelihood of being held in violation of a criminal statute? *Cf.* Model Penal Code § 2.02(2)(b)(ii) (defining "knowingly" in the case of a conduct element as being "aware that it is practically certain that his conduct will cause such a result").

4. *Willfulness and the Digital Millennium Copyright Act.* The Digital Millennium Copyright Act (DMCA), Pub. L. No. 105–304 (1998), is an effort to maintain the effectiveness of technological restrictions that copyright owners may place on access to their copyrighted works to prevent unauthorized copying and distribution. In response to the tendency of digital technologies and the Internet to facilitate copyright infringement, some copyright owners have placed technological controls on their copyrighted works. Instead of hoping that users will follow the rules of copyright law, these copyright owners have used computer code to place the digital equivalent of "locks" around their copyrighted works to prevent unauthorized copying and distribution. Unsurprisingly, the presence of digital locks around copyrighted works has generated new digital lockpicking tools—computer programs that can be used to circumvent the technological restrictions on access and copying of copyrighted works.

The DMCA prohibits possession and distribution of digital lock-picking tools designed to circumvent technological restrictions on access to copyrighted works. By restricting access to digital lockpicking tools, the thinking goes, the DMCA will result in fewer picked locks. Fewer picked locks will mean more enforceable restrictions on copying and distributing copyrighted works, counterbalancing the Internet's ability to facilitate copyright infringement. Criminal liability under the DMCA resembles criminal liability for copyright law: it also contains a requirement that the infringement must be "willful." 17 U.S.C. § 1204(a).

The meaning of willfulness played an important role in the first criminal prosecution brought under the anticircumvention provisions of the DMCA. A Russian software company, ElcomSoft, created a program called the "Advanced eBook Processor" that cracked the protections on Adobe Systems' eBooks. The FBI arrested ElcomSoft employee Dmitry Sklyarov for his role in creating the Advanced eBook Processor, and Sklyarov eventually agreed to testify for the government against ElcomSoft. The two-week trial focused on ElcomSoft's state of mind in creating and distributing their product. Sklyarov and ElcomSoft President Alexander Katalov testified that they did not believe their software was illegal and had no intent for it to be used for illegal purposes.

The jury rendered a verdict of not guilty. According to press accounts, the jury acquitted because they did not believe the company acted willfully:

> Jury foreman Dennis Strader said the jurors agreed ElcomSoft's product was illegal but acquitted the company because they believed the company didn't mean to violate the law.

> "We didn't understand why a million-dollar company would put on their Web page an illegal thing that would ruin their whole business if they were caught," he said in an interview after the verdict. Strader added that the panel found the DMCA itself confusing, making it easy for jurors to believe that executives from Russia might not fully understand it.

Lisa M. Bowman, *Elcomsoft Verdict: Not Guilty*, CNET News.com, Dec. 17, 2002.

5. *Aiding and abetting liability and the Megaupload case.* In 2012, the United States Department of Justice filed criminal copyright charges against seven individuals who had operated one of the most popular websites on the Internet, a file-sharing site available at megaupload.com. Among the charges in the 72-page indictment was that the owners of megaupload.com had aided and abetted the willful copyright infringement of its millions of users.

The owners of megaupload.com portrayed the site as a legitimate website that allowed individuals to post and share content. According to the government, however, the site was an illegal moneymaking enterprise based entirely on encouraging blatant criminal copyright infringement. According to the indictment, the owners knew and hoped that users of the site would post infringing material that other users would seek out and access.

Megaupload.com generated its income by selling advertising on the site and by selling subscriptions that enabled users to obtain full access to the site's contents.

Assume that the allegations in the indictment are correct, and that the primary purpose of megaupload.com was to make money by encouraging users to engage in copyright infringement. Also assume that among the several million users of megaupload, at least some of those users acted willfully and knew that their acts of infringement were illegal. Are the owners of megaupload.com guilty of aiding and abetting willful copyright infringement? What kind of proof should be required to evaluate that question at trial?

c) Total Retail Value

Criminal liability under the copyright laws can depend on the total retail value of the works copied. The next case considers what "total retail value" means and how it can be established.

UNITED STATES v. ARMSTEAD
United States Court of Appeals for the Fourth Circuit, 2008.
524 F.3d 442.

NIEMEYER, CIRCUIT JUDGE:

After selling 100 "bootleg" DVDs of unreleased movies to an undercover federal agent on June 11, 2003, and then selling 200 more to the same agent on January 13, 2004, David Armstead was indicted and convicted on two felony counts of willful copyright infringement for private financial gain by distributing at least 10 unauthorized DVDs on each occasion, having "a total retail value of more than $2,500," in violation of 17 U.S.C. § 506(a)(1) and 18 U.S.C. § 2319(b)(1). At trial, Armstead contested only the total retail value of the DVDs sold and urged that he be convicted of only misdemeanors for selling DVDs with a total retail value of $2,500 or less. *See* 18 U.S.C. § 2319(b)(3). The jury, however, convicted Armstead of the felony charges, and he was sentenced to six months' home detention.

On appeal, Armstead focuses on the fact that he sold the DVDs in the first transaction for a total of $500 and in the second transaction for a total of $1,000, and that the government offered no adequate alternative value to prove that the "total retail value" of the DVDs sold in each transaction was more than $2,500, as required for felony convictions. He requests that we vacate the felony convictions and enter judgments for misdemeanor offenses, remanding the case for resentencing accordingly.

As a matter of first impression, we hold that "retail value" as used in 18 U.S.C. § 2319(b)(1) refers to the value of copies of the copyrighted material at the time the defendant committed the violation and sold the copies and that the retail value is determined by taking the highest of the "face value," "par value," or "market value" of copies of the copyrighted material in a retail context. *See* 18 U.S.C. § 2311. Because the evidence of retail value, so construed, supported felony convictions, we affirm.

I

On June 11, 2003, Armstead sold 100 illicit movies in DVD format for $500 ($5 per DVD) to an undercover agent of the Bureau of Immigration and Customs Enforcement ("ICE") at the parking lot of the Springfield Mall in northern Virginia. The 100 bootleg DVDs included 25 copies of "2 Fast 2 Furious"; 25 copies of "The Matrix Reloaded"; 25 copies of "Finding Nemo"; 15 copies of "The Italian Job"; and 10 copies of "Wrong Turn." Again on January 13, 2004, Armstead sold the same agent more illicit movies in DVD format, this time 200 DVDs for $1,000 (again $5 per DVD). The 200 bootleg DVDs included 75 copies of "Lord of the Rings: The Return of the King"; 75 copies of "Paycheck"; 25 copies of "Bad Santa"; 15 copies of "My Baby's Daddy"; and 10 copies of "Gang of Roses."

The copies sold on both occasions were, for the most part, made by using a hand-held camcorder to record the films as they played in movie theaters and were, with a few exceptions, of poor quality. At the time, however, better copies of the DVD movies sold to the undercover agent were not available, as the movies were only in the "theatrical release" stage and authorized DVDs were not yet available. According to the undercover agent, legitimate DVDs would not be available until three to six months after the movie was released to theaters.

Armstead was indicted in two felony counts, one for each occasion on which he sold DVDs to the undercover agent.

At trial, Armstead conceded all elements of the offenses against him except the "total retail value" of the DVDs, claiming that their total value on each date was far less than $2,500, the threshold amount for felony liability under 18 U.S.C. § 2319(b)(1). He contended that with the proper finding of retail value, he could be convicted of only misdemeanors. He grounded his retail value assertions on the fact that the only hard evidence of retail value was the price of the DVDs in the "thieves' market," which priced the DVDs at $500 on the first occasion and $1,000 on the second.

Although the jury was instructed that if it found every element of the crime other than a retail value of over $2,500, it could return only misdemeanor convictions, it returned felony convictions on both counts. The district court sentenced Armstead to six months' home detention, five years' probation, and ordered him to pay $1,500 in restitution.

On appeal, Armstead presents the single issue of retail value and argues that "retail value," as used in § 2319(b)(1), refers to "the price a willing buyer would pay a willing seller at the time and in the market in which the infringing DVDs are sold—the thieves' market." With that definition of "retail value," Armstead contends that the evidence at trial was insufficient to support felony convictions.

II

The Copyright Act, in relevant part, provides that "[a]ny person who willfully infringes a copyright shall be punished as provided under section 2319 of title 18, if the infringement was committed—(A) for purposes of commercial advantage or private financial gain." 17 U.S.C. § 506(a)(1)(A). Section 2319 of Title 18, in turn, provides in relevant part:

> Any person who commits an offense under section 506(a)(1)(A) of title 17—shall be imprisoned not more than 5 years, or fined in the amount set forth in this title, or both, if the offense consists of the reproduction or distribution, including by electronic means, during any 180-day period, of at least 10 copies or phonorecords, of 1 or more copyrighted works, *which have a total retail value of more than $2,500.*

18 U.S.C. § 2319(b)(1) (emphasis added). Section 2319 also provides that if the $2,500-retail-value element is not satisfied, the defendant is to be punished for a misdemeanor. *See id.* § 2319(b)(3).

Armstead's argument that the government failed to produce sufficient evidence that the DVDs he sold to the undercover agent had an aggregate retail value of more than $2,500 hinges on the meaning of "retail value" as used in § 2319(b)(1). He asserts that retail value, as used in the statute, means "the price a willing buyer would pay a willing seller at the time and in the market in which it is sold—the thieves' market." With this definition of "retail value," he argues that what a willing buyer would pay a willing seller at the time was evidenced by what the undercover agent paid him and therefore that the retail value amount was insufficient to satisfy the felony threshold amount of $2,500.

The government contends that "retail value" refers to the higher value of what a willing buyer would pay a willing seller for a *legitimate* copy of the infringed item, such as an authentic, authorized DVD of the same movie. The government states that retail value as used in the statute is not the " 'bootleg value' the defendant received on the black market." It argues, "if the Congress had meant to use the 'bootleg value' or 'wholesale value' of counterfeit products, it certainly would have used that or similar language; instead, the Congress used the phrase 'total retail value' of the copyright works." Both parties seem to be arguing about a "market value," debating whether the relevant "market" from which to draw this market value refers to the market for bootleg products or the market for legitimate products. But their debate fails to account for the statutory language, which produces a broader formulation of "retail value."

"Retail value," as a phrase, is not defined in the statute, but "value" is. Section 2311, which provides definitions for chapter 113 of Title 18 (addressing "Stolen Property") defines "value" for the entire chapter (in which § 2319 is included) as "the face, par, or market value, *whichever is the greatest.*" 18 U.S.C. § 2311 (emphasis added). Thus, "value" is measured not only by actual transactions that define a market, but also by face or par values assigned to commodities or goods before reaching the market, and the statute instructs that the greatest of those "values" be used. "Retail," which is not defined at all, refers, in its ordinary meaning, to sales transactions of commodities or goods in small quantities to ultimate consumers. *See, e.g.,* Webster's Third New International Dictionary 1938 (1993). As distinct from "retail," "wholesale" refers to sales transactions of goods and commodities in quantity for resale. It follows, accordingly, that retail prices are higher than wholesale prices.

Thus considering "retail" and "value" as component terms that are individually defined by common understanding and by § 2311, respectively, we conclude that "retail value" refers to the greatest of any face value, par value, or market value of commodities or goods in reference to actual or potential sales to ultimate consumers. Thus, while market value—a value determined by the price that a willing buyer would pay a willing seller—is included in the class of values defined as "retail value," it is not the exclusive determinant. It follows that if a manufacturer of DVDs sells its DVDs at wholesale with a suggested retail price of $29 and the retailer actually sells the DVDs to the consumer at the discounted price of $19, the "retail value" as used in § 2319(b)(1) refers to the greater of the two numbers, or $29 per DVD. Of course, if the prices paid in actual retail transactions were the *only* evidence presented to support a prosecution under § 2319(b)(1), those prices could be considered as evidence of an actual "market value," which would be a permissible value for consideration as the "retail value."

In this case, while the parties agree that a "market value" may be determined by the price that a willing buyer would pay a willing seller, they disagree on whether that market value may be determined by sales in a "thieves' market." The government provides no authority to support the position that prices paid in a "thieves' market" cannot be a market value. Indeed, its only definition—the price of a movie "if it were sold to a member of the public"—would seem to include any market, except for the fact that the government argues for a value determined only by a market of "legitimate" copies. The government's assertion that the market for illicit goods is not determinative of "retail value" may be correct, but only if there is other evidence of a higher "value." *See* 18 U.S.C. § 2311. Otherwise, a black market for illegitimate goods undoubtedly may provide evidence of a "market value." And § 2311 directs that the criterion for satisfying the threshold amount for a felony conviction be the "greatest" of the permissible values in evidence.

It remains undisputed by the parties that whatever value is used, it must be a value applicable at the time the violations occurred and the transactions in question took place—in this case, June 2003 and January 2004.

Accordingly, retail value, as used in § 2319(b)(1), refers to prices assigned to commodities and goods for sale at the retail level at the time of sales at issue, representing face value or par value, *or* prices of commodities and goods determined by actual transactions between willing buyers and willing sellers at the retail level—*whichever is the greatest.* This understanding of "retail value," which is derived from §§ 2311 and 2319, is confirmed by the House Committee Report that accompanied enactment of § 2319. That Report provided:

> The term "retail value" is deliberately undefined, since in most cases it will represent the price at which the work is sold through normal retail channels. At the same time, *the Committee recognizes that copyrighted works are frequently infringed before a retail value has been established,* and that in some cases, copyrighted works are not marketed through normal retail channels. Examples include motion pictures prints distributed only for theatrical release, and beta-test versions of computer programs. *In such cases, the courts may look to the suggested retail price, the wholesale price, the replacement cost of the item, or financial injury caused to the copyright owner.*

H.R.Rep. No. 102–997, at 6–7 (1992), *as reprinted in* 1992 U.S.C.C.A.N. 3569, 3574–75.

III

In this case, Armstead sold the illicit DVDs to an undercover agent when the movies recorded on them had only been distributed for theatrical release (and perhaps for hotel and airline release) but certainly before they had been released on DVDs to the public. Thus, at the time of the illicit transactions, there was no legitimate retail market for the sale of DVDs except as evidenced by the occasional and sporadic illicit transactions of the kind represented in this case. As noted, prices paid in those illicit transactions might be evidence of a market value. But in this case, the "thieves' market" prices were not the only evidence. The government presented evidence of other kinds of value that related to retail value during the theatrical release stage of the movies when the illegal transactions occurred.

First, the government offered the testimony of two different witnesses who indicated that, based on information from the Motion Picture

Association of America, a single copy of a motion picture sold during the prerelease stage to hotels and airlines carries a price of at least $1,000 per copy, and, depending on the movie, up to $50,000 per copy. As one ICE agent explained, this was so because "at the time that these films are released in theaters, there is no legitimate market for the public to get DVDs. And the only people who can get a licensed copy of this film while it's in theaters is a hotel chain or an airline." The witness explained further that $1,000 was the price for the low-end films, and the more popular films could cost anywhere from $25,000 to $50,000 a copy. A piracy investigator for the Motion Picture Association of America then gave his opinion that there was "a good argument" to be made that the actual bootleg copies sold by Armstead "had a retail value of $1,000 a copy, as much as $50,000 a copy," even though he acknowledged that the number might be reduced somewhat to accommodate deficiencies in quality.

The government also presented testimony that after a movie was released to the public through DVDs—when prices for DVDs are much lower than prerelease values—the average retail price of the 10 DVD movies involved in this case would be "in every instance higher than $19" per DVD.

Finally, the government proffered evidence that the "suggested retail price" of each of the DVDs sold by Armstead was between $25 and $30 per copy, but the district court excluded that evidence precisely because it was only suggested, and not actual. This was error, however, because the suggested retail price was relevant to determine a "face value" or "par value" that would be especially relevant to determining prerelease retail value. Indeed, the House Report that accompanied the bill for § 2319 explicitly noted that for unreleased movies, courts could look at suggested retail prices. H.R.Rep. No. 102–997, at 6–7. And since there would be evidence of both face value (had the court properly allowed it) and market value, the higher would be applicable in determining the threshold amount for a felony conviction under § 2319(b)(1).

Based on our reading of the statute, the government's evidence of the prerelease values of copies of movies, the actual selling prices of legitimate copies of movies in the postrelease period, as well as the suggested retail prices (which were erroneously excluded by the trial court), were all appropriate evidence for a jury to consider in determining total retail value of the illicit transactions. Likewise, the evidence relied on by Armstead of the actual transaction prices in the wholesale "thieves' market" was appropriate evidence for a jury to consider. But in considering whether the evidence supports a conviction, we of course take the evidence actually presented to the jury and consider it in a view most favorable to the Government.

While the government's evidence about the wholesale cost of a single copy of a movie sold to hotels before DVDs were released to the public was not directly on point, it was a benchmark from which the jury could rationally have concluded that DVDs sold during that period had a retail value that exceeded $25 per copy. The minimum $1,000 per copy for a movie sold to hotels was a wholesale price that included payment for a license to show the movie to hotel customers. But the jury could conclude that, if there were a market for the retail sale of such DVDs, it would be higher than the wholesale price. And even though hotels did not resell the copies they bought, they nonetheless recovered their costs and profits from multiple retail rentals in hotel rooms. In this manner, the jury could readily reason from the $1,000 threshold level to conclude that the retail value of a single DVD *before general release of the movie as a DVD* exceeded $25. This conclusion would be buttressed by the fact that the average postrelease price of DVDs in the legitimate market would be greater than $19 per copy, indicating a much greater price for such DVDs prerelease.

The fact that Armstead actually sold his DVDs in bulk for $5 per copy was also evidence that the jury could have considered. But this evidence would not be evidence of the *greatest* value; rather, it provided evidence of the lowest value that could be assigned to the DVDs. Indeed, the $5-per-copy price was a wholesale price, suggesting a "retail" value somewhat greater than $5 per copy.

Armstead makes much of the fact that the DVDs he sold were of poor quality, since most of them were recorded with camcorders in theaters. While he may be correct that the quality of the infringing copy might bear on retail value, this was something that he was able to, and did, argue to the jury, and the jury was fully able to take that into account in determining the retail value of the DVDs. But it could have recognized, for example, that at this prerelease stage, advance knowledge of the plot of a movie, the action, and how the movie ends might be far more significant to retail value than reproduction quality.

At bottom, the jury had sufficient evidence from which to conclude that each copy of the DVDs sold by Armstead to undercover agents during the period before the films' release to the public on authorized DVDs had a retail value exceeding $25 per copy and therefore that each transaction exceeded the threshold amount for a felony conviction. Moreover, with respect to the second transaction, which involved the sale of 200 DVDs, even the $19 per copy ($3,800 in total), testified to by government witnesses as a retail value for the postrelease market, exceeded the $2,500 threshold amount.

The judgment of the district court is affirmed.

NOTES AND QUESTIONS

1. Why does 18 U.S.C. § 2319 require proof that the defendant "infringed at least 10 copies of one or more copyrighted works with a total retail value of more than $2,500 within a 180-day period"? The House Report that accompanied the passage of this language contains the following explanation:

> The requirement that a requisite number of infringing copies or phonorecords be reproduced or distributed within a 180 day period serves a number of important purposes. First, it excludes from felony prosecution children making copies for friends as well as other incidental copying of copyrighted works having a relatively low retail value. Second, the requirement of reproducing or distributing at least 10 copies within a 180 day period removes the possibility that the increased penalties under the bill for computer program infringement can be used as a tool of harassment in business disputes over reverse engineering. Assuming arguendo that infringement due to unauthorized reverse engineering is established, and that the infringement was done with the requisite mens rea (which, as noted above, is unlikely), no felony liability should arise, since the Committee has been informed that reverse engineering does not require the reproduction of more than a handful of copies.

H.R. Rep. No. 102–997, at 6 (1992), *reprinted in* 1992 U.S.C.C.A.N. 3569, 3574. The Report continues:

> The phrase "of one or more copyrighted works" is intended to permit aggregation of different works of authorship to meet the required number of copies and retail value. For example, a defendant's reproduction of 5 copies of a copyrighted word processing computer program having a retail value of $1,300 and the reproduction of 5 copies of a copyrighted spreadsheet computer program also having a retail value of $1,300 would satisfy the requirement of reproducing 10 copies having a retail value of at least $2,500, if done within a 180 day period.

Id. at 3574–75.

d) Intent to Profit

Should copyright law require an intent to profit or achieve private financial gain before attaching criminal penalties? It did before 1997. In 1997, however, Congress passed the No Electronic Theft (NET) Act, Pub. L. No. 105–147 (1997), which eliminated the requirement. Under current law, intent to achieve commercial advantage or private financial gain is important for sentencing purposes but not liability. The NET Act is generally understood as a response to changing technology, and especially computers and the Internet. Was it a wise move? To evaluate this question, consider the facts from a fairly typical criminal copyright case from the early 1980s.

UNITED STATES V. SHABAZZ

United States Court of Appeals for the Eleventh Circuit, 1984.
724 F.2d 1536.

JONES, SENIOR CIRCUIT JUDGE.

The appellant was engaged in the business of reproducing and distributing pirated eight track and cassette tapes. "Bootleg" or pirated tapes are the results of the illegal and unauthorized duplication of a sound recording without the permission of the copyright owners. Pirated tapes reproduce the sound but do not reproduce the tape cover or packaging of the legitimate tapes. The creation of a copyrighted tape begins with the studio master recording in the studio. One of the first duplicates of the studio master recording accompanies the copyright application. Another is sent to the Federal Bureau of Investigation for use in copyright infringement cases. A third duplicate is used for the production of legitimate copyrighted records and tapes.

The appellant purchased sophisticated audio equipment which was used for reproduction of audio tapes. He also purchased large quantities of unrecorded eight track and cassette tapes. He ordered eight track and cassette tape labels to be printed which listed the musicians and songs. He hired three employees to reproduce eight track and cassette tapes of copyrighted sound recordings of popular music. His employees, working in his home, would review work orders and reproduce selected music tapes by use of a high speed duplicator. The employees checked the tapes to insure music selection and sound quality. The tapes were individually wrapped in cellophane, placed in boxes and then sold.

An investigation lead to the issuance of a search warrant for the appellant's home and automobile. Federal agents seized blank and legitimate copyrighted tapes, duplicating equipment, blank and preprinted eight track and cassette labels, and various business records and materials. Ten legitimate copyrighted tapes and ten pirated copies were seized. The appellant was arrested for violating United States copyright laws under Title 17, §§ 106(1) and 506(a).

At the trial the government introduced ten copyright registrations, one for each tape alleged to be an infringement. Copyright owner representatives testified to the ownership of copyrights of the music recordings and to the absence of authorization for appellant to reproduce the legitimate copyrighted tapes. They also testified that it was a regular practice to send duplicates of such copyrighted recordings to the FBI for use in criminal copyright infringement cases. However, none of the copyright owner representatives had compared the duplicate sent to the FBI with either the studio master recording or the duplicate which accompanied the application to the United States copyright office.

Two FBI agents testified to examining the tapes seized from appellant's home. One agent testified that he listened to the seized legitimate copyrighted tapes and pirated copies to make sure the music listed on the tape label or box was contained on that particular tape. The second agent, an experienced aural examiner, was qualified by the district court as an expert witness. He acknowledged that the FBI received copyright owners' duplicates to compare legitimate copyrighted tapes with pirated tapes. The expert compared the copyright owners' duplicates with the legitimate copyrighted tapes and the pirated tapes seized from appellant's home and determined that the music on all three tapes had been produced from the same original source. The expert also testified that during the course of his examination of the pirated tapes, he listened to the entire tape and found that the tape labels and boxes accurately reflected the musical contents. The expert did not compare the copyright owners duplicates or the pirated tapes with the studio master recording or the duplicate which accompanied the application to the United States Copyright Office. There was no evidence that the copyright owner duplicates were tampered with or altered in any way or contained anything other than the music indicated on the tape label or box. A jury returned a verdict of guilty to ten counts of copyright infringement.

The appellant asserts that the government failed to prove that any of the tapes introduced in evidence were made for commercial profit as required by the Statute. An employee identified specific tapes made in bulk under appellant's direction as reproduced for local and out of state sale. The appellant sold pirated tapes, solicited wholesale customers, and shipped large quantities of tapes out of state. This evidence is sufficient to show that the tapes produced were made with the intention to make a profit. It is not necessary that he actually made a profit. The only requirement is that he engaged in business "to hopefully or possibly make a profit."

NOTES AND QUESTIONS

1. *The economics of the operation in Shabazz.* Shabazz created a considerable business enterprise to copy and distribute copyrighted materials. He had to purchase sophisticated equipment and pay several employees. The case for prohibiting conduct such as the operation in *Shabazz* is easy to make: Shabazz had created his own business that competed against the operations of the legitimate copyright owners. He was trying to line his pockets with money that should have gone to the copyright holders. Further, note the direct correlation between the scope of the operation and the intent to profit. Each bootleg cassette was costly for Shabazz to produce, and it seems unlikely that he would have been willing to engage in such widespread bootlegging without an economic incentive. In that environment, the statutory requirement of intent to profit makes sense. The requirement distinguishes a case like *Shabazz* from a case of small scale or personal copying.

Next consider how the picture changes when we shift to digital reproduction and distribution of copyrighted materials. Digital technologies bring the cost of copying and distributing files close to zero. A person can set up a server, connect it to the Internet, and make copyrighted files available to thousands of people at little or no cost to himself. How should the law respond, if at all?

2. *United States v. LaMacchia and the NET Act.* The traditional rationale of the intent-to-profit requirement caught up to the new facts of the Internet with the case of David LaMacchia. In 1994, LaMacchia was a 21-year-old college student at the Massachusetts Institute of Technology. LaMacchia set up an electronic bulletin board and encouraged visitors to share popular copyrighted software such as Excel and WordPerfect. Users could both upload software they possessed and download software they wanted, all for free and without the permission of the copyright holders. LaMacchia did not have an intent to profit from his efforts, which meant that he could not be prosecuted under the then-existing criminal copyright laws.

Prosecutors instead tried to prosecute LaMacchia under the wire fraud statute, 18 U.S.C. § 1343. Judge Stearns dismissed the indictment on the ground that trying to prosecute a copyright offense using the wire fraud statute ran afoul of Dowling v. United States, 473 U.S. 207 (1985). *See* United States v. LaMacchia, 871 F. Supp. 535 (D. Mass. 1994). In *Dowling*, prosecutors charged a defendant who had manufactured "bootleg" Elvis Presley records and distributed them in interstate commerce under the Interstate Transportation of Stolen Property Act, codified at 18 U.S.C. § 2314. In an opinion by Justice Blackmun, the Court held that the government could not use the ITSP Act to punish what amounted to a scheme of copyright infringement. Doing so would allow the government to circumvent Congress's design to have only narrow criminal liability for copyright infringement.

In the *LaMacchia* case, Judge Stearns held that the same rationale blocked the government from prosecuting LaMacchia under the wire fraud statute:

> While the government's objective is a laudable one, particularly when the facts alleged in this case are considered, its interpretation of the wire fraud statute would serve to criminalize the conduct of not only persons like LaMacchia, but also the myriad of home computer users who succumb to the temptation to copy even a single software program for private use. It is not clear that making criminals of a large number of consumers of computer software is a result that even the software industry would consider desirable.

> Accordingly, I rule that the decision of the Supreme Court in *Dowling v. United States* precludes LaMacchia's prosecution for criminal copyright infringement under the wire fraud statute.

> This is not, of course, to suggest that there is anything edifying about what LaMacchia is alleged to have done. If the indictment is to be

believed, one might at best describe his actions as heedlessly irresponsible, and at worst as nihilistic, self-indulgent, and lacking in any fundamental sense of values. Criminal as well as civil penalties should probably attach to willful, multiple infringements of copyrighted software even absent a commercial motive on the part of the infringer. One can envision ways that the copyright law could be modified to permit such prosecution. But, it is the legislature, not the Court which is to define a crime, and ordain its punishment.

LaMacchia, 871 F. Supp. at 544.

Congress responded by passing the NET Act in 1997 to "reverse the practical consequences of United States v. LaMacchia." H.R. Rep. No. 105–339, at 3 (1997). Under the NET Act, individuals can receive criminal punishments for copyright infringement even if they do not have commercial motives. Any person who commits willful copyright infringement can be:

imprisoned not more than 3 years, or fined in the amount set forth in this title, or both, if the offense consists of the reproduction or distribution of 10 or more copies or phonorecords of 1 or more copyrighted works, which have a total retail value of $2,500 or more.

18 U.S.C. § 2319(c)(1). If the government can show that the infringement took place "for purposes of commercial advantage or private financial gain," 17 U.S.C. § 506(a)(1), the maximum penalty is raised from three years to five years. *See* 18 U.S.C. § 2319(b)(1). The NET Act also redefined the term "financial gain" so that it now "includes receipt, or expectation of receipt, of anything of value, including the receipt of other copyrighted works." 17 U.S.C. § 101.

3. *Is the NET Act too broad?* Consider:

Even if comfort is found in relying on prosecutorial discretion to curb the possible over-breadth of the NET Act, the mere threat of criminal prosecution will deter at least some lawful uses of copyrighted works. Unfortunately some of these lawful uses are precisely the types of conduct that the policies underlying copyright law seek to encourage, not discourage.

Lydia Pallas Loren, *Digitization, Commodification, Criminalization: The Evolution of Criminal Copyright Infringement and the Importance of the Willfulness Requirement*, 77 Wash. U. L.Q. 835, 871 (1999).

4. *Is criminal copyright law needed at all?* The NET Act expands the scope of criminal liability to counter the effect of technological developments. But do those same technological developments alter the potential harms that follow from copyright infringement, and if so, what effect should that have on the scope of criminal liability?

Technological change * * * suggests it is time to revisit [the need for criminal copyright law]. It may no longer be necessary to rely so heavily on law to provide an incentive to create. The tools of digitization, broadband capacity, and the Internet make low-cost distribution a reality that may stimulate creation. Although in its infant stages, Internet commerce allows authors, musicians, and others to sell their work directly to consumers. Avoiding the added costs imposed by distribution companies may decrease costs to consumers.

Geraldine Szott Moohr, *The Crime Of Copyright Infringement: An Inquiry Based On Morality, Harm, And Criminal Theory*, 83 B.U. L. Rev. 731, 758 (2003).

5.   *Private financial gain and the DMCA.* It is interesting to note, in light of *LaMacchia* and the NET Act, that the criminal provisions of the Digital Millennium Copyright Act apply only to willful conduct committed "for purposes of commercial advantage or private financial gain." 17 U.S.C. § 1204(a). In addition, the criminal prohibitions cannot apply to any "nonprofit library, archives, educational institution, or public broadcasting entity." 17 U.S.C. § 1204(b). Why did Congress use a narrower criminal prohibition for the DMCA than for copyright law?

e) Prosecutorial Discretion

The broad scope of criminal copyright liability places a premium on prosecutorial discretion. The law permits prosecutors to charge a large number of infringers. Should they? Who should be targeted?

UNITED STATES DEPARTMENT OF JUSTICE—ILLEGAL "WAREZ" ORGANIZATIONS AND INTERNET PIRACY

In the early 1990s, groups of individuals working in underground networks organized themselves into competitive gangs that obtained software, "cracked," or "ripped" it (i.e. removed various forms of copy protections) and posted it on the Internet for other members of the group. This network of individuals and groups, numbering in the thousands, evolved into what is today loosely called the "warez scene" or community.

At the top of the warez scene are a handful of "release" groups that specialize in being the first to obtain, crack (i.e., remove or circumvent copyright protections), and distribute or release the latest software, games, movies, or music to the warez scene. Frequently, these new "releases" reach the Internet days or weeks before the product is commercially available. Release groups compete against each other to attain a reputation as the fastest providers of the highest quality, free pirated software, including utility and application software, computer and console games, and movies.

As technology has advanced, the top warez groups have become more technologically sophisticated and security conscious to avoid detection by law enforcement. Many of the elite groups communicate about warez business only through private e-mail servers, sometimes using encryption, and in closed, invite-only IRC channels. Additionally, most members disguise their true IP addresses (and thus their true locations) when communicating in IRC by routing their communications through "virtual hosts" or bounce boxes. Finally, many warez groups protect their large FTP archive sites—which can contain tens of thousands of copies of software, games, music, and music for free downloading—through a combination of security measures that include bounce sites, automated programs for IP address and user password verification, and the use of non-standard ports for FTP traffic.

The specific reasons that an individual becomes and remains involved in the top warez "release" or "courier" organizations may vary. However, it is almost always the case that a primary motivator is the desire to gain access to a virtually unlimited amount of free software, game, movie, and/or music titles available on the huge file storage and transfer sites (FTP sites) maintained by, or offering user privileges to, these elite warez groups. These computer sites not only offer a tremendous variety of quality copyrighted works, but they also generally have extremely fast Internet connections for rapid, efficient download and uploading. Other possible motivators or enticements for warez group members may include: (1) the thrill and social comradery they obtain through clandestine participation in illegal activity; (2) the improved personal reputation or fame in the warez scene that comes with membership in the "top" groups, and in helping to keep those groups on top; and (3) financial profit, as some involved in the larger warez organizations take the pirated products and sell them for commercial gain.

Today it is estimated that approximately 8–10 of the largest warez "release" groups in the world are responsible for the majority of the pirated software, games, and movies available on the Internet. These highly organized "release" groups specialize in being the first to release new pirated software, games, and movies to the warez community for unauthorized reproduction and further distribution worldwide. Individual groups generally specialize in "releasing" only certain types of copyrighted works; for instance, two of the oldest groups, DrinkOrDie and Razor1911, specialize in releasing application software and PC or console games, respectively. In addition to their release work, these warez groups also maintain large FTP archive (or "leech") sites for the benefit of their members and others engaged in Internet software piracy. An average FTP archive site may contain between 10,000 to 25,000 individual titles of software, games, movies, and music, all of which is made available for free downloading ("leeching") by group members and valued warez associates or contributors to the site.

The top-level release groups are highly structured organizations with defined roles and leadership hierarchy. These organizations generally have a Leader, who oversees and directs all aspects of the group; three Council members or Senior Staff, who direct and manage the day-to-day operations of the group; 10 to 15 Staff, who frequently are the most active and skilled contributors to the group's day to day "release" work; and finally, the general membership, whose functions and involvement in the group vary. Members generally only interact via the Internet and know each other only by their screen nicknames, such as "bandido," "hackrat," "erupt," or "doodad."

A pirated version of a software application, game or movie is frequently available worldwide even before it is made commercially available to the public. In many instances, warez groups illegally obtain advanced copies of copyrighted products from company or industry insiders, then crack the copyright protections before distributing the pirated versions on the Internet to an ever-expanding web of FTP sites worldwide. Within hours of first being posted on the Internet, a pirated version of a copyrighted product can be found on thousands of Internet sites worldwide. Eventually, these pirated versions find their way onto pay-for-access websites from China to the U.S., where users are charged monthly or per-purchase fees for downloading the unauthorized copies.

Additionally, these warez "releases" provide an unending supply of new product to counterfeit hard goods criminal organizations. For instance, almost every new PC and console game is "cracked" and available on warez sites either before or within 24 hours of their commercial release ("0-Day" releases). Hard good pirate syndicates in Asia and Russia (for example) will download a "warez" 0-Day game release and mass produce it at optical disc manufacturing facilities. These counterfeit hard goods are then illegally sold in foreign markets often weeks before the manufacturer ships the authentic goods for the official release date in those particular markets. This can cripple the market for the legitimate products.

The "Release" Process:

Speed and efficiency are essential to the process for preparing and packaging new pirated software for release and distribution to the warez community. The process generally has four stages and can occur within a matter of hours:

SUPPLY: First, a group member known as a supplier will post an original digital copy of new computer software to the group's Internet drop site, which is a computer where software is posted for retrieval by members of the group. Frequently, warez suppliers are company insiders who have access to final versions of the company's new software products before their public release date.

CRACK: Once the new supply is posted to the drop site, another group member, known as a cracker, retrieves the software and removes or circumvents all embedded copyright protection controls (e.g., serial numbers, tags, duplication controls, dongle protections, security locks).

TESTING and PACKING: Following a successful crack, the software must be tested to ensure that it is still fully operational. Following testing, the software is then "packed," or broken into file packets that are more easily distributed by other group members.

PRE-RELEASE/COURIER: After the software has been cracked, tested and packed, it is returned to the drop site, where individuals who will transfer or distribute the pirated copy across the Internet are waiting for new arrivals. Once picked up by the "preers," the illegal product is distributed to warez locations around the world in a matter of minutes. In each instance, the new "release" will include an information file (aka ".nfo file") which, among other things, proclaims and attributes credit for the release to the originating warez group. These messages allow groups and their members to get the credit they crave and develop not only their own reputations within the scene, but also that of the group.

NOTES AND QUESTIONS

1.　*The role of prosecutorial discretion.* Should members of warez groups be prosecuted? Would such prosecutions advance the goals of deterrence, retribution, or incapacitation? When picking which cases to bring, prosecutors of intellectual property crimes generally consider factors such as the amount of loss, the blatancy of the piracy, and the adequacy of civil remedies. See Kent Walker, *Federal Criminal Remedies for the Theft of Intellectual Property,* 16 Hastings Comm. & Ent. L.J. 681, 689 (1994). How should these factors play out in warez cases?

2.　*Copyright, criminal punishment, and the separation of powers.* Criminal copyright liability is broad in theory, but very few prosecutions are brought. Cases that are prosecuted tend to involve egregious facts far from the thresholds of liability.

The gap between the law and its enforcement owes largely to the different roles of legislators and prosecutors. Prosecutors tend to pick cases in which the defendant is morally culpable and societal losses are clear. The social norms surrounding copyright are unclear, however. Some people analogize infringement to theft, but others analogize it to sharing. In this environment, few prosecutors will be interested in prosecuting copyright cases. Indeed, the federal government has not brought *any* criminal prosecutions against individuals for using the Internet to obtain copyrighted materials without permission for their personal use. Copyright owners have brought civil lawsuits against users, and prosecutors have charged warez group members, but prosecutors have not charged mere users.

The legislative picture is quite different. Legislators decide what is a crime and what is not a crime. Legislators give prosecutors the tools to bring prosecutions when prosecutors wish to do so. When Congress wants to encourage more prosecutions, however, its options are limited. Members of Congress cannot order prosecutors to indict particular kinds of cases. Congress can fund task forces and provide money to hire prosecutors in particular areas, but even then it cannot determine what cases are brought. Legislators are also influenced by powerful lobbying groups, including those of copyright owners and their representatives. If Congress wants to "do something" to address copyright infringement, its primary option in the context of criminal law is to broaden the scope of criminality. Congress can expand the scope of what is criminal even if few if any prosecutors want to bring the cases that Congress has permitted them to bring.

This dynamic may explain the basic contour of criminal copyright law. The law is tremendously broad on paper, and penalties are harsh. But the law is actually used only very rarely. If you could design a regime of enforcing copyrights from scratch, would you propose something like the current system? Or would you favor less draconian laws combined with more enforcement?

3. *Peer-to-peer filesharing and criminal copyright infringement.* Starting in the late 1990s, peer-to-peer technologies began to transform how individuals obtain copies of copyrighted works online. Peer-to-peer technologies have generated civil lawsuits against the owners and creators of the technologies. *See, e.g.,* A & M Records, Inc. v. Napster, Inc., 239 F.3d 1004 (9th Cir. 2001). These technologies have not led to few criminal indictments for copyright infringement, however. Why not? Is the barrier the willfulness requirement? Or is the reason that copyright owners can bring civil suits, and law enforcement intervention may not be necessary?

The design of different peer-to-peer technologies may also influence the role of criminal law. Napster's file-sharing technology was centralized. The Napster company ran centralized servers, providing a clear target for civil or criminal legal action. The next generation of file-sharing technologies is distributed. Programs such as Gnutella and Freenet allow users to make their own files available to others, as well as to access the files of others who use the software. No centralized database exists.

Do distributed file-sharing programs make it impossible for the government to enforce copyright laws? One option would be for prosecutors to use techniques modeled on the enforcement of speeding laws over the "distributed network" of public highways. Every state has laws that regulate the speed of cars driven on public roads. These laws are difficult to enforce, however, as the roads are decentralized and a single police officer can at most monitor one location on one road at any given time. However, the possibility (however low) that a driver will be ticketed for speeding does appear to impact the speed at which most people drive. Although most drivers speed, they presumably speed less often and less egregiously than they would if they knew that the government was not policing the roads. Should the government mirror this strategy to enforce copyright laws on the Internet? If so, how?

B. CRIMES AGAINST PERSONS

There are two major types of computer crimes that can be categorized as crimes against persons. The first type covers threats and harassment, and the second covers invasion of privacy crimes such as wiretapping. These crimes address harms to individuals that violate their sense of privacy and safety. They raise a difficult question: What kinds of online conduct violate an individual's sense of privacy and safety enough that it should be declared a crime? How can we draw lines between criminal and non-criminal conduct in light of the contingent and rapidly evolving norms of computer usage? Most of the materials focus on threats and harassment law. Invasion of privacy crimes will be covered briefly in this section, and a detailed discussion appears in Chapter 6.

1. THREATS AND HARASSMENT

Criminal laws that prohibit threats and harassment attempt to balance two policy concerns. On one hand, the laws try to deter and punish the social harms associated with threats and harassment. Those harms include both inducing fear that threats will be carried out and the harms that follow if they actually are. On the other hand, the First Amendment's protection of free speech sharply restricts the government's ability to punish threats and harassment. Threats can be a form of speech, and the Supreme Court has held that governments can only punish threats that amount to "true threats." In light of this balance, understanding threat and harassment law requires understanding two sources of law: the statutory laws that create the prohibitions and the constitutional doctrines that limit their application.

a) Statutory Issues

Federal law includes many different statutes that prohibit various kinds of threats and harassment. Some of the threat statutes are general. For example, 18 U.S.C. § 875 broadly prohibits interstate threats to harm a person. On the other hand, some threat statutes are quite specific. For example, 18 U.S.C. § 115(a)(1)(B) prohibits threatening United States government officials with the intent to influence their official duties. Although a comprehensive review of all of the federal threat statutes is beyond the scope of this book, it is helpful to focus on three statutes that address online threats and harassment.

The most important is 18 U.S.C. § 875, and specifically 18 U.S.C. § 875(c). This section broadly prohibits interstate threats to harm a person:

> Whoever transmits in interstate or foreign commerce any communication containing any threat to kidnap any person or any threat to injure the person of another, shall be fined under this title or imprisoned not more than five years, or both.

Section 875(d) also covers extortionate threats to harm property, and it is supplemented by the computer-specific extortionate threat prohibition found in 18 U.S.C. § 1030(a)(7).

A second statute that prohibits both threats and harassment is 47 U.S.C. § 223. Section 223 was originally enacted as a telephone misuse and harassment statute passed as part of the federal Communications Act of 1934. Over time, its scope has expanded from telephones to other communications devices. The statute in its current form is complex and quite long, and some of the sections are dormant due to obvious First Amendment difficulties. (The Supreme Court's decision in Reno v. ACLU, 521 U.S. 844 (1997), invalidated parts of § 223 that were amended by a part of the Telecommunications Act of 1996 known as the Communications Decency Act.) Two provisions in § 223 are occasionally used to prosecute Internet threats and harassment. These two provisions, 47 U.S.C. § 223(a)(1)(C) and § 223(a)(1)(E), punish whoever:

> (C) makes a telephone call or utilizes a telecommunications device, whether or not conversation or communication ensues, without disclosing his identity and with intent to annoy, abuse, threaten, or harass any person at the called number or who receives the communications; . . . or

> (E) makes repeated telephone calls or repeatedly initiates communication with a telecommunications device, during which conversation or communication ensues, solely to harass any person at the called number or who receives the communication.

The third federal statute relevant here is the federal stalking statute first enacted in 1996 codified at 18 U.S.C. § 2261A. The statute was expanded in 2000 specifically to address "cyberstalking," the use of computers and the Internet to engage in stalking activity. The most important part of the statute for our purposes is § 2261A(2)(B), which punishes one who,

> with the intent . . . to place a person in another State or tribal jurisdiction, or within the special maritime and territorial jurisdiction of the United States, in reasonable fear of the death of, or serious bodily injury to—

> (i) that person;

> (ii) a member of the immediate family (as defined in section 115) of that person; or

> (iii) a spouse or intimate partner of that person,

> uses the mail or any facility of interstate or foreign commerce to engage in a course of conduct that places that person in reasonable

fear of the death of, or serious bodily injury to, any of the persons described in clauses (i) through (iii).

Taken together, these three statutes offer relatively broad coverage of threats and harassing conduct that can occur via computers and the Internet. Of course, the fact that the statutes are relatively broad does not mean that they are limitless—or that the meaning of the various terms in the statutes is always clear.

ELONIS V. UNITED STATES

Supreme Court of the United States, 2015.
135 S.Ct. 2001.

CHIEF JUSTICE ROBERTS delivered the opinion of the Court.

Federal law makes it a crime to transmit in interstate commerce "any communication containing any threat . . . to injure the person of another." 18 U.S.C. § 875(c). Petitioner was convicted of violating this provision under instructions that required the jury to find that he communicated what a reasonable person would regard as a threat. The question is whether the statute also requires that the defendant be aware of the threatening nature of the communication.

I

A

Anthony Douglas Elonis was an active user of the social networking Web site Facebook. Users of that Web site may post items on their Facebook page that are accessible to other users, including Facebook "friends" who are notified when new content is posted. In May 2010, Elonis's wife of nearly seven years left him, taking with her their two young children. Elonis began listening to more violent music and posting self-styled "rap" lyrics inspired by the music. Eventually, Elonis changed the user name on his Facebook page from his actual name to a rap-style nom de plume, "Tone Dougie," to distinguish himself from his on-line persona. The lyrics Elonis posted as "Tone Dougie" included graphically violent language and imagery. This material was often interspersed with disclaimers that the lyrics were "fictitious," with no intentional "resemblance to real persons." Elonis posted an explanation to another Facebook user that "I'm doing this for me. My writing is therapeutic."

Elonis's co-workers and friends viewed the posts in a different light. Around Halloween of 2010, Elonis posted a photograph of himself and a co-worker at a "Halloween Haunt" event at the amusement park where they worked. In the photograph, Elonis was holding a toy knife against his co-worker's neck, and in the caption Elonis wrote, "I wish." Elonis was not Facebook friends with the co-worker and did not "tag" her, a Facebook feature that would have alerted her to the posting. But the chief of park security was a Facebook "friend" of Elonis, saw the photograph, and fired him.

In response, Elonis posted a new entry on his Facebook page:

"Moles! Didn't I tell y'all I had several? Y'all sayin' I had access to keys for all the f***in' gates. That I have sinister plans for all my friends and must have taken home a couple. Y'all think it's too dark and foggy to secure your facility from a man as mad as me? You see, even without a paycheck, I'm still the main attraction. Whoever thought the Halloween Haunt could be so f***in' scary?"

This post became the basis for Count One of Elonis's subsequent indictment, threatening park patrons and employees.

Elonis's posts frequently included crude, degrading, and violent material about his soon-to-be ex-wife. Shortly after he was fired, Elonis posted an adaptation of a satirical sketch that he and his wife had watched together. In the actual sketch, called "It's Illegal to Say . . . ," a comedian explains that it is illegal for a person to say he wishes to kill the President, but not illegal to explain that it is illegal for him to say that. When Elonis posted the script of the sketch, however, he substituted his wife for the President. The posting was part of the basis for Count Two of the indictment, threatening his wife:

"Hi, I'm Tone Elonis.

Did you know that it's illegal for me to say I want to kill my wife? . . .

It's one of the only sentences that I'm not allowed to say. . . .

Now it was okay for me to say it right then because I was just telling you that it's illegal for me to say I want to kill my wife. . . .

Um, but what's interesting is that it's very illegal to say I really, really think someone out there should kill my wife. . . .

But not illegal to say with a mortar launcher.

Because that's its own sentence. . . .

I also found out that it's incredibly illegal, extremely illegal to go on Facebook and say something like the best place to fire a mortar launcher at her house would be from the cornfield behind it because of easy access to a getaway road and you'd have a clear line of sight through the sun room. . . .

Yet even more illegal to show an illustrated diagram. [diagram of the house]. . . ."

The details about the home were accurate. At the bottom of the post, Elonis included a link to the video of the original skit, and wrote, "Art is about pushing limits. I'm willing to go to jail for my Constitutional rights. Are you?"

After viewing some of Elonis's posts, his wife felt extremely afraid for her life. A state court granted her a three-year protection-from-abuse order against Elonis (essentially, a restraining order). Elonis referred to the order in another post on his "Tone Dougie" page, also included in Count Two of the indictment:

> "Fold up your [protection-from-abuse order] and put it in your pocket
>
> Is it thick enough to stop a bullet?
>
> Try to enforce an Order that was improperly granted in the first place
>
> Me thinks the Judge needs an education on true threat jurisprudence
>
> And prison time'll add zeros to my settlement . . .
>
> And if worse comes to worse
>
> I've got enough explosives to take care of the State Police and the Sheriff's Department."

At the bottom of this post was a link to the Wikipedia article on "Freedom of speech." Elonis's reference to the police was the basis for Count Three of his indictment, threatening law enforcement officers.

That same month, interspersed with posts about a movie Elonis liked and observations on a comedian's social commentary, Elonis posted an entry that gave rise to Count Four of his indictment:

> "That's it, I've had about enough
>
> I'm checking out and making a name for myself
>
> Enough elementary schools in a ten mile radius to initiate the most heinous school shooting ever imagined
>
> And hell hath no fury like a crazy man in a Kindergarten class
>
> The only question is . . . which one?"

Meanwhile, park security had informed both local police and the Federal Bureau of Investigation about Elonis's posts, and FBI Agent Denise Stevens had created a Facebook account to monitor his online activity. After the post about a school shooting, Agent Stevens and her partner visited Elonis at his house. Following their visit, during which Elonis was polite but uncooperative, Elonis posted another entry on his Facebook page, called "Little Agent Lady," which led to Count Five:

"You know your s***'s ridiculous when you have the FBI knockin' at yo' door

Little Agent lady stood so close

Took all the strength I had not to turn the b**** ghost

Pull my knife, flick my wrist, and slit her throat

Leave her bleedin' from her jugular in the arms of her partner

[laughter]

So the next time you knock, you best be serving a warrant

And bring yo' SWAT and an explosives expert while you're at it

Cause little did y'all know, I was strapped wit' a bomb

Why do you think it took me so long to get dressed with no shoes on?

I was jus' waitin' for y'all to handcuff me and pat me down

Touch the detonator in my pocket and we're all goin'

[BOOM!]

Are all the pieces comin' together?

S***, I'm just a crazy sociopath that gets off playin' you stupid f***s like a fiddle

And if y'all didn't hear, I'm gonna be famous

Cause I'm just an aspiring rapper who likes the attention

who happens to be under investigation for terrorism

cause y'all think I'm ready to turn the Valley into Fallujah

But I ain't gonna tell you which bridge is gonna fall into which river or road

And if you really believe this s***

I'll have some bridge rubble to sell you tomorrow

[BOOM!][BOOM!][BOOM!]"

B

A grand jury indicted Elonis for making threats to injure patrons and employees of the park, his estranged wife, police officers, a kindergarten class, and an FBI agent, all in violation of 18 U.S.C. § 875(c). In the District Court, Elonis moved to dismiss the indictment for failing to allege that he had intended to threaten anyone. The District Court denied the motion, holding that Third Circuit precedent required only that Elonis intentionally made the communication, not that he intended to make a threat. At trial, Elonis testified that his posts emulated the rap lyrics of the well-known performer Eminem, some of which involve fantasies about killing his ex-wife. In Elonis's view, he had posted "nothing . . . that hasn't been said already." The Government presented as witnesses Elonis's wife and co-workers, all of whom said they felt afraid and viewed Elonis's posts as serious threats.

Elonis requested a jury instruction that "the government must prove that he intended to communicate a true threat." The District Court denied that request. The jury instructions instead informed the jury that

> "A statement is a true threat when a defendant intentionally makes a statement in a context or under such circumstances wherein a reasonable person would foresee that the statement would be interpreted by those to whom the maker communicates the statement as a serious expression of an intention to inflict bodily injury or take the life of an individual."

The Government's closing argument emphasized that it was irrelevant whether Elonis intended the postings to be threats—"it doesn't matter what he thinks." A jury convicted Elonis on four of the five counts against him, acquitting only on the charge of threatening park patrons and employees. Elonis was sentenced to three years, eight months' imprisonment and three years' supervised release.

Elonis renewed his challenge to the jury instructions in the Court of Appeals, contending that the jury should have been required to find that he intended his posts to be threats. The Court of Appeals disagreed, holding that the intent required by Section 875(c) is only the intent to communicate words that the defendant understands, and that a reasonable person would view as a threat.

II

A

An individual who "transmits in interstate or foreign commerce any communication containing any threat to kidnap any person or any threat to injure the person of another" is guilty of a felony and faces up to five years' imprisonment. 18 U.S.C. § 875(c). This statute requires that a communication be transmitted and that the communication contain a threat. It does not specify that the defendant must have any mental state with respect to these elements. In particular, it does not indicate whether the defendant must intend that his communication contain a threat.

Elonis argues that the word "threat" itself in Section 875(c) imposes such a requirement. According to Elonis, every definition of "threat" or "threaten" conveys the notion of an intent to inflict harm. *E.g.,* 11 Oxford English Dictionary 353 (1933) ("to declare (usually conditionally) one's intention of inflicting injury upon").

These definitions, however, speak to what the statement conveys—not to the mental state of the author. For example, an anonymous letter that says "I'm going to kill you" is "an expression of an intention to inflict loss or harm" regardless of the author's intent. A victim who receives that letter in the mail has received a threat, even if the author believes (wrongly) that his message will be taken as a joke.

For its part, the Government argues that Section 875(c) should be read in light of its neighboring provisions, Sections 875(b) and 875(d). Those provisions also prohibit certain types of threats, but expressly include a mental state requirement of an "intent to extort."

But that does not suggest that Congress, at the same time, also meant to exclude a requirement that a defendant act with a certain mental state in communicating a threat. The most we can conclude from the language of Section 875(c) and its neighboring provisions is that Congress meant to proscribe a broad class of threats in Section 875(c), but did not identify what mental state, if any, a defendant must have to be convicted.

In sum, neither Elonis nor the Government has identified any indication of a particular mental state requirement in the text of Section 875(c).

B

The fact that the statute does not specify any required mental state, however, does not mean that none exists. We have repeatedly held that "mere omission from a criminal enactment of any mention of criminal intent" should not be read "as dispensing with it." *Morissette v. United States*, 342 U.S. 246, 250 (1952). This rule of construction reflects the basic principle that wrongdoing must be conscious to be criminal. As Justice Jackson explained, this principle is "as universal and persistent in mature systems of law as belief in freedom of the human will and a consequent ability and duty of the normal individual to choose between good and evil." *Id.* at 250.

The central thought is that a defendant must be blameworthy in mind before he can be found guilty, a concept courts have expressed over time through various terms such as *mens rea,* scienter, malice aforethought, guilty knowledge, and the like. Although there are exceptions, the general rule is that a guilty mind is a necessary element in the indictment and proof of every crime. We therefore generally interpret criminal statutes to include broadly applicable scienter requirements, even where the statute by its terms does not contain them.

This is not to say that a defendant must know that his conduct is illegal before he may be found guilty. The familiar maxim "ignorance of the law is no excuse" typically holds true. Instead, our cases have explained that a defendant generally must know the facts that make his conduct fit the definition of the offense, even if he does not know that those facts give rise to a crime.

Morissette, for example, involved an individual who had taken spent shell casings from a Government bombing range, believing them to have been abandoned. During his trial for knowingly converting property of the United States, the judge instructed the jury that the only question was whether the defendant had knowingly taken the property without authorization. This Court reversed the defendant's conviction, ruling that he had to know not only that he was taking the casings, but also that someone else still had property rights in them. He could not be found liable if he truly believed the casings to be abandoned.

When interpreting federal criminal statutes that are silent on the required mental state, we read into the statute only that *mens rea* which is necessary to separate wrongful conduct from otherwise innocent conduct.

C

Section 875(c), as noted, requires proof that a communication was transmitted and that it contained a threat. The presumption in favor of a scienter requirement should apply to *each* of the statutory elements that criminalize otherwise innocent conduct. The parties agree that a defendant under Section 875(c) must know that he is transmitting a communication. But communicating *something* is not what makes the conduct wrongful. Here the crucial element separating legal innocence from wrongful conduct is the threatening nature of the communication. The mental state requirement must therefore apply to the fact that the communication contains a threat.

Elonis's conviction, however, was premised solely on how his posts would be understood by a reasonable person. Such a "reasonable person" standard is a familiar feature of civil liability in tort law, but is inconsistent with the conventional requirement for criminal conduct—*awareness* of some wrongdoing. Having liability turn on whether a "reasonable person" regards the communication as a threat—regardless of what the defendant thinks—reduces culpability on the all-important element of the crime to negligence, and we have long been reluctant to infer that a negligence standard was intended in criminal statutes. Under these principles, what Elonis thinks does matter.

In light of the foregoing, Elonis's conviction cannot stand. The jury was instructed that the Government need prove only that a reasonable person would regard Elonis's communications as threats, and that was error. Federal criminal liability generally does not turn solely on the results of an act without considering the defendant's mental state. That understanding took deep and early root in American soil and Congress left it intact here: Under Section 875(c), wrongdoing must be conscious to be criminal.

There is no dispute that the mental state requirement in Section 875(c) is satisfied if the defendant transmits a communication for the purpose of issuing a threat, or with knowledge that the communication will be viewed as a threat. In response to a question at oral argument, Elonis stated that a finding of recklessness would not be sufficient. Neither Elonis nor the Government has briefed or argued that point, and we accordingly decline to address it.

Justice Alito suggests that we have not clarified confusion in the lower courts. That is wrong. Our holding makes clear that negligence is not sufficient to support a conviction under Section 875(c), contrary to the view of nine Courts of Appeals. There was and is no circuit conflict over the question Justice Alito and Justice Thomas would have us decide—whether recklessness suffices for liability under Section 875(c). No Court of Appeals has even addressed that question. We think that is more than sufficient justification for us to decline to be the first appellate tribunal to do so.

The judgment of the United States Court of Appeals for the Third Circuit is reversed, and the case is remanded for further proceedings consistent with this opinion.

JUSTICE ALITO, concurring in part and dissenting in part.

The Court's disposition of this case is certain to cause confusion and serious problems. Attorneys and judges need to know which mental state is required for conviction under 18 U.S.C. § 875(c), an important criminal statute. This case squarely presents that issue, but the Court provides only a partial answer. The Court holds that the jury instructions in this case were defective because they required only negligence in conveying a threat. But the Court refuses to explain what type of intent was necessary. Did the jury need to find that Elonis had the *purpose* of conveying a true threat? Was it enough if he *knew* that his words conveyed such a threat? Would *recklessness* suffice? The Court declines to say. Attorneys and judges are left to guess.

In my view, the term "threat" in § 875(c) can fairly be defined as a statement that is reasonably interpreted as "an expression of an intention to inflict evil, injury, or damage on another." Webster's Third New International Dictionary 2382 (1976). Conviction under § 875(c) demands proof that the defendant's transmission was in fact a threat, *i.e.,* that it is reasonable to interpret the transmission as an expression of an intent to harm another. In addition, it must be shown that the defendant was at least reckless as to whether the transmission met that requirement.

I agree with the Court that we should presume that an offense like that created by § 875(c) requires more than negligence with respect to a critical element like the one at issue here. Once we have passed negligence, however, no further presumptions are defensible. In the hierarchy of mental states that may be required as a condition for criminal liability, the *mens rea* just above negligence is recklessness. Negligence requires only that the defendant "should [have] be[en] aware of a substantial and unjustifiable risk," ALI, Model Penal Code § 2.02(2)(d), p. 226 (1985), while recklessness exists when a person disregards a risk of harm of which he is aware. Model Penal Code § 2.02(2)(c). And when Congress does not specify a *mens rea* in a criminal statute, we have no justification for inferring that anything more than recklessness is needed. It is quite unusual for us to interpret a statute to contain a requirement that is nowhere set out in the text. Once we have reached recklessness, we have gone as far as we can without stepping over the line that separates interpretation from amendment.

JUSTICE THOMAS, dissenting.

Applying ordinary rules of statutory construction, I would read § 875(c) to require proof of general intent. To know the facts that make his conduct illegal under § 875(c), a defendant must know that he transmitted a communication in interstate or foreign commerce that contained a threat. Knowing that the communication contains a "threat"—a serious expression of an intention to engage in unlawful physical violence—does not, however, require knowing that a jury will conclude that the communication contains a threat as a matter of law. Instead, like one who mails an "obscene" publication and is prosecuted under the federal obscenity statute, a defendant prosecuted under § 875(c) must know only the words used in that communication, along with their ordinary meaning in context.

A defendant like Elonis who admits that he knew that what he was saying was violent but supposedly "just wanted to express himself," acted with the general intent required under § 875(c), even if he did not know that a jury would conclude that his communication constituted a "threat" as a matter of law.

NOTES AND QUESTIONS

1.   *The mental state issue in Elonis.* The precise issue in *Elonis* can be tricky to understand, so let's break it down. The question in the case is the correct mental state requirement associated with the fact that the communication sent would be understood as a threat—that is, as a serious expression of intent to harm. If the required mental state is intent, then the government must prove that the defendant intended that the communication would be perceived as a threat. If the mental state is knowledge, the government must prove that the defendant knew the communication would be perceived as a threat. If the required mental state is reckless, then the government must show that the defendant was reckless toward whether the communication would be viewed as a threat. If the required mental state is negligence, then the government must show that a reasonable person would realize the communication would be viewed as a threat. And if there is no

mental state requirement at all, the government need not show any awareness by the defendant of the threatening nature of the communication.

2.   *Did the mental state matter in Elonis?* On remand from the Supreme Court, the Third Circuit did not give Elonis relief. Instead, the court upheld the jury's guilty verdict on the ground that the error in the jury instruction relating to mens rea was only harmless error. In other words, the jury would have convicted Elonis anyway if the government had been required to prove that Elonis knew the threatening nature of his communications:

> The jury was erroneously instructed under an objective standard. The parties dispute whether a recklessness standard or a knowledge standard is sufficient. But under either standard, we find the District Court's error was harmless. The record contains overwhelming evidence demonstrating beyond a reasonable doubt that Elonis knew the threatening nature of his communications, and therefore would have been convicted absent the error.

United States v. Elonis, 841 F.3d 589, 598 (3d Cir. 2016).

3.   *What mens rea should courts apply when construing § 875(c)?* In *Elonis*, the Supreme Court ruled out both strict liability and negligence but left unanswered whether a reckless mental state is sufficient or if the government must prove knowledge or purpose.

In light of the Third Circuit's ruling on remand in *Elonis*, it is fair to ask how much of a difference it makes whether recklessness or knowledge is required. The ideal test case would be a prosecution in which the defendant did not intend to scare anyone but realized there was a substantial risk that he would do so. Such a defendant would have a reckless mental state about the message being understood as a threat but would not have an intentional mental state about that element.

But how often will that come up? Won't most people who don't intend to send a threat, but who realize the serious risk that their message would be interpreted as a threat, simply decide not to send the message?

4.   *The role of the Model Penal Code.* Justice Alito's approach relies on the Model Penal Code's "hierarchy of mental states" that most law students learn in their first-year classes in Criminal Law. Notably, however, Congress enacted § 875(c) several decades *before* the American Law Institute published the Model Penal Code. Does it make sense to adopt a mental state that did not exist at the time the statute was enacted?

5.   *The problem of the unknown audience.* The choice of *mens rea* is made particularly tricky in the Internet age because online speakers may not know their audience. In the physical world, a person can usually predict who will hear his speech or read his words. Online, however, the audience can be hard to predict. A person with a Twitter account that has 10 followers might expect that few will read what he tweets. But a particularly shocking or disturbing tweet can go viral and be seen by millions. Should this possibility impact what mental states courts choose?

b) Constitutional Limits

Although many criminal laws prohibit threats and harassment, the enforcement of those laws must comply with the First Amendment. The First Amendment imposes two major limitations on threat and harassment law: The "true threat" doctrine and limitations on incitement liability.

The "true threat" doctrine teaches that the government cannot punish threats that in context are mere advocacy or political hyperbole, as these are protected speech under the First Amendment. Threats can be punished only if they are "true threats." The Supreme Court has never answered exactly how to measure whether a threat is a true threat. The issue was presented to the Supreme Court in Elonis v. United States, 135 S.Ct. 2001 (2015), but the Court decided that case on statutory grounds and did not reach the First Amendment question.

Lower courts have offered different definitions of what is a "true threat." Here are a few recent definitions:

- "A statement rises to the level of a 'true threat' when it amounts to a serious expression of an intention to inflict bodily harm and is conveyed for the purpose of furthering some goal through the use of intimidation." United States v. Houston, 2017 WL 1097138 (6th Cir. 2017).

- "We hold that a true threat is a statement that, considered in context and under the totality of the circumstances, an intended or foreseeable recipient would reasonably perceive as a serious expression of intent to commit an act of unlawful violence." People In Interest of R.D., 464 P.3d 717, 721 (Colo. 2020).

- "A communication is a 'true threat' if a reasonable person would foresee that the statement would be interpreted by those to whom the maker communicates the statement as a serious expression of an intention to inflict bodily harm [or death]." United States v. Dutcher, 851 F.3d 757 (7th Cir. 2017).

- "[True] threats encompass those statements where the speaker means to communicate a serious expression of an intent to commit an act of unlawful violence to a particular individual or group of individuals, even if the speaker does not actually intend to carry out the threat." Barboza v. D'Agata, 676 Fed.Appx. 9 (2d Cir. 2017).

- "A 'true threat' is a statement that a reasonable recipient would have interpreted as a serious expression of an intent to harm or cause injury to another." United States v. Colhoff, 833 F.3d 980 (8th Cir. 2016).

The collective theme of these tests, more or less, is that a true threat is a an objectively serious expression of intent to inflict harm. But the specific test remains uncertain. As the Supreme Court of Colorado recently stated, "the proper test for true threats remains an unsolved doctrinal puzzle." *People In Interest of R.D.*, 464 P.3d at 29.

A second First Amendment limit on threats and harassment law considers incitement of illegal conduct—speech that encourages others to take action, rather than suggests an intent that the speaker will act. In Brandenburg v. Ohio, 395 U.S. 444, 447 (1969) (per curiam), twelve hooded members of the KKK held a rally. One of the members of the Klan gave a speech that included the following warning:

> We're not a revengent organization, but if our President, our Congress, our Supreme Court, continues to suppress the white, Caucasian race, it's possible that there might have to be some revengeance taken.

The Supreme Court held that this warning of possible "revengeance" could not be punished under an Ohio law that punished advocating violence to achieve political goals. According to the Court, "the constitutional guarantees of free speech and free press do not permit a State to forbid or proscribe advocacy of the use of force or of law violation except where such advocacy is directed to inciting or producing imminent lawless action and is likely to incite or produce such action." *Id.* at 447–48.

The difficult question is how to apply the true threat doctrine and incitement doctrine to the Internet. How can a person judge if a threat on the Internet is a true threat? Internet message boards often include hyperbole and false claims. When are such discussions sufficiently worrisome to constitute threats that can be punished? Similarly, a speech delivered in person may be likely to produce "imminent lawless action." Is equivalent speech that appears on a website likely to do so? Who is the relevant audience, and how can a court measure when that audience is likely to be inspired to act?

UNITED STATES V. CARMICHAEL

United States District Court for the Middle District of Alabama, 2004.
326 F. Supp.2d 1267.

MYRON H. THOMPSON, DISTRICT JUDGE.

Carmichael was arrested in November 2003 in Montgomery, Alabama, after Gary Wayne George and Robert Patrick Denton—themselves under arrest for marijuana distribution—informed Drug Enforcement Administration (DEA) Task Force Agent R. David DeJohn that Carmichael had employed them to assist in his marijuana-distribution activities. On the day of his arrest, Denton told Agent DeJohn that Carmichael had been expecting a shipment of several hundred pounds of marijuana the previous day and that Carmichael had told him to assist Freddie Williams with re-packaging the marijuana. Denton's information led to a search of Williams's residence later that day; the search turned up eleven duffle bags filled with marijuana. Carmichael was arrested the same day by DEA Agent Thomas Halasz.

As stated, Carmichael is charged with one count of conspiracy to possess marijuana with the intent to distribute, and one count of conspiracy to commit money laundering. The conspiracy count alleges that, since 1993, Carmichael and others have conspired to possess with the intent to distribute 1000 kilograms or more of marijuana. Williams, Carmichael's co-defendant, is also named in the conspiracy count.

The Website

The Internet website at issue in this case is www.carmichaelcase.com. The website first appeared in December 2003 and first came to the attention of law enforcement in January 2004. The site has gone through roughly three versions. The original version contained a picture of the Montgomery federal courthouse, and it stated that the media had misrepresented the case. The site allowed users to post comments about the case, and it contained links to articles about the case, including an article from a local weekly newspaper that identified Denton by name and listed his home address. The site also included a statement to the effect that Denton had been charged with six felonies.

Sometime in February 2004, the website was changed. The second version showed a picture of the scales of justice on the left side of the page below the words "we are under construction." On the right side of the page, the site displayed the statement, "Look for a new look at this very important case. We will have photos and information on all of the courtroom participants: Defendant, Defense Attorneys, U.S. Attorneys, DEA Agents, Informants." At some point prior to the end of February, this version of the site was amended to include a picture of Carmichael and the statement, "Only public records will be published on this site. This includes all participants, in this case, including their names, pictures, and statements."

Sometime around the beginning of April 2004, the website was changed to its current format. At the top of the site is the word "Wanted" in large, red letters, beneath which are the words "Information on these Informants and Agents." Underneath this header are eight boxes, each containing the name of a witness or agent involved in the case and, in parentheses, the word "Agent" or "Informant." The four "informants" listed are Denton, George, Sherry D. Pettis, and Walace Salery. The four "agents" listed are DeJohn, Halasz, Devin Whittle, and Robert Greenwood. As the site appeared on April 27, 2004, three of the eight boxes contained pictures of the named individuals; the individuals pictured were Denton, Pettis, and George. Currently, a fourth "informant"—Salery—is pictured as well. In the boxes without pictures, the words "Picture Coming" appear in parentheses.

Beneath the eight boxes, this statement appears: "If you have any information about these informants and agents, regardless of how insignificant you may feel it is, Please contact"; the statement is followed by a list of Carmichael's attorneys and their telephone numbers. At one point, only one of Carmichael's attorneys was listed. Currently, four of his attorneys are listed.

This latest version of the site was modified in the middle of April to include, at the bottom of the page, the following language:

> "This website, or any posters and advertisements concerning the Carmichael Case, is definitely not an attempt to intimidate or harass any informants or agents, but is simply an attempt to seek information. The Carmichael Case will not be a 'closed door' case.

> "Pictures (when available), names and testimonies of informants, agents and witnesses will be on television, on the web site, on the radio and published in newspapers. Carmichael maintains his innocence, and wants the public to know all the facts as well as the participants in this case."

This disclaimer was removed around the end of April. The current version of the website, however, now contains a similarly worded disclaimer.

Carmichael argues that the protective order sought by the government would infringe his free-speech rights under the First Amendment. The first question is whether Carmichael's website is protected speech. Because threats are not protected by the First Amendment, the court can issue a protective order shutting the site down or otherwise restricting it if the site is a 'true threat.' If the site is protected by the First Amendment, the court can issue the protective order sought by the government only if the government satisfies the constitutional rules for imposing prior restraints on the speech of trial participants.

As stated, true threats are not protected by the First Amendment. *Virginia v. Black*, 538 U.S. 343, 359 (2003); *Watts v. United States*, 394 U.S. 705, 707 (1969) (per curiam). True threats encompass those statements where the speaker means to communicate a serious expression of an intent to commit an act of unlawful violence to a particular individual or group of individuals. The prohibition on true threats protects individuals from the fear of violence and from the disruption that fear engenders, in addition to protecting people from the possibility that the threatened violence will occur.

Watts is the origin of the true threat doctrine. In *Watts*, the petitioner appealed his conviction for violating 18 U.S.C. § 871, which prohibits any person from knowingly and willfully making any threat to take the life of or to inflict bodily harm upon the President of the United States. The basis of petitioner's conviction was a statement he made during a 1966 anti-Vietnam War rally on the mall in Washington: "They always holler at us to get an education. And now I have already received my draft classification as 1-A and I have got to report for my physical this Monday coming. I am not going. If they ever make me carry a rifle the first man I want to get in my sights is L.B.J."

The Supreme Court, per curiam, reversed on the ground that petitioner's speech was not a threat. After noting that the government's valid, "even overwhelming," interest in the life of the President, the Court wrote: "Nevertheless, a statute such as this one, which makes criminal a form of pure speech, must be interpreted with the commands of the First Amendment clearly in mind. What is a threat must be distinguished from what is constitutionally protected speech."

"Against the background of a profound national commitment to the principle that debate on public issues should be uninhibited, robust, and wide open, and that it may well include vehement, caustic, and sometimes unpleasantly sharp attacks on government and public officials," the Court interpreted § 871 not to reach "the kind of political hyperbole indulged in by petitioner." The Court held that the petitioner's speech was not a true threat and was thus protected by the First Amendment.

The Supreme Court has not settled on a definition of a true threat, but the United States Court of Appeals for the Eleventh Circuit has:

> A communication is a threat when in its context it would have a reasonable tendency to create apprehension that its originator will act according to its tenor. In other words, the inquiry is whether there was sufficient evidence to prove beyond a reasonable doubt that the defendant intentionally made the statement under such circumstances that a reasonable person would construe them as a serious expression of an intention to inflict bodily harm. Thus, the offending remarks must be measured by an objective standard.

United States v. Alaboud, 347 F.3d 1293, 1296–97 (11th Cir. 2003). The Eleventh Circuit's objective approach accords with that taken by the majority of the United States Courts of Appeals.

A number of factors are relevant to determine whether speech is a threat proscribable under the First Amendment. First, the court must consider the language itself. Second, the court must look at the context in which the communication was made to determine if it would cause a reasonable person to construe it as a serious intention to inflict bodily harm. Third, testimony by the recipient of the communication is relevant to determining whether it is a threat or an act of intimidation.

a. The Website Itself

The language of Carmichael's website does not make out a threat. There is no explicit threat on the site, and neither the request for information nor the list of Carmichael's attorneys is threatening or intimidating. The statement that "Mr. Carmichael maintains his innocence and wants the public to know all the facts as well as all the participants in this case" is similarly unmenacing. Furthermore, the site actually disclaims any intent to threaten; the site includes the following statement at the bottom of the page: "This web site, or any posters, and advertisements concerning the Carmichael Case, is definitely not an attempt to intimidate or harass any informants or agents, but is simply an attempt to seek information." Indeed, these elements make the site appear to be just what Carmichael maintains it is: another way of gathering information to prepare his defense.

b. Context

The court must also consider the context in which the website operates in order to determine whether the reasonable viewer would see it as a threat. The importance of context is vividly illustrated by cases arising under the Freedom of Access to Clinics Entrances Act (FACE), 18 U.S.C. § 248. FACE provides criminal penalties for

> whoever by force or threat of force or by physical obstruction, intentionally injures, intimidates or interferes with or attempts to injure, intimidate or interfere with any person because that person is or has been, or in order to intimidate such person or any other person or any class of persons from, obtaining or providing reproductive health services.

18 U.S.C. § 248(a)(1). FACE also provides for a private right of action for "any person aggrieved by reason of the conduct prohibited by subsection (a)." 18 U.S.C. § 248(c)(1)(A). These cases are helpful because they involve statements which surely lie at the outside edge of the definition of 'true threats.'

In *Planned Parenthood of the Columbia/Willamette, Inc. v. American Coalition of Life Activists*, 290 F.3d 1058 (9th Cir. 2002) (en banc), four doctors who provide abortions—Drs. Hern, Crist, Elizabeth Newhall, and James Newhall—and two abortion clinics brought a lawsuit under FACE's private cause-of-action provision against the American Coalition of Life Activists, Advocates of Life Ministries, and a number of individuals associated with these two groups. The plaintiffs' claim was that two posters and an Internet website produced by the defendants constituted "threats of force" under FACE. A jury found for the plaintiffs and awarded them substantial damages, including nearly $80 million in punitive damages. The trial court also permanently enjoined the defendants from publishing or distributing its posters and from providing material to the website. On appeal, the defendants argued that the posters and website were not 'true threats' and were thus protected by the First Amendment.

Like the www.carmichaelcase.com website, neither the posters nor the website in *Planned Parenthood* expressly threatened the plaintiffs. The first poster, published in January 1995, was captioned "GUILTY," beneath which were the words "OF CRIMES AGAINST HUMANITY." Under the heading "THE DEADLY DOZEN," the poster identified 13 doctors, including three of the plaintiffs, and listed their home addresses. At the bottom, the poster bore the legend "ABORTIONIST" in large, bold typeface. The second poster, released in August 1995, identified one of the plaintiff doctors and bore the word "GUILTY" in large bold letters at the top followed by the words "OF CRIMES AGAINST HUMANITY." The poster gave the doctor's home and work address, and it also bore the legend "ABORTIONIST" in large bold type at the bottom.

The website at issue was put up on the Internet in January 1997. It was called the "Nuremberg Files" in reference to the location of the post-World War II Nazi war crimes trial, and it listed information on abortion-providers, judges and politicians, and prominent abortion-rights supporters. The website listed the names of approximately 400 individuals and provided the following legend to interpret the font in which each name was listed: "Black font (working); Greyed-out Name (wounded); Strikethrough (fatality)." The names of three abortion providers who had been murdered between March 1993 and July 1994—Drs. Gunn, Patterson, and Britton—were struck through.

Applying roughly the same standard for determining when speech is a threat that the Eleventh Circuit applies, the United States Court of Appeals for the Ninth Circuit, sitting en banc, held that the two posters and the "Nuremberg Files" website constituted 'true threats' and affirmed the jury's verdict in favor of the plaintiffs. The court's reasoning was based on the history of violence directed against abortion-providers prior to the defendants' creation of the posters and the website. The court described how in the two years prior to January 1995, when the defendants produced the first poster, three abortion providers—Drs. Gunn, Patterson, and Britton—were killed after they appeared on similar posters which gave information about them and bore headings like "WANTED" and "unWANTED." The court described its reasoning this way:

> It is use of the 'wanted'-type format in the context of the poster pattern—poster followed by murder—that constitutes the threat. Because of the pattern, a 'wanted'-type poster naming a specific doctor who provides abortions was perceived by physicians, who

are providers of reproductive health services, as a serious threat of death or bodily harm. After a 'WANTED' poster on Dr. David Gunn appeared, he was shot and killed. After a 'WANTED' poster on Dr. George Patterson appeared, he was shot and killed. After a 'WANTED' poster on Dr. John Britton appeared, he was shot and killed. None of these 'WANTED' posters contained threatening language, either. Neither did they identify who would pull the trigger. But knowing this pattern, knowing that unlawful action had followed 'WANTED' posters on Gunn, Patterson and Britton, and knowing that 'wanted'-type posters were intimidating and caused fear of serious harm to those named on them, ACLA published a 'GUILTY' poster in essentially the same format on Dr. Crist and a Deadly Dozen 'GUILTY' poster in similar format naming Dr. Hern, Dr. Elizabeth Newhall and Dr. James Newhall because they perform abortions. Physicians could well believe that ACLA would make good on the threat. One of the other doctors on the Deadly Dozen poster had in fact been shot before the poster was published. In the context of the poster pattern, the posters were precise in their meaning to those in the relevant community of reproductive health service providers. They were a true threat.

Thus, even though the defendants were responsible neither for the earlier 'wanted posters' nor the earlier killings, the context created by those posters and killings gave the defendants' posters and website a threatening meaning.

The present case is obviously different because Carmichael's website was not put up in the context of a recent string of murders linked to similar publications. The crucial circumstance for the court in *Planned Parenthood* was the pattern of posters followed by murders that pre-dated the defendants' publication of their posters. The analogous situation in this case would be if there were a history of witnesses or government agents being threatened or killed after the release of 'wanted-style' posters on which they were pictured. Such a pattern does not exist here, so the case that www.carmichaelcase.com is a threat is not in any way as strong as that in *Planned Parenthood*.

This case is not totally dissimilar from *Planned Parenthood*, however. Just as the court in *Planned Parenthood* considered the history of violence against abortion providers, this court considers the history of violence committed against informants in drug-distribution cases generally. A brief search of recent reported decisions in the Federal Reporter reveals numerous cases involving the murder of informants in drug-conspiracy cases. This is the broad context in which Carmichael's site exists.

The facts of the present case are similar to those in the cases cited above. Carmichael is accused of heading a far-flung, long-running drug-distribution conspiracy. Denton and George—two of the 'informants' pictured on the site—have admitted to involvement in such a drug conspiracy, and marijuana and firearms have already been seized in this case.

Viewed in light of the general history of informants being killed in drug conspiracy cases and the evidence of a drug-conspiracy and other criminal activity in this case, www.carmichaelcase.com looks more like a threat. Indeed it may be that it is only this context that gives the site a threatening meaning. To illustrate how much of the website's threatening meaning is derived from the factual context of this case, imagine the same website put up by a defendant in a securities-fraud case. In the context of a white-collar crime prosecution, the same site might be an annoyance, but, absent other circumstances, it would be nearly impossible to conclude that it is a threat.

Nevertheless, it is important to recall that the inquiry here is whether a reasonable person would view Carmichael's website as "a serious expression of an intention to inflict bodily harm," *Alaboud*, 347 F.3d 1297, not whether the site calls to mind other cases in which harm has come to government informants, not whether it would be reasonable to think that Carmichael would threaten an informant, and not whether Carmichael himself is somehow threatening. Context can help explain the website's meaning, but it is the website that is the focus of the court's inquiry. Although the broad social context makes the case closer, the background facts described above are too general to make the Carmichael case site a 'true threat.'

The government's strongest argument based on context may not be that the Carmichael site is a direct threat that he will inflict harm on the 'informants' and 'agents,' but that the website is meant to encourage others to inflict harm on them. Agent Borland of the DEA suggested this interpretation when he testified that the website looked to him like a solicitation for others to inflict harm on the witnesses and agents.

The problem with this argument is that implicates the Supreme Court's stringent 'incitement' doctrine. *Brandenburg v. Ohio*, 395 U.S. 444, 447 (1969). *Brandenburg* stands for the proposition that, as a general rule, "the constitutional guarantees of free speech and free press do not permit a State to forbid or proscribe advocacy of the use of force or of law violation." To fall outside the First Amendment's protection, advocacy of violence must be "directed to inciting or producing imminent lawless action and [be] likely to incite or produce such action." There is no evidence that Carmichael's site meets the imminency requirement of *Brandenburg*. Indeed, in *Planned Parenthood*, Judge Kozinski in dissent noted that there was so little chance of proving that the posters and website in that case met the imminency requirement in *Brandenburg* that the plaintiffs did not even raise the argument. 290 F.3d at 1092 n. 5 (Kozinski, J., dissenting). Thus, the court cannot proscribe Carmichael's site as constitutionally unprotected advocacy of violence.

A final piece of 'context' evidence relevant to determining if the www.carmichaelcase.com website is a threat is the very fact that it is a website posted on the Internet. Courts and commentators have noted the unique features of the Internet, *see, e.g. Reno v. American Civil Liberties Union*, 521 U.S. 844, 851 (1997); Scott Hammack, *The Internet Loophole: Why Threatening Speech On-Line Requires a Modification of the Courts' Approach to True Threats and Incitement*, 36 Colum. J.L. & Soc. Probs. 65, 81–86 (2002), and a number of commentators have argued that these features make content posted on the Internet more likely to be threatening, *see, e.g.*, Hammack, *supra*; Jennifer L. Brenner, *True Threats—A More Appropriate Standard for Analyzing First Amendment Protection and Free Speech When Violence is Perpetrated Over the Internet*, 78 N.D. L. Rev. 753, 763–64 (2002). In fact, DEA Agent Borland testified at this court's hearing that one of his concerns about Carmichael's 'wanted poster' is that it is posted on the world-wide web.

That Carmichael's 'wanted poster' is on the Internet, however, is not enough to transform it into a true threat. First, notwithstanding the commentary cited above, the Supreme Court has held that speech on the Internet is subject to no greater or lesser constitutional protection than speech in more traditional media. Second, the general rule in the case law is that speech that is broadcast to a broad audience is less likely to be a true threat, not more. Thus, to the extent that the government's concern is that Carmichael's website will be seen by a lot of people, that fact makes the site look less like a true threat, not more.

Based on all of the above factors and the evidence presented, the court holds that Carmichael's website is not a true threat and is thus protected by the First Amendment.

NOTES AND QUESTIONS

1. *Assessing the seriousness of a threat.* How does a reasonable observer determine whether a statement posted on a website is a serious expression of an intent to inflict bodily harm? Does it depend on the appearance of the page, which can vary depending on the browser used? Does it depend on the URL? On the other sites that link to the statement? On how much traffic the site receives? Is a reasonable observer a savvy Internet user or an Internet novice?

2. *How can a court determine the immediacy of a threat posted on the Internet?* In People v. Neuman, 2002 WL 800516 (Cal. App. 2002), a man was convicted of making criminal threats for posting a webpage about a police officer who had given the defendant several traffic tickets and had impounded the defendant's car. The defendant added the page to his personal website that described his views about the illegitimacy of the government. The page stated:

> WANTED! Dead or Alive! (Reward) For Grand Theft Auto on 12/23/1998. J. Giles; Badge #233 VENTURA POLICE DEPARTMENT Height 6'3", Weight; approx. 280 lbs. Race: Aff. Amer. Last seen 12/29/1998 under HWY 101 Bridge/Johnston Rd. exit on a motorcycle. This Rogue Police Officer has been indicted and found guilty of Grand theft Auto. But has yet to be captured and brought to justice. THIS MAN IS ARMED AND DANGEROUS! USE EXTREME PREJUDICE IN APPREHENDING!

On appeal following his conviction, the defendant argued that the fact that he had posted this message on his website meant that it lacked the immediacy of a threat. According to the defendant, the message was "buried in an obscure web page, undelivered," and was therefore "too attenuated to convey a gravity of purpose and an immediate prospect of execution of the threat." *Id.* at *4. The state appellate court disagreed:

> We cannot agree that the "WANTED" notice was "buried" when it was prominently posted on a Web site accessible to millions of Internet users. The prosecution's computer expert testified that appellant's Web site had been indexed on three Internet search engines that would allow users to find it if they typed in key words such as "freedom" and "liberty."

Id. Doesn't this description apply to most things posted on the Web? Does this mean that every threat posted online is an immediate threat? What test would you devise for distinguishing immediate from non-immediate threats posted online?

    3. *Can a largely unnoticed Internet comment be a "true threat"?* In United States v. Dutcher, 851 F.3d 757 (7th Cir. 2017), the defendant learned that President Obama would be giving a speech in nearby La Crosse, Wisconsin. The defendant posted on his Facebook page: "thats [sic] it! Thursday I will be in La Crosse. hopefully I will get a clear shot at the pretend president. killing him is our CONSTITUTIONAL DUTY!" He later added another update: "I have been praying on [sic] going to D.C. for 3 months and now the usurper is coming HERE. . . . pray for me to succeed in my mission." The defendant then traveled to LaCrosse where he informed others that he was there to assassinate the President. The defendant was arrested and convicted of threatening to kill the President based on his Facebook posts and comments in LaCrosse.

    On appeal, the defendant argued that his Facebook posts could not be a true threat because they did not frighten anyone. The Seventh Circuit disagreed:

> Nothing in *Elonis* excludes the possibility of an unreported true threat. Other evidence indicates that some of Dutcher's readers took him seriously. Gregory Remen, for one, responded to the charged post by encouraging Dutcher to "try voting" and asked "how will killing the pres change anything then?" The apprehensive response to

Dutcher's follow-up posts underscores the point—one reader urged him to "Stay calm my friend. Please!" The jury was entitled to rely on these responses, along with Dutcher's later behavior, to find that the threats were genuine.

Id. at 762.

4.   *Deleting the communication and expressing remorse.* In State v. Taylor, 841 S.E.2d 776 (N.C.App. 2020), the defendant Taylor was upset about a prosecution decision made by the local District Attorney. Taylor went on Facebook and posted that the District Attorney would "be the first to go" when the "rebellion against our government" came. He added that "it is up to the people to administer justice," and that "they make new ammo everyday!" Taylor's posts were up for a few hours before he decided to delete them. During the time they were up, however, someone who was Facebook friends with both Taylor and the District Attorney took screenshots of the posts and sent them to the District Attorney.

When Taylor was contacted by an investigator about his Facebook posts, he expressed remorse. Taylor explained that he took the posts down "because he did not want people to think he was threatening anyone or taking things the wrong way." Taylor told the investigator that "he had no intention of making anyone feel threatened and that was the last thing that he wanted to do." He also asked the investigator to apologize to the District Attorney when he next saw her, and to let her know Taylor had not intended to make her feel threatened.

Taylor was prosecuted for making a threat and a jury convicted him. The Court of Appeals reversed, however, holding that his messages had not been a true threat. According to the Court of Appeals, Taylor's deleting the posts and expressing remorse were significant reasons why his acts were not a true threat:

> A person with an actual intent to threaten to kill someone is unlikely to delete the alleged threats within a couple of hours of posting them, and then politely ask a law enforcement officer to convey his apology to the alleged intended victim. Absent additional facts suggesting otherwise, Defendant's decision to delete the posts shortly after making them greatly diminishes the likelihood that a reasonable person who read the posts on Facebook would construe them to contain any true threat to kill D.A. Welch.

Id. at 838.

5.   *Threats against federal judges.* In 2009, a white supremacist blogger and Internet radio talk show host named Hal Turner posted two blog posts about a then-recent Seventh Circuit decision at his blog, *Turner Radio Network*, http://turnerradionetwork.blogspot.com. The decision, written by Chief Judge Frank Easterbrook and joined by Judges Richard Posner and William Bauer, had ruled that the Second Amendment did not apply to the

states. Turner responded with a blog post titled "OUTRAGE: Chicago Gun Ban UPHELD." After describing the opinion, Turner wrote:

> The government—and especially these three Judges—are cunning, ruthless, untrustworthy, disloyal, unpatriotic, deceitful scum. Their entire reason for existing is to accrue unto themselves, power over everything.
>
> The only thing that has ever stood in the way of their achieving ultimate power is the fact that We The People have guns. Now, that is very much in jeopardy. Government lies, cheats, manipulates, twists and outright disobeys the supreme law and founding documents of this land because they have not, in our lifetime, faced REAL free men willing to walk up to them and kill them for their defiance and disobedience.
>
> Thomas Jefferson, one of our Founding Fathers, told us "The tree of liberty must be replenished from time to time with the blood of tyrants and patriots." It is time to replenish the tree!
>
> Let me be the first to say this plainly: These Judges deserve to be killed. Their blood will replenish the tree of liberty. A small price to pay to assure freedom for millions.
>
> This is not the first politically-motivated trash to come out of the Seventh U.S. Circuit Court of Appeals. In fact, it was the Seventh U.S. Circuit Court of Appeals that decided in the Matt Hale Case, that a group which fraudulently trademarked the name "World Church of the Creator" despite the fact they knew that name had been used by a Church for 30 years, could KEEP the name because the church who had used it for 30 years didn't challenge the Trademark filing!
>
> By not challenging the Trademark registration, the people who had used the name for years LOST IT.
>
> That decision led to an order by a lower court for the Church to "surrender its Bibles for destruction because they infringed on the trademark" given to the fraudsters. Shortly thereafter, a gunman entered the home of that lower court Judge and slaughtered the Judge's mother and husband. Apparently, the 7th U.S. Circuit court didn't get the hint after those killings. It appears another lesson is needed.
>
> These Judges are traitors to the United States of America. They have intentionally violated the Constitution. They have now also intentionally ignored a major ruling by the US Supreme Court. If they are allowed to get away with this by surviving, other Judges will act the same way.
>
> These Judges deserve to made such an example of as to send a message to the entire judiciary: Obey the Constitution or die.

The next day, Turner added a second post providing the work addresses and contact information of the three judges, as well as a promise that their home addresses would follow. The post included names, photographs, phone numbers and chambers addresses of the three judges. Turner also posted a picture of the federal courthouse in which the judges worked, together with markings of where security barriers were located that could stop a truck bomb.

Turner was charged under 18 U.S.C. § 115(a)(1)(B), which punishes threatening "to assault, kidnap, or murder" a federal government official to interfere with or retaliate for his official conduct. Turner was tried three times. The first two juries could not agree on a verdict. The third jury rendered a verdict of guilty. Following the guilty verdict, Turner's mother told a reporter: "There goes the First Amendment for everyone. These judges, their job is to protect the Constitution, not shred it." Dave Goldiner, *Conservative Internet Shock Jock Harold (Hal) Turner Convicted Of Threatening To Kill Chicago Judges*, N.Y. Daily News, August 13, 2010.

The Court of Appeals affirmed Turner's conviction by a 2–1 vote. *See* United States v. Turner, 720 F.3d 411 (2d Cir. 2013). The majority ruled that the evidence was sufficient to constitute a true threat:

> The full context of Turner's remarks reveals a gravity readily distinguishable from mere hyperbole or common public discourse. In his blog post, Turner not only wrote that these three judges should be killed, but also explained how Judge Lefkow had ruled against Matt Hale and how, "shortly thereafter, a gunman entered the home of that lower court Judge and slaughtered the Judge's mother and husband. Apparently, the 7th U.S. Circuit court didn't get the hint after those killings. It appears another lesson is needed." Judges Easterbrook, Bauer, and Posner were of course familiar with those murders, with Judge Lefkow, and with Matt Hale's subsequent prosecution for soliciting someone to kill Judge Lefkow. Such serious references to actual acts of violence carried out in apparent retribution for a judge's decision would clearly allow a reasonable juror to conclude that Turner's statements were a true threat.

> Turner posted on his website that "Judge Lefkow made a ruling in court that I opined made her 'worthy of death,' and after I said that, someone went out and murdered her husband and mother inside the Judges Chicago house." Given that Turner's statements publicly implied a causal connection between Turner's calls for judges' deaths and actual murders, his statements about Judges Easterbrook, Bauer, and Posner, were quite reasonably interpreted by the jury as the serious expression of intent that these judges, too, come to harm. The seriousness of the threat, moreover, was further shown by Turner's posting of the judges' photographs and work addresses. Coupled with Turner's admission in an email a few weeks earlier that releasing addresses was an "effective way to cause otherwise immune public servants to seriously rethink how they use their power," the

jury had abundant evidence from which to conclude that Turner was threatening the judges in retaliation for their ruling, rather than engaging in mere political hyperbole.

Judge Pooler dissented. According to Judge Pooler, Turner's speech may have constituted incitement of others under the *Brandenburg* test. However, because Turner was charged only with making a threat and not with incitement, Judge Pooler reasoned that there was insufficient evidence that he had made a threat:

> I would hold that Turner's communications were advocacy of the use of force and not a threat. It is clear that Turner wished for the deaths of Judges Easterbrook, Posner, and Bauer. But I read his statements, made in the passive voice, as an exhortation toward "free men willing to walk up to them and kill them" and not as a warning of planned violence directed toward the intended victims. This reading is furthered by the fact that Turner's words were posted on a blog on a publicly accessible website, and had the trappings of political discourse, invoking Thomas Jefferson's famous quotation that "the tree of liberty must be replenished from time to time with the blood of tyrants and patriots." Although vituperative, there is no doubt that this was public political discourse. His speech might be subject to a different interpretation if, for example, the statements were sent to the Judges in a letter or email. However, Turner's public statements of political disagreement are different from a threat.

6. *A threat comparison.* Compare the Hal Turner case to United States v. O'Dwyer, 2010 WL 26006657 (E.D. La. 2010), *aff'd* 443 Fed.Appx. 18 (5th Cir. 2011). O'Dwyer was the subject of personal bankruptcy proceedings before a federal bankruptcy judge. At some point while his case was pending, he sent several e-mails to an employee of the bankruptcy court. One e-mail mentioned security breaches at "500 Poydras Street," the address of the federal courthouse. It stated:

> I have been totally without money since the weekend of January 8, 9, and 10, and that I have been without my anti-depressant medication, for which I have sought leave to pay Walgreen's from my most recent Social Security check, since last weekend. I could not sleep last night, which I attribute to the effects of abruptly stopping my medication on Sunday, the 24th (my pills "ran out", and I have no money to purchase more). Maybe my creditors would benefit from my suicide, but suppose I become "homicidal"? Given the recent "security breach" at 500 Poydras Street, a number of scoundrels might be at risk if I DO become homicidal. Please ask His Honor to consider allowing me to refill my prescription at Walgreen's, and allowing me to pay them, which is a condition for my obtaining a refill. Please communicate this missive to creditors and their counsel. Thank you.

O'Dwyer was arrested that day and charged with making a threat. The District Court dismissed the indictment, ruling as a matter of law that the e-mail was not a threat: "Phrases taken out of context could suggest a threat, but reading the sentences as a whole, no threat as a matter of law was made." *Id.* at *2.

7.   *Application to Craigslist postings.* In United States v. Stock, 2012 WL 202761 (W.D.Pa. 2012), the defendant posted the following message on Craigslist about a local police officer:

> I went home loaded in my truck and spend the past 3 hours looking for this douche with the expressed intent of crushing him in that little piece of shit under cover gray impala hooking up my tow chains and dragging his stupid ass down to creek hills and just drowning him in the falls. but alas I can't fine that bastard anywhere. I really wish he would die, just like the rest of these stupid fucking asshole cops. So if you read this I hope you burn in hell. I only wish I could have been the one to send you there.

The defendant was charged with making a threat under 18 U.S.C. § 875(c), and he moved to dismiss the indictment before trial on the ground that his posting was not a true threat as a matter of law. The district court declined to dismiss the indictment on the ground that whether the message was a true threat was a question for the jury. *See id.* at *10. The court distinguished *O'Dwyer* on the ground that Stock's statements were specific, detailed, and directed at a specific individual, while O'Dwyer "only made a general statement that he may become homicidal which was not directed to any specific individual." *Id.*

8.   *Threats on Twitter.* In United States v. Cassidy, 814 F. Supp.2d 574 (D.Md. 2011), the defendant joined a Buddhist sect and befriended a leader of the sect, A.Z. When it became clear that the defendant did not actually believe in Buddhist principles, A.Z. confronted him and he left the sect. The defendant then opened up a Twitter account, "Vajragurl," and he wrote several hundred tweets about A.Z. The tweets included the following:

> A.Z. you are a liar & a fraud & you corrupt Buddhism by your very presence: go kill yourself.

> want it to all be over soon sweetie?

> A.Z. IS A SATANIC CORRUPTER OF DHARMA: A SHE-DEMON WHO MASQUERADES AS A "TEACHER"

> ho bitch so ugly that when she was born the doctor slapped her mother

> I have just one thing I want to say to A.Z., and its form the heart: do the world a favor and go kill yourself. P.S. Have a nice day.

> I have this *amazing* present for a group of people who really, really deserve something *amazing*. Long time in preparation. Wait for it.

The District Court ruled that these tweets were protected by the First Amendment:

> It is clear that the Government's Indictment is directed at protected speech that is not exempted from protection by any of the recognized

areas just described. First, A.Z. is a well-known religious figure. Martha Sherrill, a Washington Post journalist wrote a critical non-fiction book about A.Z. entitled *The Buddha from Brooklyn*. Second, although in bad taste, Mr. Cassidy's Tweets and Blog posts about A.Z. challenge her character and qualifications as a religious leader. And, while Mr. Cassidy's speech may have inflicted substantial emotional distress, the Government's Indictment here is directed squarely at protected speech: anonymous, uncomfortable Internet speech addressing religious matters. Tellingly, the Government's Indictment is not limited to categories of speech that fall outside of First Amendment protection—obscenity, fraud, defamation, true threats, incitement or speech integral to criminal conduct. Because this speech does not fall into any of the recognized exceptions, the speech remains protected.

Id. at 583.

9. *Cyberbullying and the First Amendment.* In People v. Marquan M., 119 N.E.3d 480 (N.Y. 2014), the New York Court of Appeals struck down an Albany County cyberbullying statute on First Amendment grounds. The statute had recognized a new crime, cyberbullying, defined as:

> any act of communicating or causing a communication to be sent by mechanical or electronic means, including posting statements on the internet or through a computer or email network, disseminating embarrassing or sexually explicit photographs; disseminating private, personal, false or sexual information, or sending hate mail, with no legitimate private, personal, or public purpose, with the intent to harass, annoy, threaten, abuse, taunt, intimidate, torment, humiliate, or otherwise inflict significant emotional harm on another person.

Local Law No. 11 [2010] of County of Albany § 2. Under the statute, knowingly cyberbullying any person was a misdemeanor punishable by up to one year in jail and a $1,000 fine. *See id.* at § 4.

The New York Court of Appeals ruled that the statute violated the First Amendment:

> Based on the text of the statute at issue, it is evident that Albany County created a criminal prohibition of alarming breadth. The language of the local law embraces a wide array of applications that prohibit types of protected speech far beyond the cyberbullying of children. As written, the Albany County law in its broadest sense criminalizes "any act of communicating . . . by mechanical or electronic means . . . with no legitimate . . . personal . . . purpose, with the intent to harass or annoy . . . another person." On its face, the law covers communications aimed at adults, and fictitious or corporate entities, even though the county legislature justified passage of the

provision based on the detrimental effects that cyberbullying has on school-aged children.

The county law also lists particular examples of covered communications, such as "posting statements on the internet or through a computer or email network, disseminating embarrassing or sexually explicit photographs; disseminating private, personal, false or sexual information, or sending hate mail." But such methods of expression are not limited to instances of cyberbullying—the law includes every conceivable form of electronic communication, such as telephone conversations, a ham radio transmission or even a telegram. In addition, the provision pertains to electronic communications that are meant to "harass, annoy . . . taunt . . . or humiliate" any person or entity, not just those that are intended to "threaten, abuse . . . intimidate, torment . . . or otherwise inflict significant emotional harm on" a child. In considering the facial implications, it appears that the provision would criminalize a broad spectrum of speech outside the popular understanding of cyberbullying, including, for example: an email disclosing private information about a corporation or a telephone conversation meant to annoy an adult.

It is undisputed that the Albany County statute was motivated by the laudable public purpose of shielding children from cyberbullying. The text of the cyberbullying law, however, does not adequately reflect an intent to restrict its reach to the three discrete types of electronic bullying of a sexual nature designed to cause emotional harm to children.

Id. at 486.

10. *Interstate harassment and the First Amendment.* The federal interstate harassment statute, 18 U.S.C. § 2261A, generally prohibits a course of conduct to place another person in fear in another state. The statute has been upheld under the First Amendment. Consider the Eighth Circuit's explanation from United States v. Petrovic, 701 F.3d 849 (8th Cir. 2012):

In the First Amendment context a law may be invalidated as overbroad if a substantial number of its applications are unconstitutional, judged in relation to the statute's plainly legitimate sweep. An overbreadth challenge like Petrovic's will rarely succeed against a law or regulation that is not specifically addressed to speech or to conduct necessarily associated with speech (such as picketing or demonstrating).

Section 2261A(2)(A) is directed toward "courses of conduct," not speech, and the conduct it proscribes is not necessarily associated with speech. Because the statute requires both malicious intent on the part of the defendant and substantial harm to the victim, see § 2261A(2)(A), it is difficult to imagine what constitutionally-protected speech would fall under these statutory prohibitions. Most, if not all, of the statute's legal applications are to conduct that is not protected by the First Amendment. The rare application of the statute that offends the First Amendment can still be remedied through as-applied litigation. Because a substantial number of the statute's applications will not be unconstitutional, we decline to use the strong medicine of overbreadth to invalidate the entire statute.

Id. at 856.

c) Nonconsensual Pornography Laws

In the last ten years, most states have enacted new criminal laws on nonconsensual pornography (sometimes known as "revenge pornography," or "revenge porn"). The elements of the laws differ, but generally speaking they punish the nonconsensual distribution of pornographic materials.

DANIELLE KEATS CITRON & MARY ANNE FRANKS— CRIMINALIZING REVENGE PORN
49 Wake Forest L. Rev. 345 (2014).

"Jane" allowed her ex-boyfriend to photograph her naked because, as he assured her, it would be for his eyes only. After their breakup, he betrayed her trust. On a popular "revenge porn" site, he uploaded her naked photo along with her contact information. Jane received e-mails, calls, and Facebook friend requests from strangers, many of whom wanted sex.

According to the officers, nothing could be done because her ex had not violated her state's criminal harassment law. One post was an isolated event, not a harassing course of conduct as required by the law. Also, her ex had not threatened her or solicited others to stalk her. If Jane's ex had secretly photographed her, he might have faced prosecution for publishing the illegally obtained image. In her state, however, it was legal to publish Jane's naked photo taken with her consent even though her consent was premised on the promise the photo would remain private.

Nonconsensual pornography involves the distribution of sexually graphic images of individuals without their consent. This includes images originally obtained without consent (e.g., hidden recordings or recordings of sexual assaults) as well as images originally obtained with consent, usually within the context of a private or confidential relationship (e.g., images consensually given to an intimate partner who later distributes them without consent, popularly referred to as "revenge porn"). Because the term "revenge porn" is used so frequently as shorthand for all forms of nonconsensual pornography, we will use it interchangeably with nonconsensual porn.

Publishing Jane's nude photo without her consent was an egregious privacy violation that deserves criminal punishment. Criminalizing privacy invasions is not new. In their groundbreaking article *The Right to Privacy*, published in 1890, Samuel Warren and Louis Brandeis argued that "it would doubtless be desirable that the privacy of the individual should receive the added protection of the criminal law."

Over the past hundred years, state and federal legislators have taken Warren and Brandeis's advice and criminalized many privacy invasions. The Privacy Act of 1974 includes criminal penalties for the disclosure of agency records containing individually identifiable information to any person or agency not entitled to receive it. Federal laws against identity theft criminalize, inter alia, the transfer or use of another person's means of identification in connection with any state felony or violation of federal law. Federal laws prohibit the wrongful disclosure of individually identifiable health information. The federal Video Voyeurism Prevention Act of 2004 bans intentionally recording or broadcasting an image of another person in a state of undress without that person's consent under circumstances in which the person enjoys a reasonable expectation of privacy. Many state voyeurism laws criminalize the viewing or recording of a person's intimate parts without permission.

Why, then, are there so few laws banning nonconsensual pornography to date? A combination of factors is at work: lack of understanding about the gravity, scope, and dynamics of the problem; historical indifference and hostility to women's autonomy; inconsistent conceptions of contextual privacy; and misunderstandings of First Amendment doctrine.

Revenge porn victims have only recently come forward to describe the grave harms they have suffered, including stalking, loss of professional and educational opportunities, and psychological damage. As with domestic violence and sexual assault, victims of revenge porn suffer negative consequences for speaking out, including the risk of increased harm. We are only now beginning to get a sense of how large the problem of revenge porn is now that brave, outspoken victims have opened a space for others to tell their stories. The fact that nonconsensual porn so often involves the Internet and social media, the public, law enforcement, and the judiciary sometimes struggle to understand the mechanics of the conduct and the devastation it can cause.

Our society has a poor track record in addressing harms that take women and girls as their primary targets. Though much progress has been made towards gender equality, much social, legal, and political power remains in the hands of men. The fight to recognize domestic violence, sexual assault, and sexual harassment as serious issues has been long and difficult, and the tendency to tolerate, trivialize, or dismiss these harms persists. As revenge porn affects women and girls far more frequently than men and boys, and creates far more serious consequences for them, the eagerness to minimize its harm is sadly predictable. . . .

In this Article we make the case for the direct criminalization of nonconsensual pornography. Current civil law remedies, including copyright remedies, are an ineffective deterrent to revenge porn. If they were, we would likely not be witnessing the rise in reports of victimization as well as the proliferation in revenge porn websites. According to attorney Mitchell Matorin, who has represented revenge porn victims, "In the real world, civil lawsuits are no remedy at all." Among the reasons that civil litigation is ineffective is the fact that even a successful suit cannot stop the spread of an image already disclosed, and most disclosers know they are unlikely ever to be sued. Most victims do not have either the time or money to bring claims, and litigation may make little sense even for those who can afford to sue if perpetrators have few assets. While perpetrators may have little fear of civil litigation or copyright claims, the threat of criminal penalties is a different matter. Since criminal convictions in most cases stay on one's record forever, they are much less likely to be ignored. While some existing criminal laws can be mobilized against revenge porn, on the whole, existing criminal laws simply do not effectively address the issue.

Criminalizing nonconsensual pornography is also appropriate and necessary to convey the proper level of social condemnation for this behavior. . . .

Understanding Revenge Porn's Damage

In 2007, a man allegedly made numerous copies of DVDs of his ex-girlfriend performing sex acts and distributed them on random car windshields, along with the woman's name, address, and phone number. He was angry that the woman had broken off their relationship. The woman, who had not known that the intimate acts had been recorded, began receiving visits and phone calls from strange men who took the video as a sexual proposition.

Today, intimate photos are increasingly being distributed online, potentially reaching thousands, even millions of people, with a click of a mouse. A person's nude photo can be uploaded to a website where thousands of people can view and repost it. In short order, the image can appear prominently in a search of the victim's name. It can be e-mailed or otherwise exhibited to the victim's family, employers, coworkers, and friends. The Internet provides a staggering means of amplification, extending the reach of content in unimaginable ways.

Revenge porn's serious consequences warrant its criminalization. Nonconsensual pornography raises the risk of offline stalking and physical attack. In a study of 1,244 individuals, over 50% of victims reported that their naked photos appeared next to their full name and social network profile; over 20% of victims reported that their e-mail addresses and telephone numbers appeared next to their naked photos. Posting naked images next to a person's contact information often encourages strangers to confront the person offline. Many revenge porn victims like Jane rightly worry that anonymous callers and e-mailers would follow up on their sexual demands in person.

Victims' fear can be profound. They do not feel safe leaving their homes. Jane, for example, did not go to work for days after she discovered the postings. Hollie Toups, a thirty-three-year-old teacher's aide, explained that she was afraid to leave her home after someone posted her nude photograph, home address, and Facebook profile on a porn site. "I don't want to go out alone," she explained, "because I don't know what might happen."

Victims struggle especially with anxiety, and some suffer panic attacks. Anorexia nervosa and depression are common ailments for individuals who are harassed online. Researchers have found that cyber harassment victims' anxiety grows more severe over time. Victims have difficulty thinking positive thoughts and doing their work. According to a study conducted by the Cyber Civil Rights Initiative, over 80% of revenge porn victims experience severe emotional distress and anxiety.

Revenge porn is often a form of domestic violence. Frequently, the intimate images are themselves the result of an abuser's coercion of a reluctant partner. In numerous cases, abusers have threatened to disclose intimate images of their partners when victims attempt to leave the relationship. Abusers use the threat of disclosure to keep their partners under their control, making good on the threat once their partners find the courage to leave.

The professional costs of revenge porn are steep. Because Internet searches of victims' names prominently display their naked images or videos, many lose their jobs. Schools have terminated teachers whose naked pictures appeared online. A government agency ended a woman's employment after a coworker circulated her nude photograph to colleagues.

Victims may be unable to find work at all. Most employers rely on candidates' online reputations as an employment screen. According to a 2009 study commissioned by Microsoft, nearly 80% of employers consult search engines to collect intelligence on job applicants, and, about 70% of the time, they reject applicants due to their findings. Common reasons for not interviewing and hiring applicants include concerns about their "lifestyle," "inappropriate" online comments, and "unsuitable" photographs, videos, and information about them.

Recruiters do not contact victims to see if they posted the nude photos of themselves or if someone else did in violation of their trust. The "simple but regrettable truth is that after consulting search results, employers don't call revenge porn victims to schedule" interviews or to extend offers. Employers do not want to hire individuals whose search results might reflect poorly on the employer.

To avoid further abuse, targeted individuals withdraw from online activities, which can be costly in many respects. Closing down one's blog can mean a loss of income and other career opportunities. In some fields, blogging is key to getting a job. According to technology blogger Robert Scoble, people who do not blog are "never going to be included in the [technology] industry." When victims shut down their profiles on social media platforms like Facebook, LinkedIn, and Twitter, they are saddled with low social media influence scores that can impair their ability to obtain employment. Companies like Klout measure people's online influence by looking at their number of social media followers, updates, likes, retweets, and shares. Not uncommonly, employers refuse to hire individuals with low social media influence scores.

Aside from these traditional harms, revenge porn can also amount to a degrading form of sexual harassment. It exposes victims' sexuality in humiliating ways. Victims' naked photos appear on slut-shaming sites, such as Cheaterville.com and MyEx.com. Once their naked images are exposed, anonymous strangers can send e-mail messages that threaten rape. Some have said: "First I will rape you, then I'll kill you." Victims internalize these frightening and demeaning messages. Women would more likely suffer harm as a result of the posting of their naked images than their male counterparts. Gender stereotypes help explain why-- women would be seen as immoral sluts for engaging in sexual activity, whereas men's sexual activity is generally a point of pride.

While nonconsensual pornography can affect both men and women, empirical evidence indicates that nonconsensual pornography primarily affects women and girls. In a study conducted by the Cyber Civil Rights Initiative, 90% of those victimized by revenge porn were female. Nonconsensual pornography, like rape, domestic violence, and sexual harassment, belongs to the category of violence that violates legal and social commitments to equality. It denies women and girls control over their own bodies and lives. Not only does it inflict serious and, in many cases, irremediable injury on individual victims, it constitutes a vicious form of sex discrimination.

Revenge porn is a form of cyber harassment and cyber stalking whose victims are predominantly female. The U.S. National Violence Against Women Survey reports that 60% of cyber stalking victims are women. For over a decade, Working to Halt Online Abuse ("WHOA") has collected information from cyber harassment victims. Of the 3,787 individuals reporting cyber harassment to WHOA from 2000 to 2012, 72.5% were female, 22.5% were male, and 5% were unknown. A victim's actual or perceived sexual orientation seems to play a role as well. Research suggests that sexual minorities are more vulnerable to cyber harassment than heterosexuals.

NOTES AND QUESTIONS

1. *The widespread adoption of nonconsensual pornography statutes.* Following the publication of the Citron & Franks article in 2014, almost every state enacted a nonconsensual pornography statute. As of the publication of this casebook, 48 states plus the District of Columbia and the Territory of Guam have enacted such a law. *See generally* https://www.cybercivilrights.org/revenge-porn-laws/ (last visited August 1, 2021).

2. *Introduction to the First Amendment issues.* Several state nonconsensual pornography laws have been challenged on First Amendment grounds. The First Amendment issues raised by nonconsensual pornography laws are complex and remain somewhat disputed. *See generally* Andrew Koppelman, *Revenge Pornography and First Amendment Exceptions*, 65 Emory L.J. 661 (2016); John A. Humbach, *The Constitution and Revenge Porn*, 35 Pace L. Rev. 215 (2014). Before we read a case addressing the issues, a few guideposts may be worth keeping in mind.

First, the Supreme Court has carved out a few categories of communicative material from First Amendment protection. Examples include obscenity, true threats, child pornography, incitement, and fighting words. One issue to be considered is whether nonconsensual pornography laws should be categorically exempt from First Amendment scrutiny on a similar basis.

Second, if no categorical exclusion applies, the next question is whether laws regulating expression are content-based or content-neutral. That is, do the laws regulate speech with regard to their contents? "Content-based laws—those that target speech based on its communicative content—are presumptively unconstitutional and may be justified only if the government proves that they are narrowly tailored to serve compelling state interests." Reed v. Town of Gilbert, 576 U.S. 155, 163 (2015).

In contrast, content-neutral laws are subject to intermediate scrutiny. "Under intermediate scrutiny, the Government may employ the means of its choosing so long as the regulation promotes a substantial governmental interest that would be achieved less effectively absent the regulation, and does not burden substantially more speech than is necessary to further that interest." Turner Broadcasting System, Inc. v. F.C.C., 520 U.S. 180, 213–14 (1997).

STATE V. VAN BUREN
Vermont Supreme Court, 2019.
214 A.3d 791.

ROBINSON, J.

This case raises a facial challenge to Vermont's statute banning disclosure of nonconsensual pornography, 13 V.S.A. § 2606. We conclude that the statute is constitutional on its face and grant the State's petition for extraordinary relief.

VERMONT'S STATUTE

Vermont's law, enacted in 2015, makes it a crime punishable by not more than two years' imprisonment and a fine of $2,000 or both to "knowingly disclose a visual image of an identifiable person who is nude or who is engaged in sexual conduct, without his or her consent, with the intent to harm, harass, intimidate, threaten, or coerce the person depicted, and the disclosure would cause a reasonable person to suffer harm." 13 V.S.A. § 2606(b)(1). "Nude" and "sexual conduct" are both expressly defined. The law makes clear that "consent to recording of the visual image does not, by itself, constitute consent for disclosure of the image." *Id.* Violation of § 2606(b)(1) is a misdemeanor, unless a person acts "with the intent of disclosing the image for financial profit," in which case it is a felony.

Section 2606 does not apply to:

(1) Images involving voluntary nudity or sexual conduct in public or commercial settings or in a place where a person does not have a reasonable expectation of privacy.

(2) Disclosures made in the public interest, including the reporting of unlawful conduct, or lawful and common practices of law enforcement, criminal reporting, corrections, legal proceedings, or medical treatment.

(3) Disclosures of materials that constitute a matter of public concern.

(4) Interactive computer services, as defined in 47 U.S.C. § 230(f)(2), or information services or telecommunications services, as defined in 47 U.S.C. § 153, for content solely provided by another person. This subdivision shall not preclude other remedies available at law.

Id. § 2606(d)(1)–(4).

FACTS AND PROCEEDINGS BEFORE THE TRIAL COURT

In late 2015, defendant was charged by information with violating 13 V.S.A. § 2606(b)(1). The police officer averred as follows. Complainant contacted police after she discovered that someone had posted naked pictures of her on a Facebook account belonging to Anthony Coon and "tagged" her in the picture. Complainant called Mr. Coon and left a message asking that the pictures be deleted. Shortly thereafter, defendant called complainant back on Mr. Coon's phone; she called complainant a "moraless pig" and told her that she was going to contact complainant's employer, a child-care facility. When complainant asked defendant to remove the pictures, defendant responded that she was going to ruin complainant and get revenge.

Complainant told police that she had taken naked pictures of herself and sent them to Mr. Coon through Facebook Messenger. She advised that the pictures had been sent privately so that no one else could view them. Defendant admitted to the officer that she saw complainant's pictures on Mr. Coon's Facebook account and that she posted them on Facebook using Mr. Coon's account. Defendant asked the officer if he thought complainant had "learned her lesson."

In her sworn statement, complainant provided additional details concerning the allegations above. She described her efforts to delete the pictures from Facebook and to delete her own Facebook account. Complainant stated that the night before the pictures were publicly posted, she learned through a friend that defendant was asking about her. Defendant described herself as Mr. Coon's girlfriend. Complainant asked Mr. Coon about defendant, and Mr. Coon said that defendant was obsessed with him and that he had never slept with her. Complainant "took it as him being honest so we moved on." The next day, complainant discovered that defendant posted her nude images on Mr. Coon's Facebook page.

FACIAL VALIDITY OF SECTION 2606

The State argues that nonconsensual pornography, as defined in the Vermont statute, falls outside of the realm of constitutionally protected speech for two reasons: such speech amounts to obscenity, and it constitutes an extreme invasion of privacy unprotected by the First Amendment. Second, the State argues that even if nonconsensual pornography falls outside of the categorical exclusions to the First Amendment's protection of free speech, the statute is narrowly tailored to further a compelling State interest. Defendant counters each of these points.

For the reasons set forth below, we conclude that "revenge porn" does not fall within an established categorical exception to full First Amendment protection, and we decline to predict that the U.S. Supreme Court would recognize a new category. However, we conclude that the Vermont statute survives strict scrutiny as the U.S. Supreme Court has applied that standard.

A.   Categorical Exclusions

1.   Obscenity

Although some nonconsensual pornography may meet the constitutional definition of obscenity, we reject the State's contention that the Vermont statute categorically regulates obscenity and is thus permissible under the First Amendment. The purposes underlying government regulation of obscenity and of nonconsensual pornography are distinct, the defining characteristics of the regulated speech are accordingly quite different, and we are mindful of the U.S. Supreme Court's recent rejection of efforts to expand the definition of obscenity to include new types of speech that may engender some of the harms of obscenity.

The Supreme Court has recognized the government's "legitimate interest in prohibiting dissemination or exhibition of obscene material when the mode of dissemination carries with it a significant danger of offending the sensibilities of unwilling recipients or of exposure to juveniles." *Miller v. California*, 413 U.S. 15, 18–19 (1973). The Court has consistently recognized that a state's interest in regulating obscenity relates to protecting the sensibilities of those exposed to obscene works, as opposed to, for example, protecting the privacy or integrity of the models or actors depicted in obscene images. By contrast, a state's interest in regulating nonconsensual pornography has little to do with the sensibilities of the people exposed to the offending images; the State interest in this case focuses on protecting the privacy, safety, and integrity of the victim subject to nonconsensual public dissemination of highly private images.

In that sense, Vermont's statute is more analogous to the restrictions on child pornography that the Supreme Court has likewise categorically excluded from full First Amendment protection. Given these disparate interests, the test for obscenity that may be regulated consistent with the First Amendment is different from that for nonconsensual pornography under the Vermont statute. In considering whether expression is obscene for the purposes of the categorical exclusion from the full protections of the First Amendment, a trier of fact must consider:

> (a) whether "the average person, applying contemporary community standards" would find that the work, taken as a whole, appeals to the prurient interest; (b) whether the work depicts or describes, in a patently offensive way, sexual conduct specifically defined by the applicable state law; and (c) whether the work, taken as a whole, lacks serious literary, artistic, political or scientific value.

Miller, 413 U.S. at 24 (quotation and citations omitted).

The offending disclosures pursuant to Vermont's statute, by contrast, need not appeal to the prurient interest or be patently offensive. Typically, their purpose is to shame the subject, not arouse the viewer. *See* 13 V.S.A. § 2606(b)(1) (disclosure is prohibited if undertaken with intent to "harm, harass, intimidate, threaten, or coerce the person depicted"). Although, by definition, the nonconsensual pornography must include images of genitals, the pubic area, anus, or female nipple, or depictions of sexual conduct as defined in 13 V.S.A. §§ 2606(a)(3)–(4), those depictions need not appeal to the prurient interest applying contemporary community standards or be patently offensive in and of themselves.

We agree with the State's assertion that the privacy invasion and violation of the consent of the person depicted in revenge porn are offensive, but the viewer of the images need not know that they were disseminated without the consent of the person depicted in order to satisfy the revenge porn statute. Although the context in which images are disseminated may inform the obscenity analysis, the circumstances of their procurement and distribution fall outside of the typical obscenity assessment. For these reasons, the category of obscenity is ill-suited to include the nonconsensual pornography regulated here.

Given the ill fit between nonconsensual pornography and obscenity, and the Supreme Court's reluctance to expand the contours of the category of obscenity, we conclude that the speech restricted by Vermont's statute cannot be fairly categorized as constitutionally unprotected obscenity.

2.   Extreme Invasion of Privacy

Although many of the State's arguments support the proposition that the speech at issue in this case does not enjoy full First Amendment protection, we decline to identify a new categorical exclusion from the full protections of the First Amendment when the Supreme Court has not yet addressed the question.

The Supreme Court recognized in *United States v. Stevens*, 559 U.S. 460 (2010), that there may be "some categories of speech that have been historically unprotected, but have not yet been specifically identified or discussed as such in our case law." In deciding whether to recognize a new category outside the First Amendment's full protections for depictions of animal cruelty, the Court focused particularly on the absence of any history of regulating such depictions, rather than the policy arguments for and against embracing the proposed new category.

Notwithstanding these considerations, we decline to predict that the Supreme Court will add nonconsensual pornography to the list of speech categorically excluded. We base our declination on two primary considerations: The Court's recent emphatic rejection of attempts to name previously unrecognized categories, and the oft-repeated reluctance of the

Supreme Court to adopt broad rules dealing with state regulations protecting individual privacy as they relate to free speech.

More than once in recent years, the Supreme Court has rebuffed efforts to name new categories of unprotected speech. In *Stevens*, the Court emphatically refused to add depictions of animal cruelty to the list, rejecting the notion that the court has "freewheeling authority to declare new categories of speech outside the scope of the First Amendment." The Court explained, "Maybe there are some categories of speech that have been historically unprotected, but have not yet been specifically identified or discussed as such in our case law. But if so, there is no evidence that 'depictions of animal cruelty' is among them." A year later, citing *Stevens*, the Court declined to except violent video games sold to minors from the full protections of the First Amendment. And a year after that, the Court declined to add false statements to the list.

More significantly, in case after case involving a potential clash between the government's interest in protecting individual privacy and the First Amendment's free speech protections, the Supreme Court has consistently avoided broad pronouncements, and has defined the issue at hand narrowly, generally reconciling the tension in favor of free speech in the context of speech about matters of public interest while expressly reserving judgment on the proper balance in cases where the speech involves purely private matters. The considerations that would support the Court's articulation of a categorical exclusion in this case may carry great weight in the strict scrutiny analysis, see below. But we leave it to the Supreme Court in the first instance to designate nonconsensual pornography as a new category of speech that falls outside the First Amendment's full protections.

B.   Strict Scrutiny

Our conclusion that nonconsensual pornography does not fall into an existing or new category of unprotected speech does not end the inquiry. The critical question is whether the First Amendment permits the regulation at issue. The remaining question is whether § 2606 is narrowly tailored to serve a compelling State interest.

1.   Compelling Interest

We conclude that the State interest underlying § 2606 is compelling. We base this conclusion on the U.S. Supreme Court's recognition of the relatively low constitutional significance of speech relating to purely private matters, evidence of potentially severe harm to individuals arising from nonconsensual publication of intimate depictions of them, and a litany of analogous restrictions on speech that are generally viewed as uncontroversial and fully consistent with the First Amendment.

Although we decline to identify a new category of unprotected speech on the basis of the above cases, the decisions are relevant to the compelling interest analysis in that they reinforce that the First Amendment limitations on the regulation of speech concerning matters of public interest do not necessarily apply to regulation of speech concerning purely private matters. Time and again, the Supreme Court has recognized that speech concerning purely private matters does not carry as much weight in the strict scrutiny analysis as speech concerning matters of public concern, and may accordingly be subject to more expansive regulation.

The proscribed speech in this case has no connection to matters of public concern. By definition, the proscribed images must depict nudity or sexual conduct, § 2606(b)(1); must be disseminated without the consent of the victim, *id.*; cannot include images in settings in which a person does not have a reasonable expectation of privacy, *id.* § 2606(d)(1); cannot include disclosures made in the public interest, including reporting concerning various specified matters, *id.* § 2606(d)(2); and may not constitute a matter of public concern, *id.* § 2606(d)(3). By definition, the speech subject to regulation under § 2606 involves the most private of matters, with the least possible relationship to matters of public concern.

The harm to the victims of nonconsensual pornography can be substantial. Images and videos can be directly disseminated to the victim's friends, family, and employers; posted and "tagged" (as in this case) so they are particularly visible to members of a victim's own community; and posted with identifying information such that they catapult to the top of the results of an online search of an individual's name. In the constellation of privacy interests, it is difficult to imagine something more private than images depicting an individual engaging in sexual conduct, or of a person's genitals, anus, or pubic area, that the person has not consented to sharing publicly. The personal consequences of such profound personal violation and humiliation generally include, at a minimum, extreme emotional distress. Amici cited numerous instances in which the violation led the victim to suicide.

Finally, the government's interest in preventing the nonconsensual disclosure of nude or sexual images of a person obtained in the context of a confidential relationship is at least as strong as its interest in preventing the disclosure of information concerning that person's health or finances obtained in the context of a confidential relationship; content-based restrictions on speech to prevent these other disclosures are uncontroversial and widely accepted as consistent with the First Amendment. From a constitutional perspective, it is hard to see a distinction between laws prohibiting nonconsensual disclosure of personal information comprising images of nudity and sexual conduct and those prohibiting disclosure of other categories of nonpublic personal information. The government's interest in protecting all from disclosure is strong.

For the above reasons, we conclude that the State interest underlying § 2606 is compelling.

2.　　Narrowly Tailored

Section 2606 defines unlawful nonconsensual pornography narrowly, including limiting it to a confined class of content, a rigorous intent element that encompasses the nonconsent requirement, an objective requirement that the disclosure would cause a reasonable person harm, an express exclusion of images warranting greater constitutional protection, and a limitation to only those images that support the State's compelling interest because their disclosure would violate a reasonable expectation of privacy. Our conclusion on this point is bolstered by a narrowing interpretation of one provision that we offer to ensure that the statute is duly narrowly tailored.

The images subject to § 2606 are precisely defined, with little gray area or risk of sweeping in constitutionally protected speech. Moreover, disclosure is only criminal if the discloser knowingly discloses the images without the victim's consent. We construe this intent requirement to require knowledge of both the fact of disclosing, and the fact of nonconsent. Individuals are highly unlikely to accidentally violate this statute while engaging in otherwise permitted speech. In fact, § 2606 goes further, requiring not only knowledge of the above elements, but a specific intent to harm, harass, intimidate, threaten, or coerce the person depicted or to profit financially.

In addition, the disclosure must be one that would cause a reasonable person "physical injury, financial injury, or serious emotional distress." *Id.* § 2606(a)(2), (b)(1). The statute is not designed to protect overly fragile sensibilities, and does not reach even knowing, nonconsensual disclosures of images falling within the narrow statutory parameters unless disclosure would cause a reasonable person to suffer harm.

Two additional limitations assuage any concern that some content meeting all of these requirements may nonetheless implicate a matter of public concern. First, the statute does not purport to reach "disclosures made in the public interest, including the reporting of unlawful conduct, or lawful and common practices of law enforcement, criminal reporting, corrections, legal proceedings, or medical treatment." *Id.* § 2606(d)(2). This broad and nonexclusive list of permitted disclosures is designed to exclude from the statute's reach disclosures that do implicate First Amendment concerns—those made in the public interest.

Second, even if a disclosure is not made "in the public interest," if the materials disclosed "constitute a matter of public concern," they are excluded from the statute's reach. *Id.* § 2606(d)(3). The Legislature has made every effort to ensure that its prohibition is limited to communication of purely private matters with respect to which the State's interest is the strongest and the First Amendment concerns the weakest.

Finally, to ensure that the statute reaches only those disclosures implicating the right to privacy the statute seeks to protect, it expressly excludes "images involving voluntary nudity or sexual conduct in public or commercial settings or in a place where a person does not have a reasonable expectation of privacy." *Id.* § 2606(d)(1). Where an individual does not have a reasonable expectation of privacy in an image, the State's interest in protecting the individual's privacy interest in that image is minimal. The statute recognizes this fact.

In connection with this factor, we offer a narrowing construction, or clarification of the statute to ensure its constitutional application while promoting the Legislature's goals. The statute's exclusion of otherwise qualifying images involving voluntary nudity or sexual conduct in settings in which a person does not have a reasonable expectation of privacy, 13 V.S.A. § 2606(d)(1), does not clearly reach images recorded in a private setting but distributed by the person depicted to public or commercial settings or in a manner that undermines any reasonable expectation of privacy. From the perspective of the statute's goals, there is no practical difference between a nude photo someone voluntarily poses for in the public park and one taken in private that the person then voluntarily posts in that same public park.

Given the Legislature's clear intent to protect peoples' reasonable expectations of privacy in intimate images of them, and to exclude from the statute's reach those images in which a person has no such reasonable expectation, it seems clear that the Legislature intends its exclusion to apply to images the person has distributed to the public, as well as those recorded in public. This construction also ensures that the scope of the statute is no broader than necessary to advance the State's interest in protecting reasonable expectations of privacy with respect to intimate images.

Given this narrowing construction, as well as all the express limitations on the statute's reach built into § 2606, we conclude that it is narrowly tailored to advance the State's compelling interest.

For the above reasons, the statute is narrowly tailored to advance the State's interests, does not penalize more speech than necessary to accomplish its aim, and does not risk chilling protected speech on matters of public concern. We accordingly conclude that 13 V.S.A. § 2606 is constitutional on its face.

* * *

We now resolve the question of whether the trial court's dismissal of the State's charge against defendant for nonconsensual disclosure of images of an identifiable nude person under 13 V.S.A. § 2606 was proper on the basis that the State failed to present sufficient evidence to show that complainant, the person depicted in the images, had a reasonable expectation of privacy in those images.

We conclude that because the State's evidence, taken in the light most favorable to the State, does not establish that complainant had a reasonable expectation of privacy in the images, the State has failed to make out a prima facie case. Accordingly, we affirm the dismissal of the charge pursuant to Vermont Rule of Criminal Procedure 12(d) and deny the State's petition for relief.

The evidence before the trial court in connection with the motion to dismiss reflects the following. Complainant sent nude pictures of herself to Anthony Coon via Facebook Messenger, Facebook's private messaging service. Her sworn statement reflects that on October 8, 2015, multiple people contacted her to report that the nude photos of her had been publicly posted on Mr. Coon's Facebook page and she had been tagged in them. Complainant initially tried to untag herself but was unable to. She eventually deleted her account. She left Mr. Coon a telephone message asking that he delete the pictures from Facebook.

Complainant then received a call from Mr. Coon's phone number. The caller was defendant. Defendant called complainant a pig and said she was going to tell complainant's employer, a child-care facility, about "what kind of person worked there." Defendant said that she had left her "ex" for Mr. Coon. Complainant asked defendant to remove the pictures from Facebook, and defendant replied that she was going to "ruin" complainant and "get revenge." After that call ended, complainant contacted the police.

Complainant reported that the night before the pictures were publicly posted, a friend told her defendant was asking about her and claiming Mr. Coon was her boyfriend. Upon learning this, complainant asked Mr. Coon about defendant, and Mr. Coon said that defendant was obsessed with him and he never slept with her. Complainant "took it as him being honest so we moved on."

The investigating officer spoke with defendant over the phone. Defendant admitted that she saw the nude pictures of complainant through Mr. Coon's Facebook account and that she posted the pictures on Facebook through Mr. Coon's account. Defendant stated to the officer, "you think she learned her lesson."

In reviewing the State's motion, the trial court later asked the parties to stipulate to additional facts, if possible, concerning when the photographs were sent, whether complainant sent them while in or after ending a relationship with Mr. Coon, and how defendant had access to Mr.

Coon's Facebook account. The parties stipulated that complainant sent Mr. Coon the photos on October 7, and they were posted on a public Facebook page on October 8. They further stipulated that "complainant was not in a relationship with Mr. Coon at the time the photographs were sent to Mr. Coon." Finally, they stipulated that defendant did not have permission to access Mr. Coon's Facebook account, and Mr. Coon believes defendant gained access to his account through her phone, which had his Facebook password saved on it.

We conclude that dismissal is appropriate because the State has not established that it has evidence showing that complainant had a reasonable expectation of privacy in the images she sent to Mr. Coon. The statutory exception for images taken in a setting where there was no reasonable expectation of privacy, or previously distributed in a manner that undermined that expectation of privacy, is fundamental to the constitutionality and purpose of this statute, and must be understood as an element of the crime. The State bears the burden of establishing that it has evidence as to each element of the offense, including this one. Because the State has stipulated that complainant and Mr. Coon were not in a relationship at the time complainant sent Mr. Coon the photo, and there is no evidence in the record showing they had any kind of relationship engendering a reasonable expectation of privacy, we conclude the State has not met its burden.

The requirement that the images at issue be subject to a reasonable expectation of privacy is central to the statute's constitutional validity under a strict-scrutiny standard. A content-based restriction on First Amendment-protected speech like § 2606 can withstand strict scrutiny only if it is narrowly tailored to serve a compelling state interest. Because the protection of reasonable expectations of privacy in intimate images is central to the statute's constitutionality and purpose, the reasonable-expectation-of-privacy provision must be understood as an element of the crime.

We acknowledge that the structure of § 2606, as set forth below, weighs in favor of finding the reasonable-expectation-of-privacy requirement to be a defense because its positioning makes it appear to be an excuse or exception to the definition of the crime. But the very essence of this crime is that it is a violation of the depicted person's reasonable expectation of privacy. As the State aptly put it in its opening brief, "the conduct regulated by 13 V.S.A. § 2606" is "publicly disseminating someone's private nude pictures without their consent" and "Section 2606 thus generally prohibits disclosing a person's nude or sexually explicit pictures if the person had a reasonable expectation of privacy in the picture and did not consent to its disclosure." Although phrased as an exception, it is an essential ingredient which constitutes the offense." It is an element of the crime.

The State has not shown it has evidence that complainant had a reasonable expectation of privacy in the images she sent to Mr. Coon. We understand this to be an objective standard, and find no evidence in the record showing that complainant had such a relationship with Mr. Coon that distributing the photos to him did not undermine any reasonable expectation of privacy that she had in them.

We interpret the reasonable-expectation-of-privacy standard as a purely objective one because the Legislature specified that the statute shall not apply to "images involving voluntary nudity or sexual conduct where a person does not have a reasonable expectation of privacy." § 2606(d)(1) This reflects a decision by the Legislature that the expectation-of-privacy determination should be based on what a reasonable person would think, not what the person depicted thought.[15] We do not attempt to precisely define here where and when a person may have a reasonable expectation of privacy for the purposes of § 2606(d)(1), except to note that it generally connotes a reasonable expectation of privacy within a person's most intimate spheres. Privacy here clearly does not mean the exclusion of all others, but it does mean the exclusion of everyone but a trusted other or few.

We conclude that the State has not shown, as we held it must, that the images were not distributed by the person depicted in a manner that undermined any reasonable expectation of privacy. As the State acknowledged in its briefing, "it is difficult to see how a complainant would have a reasonable expectation of privacy in pictures sent to a stranger." But the State has not presented evidence to demonstrate that, in contrast to a stranger, Mr. Coon had a relationship with complainant of a sufficiently intimate or confidential nature that she could reasonably assume that he would not share the photos she sent with others. Nor has it offered evidence of any promise by Mr. Coon, or even express request by complainant, to keep the photos confidential.

The State stipulated that complainant and Mr. Coon were not in a relationship at the time complainant sent the pictures. In the face of this stipulation, the facts that complainant and Mr. Coon apparently knew each other, had each other's contact information, and had a conversation about whether Mr. Coon was sleeping with defendant, are not sufficient to support an inference that she had a reasonable expectation of privacy. In sum, the State has not offered sufficient evidence to permit a jury to

---

[15] We note that case law construing a criminal defendant's reasonable expectation of privacy for the purposes of the Fourth Amendment is of little help in determining whether the subject of an image has a reasonable expectation of privacy under § 2606(d)(1). Because a reasonable expectation of privacy under § 2606(d)(1) requires no analogous balancing of legitimate law-enforcement interests, the tests are fundamentally different. Although we are using the same phrase—"reasonable expectation of privacy"—it does not necessarily have the same meaning in this context that it would in the Fourth Amendment setting.

conclude beyond a reasonable doubt that complainant had a reasonable expectation of privacy in the photos she sent to Mr. Coon.

The petition for extraordinary relief is denied, and the decision below is affirmed.

NOTES AND QUESTIONS

1. *The case for a categorical exclusion.* Should the U.S. Supreme Court carve out a new categorical exclusion from First Amendment scrutiny for nonconsensual pornography? If so, how far should it extend?

2. *The Vermont law's narrow tailoring.* VanBuren concludes that Vermont's statute survives strict scrutiny under the First Amendment because it advances a compelling interest and is narrowly tailored to advance the State's interests, it does not penalize more speech than necessary to accomplish its aim, and it does not risk chilling protected speech on matters of public concern. Are you convinced? If so, could the law be drafted more broadly than it is and still survive strict scrutiny? If not, is there a way to narrow the law to have it pass strict scrutiny?

3. *The debate over including an intent-to-harm element.* The Vermont law applies to one who "knowingly disclose[s] a visual image of an identifiable person who is nude or who is engaged in sexual conduct, without his or her consent, with the intent to harm, harass, intimidate, threaten, or coerce the person depicted." 13 V.S.A. § 2606(b)(1). Unlike the Vermont law, several state revenge pornography laws do not include an intent-to-harm element. As a matter of policy, which is better: The narrower laws that include an intent-to-harm element, or the broader laws that do not include this as an element?

Consider one argument for not including an intent-to-harm element:

Consider what it would look like if laws protecting other forms of private information were treated similarly. Imagine allowing doctors to post patients' pre-op photos to Facebook—photos in which the patients are clearly identifiable by face or name or other identifying information—to amuse friends, make money, or provide sexual gratification, or any other motive other than to harm the patient. If that seems absurd, it is no less absurd here.

Danielle Citron & Mary Anne Franks, *Evaluating New York's "Revenge Porn" Law: A Missed Opportunity to Protect Sexual Privacy*, Harvard Law Review Blog, March 19, 2019. On the other hand, is it currently a crime for a doctor to post patients' pre-op photos to Facebook? If so, what crime is it? And is the case for criminalizing a physician's disclosure of patient photographs based on doctors having special responsibilities over the medical records of their patients, or is it because people should have an inherent right to control their photos?

Next consider the First Amendment implications of including an intent-to-harm element. *Van Buren* upholds the Vermont law that includes an intent-to-harm element. If the Vermont legislature removed that element, would the Vermont Supreme Court still rule that the statute was narrowly tailored and therefore constitutional? Or, based on the *Van Buren* decision, does the First Amendment require the intent-to-harm element?

4.   *Content-based or content-neutral?* Are nonconsensual pornography laws better understood as content-based speech restrictions (ordinarily subject to strict scrutiny) or as content-neutral speech restrictions (ordinarily subject only to intermediate scrutiny)?

On one hand, the Texas Court of Criminal Appeals has held that the Texas statute is a content-based speech restriction because it applies to the disclosure only of sexual images:

> Section 21.16(b) is content based on its face. The statute does not penalize all intentional disclosure of visual material depicting another person. Rather, it penalizes only a subset of disclosed images—those which depict another person with the person's intimate parts exposed or engaged in sexual conduct. That subset is drawn according to the subject matter—nudity and sex. At the same time, it places absolutely no restriction on non-sexual utterances that violate another person's privacy interests. Therefore, Section 21.16(b) applies to particular speech because of the topic discussed or the idea or message expressed.

Ex parte Brown, 2021 WL 2126172 at *6 (Tex. Ct. Crim. App. 2021).

On the other hand, the Supreme Court of Illinois has held that the Illinois statute is content-neutral because it is violated only when additional elements beyond the content of the images have been met:

> 720 ILCS 11–23.5(b) is justified on the grounds of protecting privacy. Section 11–23.5(b) distinguishes the dissemination of a sexual image not based on the content of the image itself but, rather, based on whether the disseminator obtained the image under circumstances in which a reasonable person would know that the image was to remain private and knows or should have known that the person in the image has not consented to the dissemination. 720 ILCS 5/11–23.5(b)(2), (b)(3) (West 2016). There is no criminal liability for the dissemination of the very same image obtained and distributed with consent. The *manner* of the image's acquisition and publication, and not its *content*, is thus crucial to the illegality of its dissemination.

People v. Austin, 155 N.E.3d 439, 457 (Ill. 2019) (emphasis in original). Which of these views is more persuasive?

5.   *Texas's narrowing interpretation.* The Texas Court of Criminal Appeals has upheld the Texas nonconsensual pornography statute as it existed in 2017, but construed the statute narrowly to do that:

> There does not seem to be a dispute that the classic "revenge porn" scenario—two people take intimate sexual photographs, and one

person decides to post them on the Internet without the consent of the other—could be a viable set of facts to support the prosecution of the person who disseminates the pictures. But what about when someone who wasn't involved in that encounter sees the pictures and shares them with other people? Can the State prosecute that person without violating the First Amendment? That is the difficulty with analyzing Section 21.16(b) of the Penal Code, at least as it existed in 2017.1 But, interpreting Section 21.16(b) as alleged in the indictment, we hold that the statute only covers the intentional disclosure of sexually explicit material by third parties when that third party (1) obtained the material under circumstances in which the depicted person had a reasonable expectation that the image would remain private; (2) knew or was aware of but consciously disregarded a substantial and unjustifiable risk that he did not have effective consent of the depicted person; and (3) knowingly or recklessly identified the depicted person and caused that person harm through the disclosure. Properly construed, the statute does not violate the First Amendment.

Ex parte Brown, 2021 WL 2126172 (Tex. Ct. Crim. App. 2021).

2. INVASION OF PRIVACY CRIMES

Congress has enacted three federal crimes to deter and punish personal invasions of privacy involving computers and the Internet. The offenses criminalize invasions of privacy involving a person's data online. The most important statute is the felony criminal prohibition found in the Wiretap Act, 18 U.S.C. § 2511, and the remaining two statutes are the misdemeanor criminal prohibitions found in the Stored Communications Act, 18 U.S.C. § 2701, and the Pen Register statute, 18 U.S.C. § 3121.

The Wiretap Act, Stored Communications Act, and Pen Register statute are complex surveillance statutes that were enacted to create a statutory form of the Fourth Amendment applicable to computer networks. The criminal prohibitions contained in these three statutes are best (and perhaps only) understood in the context of a broader study of surveillance law. Each of the statutes sets up both a regime of criminal procedure and a related criminal prohibition, and it helps to study the former to understand the latter. Chapter Six explores all three statutes in considerable detail, so a complete study of the three criminal offenses must await those materials.

For now, however, it is helpful to get just a flavor. The most important provision is the criminal prohibition contained in the Wiretap Act, codified at 18 U.S.C. § 2511. Section 2511(1)(a) penalizes one who "intentionally intercepts, endeavors to intercept, or procures any other person to intercept or endeavor to intercept, any wire, oral, or electronic communication." The statute defines "intercept" as "the aural or other acquisition of the contents of any wire, electronic, or oral communication through the use of any electronic, mechanical, or other device." 18 U.S.C. § 2510(4). The basic idea is that it is a crime to intentionally wiretap a private person's telephone or Internet communications. For example, a person who installs a "sniffer" Internet surveillance tool that reads an Internet user's e-mail in "real time" generally violates the Wiretap Act. If the person installs the sniffer intending to intercept a person's communications, he can be charged with criminal wiretapping. The Wiretap Act also contains criminal prohibitions against using and disclosing intercepted communications in a number of circumstances, but they are less often charged and also can raise First Amendment problems. *See* 18 U.S.C. § 2511(1)(b)–(e); Bartnicki v. Vopper, 532 U.S. 514 (2001).

The prohibition contained in the Pen Register statute resembles that of the Wiretap Act. There are two key differences. First, violations of the Pen Register statute are only misdemeanors, *see* 18 U.S.C. § 3121(d), and are only very rarely prosecuted. Second, while violations of the Wiretap Act involve interception of the contents of information such as telephone calls and e-mail, the Pen Register statute is violated when a person obtains in real time the dialing, routing, addressing, and signaling information relating to an individual's telephone calls or Internet communications. The Pen Register statute's criminal prohibition appears in 18 U.S.C. § 3121(a) and (d), and states that one who knowingly "install[s] or use[s] a pen register or a trap and trace device without first obtaining a court order" can be prosecuted. The statute defines both pen registers and trap and trace devices in 18 U.S.C. § 3127(3)–(4), and defines those terms as devices that obtain dialing, routing, addressing, and signaling information relating to telephone and Internet communications. Put together, the statute prohibits knowingly using a device to obtain in real-time the dialing, routing, addressing, or signaling information relating to Internet communications of another person.

The criminal prohibition contained in the Stored Communications Act was discussed briefly in Chapter 2. The prohibition is a specific type of unauthorized access law, punishing one who "intentionally accesses without authorization a facility through which an electronic communication service is provided, [or] intentionally exceeds an authorization to access that facility; and thereby obtains, alters, or prevents authorized access to a wire or electronic communication while it is in electronic storage in such system." 18 U.S.C. § 2701(a). This prohibition is a close cousin of § 1030(a)(2). To be a bit imprecise, it is an unauthorized access law that applies specifically to Internet service providers. The statute is largely redundant in light of the broad scope of 18 U.S.C. § 1030(a)(2)(C).

C. VICE CRIMES

Offenses involving pornography, narcotics, prostitution, and gambling are sometimes labeled "vice crimes." As a historical matter, such crimes exist because they are believed by many to relate to moral vices. Vice crimes can be controversial, as one person's upholding the moral fabric is another person's interfering with private affairs.

Computers often alter the ways in which vice crimes are committed. Traditionally, a person wishing to commit a vice crime needed to meet face-to-face with the person providing the sought-after goods or services. Some transactions could occur via postal mail (such as purchasing obscene books), and others could occur via the telephone (such as placing bets), but most vice crimes tended to occur face-to-face. Computers and the Internet change that. The transaction is no longer person-to-person; it is now person-to-computer. An individual sits at her computer, often in the comfort and privacy of her own home, and interacts with machines located hundreds or thousands of miles away.

The shift to digital vice crimes raises two difficult policy questions. The first is whether the new factual environment changes basic assumptions of the legal doctrine. Vice prohibition is often justified by its effect on the local physical environment. For example, a local prohibition on gambling may be a way to protect a neighborhood from illegal activities sometimes associated with gambling, such as organized crime and prostitution. The Internet brings new facts, and it is worth considering whether the new facts justify new law.

Second, the Internet may make it more difficult to enforce vice crime laws effectively. The enforcement of person-to-person vice crimes in the physical world focuses on particular places, which can help law enforcement allocate resources. Prostitutes may be known to walk a particular neighborhood or street; a particular park may be known for its narcotics market; an organized crime gang may run an illegal casino in a basement apartment. To commit a physical vice crime, a person must ordinarily go to a particular place in the physical world. The police can concentrate their enforcement efforts on those physical places.

In contrast, vice crimes online simply require a server, an Internet connection, and a user. The user and the server can be anywhere in the world. To investigate the offense, the police will have to conduct surveillance of the user or the server. Is this possible? Imagine that a defendant in Kansas likes to gamble online using a website that hosts its servers in the Cayman Islands. If you are a Kansas police officer, how can you gather sufficient evidence to charge the defendant in a Kansas court? Given your limited resources, are you likely to focus your efforts on investigating illegal online gambling happening in your state? Is it a coincidence that in the case of both Internet gambling and obscenity law, the legal prohibitions are broad but prosecutions remain quite rare?

1. INTERNET GAMBLING

RONALD J. RYCHLAK—LEGAL PROBLEMS WITH ON-LINE GAMBLING
Engage, May 2005, at 36.

Introduction

Not long ago, Nevada and Atlantic City, New Jersey stood out from the rest of the nation as jurisdictions where one could bet legally. With the emergence of Indian gaming, state lotteries, riverboat gambling, and other forms of legal wagering, today two states (Utah and Hawaii) stand alone as the only jurisdictions without some form of legalized gaming. In fact, today anyone with a computer and Internet access can go to a "virtual casino" and gamble on almost any casino-style game or place bets on professional and collegiate sporting events.

Online gaming is emerging as a major enterprise for the Internet, and a serious concern for lawmakers. There are presently more than 1,400 gambling sites on the web. With about 14.5 million patrons, it is estimated that global revenues for Internet gaming were about $4.2 billion in 2003. Many observers believe that Internet gaming is well on its way to becoming a $100 billion-a-year industry.

Despite its prevalence, Internet gambling is illegal in all fifty states. Several foreign nations, however, either sanction Internet gaming or do not enforce laws against it. Since web pages do not recognize international borders, a gaming site operated in any nation can attract gamblers from every other nation. Most Internet gamblers are from the United States, and that is a serious concern for American lawmakers.

Gambling, of course, has traditionally been seen as a vice, and in the United States it has a history associated with organized crime. As states have moved toward legalization, they have also instituted strict regulatory schemes designed to keep the games fair and the ownership honest. With Internet gaming, however, this may be impossible. One of the most heavily regulated industries in the world has crashed with full force into one of the most unregulated, and inherently unregulatable, phenomenon of modern times.

Several different concerns lead to the call for regulation or prohibition of Internet gambling:

- Concern about underage gamblers. Obviously, it is harder to verify age over the Internet than in person.

- Concern about fraud by Internet casino operators. Internet casino operators have already avoided paying their customers either by refusing to pay or by moving their website to another address and changing the name.

- Concern that video gambling (whose addictive nature has been compared to crack cocaine) from the privacy of one's own home will lead to an increase in gambling addiction.

- Concern that Internet casinos will negatively affect state tax revenues by taking business away from brick-and-mortar casinos that pay taxes.

These reasons for wanting to control Internet gaming, however, do not translate easily into action. When it comes to regulation or prohibition, there are two basic lines of thought. One line holds that Internet gambling cannot be entirely stopped, so it has to be regulated. The opposing argument is that it cannot be regulated, so it must be prohibited. Unfortunately, both groups are partially correct: Internet gaming is very difficult to regulate or to prohibit.

Since many of the Internet gaming web pages are sanctioned by some foreign government, one possibility would be simply to rely upon the regulatory authority provided by that nation. An obvious problem with that solution is that regulation in another nation is unlikely to protect American gamblers. More importantly, many (but not all) of the sanctioned virtual casinos are located in small, island nations that provide virtually no actual regulation; they just charge a fee. Consider:

> In Nevada and New Jersey the applicant for an unrestricted gaming license can expect the process to take one to two years. The applicant has the burden of proving to the licensing authorities that it is legitimate and has the necessary skills available to operate a casino in compliance with the law. The applicant must pay the costs of the independent investigation undertaken to test the accuracy and complete truthfulness of its responses to the myriad questions answered in filling out the application. These costs routinely amount to between $500,000 and $1,000,000. There are public hearings to delve into personal and business transgressions admitted in the application or turned up in the investigation. These amounts do not take into consideration the legal fees that each applicant incurs in getting help and advice in connection with the process.

In contrast, most of the off-shore nations that license Internet casinos charge between $8,000 and $20,000, and the time to obtain the license is between one and five weeks. Obviously, these other nations do not devote as much time and effort to gaming regulation as is expected in the United

States. As such, reliance on the laws of other nations will not meet the needs of American lawmakers.

Since gambling has traditionally been a matter of state concern, some individual states have taken action to try to stop Internet gambling. In 2001, for instance, New Jersey's Attorney General filed civil suits against three offshore casinos. This is in line with similar actions taken by officials in New York, Minnesota, and Missouri. In Florida, the Attorney General distributed "cease and desist" letters to at least ten media companies providing publishing or broadcasting advertisements for offshore computer gambling sites.

The Attorney Generals of Indiana, Minnesota, and Texas have all issued opinions specifically declaring Internet gambling illegal under the laws of their respective states, and other states are putting new legislation in place. Legal actions, however, are very difficult to bring. The Internet casino operations are usually located beyond the state's jurisdictional limits, and even if the necessary evidence could be uncovered, prosecutors are unlikely to go after individual gamblers. As such, states have been unable to significantly impact online betting.

Conclusion

In 2002, the United States General Accounting Office performed a survey of Internet gambling web sites. The findings showed that current federal statutes are not effective in controlling Internet gambling. Recent legislative proposals that have focused on ISPs or financial institutions also have difficulties. Must, then, American lawmakers resign themselves to permanent, unregulated Internet casinos? Maybe not.

Since Internet casinos cannot be stopped as long as they are legal in other nations, American lawmakers should focus on a certification process for online casinos. Those casinos that are already operating traditional gambling establishments within the United States could be given the opportunity to develop online casinos which would be accessible through a regulatory gateway page. These online casinos would face competition from unregulated virtual casinos, which might be able to operate at a lower cost than the regulated web pages. Gamblers wanting assurance of fair games, however, would presumably be interested in using the regulated pages, particularly when they are linked to well-established casino brand names. Regulators (and tax authorities) would have substantial control over these online casinos, because of the brick-and-mortar casinos over which they also have control. As such, reasonable regulations could be put in place to assure fair games, verify the age of gamblers, collect taxes, and minimize the risk to problem gamblers (to the extent that is possible). Unregulated online gaming would still exist, but if this regulation were done correctly, these officially sanctioned web pages should be able to capture a significant portion of the market. Consumers would have the choice of betting with casinos that are regulated and fair, or they could take their risks with other entities that are less secure but might offer better odds. In the end, the market could play a significant role in bringing online gaming under control.

NOTES AND QUESTIONS

1. *Internet gambling versus in-person gambling.* Consider some of the ways Internet gambling is different from traditional forms of gambling. If you visit a casino, you first have to travel to it. You will subject yourself to the legal rules applicable in the jurisdiction where the casino is located; the casino will be a known business with physical assets and employees that can be audited and taxed; and the presence of the casino is likely to have spillover effects (whether negative or positive) on the physical neighborhood surrounding the casino. When you log on to a gambling website, however, you do not need to travel. You may not know what legal regime regulates the gambling transaction or where the company is located; you may not know anything about the gambling site; and the site will not have spillover effects in any physical neighborhood. Do these differences justify regulating Internet gambling differently than traditional forms of gambling?

2. *The Unlawful Internet Gambling Enforcement Act.* The difficulty of enforcing gambling prohibitions over the Internet led Congress to enact the Unlawful Internet Gambling Enforcement Act, Pub.L. No. 109–347 (2006) ("UIGEA"). The UIGEA states in relevant part:

> No person engaged in the business of betting or wagering may knowingly accept, in connection with the participation of another person in unlawful Internet gambling—
>
> (1)   credit, or the proceeds of credit, extended to or on behalf of such other person (including credit extended through the use of a credit card);
>
> (2)   an electronic fund transfer, or funds transmitted by or through a money transmitting business, or the proceeds of an electronic fund transfer or money transmitting service, from or on behalf of such other person; [or]
>
> (3)   any check, draft, or similar instrument which is drawn by or on behalf of such other person and is drawn on or payable at or through any financial institution.

31 U.S.C. § 5363. The statute also requires the Board of Governors of the Federal Reserve System and the Secretary of the Department of the Treasury acting jointly to enact regulations

> requiring each designated payment system, and all participants therein, to identify and block or otherwise prevent or prohibit restricted transactions through the establishment of policies and procedures reasonably designed to identify and block or otherwise

prevent or prohibit the acceptance of restricted transactions in any of the following ways:

(1)   The establishment of policies and procedures that—

(A)   allow the payment system and any person involved in the payment system to identify restricted transactions by means of codes in authorization messages or by other means; and

(B)   block restricted transactions identified as a result of the policies and procedures developed pursuant to subparagraph (A).

(2)   The establishment of policies and procedures that prevent or prohibit the acceptance of the products or services of the payment system in connection with a restricted transaction.

31 U.S.C. § 5364(a). The regulations appear at 12 C.F.R. § 233.1–233.7, and they contain fairly detailed rules on what designated payment systems can and cannot do.

The basic idea behind the UIGEA is to make it more difficult for individual bettors to finance their illegal bets. Credit card companies will not accept purchases of credits at Internet betting sites, and the betting sites cannot accept the transactions on their end, either. Put another way, the idea is to deter criminal conduct by making it more difficult to commit the crime rather than through the threat of criminal punishment. Is this a more promising way to deter Internet gambling than through criminal prosecutions?

3.   *Criminal law without (much) enforcement.* If the federal government and state and local governments cannot enact an effective ban on Internet gambling, what should they do? Is there value to having a law on the books even if many violate that law? If state gambling laws are ineffective, why do all fifty states prohibit Internet gambling?

The following case involves one of the few prosecutions for operating an Internet gambling operation.

UNITED STATES V. COHEN

United States Court of Appeals for the Second Circuit, 2001.
260 F.3d 68.

KEENAN, DISTRICT JUDGE.

In 1996, the Defendant, Jay Cohen was young, bright, and enjoyed a lucrative position at Group One, a San Francisco firm that traded in options and derivatives. That was not all to last, for by 1996 the Internet revolution was in the speed lane. Inspired by the new technology and its potential, Cohen decided to pursue the dream of owning his own e-business. By year's end he had left his job at Group One, moved to the Caribbean island of Antigua, and had become a bookmaker.

Cohen, as President, and his partners, all American citizens, dubbed their new venture the World Sports Exchange ("WSE"). WSE's sole business involved bookmaking on American sports events, and was purportedly patterned after New York's Off-Track Betting Corporation. WSE targeted customers in the United States, advertising its business throughout America by radio, newspaper, and television. Its advertisements invited customers to bet with WSE either by toll-free telephone or by Internet.

WSE operated an "account-wagering" system. It required that its new customers first open an account with WSE and wire at least $300 into that account in Antigua. A customer seeking to bet would then contact WSE either by telephone or Internet to request a particular bet. WSE would issue an immediate, automatic acceptance and confirmation of that bet, and would maintain the bet from that customer's account.

In one fifteen-month period, WSE collected approximately $5.3 million in funds wired from customers in the United States. In addition, WSE would typically retain a "vig" or commission of 10% on each bet. Cohen boasted that in its first year of operation, WSE had already attracted nearly 1,600 customers. By November 1998, WSE had received 60,000 phone calls from customers in the United States, including over 6,100 from New York.

In the course of an FBI investigation of offshore bookmakers, FBI agents in New York contacted WSE by telephone and Internet numerous times between October 1997 and March 1998 to open accounts and place bets. Cohen was arrested in March 1998 under an eight-count indictment charging him with conspiracy and substantive offenses in violation of 18 U.S.C. § 1084. That statute reads as follows:

(a) Whoever being engaged in the business of betting or wagering knowingly uses a wire communication facility for the transmission in interstate or foreign commerce of bets or wagers or information assisting in the placing of bets or wagers on any sporting event or contest, or for the transmission of a wire communication which entitles the recipient to receive money or credit as a result of bets or wagers, or for information assisting in the placing of bets or wagers, shall be fined under this title or imprisoned not more than two years, or both.

(b) Nothing in this section shall be construed to prevent the transmission in interstate or foreign commerce of information for use in news reporting of sporting events or contests, or for the transmission of information assisting in the placing of bets or wagers on a sporting event or contest from a State or foreign country where betting on that sporting event or contest is legal into a State or foreign country in which such betting is legal.

See § 1084(a)–(b). In the conspiracy count (Count One) and in five of the seven substantive counts (Counts Three through Six, and Eight), Cohen was charged with violating all three prohibitive clauses of § 1084(a)(1) transmission in interstate or foreign commerce of bets or wagers, (2) transmission of a wire communication which entitles the recipient to receive money or credit as a result of bets or wagers, (3) information assisting in the placement of bets or wagers). In two counts, Counts Two and Seven, he was charged only with transmitting "information assisting in the placing of bets or wagers."

Cohen was convicted on all eight counts on February 28, 2000 after a ten-day jury trial before Judge Thomas P. Griesa. The jury found in special interrogatories that Cohen had violated all three prohibitive clauses of § 1084(a) with respect to the five counts in which those violations were charged. Judge Griesa sentenced Cohen on August 10, 2000 to a term of twenty-one months' imprisonment. He has remained on bail pending the outcome of this appeal.

Cohen appeals the district court for instructing the jury to disregard the safe-harbor provision contained in § 1084(b). That subsection provides a safe harbor for transmissions that occur under both of the following two conditions: (1) betting is legal in both the place of origin and the destination of the transmission; and (2) the transmission is limited to mere information that assists in the placing of bets, as opposed to including the bets themselves. *See* § 1084(b).

The district court ruled as a matter of law that the safe-harbor provision did not apply because neither of the two conditions existed in the case of WSE's transmissions. Cohen disputes that ruling and argues that both conditions did, in fact, exist. He argues that betting is not only legal in Antigua, it is also "legal" in New York for the purposes of § 1084. He also argues that all of WSE's transmissions were limited to mere information assisting in the placing of bets. We agree with the district court's rulings on both issues.

A.   "Legal" Betting

There can be no dispute that betting is illegal in New York. New York has expressly prohibited betting in both its Constitution, *see* N.Y. Const. art. I, § 9 ("no . . . bookmaking, or any other kind of gambling [with certain exceptions pertaining to lotteries and horseracing] shall hereafter be authorized or allowed within this state"), and its General Obligations Law, *see* N.Y. Gen. Oblig. L. § 5–401 ("All wagers, bets or stakes, made to depend on any race, or upon any gaming by lot or chance, or upon any lot, chance, casualty, or unknown or contingent event whatever, shall be unlawful"). Nevertheless, Cohen argues that Congress intended for the safe-harbor provision in § 1084(b) to exclude only those transmissions sent to or from jurisdictions in which betting was a crime. Cohen concludes that because the placing of bets is not a crime in New York, it is "legal" for the purposes of § 1084(b).

By its plain terms, the safe-harbor provision requires that betting be "legal," *i.e.,* permitted by law, in both jurisdictions. *See* § 1084(b); *see also* Black's Law Dictionary 902 (7th ed. 1999); Webster's 3d New Int'l Dictionary 1290 (1993). The plain meaning of a statute should be conclusive, except in the rare cases in which the literal application of a statute will produce a result demonstrably at odds with the intentions of its drafters. This is not the rare case.

Although, as Cohen notes, the First Circuit has stated that Congress "did not intend for § 1084 to criminalize acts that neither the affected states nor Congress itself deemed criminal in nature," it did not do so in the context of a § 1084 prosecution. *See Sterling Suffolk Racecourse Ltd. P'ship v. Burrillville Racing Ass'n,* 989 F.2d 1266, 1273 (1st Cir. 1993). Instead, that case involved a private bid for an injunction under RICO and the Interstate Horseracing Act ("IHA"). It does not stand for the proposition that § 1084 permits betting that is illegal as long as it is not criminal.

In *Sterling,* the defendant was an OTB office in Rhode Island that accepted bets on horse races from distant tracks and broadcasted the races. The office typically obtained the various consents required under the IHA, *i.e.,* from the host track, the host racing commission, and its own racing commission. However, it would often neglect to secure the consent of the plaintiff, a live horse-racing track located within the statutory sixty-mile radius from the OTB office. The plaintiff sought an injunction against the OTB office under RICO, alleging that it was engaged in a pattern of racketeering activity by violating § 1084 through its noncompliance with the IHA.

The *Sterling* court affirmed the district court's denial of the RICO injunction. It noted first that because the OTB office's business was legitimate under all applicable state laws, it fell under the safe-harbor provision in § 1084(b). Furthermore, the court held that in enacting the IHA, Congress had only created a private right of action for damages on the part of certain parties; it did not intend for any Government enforcement of the IHA. Consequently, the plaintiff could not use the IHA together with § 1084 to transform an otherwise legal OTB business into a criminal racketeering enterprise.

Neither *Sterling* nor the legislative history behind § 1084 demonstrates that Congress intended for § 1084(b) to mean anything other than what it says. Betting is illegal in New York, and thus the safe-harbor provision in § 1084(b) cannot not apply in Cohen's case as a matter of law. As a result, the district court was not in error when it instructed the jury to disregard that provision.

B.   Transmission of a Bet, Per Se

Cohen appeals the district court's instructions to the jury regarding what constitutes a bet *per se*. Cohen argues that under WSE's account-wagering system, the transmissions between WSE and its customers contained only information that enabled WSE itself to place bets entirely from customer accounts located in Antigua. He argues that this fact was precluded by the district court's instructions. We find no error in those instructions.

Judge Griesa repeatedly charged the jury as follows:

If there was a telephone call or an Internet transmission between New York and [WSE] in Antigua, and if a person in New York said or signaled that he or she wanted to place a specified bet, and if a person on an Internet device or a telephone said or signaled that the bet was accepted, this was the transmission of a bet within the meaning of Section 1084. Congress clearly did not intend to have this statute be made inapplicable because the party in a foreign gambling business deemed or construed the transmission as only starting with an employee in an Internet mechanism located on the premises in the foreign country.

Jury instructions are not improper simply because they resemble the conduct alleged to have occurred in a given case; nor were they improper in this case. It was the Government's burden in this case to prove that someone in New York signaled an offer to place a particular bet and that someone at WSE signaled an acceptance of that offer. The jury concluded that the Government had carried that burden.

Most of the cases that Cohen cites in support of the proposition that WSE did not transmit any bets involved problems pertaining either to proof of the acceptance of transmitted bets, or to proof of the locus of a betting business for taxation purposes.

No such problems existed in this case. This case was never about taxation, and there can be no dispute regarding WSE's acceptance of customers' bet requests. For example, a March 18, 1998 conversation between Spencer Hanson, a WSE employee, and a New York-based undercover FBI agent occurred as follows:

Agent: Can I place a bet right now?

Hanson: You can place a bet right now.

Agent: Alright, can you give me the line on the um Penn State/ Georgia Tech game, it's the NIT Third Round game tonight.

Hanson: It's Georgia Tech minus 7 1/2, total is 147.

Agent: Georgia Tech minus 7 1/2, umm I wanna take Georgia Tech. Can I take 'em for 50?

Hanson: Sure.

WSE could only book the bets that its customers requested and authorized it to book. By making those requests and having them accepted, WSE's customers were placing bets. So long as the customers' accounts were in good standing, WSE accepted those bets as a matter of course.

Moreover, the issue is immaterial in light of the fact that betting is illegal in New York. Section 1084(a) prohibits the transmission of information assisting in the placing of bets as well as the transmission of bets themselves. This issue, therefore, pertains only to the applicability of § 1084(b)'s safe-harbor provision. As we have noted, that safe harbor excludes not only the transmission of bets, but also the transmission of betting information to or from a jurisdiction in which betting is illegal. As a result, that provision is inapplicable here even if WSE had only ever transmitted betting information.

NOTES AND QUESTIONS

1. *The Wire Act is limited to sports-related betting.* It is not clear from the text of the Wire Act whether it applies only to sports-related gambling or if it also extends to non-sports gambling such as online casinos. The statutory text covers "bets or wagers or information assisting in the placing of bets or wagers on any sporting event or contest, or . . . the transmission of a wire communication which entitles the recipient to receive money or credit as a result of bets or wagers, or . . . information assisting in the placing of bets or wagers" 18 U.S.C. § 1084(a). Should the limitation "on any sporting event or contest" be read to apply to all of the clauses above, or only to the first clause?

In New Hampshire Lottery Commission v. Rosen, 986 F.3d 38 (1st Cir. 2021), the First Circuit ruled that the Wire Act is limited to bets or wagers on sporting events or contests. In so holding, the court rejected the government's view that the Wire Act applies to all forms of betting over wires:

> We find the text of §1084 not entirely clear on the matter at hand, and we find that the government's resolution of the Wire Act's ambiguity would lead to odd and seemingly inexplicable results.

> The legislative history provides further support for our judgment that Congress likely did not intend the strange results inherent in the government's reading. In fact, the legislative history contains strong indications that Congress did indeed train its efforts solely on sports gambling. The statute as originally presented to Congress plainly aimed only at sports gambling. The language then contained only one clause, and it used commas to clearly indicate its focus on sports gambling. *See* S. 1656, 87th Cong. § 2 (1961) ("the transmission in interstate or foreign commerce of bets or wagers, or information assisting in the placing of bets or wagers, on any sporting event or contest"). The government argues that Congress broadened its aim beyond sports gambling when the original draft was amended, most

particularly when the commas bracketing the words "or information assisting in the placing of bets or wages" disappeared. But as the district court explained, the absence of both commas merely created an ambiguity. The Senate report describing the amendments offered no hint that a major change was made or intended. *See* S. Rep. No. 87–588, at 1–2S. Rep. No. 87–588, at 1–2 (1961). And there is nothing in any of the committee reports to suggest any reason at all for the inconsistent scope of the prohibitions that the government's present position would require us to assume.

The text of the Wire Act is not so clear as to dictate in favor of either party's view. The government's reading of the statute, however, would most certainly create an odd and unharmonious piece of criminal legislation.

Id. at 60–61.

2.　*Engaged in the business of betting or wagering.* The Wire Act applies only to those "engaged in the business of betting or wagering." What does that mean? Case law indicates that the phrase is designed to refer to bookmakers, also known as "bookies." *See, e.g.,* United States v. Tomeo, 459 F.2d 445, 447 (10th Cir. 1972). It can also refer to those who have a business relationship with bookmakers. For example, in United States v. Scavo, 593 F.2d 837 (8th Cir. 1979), the defendant established a working relationship with Dwight Mezo, who operated a substantial bookmaking business in the Minneapolis area. The defendant, Scavo, then a resident of Las Vegas, Nevada, provided Mezo with "line" information. Line information refers to the odds or point spread established for various sporting events. The Eighth Circuit concluded that this was sufficient to make Scavo one who was "engaged in the business of betting or wagering":

> [The Wire Act] is not limited to persons who are exclusively engaged in the business of betting or wagering and the statute does not distinguish between persons engaged in such business on their own behalf and those engaged in the business on behalf of others.

> Although we reject appellant's blanket assertion that suppliers of line information are outside the scope of § 1084(a), we must nevertheless determine whether the government introduced evidence sufficient to show that appellant was "engaged in the business of betting and wagering." At trial, the government proceeded on the theory that appellant was part of Mezo's bookmaking business and on this aspect of the case the authorities relied upon by appellant are relevant to a prosecution under § 1084(a). They are not controlling, however, because the evidence adduced showed more than a mere occasional exchange of line information between appellant and Mezo.

> Viewed in the light most favorable to the government, the evidence showed that appellant furnished line information to Mezo on a regular basis; that Mezo relied on this information; that some sort of

financial arrangement existed between appellant and Mezo; that appellant was fully aware of Mezo's bookmaking operation; and that accurate and up-to-date line information is of critical importance to any bookmaking operation.

Id. at 841–42.

3. *Other federal statutes.* The Wire Act is not the only federal criminal law that regulates gambling. In United States v. Gotti, 459 F.3d 296 (2d Cir. 2006), a defendant named Bondi was charged with gambling offenses under 18 U.S.C. § 1955 for running a set of computer poker machines. 18 U.S.C. § 1955 provides for criminal punishment of "whoever conducts, finances, manages, supervises, directs, or owns all or part of an illegal gambling business." The question in *Gotti* was whether the poker machines constituted an illegal gambling business. New York law prohibited gambling, and defined gambling in relevant part as the staking or risking of "something of value upon the outcome of a contest of chance." N.Y. Penal Law § 225.00(2). A "contest of chance" was in turn defined as a game "in which the outcome depends in a material degree upon an element of chance, notwithstanding that the skill of the contestants may also be a factor therein." N.Y. Penal Law § 225.00(1). Bondi argued that the poker machines were not illegal because poker is a game of skill rather than a contest of chance. The Second Circuit disagreed:

> As to Bondi's argument that the games were games of skill rather than chance, he fails to recognize that a "contest of chance" encompasses games in which the skill of the contestants may play a role, as long as the outcome depends in a material degree on chance. Bondi concedes that the games in question had the theme of poker, and he has not contended in his brief that chance does not play a material role in the outcome of a poker game.

Id. at 342.

2. OBSCENITY

State and federal law has long punished the distribution and display of obscene materials with the goal of maintaining moral order. To oversimplify a very complex history, the thinking has been that there are some types of pornography and other types of displays and images that have no redeeming social value but that can corrupt and coarsen the moral fabric of society. To protect that social order and express society's disgust for the corrupting materials, the law prohibits the display and distribution of obscene materials.

Does obscenity law have a place in the Internet age? And if so, what should that place be? To understand the current state of the law, it is necessary to look at the Supreme Court decisions that have cut back on the definition of obscenity and the government's power to prosecute obscenity-related crimes. The starting point is Roth v. United States, 354 U.S. 476 (1957), an opinion by Justice Brennan that held that obscenity is categorically beyond First Amendment protection. Under *Roth*, the key question is defining the scope of what can be labeled "obscene" under the First Amendment. The definition of obscenity becomes a constitutional question for the Supreme Court; if an item falls within the definition of obscenity, the First Amendment does not apply. Over time, the Supreme Court has used a variety of different definitions to describe obscene materials. The present definition was announced in the following case.

MILLER V. CALIFORNIA
Supreme Court of the United States, 1973.
413 U.S. 15.

MR. CHIEF JUSTICE BURGER delivered the opinion of the Court.

This is one of a group of 'obscenity-pornography' cases being reviewed by the Court in a re-examination of standards enunciated in earlier cases involving what Mr. Justice Harlan called 'the intractable obscenity problem.'

Appellant conducted a mass mailing campaign to advertise the sale of illustrated books, euphemistically called 'adult' material. After a jury trial, he was convicted of violating California Penal Code § 311.2(a), a misdemeanor, by knowingly distributing obscene matter, and the Appellate Department, Superior Court of California, County of Orange, summarily affirmed the judgment without opinion. Appellant's conviction was specifically based on his conduct in causing five unsolicited advertising brochures to be sent through the mail in an envelope addressed to a restaurant in Newport Beach, California. The envelope was opened by the manager of the restaurant and his mother. They had not requested the brochures; they complained to the police.

The brochures advertise four books entitled 'Intercourse,' 'Man-Woman,' 'Sex Orgies Illustrated,' and 'An Illustrated History of Pornography,' and a film entitled 'Marital Intercourse.' While the brochures contain some descriptive printed material, primarily they consist of pictures and drawings very explicitly depicting men and women in groups of two or more engaging in a variety of sexual activities, with genitals often prominently displayed.

I

This case involves the application of a State's criminal obscenity statute to a situation in which sexually explicit materials have been thrust by aggressive sales action upon unwilling recipients who had in no way indicated any desire to receive such materials. This Court has recognized that the States have a legitimate interest in prohibiting dissemination or exhibition of obscene material when the mode of dissemination carries with it a significant danger of offending the sensibilities of unwilling recipients or of exposure to juveniles. It is in this context that we are called on to define the standards which must be used to identify obscene material that a State may regulate without infringing on the First Amendment as applicable to the States through the Fourteenth Amendment.

Since the Court now undertakes to formulate standards more concrete than those in the past, it is useful for us to focus on two of the landmark cases in the somewhat tortured history of the Court's obscenity decisions. In *Roth v. United States*, 354 U.S. 476 (1957), the Court sustained a conviction under a federal statute punishing the mailing of 'obscene, lewd, lascivious or filthy' materials. The key to that holding was the Court's rejection of the claim that obscene materials were protected by the First Amendment. Five Justices joined in the opinion stating:

> 'All ideas having even the slightest redeeming social importance— unorthodox ideas, controversial ideas, even ideas hateful to the prevailing climate of opinion—have the full protection of the (First Amendment) guaranties, unless excludable because they encroach upon the limited area of more important interests. But implicit in the history of the First Amendment is the rejection of obscenity as utterly without redeeming social importance. . . This is the same judgment expressed by this Court in Chaplinsky v. New Hampshire, 315 U.S. 568, 571–572:

> '. . . There are certain well-defined and narrowly limited classes of speech, the prevention and punishment of which have never been thought to raise any Constitutional problem. These include the lewd and obscene. *It has been well observed that such utterances are no essential part of any exposition of ideas, and are of such slight social value as a step to truth that any benefit that may be derived from them is clearly outweighed by the social interest in order and morality. . .'* (Emphasis by Court in *Roth* opinion.)

> 'We hold that obscenity is not within the area of constitutionally protected speech or press.'

Nine years later, in *Memoirs v. Massachusetts*, 383 U.S. 413 (1966), the Court veered sharply away from the *Roth* concept and, with only three Justices in the plurality opinion, articulated a new test of obscenity. The plurality held that under the *Roth* definition

> 'as elaborated in subsequent cases, three elements must coalesce: it must be established that (a) the dominant theme of the material taken as a whole appeals to a prurient interest in sex; (b) the material is patently offensive because if affronts contemporary community standards relating to the description or representation of sexual matters; and (c) the material is utterly without redeeming social value.'

While *Roth* presumed 'obscenity' to be 'utterly without redeeming social importance,' *Memoirs* required that to prove obscenity it must be affirmatively established that the material is 'utterly without redeeming social value.' Thus, even as they repeated the words of *Roth*, the *Memoirs* plurality produced a drastically altered test that called on the prosecution to prove a negative, i.e., that the material was 'utterly without redeeming social value'—a burden virtually impossible to discharge under our criminal standards of proof. Such considerations caused Mr. Justice Harlan to wonder if the 'utterly without redeeming social value' test had any meaning at all.

Apart from the initial formulation in the *Roth* case, no majority of the Court has at any given time been able to agree on a standard to determine what constitutes obscene, pornographic material subject to regulation under the States' police power. This is not remarkable, for in the area of freedom of speech and press the courts must always remain sensitive to any infringement on genuinely serious literary, artistic, political, or scientific expression. This is an area in which there are few eternal verities.

II

This much has been categorically settled by the Court, that obscene material is unprotected by the First Amendment. We acknowledge, however, the inherent dangers of undertaking to regulate any form of expression. State statutes designed to regulate obscene materials must be carefully limited. As a result, we now confine the permissible scope of such regulation to works which depict or describe sexual conduct. That conduct must be specifically defined by the applicable state law, as written or authoritatively construed. A state offense must also be limited to works which, taken as a whole, appeal to the prurient interest in sex, which portray sexual conduct in a patently offensive way, and which, taken as a whole, do not have serious literary, artistic, political, or scientific value.

The basic guidelines for the trier of fact must be: (a) whether 'the average person, applying contemporary community standards' would find that the work, taken as a whole, appeals to the prurient interest; (b) whether the work depicts or describes, in a patently offensive way, sexual conduct specifically defined by the applicable state law; and (c) whether the work, taken as a whole, lacks serious literary, artistic, political, or scientific value. We do not adopt as a constitutional standard the 'utterly without redeeming social value' test of *Memoirs v. Massachusetts*, 383 U.S. at 419; that concept has never commanded the adherence of more than three Justices at one time. If a state law that regulates obscene material is thus limited, as written or construed, the First Amendment values applicable to the States through the Fourteenth Amendment are adequately protected by the ultimate power of appellate courts to conduct an independent review of constitutional claims when necessary.

We emphasize that it is not our function to propose regulatory schemes for the States. That must await their concrete legislative efforts. It is possible, however, to give a few plain examples of what a state statute could define for regulation under part (b) of the standard announced in this opinion, supra:

(a) Patently offensive representations or descriptions of ultimate sexual acts, normal or perverted, actual or simulated.

(b) Patently offensive representation or descriptions of masturbation, excretory functions, and lewd exhibition of the genitals.

Sex and nudity may not be exploited without limit by films or pictures exhibited or sold in places of public accommodation any more than live sex and nudity can be exhibited or sold without limit in such public places. At a minimum, prurient, patently offensive depiction or description of sexual conduct must have serious literary, artistic, political, or scientific value to merit First Amendment protection. For example, medical books for the education of physicians and related personnel necessarily use graphic illustrations and descriptions of human anatomy. In resolving the inevitably sensitive questions of fact and law, we must continue to rely on the jury system, accompanied by the safeguards that judges, rules of evidence, presumption of innocence, and other protective features provide, as we do with rape, murder, and a host of other offenses against society and its individual members.

Under the holdings announced today, no one will be subject to prosecution for the sale or exposure of obscene materials unless these materials depict or describe patently offensive 'hard core' sexual conduct specifically defined by the regulating state law, as written or construed. We are satisfied that these specific prerequisites will provide fair notice to a dealer in such materials that his public and commercial activities may bring prosecution. If the inability to define regulated materials with ultimate, god-like precision altogether removes the power of the States or the Congress to regulate, then 'hard core' pornography may be exposed without limit to the juvenile, the passerby, and the consenting adult alike, as, indeed, Mr. Justice Douglas contends. In this belief, however, Mr. Justice Douglas now stands alone.

III

Under a National Constitution, fundamental First Amendment limitations on the powers of the States do not vary from community to community, but this does not mean that there are, or should or can be, fixed, uniform national standards of precisely what appeals to the 'prurient interest' or is 'patently offensive.' These are essentially questions of fact, and our Nation is simply too big and too diverse for this Court to reasonably expect that such standards could be articulated for all 50 States in a single formulation, even assuming the prerequisite consensus exists. When triers of fact are asked to decide whether 'the average person, applying contemporary community standards' would consider certain materials 'prurient,' it would be unrealistic to require that the answer be based on some abstract formulation. The adversary system, with lay jurors as the usual ultimate factfinders in criminal prosecutions, has historically permitted triers of fact to draw on the standards of their community, guided always by limiting instructions on the law. To require a State to structure obscenity proceedings around evidence of a national 'community standard' would be an exercise in futility.

As noted before, this case was tried on the theory that the California obscenity statute sought to incorporate the tripartite test of *Memoirs*. This, a 'national' standard of First Amendment protection enumerated by a plurality of this Court, was correctly regarded at the time of trial as limiting state prosecution under the controlling case law. The jury, however, was explicitly instructed that, in determining whether the 'dominant theme of the material as a whole . . . appeals to the prurient interest' and in determining whether the material 'goes substantially beyond customary limits of candor and affronts contemporary community standards of decency,' it was to apply 'contemporary community standards of the State of California.'

We conclude that neither the State's alleged failure to offer evidence of 'national standards,' nor the trial court's charge that the jury consider state community standards, were constitutional errors. Nothing in the First Amendment requires that a jury must consider hypothetical and unascertainable 'national standards' when attempting to determine whether certain materials are obscene as a matter of fact.

It is neither realistic nor constitutionally sound to read the First Amendment as requiring that the people of Maine or Mississippi accept public depiction of conduct found tolerable in Las Vegas, or New York City. People in different States vary in their tastes and attitudes, and this diversity is not to be strangled by the absolutism of imposed uniformity. The primary concern with requiring a jury to apply the standard of 'the average person, applying contemporary community standards' is to be certain that, so far as material is not aimed at a deviant group, it will be judged by its impact on an average person, rather than a particularly susceptible or sensitive person—or indeed a totally insensitive one. We hold that the requirement that the jury evaluate the materials with reference to 'contemporary standards of the State of California' serves this protective purpose and is constitutionally adequate.

IV

The dissenting Justices sound the alarm of repression. But, in our view, to equate the free and robust exchange of ideas and political debate with commercial exploitation of obscene material demeans the grand conception of the First Amendment and its high purposes in the historic struggle for freedom. It is a misuse of the great guarantees of free speech and free press. The First Amendment protects works which, taken as a whole, have serious literary, artistic, political, or scientific value, regardless of whether the government or a majority of the people approve of the ideas these works represent. The protection given speech and press was fashioned to assure unfettered interchange of ideas for the bringing about of political and social changes desired by the people, but the public portrayal of hard-core sexual conduct for its own sake, and for the ensuing commercial gain, is a different matter.

MR. JUSTICE DOUGLAS, dissenting.

Today we leave open the way for California to send a man to prison for distributing brochures that advertise books and a movie under freshly written standards defining obscenity which until today's decision were never the part of any law.

Today the Court retreats from the earlier formulations of the constitutional test and undertakes to make new definitions. This effort, like the earlier ones, is earnest and well intentioned. The difficulty is that we do not deal with constitutional terms, since 'obscenity' is not mentioned in the Constitution or Bill of Rights. And the First Amendment makes no such exception from 'the press' which it undertakes to protect nor, as I have said on other occasions, is an exception necessarily implied, for there was no recognized exception to the free press at the time the Bill of Rights was adopted which treated 'obscene' publications differently from other types of papers, magazines, and books. So there are no constitutional guidelines for deciding what is and what is not 'obscene.' The Court is at large because we deal with tastes and standards of literature. What shocks me may be sustenance for my neighbor. What causes one person to boil up in rage over one pamphlet or movie may reflect only his neurosis, not shared by others. We deal here with a regime of censorship which, if adopted, should be done by constitutional amendment after full debate by the people.

While the right to know is the corollary of the right to speak or publish, no one can be forced by government to listen to disclosure that he finds offensive. No one is being compelled to look or to listen. Those who enter newsstands or bookstalls may be offended by what they see. But they are not compelled by the State to frequent those places; and it is only state or governmental action against which the First Amendment, applicable to the States by virtue of the Fourteenth, raises a ban.

The idea that the First Amendment permits government to ban publications that are 'offensive' to some people puts an ominous gloss on freedom of the press. That test would make it possible to ban any paper or any journal or magazine in some benighted place. The First Amendment was designed to invite dispute, to induce a condition of unrest, to create dissatisfaction with conditions as they are, and even to stir people to anger. The idea that the First Amendment permits punishment for ideas that are 'offensive' to the particular judge or jury sitting in judgment is astounding. No greater leveler of speech or literature has ever been designed. To give the power to the censor, as we do today, is to make a sharp and radical break with the traditions of a free society.

NOTES AND QUESTIONS

1.   *Should the Supreme Court revisit Miller v. California?* At the time *Miller* was decided, an adult could purchase pornography by buying a copy of *Playboy* at a local magazine store, but access to more hard-core pornography was often more difficult. The *Miller* test seems to target hard-core pornography that was relatively rare and difficult to find at the time. Today, however, anyone can access hard-core pornography via the Internet. Does the *Miller* test work in a world in which hard core pornography is readily available over the Internet? Has the Internet rendered *Miller* obsolete? Alternatively, does the ready availability of materials that would seem to be prohibited under the *Miller* test make obscenity prosecutions more important, not less?

2.   *Do "community standards" make sense today?* The *Miller* obscenity standard assumes the existence of distinct local community standards. Residents of New York City will have one standard, residents of Utah will have another, and residents of Boston will have a third. The local standard test used in *Miller* is designed to ensure that persons in New York are not judged by the standards of Utah. Is this assumption sensible in an age when many individuals derive their standards from peers and the Internet? What effect has the Internet had on "community" standards? Has the global Internet reduced the local variation in community standards? And how could this be measured?

In a concurring opinion in Ashcroft v. American Civil Liberties Union, 535 U.S. 564, 590–91 (2002), Justice Breyer argued that Congress's use of the phrase "community standards" in the context of the Child Online Protection Act should be read to mean a national standard rather than a community standard. He offered the following argument in support of his approach:

> This view of the statute avoids the need to examine the serious First Amendment problem that would otherwise exist. To read the statute as adopting the community standards of every locality in the United States would provide the most puritan of communities with a heckler's Internet veto affecting the rest of the Nation. The technical difficulties associated with efforts to confine Internet material to particular geographic areas make the problem particularly serious. And these special difficulties also potentially weaken the authority of prior cases in which they were not present. A nationally uniform adult-based standard * * * significantly alleviates any special need for First Amendment protection. Of course some regional variation

may remain, but any such variations are inherent in a system that draws jurors from a local geographic area and they are not, from the perspective of the First Amendment, problematic.

Does a "community standard" based on the concept of a physical-world community make sense if allegedly obscene images are obtained and distributed online?

3.   *Stanley v. Georgia.* The Supreme Court held that the government cannot criminalize mere private possession of obscenity in a pre-*Miller* case, Stanley v. Georgia, 394 U.S. 557 (1969). *Stanley* reasoned that the state had no legitimate interest in controlling what people read in the confines of their own homes. Consider this excerpt from the Court's opinion:

> Whatever may be the justifications for other statutes regulating obscenity, we do not think they reach into the privacy of one's own home. If the First Amendment means anything, it means that a State has no business telling a man, sitting alone in his own house, what books he may read or what films he may watch. Our whole constitutional heritage rebels at the thought of giving government the power to control men's minds.

> And yet, in the face of these traditional notions of individual liberty, Georgia asserts the right to protect the individual's mind from the effects of obscenity. We are not certain that this argument amounts to anything more than the assertion that the State has the right to control the moral content of a person's thoughts. To some, this may be a noble purpose, but it is wholly inconsistent with the philosophy of the First Amendment. Nor is it relevant that obscene materials in general, or the particular films before the Court, are arguably devoid of any ideological content. The line between the transmission of ideas and mere entertainment is much too elusive for this Court to draw, if indeed such a line can be drawn at all. Whatever the power of the state to control public dissemination of ideas inimical to the public morality, it cannot constitutionally premise legislation on the desirability of controlling a person's private thoughts.

> Perhaps recognizing this, Georgia asserts that exposure to obscene materials may lead to deviant sexual behavior or crimes of sexual violence. There appears to be little empirical basis for that assertion. But more important, if the State is only concerned about printed or filmed materials inducing antisocial conduct, we believe that in the context of private consumption of ideas and information we should adhere to the view that 'among free men, the deterrents ordinarily to be applied to prevent crime are education and punishment for violations of the law.' Given the present state of knowledge, the State may no more prohibit mere possession of obscene matter on the ground that it may lead to antisocial conduct than it may prohibit possession of chemistry books on the ground that they may lead to the manufacture of homemade spirits.

Finally, we are faced with the argument that prohibition of possession of obscene materials is a necessary incident to statutory schemes prohibiting distribution. That argument is based on alleged difficulties of proving an intent to distribute or in producing evidence of actual distribution. We are not convinced that such difficulties exist, but even if they did we do not think that they would justify infringement of the individual's right to read or observe what he pleases. Because that right is so fundamental to our scheme of individual liberty, its restriction may not be justified by the need to ease the administration of otherwise valid criminal laws.

Id. at 565–67. The Supreme Court has taken a very different path in the context of criminal laws that prohibit the *distribution* of obscene materials. In United States v. Reidel, 402 U.S. 351 (1971), decided soon after *Stanley*, the Court reaffirmed pre-*Stanley* law that the government could criminalize distributing obscene materials. The Court distinguished *Stanley* in the following way:

The right *Stanley* asserted was "the right to read or observe what he pleases—the right to satisfy his intellectual and emotional needs in the privacy of his own home." The Court's response was that "a State has no business telling a man, sitting alone in his own house, what books he may read or what films he may watch. Our whole constitutional heritage rebels at the thought of giving government the power to control men's minds." The focus of this language was on freedom of mind and thought and on the privacy of one's home. It does not require that we fashion or recognize a constitutional right in people like Reidel to distribute or sell obscene materials. The personal constitutional rights of those like Stanley to possess and read obscenity in their homes and their freedom of mind and thought do not depend on whether the materials are obscene or whether obscenity is constitutionally protected. Their rights to have and view that material in private are independently saved by the Constitution.

Reidel is in a wholly different position. He has no complaints about governmental violations of his private thoughts or fantasies, but stands squarely on a claimed First Amendment right to do business in obscenity and use the mails in the process. But Roth v. United States, 354 U.S. 476 (1957), has squarely placed obscenity and its distribution outside the reach of the First Amendment and they remain there today. *Stanley* did not overrule *Roth* and we decline to do so now.

402 U.S. at 355–56.

Is this rationale persuasive? Does it make sense for distribution to be a crime if the possession that follows from the distribution is constitutionally protected? One possible explanation for this otherwise puzzling result is that it channels law enforcement efforts by allowing the government to prosecute distributors but not users. Is that a desirable result?

4.   *The impact of Lawrence v. Texas.* In Lawrence v. Texas, 539 U.S. 558 (2003), the Supreme Court invalidated a Texas statute that criminalized consensual sodomy on the ground that it was inconsistent with the Due Process clause. In its briefs to the Court, Texas had attempted to justify the statute under rational basis scrutiny as an effort to advance and recognize societal mores relating to sexuality and decency. In ruling against Texas, Justice Kennedy's opinion for the Court agreed with Justice Stevens' dissenting position in Bowers v. Hardwick, 478 U.S. 186 (1986), that "the fact that the governing majority in a State has traditionally viewed a particular practice as immoral is not a sufficient reason for upholding a law prohibiting the practice." Writing in dissent in *Lawrence*, Justice Scalia argued that the Court's decision implicitly signaled that other legislation premised on "majoritarian sexual morality," including laws against obscenity, might also be unconstitutional:

> The Texas statute undeniably seeks to further the belief of its citizens that certain forms of sexual behavior are "immoral and unacceptable,"—the same interest furthered by criminal laws against fornication, bigamy, adultery, adult incest, bestiality, and obscenity. *Bowers* held that this *was* a legitimate state interest. The Court today reaches the opposite conclusion. The Texas statute, it says, "furthers *no legitimate state interest* which can justify its intrusion into the personal and private life of the individual." The Court embraces instead Justice Stevens' declaration in his *Bowers* dissent, that "the fact that the governing majority in a State has traditionally viewed a particular practice as immoral is not a sufficient reason for upholding a law prohibiting the practice." This effectively decrees the end of all morals legislation. If, as the Court asserts, the promotion of majoritarian sexual morality is not even a *legitimate* state interest, none of the above-mentioned laws can survive rational-basis review.

Id. at 559 (Scalia, J., dissenting).

Does *Lawrence* compel the invalidation of obscenity laws, effectively overruling United States v. Reidel, 402 U.S. 351 (1971)? In United States v. Extreme Assocs., Inc., 352 F. Supp.2d 578 (W.D. Pa. 2005), a district court concluded that it did:

> It cannot be seriously disputed that, historically, the government's purpose in completely banning the distribution of sexually explicit obscene material, including to consenting adults, was to uphold the community sense of morality. That is, to prevent, to the extent possible, individuals from entertaining lewd or lustful thoughts stimulated by viewing material that appeals to one's prurient interests. Harboring such thoughts, the government deems, is immoral conduct even when done by consenting adults in private.

> After *Lawrence*, however, upholding the public sense of morality is not even a legitimate state interest that can justify infringing one's liberty interest to engage in consensual sexual conduct in private. Therefore, this historically asserted state interest certainly cannot

rise to the level of a compelling interest, as is required under the strict scrutiny test.

Id. at 592–93.

The Third Circuit reversed, however, on the ground that the district had overstepped its bounds. Under established Supreme Court precedent, it is up to the Supreme Court to overturn its decisions; a lower court cannot rule that an older Supreme Court decision on the books is no longer in effect because it is inconsistent with the reasoning of more recent Supreme Court decisions. As a result, *Reidel* is still good law unless or until the U.S. Supreme Court overturns it. *See* United States v. Extreme Assocs., Inc., 431 F.3d 150 (3d Cir. 2005).

The Third Circuit also rejected the argument that the facts of the Internet compelled a different approach to obscenity:

> Extreme Associates argues that the relevant cases are distinguishable because they were all decided before the advent of the Internet, suggesting that the commercial transportation of obscenity considered by the Court in those cases was of a more public variety than the Internet commerce at issue here. As such, the concern for community decency and order that arose in the other obscenity cases is irrelevant to this prosecution.

> We decline to join appellees in that analytical leap. The mere fact, without more, that the instant prosecution involves Internet transmissions is not enough to render an entire line of Supreme Court decisions inapplicable given their analytical and other factual similarities to this case.

> The [Supreme] Court thus far has not suggested that obscenity law does not apply to the Internet or even that a new analytical path is necessary in Internet cases. If the Supreme Court wishes to treat all Internet obscenity cases as *sui generis* for purposes of federal obscenity law analysis, it has not yet said so, "tacitly" or otherwise.

> The Internet is a channel of commerce covered by the federal statutes regulating the distribution of obscenity. Extreme Associates was indicted for engaging in commercial transactions that its own brief on appeal describes as "Internet commerce." This case cannot be meaningfully distinguished merely because it involves the Internet.

Id. at 160–61.

––––––––––

The federal obscenity statutes are codified at 18 U.S.C. §§ 1460–70. The statutes prohibit a range of offenses, ranging from selling obscene materials on federal land, 18 U.S.C. § 1460, to using a means of interstate commerce to transfer obscene materials to a minor, 18 U.S.C. § 1470. Owing to their pre-*Miller* heritage, the language of these statutes is quite archaic, and much broader than the modern first Amendment would allow. For example, many of the statutes refer to material that is not merely "obscene," but also "lewd, lascivious, or filthy." Only obscene materials can be prohibited under the First Amendment, however, so the statutes can be read as effectively being limited to obscene materials.

In the context of Internet-related crimes, the two key federal obscenity provisions are 18 U.S.C. § 1462 and 18 U.S.C. § 1465. Both sections prohibit a range of activities involving obscene materials that include using an "interactive computer service" to carry, receive, or transport obscene materials in interstate commerce. The phrase "interactive computer service" is defined in 47 U.S.C. § 230(f)(2):

> The term "interactive computer service" means any information service, system, or access software provider that provides or enables computer access by multiple users to a computer server, including specifically a service or system that provides access to the Internet and such systems operated or services offered by libraries or educational institutions.

This broad definition encompasses essentially all use of computer networks and the Internet. *See* Carafano v. Metrosplash.com, Inc., 339 F.3d 1119, 1123 (9th Cir. 2003).

UNITED STATES V. EXTREME ASSOCIATES, INC.

United States District Court for the Western District of Pennsylvania, 2009.
2009 WL 113767.

GARY L. LANCASTER, DISTRICT JUDGE.

This is a criminal prosecution in which the United States has charged defendants with distribution of obscene material via the mails and the Internet. Defendants have filed a motion asking the court to issue a pretrial ruling regarding how the "as a whole" and "community standards" elements of the *Miller* test will be applied in this case.

Defendants have been charged with ten counts of violating the federal obscenity statutes. In particular, defendants have been charged with mailing three video tapes to an undercover United States postal inspector in Pittsburgh and delivering six digital video clips over the Internet to that same undercover postal inspector. The Inspector ordered the video tapes through Extreme Associates' publicly available website and accessed the video clips after purchasing a monthly membership to the members-only section of Extreme Associates' website.

The Supreme Court has established a three part test to be used when determining whether material is legally obscene. Under this test, referred to as "the *Miller* test," material is obscene if:

1.   The average person, applying contemporary community standards, would find that the work, taken as a whole, appeals to the prurient interest;

2.   The average person, applying contemporary community standards, would find that the work depicts or describes sexual conduct in a patently offensive way; and

3.   A reasonable person would find, taking the work as a whole, that it lacks serious literary, artistic, political, or scientific value.

Miller v. California, 413 U.S. 15, 24–25 (1973).

A.   *As a Whole*

Defendants allege that the "as a whole" element of the *Miller* test as applied to the digital video clip charges should be the "entire Extreme Associates Website," including all web pages to which it is linked. Defendants' only support for this position is a concurring opinion authored by Justice Kennedy in the first case challenging the Child Online Protection Act. *Ashcroft v. American Civil Liberties Union,* 535 U.S. 564, 593 (2002). Justice Kennedy's concurrence is not controlling law, nor does it address the exact issue raised in this case.

Instead, we must apply existing obscenity case law regarding the "as a whole" element to these digital video clips. Although this may be unchartered territory, our task is not as difficult as it may appear to be. The "as a whole" element was established in *Roth v. United States,* 354 U.S. 476 (1957), in which the Supreme Court rejected the previously accepted proposition that obscenity could be judged on the basis of an isolated, detached, or separate excerpt from a larger work because it was unconstitutionally restrictive of the freedoms of speech and press.

The Supreme Court more recently reiterated the notion that individual scenes cannot be judged in isolation under the "as a whole" test if they are presented in conjunction with, or as part of, a larger work. *Ashcroft v. Free Speech Coalition,* 535 U.S. 234, 248 (2002) (stating that "where the scene is part of the narrative, the work itself does not for this reason become obscene, even though the scene in isolation might be offensive"). On the other hand, where a person removes passages from other works, and combines them into a new, free-standing compilation, that compilation becomes the new work "as a whole."

Under these standards, we must view the context and manner in which the material has been created, packaged, and presented by the author to the intended audience in order to decide what the work "as a whole" is for purposes of the *Miller* test.

As the government demonstrated at the December 2008 hearing, the digital video clips are presented to the audience as independent videos, complete in and of themselves, and unrelated in content to any other material around them. The charged clips are found on individual fetish web pages within the members-only website. These fetish pages are comprised of numerous individual still pictures, arranged in rows and columns, with a text title below each picture. The text title acts as a link to the digital video clip represented by the still picture appearing above the title. In order to view any particular video clip on the page, the user must click on the title associated with the clip. The clips are related to each other only by general fetish subject matter, and are not presented by defendants as being interconnected to each other, or to any other section of the Extreme Associates website. Nor do defendants indicate to their audience that the clips are part of another, larger work.

As such, regardless of whether the digital video clips are scenes from longer films, given the manner in which the defendants excerpted and posted the clips we find that they are themselves free standing, independent works. Therefore, the work "as a whole" will be each individual digital video clip referenced in the indictment.

B. *Community Standards*

Defendants contend that the applicable community for determining community standards for purposes of this case should be "the World Wide Web," or at least the entire United States. Defendants explicitly acknowledged at oral argument that defining the community in this way would be an "expansion" of existing law, but argued that such an expansion was warranted because "times have changed" due to the advent of the Internet. The Court of Appeals for the Third Circuit has already rejected this exact argument in this case. In its opinion reversing our order dismissing the indictment, the Court of Appeals stated that "the Supreme Court has not suggested that obscenity law does not apply to the Internet or even that a new analytical path is necessary in Internet cases." *United States v. Extreme Associates, Inc., et al.,* 431 F.3d 150, 160–61 (3d Cir. 2005). Under the explicit direction of the Court of Appeals, we decline defendants' invitation to expand existing Supreme Court precedent simply because this case involves the Internet.

However, even were we to entertain defendants' arguments in support of creating new law in this case, we would not find them persuasive under the facts of this case. At its core, defendants' argument is that the Internet is different than any other method of delivering sexually explicit materials because material available on the Internet can be viewed from anywhere in the world, without the publisher knowing where the viewer is located. Defendants contend that it is unconstitutional to hold Internet publishers to differing community standards when they have no control over, or knowledge of, from where their material is being viewed. Thus, defendants advocate the creation of a new World Wide Web, or at least national, community standard for any content provided over the Internet. Alternatively, defendants argue that the place of publication should be used to determine the community standard for Internet content providers because that is the only place that the publisher has knowingly conducted business.

The flaw in defendants' argument is that the government has not charged defendants with violating the obscenity statutes by displaying materials on their publicly available website. Instead, for the video tape counts, the materials were delivered through the mail to a Pittsburgh address. For the digital video clip counts the material was provided to a user who had previously purchased access to the members-only section of the Extreme Associates website, by, among other things, providing defendants with a credit card and a Pittsburgh address. Thus, in both instances, defendants knew where their audience was located, and the basic premise of their argument fails.

Instead, this case falls within the parameters of existing Supreme Court precedent that has rejected the need to create a national community standard for speakers who choose to send their material into many communities, each with differing community standards. As such, as in those cases, the standards of the community from which the jurors are drawn will be used in this case. Therefore, the relevant community for both the video tape charges and the digital video clip charges will be those areas within the jurisdiction of the Pittsburgh Division of the United States District Court for the Western District of Pennsylvania.

NOTES AND QUESTIONS

1.　*Revisiting Miller.* Under the law as articulated in *Extreme Associates*, courts must continue to apply the traditional obscenity test from *Miller v. California* to cases involving Internet obscenity. If the defendants are convicted, they can then argue on appeal there was insufficient evidence to support the verdict under the *Miller* standard. *See, e.g.*, Varkonyi v. State, 276 S.W.3d 27 (Tex. App. El Paso 2008) (denying such a motion). If such arguments are unsuccessful, they can then ask the Supreme Court to review the conviction and reconsider whether the traditional *Miller* test should apply to the Internet. So far, however, the Supreme Court has not taken up the invitation. Should it?

2.　*The Ninth Circuit's national standard for Internet-based obscenity.* In United States v. Kilbride, 584 F.3d 1240 (9th Cir. 2009), the Ninth Circuit concluded that the local community standard must be replaced by a national standard when obscene materials are distributed over the Internet. The Ninth Circuit derived this conclusion from various concurring opinions in Ashcroft v. ACLU, 535 U.S. 564 (2002), including the concurring opinion of Justice Breyer. The shared reasoning of the concurring opinions is that the variation in standards among different localities makes it too difficult for a person disseminating potentially obscene materials to know whether the material would be deemed obscene in the location where the materials are being sent. The Ninth Circuit concluded that in light of the serious First Amendment problems such variation would raise, the court would construe obscenity in the federal obscenity statutes to refer to obscenity as measured by national standards for any obscenity prosecutions involving the Internet:

> A national community standard must be applied in regulating obscene speech on the Internet, including obscenity disseminated via email. The constitutional problems with applying local community standards to regulate Internet obscenity certainly generate grave constitutional doubts as to the use of such standards in applying §§ 1462 and 1465 to Defendants' activities. Furthermore, the Court has never held that a jury may in no case be instructed to apply a national community standard in finding obscenity. To avoid the need to examine the serious First Amendment problem that would otherwise exist, we construe obscenity as regulated by §§ 1462 and 1465 as defined by reference to a national community standard when disseminated via the Internet.

Id. at 1254. *But see* United States v. Little, 365 Fed.Appx. 159, 164 (11th Cir. 2010) ("We decline to follow the reasoning of *Kilbride* in this Circuit. The portions of the *Ashcroft* opinion and concurrences that advocated a national community standard were dicta, not the ruling of the Court.")

Do you agree with the Ninth Circuit? If so, what is the "national community standard" for obscenity?

3.   *United States v. Stagliano.* In 2010, the first obscenity case brought in Washington, DC, in two decades went to trial against defendant John Stagliano and his pornography company Evil Angel Productions. At the end of the government's case, District Judge Richard Leon granted the defense's motion to dismiss the charges on the technical ground that the government had failed to link the defendants to the two DVD videos that formed the basis of the obscenity charges against them. In dismissing the charges, Judge Leon added the following comment:

> "I hope the government will learn a lesson from its experience," Leon said in a rebuke. He cited a string of "difficult, challenging and novel questions" raised in the case concerning decades-old federal obscenity statutes, the Internet, free speech and criminal defendants' rights.

> "I hope that [higher] courts and Congress will give greater guidance to judges in whose courtrooms these cases will be tried," he said.

Spencer S. Hsu, *U.S. District Judge Drops Porn Charges Against Video Producer John A. Stagliano*, Washington Post, July 17, 2010. Stagliano remained defiant, commenting to reporters that "This is bad for my autobiography. . . I was hoping for a better fight than they put on." *Id.*

4.   *Venue in obscenity cases.* Given the role of community standards in obscenity law, the venue of the trial has obvious importance. The venue of the

trial refers to the federal district in which the prosecution is brought. Venue in federal criminal cases is ordinarily governed by 18 U.S.C. § 3237(a):

> Except as otherwise expressly provided by enactment of Congress, any offense against the United States begun in one district and completed in another, or committed in more than one district, may be inquired of and prosecuted in any district in which such offense was begun, continued, or completed.

> Any offense involving the use of the mails, transportation in interstate or foreign commerce, or the importation of an object or person into the United States is a continuing offense and, except as otherwise expressly provided by enactment of Congress, may be inquired of and prosecuted in any district from, through, or into which such commerce, mail matter, or imported object or person moves.

This rule allows the government to set up an undercover investigation in the district of its choice; have the defendant send potentially obscene materials into that district; and then bring the prosecution in that district. *See e.g.,* United States v. Thomas, 74 F.3d 701, 711–12 (6th Cir. 1996).

Is that a fair approach? Does it depend on whether the defendant knew that the item passed through that district? Imagine a person in New York e-mails a pornographic image to another person in San Francisco, and the e-mail just happens to be routed through a server in Utah. No person in Utah ever sees the image. Does § 3237(a) allow an obscenity prosecution in Utah under the community standards of Utah?

5. *Challenging venue through vindictive prosecution claims.* In United States v. Harb, 2009 WL 499467 (D. Utah 2009), a Department of Justice obscenity task force in Washington, DC, was investigating individuals in Ohio who sold pornographic materials. The task force selected Utah as the site of the undercover location and purchased materials that were then sent to Utah for delivery. The defendants were charged with obscenity offenses in Utah, and they moved to dismiss the indictment on grounds of vindictive prosecution. According to the defendants, the government had picked Utah because Utah is known for its strict community standards. The purpose of the investigation, the defendants argued, was to deprive them of their First Amendment rights. The district court disagreed:

> Defendants' main argument is that the choice to order the material into this district and to thereafter prosecute this district shows overreaching and a likelihood of vindictiveness simply because Defendants argue that this district has more restrictive community standards. The Court finds that the Defendants do not establish either actual or likely vindictiveness by arguing or establishing that there are more restrictive community standards in this district than the district where they operate their business. There is no requirement that the government be able to show a parity in the

community standards between the district from which and the district into which the material moved in order to avoid a presumption of vindictiveness. Otherwise, the provision of § 3237(a) allowing these types of continuing offenses to be prosecuted in any district into which the material allegedly moves would be rendered null. It has been long established that the fact that distributors of allegedly obscene materials may be subjected to varying community standards in the various federal judicial districts into which they transmit the materials does not render a federal statute unconstitutional because of the failure of application of uniform national standards of obscenity. This rule cannot be avoided by imposing a parity of community standards limitation on the prosecution's exercise of its prerogative to seek indictments in districts as permitted by § 3237(a).

Id. at *3–*4.

6. *Online obscenity and Internet gambling compared.* In some ways, the regulation of Internet gambling and the regulation of online obscenity raise similar issues. The law has traditionally regulated a transaction that in the past occurred person-to-person, whether by meeting in person, through the mail, or by telephone. Computers and the Internet replace that with a person-to-computer transaction, and the computer need not be in the United States. In some ways, the relevance of the switch in fact patterns is similar. For example, policy arguments for preexisting law rooted in the community impact of the conduct regulated may be less powerful, and policy arguments rooted in the effects of the conduct on the individual in isolation may be strengthened. The law seems harder to enforce, and prosecutions are rare. Given these similarities, do you think the future of the law of Internet gambling and obscenity law will or should be the same? Or do the two present different problems?

7. *Can mere words constitute obscenity?* Courts have held that mere words can be legally obscene. *See* United States v. Whorley, 550 F.3d 326, 335 (4th Cir. 2008); Kaplan v. California, 413 U.S. 115, 199 (1973) ("Obscenity can, of course, manifest itself in conduct, in the pictorial representation of conduct, or in the written and oral description of conduct. The Court has applied similarly conceived First Amendment standards to moving pictures, to photographs, and to words in books."). Obscenity prosecutions for mere text are rare, but they have occurred. *See, e.g.,* Paula Reed Ward, *Afraid of Public Trial, Author to Plead Guilty in Online Obscenity Case,* Pittsburgh Post-Gazette, May 17, 2008 (discussing charges and guilty plea of defendant charged with distributing obscene materials for hosting website that collected written stories of sexual abuse of children). Should the First Amendment be interpreted to allow such prosecutions? Is there a constitutional difference between verbal descriptions and pictures?

8. *Minors, pornography, and the Internet.* One significant argument in favor of obscenity laws is that it allows legislatures to shield hard-core

pornography from children. In the last decade, Congress has made several efforts to protect children online by enacting criminal laws that go beyond traditional obscenity laws. For example, the Communications Decency Act (CDA), Pub. L. No. 104–104, § 502 (1996), tried to limit the exposure of children to indecent materials online. The Supreme Court invalidated the CDA in Reno v. American Civil Liberties Union, 521 U.S. 844 (1997), on the ground that the law was not narrowly tailored to its compelling state interest of protecting children.

Congress then tried again in the form of the Child Online Protection Act (COPA), Pub. L. No. 105–277, §§ 1401–06 (1998), codified at 47 U.S.C. § 231. COPA is considerably narrower than the CDA, but it has been ruled unconstitutional, as well. *See* American Civil Liberties Union v. Mukasey, 534 F.3d 181 (3d Cir. 2008). Do you think Congress should be able to regulate how minors can access non-obscene pornography and other indecent materials via the Internet? Or does attempting to regulate when minors can access pornography inevitably place an impermissible burden on the rights of adults to access non-obscene pornography?

D. CHILD EXPLOITATION CRIMES

Tragically, child exploitation offenses are among the most common computer crimes. Such crimes fall into two basic categories. The first consists of offenses involving images of child pornography. These cases involve use of a computer to send, receive, and/or possess images of minors engaged in sexual activity. The second category consists of offenses involving actual or attempted sexual contact with minors by adults. In these cases, the computer's role is facilitating the attempted or actual contact. The materials in this section begin with child pornography crimes and then turn to offenses involving attempted sexual contacts.

1. CSAM LAWS

a) Introduction

Child sexual abuse material (CSAM), also sometimes known as "child pornography," is a term generally used to describe images of persons under the age of 18 engaged in sexually explicit conduct. Before the 1960s, such images were banned under the obscenity laws. Following *Miller v. California*, however, at least some images of CSAM fell outside the definition of obscenity. In the mid-to-late 1970s, many people believed that the loosening of obscenity standards both in the United States and in Europe had gone too far. They feared that the growing availability of sexualized images of minors facilitated widespread exploitation and abuse. *See generally* Philip Jenkins, Beyond Tolerance: Child Pornography on the Internet, 30–37 (2001); Amy Adler, *The Perverse Law of Child Pornography*, 101 Colum. L. Rev. 209 (2001). Legislatures responded by enacting laws specifically addressing CSAM. By 1982, the federal government and twenty states had enacted CSAM laws, although they varied in scope considerably. *See* New York v. Ferber, 458 U.S. 747, 749 (1982). Today, the federal government and every state has CSAM laws.

CSAM laws generally address both the creation of child pornography and then its subsequent distribution, receipt, and possession. Punishments for the creation of CSAM are severe. The federal statute that prohibits the creation of CSAM is found at 18 U.S.C. § 2251, and it provides for a mandatory minimum prison term of 15 years in prison for a first offense. If the conduct results in the death of the minor, the death penalty is an available punishment. If the death penalty is not imposed, the statute provides for a mandatory minimum prison term of 30 years. *See* 18 U.S.C. § 2251(e). The materials in this section will not focus on the law governing the creation of CSAM. Instead, it will address the computer-related crimes that occur after the images are created: specifically, the distribution, receipt, and possession of the images.

Although laws governing CSAM and obscenity both involve sexual imagery of some kind, the distribution, receipt, and possession of such materials are prohibited for very different reasons. The distribution, receipt, and possession of CSAM is prohibited to protect children from sexual molestation and abuse. As the Supreme Court explained in *Ferber*, prohibiting CSAM can deter its creation. The creation of child pornography often involves sexual abuse, and distribution of the images inflicts a continuing harm on the child victim. Prohibiting the distribution, receipt, and possession of images also can help "dry up the market" for such images, lowering demand for their creation. *See id.* at 757–61. In Osborne v. Ohio, 495 U.S. 103 (1990), the Supreme Court identified two more reasons for banning possession of CSAM images. First, a ban on possession can encourage those who possess such images to destroy them. Second, pedophiles use CSAM to show to potential victims to present child sexual activity as normal, a process sometimes referred to as 'grooming.' *See id.* at 111.

b) The Proxy Rationale

Another possible rationale for CSAM offenses—albeit a rationale not used to justify their constitutionality—is the perceived correlation between possession of images and acts of child molestation. This is a difficult argument to evaluate, in large part because little reliable empirical work exists on how strong the correlation may be. *See generally* Julian Sher & Benedict Carey, *Debate on Child Pornography's Link to Molesting*, New York Times, July 19, 2007.

Consider two competing perspectives. On one hand, some people believe that those who collect CSAM are likely to engage in actual acts of molestation. They reason that knowing possession of such images signals sexual attraction to children. Given the serious criminal liability that attaches to mere possession of the images, those who collect the images are also likely to attempt actual sexual contact with children. Possession thus indicates future dangerousness. On the other hand, some people look at the problem very differently. They reason that interest in viewing CSAM is different from engaging in actual sexual contact. An interest in viewing violent movies is very different from engaging in actual acts of violence, they note, and the same distinction can be made in the context of child pornography.

Several studies have tried to measure the link between CSAM possession and acts of molestation. In one study, a group of researchers attempted to identify and analyze all of the arrests for child sex crimes that in any way involved CSAM possession that occurred in the United States in the one-year period starting July 1, 2000. *See* Janis Wolak, David Finkelhor, & Kimberly J. Mitchell, Child Pornography Possessors Arrested in Internet-Related Crimes: Findings from the National Juvenile Online Victimization Study (2005). The researchers identified 1,713 such arrests, and they studied the characteristics of the crimes and of the individuals arrested. The study concluded that within the group of individuals charged with sex crimes that included CSAM, 40% were known to have victimized a child at some point. Another 15% were known to have attempted to do so. *Id.* at 16. Among the cases that began as investigations only into child pornography possession, one in six led to discoveries that resulted in concurrent charges for actual or attempted child molestation. *Id.* at 17.

A second empirical study was conducted at the Sex Offender Treatment Program at the federal prison in Butner, North Carolina. *See* Michael L. Bourke & Andres E. Hernandez, *The 'Butner Study' Redux: A Report on the Incidence of Hands-On Child Victimization by Child Pornography Offenders*, 24 J. Family Violence 183 (2009). This study involved 155 adult males in a voluntary sex offender treatment program at a medium-security federal prison. All of the participants were serving prison time for possessing, receiving, or distributing CSAM. The sex offender treatment program encouraged participants to divulge their past sexual contacts with children as part of an intensive therapy program. The study then compared the total number of reported sexual contacts with the number of known sexual contacts at the time the defendants were sentenced for CSAM offenses. Only 26% of the participants in the study—40 out of 155—had known sexual contacts with minors at the time of their sentencing. The 40 participants with sexual contacts known at time of sentencing had a total of 75 known victims. Following therapy in the sex offender treatment program, however, 85% of the participants in the study—131 out of 155—admitted to at least one sexual contact with a minor. The 131 participants with admitted sexual contacts confessed to a total of 1,777 victims, an average of more than 13 victims per participant with admitted sexual contacts.

The results of the Bourke and Hernandez study are chilling. But are they representative? One scholar has offered several reasons why the Bourke and Hernandez figures might be unreliable. *See* Melissa Hamilton, *The Child Pornography Crusade And Its Net-Widening Effect*, 33 Cardozo L. Rev. 1679, 1696–1710 (2012). First, the study relied on self-reporting. Participants may have obtained benefits from participating in the program, and they may have lied about their contacts to remain in the program. Second, individuals who volunteered for such a program may be unrepresentative of offenders as a whole. Third, the study defined sexual contacts broadly to include "any fondling of the genitals or breasts over clothing, as well as skin-to-skin contact," and may have inadvertently included contacts when the participants were themselves minors.

An empirical study that arguably points in the opposite direction of the Bourke and Hernandez article was reported in Jérôme Endrass et al., *The Consumption of Internet Child Pornography and Violent Sex Offending,* 9 BMC Psychiatry 43 (2009). The study followed 231 Swiss CSAM defendants who were arrested in 2002 based on records indicating that they had visited a CSAM website that had been shut down in 1999. Of the 231 individuals arrested, 217 confessed to viewing CSAM. At the time of their arrest in 2002, only 8 of the individuals had prior convictions for CSAM offenses and only 2 had convictions for offenses involving actual contacts with children. The study examined the criminal records of the 231 defendants six years later, in 2008, to identify how many of the 231 defendants had been convicted or were under criminal investigation for an additional child sexual offenses. By 2008, nine of the 231 defendants had been reconvicted or were under investigation for CSAM offenses, while two had been convicted or were under investigation for offenses based on actual contact with children. The authors of the Endrass study conclude that "[t]he consumption of child pornography alone does not seem to represent a risk factor for committing hands-on sex offenses" based on their data set.

Do you agree with this conclusion? Notably, the Endrass study assumes that the Swiss police know of and investigate all crimes that the individuals in the study have committed. This is a questionable assumption given that only 8 of the 231 individuals arrested in 2002 had prior child pornography convictions over their lifetimes. Indeed, only 55% of the 231 individuals in the study were convicted of CSAM offenses following their 2002 arrests, even though 95% of them had actually confessed to the crime. Given such difficulties, does the Endrass study really suggest that CSAM possession does not correlate with actual child sexual contacts? Or does it suggest that Swiss police and prosecutors cannot or do not adequately enforce laws against child sex offenses?

c)   18 U.S.C. § 2252

The primary federal statute prohibiting CSAM distribution, receipt, and possession appears in 18 U.S.C. § 2252. It was originally enacted as part of the Protection of Children Against Sexual Exploitation Act, Pub. L. No. 95–225 (1978). In its present form, it contains four distinct offenses in §§ 2252(a)(1)–(a)(4). The first, found at § 2252(a)(1), prohibits knowingly transporting or shipping in interstate or foreign commerce a visual depiction of a minor engaging in sexually explicit conduct. The second, § 2252(a)(2), prohibits receiving or distributing such depictions that have been sent in interstate or foreign commerce, or which contain materials which have been transported in interstate commerce, or reproducing such materials for distribution in interstate or foreign commerce.

The third and fourth prohibitions, §§ 2252(a)(3) and (a)(4), deal with possession-related crimes. Section 2252(a)(3) concerns selling or having possession with intent to sell, and § 2252(a)(4) concerns mere possession of such materials and accessing such materials with intent to view them. Section 2252(a)(4) also permits defendants to raise an affirmative defense, albeit one that is invoked only rarely. If a defendant possesses only one or two "matters" containing child pornography, they can avoid criminal liability if they "promptly and in good faith, and without retaining or allowing any person, other than a law enforcement agency, to access any visual depiction or copy thereof . . . took reasonable steps to destroy each such visual depiction; or . . . reported the matter to a law enforcement agency and afforded that agency access to each such visual depiction." 18 U.S.C. § 2252(c).

Violations of §§ 2252(a)(1), (a)(2), or (a)(3) trigger a five-year mandatory minimum punishment, and can lead to higher punishments as well. *See* 18 U.S.C. § 2252(b)(1). Violations of § 2252(a)(4), the possession provision, do not trigger a mandatory minimum sentence, but permit a maximum punishment of up to ten years. *See* 18 U.S.C. § 2252(b)(2). In both cases, prior convictions will trigger higher punishments.

d)   18 U.S.C. §§ 2252A and 2256

Congress passed the Child Pornography Prevention Act, Pub. L. No. 104–208 (1996), in response to concerns that computer technologies were rendering existing CSAM laws out of date. Specifically, Congress was concerned that pedophiles could use computer software to create computer-generated CSAM, either by "morphing" a digital image of a real child's face to a computer-generated image of a child's body or by generating a life-like image entirely by computer. The CPPA was designed to expand the then-existing child pornography laws to encompass these new forms of child pornography.

Instead of amending 18 U.S.C. § 2252, Congress opted to create a new CSAM statute, 18 U.S.C. § 2252A and 18 U.S.C. § 2256. The decision to draft a new statute rather than amend the existing one was based largely on concerns that the new statute might be struck down in whole or in part under the First Amendment. If a court struck down the new statute and found that it was not severable from the preexisting language, the court's decision would leave no law on the books until Congress could act again. By creating a new statute, Congress preserved § 2252 and created new ground in 18 U.S.C. § 2252A and § 2256.

The text of 18 U.S.C. § 2252A is a modernized and expanded version of § 2252, with definitions of key terms appearing in 18 U.S.C. § 2256. Sections 2252A(a)(1), (a)(2), and (a)(3)(A) largely recreate the prohibitions in § 2252(a)(1) and (2). Sections 2252A(a)(4) and (a)(5) largely mirror §§ 2252(a)(3) and (a)(4); Section 2252A(d) mirrors the affirmative defense of § 2252(c). Sections 2252A(a)(3)(B) and 2252A(a)(6) are expansions beyond the traditional scope of CSAM laws; the former is addressed at advertising and soliciting images, and the latter at luring minors. Section 2256 provides definitions for key terms used in 2252A, most notably a definition of child pornography that goes beyond images of actual children to include morphed images of child pornography and virtual images of child pornography that are indistinguishable from real images. 18 U.S.C. § 2256(8) (2003).

e) Statutory Elements of 18 U.S.C. §§ 2252 and 2252A

When § 2252 was first enacted in 1978, materials containing images of CSAM typically appeared as physical books, magazines, and photographs. Existing law still reflects that assumption in some ways. The law prohibits conduct such as transporting, shipping, receiving, and possessing images, all conduct that is readily understood in the context of physical items. But what does it mean to "distribute" or "possess" data?

UNITED STATES V. SHAFFER
United States Court of Appeals for the Tenth Circuit, 2007.
472 F.3d 1219.

GORSUCH, CIRCUIT JUDGE.

Aaron Shaffer challenges his conviction for distribution and possession of child pornography. Mr. Shaffer claims that he did not, as a matter of law or fact, "distribute" child pornography when he downloaded images and videos from a peer-to-peer computer network and stored them in a shared folder on his computer accessible by other users of the network.

I.

Kazaa is a peer-to-peer computer application that allows users to trade computer files through the Internet. It is hardly a unique service; at any one time today, there are apparently in excess of four to five million people online sharing over 100 million files.

Users begin at Kazaa's website. There, they obtain the software necessary for file trading by clicking an installation "wizard" that walks them through a step-by-step setup process. Before installation, the wizard requires users to acknowledge and accede to Kazaa's licensing agreement. Users then identify a destination on their computers where they want the Kazaa file sharing software located, and Kazaa creates a "shortcut" icon on the user's desktop.

Upon installation, Kazaa's software walks users through certain steps to create a folder called "My Shared Folder" (hereinafter, "shared folder") on their computer's hard drive. Here, Kazaa users store the files they download from the shared folders of other Kazaa users. At the same time, anything one has in one's own Kazaa shared folder may be accessed and downloaded by other Kazaa users. Kazaa's software also shows the user in real time exactly how many of his or her files are being accessed and copied by other Kazaa users. A user can, however, select an option that precludes other users from downloading materials from his or her computer.

To download an item from another computer's shared folder, a Kazaa user simply double clicks on that file, and it is then transferred to the shared folder on the recipient user's computer. There are only two ways for items to be placed in a user's shared folder. First, one must go online, search for an item, and download the material into the shared folder. Second, one may take files already existing on his or her computer and move them into the shared folder. Either way, the placement of items in one's shared folder involves a conscious effort. A user can of course move items out of the shared folder to other folders on his or her computer, and doing so precludes other Kazaa users from accessing and downloading such material.

This case arose when Ken Rochford, an Arizona-based special agent from the United States Department of Homeland Security's Bureau of Immigration and Customs Enforcement ("ICE"), noticed that a certain Kazaa account user with the screen name shaf@Kazaa had in his shared folder accessible to other Kazaa users a large number of files containing images and videos of child pornography. Special Agent Rochford sought to download some of those images from shaf@Kazaa's computer onto his own and had no difficulty doing so.

Authorities later learned that the user associated with shaf@Kazaa was Mr. Shaffer, then a 27-year-old college student living with his mother and stepfather in Topeka, Kansas. David Zimmer, a Kansas-based ICE special agent, obtained and executed a search warrant on Mr. Shaffer's residence and computer. ICE special agents ultimately found within Mr. Shaffer's Kazaa shared folder approximately 19 image files and 25 videos containing child pornography, along with text documents describing stories of adults engaging in sex with children.

During the course of the search of his home and computer, Mr. Shaffer consented to an interview with Special Agent Zimmer. During that interview, according to Special Agent Zimmer's testimony at trial, Mr. Shaffer admitted to being the sole user of the computer in his home; employing the screen name shaf@Kazaa; and knowingly downloading through Kazaa 100 movies and 20 still photos involving child pornography, which he estimated occupied a total of approximately 10 gigabytes.

Mr. Shaffer further admitted that he stored images of child pornography in his Kazaa shared folder. He explained that he did so because, among other things, Kazaa gave him "user points" and various incentive rewards corresponding to how many images other users downloaded from his computer. Mr. Shaffer indicated he knew that other people had downloaded child pornography from him. And he stated that it takes up to 100 hours to download certain files using Kazaa, so sometimes when he went to work he would leave his computer on in order to make his images and videos available for download by other users.

Mr. Shaffer also testified at trial. He did not dispute that he gave an interview to Special Agent Zimmer or much of Special Agent Zimmer's description of that interview. Mr. Shaffer did testify, however, that he could not recall telling Special Agent Zimmer that he knew other Kazaa users had downloaded child pornography from his computer. After a four-day trial, a jury returned guilty verdicts against Mr. Shaffer for both possession and distribution of child pornography. The District Court subsequently sentenced him to 60 months of incarceration.

II.

Mr. Shaffer contends there was insufficient evidence presented at trial to sustain his conviction for distribution of child pornography. Under Section 2252A(a)(2), it is unlawful for a person knowingly to distribute child pornography by any means, including by computer.[6] Mr. Shaffer frankly concedes that he allowed, or caused, distribution by leaving files on his computer that other Kazaa users could access. He also now concedes that a rational jury could infer that he did so knowingly (and even intentionally): [His brief acknowledges that] "a reasonable jury could conclude from this evidence that Mr. Shaffer intended to allow others to take the material from his computer."

---

[6] Though it could have done so, the government did not charge Mr. Shaffer with the knowing *receipt* of child pornography under this statutory provision.

But, Mr. Shaffer argues, to "distribute" something, a person must actively transfer possession to another, such as by mail, e-mail, or handing it to another person. And here, Mr. Shaffer contends, he was only a passive participant in the process; there is no evidence that he personally completed any such transaction.

The relevant statute does not itself define the term "distribute," so we look to how the term is understood as a matter of plain meaning. Black's offers this definition: "1. To apportion; to divide among several. 2. To arrange by class or order. 3. To deliver. 4. To spread out; to disperse." Black's Law Dictionary 508 (8th ed. 2005). Webster's adds this understanding: "to divide among several or many . . . deal out . . . apportion esp. to members of a group or over a period of time . . . allot . . . dispense . . . to give out or deliver." Webster's Third New Int'l Dictionary Unabridged 660 (2002). The instruction offered by the District Court to the jury captured much the same sentiment: "To distribute something simply means to deliver or transfer possession of it to someone else."

We have little difficulty in concluding that Mr. Shaffer distributed child pornography in the sense of having delivered, transferred, dispersed, or dispensed it to others. He may not have actively pushed pornography on Kazaa users, but he freely allowed them access to his computerized stash of images and videos and openly invited them to take, or download, those items.

It is something akin to the owner of a self-serve gas station. The owner may not be present at the station, and there may be no attendant present at all. And neither the owner nor his or her agents may ever pump gas. But the owner has a roadside sign letting all passersby know that, if they choose, they can stop and fill their cars for themselves, paying at the pump by credit card. Just because the operation is self-serve, or in Mr. Shaffer's parlance, passive, we do not doubt for a moment that the gas station owner is in the business of distributing, delivering, transferring or dispersing gasoline; the *raison d'etre* of owning a gas station is to do just that. So, too, a reasonable jury could find that Mr. Shaffer welcomed people to his computer and was quite happy to let them take child pornography from it.

Indeed, Mr. Shaffer admitted that he had downloaded child pornography from other users' Kazaa shared folders and understood that file sharing was the very purpose of Kazaa. He admitted that he had child pornography stored in his computer's Kazaa shared folder. Mr. Shaffer could have, but did not, save the illicit images and videos in a computer folder not susceptible to file sharing. Likewise, he could have, but did not, activate the feature on Kazaa that would have precluded others from taking materials from his shared folder. Quite the opposite. According to Special Agent Zimmer, Mr. Shaffer acknowledged that he *knew* other people had downloaded child pornography from his shared folder. Mr.

Shaffer cannot recall making this particular admission, but we are obliged to view the facts in the light most favorable to the government, and the jury was free to credit Special Agent Zimmer's testimony and discredit Mr. Shaffer's.

The District Court's judgment is affirmed.

NOTES AND QUESTIONS

1. *Does it matter if anyone accessed the files in the shared folder?* Imagine Shaffer had placed the files in the shared folder of his computer intending that other Kazaa users could access them, but that no users had actually done so. Has Shaffer still distributed the images?

The Third Circuit answered that question "no" in United States v. Husmann, 765 F.3d 169 (3d Cir. 2014). By a vote of 2 to 1, the court concluded that the word "distribute" requires a transfer of possession from one person to another. Because that does not occur when a file is merely placed in the shared folder, the defendant is not guilty of distribution:

> Black's Law Dictionary defines "distribute" as: "to apportion; to divide among several" and "to deliver." Black's Law Dictionary 487 (9th ed. 2009). Merriam-Webster provides the following definitions, among others, for the term "distribute": "to divide among several or many" and "to give out or deliver especially to members of a group." *See* Distribute Definition, Merriam-Webster Dictionary. We find additional guidance in the definition of "distribute" set forth in the controlled substances context. Under the Model Criminal Jury Instructions for the Third Circuit, to distribute a controlled substance means "(*to deliver or to transfer*) possession or control of a controlled substance from one person to another." Model Criminal Jury Instructions for the Third Circuit § 6.21.841–2 (2014).

> The statutory context confirms that "distribute" in § 2252(a)(2) means to apportion, give out, or deliver and that distribution necessarily involves the transfer of materials to another person. Significantly, Congress legislated specific prohibitions against offering and promoting child pornography within the same statutory scheme as it prohibited distributing child pornography. *See* 18 U.S.C. § 2251(d)(1)(A) (prohibiting offers to distribute child pornography); 18 U.S.C. § 2252A(a)(3)(B) (prohibiting the advertisement and promotion of child pornography).

> Congress also penalized the attempted distribution of child pornography through specific statutory provisions. *See* 18 U.S.C. §§ 2252(b)(1), 2252A(b)(1). Because Congress has separately criminalized offering, promoting, and attempting to distribute child pornography, a broad definition of the term "distribute" would create unnecessary surplusage. To give effect to the entire statutory scheme,

"distribute" must require the transfer of possession of child pornography to another person.

> We hold that the term "distribute" in § 2252(a)(2) requires evidence that a defendant's child pornography materials were completely transferred to or downloaded by another person. Of course, knowingly placing child pornography in a shared folder on a file sharing network remains a criminal offense. *See, e.g.,* 18 U.S.C. § 2251(d)(1)(A) (prohibiting offers to distribute child pornography); 18 U.S.C. § 2252(b)(1) (prohibiting attempted distribution). It just isn't distribution. In the end, our interpretation of "distribute" in § 2252(a)(2) might affect the government's charging decisions, but it does not handicap the government's ability to prosecute child pornography offenses.

Id. at 174, 176. Judge Van Antwerpen dissented:

> Husmann placed images of child pornography into a shared folder accessible to *all global users* of the peer-to-peer file sharing program 360 Share Pro. Once in the shared folder, a search term and a click of a mouse allowed access to these images by any user on the system. My colleagues' definition of "distribution," under 18 U.S.C. § 2252, would create a system in which a person who intentionally posted child pornography on the Internet, knowing it is accessible to hundreds, if not millions, of individuals, is not "distribution." This is certainly not what Congress had in mind and following the majority's approach, the crime of distribution would not be complete until a police officer downloaded the image. This is a distinction without merit.

> Given the plain meaning of the term, the intent of Congress, and the advancement of technology, the placing of child pornography into a shared file accessible over a peer-to-peer file sharing network *alone* should constitute "distribution." Husmann took all the necessary steps to make a product available to the public in a publicly accessible location, and whether or not a party took that product is irrelevant to both the purpose of § 2252 and to his role as distributor. For that reason, the conviction of Appellant George Husmann for "distribution" under 18 U.S.C. § 2252 should be upheld.

> The ease, anonymity, and virtual untraceability with which Husmann made child pornography globally available is the engine behind § 2252, and the reason that "distribute" should be given a broader interpretation than the majority gives it. In analyzing the plain meaning of the statute, we need not define the outer boundaries of the term "distribution"; rather, we need only answer the specific question of whether placing an image of child pornography into a modern day "shared" folder as part of a peer-to-peer network is "distribution," as the District Court found.

> Looking both to Black's and Merriam-Webster's dictionaries, we find the plain meaning of "distribute" to be: "1. To apportion; to divide among several. 2. To arrange by class or order. 3. To deliver. 4. To spread out; to disperse." *Black's Law Dictionary* 487 (9th ed. 2009). Clearly the actions undertaken by Husmann, placing the images in a folder shared globally, dispersed and apportioned these images to third parties within the plain meaning of the statute.
>
> Determining that placing an image of child pornography into a shared folder constitutes "distribution" would, in light of the technological advances, encompass the plain meaning and the purpose of § 2252.

Id. at 177–78 (Van Antwerpen, J., dissenting). Which reading of the statute is more persuasive?

The majority opinion in *Husmann* suggests that placing an image of child pornography in a shared folder might (absent downloading) violate the crime of *attempting* to distribute child pornography in violation of 18 U.S.C. § 2252(b)(1). Under federal attempt law, proving attempt requires the government to show both that the accused intended to commit the underlying substantive offense and that he took a substantial step toward committing that crime. *See* United States v. Gobbi, 471 F.3d 302, 309 (1st Cir. 2006).

In your view, does placing an image in the shared folder of a peer-to-peer network necessarily establish attempted distribution of that image? What facts would you want to know to determine when placement of a file in a shared folder constitutes attempted distribution?

2. *Distribution versus receipt.* The punishment for knowingly distributing images of CSAM is the same as the punishment for knowingly receiving those images. If *A* possesses an image of CSAM, *B* asks for it, and *A* gives the image to *B*, then *A* and *B* are punished equally by the same statute. Does that make sense as a matter of policy? Does your answer depend on whether the image is a physical photograph or an electronic file? Note that if the image is a physical photograph, *A* can only distribute the image once. After *A* has given the image to *B*, *A* will no longer have a copy to distribute. In contrast, if the image is a computer file, *A* can distribute the image many times. Should that make a difference? Does your answer depend on whether distributing a single image multiple times is treated by the law as a single crime of distributing many images or as many distinct crimes of distributing a single image?

3. *Receipt versus possession.* The knowing receipt of CSAM is almost always accompanied by its possession. However, the penalties for receipt under § 2252(a)(2) are considerably more severe than the punishment for possession under § 2252(a)(4). If the conduct usually is the same, why did Congress impose two different levels of punishment?

In United States v. Richardson, 238 F.3d 837 (7th Cir. 2001), Judge Posner speculated about one possible reason:

The explanation may be that receivers increase the market for child pornography and hence the demand for children to pose as models for pornographic photographs; possessors, at least qua possessors, as distinct from receivers, though most of them are that too, do not. The possessor who creates his own pornography strictly for his personal use is not part of the interstate and international traffic in child pornography, a traffic that not only increases the demand for the production of such pornography but, by virtue of its far-flung scope, makes it extremely difficult to locate, let alone protect, the children exploited by it. Concern with the welfare of the children who are used to create pornography is part of the public concern over child pornography, and this makes the receiver a greater malefactor than the possessor.

Id. at 839.

The role of prosecutorial discretion offers another explanation. The statutory definition of child pornography arguably is quite broad, and it encompasses a number of different kinds of cases. The statutory overlap between receipt and possession crimes permits prosecutors to charge more severe cases differently than less severe cases. A prosecutor can inquire as to the nature of the images in the case and can choose whether to charge the defendant with the lesser offense of possession or the greater offense of receipt. The receipt/possession distinction may also give prosecutors an extra tool to pressure defendants to plead guilty. If the government's case is weak, a prosecutor may offer the defendant a choice between pleading guilty to possession or going to trial on more severe receipt charges.

Finally, the receipt/possession distinction may simply be an accident of history. When § 2252 was first enacted, it was unclear if the Constitution permitted criminal punishment for possession of child pornography. The initial version of § 2252 did not include such a prohibition. The federal ban on possession was added separately a few months after the Supreme Court ruled in Osborne v. Ohio, 495 U.S. 103 (1990), that such bans were constitutionally permitted. *See* Pub.L. 101–647, Title III, § 323(a), (b) (1990). Perhaps possession was punished less harshly than receipt only because it was treated as a different kind of offense after *Osborne*.

Do any of these explanations justify the different treatment of receipt and possession?

4.   *What counts as child pornography?* Federal law imposes severe punishments for knowingly possessing, distributing, or receiving child pornography. To identify whether an image of a minor counts as child pornography, courts have often relied on a six-factor test first announced in United States v. Dost, 636 F. Supp. 828 (S.D.Cal. 1986). The *Dost* test considers whether the focal point of the visual depiction is on the child's genitalia or pubic area; whether the setting of the visual depiction is sexually suggestive; whether the child is depicted in an unnatural pose or in inappropriate attire; whether the child is fully or partially clothed or nude; whether the visual

depiction suggests a willingness to engage in sexual activity; and whether the visual depiction is intended or designed to elicit a sexual response in the viewer. *See id.* at 832.

Professor Amy Adler has criticized the *Dost* test for being "extraordinarily malleable." She notes that it is unclear how many factors must be present; that each factor is difficult to apply; and that courts are deeply divided about what guidelines should be given to courts and juries trying to apply these factors. *See* Amy Adler, *The "Dost Test" in Child Pornography Law: "Trial by Rorschach Test,"* in Carissa Byrne Hessick, ed., Refining Child Pornography Law: Crime, Language, and Social Consequences 88–93 (2016). Professor Adler concludes: "Quite simply, lower courts frequently interpret *Dost* to criminalize speech that does not implicate the rationales that the Supreme Court has relied on to justify the exclusion of 'child pornography' from First Amendment protection." *Id.* at 99.

5.   *The mental state requirement.* In United States v. X-Citement Video, Inc., 513 U.S. 64 (1994), the Supreme Court considered the mens rea that applies to the statutory element of the age of the person visually depicted contained in 18 U.S.C. §§ 2252(a)(1) and (a)(2). In an opinion by Chief Justice Rehnquist, the Court held that the "knowing" mens rea applied to the person's age: As a result, it is not enough that a defendant transported or received images that happen to contain child pornography: The government must prove the defendant's knowledge that the person depicted in the image was under the age of eighteen. The Court justified this holding on a number of factors, including the odd results that would follow from a contrary approach:

> If the term "knowingly" applies only to the relevant verbs in § 2252—transporting, shipping, receiving, distributing and reproducing—we would have to conclude that Congress wished to distinguish between someone who knowingly transported a particular package of film whose contents were unknown to him, and someone who unknowingly transported that package. It would seem odd, to say the least, that Congress distinguished between someone who inadvertently dropped an item into the mail without realizing it, and someone who consciously placed the same item in the mail, but was nonetheless unconcerned about whether the person had any knowledge of the prohibited contents of the package.

> Some applications of respondents' position would produce results that were not merely odd, but positively absurd. If we were to conclude that "knowingly" only modifies the relevant verbs in § 2252, we would sweep within the ambit of the statute actors who had no idea that they were even dealing with sexually explicit material. For instance, a retail druggist who returns an uninspected roll of developed film to a customer "knowingly distributes" a visual depiction and would be criminally liable if it were later discovered that the visual depiction contained images of children engaged in sexually explicit conduct. Or, a new resident of an apartment might

receive mail for the prior resident and store the mail unopened. If the prior tenant had requested delivery of materials covered by § 2252, his residential successor could be prosecuted for "knowing receipt" of such materials. Similarly, a Federal Express courier who delivers a box in which the shipper has declared the contents to be "film" "knowingly transports" such film. We do not assume that Congress, in passing laws, intended such results.

Id. at 69.

6.	*Quantifying acts of distribution and receipt when conduct involves multiple images.* Imagine a defendant creates two websites and uses them to distribute images of CSAM. One hundred users visit each website, and each user downloads ten images during each visit. If the defendant is charged with distributing images of CSAM, has he committed one crime (for the overall conduct of creating the websites), two crimes (for the two websites), or two thousand crimes (for the total number of images downloaded)?

In United States v. Reedy, 304 F.3d 358 (5th Cir. 2002), the government argued that a defendant who creates websites to distribute CSAM commits a new and distinct offense of distribution every time an image is downloaded. Under that approach, each web query constitutes a new crime. The Fifth Circuit disagreed with the government's approach, at least based on the specific facts of the *Reedy* case. Applying the rule of lenity to an ambiguous statute, the court held that the creation and use of each individual website constitutes a single offense. In other words, a defendant who creates two websites has committed two crimes regardless of how many images the site contains or how many times the site has been visited.

Even more complex issues arise when trying to count the number of offenses of knowing receipt. For example, in United States v. Buchanan, 485 F.3d 274 (5th Cir. 2007), a defendant downloaded four images of child pornography from the Internet and was convicted of four counts of knowing receipt. The Fifth Circuit reversed on the ground that the government had not met its burden of showing four distinct acts of receiving images. Although the court rested its conclusion on the lack of evidence in the record, the court struggled to identify exactly how much distinct conduct should be sufficient to constitute a distinct act. *See id.* at 282. ("We do not resolve today whether a separate mouse click on an image to maximize its size would suffice as a separate receipt of child pornography.")

Judge Benavides filed a concurring opinion in *Buchanan* that explained the difficulty of quantifying the number of "receipts" in Internet crime cases:

Internet crimes of this sort make for complicated prosecutions. Even familiar concepts like *actus reus* and *mens rea* can present new difficulties in this context, and analogies to our precedents . . . will be imperfect at best.

There are many ways in which a defendant might receive four "visual depictions" from the web. In the simplest example, he could visit a single page that contains four large images, all of which are automatically displayed on the screen and downloaded to his hard drive. In such a case, we could debate whether the defendant had committed four separate acts of receiving an individual image, or the single act of receiving one web page. Our holding in *Reedy* strongly suggests that such a defendant has "bundled" his conduct by website, rather than by individual image, and should face only a single conviction. In a more complicated example, however, a defendant might visit a web page that has thumbnails of various images, and then individually select some of those thumbnails to enlarge them on screen. In that case, would we focus on the receipt of the first page, or the subsequent receipt of each image, or both? And what if the defendant views the same image twice during one visit? How many receipts is that?

These various scenarios—and one could easily imagine others—demonstrate that conceptualizing the "knowing receipt of any visual depiction" via the internet is much more complicated than it is in cases involving regular mail. Even with complete information about what the defendant did and what he knew at the time he did it, categorizing the criminal behavior is challenging.

Id. at 288–89 (Benavides, J., concurring).

7. *The role of the dark web.* Severe criminal punishment for CSAM offenses, combined with societal disgust directed toward those who commit such crimes, has led to the widespread use of technology to evade detection among those who collect CSAM. Consider the role of the "dark web," the name often given to websites that are available only through anonymizing services such as Tor. *See generally* Kristin Finklea, *Dark Web*, Congressional Research Service Report, July 7, 2015, available at www.fas.org/sgp/crs/misc/R44101.pdf.

Tor is a free software package that enables users to hide their true IP addresses when surfing the web. When a person surfs the web using the Tor browser, her communications are routed through a network of computers that hides her location. Further, users of Tor can access websites on the ".onion" domain that are available only through Tor. Such websites are sometimes called "hidden services," as normally they are not intended to be widely known. Such sites are not indexed and generally have hard-to-guess addresses.

There are many legal and laudatory uses for Tor, and there are also legal uses of the dark web. Unfortunately, however, the dark web also provides a free and readily available means to distribute CSAM that typically is very difficult for the government to investigate successfully. A CSAM site on the dark web will at least initially be known only to users of the site. When the government learns of a site's operation, the location of the site's server and the identity of who is running it will also be unknown. Even if the government can somehow find the server and seize it, the records kept by the site typically will not reveal accurate identifying information about any of the site's users.

These anonymity features appear to have made CSAM a leading subject of traffic on the dark web. Accurate numbers are difficult to obtain because the services and their traffic is hidden. According to one 2014 study, however, about 2% of dark web sites relate to child abuse—and those sites are responsible for about 83% of the visits to dark web sites. *See* Andy Greenberg, *Over 80 Percent of Dark-Web Visits Relate to Pedophilia, Study Finds,* Wired.com, December 30, 2014. For more on the difficulty of investigating CSAM on the dark web, *see* Susan Hennessey, *The Elephant in the Room: Addressing Child Exploitation and Going Dark,* The Hoover Institution, Aegis Paper Series No. 1701 (2017).

BARTON V. STATE
Court of Appeals of Georgia, 2007.
648 S.E.2d 660.

MILLER, JUDGE.

On appeal from the trial court's denial of his motion for a new trial, Barton asserts that the State failed to prove his knowing possession of child pornography. Finding that the State failed to prove knowing possession of child pornography, as charged in the indictment, we reverse.

The evidence shows that, after the Walker County Sheriff's Department began investigating allegations of child molestation against Barton, his wife provided authorities with Barton's laptop computer. Upon conducting a forensic examination of that computer, law enforcement retrieved 156 images they believed met the definition of child pornography stored on the computer's hard drive. Barton was indicted for sexual exploitation of children with respect to 106 of those images. Specifically, Barton was charged with "knowingly possessing" child pornography in violation of OCGA § 16–12–100(b)(8), which makes it unlawful "for any person knowingly to possess or control any material which depicts a minor or a portion of a minor's body engaged in any sexually explicit conduct."

At trial, the State sought to prove Barton's knowing possession of child pornography via the testimony of Special Agent Ben Murray of the United States Secret Service, a forensic computer analyst. Murray testified that all computers will store pictures or other information viewed over the internet on the computer's hard drive, in temporary internet file folders. There is nothing that such a user can do to prevent the computer from storing such items. Murray also explained that not everything stored in a computer's temporary internet file folders results from the affirmative conduct of a computer user. Rather, even those images which "pop-up" on a computer screen, even though neither sought nor desired by the computer user, are stored on the computer's hard drive. Furthermore, despite the fact that they are stored on the hard drive, Murray testified that no one using the computer can retrieve information stored in the temporary internet file folders without special forensic software. No such software was present on Barton's computer.

Murray testified that each of the pornographic images on Barton's computer was stored on the hard drive of his computer, in temporary internet file folders. This meant that Barton had viewed the pictures over the internet, but had taken no affirmative action to save them on his computer. Barton could not access or alter the pictures found stored on his computer's hard drive. Murray further testified that Barton had viewed all of the images within two separate time periods, totaling slightly less than four hours, on December 2 and 3, 2003. He offered no testimony as to whether the images resulted from some affirmative action by Barton, represented "pop-ups" which appeared on Barton's computer, or both. Although Murray could not tell how long Barton had spent viewing each individual image, or how long he had kept those images open on his computer, he could say that Barton had never opened any image more than once.

Barton argues that this testimony was insufficient to establish his knowing possession of child pornography because: (1) he took no affirmative action to store the images on his computer; (2) he was unaware that the computer had automatically saved those images to the hard drive; and (3) he had no ability to retrieve or access those images. Reluctantly, we must agree.

In beginning our analysis, we emphasize that the question before us is not whether the viewing of child pornography over the Internet represents the same evil sought to be eradicated by the statute prohibiting the possession of child pornography. Nor is the issue whether the legislature has the power to punish the accessing or viewing of pornographic materials over the Internet. Rather, the question is whether that conduct is punishable as "knowing possession" of child pornography, as charged in the indictment—i.e., does the mere accessing and viewing of pornographic materials over the internet, which results in those materials being stored on a computer's hard drive, constitute the knowing possession of those materials?

While this question is one of first impression in Georgia, it has been addressed by a number of state and federal courts. Each of those courts has found that possession in this context can result only where the defendant exercises "dominion and control" over the child pornography. *See* United States v. Kuchinski, 469 F.3d 853, 863 (9th Cir. 2006); United States v. Romm, 455 F.3d 990, 998 (9th Cir. 2006); United States v. Bass, 411 F.3d 1198, 1201–1202 (10th Cir. 2005); United States v. Tucker, 305 F.3d 1193, 1204 (10th Cir. 2002).

These decisions differ as to whether possession requires that a defendant take some affirmative action to download or save internet images onto his computer. None of those decisions, however, found that a defendant may be convicted of possessing child pornography stored in his computer's temporary internet file folders, also known as cache files,[4] absent some evidence that the defendant was aware those files existed. Several of those courts specifically found that there can be no possession where the defendant is unaware that the images have been saved in the cache files, reasoning that such ignorance precludes a finding that the defendant could exercise dominion or control over those images. As one federal court has explained: "Where a defendant lacks knowledge about the cache file, and concomitantly lacks access to and control over those files, it is not proper to charge him with possession of the child pornography images located in those files, without some other indication of dominion and control over the images." *Kuchinski,* supra, 469 F.3d at 863.

Georgia law requires that we reach a similar conclusion. Under Georgia law, a person who knowingly has direct physical control over a thing at a given time is in actual possession of it. A person who, though not in actual possession, knowingly has both the power and the intention at a given time to exercise dominion or control over a thing is then in constructive possession of it. In any criminal prosecution for possession, therefore, the State must prove that the defendant was *aware* he possessed the contraband at issue. Thus, in this case, the State was required to show that Barton had knowledge of the images stored in his computer's cache files.

Here, the State's brief fails to address the issue of Barton's knowledge, and we find that at trial the State failed to meet its burden on this issue. The sole witness on this issue—Agent Murray—testified that Barton took no affirmative action to save these images to his computer, a conclusion supported by the fact that all of the pictures were stored on the cache drive as "thumbnails." Murray offered no testimony indicating that Barton was aware that the computer was storing these images, but instead established only that these files were stored automatically, without Barton having to do anything. Murray also testified that Barton would have been unable to view or access these images without using software that was not present on Barton's computer. Thus, there was no way that Barton could have learned of the cache files in the normal course of using his computer. Nor did the State present any circumstantial evidence that would have allowed the jury to infer Barton's knowledge of these files-i.e., they did not show that Barton was an experienced or sophisticated computer user who would have been aware of this automatic storage process. In short, the State presented *no* evidence that Barton was aware of the existence of the files

---

[4] Temporary internet files are stored in the cache, "a storage mechanism designed to speed up the loading of internet displays." 19 Berkeley Tech L.J. 1227, 1229 (Fall 2004). The courts deciding the cases cited above, therefore, refer to the temporary internet files as the cache files.

at issue, and in doing so, they failed to prove that Barton knowingly possessed these images.

For the reasons set forth above, we find that the mere existence of pornographic images in the cache files of an individual's computer is insufficient to constitute knowing possession of those materials absent proof that the individual either: (1) took some affirmative action to save or download those images to his computer; or (2) had knowledge that the computer automatically saved those files. We are therefore compelled to conclude that the evidence was insufficient to sustain Barton's conviction for knowing possession of child pornography under OCGA § 16–12–100(b)(8), and we reverse the same.

NOTES AND QUESTIONS

1.   *The role of computer knowledge.* Does it make sense that liability for possession should hinge on whether an individual understands how computers work? Does computer expertise make the conduct more culpable, or more deserving of greater punishment?

2.   *The specific issue in Barton.* Is the issue in *Barton* whether Barton possessed the images stored in the cache? Or is the issue whether the stored images in the cache provide sufficient evidence of prior possession based on the initial downloading that would be sufficient to uphold the jury verdict?

3.   *A different view.* In Commonwealth v. Simone, 2003 WL 22994245 (Va. Cir. Ct. 2003), the defendant used an Internet search engine to locate and view CSAM. The search terms he used included "lolitas," "pre-teens," and "pedophelia." Three CSAM images were found in the cache of viewed images on his computer. However, there was no evidence that the defendant realized that the images he viewed had been saved to the cache. The court nonetheless found that there was sufficient evidence that the defendant had possessed the images. According to the court, the test for whether a defendant possessed contraband computer data should be whether he "reached out and controlled the images at issue." The court reasoned that this test best captured how the concept of possession applies in the physical world:

> If a person walks down the street and notices an item (such as child pornography or an illegal narcotic) whose possession is prohibited, has that person committed a criminal offense if they look at the item for a sufficient amount of time to know what it is and then walks away? The obvious answer seems to be "no." However, if the person looks at the item long enough to know what it is, then reaches out and picks it up, holding and viewing it and taking it with them to their home, that person has moved from merely viewing the item to knowingly possessing the item by reaching out for it and controlling it.

Id. at *7. Do you agree? Is searching for and viewing CSAM "in essence" the same as taking it home, or is it more like walking down the street, searching for contraband, and then looking at it when you find it? Does the court's approach redraft a statute that punishes knowingly possessing child pornography so that it prohibits intentionally viewing child pornography?

4. *United States v. Romm.* In United States v. Romm, 455 F.3d 990 (9th Cir. 2006), the defendant used an Internet connection from a hotel room in Las Vegas to search for images of child pornography. Romm later told federal agents that when he visited a site that contained such images, he would "save" the pictures for a few minutes and then "delete" them. A subsequent search of Romm's computer revealed 42 images of child pornography stored in the browser cache. However, government investigators did not find images outside the browser cache. A government expert witness testified at trial that it was possible for a user to access the cache and control the images stored there. However, no evidence was presented that Romm knew how to access the cache.

On appeal, the Ninth Circuit rejected Romm's claim that that there was insufficient evidence he had knowingly possessed the images. The court stated that "to possess the images in the cache, the defendant must, at a minimum, know that the unlawful images are stored on a disk or other tangible material in his possession." *Id.* at 1000. The court concluded that Romm's conduct established sufficient control over the images:

> Romm exercised control over the cached images while they were contemporaneously saved to his cache and displayed on his screen. At that moment, as the expert testimony here established, Romm could print the images, enlarge them, copy them, or email them to others. No doubt, images could be saved to the cache when a defendant accidentally views the images, as through the occurrence of a "pop-up," for instance. But that is not the case here.

> By his own admission to [federal agents], Romm repeatedly sought out child pornography over the internet. When he found images he "liked," he would "view them, save them to his computer, look at them for about five minutes and then delete them." He described his activities as the "saving" and "downloading" of the images. While the images were displayed on screen and simultaneously stored to his cache, Romm could print them, email them, or save them as copies elsewhere. Romm could destroy the copy of the images that his browser stored to his cache. And according to [the government's expert witness], Romm did just that, either manually, or by instructing his browser to do so. Forensic evidence showed that Romm had enlarged several thumbnail images for better viewing. In short, given the indicia that Romm exercised control over the images in his cache, there was sufficient evidence for the jury to find that Romm committed the act of knowing possession.

> As the record here indicates, Romm had access to, and control over, the images that were displayed on his screen and saved to his cache. He could copy the images, print them or email them to others, and did, in fact, enlarge several of the images. This control clearly

differentiates Romm's conduct from that of a visitor to the Louvre who gazes on the Mona Lisa, even if we put aside the stringent museum rules against photographing or copying without museum permission.

In short, given Romm's ability to control the images while they were displayed on screen, and the forensic and other evidence that he actually exercised this control over them, there was sufficient evidence to support the jury's finding that Romm possessed three or more images of child pornography. Coupled with Romm's conceded knowledge that the images were saved to his disk, the prosecution produced sufficient evidence to establish every element of knowingly possessing child pornography under 18 U.S.C. § 2252A.

Id. at 1000–01. Is this analysis persuasive? Does it depend on what Romm meant when he told the federal agents that he "saved" the images and later "deleted" them? Or does it depend on whether Romm knew how to access the browser cache?

5.   *Access with intent to view.* In 2008, the federal child pornography statutes were amended to add an additional prohibition beyond distribution, receipt, and possession. The new prohibition punishes anyone who "knowingly accesses" child pornography "with intent to view" it. It is now included along with the prohibition on possession in 18 U.S.C. 2252(a)(4) and 18 U.S.C. 2252A(a)(5). See Enhancing the Effective Child Pornography Prosecution Act of 2007, Pub. L. No. 110–358, § 203(b) (2008). A Senate report explained:

This section fills a gap in existing law that has led some courts to overturn convictions of possessors of child pornography. It amends the child pornography possession offense to clarify that it also covers knowingly accessing child pornography on the Internet with the intent to view child pornography. In *United States v. Kuchinski*, the Ninth Circuit ruled that such conduct is not covered by the current possession offense.

S.Rep. No. 110–332, at 5.

What do you think it means to "access" an image with an "intent to view" it? Does "access" have the same meaning as it did in 18 U.S.C. § 1030, the federal prohibition on unauthorized access to a computer? What does it mean to "access" an image—does that mean obtain possession of the image, or open the file containing the image, or something else? Or does the language in the Senate report suggest that "accessing" refers to obtaining the material on the Internet?

In United States v. Cray, 450 Fed.Appx. 923 (11th Cir. 2012), the defendant knowingly visited a website that contained child pornography and viewed some of the movies on the website. When he was interviewed by law enforcement, the defendant admitted that he had often viewed child pornography online but promised that he never downloaded or saved any images to his computer. His claim provided no defense, however, as the

Eleventh Circuit easily concluded that Cray plainly had knowingly "accessed" the movies on the website "with intent to view" them. *Id.* at 928.

One context in which "access" with "intent to view" will be clear is when a defendant created and then logs in to an account on a dedicated child pornography website. Evidence that the defendant was the one who logged in to the website will establish access. Evidence that the defendant collected child pornography then or at other times can then establish intent to view child pornography. *See, e.g.,* United States v. DeFoggi, 839 F.3d 701 (8th Cir. 2016) (affirming conviction for access with intent to view where jury had sufficient evidence to reject defendant's argument that he had accessed the child pornography website "for professional reasons").

Notably, a small number of states go beyond the prohibition on accessing child pornography with intent to view it by simply prohibiting the knowing "viewing" of child pornography. *See* Alaska Stat. § 11.61.123; Ark. Code Ann. § 5–27–602; N.J. Stat. Ann. § 2C:24–4; Ohio Rev. Code Ann. § 2907.323; 18 Pa. Cons.Stat. § 6312(d).

6. *The difference between knowing possession and knowing receipt.* Imagine a computer user is searching for CSAM, and he views some CSAM images that are then stored, without his knowledge, in his computer's browser cache. If the individual does not know how computers work, and he is unaware the images are stored on his computer, he may not be guilty of knowing possession. But is he guilty of knowing receipt of the images?

This issue arose in State v. Jensen, 173 P.3d 1046 (Ariz. App. 2008). Jensen went online and searched for CSAM, and he then viewed the images online. He was charged with sexual exploitation of a minor in violation of Arizona law, A.R.S. § 13–3553(A)(2), which prohibits knowingly receiving or knowingly possessing images of child pornography. On appeal, Jensen argued that based on his lack of knowledge of how computers work, he did not "possess" the images that he had viewed. The court concluded that whether he had possessed the images was irrelevant, because there was sufficient evidence that he had knowingly received them:

> Whether the computer automatically downloaded the images without Jensen's knowledge is irrelevant to whether Jensen knowingly "received" the images. A.R.S. § 13–3553(A)(2) criminalizes not only knowing possession, but also knowing receipt of images of child pornography.

> There is no question Jensen knowingly received such images because he actively searched for those types of images on the computer over an extended period of time, resulting in nearly 25,000 hits for websites containing certain key phrases and combinations of words often associated with child pornography and exploitation of minors.

> Jensen's knowledge of receipt of illegal pornography is implicit in his intentional searches for child pornography. Contrary to Jensen's contention, the act of intentionally searching for and accessing a

website for child pornography is not the equivalent of merely looking at a picture in a museum. Detective Core explained that in accessing a website, the computer loads a copy of the digital information available at the website into the computer's random access memory or RAM. In other words, the operator actually obtains a copy of whatever is viewed on the monitor, in this case the three images of child pornography, by the act of accessing the website. The fact that the images were contemporaneously saved automatically on the hard drive without further action by the operator is irrelevant because it does not diminish the nature and fact of the receipt of the images.

Id. at 1051–52.

In *Jensen*, the defendant argued that searching for and viewing images of CSAM was like going to a museum and looking at pictures. The court rejected the analogy on the ground that it does not accurately describe how computers work. But what if a person genuinely believes that this is how computers work? Imagine that a person goes online, searches for CSAM, and then views it, but he believes that the computer is a magic box that brings him to the images rather than the images to him. Is he guilty of knowing receipt?

7. *Liability for accidental receipt and possession.* Imagine a computer user surfs the web and innocently clicks on a link that happens to bring up CSAM. Clicking on the link causes the image of CSAM to travel across the network and store itself automatically in the user's browser cache. Is the user criminally liable, either for receipt or possession?

Consider the Seventh Circuit's answer in United States v. Watzman, 486 F.3d 1004, 1019 (7th Cir. 2007):

To be convicted of receiving, the defendant must have known the material he was receiving depicted minors engaged in sexually explicit conduct. Accordingly, a person who receives child pornography by accident (for example, if he sought adult pornography but was sent child pornography instead) is not guilty of knowingly receiving it, though he is guilty of possessing it if he retains it.

To understand why a person could be guilty of possession if he retains it, think about the meaning of possession. A person knowingly possesses contraband when he has knowledge and control over the contraband, regardless of whether he initially wanted to have that control when he first came into possession of the substance. For example, imagine *A* hands *B* a jar of leafy substance with the label "oregano." *B* believes the leafy substance is oregano. When he gets home, however, he opens the jar and realizes that the substance is marijuana. Under traditional principles of criminal law, *B* will be guilty of knowing possession as soon as he realizes that the substance is marijuana but does not take immediate steps to dispossess himself of the marijuana. Transferring that concept to digital images, a defendant has knowing possession of an accidentally downloaded image of CSAM when he realizes that the image contains CSAM and is stored in his computer but does not take immediate steps to dispossess himself of the image.

This dynamic may help explain why the safety valve clauses of 18 U.S.C. § 2252(c) and 18 U.S.C. § 2252A(d) are limited to possession and do not cover distribution or receipt. A person who accidentally comes into possession of child pornography cannot be guilty of knowingly transporting or receiving child pornography, but he may be guilty of knowing possession. The affirmative defenses in § 2252(c) and § 2252A(d) are quite narrow, however. First, they only apply if a defendant possesses one or two "matters" containing child pornography, which presumably means one or two images. Second, the defendant must "promptly and in good faith, and without retaining or allowing any person, other than a law enforcement agency, to access any visual depiction or copy thereof," either take "reasonable steps to destroy each such visual depiction" or "report[ ] the matter to a law enforcement agency and afford[ ] that agency access to each such visual depiction."

8. *Does copying a computer file containing CSAM constitute a separate crime beyond possession? Should it?* In People v. Hill, 715 N.W.2d 301 (Mich. Ct. App. 2006), a defendant downloaded CSAM images from the Internet and then saved the images on a CD. Michigan law prohibits making, possessing, and distributing child pornography, but does not prohibit receiving it. The government charged the defendant with making child pornography (a 20-year felony) instead of merely possessing child pornography (a 4-year felony) on the theory that copying the digital images onto the CD literally "made" child pornography. The defendant argued that "making" child pornography referred only to recording actual acts of child molestation, not copying digital files. A Michigan intermediate appellate court agreed with the government:

> The CD-Rs, as compiled by defendant, were defendant's own creations; he made child-pornography CD-Rs. The term "make" is defined as follows: "to bring into existence by shaping, changing, or combining material." Random House Webster's College Dictionary (2001). Defendant acquired child sexually abusive material via the Internet, and he shaped, formed, and combined the material through placement of various selected pictures, videos, and images onto specific CD-Rs, bringing into existence something that had not previously existed, i.e., distinctly created and compiled child-pornography CD-Rs.

> Given the intricacies of computer and Internet technology, we think it helpful to present an analogy, viewing a simpler scenario in which an individual obtains a magazine containing photographs of children engaging in sexual acts from another person or source. Receipt and retention of the magazine would merely reflect evidence of possession, which would give rise to a four-year felony under MCL 750.145c(4). In this scenario, the amount of child pornography in our society is not increased by the act of transferring the magazine to another and the purchaser's mere possession of the magazine. If,

however, the person in possession of the magazine makes copies and reproductions of the pornographic material, he has increased the amount of existing child pornography, or stated differently, he has engaged in acts leading to the proliferation of child pornography in our society. Under such circumstances, he would be guilty of a 20-year felony under the plain language of MCL 750.145c(2) as discussed above. This is essentially what occurred here, except it was accomplished through the use of a computer and CD-Rs.

Id. at 309–10. The Supreme Court of Michigan declined to review the decision over the dissent of Justice Markman, who argued that that the common meaning of the word "make" pointed in a different direction:

> Does a person who downloads a pirated movie "make" such a movie and would the person be subject to the same penalty as the person who originally pirated the movie? Does a person who downloads a pirated song "make" such a song and would the person be subject to the same penalty as the person who originally made available the song? Does a person who downloads a defamatory article from the Internet "make" such an article and would the person be subject to the same penalty as the original publisher of the defamation?

People v. Hill, 722 N.W.2d 665, 666 (Mich. 2006) (Markman, J., dissenting).

Under the approach of the appeals court in *Hill*, doesn't every effort to possess CSAM also involve "making" it? Or is there a legal difference between a browser's making a temporary copy as a step toward permitting the user to view a file and a user's making a permanent copy by burning a CD? As a policy matter, should burning a CD of CSAM be a distinct crime beyond mere possession? Or does the prohibition against distributing images address this concern?

9. *Law enforcement possession of contraband.* CSAM statutes do not have an explicit exception for law enforcement receipt, distribution, and possession of contraband images in the course of a criminal investigation. This presents a potential problem. If a government investigator or prosecutor must seize child pornography and must possess it in the course of a criminal investigation and prosecution, isn't it a crime to investigate or prosecute CSAM? Aren't the police and prosecutors guilty of the same offense as the defendants?

The answer is "no," thanks to an implied exception that courts have traditionally read into criminal statutes: Criminal statutes do not apply to law enforcement acting in the course of their official duties if it would lead to absurd results. This rule is sometimes referred to as the *Nardone* doctrine after its discussion in Nardone v. United States, 302 U.S. 379 (1937).

One of the cases cited in *Nardone*, State v. Gorham, 188 P. 457 (1920), provides an illustration. In *Gorham*, a sheriff on a motorcycle chased after a man who had stolen a car. In order to catch the stolen car, the sheriff had to break the speed limit. Remarkably, however, the sheriff was himself pulled over for speeding by another state police officer. The sheriff was then charged with speeding on the theory that he had been exceeding the speed limit and the statute had no express exclusion for police officers. The Washington Supreme Court overturned the conviction:

> That the enforcement of statutory or ordinance provisions limiting the speed at which a motor-propelled vehicle shall be driven over a public highway against a peace officer would have a tendency to hamper him in the performance of his official duties can hardly be doubted. The case in hand affords an illustration. Here the felon was fleeing with a stolen automobile. Naturally he would pay but little regard to the minor offense of exceeding the speed limit. And, if the sheriff must confine himself to that limit, pursuit in the manner adopted would have been useless, since the felon could not have been overtaken. The rule contended for would also hinder the public peace officer in enforcing the statutes regulating traffic upon the state highways. The statutes contain somewhat stringent regulations as to the speed a motor-propelled vehicle may be driven over them, and contain no exception in favor of the peace officers whose duty it is made to enforce them. If these officers may not pursue and overtake one violating the regulations without themselves becoming amenable to the penalties imposed by them, the old remedy of hue and cry is not available in such instances, and many offenders who are now brought to answer will escape.

Under this doctrine, law enforcement can knowingly receive, possess, and distribute CSAM in the course of their official duties investigating and prosecuting such crimes.

10. *Counting crimes when defendants possess multiple images on multiple devices.* Imagine a defendant has two computers in his home and that each computer contains twenty images of child pornography. Has the defendant committed one single crime of possessing forty images? Or has he committed two crimes of possessing twenty images each? Alternatively, has the defendant committed forty distinct crimes of possession? Put another way, should the number of crimes be determined by the number of images, the number of physical devices, or simply grouped together as a single offense?

Courts have answered these questions by applying the Double Jeopardy Clause of the Fifth Amendment, which instructs: "nor shall any person be subject for the same offense to be twice put in jeopardy of life or limb." Under this provision, a defendant cannot be punished twice for the same act. The difficult question is, what exactly is the "act" prohibited by child pornography laws? Courts have answered this question by undertaking careful and sometimes hypertechnical readings of the different laws that punish possession of child pornography. As a result, there is no one answer to the question. Instead, the answer depends on the specific statute under consideration.

In some instances, courts have held that the relevant statute makes possessing many images on multiple devices one single crime. Consider United States v. Chiaradio, 684 F.3d 265 (1st Cir. 2012), which was brought under 18 U.S.C. § 2252(a)(4)(B). A search of the defendant's home revealed a desktop computer and laptop computer. The desktop contained 5,000 images and the laptop contained 2,000 images. Both computers were connected to the defendant's home wireless network, allowing the exchange of files between them. Prosecutors charged the defendant with two counts of violating 18 U.S.C. § 2252(a)(4)(B)—that is, one count for each computer. On appeal following conviction, the First Circuit ruled that the defendant had committed only one crime rather than two.

The *Chiaradio* court reasoned that before being amended in 1998, § 2252(a)(4)(B) had prohibited only the possession of "three or more images" of child pornography. Circuit precedent at that time had held that the reference to multiple images indicated a Congressional intent to treat possession of many images as one crime. In 1998, the statute was amended to prohibit "one or more images," but the Fifth Circuit reasoned that there was no reason to treat the change in number as a change in the intent to treat possession of multiple images as a single act of possession. As a result, "at least in circumstances similar to the circumstances of this case," a person "who simultaneously possesses a multitude of forbidden images at a single time and in a single place will have committed only a single offense." *Id.* at *5.

In other instances, courts have held that the relevant statute makes possessing many images on multiple devices as many crimes as there are physical devices. Consider United States v. Hinkeldey, 626 F.3d 1010 (8th Cir. 2010), a case involving 18 U.S.C. § 2252A(a)(5). Investigators searched the defendant's home and found over 1,500 images of child pornography on six different storage devices: a computer, a zip drive, and four computer disks. The government charged the defendant with six counts of possession under § 2252A(a)(5)(B)—one for each physical storage device. Following conviction on all six counts, the Eighth Circuit affirmed the six separate convictions.

The *Hinkeldey* court emphasized the textual differences between § 2252(a)(4) and § 2252A(a)(5). Section 2252(a)(4) prohibits the collective act of possessing "one or more images" on whatever physical storage devices may exist. In contrast, § 2252A(a)(5) focuses on the distinct physical storage device, as it punishes one who knowingly possesses "any book, magazine, periodical, film, videotape, computer disk, or any other material that contains an image of child pornography." The textual difference is subtle, but the courts have found it important. Under the cases, then, prosecutors must group acts of possession of images on several physical devices as a single count of possession if they charge the case under § 2252(a)(4). On the other hand, they can charge as many counts of possession as there are physical devices that contain contraband images if they charge the case under § 2252A(a)(5).

Finally, courts have sometimes interpreted the relevant statute so that possession of each individual image constitutes its own separate crime. For a particularly extreme example, consider State v. Berger, 134 P.3d 378 (Ariz. 2006), which interpreted the Arizona child pornography statutes. As the Arizona Supreme Court explained in *Berger*, Arizona has particularly severe child pornography laws:

> Under Arizona law, a person commits sexual exploitation of a minor, a class two felony, by knowingly "distributing, transporting, exhibiting, receiving, selling, purchasing, electronically transmitting, possessing or exchanging any visual depiction in which a minor is engaged in exploitive exhibition or other sexual conduct." Ariz.Rev.Stat. ("A.R.S.") § 13–3553(A)(2) (2002). A "visual depiction," for purposes of this statute, "includes each visual image that is contained in an undeveloped film, videotape or photograph or data stored in any form and that is capable of conversion into a visual image." A.R.S. § 13–3551(11). If a depiction involves a minor under the age of fifteen, the offense is characterized as a dangerous crime against children. A.R.S. § 13–3553(C).

> Under this statutory scheme, the possession of each image of child pornography is a separate offense. Consecutive sentences must be imposed for each conviction involving children under fifteen, and each such sentence carries a minimum term of ten years, a presumptive term of seventeen years, and a maximum term of twenty-four years. A.R.S. § 13–604.01(D), (F), (G), (K). Such sentences must be served without the possibility of probation, early release, or pardon. A.R.S. § 13–3553(C) (prescribing sentencing under § 13–604.01).

Berger, 134 P.3d at 379. In *Berger*, the defendant possessed twenty images and was therefore convicted of twenty crimes. Because each crime required a ten-year sentence served consecutively, the defendant was sentenced to serve *two hundred years in jail* for possessing the twenty images. This was a greater sentence than he would have received if he had committed the actual acts of sexual assault rather than merely possessed images of them. The Arizona Supreme Court affirmed the defendant's sentence, rejecting the defendant's argument that this sentence was so disproportional that it violated the Eighth Amendment.

As a matter of policy, which is the best approach? Should the law focus on the number of images or the number of physical storage devices? Or should it treat the possession of many images on several devices as a single act of possession?

11. *The role of property concepts revisited.* The first section of this Chapter explored how property crimes involving the possession and transportation of stolen property could be applied to economic crimes involving computers. One of the major questions was how the courts could apply concepts such as "transporting" and "possessing" stolen property to cases involving unauthorized uses of data. How do the child pornography laws approach these

types of questions? Do the child pornography laws shed light on the use of stolen property laws to punish unauthorized uses of data, or vice versa?

f) Constitutional Issues

CSAM laws raise a number of important First Amendment issues. The Constitution permits the government to criminalize possession of child pornography. Osborne v. Ohio, 495 U.S. 103 (1990). At the same time, the First Amendment places constitutional limits on the definition of child pornography much like Miller v. California, 413 U.S. 15 (1973), places limits on the definition of obscenity. Those limits were explored in the following case, which considered a constitutional challenge to aspects of the Child Pornography Prevention Act of 1996 that broadly regulated "virtual" child pornography.

ASHCROFT V. FREE SPEECH COALITION
Supreme Court of the United States, 2002.
535 U.S. 234.

JUSTICE KENNEDY delivered the opinion of the Court.

We consider in this case whether the Child Pornography Prevention Act of 1996 (CPPA), 18 U.S.C. § 2251 *et seq.*, abridges the freedom of speech. The CPPA extends the federal prohibition against child pornography to sexually explicit images that appear to depict minors but were produced without using any real children. The statute prohibits, in specific circumstances, possessing or distributing these images, which may be created by using adults who look like minors or by using computer imaging. The new technology, according to Congress, makes it possible to create realistic images of children who do not exist.

By prohibiting child pornography that does not depict an actual child, the statute goes beyond *New York v. Ferber,* 458 U.S. 747 (1982), which distinguished child pornography from other sexually explicit speech because of the State's interest in protecting the children exploited by the production process. As a general rule, pornography can be banned only if obscene, but under *Ferber,* pornography showing minors can be proscribed whether or not the images are obscene under the definition set forth in *Miller v. California,* 413 U.S. 15 (1973). *Ferber* recognized that the *Miller* standard, like all general definitions of what may be banned as obscene, does not reflect the State's particular and more compelling interest in prosecuting those who promote the sexual exploitation of children.

While we have not had occasion to consider the question, we may assume that the apparent age of persons engaged in sexual conduct is relevant to whether a depiction offends community standards. Pictures of young children engaged in certain acts might be obscene where similar depictions of adults, or perhaps even older adolescents, would not. The

CPPA, however, is not directed at speech that is obscene; Congress has proscribed those materials through a separate statute. 18 U.S.C. §§ 1460–1466. Like the law in *Ferber,* the CPPA seeks to reach beyond obscenity, and it makes no attempt to conform to the *Miller* standard. For instance, the statute would reach visual depictions, such as movies, even if they have redeeming social value.

The principal question to be resolved, then, is whether the CPPA is constitutional where it proscribes a significant universe of speech that is neither obscene under *Miller* nor child pornography under *Ferber.*

I

Before 1996, Congress defined child pornography as the type of depictions at issue in *Ferber,* images made using actual minors. 18 U.S.C. § 2252 (1994 ed.). The CPPA retains that prohibition at 18 U.S.C. § 2256(8)(A) and adds three other prohibited categories of speech, of which the first, § 2256(8)(B), and the third, § 2256(8)(D), are at issue in this case. Section 2256(8)(B) prohibits "any visual depiction, including any photograph, film, video, picture, or computer or computer-generated image or picture" that "is, or appears to be, of a minor engaging in sexually explicit conduct." The prohibition on "any visual depiction" does not depend at all on how the image is produced. The section captures a range of depictions, sometimes called "virtual child pornography," which include computer-generated images, as well as images produced by more traditional means. For instance, the literal terms of the statute embrace a Renaissance painting depicting a scene from classical mythology, a "picture" that "appears to be, of a minor engaging in sexually explicit conduct." The statute also prohibits Hollywood movies, filmed without any child actors, if a jury believes an actor "appears to be" a minor engaging in "actual or simulated . . . sexual intercourse." § 2256(2).

These images do not involve, let alone harm, any children in the production process; but Congress decided the materials threaten children in other, less direct, ways. Pedophiles might use the materials to encourage children to participate in sexual activity. "A child who is reluctant to engage in sexual activity with an adult, or to pose for sexually explicit photographs, can sometimes be convinced by viewing depictions of other children 'having fun' participating in such activity." Congressional Finding note (3), notes following § 2251. Furthermore, pedophiles might "whet their own sexual appetites" with the pornographic images, "thereby increasing the creation and distribution of child pornography and the sexual abuse and exploitation of actual children." *Id.,* Findings (4), (10)(B). Under these rationales, harm flows from the content of the images, not from the means of their production. In addition, Congress identified another problem created by computer-generated images: Their existence can make it harder to prosecute pornographers who do use real minors. See *id.,* Finding (6)(A).

As imaging technology improves, Congress found, it becomes more difficult to prove that a particular picture was produced using actual children. To ensure that defendants possessing child pornography using real minors cannot evade prosecution, Congress extended the ban to virtual child pornography.

Section 2256(8)(C) prohibits a more common and lower tech means of creating virtual images, known as computer morphing. Rather than creating original images, pornographers can alter innocent pictures of real children so that the children appear to be engaged in sexual activity. Although morphed images may fall within the definition of virtual child pornography, they implicate the interests of real children and are in that sense closer to the images in *Ferber*. Respondents do not challenge this provision, and we do not consider it.

Respondents do challenge § 2256(8)(D). Like the text of the "appears to be" provision, the sweep of this provision is quite broad. Section 2256(8)(D) defines child pornography to include any sexually explicit image that was "advertised, promoted, presented, described, or distributed in such a manner that conveys the impression" it depicts "a minor engaging in sexually explicit conduct." One Committee Report identified the provision as directed at sexually explicit images pandered as child pornography. *See* S.Rep. No. 104–358, p. 22 (1996) ("This provision prevents child pornographers and pedophiles from exploiting prurient interests in child sexuality and sexual activity through the production or distribution of pornographic material which is intentionally pandered as child pornography"). The statute is not so limited in its reach, however, as it punishes even those possessors who took no part in pandering. Once a work has been described as child pornography, the taint remains on the speech in the hands of subsequent possessors, making possession unlawful even though the content otherwise would not be objectionable.

II

Congress may pass valid laws to protect children from abuse, and it has. *E.g.,* 18 U.S.C. §§ 2241, 2251. The prospect of crime, however, by itself does not justify laws suppressing protected speech. It is also well established that speech may not be prohibited because it concerns subjects offending our sensibilities.

As a general principle, the First Amendment bars the government from dictating what we see or read or speak or hear. The freedom of speech has its limits; it does not embrace certain categories of speech, including defamation, incitement, obscenity, and pornography produced with real children. While these categories may be prohibited without violating the First Amendment, none of them includes the speech prohibited by the CPPA. In his dissent from the opinion of the Court of Appeals, Judge Ferguson recognized this to be the law and proposed that virtual child pornography should be regarded as an additional category of unprotected speech. It would be necessary for us to take this step to uphold the statute.

The Government argues that speech prohibited by the CPPA is virtually indistinguishable from child pornography, which may be banned without regard to whether it depicts works of value. Where the images are themselves the product of child sexual abuse, *Ferber* recognized that the State had an interest in stamping it out without regard to any judgment about its content. The production of the work, not its content, was the target of the statute. The fact that a work contained serious literary, artistic, or other value did not excuse the harm it caused to its child participants. It was simply "unrealistic to equate a community's toleration for sexually oriented materials with the permissible scope of legislation aimed at protecting children from sexual exploitation."

Ferber upheld a prohibition on the distribution and sale of child pornography, as well as its production, because these acts were "intrinsically related" to the sexual abuse of children in two ways. First, as a permanent record of a child's abuse, the continued circulation itself would harm the child who had participated. Like a defamatory statement, each new publication of the speech would cause new injury to the child's reputation and emotional well-being. Second, because the traffic in child pornography was an economic motive for its production, the State had an interest in closing the distribution network. "The most expeditious if not the only practical method of law enforcement may be to dry up the market for this material by imposing severe criminal penalties on persons selling, advertising, or otherwise promoting the product." Under either rationale, the speech had what the Court in effect held was a proximate link to the crime from which it came.

Later, in *Osborne v. Ohio*, 495 U.S. 103 (1990), the Court ruled that these same interests justified a ban on the possession of pornography produced by using children. "Given the importance of the State's interest in protecting the victims of child pornography," the State was justified in "attempting to stamp out this vice at all levels in the distribution chain." *Osborne* also noted the State's interest in preventing child pornography from being used as an aid in the solicitation of minors. The Court, however, anchored its holding in the concern for the participants, those whom it called the "victims of child pornography." It did not suggest that, absent this concern, other governmental interests would suffice.

In contrast to the speech in *Ferber,* speech that itself is the record of sexual abuse, the CPPA prohibits speech that records no crime and creates no victims by its production. Virtual child pornography is not "intrinsically related" to the sexual abuse of children, as were the materials in *Ferber.* While the Government asserts that the images can lead to actual instances of child abuse, the causal link is contingent and indirect. The harm does not necessarily follow from the speech, but depends upon some unquantified potential for subsequent criminal acts.

The Government says these indirect harms are sufficient because, as *Ferber* acknowledged, child pornography rarely can be valuable speech. This argument, however, suffers from two flaws. First, *Ferber's* judgment about child pornography was based upon how it was made, not on what it communicated. The case reaffirmed that where the speech is neither obscene nor the product of sexual abuse, it does not fall outside the protection of the First Amendment.

The second flaw in the Government's position is that *Ferber* did not hold that child pornography is by definition without value. On the contrary, the Court recognized some works in this category might have significant value, but relied on virtual images—the very images prohibited by the CPPA—as an alternative and permissible means of expression: If it were necessary for literary or artistic value, a person over the statutory age who perhaps looked younger could be utilized. Simulation outside of the prohibition of the statute could provide another alternative. *Ferber,* then, not only referred to the distinction between actual and virtual child pornography, it relied on it as a reason supporting its holding. *Ferber* provides no support for a statute that eliminates the distinction and makes the alternative mode criminal as well.

III

Finally, the Government says that the possibility of producing images by using computer imaging makes it very difficult for it to prosecute those who produce pornography by using real children. Experts, we are told, may have difficulty in saying whether the pictures were made by using real children or by using computer imaging. The necessary solution, the argument runs, is to prohibit both kinds of images. The argument, in essence, is that protected speech may be banned as a means to ban unprotected speech. This analysis turns the First Amendment upside down.

The Government may not suppress lawful speech as the means to suppress unlawful speech. Protected speech does not become unprotected merely because it resembles the latter. The Constitution requires the reverse. The possible harm to society in permitting some unprotected speech to go unpunished is outweighed by the possibility that protected speech of others may be muted. The overbreadth doctrine prohibits the Government from banning unprotected speech if a substantial amount of protected speech is prohibited or chilled in the process.

In sum, § 2256(8)(B) covers materials beyond the categories recognized in *Ferber* and *Miller,* and the reasons the Government offers in support of limiting the freedom of speech have no justification in our precedents or in the law of the First Amendment. The provision abridges the freedom to engage in a substantial amount of lawful speech. For this reason, it is overbroad and unconstitutional.

JUSTICE THOMAS, concurring in the judgment.

In my view, the Government's most persuasive asserted interest in support of the Child Pornography Prevention Act of 1996 is the prosecution rationale—that persons who possess and disseminate pornographic images of real children may escape conviction by claiming that the images are computer generated, thereby raising a reasonable doubt as to their guilt. At this time, however, the Government asserts only that defendants *raise* such defenses, not that they have done so successfully. In fact, the Government points to no case in which a defendant has been acquitted based on a "computer-generated images" defense. While this speculative interest cannot support the broad reach of the CPPA, technology may evolve to the point where it becomes impossible to enforce actual child pornography laws because the Government cannot prove that certain pornographic images are of real children. In the event this occurs, the Government should not be foreclosed from enacting a regulation of virtual child pornography that contains an appropriate affirmative defense or some other narrowly drawn restriction.

The Court suggests that the Government's interest in enforcing prohibitions against real child pornography cannot justify prohibitions on virtual child pornography, because "this analysis turns the First Amendment upside down. The Government may not suppress lawful speech as the means to suppress unlawful speech." But if technological advances thwart prosecution of "unlawful speech," the Government may well have a compelling interest in barring or otherwise regulating some narrow category of "lawful speech" in order to enforce effectively laws against pornography made through the abuse of real children. The Court does leave open the possibility that a more complete affirmative defense could save a statute's constitutionality, implicitly accepting that some regulation of virtual child pornography might be constitutional. I would not prejudge, however, whether a more complete affirmative defense is the only way to narrowly tailor a criminal statute that prohibits the possession and dissemination of virtual child pornography. Thus, I concur in the judgment of the Court.

NOTES AND QUESTIONS

1. *The role of obscenity law. Free Speech Coalition* holds that the government may not prohibit the possession of "virtual" child pornography, and that such images are protected by the First Amendment unless they fall within the definition of obscenity from *Miller v. California.* This leaves open the possibility that virtual child pornography can be prosecuted as obscenity if it meets the standard of *Miller.* As a result, one effect of *Free Speech Coalition*

is a likely increase in the frequency of obscenity prosecutions. Is this a positive development?

2. *The PROTECT Act's revisions to the definition of "child pornography."* Congress passed the PROTECT Act, Pub. L. No. 108–21 (2003), a year after the *Free Speech Coalition* decision. Section 502(a) of the PROTECT Act reworked the definition of 18 U.S.C. § 2256(8) so that it now defines "child pornography" for use in § 2252A as follows:

> any visual depiction, including any photograph, film, video, picture, or computer or computer-generated image or picture, whether made or produced by electronic, mechanical, or other means, of sexually explicit conduct, where—
>
> (a) the production of such visual depiction involves the use of a minor engaging in sexually explicit conduct;
>
> (b) such visual depiction is a digital image, computer image, or computer-generated image that is, or is indistinguishable from, that of a minor engaging in sexually explicit conduct; or
>
> (c) such visual depiction has been created, adapted, or modified to appear that an identifiable minor is engaging in sexually explicit conduct.

Note that § 2256(8)(A), involving actual minors, and § 2256(8)(C), which involves so-called "morphed" images, both remain unchanged from the original 1996 Act. Section 2256(8)(D), struck down in *Free Speech Coalition*, has been repealed. Section 2256(8)(B), also invalidated in *Free Speech Coalition*, has been replaced with a much narrower version that applies only to virtual images "indistinguishable from" actual minors. Do you think that the PROTECT Act's narrow definition of virtual child pornography used in § 2256(8)(B) is constitutional?

3. *Morphed images.* Lower courts have so far rejected constitutional challenges to CSAM prosecutions involving "morphed" images. Several circuits have ruled that morphed images are categorically unprotected under the First Amendment. *See, e.g.,* United States v. Mecham, 950 F.3d 257 (5th Cir. 2020); Doe v. Boland, 698 F.3d 877 (6th Cir. 2012); United States v. Hotaling, 634 F.3d 725 (2d Cir. 2011). These circuits have reasoned that morphed images cause children reputational and emotional harms even if they were created in ways that did not involve the sexual abuse of minors. "By using identifiable features of children, [morphed images] place actual minors at risk of reputational harm and are thus not protected expressive speech under the First Amendment." *Boland,* 698 F.3d at 884 (quoting *Hotaling,* 634 F.3d at 729–30).

The Eighth Circuit has taken a somewhat different approach. The Eighth Circuit has ruled that morphed images are categorically outside First Amendment protection only if their creation depicts an underlying crime of sexual abuse of a minor. *See* United States v. Anderson, 759 F.3d 891, 894–95 (8th Cir. 2014). If a morphed image was created without that underlying crime occurring (such as an image of a face of a known and identifiable minor superimposed on the body of an unidentified nude adult), the prosecution must satisfy strict scrutiny in an as-applied First Amendment challenge. Notably, however, the Eighth Circuit ruled that standard satisfied in *Anderson*:

> Even though there is no contention that the nude body actually is that of M.A., a lasting record has been created of her seemingly engaged in sexually explicit activity. She is thus victimized every time the picture is displayed. Although subjects of morphed images like M.A. do not suffer the direct physical and psychological effects of sexual abuse that accompany the production of traditional child pornography, the morphed images' continued existence causes the child victims continuing harm by haunting the children in years to come. Morphed images are like traditional child pornography in that they are records of the harmful sexual exploitation of children. The children, who are identifiable in the images, are violated by being falsely portrayed as engaging in sexual activity.

> Anderson compares this psychological and reputational injury to the "indirect harms" of virtual child pornography—its potential use in seducing minors and its effect on the market for real child pornography—that the Supreme Court found insufficiently compelling in *Free Speech Coalition*. But unlike those harms, which depended upon some unquantified potential for subsequent criminal acts, the damage from a morphed image is felt directly by the identifiable minor and necessarily follows from the speech itself. The government thus has a compelling interest in protecting innocent minors from the significant harms associated with morphed images.

Id. at 895–96.

4.   *The pandering statute.* In United States v. Williams, 553 U.S. 285 (2008), the Supreme Court rejected a First Amendment challenge to 18 U.S.C. § 2252A(a)(3)(B), the so-called "pandering" statute. The statute prohibits presenting, promoting, or advertising materials in a way that leaves the impression that they are CSAM even if they are not. The Court held that the statute was distinguishable from *Free Speech Coalition* and did not violate the First Amendment:

> Offers to engage in illegal transactions are categorically excluded from First Amendment protection. Offers to provide or requests to obtain unlawful material, whether as part of a commercial exchange or not, are similarly undeserving of First Amendment protection. It would be an odd constitutional principle that permitted the government to prohibit offers to sell illegal drugs, but not offers to give them away for free.

> To be sure, there remains an important distinction between a proposal to engage in illegal activity and the abstract advocacy of illegality. The Act before us does not prohibit advocacy of child

pornography, but only offers to provide or requests to obtain it. There is no doubt that this prohibition falls well within constitutional bounds. The constitutional defect we found in the pandering provision at issue in *Free Speech Coalition* was that it went *beyond* pandering to prohibit possession of material that could not otherwise be proscribed.

In sum, we hold that offers to provide or requests to obtain child pornography are categorically excluded from the First Amendment.

Id. at 298–300.

5. *Knowledge that an image depicts a minor.* The Supreme Court held in United States v. X-Citement Video, Inc., 513 U.S. 64 (1994), that 18 U.S.C. §§ 2252(a)(1) and (a)(2), which require that the defendant acts "knowingly," require proof that the defendant knew the images were of a minor. A defendant who genuinely believes that an image is only computer-generated presumably does not act "knowingly" that an image depicts a minor. Putting *Free Speech Coalition* and *X-Citement Video* together suggests that the government must do more than prove that an image was of an actual minor: It must also prove the defendant *knew* the image was of an actual minor. How can the government satisfy this burden? The following case explores these issues.

UNITED STATES V. MARCHAND

United States District Court for the District of New Jersey, 2004.
308 F. Supp.2d 498.

HOCHBERG, DISTRICT JUDGE.

The Defendant, Anthony Marchand, is accused of possessing Child Pornography, in violation of the Child Pornography Prevention Act, 18 U.S.C. § 2252A(a)(5)(B). The Defendant knowingly and voluntarily waived his right to a jury trial. Therefore, this Court is responsible for both findings of fact and conclusions of law. The issues for this Court are: 1) whether the images that the Defendant possessed depicted real minors and 2) whether the Defendant knew that the images he possessed depicted real minors.

I. Findings of Fact

A. Background

Dr. Anthony Marchand was employed by Atlantic Health Systems ("AHS") as director of the pathology lab at Overlook Hospital in Summit, New Jersey. In October or November of 2000, the hospital experienced substantial problems with its computer network. During an investigation into the cause of these problems, a network engineer for the hospital noticed that Dr. Marchand's computer was accessing and downloading imagery from the Internet, resulting in massive re-transmissions on the network. These re-transmissions would cause the network to crash. In

April 2001, new firewall software was installed, due to the problems the hospital had experienced with the network. In addition, AHS installed a sniffer to monitor traffic through the AHS firewall in an effort to identify Internet use that violated AHS' policy.

Dr. Marchand used a computer designated OBE, with the password "amarchand" in his office at Overlook. Between April and August 2001, the OBE computer generated sniffer alerts several times a week while being operated by Dr. Marchand. AHS then assigned a static IP address to Computer OBE to make it easier for the sniffer to trace information to and from Computer OBE and the Internet. Monitoring of the sniffer revealed that Dr. Marchand accessed a variety of web sites that appeared to display child pornography. For example, the sniffer program indicated that the web sites accessed by the OBE computer contained information such as "free illegal site," "free illegal kds," "illegal ki( )s porno video," "illegally shocking 3–11y.o," and "_real_illegal_lolitas archive."

AHS contacted the Federal Bureau of Investigation, and on March 14, 2002, pursuant to a search warrant, the Government conducted a search of Dr. Marchand's office and office computer. When Dr. Marchand was informed that a search warrant for child pornography was being executed in his office, he accompanied the FBI agents and hospital staff to another office where he answered questions. He also handed several computer disks to Special Agent William DeSa ("Agent DeSa"). Later in the interview, Agent DeSa stated that his use of the term child pornography referred to "actual kids engaging in sexual activity, either with children or with adults." During the interview at the hospital, Dr. Marchand stated that he had additional images at home, and that he thought he had approximately 500 images of child pornography. Dr. Marchand then accompanied Agent DeSa and Special Agent Tanya Lamb DeSa ("Agent Lamb") to his home, where he turned over several additional CDs and a computer. In total, the agents retrieved six CDs from Dr. Marchand's office and home as well as the central processing unit from Dr. Marchand's home computer. Dr. Marchand told Agent Lamb that collecting these images "was a hobby, that he didn't realize that it was illegal or improper for him to have for personal enjoyment." Dr. Marchand also explained to Agent Lamb "that some of the images on the CDs were images that he had morphed."

B. The Images

The Government introduced into evidence 35 images from the total number seized. The evidence depicts prepubescent children engaged in sexually explicit conduct.

The children in each of the 35 images look real to the viewer. There is no indication in any of the pictures to alert the viewer that the image was created other than with the use of real children. The lighting in the images appears as it would in a photograph. The children's physical characteristics and their often highly expressive facial features are visible in great detail. A staple is visible in one of the images, indicating that the picture was taken from a compilation of multiple pages, such as a centerfold from a magazine. Some of the children are the subjects of a series of pictures. In each of the pictures within one series, the child depicted has the same appearance, and other details of the images do not vary.

The children in the images range in age from three to fifteen. The Government's expert, Dr. Robert Johnson, estimated the age of the children by comparing the level of development of the children depicted in the images with the stages of sexual maturation designed by John Tanner ("the Tanner Scale"). The Tanner Scale shows pubic hair at specific stages and the age at which it is most likely to occur and the breast development in females and the genitalia, penis, and testicle development in males.

Eleven of the images introduced were earlier published as photographs in child pornography magazines that were printed prior to 1986, a date when computer technology to create realistic virtual images of human beings did not exist. Eight of the images introduced depict actual identified and named children from the United States, England, and Brazil, who had been the subject of investigations by law enforcement into the sexual abuse they suffered. Six of the images were part of two different series of photographs. Each of the images had a file name, and Dr. Marchand organized them into folders. He named the subdirectory containing these folders, "child."

C.   Technology for Virtual Images

Defense Counsel maintained a thorough, creative, and vigorous defense, attacking the Government's case. The main thrust of the Defense was to show that technology exists to create realistic virtual images of child pornography that are indistinguishable from real images of child pornography, and that nothing in the bit structure of the digitized computer image would inform a diligent observer that the image was real rather than virtual. This defense was presented in order to rebut the Government's proofs that the images possessed by the Defendant were of real human children and to create reasonable doubt as to whether Dr. Marchand knew that the images were real rather than virtual from information available to him at the time he possessed the images.

Computer software such as POSER was presented by the Defense. POSER is a tool for artists to use in creating virtual images of people. Although the Defense did not submit any images that had been created using POSER, the Government introduced a limited number of virtual images of clothed adults as examples of what POSER can do. Two of these images were part of a recent contest held by POSER. No nude adults or children were adduced nor were any virtual images of sexually aroused body parts.

The degree to which the images created with POSER appear real and the accuracy of the details depend on the skill of the artist. For example, the software does not create details such as hair growth or vein visibility through skin, although POSER will adjust the size of each body part to be in proportion with the size of the overall human figure. Unlike images that are created by manipulating and "cutting and pasting" pre-existing images, images created with POSER will not contain internal inconsistencies in the background, known as artifacts, which indicate that the pictures are not real. However, when backgrounds other than those created by POSER are imported into the images, POSER will not automatically create proper lighting effects, leaving it to the artist to ensure that the lighting effects, such as shadows cast by one body upon an adjacent figure or upon the ground, appear realistic. The pictures that the Defendant's expert characterized as indicative of pictures created with POSER do not appear at all realistic to the viewer.

II. Application of the Facts to the Law

A. The Charges Against the Defendant

Dr. Marchand is charged with violating 18 U.S.C. § 2252A(a)(5)(B) by knowingly and willfully possessing six computer disks which contained at least three images of child pornography as defined in 18 U.S.C. § 2256(8)(A), which images were shipped and transported in interstate and foreign commerce and which were produced using materials that had been shipped and transported in interstate and foreign commerce.

B. The Elements of the Crime of Possession of Child Pornography under the CPPA

The Government must prove: 1) that the Defendant possessed at least one image of a real minor engaged in sexually explicit conduct; and 2) that the Defendant knew that at least one of the images contained a picture of a real minor engaged in sexually explicit conduct.

To prosecute a defendant under this section, the Government first must prove beyond a reasonable doubt that the image depicts a real child. Prior to the U.S. Supreme Court's decision in *Free Speech Coalition et al. v. Ashcroft,* 535 U.S. 234 (2002), the definition of child pornography included a visual depiction which appeared to be a minor engaging in sexually explicit conduct. 18 U.S.C. § 2256(8)(B). To the extent that this definition encompassed images that were generated entirely by computer, without the use of any actual minors, the Supreme Court held in *Free Speech Coalition* that, absent an obscenity charge, such material was protected by the First Amendment. Thus, the possession of virtual images of minors engaged in sexually explicit conduct is not a crime under the statute charged in this case.

The Government must also prove beyond a reasonable doubt that the Defendant knew that the images he possessed depicted real minors engaged in sexually explicit conduct. *United States v. X-Citement Video, Inc.,* 513 U.S. 64, 78 (1994). In *X-Citement Video,* the Court held that the term "knowingly" refers to the minority age of the persons depicted and the sexually explicit nature of the material. Thus, *Free Speech Coalition* and *X-Citement Video,* read together, require the Government to prove that the defendant knew the images he possessed depicted real children engaged in sexually explicit conduct.

C. *Proofs That the Images Depicted Real Minors*

The Government presented evidence that: 1) eleven of the images were taken from magazines created prior to the invention of computer technology that might make it possible to digitally create such images; 2) law enforcement agents from the U.S., England, and Brazil could positively identify by name the children in eight of the pictures as children whom they had met in person at a time not distant from the age that the child was when he or she was photographed; and 3) an opinion, from a qualified expert who reliably studied the images, that the physical development of the children depicted in the 35 images corresponds to the Tanner scale designed to show the level of physical development that children reach at different ages.

The Government linked the pre-1986 magazine photographs to the images that the Defendant downloaded from the Internet. The Government's computer expert testified that one of the ways to determine whether an image depicts real children is to compare the image to those in the FBI's Child Exploitation and Obscenity Reference File ("Reference File"). The Reference File contains approximately 10,000 images of scanned child pornography that were taken when computer technology was so primitive that a sound inference could be drawn that an image found in the Reference File depicts a real child. Eleven images possessed by Dr. Marchand matched the images in the Reference File and are found to be images of real minors engaged in sexually explicit conduct.

The Government also adduced proof in the form of direct witness identification of real children in eight of the images in evidence. These witnesses identified the children who appeared in the pictures, having met the children during law enforcement investigations into the abuse that these children had suffered.

Officer James Feehan of the Police Department in Peoria, Illinois positively identified the child in G122 as Melissa, who was between nine and ten years old when her father took pornographic pictures of her and distributed them over the Internet. During his investigation, Officer Feehan met Melissa when she was fifteen years old. He testified that

Melissa looked nearly the same at that age as she had looked five or six years earlier when the pornographic pictures were taken.

This evidence leaves no reasonable doubt that the images depict real children. Through direct identification of children, both by law enforcement and by comparison with the FBI Reference File, and through evidence of the appropriate level of development of each of the children depicted, the Government has proven beyond reasonable doubt that the files Dr. Marchand possessed contain pictures of real children.

D.　The Defendant's State of Knowledge

The Court has reviewed evidence regarding: 1) the appearance of the images; 2) the number of images; 3) the number and identity of web sites the Defendant accessed; 4) the language used in the web sites; 5) the mode and manner by which the Defendant viewed and stored the images; 6) the Defendant's state of mind; and 7) the available computer technology and manual skill required to create realistic virtual images, including a small sample of such images posted on the Internet and created with the software most frequently discussed by the Defense. From this evidence, this Court must determine whether there is sufficient evidence from which an inference can be drawn beyond a reasonable doubt that the Defendant knew that the images he possessed were of real children engaged in sexually explicit conduct.

The knowledge element can be proven through direct and/or circumstantial evidence of actual knowledge and through a finding of willful blindness. A Defendant acts knowingly if the fact finder finds beyond reasonable doubt that the Defendant acted with deliberate disregard of the truth. The Government may prove that a person acted knowingly by proving beyond a reasonable doubt that that person deliberately closed his eyes to what otherwise would have been obvious to him. One cannot avoid responsibility for an offense by deliberately ignoring what is obvious. To find knowledge based on willful blindness, it is not enough that a reasonable person would have been aware of the high probability of the truth. The Defendant himself must have been aware of the high probability that the images depicted real children. The Defendant's stupidity or negligence in not knowing is not sufficient to support a finding of knowledge based on willful blindness.

The crux of the issue in this case is whether the Government's evidence proved beyond a reasonable doubt that the Defendant knew that the pictures were of real children. Among other evidence, the Court considers: the details of each image, the staple that appeared in one of the images, a file name that includes the age of the child, the large number of images and the substantial number of separate web sites from which the pictures were downloaded, the fact that certain images showed the same child over and over again as part of a series, the very real facial expressions of the children (sometimes multiple children in the same image), the extremely detailed close-up [of various sexual acts], and the background in the photographs depicting highly detailed furniture, rumpled bedding, general household clutter, and extremely realistic lighting effects.

The circumstantial evidence from which an inference of knowledge may be drawn includes the appearance and number of images which were proven to depict real children. *United States v. Pabon-Cruz,* 255 F. Supp.2d 200, 207 (S.D.N.Y. 2003) (holding that jurors could determine from the appearance and number of images possessed that the defendant could not have believed they were all produced using digital technology rather than real children). The Government presented this Court with fewer images than it presented to the jury in *Pabon-Cruz.* However, *Pabon-Cruz* is still instructive regarding the type of evidence from which an inference of knowledge may be drawn. The appearance of the images and the number of them, once they are proven to depict real children, is appropriate circumstantial evidence that this Court may use to draw an inference of knowledge, including whether or not there is reasonable doubt that Dr. Marchand knew that at least one of the 35 images in evidence depicted a real child engaged in sexually explicit conduct.

This Court has viewed the images itself in considering whether reasonable doubt exists as to Dr. Marchand's knowledge that the children depicted in the images were real. All of the children in the 35 images look utterly real. The level of detail of the children's features in all of the images contrasts startlingly with the sample of POSER virtual images adduced as evidence of the best examples of what virtual-image technology can do.

The multiplicity of images and the fact that the Defendant downloaded them from different web sites also supports a finding that Dr. Marchand knew that at least one of the images depicted a real child. The Court considers all of the evidence, including logical inferences therefrom, based on human experience. Could the Defendant have thought that each of the 35 images, downloaded from many unrelated web sites, was each digitally created by an artist who was skillful enough to complete the task so extraordinarily realistically? It is not as though Dr. Marchand confined himself to one web site which he believed was dedicated to virtual images. Is there reasonable doubt that this Defendant knew that in surfing the web for diverse child pornography sites, he would find at least one picture of a real child engaged in sexually explicit conduct?

In addition to the 35 images themselves, the Government also presented direct evidence regarding the Defendant's state of mind. Dr. Marchand defended himself in his interview with Agent Lamb by saying, *inter alia,* that he did not know it was illegal to possess the images and that some of the images were morphed (digitally manipulated using parts of different real children) on the CDs that he created. By distinguishing between pictures that were morphed and those that were not, the Defendant certainly implied that he believed that the "un-morphed" images depicted real children. Dr. Marchand attempted to exculpate his conduct by claiming that some images were morphed, but his effort at exculpation never claimed that some of the images were virtual. Moreover, the FBI agents told Dr. Marchand that they were interested in pictures of "actual kids engaging in sexual activity, either with children or with adults," and Dr. Marchand responded by saying that he had about 500 images of child pornography. This also sheds light on his state of mind. The Defendant's characterization of 500 of his images as child pornography, especially in light of his effort to distinguish between those that were morphed and those that were not, supports a strong inference that he knew that at least one depicted a real child.

In an effort to rebut the Government's proof as to the Defendant's state of mind, the Defendant points to evidence that he had labeled some of the disks that were seized "Yoda." Defendant argues that this indicates that he believed the children in the images were not real, just as Yoda, a fictional character from the movie Star Wars, is not a real person. This label does not shed light on Defendant's knowledge of the content of the pictures he downloaded, because Yoda was his pet name for the very large computer play station that he used to view the images, and bears no relationship to the images themselves.

The Defense did prove that software like POSER exists and can be used to create virtual images. In order to be persuaded by the Defendant's argument that the existence of POSER creates reasonable doubt, the fact finder must consider whether the Defendant believed that this virtual software was so widely used in 2002, with such consistent skill, that 35 different realistic action images of nude children and adults, including several in a single image, would appear on a wide range of child pornographic web sites. The Government introduced proof that POSER-created images do not look even remotely realistic. No POSER-created image was adduced of a single realistic-looking human, even fully clothed. No evidence of virtual, nude, sexually-aroused adults or virtual, nude, prepubescent children was adduced. No virtual action image was introduced. When asked whether the POSER images introduced into evidence were typical of the type of images that could be created using POSER, the Defendant's computer and Internet technology expert testified that the images were indicative, though not necessarily typical, of the kind of images that could be created using POSER. Not one looked like a real person. Yet, every picture that the Defendant possessed appears absolutely real. Even the lighting and the shadows in each of the pictures is perfectly consistent with the various backgrounds contained in the images, a highly difficult feat to accomplish virtually. Even the Defendant's computer expert, when asked to point out those images that did not look like real photographs, could only point to one image, G121, and no others. Moreover, the expert conceded that when he looked at the pictures, he thought they were real.

Conclusion

The Government has proved beyond a reasonable doubt each element of the crime of possession of child pornography by Dr. Marchand. While *Free Speech Coalition* now imposes a heavy burden on the Government in its proofs, in this case, that burden has been satisfied.

NOTES AND QUESTIONS

1.   *Proving that an image depicts a real child.* Proving that a defendant possessed at least one image that depicted a real child is not difficult for the government in most child pornography cases. Many images of child pornography are from collections that are well known to collectors of child pornography as well as to law enforcement. Some images are known to have been created in a period before computer animation was well-established, often in the 1970s. *See* Philip Jenkins, Beyond Tolerance 80–83 (2001). Others involve known victims. In a case involving a collection of many images of child pornography, the government can search the defendant's computer and select a subset of the images known to involve a real child.

2.   *Proving knowledge that an image depicts a real child.* Establishing that a defendant knew an image involved a real child presents a more difficult task. Imagine that a collector of child pornography reads *Marchand* and takes defensive action based on its teachings. He labels the real child pornography he receives "virtual1," "virtual2," "virtual3," etc.; adds the prefix "virtual" to everything he says or writes regarding pornography; and buys a book on computer-generated images and places it next to his computer. Imagine that the defendant is later arrested and he asserts his Fifth Amendment privilege. If you are the defense attorney, what are your chances of creating reasonable doubt that your client didn't know the images depicted real children? Alternatively, if you are the prosecutor, how might you try to prove beyond a reasonable doubt that the "virtual" defense is a sham?

Marchand offers a number of suggestions for prosecutors. To prove the elements of the offense, the government must present proof beyond a reasonable doubt that the defendant knew at least one of the images was of a real child. To do this, the government can base its case on a group of images that are particularly real-looking. The government may be able to retrieve information from the defendant's computer indicating the source of the images, and it may be able to show that the images saved as "virtual1" and "virtual2" were not retrieved with such filenames. Further, the government may be able to find evidence that the defendant planned a sham virtual defense. As with any such effort, an unintended inconsistency may expose the defendant's scheme.

Finally, imagine a person is interested in collecting only virtual child pornography. He makes an earnest attempt to collect only virtual images, all of which are protected under the First Amendment. Within the collection of mostly virtual images, however, the person ends up with a handful of images that (unbeknownst to him) depict real children. Assume that a prosecutor wrongly concludes that this is a "sham" virtual pornography case, and the prosecutor believes that the virtual collector has knowledge that the images depicted real children. He indicts the collector, and you are appointed to defend him against the charges. What is your trial strategy to show the jury that your client lacks the required mens rea?

3. *The specific standard when many images exist.* Imagine that the government searches a suspect's computer hard drive and discovers 500 images of child pornography. The government selects twenty particularly real looking images and another twenty known images to offer as evidence of possession. Assume that there is some overlap between the two groups; some of the known images also look particularly real. Is it sufficient that the government can prove beyond a reasonable doubt that at least one of the images in the group was real and that the defendant believed one of the images in the group was real? Or must the government prove beyond a reasonable doubt that at least one of the images was both real and believed to be real? If you are a defense attorney in such a case, do you want the trier of fact to be a judge or a jury?

4. *The "indistinguishable" doctrine.* As modified by the PROTECT Act of 2003, federal law prohibits the possession, receipt, and distribution of virtual child pornography if it is "indistinguishable" from images of actual children. *See* 18 U.S.C. §§ 2252A, 2256(8)(B) (2003). Assuming this law is constitutional, what must the government prove to establish a violation for possessing, distributing, or receiving virtual child pornography? Must the government prove that the image looks real, and that the defendant actually believed it was real? Or is it sufficient for the government to prove that the image looks real, and the defendant knew that it looked real? As a matter of statutory interpretation, does the combination of 18 U.S.C. §§ 2252A and 2256(8)(B) require proof of knowledge that the image involves a real child, or is the statute satisfied by knowledge that the image is virtual but indistinguishable from an image of a real child? If the latter, what exactly does it mean to know that a virtual image is indistinguishable from an image of a minor?

5. *The role of the jury.* If it is difficult for a juror to know whether an image is real or computer-generated, does that difficulty render child pornography laws unconstitutionally vague? In United States v. Boehman, 2009 WL 1210989 (W.D. Ky. 2009), the district court held that the answer is "no." Whether the image is real or computer-generated is a factual issue for the jury, the court concluded, and does not render the statute vague. Note that courts have also concluded that expert testimony is not required to assist the jury: Although either side may wish to put on an expert to testify as to whether the images are real, no experts are required. *See, e.g.,* United States v. Salcido, 506 F.3d 729, 734 (9th Cir. 2007).

6. *The role of technological change.* In the past, realistic computer generated images were relatively rare. Today, however, technological advances are leading to the creation of more realistic computer-generated images and video. *See generally* Robert Chesney & Danielle Keats Citron, *Deep Fakes: A Looming Challenge for Privacy, Democracy, and National Security,* 107 Cal. L. Rev. 1753 (2019).

Assume this trend continues, and imagine the year is 2050. It is now easy to use a computer to generate a picture that looks real. There is no way to distinguish real photographs from computer-generated ones, and all photographs are presumed to be fake. In fact, one popular software program permits a user to scan in a set of photographs of a person, and the computer can then use those images to construct a computer-generated composite. The computer can output an endless series of entirely realistic images of that person, at any age, performing a wide range of acts as directed by the user.

If this future becomes reality, what will happen to CSAM laws?

2. TRAVELER CASES AND ENTRAPMENT

A second type of child exploitation offense involves so-called "traveler" cases. Traveler cases trace their lineage to the Mann Act, Pub. L. No. 61–277 (1910). The Mann Act was passed during a period of tremendous public concern that young girls, many of them recent immigrants, were being kidnapped and forced into lives of prostitution. Given the limits of federal court jurisdiction, especially at the time, Congress responded by passing a law that focused liability on the crossing of state lines with the purpose of engaging in illegal sexual activities. For example, the key provisions of the Act prohibited transporting women across interstate lines and enticing women and younger girls to cross state lines with the intent of having them engage in "prostitution or debauchery, or for any other immoral purpose."

The modern version of the Mann Act appears at 18 U.S.C. § 2421 *et seq.*, and contains a number of prohibitions that are often used in child exploitation cases involving the Internet. The statutes harness state law, and particular state statutory rape law, which generally prohibits sexual contact with a person under the age of consent as determined in that state. For example, 18 U.S.C. § 2422(b) prohibits using "the mail or any facility or means of interstate or foreign commerce" to entice a minor to engage in illegal sexual activity. The Internet obviously is such a means, which permits § 2422(b) to be used widely in cases involving the luring of children online. Similarly, 18 U.S.C. § 2423(a) prohibits enticing a minor to travel in interstate commerce to engage in "any sexual activity for which any person can be charged with a criminal offense," and § 2423(b) prohibits traveling in interstate commerce with the purpose of engaging in such an activity. This means that if an adult uses the Internet to contact a young girl, and then either travels across state lines to meet her or has her travel to meet him, the traveling or enticing violates § 2423.

The federal government prosecutes several hundred traveler cases every year. Many of the cases arise from undercover operations which begin with law enforcement officers posing as minors in Internet chat rooms. In many cases, the defendant contacts the undercover agent and asks to meet to engage in a sexual act. He then travels across state lines with the intent to meet the young victim. Upon crossing state lines, the defendant is arrested. In such cases, the elements of the offense are usually easy for the government to prove and difficult for a defense attorney to challenge. The traveling in interstate commerce is easy to show, and the government's case tends to focus on proving the defendant's intent to engage in sexual activity with a minor. Proving intent is straightforward in most cases. The combination of the chat room logs and items in the defendant's possession at the time of his arrest normally will establish the defendant's intent beyond a reasonable doubt.

The primary legal issue raised by traveler cases is the entrapment defense. Entrapment is not a constitutional claim, which means that federal and state standards for entrapment can and do vary. Generally speaking, however, there are two different aspects to entrapment law. The first aspect is inducement, which occurs when a government agent pressures or encourages a suspect to commit a crime. It is not enough for the agent to merely provide the suspect with an opportunity to commit the crime. Rather, the government must actively encourage or promote the offense. *See* United States v. Gendron, 18 F.3d 955, 961 (1st Cir. 1994).

The second aspect of entrapment is predisposition, which looks at whether facts known about the suspect suggest that he was unusually likely to have agreed to commit the offense absent the inducement. Predisposition might be established by past criminal convictions; if a defendant has committed the same offense in the past, it will often show a predisposition to commit the same offense again. Predisposition might also be established by statements or acts by the defendant establishing his interest in the offense before any inducement occurred.

Exactly how the two aspects of entrapment relate to each other can vary based on the jurisdiction. Some jurisdictions focus entirely on inducement. Others look to both inducement and predisposition. Under federal law, the defendant must put forward evidence of inducement and lack of predisposition before being entitled to an instruction on entrapment. If some evidence is put forward by the defendant, then the government bears the burden of proving beyond a reasonable doubt that the defendant either was not induced to commit the crime or was predisposed to commit the offense.

STATE V. DAVIES

Court of Appeals of Arizona, 2008.
2008 WL 4965306.

SWANN, JUDGE.

Russell Paul Davies appeals his conviction for Luring a Minor for Sexual Exploitation because the trial court refused to instruct the jury regarding the affirmative defense of entrapment. We agree that the jury should have been so instructed. We, therefore, reverse his conviction and remand for a new trial.

Facts

On July 31, 2006, the State of Arizona charged Defendant with one count of Luring a Minor for Sexual Exploitation, a class three felony and a dangerous crime against children. The charge stemmed from events occurring on July 27, 2006, when Defendant engaged in an Internet chat with a Phoenix detective, who was posing as a fourteen-year-old girl. The chat became sexual in nature, and Defendant was taken into custody when he arrived to meet the fictitious girl in an apartment complex parking lot.

Defendant entered a plea of not guilty and the matter proceeded to its first trial in the Maricopa County Superior Court on March 20, 2007. There, the trial court included an instruction on the entrapment defense. The jury was unable to reach a verdict and a mistrial was declared.

The case proceeded to trial for a second time before a different judge on August 23, 2007. As in the first trial, the evidence presented by the State included a transcript of the Internet chat and a videotaped interview of Defendant conducted by police the night he was taken into custody. Also, as in the first trial, the evidence included the testimony of the detective who had posed as the minor.

Before the cross examination of the detective in the second trial, Defendant requested that the trial court instruct the jury on the entrapment defense. Defendant argued that the transcript of the Internet chat presented by the State could be interpreted in a manner that would constitute sufficient evidence of entrapment to entitle him to the jury instruction. The State conceded that "as far as predisposition goes, we don't believe that there's been any evidence that he had a predisposition to this type of crime," but argued that there was, nonetheless, no entrapment because the idea to commit the offense did not originate with the detective and because the detective did not urge or induce Defendant to commit the offense.

The trial court denied the request and refused to include the entrapment instruction.

The defendant exercised his right against self-incrimination and did not testify. The court did not reconsider the request for the entrapment instruction.

On August 29, 2007, the jury found Defendant guilty of the charged offense. He was subsequently sentenced to ten years of probation, with conditions including five months of jail time, sex offender registration, and GPS monitoring.

Discussion

On appeal, Defendant contends that the trial court abused its discretion in refusing to instruct the jury on entrapment. The State disagrees. The State also argues that even if there was error, it was harmless error, and therefore Defendant is not entitled to a reversal of his conviction.

The issue whether a defendant asserting entrapment has met his burden as to the elements of the affirmative defense is normally an issue of fact for the jury to decide. It is an abuse of discretion for the trial court to decide the issue, unless there is no evidence to support the defense of entrapment or there is uncontradicted evidence of entrapment.

In Arizona, a defendant is entitled to a jury instruction on any theory of defense recognized by law, so long as that theory is reasonably supported by the evidence. This is not a demanding standard—while a Defendant must show more than a mere scintilla of evidence, an instruction *must* be given if there is evidence upon which the jury could rationally sustain the defense. If the standard is satisfied, but the trial court refuses to give the instruction, then there is reversible error.

Under A.R.S. § 13–206, to prevail on an entrapment defense, the defendant must prove the following elements by clear and convincing evidence:

1. The idea of committing the offense started with law enforcement officers or their agents rather than with the person.

2. The law enforcement officers or their agents urged and induced the person to commit the offense.

3. The person was not predisposed to commit the type of offense charged before the law enforcement officers or their agents urged and induced the person to commit the offense.

The record reveals that there was not an absence of evidence supporting entrapment; rather, there was some evidence reasonably supporting the defense. Therefore, the issue of whether Defendant was entrapped was for the jury to decide, and the trial court abused its discretion by deciding the issue based upon its own evaluation of the facts.

The transcript[4] of the Internet chat could reasonably be interpreted as supporting the elements of the entrapment defense. The exchanges recorded between Defendant and the fictitious minor are not unambiguous, and a reasonable juror could conclude that the idea of sexualizing the conversation originated with the detective rather than Defendant.[5] Specifically, a reasonable juror could conclude that Defendant was not asking about sex (much less sex with a minor) when he asked: "Russell D: you have a bf or too young? Lol."

There is evidence from which a reasonable juror could also find that when Defendant asked about dates with an ex-boyfriend, he was not asking about sex. The juror could then find that the detective was therefore the first to bring up the topic of sex when he used the phrases "bf and gf stuff" and "kiss and stuff," phrases that at trial he acknowledged as referring to sex:

Russell D: where'd you and your bf go on dates to?

sweetgirlinaz2006: movies the mall stuff like that

sweetgirlinaz2006: he come over here sometimes

sweetgirlinaz2006: when mom not home

Russell D: why when mom not home?

Russell D: she not like him?

sweetgirlinaz2006: not alot

Russell D: what would you do over there?

sweetgirlinaz2006: hang out

Russell D: cool

Russell D: kinda boring jk lol

sweetgirlinaz2006: lol

sweetgirlinaz2006: we would do bf and gf stuff

Russell D: at 14 what do bfs and gf's do? lol

sweetgirlinaz2006: kiss and stuff

A juror could also find that the idea of meeting originated with the detective rather than Defendant. The juror could find that Defendant spoke in jest when he brought up the topic of meeting because he used acronyms such as "lol" for "laughing out loud" and "jk" for "just kidding." The juror

---

   [4]   Portions of the transcript are reproduced below. The screen name "Russell D" is Defendant and "sweetgirlinaz2006" is the detective. Original spelling, punctuation, acronyms, and abbreviations are preserved to avoid confusion.

   [5]   The conversation took place in a chat room that was neither explicitly sexual by nature nor suggestive of the presence of minors.

could find that it was the detective who first addressed the topic seriously and who asked whether Defendant wanted to meet:

> Russell D: your mom would be really mad if I showed up at your place LoL
>
> sweetgirlinaz2006: yea
>
> sweetgirlinaz2006: lol
>
> sweetgirlinaz2006: shes not here
>
> sweetgirlinaz2006: shes at work then goin out with bf
>
> Russell D: so you inviting me over? jk haha
>
> sweetgirlinaz2006: lol
>
> sweetgirlinaz2006: u leeve
>
> Russell D: no I'm still here lol
>
> sweetgirlinaz2006: k
>
> Russell D: you still here? jk lol
>
> sweetgirlinaz2006: yep
>
> Russell D: YaY
>
> Russell D: thought may of scared you away lol
>
> sweetgirlinaz2006: no why
>
> Russell D: I don't know
>
> Russell D: saying if you were inviting me over LoL that was kinda weird
>
> sweetgirlinaz2006: oh
>
> sweetgirlinaz2006: u want ot come over

Moreover, there is evidence on the record from which a reasonable juror could find that the idea of engaging in illegal sexual conduct originated with the detective rather than Defendant, and also that the detective urged and induced Defendant to commit the offense. The juror could find that Defendant initially only wanted to "hang out" and kiss, and it was only after the detective urged and induced Defendant that he offered to engage in sexual conduct. Kissing is not proscribed by the statute under which Defendant was charged. A.R.S. §§ 13–3554 (defining the offense of Luring a Minor for Sexual Exploitation as the solicitation or offering of "sexual conduct" with a minor), –3551(9) (2001) (omitting "kissing" as a type of "sexual conduct").

sweetgirlinaz2006: what all we gonna do

Russell D: we can kiss and go from there. whatever you are comfortable with

sweetgirlinaz2006: tell me so i know what ur thinkin is all russell

sweetgirlinaz2006: just want to knwo what ur thinkin is all

sweetgirlinaz2006: what we gonna do

Russell D: hang out

sweetgirlinaz2006: and do what

Russell D: watch tv or something

sweetgirlinaz2006: nevermind russell ur not bein straight with me

sweetgirlinaz2006: take it easy

Russell D: what do you mean?

sweetgirlinaz2006: bye russell

Russell D: what don't go

Russell D: I want to meet you

Russell D: if we hit it off we can kiss

sweetgirlinaz2006: k

Russell D: is that ok?

sweetgirlinaz2006: what else I just wnat to know what im gettin in to is all

Russell D: I think we should just kiss for now

sweetgirlinaz2006: k

Russell D: are you ok with that?

sweetgirlinaz2006: i think ur lyin about what we gonna do

sweetgirlinaz2006: i just dont wnat to get into somthin without knowin before is all

Russell D: I didn't want to say anything specific cause if I go and you decide we don't hit it off and don't want to kiss me then I don't want you to feel bad

sweetgirlinaz2006: but what would u wanna do

Russell D: thats something we'd have to decide together at the moment

Russell D: at a minimum I want to meet you

Russell D: we can talk for a little bit and if you like me we can start to kiss

sweetgirlinaz2006: k

sweetgirlinaz2006: what else

Russell D: for now thats all I want to do

sweetgirlinaz2006: tonite thats all

Russell D: yeah

Russell D: then if we get together well e can meet up again

Russell D: is that okay with you?

sweetgirlinaz2006: no i dont want to risk u coming over just for that

sweetgirlinaz2006: thx for bein honest

sweetgirlinaz2006: russell

Russell D: what more would you like to do?

sweetgirlinaz2006: i appreciate it

Russell D: I really don't know what else you're looking for

Russell D: I don't want to scare you away

Russell D: How is that risking it just for that?

Russell D: I could do more if you are willing

sweetgirlinaz2006: like what

Russell D: are you willing

Russell D: ?

sweetgirlinaz2006: to do what

Russell D: we could touch each other

sweetgirlinaz2006: where

Russell D: inbetween legs

A reasonable juror could also find (as the State conceded at trial) that Defendant met his burden to show that he was not predisposed to commit the offense. This possibility is bolstered by the State's admission at trial that there was no evidence of predisposition. A reasonable juror could find that the detective's testimony at trial about the common characteristics of online sexual predators that were lacking in Defendant, combined with a cumulative reading of the chat transcript, show that Defendant was not predisposed.

Although it is undoubtedly true that a reasonable juror could review the transcript and other evidence and come to the conclusion that Defendant failed to carry his burden on the defense of entrapment, the record confirms the existence of "some evidence" reasonably supporting the defense and the requested instruction. There is some evidence that the idea to commit the offense originated with the detective, that the detective urged and induced Defendant, and that Defendant was not predisposed.

The trial court therefore erred in refusing to instruct the jury regarding the entrapment defense.

We review a trial court's error in refusing to give a jury instruction for harmless error. Harmless error exists when we can conclude beyond a reasonable doubt that [the error] did not influence the verdict.

In this case, there were two trials. In the first trial, the jury, considering essentially the same evidence as the jury in the second trial, was given the entrapment instruction and was unable to agree on a verdict. It is possible that this jury was unable to agree because it had been given the entrapment instruction, which was the core of the defense. Accordingly, we cannot conclude beyond a reasonable doubt that the trial court's error in refusing to give the instruction in the second trial, in which Defendant was convicted, did not influence the verdict.

Therefore, the error was not harmless and we must reverse Defendant's conviction.

NOTES AND QUESTIONS

1.   *The merits question.* Imagine you are a juror in the next round of the *Davies* case, and you are instructed on the entrapment defense. Would you conclude that Davies was entrapped?

2.   *The nature of the chat room.* Footnote 5 of *Davies* states that the conversation between Davies and the undercover officer "took place in a chat room that was neither explicitly sexual by nature nor suggestive of the presence of minors." Imagine the chatroom conversation had instead been initiated in a chatroom called "oldermenwholikegirls." Would that fact make a difference? Would the name of the chatroom show predisposition?

3.   *Law enforcement policies to avoid an entrapment defense.* Imagine you are a lawyer in the Office of the General Counsel at the Federal Bureau of Investigation. What guidelines would you put in place to regulate FBI online undercover operations to avoid entrapment issues in future prosecutions for child exploitation crimes? For example, would you permit your agents to pose on social media as young children? If you permit agents to visit chatrooms posing as minors, would you let them contact individuals in the chatrooms, or would you require them to wait to be contacted by others?

4.   *Accountability for online entrapment.* Do the dynamics of online interactions indicate a need for changes in entrapment doctrine? Consider Dru

Stevenson, *Entrapment by Numbers*, 16 U. Fla. J.L. & Pub. Pol'y 1, 69–70 (2005):

> There is less accountability for government where the enforcement method is cheap and relatively invisible when orchestrated. Traditional stings typically require a host of armed "backup" agents nearby in case the primary undercover operative encounters trouble. Catching pedophiles can be done mostly from a cubicle in an office. In addition, the Internet enables a single officer to entrap multiple individuals at once, as through on-line bulletin board postings. This feature of on-line entrapment may not be undesirable from a policy perspective, but it is a significant change from the traditional arrangement that the entrapment defense contemplated. Third, the inexpensive, relatively invisible nature of such operations also permits private entrapment to become rampant, which is not the case in off-line settings or with other crimes. On-line vigilantism against pedophiles, in fact, has taken on unexpected proportions.

Do you agree that there is less police accountability online? If an agent turns on a logging function so that every word in a chat room or IM exchange is recorded, isn't there greater accountability online rather than less? Won't agents turn on that function to collect evidence against the defendant? And if there is more private entrapment online, is that a good thing or a bad one?

5. *Private entrapment.* There is no defense of private entrapment. The legal defense of entrapment can only be raised if the inducement was made by a government actor or a private person acting as an agent of the government. Is this sound as a matter of policy?

6. *The role of state law in federal prosecutions.* Prosecutions under 18 U.S.C. § 2422 and § 2423(a) normally require a violation or attempted violation of state law. The statutes prohibit traveling or enticing with intent to engage in sexual activity "for which any person can be charged with a criminal offense," which generally requires an analysis of state sexual assault law. State sexual assault laws can vary, however, which may create issues as to whether particular conduct is prohibited by state law in that jurisdiction.

Consider the facts of United States v. Patten, 397 F.3d 1100 (8th Cir. 2005). A police officer in West Fargo, North Dakota, posed in an Internet chat room as a 16-year-old girl. The defendant, 26-year-old Casey Patten, visited the chat room from his home in nearby Moorhead, Minnesota. The officer persuaded Patten to come to a grocery store in West Fargo, where the defendant was arrested. The law of North Dakota and Minnesota differ in a critical respect: in Minnesota, consensual sexual conduct between a 26-year-old man and a 16-year-old girl is legal, whereas the same conduct is illegal in North Dakota.

The defendant argued that there was insufficient evidence that he had intended to engage in sexual activity in North Dakota, and therefore that he had not violated the federal statute. According to the defendant, he had planned to engage in the activity in Minnesota, where it would have been legal. The Eighth Circuit affirmed the conviction, ruling that there was sufficient evidence from the facts of the case for a reasonable juror to conclude that the defendant intended to persuade the girl to engage in sexual activity in North Dakota. *See id.* at 1103–04.

7.   *The impossibility defense.* Defendants in Internet undercover cases sometimes try to raise the impossibility defense. They argue that although they did try to meet a child to engage in sexual activity, they cannot be prosecuted because no actual child was involved. The offense was "impossible," the argument runs, because the child was actually an adult officer. Such defenses have been universally rejected, consistent with the modern trend away from recognizing an impossibility defense in other contexts. Courts have reasoned that the presence of a child is irrelevant because the liability is for attempt rather the substantive crime of engaging in sexual activities with a minor. *See, e.g.*, People v. Thousand, 631 N.W.2d 694 (Mich. 2001) (en banc).

CHAPTER 4

SENTENCING

■ ■ ■

When a defendant is convicted, a court must next impose a sentence. The law of criminal sentencing tends to focus on two issues. The first issue is whether to impose a prison term, and the length of any prison term imposed. The second issue is the conditions of any period of probation or post-incarceration supervised release.

The materials in this chapter consider sentencing law for computer crimes. The first part considers as a policy matter whether sentences for computer-related crimes should be different from sentences for equivalent physical crimes. The second part introduces the reader to the United States Sentencing Guidelines, and explores how the guidelines apply in child pornography cases. The third part considers how the Sentencing Guidelines apply in cases brought under 18 U.S.C. § 1030. The fourth section covers restrictions on computer use imposed in federal court as a condition of probation or supervised release.

A. ARE COMPUTER CRIMES DIFFERENT?

NEAL KUMAR KATYAL—CRIMINAL LAW IN CYBERSPACE
149 U. Pa. L. Rev. 1003, 1042–47, 1071–75 (2001).

Before computers, a criminal typically needed to work with other individuals to conduct serious criminal activity. Group crime arose for obvious reasons, from economies of scale to specialization of the labor pool. For example, it is nearly impossible for one person to rob a bank successfully. Several individuals are needed to carry weapons and provide firepower (economies of scale); someone needs to plan the operation (a form of specialization of labor); another must serve as a lookout (specialization again); and many people are needed to carry the money. Working together with others, whether in the criminal or corporate world, creates obvious efficiencies, as Ronald Coase explains in his pathbreaking article about why firms develop.

But computers change all this, and undermine the need for criminal conspiracy. * * * [A] cyberthief can, by herself, design a program to steal money from an electronic bank account or data from the Defense Department, rather than enlist a team to do so. A fraud artist can, by herself, send thousands of e-mails to unsuspecting recipients to create a Ponzi scheme. A child pornographer can create, store, and distribute images, and receive royalties or access fees without assistance. In these situations, a computer enables a single individual to launch a crime: No individual in realspace could break and enter a physical premise, and remove and steal the classified material without detection, perpetrate all the aspects of a Ponzi scheme, or run a child pornography ring. Cyberspace, however, is different. The electronic walls that secure money and data are pierced, not by additional thugs, but, rather, by additional computer power. In addition, cyberspace avoids the physical constraints of realspace (a burglar can only carry away a certain amount of loot and be in one place at a time).

If [the goal of criminal punishment is to deter harm], then it makes sense to punish the use of a computer to carry out a crime as if the computer were a quasi-conspirator. Doing so will deter the greater damage computer crime can incur per unit of investment in the enterprise.

In sum, the law might develop penalties for using computers to aid a criminal offense. The case for criminalization proceeds from the fact that computers and co-conspirators are substitutes for each other. The solution proposed would not necessarily require treating computers as full co-conspirators, but it would require eliminating the law's current conceptualization of a computer as simply a method of crime, not a type of (or substitute for) a participant in crime.

A separate form of reduced costs to the criminal in cyberspace is the ease of escape. Because computer crime can be perpetrated by anyone, even someone who has never set foot near the target, the range of potential suspects is huge. This is unlike traditional crime, in which there is a high likelihood that a crime is committed by someone known to or seen by either the victim or the community in which the crime took place. A criminal in realspace has to be physically present to rob a bank, but a cybercriminal can be across the globe. This makes the crime easier to carry out, easier to conceal, and tougher to prosecute.

Despite some indications of the government's ability to trace criminal suspects online, the truth is that tracing is very difficult. A criminal may leave behind a trail of electronic footprints, but the footprints often end with a pseudonymous e-mail address from an ISP that possesses no subscriber information. Moreover, finding the footprints is often very difficult. Criminals can be sophisticated at weaving their footprints through computers based in several countries, which makes getting permission for real-time tracing very difficult. Unlike a criminal who needs to escape down a particular road, a criminal in cyberspace could be on any road, and these roads are not linked together in any meaningful fashion. The internet works by sending packets of data through whatever electronic pathway it finds most efficient at a given time. The protocol moves these packets a step closer to their destination, an electronic hop, without trying to map out a particular course for the next node to use when the packet arrives. Each hop ends in a host or router, which in turn sends the information on to the next host. What's more, sometimes large packets divide into smaller packets to be reassembled by the end-user when all the packets show up. Sometimes packets never arrive, due to network congestion and mistakes.

The upshot is that it is very difficult for law enforcement to find a criminal after an attack, particularly when the criminal can be on any road and evidence of her crime can be split into numerous subparcels, each of which is not itself incriminating. Even in those cases in which law enforcement has the technology and permission under applicable law to trace an attack, the investigators must be skilled at carrying out such a trace in order for it to be successful, and they must have knowledge about how to preserve the data trails in such a way that they will be admissible evidence in a criminal trial. Regular and frequent training of law enforcement is a necessity, as is up-to-date technological equipment. Government prosecutors and police must also be trained in the application of constitutional and statutory liberties in the internet context. Furthermore, the contraband and materials can be physically stored anywhere on the planet, making such evidence difficult to find and difficult to introduce in a court. Incriminating files of a criminal organization, such as the profits made from drug dealing, may be stored thousands of miles away. Alternatively, the evidence could reside in the United States but be moved abroad literally with a keystroke—whenever a person or an entity comes under criminal suspicion. Computers could also make it easier for criminals to disrupt law enforcement by spying on informants and sabotaging networks.

Because these factors lower the probability of successful enforcement, it may be appropriate to offset this lowered probability by increasing the magnitude of the criminal sanction.

NOTES AND QUESTIONS

1. *When should using a tool to commit a crime lead to greater punishment?* Every technological tool has the capacity to facilitate criminal activity. Imagine a man robs a bank while wearing a ski mask (to avoid being identified) and while carrying a gun (to encourage compliance with his demands). Should the defendant receive a higher punishment because he wore the ski mask? Should he receive a higher punishment because he carried the gun? Are the gun and ski mask "quasi-conspirators" in the bank robbery? What general principle explains our intuitions about when use of a tool to facilitate a crime should change the appropriate punishment? How do computers fit in to that picture?

2. *A realistic view of deterrence.* Professor Katyal argues that higher punishments are needed for computer crimes to offset the ways computers facilitate crime. The thinking is that defendants will know they are facing greater punishments for computer crimes, and the fear of greater punishment will deter criminal behavior. Is this view of deterrence realistic?

3. *Are new approaches needed?* Sentencing schemes usually factor in the amount of loss or damage caused by a particular criminal offense. If a crime causes greater damage, it leads to greater punishment regardless of how the crime was committed. This means that if computers help wrongdoers commit crimes on a broader scale than before, computer crimes will trigger higher punishment even without special rules for computer-related offenses. Does this make it unnecessary to have new rules for punishing computer crimes?

4. *Retribution and computer crime.* Deterrence is one goal of criminal punishment; retribution is another. What kinds of punishment are appropriate for computer crimes from a retributive perspective?

Retributivists might argue that a person who consciously confronts the wrongfulness of his conduct but continues with the offense is more culpable than one who does not fully appreciate the wrongfulness of his behavior. Computer-related crimes may seem more virtual, less harmful, and less real than their offline equivalents. From a retributive perspective, is someone who commits a computer-related crime likely to be *less* deserving of punishment than someone who commits an otherwise equivalent physical crime?

Imagine John breaks into a closed store at night and snoops around. That same night, Jane goes online and hacks into a server at an e-commerce site and looks through various files. It takes John two days to plan the physical crime and three hours to commit it; it takes Jane thirty minutes to plan and commit the digital version of the offense. To John, the offense is very real; to Jane, it feels like a computer game. Should Jane receive a higher sentence than John because computer crimes are easier to commit and harder to detect? Or should John receive a higher sentence because he fully appreciated the wrongfulness of his conduct?

If deterrence theory points in the direction of greater punishments for cybercrimes, and retributive theory points in the opposite direction, which theory should win out? Should we call it a tie?

5. *Anonymity and deterrence.* Does the relative anonymity of the Internet encourage unlawful behavior? Researchers tried to answer this question using a decoy website. *See* Christina Demetriou & Andrew Silke, *A Criminological Internet "Sting": Experimental Evidence of Illegal and Deviant Visits to a Website Trap*, 43 Brit. J. Criminology 213 (2003).

The designers of the study set up a website called "Cyber Magpie," and turned on logging functions that recorded every visit to the site. They advertised the site on newsgroups, promoting it as a legal source of "excellent freeware and shareware games." Upon entering the site, however, visitors were offered a choice of both legal and illegal materials. The site was configured to show visitors seven links: 1) a legal disclaimer, 2) shareware and freeware, 3) games (both free and hacked), 4) illegally obtained commercial software, 5) soft-core pornography, 6) hard-core pornography, and 7) stolen passwords that could be used to access pornographic sites. (The site did not actually distribute such materials; users who attempted to access them would encounter a message that the materials were unavailable.)

The Cyber Magpie site was available for 88 days, and during that time it logged 803 visitors. The researchers determined that 93% of the visitors initially accessed the site looking for legal shareware or freeware games. However, the most popular link turned out to be hard-core pornography: 60% of visitors to Cyber Magpie clicked on the link to try to view it. Further, 45% of users accessed the portion of the site that hosted soft-core pornography; 41% attempted to access the part of the site containing illegal copyrighted commercial software; and 38% accessed the portion of the site that claimed to have illegally hacked games. Roughly similar numbers accessed the parts of the website that featured the shareware and freeware games and other legally accessible software. Only 2% of visitors viewed the legal disclaimer.

Are you surprised by these results? The authors of the study comment, *id.* at 220:

> The acts observed in this study occurred in a situation of perceived anonymity for the perpetrators, and there were immediate personal rewards for the visitors to do what they did. Such a combination of factors creates a situation where deviant behavior is not simply common, it actually becomes the norm. Only a minority of visitors to Cyber Magpie avoided the illegal or pornographic sections. Such findings have disturbing implications with regard to how we think about—and respond to—crime and deviancy in cyberspace. As more and more people access and use the Internet on an increasingly regular basis, we can expect more people to become aware of, and exposed to, a range of opportunities to commit various illegal and socially questionable behaviours. Worryingly, this research suggests that a majority of Internet users will not resist temptation. The implications of this loom large for those charged with policing the Internet and with developing policy on how it should and can be governed.

Are the authors' concerns valid? Are Internet users who choose to visit a freeware site called "Cyber Magpie" representative of Internet users as a whole? On the other hand, if the authors are correct that "the majority of Internet users will not resist temptation" to engage in criminal activity online, how should the law respond?

6.   *Higher sentences for some computer crimes under the United States Sentencing Guidelines.* In federal court, criminal sentences are imposed under the complex structure of the United States Sentencing Guidelines. Materials later in this chapter consider in detail how the Sentencing Guidelines apply to computer crimes. For now, however, it is worth noting that Congress and the

Sentencing Commission have treated computer crimes differently from analogous physical crimes in a number of ways.

For example, provisions of the Sentencing Guidelines applicable to child pornography offenses provide for an enhanced sentence "[i]f the offense involved the use of a computer or an interactive computer service for the possession, transmission, receipt, or distribution of the material." U.S.S.G. § 2G2.2(b)(6). This enhancement was first enacted in 1995. The House Report accompanying the legislation that led to this enhancement explained the rationale:

> Distributing child pornography through computers is particularly harmful because it can reach an almost limitless audience. Because of its wide dissemination and instantaneous transmission, computer-assisted trafficking is also more difficult for law enforcement officials to investigate and prosecute. Additionally, the increasing use of computers to transmit child pornography substantially increases the likelihood that this material will be viewed by, and thus harm, children. Finally, the Committee notes with particular concern the fact that pedophiles may use a child's fascination with computer technology as a lure to drag children into sexual relationships. In light of these significant harms, it is essential that those who are caught and convicted for this conduct be punished severely.

H.R. Rep. No. 104–90, at 3–4 (1995), *reprinted in* 1995 U.S.C.C.A.N. 759, 760–61. Do you agree? Most child pornography offenses prosecuted today involve computers. Does this make the case for an enhancement stronger or weaker today than in 1995, when Congress first enacted the enhancement?

7.   *Use of a special skill.* The Sentencing Guidelines allow sentencing judges to increase the punishment when a defendant uses a special skill to facilitate the commission of an offense. The use of a special skill leads to an increase in the defendant's offense level, which, as we will see, corresponds to a higher sentence. The section, U.S.S.G. § 3B1.3, applies broadly across federal crimes:

> If the defendant abused a position of public or private trust, or used a special skill, in a manner that significantly facilitated the commission or concealment of the offense, increase by 2 levels. This adjustment may not be employed if an abuse of trust or skill is included in the base offense level or specific offense characteristic[.]

Application Note 3 then explains that special skills "refers to a skill not possessed by members of the general public and usually requiring substantial education, training or licensing. Examples would include pilots, lawyers, doctors, accountants, chemists, and demolition experts."

When is using a computer in a crime "use of a special skill"? Are computer skills "special"? If a defendant commits a computer crime, does he necessarily deserve greater punishment?

UNITED STATES V. LEE

United States Court of Appeals for the Ninth Circuit, 2002.
296 F.3d 792.

KLEINFELD, CIRCUIT JUDGE.

This case involves application of the special skills sentencing adjustment to the use of a computer.

Facts

The Honolulu Marathon Association has a web site at "www.honolulu-marathon.org." During the relevant time, U.S. residents could use the site to register for the Honolulu Marathon and pay the registration fee online. Although many Japanese enter the race, the site did not permit online registration from Japan, but told Japanese entrants to register through an office in Japan.

The appellant, Kent Aoki Lee, lived in Honolulu, where he owned a video rental store. Lee came up with a scheme to sell marathon services to the marathon's Japanese market. Lee owned a computer server, which he kept on the premises of an internet service provider with whom he had a dial-up internet account. He registered the domain name "www.honolulu-marathon.org" and created a site almost identical to the official Honolulu Marathon site by copying its files onto his server. While the official site did not permit online registration from Japan, Lee's site contained an online registration form written in Japanese on which runners could enter personal information and credit card information. While the official registration fee was $65, Lee's site charged $165. The extra $100 over the registration fee covered a package including transportation to the race site, a meal, and a tour. Of course, none of this was legitimate, since Lee's web site and registration package were not authorized by the Honolulu Marathon Association. Seventeen people tried to register through Lee's site.

Lee's scheme was uncovered and he pleaded guilty to one count of wire fraud and one unrelated count of selling Viagra without a prescription. The main issue at sentencing was whether the district court could impose the special skills adjustment based on Lee's use of computer skills in creating his phony site.

Lee created his phony site by copying the legitimate site's files onto his computer server. Web sites consist of multiple web pages, which consist of individual computer files written in "hypertext markup language," or "HTML." The HTML files constituting a web site are located through a directory on a computer server. A computer directory is like a card in an old-fashioned library catalog, that tells where to find a book on a shelf. However a site's HTML files are referenced, they are linked together in the directory to create the whole web site. These links reflect the specific location of individual files within the server's structure of directories and subdirectories. The graphics on a web page are actually individual computer files to which that page's HTML file links, causing them to appear when the web page is displayed. An individual graphic file may be in the same directory as the HTML file to which it's linked, or in a subdirectory, or on another computer server altogether, and the link reflects that specific location. To copy a web site onto another computer server, it's not enough to copy the HTML file and the graphics for each web page. The copier must also recreate the directory structure of the original site or edit the links in the HTML files to reflect the different directory structure.

The creator of the genuine Honolulu Marathon site testified that Lee could have copied most of the site without knowing much about its directory structure, by using off-the-shelf software such as Microsoft's *FrontPage 98,* aided by a general circulation book such as *FrontPage 98 for Dummies.* She also testified that a program like *FrontPage* would have written a line of code into the fake site's HTML files, indicating that it had been used. There weren't any such lines of code in the HTML files on Lee's site, suggesting that he didn't use this easy approach to copying the site. The creator of the authorized web site also testified that Lee could have pirated the site, much more slowly and laboriously, by using a text editor to copy it page by page (there were 130 individual web pages) and recreating the original site's directory structure so that each web page would properly display graphics and link to the other pages on the site. The legitimate site had two features, databases containing entrants' registration information and a list of past race results, that Lee could not copy onto his phony site, so he linked to those features on the genuine site so that they would appear to be part of his fake web site.

Lee's phony site contained one feature that was not on the genuine site, the online entry form that allowed residents of Japan to sign up for the marathon and provide a credit card account number to be billed for payment of the entry fee. The information entered on this form was processed using a "script," which is a program written in "common gateway interface," or "CGI," a programming language. The CGI script used by Lee's phony site didn't directly charge credit cards. It just stored the credit card data in a file on Lee's server, so that Lee could manually charge the cards later. (This database file was password protected, which the government's witness testified would require some knowledge of the server's operating system.) An excerpt of *FrontPage 98 for Dummies* that was read into the record told readers that to do CGI scripts, they should get help from someone experienced with computer programming. The official site's creator testified that writing a CGI form-handling script from scratch would have required significant programming expertise, but that modifying an existing script would have been much easier. She also testified that CGI scripts could be downloaded from the internet, and that web sites could be found that advised how to modify scripts to suit particular online forms.

The district court did not make a finding as to whether Lee copied the web site the easy way, such as by using *FrontPage 98* and *FrontPage 98 for Dummies* (and perhaps deleting the software's identifying code using a text editor), or the hard way, using a text editor to copy the web site's HTML files page by page and figuring out the original site's directory structure. Nor did the court make a finding as to whether Lee downloaded the CGI script for his online form from the internet or made it himself from scratch, and if so, whether he had any expert assistance. Nor did the court make a finding as to whether Lee or his internet service provider maintained his server. The district court found that Lee "was skilled at accessing and manipulating computer systems" and imposed the special skills enhancement. The adjustment raised the guideline sentencing range from six to twelve months to ten to sixteen months. This increase deprived the district court of the sentencing option of imposing no imprisonment.

Although Lee pleaded guilty, he reserved his right to appeal if the district court imposed the two-level special skill adjustment under U.S.S.G. § 3B1.3. Serving of the sentence awaits disposition of this appeal.

Analysis

The special skill adjustment provides for a two-level increase "[i]f the defendant abused a position of public or private trust, or used a special skill, in a manner that significantly facilitated the commission or concealment of the offense." The abuse of a position of trust part of the adjustment applies to positions "characterized by professional or managerial discretion," such as an attorney serving as a guardian who embezzles the client's money, a bank executive's fraudulent loan scheme, or a physician who sexually abuses a patient under the guise of an examination, but not to embezzlement by a bank teller or hotel clerk. The application note defining "special skill" says that it is "a skill not possessed by members of the general public and usually requiring substantial education, training, or licensing. Examples would include pilots, lawyers, doctors, accountants, chemists, and demolition experts."

The district court based its imposition of the adjustment on our decision in *United States v. Petersen,* 98 F.3d 502 (9th Cir. 1996). The issue in the case at bar is whether Lee was more like the defendant in *Petersen,* or more like the defendant in another of our special skills cases, going the other way, *United States v. Green,* 962 F.2d 938 (9th Cir. 1992). We conclude that the scope of discretion was not broad enough, in view of the limited findings, to treat this case like *Petersen,* and that it has to be put in the same class as *Green,* where we held that it was an abuse of discretion to impose the special skills adjustment. This conclusion keeps our circuit's law consistent with that of the Sixth Circuit, which held in *United States v. Godman*, 223 F.3d 320 (6th Cir. 2000), that a level of computer expertise like Lee's did not justify imposition of the adjustment.

The defendant in *United States v. Petersen*, which upheld the adjustment, was an expert hacker. He hacked into a national credit reporting agency's computer system and stole personal information that he used to order fraudulent credit cards. Then he hacked into a telephone company's computers, seized control of the telephone lines to a radio station, and arranged for himself and his confederates to be the callers who "won" two Porsches, $40,000, and two trips to Hawaii in a radio call-in contest. Then he hacked into a national commercial lender's computer and got it to wire $150,000 to him through two other banks. This goes far beyond the computer skills of a clever high school youth or even many people who earn their livings as computer technicians and software engineers.

The district court found that Petersen had "extraordinary knowledge of how computers work and how information is stored, how information is retrieved, and how the security of those systems can be preserved or invaded" and imposed the special skill adjustment. We affirmed, holding that "despite Petersen's lack of formal training or licensing, his sophisticated computer skills reasonably can be equated to the skills possessed by pilots, lawyers, chemists, and demolition experts" for purposes of the special skills adjustment.

In a footnote, we went out of our way in *Petersen* to caution against routine application of the special skills enhancement to people with computer skills:

> We do not intend to suggest that the ability to use or access computers would support a special skill adjustment under all circumstances. Computer skills cover a wide spectrum of ability. Only where a defendant's computer skills are particularly sophisticated do they correspond to the Sentencing Commission's examples of special skills—lawyer, doctor, pilot, etc. Courts should be particularly cautious in imposing special skills adjustments where substantial education, training, or licensing is not involved.

This footnote distinguishes *Petersen* from the case at bar, because Lee's skills are not "particularly sophisticated" like Petersen's, and unlike Petersen's, don't correspond to the Sentencing Commission's examples of special skills—lawyer, doctor, pilot, etc. As we said in *Petersen*, where substantial education, training or licensing is not involved, district courts must be especially cautious about imposing the adjustment.

Petersen distinguished *United States v. Green*, where we reversed a special skills adjustment. Green took graphic design classes, learned from an instructor about paper that could be used for currency and about how it could be properly cut, ordered the special paper from a paper company (which tipped off the Secret Service), and took numerous photographs of currency, in the course of his counterfeiting scheme. We held that the printing and photographic skills were not so special as to permit the district court to impose the adjustment, saying it's not enough that "the offense was difficult to commit or required a special skill to complete."

In *United States v. Godman,* the Sixth Circuit considered *Petersen* and quoted and followed our limiting footnote that we quote above. Like Green, Godman was a counterfeiter, but Godman used an off-the-shelf professional page publishing program, Adobe PageMaker, with a scanner and a color inkjet printer. He'd learned PageMaker in a week, and had specialized computer experience preparing and repeatedly updating a color catalog. Godman held that the special skills adjustment could not properly be imposed, because Godman's level of computer skills was not analogous to the level of skill possessed by the lawyers, doctors, pilots, etc. listed in the application note. The Sixth Circuit held that the district court erred by stressing "overmuch" that Godman's skills were not shared by the general public: "As the Application Note's reference to the substantial training of such professionals as doctors and accountants suggests, emphasis is better placed on the difficulty with which a particular skill is acquired." The Sixth Circuit emphasized that "such skills are acquired through months (or years) of training, or the equivalent in self-tutelage."

Our own cases have suggested factors that might make a skill "special" for purposes of this sentencing adjustment, including a "public trust" rationale, the level of sophistication, and special educational or licensing requirements. But this adjustment becomes open-ended to the point of meaninglessness if the phrase "special skill" is taken out of its context. There probably isn't an occupation on earth that doesn't involve some special skill not possessed by people outside it, and few of us who sit as judges would know how to do the work of most of the people who appear before us. So asking whether a skill is "special," in the sense of not being common among the adult population, like driving a car, doesn't get us very far toward deciding any cases.

And focusing much on the "specialness" of a skill is also hard to reconcile with our precedents. In *United States v. Harper,* 33 F.3d 1143 (9th Cir. 1994), the defendant's skills were very special indeed. The robber had worked for both a bank and an ATM service company, and used the knowledge gained in both occupations to come up with a unique scheme to rob an ATM. At just the right time for the last service call of the day, when the ATM service office would empty out while the robbery was going on, she made a withdrawal from an ATM but didn't take the money. She knew that leaving the cash would cause the ATM to shut itself down and generate a service call, which would put technicians on the site, and that they would open the machine so that she and her confederates could rob it. As skills go, Harper's were quite special, but we reversed the sentence because they weren't like those of pilots, lawyers, doctors, accountants, chemists and demolition experts.

Our cases are best reconciled, and this sentencing guideline is best read, as a two-part test. The test is not just whether the skill is "not possessed by members of the general public," but also, as a *sine qua non*, whether it is a skill "usually requiring substantial education, training, or licensing." The application note's reference to "pilots, lawyers, doctors, accountants, chemists, and demolition experts" requires reasoning by analogy, not just reference to dictionary definitions of "special" and "skill." The special skill adjustment falls within the same guideline as an adjustment for people who abuse a "position of public or private trust, or used a special skill." The application notes limit the position of trust adjustment to people with "professional or managerial discretion," analogous to attorneys who hold their clients' money in trust, physicians who treat patients, and "executives" (but not tellers) who manage a bank's loans. The application note for special skills parallels the application note for positions of trust in its reference to people trained or employed at a high level.

Lee was a video rental store operator who copied a web site. The findings don't establish whether he used off-the-shelf software or had to know more about programming, but it doesn't matter because either way, his level of sophistication was nothing like Petersen's. His skills were more like Green's or Godman's than Petersen's, and not in the class of "pilots, lawyers, doctors, accountants, chemists, and demolition experts." Thus, under our precedents and the guideline's application notes, the district court's imposition of the special skills adjustment was not supported by the findings. We therefore reverse and remand for resentencing.

NOTES AND QUESTIONS

1. *Use of a special skill as abuse of trust.* In United States v. Mainard, 5 F.3d 404, 406 (9th Cir. 1993), the Ninth Circuit contended that the purpose of the special skills enhancement is "to add to the punishment of those who turn legitimate special skills to the perpetration of evil deeds":

> In a sense, abuse of a special skill is a special kind of abuse of trust. It is a breach of the trust that society reposes in a person when it enables him to acquire and have a skill that other members of society do not possess. That special societal investment and encouragement allows a person to acquire skills that are then held in a kind of trust for all of us. When the person turns those skills to evil deeds, a special wrong is perpetrated upon society, just as other abuses of trust perpetrate a special wrong upon their victims.

Do you find this retributive rationale persuasive? How does it apply to computer skills?

2.   *What kinds of computer skills should count as special skills?* In 1985, was reasonable proficiency in the use of a personal computer a special skill? How about today? Does the answer depend on the defendant's age? For example, an average set of computer skills among 18-year-olds might be exceptional among 75-year-olds. What standard should govern? Is the best answer a "reasonable person" standard at the time of the offense? Or should computer skills be categorically exempt from the special skills enhancement?

3.   *When technical skill is needed to commit the crime.* Technical skills may be needed to commit a particular crime. Can those skills also constitute "special skills" that justify a higher sentence following conviction? In United States v. Young, 932 F.2d 1510 (D.C. Cir. 1991), the defendant was convicted of conspiring to manufacture and distribute 100 grams or more of pure phencyclidine ("PCP"). Manufacturing PCP requires following a complex chemical process, and the defendant had set up a laboratory to manufacture the drug. The government argued that the understanding of chemistry needed to manufacture PCP amounted to special skills justifying an enhancement.

The D.C. Circuit disagreed, ruling that the defendant did not deserve the enhancement because he was not a trained chemist. Understanding chemistry just enough to commit the offense was insufficient:

> Section 3B1.3 provides a two-level enhancement if the defendant used a special skill, in a manner that significantly facilitated the commission or concealment of the offense. The use of the word "facilitate"—which means "to make easier," see Webster's New Collegiate Dictionary (1977)—is important in this context. It indicates to us that the Sentencing Commission assumed that the defendant knows how to commit the offense in the first place and that he uses a special skill to make it easier to commit the crime. Thus, the special skill necessary to justify a § 3B1.3 enhancement must be more than the mere ability to commit the offense; it must constitute an additional, pre-existing skill that the defendant uses to facilitate the commission or concealment of the offense.

> Nothing in the commentary suggests that § 3B1.3 applies to a criminal who, like appellant, bones up on the tricks of his trade and becomes adept at committing a crime that the general public does not know how to commit. To the contrary, the commentary indicates that § 3B1.3 was intended to punish those who abuse their special skills by using them to facilitate criminal activity rather than legal, socially beneficial activity.

Id. at 1512–13.

How should this apply to computer crimes? Does it matter that most Americans have some computer skills, and that given the broad scope of 18 U.S.C. § 1030, most Americans are also capable of accessing a computer without authorization or exceeding authorized access? Does applying the special skills enhancement to a computer crime amount to double-counting?

4.   *Whose skills matter?* Imagine that *A* is a skilled programmer who creates a new and dangerous computer virus. *B* is *A*'s friend and a novice computer user. *A* shares the virus with *B*, and both *A* and *B*, acting individually, send out the virus in a series of e-mails. Is *A* more culpable than *B*, assuming that they have the same intent to cause damage? Would *A* receive the special skills enhancement under prevailing law?

5.   *Obstruction of justice convictions under 18 U.S.C. § 1519.* In 2002, Congress enacted a new criminal law, 18 U.S.C. § 1519, that prohibits obstruction of justice in investigations by federal agencies:

> Whoever knowingly alters, destroys, mutilates, conceals, covers up, falsifies, or makes a false entry in any record, document, or tangible object with the intent to impede, obstruct, or influence the investigation or proper administration of any matter within the jurisdiction of any department or agency of the United States or any case filed under title 11, or in relation to or contemplation of any such matter or case, shall be fined under this title, imprisoned not more than 20 years, or both.

This law has particular relevance to computer crime cases because the forensic examination of a computer often reveals very precise details about what a criminal suspect did to try to delete evidence. Those details can support a second criminal charge that amounts in practice to a sentencing enhancement. In addition to charging the crime under investigation, the government can charge the defendant with obstructing justice under § 1519.

For example, in United States v. Kernell, 667 F.3d 746 (6th Cir. 2012), a college student named David Kernell hacked into the personal e-mail account of Alaska Governor Sarah Palin. Palin was the Republican nominee for Vice-President at the time, and Kernell hoped that he could find dirt on Palin that could hurt the Republican ticket in the upcoming presidential election. After the hack, Kernell bragged about his exploit on the Internet message board 4chan.org. One user of 4chan alerted the FBI, and another alerted the Palin campaign. The next day, Kernell realized that he was in trouble:

> Kernell returned to 4chan and began a new thread that began "Hello, /b/" ("the Hello post"). In this thread, Kernell took credit for hacking the Palin email account, and described in detail how he accomplished the task. Kernell claims that he disclosed the password to the 4chan community because he wanted the information "out there," and claimed to have deleted information from his computer as a result of his fear of being investigated. Kernell also criticized the individual who alerted the Palin staffer to the hack.

> At some point between the initial post on 4chan and the evening of September 18, Kernell cleared the cache on his Internet Explorer browser, removing the record of websites he had visited during that

period. He also uninstalled the Firefox internet browser, which more thoroughly removed the record of his internet access using that browser, and ran the disk defragmentation program on his computer, which reorganizes and cleans up the existing space on a hard drive, and has the effect of removing many of the remnants of information or files that had been deleted. Finally, Kernell deleted a series of images that he had downloaded from the Palin email account.

Id. at 749. A jury convicted Kernell of unauthorized access to a protected computer under 18 U.S.C. § 1030 and obstruction of justice under 18 U.S.C. § 1519. On appeal, the Sixth Circuit ruled that § 1519 was not unconstitutionally vague and that there was sufficient evidence to sustain the jury verdict in his case:

> For the government to support a conviction under § 1519, as it relates to Kernell, it must show (1) that he knowingly deleted or altered the information on his computer (2) with the intent to impede, obstruct or influence an investigation that (3) he contemplated at the time of the deletion or alteration. The government has put forward sufficient evidence on each of these points.
>
> Kernell does not dispute the first element. He does not contend that deletion of files or the running of the hard drive defragmenter was done accidentally, instead conceding that he initiated the actions on his computer which removed the information. Kernell does dispute the second element, and contends that there is insufficient evidence to support the conclusion that he deleted the information with obstructive intent. In support of this claim, Kernell essentially argues that nothing that is written on the internet can be taken seriously, so the entire content of the postings Kernell made should be discounted. Kernell is correct that we should exercise caution when interpreting internet postings literally, given that they are often "jargon-heavy," containing obscure references and inside jokes. However, in this case, Kernell's "Hello" posting on 4chan does not require in-depth knowledge of internet culture to interpret. Kernell expressly states that he deleted the information on his computer out of a fear that the FBI would find it, plainly showing that he took his actions with the intent to hinder an investigation. Even with proper skepticism directed toward claims made on the internet, a self-incriminating statement such as Kernell's provides sufficient evidence for a reasonable jury to conclude that he acted with obstructive intent.
>
> Finally, Kernell challenges the sufficiency of the evidence establishing that he contemplated a government investigation when he removed the evidence from his computer. Again, the "Hello" post makes clear that he believed a federal investigation was at least the possible outcome of his actions. That is sufficient to sustain the government's burden under § 1519.

Id. at 756.

B. SENTENCING IN CSAM CASES

Criminal sentences imposed for federal crimes are determined under a framework set up by the United States Sentencing Guidelines. The Sentencing Guidelines are complicated, and studying how they apply in every detail would require a course of its own. For our purposes, however, we can quickly and profitably appreciate the basics of the Guidelines that arise in federal computer crime cases. This will let us see how courts determine the length of prison terms in most cases, even if it glosses over some of the details.

The Sentencing Guidelines are very important because substantive criminal law typically leaves open a wide range of criminal punishments that a court can impose following conviction. Every crime has a statutory maximum punishment, such as five years imprisonment or twenty years imprisonment. A small number of crimes also have mandatory minimum punishments that courts must impose regardless of the circumstances. In most cases, however, substantive statutory law leaves trial judges a great deal of sentencing discretion. For example, if a defendant is convicted of violating a crime with a ten-year statutory maximum punishment and no mandatory minimum punishment, the sentencing judge can in theory impose any prison sentence from zero days up to ten years.

The Sentencing Guidelines were enacted to limit this discretion and to ensure more uniform sentences. The basic idea is that factors relevant to sentencing are considered explicitly by the Guidelines, and this consideration leads sentencing judges to a very specific range of sentences that can be imposed in that particular case. For each case, the judge calculates the "offense level" for the case, calculates the defendant's criminal history category, and then matches up the offense level and criminal history category with a set range of prison time as measured in months.

Under the Supreme Court's decision in United States v. Booker, 543 U.S. 220 (2005), Guidelines determinations are not binding on sentencing judges. Instead, courts must calculate the Guidelines sentence and then consider 18 U.S.C. § 3553. Under § 3553, a court "shall impose a sentence sufficient, but not greater than necessary, to comply" with the following goals of punishment:

(A) to reflect the seriousness of the offense, to promote respect for the law, and to provide just punishment for the offense;

(B) to afford adequate deterrence to criminal conduct;

(C) to protect the public from further crimes of the defendant; and

(D) to provide the defendant with needed educational or vocational training, medical care, or other correctional treatment in the most effective manner;

(3) the kinds of sentences available;

(4) the kinds of sentence and the sentencing range established for—

(A) the applicable category of offense committed by the applicable category of defendant as set forth in the guidelines . . . issued by the Sentencing Commission

(b) Application of guidelines in imposing a sentence.—(1) In general[, . .] the court shall impose a sentence of the kind, and within the range, referred to in subsection (a)(4) unless the court finds that there exists an aggravating or mitigating circumstance of a kind, or to a degree, not adequately taken into consideration by the Sentencing Commission in formulating the guidelines that should result in a sentence different from that described.

Under this statute, the Guidelines continue to be the primary authority used to determine the length of federal sentences. Although the Guidelines are not the entire story, they do provide the starting point.

Applying the Guidelines generally involves six steps:

1) Select the offense guideline.

The first step is to select the proper offense conduct guideline for the specific criminal offenses that the defendant violated. Chapter Two of the Guidelines contains the offense conduct guidelines that are applicable in different types of criminal offenses. Each offense conduct guideline explains how to calculate the offense level for that type of offense. For example, U.S.S.G. § 2A1.1 is the offense conduct guideline for first-degree murder cases, U.S.S.G. § 2A1.2 is for second-degree murder cases, and U.S.S.G. § 2A1.3 is for manslaughter cases. An appendix associated with the Guidelines contains a chart connecting most federal criminal statutes to their relevant offense conduct guidelines.

The Chapter Two offense guidelines that are most important in computer crime cases are U.S.S.G. § 2G2.2, applicable in child pornography offenses, and U.S.S.G. § 2B1.1, applicable in most economic crime cases including most computer misuse offenses. Because these are the two most important offense guidelines, the remainder of the material in this chapter will focus on their application.

2) Determine the offense level for the crime.

The next step is to determine the offense level for the crime by applying the relevant offense guideline from Chapter Two. To calculate this, start with the base offense level and then adjust that number by applying the special offense characteristics. This excerpt from § 2G2.2 provides the key guidance used to calculate sentences in most child pornography offenses:

(a) Base Offense Level:

(1) 18, if the defendant is convicted of 18 U.S.C. § 2252(a)(4), § 2252A(a)(5), or § 2252A(a)(7).

(2) 22, otherwise.

(b) Specific Offense Characteristics

(1) If (A) subsection (a)(2) applies; (B) the defendant's conduct was limited to the receipt or solicitation of material involving the sexual exploitation of a minor; and (C) the defendant did not intend to traffic in, or distribute, such material, decrease by 2 levels.

(2) If the material involved a prepubescent minor or a minor who had not attained the age of 12 years, increase by 2 levels.

(3) (Apply the greatest) If the offense involved:

(A) Distribution for pecuniary gain, increase by the number of levels from the table in § 2B1.1 (Theft, Property Destruction, and Fraud) corresponding to the retail value of the material, but by not less than 5 levels.

(B) Distribution for the receipt, or expectation of receipt, of a thing of value, but not for pecuniary gain, increase by 5 levels.

(C) Distribution to a minor, increase by 5 levels.

(D) Distribution to a minor that was intended to persuade, induce, entice, or coerce the minor to engage in any illegal activity, other than illegal activity covered under subdivision (E), increase by 6 levels.

(E) Distribution to a minor that was intended to persuade, induce, entice, coerce, or facilitate the travel of, the minor to engage in prohibited sexual conduct, increase by 7 levels.

(F) Distribution other than distribution described in subdivisions (A) through (E), increase by 2 levels.

(4) If the offense involved material that portrays (A) sadistic or masochistic conduct or other depictions of violence; or (B) sexual abuse or exploitation of an infant or toddler, increase by 4 levels.

(5) If the defendant engaged in a pattern of activity involving the sexual abuse or exploitation of a minor, increase by 5 levels.

(6) If the offense involved the use of a computer or an interactive computer service for the possession, transmission, receipt, or distribution of the material, or for accessing with intent to view the material, increase by 2 levels.

(7) If the offense involved—

(A) at least 10 images, but fewer than 150, increase by 2 levels;

(B) at least 150 images, but fewer than 300, increase by 3 levels;

(C) at least 300 images, but fewer than 600, increase by 4 levels; and

(D) 600 or more images, increase by 5 levels.

Notably, the Sentencing Guidelines direct the sentencing court to include all "relevant conduct" in the court's calculations, even if that conduct was not charged in the indictment, admitted in a guilty plea, or proved at trial. *See* U.S.S.G. § 1B1.3. As a result, when considering what conduct the offense "involved," you should include all of the defendant's acts that relate to the crime, not just the specific facts that led to the conviction.

An example will help illustrate how these rules work in practice. Imagine an undercover agent is in an Internet chat room posing as a collector of child pornography, and that a suspect sends the agent one image of child pornography. The agent obtains the suspect's Internet records, finds out where he lives, and then searches his home to seize his computer. A search of the suspect's home computer reveals 200 images of child pornography. The suspect then pleads guilty to possessing child pornography.

What offense level should be reached in such a case? Begin with a base offense level of 18 under § 2G.2.2(a)(1) because the defendant pled guilty to possession instead of receipt or distribution. Second, increase two levels under § 2G2.2(b)(3)(F) because the relevant conduct included distributing the image to an undercover police officer. Next, increase two levels under § 2G.2.2(b)(6) because the crime involved a computer. Finally, increase another three levels under § 2G.2.2(b)(7)(B) because of the quantity of images. The resulting offense level should be 25.

3) *Apply upward or downward adjustments.*

Chapter Three of the Sentencing Guidelines contains adjustments to the offense level that a court can make to reflect the specific circumstances of the crime, the defendant, and the victim. These adjustments apply to all crimes, not just crimes covered in a specific offense conduct guideline. For example, a defendant who had a major role in a conspiracy can receive an increase in the offense level, *see* U.S.S.G. § 3B1.1, while a defendant who played only a minor role in a conspiracy can receive a decrease in the offense level, *see* U.S.S.G. § 3B1.2. As noted earlier, a defendant who used special skills in the commission of an offense can receive an increase in the offense level pursuant to U.S.S.G. § 3B1.3.

One downward adjustment that is applied in a majority of cases is the adjustment for acceptance of responsibility, U.S.S.G. § 3E1.1. This adjustment usually applies when a defendant elects to plead guilty rather than go to trial:

> (a) If the defendant clearly demonstrates acceptance of responsibility for his offense, decrease the offense level by 2 levels.
>
> (b) If the defendant qualifies for a decrease under subsection (a), the offense level determined prior to the operation of subsection (a) is level 16 or greater, and the defendant has assisted authorities in the investigation or prosecution of his own misconduct by taking one or more of the following steps: (1) timely providing complete information to the government concerning his own involvement in the offense; or (2) timely notifying authorities of his intention to enter a plea of guilty, thereby permitting the government to avoid preparing for trial and permitting the court to allocate its resources efficiently, decrease the offense level by 1 additional level.

Application Note 2 to this provision explains that "[t]his adjustment is not intended to apply to a defendant who puts the government to its burden of proof at trial by denying the essential factual elements of guilt, is convicted, and only then admits guilt and expresses remorse."

The Guidelines also include rules on grouping offenses when a defendant is convicted of multiple offenses. Such rules are necessary because a defendant may be convicted of multiple crimes, some of which are related to each other and others of which are not, and each crime will lead to its own offense level. The grouping rules appear in Chapter Three, Part D of the Guidelines, and explain how the different crimes and offense levels should be resolved to create a single offense level. The rules are quite complicated when considered in detail, but here is the basic approach:

> (1) When the conduct involves fungible items, e.g., separate drug transactions or thefts of money, the amounts are added and the guidelines apply to the total amount.
>
> (2) When nonfungible harms are involved, the offense level for the most serious count is increased (according to a somewhat diminishing scale) to reflect the existence of other counts of conviction.

United States Sentencing Commission, Guidelines Manual 6–7 (2005).

4)   Determine the defendant's criminal history category.

Chapter Four of the Guidelines contains the rules for calculating a defendant's criminal history category. Criminal history categories range from I to VI, and are based on the number of criminal history "points" revealed by the defendant's record of past convictions. Criminal history is a very important part of criminal sentencing: If two defendants are convicted of the same crime, the defendant with a significant criminal history normally will receive a greater prison sentence than the defendant without such a history.

The general rule is that a defendant receives three points of criminal history for every past conviction that led to a sentence of greater than one year in prison; two points of criminal history for every past conviction that led to a sentence between sixty days and a year of prison; and one point for every other criminal conviction up to four points. *See* U.S.S.G. § 4A1.1. A defendant with zero or one criminal history points will have a criminal history category of I; a defendant with two or three points will have a criminal history category of II; four, five, or six points will be category III; and so forth.

    5)   *Find the sentencing range from the sentencing table.*

Chapter Five of the Guidelines contains a sentencing table that assigns a presumptive sentencing range based on the defendant's offense level and criminal history category. The table indicates the range of recommended sentences in months:

Sentencing Table
(in months of imprisonment)

Offense Level	Criminal History Category (Criminal History Points)					
	I (0 or 1)	II (2 or 3)	III (4, 5, 6)	IV (7, 8, 9)	V (10, 11, 12)	VI (13 or more)
1	0–6	0–6	0–6	0–6	0–6	0–6
2	0–6	0–6	0–6	0–6	0–6	1–7
3	0–6	0–6	0–6	0–6	2–8	3–9
4	0–6	0–6	0–6	2–8	4–10	6–12
5	0–6	0–6	1–7	4–10	6–12	9–15
6	0–6	1–7	2–8	6–12	9–15	12–18
7	0–6	2–8	4–10	8–14	12–18	15–21
8	0–6	4–10	6–12	10–16	15–21	18–24
9	4–10	6–12	8–14	12–18	18–24	21–27
10	6–12	8–14	10–16	15–21	21–27	24–30
11	8–14	10–16	12–18	18–24	24–30	27–33
12	10–16	12–18	15–21	21–27	27–33	30–37
13	12–18	15–21	18–24	24–30	30–37	33–41
14	15–21	18–24	21–27	27–33	33–41	37–46
15	18–24	21–27	24–30	30–37	37–46	41–51
16	21–27	24–30	27–33	33–41	41–51	46–57
17	24–30	27–33	30–37	37–46	46–57	51–63
18	27–33	30–37	33–41	41–51	51–63	57–71
19	30–37	33–41	37–46	46–57	57–71	63–78
20	33–41	37–46	41–51	51–63	63–78	70–87
21	37–46	41–51	46–57	57–71	70–87	77–96
22	41–51	46–57	51–63	63–78	77–96	84–105
23	46–57	51–63	57–71	70–87	84–105	92–115
24	51–63	57–71	63–78	77–96	92–115	100–125
25	57–71	63–78	70–87	84–105	100–125	110–137
26	63–78	70–87	78–97	92–115	110–137	120–150
27	70–87	78–97	87–108	100–125	120–150	130–162
28	78–97	87–108	97–121	110–137	130–162	140–175
29	87–108	97–121	108–135	121–151	140–175	151–188
30	97–121	108–135	121–151	135–168	151–188	168–210
31	108–135	121–151	135–168	151–188	168–210	188–235
32	121–151	135–168	151–188	168–210	188–235	210–262
33	135–168	151–188	168–210	188–235	210–262	235–293
34	151–188	168–210	188–235	210–262	235–293	262–327
35	168–210	188–235	210–262	235–293	262–327	292–365
36	188–235	210–262	235–293	262–327	292–365	324–405
37	210–262	235–293	262–327	292–365	324–405	360–life
38	235–293	262–327	292–365	324–405	360–life	360–life
39	262–327	292–365	324–405	360–life	360–life	
40	292–365	324–405	360–life	360–life	360–life	
41	324–405	360–life	360–life	360–life	360–life	
42	360–life	360–life	360–life	360–life	360–life	
43	life	life	life	life	life	

6)   Consider whether a non-guidelines sentence is appropriate.

The last step is to consider whether a non-guidelines sentence is appropriate. Chapter Five of the Guidelines contains provisions that permit a judge to depart from the Guidelines range in special circumstances. For example, a defendant who provided substantial assistance to the prosecution can receive a downward departure under U.S.S.G. § 5K1.1. More broadly, the Supreme Court's decision in United States v. Booker, 543 U.S. 220 (2005), permits sentencing judges to sentence defendants to prison terms outside the relevant Guidelines range so long as the departures from the Guidelines range are "reasonable." *Id.* at 261–62.

NOTES AND QUESTIONS

1.   *More tips on grouping "relevant conduct."* As noted earlier, the Sentencing Guidelines group relevant conduct when calculating the proper offense level. U.S.S.G. § 1B1.3(a)(1) explains that, in determining relevant conduct, courts should include the following:

> (A) all acts and omissions committed, aided, abetted, counseled, commanded, induced, procured, or willfully caused by the defendant; and

> (B) in the case of a jointly undertaken criminal activity (a criminal plan, scheme, endeavor, or enterprise undertaken by the defendant in concert with others, whether or not charged as a conspiracy), all reasonably foreseeable acts and omissions of others in furtherance of the jointly undertaken criminal activity, that occurred during the commission of the offense of conviction, in preparation for that offense, or in the course of attempting to avoid detection or responsibility for that offense;

Further, U.S.S.G. § 1B1.3(a)(2) explains that when the additional evidence constitutes an offense that "would require grouping of multiple counts," the relevant conduct should include "all acts and omissions described in subdivisions (1)(A) and (1)(B) above that were part of the same course of conduct or common scheme or plan as the offense of conviction."

An example shows how this rather complex language applies. In United States v. Fowler, 216 F.3d 459 (5th Cir. 2000), the defendant was convicted of transporting child pornography in violation of 18 U.S.C. § 2252(a)(1) after he sent an image of child pornography to an undercover police officer. A search of Fowler's house revealed two images of child pornography that portrayed violent conduct and that had been stored on Fowler's computer for about two years. The District Court enhanced Fowler's offense level under § 2G2.2, which provides for an increase in the offense level "[i]f the offense involved material that portrays sadistic or masochistic conduct or other depictions of violence." The Fifth Circuit reversed and held that the enhancement could not apply because the "offense" did not include the possession of the violent image:

The electronic mailing of the image that was the basis of the count of conviction occurred at a discrete moment, and Fowler's receipt of the other, sadistic images did not occur "during the commission of the offense of conviction." Further, there was no proof that the sadistic images were part of preparing for the offense of conviction or avoiding detection of the crime.

Id. at 461–62.

On the other hand, slight factual differences can lead to a different result. For example, where a defendant is convicted of possessing images instead of distributing them, the fact that some of the images possessed satisfy § 2G2.2(b)(3) generally will trigger the enhancement as relevant conduct. *See, e.g.,* United States v. Buchanan 485 F.3d 274, 286–87 (5th Cir. 2007).

2. *What are the practical consequences of an extra offense level in terms of the jail time a defendant receives?* The actual impact of an extra offense level depends on whether the offense level is at the high end of the Guidelines or the low end, as well as the defendant's criminal record. Assuming a defendant has no criminal record, each added offense level generally translates to about two months of extra jail time at the low end of the Guidelines, but an extra seven or eight months at the high end. If the defendant has a significant criminal history, the impact of an extra offense level is substantially greater.

3. *The policy question.* Do you agree with the policy choices embodied in U.S.S.G. § 2G2.2? Under § 2G2.2, the length of the prison term depends on factors such as the types of images, the number of images, and what the defendant did with the images. For example, under § 2G2.2(b)(7), a defendant who possessed fifty images of child pornography will generally face a prison term about ten months longer than a defendant who possessed five images (that is, two extra levels); a defendant who possesses 200 images will face about five more months in prison than one who possessed fifty images (one extra level); and a defendant who possessed 1,000 images will face about ten more months in prison than the defendant who possessed 200 images (two extra levels).

Do these numbers make sense? Are the punishments imposed by the Guidelines in child pornography cases too light, too heavy, or about right? Keep in mind that several child pornography offenses contain mandatory minimum punishments. If the Guidelines range is less than the statutory minimum, the statutory minimum trumps the Guidelines range.

4. *What federal judges think about sentencing guidelines for CSAM offenses.* Many federal trial judges believe that the sentencing guidelines for CSAM offenses are too harsh. In 2010, the United States Sentencing Commission published the results of a survey of federal district court judges on their personal views about the appropriateness of sentences under the Sentencing Guidelines. *See* United States Sentencing Commission, Results of Survey of United States District Judges, January 2010 through March 2010. Over half of the active District Court judges completed the survey. Although

the judges generally approved of the Guidelines ranges for most crimes, the child pornography laws proved a major exception. A large majority of judges believed that the prison sentences for possessing and receiving child pornography were too long.

Specifically, 70% of the judges thought that the punishment for possession was too severe, while 3% thought the punishment was too lenient and 26% thought it was about right. The survey results for receipt were nearly identical to those for possession: 69% of the judges thought that the punishment for receipt was too severe, while 3% thought it was too lenient and 28% thought it was about right. The punishment for distribution was significantly more popular. Based on the survey, 30% of the judges thought that the punishment for distribution was too severe, while 8% thought it was too lenient and 62% thought it was about right.

5. *Video clips as images.* Section 2G2.2(b)(7) provides a sentencing enhancement based on the number of images found. In many cases, however, a defendant will possess video clips of child pornography in addition to (or instead of) still images. This raises an almost-metaphysical question: How many "images" are in a video? Fortunately, Application Note 4.B.ii provides an answer: "Each video, video-clip, movie, or similar visual depiction shall be considered to have 75 images. If the length of the visual depiction is substantially more than 5 minutes, an upward departure may be warranted." Under this Application Note, the number of images can accumulate very quickly. A defendant with ten short clips will be deemed to have 750 images, justifying a 5 level enhancement.

Did the Sentencing Commission choose a sound way to translate video clips into images?

6. *Duplicate images.* If a defendant possesses multiple copies of a single image, does that count as multiple images or a single image for purposes of counting images under 2G2.2(b)(7)? In United States v. Ardolf, 683 F.3d 894 (8th Cir. 2012), the defendant stored multiple copies of two different images. Because he had stored multiple copies, he possessed a total of ten images. The Eighth Circuit affirmed the trial court's enhancement for possessing between 10 and 150 images on the ground that every copy of an image constituted its own image. The court relied on Application Note 4.B.i, which states: "Each photograph, picture, computer or computer-generated image, or any similar visual depiction shall be considered to be one image."

C. SENTENCING IN COMPUTER MISUSE CASES

The offense conduct guideline that applies in most computer misuse cases is U.S.S.G. § 2B1.1. This provision is known as the "economic crimes" guideline because it is broadly applicable in economic crime cases involving theft or fraud. *See generally* Frank O. Bowman, III, *The 2001 Federal Economic Crime Sentencing Reforms: An Analysis and Legislative History,* 35 Ind. L. Rev. 5 (2001).

The fact that computer misuse crimes are sentenced along with other economic crimes provides the answer to one basic question about how the Guidelines might apply. For the most part, computer misuse offenses are sentenced just like any other economic crime. At the same time, U.S.S.G. § 2B1.1 contains a number of special wrinkles that apply only in computer misuse cases.

The base offense level in § 2B1.1 ordinarily is 6. An exception exists, however: If the offense of conviction has a statutory maximum term of imprisonment of 20 years, the base offense level is 7. The loss chart contained in § 2B1.1(b)(1) adds to the base offense level depending on the dollar amount of the loss involved:

If the loss exceeded $6,500, increase the offense level as follows:

Loss (apply the greatest)	Increase in level
(A) $6,500 or less	no increase
(B) More than $6,500	add 2
(C) More than $15,000	add 4
(D) More than $40,000	add 6
(E) More than $95,000	add 8
(F) More than $150,000	add 10
(G) More than $250,000	add 12
(H) More than $550,000	add 14
(I) More than $1,500,000	add 16
(J) More than $3,500,000	add 18
(K) More than $9,500,000	add 20
(L) More than $25,000,000	add 22
(M) More than $65,000,000	add 24
(N) More than $150,000,000	add 26
(O) More than $250,000,000	add 28
(P) More than $550,000,000	add 30

As the loss chart suggests, the dollar value of loss is a critical factor used to determine the sentence in a computer misuse case. Application Note 3(a) to U.S.S.G. § 2B1.1 provides specific guidance on calculating loss, including a special rule for § 1030 cases. According to the application note, "loss is the greater of actual loss or intended loss." Actual loss and intended loss are defined as follows:

(i) Actual Loss.—"Actual loss" means the reasonably foreseeable pecuniary harm that resulted from the offense.

(ii) Intended Loss.—"Intended loss" (I) means the pecuniary harm that was intended to result from the offense; and (II) includes intended pecuniary harm that would have been impossible or unlikely to occur (e.g., as in a government sting operation, or an insurance fraud in which the claim exceeded the insured value).

(iii) Pecuniary Harm.—"Pecuniary harm" means harm that is monetary or that otherwise is readily measurable in money. Accordingly, pecuniary harm does not include emotional distress, harm to reputation, or other non-economic harm.

(iv) Reasonably Foreseeable Pecuniary Harm.—For purposes of this guideline, "reasonably foreseeable pecuniary harm" means pecuniary harm that the defendant knew or, under the circumstances, reasonably should have known, was a potential result of the offense.

Section 2B1.1 then excludes the following from loss calculations:

Loss shall not include . . . Costs to the government of, and costs incurred by victims primarily to aid the government in, the prosecution and criminal investigation of an offense.

Section 2B1.1 next includes has a special rule of construction in CFAA cases found in Application Note 3(A)(v)(III):

Offenses Under 18 U.S.C. § 1030.—In the case of an offense under 18 U.S.C. § 1030, actual loss includes the following pecuniary harm, regardless of whether such pecuniary harm was reasonably foreseeable: Any reasonable cost to any victim, including the cost of responding to an offense, conducting a damage assessment, and restoring the data, program, system, or information to its condition prior to the offense, and any revenue lost, cost incurred, or other damages incurred because of interruption of service.

Note that the special rule of construction for offenses under 18 U.S.C. § 1030 defines "actual loss" using the statutory definition of loss from 18 U.S.C. § 1030(e)(11), which itself attempted to codify United States v. Middleton, 231 F.3d 1207 (9th Cir. 2000). As a result, the methodology used to measure the statutory $5,000 loss requirement for 18 U.S.C. § 1030(a)(5) cases is also used to calculate loss at sentencing, and is used even if the case was not charged under § 1030(a)(5). The loss need not have been reasonably foreseeable, unlike the loss used for other types of cases.

U.S.S.G. § 2B1.1(b)(10), (b)(18), and (b)(19) also contain a few enhancements that are particularly relevant to 18 U.S.C. 1030 crimes:

(10) If ... (C) the offense otherwise involved sophisticated means, increase by 2 levels. If the resulting offense level is less than level 12, increase to level 12.

(18) If (A) the defendant was convicted of an offense under 18 U.S.C. 1030, and the offense involved an intent to obtain personal information, or (B) the offense involved the unauthorized public dissemination of personal information, increase by 2 levels.

(19)(A) (Apply the greatest) If the defendant was convicted of an offense under:

> **(i)** 18 U.S.C. 1030, and the offense involved a computer system used to maintain or operate a critical infrastructure, or used by or for a government entity in furtherance of the administration of justice, national defense, or national security, increase by 2 levels.
>
> **(ii)** 18 U.S.C. 1030(a)(5)(A), increase by 4 levels.
>
> **(iii)** 18 U.S.C. 1030, and the offense caused a substantial disruption of a critical infrastructure, increase by 6 levels.

(B) If subdivision (A)(iii) applies, and the offense level is less than level 24, increase to level 24.

The Application Notes to U.S.S.G. § 2B1.1 then provide more specific guidance on several of the terms used:

> For purposes of subsection (b)(10)(C), 'sophisticated means' means especially complex or especially intricate offense conduct pertaining to the execution or concealment of an offense. For example, in a telemarketing scheme, locating the main office of the scheme in one jurisdiction but locating soliciting operations in another jurisdiction ordinarily indicates sophisticated means. Conduct such as hiding assets or transactions, or both, through the use of fictitious entities, corporate shells, or offshore financial accounts also ordinarily indicates sophisticated means.

> "Critical infrastructure" means systems and assets vital to national defense, national security, economic security, public health or safety, or any combination of those matters. A critical infrastructure may be publicly or privately owned. Examples of critical infrastructures include gas and oil production, storage, and delivery systems, water supply systems, telecommunications networks, electrical power delivery systems, financing and banking systems, emergency services (including medical, police, fire, and rescue services), transportation systems and services (including highways, mass transit, airlines, and airports), and

government operations that provide essential services to the public.

"Government entity" has the meaning given that term in 18 U.S.C. § 1030(e)(9).

"Personal information" means sensitive or private information (including such information in the possession of a third party), including (i) medical records; (ii) wills; (iii) diaries; (iv) private correspondence, including e-mail; (v) financial records; (vi) photographs of a sensitive or private nature; or (vii) similar information.

Finally, Application Note 21 to § 2B1.1 provides special guidance on when an upward departure may be needed to account for non-monetary harms. The guidance is general, but some of it relates specifically to 18 U.S.C. § 1030 offenses:

> There may be cases in which the offense level determined under this guideline substantially understates the seriousness of the offense. In such cases, an upward departure may be warranted. The following is a nonexhaustive list of factors that the court may consider in determining whether an upward departure is warranted:
>
> * * *
>
> (ii) The offense caused or risked substantial non-monetary harm. For example, the offense caused physical harm, psychological harm, or severe emotional trauma, or resulted in a substantial invasion of a privacy interest (through, for example, the theft of personal information such as medical, educational, or financial records). An upward departure would be warranted, for example, in an 18 U.S.C. § 1030 offense involving damage to a protected computer, if, as a result of that offense, death resulted. * * *
>
> (v) In a case involving stolen information from a "protected computer", as defined in 18 U.S.C. § 1030(e)(2), the defendant sought the stolen information to further a broader criminal purpose.

This application note gives courts relatively wide discretion to fashion appropriate sentences to account for privacy harms in computer misuse cases.

UNITED STATES V. STRATMAN

United States District Court for the District of Nebraska, 2014.
2014 WL 3109805.

JOHN M. GERRARD, DISTRICT JUDGE.

This case is before the Court with respect to the loss calculation for purposes of sentencing. The defendant pleaded guilty to one count of violating the Computer Fraud and Abuse Act (CFAA)—specifically, 18 U.S.C. § 1030(a)(5)(A)—based on an intrusion into a protected computer system or systems that began in approximately May 2012. As directed by the Court in its Amended Order on Sentencing Schedule, the parties submitted a statement of uncontroverted facts, and a hearing was held at which evidence was adduced and submitted of losses allegedly incurred by the two primary victims in this case: the University of Nebraska and the Nebraska State College System.

The burden is on the government to prove the factual basis for a sentencing enhancement by a preponderance of the evidence. For purposes of § 2B1.1(b), loss is calculated as the greater of the actual or intended loss. Actual loss is defined as the "reasonably foreseeable pecuniary harm that resulted from the offense." § 2B1.1 cmt. n. 3(A)(i). And "reasonably foreseeable pecuniary harm" is further defined as that harm that the defendant knew, or under the circumstances, reasonably should have known, was a potential result of the offense. Id. cmt. n. 3(A)(iv). Intended loss, by comparison, includes any "pecuniary harm that was intended to result from the offense," including harm that was "impossible or unlikely to occur." Id. cmt. n. 3(A)(ii). Ultimately, this Court needs to make a "reasonable estimate of the loss." Id. cmt. n. 3(C).

For violations of the CFAA, the victim's "loss" may include "any reasonable cost to any victim, including the cost of responding to an offense, conducting a damage assessment, and restoring the data, program, system, or information to its condition prior to the offense, and any revenue lost, cost incurred, or other consequential damages incurred because of interruption of service."18 U.S.C. § 1030(e)(11).

The losses at issue in this case involve the costs of investigating the defendant's intrusion into the victims' computer systems. There is, for instance, no evidence that the victims incurred meaningful costs *repairing* damage to their systems. Instead, the evidence relates to the substantial time and expense that the victims incurred investigating the breach after it was discovered, and in attempting to ascertain the scope of their exposure. The bulk of the costs are in four categories: hours worked by University information technology (IT) department workers in response to the breach; similar hours worked by State Colleges IT workers; the cost of investigative services provided by Fishnet Services, Inc., a third-party IT consultant hired by the University; and the cost of investigative services provided by Kroll Advisory Solutions, a third-party consultant hired by the State Colleges' insurance company.

The Court accepts, as a general proposition, that the costs of investigating the scope of an intrusion into a computer system may be losses for purposes of sentencing and restitution. Such costs may be included when incurred by a private investigation conducted by the victim or consultants hired by the victim. Such losses may also, in principle, include the expense of notifying those whose personal information was compromised by the breach.

But the costs incurred must be reasonable. The CFAA defines "loss" in terms of "reasonable cost," and it cannot be said that unreasonable expenses are either caused by the offense of conviction for purposes of restitution, or reasonably foreseeable within the meaning of § 2B1.1.

The Court agrees with the defendant that part of the government's burden of proving loss for purposes of sentencing and restitution is showing that the costs incurred by the victims were *reasonably* incurred.

The Court begins with the easy part: the defendant has not objected to the University's Fishnet bills, with the exception of some reservations about whether some of those bills involved double counting. The Court has reviewed Fishnet's invoices carefully and found that each line item was unique, and that the total matched that represented by the University. The Court therefore finds that the Fishnet bills represent losses for purposes of sentencing and restitution, totaling $107,722.58.[4]

The same cannot be said of the Kroll invoices. The government's witnesses—primarily University employees—were clear about why Fishnet was hired and what Fishnet's services eventually produced for the University. Kroll was initially retained to help the State Colleges, but soon they and their insurer agreed to share the Fishnet forensic analysis with the University. The lion's share of Kroll's billing—over $308,000, as set forth in Exhibit 24—is attributed to notification services, *i.e.,* informing people whose personal information might have been compromised. But the Court cannot determine why that was so expensive for the State Colleges, or how it was determined that approximately 185,000 people needed to be notified.

The government has provided affidavits from two Kroll employees, and one employee of the insurer that hired Kroll, which generally describe the contents of Kroll's invoices and conclude that the services and expenses were fair and reasonable. But the Court does not find those conclusory opinions persuasive. Kroll's forensic analysis (which was presumably cut short when Fishnet became the primary investigator) essentially concludes that there

---

[4]   To be clear—the Court also finds based on the evidence that Fishnet's costs, while substantial, were reasonable given the services performed, and that it was reasonable for the University to retain those services when it did, shortly after the breach, when the scope of the intrusion was still unclear.

was no evidence of exfiltration or access to personal information from the PeopleSoft database, but it was hard to be sure.

The only apparent source for the number of people to be notified, 185,000+, is also in Exhibit 28—an "audit" that was conducted by Kroll "to re-mail any records that mailed in error."(Whatever that means.) The import of the audit, as the Court understands it after puzzling over it for a bit, seems to be that some of the 185,000+ client records were duplicated, and only 117,845 were actually unique. So in Exhibit 31, Kroll's employee witness talks about Kroll's services including "the facilitation of mailing letters to each of approximately 185,000 potential victims of the breach," but the only substantiation in the record for that number is an audit that contradicts it. In sum, the Court is left with considerable uncertainty about how many people the State Colleges actually needed to notify, how many actually were notified, and how the costs for doing so were determined. Given that uncertainty, the Court finds that the reasonability of those expenses has not been proven.

The Court has similar questions about the employee hours devoted to the intrusion by employees of the University and the State Colleges. No doubt an appropriate response was necessary—and in the immediate wake of the breach, "all hands on deck" might well have been warranted. But at some point, after the defendant was locked out (and quickly indicted), the actual depth of the intrusion would have been clear, and an all-out effort would no longer have been necessary. The record, as it stands, does not permit the Court to determine what the victims knew and when they knew it, nor does it permit the Court to compare the victims' knowledge with the intensity of their ongoing efforts related to the breach. The record also contains very little from which the Court could determine that the victims' employees performed with reasonable efficiency and were compensated at a reasonable rate.[6]

The victims' calculations for costs attributed to employee hours consist of the time spent on tasks associated with the breach, multiplied by that employee's hourly wage. But, for instance, if the Court was awarding attorney fees, the Court would have to ask what tasks were performed, whether the number of hours spent on each task was appropriate, and whether the attorney's billing rate for performing the task was fair and reasonable. The Court does not see why similar questions should not be asked under these circumstances—and the Court cannot find the answer in the record.

It is also not entirely clear whether all those hours are attributable to the *defendant* for purposes of sentencing and restitution. For instance, the

---

[6]   To be clear—the Court is not criticizing the victims' employees, or suggesting that they are inefficient or overpaid. The Court would prefer to assume that they are all capable, and compensated appropriately. But the Court needs evidence, not assumptions.

University's former information security officer testified that some of that time was spent implementing recommendations from the Fishnet report, and "cleaning up some of the incidents." He did testify that all the activities reflected in the government's evidence were "related to" the defendant's intrusion. But that may or may not be the same as "caused by" the defendant's intrusion.

A simple example will illustrate the point. A homeowner has a broken lock on her front door. A thief finds out and uses the vulnerability to enter the home and steal property. The losses from that crime include the value of the stolen property. They might even include investigating the crime. But they would not include repairing the lock, which was broken before the thief ever came along. The repair might be "related to" the theft, because the theft called attention to the vulnerability. But the thief didn't break the lock, and wouldn't have to pay to fix it.

Similarly, the victims no doubt learned, from the defendant's intrusion, about vulnerabilities in their computer systems. But the defendant is not responsible for creating those vulnerabilities, and he isn't liable for the cost of fixing them—or, more to the point, those costs are not the result of the offense of conviction. It is hard for the Court to conclude, on the evidence presented, that over 3,600 hours of employee time was a foreseeable consequence of the crime. And from the evidence presented, the Court cannot parse out how much time the victims' employees spent securing the system from the defendant specifically, and how much time they spent addressing the vulnerabilities he had called to their attention. The victims' exhibits reflect dozens of employees spending thousands of hours on tasks that are mostly unclear from the record. The only evidence to connect most of those hours to the defendant is that they were recorded with a project billing code that was created in response to the breach, and that the employees were verbally instructed to use for "anything related" to the defendant's intrusion.

For instance, one of the government's primary witnesses—the University's former information security officer—was listed in the government's exhibits as having spent 351 hours on the project initiated by the defendant's breach. But he was unable to say specifically how long he continued to log time on the project, other than that his "best guess" was that he was working on the project through October.

And there is even less evidence with respect to other employees and how they were spending their time—the summaries provided by the victims, and adduced by the government, simply total the hours worked by each employee between May 20, 2012, and June 4, 2013. The breach was detected by the University on May 23–24, 2012, and even if the Court was willing to presume that the hours spent on the project in the immediate wake of the breach were sufficiently connected to the defendant's crime (a fair presumption), there is no way for the Court to determine from the evidence how many hours were worked during that timeframe. That, the Court finds, is insufficient evidence to prove *which* hours represent losses that can be causally connected to the defendant's crime for purposes of sentencing and restitution. The Court has no basis to estimate, or even guess, at how many hours would be attributable to the defendant—any attempt to pick a number would be unsatisfactorily arbitrary.

Finally, there is some evidence of other expenses—for example, the EnCase forensic analysis tool that the University purchased to help investigate the breach. While the Court has no particular reason to doubt those expenses, there is also little to establish that they were reasonable or necessary. It is also unclear whether the victims' purchases are of ongoing utility to them, which would preclude characterizing the entirety of those costs as "losses" for purposes of sentencing and restitution.

In sum, the Court finds that except for the Fishnet invoices, the evidence is not sufficient to prove that the victims' costs were "losses" for purposes of sentencing and restitution. The Court finds that based on the evidence before the Court, the appropriate loss calculation figure, for purposes of sentencing and restitution, is $107,722.58.

NOTES AND QUESTIONS

1.   *Foreseeable and unforeseeable losses. Stratman* states that "it is hard for the Court to conclude, on the evidence presented, that over 3,600 hours of employee time was a foreseeable consequence of the crime." Notably, however, § 2B1.1 does not require that all victim costs be foreseeable in § 1030 offenses.

Instead, § 2B1.1 allows two kinds of losses in Section 1030 cases. First, as in all cases sentenced under § 2B1.1, losses can include the "reasonably foreseeable pecuniary harm[s] that resulted from the offense." Second, under the special rule of construction just for § 1030 cases, losses also can include certain kinds of pecuniary harm regardless of whether it was foreseeable: "Any reasonable cost to any victim, including the cost of responding to an offense, conducting a damage assessment, and restoring the data, program, system, or information to its condition prior to the offense, and any revenue lost, cost incurred, or other damages incurred because of interruption of service."

2.   *Losses to aid the government in the investigation and prosecution of criminal activity.* Section 2B1.1 provides arguably conflicting guidance on whether losses incurred by § 1030 victims to aid the government in the investigation and prosecution of criminal activity can be included in the loss calculation. On one hand, the special rule of construction for § 1030 cases includes "any reasonable cost," including "the cost of responding to an offense" and "conducting a damage assessment." On the other hand, in its general guidance, § 2B1.1 expressly excludes "costs incurred by victims primarily to aid the government in, the prosecution and criminal investigation of an offense." In a § 1030 case, which governs?

In United States v. Schuster, 467 F.3d 614 (7th Cir. 2006), the court ruled that the general guidance governs and such losses must be excluded from the loss calculation. The victim in *Schuster* spent $2,700 to travel to an FBI office to meet with the FBI and to assist with the FBI's investigation of the offense. Such costs should not be included as losses, the Seventh Circuit ruled:

> Courts must interpret the sentencing guidelines so no words are discarded as meaningless, redundant or surplusage. Allowing victims to recover as "reasonable costs" those costs primarily associated with their assistance of the government, even with regard to offenses in connection with computer-related fraud and similar activities, would render the commentary to § 2B1.1 meaningless. We cannot countenance such a result.

> Application note 3(A)(v)(III) specifies the types of reasonable costs that are recoverable: "the cost of responding to an offense, conducting a damage assessment, and restoring the data, program, system, or information to its condition prior to the offense, and any revenue lost, cost incurred, or other damages incurred because of the interruption of service." Such costs are those attributable to identifying and correcting the technological problems resulting from the offense. Costs associated with assisting the government, by contrast, are unrelated to these functions and, as a consequence, excluded from the purview of application note 3(A)(v)(III).

> The $2,700 loss incurred by victims for their travel to an FBI office to meet with the FBI and assist with the FBI's investigation of the offense easily falls within the exclusion in the commentary to § 2B1.1. The victims incurred these costs while assisting the government in building its case against Schuster. The district court erred by including the $2,700 in its calculation of the loss amount.

Id. at 620–21.

3.   Are sentences for federal computer misuse crimes too low, too high, or about right? How do sentences for typical 18 U.S.C. § 1030 offenses compare with sentences for typical child pornography offenses?

4.   Why do you think the sentencing guidelines have special rules for calculating "actual loss" in 18 U.S.C. § 1030 cases? Why should unforeseeable pecuniary harms be included in § 1030 cases but not for any other type of criminal offense? Is the idea that any loss resulting from a § 1030 offense is actually foreseeable? If so, is it fair for a defendant to have his sentence increased under § 2B1.1 if he commits a § 1030 offense that leads to truly unforeseeable harms? Is the defendant more culpable in such cases? Is a defendant more responsible for unforeseeable harms in § 1030 cases than in other cases? Or is the idea to punish those who commit computer misuse crimes more harshly than those who commit other crimes because computer misuse crimes are more dangerous?

5. *Should CFAA crimes be punished under § 2B1.1?* Consider a typical fraud case. For the most part, the victim's loss will equal the defendant's gain. If *A* defrauds *B* out of $50,000, *B* has lost the money and *A* has gained it. In all likelihood, *A* will have controlled the extent of the loss, and *A* will benefit more and more as losses increase. *B*'s loss is a good proxy for *A*'s culpability.

In a computer misuse case, however, the victim's loss generally will not equal the defendant's gain. If *A* hacks into *B*'s server, and *B* suffers $50,000 in loss from the interruption of service, *A* does not gain anything from *B*'s loss. In all likelihood, *A* will have little to no control over the extent of the loss, and *A* will not benefit as *B*'s losses mount. *B*'s loss may no longer be a good proxy for *A*'s culpability.

The sentencing guidelines do not distinguish between these two scenarios. At sentencing, the victim's loss in a computer misuse case is treated the same as the victim's loss in a fraud case. Does that make sense?

6. *Problem.* Imagine that the Smith family has three brothers: Larry, Moe, and Curly. All three brothers are skilled computer hackers. One day, each of the three brothers hacks into a server operated by a different local e-commerce company. Assume that all three intrusions are essentially the same, but that the responses of the system administrators in charge of the three victim networks are very different. The system administrator at the company targeted by Larry notices the attack but decides to ignore it. The system administrator at the company that Moe attacks takes the intrusion seriously, and his response to the offense racks up $50,000 in loss. The system administrator at the company that Curly hacks into also takes the intrusion extremely seriously, and responding to the offense racks up $250,000 in loss.

Assume that Larry, Moe, and Curly are all charged and convicted of violating § 1030. Based on the loss chart of § 2B1.1(b)(1), Moe's offense level will be six points higher than Larry's, and Curly's will be six offense levels higher than Moe's. This works out on average to about an extra year in prison for Moe, and an extra two years in prison for Curly, all based on the response of the system administrator. Is this a sensible result?

7. *Do development costs of stolen databases count as "loss"?* In United States v. Snowden, 806 F.3d 1030 (10th Cir. 2015), the defendant, Blake Snowden, was a former employee of a physician-staffing company called Onyx. After leaving Onyx, Snowden decided to steal a copy of Onyx's master database of physicians, called "Bullhorn," so he could open a new business that would compete against Onyx. After obtaining a username and password from a current Onyx employee, Snowden repeatedly logged in to Onyx's network and downloaded a copy of Bullhorn. Snowden tried to use Bullhorn to compete against Onyx. Snowden's effort was a failure, however, as he was unable to place a single Onyx physician.

Onyx noticed the intrusion, and the FBI traced it to Snowden. Snowden was then convicted of violating the CFAA. At sentencing, the district court considered whether the $1.5 million cost of creating the Bullhorn database was a "loss" for purposes of the § 2B1.1 loss calculation. The district court concluded that it was, but the Tenth Circuit disagreed and ruled that the development cost of the database could not be considered loss:

> We have some sympathy with the district court's calculation of the offense level. Development costs seem to us to be a reasonable measure of the severity of offenses such as Defendant's. He appropriated to his own use information that cost Onyx $1.5 million to develop. One's sense of outrage at the nonconsensual copying of a proprietary database is likely to be proportional to the time, effort, and expense incurred in creating the database. Indeed, this measure of severity has been adopted in the statute under which Defendant was convicted. Whether a violation of 18 U.S.C. § 1030(a)(2)(C) is a misdemeanor or a felony can depend entirely on whether "the value of the information obtained exceeds $5,000," 18 U.S.C. § 1030(c)(2)(B)(iii); and the cost of development is a reasonable (if rough) measure of value.

> Nevertheless, the guideline requires proof of *loss,* and the guideline commentary does not depart from that approach. To be sure, the loss caused by a theft will typically be the value of the property stolen. Thus, the note relied on by the district court allows the "estimate of the *loss*" to "*tak[e] into account,* as appropriate ..., the cost of developing" the stolen proprietary information. USSG § 2B1.1 cmt. n.3(C) (emphasis added). But we do not read that language in the commentary as contradicting the guideline by substituting *cost of development* for *loss* in calculating the offense level; and the evidence before the district court was that Onyx did not suffer any business loss from Defendant's acts. Perhaps one could assess Onyx's loss by treating Defendant's theft as an involuntary sale of the data by Onyx and estimating the price that Onyx would reasonably demand if it had to share its database; but neither the district court nor the government has suggested this approach or what that reasonable price would be.

Id. at 1033.

8. *Costs of notifying users as "loss."* In United States v. Auernheimer, 748 F.3d 525 (3d Cir. 2014), the district court at sentencing held that the defendant's intrusion caused $78,000 of loss based on the costs of notifying victims of the crime. The defendant had helped collect more than 100,000 customer e-mail addresses of AT&T customers from AT&T's website. Initially, AT&T had sent out an e-mail to its customers notifying them that their e-mail addresses had been collected. Next, AT&T spent $78,000 in printing and mailing costs following up the e-mail notification with postal letter notification. The district court held that the printing and mailing costs of the postal letter were caused by the intrusion and were reasonable costs for purposes of calculating loss. The defendant was sentenced to 41 months in prison in

significant part based on the district court's finding that he had caused $78,000 in loss.

The defendant challenged that ruling on appeal, but the Third Circuit vacated the conviction without ruling on the question. If the Third Circuit had reached the issue, should it have allowed the higher sentence based on $78,000 in loss?

9.   *Lost business as "loss."* In United States v. Musacchio, 590 Fed.Appx. 359 (5th Cir. 2014), the defendant left his former company and started a competing business. Unbeknownst to the former company, the defendant maintained access to its servers and used that secret access to compete against and undercut the company in its search for new business. When the former company realized that someone was accessing its secrets, the company paid $322,000 to a computer forensic firm to investigate the intrusion and identify the defendant as the wrongdoer. At sentencing, the trial court estimated that the former company also lost $1 million in business because of the defendant's intrusions into his former company's servers. The $1 million of additional loss substantially increased the defendant's sentence under the § 2B1.1 loss chart.

On appeal, the defendant argued that the "loss" of his computer hacking crime should be limited to the $322,000 fee to the forensic firm and that it should exclude the $1 million in estimated lost business. The Fifth Circuit disagreed:

> The use of the word "includes" in Note 3(A)(v)(III) indicates the loss described in that provision should be considered in addition to actual loss, as defined in Note 3(A)(i). Nothing in Note 3(A)(v)(III) suggests it replaces or limits the general process for calculating loss discussed in Note 3(A)(i)–(ii). The Sentencing Commission's report is consistent with this interpretation. According to the report, Note 3(A)(v)(III) was "designed to *more fully* account for specific factors relevant to computer offenses." U.S. Sentencing Comm'n, Report To The Congress: Increased Penalties For Cyber Security Offenses 1 (2003). The addition of Note 3(A)(v)(III) was necessary because the costs described in that provision otherwise would not have been included in the loss unless they were reasonably foreseeable.

> Moreover, the caselaw is contrary to Musacchio's position. The decision in *United States v. Schuster,*467 F.3d 614 (7th Cir. 2006), actually favors the government's position. Musacchio notes that *Schuster* found costs associated with assisting the government should not be considered under Note 3(A)(v)(III) because the Note does not explicitly list them. That case did, however, analyze whether those costs should be considered as actual losses, indicating Note 3(A)(v)(III) does not replace or limit the general process for calculating loss set out in Note 3(A)(i)–(ii).

> *Schuster* characterized the relationship between the two Notes as follows:

> "Actual loss" under the sentencing guidelines, means the reasonably foreseeable pecuniary harm that resulted from the offense. *Additionally,* in cases involving fraud and related activity in connection with computers, the sentencing guidelines *include* in the calculation of actual loss the costs described in Note 3(A)(v)(III), regardless of whether such pecuniary harm was reasonably foreseeable.

Under *Schuster,* then, the loss includes both foreseeable harm and the costs listed in Note 3(A)(v)(III). Other cases have interpreted the guidelines similarly. In light of this caselaw and the guideline language, the court properly considered business losses.

Id. at 365–66.

10. *Calculating distributed loss.* How should courts calculate "actual loss" in cases involving losses distributed around the world? Imagine a case involving a global computer virus or worms. The losses might be distributed among thousands or even millions of victims. It is presumably impractical to measure the losses from each individual victim.

What to do? Application Note 3(c) to U.S.S.G. § 2B1.1 states that the court may estimate the loss by considering "the approximate number of victims multiplied by the average loss to each victim." *Id.* cmt. n.3(c)(iii). What guidance does this provide in computer worm or virus cases? Do victims outside the United States count, or are only losses suffered inside the United States relevant?

11. *Enhancements for "substantial disruption of a critical infrastructure."* Section 2B1.1(b)(19)(A)(iii) provides a six-level enhancement for a violation of § 1030 that causes a "substantial disruption of a critical infrastructure." The harsh extra penalty when a § 1030 violation substantially disrupts a critical infrastructure prompts two questions: When does a computer count as a critical infrastructure, and what is the standard for when a CFAA violation substantially disrupts it?

The Fifth Circuit answered these questions in United States v. Brown, 884 F.3d 281 (5th Cir. 2018). The defendant, a system specialist at Citibank's Global Control Center, reacted to a negative review of his job performance by sending commands that intentionally disrupted network traffic on Citibank's network. The defendant's act of sabotage, which started at about 6pm, resulted in a loss of connectivity to some but not all of Citibank's North American data centers, campuses, call centers, and sixty-nine ATMs. By about 10 p.m., Citibank was able to restore ninety percent of the lost connectivity. By 4:30 a.m. the next morning, the network was back up and running normally. At sentencing, the trial court applied the enhancement for substantial disruption of a critical infrastructure.

On appeal, the Fifth Circuit ruled that this enhancement was improperly applied to the facts of Brown's case. On one hand, it was clear from the

Guidelines definition that Citibank's computers involved critical infrastructure:

> The commentary to the 2015 Sentencing Guidelines defines "critical infrastructure" as "systems and assets vital to national defense, national security, economic security, public health or safety, or any combination of these matters." U.S. Sentencing Guidelines Manual § 2B1.1(b)(18) cmt. n.14 (U.S. Sentencing Comm'n 2015). The enumerated examples include public and private "financing and banking systems."

Id. at 285. Despite this, the enhancement was improperly applied because Brown's conduct did not cause a "substantial disruption" of that critical infrastructure:

> Brown's conduct did not constitute a substantial disruption of a critical infrastructure. There is no indication that Brown's conduct affecting a portion of Citibank's operations for a short period of time could have had a serious impact on national economic security. As a result of Brown's actions, Citibank suffered relatively minor financial losses and was temporarily unable to optimally serve its customers. Neither of these harms threatened to disrupt the nation's economy, and, in light of Citibank's demonstrated ability to quickly resolve the disruption and mitigate in the interim, there is no other evidence that Brown's conduct had the potential to do so. Accordingly, we hold that the district court erred by applying an enhancement that we conclude is reserved for conduct that disrupts a critical infrastructure in a way that could have a serious impact on national economic security.

Id. at 287.

D. SUPERVISED RELEASE AND PROBATION RESTRICTIONS

The federal court system generally uses three different forms of punishment: prison time, fines, and probation or supervised release. Probation and supervised release are similar. Each permits a defendant to avoid prison time, contingent upon the defendant's compliance with terms of probation or supervised release. The difference between probation and supervised release primarily relates to timing. Probation is in lieu of jail time, whereas supervised release follows jail time. For example, a defendant may be sentenced to a period of probation, or may be sentenced to a prison term followed by a period of supervised release. If a defendant violates the terms of probation or supervised release, the defendant may at the discretion of the trial judge be sent to prison to serve out the remaining period of the sentence.

Under federal law, sentencing judges can impose conditions of probation or supervised release when two conditions are met. First, the conditions must be "reasonably related" to the goals of punishment set forth in § 18 U.S.C. 3553, which include deterrence and retribution. Second, the conditions must "involve only such deprivations of liberty or property as are reasonably necessary" to achieve those goals. *See* 18 U.S.C. § 3563(b) (conditions of probation); 18 U.S.C. § 3583(d) (conditions of supervised release).

Supervised release and probation raise an interesting computer-related question: What kinds of restrictions on computer and Internet use can a court impose as a condition of probation or supervised release?

UNITED STATES V. DUKE

United States Court of Appeals for the Fifth Circuit, 2015.
788 F.3d 392.

PER CURIAM:

Elliot Duke pled guilty to one count of receipt of child pornography in violation of 18 U.S.C. § 2252A(a)(2)(B). The district court sentenced Duke to 240 months in prison, the statutory maximum, and imposed several special conditions of supervised release, including one unconditional, lifetime ban on accessing computers capable of Internet access.

I.

On May 14, 2013, detectives from the Vernon Parish Sheriff's Department in Leeville, Louisiana, were contacted by an individual claiming that his landlord, Duke, had been viewing child pornography. Duke's tenant reported seeing several sexually explicit images on Duke's laptop.

Based on this information, detectives secured a search warrant for Duke's residence. Once advised that the detectives were at his residence to execute a search warrant, Duke expressed his willingness to cooperate and consented to the search. He admitted to possessing child pornography on his computer and to trading such images with other individuals over the Internet. After verifying that his computer contained images of child pornography, detectives took Duke into custody for further questioning.

Pursuant to a written plea agreement, Duke pled guilty to one count of receipt of child pornography. Duke objected at sentencing to [a] special condition of supervised release that he is "not to have access to any computer that is capable of internet access."

II.

Duke argues that the special condition prohibiting him from "having access to any computer that is capable of internet access" is overly broad. Duke acknowledges that the district court could impose restrictions on his

Internet access, but maintains that a blanket prohibition of all Internet usage is an unduly broad condition.

No circuit court of appeals has ever upheld an absolute, lifetime Internet ban. In fact, the Third and Seventh Circuits have refused to allow such bans. *See United States v. Heckman,* 592 F.3d 400, 409 (3d Cir. 2010); *United States v. Voelker,* 489 F.3d 139, 150 (3d Cir. 2007); *United States v. Holm,* 326 F.3d 872, 877 (7th Cir. 2003). While we have approved absolute Internet bans for limited durations of time, and lifetime Internet restrictions that conditioned Internet usage on probation officer or court approval, we have not addressed whether absolute bans, imposed for the rest of a defendant's life, are permissible conditions. We conclude that they are not.

First, it is hard to imagine that such a sweeping, lifetime ban could ever satisfy § 3583(d)'s requirement that a condition be narrowly tailored to avoid imposing a greater deprivation than reasonably necessary. Indeed, an unconditional, lifetime ban is the antithesis of a 'narrowly tailored' sanction. Moreover, our case law requires that Internet bans be narrowly tailored either by scope or by duration.

For example, in *United States v. Paul,* 274 F.3d 155 (5th Cir. 2001), we upheld an absolute Internet ban that prohibited the defendant from having, possessing, or having access to computers and the Internet during the three-year term of his supervised release. We have subsequently reasoned that the broad scope of the absolute ban in *Paul* was able to stand, in part, because of the short duration of the supervised release term.

Further, we have upheld Internet restrictions imposed for long durations of time based on their narrow scope. For instance, in *United States v. Miller,* 665 F.3d 114 (5th Cir. 2011), we upheld a conditional, 25-year computer and Internet restriction that prohibited the defendant from using any computer or any phone or electronic device capable of accessing the Internet without prior written approval from a probation officer. The 25-year term of the Internet restriction withstood the defendant's challenge, in part, because the ban was not absolute or unconditional.

Finally, in *United States v. Ellis,* 720 F.3d 220 (5th Cir. 2013), the court addressed a conditional, lifetime Internet restriction that prevented the defendant from possessing, having access to, or utilizing a computer or internet connection device without prior approval of the court. There, the court further narrowed the scope of the conditional restriction by excluding electronic devices that fell outside the commonsense definition of the term "computers." Unlike the conditions imposed in *Paul, Miller,* and *Ellis,* the absolute, lifetime ban at issue here is narrowed neither by scope nor by duration.

Second, the ubiquity and importance of the Internet to the modern world makes an unconditional, lifetime ban unreasonable. Although this court has not found the Internet to be so integral to modern life that a district court may not restrict its use, it has observed, along with many sister circuits, that computers and the internet have become significant and ordinary components of modern life as we know it.

Indeed, recently, in *United States v. Sealed Juvenile*, 781 F.3d 747, 752 (5th Cir. 2015), we concluded that an Internet condition requiring a defendant to request permission from his probation officer every time that he wanted to access a computer or the Internet was unreasonably restrictive based on the recognition that access to computers and the Internet is *essential* to functioning in today's society. While we ultimately affirmed the condition, we did so subject to the admonition that it was not to be construed or enforced in such a manner that the defendant would be required to seek prior written approval every single time he must use a computer or access the Internet.

Here, the absolute computer and Internet ban would completely preclude Duke from meaningfully participating in modern society for the rest of his life. It would prevent him from using a computer for benign purposes such as word processing, because as Duke argues, in our modern world all computers are *capable* of Internet access. Moreover, Duke would be prohibited from using the Internet for other innocent purposes such as paying a bill online, taking online classes, or video chatting and emailing with his family in the United Kingdom. While access to the Internet could also allow Duke to view and trade despicable images of child pornography, there are means far short of an absolute, lifetime ban to prevent him from using the Internet for this purpose.

The Government offers future modification as a means to alleviate any potential concern with the Internet ban's scope or duration. While 18 U.S.C. § 3583(e)(2) and Federal Rule of Criminal Procedure 32.1(c) provide a vehicle by which Duke can seek future modification of the Internet ban, the possibility of future modification has no bearing on whether the district court abused its discretion today. As the First Circuit explained:

> The authority of a future court to modify a sweeping ban on computer or internet use does not immunize the ban from an inquiry that evaluates the justification for the ban in the first instance. Otherwise, in the guise of delegation to a future decision-maker, sentencing courts could abdicate their responsibility to assess the compatibility of supervised release conditions with the goals of sentencing. To approve problematic conditions because a judge might, in her or his discretion, relax them in the future, undermines the command to sentencing courts to not deprive offenders of more liberty than is necessary to carry out the goals of supervised release.

United States v. Ramos, 763 F.3d 45, 61 (1st Cir. 2014).

In sum, the district court abused its discretion by imposing a condition of supervised release that prohibited Duke from accessing computers or the Internet for the rest of his life. Such a condition is not narrowly tailored and therefore imposes a greater deprivation than reasonably necessary to prevent recidivism and protect the public, especially in light of the ubiquity and importance of the Internet.

NOTES AND QUESTIONS

1. In United States v. Scott, 316 F.3d 733, 736–37 (7th Cir. 2003), Judge Easterbrook offered the following response to the defendant's claim that limitations on Internet access could never be imposed as conditions of supervised release:

> That is not a tenable argument. Computers and the Internet may be used to commit crimes, of which child pornography and fraud are only two examples. Inveterate hackers who have used access to injure others may be ordered to give up the digital world. If full access posed an unacceptable risk of recidivism, yet all controls on access were forbidden, then a judge would have little alternative but to increase the term of imprisonment in order to incapacitate the offender. Few defendants would deem that a beneficial exchange; most would prefer the conditional freedom of supervised release, even with restrictions on using the Internet, to the more regimented life in prison.
>
> This is not to gainsay the point that because the Internet is a medium of communication a total restriction rarely could be justified. The Internet is a vast repository, offering books, newspapers, magazines, and research tools along with smut. A judge who would not forbid [the defendant] to enter a video rental store (which may have an adult-video section) also should not forbid [him] to enter the Internet, even though Disney's web site coexists with others offering filthy pictures or audio files circulated in violation of the copyright laws. A judge who would not forbid a defendant to send or receive postal mail or use the telephone should not forbid that person to send or receive email or to order books at Amazon.com. [The defendant] does not have a record of extensive abuse of digital communications that could justify an outright ban.

Is forbidding the use of computers like forbidding the use of telephones? Or is it more like forbidding a person to drive a car, which is a common condition of probation in drunk driving cases? Or is it more like forbidding a person to leave his home?

2. *The timing of judicial review.* When should sentencing courts decide on the terms of supervised release relating to a defendant's computer use? In United States v. Balon, 384 F.3d 38 (2d Cir. 2004), the defendant was sentenced to a five-year prison term, followed by a period of supervised released. The terms of supervised release contained a number of restrictions

involving computer and Internet use. The court held that the defendant's challenge to the computer and Internet-related aspects of his supervised release was not yet ripe for review:

> The technology that holds the key to whether the special condition in this case involves a greater deprivation of liberty than reasonably necessary is constantly and rapidly changing. Because Balon will not begin his term of supervised release for three years, it is impossible to evaluate at this time whether one method or another, or a combination of methods, will occasion a greater deprivation of his liberty than necessary in light of the special needs of supervised release.

> We therefore dismiss this portion of the appeal but instruct the district court to reconsider the special conditions regarding monitoring of Balon's computer at a time closer to Balon's term of supervised release.

Id. at 46–47. *See also* United States v. Ford, 882 F.3d 1279, 1284–85 (10th Cir. 2018) (discussing caselaw on the ripeness of computer restrictions).

Is this a sensible approach? Should the law be changed so that terms of supervised release are set soon before the supervised released begins, rather than when the defendant is sentenced following conviction?

CHAPTER 5

THE FOURTH AMENDMENT

■ ■ ■

This chapter considers how the Fourth Amendment governs law enforcement investigations of computer crimes. It analyzes the constitutional limits on the government's ability to gather digital evidence, identify a suspect, and establish beyond a reasonable doubt that the defendant has committed the offense. The Fourth Amendment states:

> The right of the people to be secure in their persons, houses, papers, and effects, against unreasonable searches and seizures, shall not be violated, and no Warrants shall issue, but upon probable cause, supported by Oath or affirmation, and particularly describing the place to be searched, and the persons or things to be seized.

The overall framework of Fourth Amendment law is simple to state. The Fourth Amendment prohibits unreasonable searches and seizures. To determine if government conduct violates the Fourth Amendment, one must first identify whether searches or seizures have occurred, and if so, whether they are reasonable or unreasonable. A search or seizure is reasonable if it was authorized by a valid search warrant or if one of the exceptions to the warrant requirement applies.

A search warrant is a judicial order authorizing the police to execute a search or seizure. A warrant is valid if it is based on probable cause and particularly describes the property to be searched and the items to be seized. The usual remedy for violations of the Fourth Amendment is suppression of evidence obtained in any subsequent criminal case. While there are many exceptions and caveats to this rule, the basic idea is that the government cannot use the "fruits" of illegal government searches and seizures.

The meaning of the Fourth Amendment is relatively well-established for investigations involving physical evidence. Entering a house or opening a person's private packages constitutes a "search" of that house or package. Taking physical property away "seizes" it. The Fourth Amendment thus requires the police to obtain a warrant or to satisfy an exception to the warrant requirement before they can enter private spaces or take away physical property. The exceptions to the warrant requirement include consent, exigent circumstances, searches incident to a valid arrest, and border searches. All of these exceptions permit investigators to search or seize private property without a warrant.

The central question of this chapter is how these legal doctrines should apply when the government wishes to access digital evidence stored in a computer. In some cases, the searches will occur on-site, without moving the computer itself (at least until after the search). A police officer might come across a computer that he believes contains evidence, and he might want to look through the computer for the evidence. The question is, when can he look through the computer?

In other cases, the searches will occur off-site. Analyzing a single computer may take anywhere from a few hours to a few weeks, and it often requires specialized tools and expert training. In such cases, it is impractical to require agents to search computers onsite. Instead, the searches will often occur off-site at a government computer laboratory. Officers will seize computers from the target's home or possession and bring them to the government's computer lab. Next, they use special equipment to generate a "bitstream copy" (also known as an "image") of the storage device onto a government computer. The investigators then conduct their search on the bitstream copy instead of the original to ensure the evidentiary integrity of the original computer. The question is, when does the Fourth Amendment allow the government to seize computers, generate images, and search the images for evidence?

In still other cases, officers will obtain records and contents from network providers such as Facebook or Google. These companies provide network services such as e-mail, messaging, and cloud storage for users around the world. When the government seeks records or the contents of communications about a suspect from one of these providers, investigators typically will serve court orders on these providers requiring them to turn over the listed information so the government can search it for evidence. The question is, what are the Fourth Amendment limits on the government obtaining and searching through that information for evidence?

The materials in this chapter consider all of these questions. They start with the requirement of government action, and then turn to the meaning of "searches" and "seizures." They next turn to exceptions to the warrant requirement, and they conclude with the law of searches pursuant to warrants.

A. THE REQUIREMENT OF GOVERNMENT ACTION

The Fourth Amendment only regulates searches and seizures by the government or agents of the government. As the Supreme Court stated in United States v. Jacobsen, 466 U.S. 109, 113 (1984), the Fourth Amendment is "wholly inapplicable to a search or seizure, even an unreasonable one, effected by a private individual not acting as an agent of the Government or with the participation or knowledge of any governmental official."

The requirement of government action to trigger Fourth Amendment protection focuses attention on the distinction between government action and private action. Where is the line between the two?

UNITED STATES V. JARRETT
United States Court of Appeals for the Fourth Circuit, 2003.
338 F.3d 339.

DIANA GRIBBON MOTZ, CIRCUIT JUDGE.

In this case, the Government used information provided by an anonymous computer hacker to initiate a search which produced evidence that William Jarrett violated federal statutes prohibiting the manufacture and receipt of child pornography. The district court suppressed this evidence on the ground that the hacker acted as a Government agent, and so violated the Fourth Amendment, when he procured pornographic files from Jarrett's computer. The Government appeals. Because the Government did not know of, or in any way participate in, the hacker's search of Jarrett's computer at the time of that search, the hacker did not act as a Government agent. Accordingly, we reverse and remand for further proceedings.

I.

The parties do not dispute the underlying facts. Prior to his involvement in the case at hand, the hacker, referred to as Unknownuser, provided information through emails during July 2000 to the FBI and law enforcement agents in Alabama regarding a child pornographer, Dr. Bradley Steiger. In an early email, Unknownuser identified himself only as someone "from Istanbul, Turkey," who could not "afford an overseas phone call and cannot speak English fluently."

Employing the same method that he would later use to hack into Jarrett's computer, Unknownuser obtained access to Steiger's computer via a so-called Trojan Horse program that Unknownuser had attached to a picture he posted to a news group frequented by pornography enthusiasts. When Steiger downloaded the picture to his own computer, he inadvertently downloaded the Trojan Horse program, which then permitted Unknownuser to enter Steiger's computer undetected via the Internet. *See* United States v. Steiger, 318 F.3d 1039, 1044 (11th Cir. 2003). After searching Steiger's hard drive and finding evidence of child pornography, Unknownuser copied certain files and then emailed the information to the law enforcement officials who used it to identify and apprehend Steiger. A jury convicted Steiger of violating various federal statutes prohibiting the sexual exploitation of minors. He was sentenced to 210 months in prison.

Shortly after Steiger was indicted, in late November 2000, FBI Special Agent James Duffy, who served as Legal Attache for the FBI in Turkey, contacted Unknownuser via email and phone. In addition to informing Unknownuser that he would not be prosecuted for his assistance in apprehending Steiger, Duffy requested a meeting and posed a series of questions to Unknownuser, with the hope that Unknownuser would reveal his identity and perhaps agree to testify at Steiger's trial. Although Unknownuser was quite forthcoming in his responses, he refused to meet with Agent Duffy, stating emphatically that he would never allow himself to be identified. Agent Duffy closed this exchange (in an email dated December 4, 2000) by thanking Unknownuser for his assistance and stating that "If you want to bring other information forward, I am available."

Five months later, Agent Duffy contacted Unknownuser via email, informing him of a postponement in the Steiger trial, thanking him again for his assistance, and assuring him that he would not be prosecuted for his actions should he decide to serve as a witness in the Steiger trial. Unknownuser responded, repeating that he had no intention of revealing his identity.

The next contact between Unknownuser and law enforcement did not occur until December 3, 2001, almost seven months later, when Unknownuser sent an unsolicited email to his contact at the Montgomery, Alabama Police Department, Kevin Murphy, informing Murphy that he had "found another child molester from Richmond, VA" and requesting contact information for someone at the FBI dealing with these sorts of crimes. The alleged child molester referred to in the email was William Jarrett.

After contacting the FBI, Murphy informed Unknownuser that the FBI preferred that Unknownuser send the new information to Murphy's email address. On December 4, 2001, Unknownuser sent thirteen email messages to Murphy, including a ten-part series of emails with some forty-five attached files containing the "evidence" that Unknownuser had collected on Jarrett. Murphy forwarded the information to agents at the FBI, who initiated an investigation.

Based on the information provided by Unknownuser, the Government filed a criminal complaint and application for a search warrant against Jarrett on December 13, 2001. After receiving authorization from the district court, the FBI promptly executed the search warrant and arrested Jarrett.

Several days after Jarrett's arrest, on December 16, 2001, Agent Duffy sent Unknownuser an email informing him of Steiger's sentence and thanking Unknownuser for his assistance in the case. At the time, Duffy was unaware of the Jarrett investigation. The next day, Unknownuser replied, informing Duffy of his efforts to identify Jarrett and inquiring why he had heard nothing since he sent the Jarrett files to Murphy on December 4. Unknownuser sent a similar message the following day (December 18) indicating that he had read about Jarrett's arrest in the newspaper and asking Agent Duffy to have Agent Margaret Faulkner—a special agent based in Alabama who had been involved in the Steiger investigation—contact him. On December 19, 2001, Agent Duffy sent an email to Unknownuser thanking him again for his assistance, providing information on the Jarrett investigation and prosecution, and requesting that Unknownuser maintain email contact with Agent Faulkner via her personal email address.

Three weeks later, on January 9, 2002, a grand jury indicted Jarrett on one count of manufacturing child pornography in violation of 18 U.S.C. § 2251(a) and seven counts of receiving child pornography in violation of 18 U.S.C. § 2252A(a)(2)(A). Jarrett moved to suppress the evidence obtained through the execution of the search warrant on the ground that the Government violated his Fourth Amendment rights in using the information provided by Unknownuser to secure the search warrant. The district court denied the motion. Jarrett then entered a conditional guilty plea to a one-count criminal information charging him with manufacturing child pornography.

Prior to sentencing, however, Jarrett moved to reconsider his earlier motion to suppress on the basis of new evidence—a series of emails exchanged between Unknownuser and FBI agent Faulkner, beginning shortly after Jarrett's arrest and extending for almost two months. The Government did not disclose these emails until after Jarrett had entered his guilty plea.

In the initial email in this series, dated December 19, 2001, Agent Faulkner explicitly thanked Unknownuser for providing the information to law enforcement officials. She then engaged in what can only be characterized as the proverbial "wink and a nod":

> I can not ask you to search out cases such as the ones you have sent to us. That would make you an agent of the Federal Government and make how you obtain your information illegal and we could not use it against the men in the pictures you send. But if you should happen across such pictures as the ones you have sent to us and wish us to look into the matter, please feel free to send them to us. We may have lots of questions and have to email you with the questions. But as long as you are not 'hacking' at our request, we can take the pictures and identify the men and take them to court. We also have no desire to charge you

with hacking. You are not a U.S. citizen and are not bound by our laws.

Over the course of the next two months, Agent Faulkner sent at least four additional email messages, which constituted, in the words of the district court, a "pen-pal type correspondence" with Unknownuser. In addition to expressing gratitude and admiration for Unknownuser, Faulkner repeatedly sought to reassure Unknownuser that he was not a target of law enforcement for his hacking activities. For example, in an email dated January 29, 2002, she stated that

> the FACT still stands that you are not a citizen of the United States and are not bound by our laws. Our Federal attorneys have expressed NO desire to charge you with any CRIMINAL offense. You have not hacked into any computer at the request of the FBI or other law enforcement agency. You have not acted as an agent for the FBI or other law enforcement agency. Therefore, the information you have collected can be used in our criminal trials.

In his responses to Agent Faulkner, Unknownuser spoke freely of his "hacking adventures" and suggested in no uncertain terms that he would continue to search for child pornographers using the same methods employed to identify Steiger and Jarrett. As found by the district court, Agent Faulkner, despite her knowledge of Unknownuser's illegal hacking, never instructed Unknownuser that he should cease hacking.

Upon consideration of this series of emails, the district court reversed its earlier decision and suppressed the evidence obtained during the search of Jarrett's residence. At the same time, the court deemed Jarrett's motion to reconsider as a motion to withdraw his guilty plea, which it promptly granted. The court reasoned that the "totality of all the contact between law enforcement and Unknownuser encouraged Unknownuser to continue his behavior and to remain in contact with the FBI." The district court thus concluded that the Government and Unknownuser had "expressed their consent to an agency relationship," thereby rendering any evidence obtained on the basis of Unknownuser's hacking activities inadmissible on the ground that it was procured in violation of Jarrett's Fourth Amendment rights.

II.

The Fourth Amendment protects against unreasonable searches and seizures by Government officials and those private individuals acting as instruments or agents of the Government. *See* U.S. Const. amend. IV; *Coolidge v. New Hampshire,* 403 U.S. 443, 487 (1971). It does not provide protection against searches by private individuals acting in a private capacity. *See United States v. Jacobsen,* 466 U.S. 109, 113 (1984) (holding that the Fourth Amendment is "wholly inapplicable to a search or seizure, even an unreasonable one, effected by a private individual not acting as an agent of the Government or with the participation or knowledge of any governmental official"). Thus, evidence secured by private searches, even if illegal, need not be excluded from a criminal trial.

Determining whether the requisite agency relationship exists "necessarily turns on the degree of the Government's participation in the private party's activities, a question that can only be resolved in light of all the circumstances." *Skinner v. Railway Labor Executives' Ass'n*, 489 U.S. 602, 614–15 (1989). This is a fact-intensive inquiry that is guided by common law agency principles. The defendant bears the burden of proving that an agency relationship exists.

In order to run afoul of the Fourth Amendment, therefore, the Government must do more than passively accept or acquiesce in a private party's search efforts. Rather, there must be some degree of Government participation in the private search. In *Skinner*, for example, the Supreme Court found that private railroads, in performing drug tests on their employees in a manner expressly encouraged and authorized under Government regulations, acted as Government agents sufficient to implicate the Fourth Amendment. As the Court concluded, "specific features of the regulations combine to convince us that the Government did more than adopt a passive position toward the underlying private conduct."

Following the Supreme Court's pronouncements on the matter, the Courts of Appeals have identified two primary factors that should be considered in determining whether a search conducted by a private person constitutes a Government search triggering Fourth Amendment protections. These are: (1) whether the Government knew of and acquiesced in the private search; and (2) whether the private individual intended to assist law enforcement or had some other independent motivation. Although we have never articulated a specific "test," we too have embraced this two-factor approach.

In this case, the Government concedes the existence of the second factor—that Unknownuser's motivation for conducting the illicit searches stemmed solely from his interest in assisting law enforcement authorities. Thus, the only question before us concerns the first factor—did the Government know of and acquiesce in Unknownuser's search in a manner sufficient to transform Unknownuser into an agent of the Government, and so render the search unconstitutional.

In seeking to give content to this factor, we have required evidence of more than mere knowledge and passive acquiescence by the Government before finding an agency relationship.

Viewed in the aggregate, three major lessons emerge from the case law. First, courts should look to the facts and circumstances of each case in determining when a private search is in fact a Government search. Second, before a court will deem a private search a Government search, a defendant must demonstrate that the Government knew of and acquiesced in the private search and that the private individual intended to assist law enforcement authorities. Finally, simple acquiescence by the Government does not suffice to transform a private search into a Government search. Rather, there must be some evidence of Government participation in or affirmative encouragement of the private search before a court will hold it unconstitutional. Passive acceptance by the Government is not enough.

With these principles in mind, we turn to the case at hand.

III.

With respect to fact finding, the district court found the facts as we have recounted them above. The record adequately supports these findings; certainly they are not clearly erroneous.

The district court's conclusions of law, however, present problems. The court concluded that Unknownuser's extensive post-search email exchange with Agent Faulkner, together with the brief exchanges between Unknownuser and Agent Duffy in November and December 2000 (one year prior to the Jarrett search) and May 2001 (seven months prior to the Jarrett search), demonstrated that the Government had an "ongoing relationship" with Unknownuser sufficient to make Unknownuser an agent of the Government. Specifically, the court held that in light of the Government's collective efforts to praise Unknownuser for his assistance, its repeated requests for further assistance, its assurances that Unknownuser would not be prosecuted for his hacking activities, and its refusal to suggest that Unknownuser should cease hacking, "there was far more than mere knowledge on the government's part."

Although, as the Government conceded at oral argument, the Faulkner email exchange probably does constitute the sort of active Government participation sufficient to create an agency relationship going forward (absent other countervailing facts), the district court erred in relying on this exchange to find that the Government knew of and acquiesced in the Jarrett search. This is so because Unknownuser's email exchange with Faulkner took place after Unknownuser had hacked into Jarrett's computer, after the fruits of Unknownuser's hacking had been made available to the FBI, after Jarrett's home and computer had been searched, and after Jarrett himself had been arrested. Thus, Faulkner's knowledge and acquiescence was entirely post-search. Such after-the-fact conduct cannot serve to transform the prior relationship between Unknownuser and the Government into an agency relationship with respect to the search of Jarrett's computer.

Although the Government operated close to the line in this case, it did not (at least on the evidence before the district court) demonstrate the requisite level of knowledge and acquiescence sufficient to make Unknown user a Government agent when he hacked into Jarrett's computer. When

Unknownuser came forward with the Jarrett information, he had not been in contact with the Government for almost seven months, and nothing indicates that the Government had any intention of reestablishing contact with him. The only communications that could possibly be construed as signaling an agency relationship prior to the search of Jarrett's computer (the Duffy communications from November–December 2000 and May 2001) were simply too remote in time and too tenuous in substance to bring the Jarrett search within the scope of an agency relationship.

That the Government did not actively discourage Unknownuser from engaging in illicit hacking does not transform Unknownuser into a Government agent. Although the Government's behavior in this case is discomforting,[5] the Government was under no special obligation to affirmatively discourage Unknownuser from hacking.

At the end of the day, in order to bring Unknownuser within the grasp of an agency relationship, Jarrett would have to show that the Government made more explicit representations and assurances (as in the post-hoc Faulkner emails) that it was interested in furthering its relationship with Unknownuser and availing itself of the fruits of any information that Unknownuser obtained. Although evidence of such "encouragement" would not have to target a particular individual, it would have to signal affirmatively that the Government would be a ready and willing participant in an illegal search.

As the facts in this case make clear, no such relationship existed between Unknownuser and the Government when Unknownuser hacked into Jarrett's computer. Accordingly, we hold that the district court erred when it found that Unknownuser acted as an agent of the Government when he hacked into Jarrett's computer.

NOTES AND QUESTIONS

1. *Who was that unknown user?* Do you believe that Unknownuser was a resident of Istanbul, Turkey? If Unknownuser had been a local Virginia police officer, would the FBI agents who investigated the case necessarily realize it?

2. *Do private searches of computer data create a greater privacy threat than private searches of homes and other physical property?* In the physical world, private searches are most often conducted by co-workers, spouses, and roommates. None are particularly likely to report the fruits of their searches to the police. Private searches by strangers are also relatively unlikely to be reported to the police. For example, a burglar is not likely to risk being caught by reporting evidence of crime that he finds inside a victim's home.

---

[5] Notwithstanding the Government's assumptions, nothing in the record establishes that Unknownuser is a foreign national and, even if he is, of course, foreign nationals can, as the Government conceded, be prosecuted in the United States for sending and receiving child pornography. Unauthorized hacking also violates United States law.

Are computer searches different? The anonymity of the Internet may make private searches by perfect strangers significantly more common, and may increase the odds that strangers will report discovered evidence to law enforcement. Any computer user located anywhere in the world can hack in to a person's computer when it is online, and can search the computer for evidence and share what he finds with the police without revealing his identity. Should the private search doctrine be reworked so that the Fourth Amendment regulates computer searches conducted by anonymous hackers? Should the government have the burden of proving that an anonymous hacker was *not* a state actor?

3. *Computer repair cases.* A number of reported child pornography convictions followed searches by computer repairmen. In these cases, the defendant brought his personal computer to a local repairman because the computer was malfunctioning. In the course of diagnosing the problem, the repairman looked through the files on the computer, found child pornography, and contacted the police. These cases have held that the repairman's search of the computer and discovery of contraband did not violate the Fourth Amendment because the repairman was a private actor. *See, e.g.,* United States v. Hall, 142 F.3d 988, 993 (7th Cir. 1998).

4. *Reenacting a private search.* According to United States v. Jacobsen, 466 U.S. 109 (1984), government agents who learn of evidence discovered by a private search can reenact the original private search without implicating the Fourth Amendment. The agents cannot "exceed the scope of the private search" without a warrant, *id.* at 115, but they can trace the steps of the prior search with the permission of the private party.

How does this apply to a computer search? If a private party searches a computer and opens a few files, finds evidence of crime, and gives the computer to the police, can the police search the entire computer without a warrant? Or does viewing more than the exact files that were opened by the private party "exceed the scope" of the private search under *Jacobsen*? Put another way, what is the unit that is "searched" when a private party sees data on a computer: Just the data observed, the file that contained it, the folder, or the entire physical computer?

The federal circuit courts are divided on the answer. Some courts have held that when a private party sees a file, the entire physical computer has been searched. For example in United States v. Runyan, 275 F.3d 449 (5th Cir. 2001), an estranged wife looked through some of her husband's computer disks and found contraband images. She turned over the entire set of disks to the police, and the police later conducted an extensive search of all of the disks without a warrant. The Fifth Circuit concluded that the police officers did not exceed the scope of the private search when they looked through the disks that the wife had accessed, even though the police viewed files that the wife had not seen. The governmental viewing had merely examined the disks "more thoroughly than did the private parties." *Id.* at 464. The police could not search the disks that the wife had not accessed, however, as viewing files on those disks exceeded the scope of the private search. *Id.*

In contrast, the Sixth Circuit adopted the unit of data or a file in United States v. Lichtenberger, 786 F.3d 478 (6th Cir. 2015). The defendant's girlfriend searched his computer on her own and found child pornography. When she reported the discovery to the police, an officer asked her to show him the images she had seen. She opened up several files on the computer and found child pornography that later led to a warrant and a subsequent law enforcement search. Importantly, however, the defendant's girlfriend was not sure that the specific files that she discovered the second time were the same as the files she had found the first time. *Held*: The officer exceeded the private search in violation of the Fourth Amendment when he directed the girlfriend to conduct a search that led to the discovery of files not proven to have been observed previously. Here's the key passage:

> As with any Fourth Amendment inquiry, we must weigh the government's interest in conducting the search of Lichtenberger's property against his privacy interest in that property. That the item in question is an electronic device does not change the fundamentals of this inquiry. But . . . the nature of the electronic device greatly increases the potential privacy interests at stake, adding weight to one side of the scale while the other remains the same.

> All the photographs Holmes showed Officer Huston contained images of child pornography, but there was no virtual certainty that would be the case. The same folders—labeled with numbers, not words—could have contained, for example, explicit photos of Lichtenberger himself: legal, unrelated to the crime alleged, and the most private sort of images. Other documents, such as bank statements or personal communications, could also have been discovered among the photographs. So, too, could internet search histories containing anything from Lichtenberger's medical history to his choice of restaurant. The reality of modern data storage is that the possibilities are expansive.

Id. at 488–89. *See also* United States v. Sparks, 806 F.3d 1323 (11th Cir. 2015) (offering a similar analysis).

5. *The state action requirement and Internet provider scanning for CSAM.* Several major providers of Internet service in the United States have enacted voluntary programs by which their software scans messages and their attachments in and out of their networks for CSAM images. When providers discover a known image, federal law requires that they must report their finding to the National Center for Missing and Exploited Children (NCMEC). *See* 18 U.S.C. § 2258A. Upon receiving images, NCMEC can conduct a further investigation.

This arrangement raises two important legal questions under the state action doctrine. First, are Internet providers that scan for CSAM images private actors or state actors for Fourth Amendment purposes? Second, is NCMEC a private actor or a state actor for Fourth Amendment purposes?

Circuit courts have held that the Internet providers are private actors. They have reasoned that Congress has not mandated monitoring, and that the decision to monitor is the provider's, not the government's. *See, e.g.,* United States v. Miller, 982 F.3d 412, 423–25 (6th Cir. 2020) ("Google's decision to scan its customers' files is instead like the utility's decision to disconnect its customers' electricity: The initiative to take both actions comes from the private party, not the government."). Congress has mandated reporting if a provider chooses to monitor and finds CSAM, but the "search" is the provider-motivated monitoring, not the government-compelled reporting. *See id.*

On the other hand, NCMEC has been held to be a government actor under the Fourth Amendment. *See* United States v. Ackerman, 831 F.3d 1292 (10th Cir. 2016) (Gorsuch, J.). According to the Tenth Circuit, "NCMEC's law enforcement powers extend well beyond those enjoyed by private citizens—and in this way it seems to mark it as a fair candidate for a governmental entity." *Id.* at 1296. The court continued:

> NCMEC's two primary authorizing statutes—18 U.S.C. § 2258A and 42 U.S.C. § 5773(b)—mandate its collaboration with federal (as well as state and local) law enforcement in over a dozen different ways, many of which involve duties and powers conferred on and enjoyed by NCMEC but no other private person.
>
> For example, NCMEC is statutorily obliged to operate the official national clearinghouse for information about missing and exploited children, to help law enforcement locate and recover missing and exploited children, to "provide forensic technical assistance to law enforcement" to help identify victims of child exploitation, to track and identify patterns of attempted child abductions for law enforcement purposes, to "provide training to law enforcement agencies in identifying and locating non-compliant sex offenders," and of course to operate the CyberTipline as a means of combating Internet child sexual exploitation. 42 U.S.C. § 5773(b). Responsibilities and rights Congress has extended to NCMEC alone "under Federal law" and done so specifically "to assist or support law enforcement agencies in administration of criminal justice functions." *Id.* § 16961(a)(1).
>
> This special relationship runs both ways, too, for NCMEC is also empowered to call on various federal agencies for unique forms of assistance in aid of its statutory functions. *See* 18 U.S.C. § 3056(f) (authorizing the U.S. Secret Service to provide, "at the request of" NCMEC, "forensic and investigative assistance in support of any investigation involving missing or exploited children").

Id. As a result, NCMEC's investigations are governed by the limits of the Fourth Amendment.

B. DEFINING SEARCHES AND SEIZURES

1. SEARCHES

a) Introduction to Fourth Amendment "Searches"

A Fourth Amendment "search" can occur in two situations. First, a search occurs when the government physically trespasses on to persons, houses, papers, or effects with intent to obtain information. *See* United States v. Jones, 565 U.S. 400 (2012). Second, a search occurs when a person manifests a subjective expectation of privacy that society recognizes as reasonable. *See* Smith v. Maryland, 442 U.S. 735, 740 (1979).

The reasonable expectation of privacy test originated in Justice Harlan's concurrence in Katz v. United States, 389 U.S. 347 (1967). In *Katz*, FBI agents taped a microphone to the top of a public pay phone booth that Katz used to place illegal bets. When Katz entered the phone booth, agents turned on the microphone and recorded his half of the communication. Justice Stewart's majority opinion ruled that the warrantless surveillance of the phone booth was impermissible:

> One who occupies [a public phone booth], shuts the door behind him, and pays the toll that permits him to place a call is surely entitled to assume that the words he utters into the mouthpiece will not be broadcast to the world. To read the Constitution more narrowly is to ignore the vital role that the public telephone has come to play in private communication.
>
> The Government contends, however, that the activities of its agents in this case should not be tested by Fourth Amendment requirements, for the surveillance technique they employed involved no physical penetration of the telephone booth from which the petitioner placed his calls. But the premise that property interests control the right of the Government to search and seize has been discredited. Once this much is acknowledged, and once it is recognized that the Fourth Amendment protects people—and not simply "areas"—against unreasonable searches and seizures, it becomes clear that the reach of that Amendment cannot turn upon the presence or absence of a physical intrusion into any given enclosure.
>
> The Government's activities in electronically listening to and recording the petitioner's words violated the privacy upon which he justifiably relied while using the telephone booth and thus constituted a "search and seizure" within the meaning of the Fourth Amendment. The fact that the electronic device employed to achieve that end did not happen to penetrate the wall of the booth can have no constitutional significance.

Id. at 352–53.

Justice Harlan's concurrence in *Katz* offered a somewhat narrower approach than Justice Stewart's majority opinion:

> As the Court's opinion states, "the Fourth Amendment protects people, not places." The question, however, is what protection it affords to those people. Generally, as here, the answer to that question requires reference to a "place." My understanding of the rule that has emerged from prior decisions is that there is a twofold requirement, first that a person have exhibited an actual (subjective) expectation of privacy and, second, that the expectation be one that society is prepared to recognize as "reasonable." Thus a man's home is, for most purposes, a place where he expects privacy, but objects, activities, or statements that he exposes to the "plain view" of outsiders are not "protected" because no intention to keep them to himself has been exhibited. On the other hand, conversations in the open would not be protected against being overheard, for the expectation of privacy under the circumstances would be unreasonable.

> The critical fact in this case is that "one who occupies [a telephone booth], shuts the door behind him, and pays the toll that permits him to place a call is surely entitled to assume" that his conversation is not being intercepted. The point is not that the booth is "accessible to the public" at other times, but that it is a temporarily private place whose momentary occupants' expectations of freedom from intrusion are recognized as reasonable.

Id. at 361 (Harlan, J., concurring). Justice Harlan's formulation was later adopted by the full Supreme Court. As a result, the *Katz* test is generally said to have two parts: First, a subjective prong, which asks whether the person demonstrated an actual expectation of privacy; and second, an objective prong, which asks whether that expectation was one that society is prepared to recognize as reasonable.

In Rakas v. Illinois, 439 U.S. 128 (1978), then-Justice Rehnquist offered this explanation of when an expectation of privacy is constitutionally "reasonable" or "legitimate":

> A legitimate expectation of privacy by definition means more than a subjective expectation of not being discovered. A burglar plying his trade in a summer cabin during the off season may have a thoroughly justified subjective expectation of privacy, but it is not one which the law recognizes as legitimate. His presence . . . is wrongful; his expectation is not one that society is prepared to recognize as reasonable. And it would, of course, be merely tautological to fall back on the notion that those expectations of

> privacy which are legitimate depend primarily on cases deciding
> exclusionary-rule issues in criminal cases. Legitimation of
> expectations of privacy by law must have a source outside of the
> Fourth Amendment, either by reference to concepts of real or
> personal property law or to understandings that are recognized
> and permitted by society.

Id. at 144 n.12.

The *Katz* test is a common source of confusion for law students. The problem is that the Supreme Court has refused to say what makes an expectation of privacy "reasonable." You might be wondering, who is "society," and how are Supreme Court Justices supposed to know what it thinks?

Given these uncertainties, the best way to understand when a person has a reasonable expectation of privacy is to reason by analogy. The Supreme Court has decided many cases involving Fourth Amendment rights in the contents of containers such as letters, packages, boxes, and trunks. The basic rule emerging from these cases is that individuals have a Fourth Amendment reasonable expectation of privacy in the contents of their sealed containers. *See, e.g.*, Robbins v. California, 453 U.S. 420, 427 (1981) (Stewart, J., plurality opinion). The same rule applies across a wide range of different types of containers:

> Even though such a distinction [among different containers] perhaps could evolve in a series of cases in which paper bags, locked trunks, lunch buckets, and orange crates were placed on one side of the line or the other, the central purpose of the Fourth Amendment forecloses such a distinction. For just as the most frail cottage in the kingdom is absolutely entitled to the same guarantees of privacy as the most majestic mansion, so also may a traveler who carries a toothbrush and a few articles of clothing in a paper bag or knotted scarf claim an equal right to conceal his possessions from official inspection as the sophisticated executive with the locked attache case.

United States v. Ross, 456 U.S. 798, 822 (1982). In contrast, "[w]hat a person knowingly exposes to the public, even in his own home or office, is not a subject of Fourth Amendment protection." Katz v. United States, 389 U.S. 347, 351 (1967).

In United States v. Jones, 565 U.S. 400 (2012), the Supreme Court added an additional way in which government action can be a search. Under *Jones*, a search occurs if the government physically trespasses onto an individual's person, house, papers, or effects with intent to obtain information. The police installed a GPS device on the bottom of the car Jones drove and monitored its location for 28 days. The majority ruled that the installation and use of the GPS device was a search because it trespassed onto the car:

> The Government physically occupied private property for the purpose of obtaining information. We have no doubt that such a physical intrusion would have been considered a "search" within the meaning of the Fourth Amendment when it was adopted. The text of the Fourth Amendment reflects its close connection to property, since otherwise it would have referred simply to "the right of the people to be secure against unreasonable searches and seizures"; the phrase "in their persons, houses, papers, and effects" would have been superfluous.

Id. at 405. Concurring opinions by Justice Sotomayor and Justice Alito concurred and offered a different rationale, that the collective public monitoring over time was a search that violated a reasonable expectation of privacy. Consider the concurring opinion of Justice Alito:

> Relatively short-term monitoring of a person's movements on public streets accords with expectations of privacy that our society has recognized as reasonable. But the use of longer term GPS monitoring in investigations of most offenses impinges on expectations of privacy. For such offenses, society's expectation has been that law enforcement agents and others would not—and indeed, in the main, simply could not—secretly monitor and catalogue every single movement of an individual's car for a very long period.

Id. at 430 (Alito, J., concurring). Justice Sotomayor also concurred:

> GPS monitoring generates a precise, comprehensive record of a person's public movements that reflects a wealth of detail about her familial, political, professional, religious, and sexual associations. The Government can store such records and efficiently mine them for information years into the future. And because GPS monitoring is cheap in comparison to conventional surveillance techniques and, by design, proceeds surreptitiously, it evades the ordinary checks that constrain abusive law enforcement practices: limited police resources and community hostility.
>
> I would take these attributes of GPS monitoring into account when considering the existence of a reasonable societal expectation of privacy in the sum of one's public movements. I would ask whether people reasonably expect that their movements will be recorded and aggregated in a manner that enables the Government to ascertain, more or less at will, their political and religious beliefs, sexual habits, and so on. I do not regard as dispositive the fact that the Government might obtain

the fruits of GPS monitoring through lawful conventional surveillance techniques. I would also consider the appropriateness of entrusting to the Executive, in the absence of any oversight from a coordinate branch, a tool so amenable to misuse, especially in light of the Fourth Amendment's goal to curb arbitrary exercises of police power to and prevent a too permeating police surveillance.

Id. at 415–16 (Sotomayor, J., concurring).

The following materials consider how these general principles apply to searches of computers. They begin by considering the stand-alone environment, when the government is obtaining information from a physical device such as a laptop, thumb drive, or cell phone that is not connected to the Internet. The materials then turn to searches in the network context.

b)   Searches of Stand-Alone Computers

UNITED STATES V. DAVID

United States District Court for the District of Nevada, 1991.
756 F. Supp. 1385.

LAWRENCE R. LEAVITT, UNITED STATES MAGISTRATE JUDGE.

On June 21, 1990, the federal grand jury returned a one-count Indictment charging the defendant, Artem Bautista David, with conspiracy to import more than 20 kilos of heroin into the United States.

An evidentiary hearing was conducted before the undersigned Magistrate Judge on September 12, 1990. The testimony established that in late April, 1990, David flew from Hong Kong to Las Vegas and was taken into custody by Customs agents on a charge of conspiracy to smuggle heroin into the United States. Government counsel engaged in discussions with David's then counsel, John R. Lusk, with a view toward enlisting David's cooperation in exchange for a favorable plea bargain. An agreement was reached whereby David, who would remain in custody under a detention order, would meet periodically with the agents in their office and make full disclosure of his knowledge of drug trafficking activities in an "off the record" proffer. The agreement also provided that at the agents' direction, David would place consensually monitored telephone calls to his criminal associates. The telephone numbers of those associates were kept in David's computer memo book, access to which required the use of a password—"fortune"—which was known only to David.

During one such meeting in early May, 1990, which Lusk attended, David retrieved and disclosed certain information contained in the book. At the time, the agents were sitting across the table from him and were unable to see the password which David used or the information displayed on the book's screen. David did not volunteer the password to the agents, or offer to show them the book.

Jail regulations prohibited David from taking the book back to the jail at night. For the sake of convenience, Lusk permitted the agents to maintain custody of the book at the end of each session. Lusk did not, however, give them permission to access the book. Neither did David. Nor, as noted above, did the assistance agreement itself expressly permit the agents to gain access to the book or, for that matter, to any other property in David's possession.

At the next meeting on May 7, 1990, David met with Customs Special Agent Eric Peterson and DEA Special Agent Don Ware. Lusk did not attend this meeting. According to David's testimony, when he initially accessed the book at this meeting, Agent Peterson got up and stood directly behind him. David was aware that Peterson was looking over his shoulder, but did not feel that he could demand that Peterson move away. David did, however, try to position the book so as to minimize Peterson's view of it.

According to David's testimony, after he made two telephone calls for the agents, Peterson grabbed the book and accused David of deleting certain information. David demanded the book back, but Peterson refused. At the evidentiary hearing, David denied having deleted information from the book. Agent Peterson's version of what occurred at the meeting is a little different. Peterson testified that on May 7, 1990, he first requested the access code from David, but David was unresponsive. Peterson admitted that he then stood behind David and observed David use the password "fortune" to access the book. A little later, while Agent Ware was criticizing David for not cooperating fully during a consensually monitored phone call, Peterson, without requesting David's permission, used the password "fortune" and accessed the book himself. He then reviewed several of its entries. David saw Peterson doing this, but said nothing. Peterson came across an entry which read "1 = 12,000; 2 = 23,000," which, based on his experience as a Customs agent, he knew to be a heroin price list per kilo in Thailand. He then turned off the computer and returned it to David.

The Fourth Amendment provides that the "right of the people to be secure in their persons, houses, papers, and effects, against unreasonable searches and seizures, shall not be violated." The Supreme Court has defined a *search* as an infringement of "an expectation of privacy that society is prepared to consider reasonable." United States v. Jacobsen, 466 U.S. 109, 113 (1984). Hence, a law enforcement officer who looks at something has not engaged in a "search" within the meaning of the Fourth Amendment unless someone else has a right to expect that the thing which is seen will remain private.

In evaluating the factual scenario described above, we begin by identifying those events which may have Fourth Amendment implications. The *first* such event occurred when Agent Peterson deliberately looked over David's shoulder to see the password to the book. David himself voluntarily accessed the book at a time when the agents were in close proximity to him. Agent Peterson was not required to stay seated across the table from David. Nor did David have a reasonable expectation that Peterson would not walk behind him, or remain outside of some imaginary zone of privacy within the enclosed room. It was Peterson's office, and he could move about in it wherever he pleased. The Court therefore finds that under the circumstances David had no reasonable expectation of privacy in the display that appeared on the screen, and accordingly concludes that Peterson's act of looking over David's shoulder to see the password did not constitute a search within the meaning of the Fourth Amendment.

Peterson's act of accessing the book did constitute a search, however, if, under the circumstances, David had a reasonable expectation that when he turned the book off, its contents would remain private. For the purposes of this discussion, the book, in the Court's view, is indistinguishable from any other closed container, and is entitled to the same Fourth Amendment protection. *Robbins v. California,* 453 U.S. 420, 427 (1981); *United States v. Ross,* 456 U.S. 798 (1982). The Court does not question Agent Peterson's testimony that based on David's cooperation agreement with the government, Peterson had a good faith belief that he had the right to access the book. Peterson testified that in his mind the cooperation agreement implied that David would withhold nothing from the agents, including the contents of his memo book. But David's attempt to prevent Peterson from seeing the password, and his deletion of the heroin price list and attempted deletion of the firearms price list, clearly reflect that at the very least David did not *want* to share all of the contents of the book with the agents.

Accordingly, the government should not be allowed to use as evidence the information which Agent Peterson obtained from the book when he accessed it without David's express consent.

NOTES AND QUESTIONS

1.   *The container analogy.* A person ordinarily retains a reasonable expectation of privacy in the contents of his opaque containers when the containers are at home, in his possession, or are stored in a space that he legitimately controls. Opening such a container constitutes a Fourth Amendment search. Under the container analogy followed in *David,* an individual will retain a reasonable expectation of privacy in the contents of his computers in the same circumstances. When a government agent retrieves contents from the individual's computer, that retrieval is a Fourth Amendment search that ordinarily requires a warrant or a specific exception to the warrant requirement.

2. *Expectations of privacy in computer-stored information.* In Riley v. California, 134 S.Ct. 2473 (2014), which appears in the main text starting on page 485, the Supreme Court indicated that computer-stored information is highly protected under the Fourth Amendment. *Riley* involved searches of cell phones, which the Court noted was "itself misleading shorthand; many of these devices are in fact minicomputers that also happen to have the capacity to be used as a telephone." *Id.* at 2489. In light of that, the Court's discussion of privacy rights in cell phones is likely applicable to computer-stored information generally:

> One of the most notable distinguishing features of modern cell phones is their immense storage capacity. The current top-selling smart phone has a standard capacity of 16 gigabytes (and is available with up to 64 gigabytes). Sixteen gigabytes translates to millions of pages of text, thousands of pictures, or hundreds of videos. Cell phones couple that capacity with the ability to store many different types of information: Even the most basic phones that sell for less than $20 might hold photographs, picture messages, text messages, Internet browsing history, a calendar, a thousand-entry phone book, and so on. We expect that the gulf between physical practicability and digital capacity will only continue to widen in the future.

> The storage capacity of cell phones has several interrelated consequences for privacy. First, a cell phone collects in one place many distinct types of information—an address, a note, a prescription, a bank statement, a video—that reveal much more in combination than any isolated record. Second, a cell phone's capacity allows even just one type of information to convey far more than previously possible. The sum of an individual's private life can be reconstructed through a thousand photographs labeled with dates, locations, and descriptions; the same cannot be said of a photograph or two of loved ones tucked into a wallet. Third, the data on a phone can date back to the purchase of the phone, or even earlier. A person might carry in his pocket a slip of paper reminding him to call Mr. Jones; he would not carry a record of all his communications with Mr. Jones for the past several months, as would routinely be kept on a phone.

> Although the data stored on a cell phone is distinguished from physical records by quantity alone, certain types of data are also qualitatively different. An Internet search and browsing history, for example, can be found on an Internet-enabled phone and could reveal an individual's private interests or concerns—perhaps a search for certain symptoms of disease, coupled with frequent visits to WebMD. Data on a cell phone can also reveal where a person has been. Historic location information is a standard feature on many smart phones and can reconstruct someone's specific movements down to the minute, not only around town but also within a particular building.

Mobile application software on a cell phone, or "apps," offer a range of tools for managing detailed information about all aspects of a person's life. There are apps for Democratic Party news and Republican Party news; apps for alcohol, drug, and gambling addictions; apps for sharing prayer requests; apps for tracking pregnancy symptoms; apps for planning your budget; apps for every conceivable hobby or pastime; apps for improving your romantic life. There are popular apps for buying or selling just about anything, and the records of such transactions may be accessible on the phone indefinitely. There are over a million apps available in each of the two major app stores; the phrase "there's an app for that" is now part of the popular lexicon. The average smart phone user has installed 33 apps, which together can form a revealing montage of the user's life.

In 1926, Learned Hand observed that it is "a totally different thing to search a man's pockets and use against him what they contain, from ransacking his house for everything which may incriminate him." *United States v. Kirschenblatt*, 16 F.2d 202, 203 (C.A.2). If his pockets contain a cell phone, however, that is no longer true. Indeed, a cell phone search would typically expose to the government far *more* than the most exhaustive search of a house: A phone not only contains in digital form many sensitive records previously found in the home; it also contains a broad array of private information never found in a home in any form—unless the phone is.

Id. at 2489–91.

3.   *Taking a computer out of screensaver mode.* In United States v. Musgrove, 845 F. Supp.2d 932 (E.D. Wisc. 2011), officers came to Musgrove's apartment to investigate reports of a threat. Musgrove invited the officers inside. Once inside, officers saw Musgrove's computer "on" but with the screensaver engaged. An officer walked over to the computer and either pressed a key or moved the mouse. Doing so disengaged the screensaver, revealing Musgrove's Facebook wall which contained threatening comments. Musgrove moved to suppress the contents of the Facebook wall on the ground that the officer had searched his computer without a warrant by disengaging the screensaver. The court agreed:

Whether there is a search here is a close call because the officer did not actively open any files. A truly cursory inspection—one that involves merely looking at what is already exposed to view, without disturbing it—is not a "search" for Fourth Amendment purposes. However, this is not such a case. By touching a key or moving the mouse, the officer put into view the Facebook wall, which was not previously in view. Though a close call, the Court concludes that this was a search, however minimal, which required further authority, a warrant or consent.

See id. at 949.

4.   *Opening a flip phone.* In United States v. Bell, 2016 WL 1588098 (C.D.Ill. 2016), an arrested suspect charged with illegally possessing a gun owned a "flip phone" that had to be flipped opened in order to be used. An officer flipped open the phone, purportedly to turn it off, and noticed that the home screen contained a picture of the defendant's gun. *Held*: Flipping open the phone to turn it off, which exposed the home screen, was a search:

> While it is true that a "cursory inspection—one that involves merely looking at what is already exposed to view, without disturbing it—is not a search for Fourth Amendment purposes," [the officer's] opening of [the suspect's] cell phone exceeded a cursory inspection because he exposed to view concealed portions of the object—i.e., the screen. See *Arizona v. Hicks*, 480 U.S. 321, 328–29 (1987). The Supreme Court specifically addressed this issue in *Hicks*, noting that the "distinction between 'looking' at a suspicious object in plain view and 'moving' it even a few inches is much more than trivial for purposes of the Fourth Amendment." *Id.* at 325. [The officer's] opening of the flip phone, like the officer moving the stereo equipment in *Hicks*, exposed to view concealed portions of the object and thus produced a new invasion of defendant's privacy.

Id. at *3.

5.   *Powering on a cell phone.* In United States v. Sam, CR19-0115-JCC (W.D. Wash. May 18, 2020), an officer took the defendant's cell phone out of police inventory, powered it on, and took a photograph of the lock screen. The district court ruled that powering on the cell phone was a Fourth Amendment search under the physical intrusion test of United States v. Jones, 565 U.S. 400 (2012):

> The FBI physically intruded on Mr. Sam's personal effect when the FBI powered on his phone to take a picture of the phone's lock screen. See United States v. Jones, 565 U.S. 400, 410 (2012) (holding Government searched a car by attaching a GPS device to the car); Bond v. United States, 529 U.S. 334, 337 (2000) (concluding Border Patrol agent searched a bag by squeezing it); Arizona v. Hicks, 480 U.S. 321, 324–25 (1987) (holding officer searched stereo equipment by moving it so that the officer could view concealed serial numbers). The FBI therefore "searched" the phone within the meaning of the Fourth Amendment.

6.   *Locating a phone by calling it to make it ring.* In United States v. Katana, 2021 WL 185547 (D.Mass. 2021), officers arrested Katana at his home. Katana was not carrying his cell phone. Officers knew his cell phone's number, so they called the phone to locate it. The phone rang from inside the pants pocket of Katana's brother, who was also present. The court held that calling the phone to locate it was not a search:

> A person has no legitimate expectation of privacy in their phone number given that it is shared with cellphone providers and other

users. Thus, while the Katana phone was not in plain view when it was dialed, the act of dialing the defendant's phone number does not constitute a search under the Fourth Amendment. If a person wanted to keep their cell phone's location private, they could do so by turning off the phone. By having the phone turned on, a person allows any third party to call them. Because a person has no reasonable expectation of privacy in their phone number, dialing that number does not constitute a search under the Fourth Amendment.

Id. at *2.

7.   *Calling 911 from a locked phone to learn its number.* Officers who seize a locked cell phone may want to know its number to identify its owner. Modern phones allow anyone to place an emergency call to 911 without unlocking the phone. Because 911 operators work with the police, the police can call 911 from a locked phone and ask the operator to tell them the calling number.

Courts are divided on whether this causes a Fourth Amendment search. *Compare* State v. Hill, 789 S.E.2d 317 (Ga.App. 2016) (holding that no search occurs because the "the officer did not access any files on [the] phone" or "attempt to retrieve any information from within the phone") *with* United States v. Jones, 2021 WL 22176 at *4 (E.D.Wisc. 2021) (holding that a search occurs because the officer "had to push buttons . . . to obtain information that was not otherwise visible"). Which view is more persuasive?

8.   *Enlarging a thumbnail image.* If an officer sees a computer screen containing thumbnail-sized images in plain view, and he clicks on one of the thumbnails to make the image larger, does clicking on the thumbnail to see the larger image constitute a search? No court has answered this question directly. Should the answer depend on whether the larger image contains important details that were not observable from the thumbnail? *Cf.* United States v. Tosti, 733 F.3d 816 (9th Cir. 2013) (holding that when an officer reconstructed a private search, clicking on a thumbnail and seeing the larger image did not exceed the scope of the private search where "the police learned nothing new through their actions").

9.   *Pressing a button on a key fob to locate and unlock a car.* Modern cars typically can be opened at a distance using a button on a key fob. If the fob is in the area of the car, pressing the "unlock" button will cause the car to unlock its doors. This is useful when the police recover a key fob. If police want to locate the car associated with the fob, they can press the button on the fob to see if a nearby car unlocks.

Is pressing the unlock button to locate the car a Fourth Amendment search, assuming that the car is in the area and responds by unlocking? Although the precedents are not entirely clear, cases so far suggest that using the key fob to locate a car is not a search. *See, e.g.,* United States v. Burgess, 425 F. Supp.3d 413 (E.D.Pa. 2019) (suggesting that using a key fob is not a search because pressing the button merely transmits a signal to the car much like a flashlight and is similarly widely available); United States v. Cowan, 674 F.3d 947, 955–57 (8th Cir. 2012) (holding that the use of a key fob to locate a car is not a search or seizure because "the fob merely would identify the vehicle" and the defendant "did not have a reasonable expectation of privacy in the identity of his car"); Commonwealth v. Harvard, 64 A.3d 690, 696 (Pa. Super. Ct. 2013) (use of a key fob was not a search).

10. *Generating a hash, and opening the item when a hash matches with a known file.* Imagine the police obtain a computer that contains thousands of files, and they want to search through the computer to determine if it has a particular file. One way to do this is through a mathematical process known as a hash function. A hash function is a mathematical program that generates a unique alphanumeric value—a digital fingerprint, or "digital DNA"—for each file. To determine if a known file exists on a particular device, a computer analyst can generate a hash for each of the files on the device and then compare the resulting alphanumeric values to those of known files.

Is it a search to run a hash to look for matches with known files? And if a match occurs, it is a search to open the file to visually confirm the match?

In United States v. Crist, 627 F. Supp.2d 575 (M.D. Pa. 2008), the court held that running a hash on the files on a suspect's personal computer using a forensic program called EnCase was a Fourth Amendment search:

> The Government argues that no search occurred in running the EnCase program because the agents didn't look at any files, they simply accessed the computer. The Court rejects this view and finds that the "running of hash values" is a search protected by the Fourth Amendment. By subjecting the entire computer to a hash value analysis, every file, internet history, picture, and "buddy list" became available for Government review. Such examination constitutes a search.

Id. at *9.

Should it matter if the files are CSAM? In Illinois v. Caballes, 543 U.S. 405 (2005), the Supreme Court held that using a drug-sniffing dog to alert to drugs inside the car is not a search because "any interest in possessing contraband cannot be deemed 'legitimate,' and thus, governmental conduct that only reveals the possession of contraband compromises no legitimate privacy interest." *Id.* at 408. Does the rationale of *Caballes* apply to digital CSAM, such that generating a hash of a CSAM file should not be a search? *See generally* Richard P. Salgado, *Fourth Amendment Search and the Power of the Hash*, 119 Harv. L. Rev. F. 38, 45–46 (2006) (debating this question).

Next imagine a private party conducts the hash, finds a match, and gives the file to the government. Can a government agent open the hashed file to confirm the match? This issue arises when Internet providers scan the hashes of user files for matches with hashes of known images of CSAM. If the provider finds a hash match with that of a known CSAM image, and it sends the image to the government, can the government open the file without a "search" occurring?

Circuit courts have divided on this question. The Fifth Circuit and the Sixth Circuit have ruled that the government can open the file without a new search occurring, at least as long as agents only open the particular file that was hashed and the private party's hashing function is reliable. The identity of the file is a virtual certainty in those circumstances, these courts reason, so the government is merely reconstructing a private search. *See* United States v. Reddick, 900 F.3d 636, 637 (5th Cir. 2018); United States v. Miller, 982 F.3d 412, 431 (6th Cir. 2020).

On the other hand, the Ninth Circuit has ruled that the government opening a file based on a hash match with a known image of CSAM is a search unless a non-government person has earlier opened the file to confirm its contents. In United States v. Wilson, ___ F.4th ___, 2021 WL 4270847 (9th Cir. 2021), Google's CyberTip scanning program identified a hash match between an attachment to Wilson's e-mail and a known image of CSAM. Google sent the e-mail to NCMEC, and NCMEC forwarded it to Agent Thompson of the San Diego Internet Crimes Against Children Task Force. Agent Thompson opened the e-mail and confirmed its contents. According to the Ninth Circuit, this was a search because no one at Google had opened the file first:

> Viewing Wilson's email attachments substantively expanded the information available to law enforcement far beyond what the label alone conveyed, and was used to provide probable cause to search further and to prosecute. The government learned at least two things above and beyond the information conveyed by the CyberTip by viewing Wilson's images: First, Agent Thompson learned exactly what the image showed. Second, Agent Thompson learned the image was in fact child pornography. Until he viewed the images, they were at most suspected child pornography. To prosecute Wilson, it was necessary for Agent Thompson to view the images no Google employee had opened. Until Agent Thompson viewed Wilson's images, no one involved in enforcing the child pornography ban had seen them. Only by viewing the images did the government confirm, and convey to the fact finder in Wilson's criminal case, that they depicted child pornography under the applicable federal standard.

Id. Which is more persuasive, the Fifth Circuit in *Reddick* and the Sixth Circuit in *Miller* or the Ninth Circuit in *Wilson*?

11. *Swiping a credit card to learn the number programmed in the magnetic strip.* Traditional credit cards have a magnetic strip along the back that ordinarily stores the information printed on the front of the card. The magnetic strip contains the account number, bank identification number, the card expiration date, the three digit "CSC" code, and the cardholder's first and last name. The magnetic strip makes it easy for the cardholder to share credit card information with a vendor: Swiping the card transmits the information.

In *United States v. Bah*, 794 F.3d 617 (6th Cir. 2015), the Sixth Circuit considered whether accessing the data stored in the magnetic strip of a credit card is a Fourth Amendment search. Investigators came across a stash of credit cards in an impounded rental car. The investigators suspected that the credit cards might have been stolen and reprogrammed with new credit card numbers in the magnetic strip. To determine this, the investigators ran the cards through a magnetic card reader. Doing so confirmed their suspicions: The information on the front and back of the cards did not match.

The Sixth Circuit ruled that accessing the data stored in the magnetic strip was not a Fourth Amendment search. The court relied heavily on a set of mostly-unpublished district court opinions that had reached the same result:

> Because the information on the magnetic strips, with the possible exception of a few other additional, unique identifiers, mirrors that information provided on the front and back of a physical credit, debit or gift card, and the magnetic strips are routinely read by private parties at gas stations, restaurants, and grocery stores to accelerate financial transactions, such an expectation of privacy is not one that society is prepared to consider reasonable.

> Every court to have addressed this question has reached the same conclusion. Some courts have stressed that there can be no reasonable expectation of privacy in an account number—and consequently, magnetic strip—that is routinely shared with cashiers every time the card is used.

> Other courts have emphasized the fact that the scan of the magnetic strip reveals little—to potentially nothing—that cannot be viewed on the front and back of the physical card; consequently, these courts have reasoned that once law enforcement personnel have lawful, physical possession of the card, the scan does not constitute a separate "search."

> Finally, other courts focus on the fact that a scan of the magnetic strip will usually only disclose the presence or absence of activity that is not legal. The reasonable-expectation-of-privacy test in concept presupposes an innocent person, and government conduct that only reveals the possession of contraband compromises no legitimate privacy interests.

> Similar to a drug sniff alerting the handler only to the presence of narcotics—information about illegal activity—scanning credit and debit cards to read the information contained on the magnetic strips, when law enforcement already has physical possession of the cards, will disclose "only the presence or absence of" illegal information: either the information disclosed is the same information on the outside of the credit and debit cards, or is information about a different account, used to commit credit card fraud. Such a limited investigatory technique to quickly and obviously provide information

whether the payment form is being used criminally does not violate the Defendant's right to be secure in their person, house, papers, or effects.

Is the reasoning of *Bah* persuasive? Isn't accessing the magnetic strip just like accessing the information stored in the computer memo book in *David*? It is true that technology limits the amount of information stored in a traditional credit card—specifically, to 79 letters and 147 numbers. But why does this relatively small amount of information make accessing the numbers any less of a search? And why does the fact that the information can be shared with others eliminate Fourth Amendment protection when there is no evidence it actually has been so shared?

Consider the dissenting opinion of Judge Jane Kelly in United States v. DE L'Isle, 825 F.3d 426 (8th Cir. 2016), which had facts similar to *Bah* and which reached the same result. According to Judge Kelly, whether a person has a reasonable expectation of privacy in the contents of magnetic strips on credit cards in their possession "depends on whether there are significant technological barriers to an individual rewriting information on the magnetic stripe of their cards:"

> If the information on the magnetic stripe can be modified without much difficulty, the cardholder may indeed have a reasonable expectation of privacy in the contents of the stripe, based on the straightforward principle that law enforcement conducts a Fourth Amendment "search" when it reads the contents of rewritable digital storage media. That principle is implicit in the fact that both this court and the Supreme Court have consistently required searches of storage devices like hard drives and CDs to be justified either by a warrant or an applicable exception to the warrant requirement. If a magnetic stripe card is a digital storage device, albeit one whose storage capacity is limited, reading the data on it is a Fourth Amendment search. Accessing the data on the stripe would simply be a special case of the general rule that reading a digital storage device constitutes a Fourth Amendment search.

Id. at 434–36 (Kelly, J., dissenting).

12. *When does leaving a cell phone behind mean it is "abandoned," therefore eliminating its user's Fourth Amendment rights?* People normally have Fourth Amendment rights in their property. But they can give up those rights if they abandon their property. When people abandon property, they give up any claim to its continued possession and leave it for others even if they hoped that others would not search the property. At that point, the cases say, people give up their claim to Fourth Amendment protection. *See, e.g.*, United States v. Juszczyk, 844 F.3d 1213 (10th Cir. 2017) (holding that a man who threw his backpack onto someone else's roof when he realized the police were approaching had abandoned the backpack when there was no reason to believe that the homeowner would have returned the property to him).

Should this abandonment doctrine apply to searching a discovered cell phone? If so, how?

In State v. Brown, 815 S.E.2d 761 (S.C. 2018), a couple returned to their condominium apartment after dinner and heard an unfamiliar cell phone ringing in the hallway. It turned out that, in their absence, their apartment had been burglarized. The burglar had inadvertently left his cell phone behind. The couple called the police, and the police seized the cell phone and placed it in police custody. The police then waited six days, during which no one had tried to recover the phone.

After the six days had elapsed, the government searched the phone without a warrant. The phone was locked, but an officer guessed the passcode (which was 1-2-3-4) and searched the phone for information about the owner's identity. A look through the contacts stored in the phone established that the defendant was the phone's owner. A divided Supreme Court of South Carolina ruled that, by the time of the search, Brown's cell phone had been abandoned and the warrantless search was therefore lawful:

> We begin our review of the trial court's finding that Brown abandoned his phone with the factual premise of *Riley*, that cell phones hold the privacies of life. Brown's expectation that this privacy would be honored—at least initially—is supported by the fact he put a lock on the screen of the phone. At least until the time of the burglary, therefore, Brown enjoyed Fourth Amendment protection for the digital information stored on his phone.

> Additionally, we can presume Brown did not intentionally leave his cell phone at the scene of the crime, for he must have known that doing so would lead to the discovery that he was the burglar. Thus, it is unlikely a police officer would believe the mere act of leaving the phone at the scene of the crime was an intentional relinquishment of his privacy. For at least a short period of time after the crime, therefore, the phone might not yet have been abandoned. However, when a person loses something of value—whether valuable because it is worth money or because it holds privacies—the person who lost it will normally begin to look for the item.

> In this case, the phone sat in the evidence locker at the police station for six days. The record contains no evidence Brown did anything during this time to try to recover his phone. While Brown might have taken action to protect his privacy before he left it at the victim's condominium, there is no evidence he did anything after that to retain the privacy he previously had in the phone's digital contents.

> There is no evidence he tried to call the phone to see if someone would answer. There is no evidence he attempted to text the phone in hopes the text would show on the screen, perhaps with an alternate number where Brown could be reached, or perhaps even with a message that he did not relinquish his privacy in the contents of the phone. There

is no evidence he attempted to contact the service provider for information on the whereabouts of the phone. Instead, he contacted his service provider and canceled his cellular service to the phone. And there is certainly no evidence he went back to the scene of the crime to look for it, or that he attempted to call the police to see if they had it.

We would expect that a person who lost a cell phone that has value because of the privacies it holds would look for the phone in one or more of the ways described above. On the other hand, the reason a burglar would not look too hard to find a phone he lost during a burglary is obvious. Brown put himself in the difficult position of having to balance the risk that finding the phone would incriminate him against the benefit of retrieving the private digital information stored in it.

Looking at these facts objectively, any police officer would assume after six days of no efforts by the owner to recover this phone—especially under the circumstance that the owner left the phone at the scene of a burglary—that the owner had decided it was too risky to try to recover it. Brown's decision not to attempt to recover the phone equates to the abandonment of the phone.

Id. at 524–26.

Chief Justice Beatty dissented. He would have ruled that under Riley v. California, 573 U.S. 373 (2014), the abandonment doctrine does not apply to a cell phone:

I believe *Riley* creates a categorical rule that, absent exigent circumstances, law enforcement must procure a search warrant before searching the data contents of a cell phone. Even though the decision in *Riley* arose out of a search incident to an arrest, I discern no reason why the Supreme Court's rationale is not equally applicable with respect to the abandonment exception to the Fourth Amendment. I believe the defendant's expectation of privacy in the digital contents of a cell phone remains the same in either context.

As one legal scholar explained:

The logic behind the Supreme Court's need to protect cell phones during arrests applies just as convincingly to cell phones left behind by their users. Categorically, the Supreme Court clearly identified that cell phones implicate privacy concerns far beyond those implicated by the search of any other nondigital physical item or container because of cell phones' immense storage capacity and variety of detailed information. The same invasion of privacy occurs during a warrantless search of a cell phone, regardless of whether that phone is found during an arrest or left behind by its owner. In light of the modern developments of personal technological devices and the Court's analysis in *Riley*, courts should develop a carve-out for cell phones from the abandonment exception to the Fourth Amendment and require police officers to obtain a search warrant before searching cell phones left behind by their owners.

Abigail Hoverman, Note, *Riley and Abandonment: Expanding Fourth Amendment Protection of Cell Phones*, 111 Nw. U. L. Rev. 517, 543 (2017).

I agree with this assessment and believe that any interpretation limiting the holding in *Riley* effectively negates its precedential value.

Id. at 530–31 (Beatty, C.J., dissenting). Which view is more persuasive?

c)   Searches in the Network Context

The materials above considered Fourth Amendment limitations on government access to computers and data under their owners' control. In many cases, however, data will not be stored with its owner. Computer users routinely send information over local, national, or even international computer networks. When computer networks are used to commit criminal acts, investigators may wish to collect evidence directly from those networks without approaching the suspect or his home.

This section considers how the Fourth Amendment applies to the collection of computer data sent over or stored on remote computers. To appreciate the difficult questions of Fourth Amendment law raised by network surveillance, it helps to review a few basic features about how computer networks (and specifically, today's Internet protocols) work. Individuals normally connect to networks and the Internet by having an account with a server that is connected to a broader network. For example, a home user may have an Internet service provider that serves as the user's contact point with the network. Every communication sent or received by the user is routed through the user's Internet provider.

Internet communications are sent across the network by being broken into "packets," individual chunks of data that contain about a page's worth of information. Internet packets are streams of data that act as the computer equivalent of letters between computers. Each packet begins with a IP (Internet protocol) header, a computer-generated envelope that contains the packet's originating and destination address along with information about the type and size of the information the packet carries. The IP header (also referred to as a packet header) is created when the communication is sent, and is used by the network to ensure delivery of the payload. The communication itself becomes the "payload" of the packet, and appears after the header. The header is automatically discarded by the receiving computer when the packet arrives at its destination. The receiving computer then reassembles the various packets into the original file that was sent.

Packet headers are not the only kind of addressing information generated by computers. Sending an e-mail generates an "e-mail header" that contains originating and destination e-mail addresses, as well as a brief history of where and when the e-mail was sent in the course of delivery. Many types of e-mail programs permit you to view the entire e-mail header of e-mails in your inbox; the header is akin to the envelope of a letter, complete with an electronic version of a postmark.

The existence of packet headers, e-mail headers, and other types of Internet communications means that the Fourth Amendment rules that govern network surveillance must consider a very wide range of different communications and surveillance techniques. Information relating to an individual's computer use may include the contents of e-mails, requests for web pages, e-mail headers, IP headers, and many other kinds of information. That information can be monitored in real-time or collected from storage from a wide range of places across the network.

Our question is, when does a particular network surveillance technique trigger Fourth Amendment protection? We will begin by reviewing precedents from earlier technologies. We will then turn to the rules for obtaining the contents of user communications, and then turn to the rules for obtaining non-content account information (also known as "metadata").

(1) An Overview of Precedents Involving Speech, the Postal Network, and the Telephone Network

Reasoning by analogy is an important tool to help understand how the Fourth Amendment might apply to collecting information from computer networks. The courts have decided many cases applying the Fourth Amendment to earlier communications technologies such as the telephone network and the postal mail network. One way to understand the Fourth Amendment in the context of computer networks is by reasoning from analogy to these earlier technologies. In particular, consider three possible analogies: speech, postal letters, and telephone calls.

The Speech Analogy

Is sending computer data to a remote computer akin to speaking to that computer? When you send e-mail and surf the web, are you telling your ISP to send the information for you and then hearing from your ISP as to what information it received on your behalf? From this perspective, we might model computers as if they were people, and model transmission of information among computers as if it were an open sharing of information among them.

Is this analogy persuasive? If it is, sending data to a remote server likely eliminates a reasonable expectation of privacy in the data. The Supreme Court has consistently held that a person's Fourth Amendment rights are not violated if he reasonably but mistakenly tells another person his secrets and the person then relays that secret to the government.

For example, in Hoffa v. United States, 385 U.S. 293 (1966), James Hoffa admitted criminal activity to a confidant, Partin. Partin turned out to be a paid government informer, and he transmitted the information to the FBI. Hoffa objected, arguing that his Fourth Amendment rights had been violated when Partin shared Hoffa's private information with the police. The Court rejected this argument:

> Neither this Court nor any member of it has ever expressed the view that the Fourth Amendment protects a wrongdoer's misplaced belief that a person to whom he voluntarily confides his wrongdoing will not reveal it. The risk of being overheard by an eavesdropper or betrayed by an informer or deceived as to the identity of one with whom one deals is probably inherent in the conditions of human society. It is the kind of risk we necessarily assume whenever we speak.

Id. at 302–03. Under *Hoffa*, a person assumes the risk that those within earshot of their speech will hear and understand the speech and will share it with the police. However unlikely it is, the person's Fourth Amendment rights are not violated if it happens.

This is true even if the person does not intend for others overhearing the speech to listen in or understand it. Consider the unpleasant surprise encountered by the Spanish-speaking members of the narcotics conspiracy in United States v. Longoria, 177 F.3d 1179 (10th Cir. 1999). Because the co-conspirators were the only individuals nearby who spoke or understood Spanish, they discussed their criminal activity to each other in Spanish in the presence of outsiders. One such outsider turned out to be a government informant who recorded the defendant's Spanish conversations using audio equipment. The informant did not understand Spanish, but government translators did. They translated the tapes into English and used the translations at trial. The Tenth Circuit rejected the notion that the co-conspirators had a reasonable expectation of privacy because they spoke in a foreign tongue that others present did not comprehend. "[O]ne exposing conversations to others must necessarily assume the risk his statements will be overheard and understood," the court reasoned. "[The defendant] exposed his statements by speaking in a manner clearly audible by the informant. His hope that the informant would not fully understand the contents of the conversation is not an expectation society is prepared to recognize as reasonable." *Id.* at 1182.

Courts have analogized Internet communications to speech in the context of online undercover operations. For example, in State v. Moller, 2002 WL 628634 (Ohio Ct. App. 2002), a police officer entered a chat room for older men posing as a 14-year-old girl. Defendant Moller contacted the officer and the two eventually arranged for Moller to drive 200 miles to meet the "girl" for sexual activities. Following his arrest, Moller argued that the officer's conduct violated his Fourth Amendment rights. The Court disagreed, relying on the rationale of *Hoffa*:

> Like Hoffa, Moller took the risk that the 14 year old he thought he was talking to, and planning to engage in sex with, was not who she seemed to be, but was in reality a police officer. This is a risk that anyone visiting a chat room necessarily takes when communicating with strangers. It is easy for anyone using the Internet to adopt a false persona, whether for purposes of law enforcement, or for other and nefarious purposes. It was unreasonable for Moller to assume that his unsuitable conversations would be kept private. Thus, in our view, his statements made in the chat room to a stranger are not entitled to protection under the Fourth Amendment.

Id. at *5.

The Letter or Package Analogy

Is sending computer data to a remote location like sending a document, letter or package? Existing Fourth Amendment law teaches that individuals who send letters and packages retain a reasonable expectation of privacy in the contents of their sealed containers but not in the exposed exteriors of those containers. Fourth Amendment protections track what is exposed and what is sealed away from view. For example, individuals do not retain a reasonable expectation of privacy in the outside of their letters or packages, or in documents disclosed to others. The police can observe the outside of packages, take pictures of envelopes, read postcards, and analyze disclosed documents all without implicating the Fourth Amendment. On the other hand, opening a sealed letter or package during transit to view its contents is a Fourth Amendment search that implicates the Fourth Amendment rights of the sender and receiver. It requires a warrant or an exception to the warrant requirement.

The Fourth Amendment's protection of postal letters dates back to dicta in Ex parte Jackson, 96 U.S. 727 (1877), a decision involving the power of Congress to regulate the postal system. Justice Field wrote the following about the privacy of items sent through the postal system, *id.* at 733:

> Letters and sealed packages in the mail are as fully guarded from examination and inspection, except as to their outward form and weight, as if they were retained by the parties forwarding them in

their own domiciles. The constitutional guaranty of the right of the people to be secure in their papers against unreasonable searches and seizures extends to their papers, thus closed against inspection, wherever they may be. Whilst in the mail, they can only be opened and examined under like warrant, issued upon similar oath or affirmation, particularly describing the thing to be seized, as is required when papers are subjected to search in one's own household. No law of Congress can place in the hands of officials connected with the postal service any authority to invade the secrecy of letters and such sealed packages in the mail; and all regulations adopted as to mail matter of this kind must be in subordination to the great principle embodied in the Fourth Amendment of the Constitution.

The basic principle of *Ex parte Jackson* has been construed fairly broadly. Leaving a sealed package with a trustworthy bailee generally preserves the bailor's Fourth Amendment protections in the package's contents. For example, individuals have been held to retain a reasonable expectation of privacy in the contents of opaque packages when they send packages via private carriers, *see* Walter v. United States, 447 U.S. 649, 651 (1980); when they leave packages with store clerks, *see* United States v. Most, 876 F.2d 191, 197–98 (D.C. Cir. 1989); when they are stored with airport baggage counters, *see* United States v. Barry, 853 F.2d 1479, 1481–83 (8th Cir. 1988); and when they leave packages with their friends for safekeeping, *see* United States v. Presler, 610 F.2d 1206, 1213–14 (4th Cir. 1979). In all of these cases, governmental opening of the sealed package violates the owner's reasonable expectation of privacy.

However, there are two important limits on this principle. First, the sender's reasonable expectation of privacy in a sealed package or letter is eliminated when the package or letter reaches its destination. When the item is delivered and the letter becomes the property of the recipient, governmental access no longer implicates the sender's Fourth Amendment rights. For example, the search of a home that uncovers letters mailed to that address will not implicate the Fourth Amendment rights of the individuals who sent the letters. *See* United States v. King, 55 F.3d 1193, 1196 (6th Cir. 1995).

Second, a person does not have a reasonable expectation of privacy in letters or packages in the course of transit when the carrier has the right to access the contents of the letters or packages. For example, the United States Postal Service has traditionally had a category of mail known as fourth class mail. The postal service retains a right to open letters and packages sent fourth class mail. Courts have held that an individual does not retain a reasonable expectation of privacy in their fourth class mail, as sending a package when the postal service retains a right to open it constitutes consent to opening it that is inconsistent with Fourth

Amendment protection. *See, e.g.,* United States v. Huie, 593 F.2d 14, 15 (5th Cir. 1979).

How should these principles apply to computer data sent remotely over a network? Is computer data "sealed"? Do ISPs have a right to "open" it? What is the "destination" of an e-mail or a request for a web page?

The Telephone Analogy

Instead of analogizing computer network communications to speech or letters, we might try to analogize them to telephone calls. The Fourth Amendment framework that governs telephone calls ends up being very similar to the legal framework that governs letters and packages.

The Supreme Court's first decision on how the Fourth Amendment applies to telephone calls was Olmstead v. United States, 277 U.S. 438 (1928). Roy Olmstead was the leader of a massive Prohibition-era conspiracy to import illegal alcohol into the United States. Agents tapped the telephone lines to Olmstead's house and offices and then listened in on the calls to gather evidence against him. The Supreme Court ruled 5–4 that this wiretapping did not constitute a Fourth Amendment search. Writing for the majority, Chief Justice Taft rejected the letter analogy:

> The Fourth Amendment may have proper application to a sealed letter in the mail, because of the constitutional provision for the Postoffice Department and the relations between the government and those who pay to secure protection of their sealed letters. It is plainly within the words of the amendment to say that the unlawful rifling by a government agent of a sealed letter is a search and seizure of the sender's papers or effects. The letter is a paper, an effect, and in the custody of a government that forbids carriage, except under its protection.

> The United States takes no such care of telegraph or telephone messages as of mailed sealed letters. The amendment does not forbid what was done here. There was no searching. There was no seizure. The evidence was secured by the use of the sense of hearing and that only. There was no entry of the houses or offices of the defendants.

> By the invention of the telephone 50 years ago, and its application for the purpose of extending communications, one can talk with another at a far distant place.

> The language of the amendment cannot be extended and expanded to include telephone wires, reaching to the whole world from the defendant's house or office. The intervening wires are not part of his house or office, any more than are the highways along which they are stretched.

Id. at 464–65. Chief Justice Taft construed telephone calls as more akin to human speech than letters:

> The reasonable view is that one who installs in his house a telephone instrument with connecting wires intends to project his voice to those quite outside, and that the wires beyond his house, and messages while passing over them, are not within the protection of the Fourth Amendment. Here those who intercepted the projected voices were not in the house of either party to the conversation.

Id. at 466.

In his famous dissent, Justice Louis Brandeis presented a very different picture of the Fourth Amendment and the role of wiretapping:

> When the Fourth and Fifth Amendments were adopted, the form that evil had theretofore taken had been necessarily simple. Force and violence were then the only means known to man by which a government could directly effect self-incrimination. It could compel the individual to testify—a compulsion effected, if need be, by torture. It could secure possession of his papers and other articles incident to his private life—a seizure effected, if need be, by breaking and entry. Protection against such invasion of the sanctities of a man's home and the privacies of life was provided in the Fourth and Fifth Amendments by specific language. But time works changes, brings into existence new conditions and purposes. Subtler and more far-reaching means of invading privacy have become available to the government. Discovery and invention have made it possible for the government, by means far more effective than stretching upon the rack, to obtain disclosure in court of what is whispered in the closet.
>
> Moreover, in the application of a Constitution, our contemplation cannot be only of what has been, but of what may be. The progress of science in furnishing the government with means of espionage is not likely to stop with wire tapping. Ways may some day be developed by which the government, without removing papers from secret drawers, can reproduce them in court, and by which it will be enabled to expose to a jury the most intimate occurrences of the home. Advances in the psychic and related sciences may bring means of exploring unexpressed beliefs, thoughts and emotions. 'That places the liberty of every man in the hands of every petty officer' was said by James Otis of much lesser intrusions than these. To Lord Camden a far slighter intrusion seemed 'subversive of all the comforts of society.' Can it be that the Constitution affords no protection against such invasions of individual security?

In *Ex parte Jackson*, it was held that a sealed letter intrusted to the mail is protected by the amendments. The mail is a public service furnished by the government. The telephone is a public service furnished by its authority. There is, in essence, no difference between the sealed letter and the private telephone message. As Judge Rudkin said below: "True, the one is visible, the other invisible; the one is tangible, the other intangible; the one is sealed, and the other unsealed; but these are distinctions without a difference."

The evil incident to invasion of the privacy of the telephone is far greater than that involved in tampering with the mails. Whenever a telephone line is tapped, the privacy of the persons at both ends of the line is invaded, and all conversations between them upon any subject, and although proper, confidential, and privileged, may be overheard. Moreover, the tapping of one man's telephone line involves the tapping of the telephone of every other person whom he may call, or who may call him. As a means of espionage, writs of assistance and general warrants are but puny instruments of tyranny and oppression when compared with wire tapping.

The makers of our Constitution undertook to secure conditions favorable to the pursuit of happiness. They recognized the significance of man's spiritual nature, of his feelings and of his intellect. They knew that only a part of the pain, pleasure and satisfactions of life are to be found in material things. They sought to protect Americans in their beliefs, their thoughts, their emotions and their sensations. They conferred, as against the government, the right to be let alone—the most comprehensive of rights and the right most valued by civilized men. To protect that right, every unjustifiable intrusion by the government upon the privacy of the individual, whatever the means employed, must be deemed a violation of the Fourth Amendment.

Id. at 473–76, 478–79 (Brandeis, J., dissenting).

The Supreme Court effectively overruled *Olmstead* in two cases, Berger v. New York, 388 U.S. 41 (1967), and Katz v. United States, 389 U.S. 347 (1967). *Berger* invalidated a New York state wiretapping law on the ground that it did not provide sufficient Fourth Amendment safeguards. The majority opinion did not directly hold that the wiretapping violated the rights of the person whose phone was tapped. Instead, the opinion took the opportunity to articulate general Fourth Amendment requirements for wiretapping statutes. Unlike *Berger*, *Katz* was not a wiretapping case. *Katz* involved a microphone taped to a public phone booth, not the intercept of any calls. However, a passage in the majority opinion announced the end of the *Olmstead* regime:

> Although a closely divided Court supposed in *Olmstead* that surveillance without any trespass and without the seizure of any material object fell outside the ambit of the Constitution, we have since departed from the narrow view on which that decision rested. Indeed, we have expressly held that the Fourth Amendment governs not only the seizure of tangible items, but extends as well to the recording of oral statements, over-heard without any technical trespass under local property law. Once this much is acknowledged, and once it is recognized that the Fourth Amendment protects people—and not simply "areas"—against unreasonable searches and seizures, it becomes clear that the reach of that Amendment cannot turn upon the presence or absence of a physical intrusion into any given enclosure.

> We conclude that the underpinnings of *Olmstead* have been so eroded by our subsequent decisions that the "trespass" doctrine there enunciated can no longer be regarded as controlling.

Katz, 389 U.S. at 352–53. The combination of *Berger* and *Katz* indicates that wiretapping an individual's telephone calls normally amounts to a Fourth Amendment "search."

Lower courts have held that this rule does not apply in the case of cordless telephones, however. In the 1980s, companies began offering cordless telephones for sale to the public. Cordless telephones work by broadcasting FM radio signals between the base of the phone and the handset. Each phone has two radio transmitters that work at the same time: the base transmits the incoming call signal to the handset, and the handset transmits the outgoing call signal to the base. Before the mid-1990s, cordless phones generally used analog FM signals that were easy to intercept. Government agents would occasionally use widely available FM radio scanners to listen in on the cordless telephone calls of suspects without a warrant.

Courts that have addressed this issue have rejected claims of Fourth Amendment protection in the contents of cordless telephone calls. Because cordless-phone intercepting devices merely pick up a signal that has been "broadcast over the radio waves to all who wish to overhear," the interception was held not to violate any reasonable expectation of privacy. McKamey v. Roach, 55 F.3d 1236, 1239–40 (6th Cir. 1995). *See also* Tyler v. Berodt, 877 F.2d 705, 707 (8th Cir. 1989); Price v. Turner, 260 F.3d 1144, 1149 (9th Cir. 2001). Courts reached the same result when the suspect was using a traditional landline telephone and happened to engage in conversation with someone who was using a cordless phone. *See* United States v. McNulty, 47 F.3d 100, 104–106 (4th Cir. 1995).

You may recall from the discussion of letters and packages that the contents of letters or packages are ordinarily protected by the Fourth Amendment, while the outside of the envelopes and packages are not. The Supreme Court created a similar distinction for telephone calls in Smith v. Maryland, 442 U.S. 735 (1979). The police in *Smith* were investigating a robbery, and they had reason to believe that the victim of the robbery was being harassed by the robber through threatening telephone calls. The police suspected that Smith was the robber, and they asked the telephone company to install a device known as a "pen register" on Smith's telephone. In the telephone technology of the 1970s, a pen register was a device that recorded the numbers dialed from a particular telephone line. The pen register did not record the actual contents of the communications, but rather only the telephone numbers dialed to complete the call. The telephone company installed the pen register on Smith's phone line, and it recorded Smith's home telephone line being used to dial the number of the robbery victim.

The Supreme Court concluded in *Smith* that recording the numbers dialed from Smith's phone line was not protected by the Fourth Amendment:

First, we doubt that people in general entertain any actual expectation of privacy in the numbers they dial. All telephone users realize that they must "convey" phone numbers to the telephone company, since it is through telephone company switching equipment that their calls are completed. All subscribers realize, moreover, that the phone company has facilities for making permanent records of the numbers they dial, for they see a list of their long-distance (toll) calls on their monthly bills. In fact, pen registers and similar devices are routinely used by telephone companies for the purposes of checking billing operations, detecting fraud and preventing violations of law. Electronic equipment is used not only to keep billing records of toll calls, but also to keep a record of all calls dialed from a telephone which is subject to a special rate structure.

Second, even if petitioner did harbor some subjective expectation that the phone numbers he dialed would remain private, this expectation is not one that society is prepared to recognize as 'reasonable.' This Court consistently has held that a person has no legitimate expectation of privacy in information he voluntarily turns over to third parties. This analysis dictates that petitioner can claim no legitimate expectation of privacy here. When he used his phone, petitioner voluntarily conveyed numerical information to the telephone company and "exposed" that information to its equipment in the ordinary course of business. In so doing, petitioner assumed the risk that the company would reveal to police the numbers he dialed. The switching equipment that processed those numbers is merely the modern counterpart of the operator who, in an earlier day, personally completed calls for the subscriber. Petitioner concedes that if he had placed his calls through an operator, he could claim no legitimate expectation of privacy. We are not inclined to hold that a different constitutional result is required because the telephone company has decided to automate.

Petitioner argues, however, that automatic switching equipment differs from a live operator in one pertinent respect. An operator, in theory at least, is capable of remembering every number that is conveyed to him by callers. Electronic equipment, by contrast can "remember" only those numbers it is programmed to record, and telephone companies, in view of their present billing practices, usually do not record local calls. Since petitioner, in calling McDonough, was making a local call, his expectation of privacy as to her number, on this theory, would be "legitimate."

This argument does not withstand scrutiny. The fortuity of whether or not the phone company in fact elects to make a quasi-permanent record of a particular number dialed does not in our view, make any constitutional difference. Regardless of the phone company's election, petitioner voluntarily conveyed to it information that it had facilities for recording and that it was free to record. In these circumstances, petitioner assumed the risk that the information would be divulged to police.

Justice Marshall dissented:

In my view, whether privacy expectations are legitimate within the meaning of *Katz* depends not on the risks an individual can be presumed to accept when imparting information to third parties, but on the risks he should be forced to assume in a free and open society.

The use of pen registers, I believe, constitutes such an extensive intrusion. To hold otherwise ignores the vital role telephonic communication plays in our personal and professional relationships as well as the First and Fourth Amendment interests implicated by unfettered official surveillance. Privacy in placing calls is of value not only to those engaged in criminal activity. The prospect of unregulated governmental monitoring will undoubtedly prove disturbing even to those with nothing illicit to hide. Many individuals, including members of unpopular political organizations or journalists with confidential sources, may legitimately wish to avoid disclosure of their personal contacts. Permitting governmental access to telephone records on less than probable cause may thus impede certain forms of political affiliation and journalistic endeavor that are the hallmark of a truly free society. Particularly given the Government's previous reliance on warrantless telephonic surveillance to trace reporters' sources and monitor protected political activity, I am unwilling to insulate use of pen registers from independent judicial review.

Summarizing the law of how the Fourth Amendment applies to telephone communications, the Fourth Amendment ordinarily protects the contents of calls (with the exception of cordless phone calls) but does not protect the numbers dialed.

(2) Contents of Computer Communications

We now consider what Fourth Amendment rules should apply to government access to the contents of computer communications, such as e-mails and text messages.

UNITED STATES V. WARSHAK

United States Court of Appeals for the Sixth Circuit, 2010.
631 F.3d 266.

BOGGS, CIRCUIT JUDGE.

Berkeley Premium Nutraceuticals was an incredibly profitable company that served as the distributor of Enzyte, an herbal supplement purported to enhance male sexual performance. In this appeal, defendants Steven Warshak, Harriet Warshak, and TCI Media, Inc., challenge their convictions stemming from a massive scheme to defraud Berkeley's customers.

Steven Warshak owned and operated Berkeley Premium Nutraceuticals, Inc. In the latter half of 2001, Berkeley launched Enzyte, its flagship product. At the time of its launch, Enzyte was purported to increase the size of a man's erection. The product proved tremendously popular, and business rose sharply. By 2004, demand for Berkeley's products had grown so dramatically that the company employed 1500 people, and the call center remained open throughout the night, taking orders at breakneck speed.

The popularity of Enzyte appears to have been due in large part to Berkeley's aggressive advertising campaigns. The vast majority of the advertising—approximately 98%—was conducted through television spots. Around 2004, network television was saturated with Enzyte advertisements featuring a character called "Smilin' Bob," whose trademark exaggerated smile was presumably the result of Enzyte's efficacy. The "Smilin' Bob" commercials were rife with innuendo and implied that users of Enzyte would become the envy of the neighborhood.

In 2001, just after Enzyte's premiere, advertisements appeared in a number of men's interest magazines. At Warshak's direction, those advertisements cited a 2001 independent customer study, which purported to show that, over a three-month period, 100 English-speaking men who took Enzyte experienced a 12 to 31% increase in the size of their penises. [Former employee] James Teegarden later testified that the survey was bogus. A number of advertisements also indicated that Enzyte boasted a 96% customer satisfaction rating. Teegarden testified that that statistic, too, was totally spurious.

II.

Email was a critical form of communication among Berkeley personnel. As a consequence, Warshak had a number of email accounts with various ISPs, including an account with NuVox Communications. In October 2004, the government formally requested that NuVox prospectively preserve the contents of any emails to or from Warshak's email account. The request was made pursuant to 18 U.S.C. § 2703(f) and it instructed NuVox to preserve all future messages. NuVox acceded to the government's request and began preserving copies of Warshak's incoming and outgoing emails-copies that would not have existed absent the prospective preservation request. Per the government's instructions, Warshak was not informed that his messages were being archived.

In January 2005, the government obtained a subpoena under § 2703(b) and compelled NuVox to turn over the emails that it had begun preserving the previous year. In May 2005, the government served NuVox with an *ex parte* court order under § 2703(d) that required NuVox to surrender any additional email messages in Warshak's account. In all, the government compelled NuVox to reveal the contents of approximately 27,000 emails. Warshak did not receive notice of either the subpoena or the order until May 2006.

III.

The Fourth Amendment's protections hinge on the occurrence of a 'search,' a legal term of art whose history is riddled with complexity. A "search" occurs when the government infringes upon an expectation of privacy that society is prepared to consider reasonable. This standard breaks down into two discrete inquiries: first, has the target of the investigation manifested a subjective expectation of privacy in the object of the challenged search? Second, is society willing to recognize that expectation as reasonable?"

Turning first to the subjective component of the test, we find that Warshak plainly manifested an expectation that his emails would be shielded from outside scrutiny. As he notes in his brief, his "entire business and personal life was contained within the emails seized." Appellant's Br. at 39–40. Given the often sensitive and sometimes damning substance of his emails, we think it highly unlikely that Warshak expected them to be made public, for people seldom unfurl their dirty laundry in plain view.

The next question is whether society is prepared to recognize that expectation as reasonable. This question is one of grave import and enduring consequence, given the prominent role that email has assumed in modern communication. Since the advent of email, the telephone call and the letter have waned in importance, and an explosion of Internet-based communication has taken place. People are now able to send sensitive and intimate information, instantaneously, to friends, family, and colleagues half a world away. Lovers exchange sweet nothings, and businessmen swap ambitious plans, all with the click of a mouse button.

Commerce has also taken hold in email. Online purchases are often documented in email accounts, and email is frequently used to remind patients and clients of imminent appointments. In short, "account" is an apt word for the conglomeration of stored messages that comprises an email account, as it provides an account of its owner's life. By obtaining access to someone's email, government agents gain the ability to peer deeply into his activities. Much hinges, therefore, on whether the government is permitted to request that a commercial ISP turn over the contents of a subscriber's emails without triggering the machinery of the Fourth Amendment.

In confronting this question, we take note of two bedrock principles. First, the very fact that information is being passed through a communications network is a paramount Fourth Amendment consideration. Second, the Fourth Amendment must keep pace with the inexorable march of technological progress, or its guarantees will wither and perish.

With those principles in mind, we begin our analysis by considering the manner in which the Fourth Amendment protects traditional forms of communication. In *Katz,* the Supreme Court was asked to determine how the Fourth Amendment applied in the context of the telephone. There, government agents had affixed an electronic listening device to the exterior of a public phone booth, and had used the device to intercept and record several phone conversations. The Supreme Court held that this constituted a search under the Fourth Amendment, notwithstanding the fact that the telephone company had the capacity to monitor and record the calls, In the eyes of the Court, the caller was "surely entitled to assume that the words he uttered into the mouthpiece would not be broadcast to the world." *Katz,* 389 U.S. at 352. The Court's holding in *Katz* has since come to stand for the broad proposition that, in many contexts, the government infringes a reasonable expectation of privacy when it surreptitiously intercepts a telephone call through electronic means.

Letters receive similar protection. *Ex Parte Jackson,* 96 U.S. 727, 733 (1877). While a letter is in the mail, the police may not intercept it and examine its contents unless they first obtain a warrant based on probable cause. This is true despite the fact that sealed letters are handed over to perhaps dozens of mail carriers, any one of whom could tear open the thin paper envelopes that separate the private words from the world outside. Put another way, trusting a letter to an intermediary does not necessarily defeat a reasonable expectation that the letter will remain private.

Given the fundamental similarities between email and traditional forms of communication, it would defy common sense to afford emails lesser Fourth Amendment protection. Email is the technological scion of tangible mail, and it plays an indispensable part in the Information Age. Over the last decade, email has become so pervasive that some persons may consider it to be an essential means or necessary instrument for self-expression, even self-identification. It follows that email requires strong protection under the Fourth Amendment; otherwise, the Fourth Amendment would prove an ineffective guardian of private communication, an essential purpose it has long been recognized to serve. As some forms of communication begin to diminish, the Fourth Amendment must recognize and protect nascent ones that arise.

If we accept that an email is analogous to a letter or a phone call, it is manifest that agents of the government cannot compel a commercial ISP to turn over the contents of an email without triggering the Fourth Amendment. An ISP is the intermediary that makes email communication possible. Emails must pass through an ISP's servers to reach their intended recipient. Thus, the ISP is the functional equivalent of a post office or a telephone company. As we have discussed above, the police may not storm the post office and intercept a letter, and they are likewise forbidden from using the phone system to make a clandestine recording of a telephone call-unless they get a warrant, that is. It only stands to reason that, if government agents compel an ISP to surrender the contents of a subscriber's emails, those agents have thereby conducted a Fourth Amendment search, which necessitates compliance with the warrant requirement absent some exception.

The government argues that this conclusion is improper, pointing to the fact that NuVox contractually reserved the right to access Warshak's emails for certain purposes. While we acknowledge that a subscriber agreement might, in some cases, be sweeping enough to defeat a reasonable expectation of privacy in the contents of an email account, we doubt that will be the case in most situations, and it is certainly not the case here.

As an initial matter, it must be observed that the mere *ability* of a third-party intermediary to access the contents of a communication cannot be sufficient to extinguish a reasonable expectation of privacy. In *Katz,* the Supreme Court found it reasonable to expect privacy during a telephone call despite the ability of an operator to listen in. Similarly, the ability of a rogue mail handler to rip open a letter does not make it unreasonable to assume that sealed mail will remain private on its journey across the country. Therefore, the threat or possibility of access is not decisive when it comes to the reasonableness of an expectation of privacy.

Our conclusion finds additional support in the application of Fourth Amendment doctrine to rented space. Hotel guests, for example, have a reasonable expectation of privacy in their rooms. This is so even though maids routinely enter hotel rooms to replace the towels and tidy the furniture. Similarly, tenants have a legitimate expectation of privacy in their apartments. That expectation persists, regardless of the incursions of handymen to fix leaky faucets. Consequently, we are convinced that some degree of routine access is hardly dispositive with respect to the privacy question.

We recognize that our conclusion may be attacked in light of the Supreme Court's decision in *United States v. Miller,* 425 U.S. 435 (1976). In *Miller,* the Supreme Court held that a bank depositor does not have a reasonable expectation of privacy in the contents of bank records, checks, and deposit slips. The Court's holding in *Miller* was based on the fact that bank documents, including financial statements and deposit slips, contain only information voluntarily conveyed to the banks and exposed to their employees in the ordinary course of business The Court noted: "The depositor takes the risk, in revealing his affairs to another, that the information will be conveyed by that person to the Government. The Fourth Amendment does not prohibit the obtaining of information revealed to a third party and conveyed by him to Government authorities, even if the information is revealed on the assumption that it will be used only for a limited purpose and the confidence placed in the third party will not be betrayed."

But *Miller* is distinguishable. First, *Miller* involved simple business records, as opposed to the potentially unlimited variety of "confidential communications" at issue here. Second, the bank depositor in *Miller* conveyed information to the bank so that the bank could put the information to use "in the ordinary course of business." By contrast, Warshak received his emails through NuVox. NuVox was an *intermediary,* not the intended recipient of the emails. Thus, *Miller* is not controlling.

Accordingly, we hold that a subscriber enjoys a reasonable expectation of privacy in the contents of emails that are stored with, or sent or received through, a commercial ISP. The government may not compel a commercial

ISP to turn over the contents of a subscriber's emails without first obtaining a warrant based on probable cause. Therefore, because they did not obtain a warrant, the government agents violated the Fourth Amendment when they obtained the contents of Warshak's emails.

NOTES AND QUESTIONS

1.   *Other courts agree with Warshak.* The United States Supreme Court has not directly addressed whether it agrees with *Warshak.* Lower courts have agreed with the decision, however. *See, e.g.,* In re Grand Jury Subpoena, 828 F.3d 1083, 1090 (9th Cir. 2016) ("Emails are to be treated as closed, addressed packages for expectation-of-privacy purposes"); United States v. Ackerman, 831 F.3d 1292 (10th Cir. 2016).

2.   *Contents posted on the World Wide Web, both without password protection and with it.* Imagine a person posts a photograph on the Web. Does the Fourth Amendment protect access to it? If the photograph is available for all to see without password protection, the answer is "no." *See* United States v. Gines-Perez, 214 F. Supp.2d 205 (D.P.R. 2002) ("It strikes the Court as obvious that a claim to privacy is unavailable to someone who places information on an indisputably, public medium, such as the Internet, without taking any measures to protect the information."). On the other hand, the Fourth Amendment protects contents hidden by a password. *See, e.g.,* United States v. D'Andrea, 497 F. Supp.2d 117, 121 (D. Mass. 2007) ("Reliance on protections such as individual computer accounts, password protection, and perhaps encryption of data should be no less reasonable than reliance upon locks, bolts, and burglar alarms, even though each form of protection is penetrable.").

3.   *Placing files in a shared folder for a peer-to-peer network.* In United States v. Ganoe, 538 F.3d 1117 (9th Cir. 2008), an undercover agent used the file-sharing program LimeWire to find a movie containing CSAM. LimeWire allows users to share various files with other users who have downloaded the free LimeWire software. Ganoe had installed LimeWire on his home computer, and he used the program to find music files. Unbeknownst to him, however, the software was configured to reveal several movies containing CSAM located on his home computer. An undercover agent using LimeWire to look for CSAM found it stored on Ganoe's computer, leading to charges against Ganoe.

The Ninth Circuit held that the undercover agent's use of LimeWire to search Ganoe's computer did not violate Ganoe's Fourth Amendment rights:

> Although as a general matter an individual has an objectively reasonable expectation of privacy in his personal computer, we fail to see how this expectation can survive Ganoe's decision to install and use file-sharing software, thereby opening his computer to anyone else with the same freely available program. The crux of Ganoe's argument is that he simply did not know that others would be able to access files stored on his own computer. But he knew he had file-sharing software on his computer; indeed, he admitted that he used it—he says to get music. Moreover, he was explicitly warned before

> completing the installation that the folder into which files are downloaded would be shared with other users in the peer-to-peer network.

> Ganoe thus opened up his download folder to the world, including [the undercover agent]. To argue that Ganoe lacked the technical savvy or good sense to configure LimeWire to prevent access to his pornography files is like saying that he did not know enough to close his drapes. Having failed to demonstrate an expectation of privacy that society is prepared to accept as reasonable, Ganoe cannot invoke the protections of the Fourth Amendment.

Id. at 1127. Is the analogy to closing the drapes persuasive? Everyone knows how to close the drapes. Does everyone know how to configure a computer program to avoid inadvertently exposing files? How much computer savvy should courts assume when identifying when an expectation of privacy is reasonable?

4. *Does connecting to a university network eliminate a student's reasonable expectation of privacy?* In United States v. Heckenkamp, 482 F.3d 1142 (9th. Cir. 2007), a student at the University of Wisconsin used the university's computer network to hack into computers from his dorm room. A system administrator of the university network knew the student's username and password, and he accessed the student's computer remotely to confirm that it was the suspect's computer that was responsible. The court held that the student had a reasonable expectation of privacy in the contents of his personal computer even though it was connected to the network:

> The salient question is whether the defendant's objectively reasonable expectation of privacy in his computer was eliminated when he attached it to the university network. We conclude under the facts of this case that the act of attaching his computer to the network did not extinguish his legitimate, objectively reasonable privacy expectations.

> A person's reasonable expectation of privacy may be diminished in transmissions over the Internet or e-mail that have already arrived at the recipient. However, the mere act of accessing a network does not in itself extinguish privacy expectations, nor does the fact that others may have occasional access to the computer.

> We must reject the government's contention that [the student] had no objectively reasonable expectation of privacy in his personal computer, which was protected by a screen-saver password, located in his dormitory room, and subject to no policy allowing the university actively to monitor or audit his computer usage.

Id. at 1146–47.

5. *Fourth Amendment rights in unintentionally shared files.* In United States v. Ahrndt, 2013 WL 179326 (D.Or. 2013), a woman known as JH opened her laptop and found that she could see an unfamiliar iTunes folder named

"Dad's LimeWire Tunes." Unbeknownst to JH, her laptop had automatically hopped on the unsecured wireless network of her neighbor, Ahrndt. Ahrndt's computer was programmed to share his iTunes folder with anyone on Arndt's network. JH looked through a few files in the "Dad's LimeWire Tunes" folder and was sufficiently concerned to call the police. A police officer arrived and opened additional images in the folder.

The court held that the officer's opening of files in the folder violated Ahrndt's Fourth Amendment rights:

> There is no evidence Ahrndt was using iTunes software or any other program to deliberately share files. The evidence is that he had media-enabled files that JH was able to view using her own iTunes program because Ahrndt's files made themselves available, by default, through JH's iTunes. There is no evidence Ahrndt intentionally enabled sharing of his files over his wireless network, and there is no evidence he knew or should have known that others could access his files by connecting to his wireless network. [The officer's] action of clicking on the image in JH's iTunes directory to open the image violated Ahrndt's Fourth Amendment rights.

Id. at *8. Can you reconcile *Heckencamp*, *Ganoe*, and *Ahrndt*?

6.   *Intercepting wireless transmissions, either encrypted or unencrypted.* Is it a Fourth Amendment "search" for the government to intercept wireless communications? Imagine a criminal suspect is known to use the wi-fi at a local coffee shop. The shop's wi-fi does not require a password, so it does not encrypt communications between the user's computer and the coffee shop's router. If the government intercepts and reads the wireless communications, is that a search? Which matters more: The fact that the communications are contents under *Warshak* (suggesting interception is a search), or the fact that the signals are openly available to the public (suggesting interception is not a search)? Now imagine that the coffee shop requires a password so that communications are now encrypted. If the government intercepts the encrypted traffic and finds a way to decrypt it, has a search occurred? *See* Orin Kerr, *The Fourth Amendment in Cyberspace: Can Encryption Create a "Reasonable Expectation of Privacy"?*, 33 Conn. L. Rev. 503 (2001) (arguing that decryption is not a search).

7.   *The possible impact of terms of service.* Should terms of service have an effect on a person's Fourth Amendment rights? Imagine an individual uses an e-mail provider that has the following term of service: "As a condition of having an account, you agree that you have no privacy rights in your messages." Should this language eliminate Fourth Amendment rights? *Cf.* Byrd v. United States, 138 S.Ct. 1518, 1529 (2018) (considering whether the breach of a rental car contract alters a driver's Fourth Amendment rights in a rental car).

8.   *Data mining and the Fourth Amendment.* Imagine the government collects data, enters it into a database, and then mines the data for

information. Analysis of the data in the database reveals important information that the government then uses in criminal cases. Does this datamining trigger the Fourth Amendment?

Consider three relevant cases. First, in State v. Sloane, 939 A.2d 796 (N.J. 2008), the defendant challenged a government query of the federal database that contains criminal records known as the National Crime Information Center (NCIC). The query revealed Sloane's past criminal record and warrants out for his arrest. The Supreme Court of New Jersey rejected Sloane's Fourth Amendment challenge on the ground that the information in the NCIC database was not itself protected by the Fourth Amendment:

> An NCIC check is not a search under the federal or state constitutions. Critical to our analysis is the fact that the NCIC database is comprised of matters of public record. Because Sloane had no reasonable expectation of privacy in the public records maintained in NCIC—such as his two outstanding warrants and record of a parole violation—a check of the NCIC database was not a search.

Id. at 803–04. Under Sloane, datamining ordinarily will not trigger the Fourth Amendment because the information entered into the database itself will not be protected by the Fourth Amendment. If information is not protected by the Fourth Amendment, analysis of it inside a database normally will not trigger the Fourth Amendment's restrictions.

Next consider United States v. Hasbajrami, 945 F.3d 641 (2d Cir. 2019). Under § 702 of the Foreign Intelligence Surveillance Act, codified at 50 U.S.C. § 1881a, the government can intercept communications inside the United States when they target "persons reasonably believed to be located outside the United States" in order "to acquire foreign intelligence information." When the government collects communications pursuant to this section, it collects contents of communications without listening to or reading them and stores them in a database. Hasbajrami ruled that subsequently querying the database for contents of communications is a search:

> Querying that stored data has important Fourth Amendment implications, and those implications counsel in favor of considering querying a separate Fourth Amendment event that, in itself, must be reasonable. Our reasoning is based on three considerations.

> First, courts have increasingly recognized the need for additional probable cause or reasonableness assessments to support a search of information or objects that the government has lawfully collected. It is true that the FBI does not need an additional warrant to go down to its evidence locker and look through a box of evidence it collected from a crime scene. But lawful collection alone is not always enough to justify a future search.

> Second, Section 702 is sweeping in its technological capacity and broad in its scope. If such a vast body of information is simply stored in a database, available for review by request from domestic law

enforcement agencies solely on the speculative possibility that evidence of interest to agents investigating a particular individual might be found there, the program begins to look more like a dragnet, and a query more like a general warrant, and less like an individual officer going to the evidence locker to check a previously-acquired piece of evidence against some newfound insight.

Third, as a practical matter, querying is problematic because it may make it easier to target wide-ranging information about a given United States person at a point when the government knows it is investigating such a person. To permit that information to be accessed indiscriminately, for domestic law enforcement purposes, without any reason to believe that the individual is involved in any criminal activity and or even that any information about the person is likely to be in the database, just to see if there is anything incriminating in any conversations that might happen to be there, would be at odds with the bedrock Fourth Amendment concept that law enforcement agents may not invade the privacy of individuals without some objective reason to believe that evidence of crime will be found by a search.

Id. at 670–72. This holding is consistent with Fourth Amendment rules for searching an image copy of a computer. When agents seize a personal computer and image the hard drive, courts have assumed that the Fourth Amendment rules that apply to searching the image are the same as the rules that apply to searching the original. The fact that a copy has been made does not alter the Fourth Amendment test. When the contents have not yet been analyzed or exposed, which itself would be a search requiring Fourth Amendment justification, the contents presumably retain their Fourth Amendment protection whether or not they have been added to a large database or copied on to a government machine. A subsequent query through that database is a "search."

Finally, consider Commonwealth v. Yusuf, 488 Mass. 379 (2021). An officer who was wearing a body-worn camera entered Yusuf's home with the consent of Yusuf's sister to investigate a domestic disturbance inside. The video footage from the body-worn camera was then stored by the police. Later, the footage was examined by another officer who was investigating Yusuf for an unrelated firearms offense. The second officer's review of the stored video footage revealed a distinctive set of curtains in a room that exactly matched the background of a photograph Yusuf had posted on social media showing him unlawfully possessing a firearm. The matching background enabled the government to establish probable cause for a warrant to search Yusuf's home for the illegal firearm.

In *Yusuf*, the Massachusetts Supreme Judicial Court made two relevant holdings. First, the Court held that using the camera to record what the officer observed inside the house was not an additional search: "Where, as here, the officer was lawfully present in the home and the body-worn camera captured only the areas and items in the plain view of the officer as he or she traversed the home, in a manner consistent with the reasons for the officer's lawful presence, the recording is not a search in the constitutional sense and does not violate the Fourth Amendment."

Second, the Court ruled that it *was* a search for the second officer to later review the stored camera footage for an unrelated reason:

> Unlike the recording of the plain view observations attendant to the initial and lawful entry into the defendant's home, this subsequent review for investigatory and unrelated reasons cannot be justified as a limited extension of the officer's plain view observations. The home is not a place to which the public has access, or where an individual might expect a recording made during a lawful police visit would be preserved indefinitely, accessed without restriction, and reviewed at will for reasons unrelated to the purposes of the police visit.

> Both this court and the United States Supreme Court have been careful to guard against the power of technology to shrink the realm of guaranteed privacy by emphasizing that privacy rights cannot be left at the mercy of advancing technology but rather must be preserved and protected as new technologies are adopted and applied by law enforcement. It is the duty of courts to be watchful for the constitutional rights of the citizen, and against any stealthy encroachments thereon.

> Consistent with these principles, we conclude that while the plain view observation doctrine extended to the officer's recording of his interactions in the defendant's home in response to the domestic disturbance call, that doctrine cannot be stretched to sanction the subsequent review of the footage for reasons unrelated to the call. The ability of police officers, at any later point, to trawl through video footage to look for evidence of crimes unrelated to the officers' lawful presence in the home when they were responding to a call for assistance is the virtual equivalent of a general warrant. A database of body-worn camera footage of the places where officers are called upon to assist residents, reviewable at will and without a warrant, for unrelated investigations, renders technologically feasible the Orwellian Big Brother.

> Because protecting the home from such arbitrary government invasion always has been a central aim of [the Fourth Amendment], we decline to extend the plain view observation doctrine to the subsequent, unrelated review of body-worn camera footage of the defendant's home.

Is *Yusuf* consistent with *Sloane* and *Hasbajrami*? Does it depend on whether you construe the first holding of *Yusuf* as saying that it was permissible to generate the video footage but that it still contained constitutionally-protected data, or, alternatively, that the video footage was unprotected by the Fourth Amendment when it was made but only became protected after it was stored?

(3) Non-Content Account Records

The next question is how the Fourth Amendment applies to government access to non-content account records, sometimes known as "metadata." Metadata consists of records about an account other than the contents of communications. Metadata can include information such as who registered the account; when it was registered; when it was used; to whom and from whom communications were sent; the length or duration of communications that were sent and received; what addresses were used to sign into the account at various times; and the location of the device used.

Two points are worth keeping in mind. First, the Fourth Amendment rules for accessing non-content account records are uncertain following Carpenter v. United States, 138 S.Ct. 2206 (2018). Before *Carpenter*, lower courts had held that the Fourth Amendment does not apply to compelled government access to computer account metadata. In 2018, however, *Carpenter* held that the Fourth Amendment requires a warrant for the government to compel at least longer-term historical cell-site location information (CSLI), which is one form of metadata. Following *Carpenter*, courts are still figuring out when metadata is covered by the prior rule and when it is covered by *Carpenter*. To help explore that, the materials below start with a pre-*Carpenter* case and then turn to *Carpenter* and the cases interpreting it.

A second point to keep in mind is that Congress and state legislatures have enacted statutory privacy law that also regulate access to metadata. As a practical matter, the rules for access are governed by whatever is the most strict among the different sources of protection. The statutory rules under federal law will be covered in Chapter 6, and Chapter 7 will address some of the state rules.

UNITED STATES V. FORRESTER

United States Court of Appeals for the Ninth Circuit, 2007.
495 F.3d 1041.

FISHER, CIRCUIT JUDGE:

Defendants-appellants Mark Stephen Forrester and Dennis Louis Alba were charged with various offenses relating to the operation of a large Ecstasy-manufacturing laboratory, and were convicted on all counts following a jury trial. They now appeal their convictions and sentences.

Alba challenges the validity of computer surveillance that enabled the government to learn the to/from addresses of his e-mail messages, the

Internet protocol ("IP") addresses of the websites that he visited and the total volume of information transmitted to or from his account. We conclude that this surveillance was analogous to the use of a pen register that the Supreme Court held in *Smith v. Maryland*, 442 U.S. 735 (1979), did not constitute a search for Fourth Amendment purposes.

I. Background

Following a lengthy government investigation, Forrester and Alba were indicted on October 26, 2001, and arraigned shortly thereafter. Forrester was charged with one count of conspiracy to manufacture and distribute 3, 4-methylenedioxymethamphetamine ("Ecstasy"). Alba was also charged with that offense, as well as with engaging in a continuing criminal enterprise, conspiracy to transfer funds outside the United States in promotion of an illegal activity, and conspiracy to conduct financial transactions involving the proceeds of an illegal activity. Both defendants pleaded not guilty to all charges.

During its investigation of Forrester and Alba's Ecstasy-manufacturing operation, the government employed various computer surveillance techniques to monitor Alba's e-mail and Internet activity. The surveillance began in May 2001 after the government applied for and received court permission to install a pen register analogue known as a "mirror port" on Alba's account with PacBell Internet. The mirror port was installed at PacBell's connection facility in San Diego, and enabled the government to learn the to/from addresses of Alba's e-mail messages, the IP addresses of the websites that Alba visited and the total volume of information sent to or from his account. Later, the government obtained a warrant authorizing it to employ imaging and keystroke monitoring techniques, but Alba does not challenge on appeal those techniques' legality or the government's application to use them.

Forrester and Alba were tried by jury. At trial, the government introduced extensive evidence showing that they and their associates built and operated a major Ecstasy laboratory. Witnesses described the lab as "very, very large," and seized documents show that it was intended to produce approximately 440 kilograms of Ecstasy (and $10 million in profit) per month. The government also presented evidence that Alba purchased precursor chemicals for Ecstasy, that Forrester met with a Swedish chemist in Stockholm to learn about manufacturing Ecstasy, that the defendants first tried to construct the lab in two other locations before settling on Escondido, California and that the Escondido lab was located inside an insulated sea/land container and contained an array of devices and chemicals used to make Ecstasy.

The jury convicted Forrester and Alba on all counts. The district court sentenced them each to 360 months in prison and six years of supervised release.

II.   Computer Surveillance

Alba contends that the government's surveillance of his e-mail and Internet activity violated the Fourth Amendment.[4] We hold that the surveillance did not constitute a Fourth Amendment search and thus was not unconstitutional.

The Supreme Court held in *Smith v. Maryland,* 442 U.S. 735 (1979), that the use of a pen register (a device that records numbers dialed from a phone line) does not constitute a search for Fourth Amendment purposes. According to the Court, people do not have a subjective expectation of privacy in numbers that they dial because they realize that they must 'convey' phone numbers to the telephone company, since it is through telephone company switching equipment that their calls are completed. Even if there were such a subjective expectation, it would not be one that society is prepared to recognize as reasonable because a person has no legitimate expectation of privacy in information he voluntarily turns over to third parties." Therefore the use of a pen register is not a Fourth Amendment search.

Importantly, the Court distinguished pen registers from more intrusive surveillance techniques on the ground that pen registers do not acquire the *contents* of communications but rather obtain only the addressing information associated with phone calls.

Neither this nor any other circuit has spoken to the constitutionality of computer surveillance techniques that reveal the to/from addresses of e-mail messages, the IP addresses of websites visited and the total amount of data transmitted to or from an account. We conclude that these techniques are constitutionally indistinguishable from the use of a pen register that the Court approved in *Smith*.

First, e-mail and Internet users, like the telephone users in *Smith,* rely on third-party equipment in order to engage in communication. *Smith* based its holding that telephone users have no expectation of privacy in the numbers they dial on the users' imputed knowledge that their calls are completed through telephone company switching equipment. Analogously, e-mail and Internet users have no expectation of privacy in the to/from addresses of their messages or the IP addresses of the websites they visit because they should know that these messages are sent and these IP addresses are accessed through the equipment of their Internet service provider and other third parties. Communication by both Internet and

---

[4]   As mentioned earlier, Alba complains only about the initial surveillance through which the government obtained the to/from addresses of his e-mail messages, the IP addresses of the websites that he visited and the total volume of information sent to or from his account. He does not challenge the more intrusive imaging and keystroke monitoring that subsequently took place (though he does argue that the information obtained through those techniques should be suppressed as tainted derivative evidence).

telephone requires people to voluntarily turn over information to third parties.

Second, e-mail to/from addresses and IP addresses constitute addressing information and reveal no more about the underlying contents of communication than do phone numbers. When the government learns the phone numbers a person has dialed, it may be able to determine the persons or entities to which the numbers correspond, but it does not know what was said in the actual conversations. Similarly, when the government obtains the to/from addresses of a person's e-mails or the IP addresses of websites visited, it does not find out the contents of the messages or the particular pages on the websites the person viewed. At best, the government may make educated guesses about what was said in the messages or viewed on the websites based on its knowledge of the e-mail to/from addresses and IP addresses—but this is no different from speculation about the contents of a phone conversation on the basis of the identity of the person or entity that was dialed. The distinction between mere addressing and more content-rich information drawn by the Court in *Smith* and *Katz v. United States*, 389 U.S. 347 (1967), is thus preserved, because the computer surveillance techniques at issue here enable only the discovery of addressing information.[6]

The government's surveillance of e-mail addresses also may be technologically sophisticated, but it is conceptually indistinguishable from government surveillance of physical mail. In a line of cases dating back to the nineteenth century, the Supreme Court has held that the government cannot engage in a warrantless search of the contents of sealed mail, but can observe whatever information people put on the outside of mail, because that information is voluntarily transmitted to third parties. E-mail, like physical mail, has an outside address "visible" to the third-party carriers that transmit it to its intended location, and also a package of content that the sender presumes will be read only by the intended recipient. The privacy interests in these two forms of communication are identical. The contents may deserve Fourth Amendment protection, but the address and size of the package do not.

Finally, the pen register in *Smith* was able to disclose not only the phone numbers dialed but also the number of calls made. There is no difference of constitutional magnitude between this aspect of the pen

---

[6] Surveillance techniques that enable the government to determine not only the IP addresses that a person accesses but also the uniform resource locators ("URL") of the pages visited might be more constitutionally problematic. A URL, unlike an IP address, identifies the particular document within a website that a person views and thus reveals much more information about the person's Internet activity. For instance, a surveillance technique that captures IP addresses would show only that a person visited the New York Times' website at http://www.nytimes.com, whereas a technique that captures URLs would also divulge the particular articles the person viewed. *See In re Application of the United States of America*, 396 F. Supp.2d 45, 49 (2005) ("[I]f the user then enters a search phrase [in the Google search engine], that search phrase would appear in the URL after the first forward slash. This would reveal content. . . .").

register and the government's monitoring here of the total volume of data transmitted to or from Alba's account. Devices that obtain addressing information also inevitably reveal the amount of information coming and going, and do not thereby breach the line between mere addressing and more content-rich information.

We therefore hold that the computer surveillance techniques that Alba challenges are not Fourth Amendment searches. However, our holding extends only to these particular techniques and does not imply that more intrusive techniques or techniques that reveal more content information are also constitutionally identical to the use of a pen register.

CARPENTER V. UNITED STATES

Supreme Court of the United States, 2018.
138 S.Ct. 2206.

CHIEF JUSTICE ROBERTS delivered the opinion of the Court.

This case presents the question whether the Government conducts a search under the Fourth Amendment when it accesses historical cell phone records that provide a comprehensive chronicle of the user's past movements.

I

A

There are 396 million cell phone service accounts in the United States—for a Nation of 326 million people. Cell phones perform their wide and growing variety of functions by connecting to a set of radio antennas called "cell sites." Although cell sites are usually mounted on a tower, they can also be found on light posts, flagpoles, church steeples, or the sides of buildings. Cell sites typically have several directional antennas that divide the covered area into sectors.

Cell phones continuously scan their environment looking for the best signal, which generally comes from the closest cell site. Most modern devices, such as smartphones, tap into the wireless network several times a minute whenever their signal is on, even if the owner is not using one of the phone's features. Each time the phone connects to a cell site, it generates a time-stamped record known as cell-site location information (CSLI). The precision of this information depends on the size of the geographic area covered by the cell site. The greater the concentration of cell sites, the smaller the coverage area. As data usage from cell phones has increased, wireless carriers have installed more cell sites to handle the traffic. That has led to increasingly compact coverage areas, especially in urban areas.

Wireless carriers collect and store CSLI for their own business purposes, including finding weak spots in their network and applying "roaming" charges when another carrier routes data through their cell sites. In addition, wireless carriers often sell aggregated location records to data brokers, without individual identifying information of the sort at issue here. While carriers have long retained CSLI for the start and end of incoming calls, in recent years phone companies have also collected location information from the transmission of text messages and routine data connections. Accordingly, modern cell phones generate increasingly vast amounts of increasingly precise CSLI.

B

In 2011, police officers arrested four men suspected of robbing a series of Radio Shack and (ironically enough) T-Mobile stores in Detroit. One of the men confessed that, over the previous four months, the group (along with a rotating cast of getaway drivers and lookouts) had robbed nine different stores in Michigan and Ohio. The suspect identified 15 accomplices who had participated in the heists and gave the FBI some of their cell phone numbers; the FBI then reviewed his call records to identify additional numbers that he had called around the time of the robberies.

Based on that information, the prosecutors applied for court orders under the Stored Communications Act to obtain cell phone records for petitioner Timothy Carpenter and several other suspects. That statute, as amended in 1994, permits the Government to compel the disclosure of certain telecommunications records when it "offers specific and articulable facts showing that there are reasonable grounds to believe" that the records sought "are relevant and material to an ongoing criminal investigation." 18 U.S.C. § 2703(d). Federal Magistrate Judges issued two orders directing Carpenter's wireless carriers—MetroPCS and Sprint—to disclose cell/site sector information for Carpenter's telephone at call origination and at call termination for incoming and outgoing calls during the four-month period when the string of robberies occurred. The first order sought 152 days of cell-site records from MetroPCS, which produced records spanning 127 days. The second order requested seven days of CSLI from Sprint, which produced two days of records covering the period when Carpenter's phone was "roaming" in northeastern Ohio. Altogether the Government obtained 12,898 location points cataloging Carpenter's movements—an average of 101 data points per day.

Carpenter was charged with six counts of robbery and an additional six counts of carrying a firearm during a federal crime of violence. At trial, seven of Carpenter's confederates pegged him as the leader of the operation. In addition, FBI agent Christopher Hess offered expert testimony about the cell-site data. Hess explained that each time a cell phone taps into the wireless network, the carrier logs a time-stamped record of the cell site and particular sector that were used. With this information, Hess produced maps that placed Carpenter's phone near four of the charged robberies. In the Government's view, the location records clinched the case: They confirmed that Carpenter was "right where the robbery was at the exact time of the robbery." App. 131 (closing argument). Carpenter was convicted on all but one of the firearm counts and sentenced to more than 100 years in prison.

The Court of Appeals for the Sixth Circuit affirmed. The court held that Carpenter lacked a reasonable expectation of privacy in the location information collected by the FBI because he had shared that information with his wireless carriers. Given that cell phone users voluntarily convey cell-site data to their carriers as "a means of establishing communication," the court concluded that the resulting business records are not entitled to Fourth Amendment protection. (quoting *Smith v. Maryland,* 442 U.S. 735, 741 (1979)).

II

A

As technology has enhanced the Government's capacity to encroach upon areas normally guarded from inquisitive eyes, this Court has sought to "assure preservation of that degree of privacy against government that existed when the Fourth Amendment was adopted." *Kyllo v. United States,* 533 U.S. 27, 34 (2001). For that reason, we rejected in *Kyllo* a mechanical interpretation of the Fourth Amendment and held that use of a thermal imager to detect heat radiating from the side of the defendant's home was a search. Because any other conclusion would leave homeowners at the mercy of advancing technology, we determined that the Government—absent a warrant—could not capitalize on such new sense-enhancing technology to explore what was happening within the home.

Likewise in *California v. Riley,* 134 S.Ct. 2473 (2014), the Court recognized the immense storage capacity of modern cell phones in holding that police officers must generally obtain a warrant before searching the contents of a phone. We explained that while the general rule allowing warrantless searches incident to arrest strikes the appropriate balance in the context of physical objects, neither of its rationales has much force with respect to the vast store of sensitive information on a cell phone.

B

The case before us involves the Government's acquisition of wireless carrier cell-site records revealing the location of Carpenter's cell phone whenever it made or received calls. This sort of digital data—personal location information maintained by a third party—does not fit neatly under existing precedents. Instead, requests for cell-site records lie at the intersection of two lines of cases, both of which inform our understanding of the privacy interests at stake.

The first set of cases addresses a person's expectation of privacy in his physical location and movements. In *United States v. Knotts,* 460 U.S. 276 (1983), we considered the Government's use of a "beeper" to aid in tracking a vehicle through traffic. Police officers in that case planted a beeper in a container of chloroform before it was purchased by one of Knotts's co-conspirators. The officers (with intermittent aerial assistance) then followed the automobile carrying the container from Minneapolis to Knotts's cabin in Wisconsin, relying on the beeper's signal to help keep the vehicle in view. The Court concluded that the augmented visual surveillance did not constitute a search because a person traveling in an automobile on public thoroughfares has no reasonable expectation of privacy in his movements from one place to another. Since the movements of the vehicle and its final destination had been voluntarily conveyed to anyone who wanted to look, Knotts could not assert a privacy interest in the information obtained.

This Court in *Knotts,* however, was careful to distinguish between the rudimentary tracking facilitated by the beeper and more sweeping modes of surveillance. The Court emphasized the limited use which the government made of the signals from this particular beeper during a discrete automotive journey. Significantly, the Court reserved the question whether different constitutional principles may be applicable if twenty-four hour surveillance of any citizen of this country were possible.

Three decades later, the Court considered more sophisticated surveillance of the sort envisioned in *Knotts* and found that different principles did indeed apply. In *United States v. Jones,* 565 U.S. 400 (2012), FBI agents installed a GPS tracking device on Jones's vehicle and remotely monitored the vehicle's movements for 28 days. The Court decided the case based on the Government's physical trespass of the vehicle. At the same time, five Justices agreed that related privacy concerns would be raised by, for example, surreptitiously activating a stolen vehicle detection system in Jones's car to track Jones himself, or conducting GPS tracking of his cell phone. *Id.,* at 426, 428 (Alito, J., concurring in judgment); *id.,* at 415 (Sotomayor, J., concurring). Since GPS monitoring of a vehicle tracks every movement a person makes in that vehicle, the concurring Justices concluded that longer term GPS monitoring in investigations of most offenses impinges on expectations of privacy—regardless whether those movements were disclosed to the public at large. *Id.,* at 430, (opinion of Alito, J.); *id.,* at 415 (opinion of Sotomayor, J.).

In a second set of decisions, the Court has drawn a line between what a person keeps to himself and what he shares with others. We have previously held that a person has no legitimate expectation of privacy in information he voluntarily turns over to third parties. *Smith v. Maryland,* 442 U.S. 735, 743–744 (1979). That remains true even if the information is revealed on the assumption that it will be used only for a limited purpose.

United States v. Miller, 425 U.S. 435, 443 (1976). As a result, the Government is typically free to obtain such information from the recipient without triggering Fourth Amendment protections.

This third-party doctrine largely traces its roots to *Miller.* While investigating Miller for tax evasion, the Government subpoenaed his banks, seeking several months of canceled checks, deposit slips, and monthly statements. The Court rejected a Fourth Amendment challenge to the records collection. For one, Miller could assert neither ownership nor possession of the documents; they were business records of the banks. For another, the nature of those records confirmed Miller's limited expectation of privacy, because the checks were not confidential communications but negotiable instruments to be used in commercial transactions, and the bank statements contained information exposed to bank employees in the ordinary course of business. The Court thus concluded that Miller had taken the risk, in revealing his affairs to another, that the information would be conveyed by that person to the Government.

Three years later, *Smith* applied the same principles in the context of information conveyed to a telephone company. The Court ruled that the Government's use of a pen register—a device that recorded the outgoing phone numbers dialed on a landline telephone—was not a search. Noting the pen register's limited capabilities, the Court doubted that people in general entertain any actual expectation of privacy in the numbers they dial. Telephone subscribers know, after all, that the numbers are used by the telephone company for a variety of legitimate business purposes, including routing calls. And at any rate, the Court explained, such an expectation is not one that society is prepared to recognize as reasonable. When Smith placed a call, he voluntarily conveyed the dialed numbers to the phone company by exposing that information to its equipment in the ordinary course of business. Once again, we held that the defendant assumed the risk that the company's records would be divulged to police.

III

The question we confront today is how to apply the Fourth Amendment to a new phenomenon: the ability to chronicle a person's past movements through the record of his cell phone signals. Such tracking partakes of many of the qualities of the GPS monitoring we considered in *Jones.* Much like GPS tracking of a vehicle, cell phone location information is detailed, encyclopedic, and effortlessly compiled.

At the same time, the fact that the individual continuously reveals his location to his wireless carrier implicates the third-party principle of *Smith* and *Miller.* But while the third-party doctrine applies to telephone numbers and bank records, it is not clear whether its logic extends to the qualitatively different category of cell-site records. After all, when *Smith* was decided in 1979, few could have imagined a society in which a phone goes wherever its owner goes, conveying to the wireless carrier not just dialed digits, but a detailed and comprehensive record of the person's movements.

We decline to extend *Smith* and *Miller* to cover these novel circumstances. Given the unique nature of cell phone location records, the fact that the information is held by a third party does not by itself overcome the user's claim to Fourth Amendment protection. Whether the Government employs its own surveillance technology as in *Jones* or leverages the technology of a wireless carrier, we hold that an individual maintains a legitimate expectation of privacy in the record of his physical movements as captured through CSLI. The location information obtained from Carpenter's wireless carriers was the product of a search.[3]

A

A person does not surrender all Fourth Amendment protection by venturing into the public sphere. To the contrary, what one seeks to preserve as private, even in an area accessible to the public, may be constitutionally protected. A majority of this Court has already recognized that individuals have a reasonable expectation of privacy in the whole of their physical movements. *Jones*, 565 U.S., at 430 (Alito, J., concurring in judgment); *id.*, at 415 (Sotomayor, J., concurring). Prior to the digital age, law enforcement might have pursued a suspect for a brief stretch, but doing so for any extended period of time was difficult and costly and therefore rarely undertaken. For that reason, society's expectation has been that law enforcement agents and others would not—and indeed, in the main, simply could not—secretly monitor and catalogue every single movement of an individual's car for a very long period.

Allowing government access to cell-site records contravenes that expectation. Although such records are generated for commercial purposes, that distinction does not negate Carpenter's anticipation of privacy in his physical location. Mapping a cell phone's location over the course of 127 days provides an all-encompassing record of the holder's whereabouts. As with GPS information, the time-stamped data provides an intimate window into a person's life, revealing not only his particular movements, but through them his familial, political, professional, religious, and sexual associations. These location records hold for many Americans the privacies of life. And like GPS monitoring, cell phone tracking is remarkably easy, cheap, and efficient compared to traditional investigative tools. With just

---

[3] The parties suggest as an alternative to their primary submissions that the acquisition of CSLI becomes a search only if it extends beyond a limited period. As part of its argument, the Government treats the seven days of CSLI requested from Sprint as the pertinent period, even though Sprint produced only two days of records. We need not decide whether there is a limited period for which the Government may obtain an individual's historical CSLI free from Fourth Amendment scrutiny, and if so, how long that period might be. It is sufficient for our purposes today to hold that accessing seven days of CSLI constitutes a Fourth Amendment search.

the click of a button, the Government can access each carrier's deep repository of historical location information at practically no expense.

In fact, historical cell-site records present even greater privacy concerns than the GPS monitoring of a vehicle we considered in *Jones*. Unlike the bugged container in *Knotts* or the car in *Jones*, a cell phone— almost a feature of human anatomy—tracks nearly exactly the movements of its owner. While individuals regularly leave their vehicles, they compulsively carry cell phones with them all the time. A cell phone faithfully follows its owner beyond public thoroughfares and into private residences, doctor's offices, political headquarters, and other potentially revealing locales. Accordingly, when the Government tracks the location of a cell phone it achieves near perfect surveillance, as if it had attached an ankle monitor to the phone's user.

Moreover, the retrospective quality of the data here gives police access to a category of information otherwise unknowable. In the past, attempts to reconstruct a person's movements were limited by a dearth of records and the frailties of recollection. With access to CSLI, the Government can now travel back in time to retrace a person's whereabouts, subject only to the retention polices of the wireless carriers, which currently maintain records for up to five years. Critically, because location information is continually logged for all of the 400 million devices in the United States— not just those belonging to persons who might happen to come under investigation—this newfound tracking capacity runs against everyone. Unlike with the GPS device in *Jones*, police need not even know in advance whether they want to follow a particular individual, or when.

Whoever the suspect turns out to be, he has effectively been tailed every moment of every day for five years, and the police may—in the Government's view—call upon the results of that surveillance without regard to the constraints of the Fourth Amendment. Only the few without cell phones could escape this tireless and absolute surveillance.

The Government and Justice Kennedy contend [in dissent] that the collection of CSLI should be permitted because the data is less precise than GPS information. Not to worry, they maintain, because the location records did not on their own suffice to place Carpenter at the crime scene; they placed him within a wedge-shaped sector ranging from one-eighth to four square miles. . . . [But] the rule the Court adopts must take account of more sophisticated systems that are already in use or in development. While the records in this case reflect the state of technology at the start of the decade, the accuracy of CSLI is rapidly approaching GPS-level precision. As the number of cell sites has proliferated, the geographic area covered by each cell sector has shrunk, particularly in urban areas. In addition, with new technology measuring the time and angle of signals hitting their towers, wireless carriers already have the capability to pinpoint a phone's location within 50 meters. Brief for Electronic Frontier Foundation et al. as *Amici Curiae* 12 (describing triangulation methods that estimate a device's location inside a given cell sector).

Accordingly, when the Government accessed CSLI from the wireless carriers, it invaded Carpenter's reasonable expectation of privacy in the whole of his physical movements.

B

The Government's primary contention to the contrary is that the third-party doctrine governs this case. In its view, cell-site records are fair game because they are "business records" created and maintained by the wireless carriers. The Government (along with Justice Kennedy) recognizes that this case features new technology, but asserts that the legal question nonetheless turns on a garden-variety request for information from a third-party witness.

The Government's position fails to contend with the seismic shifts in digital technology that made possible the tracking of not only Carpenter's location but also everyone else's, not for a short period but for years and years. Sprint Corporation and its competitors are not your typical witnesses. Unlike the nosy neighbor who keeps an eye on comings and goings, they are ever alert, and their memory is nearly infallible. There is a world of difference between the limited types of personal information addressed in *Smith* and *Miller* and the exhaustive chronicle of location information casually collected by wireless carriers today. The Government thus is not asking for a straightforward application of the third-party doctrine, but instead a significant extension of it to a distinct category of information.

The third-party doctrine partly stems from the notion that an individual has a reduced expectation of privacy in information knowingly shared with another. But the fact of diminished privacy interests does not mean that the Fourth Amendment falls out of the picture entirely. *Smith* and *Miller,* after all, did not rely solely on the act of sharing. Instead, they considered the nature of the particular documents sought to determine whether there is a legitimate 'expectation of privacy' concerning their contents. *Smith* pointed out the limited capabilities of a pen register; as explained in *Riley,* telephone call logs reveal little in the way of identifying information. *Miller* likewise noted that checks were not confidential communications but negotiable instruments to be used in commercial transactions. In mechanically applying the third-party doctrine to this case, the Government fails to appreciate that there are no comparable limitations on the revealing nature of CSLI.

The Court has in fact already shown special solicitude for location information in the third-party context. In *Knotts,* the Court relied on *Smith* to hold that an individual has no reasonable expectation of privacy in public movements that he "voluntarily conveyed to anyone who wanted to look. But when confronted with more pervasive tracking, five Justices [in *Jones*] agreed that longer term GPS monitoring of even a vehicle traveling on public streets constitutes a search. [T]his case is not about "using a phone" or a person's movement at a particular time. It is about a detailed chronicle of a person's physical presence compiled every day, every moment, over several years. Such a chronicle implicates privacy concerns far beyond those considered in *Smith* and *Miller*.

Neither does the second rationale underlying the third-party doctrine—voluntary exposure—hold up when it comes to CSLI. Cell phone location information is not truly "shared" as one normally understands the term. In the first place, cell phones and the services they provide are such a pervasive and insistent part of daily life that carrying one is indispensable to participation in modern society. Second, a cell phone logs a cell-site record by dint of its operation, without any affirmative act on the part of the user beyond powering up. Virtually any activity on the phone generates CSLI, including incoming calls, texts, or e-mails and countless other data connections that a phone automatically makes when checking for news, weather, or social media updates. Apart from disconnecting the phone from the network, there is no way to avoid leaving behind a trail of location data. As a result, in no meaningful sense does the user voluntarily assume the risk of turning over a comprehensive dossier of his physical movements.

We therefore decline to extend *Smith* and *Miller* to the collection of CSLI. Given the unique nature of cell phone location information, the fact that the Government obtained the information from a third party does not overcome Carpenter's claim to Fourth Amendment protection. The Government's acquisition of the cell-site records was a search within the meaning of the Fourth Amendment.

* * *

Our decision today is a narrow one. We do not express a view on matters not before us: real-time CSLI or "tower dumps" (a download of information on all the devices that connected to a particular cell site during a particular interval). We do not disturb the application of *Smith* and *Miller* or call into question conventional surveillance techniques and tools, such as security cameras. Nor do we address other business records that might incidentally reveal location information. Further, our opinion does not consider other collection techniques involving foreign affairs or national security.

As Justice Brandeis explained in his famous dissent, the Court is obligated—as "subtler and more far-reaching means of invading privacy have become available to the Government"—to ensure that the "progress of science" does not erode Fourth Amendment protections. *Olmstead v.*

United States, 277 U.S. 438, 473–474 (1928). Here the progress of science has afforded law enforcement a powerful new tool to carry out its important responsibilities. At the same time, this tool risks Government encroachment of the sort the Framers, after consulting the lessons of history, drafted the Fourth Amendment to prevent.

We decline to grant the state unrestricted access to a wireless carrier's database of physical location information. In light of the deeply revealing nature of CSLI, its depth, breadth, and comprehensive reach, and the inescapable and automatic nature of its collection, the fact that such information is gathered by a third party does not make it any less deserving of Fourth Amendment protection. The Government's acquisition of the cell-site records here was a search under that Amendment.

JUSTICE KENNEDY, with whom JUSTICE THOMAS and JUSTICE ALITO join, dissenting.

This case involves new technology, but the Court's stark departure from relevant Fourth Amendment precedents and principles is, in my submission, unnecessary and incorrect, requiring this respectful dissent.

The new rule the Court seems to formulate puts needed, reasonable, accepted, lawful, and congressionally authorized criminal investigations at serious risk in serious cases, often when law enforcement seeks to prevent the threat of violent crimes. And it places undue restrictions on the lawful and necessary enforcement powers exercised not only by the Federal Government, but also by law enforcement in every State and locality throughout the Nation. Adherence to this Court's longstanding precedents and analytic framework would have been the proper and prudent way to resolve this case.

The Court has twice held that individuals have no Fourth Amendment interests in business records which are possessed, owned, and controlled by a third party. *United States v. Miller,* 425 U.S. 435 (1976); *Smith v. Maryland,* 442 U.S. 735 (1979). This is true even when the records contain personal and sensitive information. So when the Government uses a subpoena to obtain, for example, bank records, telephone records, and credit card statements from the businesses that create and keep these records, the Government does not engage in a search of the business's customers within the meaning of the Fourth Amendment.

Petitioner acknowledges that the Government may obtain a wide variety of business records using compulsory process, and he does not ask the Court to revisit its precedents. Yet he argues that, under those same precedents, the Government searched his records when it used court-approved compulsory process to obtain the cell-site information at issue here. Cell-site records, however, are no different from the many other kinds of business records the Government has a lawful right to obtain by compulsory process. Customers like petitioner do not own, possess, control, or use the records, and for that reason have no reasonable expectation that they cannot be disclosed pursuant to lawful compulsory process.

The Court today disagrees. It holds for the first time that by using compulsory process to obtain records of a business entity, the Government has not just engaged in an impermissible action, but has conducted a search of the business's customer. The Court further concludes that the search in this case was unreasonable and the Government needed to get a warrant to obtain more than six days of cell-site records.

In concluding that the Government engaged in a search, the Court unhinges Fourth Amendment doctrine from the property-based concepts that have long grounded the analytic framework that pertains in these cases. In doing so it draws an unprincipled and unworkable line between cell-site records on the one hand and financial and telephonic records on the other. According to today's majority opinion, the Government can acquire a record of every credit card purchase and phone call a person makes over months or years without upsetting a legitimate expectation of privacy. But, in the Court's view, the Government crosses a constitutional line when it obtains a court's approval to issue a subpoena for more than six days of cell-site records in order to determine whether a person was within several hundred city blocks of a crime scene. That distinction is illogical and will frustrate principled application of the Fourth Amendment in many routine yet vital law enforcement operations.

It is true that the Cyber Age has vast potential both to expand and restrict individual freedoms in dimensions not contemplated in earlier times. However, there is simply no basis here for concluding that the Government interfered with information that the cell phone customer, either from a legal or commonsense standpoint, should have thought the law would deem owned or controlled by him.

JUSTICE GORSUCH, dissenting.

Today the Court suggests that *Smith* and *Miller* distinguish between *kinds* of information disclosed to third parties and require courts to decide whether to "extend" those decisions to particular classes of information, depending on their sensitivity. But as the Sixth Circuit recognized and Justice Kennedy explains, no balancing test of this kind can be found in *Smith* and *Miller*. Those cases announced a categorical rule: Once you disclose information to third parties, you forfeit any reasonable expectation of privacy you might have had in it. And even if *Smith* and *Miller* did permit courts to conduct a balancing contest of the kind the Court now suggests, it's still hard to see how that would help the petitioner in this case. Why is someone's location when using a phone so much more sensitive than who he was talking to (*Smith*) or what financial transactions he engaged in (*Miller*)? I do not know and the Court does not say.

I cannot fault the Sixth Circuit for holding that *Smith* and *Miller* extinguish any *Katz*-based Fourth Amendment interest in third party cell-site data. That is the plain effect of their categorical holdings. Nor can I fault the Court today for its implicit but unmistakable conclusion that the rationale of *Smith* and *Miller* is wrong; indeed, I agree with that. The Sixth Circuit was powerless to say so, but this Court can and should. At the same time, I do not agree with the Court's decision today to keep *Smith* and *Miller* on life support and supplement them with a new and multilayered inquiry that seems to be only *Katz*-squared. Returning there, I worry, promises more trouble than help. Instead, I would look to a more traditional Fourth Amendment approach. Even if *Katz* may still supply one way to prove a Fourth Amendment interest, it has never been the only way. Neglecting more traditional approaches may mean failing to vindicate the full protections of the Fourth Amendment.

NOTES AND QUESTIONS

1. *New versus traditional surveillance techniques.* The Supreme Court's *Carpenter* decision draws a distinction between new technologies that cause "seismic shifts" in the government's power and "traditional surveillance techniques" that are not called into question by the Court's reasoning. On one hand, *Carpenter* directs that use of "seismic shift" technologies can be a search to prevent the government from having too much surveillance power as a result of technological change. On the other hand, *Carpenter* suggests that traditional surveillance techniques that were not a search under traditional Fourth Amendment principles remain a non-search. How should courts apply this distinction to Internet surveillance?

2. *Translating Carpenter's physical expectations to the Internet.* *Carpenter* is based on an understanding of traditional expectations in the physical world. In the past, the Court reasons, you wouldn't expect others to monitor your every single movement in physical space for a long period of time because it would be technologically impossible. New technology has changed that expectation, *Carpenter* explains. Technology has enabled perfect location surveillance that previously didn't exist. The law must declare that monitoring a search, the Court reasons, to restore the earlier balance of government power.

But how does that apply to Internet surveillance? There is likely no established past set of societal expectations about how much Internet surveillance power the government has. Given that, how can you tell if technological changes in Internet surveillance power have changed a previous expectation? Or is the idea that the entire Internet, viewed as a whole, works a "seismic shift" in the amount of surveillance power the government has relative to the pre-Internet age? If so, what were the old expectations about government power, and what is the new reality? And what legal rules are needed to restore the old reality of government power by changing Fourth Amendment doctrine?

3. *Obtaining basic subscriber information.* Courts have held, both before *Carpenter* and after, that the government can collect identity information about who registered an account—sometimes called "basic subscriber information"—without triggering the Fourth Amendment. If the government obtains a subpoena or court order requiring the Internet provider to disclose the name and address of who registered an account, the Fourth Amendment does not apply and no warrant is needed. *See, e.g.,* United States v. Hambrick, 225 F.3d 656 (4th Cir. 2000) (before *Carpenter*); United States v. VanDyck, 776 Fed.Appx. 495 (9th Cir. 2019) (after *Carpenter*).

4. *Obtaining the IP addresses that a suspect used.* Investigators who are monitoring a suspicious Internet account may want to know what IP addresses were used to access the account at a particular time. If the suspect did not use a virtual private network or other anonymizing software, the IP address used to access the account may tell the government who the user is or where he is located. Is access to such records governed by *Carpenter*?

Courts have held that *Carpenter* does not apply. For example, in United States v. Hood, 920 F.3d 87 (1st Cir. 2019), the government had reason to believe that someone using a particular Kik account with the associated name "Rusty Hood" had recently used the account to commit a crime. In an effort to identify the suspect, investigators asked Kik to disclose the IP addresses used to log in to the account recently. Kik disclosed the IP addresses used over a four-day period, and that led to the identification and prosecution of the user, Mr. Rusty Hood. Hood argued that obtaining his IP addresses was a Fourth Amendment search under *Carpenter*. The First Circuit disagreed:

> An internet user generates the IP address data that the government acquired from Kik in this case only by making the affirmative decision to access a website or application. By contrast, as the Supreme Court noted in *Carpenter*, every time a cell phone receives a call, text message, or email, the cell phone pings CSLI to the nearest cell site tower without the cell phone user lifting a finger. In fact, those pings are recorded every time a cell phone application updates of its own accord, possibly to refresh a news feed or generate new weather data, such that even a cell phone sitting untouched in a suspect's pocket is continually chronicling that user's movements throughout the day.

> Moreover, the IP address data that the government acquired from Kik does not itself convey any location information. The IP address data is merely a string of numbers associated with a device that had, at one time, accessed a wireless network. By contrast, CSLI itself reveals—without any independent investigation—the (at least approximate) location of the cell phone user who generates that data simply by possessing the phone.

> Thus, the government's warrantless acquisition from Kik of the IP address data at issue here in no way gives rise to the unusual concern that the Supreme Court identified in *Carpenter* that, if the third-

party doctrine were applied to the acquisition of months of Carpenter's CSLI, only the few without cell phones could escape tireless and absolute surveillance. Accordingly, we conclude that Hood did not have a reasonable expectation of privacy in the information that the government acquired from Kik without a warrant.

Id. at 91–92. *See also* United States v. Morel, 922 F.3d 1 (1st Cir. 2019); United States v. Wellbeloved-Stone, 777 Fed.Appx. 605 (4th Cir. 2019). Are you persuaded?

5.   *Obtaining the IP addresses of websites that a computer account was used to visit.* How does *Carpenter* apply to the facts of *United States v. Forrester* above? In *Forrester*, the government monitored a home Internet connection and obtained the IP addresses of the websites visited from the account. Note the key difference between the facts of *Forrester* and the facts of *Hood*. In *Hood*, the IP addresses collected were those assigned to Hood's account. In *Forrester*, the IP addresses collected were those of every website visited using the home's account. Should that make a difference?

This issue arose in United States v. Soybel, ___ F.4th ___, 2021 WL 4076759 (7th Cir. 2021), which had facts materially identical to those of *Forrester*. The government used a pen register order to collect the IP addresses of the websites that visited from Soybel's home Internet account. The Seventh Circuit ruled that no search occurred and that the case was governed by *Smith v. Maryland* instead of *Carpenter*:

> The unique features of historical CSLI are absent for IP-address data. The pen register was stationary and could not capture the whole of Soybel's physical movements. As was true in *Smith*, a recorded connection at most incidentally revealed when Soybel may have been in his apartment. But even that's not a given because the data was impersonal. A recording of the existence of connections between communications devices shows only that someone in Soybel's unit was using the internet. It could not reveal the identity of the user— whether it be Soybel, his mother, or an unidentified guest. The same cannot be said for CSLI, unless the cell phone's owner takes the unusual step of giving it to someone else.

> Moreover, routing information obtained via a pen register isn't retrospective. The government could not effectively "travel back in time" by using an IP pen register. A pen register is only forward-looking; its usefulness extends only so far as it is installed and no further. And here, the government would have had to seek a renewal of the 60-day order if it needed data beyond that point. CSLI, in contrast, is continuously collected and available for the government's ready use so long as the cell carrier retains the records, which could be up to five years.

Id. at *6–*7. Do you agree? Is watching every website a suspect visits merely "stationary" surveillance that shows a person was using the Internet, as the Seventh Circuit says? Or is it effectively watching the person as they virtually travel all around the Internet in a way that gathers a comprehensive picture of their lives?

6. *Obtaining wireless network login records.* In Commonwealth v. Dunkins, 229 A.3d 622 (Pa. Super. 2020), the police were investigating a robbery by two men in ski masks at a dormitory at Moravian College. The campus police suspected that the robbers might be students, and that, if so, they might have been carrying cell phones that had automatically logged into the dormitory's wireless network. The police asked the Moravian College IT director to turn over a list of students who were logged into the network near the dormitory's wireless access point at the time of the robbery. When the IT director produced the list, it turned out that only one male student was logged into the network who did not live in the dorm. Further investigation revealed that the student, Dunkins, was one of the robbers.

Dunkins moved to suppress the evidence of his logins under *Carpenter*, arguing that a warrant was needed before his wireless access records could be collected by the police. The Superior Court disagreed:

> Whereas CSLI tracks an individual's movements at all times of the day regardless of where he travels, the WiFi data in this case is only collected when an individual logs onto the campus wireless network and is present on the Moravian campus.

> We agree with the trial court's observation that the Moravian WiFi network is confined to the college campus and offered as an available option to students and faculty. When college officials seek to determine which students are logged on to the network near a particular wireless access point at a particular time, the private wireless network functions similarly to a security camera that may exist at the college. As such, the decision in *Carpenter* does not invalidate the warrantless search in this case.

Id. at *5.

7. *Obtaining cell tower dumps.* The government may want to know what cell phones were connected in the past to a particular cell tower when a crime occurred near it. To do this, they may ask the cell phone provider for a so-called "tower dump," a list of every phone connected to that tower at that time. Investigators can then study the list of connected phones for clues about possible suspects.

Is a tower dump a Fourth Amendment search? *Carpenter* expressly declined to say. Courts so far have answered "no." Consider United States v. Walker, 2020 WL 4065980 (E.D.N.C. 2020):

> Here, the orders capture CLSI not for one targeted individual for an extended time, chronicling that individual's private life for days, but rather capture CLSI for a particular *place* at a *limited time*. In this

manner, the privacy concerns underpinning the court's holding in *Carpenter* do not come into play here, where the search for data focuses not on the whole of an individual's physical movements but rather on the data that was left behind at a particular time and place by virtue of cell phone tower locations.

Instead, the CLSI tower dump information gathered here is more akin to conventional surveillance techniques and tools, such as security cameras and fingerprint collections, which capture data from every individual who came into contact with the crime scene in the manner revealed by the technology at issue. In light of the significant differences between a tower dump CLSI and long term CSLI targeted at the whole of an individual's movements, as highlighted by the court's decision in *Carpenter*, the court finds no basis for attaching a Fourth Amendment interest to tower dump CLSI.

See also United States v. Rhodes, 2021 WL 1541050 (N.D.Ga. 2021) (same).

8. *Blockchain technologies and monitoring Bitcoin transactions.* Bitcoin is a virtual currency sometimes used in criminal activity. All Bitcoin transactions are public and are recorded on a public list known as a blockchain. Although the blockchain is public, using Bitcoin offers significant amounts of anonymity because the blockchain records only include the anonymous addresses (similar to bank account numbers) for both the buyer and seller as well as the amount of Bitcoin transferred. Although anyone can know that an amount of Bitcoin was transferred from a buyer at one account address to a seller at another account address, it can be very difficult for the government to figure out who is the buyer and who is the seller.

In United States v. Gratkowski, 964 F.3d 307 (5th Cir. 2020), the government was investigating an illegal website that sold services using Bitcoin. The government analyzed the publicly viewable Bitcoin blockchain and identified a group of Bitcoin addresses controlled by the illegal website. The government then approached Coinbase, a popular virtual currency exchange, and served a subpoena on Coinbase for account records of any Coinbase accounts that sent Bitcoin to any of the addresses controlled by the illegal website.

Coinbase complied with the subpoena, revealing Gratkowski as one of the customers who had purchased items from the website using Bitcoin. That in turn led to a search of Gratkowski's home and the discovery of evidence stored there. When criminal charges followed, Gratkowski moved to suppress the evidence on Fourth Amendment grounds.

Gratkowski first argued that he had a reasonable expectation of privacy in the public blockchain under *Carpenter*, such that analyzing his transactions on the public blockchain was a search. The Fifth Circuit disagreed:

> The information on Bitcoin's blockchain is far more analogous to the bank records in *Miller* and the telephone call logs in *Smith* than the CSLI in *Carpenter*. The nature of the information on the Bitcoin

blockchain and the voluntariness of the exposure weigh heavily against finding a privacy interest in an individual's information on the Bitcoin blockchain. The Bitcoin blockchain records (1) the amount of Bitcoin transferred, (2) the Bitcoin address of the sending party, and (3) the Bitcoin address of the receiving party. The information is limited.

Further, Bitcoin users are unlikely to expect that the information published on the Bitcoin blockchain will be kept private, thus undercutting their claim of a legitimate expectation of privacy. Granted, they enjoy a greater degree of privacy than those who use other money-transfer means, but it is well known that each Bitcoin transaction is recorded in a publicly available blockchain. Every Bitcoin user has access to the public Bitcoin blockchain and can see every Bitcoin address and its respective transfers. Due to this publicity, it is possible to determine the identities of Bitcoin address owners by analyzing the blockchain. Gratkowski thus lacked a privacy interest in his information on the Bitcoin blockchain.

Next, Gratkowski argued that he had Fourth Amendment rights under *Carpenter* in his Coinbase records. Again, the Fifth Circuit disagreed:

Like the Blockchain, we hold that the Coinbase records are more akin to the bank records in *Miller* than the CSLI in *Carpenter*.

The nature of the information and the voluntariness of the exposure weigh heavily against finding a privacy interest in Coinbase records. First, Coinbase records are limited. Having access to Coinbase records does not provide agents with an intimate window into a person's life; it provides only information about a person's virtual currency transactions. Second, transacting Bitcoin through Coinbase or other virtual currency exchange institutions requires an affirmative act on part of the user.

Bitcoin users have the option to maintain a high level of privacy by transacting without a third-party intermediary. But that requires technical expertise, so Bitcoin users may elect to sacrifice some privacy by transacting through an intermediary such as Coinbase. Gratkowski thus lacked a privacy interest in the records of his Bitcoin transactions on Coinbase.

The lesson of *Gratkowski* seems simple enough. Although buying illegal goods using Bitcoin may make the transaction difficult to trace, the difficulty is practical, not legal.

9.   *Short-term vs. long-term surveillance.* Footnote 3 of *Carpenter* states that the Court "need not decide whether there is a limited period for which the Government may obtain an individual's historical CSLI free from Fourth Amendment scrutiny, and if so, how long that period might be." The distinction between long-term and short-term surveillance was the basis of Justice Alito's concurring opinion in *Jones*, on which the reasoning of *Carpenter* is based. In

Jones, the government installed a physical GPS device on a car the suspect was driving and tracked the car's location for 28 days. Justice Alito reasoned that using the GPS device only briefly was not a search because that was the kind of government surveillance people have traditionally expected. Longer term surveillance became a search, Justice Alito reasoned, because it was the kind of surveillance that people wouldn't expect the government to be able to conduct. Here's the key language from Justice Alito's *Jones* concurrence:

> Relatively short-term monitoring of a person's movements on public streets accords with expectations of privacy that our society has recognized as reasonable. But the use of longer term GPS monitoring in investigations of most offenses impinges on expectations of privacy. For such offenses, society's expectation has been that law enforcement agents and others would not—and indeed, in the main, simply could not—secretly monitor and catalogue every single movement of an individual's car for a very long period. In this case, for four weeks, law enforcement agents tracked every movement that respondent made in the vehicle he was driving.

> We need not identify with precision the point at which the tracking of this vehicle became a search, for the line was surely crossed before the 4-week mark. Other cases may present more difficult questions. But where uncertainty exists with respect to whether a certain period of GPS surveillance is long enough to constitute a Fourth Amendment search, the police may always seek a warrant. We also need not consider whether prolonged GPS monitoring in the context of investigations involving extraordinary offenses would similarly intrude on a constitutionally protected sphere of privacy. In such cases, long-term tracking might have been mounted using previously available techniques.

> For these reasons, I conclude that the lengthy monitoring that occurred in this case constituted a search under the Fourth Amendment.

United States v. Jones, 565 U.S. 400, 430–31 (Alito, J., concurring in the judgment).

If *Carpenter* is based on the reasoning of Justice Alito's *Jones* concurrence, does that mean that some kind of short-term collection of records is not a search? If so, how short is short enough not to be a search?

In Kinslow v. State, 129 N.E.3d 810 (Ind. Ct. App. 2019), investigators placed a GPS device inside a package that Kinslow later picked up and placed in his car. The police tracked the location of Kinslow's car as it drove around for about six hours. The Indiana Court of Appeals held that no search occurred under *Carpenter*:

> While the United States Supreme Court found that tracking such information violated Carpenter's expectation of privacy, we read the Court's holding to apply to records, such as cellphone tracking data,

that hold for many Americans the 'privacies of life.' Cell phone location data provides an intimate window into a person's life, revealing not only his particular movements, but through them his professional, political, religious, and sexual associations. Because the tracking of Kinslow lasted only approximately six hours and because the electronic devices used here do not provide an intimate window into a person's life, we find that *Carpenter* has no bearing on this case.

Id. at *3 n.6. *See also* Sims v. State, 569 S.W.3d 634 (Tex. Ct. Crim. App. 2019) (holding that *Carpenter* applies to real-time cell-site pinging, but that obtaining real-time location with five pings over less than three hours was insufficient to trigger a *Carpenter* search).

Contrast *Kinslow* and *Sims* with the Washington Supreme Court's decision in State v. Muhammad, 451 P.3d 1060 (Wash. 2019). In *Muhammad*, the police were looking for the defendant and sent a one-time ping to his cell phone to locate it. The Washington Supreme Court held that the one-time ping was a search, and that trying to create a rule that permitted some amount of pinging without it rising to the level of a search was unworkable:

> The argument that an isolated cell phone ping offers limited information and therefore does not implicate the Fourth Amendment appears to advance what federal courts have deemed the "mosaic" theory. Under this theory, discrete acts of law enforcement surveillance may be lawful in isolation but may otherwise intrude on reasonable expectations of privacy in the aggregate because they paint an intimate picture of a defendant's life.

> At first glance, the mosaic theory presents an attractive answer to whether a singular cell phone ping constitutes a Fourth Amendment search. But federal courts have recognized the practical problems inherent in this theory when traditional surveillance becomes a search only after some specific period of time elapses. As United States v. Graham, 846 F. Supp. 2d 384, 401–03 (D. Md. 2012), noted, "discrete acts of law enforcement are either constitutional or they are not."

> For instance, to conclude that one cell phone ping is not a search, provided it lasts less than six hours, yet hold multiple or longer pings do qualify as search is not a workable analysis. There is no rational point to draw the line; it is arbitrary and unrelated to a reasonable expectation of privacy.

> Rather than offering analysis based on a reasonable expectation of privacy, the mosaic theory instead requires a case-by-case, ad hoc determination of whether the length of time of a cell phone ping violated the Fourth Amendment. It offers little guidance to courts or law enforcement and presents the danger that constitutional rights will be arbitrarily and inequitably enforced.

Id. at 1072–73. Should the Fourth Amendment recognize this "mosaic theory," and if so, what lines should it draw to say how much surveillance is enough? *See generally* Orin S. Kerr, *The Mosaic Theory of the Fourth Amendment*, 111 Mich. L. Rev. 311 (2012).

10. *Identifying the stage of surveillance that counts as a potential Carpenter search.* Imagine the government collects data into a database, later retrieves some of the data, analyzes it, and uses it in a criminal case. For *Carpenter* purposes, exactly which of these stages is relevant to when a "search" may have occurred? Is the initial collection of information the potential search? The retrieval? The analysis? The use?

The answer matters because the government often starts by collecting a massive amount of data that it then winnows down through retrieval and analysis to only a small number of records that are actually used. If courts adopt the mosaic theory of *Carpenter,* by which government acts concerning small amounts of data are not a search but that acts concerning large amounts of data may become one, identifying the exact stage to examine to know if a *Carpenter* search occurred becomes very important.

Consider two cases on this question.

The first case, Commonwealth v. McCarthy, 142 N.E.3d 1090 (Mass. 2020), involves government automated license plate readers (ALPRs). ALPRs take pictures of the license plates of cars on the road. In some cases, the ALPRs are in fixed locations. In other cases, the ALPRs are mounted on police squad cars. In both cases, the government can use ALPRs to create massive databases of where cars are located on the road at various times. They can use these databases to try to reconstruct where cars were in the past based on license plate "hits" in the database, or else they can try to find out where cars are at present when a plate registers in the database in real time.

In *McCarthy*, the government was tracking a suspected drug dealer who often drove to a co-conspirator's home. There were only two roads to that home, each of which went over a different bridge. Both sides of each bridge had a state ALPR affixed to it. The police created an alert telling investigators whenever McCarthy's car drove over either bridge. For two and a half months, the police learned the precise dates, times, directions, and specific lanes that McCarthy's car traveled on the two bridges.

The court first ruled that the search did not depend on what was actually admitted in court. Further, ideally, whether a search occurred under *Carpenter* should consider every ALPR record collected by the government for McCarthy's car whether it was actually retrieved:

> In determining whether a reasonable expectation of privacy has been invaded, it is not the amount of data that the Commonwealth seeks to admit in evidence that counts, but, rather, the amount of data that the government collects or to which it gains access. In *Carpenter*, the relevant period was the 127 days of CSLI data, not the data that placed the defendant near the robberies on four particular days.

> For this reason, our constitutional analysis ideally would consider every ALPR record of a defendant's vehicle that had been stored and collected by the government up to the time of the defendant's arrest. That information, however, is not in the record before us.
>
> On this record, we need not, and indeed cannot, determine how pervasive a system of ALPRs would have to be to invade a reasonable expectation of privacy. While a testifying expert alluded to cameras all over the state, the record is silent as to how many of these cameras currently exist, where they are located, and how many of them detected the defendant.

Id. at 1103–04, 1105. Because that information was not available, the court focused instead on how much information was actually observed by the government. In other words, how complete a picture was the government able to assemble from the records it obtained from the database? Because the picture was insufficiently comprehensive, the court ruled, no search had occurred:

> The cameras in question here gave police only the ability to determine whether the defendant was passing [over one of the bridges] at a particular moment, and when he had done so previously. This limited surveillance does not allow the Commonwealth to monitor the whole of the defendant's public movements, or even his progress on a single journey.
>
> These particular cameras make this case perhaps more analogous to CSLI, if there were only two cellular telephone towers collecting data. Such a limited picture does not divulge the whole of the defendant's physical movements, or track enough of his comings and goings so as to reveal the privacies of life.
>
> While we cannot say precisely how detailed a picture of the defendant's movements must be revealed to invoke constitutional protections, it is not that produced by four cameras at fixed locations on the ends of two bridges. Therefore, we conclude that the limited use of ALPRs in this case does not constitute a search within the meaning of the Fourth Amendment.

Id. at 508–09.

A second case to consider is United States v. George, 2020 WL 1689715 (E.D.Cal. 2020). The officers in *George* served a non-warrant SCA order on AT&T for CSLI a month before *Carpenter* was handed down. AT&T responded a few weeks later, sending the CSLI to the officers just a week before *Carpenter* was decided. The officers did not review and analyze the CSLI until after *Carpenter* was published. When the defendant moved to suppress the evidence obtained without a warrant, the government argued that it could rely on the good faith exception to the exclusionary rule because the search had occurred before *Carpenter* was handed down. (The timing mattered because the good-faith exception is time-focused: It applies when appellate precedents existing at the time the search occurred say the government's act was lawful.)

The district court held that the search had been completed "when AT&T searched through its records and provided defendant's CSLI to the government" in response to the court order:

> Orders or warrants to produce information under the SCA are executed when a law enforcement agent delivers the warrant to the service provider. The service provider, not the agent, performs the 'search'; the service provider 'produces' the relevant material to the agent. Defendant has provided no authority, and the court is unaware of any, which would require law enforcement or the government to obtain a warrant to use or analyze evidence that was already in its possession, where subsequent court decisions made it clear that a warrant was now required to obtain such evidence. Simply put, analyzing data obtained via a court order has never been considered a separate search under the Fourth Amendment.

Id. at *3.

Are *McCarthy* and *George* consistent? Are they correct?

11. *Searching for Internet Protocol addresses inside a person's home computer or local network.* The *Forrester* case rules that individuals do not have a reasonable expectation of privacy in their IP addresses collected from a service provider. But what about IP addresses that may be collected from a user's computer or local network?

In United States v. Horton, 863 F.3d 1041 (8th Cir. 2017), the FBI obtained a warrant authorizing use of a "network investigative technique" (NIT)— specifically, the installation of government malware—on the computers of visitors to a CSAM website. The website operated on the dark web, and as such the true IP addresses of visitors were concealed. The warrant permitted the government to use the NIT when a user visited the site: The malware would be installed on the user's home network and would surreptitiously report the user's actual IP address and some other identifying information to an FBI computer.

Horton ruled that installation of malware on a suspect's computer to retrieve an IP address constitutes a search:

> The government is not permitted to conduct a warrantless search of a place in which a defendant has a reasonable expectation of privacy simply because it intends to seize property for which the defendant does not have a reasonable expectation of privacy.

> This case differs from cases in which an IP address is voluntarily provided to third parties. In this case, the FBI sent computer code to the defendants' respective computers that searched those computers for specific information and sent that information back to law enforcement. Even if a defendant has no reasonable

expectation of privacy in his IP address, he has a reasonable expectation of privacy in the contents of his personal computer.

Id. at 1046–47.

2. SEIZURES

The Supreme Court has defined a "seizure" of property as "some meaningful interference with an individual's possessory interest in [the individual's] property." United States v. Jacobsen, 466 U.S. 109, 113 (1984). Under this definition, a seizure occurs when the police take property away, block a person from being able to control her property in a meaningful way, or interfere with the path of property in transit. For example, if a package is sent through the mail, the police "seize" the package if they go to the mail room and take the package out of the stream of delivery. *See* United States v. Van Leeuwen, 397 U.S. 249 (1970). It is easy to apply these principles to computers in the case of physical storage devices. Under the container analogy, taking a computer away from its owner "seizes" it. This means that if the police want to take a person's computer away, they must ordinarily obtain a warrant to justify the seizure.

The legal question becomes more complicated when computer data is no longer linked to a physical container. For example, imagine that a police officer enters a coffee shop, orders a decaf latte, and sits down at a table. A patron at the table next to him has left his laptop computer on the table while he is away for a few minutes, and the officer sees what appears to be evidence of credit card fraud on the computer's monitor. If the officer writes down the text of what he sees, has he "seized" that data? What if the officer inserts a storage device into an input/output port in the back of the computer and copies the file that appears on the screen? Has he seized the file? Imagine the officer brings more sophisticated equipment and copies the entire computer hard drive. Does that copying seize the entire hard drive? More broadly, if a police officer copies data but does not otherwise interfere with the owner's possessory interest in the physical storage device, is that copying a "seizure"?

The courts have not yet definitively answered such questions. The precedents from earlier technologies are mixed. On one hand, cases like United States v. New York Telephone Co., 434 U.S. 159 (1977), suggest that copying a file seizes it. In *New York Telephone*, the Supreme Court held that Federal Rule of Criminal Procedure 41 authorized the government to apply for a search warrant to install a monitoring device known as a pen register. Rule 41 is the statutory rule that authorizes federal investigators to obtain search warrants "to search for and seize" evidence of criminal activity; a pen register is a device that records the outgoing numbers dialed from a telephone. Although *New York Telephone* involved interpretation of a statutory rule, not the Fourth Amendment, the

Court's language is suggestive. The Court ruled that Rule 41 "is broad enough to encompass a 'search' designed to ascertain the use which is being made of a telephone suspected of being employed as a means of facilitating a criminal venture and the 'seizure' of evidence which the 'search' of the telephone produces. Rule 41 is sufficiently broad to include seizures of intangible items such as dial impulses recorded by pen registers as well as tangible items." *Id.* at 169–70.

On the other hand, consider Arizona v. Hicks, 480 U.S. 321 (1987), which points in the opposite direction. In *Hicks*, an officer came across stereo equipment that he believed was stolen. The officer wrote down the serial numbers he observed on the equipment, and he then called in the numbers to the police station to confirm that the equipment was stolen. The Supreme Court held that the act of copying the numbers was not a seizure:

> We agree that the mere recording of the serial numbers did not constitute a seizure. To be sure, that was the first step in a process by which respondent was eventually deprived of the stereo equipment. In and of itself, however, it did not "meaningfully interfere" with respondent's possessory interest in either the serial numbers or the equipment, and therefore did not amount to a seizure.

Id. at 327.

Is copying computer data more like recording a number as in *Hicks* or recording a dialed impulse as in *New York Telephone*? Are these cases reconcilable?

UNITED STATES V. JEFFERSON
United States District Court for the Eastern District of Virginia, 2008.
571 F. Supp.2d 696.

T.S. ELLIS, III, DISTRICT JUDGE.

A sixteen-count indictment charges defendant William J. Jefferson, a sitting member of the United States House of Representatives, with a variety of crimes including bribery, conspiracy, wire fraud, foreign corrupt practices, money laundering, obstruction of justice, and racketeering. As part of the investigation leading to the Indictment, Federal Bureau of Investigation agents executed a search warrant at defendant's residence at 1922 Marengo Street in New Orleans, Louisiana on August 3, 2005.

I.

Defendant is the currently sitting member of the United States House of Representatives representing Louisiana's 2nd Congressional District, an office he has held since 1991. The Indictment alleges that beginning in or about January 2001, defendant used his office to advance the business interests of various individuals and corporations in return for money and other things of value paid either directly to defendant or via "nominee companies," i.e., companies ostensibly controlled by one of defendant's family members, but in fact controlled by defendant himself.

As part of the investigation leading to the Indictment in this case, agents from the FBI went to defendant's residence at 1922 Marengo Street in New Orleans, Louisiana on the morning of August 3, 2005 to execute a search warrant and to interview defendant. Following the conclusion of the interview, FBI agents executed a search of defendant's residence pursuant to the terms of a warrant issued by the United States District Court for the Eastern District of Louisiana. Schedule B to the search warrant listed "items to be seized from" the Marengo Street residence in four general categories: (1) records and documents related to various corporate entities, (2) records and documents related to specific correspondence or communications between certain individuals, (3) records and documents related to travel to Ghana and/or Nigeria by certain individuals, and (4) records and documents related to appointments, visits, and telephone messages to or for defendant.

During the course of the search, which lasted roughly seven-and-a-half hours, FBI agents seized and removed approximately 1,400 pages of documents from defendant's residence. Defendant has not challenged the seizure and removal of any of those 1,400 pages of documents. In addition to these seizures, an FBI photographer took high-resolution photographs of thirteen separate items,[22] and agents conducting the search took cursory notes of the contents of certain documents not seized or photographed as well as bank account information discovered during the search but not

---

[22] Specifically, photographs were taken of the following items:

1. A hand-written list of topics relating to Multimedia Broadband Services, Inc.

2. A document relating to iGate, Inc. and containing a telephone message.

3. A twenty-two page document relating to iGate, Inc.

4. A document containing telephone numbers and messages.

5. An e-mail from B.K. Son to Defendant regarding Multimedia Broadband Services, Inc.

6. A printout of a power-point presentation entitled "E-Star Wireless Broadband Network Business Opportunity."

7. E-mails between B.K. Son, Darren Purifoy, and Defendant and accompanying technical data.

8. Business cards of Nigerian government officials.

9. A non-circumvention and non-disclosure agreement between Arkel Sugar and Providence Lake, together with a letter from Arkel Sugar to Providence Lake written to the attention of Mose Jefferson.

10. An agreement between Providence International Petroleum Company, James Creaghan, and Procurer Financial Consultants.

11. Fifty-five pages of an address book.

12. A 1991 calendar/appointment book.

13. Documents relating to Moss Creek.

physically seized. It is the agents' photographs and notes that are the focus of defendant's suppression motion.

Agents Thibault and Horner testified that they would normally have removed the documents at issue under the "plain view" doctrine, rather than photographing them or taking notes of their contents. But according to these agents, attorneys with the U.S. Attorney's Office for the Eastern District of Virginia had instructed them to seize and remove only evidence that was directly responsive to the list of items in the warrant's Schedule B. Both agents testified they understood this instruction to be a prudential limit on their ability to remove evidence that they were nonetheless constitutionally permitted to search and seize under the plain view doctrine, and that the photographs and notes were taken in an effort to comply with the prosecutors' instructions while still giving effect to the plain view doctrine.

II.

It is necessary to determine whether (i) taking high-resolution photographs of documents or (ii) taking notes of the contents of documents constitutes either a search or a seizure under the Fourth Amendment.

The Fourth Amendment protects the "right of the people to be secure in their persons, houses, papers, and effects against unreasonable searches and seizures." U.S. Const. amend. IV. Accordingly, it is first necessary to determine whether photographing documents or taking notes of the contents of documents constitutes either a search or a seizure as those terms are used in the Fourth Amendment context. A "search" occurs when "an expectation of privacy that society is prepared to consider reasonable is infringed." A "seizure" occurs when "there is some meaningful interference with an individual's possessory interests in the property seized." The question, then, is whether taking photographs or notes constitutes a meaningful interference with an individual's possessory privacy interest in the property seized.

Importantly in this respect, the Supreme Court has extended the Fourth Amendment's protections to intangible as well as tangible possessory interests. *See Hoffa v. United States*, 385 U.S. 293 (1966). In *Hoffa*, a paid government informant overheard the defendant make numerous incriminating statements and reported those statements to law enforcement officials. Following his conviction, the defendant challenged the use of those statements on the ground that they had been unconstitutionally seized by the paid informant. The Supreme Court made clear that the Fourth Amendment's protections were surely not limited to tangibles, but can extend as well to oral statements. Nevertheless, the Supreme Court affirmed the conviction, holding that the defendant had no expectation of privacy in statements he made in public and to people he mistakenly took into his confidence.

The Supreme Court again addressed the Fourth Amendment's applicability to intangible matters in *Katz v. United States*, 389 U.S. 347 (1967). There, the defendant had been convicted of transmitting wager information by telephone across state lines, based in part on a recording of the defendant's phone call which the FBI had obtained by placing an electronic listening device on the phone booth from which defendant placed his call. Reversing the defendant's conviction, the Supreme Court held that the defendant had a reasonable expectation of privacy in his telephone conversation, even though he placed his call from a public telephone booth. In so holding, the Supreme Court reaffirmed the applicability of the Fourth Amendment to intangible matters such as oral statements.

Both *Hoffa* and *Katz* therefore support the proposition that an individual has a possessory privacy interest in intangible information which he or she discloses orally, provided that such disclosure is done in manner reasonably expected to be private. In *United States v. New York Telephone Co.*, 434 U.S. 159 (1977), the Supreme Court extended this line of reasoning beyond oral statements to information recorded electronically, namely pen registers which record all numbers dialed by a particular telephone. Citing *Katz*, the Supreme Court held that the electronic recording of telephone numbers by means of a pen register constituted a permissible search and seizure of such information under the Fourth Amendment and Rule 41, Fed.R.Crim.P.

Taken together, therefore, *Hoffa*, *Katz*, and *New York Telephone Co.* stand for the proposition that the Fourth Amendment protects an individual's possessory interest in information itself, and not simply in the medium in which it exists. In essence these cases recognize that the Fourth Amendment privacy interest extends not just to the paper on which the information is written or the disc on which it is recorded but also to the information on the paper or disc itself. It follows from this that recording the information by photograph or otherwise interferes with this possessory privacy interest even if the document or disc is not itself seized.

In sum, *Hoffa*, *Katz*, and *New York Telephone Co.* all support the proposition that individuals possess a constitutionally protected right to preserve the privacy of information recorded in books and documents against government attempts to photograph, transcribe, or otherwise copy the information. This conclusion is convincingly confirmed by recognizing that a contrary rule would significantly degrade the right to privacy protected by the Fourth Amendment. Thus, if Fourth Amendment protection did not extend to the information reflected in books and documents, then there would be no constitutional bar to police entering an individual's home pursuant to a lawful warrant and then evading the warrant's limits by recording every detail of the premises and its contents by way of high-resolution photographs and notes, all in a search for evidence of crimes unrelated to the matter giving rise to the warrant. To put this point more concretely, failure to recognize that photographing or taking notes of private information, without seizing the medium on which the information exists, constitutes a seizure under the Fourth Amendment would allow the government to ignore a narrowly circumscribed warrant in searching a premises containing volumes of documents by simply photographing the documents without removing them, and then reviewing the documents at length back at the station house.

Of course, the agents are not required to erase from their memories what they saw in the documents, and if they subsequently obtain information that, coupled with what they saw, gives them probable cause to seize the documents, they may then seek a warrant to seize the documents.

These principles, applied here, compel the conclusion that (i) taking high-resolution photographs of documents and (ii) taking notes of the contents of documents each constitute both a search and a seizure of the information contained in those documents for Fourth Amendment purposes.

NOTES AND QUESTIONS

1. *The contrary view.* Contrast the reasoning of *Jefferson* with that of United States v. Gorshkov, 2001 WL 1024026 (W.D. Wash. 2001). In *Gorshkov*, an FBI agent knew the online username and password used by a Russian hacker. The agent went online and made a copy of the files in the hacker's account to show that the account contained hacker tools. Before looking through the copied files, the agent obtained a warrant. When charges were filed, the hacker moved to suppress the contents of the account on the ground that copying the account before obtaining a warrant was a Fourth Amendment seizure. The district court disagreed:

> The agents' act of copying the data on the Russian computers was not a seizure under the Fourth Amendment because it did not interfere with Defendant's or anyone else's possessory interest in the data. The data remained intact and unaltered. It remained accessible to Defendant and any co-conspirators or partners with whom he had shared access. The copying of the data had absolutely no impact on his possessory rights. Defendant argues that the Government seized the data on the Russian computers because the *tar* command [used to copy the files] blocks other users from accessing the data. After hearing the testimony on this subject, the Court is convinced that no authorized user is prevented from accessing the files that are being [copied]. Therefore it was not a seizure under the Fourth Amendment. *See* Arizona v. Hicks, 480 U.S. 321, 324 (1987) (recording of serial number on suspected stolen property was not seizure because it did not "meaningfully interfere" with respondent's possessory interest in either the serial number or the equipment);

Bills v. Aseltine, 958 F.2d 697, 707 (6th Cir. 1992) (officer's photographic recording of visual images of scene was not seizure because it did not "meaningfully interfere" with any possessory interest).

A second case that takes the same view as *Gorshkov* is In re Application of the United States for a Search Warrant for the Contents of Electronic Mail, 665 F. Supp.2d 1210 (D. Or. 2009). In that case, the district court considered whether the Fourth Amendment or the Federal Rules of Criminal Procedure require that the government notify an account holder when the government obtains a copy of a suspect's e-mails from his Internet service provider. The federal statute governing search warrants, Federal Rule of Criminal Procedure 41, states that notice of the warrant must be given to the person from whose premises the property at issue was "seized."

The district court concluded that neither the Fourth Amendment nor Rule 41 requires notice to a suspect when the government obtains a warrant to obtain copies of a suspect's e-mails. Among the reasons for this holding was the court's conclusion that "no property is actually taken or seized as that term is used in the Fourth Amendment" when the government obtains a suspect's e-mail:

> The Supreme Court has stated that a 'seizure' of property occurs when there is some meaningful interference with an individual's possessory interests in that property. Here, there was no such meaningful interference due to the nature of electronic information, which can be accessed from multiple locations, by multiple people, simultaneously. More specifically for the purposes of Rule 41, if no property was taken, there is no person from whom, or from whose premises, the property was taken. Thus, under the plain language of Rule 41 there would not appear to be any requirement that a warrant be left with or a receipt be provided to anyone.

Id. at 1222.

Which is more persuasive: *Gorshkov*'s view that copying does not constitute a seizure or *Jefferson*'s view that it does?

2.   *Elephants all the way down.* If making a digital copy of data constitutes a seizure, does copying the copy also constitute a seizure? If the police make ten copies of a lawfully obtained file, has the file been seized ten times? Once? Never?

3.   *United States v. Ganias.* The Second Circuit considered the meaning of "seizures" in the context of digital copying in United States v. Ganias, 755 F.3d 125 (2d Cir. 2014), which was later vacated by the court when the decision was reheard en banc. In *Ganias*, the government executed a search warrant for digital evidence by making electronic copies of all of the defendant's files on his computer hard drives without physically removing any of the hard drives from the defendant's home. The government then held the copies in law

enforcement custody, including the files that were not responsive to the warrant, for over two years.

The Second Circuit ruled that copying the files and retaining the copies was a continuing Fourth Amendment seizure. "The Government's retention of copies of Ganias's personal computer records for two-and-a-half years deprived him of exclusive control over those files," the court noted. "This was a meaningful interference with Ganias's possessory rights in those files and constituted a seizure within the meaning of the Fourth Amendment." *Id.* at 137. The Second Circuit later vacated the panel decision, however, and the en banc decision of the Court did not resolve that question on rehearing. *See* United States v. Ganias, 824 F.3d 199 (2d Cir. 2016) (en banc).

4. *A proposed test.* Consider the argument that "copying data 'seizes' it under the Fourth Amendment when copying occurs without human observation and interrupts the course of the data's possession or transmission." Orin S. Kerr, *Fourth Amendment Seizures of Computer Data*, 119 Yale L.J. 700, 703 (2010):

> Generating an electronic copy of data freezes that data for future use just like taking physical property freezes it. From the standpoint of regulating the government's power to collect and use evidence, generating an electronic copy is no different from controlling access to a house or making an arrest: it ensures that the government has control over the person, place, or thing that it suspects has evidentiary value.

> Granted, an important difference separates physical seizures from electronic seizures. When the government conducts a physical seizure, it interferes with the owner's right to control the item seized. If the government seizes a person's car, the person cannot drive it; if the government arrests a person, he cannot walk away. Only one person can control the physical item at a time, and freezing by the government means that the suspect loses control. That is not true with data, of course. Data is nonrivalrous, so the government can create a copy of the data in a way that does not take away the suspect's possession of his own copy. As a result, computer data severs the connection between the information and the storage device. The question is, should the law focus on when a person loses exclusive rights to the device, or when a person loses exclusive rights to the data?

> The law should focus on when the person loses exclusive rights to the data. The reason is that computer environments are data environments. In a world of data, whether an individual has access to a particular copy of her data has much less significance than whether the government has obtained a copy of the data for possible government use in the future. In an environment of data, data is simply more important than hardware. Hardware is increasingly fungible. Hard drives crash. Thumb drives get lost. Networks go

down. To most users, what matters is the data. Users often generate multiple copies of their most valuable data to ensure that their data is protected from destruction no matter what happens to the hardware that happens to store it. Given the importance of data, and the frequent existence of multiple copies of it, there is little difference between (a) taking a physical device that contains data and (b) copying the data without taking the device.

Id. at 711–12. The author then imposes two limitations on this conclusion. First, the rule that copying counts as a seizure should apply only to copying without human observation. As a result, writing down information or taking a photograph should not be a seizure while making an electronic copy should be a seizure:

Electronic copying of computer files is different in a critical way from writing down information or taking a photograph. Writing down information or taking a photograph merely preserves the human observation in a fixed form. In contrast, electronic copying adds to the information in the government's possession by copying that which the government has not observed. The two types of copying should be treated differently; the former should not be treated as a seizure while the latter should.

Id. at 714. Second, "copying data in the ordinary course of use will not constitute a seizure. A seizure of moving or movable property occurs only when government action alters the path or timing of its intended possession or transmission." *Id.* at 721.

C. EXCEPTIONS TO THE WARRANT REQUIREMENT

If government action is a Fourth Amendment search or seizure, its legality hinges on whether the search or seizure is constitutionally "reasonable." Searches and seizures are reasonable if authorized by a valid warrant or an exception to the warrant requirement applies.

The following materials consider the most important exceptions to the warrant requirement. The materials consider five exceptions in the following order:

(1) Search incident to arrest

(2) Exigent circumstances

(3) Consent

(4) Border searches

(5) Government workplace computers

The materials begin with Riley v. California, 134 S.Ct. 2473 (2014), a Supreme Court decision that suggests a new path for how the Fourth Amendment applies to computer searches.

1. SEARCH INCIDENT TO ARREST

RILEY V. CALIFORNIA
Supreme Court of the United States, 2014.
573 U.S. 373.

CHIEF JUSTICE ROBERTS delivered the opinion of the Court.

These two cases raise a common question: whether the police may, without a warrant, search digital information on a cell phone seized from an individual who has been arrested.

I

A

In the first case, petitioner David Riley was stopped by a police officer for driving with expired registration tags. In the course of the stop, the officer also learned that Riley's license had been suspended. The officer impounded Riley's car, pursuant to department policy, and another officer conducted an inventory search of the car. Riley was arrested for possession of concealed and loaded firearms when that search turned up two handguns under the car's hood.

An officer searched Riley incident to the arrest and found items associated with the "Bloods" street gang. He also seized a cell phone from Riley's pants pocket. According to Riley's uncontradicted assertion, the phone was a "smart phone," a cell phone with a broad range of other functions based on advanced computing capability, large storage capacity, and Internet connectivity. The officer accessed information on the phone and noticed that some words (presumably in text messages or a contacts list) were preceded by the letters "CK"—a label that, he believed, stood for "Crip Killers," a slang term for members of the Bloods gang.

At the police station about two hours after the arrest, a detective specializing in gangs further examined the contents of the phone. The detective testified that he went through Riley's phone looking for evidence, "because gang members will often video themselves with guns or take pictures of themselves with the guns." Although there was "a lot of stuff" on the phone, particular files that caught the detective's eye included videos of young men sparring while someone yelled encouragement using the moniker "Blood." The police also found photographs of Riley standing in front of a car they suspected had been involved in a shooting a few weeks earlier.

Riley was ultimately charged, in connection with that earlier shooting, with firing at an occupied vehicle, assault with a semiautomatic firearm, and attempted murder. The State alleged that Riley had committed those crimes for the benefit of a criminal street gang, an aggravating factor that carries an enhanced sentence. Prior to trial, Riley moved to suppress all evidence that the police had obtained from his cell phone. He contended that the searches of his phone violated the Fourth Amendment, because they had been performed without a warrant and were not otherwise justified by exigent circumstances. The trial court rejected that argument. At Riley's trial, police officers testified about the photographs and videos found on the phone, and some of the photographs were admitted into evidence. Riley was convicted on all three counts and received an enhanced sentence of 15 years to life in prison.

B

In the second case, a police officer performing routine surveillance observed respondent Brima Wurie make an apparent drug sale from a car. Officers subsequently arrested Wurie and took him to the police station. At the station, the officers seized two cell phones from Wurie's person. The one at issue here was a "flip phone," a kind of phone that is flipped open for use and that generally has a smaller range of features than a smart phone. Five to ten minutes after arriving at the station, the officers noticed that the phone was repeatedly receiving calls from a source identified as "my house" on the phone's external screen. A few minutes later, they opened the phone and saw a photograph of a woman and a baby set as the phone's wallpaper. They pressed one button on the phone to access its call log, then another button to determine the phone number associated with the "my house" label. They next used an online phone directory to trace that phone number to an apartment building.

When the officers went to the building, they saw Wurie's name on a mailbox and observed through a window a woman who resembled the woman in the photograph on Wurie's phone. They secured the apartment while obtaining a search warrant and, upon later executing the warrant, found and seized 215 grams of crack cocaine, marijuana, drug paraphernalia, a firearm and ammunition, and cash.

Wurie was charged with distributing crack cocaine, possessing crack cocaine with intent to distribute, and being a felon in possession of a firearm and ammunition. He moved to suppress the evidence obtained from the search of the apartment, arguing that it was the fruit of an unconstitutional search of his cell phone.

II

The two cases before us concern the reasonableness of a warrantless search incident to a lawful arrest. In 1914, this Court first acknowledged in dictum "the right on the part of the Government, always recognized under English and American law, to search the person of the accused when legally arrested to discover and seize the fruits or evidences of crime." *Weeks v. United States,* 232 U.S. 383, 392 (1914). Since that time, it has been well accepted that such a search constitutes an exception to the warrant requirement. Indeed, the label "exception" is something of a misnomer in this context, as warrantless searches incident to arrest occur with far greater frequency than searches conducted pursuant to a warrant.

Although the existence of the exception for such searches has been recognized for a century, its scope has been debated for nearly as long. That debate has focused on the extent to which officers may search property found on or near the arrestee. Three related precedents set forth the rules governing such searches:

The first, *Chimel v. California,* 395 U.S. 752 (1969), laid the groundwork for most of the existing search incident to arrest doctrine. Police officers in that case arrested Chimel inside his home and proceeded to search his entire three-bedroom house, including the attic and garage. In particular rooms, they also looked through the contents of drawers.

The Court crafted the following rule for assessing the reasonableness of a search incident to arrest:

> When an arrest is made, it is reasonable for the arresting officer to search the person arrested in order to remove any weapons that the latter might seek to use in order to resist arrest or effect his escape. Otherwise, the officer's safety might well be endangered, and the arrest itself frustrated. In addition, it is entirely reasonable for the arresting officer to search for and seize any evidence on the arrestee's person in order to prevent its concealment or destruction. There is ample justification, therefore, for a search of the arrestee's person and the area 'within his immediate control'—construing that phrase to mean the area from within which he might gain possession of a weapon or destructible evidence.

The extensive warrantless search of Chimel's home did not fit within this exception, because it was not needed to protect officer safety or to preserve evidence.

Four years later, in *United States v. Robinson,* 414 U.S. 218 (1973), the Court applied the *Chimel* analysis in the context of a search of the arrestee's person. A police officer had arrested Robinson for driving with a revoked license. The officer conducted a patdown search and felt an object that he could not identify in Robinson's coat pocket. He removed the object, which turned out to be a crumpled cigarette package, and opened it. Inside were 14 capsules of heroin.

The Court of Appeals concluded that the search was unreasonable because Robinson was unlikely to have evidence of the crime of arrest on his person, and because it believed that extracting the cigarette package and opening it could not be justified as part of a protective search for weapons. This Court reversed, rejecting the notion that "case-by-case adjudication" was required to determine "whether or not there was present one of the reasons supporting the authority for a search of the person incident to a lawful arrest." *Id.* at 235. As the Court explained,

> the authority to search the person incident to a lawful custodial arrest, while based upon the need to disarm and to discover evidence, does not depend on what a court may later decide was the probability in a particular arrest situation that weapons or evidence would in fact be found upon the person of the suspect. Instead, a custodial arrest of a suspect based on probable cause is a reasonable intrusion under the Fourth Amendment; that intrusion being lawful, a search incident to the arrest requires no additional justification.

The Court thus concluded that the search of Robinson was reasonable even though there was no concern about the loss of evidence, and the arresting officer had no specific concern that Robinson might be armed. In doing so, the Court did not draw a line between a search of Robinson's person and a further examination of the cigarette pack found during that search. It merely noted that, "having in the course of a lawful search come upon the crumpled package of cigarettes, the officer was entitled to inspect it." A few years later, the Court clarified that this exception was limited to "personal property immediately associated with the person of the arrestee." *United States v. Chadwick,* 433 U.S. 1, 15 (1977) (200-pound, locked footlocker could not be searched incident to arrest), abrogated on other grounds by *California v. Acevedo,* 500 U.S. 565 (1991).

The search incident to arrest trilogy concludes with *Arizona v. Gant,* 556 U.S. 332 (2009), which analyzed searches of an arrestee's vehicle. *Gant,* like *Robinson,* recognized that the *Chimel* concerns for officer safety and evidence preservation underlie the search incident to arrest exception. As a result, the Court concluded that *Chimel* could authorize police to search a vehicle "only when the arrestee is unsecured and within reaching distance of the passenger compartment at the time of the search." *Gant* added, however, an independent exception for a warrantless search of a vehicle's passenger compartment "when it is 'reasonable to believe evidence relevant to the crime of arrest might be found in the vehicle.'" That exception stems not from *Chimel,* the Court explained, but from "circumstances unique to the vehicle context."

III

These cases require us to decide how the search incident to arrest doctrine applies to modern cell phones, which are now such a pervasive and insistent part of daily life that the proverbial visitor from Mars might conclude they were an important feature of human anatomy. A smart phone of the sort taken from Riley was unheard of ten years ago; a significant majority of American adults now own such phones. Even less sophisticated phones like Wurie's, which have already faded in popularity since Wurie was arrested in 2007, have been around for less than 15 years. Both phones are based on technology nearly inconceivable just a few decades ago, when *Chimel* and *Robinson* were decided.

Absent more precise guidance from the founding era, we generally determine whether to exempt a given type of search from the warrant requirement by assessing, on the one hand, the degree to which it intrudes upon an individual's privacy and, on the other, the degree to which it is needed for the promotion of legitimate governmental interests. Such a balancing of interests supported the search incident to arrest exception in *Robinson,* and a mechanical application of *Robinson* might well support the warrantless searches at issue here.

But while *Robinson*'s categorical rule strikes the appropriate balance in the context of physical objects, neither of its rationales has much force with respect to digital content on cell phones. On the government interest side, *Robinson* concluded that the two risks identified in *Chimel*—harm to officers and destruction of evidence—are present in all custodial arrests. There are no comparable risks when the search is of digital data. In addition, *Robinson* regarded any privacy interests retained by an individual after arrest as significantly diminished by the fact of the arrest itself. Cell phones, however, place vast quantities of personal information literally in the hands of individuals. A search of the information on a cell phone bears little resemblance to the type of brief physical search considered in *Robinson*.

We therefore decline to extend *Robinson* to searches of data on cell phones, and hold instead that officers must generally secure a warrant before conducting such a search.

A

We first consider each *Chimel* concern in turn. In doing so, we do not overlook *Robinson*'s admonition that searches of a person incident to arrest, "while based upon the need to disarm and to discover evidence," are reasonable regardless of "the probability in a particular arrest situation that weapons or evidence would in fact be found." Rather than requiring the "case-by-case adjudication" that *Robinson* rejected, we ask instead whether application of the search incident to arrest doctrine to this particular category of effects would untether the rule from the justifications underlying the *Chimel* exception.

1

Digital data stored on a cell phone cannot itself be used as a weapon to harm an arresting officer or to effectuate the arrestee's escape. Law enforcement officers remain free to examine the physical aspects of a phone to ensure that it will not be used as a weapon—say, to determine whether there is a razor blade hidden between the phone and its case. Once an officer has secured a phone and eliminated any potential physical threats, however, data on the phone can endanger no one.

Perhaps the same might have been said of the cigarette pack seized from Robinson's pocket. Once an officer gained control of the pack, it was unlikely that Robinson could have accessed the pack's contents. But unknown physical objects may always pose risks, no matter how slight, during the tense atmosphere of a custodial arrest. The officer in *Robinson* testified that he could not identify the objects in the cigarette pack but knew they were not cigarettes. Given that, a further search was a reasonable protective measure. No such unknowns exist with respect to digital data. As the First Circuit explained, the officers who searched Wurie's cell phone knew exactly what they would find therein: data. They also knew that the data could not harm them.

The United States and California both suggest that a search of cell phone data might help ensure officer safety in more indirect ways, for example by alerting officers that confederates of the arrestee are headed to the scene. There is undoubtedly a strong government interest in warning officers about such possibilities, but neither the United States nor California offers evidence to suggest that their concerns are based on actual experience. The proposed consideration would also represent a broadening of *Chimel*'s concern that an *arrestee himself* might grab a weapon and use it against an officer "to resist arrest or effect his escape." And any such threats from outside the arrest scene do not "lurk in all custodial arrests." *Chadwick*, 433 U.S., at 14–15. Accordingly, the interest in protecting officer safety does not justify dispensing with the warrant requirement across the board. To the extent dangers to arresting officers may be implicated in a particular way in a particular case, they are better addressed through consideration of case-specific exceptions to the warrant requirement, such as the one for exigent circumstances.

2

The United States and California focus primarily on the second *Chimel* rationale: preventing the destruction of evidence.

Both Riley and Wurie concede that officers could have seized and secured their cell phones to prevent destruction of evidence while seeking a warrant. And once law enforcement officers have secured a cell phone, there is no longer any risk that the arrestee himself will be able to delete incriminating data from the phone.

The United States and California argue that information on a cell phone may nevertheless be vulnerable to two types of evidence destruction unique to digital data—remote wiping and data encryption. Remote wiping occurs when a phone, connected to a wireless network, receives a signal that erases stored data. This can happen when a third party sends a remote signal or when a phone is preprogrammed to delete data upon entering or leaving certain geographic areas (so-called "geofencing"). See Dept. of Commerce, National Institute of Standards and Technology, R. Ayers, S. Brothers, & W. Jansen, Guidelines on Mobile Device Forensics (Draft) 29, 31 (SP 800–101 Rev. 1, Sept. 2013). Encryption is a security feature that some modern cell phones use in addition to password protection. When such phones lock, data becomes protected by sophisticated encryption that renders a phone all but "unbreakable" unless police know the password.

As an initial matter, these broader concerns about the loss of evidence are distinct from *Chimel*'s focus on a defendant who responds to arrest by trying to conceal or destroy evidence within his reach. With respect to remote wiping, the Government's primary concern turns on the actions of third parties who are not present at the scene of arrest. And data encryption is even further afield. There, the Government focuses on the ordinary operation of a phone's security features, apart from *any* active attempt by a defendant or his associates to conceal or destroy evidence upon arrest.

We have also been given little reason to believe that either problem is prevalent. The briefing reveals only a couple of anecdotal examples of remote wiping triggered by an arrest. Similarly, the opportunities for officers to search a password-protected phone before data becomes encrypted are quite limited. Law enforcement officers are very unlikely to come upon such a phone in an unlocked state because most phones lock at the touch of a button or, as a default, after some very short period of inactivity. See, *e.g.,* iPhone User Guide for iOS 7.1 Software 10 (2014) (default lock after about one minute). This may explain why the encryption argument was not made until the merits stage in this Court, and has never been considered by the Courts of Appeals.

Moreover, in situations in which an arrest might trigger a remote-wipe attempt or an officer discovers an unlocked phone, it is not clear that the ability to conduct a warrantless search would make much of a difference. The need to effect the arrest, secure the scene, and tend to other pressing matters means that law enforcement officers may well not be able to turn their attention to a cell phone right away. Cell phone data would be vulnerable to remote wiping from the time an individual anticipates arrest to the time any eventual search of the phone is completed, which might be at the station house hours later. Likewise, an officer who seizes a phone in an unlocked state might not be able to begin his search in the short time remaining before the phone locks and data becomes encrypted.

In any event, as to remote wiping, law enforcement is not without specific means to address the threat. Remote wiping can be fully prevented by disconnecting a phone from the network. There are at least two simple ways to do this: First, law enforcement officers can turn the phone off or remove its battery. Second, if they are concerned about encryption or other potential problems, they can leave a phone powered on and place it in an enclosure that isolates the phone from radio waves. Such devices are commonly called "Faraday bags," after the English scientist Michael Faraday. They are essentially sandwich bags made of aluminum foil: cheap, lightweight, and easy to use. They may not be a complete answer to the problem, but at least for now they provide a reasonable response. In fact, a number of law enforcement agencies around the country already encourage the use of Faraday bags. See, *e.g.*, Dept. of Justice, National Institute of Justice, Electronic Crime Scene Investigation: A Guide for First Responders 14, 32 (2d ed. Apr. 2008).

To the extent that law enforcement still has specific concerns about the potential loss of evidence in a particular case, there remain more targeted ways to address those concerns. If the police are truly confronted with a 'now or never' situation—for example, circumstances suggesting that a defendant's phone will be the target of an imminent remote-wipe attempt—they may be able to rely on exigent circumstances to search the phone immediately. Or, if officers happen to seize a phone in an unlocked state, they may be able to disable a phone's automatic-lock feature in order to prevent the phone from locking and encrypting data.

B

The search incident to arrest exception rests not only on the heightened government interests at stake in a volatile arrest situation, but also on an arrestee's reduced privacy interests upon being taken into police custody. Put simply, a patdown of Robinson's clothing and an inspection of the cigarette pack found in his pocket constituted only minor additional intrusions compared to the substantial government authority exercised in taking Robinson into custody.

The United States asserts that a search of all data stored on a cell phone is "materially indistinguishable" from searches of physical items. That is like saying a ride on horseback is materially indistinguishable from a flight to the moon. Both are ways of getting from point A to point B, but little else justifies lumping them together. Modern cell phones, as a category, implicate privacy concerns far beyond those implicated by the search of a cigarette pack, a wallet, or a purse. A conclusion that inspecting the contents of an arrestee's pockets works no substantial additional intrusion on privacy beyond the arrest itself may make sense as applied to physical items, but any extension of that reasoning to digital data has to rest on its own bottom.

Cell phones differ in both a quantitative and a qualitative sense from other objects that might be kept on an arrestee's person. The term "cell phone" is itself misleading shorthand; many of these devices are in fact minicomputers that also happen to have the capacity to be used as a telephone. They could just as easily be called cameras, video players, rolodexes, calendars, tape recorders, libraries, diaries, albums, televisions, maps, or newspapers.

One of the most notable distinguishing features of modern cell phones is their immense storage capacity. Before cell phones, a search of a person was limited by physical realities and tended as a general matter to constitute only a narrow intrusion on privacy. Most people cannot lug around every piece of mail they have received for the past several months, every picture they have taken, or every book or article they have read—nor would they have any reason to attempt to do so. And if they did, they would have to drag behind them a trunk of the sort held to require a search warrant in *Chadwick, supra,* rather than a container the size of the cigarette package in *Robinson.*

But the possible intrusion on privacy is not physically limited in the same way when it comes to cell phones. The current top-selling smart phone has a standard capacity of 16 gigabytes (and is available with up to 64 gigabytes). Sixteen gigabytes translates to millions of pages of text, thousands of pictures, or hundreds of videos. Cell phones couple that capacity with the ability to store many different types of information: Even the most basic phones that sell for less than $20 might hold photographs, picture messages, text messages, Internet browsing history, a calendar, a thousand-entry phone book, and so on. We expect that the gulf between physical practicability and digital capacity will only continue to widen in the future.

The storage capacity of cell phones has several interrelated consequences for privacy. First, a cell phone collects in one place many distinct types of information—an address, a note, a prescription, a bank statement, a video—that reveal much more in combination than any isolated record. Second, a cell phone's capacity allows even just one type of information to convey far more than previously possible. The sum of an individual's private life can be reconstructed through a thousand photographs labeled with dates, locations, and descriptions; the same cannot be said of a photograph or two of loved ones tucked into a wallet. Third, the data on a phone can date back to the purchase of the phone, or even earlier. A person might carry in his pocket a slip of paper reminding him to call Mr. Jones; he would not carry a record of all his communications with Mr. Jones for the past several months, as would routinely be kept on a phone.

Finally, there is an element of pervasiveness that characterizes cell phones but not physical records. Prior to the digital age, people did not typically carry a cache of sensitive personal information with them as they went about their day. Now it is the person who is not carrying a cell phone, with all that it contains, who is the exception. According to one poll, nearly three-quarters of smart phone users report being within five feet of their phones most of the time, with 12% admitting that they even use their phones in the shower. See Harris Interactive, 2013 Mobile Consumer Habits Study (June 2013). A decade ago police officers searching an arrestee might have occasionally stumbled across a highly personal item such as a diary. But those discoveries were likely to be few and far between. Today, by contrast, it is no exaggeration to say that many of the more than 90% of American adults who own a cell phone keep on their person a digital record of nearly every aspect of their lives—from the mundane to the intimate. Allowing the police to scrutinize such records on a routine basis is quite different from allowing them to search a personal item or two in the occasional case.

Although the data stored on a cell phone is distinguished from physical records by quantity alone, certain types of data are also qualitatively different. An Internet search and browsing history, for example, can be found on an Internet-enabled phone and could reveal an individual's private interests or concerns—perhaps a search for certain symptoms of disease, coupled with frequent visits to WebMD. Data on a cell phone can also reveal where a person has been. Historic location information is a standard feature on many smart phones and can reconstruct someone's specific movements down to the minute, not only around town but also within a particular building.

Mobile application software on a cell phone, or "apps," offer a range of tools for managing detailed information about all aspects of a person's life. There are apps for Democratic Party news and Republican Party news; apps for alcohol, drug, and gambling addictions; apps for sharing prayer requests; apps for tracking pregnancy symptoms; apps for planning your budget; apps for every conceivable hobby or pastime; apps for improving your romantic life. There are popular apps for buying or selling just about anything, and the records of such transactions may be accessible on the phone indefinitely. There are over a million apps available in each of the two major app stores; the phrase "there's an app for that" is now part of the popular lexicon. The average smart phone user has installed 33 apps, which together can form a revealing montage of the user's life. See Brief for Electronic Privacy Information Center as *Amicus Curiae* in No. 13–132, p. 9.

In 1926, Learned Hand observed (in an opinion later quoted in *Chimel*) that it is "a totally different thing to search a man's pockets and use against him what they contain, from ransacking his house for everything which may incriminate him." *United States v. Kirschenblatt*, 16 F.2d 202, 203 (C.A.2). If his pockets contain a cell phone, however, that is no longer true. Indeed, a cell phone search would typically expose to the government far *more* than the most exhaustive search of a house: A phone not only contains in digital form many sensitive records previously found in the home; it also contains a broad array of private information never found in a home in any form—unless the phone is.

IV

We cannot deny that our decision today will have an impact on the ability of law enforcement to combat crime. Cell phones have become important tools in facilitating coordination and communication among members of criminal enterprises, and can provide valuable incriminating information about dangerous criminals. Privacy comes at a cost.

Our holding, of course, is not that the information on a cell phone is immune from search; it is instead that a warrant is generally required before such a search, even when a cell phone is seized incident to arrest.

Moreover, even though the search incident to arrest exception does not apply to cell phones, other case-specific exceptions may still justify a warrantless search of a particular phone.

In light of the availability of the exigent circumstances exception, there is no reason to believe that law enforcement officers will not be able to address some of the more extreme hypotheticals that have been suggested: a suspect texting an accomplice who, it is feared, is preparing to detonate a bomb, or a child abductor who may have information about the child's location on his cell phone. The defendants here recognize—indeed, they stress—that such fact-specific threats may justify a warrantless search of cell phone data. The critical point is that, unlike the search incident to arrest exception, the exigent circumstances exception requires a court to examine whether an emergency justified a warrantless search in each particular case.

Modern cell phones are not just another technological convenience. With all they contain and all they may reveal, they hold for many Americans the privacies of life. The fact that technology now allows an individual to carry such information in his hand does not make the information any less worthy of the protection for which the Founders fought. Our answer to the question of what police must do before searching a cell phone seized incident to an arrest is accordingly simple—get a warrant.

NOTES AND QUESTIONS

1.   *The life of Riley.* Although *Riley* speaks of cell phones, its reasoning presumably applies to all digital storage devices. If a suspect has a thumb drive on his key chain, for example, *Riley* would block a warrantless search incident to arrest of the thumb drive. Under *Riley*, then, the search-incident-to-arrest exception applies to physical storage devices but not electronic storage devices.

2.   *Digital is different, but how different?* The reasoning of *Riley* seems to be that digital searches are different. New facts may require new rules. But how different are digital searches? Does *Riley* give lower courts free license to devise new Fourth Amendment rules involving digital evidence? Or should "*Riley* moments" be limited to occasional cases in which digital technologies have dramatically changed the implications of preexisting rules?

3.   *Search of a phone's SIM card.* A cell phone generally requires a SIM card to operate. SIM stands for Subscriber Identity Module. A SIM card is a memory chip that contains the phone's number, the service provider's information, and some records of data usage. You might have encountered your phone's SIM card when you upgraded your phone: You probably removed your SIM card from your old phone and inserted it in the new phone to continue your new service with your old number.

If the government wants to remove a SIM card and search it incident to arrest, does *Riley* require a warrant? In State v. Moore, 839 S.E.2d 882 (S.C.2020), the Supreme Court of South Carolina held that *Riley* does not apply to searching SIM cards from flip phones to obtain their numbers: "We conclude searching a SIM card is fundamentally distinct from searching the full contents of an unlocked cell phone, making much of the language in *Riley* concerning the privacy implications for searching a cell phone inapplicable or, at best, greatly diminished here." *Id.* at 475.

4.   *Searching phones found in cars.* Under the so-called "automobile exception" to the warrant requirement, the police do not need a warrant to search an automobile. Probable cause is required to search the car, but no warrant is needed. Now imagine how the Fourth Amendment applies when the police search a car with probable cause (but no warrant) and they come across a cell phone. Can agents search the phone without a warrant under the automobile exception, or is a warrant needed under Riley?

In United States v. Camou, 773 F.3d 932 (9th Cir. 2014) (Pregerson, J.), the Ninth Circuit held that a warrant was required to search a cell phone found in a car. Put another way, the automobile exception does not permit computer searches:

> Given [*Riley*'s] extensive analysis of cell phones as "containers" and cell phone searches in the vehicle context, we find no reason not to extend the reasoning in *Riley* from the search incident to arrest exception to the vehicle exception. Just as cell phones differ in both a quantitative and a qualitative sense from other objects that might be kept on an arrestee's person, so too do cell phones differ from any

other object officers might find in a vehicle. Today's cell phones are unlike any of the container examples the Supreme Court has provided in the vehicle context.

We further note that the privacy intrusion of searching a cell phone without a warrant is of particular concern in the vehicle exception context because the allowable scope of the search is broader than that of an exigency search, or a search incident to arrest. Whereas exigency searches are circumscribed by the specific exigency at hand and searches incident to arrest are limited to areas within the arrestee's immediate control or to evidence relevant to the crime of arrest, vehicle exception searches allow for evidence relevant to criminal activity broadly. If cell phones are considered containers for purposes of the vehicle exception, officers would often be able to sift through all of the data on cell phones found in vehicles because they would not be restrained by any limitations of exigency or relevance to a specific crime.

We therefore conclude that cell phones are *non*-containers for purposes of the vehicle exception to the warrant requirement, and the search of Camou's cell phone cannot be justified under that exception.

Id. at 942–43.

2. EXIGENT CIRCUMSTANCES

The exigent circumstances exception permits the government to conduct warrantless searches or seizures when immediately necessary to protect public safety or preserve evidence. *See, e.g.,* Mincey v. Arizona, 437 U.S. 385 (1978). This long-established exception applies when circumstances "would cause a reasonable person to believe" that a search or seizure "was necessary to prevent physical harm to the officers or other persons, the destruction of relevant evidence, the escape of the suspect, or some other consequence improperly frustrating legitimate law enforcement efforts." United States v. McConney, 728 F.2d 1195, 1199 (9th Cir. 1984) (en banc).

The Supreme Court has never articulated a clear test for exigent circumstances. Some lower courts have required the agents to show probable cause that the item seized is or contains evidence or contraband. *See, e.g.,* United States v. Cisneros-Gutierrez, 598 F.3d 997, 1004 (8th Cir. 2010). Beyond requiring probable cause, lower courts generally have applied a general balancing of interests to determine when and how broadly the exigent circumstances exception applies. As a general matter, interests to be balanced include the degree of urgency involved, whether a warrant could have been obtained, the seriousness of the crime investigated, the possibility of danger, the likelihood evidence may be destroyed, and the availability of alternative means of obtaining or securing evidence or protecting public safety. Further, an exigent circumstances search must be "strictly circumscribed by the exigencies which justify its initiation." Terry v. Ohio, 392 U.S. 1, 25–36 (1968).

UNITED STATES V. TROWBRIDGE

United States District Court for the Northern District of Texas, 2007.
2007 WL 4226385.

JANE J. BOYLE, DISTRICT JUDGE.

On January 24, 2007, FBI Special Agents Lynd and Sabol attempted to conduct a "knock and talk" at Jason Trowbridge's Houston, Texas home to obtain information about Guadalupe Martinez, a suspect who had recently been arrested. The agents were also investigating a conspiracy involving Martinez, Trowbridge, Chad Ward, and Stuart Rosoff in which these individuals allegedly exceeded authorized computer access to a commercial database to obtain personal identification information on individuals on telephone partylines, so that the conspirators could harass them by making threatening phone calls, disrupting telephone service and making false 911 calls to elicit response by police, fire and ambulance to residences. In the world of cyber-crime, this activity is known as "swatting."

Agent Lynd testified that there was some urgency to their "knock and talk" with Trowbridge because Martinez had been arrested in the presence of another party line member who told others about his arrest. After traveling to two locations, the agents discovered that they had incorrect information about where Trowbridge lived. At around noon, the agents proceeded to Ward's home and interviewed him. Ward confirmed Trowbridge's address and stated that Trowbridge had a girlfriend who lived with him, that Trowbridge had instructed him to destroy evidence on one occasion, that Trowbridge had seven computers in his home, and that Trowbridge was anti-government and could take care of himself if law enforcement arrived. He also told the agents that Trowbridge had access to a commercial database in his business but did not state whether this database was used at Trowbridge's residence.

The agents proceeded to Trowbridge's town home at about 3:00pm to perform their "knock and talk." At this time, they believed that they did not have probable cause to search Trowbridge's residence. The agents observed a car that they believed to be associated with Trowbridge and saw a business card with his name on it inside the car. When the agents knocked on Trowbridge's door, identified themselves, and called out Trowbridge's name, the music inside the home stopped playing. Agent Sabol noticed a cell phone on the balcony and went to the back of the building where he observed two individuals, who did not fit Trowbridge's description, exit the residence and jump over an eight to ten foot fence. When Sabol returned to the front of the home, the cell phone he had previously observed was no longer on the balcony causing him to believe that there might be someone inside the home.

Angela Roberson, Trowbridge's girlfriend who lived with him, eventually answered the door and told the agents that Trowbridge was not home. She agreed to talk to the agents about Martinez and allowed them to come inside. The agents remained on the first floor of the three-level town house during this interview. During the course of the interview, Roberson told the agents that she had exchanged instant messages with Martinez regarding his swatting activities on various computers in the home, that spoof cards had been purchased using computers in the home, and that Trowbridge had computer access to a commercial database at the home. The agents also smelled marijuana and observed drug paraphernalia.

Officer Lynd observed a wireless router that he explained would allow a person within a few hundred yards to access the computers and erase or change them. Officer Lynd testified that if he had access to the computers he could determine whether the allegedly criminal phone calls had been made using spoof cards purchased on Trowbridge's computers. During the interview, the officers noticed three computers downstairs, and Roberson said that there were three upstairs. At the agents' request, Roberson called Trowbridge's cell phone, and the agents heard the phone ring upstairs. Roberson hung up the phone stating that Trowbridge did not answer. At this point, the agents believed that Trowbridge was hiding upstairs but did not know how many people were upstairs, if there were any weapons, or if the individuals who had fled would be returning. Agent Lynd then called and spoke with Trowbridge who said he was not home and that Lynd could make an appointment to speak with him and his attorney. Agent Sabol testified that the design of the multiple level town house would allow someone from upstairs to approach the agents without being discovered.

At some point during the conversation with Roberson, the agents developed probable cause to search the computer hard drives because she identified the computers as being used to have conversations with Martinez and to purchase spoof cards. The agents then spoke with the U.S. Attorney's Offices in Dallas and Houston and determined that exigent circumstances existed to seize the computers. The U.S. Attorney's Office advised them that it would be difficult to get a search warrant in the late afternoon around 4:30 because of Houston traffic.

Agent Lynd testified that in his experience individuals involved in computer crimes had attempted to destroy computer evidence and that Martinez had given a computer away to prevent the agents from obtaining evidence. He also testified that computer evidence is more fragile than drug evidence. It can be destroyed by turning off the computer, smashing it with a hammer, using a magnet, or throwing it into a fire. He stated that software is available to destroy evidence on a computer and that a hard drive is easy to remove and hide. Lynd said that he was sure the evidence would be gone in a few minutes if the agents left.

Both agents testified that they did not believe it would be safe to leave one agent at the residence while the other secured a search warrant. Officer Lynd based this fear on the fact that Roberson and Trowbridge were concealing Trowbridge's presence upstairs, people had fled the residence, the residence smelled like marijuana, and they could not see what was occurring upstairs. Agent Sabol also knew Trowbridge had been affiliated with an anarchist group. Lynd testified that he was concerned that Ward had called Trowbridge to warn him that the agents were coming.

The agents asked Roberson for a copy of the computers and when she refused informed her that they would seize the computers to prevent the destruction of evidence. At this point Roberson for the first time asked the agents to leave. Trowbridge and Trowbridge's attorney also spoke with the agents on the phone. When Houston police department officers arrived to perform a safety sweep, Roberson told them that Trowbridge was upstairs. The police officers escorted him downstairs. Then additional agents arrived and seized the computers. Trowbridge's attorney also arrived. The agents checked the computers into the evidence control room in Houston, obtained a search warrant, shipped the computers to the Dallas evidence control room, and then delivered them to the North Texas forensic lab. The agents seized only the computers and did not search anything else in the home. They also left two inventories of what was taken from the home.

On June 19, 2007, a grand jury charged Trowbridge with "Conspiracy to Use Access Devices to Modify Telecommunications Instruments and to Access Protected Telecommunications Computers" [in violation of 18 U.S.C. § 371, 18 U.S.C. §§ 1029(a)(9), and 1030(a)(5)(A)(ii)]." Trowbridge moved to suppress all evidence obtained as a result of the January 24, 2007 search of his residence because the search violated his right to be free from unlawful searches and seizures under the Fourth Amendment.

A warrantless intrusion into an individual's home is presumptively unreasonable unless the person consents or probable cause and exigent circumstances justify the encroachment. The government bears the burden of proving that an exigency exists. Whether exigent circumstances exist is a question of fact, reversible only if the district court's factual findings are clearly erroneous. We look to the totality of the circumstances surrounding the officers' actions, mindful that our review is more akin to examining a video tape by instant replay than to examining a snapshot.

Exigent circumstances include: (1) reasonable fear for officer's safety; (2) presence of firearms; (3) risk of a criminal suspect escaping; or (4) fear of destruction of evidence. The Court will consider the following factors to determine whether an exigency exists: (1) the degree of urgency involved and amount of time necessary to obtain a warrant; (2) the reasonable belief that contraband is about to be removed; (3) the possibility of danger to the police officers guarding the site of contraband while a search warrant is sought; (4) information indicating that the possessors of the contraband are aware that the police are on their trail; and (5) the ready destructibility of the contraband and the knowledge that efforts to dispose of narcotics and to escape are characteristic behavior of persons engaged in the narcotics traffic.

Applying the first factor to the present case, the degree of urgency and the time required to obtain a warrant, the situation was urgent because the officers believed that Trowbridge was upstairs and could quickly destroy the evidence. Lynd testified that he was sure that the evidence would be gone in a few minutes. The agents also testified that they feared for their safety. With respect to the time it would take to obtain a warrant, the U.S. Attorney's Office told the agents that due to afternoon traffic, it would be difficult to obtain a search warrant that day. As for the second factor, the reasonable belief that contraband will be removed, the officers believed that Trowbridge was hiding upstairs and had access to the computers. They had also been told that Trowbridge had instructed Ward to destroy evidence in the past.

The next factor for the Court to consider is whether it would be dangerous for police officers to guard the site while a search warrant is sought. Both officers credibly testified that they did not believe it would be safe to leave one agent at the residence while the other secured a warrant. Agent Sabol testified about his concern regarding the layout of the town house. He stated that it would be easy for someone to approach the officers without being detected. The officers believed that Roberson and Trowbridge were deceiving them by concealing Trowbridge's presence in the home. Agent Sabol had seen two individuals fleeing the house and was unaware whether they might return or whether there were other individuals or weapons in the home. Ward also told the agents that Trowbridge was anti-government and could take care of himself if law enforcement arrived. The smell of marijuana and the knowledge that Trowbridge was allegedly affiliated with an anarchist group also alarmed the agents. These facts support a finding that it would have been dangerous for one of the officers to guard the residence.

Considering the fourth factor, an indication that the possessors are aware that the police are approaching, Lynd testified that Martinez had recently been arrested and news of this arrest may have been available to party line members. The agents had spoken with Ward, another suspect. They were concerned that he would call Trowbridge to warn him that they were coming. When Roberson called Trowbridge's cell phone, the officers heard the phone ring upstairs. This indicated to the officers that Trowbridge was upstairs and was aware of their presence. The presence of a car that they associated with Trowbridge and the disappearance of the cell phone from the balcony also indicated that Trowbridge might be in the home. In addition, the agents had spoken with Trowbridge on the phone, confirming that he knew of their presence.

Finally, the Court will consider the ready destructibility of the contraband and the knowledge that efforts to dispose of narcotics and to escape are characteristic behaviors of persons engaged in the narcotics traffic. Officer Lynd testified that computer evidence is easier to destroy than drug evidence. Trowbridge argued that even if electronic data may be easily destroyed, one may not assume that the suspect has the means, knowledge, or wherewithal to destroy it. However, the Court found that based on the agents' testimony, there was reason to believe that Trowbridge would destroy the evidence. Ward informed the officers that Trowbridge had instructed him to destroy evidence in the past; therefore, the destruction of computer evidence may be characteristic of his behavior. While this was not a narcotics case, Agent Lynd testified that individuals accused of computer crimes had attempted to destroy evidence in his experience and that Martinez had disposed of computer evidence. In conclusion, the Government has presented sufficient facts to support each factor.

This Court determines, based on the agents' credible testimony and the totality of the circumstances, that an exigency existed because of the likelihood that the computer evidence would be destroyed.

NOTES AND QUESTIONS

1.   *Exigent seizures versus exigent searches.* The issue in *Trowbridge* was whether the investigators could initially seize Trowbridge's computers, not whether the investigators could then search the computers. The latter issue was not raised because the police obtained a search warrant before they searched the computers that had been seized. If investigators had not obtained a warrant to search the computers, would exigent circumstances have allowed the investigators to search the computers that had been seized?

This question arose in United States v. David, 756 F. Supp. 1385 (D. Nev. 1991), parts of which appeared earlier in this chapter. At one point, the FBI agent investigating the case saw the defendant deleting files from his computer memo book. The FBI agent, Agent Peterson, quickly seized the computer from David to stop him from deleting evidence of his crimes. Peterson later searched the computer without a warrant. The court held that the seizure was justified but the search was not:

> When destruction of evidence is imminent, a warrantless seizure of that evidence is justified if there is probable cause to believe that the item seized constitutes evidence of criminal activity. Here, Agent Peterson saw David destroying evidence. David's use of the book in retrieving telephone numbers of criminal associates provided ample

probable cause that the book contained information relative to criminal activity. Peterson therefore reasonably believed that prompt action was necessary to prevent further destruction of relevant evidence.

Although Peterson had the authority to seize and hold the book due to the exigency at hand, his authority to examine its contents is a different matter. The seizure of the book affected only David's possessory interests. It did not affect the privacy interests vested in the contents of the book.

Once he took the book from David the exigency which justified the seizure came to an end. Nevertheless, without seeking a warrant, Peterson conducted a complete search of the book's contents. The seizure of the book did not justify the invasion of privacy involved in the subsequent search.

Id. at 1392–93. In a footnote, the court rejected the government's argument that exigent circumstances justified the search because the computer's batteries might have failed and its memory might have been lost:

The government argues, lamely, that the exigency continued even after the seizure, because Agent Peterson did not know how much longer the book's batteries would live. It was therefore imperative, according to the government, that Peterson access the book before the batteries died and the information was erased. At the evidentiary hearing, however, no evidence was offered to substantiate this concern. In fact, Peterson testified that he successfully accessed the book at a later time without changing the batteries. The government bears a heavy burden of establishing exigent circumstances. Speculation is insufficient to carry that burden. The government has not met its burden here.

Id. at 1392 n.2.

As these passages from *David* suggest, exigent circumstances to seize a computer are very different from exigent circumstances to search it. Once the computer is secured, it usually will be the case that the exigency is over and a warrant can then be obtained. *See also* Commonwealth v. Kaupp, 899 N.E.2d 809, 814, n.7 (Mass. 2009).

2. *Does the exigent circumstances exception permit confronting a suspect about his computer crimes and then seizing his computers to avoid destruction of evidence?* In United States v. Bradley, 2012 WL 2580807 (6th Cir. 2012), an investigator named Bell had probable cause to believe that Bradley had used his laptop computer to distribute CSAM. Bell came to Bradley's office and told Bradley of his investigation. Bell then confronted Bradley about his belief that Bradley's computer stored contraband images. Fearing that Bradley might later delete the evidence, Bell seized the laptop under the exigent circumstances exception and later searched it pursuant to a warrant. The Sixth Circuit held that seizing the computer was justified by exigent circumstances,

at least in light of the district court's factual findings that Bell had a reasonable belief that evidence would be destroyed:

> We cannot say that the district court's determination that Bell reasonably feared Bradley would attempt to destroy the laptop or evidence on the laptop was clearly erroneous. Courts have doubted the wisdom of leaving the owner of easily-destructible contraband in possession of that contraband once the owner is aware that law-enforcement agents are seeking a search warrant. Had Bell left the laptop in Bradley's possession, Bradley could have attempted to destroy any computer files or the laptop itself. We agree with the district court below that it is objectively reasonable to seize a container an officer has probable cause to believe contains evidence of a crime, rather than leave it unguarded in the hands of a suspect who knows that it will be searched.

> Having determined that Bell's imminent fear that evidence would be destroyed was objectively reasonable, we next weigh the governmental interest being served by the intrusion against the individual's interest protected by requiring a warrant. First, we recognize that courts are still struggling to conceptualize Fourth Amendment jurisprudence as applied to computers and the variety of interests implicated by seizures and searches of personal electronics. Some have analogized computers to closed containers. However, owners often have more interest in their computers than they have in traditional closed containers like suitcases or trunks. A laptop is likely to contain non-contraband information of exceptional value to its owner. In addition, we consider the fact that the governmental interest in protecting evidence from destruction is particularly high where digital evidence is involved, because such evidence is inherently ephemeral and easily destructible. Thus, we note that, although there are strong personal interests that demand caution by police in seizing personal computers, the government's interest in preventing the destruction of evidence is equally strong when electronic evidence is at issue.

> Second, we note that the government's interest in deterring the production and dissemination of child pornography is significant. Finally, because Bell seized Bradley's computer but did not search it until he had acquired a search warrant, the initial seizure affected only Bradley's possessory interest in the laptop and did not implicate a privacy interest. Courts have considered this lesser interference as a factor when upholding warrantless seizures. In addition, the district court correctly noted that, unlike luggage-seizure cases, no liberty interest was impinged by the seizure of Bradley's laptop. Thus, although the Fourth Amendment protects individuals from unreasonable interference with their possessory interests, in deciding what is reasonable, interference with possessory interests may well be less significant that interference with other rights.

In sum, we agree with the district court's determination that exigent circumstances—together with probable cause to believe that the laptop contained evidence of a crime—justified a warrantless seizure.

Id. at *4–5.

3. *How long can a seized computer be held without a warrant?* When the police seize a computer based on exigent circumstances, they often will hold the computer for a period before obtaining a warrant to search it. Does the Fourth Amendment impose any limits on how long the police can hold the computer before searching it pursuant to a warrant? If so, how long a period is constitutionally reasonable?

In United States v. Mitchell, 565 F.3d 1347 (11th Cir. 2009), a suspect admitted to federal agent Thomas West that his computer contained child pornography. Agent West seized the computer's hard drive without a warrant. A few days later, West left the office to attend a two-week training program. A few days after West returned from his training program, he obtained a warrant, searched the computer, and found the expected images. A total of 21 days passed between the time West seized the computer and when he obtained a search warrant authorizing its search. According to West, he waited to obtain the warrant because the defendant had already admitted that the computer contained contraband. As a result, West did not "see any urgency of the fact that there needed to be a search warrant during the two weeks that he was gone."

The Eleventh Circuit held that 21 days was too long a delay before obtaining a warrant, and therefore that the warrantless seizure was unreasonable and the images found should be suppressed:

> Even a seizure based on probable cause is unconstitutional if the police act with unreasonable delay in securing a warrant. The reasonableness of the delay is determined in light of all the facts and circumstances, and on a case-by-case basis. The reasonableness determination will reflect a careful balancing of governmental and private interests.

> Computers are relied upon heavily for personal and business use. Individuals may store personal letters, e-mails, financial information, passwords, family photos, and countless other items of a personal nature in electronic form on their computer hard drives. Thus, the detention of the hard drive for over three weeks before a warrant was sought constitutes a significant interference with Mitchell's possessory interest.

> Nor was that interference eliminated by admissions Mitchell made that provided probable cause for the seizure. A defendant's possessory interest in his computer is diminished but not altogether eliminated by such an admission for two reasons: (1) a home computer's hard drive is likely to contain other, non-contraband information of exceptional value to its owner, and (2) until an agent

examines the hard drive's contents, he cannot be certain that it actually contains child pornography, for a defendant who admits that his computer contains such images could be lying, factually mistaken, or wrong as a matter of law (by assuming that some image on the computer is unlawful when in fact it is not).

While the possessory interest at stake here was substantial, there was no compelling justification for the delay.

We find [the government's] arguments unpersuasive because they are predicated on the premise that Agent West's attendance at the training session would have provided an excuse for the delay in applying for the warrant and, if a warrant had been obtained, it would have justified a delay in commencing the search of the hard drive until three weeks after its seizure. We reject this premise.

The United States magistrate judge correctly observed that "the purpose of securing a search warrant soon after a suspect is dispossessed of a closed container reasonably believed to contain contraband is to ensure its prompt return should the search reveal no such incriminating evidence, for in that event the government would be obligated to return the container (unless it had some other evidentiary value). In the ordinary case, the sooner the warrant issues, the sooner the property owner's possessory rights can be restored if the search reveals nothing incriminating." If anything, this consideration applies with even greater force to the hard drive of a computer, which is the digital equivalent of its owner's home, capable of holding a universe of private information.

Under these circumstances, the excuse offered for the three-week delay in applying for a warrant is insufficient. If Agent West's attendance at the training seminar could not have been postponed to a later date, an issue as to which no evidence was offered, there is no reason why another agent involved in this nationwide investigation, who possessed qualifications similar to that of Agent West, could not have been assigned the task of conducting the forensic search of the hard drive. The fact that Agent West did all of the forensic examinations in Savannah does not provide a basis for undermining the significant Fourth Amendment interests at stake here.

No effort was made to obtain a warrant within a reasonable time because law enforcement officers simply believed that there was no rush. Under these circumstances, the twenty-one-day delay was unreasonable.

Id. at 1350–53.

3. CONSENT

The consent exception is a powerful exception to the warrant requirement. Voluntary consent by a person with a right to consent makes a warrantless search reasonable and therefore constitutional. Whether consent is voluntary is determined by a totality of the circumstances. *See* Schnekloth v. Bustamonte, 412 U.S. 218 (1973).

Consent doctrine raises three basic questions. First, how should courts interpret the scope of consent? Second, when can a third party consent? Third, when can the police reasonably rely on the apparent authority of a third party to consent?

a) Scope of Consent

UNITED STATES V. AL-MARRI
United States District Court for the Southern District of New York, 2002.
230 F. Supp.2d 535.

MARRERO, DISTRICT JUDGE.

Al-Marri arrived in the United States from Qatar on September 10, 2001 to enroll in a graduate program in computer science at Bradley University in Illinois, from which he had received a bachelor's degree in 1991. In the wake of the September 11 attacks, the Federal Bureau of Investigation received calls reporting that Al-Marri may have been implicated in possible suspicious activity. In response, FBI agents visited Al-Marri twice at his home in Peoria, Illinois.

At the Court's September 5, 2002 evidentiary hearing on the Motion, Nicholas Zambeck and Robert Brown, the two FBI agents who conducted the interviews with Al-Marri and the search of his home and car, testified in person. They stated that during the first visit on October 2, 2001, they asked Al-Marri a series of questions concerning his background, travels, and eventual arrival in the United States. Al-Marri satisfactorily answered the agents' questions and consented to a search of his steamer trunk, which had been mentioned in one of the leads received by the FBI. The agents then ended the interview.

Two months later, at about 4:00 p.m. on December 11, 2001, Zambeck and Brown returned to Al-Marri's home. At the door, Zambeck explained that they had additional questions regarding his date of birth and enrollment at Bradley. It is undisputed that the agents asked permission to enter Al-Marri's home and he agreed, but Al-Marri asked for a few minutes so he could move his wife, who was in an unveiled state and could not be viewed by men, into another part of the house. The agents allowed Al-Marri to do this, and then entered the house.

Once inside, the agents explained that they wanted to conduct the interview back at their office. They contend that Al-Marri agreed to this request. The agents then asked for permission to look around the house, to which they maintain Al-Marri consented. Al-Marri accompanied the agents as they conducted a search of the apartment room by room.

Upon seeing Al-Marri's laptop computer, which was located on a table in the master bedroom and turned on, the agents asked whether they could take it to their office "to take a look at it" because they did not have the skills nor the time to conduct such an examination at the house. According to the agents, Al-Marri agreed to this request, and proceeded to power the computer down. By the agents' account, as he turned the computer off, Al-Marri suggested that the agents carry the computer in his traveling carrying case. Al-Marri retrieved the case from a closet, placed the computer inside and handed it to the agents. On the table, the agents also saw several CDs and diskettes stored inside a container. They testified that they asked Al-Marri if they could take those as well and that Al-Marri agreed. In addition, the agents claimed that Al-Marri gave them permission to search his car, from which they seized additional items of evidence.

The agents then brought Al-Marri back to their office in order to question him further, and arrived at the office at approximately 4:30 p.m. They brought him to an unlocked interview room, offered him a refreshment, and began the interview by requesting that he sign a consent form indicating he had approved the search. Al-Marri declined to sign the form at that point, and asked the agents to set the form aside for the time being. Towards the end of the interview, the conversation grew contentious, and Zambeck reminded Al-Marri of the consequences of lying to an FBI agent. When the interview ended at approximately 10:00 p.m., the agents asked Al-Marri to return the next day to take a polygraph test to verify the information he had provided. Al-Marri agreed, and then was driven home by the agents. Before he left, Al-Marri asked Brown: "Do I get my computer back tonight?" Brown replied: "No, not tonight."

Inspection of Al-Marri's computer and its carrying case, conducted from December 12 to December 23, revealed credit card numbers and other information and resources that, according to the Government charges, could be used to conduct credit card fraud. In examining the laptop, the FBI made several copies of the hard drive, analyzed the data on the computer to identify both current and deleted files, and scrutinized the internet search engine's bookmarks. These examinations revealed several files related to or containing credit card numbers and expiration dates for those numbers, along with comments on whether such numbers were still valid. In addition, the FBI found bookmarks to several web sites that could be used to assist a person conducting credit card fraud.

The evidence taken from Al-Marri's computer, in conjunction with other information gathered by the FBI, led to Al-Marri's arrest on January 28, 2002 under an indictment charging Al-Marri with unauthorized possession of access devices with intent to defraud in violation of 18 U.S.C. § 1029(a)(3).

Al-Marri claims that the scope of the consent did not extend to allowing the Government to seize his computer for inspection of its hard drive.

A warrantless search and seizure is per se unreasonable under the Fourth Amendment—subject only to a few specifically established and well-delineated exceptions. One such exception applies to consensual searches, which have consistently been approved by courts based on the logic that it is "reasonable for the police to conduct a search once they have been permitted to do so." *Florida v. Jimeno,* 500 U.S. 248, 251 (1991).

The issue presented to the Court in regard to the search entails a legal question: [given that] the FBI had consent to search Al-Marri's home, did the extensive search of his computer exceed the scope of such consent? The central requirement of all Fourth Amendment analysis is one of reasonableness. Thus, in measuring the scope of a suspect's consent under the Fourth Amendment, the Supreme Court has imposed a standard of "objective reasonableness—what would the typical reasonable person have understood by the exchange between the officer and the suspect?" *Jimeno,* 500 U.S. at 251.

In the instant case, the agents asked Al-Marri for permission to search the entirety of his home, and Al-Marri agreed to the search. When the agents asked to take his computer back to the FBI office for further examination, Al-Marri agreed to shut the computer down and even helped put the computer in a carrying case for the agents. Al-Marri did not place any explicit limitation on the scope of the search of his home, car or computer, other than to insist that his wife occupy another room in the house to prevent the agents from seeing her in an unveiled state.

Al-Marri would have realized that the examination of his computer would be more than superficial when the agents explained that they did not have the skills nor the time to perform the examination at his home. Moreover, a graduate student in computer science would clearly understand the technological resources of the FBI and its ability to thoroughly examine his computer. Based on this knowledge, Al-Marri could have provided specific instructions to the FBI about the scope of the search he had permitted, specifically whether there were any files or programs he wanted kept private. He did not offer such guidance. Viewed objectively from the perspective of the agents, it was reasonable for Zambeck and Brown to have understood that this unrestricted grant of access, combined with Al-Marri's expertise in computer technology and his helpful attitude in handing the laptop over, indicated that Al-Marri had no qualms about an extensive search of his computer.

Al-Marri's exchange with Brown at the end of the interview on December 11 also provides insight into Al-Marri's state of mind, and what

Brown reasonably could have inferred from Al-Marri's expressions regarding the scope of his consent to search the computer. Viewed objectively, Al-Marri's question "Do I get my computer back tonight?" reasonably indicated that Al-Marri did not know the length of time the FBI would retain the computer, implicitly conveyed Al-Marri's awareness and acceptance of the possibility that the agents' control over it would last beyond "tonight" and extend into an indefinite duration, and suggested that he was not insistent on demanding its immediate return. When he did not respond to Brown's answer "No, not tonight," Al-Marri further demonstrated that he felt no need to put a time limit on the FBI's possession of his laptop. If Al-Marri had any need for use of the computer, or felt any reservation or objection about the FBI's prolonged retention of it, a reasonable person would have expected Al-Marri to ask for the computer to be restored to him within a specified time frame for whatever reason justified a prompt return. Al-Marri's silence on this subject and his failure to raise the issue again the next day persuades this Court that his consent could reasonably have been understood to be open-ended and given without a limitation on time or scope.

Even assuming Al-Marri had not voluntarily handed over his computer to the FBI agents, the Supreme Court has ruled that "a lawful search of a fixed premises generally extends to the entire area where the object of the search could be found." *United States v. Ross*, 456 U.S. 798, 820 (1982). In this case, the object of the search was not made explicit. However, the circumstance that neither Al-Marri nor the agents knew precisely what the object of the search was does not change the nature of the consent.

Here, although the purpose of the FBI's search of Al-Marri's home was not specifically stated, it is clear from the totality of the circumstances that the agents' questioning of Al-Marri related to the investigation of the terrorist attacks of September 11, 2001. Al-Marri, who arrived from Qatar the day before the attacks, had already been interviewed by the same agents on October 2, 2001, exactly three weeks after the attacks. Any reasonable person in Al-Marri's position could not have lived through the events of September 11 and its aftermath and yet not realize that the FBI's questions of him so soon after—including questions about telephone calls he placed to particular individuals or numbers—related to that investigation, even if such an investigative focus was not expressly conveyed to him.

Consequently, it seems reasonably probable that federal agents involved in an investigation of international terrorist crimes who ask for permission to search a person's home under these circumstances will be understood to be looking for evidence of unlawful conduct. Thus, a reasonable person—and in particular a graduate student in computer science who is fluent in English—would have recognized the agents' request to search his home, car and computer as a search for evidence of possible criminal activities.

NOTES AND QUESTIONS

1. *Applying the "typical reasonable person" test to computers.* The test for the scope of consent is what a "typical reasonable person" would have understood the consent to have included in light of the specific facts of the case. Would a "typical reasonable person" understand consent to search a place to include consent to search computers located in that place?

Imagine a police officer visits a home in response to a reported burglary. The officer asks the homeowner if he will let the officer "look around for evidence." The homeowner responds, "sure, officer, do whatever you want." Would a reasonable person understand this exchange to permit the officer to search any computers found inside the home? Does it matter whether the officer is searching for evidence of the burglary or evidence of some other crime?

Also consider how this test applies when a suspect consents to a search of a specific computer storage device. Does the consent ordinarily limit the type of evidence the officer may try to find? Does it limit the thoroughness of the search? If a target permits an officer to "look through" his computer, is the officer restricted in terms of what kind of search he can conduct? Or would a "typical reasonable person" understand that permitting an officer to search a computer permits the officer to look for any evidence using any technique?

More broadly, how do you apply a "typical reasonable person" test to a computer forensics process that most people do not understand?

2. *The scope of consent and files in the recycle bin.* In State v. Jereczek, 961 N.W.2d 70 (Wisc. App. 2021), officers obtained Jereczek's limited consent to search only the files stored in his son's user profile on their family-owned computer that had the Windows 7 operating system installed. A computer forensic agent, Behling, began his search by looking in the "recycle bin" of the computer. In Windows 7, the recycle bin stores deleted files from all user profiles together. Behling found two deleted CSAM files, one of which had originated from Jereczek's user profile and one that had originated in his son's user profile. Behling used this discovery to obtain a warrant to search the entire computer for CSAM.

The Wisconsin Court of Appeals ruled that "Behling plainly violated the scope of Jereczek's consent, which gave police authority to search only his son's user account":

> Behling began his search of the computer in the recycle bin, a location where he knew he was likely to find—and did find—not just files deleted from the son's user account, but the deleted files of the computer's other users as well. Indeed, further investigative efforts were necessary to determine precisely from which account each item of child pornography in the recycle bin had come. A search of the

shared recycle bin container was therefore not a search of "the son's account," and it exceeded the scope of the consent that Jereczek had given law enforcement.

Our conclusion in this regard gives effect to what a reasonable person would have understood the consent limitation to mean. *See Jimeno*, 500 U.S. at 251, Objectively speaking, when a person thinks of a particular user account on a computer, he or she is not likely thinking about where specific items of data are stored on the physical hard drive disc. Rather, the commonly understood meaning of a user account is an interface through which a user can access his or her own files, folders and personalization options. A search of a user account, therefore, is functionally a limited search of a particular area of a computer—i.e., everything accessible by that user account.

Nor do technical difficulties in adhering to the scope of consent justify a broader search. Behling was aware it would be difficult, although not impossible, to tailor his search to the contents of only one user profile. Indeed, he testified he would usually seek a warrant initially for single-user searches of computers with multiple user accounts. But Behling did not inform the referring detective that he thought it was necessary to view data from other accounts during his review, nor did he seek to clarify the scope of consent with Jereczek himself. Law enforcement cannot rely on technical limitations of their forensic software to expand the scope of consent beyond those areas that are reasonably implied by the terms of the consent.

Id. at 76, 78.

3.   *Written consent forms (usually) make it easy.* Government agents often ask suspects to sign a written consent form. In some cases, those written consent forms will be drafted by government lawyers and will specifically mention that computers are included in the scope of consent. So long as the officers do not make any oral representations that the search will be more limited, courts generally will conclude that the written consent permits a seizure and subsequent search of computers located in the place to be searched. *See, e.g.,* United States v. Long, 425 F.3d 482, 487 (7th Cir. 2005). In other cases, officers may simply write up a written consent form from a blank piece of paper. The scope of consent will normally be based on what the paper form says. *See, e.g.,* United States v. Luken, 560 F.3d 741, 644–45 (8th Cir. 2009) (handwritten statement in which suspect writes, "I, Jon Luken, give law enforcement the permission to seize & view my Gateway computer" construed to permit extensive computer forensic analysis of computer).

On the other hand, if agents leave the impression that the search will be limited, courts may then construe the consent as limited. This is particularly likely if the agents create the impression that they are looking for one kind of evidence but they search for a different kind of evidence. For example, in United States v. Turner, 169 F.3d 84 (1st Cir. 1999), detectives were investigating a physical assault of a woman named Thomas that had occurred inside her apartment. Thomas's neighbor, a man named Turner, had reported the assault to the police when he had heard it occurring next door. A brief investigation revealed blood stains on the window sill of Turner's apartment, suggesting that the man who committed the assault had escaped by breaking into Turner's apartment. The police then asked Turner if they could look around his apartment to find more clues that may have been left behind. Turner agreed, and he signed a broad consent form allowing the police to search his apartment. An officer searched Turner's computer and found child pornography. The First Circuit held that the search of the computer was beyond the scope of consent:

> We think that an objectively reasonable person assessing in context the exchange between Turner and these detectives would have understood that the police intended to search only in places where an *intruder* hastily might have disposed of any *physical evidence of the Thomas assault* immediately after it occurred; for example, in places where a fleeing suspect might have tossed a knife or bloody clothing. Whereas, in sharp contrast, it obviously would have been impossible to abandon physical evidence of this sort in a personal computer hard drive, and bizarre to suppose—nor has the government suggested— that the suspected intruder stopped to enter incriminating evidence into the Turner computer.

Id. at 88.

4.   *Social norms and new technologies.* When a technology is new, it can be difficult to tell how a "typical reasonable person" would interpret a statement permitting a search. The difficulty is demonstrated by United States v. Blas, 1990 WL 265179 (E.D. Wis. 1990), a case involving consent to look at a telephone pager. In 1990, before the widespread use of cell phones, pagers were a useful if rather expensive way to keep in touch with others. Those seeking to contact the pager owner would call the pager telephone number, and the telephone number would appear on the pager device. The pager owner would then find a telephone and call back the initial caller at the number stored in the pager. In 1990, few people carried pagers. They were known to be used mostly by physicians and drug dealers, both members of professions that require constant contact with clients and patients.

The officers in *Blas* were investigating narcotics traffickers, and they saw a suspect driving a van. They pulled over the van for a traffic violation. During the traffic stop, an officer saw a telephone pager hanging on the suspect's belt. The officer asked the suspect if the pager was his; the suspect replied that it was. The officer then asked, "Can I look at your pager?" The suspect agreed, and he handed the officer the pager. The officer then clicked through the phone numbers stored in the pager and discovered telephone numbers that were valuable to the investigation. After charges were filed, the suspect argued that retrieving the numbers was beyond the scope of consent and that the numbers should be suppressed. The court agreed:

When the ordinary person asks to look *at* a telephone diary, that person is asking to inspect the physical object. It is commonly understood that the person is asking to see the physical object which includes the pages of numbers contained in the diary. The outside of personal telephone diaries in which numbers are written are commonplace to the general populace and of little interest.

A pager, on the other hand, while gaining in popularity, is still a device common only amongst certain occupations or professions, albeit drug dealers are included. In any event, when a person asks to look *at* a pager, that person is likely to be interested in what the device is, or how small it is, or what brand of pager it may be. Seldom is the person who asks to look *at* a doctor's pager, for example, asking to look inside at the contents of the pager's memory. Correspondingly, the doctor in responding to the inquiry, does not expect the person to activate the pager, in order to scan its memory bank.

To the law enforcement officer and the suspected drug dealer, a pager may have more familiarity. However, when a law enforcement officer asks, "is that your pager," or words to that effect, and next asks to look *at* it, the person who was stopped could reasonably think that the officer simply wants to confirm the fact that it is a pager, rather than a weapon.

Accordingly, this court finds that an individual has the same expectation of privacy in a pager, computer or other electronic data storage and retrieval device as in a closed container, and granting consent to "look at" the container is not a grant of consent to look into the contents of the container.

Id. at *20–21.

Compare *Blas* to a more recent case involving a cellular phone. In Lemons v. State, 98 S.W.3d 658 (Tex. App. 2009), a police officer named Thornhill learned that Lemons was suspected of having engaged in sexual relations with a 14-year-old girl. Thornhill visited Lemons at work, and he asked Lemons if he had been calling the girl on his cell phone. Shortly after, Thornhill asked Lemons if he could see his cell phone. Lemons handed the phone to Thornhill, and Thornhill pressed the "camera" button to access the part of the telephone that stored photographs. Thornhill found a nude photograph of the girl stored in the phone. The Texas Court of Appeals ruled that Lemons had consented to the search because "it is reasonable to conclude that Appellant's surrender to Thornhill of his cellular telephone in response to Thornhill's open ended request implied Appellant's grant of equally unbridled consent for Thornhill to examine the phone and the information contained therein."

Are *Blas* and *Lemons* consistent? If not, which is correct?

5.   *Withdrawn consent and the computer forensics process.* Searching a computer can alter the information it contains. As a result, when the government agents search a computer, they usually make an image of the

computer and then search the image rather than the original. The process protects the evidentiary value of the original computer. If the defendant argues that the government planted data, and that the evidence of crime allegedly found on the computer was not originally there, the government can produce the original computer with the original evidence.

What happens if the government obtains a suspect's consent, makes an image of the government's computer, and then the suspect withdraws his consent? Does the suspect retain control over the image? Or is the image copy now the property of the government, such that the suspect's rights are extinguished and the government can search the computer without limit?

This issue arose in United States v. Megahed, 2009 WL 722481 (M.D. Fla. 2009). Megahed was a college student suspected of making bombs. Agents went to Megahed's home, where he lived with his parents, and they obtained the consent of Megahed's father to remove and then search the family computer that Megahed frequently used. Agents took away the computer, generated an image, and then began searching the image for evidence.

Weeks later, Megahed's father withdrew his consent. Agents continued to search the image, however, eventually finding an Internet history file that incriminated Megahed. At trial, the government wished to use the Internet history file against Megahed. Megahed filed a motion to suppress, arguing that the file was discovered in a search that was beyond the scope of consent because consent had been withdrawn. The court agreed with the government that the Internet history file was admissible:

> Neither the defendant nor [his father] retained a reasonable expectation of privacy in the mirror image copy that the FBI had obtained already with [the father's] consent and had begun already to search. The revocation did not operate retroactively to nullify this history. See United States v. Ponder, 444 F.2d 816, 818 (5th Cir. 1971) ("A valid consent to a search carries with it the right to examine and photocopy."); Mason v. Pulliam, 557 F.2d 426, 429 (5th Cir. 1977) (affirming an order that directed the return of original records and documents voluntarily provided to an IRS agent after withdrawal of consent but agreeing that the taxpayer's "withdrawal and reinvocation does not affect the validity of [the agent's] actions prior to the time he received notice that his right to retain Mason's papers was gone. The district court correctly refused to require the return of copies made prior to the demand by Mason's attorney."); United States v. Ward, 576 F.2d 243, 244–45 (9th Cir. 1978) (adopting the reasoning of Mason as to the use of records following revocation but concluding that "any evidence gathered or copies made from the records before revocation should not be suppressed.").

Are you persuaded? Does your answer depend on whether you model a computer as a single container or as a container of containers? What result would you reach if the consent was withdrawn before agents conducted an initial search of the image?

In United States v. Sharp, 2015 WL 4641537 (N.D.Ga. 2015), agents obtained Sharp's written consent to seize and search his computers. Agents quickly imaged the computers but did not search them. Sharp then withdrew his consent to search his computers after the images were made but before the searches began. *Held*: Agents could search the images for evidence after Sharp had withdrawn his consent.

The court relied heavily on the approach courts have taken for physical papers. When agents search paper documents with proper consent, courts have allowed agents to retain and examine the copies made before consent was withdrawn. The defendant in *Sharp* argued that precedents from the context of physical paper should not be followed because paper documents are searched when they are copied. In contrast, he argued, the government makes a computer image without searching the image or knowing what is on it. The District Court held that this was insufficient reason to adopt a different rule for computers:

> Though the Court recognizes that the prior knowledge of the contents of a paper document versus an imaged hard drive may vary, Sharp cites no authority that suggests that the copies of each should be viewed differently for purposes of a later search.

Id. at *5.

6.   *What happens after consent is withdrawn?* In United States v. Ramsey, 2020 WL 2220312 (E.D.Pa. 2020), the defendant Ramsey signed a consent form permitting the FBI to search his laptop computer for evidence of insider trading. The next morning, Ramsey called the FBI and withdrew his consent. The FBI computer forensics lab immediately ceased the ongoing imaging of Ramsey's laptop.

The FBI agent on the case quickly prepared a search warrant application to authorize the search of the laptop. A judge issued the warrant just six hours after Ramsey had withdrawn his consent. The FBI lab then resumed the imaging process, completing the image a few hours later and returning the laptop to Ramsey that same day.

Ramsey later moved to suppress evidence found on the image. He argued that the FBI had acted unlawfully in holding on to the laptop after he revoked his consent. The District Court disagreed:

> The Government's seizure of the laptop after Mr. Ramsey revoked his consent was constitutional. In *United States v. Laist*, 702 F.3d 608 (11th Cir. 2012), the Government seized the defendant's laptop after obtaining his consent to search the device. The defendant revoked his consent a week later, at which point the FBI began preparing a warrant affidavit and application. The Government kept the laptop for 25 days until it obtained a warrant and could search the laptop and hard drives.

> In holding that the 25-day delay was not unreasonable, the Eleventh Circuit explained that the defendant had a significant possessory

interest in his computer and his hard drives, but (1) that possessory interest was diminished and the Government's legitimate interest in maintaining custody of the computer was increased when the defendant admitted to the presence of illicit images on the computer, and (2) the Government diligently obtained a warrant by starting the process the same day it received the notice that the defendant had revoked consent.

Here, Mr. Ramsey [had given officers probable cause to believe there was evidence on the laptop in a prior interview]. The Government also applied for a search warrant immediately after Mr. Ramsey revoked his consent, and the Government then held the laptop for only six hours. Furthermore, the fact that Mr. Ramsey knew at the time that he revoked consent that the Government wanted to search the laptop for evidence greatly increased the risk that he would attempt to remove any such evidence from the laptop had it been returned before a search could be completed. For all of these reasons, the Court finds that the Government's six-hour seizure of the laptop was supported by probable cause and was reasonable under the totality of the circumstances.

Id. at *5.

As *Ramsey* indicates, the revocation of consent to search a computer doesn't necessarily mean no search will occur. Instead, revocation may prompt the exigent circumstances question discussed in the prior section, in which agents may be able to hold on to a computer temporarily as they apply for a search warrant. But that requires probable cause for a warrant: If agents lack probable cause, normally they will be required to return the computer after consent is withdrawn.

7.   *Mistaken beliefs about the scope of consent.* In United States v. Whaley, 415 Fed.Appx. 129 (11th Cir. 2011), a court considered how to construe the scope of consent when a police officer inadvertently searches a computer beyond the scope of a suspect's consent. The suspect mentioned to a police officer named Schoenfeld that he had a flight simulator program stored on his laptop computer. Schoenfeld happened to be a pilot, and he asked to see the flight simulator program. The suspect agreed and gave Schoenfeld the laptop and told him to turn it on. When a password prompt appeared, the suspect typed in the password for Schoenfeld. Schoenfeld then looked for the flight simulator program on the desktop of the suspect's computer:

Because the mouse pad on the laptop was not working. Schoenfeld had to scroll through each icon individually. He used the "Tab" key to move from icon to icon until he reached an icon entitled, "auto racing 13." He saw the word "racing" and believed that the icon would be the flight simulator program, so he hit the "Enter" key to open it. There was another icon on the desktop entitled, "Microsoft Flight Si," but Schoenfeld explained that he did not notice it at the time. After

> Schoenfeld opened the "auto racing 13" icon, a video began to play. It immediately was apparent that the video depicted child pornography.

Id. at *2. The suspect was charged with possessing child pornography, and he moved to suppress the evidence on the ground that he had only consented to the officer viewing the flight simulator program. According to the defendant, the scope of his consent did not extent to viewing the video of child pornography.

The Eleventh Circuit held that Schoenfeld's search did not exceed the scope of the suspect's consent:

> In this case, Whaley permitted Schoenfeld to use his computer, but only for the limited purpose of viewing the flight simulator program. We discern no clear error in the magistrate's finding that Schoenfeld was, in fact, searching for the flight simulator when he opened the "auto racing 13" icon. Because the laptop's mouse pad was not working, Schoenfeld had to scroll through the icons one by one. Therefore, it is plausible that he did not notice the "Microsoft Flight Si" icon at the time. If Schoenfeld's interest in the flight simulator was actually a pretext for conducting a search for contraband, he likely would not have clicked on the "auto racing 13" icon because the file name was not suggestive of child pornography or other illegal materials. And, in fact, there were other icons on the computer with more suggestive titles that Sgt. Schoenfeld did not click on. These included "beautiful kiss," "girls gone wild9best o . . .," etc.
>
> Here, Schoenfeld discovered the child pornography inadvertently while searching, with Whaley's consent, for the flight simulator program. After Schoenfeld discovered the illicit video, the officers sought and obtained Whaley's consent before opening any additional programs. Accordingly, we conclude that the initial opening of the "auto racing 13" icon did not exceed the scope of Whaley's consent.

Id. at 133–34. Why should an officer's mistaken belief that his conduct was within the scope of consent make the search lawful? Isn't the scope of consent based on the viewpoint of a reasonable observer, not the viewpoint of a police officer who makes reasonable mistakes?

8.   *Consent to search different computer components.* In United States v. Beckmann, 786 F.3d 672 (8th Cir. 2015), an officer asked a suspect if he could search the suspect's home computer. The suspect consented. When the officer approached the computer, he observed a computer tower with two external hard drives attached to it. One of the external hard drives had its power plug disconnected from the wall. The officer connected the power plug and searched the hard drive, finding evidence of crime stored inside it.

The Eighth Circuit held that the suspect's consent to search the computer also authorized the search of the unplugged external hard drive. The general term "computer" implicitly includes "the collection of component parts involved in a computer's operation," the court concluded. Because the defendant "did not explicitly limit the scope of his consent to search the computer, nor did he object when [the officer] plugged the external hard drive into the electrical outlet and began searching," the officer "had an objectively reasonable basis to conclude that [the defendant] consented to the search of the external hard drive" when he consented to a search of the computer. *Id.* at 678–79.

b) Third-Party Consent

Criminal investigators often seek consent to search a computer from an individual other than the suspect. In these cases, the government asks a third party to consent to the search for evidence of the suspect's offenses. If the individual who consents has common authority over the property, the consent is valid. United States v. Matlock, 415 U.S. 164, 171 (1974). In *Matlock*, the Supreme Court explained that common authority to establish third-party consent requires:

> mutual use of the property by persons generally having joint access or control for most purposes, so that it is reasonable to recognize that any of the co-inhabitants has the right to permit the inspection in his own right and that the others have assumed the risk that one of their number might permit the common area to be searched.

Id. at 171 n.7. The following case considers how this rule applies to computers.

UNITED STATES V. BUCKNER

United States Court of Appeals for the Fourth Circuit, 2007.
473 F.3d 551.

DIANA GRIBBON MOTZ, CIRCUIT JUDGE.

Frank Gary Buckner appeals from an order denying his motion to suppress evidence gathered from password-protected files on the hard drive of a computer police seized from his home. The officers seized and searched the computer, without a warrant, on the basis of oral consent granted by Buckner's wife, Michelle. On appeal, Buckner contends that although Michelle's consent sufficed to give the officers permission to search the computer itself, her consent could not extend to his password-protected files.

I.

This criminal investigation began when the Grottoes, Virginia police department received a series of complaints regarding online fraud committed by someone using AOL and eBay accounts opened in the name Michelle Buckner. On July 28, 2003, police officers went to the Buckner residence to speak with Michelle, but only Frank Buckner was at home. The officers then left, asking Frank to have Michelle contact them. A short while later, Frank Buckner himself called the police, seeking more information about why they wanted to speak with Michelle. The police responded that they wanted to talk with her about some computer transactions. That evening, Michelle Buckner went to the police station and told officers that she knew nothing about any illegal eBay transactions, but that she did have a home computer leased in her name. She further stated that she only used the home computer occasionally to play solitaire.

The next day, July 29, police returned to the Buckner residence to speak further with Michelle about the online fraud. Frank Buckner was not present. Michelle again cooperated fully, telling the officers "to take whatever they needed" and that she "wanted to be as cooperative as she could be." The computer Michelle had indicated was leased in her name was located on a table in the living room, just inside the front door of the residence. Pursuant to Michelle's oral consent, the officers seized the leased home computer.

At the time the officers seized the computer, it was turned on and running, with the screen visibly lit. The officers did not, at this time, open any files or look at any information on the computer. Instead, with Michelle's blessing, they shut down the computer and took its data-storage components for later forensic analysis. This analysis consisted of "mirroring"—that is, creating a copy of—the hard drive and looking at the computer's files on the mirrored copy.

Ultimately, a grand jury indicted Frank Buckner on twenty counts of wire fraud and twelve counts of mail fraud. At a suppression hearing, Frank Buckner offered the only affirmative evidence on the password issue, testifying that a password was required to use the computer. Buckner stated that he was the only person who could sign on to the computer and the only person who knew the password necessary to view files that he had created. Nothing in the record contradicts this testimony.

In the district court, Buckner challenged both the officers' seizure of the computer and the subsequent search of password-protected files located on the computer's hard drive. On appeal, he challenges only the search.

II.

Although the Fourth Amendment generally prohibits warrantless searches, valid consent to seize and search items provides an exception to the usual warrant requirement. In responding to a defendant's motion to suppress, the Government bears the burden of establishing, by a preponderance of the evidence, that it obtained valid consent to search.

Consent to search is valid if it is (1) knowing and voluntary, and (2) given by one with authority to consent. There is no question in this case that Michelle Buckner's consent was knowing and voluntary; Frank Buckner challenges only her authority to consent. Because the Government has never contended that Michelle had primary ownership of, or sole access to, these files, this case presents an issue of third-party consent.

A third-party has authority to consent to a search of property when she possesses common authority over or other sufficient relationship to the effects sought to be inspected. *United States v. Matlock*, 415 U.S. 164, 171 (1974). "Common authority" in this context is not merely a question of property interest. Rather, it requires evidence of mutual use by one generally having joint access or control for most purposes. *Id.* at 171, n. 7. Such use makes it reasonable to recognize that any of the co-users has the right to permit the inspection in her own right and that the others have assumed the risk that one of their number might permit the common effects to be searched.

We have previously considered whether a computer user has actual authority to consent to a warrantless search of the password-protected files of a co-user. In *Trulock v. Freeh*, 275 F.3d 391 (4th Cir. 2001), when considering whether FBI agents were entitled to qualified immunity in a suit alleging a Fourth Amendment violation, we held that a co-resident of a home and co-user of a computer, who did not know the necessary password for her co-user's password-protected files, lacked the authority to consent to a warrantless search of those files. Borrowing an analogy from *United States v. Block*, 590 F.2d 535, 539 (4th Cir. 1978), we likened these private files to a "locked box" within an area of common authority. Although common authority over a general area confers actual authority to consent to a search of that general area, it does not automatically extend to the interiors of every discrete enclosed space capable of search within the area.

The logic of *Trulock* applies equally here. By using a password, Frank Buckner, like Trulock, affirmatively intended to exclude others from his personal files. For this reason, it cannot be said that Buckner, any more than Trulock, assumed the risk that a joint user of the computer, not privy to password-protected files, would permit others to search his files. Thus, under the *Trulock* rationale, Michelle Buckner did not have actual authority to consent to a search of her husband's password-protected files because she did not share mutual use, general access or common authority over those files.

NOTES AND QUESTIONS

1.   *The role of passwords.* Would the result in *Buckner* be different if the defendant had not used passwords? A number of courts have considered consent from wives to search their husbands' computer files when their husbands used a joint computer to commit crimes without password protecting their files. Courts have concluded that common authority existed to allow consent to search the files. *See, e.g.,* United States v. Mannion, 54 Fed. Appx. 372 (4th Cir. 2002).

2.   *The "common authority" standard.* United States v. Matlock, 415 U.S. 164 (1974), permits a third party to consent if the third-party has "common authority over or other sufficient relationship to the premises or effects sought to be inspected." When the "premises or effects" are computers, should courts focus on common authority over the physical hardware or common authority over specific files? Put another way, should we model the computer from the standpoint of virtual reality or physical reality?

Applying law to computers often raises a choice between modeling facts from a virtual perspective or a physical perspective. The virtual perspective is the perspective of a user who sees the computer as a window to a virtual reality. In contrast, the physical perspective sees the machine as a physical device that sends, receives, and stores zeros and ones.

The *Buckner* court adopts a virtual approach to construing the scope of consent. It assumes the perspective of a computer user, and analogizes password protected files to locked containers. From this perspective, it is natural that different users have different authority to consent to searches of different files or folders on a single computer storage device.

From a physical perspective, however, distinguishing among files or folders may seem quite artificial. When government investigators search computers, they often search them at a physical level instead of a virtual level. From this perspective, the storage device is a magnetic platter or other device with zeros and ones mixed together rather than stored in distinct virtual "folders." Analysts working from a physical perspective may be unable to tell how access to a storage device would appear to a user from a virtual perspective. From the physical perspective, it seems unnatural to say that a user has common authority over some of the data on the device but not others.

If government investigators search computers at a physical level instead of a virtual one, does it make sense for courts to approach the scope of consent from a virtual perspective? Should investigators be required to reconstruct the search from a virtual perspective, and to limit the scope of consent based on what a user would observe?

3.   *United States v. Wright.* In United States v. Wright, 838 F.3d 880 (7th Cir. 2016), the defendant Wright lived with his girlfriend Hamilton and her children. Wright owned a computer that was occasionally used by Hamilton and regularly used by her children. The record was unclear about whether access to the computer was protected by a password. Testimony indicated that Hamilton did not know of any password, but that her children must have known of any password that existed because they frequently used the computer. Hamilton consented to a law enforcement search of the computer, leading to the discovery of evidence on it and Wright's arrest.

The Seventh Circuit ruled that Hamilton had common authority to consent to the search regardless of whether it was protected by a password:

> We agree with the district judge that Hamilton exercised common authority over the computer even assuming it was password-

protected. Hamilton didn't know the password but her children did, which strongly suggests that Wright made no attempt to keep it from her. Indeed, there's no indication that Wright made any effort to prevent Hamilton from using the computer despite knowing that she and her children did so frequently. In contrast Wright did take steps to prevent Hamilton from accessing his cellphone: Hamilton told investigators that she rarely even got a look at the phone because Wright was constantly changing its passcode. In this context Hamilton's ignorance of whatever password may have been associated with the desktop computer doesn't undercut the common authority that she exercised by virtue of being able to use the computer whenever she wanted.

Id. at 886–87. Is *Wright* consistent with *Buckner*?

c) Apparent Authority

The police may reasonably rely on a third party's claim to have common authority to consent to a search, only to find out later that the third party actually lacked that common authority. Is the search constitutional? In Illinois v. Rodriguez, 497 U.S. 177 (1990), the Supreme Court held that police can rely on a false claim of authority to consent if based on "the facts available to the officer at the moment, . . . a man of reasonable caution . . . [would believe] that the consenting party had authority" to consent to a search of the premises. *Id.* at 188–89. Under this so-called apparent authority doctrine, courts will not suppress evidence if the police reasonably but incorrectly rely on third-party consent to conduct a search.

UNITED STATES v. ANDRUS

United States Court of Appeals for the Tenth Circuit, 2007.
483 F.3d 711.

MURPHY, CIRCUIT JUDGE.

Defendant-Appellant Ray Andrus was indicted on one count of possession of child pornography, in violation of 18 U.S.C. § 2252(a)(4)(B). Agents of the Bureau of Immigration and Customs Enforcement ("ICE") found pornographic images of children on Andrus' home computer after Andrus' father, Dr. Bailey Andrus, consented to a search of the Andrus home and Andrus' computer. Andrus moved to suppress the inculpatory evidence found on his computer during the search, arguing * * * that Dr. Andrus lacked both actual and apparent authority to consent to a search of the computer.

After the district court's denial of his motion, Andrus pleaded guilty to the charge against him but retained the right to appeal the district court's denial of his suppression motion. He was sentenced to seventy months' imprisonment followed by three years' supervised release. In this appeal, Andrus challenges the district court's denial of his suppression motion.

I. Background

Federal authorities first became interested in Ray Andrus during an investigation of Regpay, a third-party billing and credit card aggregating company that provided subscribers with access to websites containing child pornography. The investigation of Regpay led to an investigation of Regpay subscribers. One of the subscribers providing personal information and a credit card number to Regpay was an individual identifying himself as "Ray Andrus" at "3208 W. 81st Terr., Leawood, KS." The Andrus Regpay subscription was used to access a pornographic website called www. sunshineboys.com. Record checks with the driver's license bureau and post office indicated Ray Andrus, Bailey Andrus, and a third man, Richard Andrus, all used the West 81st Terrace address. The credit card number provided to Regpay was determined to belong to Ray Andrus. The email address provided to Regpay, "bandrus@kc.rr.com," was determined to be associated with Dr. Bailey Andrus.

The federal investigation into the Andrus household began in January 2004 and focused primarily on Ray Andrus. At least one agent conducted surveillance on the Andrus residence and knew Ray Andrus worked at the Shawnee Mission School. Eight months into the investigation, agents believed they did not have enough information to obtain a search warrant for the Andrus residence. They, therefore, attempted to gather more information by doing a "knock and talk" interview with the hope of being able to conduct a consent search. ICE Special Agent Cheatham and Leawood Police Detective Woollen arrived at the Andrus house at approximately 8:45 a.m. on August 27, 2004. ICE Special Agent Kanatzar, a forensic computer expert, accompanied Cheatham and Woollen to the residence, but waited outside in his car for Cheatham's authorization to enter the premises.

Dr. Andrus, age ninety-one, answered the door in his pajamas. Dr. Andrus invited the officers into the residence and, according to the testimony of Cheatham and Woollen, the three sat in Dr. Andrus' living room, where the officers learned that Ray Andrus lived in the center bedroom in the residence. In response to the officers' questions, Dr. Andrus indicated Ray Andrus did not pay rent and lived in the home to help care for his aging parents. Cheatham testified he could see the door to Ray Andrus' bedroom was open and asked Dr. Andrus whether he had access to the bedroom. Dr. Andrus testified he answered "yes" and told the officers he felt free to enter the room when the door was open, but always knocked if the door was closed.

Cheatham asked Dr. Andrus for consent to search the house and any computers in it. Dr. Andrus signed a written consent form indicating his willingness to consent to a premises and computer search. He led Cheatham into Ray Andrus' bedroom to show him where the computer was located. After Dr. Andrus signed the consent form, Cheatham went outside to summon Kanatzar into the residence. Kanatzar went straight into Andrus' bedroom and began assembling his forensic equipment. Kanatzar removed the cover from Andrus' computer and hooked his laptop and other equipment to it. Dr. Andrus testified he was present at the beginning of the search but left the bedroom shortly thereafter. Kanatzar testified it took about ten to fifteen minutes to connect his equipment before he started analyzing the computer.

Kanatzar used EnCase forensic software to examine the contents of the computer's hard drive. The software allowed him direct access to the hard drive without first determining whether a user name or password were needed. He, therefore, did not determine whether the computer was protected by a user name or password prior to previewing the computer's contents. Only later, when he took the computer back to his office for further analysis, did he see Ray Andrus' user profile.[23]

Kanatzar testified he used EnCase to search for .jpg picture files. He explained that clicking on the images he retrieved allowed him to see the pathname for the image, tracing it to particular folders on the computer's hard drive. This process revealed folder and file names suggestive of child pornography. Kanatzar estimated it took five minutes to see depictions of child pornography.

Ray Andrus was indicted on one count of knowingly and intentionally possessing pornographic images of minors in violation of 18 U.S.C. § 2252(a)(4)(B). Claiming a Fourth Amendment violation, Andrus moved to suppress the evidence gathered from his residence and his computer.

The district court held an evidentiary hearing at which Detective Woollen, Agent Cheatham, Agent Kanatzar, Agent Smith, Dr. Andrus, and Ray Andrus testified. At the conclusion of the hearing, the court determined Dr. Andrus' consent was voluntary, but concluded Dr. Andrus lacked actual authority to consent to a computer search. The court based its actual authority ruling on its findings that Dr. Andrus did not know how to use the computer, had never used the computer, and did not know the user name that would have allowed him to access the computer.

The district court then proceeded to consider apparent authority. It indicated the resolution of the apparent authority claim in favor of the government was a "close call." The court concluded the agents' belief that Dr. Andrus had authority to consent to a search of the computer was reasonable up until the time they learned there was only one computer in

---

[23] Kanatzar testified that someone without forensic equipment would need Ray Andrus' user name and password to access files stored within Andrus' user profile.

the house. Because Cheatham instructed Kanatzar to suspend the search at that point, there was no Fourth Amendment violation.

On appeal, Andrus contests the district court's apparent authority ruling. He contends that ambiguities in the situation facing the officers at the Andrus residence required the officers to ask further questions concerning Dr. Andrus' authority to consent to a computer search prior to commencing the search.

II. Discussion

Valid third party consent can arise either through the third party's actual authority or the third party's apparent authority. Even where actual authority is lacking, however, a third party has apparent authority to consent to a search when an officer reasonably, even if erroneously, believes the third party possesses authority to consent.

Whether apparent authority exists is an objective, totality-of-the-circumstances inquiry into whether the facts available to the officers at the time they commenced the search would lead a reasonable officer to believe the third party had authority to consent to the search. When the property to be searched is an object or container, the relevant inquiry must address the third party's relationship to the object.

The resolution of this appeal turns on whether the officers' belief in Dr. Andrus' authority was reasonable, despite the lack of any affirmative assertion by Dr. Andrus that he used the computer and despite the existence of a user profile indicating Ray Andrus' intent to exclude other household members from using the computer. For the reasons articulated below, this court concludes the officers' belief in Dr. Andrus' authority was reasonable.

The critical issue in our analysis is whether, under the totality of the circumstances known to Cheatham, Woollen, and Kanatzar, these officers could reasonably have believed Dr. Andrus had authority to consent to a search of the computer. Phrased in the negative, we must ask whether the surrounding circumstances could conceivably be such that a reasonable person would doubt Dr. Andrus' consent and not act upon it without further inquiry. If the circumstances reasonably indicated Dr. Andrus had mutual use of or control over the computer, the officers were under no obligation to ask clarifying questions, even if, as the dissent notes, the burden would have been minimal in this particular case.

We accept the following facts as true: First, the officers knew Dr. Andrus owned the house and lived there with family members. Second, the officers knew Dr. Andrus' house had internet access and that Dr. Andrus paid the Time Warner internet and cable bill. Third, the officers knew the email address bandrus@kc.rr.com had been activated and used to register on a website that provided access to child pornography. Fourth, although the officers knew Ray Andrus lived in the center bedroom, they also knew that Dr. Andrus had access to the room at will. Fifth, the officers saw the computer in plain view on the desk in Andrus' room and it appeared available for use by other household members. Furthermore, the record indicates Dr. Andrus did not say or do anything to indicate his lack of ownership or control over the computer when Cheatham asked for his consent to conduct a computer search. It is uncontested that Dr. Andrus led the officers to the bedroom in which the computer was located, and, even after he saw Kanatzar begin to work on the computer, Dr. Andrus remained silent about any lack of authority he had over the computer. Even if Ray Andrus' computer was protected with a user name and password, there is no indication in the record that the officers knew or had reason to believe such protections were in place.

Andrus argues his computer's password protection indicated his computer was "locked" to third parties, a fact the officers would have known had they asked questions of Dr. Andrus prior to searching the computer. Under our case law, however, officers are not obligated to ask questions unless the circumstances are ambiguous. *United States v. Kimoana,* 383 F.3d 1215, 1222 (10th Cir. 2004). In essence, by suggesting the onus was on the officers to ask about password protection prior to searching the computer, despite the absence of any indication that Dr. Andrus' access to the computer was limited by a password, Andrus necessarily submits there is inherent ambiguity whenever police want to search a household computer and a third party has not affirmatively provided information about his own use of the computer or about password protection.

Andrus' argument presupposes, however, that password protection of home computers is so common that a reasonable officer ought to know password protection is likely. Andrus has neither made this argument directly nor proffered any evidence to demonstrate a high incidence of password protection among home computer users. Without a factual basis on which to proceed, we are unable to address the possibility that passwords create inherent ambiguities.[8]

Viewed under the requisite totality-of-the-circumstances analysis, the facts known to the officers at the time the computer search commenced created an objectively reasonable perception that Dr. Andrus was, at least, *one* user of the computer. That objectively reasonable belief would have been enough to give Dr. Andrus apparent authority to consent to a search.

For the foregoing reasons, this court concludes Dr. Andrus had apparent authority to consent to a search of the computer in Ray Andrus'

---

[8]   If the factual basis were provided, law enforcement's use of forensic software like EnCase, which overrides any password protection without ever indicating whether such protection exists, may well be subject to question. This, however, is not that case.

bedroom. We accordingly affirm the district court's denial of Andrus' motion to suppress.

McKAY, CIRCUIT JUDGE, dissenting.

I take issue with the majority's implicit holding that law enforcement may use software deliberately designed to automatically bypass computer password protection based on third-party consent without the need to make a reasonable inquiry regarding the presence of password protection and the third party's access to that password.

The presence of security on Defendant's computer is undisputed. Yet, the majority curiously argues that Defendant's use of password protection is inconsequential because Defendant failed to argue that computer password protection is commonplace. Of course, the decision provides no guidance on what would constitute sufficient proof of the prevalence of password protection, nor does it explain why the court could not take judicial notice that password protection is a standard feature of operating systems.

The development of computer password technology no doubt presents a challenge distinct from that associated with other types of *locked* containers. But this difficulty does not and cannot negate Fourth Amendment protection to computer storage nor render an expectation of computer privacy unreasonable. The unconstrained ability of law enforcement to use forensic software such as the EnCase program to bypass password protection without first determining whether such passwords have been enabled does not "exacerbate" this difficulty; rather, it avoids it altogether, simultaneously and dangerously sidestepping the Fourth Amendment in the process. Indeed, the majority concedes that if such protection were shown to be commonplace, law enforcement's use of forensic software like EnCase "may well be subject to question." But the fact that a computer password "lock" may not be *immediately* visible does not render it unlocked. I appreciate that unlike the locked file cabinet, computers have no handle to pull. But, like the padlocked footlocker, computers do exhibit outward signs of password protection: they display boot password screens, username/password log-in screens, and/or screen-saver reactivation passwords.[3]

The fact remains that EnCase's ability to bypass security measures is well known to law enforcement. Here, ICE's forensic computer specialist found Defendant's computer turned off. Without turning it on, he hooked his laptop directly to the hard drive of Defendant's computer and ran the EnCase program. The agents made no effort to ascertain whether such security was enabled prior to initiating the search. The testimony makes

---

[3]   I recognize that the ability of users to program automatic log-ins and the capability of operating systems to "memorize" passwords poses potential problems, since these only create the appearance of a restriction without actually blocking access.

clear that such protection was discovered during additional computer analysis conducted at the forensic specialist's office.

The burden on law enforcement to identify ownership of the computer was minimal. A simple question or two would have sufficed. Prior to the computer search, the agents questioned Dr. Andrus about Ray Andrus' status as a renter and Dr. Andrus' ability to enter his 51-year-old son's bedroom in order to determine Dr. Andrus' ability to consent to a search of the room, but the agents did not inquire whether Dr. Andrus used the computer, and if so, whether he had access to his son's password. At the suppression hearing, the agents testified that they were not immediately aware that Defendant's computer was the only one in the house, and they began to doubt Dr. Andrus' authority to consent when they learned this fact. The record reveals that, upon questioning, Dr. Andrus indicated that there was a computer in the house and led the agents to Defendant's room. The forensic specialist was then summoned. It took him approximately fifteen to twenty minutes to set up his equipment, yet, bizarrely, at no point during this period did the agents inquire about the presence of any other computers.

Accordingly, in my view, given the case law indicating the importance of computer password protection, the common knowledge about the prevalence of password usage, and the design of EnCase or similar password bypass mechanisms, the Fourth Amendment and the reasonable inquiry rule, *United States v. Kimoana,* 383 F.3d 1215, 1222 (10th Cir. 2004) (collecting cases), mandate that in consent-based, warrantless computer searches, law enforcement personnel inquire or otherwise check for the presence of password protection and, if a password is present, inquire about the consenter's knowledge of that password and joint access to the computer.

NOTES AND QUESTIONS

1.   *The limited scope of Andrus.* Following the publication of the decision above, Andrus petitioned for rehearing before the en banc Tenth Circuit. The en banc court denied rehearing over the dissent of four judges in addition to Judge McKay. When the petition for rehearing was denied, the two judges who were in the majority of the original panel added a rare addendum limiting the panel opinion to its facts:

> The panel majority notes that its opinion is limited to the narrow question of the apparent authority of a homeowner to consent to a search of a computer on premises in the specific factual setting presented, including the undisputed fact that the owner had access to the computer, paid for internet access, and had an e-mail address used to register on a website providing access to the files of interest to law enforcement.

Among the questions not presented in this matter, and for which there is no factual development in the record, are the extent of capability and activation of password protection or user profiles on home computers, the capability of EnCase software to detect the presence of password protection or a user profile, or the degree to which law enforcement confronts password protection or user profiles on home computers.

United States v. Andrus, 499 F.3d 1162, 1162–63 (10th Cir. 2007).

If there had been factual development of these issues, how much should they matter?

2.   *Understanding the "reasonable inquiry" rule.* The Tenth Circuit's "reasonable inquiry rule" is based on the notion that a police officer presented with an ambiguous situation may not meet his burden of establishing valid third-party consent. If the facts do not establish that a reasonable officer would believe the third party has common authority, apparent authority does not exist. As a result, the officer has the duty to ask the third party about his relationship with the property to be searched so as to establish whether the third party has common authority over it. If the third party answers the questions in a way that would lead a reasonable officer to believe that he has common authority, the officer can rely on the third party's consent. In that sense, the "reasonable inquiry rule" does not impose a duty to ask questions. Rather, it limits the government's ability to rely on third-party authority to search until the government has clarified the third party's authority by making inquiries.

Do you think a reasonable officer in *Andrus* would believe that Andrus the elder had common authority over the files that belonged to Andrus the younger based on what the officers knew, without asking the elder Andrus questions?

3.   *Some hypotheticals.* Imagine a police officer visits a law school library and observes a law student using a laptop. The officer asks the student if she will consent to a search of the computer. At this point, do you think a reasonable officer would conclude that the student has authority to consent to the search?

Now add in some details. The officer casually looks through the computer and finds evidence of financial fraud. The officer asks the student about the files, and the student truthfully explains that the computer actually belongs to her roommate, who works in finance. She had borrowed her roommate's computer for the day when her own computer crashed, and she has no idea what files are stored on the computer.

Now reconsider the question: Before the search occurred, do you think a reasonable officer would have concluded that the student had authority to consent to the search? Does it matter where on the hard drive the evidence was stored, and whether the files are password-protected?

4.   *When a suspect has left his computer with a friend for safe-keeping, does the friend have common authority to consent to a search?* In United States

v. James, 353 F.3d 606 (8th Cir. 2003), the defendant tried to smuggle out a letter from jail to two friends asking them to contact a third man with instructions to destroy computer discs the defendant had left with him. The letter ended up in the hands of the police. The police approached the third man, Laschober, to determine if he had the defendant's computer discs and if he would consent to a police search of them. Laschober explained that he had known the defendant since childhood, and that the defendant had left a stack of computer discs with him in an envelope as storage for back-up purposes. The police asked Laschober if they could search the discs, and Laschober consented. The government searched the discs and found CSAM.

The Eighth Circuit ruled that Laschober did not have common authority over the discs:

> James did not give permission to Mr. Laschober to exercise control over the discs, or to consent to the searching of the discs. Instead, he gave the discs to Mr. Laschober for the sole purpose of storing them (except that, as the police knew, but Mr. Laschober did not, the defendant had given instructions that the discs be destroyed). The discs came to him in sealed envelopes. They were packaged within the envelope in tape. Mr. James never told Mr. Laschober "go ahead and look at these." Instead, he asked only that they be stored (and, as we have noted, that all of them be destroyed).

Id. at 614. The court also held that Laschober did not have apparent authority to consent to searching the discs:

> [The officers] knew that the discs contained in the envelope belonged to defendant and not Mr. Laschober. They knew, once the envelope had been opened, that the top disc said "confidential," "personal," "private." They knew that it took an advanced computer to view the disc's contents. And they had a piece of information that Mr. Laschober did not. They knew that his actual authority had changed. They knew, because they had intercepted and read the letter, that Mr. Laschober's only authority was to scratch and destroy the discs. This last fact is critical.

> It cannot be reasonable to rely on a certain theory of apparent authority, when the police themselves know what the consenting party's actual authority is—in this case, not to store the discs, but to destroy them.

Id. at 615. Is the relevant question the defendant's desire to keep others from seeing the contents of the disc or whether the defendant had given others authority over them? Did James give Laschober authority over the discs by sending a letter asking Laschober to destroy them?

4. BORDER SEARCHES

The Supreme Court has created a special set of Fourth Amendment rules that apply at the international border "or its functional equivalents."

United States v. Ortiz, 422 U.S. 891, 896 (1975). The following case considers how the rules apply to border searches of computers. When you cross the border, when can the police search your laptop or cell phone?

UNITED STATES V. COTTERMAN

United States Court of Appeals for the Ninth Circuit (en banc), 2013.
709 F.3d 952.

MCKEOWN, CIRCUIT JUDGE.

Every day more than a million people cross American borders, from the physical borders with Mexico and Canada to functional borders at airports such as Los Angeles (LAX), Honolulu (HNL), New York (JFK, LGA), and Chicago (ORD, MDW). As denizens of a digital world, they carry with them laptop computers, iPhones, iPads, iPods, Kindles, Nooks, Surfaces, tablets, Blackberries, cell phones, digital cameras, and more. These devices often contain private and sensitive information ranging from personal, financial, and medical data to corporate trade secrets. And, in the case of Howard Cotterman, child pornography.

Agents seized Cotterman's laptop at the U.S.-Mexico border in response to an alert based in part on a fifteen-year-old conviction for child molestation. The initial search at the border turned up no incriminating material. Only after Cotterman's laptop was shipped almost 170 miles away and subjected to a comprehensive forensic examination were images of child pornography discovered.

This watershed case implicates both the scope of the narrow border search exception to the Fourth Amendment's warrant requirement and privacy rights in commonly used electronic devices. Specifically, we consider the reasonableness of a computer search that began as a cursory review at the border but transformed into a forensic examination of Cotterman's hard drive.

Computer forensic examination is a powerful tool capable of unlocking password-protected files, restoring deleted material, and retrieving images viewed on web sites. But while technology may have changed the expectation of privacy to some degree, it has not eviscerated it, and certainly not with respect to the gigabytes of data regularly maintained as private and confidential on digital devices. Our Founders were indeed prescient in specifically incorporating "papers" within the Fourth Amendment's guarantee of "the right of the people to be secure in their persons, houses, papers, and effects." U.S. Const. amend. IV. The papers we create and maintain not only in physical but also in digital form reflect our most private thoughts and activities.

Although courts have long recognized that border searches constitute a "historically recognized exception to the Fourth Amendment's general principle that a warrant be obtained," *United States v. Ramsey,* 431 U.S. 606, 621 (1977), reasonableness remains the touchstone for a warrantless search. Even at the border, we have rejected an "anything goes" approach. *See United States v. Seljan,* 547 F.3d 993, 1000 (9th Cir. 2008) (en banc).

Mindful of the heavy burden on law enforcement to protect our borders juxtaposed with individual privacy interests in data on portable digital devices, we conclude that, under the circumstances here, reasonable suspicion was required for the forensic examination of Cotterman's laptop. Because border agents had such a reasonable suspicion, we reverse the district court's order granting Cotterman's motion to suppress the evidence of child pornography obtained from his laptop.

I. FACTUAL BACKGROUND AND PROCEDURAL HISTORY

Howard Cotterman and his wife were driving home to the United States from a vacation in Mexico on Friday morning, April 6, 2007, when they reached the Lukeville, Arizona, Port of Entry. During primary inspection by a border agent, the Treasury Enforcement Communication System ("TECS") returned a hit for Cotterman. The TECS hit indicated that Cotterman was a sex offender—he had a 1992 conviction for two counts of use of a minor in sexual conduct, two counts of lewd and lascivious conduct upon a child, and three counts of child molestation—and that he was potentially involved in child sex tourism. Because of the hit, Cotterman and his wife were referred to secondary inspection, where they were instructed to exit their vehicle and leave all their belongings in the car. The border agents called the contact person listed in the TECS entry and, following that conversation, believed the hit to reflect Cotterman's involvement "in some type of child pornography." The agents searched the vehicle and retrieved two laptop computers and three digital cameras. Officer Antonio Alvarado inspected the electronic devices and found what appeared to be family and other personal photos, along with several password-protected files.

Border agents contacted Group Supervisor Craig Brisbine at the Immigration and Customs Enforcement ("ICE") office in Sells, Arizona, and informed him about Cotterman's entry and the fact that he was a sex offender potentially involved in child sex tourism. The Sells Duty Agent, Mina Riley, also spoke with Officer Alvarado and then contacted the ICE Pacific Field Intelligence Unit, the office listed on the TECS hit, to get more information. That unit informed Riley that the alert was part of Operation Angel Watch, which was aimed at combating child sex tourism by identifying registered sex offenders in California, particularly those who travel frequently outside the United States. She was advised to review any media equipment, such as computers, cameras, or other electronic devices, for potential evidence of child pornography. Riley then spoke again to Alvarado, who told her that he had been able to review some of the photographs on the Cottermans' computers but had encountered password-protected files that he was unable to access.

Agents Brisbine and Riley departed Sells for Lukeville at about 1:30 p.m. and decided en route to detain the Cottermans' laptops for forensic examination. Upon their arrival, they gave Cotterman and his wife *Miranda* warnings and interviewed them separately. The interviews revealed nothing incriminating. During the interview, Cotterman offered to help the agents access his computer. The agents declined the offer out of concern that Cotterman might be able to delete files surreptitiously or that the laptop might be "booby trapped."

The agents allowed the Cottermans to leave the border crossing around 6 p.m., but retained the Cottermans' laptops and a digital camera. Agent Brisbine drove almost 170 miles from Lukeville to the ICE office in Tucson, Arizona, where he delivered both laptops and one of the three digital cameras to ICE Senior Special Agent & Computer Forensic Examiner John Owen. Agent Owen began his examination on Saturday, the following day. He used a forensic program to copy the hard drives of the electronic devices. He determined that the digital camera did not contain any contraband and released the camera that day to the Cottermans, who had traveled to Tucson from Lukeville and planned to stay there a few days. Agent Owen then used forensic software that often must run for several hours to examine copies of the laptop hard drives. He began his personal examination of the laptops on Sunday. That evening, Agent Owen found seventy-five images of child pornography within the unallocated space of Cotterman's laptop.[5]

On April 11, Agent Owen finally managed to open twenty-three password-protected files on Cotterman's laptop. The files revealed approximately 378 images of child pornography. Over the next few months, Agent Owen discovered hundreds more pornographic images, stories, and videos depicting children.

A grand jury indicted Cotterman for a host of offenses related to child pornography. Cotterman moved to suppress the evidence gathered from his laptop and the fruits of that evidence. The magistrate judge filed a Report and Recommendation finding that the forensic examination was an "extended border search" that required reasonable suspicion. He found that the TECS hit and the existence of password-protected files on Cotterman's laptop were suspicious, but concluded that those facts did not suffice to give rise to reasonable suspicion of criminal activity. The district judge adopted

---

[5] "Unallocated space is space on a hard drive that contains deleted data, usually emptied from the operating system's trash or recycle bin folder, that cannot be seen or accessed by the user without the use of forensic software. Such space is available to be written over to store new information." *United States v. Flyer*, 633 F.3d 911, 918 (9th Cir. 2011).

the Report and Recommendation and granted Cotterman's motion to suppress.

In its interlocutory appeal of that order, the government characterized the issue as follows: "Whether the authority to search a laptop computer *without reasonable suspicion* at a border point of entry permits law enforcement to take it to another location to be forensically examined, when it has remained in the continuous custody of the government." A divided panel of this court answered that question in the affirmative and reversed. *United States v. Cotterman*, 637 F.3d 1068 (9th Cir. 2011). The panel concluded that reasonable suspicion was not required for the search and that the district court erred in suppressing the evidence lawfully obtained under border search authority.

II. THE BORDER SEARCH

The broad contours of the scope of searches at our international borders are rooted in "the long-standing right of the sovereign to protect itself by stopping and examining persons and property crossing into this country." *Ramsey*, 431 U.S. at 616. Thus, border searches form a narrow exception to the Fourth Amendment prohibition against warrantless searches without probable cause. Because "the Government's interest in preventing the entry of unwanted persons and effects is at its zenith at the international border," *United States v. Flores-Montano*, 541 U.S. 149, 152 (2004), border searches are generally deemed reasonable simply by virtue of the fact that they occur at the border.

This does not mean, however, that at the border anything goes. Even at the border, individual privacy rights are not abandoned but balanced against the sovereign's interests. That balance is qualitatively different than in the interior and is struck much more favorably to the Government. Nonetheless, the touchstone of the Fourth Amendment analysis remains reasonableness. The reasonableness of a search or seizure depends on the totality of the circumstances, including the scope and duration of the deprivation.

In view of these principles, the legitimacy of the initial search of Cotterman's electronic devices at the border is not in doubt. Officer Alvarado turned on the devices and opened and viewed image files while the Cottermans waited to enter the country. It was, in principle, akin to the search in *Seljan*, where we concluded that a suspicionless cursory scan of a package in international transit was not unreasonable. Similarly, we have approved a quick look and unintrusive search of laptops. *United States v. Arnold*, 533 F.3d 1003, 1009 (9th Cir. 2008) (holding border search reasonable where CBP officers simply had traveler boot the laptop up, and looked at what he had inside). Had the search of Cotterman's laptop ended with Officer Alvarado, we would be inclined to conclude it was reasonable even without particularized suspicion. But the search here transformed into something far different. The difficult question we confront is the reasonableness, without a warrant, of the forensic examination that comprehensively analyzed the hard drive of the computer.

A. The Forensic Examination Was Not An Extended Border Search

Cotterman urges us to treat the examination as an extended border search that requires particularized suspicion. Although the semantic moniker "extended border search" may at first blush seem applicable here, our jurisprudence does not support such a claim. We have defined an extended border search as any search away from the border where entry is not apparent, but where the dual requirements of reasonable certainty of a recent border crossing and reasonable suspicion of criminal activity are satisfied. The key feature of an extended border search is that an individual can be assumed to have cleared the border and thus regained an expectation of privacy in accompanying belongings.

Cotterman's case is different. Cotterman was stopped and searched at the border. Although he was allowed to depart the border inspection station after the initial search, some of his belongings, including his laptop, were not. The follow-on forensic examination was not an "extended border search." A border search of a computer is not transformed into an extended border search simply because the device is transported and examined beyond the border.

B. Forensic Examination At The Border Requires Reasonable Suspicion

It is the comprehensive and intrusive nature of a forensic examination—not the location of the examination—that is the key factor triggering the requirement of reasonable suspicion here. The search would have been every bit as intrusive had Agent Owen traveled to the border with his forensic equipment. Indeed, Agent Owen had a laptop with forensic software that he could have used to conduct an examination at the port of entry itself, although he testified it would have been a more time-consuming effort. To carry out the examination of Cotterman's laptop, Agent Owen used computer forensic software to copy the hard drive and then analyze it in its entirety, including data that ostensibly had been deleted. This painstaking analysis is akin to reading a diary line by line looking for mention of criminal activity—plus looking at everything the writer may have erased.[9]

Notwithstanding a traveler's diminished expectation of privacy at the border, the search is still measured against the Fourth Amendment's

---

[9]   Agent Owen used a software program called EnCase that exhibited the distinctive features of computer forensic examination. The program copied, analyzed, and preserved the data stored on the hard drive and gave the examiner access to far more data, including password-protected, hidden or encrypted, and deleted files, than a manual user could access.

reasonableness requirement, which considers the nature and scope of the search. Significantly, the Supreme Court has recognized that the dignity and privacy interests of the person being searched at the border will on occasion demand some level of suspicion in the case of highly intrusive searches of the person. Likewise, the Court has explained that some searches of property are so destructive, particularly offensive, or overly intrusive in the manner in which they are carried out as to require particularized suspicion. The Court has never defined the precise dimensions of a reasonable border search, instead pointing to the necessity of a case-by-case analysis. As we have emphasized, reasonableness, when used in the context of a border search, is incapable of comprehensive definition or of mechanical application.

We are now presented with a case directly implicating substantial personal privacy interests. The private information individuals store on digital devices—their personal "papers" in the words of the Constitution—stands in stark contrast to the generic and impersonal contents of a gas tank [that can be searched without reasonable suspicion]. We rest our analysis on the reasonableness of this search, paying particular heed to the nature of the electronic devices and the attendant expectation of privacy.

The amount of private information carried by international travelers was traditionally circumscribed by the size of the traveler's luggage or automobile. That is no longer the case. Electronic devices are capable of storing warehouses full of information. The average 400-gigabyte laptop hard drive can store over 200 million pages—the equivalent of five floors of a typical academic library. Even a car full of packed suitcases with sensitive documents cannot hold a candle to the sheer, and ever-increasing, capacity of digital storage.

The nature of the contents of electronic devices differs from that of luggage as well. Laptop computers, iPads and the like are simultaneously offices and personal diaries. They contain the most intimate details of our lives: financial records, confidential business documents, medical records and private emails. This type of material implicates the Fourth Amendment's specific guarantee of the people's right to be secure in their "papers." U.S. Const. amend. IV. The express listing of papers reflects the Founders' deep concern with safeguarding the privacy of thoughts and ideas—what we might call freedom of conscience—from invasion by the government. These records are expected to be kept private and this expectation is one that society is prepared to recognize as 'reasonable.'

Electronic devices often retain sensitive and confidential information far beyond the perceived point of erasure, notably in the form of browsing histories and records of deleted files. This quality makes it impractical, if not impossible, for individuals to make meaningful decisions regarding what digital content to expose to the scrutiny that accompanies international travel. A person's digital life ought not be hijacked simply by crossing a border. When packing traditional luggage, one is accustomed to deciding what papers to take and what to leave behind. When carrying a laptop, tablet or other device, however, removing files unnecessary to an impending trip is an impractical solution given the volume and often intermingled nature of the files. It is also a time-consuming task that may not even effectively erase the files.

The present case illustrates this unique aspect of electronic data. Agents found incriminating files in the unallocated space of Cotterman's laptop, the space where the computer stores files that the user ostensibly deleted and maintains other "deleted" files retrieved from web sites the user has visited. Notwithstanding the attempted erasure of material or the transient nature of a visit to a web site, computer forensic examination was able to restore the files. It is as if a search of a person's suitcase could reveal not only what the bag contained on the current trip, but everything it had ever carried.

This is not to say that simply because electronic devices house sensitive, private information they are off limits at the border. The relevant inquiry, as always, is one of reasonableness. But that reasonableness determination must account for differences in property. Unlike searches involving a reassembled gas tank, or small hole in the bed of a pickup truck, which have minimal or no impact beyond the search itself—and little implication for an individual's dignity and privacy interests—the exposure of confidential and personal information has permanence. It cannot be undone. Accordingly, the uniquely sensitive nature of data on electronic devices carries with it a significant expectation of privacy and thus renders an exhaustive exploratory search more intrusive than with other forms of property.

After their initial search at the border, customs agents made copies of the hard drives and performed forensic evaluations of the computers that took days to turn up contraband. It was essentially a computer strip search. An exhaustive forensic search of a copied laptop hard drive intrudes upon privacy and dignity interests to a far greater degree than a cursory search at the border. It is little comfort to assume that the government—for now—does not have the time or resources to seize and search the millions of devices that accompany the millions of travelers who cross our borders. It is the potential unfettered dragnet effect that is troublesome.

The effort to interdict child pornography is also a legitimate one. But legitimate concerns about child pornography do not justify unfettered crime-fighting searches or an unregulated assault on citizens' private information. Reasonable suspicion is a modest, workable standard that is already applied in the extended border search, *Terry* stop, and other contexts. Its application to the forensic examination here will not impede law enforcement's ability to monitor and secure our borders or to conduct appropriate searches of electronic devices.

We have confidence in the ability of law enforcement to distinguish a review of computer files from a forensic examination. We do not share the alarm expressed by the concurrence and the dissent that the standard we announce will prove unmanageable or give border agents a "Sophie's choice" between thorough searches and *Bivens* actions. Determining whether reasonable suspicion is required does not necessitate a complex legal determination to be made on a moment-by-moment basis. Rather, it requires that officers make a commonsense differentiation between a manual review of files on an electronic device and application of computer software to analyze a hard drive, and utilize the latter only when they possess a particularized and objective basis for suspecting the person stopped of criminal activity.

International travelers certainly expect that their property will be searched at the border. What they do not expect is that, absent some particularized suspicion, agents will mine every last piece of data on their devices or deprive them of their most personal property for days (or perhaps weeks or even months, depending on how long the search takes). Such a thorough and detailed search of the most intimate details of one's life is a substantial intrusion upon personal privacy and dignity. We therefore hold that the forensic examination of Cotterman's computer required a showing of reasonable suspicion, a modest requirement in light of the Fourth Amendment.

III. REASONABLE SUSPICION

Reasonable suspicion is defined as a particularized and objective basis for suspecting the particular person stopped of criminal activity. This assessment is to be made in light of the totality of the circumstances. Even when factors considered in isolation from each other are susceptible to an innocent explanation, they may collectively amount to a reasonable suspicion. We review reasonable suspicion determinations de novo, reviewing findings of historical fact for clear error and giving due weight to inferences drawn from those facts by resident judges and local law enforcement officers.

In the district court and in supplemental briefing, the government argued that the border agents had reasonable suspicion to conduct the initial search and the forensic examination of Cotterman's computer. We agree.

The objective facts reflect that both the agents at the border and the agents who arrived later from Sells based their decision to search Cotterman's belongings on the TECS hit. Officer Alvarado was told by those in charge of administering the TECS database that he should search Cotterman's property because the TECS hit indicated "that Cotterman appeared to have been involved in some type of child pornography." Agent Riley also looked up Cotterman's criminal record and understood that he had a prior conviction for child pornography. As it turned out, Cotterman's previous conviction was not for pornography, but for child molestation. Nonetheless, the agents' *understanding* of the objective facts, albeit mistaken, is the baseline for determining reasonable suspicion.

By itself, Cotterman's 1992 conviction for child molestation does not support reasonable suspicion to conduct an extensive forensic search of his electronic devices. The TECS alert was not based merely on Cotterman's conviction—the agents were aware that the alert targeted Cotterman because he was a sex offender "who traveled frequently out of the country" and who was "possibly involved in child sex tourism." Further, Agent Riley testified that an examination of Cotterman's passport confirmed that he had traveled in and out of the country frequently since his conviction in 1992.

In further support of reasonable suspicion, the government asserts that Mexico, from which the Cottermans were returning, is a country associated with sex tourism. Cotterman's TECS alert, prior child-related conviction, frequent travels, crossing from a country known for sex tourism, and collection of electronic equipment, plus the parameters of the Operation Angel Watch program, taken collectively, gave rise to reasonable suspicion of criminal activity.

To these factors, the government adds another—the existence of password-protected files on Cotterman's computer. We are reluctant to place much weight on this factor because it is commonplace for business travelers, casual computer users, students and others to password protect their files. Law enforcement cannot rely solely on factors that would apply to many law-abiding citizens, and password protection is ubiquitous. National standards require that users of mobile electronic devices password protect their files. Computer users are routinely advised—and in some cases, required by employers—to protect their files when traveling overseas.

Although password protection of files, in isolation, will not give rise to reasonable suspicion, where, as here, there are other indicia of criminal activity, password protection of files may be considered in the totality of the circumstances. To contribute to reasonable suspicion, encryption or password protection of files must have some relationship to the suspected criminal activity. Here, making illegal files difficult to access makes perfect sense for a suspected holder of child pornography. When combined with the other circumstances, the fact that Officer Alvarado encountered at least one password protected file on Cotterman's computer contributed to the basis for reasonable suspicion to conduct a forensic examination.

For the above reasons, we conclude that the examination of Cotterman's electronic devices was supported by reasonable suspicion and that the scope and manner of the search were reasonable under the Fourth Amendment. Cotterman's motion to suppress therefore was erroneously granted.

CALLAHAN, CIRCUIT JUDGE, concurring in part, dissenting in part, and concurring in the judgment:

Whether it is drugs, bombs, or child pornography, we charge our government with finding and excluding any and all illegal and unwanted articles and people before they cross our international borders. Accomplishing that Herculean task requires that the government be mostly free from the Fourth Amendment's usual restraints on searches of people and their property. Today the majority ignores that reality by erecting a new rule requiring reasonable suspicion for any thorough search of electronic devices entering the United States. This rule flouts more than a century of Supreme Court precedent, is unworkable and unnecessary, and will severely hamstring the government's ability to protect our borders.

The majority's opinion turns primarily on the notion that electronic devices deserve special consideration because they are ubiquitous and can store vast quantities of personal information. That idea is fallacious and has no place in the border search context.

The two courts of appeals—including this court—that have had occasion to address whether electronic devices deserve special consideration have correctly concluded that they do not. In *United States v. Arnold,* 533 F.3d 1003, 1008–10 (9th Cir. 2008), we held that laptops are like other property. Similarly, in *United States v. Ickes,* 393 F.3d 501, 503–07 (4th Cir. 2005), the Fourth Circuit upheld an extensive border search of the defendant's laptop that revealed child pornography. Notably, the court held that the border agents had reasonable suspicion to search the defendant's laptop, but explained why that did not matter:

> The agents did not inspect the contents of Ickes's computer until they had already discovered marijuana paraphernalia, photo albums of child pornography, a disturbing video focused on a young ball boy, and an outstanding warrant for Ickes's arrest. As a practical matter, computer searches are most likely to occur where—as here—the traveler's conduct or the presence of other items in his possession suggest the need to search further. However, to state the probability that reasonable suspicions will give rise to more intrusive searches is a far cry from enthroning this notion as a matter of constitutional law. The essence of border search doctrine is a reliance upon the trained observations and judgments of customs officials, rather than upon constitutional

requirements applied to the inapposite context of this sort of search.

Id. at 507. Thus, the Fourth Circuit has recognized what the majority does not: electronic devices are like any other container that the Supreme Court has held may be searched at the border without reasonable suspicion. Though we are not bound by *Arnold* nor *Ickes* in this en banc proceeding, we *are* bound by what the Supreme Court has said: in the unique context of border searches, property is property and we may not chip away at the government's authority to search it by adopting a sliding scale of intrusiveness. It's the border, not the technology, that "matters."

The court erects a new bright-line rule: "forensic examination" of electronic devices "at the border requires reasonable suspicion. The majority never defines "forensic," leaving border agents to wonder exactly what types of searches are off-limits. Even if the majority means to require reasonable suspicion for any type of digital forensic border search, no court has ever erected so categorical a rule, based on so general a type of search or category of property, and the Supreme Court has rightly slapped down anything remotely similar. The majority invites—indeed, requires—the Court to do so again.

The border search exception to the Fourth Amendment may be just that—an exception—but it is, and must be, a mighty one. The government's right and duty to protect our nation's territorial integrity demand that the government have clear authority to exclude—*and thus to find*—those people and things we have decided are offensive, threatening, or otherwise unwanted. Recognizing this, the Supreme Court has only once required reasonable suspicion for border searches in the 125 years it has been reviewing them. In the remaining cases, the Court has eschewed bright-line rules, balancing tests, and sliding intrusiveness scales, alluding to the possibility of, but never finding, a "particularly offensive" search. The fact that electronic devices can store large amounts of private information, or that the government can search them forensically, does not make a thorough search of such devices "particularly offensive." Rather, the Supreme Court and this court have wisely avoided making the reasonableness of a search turn on the nature of the property being searched, for the many reasons discussed above. The result has been a clear, well-understood, efficient, and effective rule that border searches are *per se* reasonable.

Regrettably the majority, dispensing with these well-settled, sensible, and *binding* principles, lifts our anchor and charts a course for muddy waters. Now border agents, instead of knowing that they may search any and all property that crosses the border for illegal articles, must ponder whether their searches are sufficiently "comprehensive and intrusive," to require reasonable suspicion, and whether they have such suspicion. In most cases the answer is going to be as clear as, well, mud. We're due for another course correction.

NOTES AND QUESTIONS

1.   *Federal circuits divide on applying the border search exception to computers.* Recent decisions from the Fourth Circuit, the Eleventh Circuit, and the First Circuit have reached different conclusions on how to apply the border exception to computers. The decisions create a clear disagreement among lower courts that is likely to prompt eventual review from the United States Supreme Court.

First, in United States v. Kolsuz, 890 F.3d 133 (4th Cir. 2018), the Fourth Circuit held that forensic searches of computers at the border require some kind of suspicion. The Fourth Circuit did not resolve exactly how much suspicion was required—whether reasonable suspicion was sufficient as *Cotterman* had held, or if probable cause was needed, or even if the legal process of a warrant was necessary. But echoing the Ninth Circuit's decision in *Cotterman*, the Fourth Circuit in *Kolsuz* rejected the notion that forensic searches of computers could be allowed without any suspicion at all. Much of the reasoning in *Kolsuz* tracked the Ninth Circuit's reasoning in *Cotterman*, which the Fourth Circuit argued was bolstered by the Supreme Court's subsequent decision in *Riley v. California*, 573 U.S. 373 (2014):

> And then came *Riley*, in which the Supreme Court confirmed every particular of [the reasoning in *Cotterman*]. *Riley* holds that the search incident to arrest exception, which allows for automatic searches of personal effects in the possession of an arrestee, does not apply to manual searches of cell phones. The key to *Riley*'s reasoning is its express refusal to treat such phones as just another form of container, like the wallets, bags, address books, and diaries covered by the search incident exception. Instead, *Riley* insists, cell phones are fundamentally different in both a quantitative and a qualitative sense from other objects traditionally subject to government searches.

> And that is so, *Riley* explains, for precisely the reasons already identified by cases treating border searches of digital devices as nonroutine: the immense storage capacity of cell phones, putting a vastly larger array of information at risk of exposure; the special sensitivity of the kinds of information that may be stored on a phone, such as browsing history and historical location data; and, finally, the element of pervasiveness that characterizes cell phones, making them an "insistent part of daily life.

> After *Riley*, we think it is clear that a forensic search of a digital phone must be treated as a nonroutine border search, requiring some form of individualized suspicion.

Id. at 146. Notably, *Kolsuz* left open the possibility that there is also an individualized suspicion requirement for a manual search of a computer at the border. *See id.* at n.5 ("Because Kolsuz does not challenge the initial manual search of his phone at Dulles, we have no occasion here to consider whether *Riley* calls into question the permissibility of suspicionless manual searches of digital devices at the border.")

Two weeks after the Fourth Circuit handed down *Kolsuz*, the Eleventh Circuit adopted a very different approach in United States v. Touset, 890 F.3d 1227 (11th Cir. 2018). In a decision by Judge William Pryor, the Eleventh Circuit held that no suspicion is required for a border search of a computer whether it is a manual or forensic search:

> We see no reason why the Fourth Amendment would require suspicion for a forensic search of an electronic device when it imposes no such requirement for a search of other personal property. Just as the United States is entitled to search a fuel tank for drugs, it is entitled to search a flash drive for child pornography. And it does not make sense to say that electronic devices should receive special treatment because so many people now own them or because they can store vast quantities of records or effects. The same could be said for a recreational vehicle filled with personal effects or a tractor-trailer loaded with boxes of documents. Border agents bear the same responsibility for preventing the importation of contraband in a traveler's possession regardless of advances in technology. Indeed, inspection of a traveler's property at the border is an old practice and is intimately associated with excluding illegal articles from the country.

> In contrast with searches of property, we have required reasonable suspicion at the border only for highly intrusive searches of a person's body. Even though the Supreme Court has declined to decide what level of suspicion, if any, is required for such nonroutine border searches of a person, [our Eleventh Circuit caselaw has] required reasonable suspicion for a strip search or an x-ray examination. We have defined the intrusiveness of a search of a person's body that requires reasonable suspicion in terms of the indignity that will be suffered by the person being searched in contrast with whether one search will reveal more than another. And we have isolated three factors which contribute to the personal indignity endured by the person searched: (1) physical contact between the searcher and the person searched; (2) exposure of intimate body parts; and (3) use of force.

> These factors are irrelevant to searches of electronic devices. A forensic search of an electronic device is not like a strip search or an x-ray; it does not require border agents to touch a traveler's body, to expose intimate body parts, or to use any physical force against him. Although it may intrude on the privacy of the owner, a forensic search

of an electronic device is a search of property. And our precedents do not require suspicion for intrusive searches of any property at the border.

Id. at 1234. Judge Pryor's opinion in *Touset* recognizes the Eleventh Circuit disagreement with the Ninth Circuit in *Cotterman* and the Fourth Circuit's decision in *Kolsuz*.

> Although the Supreme Court stressed in *Riley* that the search of a cell phone risks a significant intrusion on privacy, *Riley* does not apply to searches at the border. And our precedent considers only the personal indignity of a search, not its extensiveness. Again, we fail to see how the personal nature of data stored on electronic devices could trigger this kind of indignity when our precedent establishes that a suspicionless search of a home at the border does not. Property and persons are different.

> We are also unpersuaded that a traveler's privacy interest should be given greater weight than the paramount interest of the sovereign in protecting its territorial integrity. The Ninth and Fourth Circuits stressed the former interest and asserted that travelers have no practical options to protect their privacy when traveling abroad. For example, the Ninth Circuit explained that it is "impractical, if not impossible, for individuals to make meaningful decisions regarding what digital content to expose to the scrutiny that accompanies international travel" and that "removing files unnecessary to an impending trip" is "a time-consuming task that may not even effectively erase the files." *Cotterman*, 709 F.3d at 965. The Fourth Circuit added that "it is neither realistic nor reasonable to expect the average traveler to leave his digital devices at home when traveling." *Kolsuz*, 890 F.3d at 145.

> But a traveler's expectation of privacy is less at the border, and the Fourth Amendment does not guarantee the right to travel without great inconvenience, even within our borders. Anyone who has recently taken a domestic flight likely experienced inconvenient screening procedures that require passengers to unpack electronic devices, separate and limit liquids, gels, and creams, remove their shoes, and walk through a full-body scanner. Travelers crossing a border are on notice that a search may be made, and they are free to leave any property they do not want searched—unlike their bodies—at home.

> In contrast with the diminished privacy interests of travelers, the government's interest in preventing the entry of unwanted persons and effects is at its zenith at the international border. Nothing in *Riley* undermines this interest. In *Riley*, the Supreme Court explained that the rationales that support the search-incident-to-arrest exception—namely the concerns of harm to officers and destruction of evidence—did not have much force with respect to

digital content on cell phones, because digital data does not pose comparable risks. But digital child pornography [involved in *Touset*] poses the same exact risk of unlawful entry at the border as its physical counterpart. If anything, the advent of sophisticated technological means for concealing contraband only heightens the need of the government to search property at the border unencumbered by judicial second-guessing.

Indeed, if we were to require reasonable suspicion for searches of electronic devices, we would create special protection for the property most often used to store and disseminate child pornography. With the advent of the internet, child pornography offenses overwhelmingly involve the use of electronic devices for the receipt, storage, and distribution of unlawful images. And law enforcement officers routinely investigate child-pornography offenses by forensically searching an individual's electronic devices. We see no reason why we would permit traditional, invasive searches of all other kinds of property, but create a special rule that will benefit offenders who now conceal contraband in a new kind of property.

Id. at 1234–35.

Finally, in Alasaad v. Mayorkas, 988 F.3d 8 (1st Cir. 2021), the First Circuit "agree[d] with the holdings of the Ninth and Eleventh circuits that basic border searches are routine searches and need not be supported by reasonable suspicion." *Id.* at 19. Further, the First Circuit "join[ed] the Eleventh Circuit in holding that advanced searches of electronic devices at the border do not require a warrant or probable cause." *Id.* at 13.

2. *Summarizing the existing circuit split in a chart.* The current circuit split on computer border searches in the Ninth, Fourth, Eleventh, and First Circuits might be summarized by the following chart:

	Ninth Circuit (Cotterman)	*Fourth Circuit (Kolsuz)*	*Eleventh Circuit (Touset)*	*First Circuit (Alasaad)*
Manual Search at the Border	No suspicion required	Undecided	No suspicion required	No suspicion required
Forensic Search at the Border	Reasonable suspicion required	Some individualized suspicion required, although undecided how much	No suspicion required	Warrant or probable cause not required

If the Supreme Court agrees to decide how the Fourth Amendment applies to border searches, how should the Supreme Court rule? Should there be a different answer for manual searches and forensic searches? Or should there be one answer for all computer searches—and if so, what should it be?

3. *The distinction between manual and forensic searches.* What exactly is the difference between "manual" and "forensic" border searches? In United States v. Kolsuz, 890 F.3d 133 (4th Cir. 2018), the court considered use of a Cellebrite Universal Forensic Extraction Device Physical Analyzer to extract 896 printed pages of data from a cell phone. The Fourth Circuit concluded that this was a forensic search, explaining the distinction by reference to a computer border search policy enacted by the Department of Homeland Security:

> Shortly after argument in this case, the Department of Homeland Security adopted a policy that treats forensic searches of digital devices as nonroutine border searches, insofar as such searches now may be conducted only with reasonable suspicion of activity that violates the customs laws or in cases raising national security concerns. U.S. Customs and Border Prot., CBP Directive No. 3340–049A, Border Search of Electronic Devices 5 (2018).

> The new policy does not use the "routine" and "nonroutine" terminology of Supreme Court case law, distinguishing instead between "basic" and "advanced" searches. But the import is the same. "Basic" searches (like those we term "manual") are examinations of an electronic device that do not entail the use of external equipment or software and may be conducted without suspicion. "Advanced" searches (like "forensic" searches) involve the connection of external equipment to a device—such as the Cellebrite Physical Analyzer used on Kolsuz's phone—in order to review, copy, or analyze its contents, and are subject to the restrictions noted above.

Id. at 146, 146 n.6. Is this a persuasive distinction?

4. *Reasonable suspicion (or probable cause) of what?* Whenever courts impose some kind of a cause restriction on warrantless border searches, such as reasonable suspicion or probable cause, the next question is, probable cause *of what*? If the standard is reasonable suspicion, for example, is that satisfied by reasonable suspicion that evidence of any crime is on the device? Alternatively, does it require reasonable suspicion that evidence of a specifically border-related crime is on the device? Or does it require evidence that contraband itself—something that is illegal to possess, distribute, import, or export—is on the device?

Courts have disagreed about this, too. In United States v. Aigbekaen, 943 F.3d 713 (4th Cir. 2019), the Fourth Circuit held that, at least in the context of a forensic search, the reasonable suspicion must be of an offense that has some nexus to the border search exception's purposes of protecting national security, collecting duties, blocking the entry of unwanted persons, or disrupting efforts to export or import contraband.

In *Aigbekaen*, a young woman had reported to law enforcement that Aigbekaen had trafficked her for sex. An investigation followed in which law enforcement learned that Aigbekaen was traveling abroad but would be returning to the United States on an upcoming flight. When Aigbekaen returned, his computers were seized at the border and subject to a forensic searched. A search of Aigbekaen's laptop revealed text messages that were evidence of Aigbekaen's sex trafficking crimes.

This search violated the Fourth Amendment, the Fourth Circuit ruled, because the reasonable suspicion was "based simply on the Government's knowledge of *domestic* crimes, would untether that exception from its well-established justifications." *Id.* at 721 (emphasis in original). The Fourth Amendment required a more specific nexus to the rationales of the border exception:

> The Government may not invoke the border exception on behalf of its generalized interest in law enforcement and combatting crime. The Government must have individualized suspicion of an offense that bears some nexus to the border search exception's purposes of protecting national security, collecting duties, blocking the entry of unwanted persons, or disrupting efforts to export or import contraband.

> Applying these principles to the facts at hand, we can only conclude that the warrantless forensic searches of Aigbekaen's devices lacked the requisite nexus to the recognized historic rationales justifying the border search exception. Of course, when Aigbekaen landed at the airport with his MacBook Pro, iPhone, and iPod in tow, agents had not only reasonable suspicion but probable cause to suspect that he had previously committed grave domestic crimes. But these suspicions were entirely unmoored from the Government's sovereign interests in protecting national security, collecting or regulating duties, blocking Aigbekaen's own entry, or excluding contraband.

Id. See also Alasaad v. Mayorkas, 988 F.3d 8, 19 (1st Cir. 2021) (concluding that "a search for evidence of either contraband or a cross-border crime furthers the purposes of the border search exception to the warrant requirement.")

The Ninth Circuit took a more restrictive approach in United States v. Cano, 934 F.3d 1002 (9th Cir. 2019). Cano was caught bringing 14 kilograms of cocaine across the Mexico border into California in his car. Agents conducted a warrantless forensic search of his cell phone for evidence of Cano's narcotics offenses. Notably, the government clearly had at least reasonable suspicion that there was evidence of Cano's narcotics trafficking offense on his phone. Under the Fourth Circuit's standard in *Aigbekaen*, this would have been enough to justify the forensic search.

But the Ninth Circuit ruled that the search violated the Fourth Amendment. According to the Ninth Circuit, the border search exception applies only if officials "reasonably suspect that the cell phone to be searched itself contains contraband." *Id.* at 2019. Reasonable suspicion about a border-related offense was not enough. Because there was no reason to think there was cocaine in the phone, searching the phone was not permitted under the border search exception.

This was the correct rule, the Ninth Circuit reasoned, because the animating purpose of the border search exception is "interdicting foreign contraband," not merely searching "for evidence that would aid in prosecuting past and preventing future border-related crimes." *Id.* at 1017. This meant that "border officials are limited to searching for contraband only," and "they may not search in a manner untethered to the search for contraband." *Id.* at 1019. A warrantless forensic border search was therefore permitted only based on reasonable suspicion that the electronic device itself contained contraband:

> Were we to rule otherwise, the government could conduct a full forensic search of every electronic device of anyone arrested at the border, for the probable cause required to justify an arrest at the border will always satisfy the lesser reasonable suspicion standard needed to justify a forensic search. Were we to give the government unfettered access to cell phones, we would enable the government to evade the protections laid out in *Riley* on the mere basis that the searches occurred at the border.

> Moreover, in cases such as this, where the individual suspected of committing the border-related crime has already been arrested, there is no reason why border officials cannot obtain a warrant before conducting their forensic search. This is particularly true in light of advances in technology that now permit the more expeditious processing of warrant applications. Indeed, in most cases the time required to obtain a warrant would seem trivial compared to the hours, days, and weeks needed to complete a forensic electronic search. We therefore conclude that border officials may conduct a forensic cell phone search only when they reasonably suspect that the cell phone to be searched itself contains contraband.

Id. at 1019–20.

5. *What is a permitted search for contraband if no suspicion is required?* Under Ninth Circuit law, a border search must be limited to contraband and yet no suspicion is required for a manual border search. This raises a puzzle: How can a search be limited to a thing without evidence that the thing exists?

This issue arose in United States v. Cano, 934 F.3d 1002 (9th Cir. 2019), Recall that *Cano* was a narcotics trafficking case: Cano was arrested trying to bring cocaine into California. During the investigation, officers conducted two manual searches of Cano's phone. First, an officer briefly conducted a manual search of the phone that revealed a "lengthy call log" but no text messages. Second, an officer conducted a second manual search that revealed additional information in the call log and uncovered two text messages on the phone that had arrived after Cano had arrived at the border. The officer also wrote down some of the numbers in the call log and took photos of the text messages.

The Ninth Circuit ruled that the first search was constitutional but that the second search violated the Fourth Amendment. According to the court, the key question was whether the search, viewed objectively, was "consistent with a search for contraband" or "went beyond a verification that the phone lacked digital contraband." *Id.* at 1019. As a practical matter, the primary form of digital contraband is child pornography. The Ninth Circuit therefore focused on whether each search was the kind of search that an officer might conduct if he were looking for child pornography. The first search was permitted because it was objectively consistent with such a goal:

> The observation that the phone contained no text messages falls comfortably within the scope of a search for digital contraband. Child pornography may be sent via text message, so the officers acted within the scope of a permissible border search in accessing the phone's text messages.

Id. The second search was forbidden because it was not consistent with that type of search. In the second search, the officer "did more than thumb through the phone consistent with a search for contraband." *Id.*

> [The agent] also recorded phone numbers found in the call log, and he photographed two messages received after Cano had reached the border. Those actions have no connection whatsoever to digital contraband. Criminals may hide contraband in unexpected places, so it was reasonable for the two officers to open the phone's call log to verify that the log contained a list of phone numbers and not surreptitious images or videos. But the border search exception does not justify [the officer's] recording of the phone numbers and text messages for further processing, because that action has no connection to ensuring that the phone lacks digital contraband.

Id.

Does this test make sense? Does it seem odd that the United States Constitution allows border agents to look through a person's phone numbers and text messages without suspicion as long as they don't write anything down?

6.   *Riley and the border search exception.* The Supreme Court held in Riley v. California, 134 S.Ct. 2473 (2014), that searching a cell phone incident to arrest ordinarily requires a warrant. No appellate court has yet concluded that the reasoning of *Riley* justifies a warrant requirement for computer border searches. Under such a rule, the border search exception simply does not apply at all to computer searches. If and when the Supreme Court decides how the border search doctrine applies to computer searches, should the Supreme Court adopt that rule?

7.   *Does the border exception matter?* Imagine that an international traveler fears that the United States government may search his computer.

Instead of crossing the border with his computer in the usual way, he could instead wipe his computer clean, travel across the border with the clean computer, and then load his files remotely onto his computer using an encrypted tunnel. In such cases, the state of Fourth Amendment law may not matter. Cloud and encryption technology may enable users to move their data around the world free from government inspection regardless of what the law says about the border search exception. If that is true, does that have any implications for the scope of the border search exception?

5. GOVERNMENT WORKPLACE SEARCHES

Many people use computers at work. When a workplace computer is used to commit a crime, the rules that regulate government access to the computer depend on whether the employer is a private company or the government. The Fourth Amendment rules regulating access to private sector workplace computers is similar to the rules regulating access to computers stored in homes, with one major caveat: Employers almost always have common authority to provide third-party consent to a search. *Compare* Chapman v. United States, 365 U.S. 610 (1961) (holding that a landlord lacks authority to consent to search of premises used by his tenant) *with* United States v. Gargiso, 456 F.2d 584 (2d Cir. 1972) (holding that an employer can consent to a search of an employee's locked workspace). When investigators want to seize and analyze a computer in a private workplace, they ordinarily will obtain the employer's authorization and then rely on that consent to seize the computers without a warrant. If the employer does not consent, however, the police ordinarily will obtain a warrant.

Computer searches at government workplaces present a very different situation. In a government workplace, employers are by definition state actors covered by the Fourth Amendment. This sets up a puzzle: If government employers are state actors, does a supervisor violate the Fourth Amendment every time he enters an employee's office without a warrant or the employee's consent? Although they are state actors, government employers normally do not act in a law enforcement capacity at work. Given that, it would be rather odd to require them to obtain a warrant to do their job. Alternatively, it may seem equally troubling to say that government employees have no privacy rights at all in their workspaces. If that were the case, government employees would forfeit all Fourth Amendment rights upon arriving at work.

The Supreme Court has resolved this tension by creating a somewhat *sui generis* framework for analyzing government employee privacy. The key case is O'Connor v. Ortega, 480 U.S. 709 (1987), which was decided in a plurality opinion by Justice O'Connor combined with a concurrence by Justice Scalia. Under *O'Connor*, Fourth Amendment rights in government workplaces are determined by a two-step framework. First, the court must apply a rather unusual version of the reasonable expectation of privacy test. Unlike the traditional reasonable expectation of privacy test used in homes and private workplaces, the version of the test applied in government workplaces looks to: (a) whether the defendant shared his space or property with others; and (b) whether legitimate workplace policies put the defendant on notice that he was denied otherwise existing Fourth Amendment rights. If a government employee shares his space with others, or legitimate workplace policies deny his privacy rights, he cannot have a reasonable expectation of privacy in the workplace.

If a government employee has a reasonable expectation of privacy under this test, the next question is whether the workplace search is "reasonable." In *O'Connor*, the Supreme Court held that this second question should be analyzed under the Supreme Court's "special needs" exception to the warrant requirement. The "special needs" exception permits state actors to dispense with the warrant requirement when acting in a non-law-enforcement capacity, such as the case of a school principal searching student lockers or mandatory drug testing by a government agency. The thinking is that the government interest beyond law enforcement must be balanced with the traditional Fourth Amendment rule, relaxing the warrant requirement when "the burden of obtaining a warrant is likely to frustrate the [non-law-enforcement] governmental purpose behind the search." Camara v. Municipal Court, 387 U.S. 523, 533 (1967). *O'Connor* brought government workplace searches within this category, permitting government employers to conduct reasonable warrantless searches even if the searches violated the employee's reasonable expectation of privacy. The employer must conduct the search for a work-related reason, rather than solely to obtain evidence in a criminal case, and the search must be justified at its inception and permissible in its scope.

LEVENTHAL V. KNAPEK

United States Court of Appeals for the Second Circuit, 2001.
266 F.3d 64.

SOTOMAYOR, CIRCUIT JUDGE:

After receiving anonymous allegations that an employee reasonably suspected to be plaintiff-appellant Gary Leventhal was neglecting his duties in the Accounting Bureau of the New York State Department of Transportation, DOT investigators, without Leventhal's consent, printed out a list of the file names found on Leventhal's office computer. The list of file names contained evidence that certain non-standard software was loaded on Leventhal's computer. This led to additional searches confirming that Leventhal had a personal tax preparation program on his office computer and to disciplinary charges against Leventhal for misconduct.

After settling the disciplinary charges, Leventhal sued defendants-appellees, challenging the legality of the searches.

We affirm the district court's grant of summary judgment to defendants. Even though, based on the particular facts of this case, Leventhal had some expectation of privacy in the contents of his computer, the searches were reasonable in light of the DOT's need to investigate the allegations of Leventhal's misconduct as balanced against the modest intrusion caused by the searches.

Background

Leventhal began his career at the DOT in 1974. At the time of the searches in question, Leventhal had risen to the position of Principal Accountant in the Accounting Bureau of the DOT, a grade 27 position. In 1996, and for several previous years, Leventhal maintained a private tax practice while employed at the DOT. He received DOT approval to make up on weekends or after normal work hours any time he missed because of his outside employment. In order to receive approval for this arrangement, Leventhal declared that his outside employment would "not interfere with the complete and proper execution of my duties with the Department of Transportation."

The DOT had a written policy prohibiting theft. The policy broadly defined theft to include:

> improper use of State equipment, material or vehicles. Examples include but are not limited to: conducting personal business on State time; using State equipment, material or vehicles for personal business; improper use of the mail, copiers, fax machines, personal computers, lincs codes or telephones and time spent on non-State business related activities during the workday.

The DOT also had an unwritten rule that only "standard" DOT software could be loaded on DOT computers. Although this rule was never officially promulgated as a DOT policy, Leventhal remarked during his interrogation that "the stated policy" was that employees were not to have personal software on a DOT computer "without permission." Nevertheless, it was known that the staff of the Accounting Bureau had loaded unlicensed copies of "non-standard" software on DOT computers and used the software to perform work-related activities due, at least in part, to the DOT's inability to purchase needed software for its employees. The DOT also had an official policy restricting office Internet access to DOT business.

In July 1996, the DOT circulated a memo from Ann Snow, the Network Administrator for the Budget and Finance Division, which stated that only original, licensed copies of software could be installed on DOT computers. Following the distribution of this memo, however, Leventhal's supervisors discussed their difficulties in complying with the memo because of the department's dependence upon the use of unlicensed software. Leventhal's immediate supervisor at the time, John Chevalier, instructed his subordinates, including Leventhal, that they could continue to use non-standard software for departmental business.

DOT computers were accessible, for certain limited purposes, by those other than their normal users. The computer support staff of the DOT engaged in troubleshooting and the upgrading of individual computers. During these maintenance operations, it was possible for the computer staff to observe whether non-standard DOT software had been loaded on an individual computer. DOT computers were also occasionally accessed without the user's knowledge to retrieve a needed document, sometimes bypassing a password prompt to obtain access. The computer staff of the DOT provided technical support for Leventhal's DOT computer upon his request three or four times between 1994 and 1996, and once, after hours, without his request, in order to change the name of the server.

On October 15, 1996, the New York State Office of the Inspector General referred to the DOT an anonymous letter it had received complaining of abuses at the DOT Accounting Bureau. This letter described specific employees by reference to their salary grades, genders, and job titles, without providing names. The letter made certain allegations concerning a grade 27 employee. Leventhal was the only grade 27 employee in the office at that time and, therefore, the DOT investigators inferred that the grade 27 employee described in the letter was Leventhal. The relevant portion of the letter states:

> The abuse of time and power is so far out of line with the intended functions of the bureau that to cite all specifics would be an endless task. The day to day operation of this bureau is a slap in the face to all good state workers. You have to see this place to believe it. I will cite a few examples. A grade 27 who is late everyday. The majority of his time is spent on non-DOT business related phone calls or talking to other personnel about personal computers. He is only in the office half the time he is either sick or on vacation.

Lawrence Knapek, the Assistant Commissioner of the DOT for the Office of Budget and Finance, met with John Samaniuk, the acting director of the Office of Internal Audit and Investigations, and Gary Cuyler, the chief investigator for that office, to discuss how to respond to the allegations made in the letter. They decided that the Office of Internal Audit and Investigation would conduct an investigation employing "such techniques as reviewing telephone records, reviewing computer records, Internet logs, that kind of thing." A "computer review" was ordered for all of the employees who could be identified from the letter. This involved printing out a list of file names found on these DOT computers to determine whether any contained non-standard software. After business hours on October 25, 1996, the investigators entered Leventhal's office through an open door, turned on his DOT computer, and reviewed the directories of files on the computer's hard drive. There was no power-on password to gain access to Leventhal's computer, but once the machine was turned on, some of the menu selections that appeared were password-protected. In order to perform their search, the investigators may have used a "boot-disk," a disk which allows the computer to start up without encountering the menus normally found there.

Having located the computer directories, the investigators printed out a list of the file names to enable the later identification of the programs loaded on Leventhal's computer without having to open each program. This included a printout of the names of the "hidden" files on Leventhal's computer. These "hidden" directories, the investigators found, contained "Morph," a type of drawing program and "PPU," a program suspected of containing tax software because of file names such as "TAX.FNT," and "CUSTTAX.DBF." On the non-"hidden" directories, the investigators found other non-standard software, including the programs Prodigy, Quicken, and Lotus Suite (although one part of Lotus Suite was standard DOT software at the time).

In February 1997, DOT management and investigators met to examine the results from these searches. Assistant DOT Commissioner Knapek attended the meeting and, aware of Leventhal's private tax practice, was particularly interested in confirming the investigators' suspicion that Leventhal had loaded tax software on his DOT office computer. They decided to conduct a further search of Leventhal's computer to determine with greater certainty whether the "PPU" directory they had discovered during the first search was part of a tax preparation program. Investigators reexamined the computer in Leventhal's office once in February 1997 and twice in April 1997. During these subsequent searches, they copied the "Morph" and "PPU" directories onto a laptop computer, obtained additional printouts of the file directories, and opened a few files to examine their contents. In the first April search, an investigator noticed that some items had been added to the PPU directory since the previous search, indicating recent activity. The PPU directory was later identified as belonging to "Pencil Pushers," a tax preparation program.

On May 2, 1997, shortly after informing Leventhal that he was under investigation and that the computer in his office would be confiscated, the Director of the DOT Employee Relations Bureau observed Leventhal appearing to delete items from his computer directories. Leventhal was then interrogated. He admitted to belonging to a group that had jointly purchased a single copy of the Pencil Pushers software that was then copied onto his computer and the computers of other members of the group.

Leventhal also admitted that he had printed out up to five personal income tax returns from the computer in his DOT office.

In September 1997, the DOT brought disciplinary charges against Leventhal under N.Y. Civ. Serv. Law § 75 charging six grounds of misconduct or incompetence. Four days after he settled the DOT disciplinary charges, Leventhal filed this action in United States District Court for the Northern District of New York.

Discussion

The Fourth Amendment protects individuals from unreasonable searches conducted by the Government, even when the Government acts as an employer. The "special needs" of public employers may, however, allow them to dispense with the probable cause and warrant requirements when conducting workplace searches related to investigations of work-related misconduct. *See O'Connor v. Ortega*, 480 U.S. 709, 719–26 (1987) (plurality opinion); *id.* at 732 (Scalia, J. concurring). In these situations, the Fourth Amendment's protection against "unreasonable" searches is enforced by "a careful balancing of governmental and private interests." *New Jersey v. T.L.O.*, 469 U.S. 325, 341 (1985). A public employer's search of an area in which an employee had a reasonable expectation of privacy is "reasonable" when "the measures adopted are reasonably related to the objectives of the search and not excessively intrusive in light of" its purpose. *O'Connor*, 480 U.S. at 726 (plurality opinion).

We begin by inquiring whether the conduct at issue infringed an expectation of privacy that society is prepared to consider reasonable. Without a reasonable expectation of privacy, a workplace search by a public employer will not violate the Fourth Amendment, regardless of the search's nature and scope. The workplace conditions can be such that an employee's expectation of privacy in a certain area is diminished. *See id.* at 717–18 (plurality opinion) (recognizing that offices that are "continually entered by fellow employees and other visitors during the workday for conferences, consultations, and other work-related visits," can be "so open to fellow employees or the public that no expectation of privacy is reasonable."). On the facts of *O'Connor*, the entire Court found a reasonable expectation of privacy with respect to the office desk and file cabinets in which the plaintiff had maintained his personal correspondence, medical files, correspondence from private patients unconnected with his employment, personal financial records, teaching aids and notes, and personal gifts and mementos. *Id.* at 718 (plurality opinion); *id.* at 731 (Scalia, J., concurring). In finding that the plaintiff had a reasonable expectation of privacy, the plurality noted that there was no evidence that the employer had "established a reasonable regulation or policy discouraging employees from storing personal papers and effects in their desks or file cabinets." *Id.* at 719 (plurality opinion).

We hold, based on the particular facts of this case, that Leventhal had a reasonable expectation of privacy in the contents of his office computer. We make this assessment in the context of the employment relation, after considering what access other employees or the public had to Leventhal's office.

Leventhal occupied a private office with a door. He had exclusive use of the desk, filing cabinet, and computer in his office. Leventhal did not share use of his computer with other employees in the Accounting Bureau nor was there evidence that visitors or the public had access to his computer.

We are aware that "public employees' expectations of privacy in their offices, desks, and file cabinets, like similar expectations of employees in the private sector, may be reduced by virtue of actual office practices and procedures, or by legitimate regulation." *Id.* Construing the evidence in favor of Leventhal, as we must in reviewing this grant of summary judgment against him, we do not find that the DOT either had a general practice of routinely conducting searches of office computers or had placed Leventhal on notice that he should have no expectation of privacy in the contents of his office computer.

Viewing the DOT anti-theft policy in the light most favorable to Leventhal, we find that it did not prohibit the mere storage of personal materials in his office computer. Rather, the anti-theft policy prohibited "using" state equipment "for personal business" without defining further these terms. John Samaniuk, acting director of the DOT's Office of Internal Audits and Investigations, testified at Leventhal's disciplinary hearing that an employee would not violate state policies by keeping a personal checkbook in an office drawer, even though it would take up space there. Under the circumstances presented here, we cannot say that the same anti-theft policy prohibited Leventhal from storing personal items in his office computer.

Although the DOT technical support staff had access to all computers in the DOT offices, their maintenance of these computers was normally announced and the one example in the record of an unannounced visit to Leventhal's computer was only to change the name of a server. DOT personnel might also need, at times, to search for a document in an unattended computer, but there was no evidence that these searches were frequent, widespread, or extensive enough to constitute an atmosphere "so open to fellow employees or the public that no expectation of privacy is reasonable." *Id.* at 718 (plurality opinion). This type of infrequent and selective search for maintenance purposes or to retrieve a needed document, justified by reference to the "special needs" of employers to pursue legitimate work-related objectives, does not destroy any underlying expectation of privacy that an employee could otherwise possess in the contents of an office computer.

Even though Leventhal had some expectation of privacy in the contents of his office computer, the investigatory searches by the DOT did not violate his Fourth Amendment rights. An investigatory search for evidence of suspected work-related employee misfeasance will be constitutionally "reasonable" if it is "justified at its inception" and of appropriate scope. *Id.* at 726 (plurality opinion). We agree with the district court that both of these requirements are satisfied here.

The initial consideration of the search's justification examines whether "there are reasonable grounds for suspecting that the search will turn up evidence that the employee is guilty of work-related misconduct." *O'Connor*, 480 U.S. at 726 (plurality opinion). Here, there were reasonable grounds to believe that the searches would uncover evidence of misconduct. The specific allegations against the grade 27 employee, who was reasonably assumed to be Leventhal, were that (1) he was "late everyday"; (2) he spent "the majority of his time on non-DOT business related phone calls or talking to other personnel about personal computers"; and that (3) "he is only in the office half the time; the other half he is either sick or on vacation." Probable cause is not necessary to conduct a search in this context, a plurality of the Court has explained, because "public employers have a direct and overriding interest in ensuring that the work of the agency is conducted in a proper and efficient manner." *Id.* at 724 (plurality opinion). The individualized suspicion of misconduct in this case justified the DOT's decision to instigate some type of search.

The scope of a search will be appropriate if reasonably related to the objectives of the search and not excessively intrusive in light of the nature of the misconduct. We conclude that the DOT search to identify whether Leventhal was using non-standard DOT software was reasonably related to the DOT's investigation of the allegations of Leventhal's workplace misconduct. Although the anonymous letter did not allege that the grade 27 employee was misusing DOT office computers, it did allege that the grade 27 employee was not attentive to his duties and spent a significant amount of work time discussing personal computers with other employees.

Leventhal argues that a search for non-standard software would be irrelevant to charges of misconduct because the DOT had, de facto, approved of the use of non-standard software needed to conduct DOT business. Even assuming that this were true, the investigation was more broadly aimed at uncovering evidence that Leventhal was using his office computer for non-DOT purposes. The searches accomplished this task by uncovering evidence that Leventhal had loaded a tax preparation program onto his office computer, a program that he later admitted he used to print out personal tax returns in his office.

We also find that the scope of the searches was not excessively intrusive in light of the nature of the misconduct. During the first search, the DOT investigators printed out a list of file names found on Leventhal's office computer. They did not run any program or open any files. The investigators entered Leventhal's office through an open door and found that Leventhal's computer had no power-on password although some menu selections were password protected. The investigators limited their search to viewing and printing file names that were reasonably related to the DOT's need to know whether Leventhal was misusing his office computer. The first search was permissible in scope.

Neither were the three subsequent searches "excessively intrusive." After the first search had established that files named "TAX.FNT" and "CUSTTAX.DBF" were loaded on Leventhal's computer, the investigators reasonably suspected that these files were part of a tax program. When DOT investigators and management met to discuss what they had found in the first search, Assistant Commissioner Knapek expressed a particular interest in confirming whether Leventhal had loaded tax preparation software on his DOT computer, aware that Leventhal had a private tax practice. Investigators reexamined the computer in Leventhal's office once in February 1997 and twice in April 1997. These searches were limited to copying onto a laptop computer the "PPU" directories that they later identified as referring to "Pencil Pushers," a tax preparation program, and the "Morph" directories, pertaining to a graphics program, to printing out additional copies of the file names, and to opening a few files to examine their contents. There is no evidence that the DOT opened and examined any computer files containing individual tax returns that may have been saved on Leventhal's computer, and, therefore, we need not address the permissibility of searching such materials. Considering that the first search yielded evidence upon which it was reasonable to suspect that a more thorough search would turn up additional proof that Leventhal had misused his DOT office computer, the DOT investigators were justified in returning to confirm the nature of the non-standard DOT programs loaded on Leventhal's computer by copying directories, printing file names, and opening selected files.

Because the DOT searches of Leventhal's office computer were not "unreasonable" under the Fourth Amendment, we affirm the district court's grant of summary judgment to defendants.

NOTES AND QUESTIONS

1. *The first step of the O'Connor test.* The first step of the *O'Connor* test considers whether the employee shared his space with others and whether legitimate workplace policies put the defendant on notice that no privacy rights should be expected. In *Leventhal v. Knapek*, the court concludes that the workplace policies and practices at the DOT were insufficient to deny

Leventhal Fourth Amendment rights. As a result, Leventhal enjoyed Fourth Amendment protection in his computer.

In many other cases, however, government employers have promulgated computer use policies that eliminate Fourth Amendment protection entirely. For example, in United States v. Thorn, 375 F.3d 679 (8th Cir. 2004), an employee of the Missouri Department of Social Services downloaded contraband images to his computer at work. When the employee had obtained computer access two years earlier, he had acknowledged a workplace policy that stated: "Employees *do not* have any personal privacy rights regarding their use of DSS information systems and technology. An employee's use of DSS information systems and technology indicates that the employee understands and *consents* to DSS's right to inspect and audit all such use as described in this policy." The Eighth Circuit held that the policy eliminated the employee's Fourth Amendment rights in his workplace computer. *Id.* at 683–84.

The powerful effect of workplace regulations under the first step of *O'Connor* encourages government employers to install network "banners" or enact Internet use policies. In the case of a banner, the employee is greeted with a privacy notice upon logging in to a workplace computer. In most cases, the notice explains that the user should have no reasonable expectation of privacy in his use of the network. Banners and Internet use policies are generally binding: if a notice says that a government employee has no privacy rights, the employee has no privacy rights. Should government employers be allowed to eliminate Fourth Amendment rights so easily?

2.   *The second step of the O'Connor test.* At stage two of the *O'Connor* test, the court must determine whether the search was reasonable in its scope and justified by non-law-enforcement needs. *Leventhal v. Knapek* focuses on whether the employer search was reasonable in its scope, and concludes that the search in that case was indeed reasonable. Other cases have focused on the line between law enforcement searches and searches for non-law-enforcement reasons. The line may be difficult to draw because government employers often serve two roles at once. The head of a government office may want to end workplace misconduct and may also control criminal investigators who can build a case against employees who break the rules. In such situations, how should courts distinguish work-related searches from law enforcement searches?

In United States v. Simons, 206 F.3d 392 (4th Cir. 2000), an employee of the Foreign Bureau of Information Services (FBIS), a division of the CIA, used his computer at work to download child pornography. Two employees of the CIA Office of Inspector General, one of whom was a criminal investigator, were sent to search the employee's office for evidence. The Fourth Circuit held that this search fell within the *O'Connor* exception to the warrant requirement even though the dominant purpose of the search was to gather evidence:

> FBIS did not lose its special need for the efficient and proper operation of the workplace, merely because the evidence obtained was

evidence of a crime. [The employee]'s violation of FBIS' Internet policy happened also to be a violation of criminal law; this does not mean that FBIS lost the capacity and interests of an employer. *See Gossmeyer v. McDonald,* 128 F.3d 481, 492–93 (7th Cir. 1997) (concluding that presence of law enforcement personnel at search of employee's office by government employer did not preclude application of *O'Connor*); *see also* 4 Wayne R. LaFave, *Search and Seizure* § 10.3(d), at 487–88 (3d ed. 1996) (noting that conclusion that warrant requirement does not apply when employer is investigating work-related criminal conduct is consistent with reasoning of *O'Connor*).

Id. at 400.

3. *Computer searches involving probationers.* The special needs doctrine also applies to searches of individuals on probation. *See* Griffin v. Wisconsin, 483 U.S. 868 (1987). For example, in United States v. Lifshitz, 369 F.3d 173 (2d Cir. 2004), the defendant pled guilty to receiving images of child pornography using his computer. The district court imposed a sentence of probation that contained the following restriction, *id.* at 177 n.3:

> The defendant shall consent to the installation of systems that enable the probation officer or designee to monitor and filter computer use, on a regular or random basis, on any computer owned or controlled by the defendant. Upon reasonable suspicion, the probation office may make unannounced examinations of any computer equipment owned or controlled by the defendant, which may result in retrieval and copying of all data from the computer(s) and any internal or external peripherals, and may involve removal of such equipment for the purpose of conducting a more thorough inspection.

The Second Circuit held that the special needs exception permitted conditioning the defendant's probation on his agreement to computer monitoring. The court remanded the case back to the district court, however, on the ground that the district court needed to craft a narrower and more specific condition that would satisfy the reasonableness requirement of the special needs doctrine given the facts of that particular case. *See id.* at 193.

D. SEARCHING AND SEIZING COMPUTERS WITH A WARRANT

Searches and seizures are constitutional when authorized by a valid and properly executed search warrant. A search warrant is a court order signed by a judge that authorizes government agents to enter a place and seize property. The Fourth Amendment's requirement for issuing a search warrant is unusually clear from its text: "no Warrants shall issue, but upon probable cause, supported by Oath or affirmation, and particularly describing the place to be searched, and the persons or things to be seized."

The Framers of the Fourth Amendment enacted these restrictions in reaction to the English and early Colonial experience with "general warrants," warrants that gave the King's officials wide discretion to execute searches as they believed necessary to enforce the law. The text of the Fourth Amendment forbids general warrants by ensuring that all warrants must be based on probable cause and must state with specificity where the police will go and what property they will seize.

The requirement that a warrant must be issued "upon probable cause" ordinarily is satisfied by a written affidavit submitted to the issuing judge. The affidavit explains the investigation and articulates the officer's probable cause that evidence of the crime will be located in the place to be searched. The proposed warrant itself is a one-page order containing the judge's authorization to enter the named place to be searched and to seize the property listed in the warrant. If the judge agrees that the affidavit establishes probable cause, and that the place to be searched and property to be seized are "particularly" described, then the judge will sign the warrant. The warrant then becomes a court order permitting the investigator or his agents to execute the search.

Both constitutional and statutory law regulate the process of obtaining and executing search warrants. Probable cause and the particularity requirement are obvious constitutional requirements governing what warrants may issue. The Fourth Amendment also imposes some restrictions on how investigators execute warrants and what property they may seize.

Beyond the Fourth Amendment, statutes regulating the warrant process impose a number of nuts-and-bolts restrictions. At the federal level, for example, Federal Rule of Criminal Procedure 41 provides a relatively detailed set of instructions governing how and when warrants must be obtained and executed. Rule 41 requires agents to execute warrants within a period of days after the judge issues the warrant. It also requires agents to leave behind a copy of the warrant when it is executed, as well as to file a "return" of the warrant with the issuing judge listing the property investigators seized. Although the materials in this section will occasionally discuss Rule 41 and associated state statutory restrictions on computer warrants, they focus primarily on constitutional rules under the Fourth Amendment.

Computer searches often involve a two-step process. Agents will first execute the physical search and take away the computers that must be analyzed. They will then execute the electronic search, searching the seized computer for evidence. The bifurcation of the one-step search process into two steps raises a number of difficult questions. For example, should the probable cause required to seize a computer focus on probable cause to believe evidence is located in the physical place where the computer is located, or probable cause that evidence is located in a particular computer? Is the "place to be searched" the physical location of the physical search, the physical location of the electronic search, or the computer itself? What legal restrictions govern the execution of the electronic search stage?

The law governing this area presently is in a state of considerable uncertainty, owing largely to the novelty of the two-step search process. The overarching question is, how can the traditional rules governing warrant searches be applied to the new facts to retain the basic function of existing law? How can the law both deter general warrants and ensure that investigators have the ability to collect digital evidence to protect public safety?

1. PROBABLE CAUSE

To obtain a search warrant, the government must first show probable cause to believe that evidence will be found in the place searched. According to the Supreme Court, probable cause is "a fair probability that contraband or evidence of a crime will be found in a particular place." Illinois v. Gates, 462 U.S. 213, 238 (1983). No special rules determine when probable cause exists. The question is whether the affidavit submitted in support of the warrant establishes a fair probability the evidence will be found in a practical, common-sense way based on the totality of the circumstances.

UNITED STATES V. GRIFFITH

United States Court of Appeals for the District of Columbia Circuit, 2017.
867 F.3d 1265.

SRINIVASAN, CIRCUIT JUDGE.

Most of us nowadays carry a cell phone. And our phones frequently contain information chronicling our daily lives—where we go, whom we see, what we say to our friends, and the like. When a person is suspected of a crime, his phone thus can serve as a fruitful source of evidence, especially if he committed the offense in concert with others with whom he might communicate about it. Does this mean that, whenever officers have reason to suspect a person of involvement in a crime, they have probable cause to search his home for cell phones because he might own one and it might contain relevant evidence? That, in essence, is the central issue raised by this case.

I.

In January 2013, police obtained a warrant to search Griffith's residence in connection with their investigation of a homicide committed more than one year earlier. Investigators concluded that the shooting related to a conflict between rival gangs. The officers knew Griffith was a member of one of the gangs and suspected he drove the getaway car, which surveillance footage had captured circling the scene. Two months after the shooting, police found a vehicle matching the surveillance footage and registered to Griffith's mother. Eight months later, a detective met with Griffith's mother, who confirmed that Griffith had been the vehicle's principal user.

During much of the year-long investigation, Griffith had been incarcerated on unrelated charges. Detectives obtained recordings of Griffith's jailhouse phone calls made on the day they interviewed his mother. Griffith initiated four calls that day: two to his home number (where his mother lived) and two to his grandmother's home phone. In one of the calls, Griffith spoke to Dwayne Hilton, another suspect in the shooting, and said, "man you know it's about that." The two briefly discussed a "whip" (slang for car), before Hilton changed the subject. In another call, Griffith's brother reported that fellow gang member Carl Oliphant needed to speak with Griffith. Oliphant did not have a cell phone, so Griffith's brother walked with a phone to Oliphant's house. Griffith then briefly explained to Oliphant that detectives had been investigating the car.

In September 2012, Griffith was released from his confinement on the unrelated charges after serving approximately 10 months. Detectives learned that Griffith moved into an apartment owned by his girlfriend, Sheree Lewis. In January 2013, police sought a warrant to search Lewis's apartment.

The bulk of the ten-page affidavit supporting the search warrant explained Griffith's suspected involvement in the homicide committed more than one year beforehand. The affiant, a 22-year veteran of the police department, recounted the evidence and expressed his belief that Griffith had been the getaway driver. The affidavit also described the evidence that Griffith now lived with Lewis in her apartment.

Two sentences in the affidavit then set out the basis for believing incriminating evidence would be discovered in the apartment. Those sentences read as follows:

> Based upon your affiant's professional training and experience and your affiant's work with other veteran police officers and detectives, I know that gang/crew members involved in criminal activity maintain regular contact with each other, even when they are arrested or incarcerated, and that they often stay advised and share intelligence about their activities through cell phones and other electronic communication devices and the Internet, to include Facebook, Twitter and E-mail accounts.

> Based upon the aforementioned facts and circumstances, and your affiant's experience and training, there is probable cause to

believe that secreted inside of [Lewis's apartment] is evidence relating to the homicide discussed above.

The affidavit then concluded by enumerating the items the officers sought to seize from the apartment, principally any cell phones and electronic devices found there.

On January 4, 2013, a magistrate judge granted the application for a search warrant. As requested in the affidavit, the warrant authorized a search for, and seizure of, the following items:

all electronic devices to include, but not limited to cellular telephone(s), computer(s), electronic tablet(s), devices capable of storing digital images (to include, but not limited to, PDAs, CDs, DVD's [and] jump/zip drives), evidence of ownership of such devices, subscriber information relating to the electronic devices, any information describing, referencing, or mentioning in any way the above-described offense, any handwritten form (such as writing to include but not limited to notes, papers, or mail matter), photographs, newspaper articles relating to the shooting death under investigation, and any indicia of occupancy of the premises described above.

Three days later, on January 7, a team of officers executed the search. When they knocked on the door and announced they had a search warrant, an officer assigned to contain the premises observed an arm throw an object out of the apartment's window. The officer determined that the object was a firearm and then glanced at the window. He saw Griffith looking back at him.

About 30 seconds after the officers knocked on the door and announced they had a search warrant, Lewis opened the door. Officers found three people inside the apartment: Lewis, Griffith, and a six-year-old child. Officers knew one of those three people had tossed the gun out of the window. Officers seized the gun, and also seized a number of cell phones recovered in the course of their search of the apartment.

Based on the containment officer's identification of him, the government charged Griffith with possession of a firearm by a convicted felon. Griffith moved to suppress all tangible evidence seized under the search warrant, including the gun. He challenged the warrant as facially invalid, arguing there was no evidence he had ever owned a cell phone or other electronic device, or that any such device would be found in the apartment.

II.

The government's argument in support of probable cause to search the apartment rests on the prospect of finding one specific item there: a cell phone owned by Griffith. Yet the affidavit supporting the warrant application provided virtually no reason to suspect that Griffith in fact owned a cell phone, let alone that any phone belonging to him and containing incriminating information would be found in the residence.

Although the warrant application sought authorization to search for items other than a cell phone, those additional items have no bearing on our assessment of probable cause to search the home. The application, for instance, encompassed the seizure of any documents, newspaper articles, photographs, or other information relating to the crime. The affiant, however, suggested no reason whatsoever to expect the presence of incriminating documents, newspaper articles, or photographs in the apartment. The affidavit in fact contained no mention of those items apart from a final sentence summarily seeking authorization to seize any of them officers might happen to discover. The government thus understandably makes no argument that there was probable cause to search the apartment due to a belief that incriminating documents, articles, or photographs would be found there.

The application also referenced electronic devices apart from cell phones, including computers, tablets, and personal digital assistants. Again, though, the affidavit provided no reason to suppose that Griffith possessed any of those devices or that any would be found in the apartment. And although we give a commonsense rather than "hypertechnical" reading to a warrant application, there is no commonsense reason simply to presume that individuals own a computer or tablet. Those sorts of devices do not approach cellphones in their ubiquity: whereas the Supreme Court, around the time of the warrant application in this case, observed that more than 90% of American adults own a cell phone, *Riley v. California*, 134 S. Ct. 2473 (2014), the same organization cited by the Court for that measure estimated the contemporaneous incidence of tablet ownership among adults at roughly 30% (2013), and of computer ownership at roughly 75%.

That brings us back to the warrant application's reliance on cell phones—in particular, on the possibility that Griffith owned a cell phone, and that his phone would be found in the home and would contain evidence of his suspected offense. With regard to his ownership of a cell phone, it is true that, as the Supreme Court recently said, cell phones are now "such a pervasive and insistent part of daily life that the proverbial visitor from Mars might conclude they were an important feature of human anatomy." *Riley*, 134 S. Ct. at 2484.

We do not doubt that most people today own a cell phone. But the affidavit in this case conveyed no reason to think that Griffith, in particular, owned a cell phone. There was no observation of Griffith's using a cell phone, no information about anyone having received a cell phone call or text message from him, no record of officers recovering any cell phone in his possession at the time of his previous arrest (and confinement) on unrelated charges, and no indication otherwise of his ownership of a cell phone at any time. To the contrary, the circumstances suggested Griffith might have been less likely than others to own a phone around the time of the search: he had recently completed a ten-month period of confinement, during which he of course had no ongoing access to a cell phone; and at least one person in his circle—his potential co-conspirator, Carl Oliphant—was known not to have a cell phone.

To justify a search of the apartment to seize any cell phone owned by Griffith, moreover, police needed reason to think not only that he possessed a phone, but also that the device would be located in the home and would contain incriminating evidence about his suspected offense. With respect to the first of those additional considerations, the affidavit set out no reason to believe the phone was likely to be found at the place to be searched. People ordinarily carry their cell phones with them wherever they go. A cell phone, after all, is nearly a "feature of human anatomy." *Riley*, 134 S. Ct. at 2484. According to one poll cited by the Supreme Court, nearly three-quarters of smart phone users report being within five feet of their phones most of the time.

In that light, the assumption that most people own a cell phone would not automatically justify an open-ended warrant to search a home anytime officers seek a person's phone. Instead, such a search would rest on a second assumption: that the person (and his cell phone) would be home. When, as here, the police execute a warrant early in the morning, such an assumption might be fair, but it entails adding another layer of inference onto an already questionable probable cause calculus. And the warrant in any event gave officers authority to search Griffith's apartment for any cell phones without regard to his presence on the scene. Indeed, the police, not knowing whether Griffith owned a cell phone, sought and obtained authority to maintain their search until they found *all* cell phones in Lewis's apartment, so that they could later assess which (if any) belonged to Griffith.

The upshot is that the information in the warrant application might well have supported an arrest warrant for Griffith—which in turn presumably would have occasioned a search of him incident to his arrest, and an ensuing seizure of any cell phone he owned in the most likely place to find it (on his person). But the government instead elected to seek license to conduct a full-scale search of his entire home based on the possibility that he owned a phone and that a phone found there might be his.

Finally, even if we assume Griffith owned a phone and that his phone would be found in the apartment, what about the likelihood that the phone would contain incriminating evidence? Because a cell phone, unlike drugs or other contraband, is not inherently illegal, there must be reason to believe that a phone may contain evidence of the crime. On that score, the affidavit in this case stated only that, in the affiant's experience, gang members "maintain regular contact with each other" and "often stay advised and share intelligence about their activities through cell phones and other electronic communication devices and the Internet."

That assessment might have added force if officers had been investigating a more recent crime. Because the information on a cell phone can enable reconstruction of the "sum of an individual's private life," *Riley*, 134 S. Ct. at 2489, the police often might fairly infer that a suspect's phone contains evidence of recent criminal activity, perhaps especially when, as here, multiple perpetrators may have coordinated the crime. But by the time police sought the warrant in this case, more than a year had elapsed since the shooting.

We require the existence of probable cause at the time that law enforcement applies for a warrant, such that the freshness of the supporting evidence is critical. Insofar as Griffith might have used a cell phone to communicate with his associates around the time of the crime, the search of the apartment would be grounded in an assumption that he continued to possess the same phone more than one year later. In the intervening period, though, he had been confined for some ten months.

What is more, even in the event that Griffith, after his release, recovered possession of the same phone he had owned at the time of the crime, he would have had ample opportunity to delete incriminating information from the device by the time of the search (which occurred more than four months after his release). He had every incentive to cleanse his phone, and also to refrain from adding any new incriminating information to it: he had become aware of the investigation of him by the time of his release.

In that light, the government gains little by relying on Griffith's making of calls to his associates on a recorded jail line upon learning of the investigation. Griffith's use of a landline phone when confined sheds minimal light on whether any cell phone he once owned would retain any incriminating information if recovered in a search of his post-release residence. Nor do Griffith's calls from jail indicate how he would communicate upon his release, when he could contact his associates, if at all, in person. The jailhouse calls also occurred in response to a specific triggering event—his learning of the investigation. And, even then, those calls took place several months before officers obtained and executed the search warrant.

In view of the limited likelihood that any cell phone discovered in the apartment would contain incriminating evidence of Griffith's suspected crime, the government's argument in favor of probable cause essentially falls back on our accepting the following proposition: because nearly everyone now carries a cell phone, and because a phone frequently contains all sorts of information about the owner's daily activities, a person's suspected involvement in a crime ordinarily justifies searching her home for any cell phones, regardless of whether there is any indication that she in fact owns one. Finding the existence of probable cause in this case, therefore, would verge on authorizing a search of a person's home almost anytime there is probable cause to suspect her of a crime. We cannot accept that proposition.

NOTES AND QUESTIONS

1. *The rates of cell phone ownership.* According to survey taken in the fall of 2016, the overall rate of cell phone ownership in the United States among adults is 95%. That result varies with age, however. Among adults from the ages of 18–29, the reported rate of cell phone ownership is 100%. From the ages of 20–49, the rate is 99%. Among adults 65 or older, the reported rate of cell phone ownership is 80%. *See* Mobile Fact Sheet, Pew Research Center, January 12, 2017, available at http://www.pewinternet.org/fact-sheet/mobile/. Assuming that Griffith was not a senior citizen, was the court wrong to require special evidence that Griffith owned a cell phone?

2. *Probable cause based on clicking on a website address from an unknown source.* In United States v. Bosyk, 933 F.3d 319 (4th Cir. 2019), the Fourth Circuit divided on whether a magistrate judge had a substantial basis for finding probable cause to search a home based on a single click of a website link.

Investigators were monitoring an online message board dedicated to child pornography referred to in the opinion as Bulletin Board A. Bulletin Board A was hosted on the Internet's "dark web," which consists of websites that are available only through anonymizing services that hide the location of the webserver and its users. On a particular day, an unknown user of Bulletin Board A posted a link to a website address on a file-sharing website. The file-sharing site was typically used for lawful content, and it permitted anyone to upload and share various media. The posting on Bulletin Board A indicated that child pornography videos were available at the specific link on the file-sharing website, and it included the password that was needed to access and view the videos.

The government could not obtain any records from Bulletin Board A about who had posted or accessed the files. Because Bulletin Board A was on the dark web, the location of its server was unknown and it was effectively unreachable. Instead, the government issued a subpoena to the file-sharing website asking for any IP addresses that had been used to visit the address at which the child pornography videos had been available on the file-sharing website. In response to the subpoena, the file-sharing website disclosed that one of the requests for files at that address that was made on the same day as the posting on Bulletin Board A was from an IP address assigned to a particular home.

Investigators obtained a warrant to search the home for child pornography. The police then executed the search, which belonged to Bosyk. The search revealed thousands of images and videos of child pornography— including the videos that were available from the link posted on Bulletin Board A.

The Fourth Circuit divided on whether the magistrate judge had a substantial basis to find probable cause to issue the warrant to search Bosyk's home. Writing for the majority, Judge Diaz concluded that probable cause existed:

> The facts in the affidavit support a reasonable inference that someone using Bosyk's IP address clicked the link knowing that it contained child pornography. This in turn makes it fairly probable that criminal evidence would have been found at Bosyk's address.
>
> The critical fact in this case is the timing. On the very day that someone clicked the link, it appeared on a website whose purpose was to advertise and distribute child pornography to its limited membership. And it appeared in a post containing text and images that unequivocally identified its contents as child pornography. The close timing between the link's appearance on Bulletin Board A and the click by a user's IP address is highly relevant: because the link was accessed on the same day it appeared on Bulletin Board A, it is at least reasonably probable that the user clicked the link having encountered it on that website.
>
> With this fair assumption, several inferences drop into place to support the magistrate judge's decision to issue the warrant. If one assumes, given the close timing, that the user accessed the link after seeing it on Bulletin Board A, it's fair to conclude that the user also knew it contained child pornography, as that much was explicit from the posting. On top of that, one can fairly conclude that the same person typed the password posted on Bulletin Board A, downloaded the content, and viewed the video contained at that URL. For why else would someone who had seen the pornographic stills and read the description on Bulletin Board A click the link if not to access its contents? Thus, if we suppose that someone accessed the link through Bulletin Board A, it's fairly probable that the same person downloaded or viewed child-pornographic images.
>
> Recall that the magistrate judge knew someone using Bosyk's home IP address had clicked the link. Given that fact—and the permissible inferences described above—we think it was fairly probable that child pornography would be found on computers or other devices within Bosyk's property. And because child pornography constitutes contraband or evidence of a crime, this is all that was needed for probable cause to search Bosyk's house.

Id. at 325–26.

Judge Wynn dissented. According to Judge Wynn, probable cause was lacking because there was no reason to think that the click on the file-sharing website had come from Bulletin Board A. That click could have come from anywhere. And without knowing where the click had come from, there was no reason to think that whoever clicked on the link had sufficient reason to realize that the link contained child pornography that would then be found on the computer in the home searched:

> Users can *encounter* URLs, or hyperlinks to URLs, in myriad ways—including through websites, emails, chats, text messages, comment threads, discussion boards, File Sharing Sites (such as DropBox, Google Drive, or Apple iCloud), tweets, Facebook posts, Instagram captions, Snapchat messages, embedded images or videos, unwanted pop-up windows, any combination thereof, or by any other digital means. And because a URL, or a hyperlink to a URL, can be copied with only a click of a button, a single URL can be copied and further disseminated through any or all of these ways millions of additional times, often in a matter of seconds.

> Thus, it is no exaggeration to state that URLs, or hyperlinks to URLs, can be posted and disseminated millions of times anywhere by anyone. Take for example, the trailer for the movie *Avengers: Endgame*—which was shared through multiple online platforms such as YouTube, Facebook, and Twitter—was viewed 289 million times in the first 24 hours after it was posted online. Todd Spangler, *'Avengers: Endgame' Trailer Smashes 24-Hour Video Views Record*, Variety (Dec. 8, 2018, 11:02 a.m.). In this matter, none of the facts alleged in the affidavit rule out any of these potentially millions of alternative paths—wholly unconnected to the Bulletin Board A post—through which someone using Defendant's IP address could have encountered the URL navigating to the child pornography on File Sharing Site.

> Additionally, users can *navigate* to a URL in numerous ways beyond clicking on a link included in a post on a particular webpage, like Bulletin Board A. For example, a user could click on a copy of the URL posted to another website, click on a bookmark, type the URL directly into a browser's navigation bar, or click a hyperlink in an email or a news article, to name only a few. That is particularly true when the URL navigates to a site on the normal Internet, like File Sharing Site, as opposed to a site, like Bulletin Board A, that can only be reached using a specialty browser, like Tor.

> Importantly, users can *unintentionally navigate* to URLs because—as is the case with the URL clicked by someone using Defendant's IP address—URLs frequently do not provide any external indication of the content to which they navigate. For example, services like YouTube and DropBox generate random URLs that provide no information about their underlying content. Other services, like

Bitly, TinyURL, and Perma shorten URLs, which may otherwise provide external indicators of their content, to generic URLs that include a standard URL base, such as "https://bit.ly/," "https://tinyurl.com/," or "https://perma.cc/," followed by a random string of alphanumeric characters. Such generic URLs offer no indication of the content to which they navigate.

Link shortening and disguising often serve beneficial purposes by, for example, permitting distribution of password-protected files, facilitating the sharing of less clunky links, or permitting simpler citation styles. And link shortening and disguising can serve other innocuous purposes. URL spoofing, for example, permits one user to disguise a hyperlink as directing to specific content or a particular website, while in reality directing the unwitting user to a distinct website altogether.

One humorous form of URL spoofing is "rickrolling," one of the Internet's oldest memes, in which individuals click on a link expecting one thing but are instead led to a video of Rick Astley singing 'Never Gonna Give You Up.' The unsuspecting individual who follows the disguised URL is said to be "rickrolled."

Thus, with a few clicks, anyone—even users with no advanced computational skills—can disguise a link and lure an unsuspecting user to click that link. In such circumstances, the user would learn of the content to which the URL navigates only *after* clicking on the link.

In sum, there are myriad ways users can encounter and navigate to a URL—including unintentionally, particularly when, as here, the text of the URL provides no indication as to the nature of the content to which it navigates. Accordingly, even if the Bulletin Board A post preceded the attempt by someone using Defendant's IP address to download child pornography from File Sharing Site—a fact not established by the affidavit—there are potentially millions of paths through which someone using Defendant's IP address could have encountered and navigated to the File Sharing Site URL hosting the child pornography other than through Bulletin Board A.

Put simply, the affidavit does not establish the probability of the single sequence of events upon which the majority opinion relies— that someone using Defendant's IP address navigated to the File Sharing Site URL after encountering it on Bulletin Board A.

Id. at 342–46 (Wynn, J., dissenting).

Can the disagreement between Judge Diaz and Judge Wynn be resolved by understanding the nature of the probable cause standard? Importantly, the relevant legal question is whether probable cause was shown that child pornography would be found in the home, not whether probable cause was shown that someone had intentionally looked for child pornography. Given that, how much does it matter whether the person who visited the specific address where child pornography would be obtained had done so intending to find child pornography?

3. *Linking an Internet account to a home.* In United States v. Gourde, 440 F.3d 1065 (9th Cir. 2006) (en banc), an undercover FBI agent discovered a website called "Lolitagurls.com." According to the agent, the site contained images of nude and partially-dressed girls, some prepubescent, along with text promising pictures of young girls 12–17 to those who paid the subscription fee of $19.95 per month. The agent purchased a subscription and con-firmed that the site hosted hundreds of CSAM images. The FBI seized the server that hosted the website and obtained the list of e-mail ad-dresses used by paid subscribers to the site. The FBI then obtained a list of customers associated with these e-mail addresses from Lancelot Security, a credit card processing company that handled credit card processing and access control for Lolitagurls.com.

The FBI later executed warrants at the homes of many of the subscribers. The sole basis for the warrants was the paid subscription with the web-site. Micah Gourde was a subscriber to Lolitagurls.com for several months, and a search of his home pursuant to a warrant led to the seizure of his computer and the discovery of CSAM inside it. Gourde challenged the warrant on the ground that his membership with the website did not establish probable cause to search his home. The en banc Ninth Circuit rejected this argument in an opinion by Judge McKeown:

> Gourde subscribed to Lolitagurls.com for over two months, from November 2001 to January 2002. As a paying member, Gourde had unlimited access to hundreds of illegal images. He clearly had the means to receive and possess images in violation of 18 U.S.C. § 2252. But more importantly, Gourde's status as a member manifested his intention and desire to obtain illegal images.

> Membership is both a small step and a giant leap. To become a member requires what are at first glance little, easy steps. It was easy for Gourde to submit his home address, email address and credit card data, and he consented to have $19.95 deducted from his credit card every month. But these steps, however easy, only could have been intentional and were not insignificant. Gourde could not have become a member by accident or by a mere click of a button. This reality is perhaps easier to see by comparing Gourde to other archetypical visitors to the site. Gourde was not an accidental browser, such as a student who came across the site after "Googling" the term "Lolita" while researching the Internet for a term paper on Nabokov's book. Nor was Gourde someone who took advantage of the free tour but, after viewing the site, balked at taking the active steps necessary to become a member and gain unlimited access to images of child pornography.

> Gourde is different still from a person who actually mustered the money and nerve to become a member but, the next morning, suffered

buyer's remorse or a belated fear of prosecution and cancelled his subscription. Instead, Gourde became a member and never looked back—his membership ended because the FBI shut down the site. The affidavit left little doubt that Gourde had paid to obtain unlimited access to images of child pornography knowingly and willingly, and not involuntary, unwittingly, or even passively. With evidence from Lancelot Security, the FBI linked the email user— "gilbert_95@yahoo.com," a known subscriber to Lolitagurls.com—to Gourde and to his home ad-dress in Castle Rock, Washington.

Having paid for multi-month access to a child pornography site, Gourde was also stuck with the near certainty that his computer would contain evidence of a crime had he received or downloaded images in violation of § 2252. Thanks to the long memory of computers, any evidence of a crime almost certainly still on his computer, even if he had tried to delete the images. FBI computer experts, cited in the affidavit, stated that "even if graphic image files have been deleted these files can easily be restored." In other words, his computer would contain at least the digital footprint of the images. It was unlikely that evidence of a crime would have been stale or missing, as less than four months had elapsed be-tween the closing of the Lolitagurls.com website and the execution of the search warrant.

Given this triad of solid facts—the site had illegal images, Gourde in-tended to have and wanted access to these images, and these images were almost certainly retrievable from his computer if he had ever received or downloaded them—the only inference the magistrate judge needed to make to find probable cause was that there was a "fair probability" Gourde had, in fact, received or downloaded images.

Id. at 1070–71. Judge Kleinfeld dissented:

There are just too many secrets on people's computers, most legal, some embarrassing, and some potentially tragic in their implications, for loose liberality in allowing search warrants. Emails and history links may show that someone is ordering medication for a disease being kept secret even from family members. Or they may show that someone's child is being counseled by parents for a serious problem that is none of anyone else's business. Or a married mother of three may be carrying on a steamy email correspondence with an old high school boyfriend. Or an otherwise respectable, middle-aged gentleman may be looking at dirty pictures.

Just as a conscientious public official may be hounded out of office because a party guest found a homosexual magazine when she went to the bathroom at his house, people's lives may be ruined because of legal but embarrassing materials found on their computers. And, in all but the largest metropolitan areas, it really does not matter whether any formal charges ensue—if the police or other visitors find the material, it will be all over town and hinted at in the newspaper within a few days.

Nor are secrets the only problem. Warrants ordinarily direct seizure, not just search, and computers are often shared by family members. Seizure of a shared family computer may, though unrelated to the law enforcement purpose, effectively confiscate a professor's book, a student's almost completed Ph.D. thesis, or a business's accounts payable and receivable. People cannot get their legitimate work done if their computer is at the police station because of someone else's suspected child pornography downloads. Sex with children is so disgusting to most of us that we may be too liberal in allowing searches when the government investigates child pornography cases. The privacy of people's computers is too important to let it be eroded by sexual disgust.

The reason [Gourde] could not be assumed to possess child pornography is that possession of child pornography is a very serious crime and the affidavit did not say he had downloaded any. He could use the site to look at child pornography without downloading it, a reasonable assumption in the absence of evidence that he had downloaded images. Common sense suggests that everyone, pervert or not, has the desire to stay out of jail. The ordinary desire to stay out of jail is a factor that must be considered in the totality of circumstances. It would be irrational to assume that an individual is indifferent between subjecting himself to criminal sanctions and avoiding them, when he can attain his object while avoiding them. To commit the crime for which the warrant sought evidence, one has to do something more than look: he must ship, produce, or at the least knowingly possess. The two child pornography statutes at issue do not say that *viewing* child pornography is a crime. Congress could perhaps make it a crime to pay to view such images, but it did not.

Id. at 1077–79.

Judge Kleinfeld's dissent hinges on the claimed distinction between looking at child pornography and possessing it. Is Judge Kleinfeld interpreting the law correctly? Also note that shortly after the *Gourde* case, Congress amended the child pornography laws to punish accessing a computer "with intent to view" child pornography. *See* Enhancing the Effective Child Pornography Prosecution Act of 2007, Pub. L. No. 110–358, § 203(b) (2008) (amending 18 U.S.C. § 2252(a)(4) and 18 U.S.C. § 2252A(a)(5)). Does the current version of the statute make the question in *Gourde* easier?

4. *Inferences from account usage to a home.* Consider the inferences a court must draw before concluding that membership in a website or online group connected to criminal activity creates probable cause to search a member's home for evidence of the crime. Satisfying this burden requires an explicit or implicit assessment of the following questions:

A. How likely is it that the defendant is the one who controlled the account when it was used to join the group?

B. How likely is it that the defendant signed up for the service with the intent to obtain evidence of crime?

C. How likely is it that the defendant obtained evidence of crime or otherwise had it on his computer?

D. How likely is it that the evidence is currently present in the home?

Are judges well-equipped to answer these questions?

5.   *Tracing IP addresses.* Investigators often try to establish probable cause to search a home for evidence of computer crimes by tracing Internet Protocol (IP) addresses. In many cases, the investigators collect evidence by linking IP addresses to accounts and then accounts to physical addresses.

The basic technology of the Internet makes IP addresses an essential tool for tracing Internet activity. Whenever a user connects to the Internet, the service provider that provides the connection will assign the user a series of numbers known as an IP address that serves as the unique identifying address of his computer for that session (and in some cases, for all of that user's sessions). As a general matter, communications sent by or to that user across the Internet will contain that IP address. This means that when investigators know the IP address used in a session of Internet activity that is linked to a crime, they will first identify the service provider known to control the block of IP addresses that includes that specific address.

When investigators know that a particular IP address was used in criminal activity, they can contact the owner/operator of the server that controls the address and try to find out more information. For example, if an IP address belongs to a specific provider, the provider's system administrator may have business records that indicate what account controlled that address when it was used in criminal activity. If the account is associated with a physical address—in the case of a home user, for example, the home address used for billing purposes—investigators can then focus their suspicion on that physical location.

6.   *Probable cause and unsecured wireless networks.* Imagine the police trace wrongdoing to an unsecured wireless access point based inside a home. Access to the network does not require a password, which means that anyone near the home can log on and use that IP address to engage in wrongdoing. Should investigators be allowed to assume that criminal acts using that network came from inside the home? Alternatively, before obtaining a warrant to search the home, should they be required to investigate the possibility that someone nearby used the network instead? *Cf.* United States v. Larson, 2011 WL 3837540 (W.D.Mo. 2011) ("The fact that someone could have sat outside defendant's residence with a laptop and downloaded child pornography certainly exists, but it does not negate the fair probability that someone inside the house downloaded that material.").

7. *Staleness*. One issue that often arises in computer crime cases is the "staleness" of the government's probable cause. Digital evidence may be present one day but erased, deleted, or removed by the next. To establish probable cause, the government must show probable cause to believe evidence of crime exists at the place to be searched at the time the warrant is issued, not just at the time the crime was committed. If too much time has elapsed after the relevant time period of the government's evidence, that evidence may become stale and may no longer satisfy the probable cause standard.

In CSAM cases, courts have rejected staleness challenge by taking judicial notice of the practices of CSAM collectors. Consider United States v. Lamb, 945 F. Supp. 441 (N.D.N.Y. 1996):

> The observation that images of child pornography are likely to be hoarded by persons interested in those materials in the privacy of their homes is supported by common sense and the cases. Since the materials are illegal to distribute and possess, initial collection is difficult. Having succeeded in obtaining images, collectors are unlikely to quickly destroy them. Because of their illegality and the imprimatur of severe social stigma such images carry, collectors will want to secret them in secure places, like a private residence. This proposition is not novel in either state or federal court: pedophiles, preferential child molesters, and child pornography collectors maintain their materials for significant periods of time.

Id. at 460.

How should courts evaluate staleness arguments in other types of computer crime cases? Imagine Sarah uses her personal, home computer to hack into a sensitive government server, and that one year later the police develop reason to believe Sarah was the intruder. The police apply for a warrant to search Sarah's house. What are the chances that Sarah's computer will continue to store evidence of the crime a year after the intrusion? Does evidence stay on a computer forever?

2.   PARTICULARITY

The Fourth Amendment requires that warrants must "particularly describ[e] the place to be searched and the persons or things to be seized." This is the so-called particularly requirement. The Supreme Court explained the purpose of the particularity requirement in Maryland v. Garrison, 480 U.S. 79, 84 (1987):

> The manifest purpose of this particularity requirement was to prevent general searches. By limiting the authorization to search to the specific areas and things for which there is probable cause to search, the requirement ensures that the search will be carefully tailored to its justifications, and will not take on the character of the wide-ranging exploratory searches the Framers intended to prohibit. Thus, the scope of a lawful search is defined

by the object of the search and the places in which there is probable cause to believe that it may be found. Just as probable cause to believe that a stolen lawnmower may be found in a garage will not support a warrant to search an upstairs bedroom, probable cause to believe that undocumented aliens are being transported in a van will not justify a warrantless search of a suitcase.

As this excerpt suggests, the probable cause and particularity requirements work together. A warrant must specify a specific place in which specific evidence of the crime is probably located, and the affidavit must establish probable cause to believe that the evidence is located in the place to be searched.

UNITED STATES V. ULBRICHT

United States Court of Appeals for the Second Circuit, 2017.
858 F.3d 71.

GERARD E. LYNCH, CIRCUIT JUDGE:

Defendant Ross William Ulbricht appeals from a judgment of conviction and sentence to life imprisonment entered in the United States District Court for the Southern District of New York. A jury convicted Ulbricht of drug trafficking and other crimes associated with his creation and operation of Silk Road, an online marketplace whose users primarily purchased and sold illegal goods and services. Because we identify no reversible error, we affirm Ulbricht's conviction.

BACKGROUND

In February 2015, a jury convicted Ross William Ulbricht on seven counts arising from his creation and operation of Silk Road under the username Dread Pirate Roberts ("DPR"). Silk Road was a massive, anonymous criminal marketplace that operated using the Tor Network, which renders Internet traffic through the Tor browser extremely difficult to trace. Silk Road users principally bought and sold drugs, false identification documents, and computer hacking software. Transactions on Silk Road exclusively used Bitcoins, an anonymous but traceable digital currency.

According to the government, between 2011 and 2013, thousands of vendors used Silk Road to sell approximately $183 million worth of illegal drugs, as well as other goods and services. Ulbricht, acting as DPR, earned millions of dollars in profits from the commissions collected by Silk Road on purchases. In October 2013, the government arrested Ulbricht, seized the Silk Road servers, and shut down the site.

Ulbricht was arrested in a San Francisco public library on October 1, 2013, after the government had amassed significant evidence identifying him as Dread Pirate Roberts. Ulbricht was arrested, and incident to that arrest agents seized his laptop.

A great deal of the evidence against Ulbricht came from the government's search of his laptop and his home after the arrest. On the day of Ulbricht's arrest, the government obtained a warrant to seize Ulbricht's laptop and search it for a wide variety of information related to Silk Road and information that would identify Ulbricht as Dread Pirate Roberts. Ulbricht moved to suppress the large quantity of evidence obtained from his laptop, challenging the constitutionality of that search warrant. Ulbricht argues on appeal that the district court erred in denying his motion to suppress.

DISCUSSION

Ulbricht contends that the warrant authorizing the search and seizure of his laptop violated the Fourth Amendment's particularity requirement. To be sufficiently particular under the Fourth Amendment, a warrant must satisfy three requirements. First, a warrant must identify the specific offense for which the police have established probable cause. Second, a warrant must describe the place to be searched. Finally, the warrant must specify the items to be seized by their relation to designated crimes.

Where, as here, the property to be searched is a computer hard drive, the particularity requirement assumes even greater importance. A general search of electronic data is an especially potent threat to privacy because hard drives and e-mail accounts may be akin to a residence in terms of the scope and quantity of private information they may contain. The seizure of a computer hard drive, and its subsequent retention by the government, can therefore give the government possession of a vast trove of personal information about the person to whom the drive belongs, much of which may be entirely irrelevant to the criminal investigation that led to the seizure.

Such sensitive records might include tax records, diaries, personal photographs, electronic books, electronic media, medical data, records of internet searches, and banking and shopping information. Because of the nature of digital storage, it is not always feasible to extract and segregate responsive data from non-responsive data, creating a serious risk that every warrant for electronic information will become, in effect, a general warrant. Thus, we have held that warrants that fail to link the evidence sought to the criminal activity supported by probable cause do not satisfy the particularity requirement because they lack meaningful parameters on an otherwise limitless search" of a defendant's electronic media.

The Fourth Amendment does not require a perfect description of the data to be searched and seized, however. Search warrants covering digital data may contain some ambiguity so long as law enforcement agents have done the best that could reasonably be expected under the circumstances, have acquired all the descriptive facts which a reasonable investigation could be expected to cover, and have insured that all those facts were included in the warrant."

Moreover, it is important to bear in mind that a search warrant does not necessarily lack particularity simply because it is broad. Since a search of a computer is akin to a search of a residence, searches of computers may sometimes need to be as broad as searches of residences pursuant to warrants. Similarly, traditional searches for paper records, like searches for electronic records, have always entailed the exposure of records that are not the objects of the search to at least superficial examination in order to identify and seize those records that are. And in many cases, the volume of records properly subject to seizure because of their evidentiary value may be vast. None of these consequences necessarily turns a search warrant into a prohibited general warrant.

The warrant authorizing the search and seizure of Ulbricht's laptop explicitly incorporated by reference an affidavit listing the crimes charged, which at the time included narcotics trafficking, computer hacking, money laundering, and murder-for-hire offenses in violation of 21 U.S.C. § 846, 18 U.S.C. §§ 1030, 1956, and 1958. The affidavit also described the workings of Silk Road and the role of Dread Pirate Roberts in operating the site and included a wealth of information supporting a finding that there was probable cause to believe that Ulbricht and DPR were the same person. Based on that information, the Laptop Warrant alleged that Ulbricht used the laptop in connection with his operation of Silk Road, and that there was probable cause to believe that evidence, fruits, and instrumentalities of the charged offenses would be found on the laptop.

Generally speaking, the Laptop Warrant divided the information to be searched for and seized into two categories. The first covered evidence concerning Silk Road that was located on the computer, including, *inter alia*, data associated with the Silk Road website, such as web content, server code, or database records; any evidence concerning servers or computer equipment connected with Silk Road; e-mails, private messages, and forum postings or other communications concerning Silk Road in any way; evidence concerning funds used to facilitate or proceeds derived from Silk Road, including Bitcoin wallet files and transactions with Bitcoin exchangers, or information concerning any financial accounts where Silk Road funds may be stored; and any evidence concerning any illegal activity associated with Silk Road.

The second category of information in the Laptop Warrant included evidence relevant to corroborating the identification of Ulbricht as the Silk Road user 'Dread Pirate Roberts.' In order to connect Ulbricht with DPR, the Laptop Warrant authorized agents to search for: any communications or writings by Ulbricht, which may reflect linguistic patterns or idiosyncrasies associated with 'Dread Pirate Roberts,' or political/economic views associated with DPR; any evidence concerning any computer equipment, software, or usernames used by Ulbricht, to allow comparison with computer equipment used by DPR; any evidence concerning Ulbricht's travel or patterns of movement, to allow comparison with patterns of online activity of DPR; any evidence concerning Ulbricht's technical expertise concerning Tor, Bitcoins, and other computer programming issues; any evidence concerning Ulbricht's attempts to obtain fake identification documents use aliases, or otherwise evade law enforcement; and any other evidence implicating Ulbricht in the subject offenses.

After careful consideration of the warrant, the supporting affidavit, and Ulbricht's arguments, we conclude that the Laptop Warrant did not violate the Fourth Amendment's particularity requirement. We note, at the outset of our review, that the warrant plainly satisfies the basic elements of the particularity requirement as traditionally understood. By incorporating the affidavit by reference, the Laptop Warrant lists the charged crimes, describes the place to be searched, and designates the information to be seized in connection with the specified offenses. Each category of information sought is relevant to Silk Road, DPR's operation thereof, or identifying Ulbricht as DPR. We do not understand Ulbricht's arguments to contest the Laptop Warrant's basic compliance with those requirements.

Rather, Ulbricht's arguments turn on the special problems associated with searches of computers which, as we have acknowledged in prior cases, can be particularly intrusive. These arguments merit careful attention. For example, Ulbricht questions the appropriateness of the protocols that the Laptop Warrant instructed officers to use in executing the search. Those procedures included opening or "cursorily reading the first few" pages of files to "determine their precise contents," searching for deliberately hidden files, using "key word searches through all electronic storage areas," and reviewing file "directories" to determine what was relevant. Ulbricht, supported by *amicus* the National Association of Criminal Defense Lawyers ("NACDL"), argues that the warrant was insufficiently particular because the government and the magistrate judge failed to specify the search terms and protocols *ex ante* in the warrant.

We cannot agree. As illustrated by the facts of this very case, it will often be impossible to identify in advance the words or phrases that will separate relevant files or documents before the search takes place, because officers cannot readily anticipate how a suspect will store information related to the charged crimes. Files and documents can easily be given misleading or coded names, and words that might be expected to occur in pertinent documents can be encrypted; even very simple codes can defeat a pre-planned word search. For example, at least one of the folders on Ulbricht's computer had a name with the misspelling "aliaces." For a more challenging example, Ulbricht also kept records of certain Tor chats in a file on his laptop that was labeled "mbsobzvkhwx4hmjt."

The agents reasonably anticipated that they would face such problems in this case. Operating Silk Road involved using sophisticated technology to mask its users' identities. Accordingly, although we acknowledge the NACDL's suggestions in its *amicus* submission for limiting the scope of such search terms, the absence of the proposed limitations does not violate the particularity requirement on the facts of this case.

The fundamental flaw in Ulbricht's (and NACDL's) argument is that it confuses a warrant's breadth with a lack of particularity. As noted above, breadth and particularity are related but distinct concepts. A warrant may be broad, in that it authorizes the government to search an identified location or object for a wide range of potentially relevant material, without violating the particularity requirement. For example, a warrant may allow the government to search a suspected drug dealer's entire home where there is probable cause to believe that evidence relevant to that activity may be found anywhere in the residence.

Similarly, when the criminal activity pervades an entire business, seizure of all records of the business is appropriate, and broad language used in warrants will not offend the particularity requirements. Ulbricht used his laptop to commit the charged offenses by creating and continuing to operate Silk Road. Thus, a broad warrant allowing the government to search his laptop for potentially extensive evidence of those crimes does not offend the Fourth Amendment, as long as that warrant meets the three particularity criteria outlined above.

It is also true that allowing law enforcement to search his writings for linguistic similarities with DPR authorizes a broad search of written materials on Ulbricht's hard drive. That fact, however, does not mean that the warrants violated the Fourth Amendment. The Laptop Warrant clearly explained that the government planned to compare Ulbricht's writings to DPR's posts to confirm that they were the same person, by identifying both linguistic patterns and distinctive shared political or economic views.

Ulbricht and the NACDL similarly claim that searching for all evidence of his travel patterns and movement violates the Fourth Amendment's particularity requirement. Again, the warrant explained that it sought information about Ulbricht's travel to allow comparison with patterns of online activity of 'Dread Pirate Roberts' and any information known about his location at particular times. Thus, the Laptop Warrant connects the information sought to the crimes charged and, more specifically, its relevance to identifying Ulbricht as the perpetrator of those crimes.

We remain sensitive to the difficulties associated with preserving a criminal defendant's privacy while searching through his electronic data and computer hard drives. In the course of searching for information related to Silk Road and DPR, the government may indeed have come across personal documents that were unrelated to Ulbricht's crimes. Such an invasion of a criminal defendant's privacy is inevitable, however, in almost any warranted search because in searches for papers, it is certain that some innocuous documents will be examined, at least cursorily, in order to determine whether they are, in fact, among those papers authorized to be seized. The Fourth Amendment limits such unwarranted intrusions upon privacy by requiring a warrant to describe its scope with particularity.

The Laptop Warrant satisfied that requirement. Ulbricht has challenged only the facial validity of the Laptop Warrant and not its execution. Because we have no reason to doubt that the officers faithfully executed the warrant, its execution did not result in an undue invasion of Ulbricht's privacy.

Finally, we note that the crimes charged in this case were somewhat unusual. This case does not involve a more typical situation in which officers searched for evidence of a physician's illegal distribution of pain medications, to use the NACDL's example, which may have electronically-stored data associated with the alleged crimes on a hard drive that largely contains non-criminal information. Here the crimes under investigation were committed largely through computers that there was probable cause to believe included the laptop at issue, and the search warrant application gave ample basis for the issuing magistrate judge to conclude that evidence related to Silk Road and Ulbricht's use of the DPR username likely permeated Ulbricht's computer.

Thus, given the nature of Ulbricht's crimes and their symbiotic connection to his digital devices, we decline to rethink the well-settled Fourth Amendment principles that the Laptop Warrant may implicate. A future case may require this Court to articulate special limitations on digital searches to effectuate the Fourth Amendment's particularity or reasonableness requirements. Such a case is not before us.

NOTES AND QUESTIONS

1.   *Particularity and the two stages of computer search warrants.* Most computer warrants are executed in two stages. First, the computer hardware is taken away; second, the computers are searched for electronic evidence. The physical search comes first and the electronic search comes second. Should the particularity requirement focus on the physical search stage, the electronic search stage, or both?

For example, imagine a warrant states with exquisite particularity exactly what kinds of computer hardware will be seized at the first stage but gives no guidance on the evidence investigators will look for when the computers are searched. Alternatively, imagine a warrant names the exact computer file that agents will look for at the second stage, but it doesn't say anything about what computers the agents plan to remove at the place to be searched. Are either of these warrants sufficiently particular?

2.   *Limiting the scope of computer search warrants to specific files sought.* In Burns v. United States, 235 A.3d 758 (D.C. 2020), the defendant Burns was charged with premeditated first-degree murder for shooting and killing his best friend Osuchukwu following a dispute over how to divide the proceeds from their joint drug dealing business. Burns claimed he had acted in self-defense. The prosecution argued that Burns had carefully planned the killing.

The government's case was based heavily on digital evidence recovered from two cell phones seized from Burns the day after Osuchukwu's death. In the days leading up to the homicide, Internet search queries made from the phones included the following:

- "Are you capable of killing your best friend?"
- "How does it feel when you kill someone for the first time?"
- "Will God forgive murderers?"
- "Shot placement for instant kill"

The evidence retrieved from the cell phone also included a text message from Burns to his cousin about Osuchukwu's arrival in town, dated the day before the killing. The message stated, "I'm clapping him today," using a slang term for shooting.

On the basis of this digital evidence, Burns was convicted of first-degree premeditated murder.

The legal issue in *Burns* was the validity of the warrants used to search the phones. The affidavits established that Burns and Osuchukwu were best friends; that Burns had been texting with Osuchukwu on the day of Osuchukwu's death, November 14th, 2015; that Burns had been waiting for Osuchukwu to arrive from out of town in a particular apartment where Osuchukwu was later shot and killed; and that Burns claimed he had left the apartment before Osuchukwu arrived and only later discovered him dead the next day, November 15th, 2015. Based on these facts, the government had obtained and executed warrants to search the two phones for "all records" that "relate" to violations of first-degree murder.

The D.C. Court of Appeals overturned the conviction on the ground that the warrants violated the Fourth Amendment:

> It is not enough for police to show there is probable cause to arrest the owner or user of the cell phone, or even to establish probable cause to believe the phone contains some evidence of a crime. To be compliant with the Fourth Amendment, the warrant must specify the particular items of evidence to be searched for and seized from the phone and be strictly limited to the time period and information or

other data for which probable cause has been properly established through the facts and circumstances set forth under oath in the warrant's supporting affidavit.

Vigilance in enforcing the probable cause and particularity requirements is thus essential to the protection of the vital privacy interests inherent in virtually every modern cell phone and to the achievement of the meaningful constraints contemplated in *Riley*. As the Supreme Court recently reiterated, judges are obligated—as subtler and more far-reaching means of invading privacy have become available to the Government—to ensure that the 'progress of science' does not erode Fourth Amendment protections.

We conclude as a matter of law that the search warrants for Mr. Burns's cell phones did not satisfy the requirements of the Warrant Clause. The facts set forth in the warrants' supporting affidavits established probable cause to believe the phones contained text messages between Mr. Burns and Mr. Osuchukwu on November 14, 2015 and a log showing the precise time of the telephone call Mr. Burns reportedly made to his cousin that night. The facts alleged in the affidavits also supplied probable cause to support a search of the GPS tracking features on the phones to determine Mr. Burns's whereabouts at pertinent times on November 14 and 15, 2015. But beyond those discrete items, the affidavits stated no facts that even arguably provided a reason to believe that any other information or data on the phones had any nexus to the investigation of Mr. Osuchukwu's death.

The warrants also lacked particularity, describing the objects of the search in the most general terms imaginable. Rather than specifying the three narrow items of evidence for which the affidavits established probable cause, the warrants broadly authorized the seizure of "any evidence" on the phones and listed, by way of examples, generic categories covering virtually all of the different types of data found on modern cell phones. The warrants imposed no meaningful limitations as to how far back in time police could go or what applications they could review and, instead, endorsed the broadest possible search without regard to the facts of the case or the limited showings of probable cause set forth in the affidavits.

Is *Burns* consistent with *Ulbricht*? If not, which is more persuasive?

3. *The need to name the crime or specific kinds of evidence.* In United States v. Riccardi, 405 F.3d 852 (10th Cir. 2005), police executed a warrant to search for and seize computers in a CSAM investigation. The warrant authorized investigators to search the defendant's home and seize his computer as well as:

all electronic and magnetic media stored therein, together with all storage devises [sic], internal or external to the computer or computer system, including but not limited to floppy disks, diskettes, hard disks, magnetic tapes, removable media drives, optical media such as CD-ROM, printers, modems, and any other electronic or magnetic devises used as a peripheral to the computer or computer system, and all electronic media stored within such devises.

The police executed the warrant, seized the defendant's home computer, and later searched it and found CSAM images. In an opinion by Judge McConnell, the Tenth Circuit held that the warrant violated the Fourth Amendment because it was not sufficiently particular: "warrants for computer searches must affirmatively limit the search to evidence of specific federal crimes or specific types of material." *Id.* at 862.

The warrant in this case was not limited to any particular files, or to any particular federal crime. By its terms, the warrant thus permitted the officers to search for anything—from child pornography to tax returns to private correspondence. It seemed to authorize precisely the kind of wide-ranging exploratory search that the Framers intended to prohibit.

Id. at 862–63.

4.   *When naming the crime is not enough.* In United States v. Shah, 2015 WL 72118 (E.D.N.C. 2015), the government obtained a warrant for all evidence of violations of the Computer Fraud and Abuse Act found in the contents of a Google e-mail account, "shahnn28@gmail.com." The district court ruled that this warrant violated the particularity requirement:

In order to satisfy particularity, the warrant must at least minimally confine the executing officers' discretion by allowing them to seize only evidence of a particular crime.

United States v. Dickerson, 166 F.3d 667, 693 (4th Cir. 1999), distinguished between evidence of a "particular crime" and evidence related to "general criminal activity" as follows: "A warrant authorizing a search for evidence relating to a broad criminal statute or general criminal activity such as wire fraud, fraud, conspiracy, or tax evasion, is overbroad because it provides no readily ascertainable guidelines for the executing officers as to what items to seize. In contrast, a warrant authorizing a search for evidence relating to a specific illegal activity, such as narcotics, or theft of fur coats is sufficiently particular."

In *Dickerson*, the warrant authorized seizure of evidence of the crime of bank robbery. The court held that bank robbery was a specific illegal activity that generates quite distinctive evidence, and thereby upheld the warrant.

A violation of the CFAA would not necessarily generate such distinctive evidence as bank robbery or narcotics. Nor would evidence necessarily be as distinctive as that of child pornography, a type of crime more commonly targeted by warrants for electronic information. Rather, a warrant authorizing collection of evidence of a CFAA violation comes closer to warrants seeking to collect evidence regarding violations of broad federal statutes prohibiting fraud or conspiracy. In these cases, limitation by reference to the broad statute fails to impose any real limitation.

The Google Warrant provides no other details to clarify the particular crime at issue. Section II(a) makes reference to "unauthorized network activity," yet gives no indication as to the meaning of this phrase, which would seem to be implicated in almost all of the activities prohibited by the CFAA. The warrant offers nothing about the time frame of the offense. Rather, it provides for the seizure of all evidence of violations of the CFAA "since account inception."

Id. at *12–*14.

5. *Are date restrictions required?* In Wheeler v. State, 135 A.3d 282 (Del. 2016), the defendant Wheeler had abused several individuals decades earlier. In July 2013, the individuals confronted Wheeler about their abuse. Wheeler acknowledged his acts but discouraged the individuals from contacting law enforcement. The government obtained search warrants to search Wheeler's home and office for evidence of witness tampering.

Agents seized several computers when they executed the warrants. A search of one computer that had not been powered on since September 2012 revealed images of child pornography, which then led to a criminal prosecution against Wheeler for possessing child pornography.

The Supreme Court of Delaware ruled that the warrants violated the particularity requirement because they did not contain a date restriction. The government should not have been permitted to search a computer that had not been used after 2012 to look for evidence of a crime that occurred in 2013:

> We hesitate to prescribe rigid rules and instead reiterate that warrants must designate the things to be searched and seized as particularly as possible. Striking the correct balance when protecting against generality and overbreadth requires vigilance on the part of judicial officers who are on the front lines of preserving constitutional rights while assisting government officials in the legitimate pursuit of prosecuting criminal activity. Where, as here, the investigators had available to them a more precise description of the alleged criminal activity that is the subject of the warrant, such information should be included in the instrument and the search and seizure should be appropriately narrowed to the relevant time period so as to mitigate the potential for unconstitutional exploratory rummaging.

> The State conceded that nothing relating to [one victim] would be found on Wheeler's property identified in the Witness Tampering Warrants. And the Affidavits do not suggest otherwise. As to the only other potential victims, the Affidavits indicate that the alleged witness tampering occurred, if it did, in or after July 2013, since that

was when they renewed contact with Wheeler. The Affidavits contain no facts suggesting that any tampering might have occurred prior to July 2013.

Yet, the Witness Tampering Warrants were boundless as to time. Sergeant Perna testified that one of the first things he did in executing the search was determine when the iMac was last used. Proceeding under the Witness Tampering Warrants, he determined that the computer had last been powered on in September 2012. However, the State unsystematically sifted through Wheeler's digital universe, even though the iMac logically could not have contained material created or recorded during the relevant time period.

A failure to describe the items to be searched for and seized with as much particularity as the circumstances reasonably allow offends the constitutional protections against unreasonable searches and seizures. Because the State was able to more precisely describe the items to be searched and seized, the Witness Tampering Warrants violated the particularity requirement.

Id. at 304–05.

The Colorado Supreme Court struck a similar note in People v. Coke, 461 P.3d 508 (Colo. 2020). The defendant was suspected of having sent text messages that indicated her involvement in a crime. The police obtained a warrant to broadly search her phone for text messages, photographs, and items showing ownership of the phone. Searching the phone revealed the expected text messages. The Colorado Supreme Court ruled that the warrant violated the particularity requirement because it was not limited to "the alleged victim or to the time period during which the assault allegedly occurred." *Id.* at 516. *But see* United States v. Richards, 76 M.J. 365, 370 (C.A.A.F. 2017) (holding that "though a temporal limitation is one possible method of tailoring a search authorization, it is by no means a requirement.").

6.   *Particularity of a warrant for historical cell-site location information (CSLI).* The Supreme Court held in Carpenter v. United States, 138 S.Ct. 2206 (2018), that the government needs a warrant to collect CSLI, at least over the longer-term, from a cell phone service provider. This prompts a particularity question: When a warrant is needed, how long a period can the warrant cover before it violates the particularity requirement?

In State v. Waters, 2020 WL 507703 (Del. Super. 2020), a home robbery turned tragic when one of the robbers shot and killed an occupant. Other occupants identified Waters as the robber that had fired the shot. The government obtained a warrant for the CSLI of Waters' cell phone starting four days before the robbery and continuing two weeks after it.

Waters moved to suppress the evidence, arguing that the warrant was overbroad because there was no reason to think that his location over the entire period of the warrant provided evidence of the robbery. The trial court agreed that the warrant was overbroad. The court concluded that the remedy was to limit the admitted evidence to the time period for which there was probable cause. According to the court, the proper time window was only the 24 hours after the crime:

> Demonstrating the whereabouts of the Defendant in the hours after the murder is certainly probative of whether he stayed within range of the cell tower for hours after the homicide—demonstrating that he remained within the locale of the crime scene or departed shortly thereafter. The Court finds that the historical CSLI for the 24 hours after the crime is a reasonable window within the probable cause laid out in the warrant.

Id. at *5. The remaining evidence outside the one-day window was suppressed. *See id.*

Is the court's approach persuasive? Recall from the Notes following *Carpenter* that it remains unclear whether *Carpenter* applies to short-term collection of CSLI. If *Carpenter* only requires a warrant for long-term collection, does it make sense that the warrant authority only permits short-term collection?

Imagine the police have probable cause that CSLI will provide evidence of a crime during a 5-minute window when a known crime occurred. If this is an insufficiently long period to trigger the Fourth Amendment under *Carpenter*, does obtaining a warrant permit the government to learn information about the suspect's location beyond the 5-minute window? If the government wants to know where a person was located over several weeks or months, perhaps to uncover other crimes they committed, is that information categorically off-limits?

7. *Probable cause and particularity for automated searches: The case of the Playpen warrant.* CSAM websites frequently operate in anonymity using the Tor network. Tor, short for "The Onion Router," is a free service that disguises user identity by bouncing traffic across different servers and using encryption to prevent traffic from being traced. When a website is accessible only using Tor, the website will ordinarily keep no records that can help trace users' identities. Because Tor masks IP addresses, investigators will have no way to find the visitors who have visited the site.

In 2014, the federal government began investigating a CSAM website known as "Playpen" that was accessible only through the Tor network. The website was located at an address that was a long random string of letters and numbers ending in ".onion." The FBI was able to take over the server that hosted Playpen. Upon doing so, however, the FBI learned that Playpen stored no records that could allow identification of any users of the site. To identify Playpen's users, the FBI obtained a search warrant allowing the government to install a "network investigative technique" ("NIT") on the computers of Playpen account holders.

The NIT was essentially a computer virus that would infect the user machines. When a Playpen visitor logged in to the site with a username and password, the NIT would be surreptitiously installed on the visitor's computer. The NIT would then send the government information about the user's computer, most importantly the computer's true IP address. The NIT was successfully installed on over 1,000 computers all around the world during the weeks it was used. The use of the NIT enabled the FBI to identify hundreds of visitors to Playpen, which then led to arrests and prosecution around the country for CSAM offenses.

District courts ruled that the warrant satisfied the probable cause and particularity requirements of the Fourth Amendment. A typical analysis is found in United States v. Allain, 2016 WL 5660452 (D.Mass. 2016). Allain's computer was searched by the NIT when he logged in to the Playpen website. Among his challenges to the warrant was that it lacked probable cause and particularity. First, the court held that probable cause existed to search Allain's computer:

> The NIT Warrant authorized the NIT to be deployed to any computer used to log into Playpen. Because logging into Playpen was not itself a crime, the warrant application needed to establish probable cause to believe that anyone logging into Playpen was doing so for the purpose of viewing or distributing child pornography.
>
> While it was possible that someone could log into Playpen and then not attempt to access child pornography, probable cause does not require certainty, and the Warrant Application and supporting affidavit established a fair probability that anyone who logged into Playpen would view or share child pornography. The appearance of Playpen's homepage was only one of the several factors supporting the magistrate's probable cause determination. Even if the homepage alone would not have established probable cause, the totality of the circumstances were sufficient to demonstrate the requisite level of proof.
>
> Playpen operated as a hidden service on the Tor network. The parties dispute how hidden websites on the Tor network can be located, but there is no question that it was difficult to find. Users first had to gain access to the Tor Network, and then somehow locate the site, despite its indecipherable web address. Therefore, the Court credits the affiant's statement in the warrant application that it would be "extremely unlikely that any user could simply stumble upon Playpen without understanding its purpose and content."
>
> Playpen was in fact a website devoted to child pornography, and the fact that users found it and then logged into it is indicative of criminal intent. While there may be legitimate reasons to use the Tor network other than masking illicit activity, the clandestine nature of the website and the challenges of finding it on the Tor Network suggests that those who logged into Playpen likely knew the purpose of the website and were entering it to access child pornography.

> Playpen's registration terms, which appeared before users setup a username and password, gave further indication of Playpen's illicit purpose. Prospective registrants were told that, "the forum operators do NOT want you to enter a real e-mail address," that users "should not post information in their profile that can be used to identify you," and that, "this website is not able to see your IP." In addition, Playpen's homepage (as it actually appeared when the warrant was issued and Allain logged in), would likely still have alerted users to the general content of the website. The homepage had a picture of a young girl scantily clad, was titled "Playpen," and required a username and password to proceed.

> Considering the totality of the circumstances—the appearance and content of Playpen, the fact that it was a hidden service on the Tor network, and its registration terms—the magistrate judge had a substantial basis for concluding that the search warrant was supported by probable cause to believe that evidence of criminal conduct would be found on computers used to log into Playpen.

Id. at *5–*7. The court also ruled that the warrant was sufficiently particular. The defendant argued that the warrant was a prohibited general warrant because it authorized a limitless number of searches all around the world. The court disagreed:

> This argument is largely duplicative of Defendant's probable cause argument. As already discussed, there was adequate support for the magistrate judge's finding that there was probable cause to search any computers that logged into Playpen. It is irrelevant how many computers were covered by the warrant, given that there was probable cause to search each one. Likewise, it is irrelevant that the warrant could have been narrower, given that the warrant as actually issued was sufficiently narrow to limit searches to computers for which there was probable cause to search.

> The NIT Warrant is not a general warrant in that it clearly limited which computers could be searched and what information could be obtained as a result of that search. Attachment A of the warrant authorized deployment of the NIT to the computer server hosting Playpen and then to computers of "any user or administrator who logs into Playpen by entering a username and password." Attachment B, in turn, imposed detailed limits on what information could be obtained from those computers by the NIT. Id., Att. B. The NIT Warrant therefore satisfied the particularity requirements of the Fourth Amendment.

Id. at *8–*9.

Is it odd that a single warrant can authorize thousands of searches all around the world and yet still not be considered a general warrant? The text of the Fourth Amendment requires warrants to state the place to be searched.

Is it sufficient to describe that "place" as wherever the computers that will log in to a particular website happen to be?

8.   *The good faith exception.* The development of caselaw on the particularity requirement for computer searches has been hindered by the good faith exception to the exclusionary rule. In United States v. Leon, 468 U.S. 897 (1984), the Supreme Court held that defects in search warrants should not lead to suppression of evidence if the government investigators have a reasonable good faith belief that the warrant satisfied the Fourth Amendment. The Court reasoned that an officer who has an objectively reasonable belief that the warrant was proper has not committed a wrong that courts must deter:

> It is the magistrate's responsibility to determine whether the officer's allegations establish probable cause and, if so, to issue a warrant comporting in form with the requirements of the Fourth Amendment. In the ordinary case, an officer cannot be expected to question the magistrate's probable-cause determination or his judgment that the form of the warrant is technically sufficient. Once the warrant issues, there is literally nothing more the policeman can do in seeking to comply with the law. Penalizing the officer for the magistrate's error, rather than his own, cannot logically contribute to the deterrence of Fourth Amendment violation. We conclude that the marginal or nonexistent benefits produced by suppressing evidence obtained in objectively reasonable reliance on a subsequently invalidated search warrant cannot justify the substantial costs of exclusion.

Because of the good faith exception, courts will often deny motions to suppress the fruits of computer searches because any defects in particularity should nonetheless not lead to suppression.

9.   *Incorporating the affidavit by reference.* One way to make a warrant more particular is for the officer or magistrate to expressly incorporate the affidavit in the statement of what is to be seized. For example, in United States v. Triplett, 684 F.3d 500 (5th Cir. 2012), agents seeking to search a home for evidence of a missing girl obtained a warrant to search the suspect's home for "for any and all articles of clothing of [the girl], bed sheets, electronic devices, electronic memory devices, cell phones, DNA, hand digging and cutting tools, vehicles, and utility vehicles." The Fifth Circuit held that the warrant was sufficiently particular because it had expressly incorporated the affidavit. The affidavit had explained the officers' reasons for seeking "electronic devices," and it explained what officers planned to search for if they found such devices in the home. The terms of the warrant could be read in light of that explanation, the Fifth Circuit held, and the explanation implicitly limited the search to the kinds of crimes described in the affidavit.

10.   *Catch-all provisions.* In some cases, search warrants will include a list of specific items to be searched for together with a general "catch-all" provision allowing the seizure of any computer and electronic storage devices. Courts generally have been rather lenient in allowing such warrants. They

have reasoned that the catch-all provision allowing the seizure of all computers is implicitly narrowed by the list of other items. As a result, the warrant should be read as allowing agents to search for the narrow items that might be found in the computers. So read, the warrants have been upheld as sufficiently particular.

Consider United States v. Burgess, 576 F.3d 1078 (10th Cir. 2009). Agents investigating a narcotics case obtained a search warrant to search premises for the following:

> Certain property and evidence to show the transportation and delivery of controlled substances, which may include but not limited to, cash, or proceeds from the sale of controlled substances, Marijuana, Cocaine, Methamphetamine, or other illegal controlled substances, along with associated paraphernalia to include but not limited to pipes, bongs, syringes, packaging material, computer records, scales, laboratory dishes, flasks, beakers, tubes, pie tins, electrical timers, containers to be used for storing, manufacturing and selling, chemicals used in the creation of illegal narcotics as well as their diluting agents, items of personal property which would tend to show conspiracy to sell drugs, including pay-owe sheets, address books, rolodexes, pagers, firearms and monies.

During the search, agents found two computers and seized them pursuant to the language in the warrant allowing the government to seize "computer records." A search of the computers revealed images of child pornography. The defendant later moved to suppress the images on the ground that the warrant was overly broad. The Tenth Circuit disagreed, reasoning that the phrase "computer records" had to be construed in light of the other items listed in the warrant:

> If the warrant is read to allow a search of all computer records without description or limitation it would not meet the Fourth Amendment's particularity requirement. *United States v. Riccardi,* 405 F.3d 852, 862 (10th Cir. 2005). But a word is known by the company it keeps. The search, in general, was limited to evidence of drugs and drug trafficking and, as it relates to the computer, was limited to the kind of drug and drug trafficking information likely to be found on a computer, to wit (as the warrant says): "pay-owe sheets, address books, rolodexes" and "personal property which would tend to show conspiracy to sell drugs."

> The affidavit explicitly included "photographs of coconspirators or photographs of illegal narcotics" among the types of items to be included in the requested search. The warrant, itself, does not explicitly instruct officers to look for image files on the hard drive, but the affidavit was incorporated into the warrant and is, at least, an aid to interpretation of the term used in the warrant—computer records.

Our reading of the scope of the "computer records" subject to search, narrowing it to looking for drug related evidence, comes from the text of the warrant, with due regard to context, coupled with the specifics of the supporting affidavit, and is reinforced by the executing officer's understanding of and respect for the narrow scope authorized by the search warrant.

Id. at 1091–92.

11. *Search protocols.* The *Ulbricht* opinion introduces the idea of limiting the scope of computer searches by imposing search protocols that detail how investigators must carry out the electronic stage of the warrant. A detailed discussion of search protocols appears later in this Chapter.

3. THE PHYSICAL SEARCH STAGE

The first stage of executing a warrant to search and seize computers is the physical search stage. At this stage, the government enters the physical place to be searched and removes the computers from the site for subsequent analysis. The key question is, what can the agents seize? Can the agents remove all the computers and search them off-site? What restrictions are there on the seizure of computers and removal to an off-site location for a subsequent electronic search?

UNITED STATES V. HILL
United States Court of Appeals for the Ninth Circuit, 2006.
459 F.3d 966.

FISHER, CIRCUIT JUDGE.

Justin Hill conditionally pled guilty to possession of child pornography subject to his challenge to the admission of evidence that he contends was seized in violation of the Fourth Amendment. We must decide whether it was reasonable under the Fourth Amendment for the police to take all of Hill's computer storage media from his home (they did not find his computer) so they could conduct their search offsite in a police laboratory, rather than carrying out the search onsite and taking only whatever evidence of child pornography they might find.

Because computers typically contain so much information beyond the scope of the criminal investigation, computer-related searches can raise difficult Fourth Amendment issues different from those encountered when searching paper files. Judge Kozinski, sitting as the district court in this case, thoughtfully addressed some of these issues in a published opinion upholding the validity of the search warrant and its execution. *United States v. Hill,* 322 F. Supp.2d 1081, 1092 (C.D.Cal. 2004). We affirm the district court's ruling in most but not all respects for the reasons Judge Kozinski stated; to the extent we do agree with that reasoning, we adopt it verbatim in this opinion. In sum, we affirm the district court's denial of the defendant's motion to suppress evidence.

I.

A computer technician was repairing defendant's computer when she discovered what she believed to be child pornography. She called Long Beach police, and the detective who took the call obtained a search warrant from a judge of the Long Beach Superior Court. The warrant authorized a search of the computer repair store and seizure of the computer, any work orders relating to the computer, all storage media belonging to either the computer or the individual identifying himself as defendant at the location, and all sexually explicit images depicting minors contained in the storage media. By the time the detective arrived at the store to execute the warrant, defendant had picked up his computer. The detective submitted an affidavit, which included the computer technician's sworn statement describing the images. On the basis of this affidavit, the officer obtained a second warrant, this one directed at defendant's home, authorizing seizure of the same items.

Officers executed the search warrant but did not find the computer in defendant's apartment.[1] In what appeared to be defendant's bedroom, they found and seized computer storage media, specifically: 22 5.25-inch floppy disks, two CD-ROMs, 124 3.5-inch floppy disks and six zip disks. Two of the zip disks were eventually determined to contain images of child pornography; officers also seized other evidence consistent with the warrant. Defendant was subsequently charged with one count of possession of child pornography, in violation of 18 U.S.C. § 2252A(a)(5)(B).

II.

The defendant argues that the search warrant was overbroad because it authorized the officers to seize and remove from his home his computer and storage media without first determining whether they actually contained child pornography.

The warrant here commanded the officers to search for and seize: "1) An IBM 'clone' medium tower personal computer . . . 3) All storage media belonging to either item #1 or the individual identifying himself as defendant at the location. 4) All sexually explicit images depicting minors contained in item #3." Defendant argues the warrant was overbroad because it authorized seizure of storage media whether or not they contained child pornography. He suggests it should have authorized seizure only of media containing child pornography. But it is impossible to tell what a computer storage medium contains just by looking at it. Rather, one has to examine it electronically, using a computer that is running the appropriate operating system, hardware and software. The police had no

---

[1]   Or anywhere else: The computer was never found.

assurance they would find such a computer at the scene—nor did they, for that matter—or that, if they found one, they could bypass any security measures and operate it.

Defendant suggests that the police could have brought their own laptop computer: Having probable cause to seize only computer storage media that contained certain types of files, the police should have been required to bring with them the equipment necessary to separate the sheep from the goats. Defendant's argument raises an important question about how police must execute seizures pursuant to a warrant. Because seizable materials are seldom found neatly separated from their non-seizable counterparts, how much separating must police do at the scene to avoid taking items that are neither contraband nor evidence of criminal activity?

As always under the Fourth Amendment, the standard is reasonableness. To take an extreme example, if police have probable cause to seize business records, the warrant could not authorize seizure of every piece of paper on the premises on the theory that the police conducting the search might not know how to read.

The court concludes that the police were not required to bring with them equipment capable of reading computer storage media and an officer competent to operate it. Doing so would have posed significant technical problems and made the search more intrusive. To ensure that they could access any electronic storage medium they might find at the scene, police would have needed far more than an ordinary laptop computer. Because computers in common use run a variety of operating systems—various versions or flavors of Windows, Mac OS and Linux, to name only the most common—police would have had to bring with them a computer (or computers) equipped to read not only all of the major media types, but also files encoded by all major operating systems. Because operating systems, media types, file systems and file types are continually evolving, police departments would frequently have to modify their computers to keep them up-to-date. This would not be an insuperable obstacle for larger police departments and federal law enforcement agencies, but it would pose a significant burden on smaller agencies.

Even if the police were to bring with them a properly equipped computer, and someone competent to operate it, using it would pose two significant problems. First, there is a serious risk that the police might damage the storage medium or compromise the integrity of the evidence by attempting to access the data at the scene. As everyone who has accidentally erased a computer file knows, it is fairly easy to make mistakes when operating computer equipment, especially equipment one is not intimately familiar with. The risk that the officer trying to read the suspect's storage medium on the police laptop will make a wrong move and erase what is on the disk is not trivial. Even if the officer executes his task flawlessly, there might be a power failure or equipment malfunction that could affect the contents of the medium being searched. For that reason, experts will make a back-up copy of the medium before they start manipulating its contents. Various other technical problems might arise; without the necessary tools and expertise to deal with them, any effort to read computer files at the scene is fraught with difficulty and risk.

Second, the process of searching the files at the scene can take a long time. To be certain that the medium in question does not contain any seizable material, the officers would have to examine every one of what may be thousands of files on a disk—a process that could take many hours and perhaps days. Taking that much time to conduct the search would not only impose a significant and unjustified burden on police resources, it would also make the search more intrusive. Police would have to be present on the suspect's premises while the search was in progress, and this would necessarily interfere with the suspect's access to his home or business. If the search took hours or days, the intrusion would continue for that entire period, compromising the Fourth Amendment value of making police searches as brief and non-intrusive as possible.

We agree with the district court that under the circumstances here, the warrant was not fatally defective in failing to require an onsite search and isolation of child pornography before removing storage media wholesale. That does not mean, however, that the government has an automatic blank check when seeking or executing warrants in computer-related searches. Although computer technology may in theory justify blanket seizures for the reasons discussed above, the government must still demonstrate to the magistrate factually why such a broad search and seizure authority is reasonable in the case at hand. There may well be situations where the government has no basis for believing that a computer search would involve the kind of technological problems that would make an immediate onsite search and selective removal of relevant evidence impracticable. Thus, there must be some threshold showing before the government may seize the haystack to look for the needle.

Our cases illustrate this principle. In *United States v. Hay*, 231 F.3d 630 (9th Cir. 2000), for example, we held permissible a "generic classification" authorizing seizure of an "entire computer system and virtually every document in the defendant's possession without referencing child pornography or any particular offense conduct" because, although officers knew that a party had sent 19 images of child pornography directly to the defendant's computer, they had no way of knowing where the images were stored. Similarly *United States v. Lacy*, 119 F.3d 742 (9th Cir. 1997), allowed "blanket seizure" of the defendant's entire computer system. We reasoned that no more specific description of the computer equipment sought was possible, because the agents did not know whether the images were stored on the hard drive or on one or more of the defendant's many computer disks.

By contrast, although the warrant in this case authorized a wholesale seizure, the supporting affidavit did not explain why such a seizure was necessary. *See* U.S. Dep't of Justice, Searching and Seizing Computers and Obtaining Electronic Evidence in Criminal Investigations 43, 69 (July 2002) (recommending that "if agents expect that they may need to seize a personal computer and search it off-site to recover the relevant evidence, the affidavit should explain this expectation and its basis to the magistrate judge. The affidavit should inform the court of the practical limitations of conducting an on-site search, and should articulate the plan to remove the entire computer from the site if it becomes necessary.").[11]

We do not approve of issuing warrants authorizing blanket removal of all computer storage media for later examination when there is no affidavit giving a reasonable explanation, such as that provided in *Hay* and *Lacy*, as to why a wholesale seizure is necessary. Without such individualized justification being presented to the magistrate, we cannot be sure that the judge was aware of the officers' intent and the technological limitations meriting the indiscriminate seizure—and thus was intelligently able to exercise the court's oversight function. An explanatory statement in the affidavit also assures us that the officers could not reasonably describe the objects of their search with more specificity. Accordingly, we hold that the warrant here was overbroad in authorizing a blanket seizure in the absence of an explanatory supporting affidavit, which would have documented the informed endorsement of the neutral magistrate.

Nonetheless, we conclude that suppression of the evidence of child pornography found on the defendant's seized zip disks is not an appropriate remedy. The pornographic images from the defendant's zip disks that he sought to exclude as evidence at trial was seized and retained lawfully because described in and therefore taken pursuant to the valid search warrant. As we have discussed above, the officers' wholesale seizure was flawed here because they failed to justify it to the magistrate, not because they acted unreasonably or improperly in executing the warrant. Because the officers were motivated by considerations of practicality rather than by a desire to engage in indiscriminate 'fishing,' we cannot say that the officers so abused the warrant's authority that the otherwise valid warrant was transformed into a general one, thereby requiring all fruits to be suppressed.

Therefore, we hold that the district court properly admitted the evidence of child pornography found on the defendant's computer storage

---

[11] In retrospect, it is clear that not all the storage media needed to be seized as evidence of criminal activity; of the 154 disks seized, only two zip disks contained lascivious images of children. There is no evidence or allegation that the officers knew of this result before they searched and seized.

media notwithstanding the lack of a sufficiently detailed supporting affidavit describing the need for wholesale seizure of such media.

III. Conclusion

We realize that judicial decisions regarding the application of the Fourth Amendment to computer-related searches may be of limited longevity. Technology is rapidly evolving and the concept of what is reasonable for Fourth Amendment purposes will likewise have to evolve. New technology may become readily accessible, for example, to enable more efficient or pinpointed searches of computer data, or to facilitate onsite searches. If so, we may be called upon to reexamine the technological rationales that underpin our Fourth Amendment jurisprudence in this technology-sensitive area of the law.

NOTES AND QUESTIONS

1.   *The boilerplate response.* The Justice Department manual on Searching and Seizing Computers that is cited in *Hill* recommends the following "sample language" that agents can insert into affidavits to explicitly permit the seizure and removal of computers at the physical search stage:

> Based upon my training and experience and information related to me by agents and others involved in the forensic examination of computers, I know that computer data can be stored on a variety of systems and storage devices including hard disk drives, floppy disks, compact disks, magnetic tapes and memory chips. I also know that during the search of the premises it is not always possible to search computer equipment and storage devices for data for a number of reasons, including the following:
>
> > a.   Searching computer systems is a highly technical process which requires specific expertise and specialized equipment.
> >
> > b.   Searching computer systems requires the use of precise, scientific procedures which are designed to maintain the integrity of the evidence and to recover "hidden," erased, compressed, encrypted or password-protected data.
> >
> > c.   The volume of data stored on many computer systems and storage devices will typically be so large that it will be highly impractical to search for data during the execution of the physical search of the premises.
> >
> > d.   Computer users can attempt to conceal data within computer equipment and storage devices through a number of methods, including the use of innocuous or misleading filenames and extensions. Therefore, a substantial amount of time is necessary to extract and sort through data that is concealed or encrypted to determine whether it is evidence, contraband or instrumentalities of a crime.

> In light of these concerns, your affiant hereby requests the Court's permission to seize the computer hardware (and associated peripherals) that are believed to contain some or all of the evidence described in the warrant, and to conduct an off-site search of the hardware for the evidence described, if, upon arriving at the scene, the agents executing the search conclude that it would be impractical to search the computer hardware on-site for this evidence.

U.S. Dep't of Justice, *Searching and Seizing Computers and Obtaining Electronic Evidence in Criminal Investigations*, Appendix F (July 2002).

If an agent inserts this form language into an affidavit, does that satisfy *Hill*? If so, how much does the *Hill* court's requirement of an explanation in the affidavit actually matter?

2. *Allowing broad seizures at the physical search stage.* Lower courts have concluded that search warrants give the police broad authority to seize computers and search them later offsite. An early example is United States v. Schandl, 947 F.2d 462 (11th Cir. 1991). In *Schandl*, investigators seized paper documents and computer discs at the suspect's home and office as part of an investigation into tax evasion. The defendant later claimed that the Fourth Amendment required investigators to search through the documents and papers onsite rather than seize them and search them offsite. The Eleventh Circuit rejected the defendant's argument:

> It was inevitable that some irrelevant materials would be seized as agents searched through numerous documents for evidence of tax evasion and failure to file, crimes that are generally only detected through the careful analysis and synthesis of a large number of documents. Indeed, it might have been far more disruptive had the agents made a thorough search of each individual document and computer disc before removing it from Schandl's home and office. To insist on such a practice would substantially increase the time required to conduct the search, thereby aggravating the intrusiveness of the search.

Id. at 465–66.

3. *Does a warrant for "documents" or "papers" allow the seizure of a computer?* If a warrant does not expressly state that it permits the seizure of computers, should courts nonetheless allow investigators to seize computers they come across during the search if they believe the computers may contain evidence described in the warrant? Imagine investigators execute a search for particular "documents" or "papers," and during the search they come across a computer. Can the investigators seize the computer because it may contain the "documents" or "papers" in electronic form?

Courts have generally allowed the seizure of computers in such circumstances. For example, in People v. Gall, 30 P.3d 145 (Colo. 2001) (en banc), the police were investigating reports that a suspect planned to kill several people at work. Investigators obtained a warrant to search the suspect's home for a number of items, including "[a]ny and all written or printed material which shows an intent to do physical harm or physical damage against any person or building" and "any documents or materials that show the occupier or possessor of the premises."

During the search, investigators came across and seized two desktop computers from the living room and five laptop computers found in individual carrying cases on the floor of one of the defendant's closets. The five laptop computers turned out to be stolen, and the defendant was charged with receiving stolen property (among other things). On appeal, the defendant argued that the seizure of the computers was impermissible because it was not authorized by the warrant. A 4–3 majority of the Colorado Supreme Court disagreed, concluding that the warrant could be construed to include the computers:

> In deciding whether items discovered during the execution of a search warrant are within the scope of the warrant, police officers are not obliged to interpret its terms narrowly. They may search the location authorized by the warrant, including any containers at that location that are reasonably likely to contain items described in the warrant. This container rationale is equally applicable to nontraditional, technological "containers" that are reasonably likely to hold information in less tangible forms. Similarly a warrant cannot be expected to anticipate every form an item or repository of information may take, and therefore courts have affirmed the seizure of things that are similar to, or the "functional equivalent" of, items enumerated in a warrant, as well as containers in which they are reasonably likely to be found.

Id. at 153. In dissent, Justice Martinez argued that courts should not permit computers to be seized unless the computers are expressly named in the warrant:

> In my view, the warrant here was insufficient to justify the seizure or search of the computers in this case because the warrant sought writings, not computers. Computers are far more complex and versatile than mere writings and their purpose is significantly different from just a container storing writings. As such, the warrant authorizing the seizure of writings was not sufficiently particularized to include computers. We require a warrant to particularly describe the things to be seized in order to avoid the harm to privacy inherent in the seizure of items that are not the subject of a search. This purpose is not served if computers are seized when writings are sought.

Id. at 160 (Martinez, J., dissenting).

Which side is more persuasive—the majority or the dissent? Should warrants that permit the seizure of writings or documents automatically be construed to permit the seizure of any computer devices that may contain such writings or documents? Should computers be seized in every case? If not, how should courts determine when the seizure of a computer is necessary? How can judges or police officers know when a computer should be seized given that they normally will not know what evidence it contains until it is searched? And how are the answers to these questions changing as more and more devices and tools are becoming computerized?

4.   *Access to files possessed because of an earlier overseizure.* Judicial approval of overseizing digital evidence at the physical search stage means that the government will have additional files in its possession that are outside the scope of the warrant. Can the government maintain possession of those non-responsive files? What happens if the government later develops probable cause to believe that the non-responsive files in its possession are evidence of a second crime? Can investigators obtain a second warrant to search the files in its possession—files that it possesses only because of the overseizure allowed by the first warrant? Or are the overseized files somehow exempt from later government access with a second warrant?

The Second Circuit addressed these questions in a panel ruling in United States v. Ganias, 755 F.3d 125 (2d Cir. 2014), that was later vacated by the Second Circuit on rehearing en banc. In its en banc decision, the Second Circuit offered tentative thoughts on the issues addressed by the panel but resolved the case on other grounds without having to take a position. *See* United States v. Ganias, 824 F.3d 199 (2d Cir. 2016) (en banc). Given the conceptual importance of the issues addressed in the panel decision, a close look at the panel decision is helpful even if its rulings are no longer Second Circuit law.

In *Ganias*, officers executed a first search warrant in 2003 for customer files stored by Ganias as part of his accounting business in an investigation into crimes by Ganias's customers. When agents executed the warrant in 2003, they made electronic copies of all three of Ganias's computer hard drives. Those copies were then stored by law enforcement. More than two years later, agents came to suspect that Ganias himself had committed different crimes and that the evidence for the different crimes would be found on the copies of Ganias's files that were already in the government's possession from the first warrant.

In 2006, agent obtained a second warrant allowing the agents to search the copies of Ganias's files in the government's possession for evidence of the second crime. A search pursuant to the 2006 warrant revealed evidence used to convict Ganias of the second crime. Further, it turned out that the evidence found in the copies stored by law enforcement for over two years were the only existing copies. In the intervening two-plus years, before the government obtained the second warrant, Ganias had deleted his own copies. As a result, the only reason the government was able to obtain the evidence sought by the 2006 warrant was because of the overseizure in carrying out the 2003 warrant.

The Second Circuit held that this procedure violated the Fourth Amendment. According to the Second Circuit, the Fourth Amendment does not permit officials who "execute a warrant for the seizure of particular data on a computer to seize and indefinitely retain every file on that computer for use in future criminal investigations." *Id.* at 137. According to the court, retaining copies of non-responsive files indefinitely was an unreasonable seizure:

> The Government had no warrant authorizing the seizure of Ganias's personal records in 2003. By December 2004, these documents had been separated from those relevant to the investigation of [Ganias's clients]. Nevertheless, the Government continued to retain them for another year-and-a-half until it finally developed probable cause to search and seize them in 2006. Without some independent basis for its retention of those documents in the interim, the Government clearly violated Ganias's Fourth Amendment rights by retaining the files for a prolonged period of time and then using them in a future criminal investigation.

> The Government offers several arguments to justify its actions, but none provides any legal authorization for its continued and prolonged possession of the non-responsive files. First, it argues that it must be allowed to make the mirror image copies as a matter of practical necessity and, according to the Government's investigators, those mirror images were "the government's property." As explained above, practical considerations may well justify a reasonable accommodation in the manner of executing a search warrant, such as making mirror images of hard drives and permitting off-site review, but these considerations do not justify the indefinite retention of non-responsive documents. Without a warrant authorizing seizure of Ganias's personal financial records, the copies of those documents could not become *ipso facto* "the government's property" without running afoul of the Fourth Amendment.

> Second, the Government asserts that by obtaining the 2006 search warrant, it cured any defect in its search of the wrongfully retained files. But this argument reduces the Fourth Amendment to a form of words. The essence of a provision forbidding the acquisition of evidence in a certain way is that not merely evidence so acquired shall not be used before the Court but that it shall not be used at all unless some exception applies. If the Government could seize and retain non-responsive electronic records indefinitely, so it could search them whenever it later developed probable cause, every warrant to search for particular electronic data would become, in essence, a general warrant.

> Third, the Government argues that it must be permitted to search the mirror images in its possession because the evidence no longer existed on Ganias's computers. But the ends, however, do not justify the means. The loss of the personal records is irrelevant in this case because the Government concedes that it never considered performing a new search of Ganias's computers and did not know that the files no longer existed when it searched the mirror images in its possession. And even if it were relevant, the Fourth Amendment

clearly embodies a judgment that some evidence of criminal activity may be lost for the sake of protecting property and privacy rights.

Fourth, the Government contends that returning or destroying the non-responsive files is "entirely impractical" because doing so would compromise the remaining data that was responsive to the warrant, making it impossible to authenticate or use it in a criminal prosecution. We are not convinced that there is no other way to preserve the evidentiary chain of custody. But even if we assumed it were necessary to maintain a complete copy of the hard drive solely to authenticate evidence responsive to the original warrant, that does not provide a basis for using the mirror image for any other purpose.

Because the Government has demonstrated no legal basis for retaining the non-responsive documents, its retention and subsequent search of those documents were unconstitutional.

Id. at 137–40.

If you read the panel opinion in *Ganias* as imposing an affirmative duty on the government to delete all non-responsive files after a warrant for digital evidence is collected, is that a correct interpretation of the Fourth Amendment? If so, when is this "right to delete" triggered? Alternatively, if you read *Ganias* as imposing a use restriction, so that if such non-responsive files must be collected they cannot be used in a different criminal case even with a second warrant, is that a better interpretation of what the Fourth Amendment requires? Or should the Fourth Amendment be interpreted to impose neither an affirmative duty to delete nor a use restriction?

United States v. Nasher-Alneam, 399 F. Supp.3d 579 (S.D.W.Va. 2019), returned to this problem. Officers executed a search warrant authorizing them to image the server of a physician's medical practice to seize evidence of intentionally overprescribing certain medication in violation of the narcotics laws. At trial, the jury could not reach a verdict. The government brought charges against the physician a second time, and this time added health care billing fraud to the list of charges.

Relying only on the first warrant, agents searched the imaged server again and collected records of health care billing fraud. The government argued that it was proper because the evidence of health care billing fraud was directly related to the evidence of narcotics violations. Because both types of charges were based on reviews of patient records, the government argued, "there's no problem and no limitation to go back and look at them later." *Id.* at 593 (quoting the prosecutor).

The district court disagreed, holding that the second search violated the Fourth Amendment. "When law enforcement personnel obtain a warrant to search for a specific crime but later, for whatever reason, seek to broaden their scope to search for evidence of another crime, a new warrant is required." Id. at 492. The warrant had authorized searches for violations of the narcotics laws, and the Fourth Amendment did not permit searching through the seized records for evidence of a different crime. *Id.* at 594.

Notably, however, the court indicated that the government could have lawfully searched the imaged server with a second warrant directed at the new evidence:

> The government should have gotten a second warrant to conduct its search for evidence of healthcare billing fraud. There was no impediment to doing so as the government was 'not in a rapidly unfolding situation or searching a location where evidence was likely to move or change, and there was no downside to halting the search to obtain a second warrant.

Id.

Should the answer to whether a second warrant is required depend on whether the actual records that the government seeks to review are the same the second time as they were the first time? Consider a hypothetical involving traditional paper records. Imagine that the government searches the computer server the first time and prints out paper copies of the records that the government believes are responsive to the warrant. Later on, the government learns that the suspect committed a second offense that can be proved by reviewing the printed paper copies of the records from the first search. Does the government need a new warrant to review the printed paper files as they are looking for evidence of a second crime? What if the government discovers the second crime while reviewing the papers for the first crime?

5.   *The two-stage computer search process and warrants for Internet accounts.* The two-stage computer search process is generally followed when the government obtains a search warrant for an Internet account such as an e-mail account. Unlike stand-alone searches, however, network searches usually involve two different entities. First, the government will obtain a warrant and serve it on the Internet provider. Next, the provider will disclose the entire contents of the account (often limited to specific date restrictions) to the government. Finally, the government will search through the disclosed e-mails for the contents responsive to the warrant. This two-step procedure is recommended by the Justice Department's manual, *Searching and Seizing Computers and Obtaining Electronic Evidence in Criminal Investigations.* The procedure is an adaptation of the two-step approach to executing warrants that courts have approved to search stand-alone computers.

But does this procedure satisfy the Fourth Amendment? In particular, does the network equivalent of the physical search stage, in which the provider collects the entire contents of the account and sends it to the government, go too far? Some magistrate judges have ruled that this process is overbroad under the Fourth Amendment, in that it gives the government access to the entirety of the suspect's account (or at least everything within a specific date range).

For example, Magistrate Judge John Facciola rejected a two-step e-mail warrant application and suggested that the Fourth Amendment might require e-mail providers to search through the contents of the account for responsive files instead of the government:

> Having an electronic communication service provider perform a search, using a methodology based on search terms such as date stamps, specific words, names of recipients, or other methodology suggested by the government and approved by the Court seems to be the only way to enforce the particularity requirement commanded by the Fourth Amendment."

> To be clear: the government must stop blindly relying on the language provided by the Department of Justice's *Searching and Seizing Computers and Obtaining Electronic Evidence in Criminal Investigations* manual. By doing so, it is only submitting unconstitutional warrant applications.

In the Matter of the Search of Information Associated with [redacted]@mac.com that is Stored at Premises Controlled by Apple, Inc., 25 F. Supp.3d 1, 8–9 (D.D.C. 2014).

Despite these occasional views from federal magistrate judges, the federal District Judges who review their decisions have uniformly disagreed and have approved two-step e-mail warrants. For example, Magistrate Judge Facciola's rejection of a warrant in the case above was reversed by Chief Judge Richard Roberts, who ruled that the two-step procedure usually followed for physical searches of computers can also be used for e-mail searches. *See* In the Matter of the Search of Information Associated with [redacted]@mac.com that is Stored at Premises Controlled by Apple, Inc., 13 F. Supp.3d 157 (D.D.C. 2014). Judge Roberts reasoned that the alternative of forcing providers to search for responsive materials presented "nettlesome problems:"

> It would be unworkable and impractical to order Apple to cull the e-mails and related records in order to find evidence that is relevant to the government's investigation. To begin with, non-governmental employees untrained in the details of the criminal investigation likely lack the requisite skills and expertise to determine whether a document is relevant to the criminal investigation. Moreover, requiring the government to train the electronic service provider's employees on the process for identifying information that is responsive to the search warrant may prove time-consuming, increase the costs of the investigation, and expose the government to potential security breaches.

Id. at 165–66.

4. THE ELECTRONIC SEARCH STAGE

At the electronic search stage, the computer has been brought to a government laboratory and is searched for evidence. The analyst normally begins by making a copy of the storage device. The analyst then searches the copy for evidence. What rules govern searching the copy of the computer for evidence? How invasive can the search be for evidence within the scope of the warrant? And what happens when the agent discovers evidence of crime outside the scope of the warrant, either inadvertently or intentionally? Is that evidence admissible?

UNITED STATES V. WILLIAMS

United States Court of Appeals for the Fourth Circuit, 2010.
592 F.3d 511.

NIEMEYER, CIRCUIT JUDGE:

In September 2007, the Fairfax Baptist Temple in Fairfax Station, Virginia, began receiving threatening e-mail messages from an individual identifying himself as "Franklin Pugh." Similar and related e-mails were later received from several other e-mail accounts, registered in the names of children attending the Fairfax Baptist Temple School, who had been referred to in the earlier e-mails. Upon investigation, the Fairfax County Police determined that at least one of the e-mail accounts from which e-mails had been received had been accessed repeatedly by an Internet account registered to Karol Williams, in Clifton, Virginia, who is the wife of the defendant, Curtis Williams. Both Karol and Curtis were active members of the Fairfax Baptist Temple. Upon learning this, the police applied for a warrant to search Karol and Curtis Williams' home.

In the affidavit supporting the warrant application, Fairfax County Detective Craig Paul summarized the e-mails, detailed the police investigation to date, and stated that the evidence supported his belief that violations of state law had occurred, particularly § 18.2–60 of the Virginia Code, prohibiting any person from communicating threats to kill or do bodily harm to persons at elementary, middle, or secondary schools, and § 18.2–152.7:1, prohibiting harassment by computer by communicating "obscene, vulgar, profane, lewd, lascivious, or indecent language, or mak[ing] any suggestion or proposal of an obscene nature." To support his concern for the safety of the boys at the school, Detective Paul highlighted the e-mail statements, "I know your boy's names. I know where they go for lunch after church. I know where they live. I know when they come and leave school."

Based on Detective Paul's affidavit, a Fairfax County magistrate issued a search warrant on October 25, 2007, that "commanded" officers to search for and seize from the home of Karol and Curtis Williams:

> Any and all computer systems and digital storage media, videotapes, videotape recorders, documents, photographs, and Instrumentalities indicative of the offense of § 18.2–152.7:1 Harassment by Computer and § 18.2–60 Threats of death or

bodily injury to a person or member of his family; threats to commit serious bodily harm to persons on school property, Code of Virginia (as amended).

Police, along with the FBI, executed the warrant the next day and seized several computers, CDs, DVDs, and other electronic media devices.

The FBI agents who had participated in the search of the Williams' house took the computers and electronic media and later searched their contents. During the course of that search, FBI Agent Michael French reported in an e-mail sent to the U.S. Attorney's Office in the Eastern District of Virginia that "we found many deleted images of young male erotica from September-October 2007. We also found that the anonymizer software TOR had been installed." He concluded by saying that he hoped to find Williams' "collection" on the lap top and USB thumbdrives the following week.

Sometime later during his search, Agent French opened a DVD that had been seized from the Williams' home, labeled with the words, "Virus Shield, Quarantined Files, Destroy." Upon opening the DVD, he observed over a thousand images in "thumbnail view" of minor boys, some of which were sexually suggestive and some of which were sexually explicit. Of the total number of images, approximately 39 constituted child pornography.

Williams filed a motion to suppress the child pornography contending that their seizure was not justified by the plain-view exception to the warrant requirement. The district court denied Williams' motion.

Williams argues that the search for and seizure of child pornography in this case [was outside the scope of the warrant and] did not fall within any recognized exception to the Fourth Amendment's warrant requirement. To apply the plain-view exception in the context of computer searches would, Williams argues, effectively read the warrant requirement out of the Fourth Amendment.

Relying heavily on *United States v. Carey,* 172 F.3d 1268, 1273 (10th Cir. 1999), which held that child pornography discovered on a computer during the course of a search for evidence of drug transactions must be suppressed because it was not "inadvertently discovered," Williams argues that the plain-view exception cannot be applied in the context of computer searches unless the files sought to be seized pursuant to the exception are discovered "inadvertently." In this case, Williams observes that the officers suspected him of possessing child pornography from the outset of their investigation and that they used the warrant's authorization to search for such materials, which, he maintains, fell outside the scope of the warrant. Such a scenario, he concludes, can hardly be thought of as "inadvertent," and thus the plain-view exception cannot justify the seizure of the images.

The government contends that if the child pornography was seized without the warrant's authorization, its seizure was nonetheless justified under the plain-view exception to the warrant requirement. It observes that the warrant authorized officers to search Williams' computer and computer storage devices and that, during the search of those items, the officers came upon the DVD containing thumbnail images of child pornography, whose nature as contraband was clear.

As a general rule, warrantless searches or seizures are per se unreasonable. But there are a few specifically established and well-delineated exceptions. One such exception is that under certain circumstances the police may seize evidence in plain view without a warrant. Under this exception, police may seize evidence in plain view during a lawful search if (1) the seizing officer is "lawfully present at the place from which the evidence can be plainly viewed"; (2) the seizing officer has "a lawful right of access to the object itself"; and (3) "the object's 'incriminating character is immediately apparent,'" *United States v. Legg,* 18 F.3d 240, 242 (4th Cir. 1994). The plain-view doctrine is grounded on the proposition that once police are lawfully in a position to observe an item first-hand, its owner's privacy interest in that item is lost; the owner may retain the incidents of title and possession *but not privacy.*

In this case, the warrant authorized a search of Williams' computers and digital media for evidence relating to the designated Virginia crimes of making threats and computer harassment. To conduct that search, the warrant impliedly authorized officers to open each file on the computer and view its contents, at least cursorily, to determine whether the file fell within the scope of the warrant's authorization—*i.e.,* whether it related to the designated Virginia crimes of making threats or computer harassment.

Once it is accepted that a computer search must, by implication, authorize at least a cursory review of each file on the computer, then the criteria for applying the plain-view exception are readily satisfied. *First,* an officer who has legal possession of the computer and electronic media and a legal right to conduct a search of it is "lawfully present at the place from which evidence can be viewed," thus satisfying the first element of the plain-view exception. *Second,* the officer, who is authorized to search the computer and electronic media for evidence of a crime and who is therefore legally authorized to open and view all its files, at least cursorily, to determine whether any one falls within the terms of the warrant, has "a lawful right of access" to all files, albeit only momentarily. And *third,* when the officer then comes upon child pornography, it becomes "immediately apparent" that its possession by the computer's owner is illegal and incriminating. And so, in this case, any child pornography viewed on the computer or electronic media may be seized under the plain-view exception.

Williams, relying on the Tenth Circuit's opinion in *United States v. Carey,* advances an argument that the plain-view exception cannot apply to searches of computers and electronic media when the evidence indicates that it is the officer's *purpose* from the outset to use the authority of the warrant to search for unauthorized evidence because the unauthorized evidence would not then be uncovered "inadvertently." *See Carey,* 172 F.3d at 1273.

This argument, however, cannot stand against the principle, well-established in Supreme Court jurisprudence, that the scope of a search conducted pursuant to a warrant is defined *objectively* by the terms of the warrant and the evidence sought, not by the *subjective* motivations of an officer. *See Maryland v. Garrison,* 480 U.S. 79, 84 (1987). *See also Whren v. United States,* 517 U.S. 806, 813 (1996) ("Subjective intentions play no role in ordinary, probable-cause Fourth Amendment analysis"). As the Court stated in *Horton v. California,* 496 U.S. 128 (1990), "the fact that an officer is interested in an [unauthorized] item of evidence and fully expects to find it in the course of a search should not invalidate its seizure if the search is confined in area and duration by the terms of a war rant or a valid exception to the warrant requirement." In that case, the Court *explicitly* rejected the very argument that Williams makes in this case, that unauthorized evidence must be suppressed because its discovery was not "inadvertent." As the *Horton* Court explained, "Even though inadvertence is a characteristic of most legitimate 'plain view' seizures, it is not a necessary condition."

While Williams relies accurately on *Carey,* which effectively imposes an "inadvertence" requirement, such a conclusion is inconsistent with *Horton.* Inadvertence focuses incorrectly on the subjective motivations of the officer in conducting the search and not on the objective determination of whether the search is authorized by the warrant or a valid exception to the warrant requirement.

In this case, because the scope of the search authorized by the warrant included the authority to open and cursorily view each file, the observation of child pornography within several of these files did not involve an intrusion on Williams' protected privacy interests beyond that already authorized by the warrant, regardless of the officer's subjective motivations. And neither did the seizure of these photographs interfere with Williams' possessory interests, for once their nature as contraband became apparent, Williams' possessory interests were forfeited.

At bottom, we conclude that the sheer amount of information contained on a computer does not distinguish the authorized search of the computer from an analogous search of a file cabinet containing a large number of documents. As the Supreme Court recognized in *Andresen,* "There are grave dangers inherent in executing a warrant authorizing a search and seizure of a person's papers that are not necessarily present in executing a warrant to search for physical objects whose relevance is more easily ascertainable." 427 U.S. at 482 n. 11. While that danger certainly counsels care and respect for privacy when executing a warrant, it does not prevent officers from lawfully searching the documents, nor should it undermine their authority to search a computer's files. *See United States v. Giberson,* 527 F.3d 882, 888 (9th Cir. 2008) (holding that "neither the quantity of information, nor the form in which it is stored, is legally relevant in the Fourth Amendment context"). We have applied these rules successfully in the context of warrants authorizing the search and seizure of non-electronic files, and we see no reason to depart from them in the context of electronic files.

Thus, the warrant in this case, grounded on probable cause to believe that evidence relating to the Virginia crimes of threatening bodily harm and computer harassment would be found on Williams' computers and digital media, authorized the officers to search these computers and digital media for files satisfying that description, regardless of the officers' motivations in conducting the search. If, in the course of conducting such a search, the officers came upon child pornography, even if finding child pornography was their hope from the outset, they were permitted to seize it as direct evidence of criminal conduct and, indeed, bring additional charges based on that evidence.

NOTES AND QUESTIONS

1. *Avoiding general warrants.* The original purpose of the Fourth Amendment was to forbid the use of general warrants. General warrants typically did not name the place to be searched or the property to be seized, and as a result permitted a general rummaging through a suspect's property. The particularity requirement was designed to prevent such general rummaging. By limiting searches to a particular place for particular evidence, the requirement limits the government's powers to conduct dragnet searches.

Does the particularity requirement continue to serve this function in a world of digital evidence? Or do traditional Fourth Amendment rules make computer warrants that are particularized in theory general warrants in practice? Consider the fact that the computer forensics process can be extremely invasive. Forensic analysts looking for evidence described in a warrant sometimes open every file and view every image. As a result, almost everything on the computer can come into plain view. Under *Williams,* any evidence outside the warrant that comes into plain view can potentially be seized under the plain view exception. Are there any limits at all to how agents can search a computer and whether they can use evidence outside the scope of the warrant that they discover?

2. *Comparing objective and subjective approaches.* The *Williams* court expressly disagrees with the Tenth Circuit's ruling in United States v. Carey,

172 F.3d 1268 (10th Cir. 1999), which adopted a subjective approach to the plain view exception. In *Carey*, an agent in a forensic lab searched a computer for evidence related to drug trafficking. During the forensic search, the agent came across images of child pornography. At that point, the agent abandoned the search for evidence of drug trafficking and instead searched for and found additional images of child pornography. The government then charged the owner of the computer with possessing child pornography, and the defendant moved to suppress the images.

The Tenth Circuit ruled in *Carey* that the files the agent opened after he had abandoned his search for evidence in the warrant went beyond the plain view exception and were not admissible. As the *Williams* court noted, *Carey* adopted a subjective test: Whether immediately incriminating evidence outside the scope of the warrant can be admitted depends on whether the agent opened the file with the intent to look for evidence beyond the scope of the warrant. The discovery of evidence outside the scope of the warrant must be inadvertent.

The *Williams* court concludes that the subjective standard from *Carey* is inconsistent with Horton v. California, 496 U.S. 128 (1990). In *Horton*, the defendant argued that an inadvertence requirement was necessary to ensure that officers would not use cause to obtain a warrant for one crime as an excuse to rummage through a suspect's property for other crimes and thus engage in general searches. The Supreme Court rejected this argument on the following grounds:

> The suggestion that the inadvertence requirement is necessary to prevent the police from conducting general searches, or from converting specific warrants into general warrants, is not persuasive because that interest is already served by the requirements that no warrant issue unless it particularly describes the place to be searched and the persons or things to be seized, and that a warrantless search be circumscribed by the exigencies which justify its initiation. Scrupulous adherence to these requirements serves the interests in limiting the area and duration of the search that the inadvertence requirement inadequately protects. Once those commands have been satisfied and the officer has a lawful right of access, however, no additional Fourth Amendment interest is furthered by requiring that the discovery of evidence be inadvertent.

Id. at 139–140.

In United States v. Loera, 923 F.3d 907 (10th Cir. 2019), the Tenth Circuit reconciled *Carey*'s subjective approach with *Horton*'s objective approach on the ground that computer searches are different: "The fundamental differences between electronic searches and physical searches, including the fact that electronic search warrants are less likely prospectively to restrict the scope of the search, justify our inclusion of that [subjective] factor." *Id*. at 919 n.3. Do you agree? Should courts restore the inadvertence requirement to narrow the scope of computer searches?

Note that even under the subjective approach adopted in *Carey*, a government agent with a search warrant apparently can search anywhere in a computer so long as he looks for material described in the warrant. If the agent comes across evidence unrelated to the crime described in the warrant, the agent can copy the unrelated evidence for use in court. The agent can then continue to search for the evidence named in the warrant and can continue to copy unrelated evidence he comes across during the search. Alternatively, the agent can use the discovery of the unrelated evidence as the basis for probable cause to obtain a second warrant to search the computer for more of the unrelated evidence. Either way, the unrelated evidence is admissible in court under these standards as long as the agent does not abandon the search for evidence described in the warrant without first obtaining another warrant.

3.   *The case for eliminating plain view for digital searches.* Should the plain view exception be abolished in computer cases so that any evidence beyond the scope of the warrant cannot be admitted in court?

> The dynamics of computer searches upset the basic assumptions underlying the plain view doctrine. More and more evidence comes into plain view, and the particularity requirement no longer functions effectively as a check on dragnet searches. In this new environment, a tightening of the plain view doctrine may be necessary to ensure that computer warrants that are narrow in theory do not become broad in practice.
>
> In time, abolishing the plain view exception may best balance the competing needs of privacy and law enforcement in light of developments in computer technology and the digital forensics process. Forensic analysis is an art, not a science; the process is contingent, technical, and difficult to reduce to rules. Eliminating the plain view exception in digital evidence cases would respect law enforcement interests by granting the police every power needed to identify and locate evidence within the scope of a warrant given the particular context-sensitive needs of the investigation. At the same time, the approach would protect privacy interests by barring the disclosure of any evidence beyond the scope of a valid warrant in most cases.
>
> It is an imperfect answer, to be sure, but it may be the best available rule. Although forensic practices may be invasive by technological necessity, a total suppression rule for evidence beyond the scope of a warrant would both remove any incentive for broad searches and neutralize the effect of broad searches that occur. It would regulate invasive practices by imposing use restrictions ex post rather than attempting to control searches ex ante, offering a long-term second-best approach to regulating the computer forensics process. In short, it would allow the police to conduct whatever search they needed to conduct (to ensure recovery) and then limit use of the evidence found (to deter abuses).

Orin S. Kerr, *Searches and Seizures in a Digital World*, 119 Harv. L. Rev. 531, 576–77, 583–84 (2005).

4. *The Oregon Supreme Court adopts a use restriction for digital warrants under the Oregon Constitution.* In State v. Mansor, 421 P.3d 323 (Or. 2018), the Oregon Supreme Court interpreted the search and seizure provision in the Oregon Constitution, Article I, Section 9, as adopting a use restriction for information outside the scope of digital warrants. If the government searches a computer based on a warrant establishing probable cause to find Evidence X, the government can use any Evidence X it finds on the computer. However, if it finds anything else of interest, including evidence of other crimes, that other evidence must be suppressed:

> In our view, the privacy interests underlying Article I, Section 9, are best protected by recognizing a necessary trade-off when the state searches a computer that has been lawfully seized. Even a reasonable search authorized by a valid warrant necessarily may require examination of at least some information that is beyond the scope of the warrant. Such state searches raise the possibility of computer search warrants becoming the digital equivalent of general warrants and of sanctioning the undue rummaging that the particularity requirement was enacted to preclude.

> Although such searches are lawful and appropriate, individual privacy interests preclude the state from benefiting from that necessity by being permitted to use that evidence at trial. We thus conclude that the state should not be permitted to use information obtained in a computer search if the warrant did not authorize the search for that information, unless some other warrant exception applies. Put differently, when the state conducts a reasonably targeted search of a person's computer for information pursuant to a warrant that properly identifies the information being sought, the state has not unreasonably invaded the person's privacy interest, and the state may use the information identified in the warrant in a prosecution or any other lawful manner. But when the state looks for other information or uncovers information that was not authorized by the warrant, Article I, section 9, prohibits the state from using that information at trial, unless it comes within an exception to the warrant requirement.

Id. at 334. Should courts adopt that approach for the federal Fourth Amendment?

5. *What does it mean for agents to search a computer in an "objectively reasonable" way?* Consider the guidance offered in United States v. Burgess, 576 F.3d 1078 (10th Cir. 2009):

> A warrant may permit only the search of particularly described places and only particularly described things may be seized. As the description of such places and things becomes more general, the

method by which the search is executed become more important—the search method must be tailored to meet allowed ends. And those limits must be functional. For instance, unless specifically authorized by the warrant there would be little reason for officers searching for evidence of drug trafficking to look at tax returns (beyond verifying the folder labeled "2002 Tax Return" actually contains tax returns and not drug files or trophy pictures).

Respect for legitimate rights to privacy in papers and effects requires an officer executing a search warrant to first look in the most obvious places and as it becomes necessary to progressively move from the obvious to the obscure. That is the purpose of a search protocol which structures the search by requiring an analysis of the file structure, next looking for suspicious file folders, then looking for files and types of files most likely to contain the objects of the search by doing keyword searches. But in the end, there may be no practical substitute for actually looking in many (perhaps all) folders and sometimes at the documents contained within those folders, and that is true whether the search is of computer files or physical files. It is particularly true with image files.

Id. at 1094.

How can a court identify when an agent must "first look in the most obvious places" for evidence as compared to when there is "no practical substitute for actually looking in many (perhaps all) folders"? If the court is to consider only what is objectively reasonable, rather than whether the officer was subjectively trying to find evidence outside the scope of the warrant, how much should the court second-guess the officer's chosen way of searching the computer?

6.　　*The role of the "immediately apparent" limitation.* The plain view exception allows law enforcement to seize evidence beyond the scope of a warrant only if the incriminating nature of that evidence is "immediately apparent." David Ziff argues that the plain view doctrine plays only a limited role in computer search cases because the incriminating nature of most digital evidence is not immediately apparent. *See* David J.S. Ziff, Note, *Fourth Amendment Limitations on the Execution of Computer Searches Conducted Pursuant to a Warrant*, 105 Colum. L. Rev. 841, 869 (2005):

A file that is not particularly described in the warrant can be seized by officers only if the file's incriminating character becomes immediately apparent before it can be determined that the contents of the file are outside of the scope of the warrant. For the vast majority of computer files, this limitation will shield private information from inspection by officers. For example, suppose an officer is searching the contents of a computer for child pornography and opens a file labeled "letter to grandma.doc." Under the proposed standard, the officer is only allowed to open and view the file to the extent necessary to determine that it is not merely a mislabeled file concealing the object of the warrant. This limitation prohibits the officer from reading the contents of the letter. Any information in the letter, including information relating to other illegal activity, remains private. Even if an individual file appears suspicious to an officer but further investigation beyond what is necessary to determine that the file is outside the scope of the warrant is required to establish probable cause as to its association with criminal activity, the item is not immediately incriminating and cannot be seized pursuant to the plain view doctrine.

Does this argument depend on how broadly the warrant is drafted? Computer warrants can be drafted in very broad ways that require agents to exercise considerable judgment as to whether a particular file is within the scope of the warrant. For example, imagine that the warrant in Ziff's hypothetical were not limited to actual images of child pornography, but instead encompassed "any documents, letters, memos, images, or other information concerning violations of child pornography crimes or child sex offenses." In that case, couldn't the officer read "letter to grandma.doc" to determine whether the letter contained any information relating to child sex offenses or child pornography? And if the letter contained discussions of unrelated crimes, couldn't the officer use the letter to prosecute the defendant for the unrelated crime under the plain view doctrine?

Also note that the "immediately apparent" limitation is only a limit on the seizure of evidence. Agents can view unrelated evidence that they come across in plain view, but they can seize the evidence only if its incriminating nature is immediately apparent. This brings us back to a question considered earlier in the chapter: Does copying digital evidence for use in court constitute a Fourth Amendment seizure? If not, does the "immediately apparent" limitation even apply in digital evidence cases?

7.   *Plain view and CSAM.* Most of the published cases involving the discovery of digital evidence beyond the scope of a warrant involve CSAM. CSAM offenses are very easy for the government to prove, and the penalties for such offenses are severe. As a result, the discovery of CSAM during a computer search for other evidence may lead prosecutors to call off the initial investigation and bring charges under CSAM statutes. Does this dynamic help explain why some courts have used a subjective test when applying the plain view exception in computer search cases?

8.   *Can courts rule out parts of an electronic storage device where evidence categorically will not be found?* In Herrera v. State, 357 P.3d 1227 (Colo. 2015), agents obtained a warrant to search the seized cell phone of a suspect, Herrera, who had contacted young girls to set up sexual encounters with them. The police obtained a narrow warrant that authorized the seizure of records identifying the phone as Herrera's as well as the seizure of communications between Herrera and an undercover police officer who had communicated with him posing as a girl named "Stazi."

In the course of searching the phone pursuant to the warrant, the detective came across a folder in the phone's instant messaging app that appeared to contain messages between Herrera and another known victim. The known victim was named "Faith W."—her full last name was excluded from the opinion because she was a minor—and the folder was labeled "Faith Fallout." The detective opened the folder to read the communications. After reading the communications, he copied them for use at trial.

The Colorado Supreme Court ruled that the officer had violated the Fourth Amendment by opening the "Faith Fallout" folder:

> In executing a search warrant, police officers may search areas in which the items identified in the warrant might reasonably be found, including closed containers. We analogize the "Faith Fallout" text message folder to a closed container, which Detective Slattery opened to discover its contents—namely, the text messages between Faith W. and Herrera. Here, the warrant authorized Detective Slattery to search for messages between "Stazi" and Herrera. The question, then, is whether the "Faith Fallout" folder was a container in which messages from "Stazi" could reasonably be found. We agree with the trial court that it was not.

> Because the evidence objectively indicated that the "Faith Fallout" folder contained messages from Faith W. and only Faith W., the police had no objective basis to conclude that the folder would contain messages from "Stazi."

Id. at 1232–33.

Is the court's analysis persuasive? On one hand, courts have widely held that agents cannot open a closed container if it could not fit the evidence described in the warrant. On the other hand, it seems that *Herrera* changed the question: Instead of asking whether the evidence described in the warrant *could* fit in the folder, the court asked whether there was a basis to think the evidence *would* be in the folder. If the Fourth Amendment rule is that the police cannot search folders if there is no reason to believe that the folder contains evidence, can a criminal simply place evidence in folders unlikely to contain evidence? Or is a cell phone special, as an instant messaging app with a particular name on the folder will almost always only contain messages with that particular user?

9. *Does the government need a second warrant for the electronic search stage?* Federal warrants to search computers generally allow a single warrant to cover both stages of the computer search process. That is, one warrant justifies both the physical search stage (retrieving the computer) and the electronic search stage (searching the computer). The federal rule on search warrants makes this explicit:

> *Warrant Seeking Electronically Stored Information.* A warrant [issued under the federal rules] may authorize the seizure of electronic storage media or the seizure or copying of electronically

stored information. Unless otherwise specified, the warrant authorizes a later review of the media or information consistent with the warrant.

Fed. R. Crim. Proc. 41(e)(2)(B).

In contrast, state practices can vary. For an example of a two-warrant approach, consider State v. Fairley, 457 P.3d 1150 (Wash. App. 2020). The police obtained a warrant to search Brown's home for evidence of a bomb threat. The list of items to be seized included Brown's cell phone. The police executed the warrant, seized Brown's phone, and then later searched it. The search through phone revealed text messages sent to that phone from Fairley, who had sent messages to the phone to Brown's daughter relating to prostitution. Fairley was later charged with misdemeanor offenses.

The Court of Appeals held that searching the phone without a second warrant was unlawful:

> It is readily apparent the warrant here did not authorize a search of the contents of Mr. Brown's cell phone. While law enforcement undoubtedly obtained the warrant in hopes of conducting a search, permission to search the phone was neither sought nor granted.
>
> To hold that authorization to search the contents of a cell phone can be inferred from a warrant authorizing a seizure of the phone would be to eliminate the particularity requirement and to condone a general warrant. This outcome is constitutionally unacceptable. The particularity requirement envisions a warrant will describe items to be seized with as much specificity as possible. Narrow tailoring is necessary to prevent overseizure and oversearching beyond the warrant's probable cause authorization.
>
> Rather than allowing law enforcement officers to operate through inferences, the Fourth Amendment demands a cell phone warrant specify the types of data to be seized with sufficient detail to distinguish material for which there is probable cause from information that should remain private. There are likely a variety of ways to meet the Fourth Amendment's particularity requirement in the context of cell phone searches. But one rule is absolute: the responsibility for setting the bounds of the search lies with the judicial officer issuing the warrant, not with the executing officer.

Id. at 1154.

Does it make sense that the government needs two warrants to search a computer? Why would a second warrant add particularity that the first warrant lacks? Or is the real problem in *Fairley* that the search for one kind of evidence led to very different evidence, raising concerns about the scope of the plain view exception?

5.　EX ANTE RESTRICTIONS ON COMPUTER WARRANTS

Some courts have tried to limit the invasiveness of warrants to search computers by imposing restrictions on the face of search warrants concerning how the warrant can be executed. These ex ante restrictions are imposed as conditions of obtaining a warrant. Magistrate judges refuse to sign warrant applications unless agents agree to the limitations. Most magistrate judges have not imposed such requirements. Among those who have, however, the specific limitations vary from judge to judge.

In some cases, the limitations require the investigators to search the computers in a specific period of time. In other cases, the limitations require investigators to follow a specific search protocol during the electronic search stage. Other conditions may require agents to return the seized computers or destroy nonresponsive data when searches are complete. Finally, some judges have imposed requirements ordering the government to waive certain rights to the use of information discovered. The purpose of all of these limitations is the same: Judges try to manage the search process ex ante to ensure that computer warrants are not executed in an overly broad manner.

We first encountered ex ante restrictions in United States v. Ulbricht, 858 F.3d 71 (2d Cir. 2017), starting on page 578. In that case, the defendant unsuccessfully argued that the warrant was defective because it lacked clear ex ante restrictions on how it was to be executed. Now we can return to the question and consider the merits *of ex ante* limitations in more depth. Are these *ex ante* limitations wise? Are they necessary? Do judges have the power to impose them? And if agents do not follow the limitations, what remedies are available to enforce them?

IN RE APPLICATION FOR A SEARCH WARRANT TO SEIZE AND SEARCH ELECTRONIC DEVICES FROM EDWARD CUNNIUS

United States District Court for the Western District of Washington, 2011.
770 F. Supp.2d 1138.

JAMES P. DONOHUE, UNITED STATES MAGISTRATE JUDGE.

I.　Introduction and Summary Conclusion

This matter comes before the Court on the government's application for a warrant to search the residence of Edward Cunnius, to seize any computers or digital devices that may be located at the premises, and to search all electronically stored information ("ESI") contained in any digital devices seized from Mr. Cunnius' residence for evidence relating to the crimes of copyright infringement or trafficking in counterfeit goods.

The United States has refused to accede to the Court's view that a filter team and forswearing reliance on the plain view doctrine are appropriate, and indeed, required in this specific case. Because the government, in this application, refuses to conduct its search of the digital devices utilizing a filter team and forswearing reliance on the plain view doctrine, the Court denies the application as seeking an overbroad or general warrant in violation of the Fourth Amendment and the law of this Circuit.

II.   Discussion

A.   *The Warrant Application to Seize and Search ESI devices*

The affidavit in support of the government's warrant application indicates that agents received information from Microsoft Corporation in October 2010 regarding an individual, Mr. Cunnius, whom they believed was advertising counterfeit Microsoft software via the internet classified advertising service Craigslist. Specifically, a Microsoft anti-piracy investigator informed agents that a shipment of counterfeit Microsoft software from China, addressed to "Edward Russell Cunnius" at 2305 Rucker Avenue # 5, Everett, Washington, had been seized by Customs and Border Protection on October 18, 2010.

The Microsoft investigator also informed the agents that Mr. Cunnius was responsible for numerous Craigslist advertisements over the past few months that offered to sell brand new, in-the-box, Microsoft software at prices well below typical retail prices for the same software. After contacting Mr. Cunnius at the phone number listed on the Craigslist advertisements, Microsoft conducted an undercover test purchase of several products from Mr. Cunnius at his home in Everett, Washington. These products were purchased at prices substantially below retail value, and upon further examination, were found to be counterfeit.

Following Microsoft's test purchase, undercover law enforcement agents conducted two test purchases from Mr. Cunnius at his apartment. During each purchase, Mr. Cunnius retrieved the boxes containing the software from a closet in the bedroom of his apartment. According to the affidavit, he was evasive in response to questions regarding the authenticity of the products, and stated that if customers complained to him, he would instruct them to go buy the products for much higher prices at retail establishments. The agents submitted the products purchased from Mr. Cunnius to Microsoft for analysis by their product identification specialists, who determined that the products were counterfeit.

The government then applied to this Court for a warrant authorizing agents to search Mr. Cunnius' apartment and seize evidence, fruits and instrumentalities of the crimes of (1) copyright infringement and/or (2) trafficking in counterfeit goods. Specifically, the government believes that evidence related to how Mr. Cunnius obtained counterfeit software, paid for it, and how he distributed the counterfeit software is likely to be discovered on digital devices located at his apartment.

The Court finds that the warrant affidavit establishes probable cause to search the digital devices located at Mr. Cunnius' residence for evidence of criminal copyright infringement and/or trafficking in counterfeit goods. In light of the sworn affidavit that Mr. Cunnius advertises the counterfeit goods by posting advertisements containing digital photographs of the products on the website Craigslist, communicates with his source by e-mail, and pays his source using electronic transfers from his bank, the Court can reasonably assume that digital devices contain evidence relating to the crimes alleged.

However, despite the existence of probable cause to search the digital devices, the Court finds the warrant requested by the government overbroad. The affidavit contains no reference to use of a filter team, and no promise to foreswear reliance on the plain view doctrine. With respect to the procedures to be employed by law enforcement personnel to execute the search of digital devices, once they have been seized, the affidavit provides:

> In order to examine the ESI in a forensically sound manner, law enforcement personnel with appropriate expertise will produce a complete forensic image, if possible and appropriate, of any digital device that is found to contain data or items that fall within the scope of Attachment B of this Affidavit. In addition, appropriately trained personnel may search for and attempt to recover deleted, hidden, or encrypted data to determine whether the data fall within the list of items to be seized pursuant to the warrant. In order to search fully for the items identified in the warrant, law enforcement personnel may then examine all of the data contained in the forensic image/s and/or on the digital devices to view their precise contents and determine whether the data falls within the list of items to be seized pursuant to the warrant.

> The search techniques that will be used will be only those methodologies, techniques and protocols as may reasonably be expected to find, identify, segregate, and/or duplicate the items authorized to be seized pursuant to Attachment B to this affidavit.

> If, after conducting its examination, law enforcement personnel determine that any digital device is an instrumentality of the criminal offense referenced above, the government may retain that device during the pendency of the case as necessary to, among other things, preserve the instrumentality evidence for trial, ensure the chain of custody, and litigate the issue of forfeiture. If law enforcement personnel determine that a device was not an instrumentality of the criminal offense referenced above, it shall

be returned to the person/entity from whom it was seized within 90 days of the issuance of the warrant, unless the government seeks and obtains authorization from the court for its retention.

Unless the government seeks an additional order of authorization from any Magistrate Judge in the District, the government will return any digital device that has been forensically copied, that is not an instrumentality of the crime, and that may be lawfully possessed by the person/entity from whom it was seized, to the person/entity from whom it was seized within 90 days of seizure.

If, in the course of their efforts to search the subject digital devices, law enforcement agents or analysts discover items outside of the scope of the warrant that are evidence of other crimes, that data/evidence will not be used in any way unless it is first presented to a Magistrate Judge of this District and a new warrant is obtained to seize that data, and/or to search for other evidence related to it. In the event a new warrant is authorized, the government may make use of the data then seized in any lawful manner.

Larson Aff. ¶ 46(c)–(g).

As discussed below, permitting the government to conduct a search along these lines would violate the Fourth Amendment and the law of this Circuit.

B.   *The Fourth Amendment Prohibits General Searches*

The instant warrant application cannot be squared with the Fourth Amendment's prohibition on general searches. The Warrant Clause of the Fourth Amendment categorically prohibits the issuance of any warrant except one particularly describing the place to be searched and the persons or things to be seized.

Here, the government seeks permission to search every bit of data contained in each digital device seized from Mr. Cunnius' residence. Contrary to the Fourth Amendment's particularity requirement limiting searches to only the specific areas and things for which there is probable cause to search, the government seeks to scour everything contained in the digital devices and information outside of the digital devices. This practice is akin to the revenue officers in colonial days who scoured "suspected places" pursuant to a general warrant.

The Court has considered the fact that the search warrant application seeks permission to search and seize evidence of the specified crimes, and a second warrant would be needed to seize evidence of other crimes for which there is no probable cause shown. However, the ability to seek a second warrant after finding evidence as to which there was no probable cause to search only magnifies the danger of the warrant constituting a general warrant. The requirement that a second warrant be obtained provides no meaningful limitation on the scope of the search conducted under the first warrant and no meaningful protection against the government obtaining evidence for which it lacks probable cause. For the first warrant would be nothing more than a "vehicle to gain access to data for which the government has no probable cause to collect." *United States v. Comprehensive Drug Testing*, 621 F.3d 1162, 1177 (9th Cir. 2010) (en banc) ("*CDT III*").[4] Indeed, the warrant the government now seeks would permit it to seize evidence found outside the scope of the first warrant whether that evidence was initially in plain view, or not.

C. *What is Involved in a Digital Search?*

A government search of even a single, non-networked computer involves searching vast quantities of ESI. As pointed out in the warrant affidavit, a single gigabyte of storage space is the equivalent of 500,000 double-spaced pages of text. Computer hard drives are now being sold for personal computers capable of storing up to two terabytes, or 2,048 gigabytes of data. If a computer is networked, this exponentially increases the volume of data being searched. Thus, the sheer volume of ESI involved distinguishes a digital search from the search of, for example, a file cabinet.

Because it is common practice for people to store innocent and deeply personal information on their personal computers, a digital search of ESI will also frequently involve searching personal information relating to the subject of the search as well as third parties.

The language in the instant warrant raises another significant constitutional concern related to the interactive nature of modern digital devices. These digital devices are not just repositories of data, but access points, or portals, to other digital devices and data, typically obtained through the internet or stored on a network. All data on the internet is both separate and one. The requested warrant is, in essence, boundless.

In addition to granting the government access to ESI that was consciously downloaded by computer users, this boundless search would reveal ESI that computer users have no way of knowing is stored on their device. A search of a file cabinet, in contrast, would include only items put in the file cabinet by a person. A conscious, even if unknowing, act is required. This act perhaps would be analogous to intentionally downloading a file. However, in contrast to the conscious act of downloading a file or storing something in a file cabinet, cache files are a

---

[4] The Ninth Circuit's initial panel decision is found at *United States v. Comprehensive Drug Testing*, 473 F.3d 915 (9th Cir. 2006). This panel decision was withdrawn and superseded by *United States v. Comprehensive Drug Testing*, 513 F.3d 1085 (9th Cir. 2008) ("*CDT I*"). The Ninth Circuit then granted rehearing *en banc*, *United States v. Comprehensive Drug Testing*, 545 F.3d 1106 (9th Cir. 2008), and issued its first *en banc* decision at *United States v. Comprehensive Drug Testing*, 579 F.3d 989 (9th Cir. 2009) ("*CDT II*"). The initial *en banc* decision was then revised and superseded by *CDT III*, 621 F.3d 1162.

set of files automatically stored on a user's hard drive by a web browser to speed up future visits to the same websites, without the affirmative action of downloading. Thus, a person's entire online viewing history can be retrieved from the cache, without any affirmative act other than visiting a web page.

Unlike information in a file cabinet that can simply be taken out and destroyed, ESI is present after attempts to destroy it. In addition to data stored in cache files, ESI can be recovered from "unallocated space" on a hard drive, which contains deleted data, usually emptied from the operating system's trash or recycle bin folder, that cannot be seen or accessed by the user without the use of forensic software.

D.   *Comprehensive Drug Testing Inc. v. United States*

With this background, the Court turns to the Ninth Circuit opinion in *CDT III*. In that case, the government obtained a warrant to search CDT's facilities limited to the records of ten baseball players for whom there was probable cause to suspect of drug use. Included in the warrant was a provision to allow seizure of computer records from CDT facilities for off-site examination and segregation of the evidence. To justify this provision, which the government acknowledged included information beyond that relevant to the investigation, the supporting affidavit contained information about the difficulty and hazards of retrieving only ESI for which the government had probable cause.

Based on these representations, a magistrate judge granted the government permission to engage in a broad seizure. However, the warrant the magistrate judge authorized also contained important restrictions on the handling of seized data, including review and segregation by noninvestigating law enforcement personnel rather than the case agents. The purpose of the segregation requirement was to prevent case agents from accessing information outside the scope of the warrant.

Utilizing this warrant, agents found at CDT's facilities the "Tracey Directory," which included, among hundreds of other documents, a spreadsheet containing the names of all the major league baseball players who had tested positive for steroids. The government had probable cause to search and seize records of ten baseball players. After deciding it was impractical to sort through the information on-site, the agents removed the data for off-site review. Although the warrant required segregation and screening, the case agent ignored this requirement and took control of the data.

Based on its search of the Tracey Directory, the government obtained additional warrants to search the facilities of CDT and Quest for information regarding more baseball players who they discovered had tested positive for steroids, and issued subpoenas demanding production of the same records it had just seized. The government claimed it was justified in obtaining this additional incriminating information, based on the plain view doctrine of evidence found outside the scope of the warrant. In response, CDT and the baseball players' association moved for return of the seized property.

The litigation in *CDT III* involved multiple district courts. Two district courts ordered the government to return the property. The judges expressed grave dissatisfaction with the government's conduct; some accused the government of manipulation and misrepresentations. As one district judge stated in rejecting the government's arguments, "whatever happened to the Fourth Amendment? Was it . . . repealed somehow?"

The government appealed to the Ninth Circuit. In a reissued decision, the panel reversed two of the district courts' orders to return the property, and held the government was bound by the third court's order containing factual determinations including the government's failure to comply with the warrant and that it had displayed a callous disregard for the rights of third parties. The case was then taken *en banc. CDT II*, 579 F.3d 989. The *en banc* panel reversed and ordered the return of all testing results, save the ten athletes named in the first warrant. The majority explored the government's improper conduct and further reflected on the balance between law enforcement's perhaps legitimate need to over-seize in conducting searches of ESI devices, with the Fourth Amendment's prohibition on general or overbroad searches. To strike this balance, the court directed magistrate judges to adhere to the following five guidelines:

1.   Magistrate Judges should insist that the government waive reliance upon the plain view doctrine in digital evidence cases.

2.   Segregation and redaction must be either done by specialized personnel or an independent third party. If segregation is to be done by government computer personnel, it must agree in the warrant application that the computer personnel will not disclose to the investigators any information other than that which is the target of the warrant.

3.   Warrants and subpoenas must disclose the actual risks of destruction of information as well as prior efforts to seize that information in other judicial fora.

4.   The government's search protocol must be designed to uncover only the information for which it has probable cause, and only that information may be examined by the case agents.

5.   The government must destroy or, if the recipient may lawfully possess it, return non-responsive data, keeping the issuing magistrate informed about when it has done so and what it has kept.

Id. at 1006.

On September 13, 2010, the Ninth Circuit issued a revised *en banc* opinion. *CDT III*, 621 F.3d 1162. The new opinion did not change the outcome of the first *en banc* decision, but the five guidelines that were previously part of the majority decision became part of a concurring opinion authored by Chief Judge Kozinski.

In the Court's view, the Ninth Circuit's final *en banc* opinion does not permit the issuance of the warrant the government seeks in this case for four reasons. First, although the five guidelines are no longer mandatory, the majority did not hold magistrate judges are prohibited from employing them or that they are improper or inappropriate. Rather the Court, exercising its independent judgment, as it must, has arrived at the conclusion that some of the guidelines should be applied based on the specifics of the present case.

Second, the warrant application in *CDT III* was drafted in a manner designed to ensure that it would be lawful and comport with the requirements of the Fourth Amendment. The warrant contained a panoply of safeguards absent here. As the Ninth Circuit stated "the magistrate judge wisely made such broad seizure subject to certain procedural safeguards." *CDT III*, 621 F.3d at 1168. Germane to the present case, these safeguards included: (1) that investigative agents not review and segregate the data; (2) that specialized forensic computer search personnel review and segregate the data and not give it to the investigative agents; and (3) seized evidence outside the scope of the warrant be returned within 60 days.

There is nothing in *CDT III* indicating it is unwise for a magistrate judge to require the warrant application contain such safeguards where requests for broad computer searches are made, that such safeguards are inappropriate, or that once such safeguards are ordered, it is permissible for the government to ignore them. These safeguards are particularly appropriate in this case. According to the affidavit, the target of the search is a disabled man who conducts business out of his home. There is no evidence he is using the computer to create illegal copies, but the computer is likely to store information regarding his supplier, customers and financial transactions. There is no suggestion that utilizing a filter team in this investigation would compromise the government's ability to prosecute this case. There is no suggestion that requiring waiver of the plain view doctrine as a *quid pro quo* for the evident over-seizing will compromise the government's ability to prosecute this case.

In contrast to the warrants issued in *CDT III*, the government, here, applies for the broadest warrant possible—the authority to search every single thing—but minus any of the procedural safeguards the Ninth Circuit in *CDT III* deemed to be wise. Perhaps the government believes that its promise to use "only those methodologies, techniques and protocols as may reasonably be expected to find, identify, segregate and/or duplicate the items authorized to be seized" is a sufficient safeguard. However, such protection is illusory and does not justify the government's request to conduct a search without a filter team and to rely on the plain view doctrine. Once the Court authorizes the government to search all data, the government can, and will.

Third, the *CDT III* opinion rejected the government's arguments that under *United States v. Tamura*, 694 F.2d 591 (9th Cir. 1982), it did not have to return any data it found about baseball players outside the scope of the first warrant because that evidence was in "plain view" when agents examined the Tracey Directory. Calling this argument "too clever by half" the Ninth Circuit found the "point of the *Tamura* procedures is to maintain the privacy of materials that are intermingled with seizable materials, and to avoid turning a limited search into a general search." *CDT III*, 621 F.3d at 1170.

The instant warrant application goes a step beyond the position it took in *CDT III*. In this case, not only does the government fail to foreswear reliance on the plain view doctrine, it requests that it be allowed to seek a warrant that permits it to obtain a second warrant to seize additional evidence whether it was found in the initial search in plain view or not.

And fourth, the Ninth Circuit's "concluding thoughts" in *CDT III* put to rest any notion the warrant sought here is appropriate. Broad searches of ESI devices create "a serious risk that every warrant for electronic information will become, in effect, a general warrant, rendering the Fourth Amendment irrelevant."

In this case, the Court finds that the requested warrant application impermissibly grants the government a general or overbroad search warrant in violation of the Constitution and the law of the Circuit. The Court also reaches this conclusion while recognizing that quite often, broad searches of digital devices and over-seizing is an inherent part of the electronic search process. However, a balance must be struck between the government's investigatory interests and the right of individuals to be free from unreasonable searches and seizures.

III. Conclusion

This Court is required under the U.S. Constitution and the law of the Circuit to deny the instant warrant application. Counterfeiting products is a serious crime and costs American intellectual property owners billions of dollars annually, results in lost jobs, and creates substantial threats to consumers of these products. Probable cause exists to search Mr. Cunnius' digital devices for evidence relating to counterfeit products. But the government asks the Court to do what the law does not permit.

NOTES AND QUESTIONS

1. *Ex ante restrictions and the plain view exception.* According to the Fourth Circuit in *United States v. Williams, supra* at pages 607–611, the plain view exception should apply in the same way to computer searches that it applies to physical searches. If this is correct, why should individual magistrate judges have the power to require prosecutors to forswear reliance on the plain view exception as a condition of obtaining a warrant? Doesn't this simply negate Fourth Amendment doctrine? And if so, why should that power be held by individual magistrate judges when reviewing warrant applications *ex ante* rather than by circuit court judges and Supreme Court Justices when reviewing warrant searches *ex post*? What do individual magistrate judges know that appellate court judges don't know?

Magistrate Judge Donohue reasons in *Cunnius* that the Fourth Amendment required him to deny the warrant application because the government insisted on following Fourth Amendment doctrine (that is, the plain view exception). A less awkward way to reach the same result would be to hold that the plain view exception does not apply in computer search cases. If appellate courts were to so hold, wouldn't such a holding implicitly write the search condition sought by Magistrate Judge Donohue into all computer warrants?

2. *Search protocols.* One way to limit the invasiveness of computer searches would be to require investigators to follow specific search protocols when a computer is searched. For example, a protocol might explain the search terms the investigators will use to locate evidence, or the specific steps investigators must follow when searching the hard drive.

Circuit courts have rejected a requirement of search protocols, although several courts have indicated that search protocols are looked upon favorably. For example, in United States v. Hill, 459 F.3d 966 (9th Cir. 2006), a defendant charged with child pornography possession challenged the warrant used to search his computer on the ground that it did not include any search protocols. He claimed that the search should have been limited to certain files that were more likely to be associated with child pornography, such as those with a ".jpg" suffix (which usually identifies files containing images) or those containing the word "sex" or other key words. The Ninth Circuit disagreed, noting that "we look favorably upon the inclusion of a search protocol; but its absence is not fatal." *Id.* at 978. The court concluded that the defendant's proposed search protocol was not reasonable in light of investigative realities:

> Computer records are extremely susceptible to tampering, hiding, or destruction, whether deliberate or inadvertent. Images can be hidden in all manner of files, even word processing documents and spreadsheets. Criminals will do all they can to conceal contraband, including the simple expedient of changing the names and extensions of files to disguise their content from the casual observer.

> Forcing police to limit their searches to files that the suspect has
> labeled in a particular way would be much like saying police may not
> seize a plastic bag containing a powdery white substance if it is
> labeled "flour" or "talcum powder." There is no way to know what is
> in a file without examining its contents, just as there is no sure way
> of separating talcum from cocaine except by testing it. The ease with
> which child pornography images can be disguised—whether by
> renaming sexyteenyboppersxxx.jpg as sundayschoollesson.doc, or
> something more sophisticated—forecloses defendant's proposed
> search methodology.

Id. (quoting United States v. Hill, 322 F. Supp.2d 1081, 1090–91 (C.D. Cal.
2004) (Kozinski, J.)).

The decision in *Hill* echoes United States v. Upham, 168 F.3d 532 (1st Cir.
1999). In *Upham*, the police recovered incriminating information by
"undeleting" files stored on the defendant's personal computer. This was
possible because information stored on a computer often continues to be
present when the machine has been reformatted or a file "deleted." The First
Circuit held that the warrant permitted investigators to find and recover the
deleted files:

> The seizure of unlawful images is within the plain language of the
> warrant; their recovery, after attempted destruction, is no different
> than decoding a coded message lawfully seized or pasting together
> scraps of a torn-up ransom note. The warrant did not prescribe
> methods of recovery or tests to be performed, but warrants rarely do
> so. The warrant process is primarily concerned with identifying *what*
> may be searched or seized—not how—and *whether* there is sufficient
> cause for the invasion of privacy thus entailed.

Id. at 537. *See also* United States v. Brooks, 427 F.3d 1246, 1251–53 (10th Cir.
2005).

Do you think search protocols should be required? If so, how detailed
should they have to be?

3.   *Reconciling ex ante restrictions with Supreme Court precedent.*
Supreme Court caselaw on executing warrants generally indicates that the
execution of the warrant is up to executive branch officers rather than the
judge who issued the warrant. Of course, judicial review of the reasonableness
of the search can occur ex post. But the warrant itself generally does not
contain guidance as to how the warrant will be executed.

For example, in Dalia v. United States, 441 U.S. 238 (1979), the
government obtained a warrant to conduct bugging surveillance. Investigators
executed the warrant by covertly entering the place to install the bug. The
Supreme Court rejected the defendant's contention that the warrant had to
state that it permitted covert entry:

> Nothing in the language of the Constitution or in this Court's
> decisions interpreting that language suggests that search warrants

also must include a specification of the precise manner in which they are to be executed. On the contrary, it is generally left to the discretion of the executing officers to determine the details of how best to proceed with the performance of a search authorized by warrant—subject of course to the general Fourth Amendment protection against unreasonable searches and seizures.

Id. at 257.

Also consider *United States v. Ross*, 456 U.S. 798, 820–21 (1982), where the Supreme Court articulated the following general guidance for executing search warrants:

A lawful search of fixed premises generally extends to the entire area in which the object of the search may be found. Thus, a warrant that authorizes an officer to search a home for illegal weapons also provides authority to open closets, chests, drawers, and containers in which the weapon might be found. A warrant to open a footlocker to search for marihuana would also authorize the opening of packages found inside. A warrant to search a vehicle would support a search of every part of the vehicle that might contain the object of the search. When a legitimate search is under way, and when its purpose and its limits have been precisely defined, nice distinctions between closets, drawers, and containers, in the case of a home, or between glove compartments, upholstered seats, trunks, and wrapped packages, in the case of a vehicle, must give way to the interest in the prompt and efficient completion of the task at hand.

Do computer warrants merit a different approach? Does it depend on whether courts retain the traditional approach to the plain view doctrine in the context of digital evidence?

4. *The policy debate.* Which is the better way to minimize the intrusiveness of computer searches: Should magistrate judges impose restrictions ex ante, or should appellate courts impose limitations ex post? Or both? For a debate on these issues, compare Orin S. Kerr, *Ex Ante Regulation of Computer Search and Seizure*, 96 Va. L. Rev. 1241 (2010) (arguing that ex ante limitations are impermissible and unwise, and that courts must develop the reasonableness of computer searches ex post) with Paul Ohm, *Massive Hard Drives, General Warrants, and the Power of Magistrate Judges*, 97 Va. L. Rev. In Brief 1 (2011) (arguing that ex ante limitations are permissible and sound policy).

5. *Enforcing ex ante restrictions.* Imagine a magistrate judge imposes an ex ante restriction on how the warrant must be executed. The government then violates the ex ante restriction in the course of executing the warrant. What is the remedy?

Richards v. Wisconsin, 520 U.S. 385 (1997), suggests that the answer may be "none." In *Richards*, agents obtained a warrant to search a hotel room for drugs. The agents asked the judge to sign a warrant permitting them to execute it without first knocking and announcing their presence. The magistrate judge signed the warrant, but he expressly rejected the request to dispense with the usual knock-and-announce requirement by affirmatively crossing out that part of the warrant. When the agents executed the warrant, however, they did not announce their presence. The defendant later moved to suppress the drugs found in the hotel room on the ground that the agents had expressly violated the terms of the warrant. Specifically, the judge had declined to let the officers dispense with the knock-and-announce requirement but the officers had done so anyway. The Supreme Court ruled that the magistrate judge's "ruling" at the time of issuing the warrant was irrelevant to the constitutionality of the entry into the hotel room:

> In arguing that the officers' entry was unreasonable, Richards places great emphasis on the fact that the magistrate who signed the search warrant for his hotel room deleted the portions of the proposed warrant that would have given the officers permission to execute a no-knock entry. But this fact does not alter the reasonableness of the officers' decision, which must be evaluated as of the time they entered the hotel room. At the time the officers obtained the warrant, they did not have evidence sufficient, in the judgment of the magistrate, to justify a no-knock warrant. Of course, the magistrate could not have anticipated in every particular the circumstances that would confront the officers when they arrived at Richards' hotel room. These actual circumstances-petitioner's apparent recognition of the officers combined with the easily disposable nature of the drugs-justified the officers' ultimate decision to enter without first announcing their presence and authority.

Despite *Richards*, lower courts have generally assumed without analysis that ex ante restrictions on warrants can be enforced by suppressing evidence obtained in violation of those restrictions. For example, in United States v. Brunette, 76 F. Supp.2d 30 (D. Me. 1999), a magistrate judge signed a warrant allowing agents to seize the defendant's computers on the condition that the forensic analysis must occur "within 30 days." When agents failed to search the computer during the time window, the court suppressed the evidence discovered on the computer after the 30-day period had elapsed. *Id.* at 42.

6.   *United States v. Mann*. Although the Ninth Circuit has generally endorsed ex ante limitations on computer warrants in cases such as *CDT*, other circuits have taken a different approach. For example, the Seventh Circuit rejected the Ninth Circuit's approach in United States v. Mann, 592 F.3d 779 (7th Cir. 2010):

> Although the Ninth Circuit's rules provide some guidance in a murky area, jettisoning the plain view doctrine entirely in digital evidence cases is an efficient but overbroad approach. There is nothing in the Supreme Court's case law (or the Ninth Circuit's for that matter) counseling the complete abandonment of the plain view doctrine in digital evidence cases. We believe the more considered approach

would be to allow the contours of the plain view doctrine to develop incrementally through the normal course of fact-based case adjudication.

We are also skeptical of a rule requiring officers to always obtain pre-approval from a magistrate judge to use the electronic tools necessary to conduct searches tailored to uncovering evidence that is responsive to a properly circumscribed warrant. Instead, we simply counsel officers and others involved in searches of digital media to exercise caution to ensure that warrants describe with particularity the things to be seized and that searches are narrowly tailored to uncover only those things described.

Id. at 785–86.

7. *Are ex ante search restrictions permitted?* In In re Search Warrant, 71 A.3d 1158 (Vt. 2012), the Vermont Supreme Court considered whether the Fourth Amendment permits magistrates to impose ex ante search restrictions on computer warrants. Vermont investigators had applied for a search warrant to search the home of a suspect for evidence of credit card fraud. The warrant requested permission to seize any computers that might be found at the home and to search the computers off-site. The magistrate signed the warrant but imposed ten ex ante restrictions with the following conditions:

(1) restricting the police from relying on the plain view doctrine to seize any incriminatory electronic record not authorized by the warrant—that is, "any digital evidence relating to criminal matters other than identity theft offenses";

(2) requiring third parties or specially trained computer personnel to conduct the search behind a "firewall" and provide to State investigatory agents only "digital evidence relating to identity theft offenses";

(3) requiring digital evidence relating to the offenses to be segregated and redacted from surrounding nonevidentiary data before being delivered to the case investigators, "no matter how intermingled it is";

(4) precluding State police personnel who are involved in conducting the search under condition (2) from disclosing their work to prosecutors or investigators;

(5) limiting the search protocol to methods designed to uncover only information for which the State has probable cause;

(6) precluding the use of specialized "hashing tools" and "similar search tools" without specific authorization of the court;

(7) allowing only evidence "relevant to the targeted alleged activities" to be copied to provide to State agents;

(8) requiring the State to return "non-responsive data" and to inform the court of this action;

(9) directing police to destroy remaining copies of electronic data absent judicial authorization otherwise; and

(10) requiring the State to file a return within the time limit of the warrant to indicate precisely what data were obtained, returned, and destroyed.

Id. at 1162–63. The police executed the warrant and seized a computer and an iPad but did not search it. Instead, the police asked the court to strike the ex ante restrictions to enable them to search the computer and iPad without complying with the restrictions. The government argued that magistrates lack the constitutional authority to impose ex ante restrictions because the constitutionality of a search pursuant to a warrant must be reviewed ex post after the search occurs, when all the facts are known.

Reviewing the magistrate's decision under an abuse of discretion standard, as dictated by Vermont law, the Vermont Supreme Court ruled that ex ante search restrictions are "sometimes acceptable" because they can be a way to ensure that searches are executed in a narrow way. The court then reviewed each of the ten restrictions to determine if they were acceptable, striking the first restriction as an abuse of discretion but upholding the remaining restrictions.

The court invalidated the first restriction—the one requiring the government to forswear the plain view exception—on the ground that it was "unnecessary for privacy protection and inappropriate." It was unnecessary because the other restrictions in the warrant made it unlikely that the government would be in a position to rely on evidence in plain view. The first restriction also was inappropriate because it amounted to an effort to overturn Supreme Court precedent:

> It is beyond the authority of a judicial officer issuing a warrant to abrogate a legal doctrine in this way. Judicial supervision of the administration of criminal justice in the courts implies the duty of establishing and maintaining civilized standards of procedure and evidence. This supervisory power does not, however, go so far as to allow a judicial officer to alter what legal principles will or will not apply in a particular case.

> This proposition was established in United States v. Payner, 447 U.S. 727 (1980), in which the trial court attempted to use its supervisory authority to suppress items seized in violation of a third party's constitutional rights, thereby avoiding the established rules for Fourth Amendment standing. In reversing, the Supreme Court concluded that, if it accepted such use of the supervisory power, it "would confer on the judiciary discretionary power to disregard the considered limitations of the law it is charged with enforcing." In this case, allowing instruction (1) would confer on a judicial officer the

authority to pick and choose what legal doctrines would apply to a particular police search. Because we do not believe that a judicial officer holds such authority, we conclude that the State's [request to invalidate the search restrictions] must be granted with regard to instruction (1).

Id. at 1174.

The court upheld the remaining restrictions. The second set of restrictions—requiring the computer to be searched by non-investigative personnel who would then set up a "wall" and not give any evidence to the investigators that was not, in their view, related to the crime under investigation—were allowed because they were efforts to try to restore particularity. "In lieu of a particular description of the files" that would ordinarily be required under the Fourth Amendment, this provisions allowed a substitute of "a procedure for identifying the relevant files and exposing them only to police investigators." According to the court, exposure of "embarrassing information to a detached third party constitutes a lesser injury" to privacy interest than does exposure to the police, so this procedure minimizes the invasiveness of a computer search and is therefore "not so wholly without basis as to constitute an abuse of discretion." (Two Justices dissented on this part of the opinion: They argued that these search restrictions were a procedure designed to frustrate the plain view exception, and thus were not permitted for the same reason that it was impermissible to force the government to forswear reliance on the plain view exception.)

The third set of restrictions was a requirement of special search protocols and a ban on using "sophisticated hashing tools" and "similar tools" without special permission. The court permitted these restrictions because they were ways to limit the scope of the search that could limit the privacy invasion. If the government searches the computer and investigators believe that there may be more evidence on the machine, the court reasoned, investigators can always apply for a second warrant to use "sophisticated" tools. The magistrate might reject the government's application, but at least the government was allowed to request permission.

The fourth set of restrictions required only responsive data to be copied, non-responsive data to be destroyed, and the search to be completed in a particular period of time. The court permitted these restrictions on the ground that they were similar to the kind of restrictions traditionally imposed by statutory rules governing warrants.

In dicta, the court expressed the view that the search restrictions "generally" are binding on law enforcement when issued, although the government can try to argue that circumstances changed and that therefore the restrictions need not be followed. The court also suggests that the fact that the restrictions are always optional and not always binding when issued means that there can still be ex post litigation to figure out what kind of search rules are constitutional as a matter of law.

8. *The "flagrant disregard" standard.* When a defendant moves to suppress evidence obtained pursuant to a facially valid warrant, the admissibility of the evidence usually depends on whether the evidence falls within the scope of the warrant. If the evidence is construed to fall beyond the scope of the warrant, the evidence is excluded unless it fits within the "plain view" exception. If the evidence fits within the scope of the warrant, however, it will be admitted unless the warrant was executed in "flagrant disregard" of the warrant's terms.

The "flagrant disregard" standard is very hard for a defense attorney to satisfy. Agents execute a warrant in "flagrant disregard" of its terms only if the search so grossly exceeds what the warrant permits that the authorized search appears to be merely a pretext for a fishing expedition through the target's private property. *See, e.g.,* United States v. Shi Yan Liu, 239 F.3d 138, 140–42 (2d Cir. 2000). Is this burden too high? What kind of search through a computer would be in "flagrant disregard" of the warrant? Should courts regulate computer searches more closely than traditional physical searches, or is the traditional "flagrant disregard" standard appropriate?

6. ENCRYPTION

Encryption is a way of transforming information into a form that cannot be read without a special code (referred to as a "key") that can return the information into readable form. The readable form is generally known as plaintext; the scrambled form is known as ciphertext. Encryption is a very powerful tool for maintaining privacy in computer data. If a target encrypts evidence of his crime, the government generally needs to obtain the key to decrypt the ciphertext and view the evidence.

The widespread use of encryption raises two interesting and difficult legal questions addressed below. First, when can the government order a target to divulge his encryption key in light of Fifth Amendment protections? Second, how much power does the government have to compel third parties to decrypt encrypted devices or files under the All Writs Act?

a) Fifth Amendment Issues

Imagine the government seizes an encrypted phone or computer belonging to a suspect, and the government wants to compel the suspect to unlock it. Does the Fifth Amendment provide the suspect with a constitutional privilege not to comply?

An overview of the Fifth Amendment privilege against self-incrimination may be helpful before we study the caselaw on this specific question. The Fifth Amendment to the United States Constitution states that no person "shall be compelled in any criminal case to be a witness against himself." The Fifth Amendment privilege is generally triggered when three requirements are met: compulsion, testimony, and incrimination.

Compulsion exists if there is a legal penalty for failure to comply with an act. In that case, the force of law "compels" the action. For example, a subpoena provides compulsion for Fifth Amendment purposes because failure to comply with a valid subpoena can lead to civil or criminal liability for obstruction of justice.

An act is generally testimonial for Fifth Amendment purposes if it requires the individual to divulge the contents of his own mind. Importantly for our purposes, an act of production can be testimonial. If the government orders a person to produce a particular item, under penalty of law, then responding to the order may provide implicit testimony about it that implicates the Fifth Amendment:

> The act of production itself may implicitly communicate statements of fact. By producing documents in compliance with a subpoena, the witness would admit that the papers existed, were in his possession or control, and were authentic. Moreover, as was true in this case, when the custodian of documents responds to a subpoena, he may be compelled to take the witness stand and answer questions designed to determine whether he has produced everything demanded by the subpoena. The answers to those questions, as well as the act of production itself, may certainly communicate information about the existence, custody, and authenticity of the documents. Whether the constitutional privilege protects the answers to such questions, or protects the act of production itself, is a question that is distinct from the question whether the unprotected contents of the documents themselves are incriminating.

United States v. Hubbell, 530 U.S. 27, 36–37 (2000).

One exception to this rule is that if the government already knows that a witness possesses a document or knows a particular piece of information exists, and it is therefore a "foregone conclusion," then it is not testimonial to compel a witness to produce the documents or state the fact. *See* Fisher v. United States, 425 U.S. 391, 411 (1976). For example, in United States v. Teeple, 286 F.3d 1047 (8th Cir. 2002), a tax protester who worked as a chiropractor failed to file tax returns for several years. The government issued a subpoena for his financial records, and he asserted his Fifth Amendment privilege. The Fifth Circuit ruled that complying with the subpoena would not be testimonial because Teeple's past conduct had already demonstrated the relevant facts to the government. Specifically, Teeple had made statements at an earlier court hearing that had essentially demonstrated his knowledge and possession of the financial records the government was seeking.

Finally, an act is incriminating if a person has "reasonable ground to apprehend danger to the witness from his being compelled to answer."

Brown v. Walker, 161 U.S. 591, 599 (1896). That is, the individual's refusal to comply must be based on "articulated real and appreciable fear" that the information to be disclosed "would be used to incriminate him, or that it would furnish a link in the chain of evidence needed to prosecute him." Hiibel v. Sixth Judicial District Court, 542 U.S. 177, 190 (2004). The notion is that the information disclosed must provide the government with evidence that helps prove a criminal case against the witness.

SEO V. STATE
Supreme Court of Indiana, 2020.
148 N.E.3d 952.

RUSH, CHIEF JUSTICE.

When Katelin Seo was placed under arrest, law enforcement took her iPhone believing it contained incriminating evidence. A detective got a warrant to search the smartphone, but he couldn't get into the locked device without Seo's assistance. So the detective got a second warrant that ordered Seo to unlock her iPhone. She refused, and the trial court held her in contempt.

We reverse the contempt order. Forcing Seo to unlock her iPhone would violate her Fifth Amendment right against self-incrimination. By unlocking her smartphone, Seo would provide law enforcement with information it does not already know, which the State could then use in its prosecution against her. The Fifth Amendment's protection from compelled self-incrimination prohibits this result. We thus reverse and remand.

Facts and Procedural History

Katelin Seo contacted her local sheriff's department claiming D.S. had raped her. Detective Bill Inglis met with Seo, and she told him that her smartphone—an iPhone 7 Plus—contained relevant communications with the accused. With Seo's consent, officers completed a forensic download of the device and returned it.

Based on the evidence recovered from the iPhone and the detective's conversations with Seo, no charges were filed against D.S. Instead, law enforcement's focus switched to Seo. D.S. told Detective Inglis that Seo stalked and harassed him, and the detective's ensuing investigation confirmed those claims.

Detective Inglis learned that Seo first contacted D.S. from the phone number associated with her iPhone. But D.S. then began receiving up to thirty calls or text messages daily from dozens of different, unassigned numbers. Yet, because the substance of the contact was consistent, the detective believed that Seo placed the calls and texts using an app or internet program to disguise her phone number. As a result of this investigation, the State charged Seo with several offenses and issued an arrest warrant.

When Detective Inglis arrested Seo, he took possession of her locked iPhone. Officers asked Seo for the device's password, but she refused to provide it. To clear this hurdle, Detective Inglis obtained two search warrants. The first authorized a forensic download of Seo's iPhone so that law enforcement could search the device for "incriminating evidence." And the second "compelled" Seo to unlock the device and stated that she would be subject "to the contempt powers of the court" if she failed to do so. After Seo again refused to unlock her iPhone, the State moved to hold her in contempt.

At the ensuing hearing, Seo argued that forcing her to unlock the iPhone would violate her Fifth Amendment right against self-incrimination. The trial court disagreed and held Seo in contempt, concluding that the act of unlocking the phone does not rise to the level of testimonial self-incrimination. Seo appealed, and the trial court stayed its contempt order.

While her appeal was pending, Seo entered into a plea agreement with the State. She pleaded guilty to one count of stalking, and the State dismissed eighteen other charged offenses without prejudice. But because the contempt citation remained in place, Seo still faced the threat of further sanction for disobeying that order. A divided panel of our Court of Appeals reversed the court's pending contempt order.

Discussion and Decision

The Fifth Amendment's Self-Incrimination Clause protects a person from being "compelled in any criminal case to be a witness against himself." U.S. Const. amend. V. Embedded within this constitutional principle is the requirement that the State produce evidence against an individual through the independent labor of its officers, not by the simple, cruel expedient of forcing it from his own lips. The privilege thus protects an accused from being forced to provide the State with even a link in the chain of evidence needed for prosecution. Yet, not all compelled, incriminating evidence falls under this constitutional protection: the evidence must also be testimonial.

To be testimonial, an accused's communication must itself, explicitly or implicitly, relate a factual assertion or disclose information. The most common form of testimony is verbal or written communications—the vast amount of which will fall within the privilege. But physical acts can also have a testimonial aspect.

When the State compels a suspect to produce physical evidence, that act is testimonial if it implicitly conveys information. In certain contexts, however, the communicative aspects of the act may be rendered nontestimonial if the State can show that it already knows the information conveyed, making it a foregone conclusion. In other words, the inquiry is whether the testimonial communications implicit in producing the evidence provide the State with something it does not already know.

Here, Seo argues that the State, by forcing her to unlock her iPhone for law enforcement, is requiring her to "assist in the prosecution of her own criminal case" and thus violating her right against self-incrimination. The State disagrees, claiming it already knows the implicit factual information Seo would convey by unlocking her iPhone—namely, that she "knows the password and thus has control and use of the phone."

We agree with Seo. The compelled production of an unlocked smartphone is testimonial and entitled to Fifth Amendment protection—unless the State demonstrates the foregone conclusion exception applies. Here, the State has failed to make that showing; and this case also highlights concerns with extending the limited exception to this context.

I.   The act of producing an unlocked smartphone communicates a breadth of factual information.

Giving law enforcement an unlocked smartphone communicates to the State, at a minimum, that (1) the suspect knows the password; (2) the files on the device exist; and (3) the suspect possesses those files. This broad spectrum of communication is entitled to Fifth Amendment protection unless the State can show that it already knows this information, making it a foregone conclusion. We make these determinations after carefully reviewing the U.S. Supreme Court precedent that has created and evaluated both the act of production doctrine and its accompanying foregone conclusion exception.

Our starting point is *Fisher v. United States*, 425 U.S. 391 (1976). There, the IRS subpoenaed several taxpayers' documents that accountants prepared and the taxpayers' attorneys possessed. The attorneys responded that complying with the subpoenas would violate their clients' rights against self-incrimination. The Court disagreed.

In reaching that conclusion, *Fisher* considered what, if any, incriminating testimony would be compelled by responding to a documentary summons. It was here that the Court created the act of production doctrine: producing documents in response to a subpoena can be testimonial if the act concedes the existence, possession, or authenticity of the documents ultimately produced. But when the government can show that it already knows this information, then the testimonial aspects of the act are a "foregone conclusion," *id.* at 411, and complying with the subpoena becomes a question "not of testimony but of surrender," *id.* This was the situation in *Fisher*—the Government knew who possessed the tax documents, and it could independently confirm the documents' existence and authenticity through the accountants who prepared them. So, the Court narrowly held that "compliance with a summons directing the taxpayer to produce the accountant's documents involved in these cases" did not implicate incriminating testimony within the Fifth Amendment's protection.

Fisher was the first, and only, Supreme Court decision to find that the testimony implicit in an act of production was a foregone conclusion. In contrast, the government failed to make that showing in the other two relevant decisions: *United States v. Doe*, 465 U.S. 605 (1984) (*Doe I*) and *United States v. Hubbell*, 530 U.S. 27 (2000).

In *Doe I*, the Government served five subpoenas commanding a business owner to produce certain documents. He refused, arguing that complying with the subpoenas would violate his right against self-incrimination. The District Court agreed, finding that compliance would compel the business owner to admit that the records exist, that they are in his possession, and that they are authentic.

The *Doe I* Court affirmed the District Court's finding that the act of producing documents would involve testimonial self-incrimination. The Court then explained that the Government was not foreclosed from producing evidence that possession, existence, and authentication were a 'foregone conclusion,' but that it had failed to make such a showing.

Similarly, the Court in *Hubbell* found that the foregone conclusion exception did not apply. There, the Government served a subpoena requesting a vast array of documents. In response, Hubbell produced 13,120 pages; and he was later indicted based on information gleaned from their contents. In finding that Hubbell's compliance with the subpoena violated his right against self-incrimination, the Court rejected two of the Government's arguments.

Hubbell first refused to equate the physical act of handing over the documents with the testimony implicit in the act. The Court agreed that the testimonial aspect of responding to a documentary summons does nothing more than establish the existence, authenticity, and custody of items that are produced." But it rebuffed the Government's "anemic view" of the act of production as a "simple physical act." The Court explained that a physical act, nontestimonial in character, cannot be entirely divorced from its 'implicit' testimonial aspect.

Hubbell also rejected the Government's argument that, under *Fisher*, the existence and possession of such records by any businessman is a 'foregone conclusion.' The Court referred to *Fisher*'s unique context and explained, "Whatever the scope of this 'foregone conclusion' rationale, the facts of this case plainly fall outside of it." Unlike in *Fisher*, the *Hubbell* Court reasoned that, because the Government failed to show "it had any prior knowledge of either the existence or the whereabouts of the documents ultimately produced," the foregone conclusion exception did not apply.

Fisher, *Doe I*, and *Hubbell* establish that the act of producing documents implicitly communicates that the documents can be physically produced, exist, are in the suspect's possession, and are authentic. And this trilogy of Supreme Court precedent further confirms that the foregone conclusion exception must consider these broad communicative aspects.

In this way, the act of production doctrine links the physical act to the documents ultimately produced. *See* Laurent Sacharoff, *What Am I Really Saying When I Open My Smartphone? A Response to Orin S. Kerr*, 97 Tex. L. Rev. Online 63, 68 (2019). And the foregone conclusion exception relies on this link by asking whether the government can show it already knows the documents exist, are in the suspect's possession, and are authentic. *Id.* True, the documents' contents are not protected by the Fifth Amendment because the government did not compel their creation. But the specific documents ultimately produced implicitly communicate factual assertions solely through their production.

When extending these observations to the act of producing an unlocked smartphone, we draw two analogies. First, entering the password to unlock the device is analogous to the physical act of handing over documents. *Sacharoff*, *supra*, at 68. And second, the files on the smartphone are analogous to the documents ultimately produced. *Id.*

Thus, a suspect surrendering an unlocked smartphone implicitly communicates, at a minimum, three things: (1) the suspect knows the password; (2) the files on the device exist; and (3) the suspect possessed those files. And, unless the State can show it already knows this information, the communicative aspects of the production fall within the Fifth Amendment's protection. Otherwise, the suspect's compelled act will communicate to the State information it did not previously know—precisely what the privilege against self-incrimination is designed to prevent.

This leads us to the following inquiry: has the State shown that (1) Seo knows the password for her iPhone; (2) the files on the device exist; and (3) she possessed those files?

II.   *The foregone conclusion exception does not apply.*

As discussed above, compelling Seo to unlock her iPhone would implicitly communicate certain facts to the State. And for those communicative aspects to be rendered nontestimonial, the State must establish that it already knows those facts.

Even if we assume the State has shown that Seo knows the password to her smartphone, the State has failed to demonstrate that any particular files on the device exist or that she possessed those files. Detective Inglis simply confirmed that he would be fishing for "incriminating evidence" from the device. He believed Seo—to carry out the alleged crimes—was using an application or internet program to disguise her phone number. Yet, the detective's own testimony confirms that he didn't know which applications or files he was searching for: "There are numerous, and there's probably some that I'm not even aware of, numerous entities out there like Google Voice and Pinger and Text Now and Text Me, and I don't know, I don't have an all-encompassing list of them, however if I had the phone I could see which ones she had accessed through Google."

In sum, law enforcement sought to compel Seo to unlock her iPhone so that it could then scour the device for incriminating information. And Seo's act of producing her unlocked smartphone would provide the State with information that it does not already know. But, as we've explained above, the Fifth Amendment's privilege against compulsory self-incrimination prohibits such a result.

Conclusion

Forcing Seo to unlock her iPhone for law enforcement would violate her Fifth Amendment right against self-incrimination. We thus reverse the trial court's order finding Seo in contempt and instruct the court to dismiss the citation.

NOTES AND QUESTIONS

1.   *The Massachusetts Supreme Judicial Court takes a different view.* Contrast *Seo* with the Massachusetts Supreme Judicial Court's opinion in Commonwealth v. Jones, 117 N.E.3d 702 (Mass. 2019). In rejecting a claim of Fifth Amendment privilege in a case with essentially identical facts to *Seo*, *Jones* offered a very different interpretation of the "foregone conclusion" doctrine:

> For the foregone conclusion exception to apply, the Commonwealth must establish that it already knows the testimony that is implicit in the act of the required production. In the context of compelled decryption, the only fact conveyed by compelling a defendant to enter the password to an encrypted electronic device is that the defendant knows the password, and can therefore access the device. The Commonwealth must therefore establish that a defendant knows the password to decrypt an electronic device before his or her knowledge of the password can be deemed a foregone conclusion under the Fifth Amendment.

> We clarify that the evidence at issue in the compelled decryption here is the password itself, not the contents of the phone. The only testimony that would be conveyed by compelling the defendant to enter the password is the fact that the defendant knows the password, and therefore has the ability to access the phone. The entry would convey no information about the contents of the phone.

The analysis would be different had the Commonwealth sought to compel the defendant to produce specific files located in the contents of the phone. If that had been the case, the production of the files would implicitly convey far more information than just the fact that the defendant knows the password. The defendant's production of specific files would implicitly testify to the existence of the files, his control over them, and their authenticity. Accordingly, the Commonwealth would be required to prove its prior knowledge of those facts.

Id. at 548, 538 n.10. *See also* State v. Pittman, 300 Or. App. 147 (2019) (adopting the same reasoning).

Note the key difference between the reasoning of *Jones* and *Seo*. According to *Seo,* the relevant question was whether the act of decryption "would provide the State with information that it does not already know." This is a causal view of the foregone conclusion doctrine, in that it asks if the government will learn something new through the compelled act. According to *Jones*, however, the relevant question is whether the compelled act implicitly testifies as to a fact that the government already knows or is trying to find out. This is a testimonial view of the foregone conclusion doctrine, as it asks only whether the government knows the facts testified to by the compelled act. Which view is more persuasive?

2. *The implicit testimony made by unlocking a device. Jones* and *Seo* disagree about what a person implicitly says when they unlock a device. According to *Jones*, the only implicit statement is that the person knows the password needed to unlock the device. According to *Seo*, the implicit testimony is that the person knows the password, that particular files on the device exist, and that the person possessed those files.

Which view rings more true? Imagine your friend calls you on the phone one day and tells you that his cell phone passcode is 1-2-3-4-5-6. The next day, your friend is arrested, but he refuses to tell the police his cell phone passcode. The government obtains a court order demanding that you enter the passcode into your friend's phone so they can search it for evidence with a search warrant. If you comply with the order, to what exactly are you testifying, if anything? Are you implicitly admitting that you know the passcode? Are you implicitly admitting that you know what evidence is on your friend's phone? Are you implicitly admitting that you possess the contents of your friend's phone?

3. *The Fifth Amendment versus the Fourth Amendment.* Do your instincts about the correct Fifth Amendment rule for permitted unlocking depend on your assumptions about what Fourth Amendment rules apply to computer warrant searches after the device is unlocked? Imagine two futures. In the first future, the Supreme Court has announced strict Fourth Amendment rules limiting the scope of computer searches pursuant to a warrant. In the second future, the Supreme Court has announced that the Fourth Amendment imposes no limits whatsoever on the scope of computer

searches as long as a warrant is obtained. Should the same Fifth Amendment rule apply in both situations?

4.   *What are the Fifth Amendment implications of disclosing a password instead of entering it? (Yet more disagreement among state supreme courts.)* Are the Fifth Amendment issues the same or different if the defendant is ordered to tell the government his password versus if he is required to enter in the password? In the former case, the government learns the password and can try entering it into additional computers to see if it works there. In the latter case, the government only sees that the defendant successfully unlocked the file or device. Should that make a difference?

State supreme courts have divided on this question. On one hand, in Commonwealth v. Davis, 220 A.3d 534, 537 (Pa. 2019), the Supreme Court of Pennsylvania ruled that a defendant cannot be compelled to disclose his password to unlock a phone. First, the court ruled that disclosing a password is testimonial:

> The revealing of a computer password is a verbal communication, not merely a physical act that would be nontestimonial in nature. There is no physical manifestation of a password, unlike a handwriting sample, blood draw, or a voice exemplar. As a passcode is necessarily memorized, one cannot reveal a passcode without revealing the contents of one's mind.

Second, the court ruled that the foregone conclusion doctrine does not apply because that doctrine is limited to compelling acts and does not apply to compelling direct testimony:

> We appreciate the significant and ever-increasing difficulties faced by law enforcement in light of rapidly changing technology, including encryption, to obtain evidence. However, unlike the documentary requests under the foregone conclusion rationale, or demands for physical evidence such as blood, or handwriting or voice exemplars, information in one's mind to "unlock the safe" to potentially incriminating information does not easily fall within this exception. Indeed, we conclude the compulsion of a password to a computer cannot fit within this exception.

On the other hand, consider the contrary decision of the Supreme Court of New Jersey in State v. Andrews, 234 A.3d 1254 (N.J. 2020). Although *Andrews* agreed with *Davis* that disclosing a passcode is testimonial, *Andrews* then ruled that the foregone conclusion doctrine applies to disclosing a passcode. Further, the test is satisfied, and the Fifth Amendment challenge defeated, *Andrews* held, when the government shows the existence, possession, and authentication of the passcode was already known:

> We view the compelled act of production in this case to be that of producing the passcodes. Although that act of production is testimonial, we note that passcodes are a series of characters without independent evidentiary significance and are therefore of "minimal

testimonial value"—their value is limited to communicating the knowledge of the passcodes. Thus, although the act of producing the passcodes is presumptively protected by the Fifth Amendment, its testimonial value and constitutional protection may be overcome if the passcodes' existence, possession, and authentication are foregone conclusions.

Where the government had a locked phone and established that the defendant knew the passcode, "the passcodes' self-authenticating nature" established a foregone conclusion and the Fifth Amendment did not pose a barrier.

Which of these approaches is more persuasive? If the United States Supreme Court agrees to review this issue, how should it rule?

5.	*Compelling biometric access.* Many people set up biometric access to unlock their encrypted devices. For example, an iPhone user might set up Touch ID, which typically uses a thumbprint to unlock the phone, or Face ID, which uses the contours of a person's face. If the government forces a user to unlock a phone by pressing the user's thumb to the biometric reader or looking into its camera, does that raise any Fifth Amendment issues?

Most courts have concluded that the Fifth Amendment is not implicated by compelled biometrics because using a body part is not "testimonial." Consider State v. Diamond, 905 N.W.2d 870 (Minn. 2018):

> Producing a fingerprint to unlock a phone, unlike the act of producing documents, is a display of the physical characteristics of the *body*, not of the mind, to the police. Because we conclude that producing a fingerprint is more like exhibiting the body than producing documents, we hold that providing a fingerprint to unlock a cellphone is *not* a testimonial communication under the Fifth Amendment.

Id. at 875–76.

A few judges have taken a different view, however. Consider the argument of Magistrate Judge Westmore that compelling biometric access is testimonial under the Fifth Amendment:

> The Court finds that utilizing a biometric feature to unlock an electronic device is not akin to submitting to fingerprinting or a DNA swab, because it differs in two fundamental ways. First, the Government concedes that a finger, thumb, or other biometric feature may be used to unlock a device in lieu of a passcode. In this context, biometric features serve the same purpose of a passcode, which is to secure the owner's content, pragmatically rendering them functionally equivalent.
>
> As the Government acknowledges, there are times when the device will not accept the biometric feature and require the user to type in the passcode to unlock the device. For example, a passcode is generally required when a device has been restarted, inactive, or has not been unlocked for a certain period of time. This is, no doubt, a

security feature to ensure that someone without the passcode cannot readily access the contents of the phone. Indeed, the Government expresses some urgency with the need to compel the use of the biometric features to bypass the need to enter a passcode.

This urgency appears to be rooted in the Government's inability to compel the production of the passcode under the current jurisprudence. It follows, however, that if a person cannot be compelled to provide a passcode because it is a testimonial communication, a person cannot be compelled to provide one's finger, thumb, iris, face, or other biometric feature to unlock that same device.

Second, requiring someone to affix their finger or thumb to a digital device is fundamentally different than requiring a suspect to submit to fingerprinting. A finger or thumb scan used to unlock a device indicates that the device belongs to a particular individual. In other words, the act concedes that the phone was in the possession and control of the suspect, and authenticates ownership or access to the phone and all of its digital contents. Thus, the act of unlocking a phone with a finger or thumb scan far exceeds the "physical evidence" created when a suspect submits to fingerprinting to merely compare his fingerprints to existing physical evidence (another fingerprint) found at a crime scene, because there is no comparison or witness corroboration required to confirm a positive match.

Instead, a successful finger or thumb scan confirms ownership or control of the device, and, unlike fingerprints, the authentication of its contents cannot be reasonably refuted. In a similar situation, the court in *In re Application for a Search Warrant* observed that "with a touch of a finger, a suspect is testifying that he or she has accessed the phone before, at a minimum, to set up the fingerprint password capabilities, and that he or she currently has some level of control over or relatively significant connection to the phone and its contents." 236 F. Supp.3d 1066, 1073 (N.D. Ill. 2017).

It is also noteworthy that many smartphone applications providing access to personal, private information—including medical records and financial accounts—now allow users to utilize biometric features in lieu of passcodes to access those records. As Judge Weisman astutely observed, using a fingerprint to place someone at a particular location is a starkly different scenario than using a finger scan to access a database of someone's most private information. Thus, the undersigned finds that a biometric feature is analogous to the nonverbal, physiological responses elicited during a polygraph test, which are used to determine guilt or innocence, and are considered testimonial.

While the Court sympathizes with the Government's interest in accessing the contents of any electronic devices it might lawfully seize, there are other ways that the Government might access the content that do not trample on the Fifth Amendment. In the instant matter, the Government may obtain any Facebook Messenger communications from Facebook under the Stored Communications Act or warrant based on probable cause. While it may be more expedient to circumvent Facebook, and attempt to gain access by infringing on the Fifth Amendment's privilege against self-incrimination, it is an abuse of power and is unconstitutional.

In the Matter of the Search of a Residence in Oakland, Cal., 354 F. Supp. 3d 1010, 1015–16 (N.D. Cal. 2019).

Are you persuaded by Magistrate Judge Westmore's analysis? Consider her argument that biometric access must be testimonial because it is "functionally equivalent" to compelling the disclosure of the passcode. Does this functional equivalence test make sense? Imagine a person sets up his phone so that there are two ways of unlocking it. The first way requires making a testimonial statement, and the second way does not. Why should the functional equivalence of these two methods from the standpoint of access to evidence mean that the Fifth Amendment must apply in the same way to both methods? And if the same standard must apply, does which standard applies depend which issue is decided first? Most courts have held that compelling biometric access is not testimonial. If courts apply a functional equivalence test, does this mean that forcing a suspect to state his passcode must now be deemed non-testimonial because it is the functional equivalent of the non-testimonial act of compelling biometric access?

6.   *Can warrants order everyone at the place to be searched to provide biometric access to seized phones?* The ubiquity of biometric access to cell phones has led some investigators to apply for search warrants that mandate assistance with biometric access for everyone found at the place to be searched. When the search warrant is executed, anyone present can be ordered to place a thumbprint on any seized phone. Is such a warrant provision legally proper? *Compare* In re Application for a Search Warrant, 236 F. Supp.3d 1066 (N.D. Ill. 2017) (rejecting a proposed warrant provision that would compel any individual present at the subject premises at the time of the search to provide his fingerprints and/or thumbprints "onto the Touch ID sensor of any Apple iPhone, iPad, or other Apple brand device in order to gain access to the contents of any such device") *with* In re Application for a Search Warrant, No. 17 M 85 at *10–11 (N.D. Ill. Sept. 18, 2017) (reviewing the application and concluding that mandatory thumbprint provisions do not implicate the Fifth Amendment).

7.   *What happens when a suspect is ordered to enter in a computer password but says he will not or cannot comply?* A witness who is ordered to enter in or disclose a password may claim to have forgotten it. What happens then? The Second Circuit has summarized the legal consequences in federal cases as follows:

Testimonial obduracy by a witness who has been ordered by the court to answer questions may take any of a number of forms. The witness may refuse categorically to answer. Or he may respond in a way that avoids providing information, as, for example, by denying memory of the events under inquiry, denying acquaintance with targets of the inquiry, or denying knowledge of facts sought to be elicited. Or he may purport to state informative facts in response to the questions while in fact testifying falsely.

Any of these three forms of obduracy may be met with the imposition of one or more judicial or governmental sanctions. For example, when the witness has refused to answer questions, he may be adjudged in civil contempt and ordered to answer, or he may be adjudged in criminal contempt and punished for his past failure to answer. In some cases both coercive and punitive sanctions have been imposed.

If the witness has responded falsely to the questions propounded, he may be subject to prosecution for a criminal offense in violation of, *e.g.,* 18 U.S.C. § 1621 (perjury), or 18 U.S.C. § 1623 (false declarations before grand jury or court). If the witness's false testimony has obstructed the court in the performance of its duty, the witness may be met with sanctions for civil contempt or criminal contempt.

The middle category of testimonial obduracy, *i.e.,* the witness's equivocal responses or disclaimers of knowledge or memory, has also been dealt with as contemptuous conduct, warranting sanctions that were coercive, punitive, or both. It has long been the practice of courts viewing such testimony as false and intentionally evasive, and as a sham or subterfuge that purposely avoids giving responsive answers, to ignore the form of the response and treat the witness as having refused to answer.

In re Weiss, 703 F.2d 653, 662–663 (2d Cir. 1983).

If a person refuses to comply because he has asserted a valid legal privilege such as the Fifth Amendment, then the court should quash the order to compel the testimony. If the person genuinely does not know the password or states truthfully that he has forgotten it, then he should not be punished. Legally speaking, he has "just cause" to not comply with the order. 28 U.S.C. § 1826(a) (civil contempt standard). *See also* 18 U.S.C. § 401 (criminal contempt standard). Whether a person is being truthful about forgetting a password is a question of fact that normally must be settled by a hearing before the trial judge.

8.   *The penalties for criminal contempt versus civil contempt.* The penalties for contempt vary by jurisdiction. In the federal system, however, the maximum period of detention that can be imposed for refusal to unlock a computer or provide a password varies considerably depending on what kind of contempt is at issue.

Generally speaking, there are two kinds of contempt sanctions. Criminal contempt is a criminal prosecution punishing the subject for failure to comply with a court order when the subject has no valid legal reason not to comply.

The purpose of the sanction is to punish the person for a past failure to comply with the order. In contrast, civil contempt is designed to persuade a person to comply with a pending order. A subject of the order is held in jail until they agree to comply. Upon complying with the order, they are freed.

In United States v. Apple MacPro Computer, 949 F.3d 102 (3d Cir. 2020), the Third Circuit ruled that the maximum period of incarceration for a person held in federal civil contempt for failure to unlock a computer is eighteen months. According to the court, such detention was governed by the federal recalcitrant witness statute, 28 U.S.C. § 1826. That provision states that a witness can be incarcerated for refusal to testify or provide information "at a suitable place until such time as the witness is willing to give such testimony or provide such information, . . but in no event shall such confinement exceed eighteen months." *Id.*

In contrast, the punishment for criminal contempt does not have a statutory cap. The criminal contempt statute, 18 U.S.C. § 401, states in relevant part:

> A court of the United States shall have power to punish by fine or imprisonment, or both, at its discretion, such contempt of its authority, and none other, as. . . Disobedience or resistance to its lawful writ, process, order, rule, decree, or command.

This is certainly unusual, as it means that criminal contempt is neither a felony nor a misdemeanor but rather a *sui generis* crime. *See* United States v. Cohn, 586 F.3d 844, 848–49 (11th Cir. 2009).

Should Congress impose a statutory cap on criminal contempt sanctions for refusal to unlock a computer? If so, what should that cap be?

b)   The All Writs Act

The government has several ways to bypass encryption. When alternative techniques fail, however, the government may seek assistance from the manufacturer of the encrypted device. The manufacturer may have a way to facilitate access to the decrypted contents of the device. This prompts the following question: What power does the government have to force a private company, such as a manufacturer of computer equipment, to assist the government in its efforts to bypass encryption?

This question issue became a matter of public debate following a terrorist shooting in San Bernardino, California, in 2015. The government sought assistance from Apple Computer, the manufacturer of the iPhone smart phone, to help decrypt a phone that was used by shooter Syed Rizwan Farook. The government had both the consent of the phone's owner and a probable cause warrant, allowing it to search the phone under the Fourth Amendment. Farook was killed in the attack, so there could be no effort to compel him to decrypt the phone that might otherwise raise Fifth Amendment issues. But the question remained whether the government could obtain Apple's assistance in enabling access to the decrypted contents of the phone.

The relevant law is the All Writs Act, 28 U.S.C. § 1651(a), a statute that gives judge the power to impose legal duties on third parties in aid of other lawful judicial orders. The Act states:

> The Supreme Court and all courts established by Act of Congress may issue all writs necessary or appropriate in aid of their respective jurisdictions and agreeable to the usages and principles of law.

Whether the All Writs Act permitted the assistance order against Apple was never resolved, as the government ended up paying a private party to decrypt the phone. With the phone successfully decrypted, the government did not need Apple's assistance and withdrew the order. But the legal question is likely to come up in another case: What power does a federal judge have to issue an assistance order under the All Writs Act to help the government bypass encryption?

UNITED STATES V. NEW YORK TELEPHONE COMPANY
Supreme Court of the United States, 1977.
429 U.S. 1072.

MR. JUSTICE WHITE delivered the opinion of the Court.

This case presents the question of whether a United States District Court may properly direct a telephone company to provide federal law enforcement officials the facilities and technical assistance necessary for the implementation of its order authorizing the use of pen registers[1] to investigate offenses which there was probable cause to believe were being committed by means of the telephone.

I

On March 19, 1976, the United States District Court for the Southern District of New York issued an order authorizing agents of the Federal Bureau of Investigation to install and use pen registers with respect to two telephones and directing the New York Telephone Co. to furnish the FBI "all information, facilities and technical assistance" necessary to employ the pen registers unobtrusively. The FBI was ordered to compensate the Company at prevailing rates for any assistance which it furnished. The order was issued on the basis of an affidavit submitted by an FBI agent which stated that certain individuals were conducting an illegal gambling enterprise at 220 East 14th Street in New York City and that, on the basis of facts set forth therein, there was probable cause to believe that two

---

[1] A pen register is a mechanical device that records the numbers dialed on a telephone by monitoring the electrical impulses caused when the dial on the telephone is released. It does not overhear oral communications and does not indicate whether calls are actually completed.

telephones bearing different numbers were being used at that address in furtherance of the illegal activity.

The District Court found that there was probable cause to conclude that an illegal gambling enterprise using the facilities of interstate commerce was being conducted at the East 14th Street address in violation of 18 U.S.C. §§ 371 and 1952, and that the two telephones had been, were currently being, and would continue to be used in connection with those offenses. Its order authorized the FBI to operate the pen registers with respect to the two telephones until knowledge of the numbers dialed led to the identity of the associates and confederates of those believed to be conducting the illegal operation or for 20 days, "whichever is earlier."

The Company declined to comply fully with the court order. It did inform the FBI of the location of the relevant "appearances," that is, the places where specific telephone lines emerge from the sealed telephone cable. In addition, the Company agreed to identify the relevant "pairs," or the specific pairs of wires that constituted the circuits of the two telephone lines. This information is required to install a pen register.

The Company, however, refused to lease lines to the FBI which were needed to install the pen registers in an unobtrusive fashion. Such lines were required by the FBI in order to install the pen registers in inconspicuous locations away from the building containing the telephones. A "leased line" is an unused telephone line which makes an "appearance" in the same terminal box as the telephone line in connection with which it is desired to install a pen register. If the leased line is connected to the subject telephone line, the pen register can then be installed on the leased line at a remote location and be monitored from that point.

The Company, instead of providing the leased lines, which it conceded that the court's order required it to do, advised the FBI to string cables from the "subject apartment" to another location where pen registers could be installed. The FBI determined after canvassing the neighborhood of the apartment for four days that there was no location where it could string its own wires and attach the pen registers without alerting the suspects, in which event, of course, the gambling operation would cease to function.

On March 30, 1976, the Company moved in the District Court to vacate that portion of the pen register order directing it to furnish facilities and technical assistance to the FBI. The District Court concluded that it had jurisdiction to authorize the installation of the pen registers upon a showing of probable cause and that both the All Writs Act and its inherent powers provided authority for the order directing the Company to assist in the installation of the pen registers.

On April 9, 1976, after the District Court and the Court of Appeals denied the Company's motion to stay the pen register order pending appeal, the Company provided the leased lines.

The Court of Appeals affirmed in part and reversed in part, with one judge dissenting on the ground that the order below should have been affirmed in its entirety. The majority held that the District Court abused its discretion in ordering the Company to assist in the installation and operation of the pen registers. It assumed, *arguendo,* that "a district court has inherent discretionary authority or discretionary power under the All Writs Act to compel technical assistance by the Telephone Company," but concluded that "in the absence of specific and properly limited Congressional action, it was an abuse of discretion for the District Court to order the Telephone Company to furnish technical assistance."

The majority expressed concern that "such an order could establish a most undesirable, if not dangerous and unwise, precedent for the authority of federal courts to impress unwilling aid on private third parties" and that "there is no assurance that the court will always be able to protect [third parties] from excessive or overzealous Government activity or compulsion."

IV.

The Court of Appeals held that even though the District Court had ample authority to issue the pen register warrant and even assuming the applicability of the All Writs Act, the order compelling the Company to provide technical assistance constituted an abuse of discretion. Since the Court of Appeals conceded that a compelling case existed for requiring the assistance of the Company and did not point to any fact particular to this case which would warrant a finding of abuse of discretion, we interpret its holding as generally barring district courts from ordering any party to assist in the installation or operation of a pen register. It was apparently concerned that sustaining the District Court's order would authorize courts to compel third parties to render assistance without limitation regardless of the burden involved and pose a severe threat to the autonomy of third parties who for whatever reason prefer not to render such assistance. Consequently the Court of Appeals concluded that courts should not embark upon such a course without specific legislative authorization.

We agree that the power of federal courts to impose duties upon third parties is not without limits; unreasonable burdens may not be imposed. We conclude, however, that the order issued here against respondent was clearly authorized by the All Writs Act and was consistent with the intent of Congress.

The All Writs Act provides:

> The Supreme Court and all courts established by Act of Congress may issue all writs necessary or appropriate in aid of their respective jurisdictions and agreeable to the usages and principles of law.

28 U.S.C. § 1651(a).

The assistance of the Company was required here to implement a pen register order which we have held the District Court was empowered to issue by Rule 41. This Court has repeatedly recognized the power of a federal court to issue such commands under the All Writs Act as may be necessary or appropriate to effectuate and prevent the frustration of orders it has previously issued in its exercise of jurisdiction otherwise obtained: This statute has served since its inclusion, in substance, in the original Judiciary Act as a legislatively approved source of procedural instruments designed to achieve the rational ends of law. Indeed, unless appropriately confined by Congress, a federal court may avail itself of all auxiliary writs as aids in the performance of its duties, when the use of such historic aids is calculated in its sound judgment to achieve the ends of justice entrusted to it.

The Court has consistently applied the Act flexibly in conformity with these principles. Although § 262 of the Judicial Code, the predecessor to § 1651, did not expressly authorize courts, as does § 1651, to issue writs "appropriate" to the proper exercise of their jurisdiction but only "necessary" writs, . . . these supplemental powers are not limited to those situations where it is "necessary" to issue the writ or order in the sense that the court could not otherwise physically discharge its appellate duties.

The power conferred by the Act extends, under appropriate circumstances, to persons who, though not parties to the original action or engaged in wrongdoing, are in a position to frustrate the implementation of a court order or the proper administration of justice, and encompasses even those who have not taken any affirmative action to hinder justice.

Turning to the facts of this case, we do not think that the Company was a third party so far removed from the underlying controversy that its assistance could not be permissibly compelled. A United States District Court found that there was probable cause to believe that the Company's facilities were being employed to facilitate a criminal enterprise on a continuing basis. For the Company, with this knowledge, to refuse to supply the meager assistance required by the FBI in its efforts to put an end to this venture threatened obstruction of an investigation which would determine whether the Company's facilities were being lawfully used.

Moreover, it can hardly be contended that the Company, a highly regulated public utility with a duty to serve the public, had a substantial interest in not providing assistance. Certainly the use of pen registers is by no means offensive to it. The Company concedes that it regularly employs such devices without court order for the purposes of checking billing operations, detecting fraud, and preventing violations of law. It also agreed to supply the FBI with all the information required to install its own pen registers. Nor was the District Court's order in any way burdensome. The order provided that the Company be fully reimbursed at prevailing rates, and compliance with it required minimal effort on the part of the Company and no disruption to its operations.

Finally, we note, as the Court of Appeals recognized, that without the Company's assistance there is no conceivable way in which the surveillance authorized by the District Court could have been successfully accomplished. The FBI, after an exhaustive search, was unable to find a location where it could install its own pen registers without tipping off the targets of the investigation. The provision of a leased line by the Company was essential to the fulfillment of the purpose—to learn the identities of those connected with the gambling operation—for which the pen register order had been issued.

The order compelling the Company to provide assistance was not only consistent with the Act but also with more recent congressional actions. Congress clearly intended to permit the use of pen registers by federal law enforcement officials. Without the assistance of the Company in circumstances such as those presented here, however, these devices simply cannot be effectively employed. Moreover, Congress provided in a 1970 amendment to Title III that "an order authorizing the interception of a wire or oral communication shall, upon request of the applicant, direct that a communication common carrier shall furnish the applicant forthwith all information, facilities, and technical assistance necessary to accomplish the interception unobtrusively." 18 U.S.C. § 2518(4).

In light of this direct command to federal courts to compel, upon request, any assistance necessary to accomplish an electronic interception, it would be remarkable if Congress thought it beyond the power of the federal courts to exercise, where required, a discretionary authority to order telephone companies to assist in the installation and operation of pen registers, which accomplish a far lesser invasion of privacy. We are convinced that to prohibit the order challenged here would frustrate the clear indication by Congress that the pen register is a permissible law enforcement tool by enabling a public utility to thwart a judicial determination that its use is required to apprehend and prosecute successfully those employing the utility's facilities to conduct a criminal venture. The contrary judgment of the Court of Appeals is accordingly reversed.

NOTES AND QUESTIONS

1.   How should *New York Telephone* apply to efforts to force Apple to assist the government in efforts to unlock an iPhone? In its briefing filed in the San Bernardino case, Apple estimated that it would take a group of 6 to 10 employees about 2 to 4 weeks to create new software to assist the government. Is this an "unreasonable burden" on Apple, which has over 100,000 employees? Alternatively, does it matter that Apple's product is marketed in part for its security, so that ordering Apple's assistance was "offensive" to Apple? How

much does it matter that Apple is a private company and not a regulated public utility?

2.   Under *New York Telephone*, the burden placed on the third party that may be forced to comply with an order is one of the most significant questions in assessing its legality under the All Writs Act. But what is the standard for measuring the burden? A company that does not want to comply with judicial orders commanding assistance, and that knows such orders may be coming, can take steps now to make any future assistance as costly as possible. Should the company's steps taken to make future assistance costly be later factored into the assessment of burden? Or should a company be allowed to thwart assistance orders by choosing to make assistance difficult?

3.   What responsibility should individuals or companies have to help the government carry out lawful orders? Consider the following footnote in *New York Telephone*:

> We are unable to agree with the Company's assertion that "it is extraordinary to expect citizens to directly involve themselves in the law enforcement process." The conviction that private citizens have a duty to provide assistance to law enforcement officials when it is required is by no means foreign to our traditions, as the Company apparently believes. See Babington v. Yellow Taxi Corp., 250 N.Y. 14, 17, 164 N.E. 726, 727 (1928) (Cardozo, C. J.) ("Still, as in the days of Edward I, the citizenry may be called upon to enforce the justice of the state, not faintly and with lagging steps, but honestly and bravely and with whatever implements and facilities are convenient and at hand"). See also In re Quarles and Butler, 158 U.S. 532, 535 (1895) ("It is the duty of every citizen, to assist in prosecuting, and in securing the punishment of, any breach of the peace of the United States").

New York Telephone, 434 U.S. at 175 n.24. Does this sense of "citizen's duty" continue today? Should it?

CHAPTER 6

STATUTORY PRIVACY PROTECTIONS

■ ■ ■

In the stand-alone computer environment, Fourth Amendment protections are the primary privacy protections that regulate government access to data. In a network environment, Fourth Amendment protections are supplemented by statutory privacy laws. This chapter covers the four federal statutory privacy laws that regulate access to computer network communications in criminal investigations. The four laws are the Wiretap Act, 18 U.S.C. §§ 2510–22; the Pen Register statute, 18 U.S.C. §§ 3121–27; the Stored Communications Act, 18 U.S.C. §§ 2701–11; and the Cybersecurity Act of 2015, 6 U.S.C. § 1501 *et seq.*

Brief History of Statutory Privacy Laws

To understand the statutory privacy laws that regulate digital evidence collection, a page of history is worth a volume of logic. That history begins with the telephone network in the period following the Supreme Court's decision in Olmstead v. United States, 277 U.S. 438 (1928). *Olmstead* held that the Fourth Amendment did not regulate telephone wiretapping. The opinion for the Court expressly invited Congress to enact statutory prohibitions on wiretapping practices: "Congress may, of course, protect the secrecy of telephone messages by making them, when intercepted, inadmissible in evidence in federal criminal trials, by direct legislation." *Id.* at 465–66.

Congress responded in 1934 with the New Deal legislation known as the Communications Act. A provision of the Communications Act codified at 47 U.S.C. § 605 became the first federal wiretapping statute (with the exception of a temporary statute passed during World War I and repealed shortly after the war). In its original form, § 605 stated that "no person not being authorized by the sender shall intercept any communication and divulge or publish the existence, contents, substance, purport, effect, or meaning of such intercepted communication to any person." In Nardone v. United States, 302 U.S. 379, 384 (1937), the Supreme Court held that the remedy for violating this statute was suppression of any evidence unlawfully obtained.

It soon became clear that the Communications Act of 1934 was poorly suited to regulate telephone wiretapping. First, the statute did not provide an exception when the government had obtained a warrant. Second, the statute prohibited only the combination of "intercepting" and "divulging or publishing," which the Justice Department interpreted as permitting wiretapping so long as the information was never used in court. The combination made the statute both under-inclusive and over-inclusive: the FBI could wiretap without restriction so long as it didn't use the evidence in court, but the government could not obtain a warrant permitting admission of wiretapping evidence in court even in the most compelling case. Finally, the law only regulated the admissibility of wiretapping evidence in federal court. It had no application when state investigators sought to introduce wiretapping evidence in state court. *See* Schwartz v. Texas, 344 U.S. 199 (1952).

Congress revisited the law regulating telephone wiretapping in the late 1960s. Congress's goal was to replace the unsatisfactory Communications Act and regulate two distinct privacy-invading practices: bugging, the use of secret recording devices in a room or physical space; and wiretapping, the interception of private telephone calls. The statutory design was heavily influenced by the Supreme Court's pair of decisions in 1967 that explained the constitutional limitations on such practices. The first case, Berger v. New York, 388 U.S. 41 (1967), articulated constitutional requirements for wiretapping. The second case, Katz v. United States, 389 U.S. 347 (1967), articulated constitutional limits on bugging.

The wiretapping law that Congress passed is generally known either as the Wiretap Act or as "Title III," so-called because the statute was passed as the third part (or "Title") of the Omnibus Crime Control and Safe Streets Act of 1968. The statute is codified at 18 U.S.C. §§ 2510–22. It regulates both government actors and private parties, and it imposes strict limitations on the use of devices to intercept "oral communications" (that is, use of a bugging device to listen in on private conversations) or "wire communications" (that is, use of a wiretapping device to tap a telephone and listen in on private telephone conversations). It also allows the government to obtain court orders permitting interception when investigators have probable cause and can satisfy a number of additional requirements. The heightened requirements of Title III beyond the usual search warrant requirement have led some to describe Title III intercept orders as "super warrants."

The Wiretap Act effectively and comprehensively regulated government access to the contents of traditional telephone calls. In the 1980s, however, it became clear that additional privacy laws were necessary. This was true for two reasons. First, the Supreme Court's decision in Smith v. Maryland, 442 U.S. 735 (1979), indicated that the Fourth Amendment did not provide robust privacy protection in the network context. *Smith* made clear that the Fourth Amendment did not regulate the use of pen registers, and the opinion left uncertain how or even whether the Fourth Amendment would apply to computer networks.

Second, the Wiretap Act was not equipped to protect computer network communications. The Wiretap Act applied only to "oral communications" and "wire communications," both of which were limited to communications containing the human voice. Further, the Wiretap Act applied only to the acquisition of communications "in transit," such as real-time wiretapping, and did not apply to accessing stored communications. This made sense for the traditional telephone network, as calls were never stored (or at least only rarely, as voicemail was in its infancy at the time). In contrast, computer communications were stored routinely, either in temporary storage pending transmission or after a communication had been delivered. *See* Office of Tech. Assessment, Federal Government Information Technology: Electronic Surveillance and Civil Liberties (1985).

In 1986, Congress passed the Electronic Communications Privacy Act, Pub. L. No. 99–508 (1986) ("ECPA"), to correct the gaps in existing legislation and respond to the new computer network technologies. ECPA included three basic parts. The first part expanded the Wiretap Act to include a new category of protected communications, "electronic communications," which broadly includes computer communications. The second part created a new statute to regulate access to stored electronic communications known as the Stored Communications Act, codified at 18 U.S.C. §§ 2701–11. The third part created a new statute, generally known as the Pen Register Statute, 18 U.S.C. §§ 3121–27, that responds to *Smith v. Maryland* and regulates the use of pen registers.

In 1986, when ECPA was passed, Congress did not know how courts might apply the Fourth Amendment to computers. As a result, the statutory privacy laws put in place by ECPA attempted to create what amounts to a statutory version of the Fourth Amendment for computer networks. In recent years, courts have begun to fill in some previously unanswered questions about how the Fourth Amendment might apply. It is therefore important to see the protections offered by the Fourth Amendment and ECPA together: The Fourth Amendment protections form a base that provides protections in some cases and not others, and the statutory protections provide additional protections beyond the constitutional baseline.

Finally, in 2015, Congress enacted the Cybersecurity Act of 2015. The Cybersecurity Act contains several surveillance rules that apply "notwithstanding any other provision of law," which means that they effectively modify the application of the Wiretap Act, the Stored Communications Act, and the Pen Register statute.

The Basic Structure of the Statutory Privacy Laws

The basic framework created by ECPA remains in place today. The framework is premised on two major distinctions: the distinction between prospective surveillance and retrospective surveillance, and the distinction between the contents of communications and non-content information.

Prospective surveillance refers to obtaining communications in the course of transmission, typically by installing a monitoring device at a particular point in the network and scanning the traffic as it passes by that point. The monitoring is prospective because the communication has not yet reached the place where the surveillance device is installed. For example, a traditional wiretapping device taps into the conversation while it is happening. Any communication sent over the line will be tapped. Similarly, an Internet wiretapping program such as a "packet sniffer" scans packets of Internet traffic at a particular place in the network where the program is directed to function.

In contrast, retrospective surveillance refers to access to stored communications that may be kept in the ordinary course of business by a third-party provider. For example, if an FBI agent issues a subpoena ordering an Internet provider to disclose basic subscriber information about a particular Internet account, that access is a type of retrospective surveillance. The Internet provider will have generated that record at some time in the past in the ordinary course of its business; the subpoena seeks the disclosure of a stored record that already has been created.

The basic distinction between the contents of communications and non-content information was introduced in the previous chapter. Contents of communications are the substance of the message communicated from sender to receiver, while non-content information refers to the information used to deliver the communications from senders to receivers and other network-generated information about the communication. In the case of a telephone call, for example, a basic difference exists between the contents of the call itself (the conversation) and mere information about the call (such as the phone numbers of the two parties and the duration of the call).

The privacy statutes reflect these two distinctions. The Wiretap Act and the Pen Register statute regulate prospective surveillance, and the Stored Communications Act regulates retrospective surveillance. Within the category of prospective surveillance, the Wiretap Act handles access to the contents of communications, and the Pen Register regulates access to non-content information. The basic framework looks like this:

	Prospective	Retrospective
Contents	Wiretap Act 18 U.S.C. §§ 2510–22	Stored Communications Act 18 U.S.C. §§ 2701–11
Non-content	Pen Register Statute 18 U.S.C. §§ 3121–27	Stored Communications Act 18 U.S.C. §§ 2701–11

Finally, the application of each of these laws can be modified by relevant provisions of the Cybersecurity Act of 2015.

Remedies and a Note About Studying the Statutory Privacy Laws

One very unusual feature of the statutory privacy laws is the remedial scheme for statutory violations. The Fourth Amendment is enforced with an exclusionary rule, but the statutory privacy laws do not include a statutory suppression remedy in the computer context. Violations of the Wiretap Act, Pen Register statute, and Stored Communications Act can lead to criminal liability, as noted on pages 262–263. Violations of the Wiretap Act and the Stored Communications Act can also lead to civil liability, including attorney's fees awards and the possibility of punitive damages. However, suppression of evidence unlawfully obtained is not an available remedy in most computer-related cases. The only statutory suppression remedy is for violations of the Wiretap Act involving the interception of human voice communications. *See* 18 U.S.C. § 2515. Because computer communications normally do not include the human voice, no statutory suppression remedy exists for their unlawful interception.

The limited statutory suppression remedy dates back to 1986, when Congress first enacted ECPA. The rationale at the time was that computer communications implicated lesser privacy concerns than telephone calls and speech involving the human voice, so that the suppression remedy imposed by the Wiretap Act for violations relating to telephone calls did not need to be extended to cases involving computers. *See* Michael S. Leib, *E-mail and the Wiretap Laws: Why Congress Should Add Electronic Communication to Title III's Statutory Exclusionary Rule and Expressly Reject a "Good Faith" Exception*, 34 Harv. J. on Legis. 393 (1997).

To modern ears, this sounds like a strange judgment. It may have been rational in 1986 to distinguish between voice transmissions and computer communications. Today it is not. Nonetheless, the law still lacks a statutory suppression remedy for communications other than voice transmissions.

The narrow scope of the statutory exclusionary rule creates a special challenge for students attempting to understand the statutory privacy laws. Because no suppression remedy exists in most cases, defense lawyers in computer crime cases ordinarily have no incentive to file statutory challenges to government surveillance practices. The absence of challenges means that few judicial opinions explain how the statutory laws apply to computer technologies. Learning how the statutes work requires careful study of statutory text and legislative history, drawing analogies from decisions involving telephone surveillance, and careful scrutiny of existing civil cases.

A. THE WIRETAP ACT

The Wiretap Act, 18 U.S.C. §§ 2510–22, prohibits the real-time interception of telephone calls and computer communications unless an exception applies or investigators have a "super warrant" interception order. The statute applies whenever a surveillance device has been installed that acquires the contents of communications during transit. The exceptions to the statute articulate specific contexts in which the surveillance can occur without a court order.

The materials begin by exploring the basic framework of the statute and its prohibition on intercepting communications in transit. They then turn to the three most important exceptions to the statute: the consent exception, the provider exception, and the computer trespasser exception.

1. THE BASIC STRUCTURE

The basic structure of the Wiretap Act is surprisingly simple. The statute envisions that an individual is exchanging communications with another person or machine. The statute makes it a crime for someone who is not a party to the communication to use an intercepting device to intentionally access the private communications in "real time."

The following case shows how the framework works in practice. Although it is based on Florida law, the case interprets portions of the Florida statute that are identical to the federal Wiretap Act.

O'BRIEN V. O'BRIEN

District Court of Appeal of Florida, Fifth District, 2005.
899 So.2d 1133.

SAWAYA, C.J.

Emanating from a rather contentious divorce proceeding is an issue we must resolve regarding application of certain provisions of the Security of Communications Act found in Chapter 934, Florida Statutes (2003). Specifically, we must determine whether the trial court properly concluded that pursuant to section 934.03(1), certain communications were inadmissible because they were illegally intercepted by the Wife who, unbeknownst to the Husband, had installed a spyware program on a computer used by the Husband that copied and stored electronic communications between the Husband and another woman.

When marital discord erupted between the Husband and the Wife, the Wife secretly installed a spyware program called Spector on the Husband's computer. It is undisputed that the Husband engaged in private on-line chats with another woman while playing Yahoo Dominoes on his computer. The Spector spyware secretly took snapshots of what appeared on the computer screen, and the frequency of these snapshots allowed Spector to capture and record all chat conversations, instant messages, e-mails sent and received, and the websites visited by the user of the computer. When the Husband discovered the Wife's clandestine attempt to monitor and record his conversations with his Dominoes partner, the Husband uninstalled the Spector software and filed a Motion for Temporary Injunction, which was subsequently granted, to prevent the Wife from disclosing the communications. Thereafter, the Husband requested and received a permanent injunction to prevent the Wife's disclosure of the communications and to prevent her from engaging in this activity in the future. The latter motion also requested that the trial court preclude introduction of the communications into evidence in the divorce proceeding. This request was also granted. The trial court, without considering the communications, entered a final judgment of dissolution of marriage. The Wife moved for rehearing, which was subsequently denied.

The Wife appeals the order granting the permanent injunction, the final judgment, and the order denying the Wife's motion for rehearing on the narrow issue of whether the trial court erred in refusing to admit evidence of the Husband's computer activities obtained through the spyware the Wife secretly installed on the computer. The Wife argues that the electronic communications do not fall under the umbra of the Act because these communications were retrieved from storage and, therefore, are not "intercepted communications" as defined by the Act. In opposition, the Husband contends that the Spector spyware installed on the computer acquired his electronic communications real-time as they were in transmission and, therefore, are intercepts illegally obtained under the Act.

The trial court found that the electronic communications were illegally obtained in violation of section 934.03(1)(a)–(e), and so we begin our analysis with the pertinent provisions of that statute, which subjects any person to criminal penalties who:

> Intentionally intercepts, endeavors to intercept, or procures any other person to intercept or endeavor to intercept any wire, oral, or electronic communication;

§ 934.03(1)(a), Fla. Stat. Enactment of these prohibitions connotes a policy decision by the Florida legislature to allow each party to a conversation to have an expectation of privacy from interception by another party to the conversation. The purpose of the Act is to protect every person's right to privacy and to prevent the pernicious effect on all citizens who would otherwise feel insecure from intrusion into their private conversations and communications.

The clear intent of the Legislature in enacting section 934.03 was to make it illegal for a person to intercept wire, oral, or electronic communications. It is beyond doubt that what the trial court excluded from evidence are "electronic communications." The core of the issue lies in whether the electronic communications were intercepted. The term "intercept" is defined by the Act as "the aural or other acquisition of the contents of any wire, electronic, or oral communication through the use of any electronic, mechanical, or other device." § 934.02(3). We discern that there is a rather fine distinction between what is transmitted as an electronic communication subject to interception and the storage of what has been previously communicated. It is here that we tread upon new ground. Because we have found no precedent rendered by the Florida courts that considers this distinction, and in light of the fact that the Act was modeled after the Federal Wiretap Act, we advert to decisions by the federal courts that have addressed this issue for guidance.

The federal courts have consistently held that electronic communications, in order to be intercepted, must be acquired contemporaneously with transmission and that electronic communications are not intercepted within the meaning of the Federal Wiretap Act if they are retrieved from storage. *See Fraser v. Nationwide Mut. Ins. Co.*, 352 F.3d 107 (3d Cir. 2003); *Theofel v. Farey-Jones*, 359 F.3d 1066 (9th Cir. 2004); *United States v. Steiger*, 318 F.3d 1039 (11th Cir. 2003); *Konop v. Hawaiian Airlines, Inc.*, 302 F.3d 868 (9th Cir. 2002). The particular facts and circumstances of the instant case reveal that the electronic communications were intercepted contemporaneously with transmission.

The Spector spyware program that the Wife surreptitiously installed on the computer used by the Husband intercepted and copied the electronic communications as they were transmitted. We believe that particular method constitutes interception within the meaning of the Florida Act, and the decision in *Steiger* supports this conclusion. In *Steiger*, an individual was able to hack into the defendant's computer via a Trojan horse virus that allowed the hacker access to pornographic materials stored on the hard drive. The hacker was successful in transferring the pornographic material from that computer to the hacker's computer. The court held that because the Trojan horse virus simply copied information that had previously been stored on the computer's hard drive, the capture of the electronic communication was not an interception within the meaning of the Federal Wiretap Act. The court did indicate, however, that interception could occur if the virus or software intercepted the communication as it was being transmitted and copied it. The court stated:

> There is only a narrow window during which an E-mail interception may occur—the seconds or milli-seconds before which a newly composed message is saved to any temporary location following a send command. Therefore, unless some type of automatic routing software is used (for example, a duplicate of all of an employee's messages are automatically sent to the

employee's boss), interception of E-mail within the prohibition of the Wiretap Act is virtually impossible.

Steiger, 318 F.3d at 1050 (quoting Jarrod J. White, E-Mail@Work.com: Employer Monitoring of Employee E-Mail, 48 Ala. L. Rev. 1079, 1083 (1997)). Hence, a valid distinction exists between a spyware program similar to that in *Steiger*, which simply breaks into a computer and retrieves information already stored on the hard drive, and a spyware program similar to the one installed by the Wife in the instant case, which copies the communication as it is transmitted and routes the copy to a storage file in the computer.

The Wife argues that the communications were in fact stored before acquisition because once the text image became visible on the screen, the communication was no longer in transit and, therefore, not subject to intercept. We disagree. We do not believe that this evanescent time period is sufficient to transform acquisition of the communications from a contemporaneous interception to retrieval from electronic storage. We conclude that because the spyware installed by the Wife intercepted the electronic communication contemporaneously with transmission, copied it, and routed the copy to a file in the computer's hard drive, the electronic communications were intercepted in violation of the Florida Act.

We must next determine whether the improperly intercepted electronic communications may be excluded from evidence under the Act. The exclusionary provisions of the Act are found in section 934.06, Florida Statutes (2003), which provides that "whenever any wire or oral communication has been intercepted, no part of the contents of such communication and no evidence derived therefrom may be received in evidence." Conspicuously absent from the provisions of this statute is any reference to electronic communications. The federal courts, which interpreted an identical statute contained in the Federal Wiretap Act, have held that because provision is not made for exclusion of intercepted electronic communications, Congress intended that such communications not be excluded under the Federal Wiretap Act. We agree with this reasoning and conclude that the intercepted electronic communications in the instant case are not excludable under the Act. But this does not end the inquiry.

Although not specifically excludable under the Act, it is illegal and punishable as a crime under the Act to intercept electronic communications. § 934.03, Fla. Stat. (2003). The trial court found that the electronic communications were illegally intercepted in violation of the Act and ordered that they not be admitted in evidence. Generally, the admission of evidence is a matter within the sound discretion of the trial court. Because the evidence was illegally obtained, we conclude that the trial court did not abuse its discretion in refusing to admit it.

We affirm the orders and the final judgment under review in the instant case.

NOTES AND QUESTIONS

1.   *An overall view of the Wiretap Act.* The *O'Brien* case interprets a Florida state law that mirrors the federal Wiretap Act, 18 U.S.C. §§ 2510–22. At this point it may be helpful to read the Wiretap Act to get an idea of its structure. Key terms used in the statute are defined in 18 U.S.C. § 2510, and § 2511(1) contains the basic prohibitions against intercepting oral, wire, and electronic communications. Section 2511(2) lists the most important exceptions to the statute, including the provider exception, § 2511(2)(a)(i), and the consent exception, § 2511(2)(c)–(d). Sections 2515 and 2518 create a statutory suppression remedy for violations involving oral and wire communications (although not violations involving electronic communications), and § 2516 lays out the requirements the government must follow to obtain Title III intercept "super warrants."

Notably, several sections of the statute are not directly relevant to our goal of understanding how the Wiretap Act works in computer crime cases. Just to give you a flavor of what you're missing, though, here is a rundown: 18 U.S.C. § 2512 prohibits possessing or distributing wiretapping devices in some circumstances; § 2513 involves the forfeiture of such devices; § 2514 has been repealed; § 2517 concerns the use and disclosure of the fruits of wiretapping; § 2519 requires the filing of annual reports on government wiretapping practices; § 2520 permits civil damages for unlawful wiretapping; § 2521 permits injunctions in civil cases; and § 2522 involves compliance with the Communications Assistance for Law Enforcement Act. It's all good stuff, but not material you need to worry about for this course.

2.   *Oral, wire, and electronic communications.* The Wiretap Act covers three distinct types of communications: wire communications, electronic communications, and oral communications. Wire communications are communications that contain the human voice and that are sent over a wire. 18 U.S.C. § 2510(1); 18 U.S.C. § 2510(18). Oral communications are "in person" recordings of the human voice that can be picked up by a bugging device or microphone when the person recorded has a reasonable expectation of privacy. 18 U.S.C. § 2510(2). Electronic communications are communications that do not contain the human voice. 18 U.S.C. § 2510(12).

For our purposes, the two most important categories are wire communications and electronic communications. To simplify matters, telephone calls count as wire communications and almost all computer transmissions count as electronic communications. Computer communications can be wire communications in narrow situations; the most obvious examples are services that transfer the human voice using Internet protocols (so-called voice-over-Internet-Protocol, or VOIP). VOIP communications are "aural transfers" under 18 U.S.C. § 2510(18), as they contain the human voice at the point of origin and reception. This makes such communications "wire communications" under 18 U.S.C. § 2510(1).

3. *Prospective and retrospective surveillance.* The Wiretap Act only applies when a surveillance device is used to "intercept" a communication. 18 U.S.C. § 2510(4) defines intercept as "the aural or other acquisition of the contents of any wire, electronic, or oral communication through the use of any electronic, mechanical, or other device." As the *O'Brien* opinion indicates, the word "acquisition" generally has been understood to mean acquisition contemporaneously with transmission rather than when the communication has been stored. This explains why the Wiretap Act regulates prospective surveillance and not retrospective surveillance.

At the same time, the line between prospective surveillance and retrospective surveillance can become fuzzy. Imagine a government agent has access to a suspect's e-mail account, and he can click a button and receive an update with all new incoming or outgoing messages. Is the access prospective or retrospective if the government agent clicks the button every hour? Every minute? Every second?

Such issues arose in United States v. Szymuszkiewicz, 622 F.3d 701 (7th Cir. 2010). Szymuszkiewicz was an IRS employee who feared he might be fired. To learn more about his employment situation, he programmed a "rule" into the Microsoft Outlook e-mail program of his supervisor, Infusino. The rule directed Outlook to forward all of Infusino's incoming messages to Szymuszkiewicz's account. When the forwarding was discovered, Szymuszkiewicz was charged with a criminal violation of the Wiretap Act. Szymuszkiewicz argued that his conduct had not "intercepted" his supervisor's e-mail because Outlook made a copy of the e-mail after it arrived in Infusino's inbox. Because Outlook copied the e-mail immediately after it arrived, he reasoned, the e-mail was no longer "in flight" and the Wiretap Act did not apply. Judge Easterbrook disagreed with the defendant's argument and affirmed the conviction:

> Several circuits have said that, to violate § 2511, an interception must be "contemporaneous" with the communication. Szymuszkiewicz sees this as support for his "in flight" reading, but it is not. "Contemporaneous" differs from "in the middle" or any football metaphor. Either the server in Kansas City or Infusino's computer made copies of the messages for Szymuszkiewicz within a second of each message's arrival and assembly; if both Szymuszkiewicz and Infusino were sitting at their computers at the same time, they would have received each message with no more than an eyeblink in between. That's contemporaneous by any standard.

Id. at 705.

4. *Contents and non-content information.* The Wiretap Act applies only to the acquisition of "contents." Contents are defined somewhat awkwardly based on what they include, rather than what they are. According to 18 U.S.C.

§ 2510(8), " 'contents', when used with respect to any wire, oral, or electronic communication, includes any information concerning the substance, purport, or meaning of that communication."

The phrase "substance, purport, or meaning" derives largely from language originally used in the Communications Act of 1934. The 1934 statute stated that "no person not being authorized by the sender shall intercept any communication and divulge or publish the existence, contents, substance, purport, effect, or meaning of such intercepted communication to any person." The existing definition of "contents" retains the inclusion of "substance, purport, or meaning," but drops the "existence" and "effect" of the communication.

The scope of "contents" under the Wiretap Act is clear in some cases. It includes e-mail messages and the subject lines of e-mails. *See* In re Application of United States for an Order Authorizing Use of A Pen Register, 396 F. Supp.2d 45, 48 (D. Mass. 2005) (stating that e-mail subject lines are contents). It presumably includes the text of any attachments to e-mails, such as document files. As we will see when we study the Pen Register statute, it also excludes "dialing, routing, addressing, or signaling information," which presumably refers to IP headers and e-mail headers (other than subject lines). *See* 18 U.S.C. § 3127(3)–(4).

Other cases are less clear. Consider the status of "Uniform Resource Locators," also known as URLs, the address lines commonly used to retrieve information on the World Wide Web. Do you think a URL entered into a web browser contains contents? Consider the following three URLs:

https://www.nytimes.com/

https://www.nytimes.com/2021/06/03/us/supreme-court-computer-crime.html

https://www.google.com/search?q=computer+crime+law

Do any of these URLs contain contents? Note that typing the first URL into a functioning browser will direct a visitor to the *New York Times* homepage; entering the second will direct the user to a particular story; and entering the third will run a Google query and return matches for it.

5.   *Websurfing and the Wiretap Act.* The Third Circuit handed down an important decision on the content/non-content distinction in In re Google Cookie Placement Consumer Privacy Litigation, 806 F.3d 125 (3d Cir. 2015). The case involved a class action lawsuit filed against Google and two online advertising companies concerning tracking cookies that could be used to determine the Internet addresses visited by a person surfing the web. The plaintiffs claimed that by collecting the URLs that the users visited, Google and the advertising companies had intercepted the contents of user communications in violation of the Wiretap Act. This claim led the Third Circuit to consider the meaning of "contents" in the context of websurfing, and in particular whether or when URLs could be considered "contents" under the Wiretap Act.

The Third Circuit ruled that "—at a minimum—some queried URLs qualify as content." *Id.* at 139. This was true even though URLs served an addressing function, as even addresses could also serve as contents of communications. "Often, a location identifier serves no routing function, but instead comprises part of a communication's substance." *Id.* at *5. The court quoted approvingly from a treatise, Wayne R. LaFave, et al., 2 Crim. Proc. § 4.4(d) (3d ed.):

> The line between content and non-content information is inherently relative. If A sends a letter to B, asking him to deliver a package to C at a particular address, the contents of that letter are contents from A to B but mere non-content addressing information with respect to the delivery of the package to C. In the case of email, for example, a list of e-mail addresses sent as an attachment to an e-mail communication from one person to another are contents rather than addressing information. In short, whether an e-mail address is content or non-content information depends entirely on the circumstances.

According to the Third Circuit, this required a contextual analysis of the role of the information in that particular communication:

> In essence, addresses, phone numbers, and URLs may be dialing, routing, addressing, or signaling information, but only when they are performing such a function. If an address, phone number, or URL is instead part of the substantive information conveyed to the recipient, then by definition it is "content."

> The different ways that an address can be used means that the line between contents and metadata is not abstract but contextual with respect to each communication. Thus, there is no general answer to the question of whether locational information is content. Rather, a "content" inquiry is a case-specific one turning on the role the location identifier played in the "intercepted" communication.

Id. at 137. The Third Circuit went on to endorse the conclusion of some other courts that post-cut-through-dialed digits constitute contents. *See* Note 6, *infra*. According to the Third Circuit, that conclusion "hints at a different reason why queried URLs might be considered content":

> URL queries bear functional analogues to [numbers dialed as part of post-cut-through dialed digits], in that different portions of a queried URL may serve to convey different messages to different audiences. For instance, the domain name portion of the URL—everything before the ".com"—instructs a centralized web server to direct the user to a particular website, but post-domain name portions of the URL are designed to communicate to the visited website which webpage content to send the user.

Id. at 139. "Because the complaint pleads a broad scheme in which the defendants generally acquired and tracked the plaintiffs' internet usage," and given the resemblance between "the information revealed by highly detailed URLs" and post-cut-through dialed digits, the court ruled that the acquisition of URLs on a broad scale "involved the collection of at least some 'content' within the meaning of the Wiretap Act." *Id.*

The court then cautioned that it was not drawing a conclusive line between contents and metadata:

> We need not make a global determination as to what is content, and why, in the context of queried URLs. Lack of consensus, the complexity and rapid pace of change associated with the delivery of modern communications, and the facileness of direct analogy to mail and telephone cases counsel the utmost care in considering what is, and what is not, "content" in the context of web queries.

Id. at 139, n.50.

6. *When do post-cut-through dialed digits constitute contents?* The Foreign Intelligence Court of Review encountered the content/non-content distinction in a case on post-cut-through dialed digits. *See* In re Certified Question of Law, No. FISCR 16–01 (For. Intell. Ct. Rev. 2016). Post-cut-through dialed digits ("PCTDD") are numbers that telephone callers may enter after a call is initially placed.

The issue arose with respect to international calling cards, which generally require a caller to first dial the calling card service number and then, when prompted, to enter in the ultimate destination phone number. The question: Is the second phone number that a user enters the contents of a communication between the caller and the calling card service, or is it only non-content metadata?

In his certification to the Court of Review, Judge Hogan reasoned that PCTDD are non-content metadata when they only contain information about the call but are contents when they contain information unrelated to the call. According to Judge Hogan, the second number entered is non-content metadata even though it is a message to the calling card service. On the other hand, if you call a bank's automated phone service and then enter in that you want to transfer funds, that entering in of information constitutes contents because it is not dialing information.

On appeal, the Court of Review rejected the argument that PCTDD are always contents because they constitute messages to the phone company. According to the Court of Review, PCTDD that consist of only dialing information are not also contents. "The fact that the provider is not the one who uses that information for dialing purposes does not alter the fact that the information is dialing information." Put another way, if a person uses a calling card, first calling the calling card service at its phone number and then entering in the number they wish to call, that second number constitutes non-content metadata instead of contents even though it is a communication to the calling card company about what number to call on the person's behalf.

Is this approach consistent with the Third Circuit's approach in *In re Google Cookie Placement Consumer Privacy Litigation*, discussed immediately above in note 5?

7. *Packet sniffers.* Many different kinds of tools can be used to intercept computer and Internet communications. One popular type of tool is known as a "packet sniffer." A packet sniffer scans the packets of network traffic passing by a particular point in the network, and it then copies the parts of the traffic that match whatever characteristics the sniffer has been programmed to copy. *See generally* David McPhie, *Almost Private: Pen Registers, Packet Sniffers, and Privacy at the Margin*, 2005 Stan. Tech. L. Rev. 1.

Packets themselves are actually just streams of zeros and ones of data, and specific patterns of zeros and ones represent specific alphanumeric symbols. For example, a packet sniffer looking for the e-mail address "bob@aol.com," will scan for the following sequence: 01100010011011110110001001010000000110001. If this particular sequence appears, the sniffer can then begin to record a particular number of digits representing the remainder of the packet. The fruits of the sniffer can then be copied to a file, and a user can access the file at a later time and reconstruct the packets into readable form.

Whether a packet sniffer intercepts the contents of communications depends on how it is programmed. A sniffer program must be programmed to scan for and record particular sequences of traffic. If a sniffer is programmed in a way such that the zeros and ones collected include parts of communications that are "contents," then the use of the sniffer implicates the Wiretap Act. On the other hand, if the sniffer is programmed such that it does not copy any data streams that represent contents, then the sniffer will not implicate the Wiretap Act.

In the late 1990s, a great deal of media attention focused on the FBI's "Carnivore" surveillance tool. Carnivore, later renamed "DCS-1000," was a packet sniffer with an unusually sophisticated filter designed specifically to comply with court orders. The Carnivore system presented the user with a graphic user interface set for "content" or "non-content" monitoring, and adjusted the filter automatically. The FBI developed Carnivore in the late 1990s because commercial packet sniffer software available at that time lacked a sophisticated filter, and the commercial software could accidentally collect some content information when the sniffer was programmed to intercept only non-content information. By 2003, improvements in commercial packet sniffer design led to a phase-out of Carnivore/DCS-1000.

For more on Carnivore, see Illinois Institute of Technology Research Institute, Independent Review of Carnivore System—Final Report (2000); Griffin S. Dunham, Note, *Carnivore, The FBI's E-Mail Surveillance System: Devouring Criminals, Not Privacy*, 54 Fed. Comm. L.J. 543 (2002).

8. *The beginning and end of the Wiretap Act.* In the case of a traditional telephone call, the beginning and end point of the Wiretap Act's protection is very clear. The Act applies from handset to handset. Information becomes a

"wire communication" when the human voice is transferred into a signal, and ceases to be a wire communication when the signal is transferred back to a human voice. In the case of computer communications such as e-mails, however, the picture is more complicated. Computer data does not change form when that data is an "electronic communication," creating interesting issues about where and when the statute's protection begins and where and when it ends.

Consider an example. Suppose Jane turns on her computer at 9 am and begins to type up an e-mail that she plans to send to her boss Catherine. Jane completes the e-mail at 9:30 am, but decides not to send it immediately. Instead, she saves the e-mail as a draft. At 2:00 pm, Jane pulls up the draft, looks it over for a few minutes, and sends it. The e-mail arrives at Catherine's ISP at 2:15 pm. Catherine logs in to her e-mail account at 3:00 pm, downloads the file unopened to her laptop at 3:15 pm, and then reads the file from her laptop at 3:30 pm. Now imagine that the government believes that the e-mail from Jane to Catherine contains evidence of a crime, and that investigators want to obtain a copy. Does the Wiretap Act apply to efforts to obtain the email at 9:30 am? 2 pm? 3 pm? At any other time?

Two different sources of law regulate this question. First, the definition of intercept requires that the collection of evidence must be contemporaneous with transmission. Second, the Wiretap Act defines "electronic communication" in relevant part as *"any transfer* of signs, signals, writing, images, sounds, data, or intelligence of any nature *transmitted* in whole or in part by a wire, radio, electromagnetic, photoelectronic or photooptical system *that affects interstate or foreign commerce"*. 18 U.S.C. § 2510(12) (emphasis added). This definition suggests that the Wiretap Act begins when data is first transferred over an interstate system, and that it ends when data reaches its destination and is no longer being transferred over an interstate system. A communication typed into a desktop computer that is not connected to the Internet should not be subject to the Wiretap Act, as the communication is not a transfer (at least yet).

Goldman v. United States, 316 U.S. 129 (1942), may provide additional insight. *Goldman* interpreted 47 U.S.C. § 605 of the 1934 Communications Act, the predecessor to the Wiretap Act that shares a number of principles with it. The *Goldman* defendants were attorneys engaged in a conspiracy relating to a bankruptcy scheme. Federal agents entered the room next door to one attorney's office, and they used a type of microphone placed against the wall to amplify the sound from the adjacent room and record the defendant's speech while he was talking on the telephone. The defendant claimed that the use of the microphone from the next room had "intercepted" the "communication" of his telephone call. The Supreme Court disagreed:

> What is protected is the message itself throughout the course of its transmission by the instrumentality or agency of transmission. Words written by a person and intended ultimately to be carried as so written to a telegraph office do not constitute a communication

within the terms of the Act until they are handed to an agent of the telegraph company. Words spoken in a room in the presence of another into a telephone receiver do not constitute a communication by wire within the meaning of the section. Letters deposited in the Post Office are protected from examination by federal statute, but it could not rightly be claimed that the office carbon of such letter, or indeed the letter itself before it has left the office of the sender, comes within the protection of the statute.

Id. at 133–34.

Did the *O'Brien* court apply these principles correctly? What is the electronic equivalent of handing a message to an agent of the telegraph company? In the case of e-mail, is it pressing "send"?

9.   *Remedies.* The *O'Brien* court comes up with a rather creative way to impose a suppression remedy. The statute itself imposes no such remedy, and a federal court in analogous circumstances would not suppress the evidence. As a matter of policy, is a suppression remedy appropriate in this case? Note that the *O'Brien* case is a civil dispute: the Wife monitored the Husband, and she wanted to use the evidence against him in a divorce proceeding.

Should the Wiretap Act include a statutory suppression remedy, either for government violations, for private violations, or for both?

10.   *The "super warrant" requirement.* The Wiretap Act permits agents to intercept communications pursuant to a court order. *See* 18 U.S.C. §§ 2516, 2518. Obtaining a Title III "super warrant" order is quite burdensome, however, as the requirements extend far beyond probable cause and involve a great deal of paperwork. The Justice Department explains:

High-level Justice Department approval is required for federal Title III applications, by statute in the case of wire communications, and by Justice Department policy in the case of electronic communications (except for numeric pagers). When authorized by the Justice Department and signed by a United States District Court or Court of Appeals judge, a Title III order permits law enforcement to intercept communications for up to thirty days. *See* § 2518.

18 U.S.C. §§ 2516–2518 imposes several formidable requirements that must be satisfied before investigators can obtain a Title III order. Most importantly, the application for the order must show probable cause to believe that the interception will reveal evidence of a predicate felony offense listed in § 2516. *See* § 2518(3)(a)–(b). For federal agents, the predicate felony offense must be one of the crimes specifically enumerated in § 2516(1)(a)–(r) to intercept wire communications, or any federal felony to intercept electronic communications. *See* 18 U.S.C. § 2516(3). The predicate crimes for state investigations are listed in 18 U.S.C. § 2516(2). The application for a Title III order also (1) must show that normal investigative procedures have been tried and failed, or that they reasonably appear

to be unlikely to succeed or to be too dangerous, *see* § 2518(1)(c); (2) must establish probable cause that the communication facility is being used in a crime; and (3) must show that the surveillance will be conducted in a way that minimizes the interception of communications that do not provide evidence of a crime.

U.S. Department of Justice, Searching and Seizing Computers and Obtaining Electronic Evidence in Criminal Investigations (2002).

The difficulty of obtaining a Title III order results in such orders being obtained only rarely. This is particularly true in computer-related cases. In a typical year, only a small Title III orders are obtained to monitor only electronic communications. The very low number of Title III orders in computer cases should direct our attention to the two main exceptions applicable in computer wiretapping cases: the consent exception, § 2511(2)(c)–(d) and the provider exception, § 2511(2)(a)(i).

2. THE CONSENT EXCEPTION

Like the Fourth Amendment, the Wiretap Act has a consent exception. 18 U.S.C. § 2511(2)(c) and (d) state:

(c) It shall not be unlawful under this chapter for a person acting under color of law to intercept a wire, oral, or electronic communication, where such person is a party to the communication or one of the parties to the communication has given prior consent to such interception.

(d) It shall not be unlawful under this chapter for a person not acting under color of law to intercept a wire, oral, or electronic communication where such person is a party to the communication or where one of the parties to the communication has given prior consent to such interception unless such communication is intercepted for the purpose of committing any criminal or tortious act in violation of the Constitution or laws of the United States or of any State.

This exception permits "a party to the communication" to give "prior consent" to interception. If a party to the communication consents to the interception, the interception does not violate the Wiretap Act. For example, an undercover government agent can record a conversation between himself and a suspect or permit others to record the call. Similarly, if a private person records his own telephone conversations with others, his consent authorizes the interception unless the commission of a criminal, tortious, or other injurious act was a determinative factor in the person's motivation for intercepting the communication. *See* United States v. Cassiere, 4 F.3d 1006, 1021 (1st Cir. 1993).

GRIGGS-RYAN V. SMITH

United States Court of Appeals for the First Circuit, 1990.
904 F.2d 112.

SELYA, CIRCUIT JUDGE.

Reaching out to touch someone, plaintiff-appellant Gerald Griggs-Ryan filed two related civil actions in the United States District Court for the District of Maine. Suing his landlady, Beulah Smith, plaintiff alleged that she unlawfully intercepted and disclosed the contents of a telephone conversation in which he participated.

I.

Plaintiff was a tenant at a campground which Smith operated in Wells. The individual units did not have telephones, but lodgers were allowed to use the landlady's telephone. During the summer of 1987, Smith was plagued by obscene calls. On the police department's advice, she began to record incoming calls through her answering machine. Because she suspected that plaintiff's friend, Paul Jackson, was responsible for the offensive overtures, Smith informed plaintiff on a number of occasions that all calls to her home were being recorded. She hoped, of course, that plaintiff would relay the message to Jackson.

On September 14, 1987, Smith answered the telephone in her bedroom. The caller identified himself as "Richard Kierstead" and asked to speak with plaintiff. Smith held the line open to maintain the connection while her daughter went to fetch plaintiff. When Griggs-Ryan picked up the office extension, Smith started to cradle her instrument. Overhearing the caller say, "Hi, it's Paul, she thinks it's Kierstead," and believing the voice to be Paul Jackson's, Smith changed her mind. She did not hang up but instead listened to and recorded the ensuing discussion.

As a result of the eavesdropping, Smith came to suspect that the overheard conversation concerned a drug transaction. She immediately contacted the authorities. At police headquarters, she played the tape for defendant Connelly. Sharing Smith's suspicions, the detective revealed the conversation's contents to the district attorney and to a local magistrate. The magistrate issued a warrant to search plaintiff's abode and the Wells police executed it, seizing marijuana. Griggs-Ryan was arrested and charged with trafficking.

A suppression hearing was held in the state superior court. Smith testified about what she told Griggs-Ryan concerning her recording practice. The judge found that plaintiff was "unaware" that Smith was listening to, or recording, the September 14 conversation, and ruled that Smith's interception of the conversation was therefore inadmissible under Maine law. On September 28, 1989, the judge suppressed the fruits of the search.

In the meantime, plaintiff had begun the instant suits in federal court. For their part, defendants argued that plaintiff, by electing to talk to Jackson after Smith's warning that all incoming calls were being recorded, effectively acquiesced in the interception.

The district court concluded that the landlady's actions were not proscribed by federal law because Smith informed Plaintiff on more than one occasion that she was recording all incoming calls and that there was no evidence that Smith qualified her statements to Plaintiff on the matter. Thus, the district court held that Plaintiff's receiving of a telephone call inside of Smith's home, when considered in light of the warning he received, manifests implied consent sufficient to trigger the prior consent exception to Title III.

II.

Although plaintiff repeatedly declaims that wire communications are "protected absolutely from illegal interception," that rallying cry—like most sloganeering—overstates the proposition. Title III was intended to prohibit all interceptions except those specifically provided for in the Act. Congress, in its wisdom, chose to insert a myriad of exceptions and restrictive definitions into Title III, purposely leaving certain wire communications unprotected. Accordingly, there is little to be gained by pejorative declamations; the question is simply whether a particular intercept runs afoul of the statute's imperatives.

18 U.S.C. § 2511(2)(d) outlines a Title III exclusion applicable where one of the parties to the communication has given prior consent to such interception. We agree with the Second Circuit that "Congress intended the consent requirement to be construed broadly." United States v. Amen, 831 F.2d 373, 378 (2d Cir. 1987). In this spirit, we—and other courts—have held that Title III affords safe harbor not only for persons who intercept calls with the explicit consent of a conversant but also for those who do so after receiving implied consent. See United States v. Willoughby, 860 F.2d 15, 19 (2d Cir. 1988); Watkins v. L.M. Berry & Co., 704 F.2d 577, 581 (11th Cir. 1983); Campiti v. Walonis, 611 F.2d 387, 393 (1st Cir. 1979). Acknowledging the doctrinal vitality of implied consent, however, does not address its parameters—nor can we suggest any pat, all-purpose definition. In the Title III milieu as in other settings, consent inheres where a person's behavior manifests acquiescence or a comparable voluntary diminution of his or her otherwise protected rights.

Of course, implied consent is not constructive consent. Rather, implied consent is "consent in fact" which is inferred from surrounding circumstances indicating that the party knowingly agreed to the surveillance. Thus, implied consent—or the absence of it—may be deduced from the circumstances prevailing in a given situation. The circumstances relevant to an implication of consent will vary from case to case, but the compendium will ordinarily include language or acts which tend to prove (or disprove) that a party knows of, or assents to, encroachments on the routine expectation that conversations are private. And the ultimate determination must proceed in light of the prophylactic purpose of Title III—a purpose which suggests that consent should not casually be inferred.

The salient facts are these. Prior to September 14, Griggs-Ryan had been repeatedly informed that all incoming calls were being monitored. Smith's affidavit in this respect stands uncontradicted and unimpeached:

> On several occasions during the course of the summer I spoke to Mr. Ryan and informed him that all incoming telephone calls to my home were being tape recorded. I had made it quite clear to Mr. Ryan by virtue of these several conversations that all of the incoming telephone calls to my home on my phones were being tape recorded.

There is no evidence that Smith, whatever her actual practice might have been, ever informed plaintiff that she would cease monitoring a call once she determined that it was not harassing. Indeed, the only record evidence speaking directly to this question is Smith's testimony at the state court suppression hearing, where the following colloquy occurred:

> Q. When you told Mr. Ryan that you were taping every phone call, did you tell him that you have stopped taping once you identified who the caller was?
>
> A. No.

We take as undisputed that (1) plaintiff was told unequivocally that all incoming calls would be recorded, and (2) Smith did not qualify the warning by telling him that she planned to listen only until she could ascertain whether the call was offensive.

It remains only for us to link applicable law to undisputed fact. The district court ruled that plaintiff, in taking the call from Jackson and conversing with him on Smith's telephone, impliedly consented to the interception. We think that this ruling was inevitable. Plaintiff had been unmistakably warned on a number of occasions that all incoming calls were being monitored. In light of so sweeping a warning, he continued to receive calls and talk unguardedly on Smith's personal line without the slightest hint of coercion or exigent circumstance. Plaintiff was free to use some other instrument; or since outgoing calls were not recorded, to return calls on Smith's telephone and thus avoid any unwanted eavesdropping. Given the circumstances prevailing, it seems altogether clear that plaintiff knowingly agreed to the surveillance. His consent, albeit not explicit, was manifest. No more was required.

Smith's conduct on September 14 fell squarely within the parameters of what she had repeatedly told plaintiff to expect, and thus, fell squarely within the bounds of plaintiff's consent. Having persisted in using Smith's telephone to converse with callers in the face of unambiguous, unqualified notice that every incoming call would be monitored, plaintiff's consent necessarily encompassed every portion of every call he accepted on his landlady's line.

Plaintiff's final fizgig, centering on the upshot of the state court suppression hearing, is equally unimpressive. It is true that the state court found plaintiff "unaware" that the call in question was being recorded. Even assuming, however, that the finding has evidentiary significance in a federal civil case involving persons not parties to the state criminal proceedings—a matter on which we do not opine—it is beside the present point. Whether a person is cognizant that a particular call is being recorded does not answer, or fully respond to, the question of whether the scope of consent previously granted was sufficiently expansive to cover a generalized practice of recording.

Because plaintiff unqualifiedly consented to Smith's interception of all incoming calls, the latter's conduct was "not unlawful" within the meaning of 18 U.S.C. § 2511(2)(d). Consequently, no cause of action could be maintained against Smith under Title III.

NOTES AND QUESTIONS

1. *Understanding the Wiretap Act's standard for consent.* In what sense did Griggs-Ryan consent to Smith's monitoring? He had been told a few times in the months leading up to the call that Smith was recording calls made to her phone. But there was no evidence that he knew this particular call was recorded. Is the key question whether Griggs-Ryan proceeded after receiving notice, or whether he actually consented to being taped? Which court was right: the state court that ruled Griggs-Ryan had not consented, or the federal court that ruled he had?

Which is the better approach as a matter of policy? Should notice of monitoring be sufficient even if the person monitored did not realize the call was being monitored?

2. *Deal v. Spears.* Compare *Griggs-Ryan* with Deal v. Spears, 980 F.2d 1153 (8th Cir. 1992). In *Spears*, owners of a packaging store suspected that an employee was involved in an earlier burglary of the store. The employee often spent much of her day flirting on the store telephone with her boyfriend, and the store owners asked the employee to cut down on her personal calls and warned that they might start recording her calls to curtail abuses. The owners later decided to record all calls to and from the store in an effort to catch the employee making an unguarded admission of her involvement in the burglary. When the monitoring recorded the employee admitting petty wrongdoing at the store, the store owners fired her. The employee then brought a wiretapping suit against the store owners. Held: The owners' warning that they "might"

begin to monitor calls was insufficient to generate consent under the Wiretap Act. *See id.* at 1157.

3. *Actual notice is required.* Does a telephone or Internet user impliedly consent to monitoring if she did not receive notice but should have known that the communications would be monitored? Cases suggest that the answer is "no." For example, in United States v. Lanoue, 71 F.3d 966 (1st Cir. 1995), the defendant was a prisoner who was monitored while making calls from a detention center that did not notify prisoners of monitoring. The First Circuit articulated the following standard to determine whether consent exists absent sufficient formal notice:

> Deficient notice will almost always defeat a claim of implied consent. Keeping in mind that implied consent is not constructive consent but 'consent in fact,' consent might be implied in spite of deficient notice, but only in a rare case where the court can conclude with assurance from surrounding circumstances that the party knowingly agreed to the surveillance. We emphasize that consent should not casually be inferred, particularly in a case of deficient notice. The surrounding circumstances must convincingly show that the party knew about and consented to the interception in spite of the lack of formal notice or deficient formal notice.

Id. at 981. Similarly, in Jandak v. Village of Brookfield, 520 F. Supp. 815, 820 n. 5 (N.D. Ill. 1981), a police officer placed a personal call from the police station to another person. The call was secretly recorded, and the court rejected the notion that one of the parties consented because they should have known that a call from the police station would be recorded:

> Consent may be implied in fact, from surrounding circumstances indicating that the party knowingly agreed to the surveillance. Defendants here are asking that the consent be implied in law, if the party reasonably should have known. This goes far beyond the language of the statute, or any indications in the legislative history, and the court declines to so expansively read the exception.

4. *Do Internet terms of service suffice to generate consent?* Imagine an Internet provider wishes to intercept a user's communications. The provider inserts a term in the terms of service that states: "We reserve the right to intercept your communications for any reason." Before using the service, the user must click on a box saying that she has read and agreed to all terms of service. Every user clicks the box, although very few actually read the terms of service and see of the interception provision.

Has a user who signs up for the service and clicks on the box, but who has not actually read the terms, consented to monitoring for Wiretap Act purposes? If the user gives her computer over to a friend or family member to use, and that person has his communication intercepted, does any consent obtained from the user also apply by extension to his friend or family member?

5. *Using banners to generate consent.* Computer owners sometimes install network banners to generate users' consent and permit monitoring. A banner is a message that greets computer users when they log on to a network; a typical banner informs users that their communications on the network may be monitored. After a user sees the banner and has knowledge of the monitoring, the computer can be monitored without violating the Wiretap Act under the consent theory of *Griggs-Ryan v. Smith.*

Banners are routinely used in government workplaces to regulate rights on government networks. In the context of government employment, computer network banners perform two functions at once. They generate consent to monitoring for purposes of Title III, and they also constitute a legitimate workplace policy that eliminates Fourth Amendment privacy rights in the network under O'Connor v. Ortega, 480 U.S. 709 (1987).

How clear must the wording of a banner be to generate a computer user's consent to monitoring? Should the banner require users to "click through" the notice? Is it sufficient if the notice of monitoring can be found somewhere in the Terms of Service or an employee manual? What if the computer user does not see the banner or does not understand it? What if the user is trying to avoid the banner and bypasses it to avoid actual notice?

6. *Computers, victims, and intermediaries as parties to the communication.* In the case of telephone calls, a "party to the communication" is usually easy to identify. Any human participant in a telephone conversation is a party to the communication. The simple framework of a two-way communication between two parties may be more difficult to apply in the case of a computer network.

> When a hacker launches an attack against a computer network, for example, he may route the attack through a handful of compromised computer systems before directing the attack at a final victim. At the victim's computer, the hacker may direct the attack at a user's network account, at the system administrator's "root" account, or at common files. Finding a "person" who is a "party to the communication"—other than the hacker himself, of course—can be a difficult (if not entirely metaphysical) task.

U.S. Department of Justice, Searching and Seizing Computers (2002).

Can a computer be a party to the communication that can consent to monitoring under the Wiretap Act? Is the owner or system administrator a party to the communication? Recall the early case of United States v. Seidlitz, 589 F.2d 152 (4th Cir. 1978), first introduced in Chapter 2. Seidlitz used a stolen account to break into computers owned and operated by OSI. Employees at OSI monitored Seidlitz's unauthorized use of the OSI computer and used that monitoring to trace the attack back to Seidlitz. At trial, Seidlitz argued that the evidence of his conduct could not be used against him because the monitoring violated the Wiretap Act. The case was decided before the passage of ECPA, and the Fourth Circuit properly rejected the claim on the ground that the computer communication was not a "wire communication" protected by the 1968 statute. The Court then suggested this secondary rationale for its holding:

> Title III specifically authorizes the interception of a wire communication by a party to the communication or by a person acting with the consent of a party to the communication. 18 U.S.C. § 2511(2)(c), (d). In our opinion OSI, which leased, housed, programmed, and maintained the computers and subscribed to the relevant telephone numbers, was for all intents and purposes a party to the communications initiated by the defendant, since in a very real sense the company used the computers solely as a medium for imparting to customers, via telephone lines, its own expertise. Insofar as OSI installed on its line a computer which was capable of recording the messages exchanged in the course of responding to a remote user's requests, we consider this case analogous to those which recognize that a party may, consistent with Title III, use a device to capture and record both sides of his telephone conversation with another party.

Id. at 158. Do you agree that OSI was a party to the communication in the *Seidlitz* case? If not, can OSI monitor intrusions into its network? As a matter of policy, what rights should the victim of a computer intrusion have to monitor attacks against it? *See also* United States v. Mullins, 992 F.2d 1472, 1478 (9th Cir. 1993) (suggesting in passing that the consent exception authorizes monitoring of computer system misuse because the owner of the victimized computer system is a party to the communication).

If you agree that OSI was a party to the communication in the *Seidlitz* case, do you reach the same conclusion with respect to intermediary computers that may be involved in computer intrusion cases? For example, if you write an e-mail to your best friend, is your ISP a party to the communication? Is your friend's ISP a party to the communication? Or are you and your friend the only parties to the communication?

A somewhat related issue came up in a case brought under 47 U.S.C. § 605, the predecessor to the Wiretap statute. In United States v. Dote, 371 F.2d 176 (7th Cir. 1966), the Illinois Bell Telephone company tipped off IRS agents that a particular telephone was being used in an illegal gambling ring. Acting at the request of IRS investigators, the company installed a pen register on the phone. The pen register led IRS investigators to the members of the gambling enterprise, who were then arrested and convicted of tax evasion. They appealed their convictions on the ground that the pen register violated 47 U.S.C. § 605. (Although the pen register did not collect contents, § 605 applied both to content and non-content information at that time.) The government defended its use of the pen register on the ground that the dial pulses of the numbers dialed from the telephone were communications to the phone company. In the parlance of the modern Wiretap Act, the government's claim was that the phone company could consent to monitoring because it was a party to the communication of the numbers dialed. The Seventh Circuit disagreed:

> We see no reason to indulge in a game of words, [on] whether the telephone company as a legal entity is sufficiently embodied in the wires and devices of its system to be an intended recipient of the dial pulse signal. No person was the intended recipient of the dial pulses, but rather the communications system through which the pulses were to be relayed as a signal to activate the telephone of the intended recipient of a telephone call. The dial telephone system does not generally require human intervention to connect two telephones. The telephone company was not therefore the intended recipient of the signal. The 'intended recipient' was the telephone of another subscriber, which would ring to notify the subscriber of a call. Ultimately, the intended human recipient of the signal was the subscriber called.

Id. at 180.

7. *All-party consent statutes.* The federal Wiretap Act is a one-party consent statute. That is, the consent of any one party to the communication permits monitoring of every other party. In contrast, some state wiretap statutes require every party to consent before the state consent exception applies. In the case of a telephone call, for example, each person on the call must authorize the monitoring.

How does an all-party consent approach apply to monitoring computer communications? In Commonwealth v. Proetto, 771 A.2d 823 (Pa. Super. Ct. 2001), *aff'd,* 837 A.2d 1163 (Pa. 2003), the defendant engaged in chat and e-mail communications with an undercover police officer who was posing as a young girl. The police officer recorded all of the communications, and printouts of the exchanges were admitted at trial. Pennsylvania's state wiretap statute requires the consent of all parties, and the defendant argued that the officer had intercepted his communications unlawfully because the defendant had not consented to the officer recording his chat and e-mail exchanges. The Pennsylvania Superior Court rejected the claim, finding the defendant's consent implicit in his use of the technology:

> This situation is unlike one in which a party is engaging in a conversation over the telephone. While engaging in a conversation over the telephone, a party would have no reason to believe that the other party was taping the conversation. Any reasonably intelligent person, savvy enough to be using the Internet, however, would be aware of the fact that messages are received in a recorded format, by their very nature, and can be downloaded or printed by the party receiving the message. By the very act of sending a communication over the Internet, the party expressly consents to the recording of the message.

See id. at 830. Is this reasoning persuasive? Does an Internet user expressly (or impliedly) permit intended recipients of his communications to make copies of his communications?

8.   *Does third-party website tracking violate the Wiretap Act, or does the consent exception categorically permit it?* Circuit courts have divided on how the Wiretap Act's consent exception applies to third-party website tracking. To understand the dispute, you need to know a little bit about how website tracking works. (This is useful not just for understanding the Wiretap Act, but also for knowing what your computer is doing as you surf the web. It's doing a lot, it turns out.) With that technological background in place, we can then cover the disagreement between the Third Circuit and the Ninth Circuit on how the Wiretap Act applies.

The best way to understand the technological problem is to start with third-party advertising. You probably know that website owners often earn money for their websites by selling advertisements. A visitor to the website will see the advertisements, and the website owner will generate revenue for ads served to the visitors. But where do the advertisements come from? These days, advertisements typically come from third-party advertisers.

Say a user visits a website, website.com, that generates income by selling ads that will be served by a third-party advertising service. When a user visits a particular page at website.com that includes an advertisement, website.com will send a message to the user's browser directing the browser to send a request for an ad to the third-party advertising service. The browser immediately sends the request, and the advertising service will send the ad to appear as part of that page at website.com.

To the casual user, this sequence is hidden. The ads may fill in at slightly different times than the rest of the page, but it all looks like it's coming from the same source. In fact, the page and the ads are coming from different sources. And note one important consequence of how this works: The third-party advertising service learns that a person using this particular browser visited the particular page at website.com that was served the ad.

Now add a complication. Third-party advertising services can sell their advertisements at higher rates if they can give advertisers a more specific profile of who is seeing a particular ad. And those third-party advertising services can create profiles by selling other ads that generate records that the user visited those other websites. Those profiles can be stored as "cookies," pieces of code, on the user's browser.

The cookies enable the third-party advertising site to keep a record of website addresses the user has visited to which the service has served ads. If a user visits website.com, twitter.com, and cnn.com, and that service was hired to serve ads to all three sites, the advertising service will know the specific pages visited on all three sites. And consider that users can visit hundreds of websites over time. The cookie created by the advertising service can generate a fairly detailed profile of who is using that browser that it can use to sell its advertisements at higher rates.

At this point you're probably wondering: What does this have to do with the consent exception of the Wiretap Act?

Class action lawsuits have been brought against advertisers and social media companies claiming that third-party website tracking can violate the Wiretap Act. The lawsuits claim that, at least in some circumstances, third-party website tracking amounts to a wiretap. The webpage addresses that the tracker learns are contents of communications, the argument runs. And the tracking company that is acquiring those contents is intercepting those contents. If the user knows about the tracking, that may be lawful under the consent exception. But what if the user doesn't know that the tracking has occurred? Is this website tracking a wiretap violation if it occurs without the user's knowledge?

This has come up in two cases. In the first case, In re Google Cookie Placement Consumer Privacy Litigation, 806 F.3d 125 (3d Cir. 2015), a class action was filed against third-party advertising services claiming that the services violated the Wiretap Act when they conducted third-party tracking that overrode browser settings designed to block tracking cookies. The plaintiff class had used browser settings designed to block third-party tracking. But the advertisers sued had allegedly conducted third-party tracking nonetheless in a way that circumvented the browser settings.

In the second case, In re Facebook, Inc. Internet Tracking Litigation, 956 F.3d 589 (9th Cir. 2020), a class action was filed against Facebook for conducting third party tracking of the webpages visited by Facebook users even when they had logged out of Facebook. Facebook does this by using "plug-ins," such as Facebook's "like" button, that owners of other websites can place on their websites so Facebook users can express their opinions about those items. These plug-ins act just like third-party advertisements. When a Facebook user visits a site that hosts a Facebook plug-in, the site sends a request to Facebook for the plug-in and Facebook notes the address in a cookie stored on the user's browser that generates a profile Facebook can sell for advertising purposes.

The difficult legal question is how the consent exception applies to the actions of the companies doing the third-party tracking, whether it is serving the advertisement (in the Third Circuit's case) or serving the Facebook plug-in (in the Ninth Circuit's case). A "party to the communication" can always consent under 18 U.S.C. § 2511(2)(d). Here's the question: Is the third-party tracking service a "party to the communication"? If it is, it cannot violate the Wiretap Act because it is consenting. If it is not, third-party website tracking may violate the Wiretap Act.

The Third Circuit held that a third-party tracking service is indeed a party to the communication. *See In re Google Cookie Placement Consumer Privacy Litigation*, 806 F.3d at 142–43. The Third Circuit reasoned that the tracking service only knows the contents of the user's communication because the user's own browser has sent it a message asking for the third-party code, a message known technically as a "GET request." Because the GET request was sent from the user's browser to the third-party tracker, it is a communication between those two parties and the third-party tracker is free to record it. Here's the Third Circuit's analysis:

> Our understanding of the plaintiffs' allegations is that the defendants acquired the plaintiffs' internet history information when, in the course of requesting webpage advertising content at the direction of the visited website, the plaintiffs' browsers sent that information directly to the defendants' servers.

> Because the defendants were the intended recipients of the transmissions at issue—i.e. GET requests that the plaintiffs' browsers sent directly to the defendants' servers—we agree that § 2511(2)(d) means the defendants have done nothing unlawful under the Wiretap Act. Tautologically, a communication will always consist of at least two parties: the speaker and/or sender, and at least one intended recipient.

> As the intended recipient of a communication is necessarily one of its parties, and the defendants were the intended recipients of the GET requests they acquired here, the defendants were parties to the transmissions at issue in this case. And under § 2511(2)(d), it is not unlawful for a private person to intercept a wire, oral, or electronic communication where such person is a party to the communication.

Id.

In contrast, the Ninth Circuit held that a third-party tracking service is not a party to the communication. *See In re Facebook, Inc. Internet Tracking Litigation*, 956 F.3d at 608. According to the Ninth Circuit, the GET request from the user's browser is not a communication from the browser but rather an "unseen auditor" that may be surreptitiously intercepting the user's contents:

> We adopt the understanding that simultaneous, unknown duplication and communication of GET requests do not exempt a defendant from liability under the party exception.

> As we have previously held, the paramount objective of the Electronic Communications Privacy Act, which amended the Wiretap Act is to protect effectively the privacy of communications. We also recognize that the Wiretap Act's legislative history evidences Congress's intent to prevent the acquisition of the contents of a message by an unauthorized third-party or "an unseen auditor." *See* S. Rep. No. 90–1097, *reprinted in* 1986 U.S.C.C.A.N. 2112, 2154, 2182. Permitting an entity to engage in the unauthorized duplication and forwarding of unknowing users' information would render permissible the most common methods of intrusion, allowing the exception to swallow the rule.

Therefore, we conclude that Facebook is not exempt from liability as a matter of law under the Wiretap Act or CIPA as a party to the communication.

In re Facebook, Inc. Internet Tracking Litigation, 956 F.3d at 608.

Which is more persuasive, the Third Circuit's approach or the Ninth Circuit's approach? Can a third-party tracking service be a "party" to a user's communication that the user does not even know is there? Or should we assume that Internet users know what their browsers are doing?

3.   THE PROVIDER EXCEPTION

The next important exception to the Wiretap Act is the provider exception, 18 U.S.C. § 2511(2)(a)(i). The provider exception is particularly important in computer misuse cases, as it allows reasonable monitoring of computer misuse. The exception states in relevant part:

> an officer, employee, or agent of a provider of wire or electronic communication service, whose facilities are used in the transmission of a wire or electronic communication, [can] intercept, disclose, or use that communication in the normal course of his employment while engaged in any activity which is a necessary incident to the rendition of his service or to the protection of the rights or property of the provider of that service.

The provider exception recognizes that providers of network services may have legitimate business reasons to tap communications within their networks. Networks can be misused or abused, and providers may need to monitor the misuse to identify the wrongdoer and stop the misconduct. The provider exception thus gives providers a limited right to monitor communications to protect their property. The basic standard is reasonableness. *See* United States v. Harvey, 540 F.2d 1345, 1350 (8th Cir. 1976). Providers are permitted to conduct reasonable monitoring to protect their rights or property and can disclose the fruits of what they obtain to the government. However, they cannot take the monitoring or disclosure too far.

UNITED STATES V. AULER
United States Court of Appeals for the Seventh Circuit, 1976.
539 F.2d 642.

FAIRCHILD, CHIEF JUDGE.

In this appeal we are once again asked to consider the scope of the authority of a common carrier to intercept and disclose wire communications, 18 U.S.C. § 2511(2)(a)(i). The appellant, Raymond Auler, was convicted for violating the Wire Fraud Statute, 18 U.S.C. § 1343, and sentenced to six months imprisonment.

I

During June 1973, a security supervisor for the Wisconsin Telephone Company, Bernard G. Schlimgen, attached a 2600 cycle detecting device to the telephone line serving Auler's residence in Milwaukee. Schlimgen believed that there was in use a device known as a "blue box" to fraudulently place toll-free long distance calls. The blue box is used to electronically bypass the telephone company's billing equipment. After engaging a wide area telephone service system (WATS), the blue box emits a 2600 cycle tone which allows the user to remain within the toll system after the WATS line has been disconnected. Subsequently, the user "key pulses" through the blue box a series of multifrequency tones, comparable to those normally generated by a long distance call. The telephone company's billing equipment only records the original toll-free call; consequently, the user is not charged for the call made with the blue box.

The 2600 cycle detector indicated that an out of state call was made by use of the blue box technique. Schlimgen informed Roger Davis, then a Special Agent for the F.B.I., of this suspected violation of the Wire Fraud Statute. Davis obtained a warrant, and accompanied by Schlimgen, searched Auler's residence. They did not find a blue box, but learned from Auler's daughter that Auler had been present earlier, but was moving to Wisconsin Dells.

On June 21, 1973, Schlimgen contacted Gary Mattila, a security agent for the General Telephone Company, the company which provides telephone service for the Wisconsin Dells area, concerning Auler's alleged use of the blue box. Mattila discovered that Auler had two telephone listings at a Wisconsin Dells residence. He further learned from another Wisconsin Telephone Company security agent that Auler was a suspected blue box user. This information was obtained by examining a computer printout list of all the toll-free calls placed in that area. On the basis of these reports, Mattila ordered on July 13, and 17, 1973 the installation of a 2600 cycle detector placed on both of Auler's Wisconsin Dells telephone lines.

After the detection of numerous 2600 cycle tones, Mattila, on July 27, 1973, ordered the attachment of magnetic tape recording devices to Auler's lines to monitor all multifrequency tones and conversations originating from Auler's residence. This taping was discontinued on one line on July 29, and on the other on July 30. General Telephone's logs indicate that the magnetic recorders also taped traffic over Auler's lines on August 2 through 3, and August 9 through 13.

On July 30 and 31, Mattila advised F.B.I. Agent Hunter that General Telephone had conducted an investigation regarding Raymond Auler, and that based on this investigation Auler was suspected of using a blue box. Hunter obtained a warrant on August 3 to search Auler's residence.

Accompanied by Mattila, Hunter executed the warrant on August 10. Immediately preceding the search Mattila had been in contact with General Telephone agents who were monitoring Auler's lines. These agents informed Mattila that they had detected a 2600 cycle tone and had recorded Auler completing a call. During the search Hunter found and seized a blue box and other equipment. Auler was subsequently tried on stipulated facts and found guilty. Prior to trial Auler had unsuccessfully sought to suppress any evidence that was the product of General Telephone's interception of his telephone lines.

II

Section 2511(2)(a)(i) provides a telephone company with the power to protect its property through limited monitoring of the lines of suspected illegal users and the subsequent immunity to disclose necessary information to law enforcement agencies.

This authority of the telephone company to intercept and disclose wire communications is not unlimited. It may only intercept a communication which is a necessary incident to the rendition of service or for the protection of the company's rights or property. Therefore, we think that any surveillance of a suspected blue box user must be restricted to a determination of (1) whether a blue box is being used; (2) the multifrequency tones of the number "dialed" by the blue box; (3) whether the call was completed; (4) the duration of the call; and (5) the identity of the caller. This information can be obtained through a 2600 cycle detector, or similar device, and a tape recording of the salutations at the beginning of the conversation. Therefore, section 2511(2)(a)(i) must reasonably be read to permit the telephone company to divulge, at least, the existence of the illegal calls and the fact that they were completed (the salutations) to law enforcement authorities. These authorized disclosures could properly be used to obtain a search warrant and would be admissible as evidence.

Auler points out that General Telephone's surveillance of his conversations extended beyond the scope of permissible interception just outlined. At oral argument, the Government conceded that during the approximately two week period of surveillance, General Telephone monitored and committed to tape all calls, whether made illicitly with a blue box or in compliance with the subscription agreement. This intrusive interception provided General Telephone with far more information than it needed to protect its interests.

However, General Telephone only disclosed to the F.B.I. the limited evidence which section 2511(2)(a)(i) reasonably permits. This consisted of edited tape recordings containing tones identified as those transmitted by a blue box, dialing signals, and salutations of the appellant. The interception of the material recorded on these tapes may be viewed apart from those more intrusive acts of surveillance which are not immunized by section 2511(2)(a)(i). The reasonable and necessary interceptions and disclosures need not be suppressed as the "fruits" of illegal surveillance. Neither the statute nor the Fourth Amendment, which does not prohibit unreasonable searches by private individuals, require lawful interceptions and disclosures to be excluded as evidence; only evidence obtained through surveillance beyond the authorization of section 2511(2)(a)(i) * * * must be suppressed. General Telephone provided no evidence stemming from excessive interception to the F.B.I., and the Government offered none at trial.[10] The edited tapes offered at trial were properly admitted. We do assume for the purpose of this discussion that General Telephone conducted excessive and therefore illegal surveillance. Any consequences to General Telephone in the context of the civil and criminal penalties imposed by [the Wiretap Act] would be the subject of an action to which General Telephone would be a party.

III

The appellant further argues that even if section 2511(2)(a)(i) permits limited telephone company surveillance, he is entitled to the protection provided by the Fourth Amendment. Auler asserts that the search warrant, executed by the F.B.I. was obtained as a result of illegal surveillance directed by Government agents. The tape recordings and the evidence secured as a result of the search of Auler's Wisconsin Dells residence should, he claims, therefore have been suppressed.

Auler relies on the principles that Government agents, state or federal, who engage in electronic eavesdropping must comply with the constitutional requirements of a reasonable search, *Katz v. United States*, 389 U.S. 347, 359 (1967), and that evidence, tangible or testimonial, which is seized without adherence to these constitutional safeguards must be excluded. *Weeks v. United States*, 232 U.S. 383, 391–92 (1914); *Wong Sun v. United States*, 371 U.S. 471, 485 (1963). Before we can apply these principles to the case before us, the appellant must demonstrate that the Government was directly or indirectly engaged in gathering the alleged illegal surveillance.

The district court found that the F.B.I. neither initiated nor directed the surveillance conducted by General Telephone. Our own search of the record supports this conclusion. Nor do we find that the F.B.I. participated in or tacitly approved of the interceptions made by General Telephone to the degree that they became a government search. Finally, we cannot agree with the circuitous reasoning that would label the surveillance permitted by section 2511(2)(a)(i) as governmental action, thereby requiring a warrant.

---

[10] Evidence which is obtained through an unreasonably broad surveillance cannot be legally disclosed to the government, regardless whether it is offered at trial.

Auler further contends that the intimate collaboration between F.B.I. Agent Hunter and General Telephone employees Mattila and Nelson constituted a government wiretap, resulting in an illegally executed search warrant. The facts stipulated by both parties do indicate that on August 10, 1973 Nelson informed Mattila that the blue box was being used and that Auler had identified himself during the illegal call. Mattila received this information while he was in the company of Agent Hunter; both men were stationed outside Auler's residence. Upon receipt of this surveillance Hunter and Mattila executed the search warrant and found the blue box.

We are aware, as was the Government at oral argument, that Government agents must not rely on telephone company employees to act on their behalf without complying with the requirements of the Fourth Amendment. In no situation may the Government direct the telephone company to intercept wire communications in order to circumvent the warrant requirements of a reasonable search. The Government may not use their ears for what it cannot do. On the morning of August 10, 1973 General Telephone was engaged in surveillance permitted by section 2511(2)(a)(i). The interceptions recorded by Nelson were part of the continuing effort by General Telephone to gather evidence concerning Auler's illegal use of the telephone lines. The disclosure of this continuing illegal conduct was in furtherance of General Telephone's attempt to protect its equipment.

Based on information supplied by General Telephone, Agent Hunter had secured a valid search warrant. He had asked Mattila to accompany him to identify any illegal equipment found during the course of the search. Mattila's disclosure, just prior to execution of the warrant, that the blue box was being used, was a disclosure of information lawfully acquired through surveillance necessary to protect company rights and property. The surveillance had been conducted independently of any governmental direction. The search warrant had been obtained on the basis of legally intercepted and disclosed information. Consequently, the final disclosure by Mattila cannot transform authorized conduct into an illegal Government search. The trial record and the district court's analysis of these facts can bear no other interpretation.

For the reasons set forth above, the judgment appealed from is affirmed.

NOTES AND QUESTIONS

1. *The scope of reasonable monitoring.* Imagine a system administrator has reason to believe that a computer hacker has intruded into his network from a particular IP address using a particular destination port. Ports enable computers to classify different types of Internet traffic. Every computer server connected to the Internet makes its functions available to those connecting to the server by using specific numbered ports. Different port numbers translate

into different services available on that server. For example, World Wide Web traffic typically is sent at port 80, and ftp (file transfer protocol) commands are sent at port 21. Most Internet packets are assigned a port number, and the port number tells the receiving computer what to do with the traffic when it arrives.

In response to the hacker's intrusion, the system administrator wants to take the following steps:

A.   Record every command from that IP address to that destination port for one week.

B.   Record every command from that IP address to any port for one week.

C.   Record every command to that port regardless of IP address for one week.

D.   Record every command into the network at every IP address and every port for 24 hours.

E.   Install intrusion detection software that will automatically record future intrusions that match known attack patterns common among computer hackers.

Which of these steps fall within the provider exception? Does it depend on the IP address, or how much traffic the network receives on that particular port? Does it depend on the intrusion detection software and how it is configured? Does it depend on what kind of communications the hacker routes through the victim network? What if the hacker sets up a private Internet chat channel from inside the network—can the system administrator monitor the Internet chat communications to identify the hacker?

2.   *Regulating interception and disclosure.* Unlike other Wiretap Act exceptions, the provider exception regulates both the interception and the disclosure of communications. If a provider wants to monitor communications and disclose them to the government under the provider exception, both steps must be independently justified. In contrast, exceptions such as the consent exception focus entirely on interception; when a communication has been intercepted permissibly under the consent exception, the Wiretap Act places no additional restrictions on its use or disclosure.

3.   *The scope of "rights or property."* How broadly should courts interpret the "rights or property" of a provider? Are rights or property limited to delivering communications and protecting the network from attack, or do they extend to the broader purposes of the network and the interests of its owner?

Suppose a university provides Internet services to its undergraduate students living in on-campus dormitories. Can the university justify wiretapping student accounts under the provider exception to protect the safety of its students? May it do so to ensure that the students are not downloading copyrighted materials without permission? Can it monitor accounts to make sure no students are taking drugs? Is the university's interest limited to providing network services, or does it extend to taking care of students?

4. *Fourth Amendment redux.* The *Auler* decision provides a helpful reminder of how statutory and constitutional issues can apply simultaneously in wiretapping investigations. Most network providers are private actors, and therefore are bound by the Wiretap Act but not the Fourth Amendment. As they collect evidence of wrongdoing, however, providers may wish to contact law enforcement investigators either to ask them for help or to forward on incriminating evidence. At some point, the private providers may become state actors under the Fourth Amendment.

Monitoring under the provider exception may raise interesting Fourth Amendment issues if a provider crosses the line and becomes a state actor. For example, does a computer hacker have a reasonable expectation of privacy against the monitoring of his communications inside the victim network? In Rakas v. Illinois, 439 U.S. 128, 143 n.12 (1978), the Supreme Court stated that: "a burglar plying his trade in a summer cabin during the off season may have a thoroughly justified subjective expectation of privacy, but it is not one which the law recognizes as legitimate. His presence is wrongful; his expectation is not one that society is prepared to recognize as reasonable." For Fourth Amendment purposes, is a hacker just an electronic burglar?

Consider the dicta relevant to this issue in United States v. Seidlitz, 589 F.2d 152 (4th Cir. 1978). Recall from Chapter 2 that Seidlitz hacked into OSI, and employees at OSI installed a surveillance tool known as the Milten Spy to recorded the intrusion. After rejecting the defendant's argument that the monitoring violated his statutory privacy rights, the Fourth Circuit added this interesting aside:

> We discern a certain speciousness which infects all of the illegal surveillance contentions made by the defendant with respect to the evidence which was obtained through use of the Milten Spy. Unlike the typical telephone user who employs the telephone merely as a convenience to converse with other persons over distances, Seidlitz used the telephone to tamper with and manipulate a machine which was owned by others, located on their premises, and obviously not intended for his use. In this sense the use by the witnesses below of the term "intruder" to describe an unauthorized user of the computers is aptly applied to the defendant, since by telephonic signal he in fact intruded or trespassed upon the physical property of OSI as effectively as if he had broken into the Rockville facility and instructed the computers from one of the terminals directly wired to the machines. Under these circumstances, having been 'caught with his hand in the cookie jar', we seriously doubt that he is entitled to raise either statutory or constitutional objections to the evidence.

Id. at 160.

McClelland v. McGrath

United States District Court for the Northern District of Illinois, 1998.
31 F. Supp.2d 616.

ASPEN, CHIEF JUDGE.

At first glance, it might seem the very definition of chutzpah for Michael McClelland to sue the City of Chicago and several of its police officers for asking a phone company to intercept a call he made on a cloned cellular phone. The user of a cloned cellular phone—a phone which has been rigged to imitate a legitimate cellular phone—is stealing from the phone company, and phone companies routinely investigate such theft.

The complication in this case is that the officers were investigating a kidnapping, not cellular service theft. Adalberto Valdavia had been abducted, and the officers asked Ameritech, the local telephone service provider, to trace the ransom calls. Ameritech determined that the calls were being made on a cellular line dedicated to Cellular One, and Cellular One informed Ameritech, who informed the officers, that the ransom calls had indeed been made on a cellular telephone and that other calls on the same line had been made almost simultaneously in another part of the state, where the cellular subscriber was located. From this Cellular One concluded that the ransom calls were being made on a cloned phone, and Cellular One indicated that it was able to monitor any conversations involving the cloned phone and to isolate its approximate location. The officers asked Cellular One to relay any information from those calls which might assist them in finding the kidnapper, and Cellular One agreed.

Late that afternoon, someone used the cloned phone to call a lifeguard station and informed the station that he would not be able to come to work that day. Cellular One intercepted the call and relayed the information to Ameritech, who informed the officers, who dispatched other officers to the lifeguard station. (No judge ever approved this intercept.) The officers learned that the caller was Michael McClelland, whom they arrested after securing Valdavia's release. McClelland was incarcerated pending trial on aggravated kidnapping charges, but for reasons unknown to us, his prosecution was terminated.

McClelland learned of the interception during his prosecution, and he filed a complaint with this Court alleging that the officers' failure to obtain judicial authorization for the interception constituted a violation of Title III of the Omnibus Crime Control and Safe Streets Act of 1968, which is codified at 18 U.S.C. §§ 2510–2520 and is popularly known as the "Wiretap Act." The defendants moved to dismiss the complaint on the ground that the Wiretap Act contains an exemption for interceptions by an employee of a phone company who intercepts, discloses, or uses that communication in the normal course of his employment while engaged in any activity which is a necessary incident to the protection of the rights or property of the provider of that service. They argued that since Cellular One intercepted the call and since Cellular one intercepts communications on cloned phones as a necessary incident to the protection of its rights or property, the interception of the call and the subsequent use of its contents was lawful.

The defendants are of course correct that Cellular One is entitled to "intercept, disclose, and use," in the words of § 2511(2)(a)(ii), communications and their contents in order to protect its rights or property. McClelland does not dispute this point—in fact he did not even sue Cellular One. And obviously he would not have had a gripe with the officers had Cellular One intercepted his cloned phone calls on its own and then turned to the officers for assistance.

What the officers do not seem to understand, however, is that *they* are not free to ask or direct Cellular One to intercept *any* phone calls or disclose their contents, at least not without complying with the judicial authorization provisions of the Wiretap Act, *regardless* of whether Cellular One would have been entitled to intercept those calls on its own initiative. This is why the courts in [other cases] go to such lengths to determine whether the phone companies in those cases were acting at the request or direction of police officers.

This case is different, for here a jury could reasonably find that Cellular One was acting as an "instrument or agent" of the government. The officers, after being informed by Cellular One that it could monitor calls made on the cloned phone, asked that Cellular One relay the contents of those calls to them. This shows both that Cellular One acted at the government's request and (ergo) that the government knew of and agreed to Cellular One's actions, two important factors in the "instrument or agent" analysis. In addition, it seems clear that Cellular One was motivated by its desire to help the officers rather than to protect its own property, another important "instrument or agent" factor, *see id.*, as the content of the communication they passed along to the officers—that the caller wouldn't be at work that day—is irrelevant to a cloned phone investigation but is very useful to a kidnapping investigation. *Cf. United States v. Auler*, 539 F.2d 642, 646 (7th Cir. 1976) (telephone companies which intercept calls pursuant to § 2511(2)(a)(i) may forward to the police no more of the content of those calls than is necessary to protect telephone company rights).

It is easy to think that McClelland, the accused kidnapper and confessed cellular service thief, has no right to sue the officers whose jobs required that they find the kidnapper with all possible speed. But anyone who cannot shake this intuition would be wise to recall the sage words of Justices Holmes and Brandeis in an early wiretap case. The former thought it a lesser evil "that some criminals should escape than the government should play an ignoble part," and the latter wrote that "In a government of laws, existence of the government will be imperiled if it fails to observe the law scrupulously," since if "the government becomes a lawbreaker, it breeds contempt for law; it invites every man to become a law unto himself; it invites anarchy." *Olmstead v. United States,* 277 U.S. 438, 469, 485 (1928) (Holmes, J., and Brandeis, J., dissenting). They dissented that day, but their view has prevailed.

NOTES AND QUESTIONS

1.   Imagine the facts of the case above had been different: Upon being contacted by the police, the provider decided to listen in on the call in an effort to combat cloned phone usage rather than to help the police find the kidnapper. Would the outcome of the case be different? What if the provider had decided on its own to monitor the calls to find the kidnapper, and it was never asked to do so by the police? Should the provider's intent matter? Should it matter whether the provider or the police came up with the idea of monitoring?

2.   Did McClelland have Fourth Amendment rights in his telephone call? If not, does it make sense that he should have statutory rights against monitoring? Note that Wiretap Act protections do not hinge on judgments as to whether a particular telephone call implicates greater or lesser legitimate privacy interests. Every call receives full privacy protection, regardless of context.

3.   Imagine that you set up a monitoring system on your home personal computer that records every communication sent from and received by your computer. You leave your computer logged on to an Internet connection 24 hours a day. One day, a burglar breaks into your apartment when you are away; after rifling through your valuables, the burglar decides to take a break and surf the web. He opens a web browser on your computer and visits a few websites. He then gathers up your valuables, puts them in a large sack, and departs. The next day, you return to your apartment and find that your valuables are missing.

Does your use of the monitoring system to record all of the burglar's communications violate the Wiretap Act? Can the burglar sue you under the Wiretap Act for violating his privacy? If not, what exception applies? *Hint:* Look carefully at the elements of 18 U.S.C. § 2511(1)(a).

4.   *The computer trespasser exception. McClelland v. McGrath* raises the possibility that government investigators may not be able to monitor hackers inside the networks of victims even when the victim network providers consent to the monitoring. In response, Congress passed the computer trespasser exception, 18 U.S.C. § 2511(2)(i), It provides:

It shall not be unlawful under this chapter for a person acting under color of law to intercept the wire or electronic communications of a computer trespasser transmitted to, through, or from the protected computer, if—

(I)   the owner or operator of the protected computer authorizes the interception of the computer trespasser's communications on the protected computer;

(II) the person acting under color of law is lawfully engaged in an investigation;

(III) the person acting under color of law has reasonable grounds to believe that the contents of the computer trespasser's communications will be relevant to the investigation; and

(IV) such interception does not acquire communications other than those transmitted to or from the computer trespasser.

18 U.S.C. § 2511(2)(i). The phrase "computer trespasser" is defined in § 2510(21):

"computer trespasser"—

(A) means a person who accesses a protected computer without authorization and thus has no reasonable expectation of privacy in any communication transmitted to, through, or from the protected computer; and

(B) does not include a person known by the owner or operator of the protected computer to have an existing contractual relationship with the owner or operator of the protected computer for access to all or part of the protected computer.

Putting the two pieces together reveals how the trespasser exception works. For the exception to apply, an investigator must already be conducting an investigation, § 2511(2)(i)(II), and must have reasonable grounds to believe that intercepting an intruder's communication will further that investigation, § 2511(2)(i)(III), § 2510(21). The trespasser exception permits investigators to intercept the intruder's communications with the provider's consent, § 2511(2)(i)(II), although the exception does not justify any other monitoring, § 2511(2)(i)(IV). So long as the government is already conducting an investigation, the government can intercept the hacker's communications with the victim provider's permission.

5.   *Honey pots and the Wiretap Act.* Computer security professionals occasionally set up "honey pot" computer networks to test security efforts and understand hacker techniques. A "honey pot" is a decoy network connected to the Internet. To an intruder, the network looks like any other network. In truth, the network is a fake; it is set up with the sole purpose of being a target for anonymous attackers. When hackers try to break in, as some inevitably will, every aspect of the intrusion will be monitored, recorded, and later analyzed.

Does the use of honey pots by a computer security professional violate the Wiretap Act? Can you justify monitoring intrusions into the honey pot under the consent exception? Under the provider exception? Under the trespasser exception? Does the legal picture change if a criminal investigator wishes to set up a honey pot to identify intruders?

6.   Are the Wiretap Act's exceptions too broad? Too narrow? Just right? Given that the Act was originally drafted for the telephone, does it still work well in the context of Internet crime investigations? Or is the difference between monitoring phone calls and monitoring Internet communications too great for the same statute to regulate both contexts?

B. THE CYBERSECURITY ACT OF 2015

The Cybersecurity Act of 2015, codified at 6 U.S.C. § 1501 *et seq.*, amends the surveillance laws by introducing a general privilege to conduct surveillance on one's own network when conducted for a cybersecurity purpose.

The Act is complicated in part because it uses a series of nested definitions. The best place to start is § 1503(a)(1), which states:

> Notwithstanding any other provision of law, a private entity may, for cybersecurity purposes, monitor—
>
> (A) an information system of such private entity;
>
> (B) an information system of another non-Federal entity, upon the authorization and written consent of such other entity;
>
> (C) an information system of a Federal entity, upon the authorization and written consent of an authorized representative of the Federal entity; and
>
> (D) information that is stored on, processed by, or transiting an information system monitored by the private entity under this paragraph.

This provision is in effect until September 2025 unless it is renewed by Congress. *See* 6 U.S.C. § 1510(1).

What does the legal privilege to conduct monitoring in § 1503(a)(1) actually mean? To see this, it's necessary to break down the individual phrases.

The first phrase, "notwithstanding any other provision of law," is important. The Supreme Court has explained that this "clearly signals the drafter's intention that the provisions . . . override conflicting provisions of any other section." Cisneros v. Alpine Ridge Group, 508 U.S. 10, 18 (1993). In other words, the section creates a legal privilege that allows monitoring even when otherwise prohibited by the Wiretap Act.

The Act defines a "private entity" to mean, in effect, a non-government entity. *See* 6 U.S.C. § 1510(15).

The Act defines "monitor" as "to acquire, identify, or scan, or to possess, information that is stored on, processed by, or transiting an information system." 6 U.S.C. § 1510(13). This includes interception as contemplated in the Wiretap Act, meaning that the § 1503(a)(1) privilege acts as an exception to the Wiretap Act. Monitoring for a "cybersecurity purpose" is legally permitted despite textual prohibitions in the Wiretap Act.

But what is a "cybersecurity purpose"? The Act defines a "cybersecurity purpose" as

> the purpose of protecting an information system or information that is stored on, processed by, or transiting an information system from a cybersecurity threat or security vulnerability.

6 U.S.C. § 1501(4). Note that this definition appears to be subjective. What matters is the subjective purpose of the monitoring, not the effect of the monitoring or what goals might seem objectively reasonable.

Embedded in the definition of "cybersecurity purpose" are three more defined terms. First, the phrase "information system" has a complex definition that essentially means any computer or network of computers. See 6 U.S.C. § 1501(4); 44 U.S.C. § 3502.

Second, the phrase "cybersecurity threat" is defined as "an action, not protected by the First Amendment to the Constitution of the United States, on or through an information system that may result in an unauthorized effort to adversely impact the security, availability, confidentiality, or integrity of an information system or information that is stored on, processed by, or transiting an information system." 6 U.S.C. § 1501(5)(A).

Third, the phrase "security vulnerability" is defined as "any attribute of hardware, software, process, or procedure that could enable or facilitate the defeat of a security control." 6 U.S.C. § 1501(17). That definition introduces yet another defined term, "security control," defined as "the management, operational, and technical controls used to protect against an unauthorized effort to adversely affect the confidentiality, integrity, and availability of an information system or its information." 6 U.S.C. § 1501(16).

Putting the pieces together, the Cybersecurity Act of 2015 makes it legal to intercept communications on one's own network, or, if on another entity's network, with the entity's permission, if the interception is undertaken with the subjective purpose of protecting the network from an unauthorized effort to impair the confidentiality, integrity, and availability of the network or information on the network.

NOTES AND QUESTIONS

1.   How should a court determine the "purpose" of monitoring? Imagine a large corporation adopts a monitoring program for its network. Assume the legality of the program hinges on whether it falls within the legal privilege of the Cybersecurity Act. How can you determine whether the monitoring was undertaken for a true cybersecurity purpose versus for some other purpose?

2.   A striking difference between the provider exception in 18 U.S.C. § 2511(2)(a)(i) and the Cybersecurity Act's privilege is that the former has been interpreted to have a scope limitation while the latter does not, at least on its face, contain one. Monitoring under the provider exception has to be reasonable, while monitoring under the Cybersecurity Act just needs to be for a cybersecurity purpose. Would you interpret the Cybersecurity Act to include at least some scope limitation?

Imagine that Mark Zuckerberg, the Chairman and CEO of Facebook, has a terrible dream one night that Facebook's network is being invaded by computer viruses. In Zuckerberg's dream, the viruses were too subtle to be detected by machine. Instead, the only way to detect them was for a person to read the messages of every user to see if any of them indicated an awareness of the virus invasion. Zuckerberg orders that every message on Facebook's network must be read by a Facebook employee to identify if any users know about the viruses. In this (fanciful) hypothetical, the monitoring would be for a cybersecurity purpose. On the other hand, the monitoring would be unreasonable in scope and based on bizarre fears from a bad dream. Does the Cybersecurity Act allow the monitoring?

3.   Imagine that executives at the ABC Corporation are worried that some ABC employees may be copying valuable proprietary data from the company's network and sending it to their personal accounts. To determine if this is occurring, the company intercepts all of their employees' incoming and outgoing communications on the company network. Is this monitoring allowed under the Cybersecurity Act? Is the monitoring designed to catch disloyal insiders undertaken for a "cybersecurity purpose"?

C. THE PEN REGISTER STATUTE

The Pen Registers and Trap and Trace Devices statute, commonly known as the Pen Register statute, is codified at 18 U.S.C. §§ 3121–27. At a very general level, the Pen Register statute can be understood as a non-content cousin of the Wiretap Act. Because it deals only with non-content information, however, the Pen Register statute generally receives substantially less attention than the Wiretap Act. Its prohibitions are weaker, its exceptions are broader, and penalties for violating the statute are modest.

The statute's history explains its rather odd structure. The Pen Register statute was designed as a legislative response to *Smith v.*

Maryland, 442 U.S. 735 (1979). As enacted in 1986, the statute prohibited the installation of pen registers and trap and trace devices without a court order unless a statutory exception applied. In the technological era of the 1960s and 1970s, pen registers were devices that could be installed to record the numbers dialed from a telephone line, and "trap and trace" devices could be used to record the incoming numbers dialed into a phone line. (They were called "trap and trace" devices because collecting incoming numbers originally required the telephone company to trace the phone line using a tool known as a "terminating trap." *See* In re United States, 610 F.2d 1148, 1151 (3d Cir. 1979)). When first passed in 1986, the Pen Register statute regulated the use of the tools that were used to collect "to" and "from" information for telephone calls, namely pen registers and trap and trace devices.

The structure of the Pen Register statute makes sense in light of this history. Section 3121 contains the basic prohibition on the use of a pen register or trap and trace device, subject to exceptions in § 3121(b); § 3122 tells investigators how to apply for court orders authorizing the use of such devices; § 3123 instructs judges on what the orders should look like and what they should say; and § 3124 tells network providers how to comply with the orders. Finally, § 3125 concerns emergency court orders, § 3126 is a reporting requirement, and § 3127 contains definitions of key terms.

The trick to understanding the modern Pen Register statute is the definition of "pen register" and "trap and trace device" in §§ 3127(3)–(4). Section 216 of the USA Patriot Act replaced the telephone-focused language of the 1986 Act with more general language that covers non-content addressing information for both telephone calls and Internet communications. Specifically, a pen register is defined as "a device or process which records or decodes dialing, routing, addressing, or signaling information transmitted by an instrument or facility from which a wire or electronic communication is transmitted, provided, however, that such information shall not include the contents of any communication." 18 U.S.C. § 3127(3). A trap and trace device is defined as "a device or process which captures the incoming electronic or other impulses which identify the originating number or other dialing, routing, addressing, and signaling information reasonably likely to identify the source of a wire or electronic communication, provided, however, that such information shall not include the contents of any communication." 18 U.S.C. § 3127(4).

Putting the new definitions into the old statutory text yields a statute that regulates the collection of non-content "dialing, routing, addressing, or signaling information" for both telephone calls and Internet communications. For example, if investigators or providers install a sniffer device that collects only non-content addressing information such as IP headers, the sniffer device acts as both a pen register (when it collects "from" information) and a trap and trace device (when it collects "to" information). Because Internet communications normally combine "to" and "from" information, the two sides usually work together; the surveillance device becomes a "pen/trap," and the court order permitting the surveillance is often referred to as a "pen/trap order."

In practice, issues involving the Pen Register statute often arise at the same time as issues involving the Wiretap Act. Which statute applies depends on the filter setting of the particular surveillance tool. For example, a sniffer device that collects contents is a wiretap device implicating the Wiretap statute; a sniffer device that only collects non-content addressing information is a pen/trap that implicates the Pen Register statute. A sniffer device that collects both content and non-content information acts as both a wiretap device and a pen/trap, and must be used in compliance with both statutes.

Although the Pen Register statute is a non-content cousin of the Wiretap Act, Congress chose to regulate non-content acquisition very differently than content acquisition. The following case explores some of the differences between the Wiretap Act and the Pen Register statute.

IN RE APPLICATION OF THE UNITED STATES OF AMERICA

United States District Court for the Middle District of Florida, 1994.
846 F. Supp. 1555.

MERRYDAY, DISTRICT JUDGE.

The magistrate judge has twice denied the United States' application for an order authorizing the installation and use of a pen register and trap and trace device. The latter of the two applications, a somewhat supplemented edition of the earlier application, states in part that:

> Applicant certifies that the Federal Bureau of Investigation, United States Customs Service, County Sheriff's Office and * * * * * Police Department are conducting a criminal investigation of * * * * *, owner/operator of * * * * *, located in * * * * *, Florida; employees of * * * * * located at * * * * *, and others known and unknown, in connection with possible violations of, inter alia, Title 21, United States Code, Sections 846 and 841(a)(1), occurring within the Middle District of Florida and elsewhere; that it is believed that the subjects of the investigation are using telephone number (* * *) * * *-* * * *, listed in the name of * * * * * and located at * * * * *, in furtherance of the subject offenses; and that the information likely to be obtained from the pen register and trap and trace device, that is, a caller ID device, is relevant to the ongoing criminal investigation being conducted by the aforementioned law enforcement agencies in that it is believed that this information will concern the aforementioned offenses.

This Court has jurisdiction to issue an order authorizing the installation and use of the requested pen register and trap and trace device in that the actual pen register equipment and trap and trace device which will be used to monitor telephone number (* * *) * * *-* * * * [and] will be installed and used at the * * * * * County Sheriff's Office located in * * * * * County, within the Middle District of Florida.

Applicant knows that there are incoming telephone calls to telephone number (* * *) * * *-* * * * and believes the identification of the calling telephone facility will be relevant to the ongoing criminal investigation and that this information will concern the aforementioned offenses.[2]

The magistrate judge premised his denial on the failure of the United States to advance a factual demonstration that the pen register is likely to disclose information relevant to an ongoing criminal investigation that has a nexus to the Middle District of Florida. The magistrate judge determined that the statute governing the installation and use of pen registers requires a demonstration of qualifying facts sufficient to establish the correctness of both the United States' assertion of this court's jurisdiction and the pen register's purpose and probable results, i.e., the discovery of information beneficial to an investigation with a nexus to the Middle District of Florida. Asserting energetically that the pen register statute envisions only perfunctory judicial involvement, the United States appeals to the district court. The magistrate judge's order is reversed because the application of the United States satisfies the requirements of the applicable statute.

II.

In 1986, Congress enacted 18 U.S.C. §§ 3121–27, which governs pen registers. Section 3121(a) provides, with a few irrelevant exceptions, that "no person may install or use a pen register or a trap and trace device without first obtaining a court order under section 3123 of this title or under the Foreign Intelligence Surveillance Act of 1978 (50 U.S.C. 1801 *et seq.*)." Pursuant to Section 3121(c), the penalty for violation of the statute is imprisonment for not more than one year, a fine, or both.

Section 3122(a) authorizes an attorney for the United States to apply for an order, "in writing, under oath or equivalent affirmation, to a court of competent jurisdiction." First, Section 3122(b)(1) requires the application to include both the identity of the applying attorney and the identity of the law enforcement agency conducting the investigation. Second, Section 3122(b)(2) requires the application to include a certification by the attorney

---

[2]   Because the original of this order is filed *in camera* and relates to an ongoing criminal investigation, any revealing and identifying words are replaced by asterisks.

"that the information likely to be obtained is relevant to an ongoing criminal investigation being conducted by that agency."

Section 3123(a) states that, after a completing an application:

> [T]he court shall enter an ex parte order authorizing the installation and use of a pen register or a trap and trace device within the jurisdiction of the court if the court finds that the attorney for the Government . . . has certified to the court that the information likely to be obtained by such installation and use is relevant to an ongoing criminal investigation.

Section 3124 requires that providers of telephone services and other persons, if the court so orders, must assist with the installation of the pen register. Section 3124(e) provides to any cooperating person a complete defense against either civil or criminal liability, if the person relies in good faith on a court order authorizing the pen register.

A review of these provisions demonstrates that Congress, absent Fourth Amendment concerns, intended to require an identified and presumably responsible official to attest the facts supporting the pen register application. The salient purpose of requiring the application to the court for an order is to affix personal responsibility for the veracity of the application (i.e., to ensure that the attesting United States Attorney is readily identifiable and legally qualified) and to confirm that the United States Attorney has sworn that the required investigation is in progress. Section 3122(b) requires only identification and certification by the official applying for the order. Section 3123(a) requires only confirmation by the court that identification and certification have occurred. No provision appears for independent judicial inquiry into the veracity of the attested facts. As a form of deterrence and as a guarantee of compliance, the statute provides instead for a term of imprisonment and a fine as punishment for a violation.

Requiring identification and certification, but nothing further, admittedly extends only minimal protection to whatever privacy expectations attend the dialing of a telephone number. On the other hand, prompt availability of pen registers usefully expedites law enforcement with no countervailing loss, the Supreme Court instructs, of the Fourth Amendment's protections against search and seizure. In other words, the statute's structure balances the need for accountability, the legitimate interest of law enforcement in advancing a criminal investigation, and the residual privacy interest of the public.

III.

A comparison of the statute governing wiretaps, 18 U.S.C. §§ 2510–21, with the statute governing pen registers demonstrates that Congress intended only minimal safeguards against the unwarranted use of a pen register. The procedure for obtaining authorization for a pen register is summary in nature and the requisite disclosure is perfunctory. In contrast, the wiretap statute provides formidable procedural protections and requires extensive and detailed information in the application. Perhaps most pertinent to this order is the presence of the following provision in Section 2518(2) of the wiretap statute:

> The judge may require the applicant to furnish additional testimony or documentary evidence in support of the application.

No similar provision for additional judicial inquiry appears in the pen register statute, indicating that Congress intended no focused judicial scrutiny of an application for a pen register (at least at the time of the application). The legislative history of the pen register statute contains a similar signal:

> To issue an order [authorizing a pen register], the court must first be satisfied that the information sought is relevant to an ongoing criminal investigation. This provision does not envision an independent judicial review of whether the application meets the relevance standard, rather the court needs only to review the completeness of the certification submitted.

S. Rep. No. 541, 99th Cong., 2d Sess. 47, *reprinted in* 1986 U.S.C.C.A.N. 3555, 3601.

Under Section 2518(1)(b) of the wiretap statute, an application must contain "a full and complete statement of the facts and circumstances relied upon by the applicant to justify his belief that an order should be issued," including details of the offense, the sites of the interception devices, the type of communication subject to interception, and the identity of the person whose communications are subject to interception. Section 2518(1)(c) requires that a wiretap application include "a full and complete statement as to whether or not other investigative procedures have been tried and failed or why they reasonably appear to be unlikely to succeed if tried or to be too dangerous." Section 2518(1)(d) requires a prediction of the duration of the wiretap and Section 2518(1)(e) requires a statement of the circumstances of any previous wiretap applications involving the same person or place. Section 2518(1)(f) provides that, if the application extends a previous authorization, the application must contain "a statement setting forth the results thus far obtained from the interception, or a reasonable explanation of the failure to obtain such results."

By comparison, an application for a pen register includes only the identification and certification required by Section 3122(b). No requirement exists for a pen register applicant to unsuccessfully attempt other investigative techniques or to explain the failure to attempt other investigative techniques. Section 3123(c)(2) permits a pen register applicant to obtain an extension of an authorizing order by providing the same identification and certification required by the initial application. The statute excludes any requirement that an applicant for an extension set forth either the results previously obtained or an explanation for the failure to obtain results.

Other comparisons are similarly instructive. To authorize a wiretap, the court must find (1) probable cause to believe that an individual has committed, is committing, or imminently will commit an offense listed in the statute, (2) probable cause to believe that the intercepted communications will relate to the alleged offense, (3) probable cause to believe (with limited exceptions) that the communications facilities subject to the wiretap are being used in connection with the offense, and (4) that other investigative procedures have failed, are likely to fail, or will be too dangerous. To authorize a pen register, the court need not find any of these facts. The pen register statute contains no requirement for a finding of "probable cause," "reasonable suspicion," or the like.

Section 2518(6) of the wiretap statute permits the court to require periodic reports by the intercepting authorities of the progress of the wiretap. Sections 2518(8)(a) and (d) of the wiretap statute require that the intercepted communications be recorded and maintained both under seal and unedited and that an inventory of the intercepted communications be provided to the subjects after termination of the wiretap. Section 2518(9) of the wiretap statute bars the use of intercepted communications at trial without advance notice. Neither these provisions nor approximations of them appear in the pen register statute.

Section 2518(10)(a) of the wiretap statute provides for suppression of evidence obtained by wiretap [of wire communications] if the evidence was obtained in violation of the statute. The pen register statute contains no exclusionary remedy, and *United States v. Thompson*, 936 F.2d 1249 (11th Cir. 1991), declines to create a common law rule of exclusion.

As punishment for an unlawfully obtained wiretap, Section 2511(4)(a) of the wiretap statute provides a maximum penalty of imprisonment for five years and a fine. As noted already, Section 3121(c) provides that the maximum penalty for violation of the pen register statute is imprisonment for one year and a fine. Section 2520 of the wiretap statute also authorizes recovery of civil damages, including statutory damages of up to $10,000, punitive damages, equitable relief, and recovery of costs and attorney fees. The pen register statute contains no provision for recovery of civil damages.

The breadth and intricacy of the wiretap statute illustrate that Congress, when electing to do so, conceived and implemented formidable safeguards, including extensive judicial review, for the protection of electronic communications. Congress elected to provide only minimal regulation of the use of pen registers. Absent recognized constitutional considerations, the court should create and implement by decisional law no more extensive restrictions on the use of pen registers than Congress has provided explicitly in the governing statute after consideration in gross of all the pertinent factors, not the least of which is privacy.

IV.

No judicial imprimatur on pen registers is required, permitted, or implied under the pen register statute. The court is not asked to "approve" the application for a pen register in the sense that the court would vouch initially for the propriety of the use of a wiretap. Congress asks the court only to confirm that the approved safety measures are observed—that is, primarily, that the responsible persons are identified and accountable if any malfeasance or misprision comes to light and that the nature of that misconduct is readily provable. Undoubtedly, Congress knew that providing to a court false information about the nature of an investigation is an offense which, especially if committed by a United States Attorney, is due for a most unforgiving penalty.

Far from compromising the judiciary, the statutory procedure removes the court from unnecessary entanglement in decisions properly residing in the first instance in law enforcement and prosecuting authorities, yet subject to judicial inquiry at the end of the day. The judiciary is not the daily supervisor of the prosecutor. The judiciary should maintain a sanitary distance from law enforcement. The more the court is insinuated unduly into an *ex parte* inquiry conducted *in camera*, the more the independence of the judiciary is compromised. Serious Fourth Amendment concerns commend, in fact compel, a routinely undesirable, *ex parte* inquiry before the authorization of an arrest, a search, or a wiretap. But this is not so for the authorization of a mere pen register, which presents no privacy issue that rises to Fourth Amendment severity. On behalf of judicial independence, the court is better kept safely apart from the investigatory function unless some constitutional matter (or statutory, if Congress so declares) warrants intrusion. Only in this way is independence and integrity maintained.

The matter of judicial integrity and independence serves, on balance, to separate my conclusion from the magistrate judge's conclusion. He concludes that authorizing a pen register based on no more than the certification of a United States Attorney and without judicial scrutiny breeds suspicion and implies a compromise of independence. I conclude that undue entanglement with the prosecutor, if not required by constitutional matters, breeds suspicion and implies compromise. *Ex parte* and *in camera* hearings, I conclude, amplify those unsavory appearances, if they exist at all.

I conclude that the independence and integrity of the judiciary is best served by preserving, free of any undue entanglement and until a later stage, the oversight function of the court. This is the general rule.

Exceptions appear for an arrest, a search, a wiretap, and for certain aspects of the grand jury's proceedings. However, at each stage for which an exception appears, the constitution appears also. Similarly, if no constitutional or statutory command appears, the courts must conform to the sharply constrained role assigned in pen register cases. To attempt after *Smith v. Maryland*, 442 U.S. 735 (1979), to raise a privacy consideration to sufficient dignity to overcome a direct Congressional limitation is to risk a form of judicial behavior likely to taint integrity more tellingly than the taint, if any, attendant to a mere application for a pen register.

V.

In the present case, the magistrate judge rejected the pen register application because the United States, in his view, failed to show that the pen register is "within the jurisdiction of the court" as required by Section 3123(a). The magistrate judge raised this concern because the pen register, which will be located in this district, will monitor a telephone located in the Southern District of Florida. The magistrate judge required "a factual demonstration that the pen register is likely to disclose information relevant to an ongoing criminal investigation that has a nexus to the Middle District of Florida." He determined that the United States failed to show the qualifying facts.

The court finds that the United States has met the requirements of the statute. The application contains the identification and certification required by Section 3122(b). In the certification, an assistant United States Attorney reports that local law enforcement agencies within this district and federal law enforcement agencies, acting in concert, are conducting within this district and within the Southern District an investigation of possible criminal offenses occurring within this district and elsewhere. Part of this investigation is prospectively a pen register installed in a county within the Middle District of Florida. This certification amply demonstrates that the pen register is "within the jurisdiction of the court." No further factual showing is necessary.

The order of the magistrate judge denying the application for a pen register is reversed. The application of the United States is granted.

NOTES AND QUESTIONS

1.   Should the threshold for obtaining a pen register order be raised? If so, what should the new standard be? Should the law require reasonable suspicion? Should it require judicial review of the facts instead of certification by the applicant?

2.   As amended by the Patriot Act, the Pen Register statute regulates the acquisition of "dialing, routing, addressing, or signaling information" relating to wire and electronic communications. But what exactly is "dialing,

routing, addressing, or signaling information," a.k.a. DRAS? DRAS clearly includes IP addresses, as well as non-content information relating to e-mails. *See* In re Application of the United States, 396 F. Supp.2d 45, 48 (D. Mass. 2005) (IP addresses); In re Application of the United States, 416 F. Supp.2d 13 (D.D.C. 2006) (non-content information relating to e-mails).

But is all non-content information DRAS by default? Or does a category of information exist beyond contents and DRAS that is not covered either by the Wiretap Act or the Pen Register statute? If there is such a category, what treatment should it receive under the statutory privacy laws?

3.   *Post-cut-through dialed digits.* In the case of In re Applications of the United States, 515 F. Supp.2d 325 (E.D.N.Y. 2007), federal investigators sought court orders allowing the collection of all dialed digits entered from a telephone line used by a particular suspect. The orders sought in the applications would have allowed the government both to record the numbers dialed to place the call as well as to record any numbers entered after the call was placed. Such numbers are known as "post-cut-through dialed digits," as they refer to digits entered after the "cut through," that is, the placing of the call. Examples include PIN numbers, account numbers, numbers entered in to navigate the maze of computerized help desks, and the like.

The Magistrate Judge granted the application as to the numbers dialed to place the call but denied the application as to the post-cut-through dialed digits. According to the Judge, digits entered after a call were very likely contents protected by the Fourth Amendment. As a result, the doctrine of constitutional avoidance counseled against interpreting the Pen Register statute as allowing the collection of such information:

> The doctrine of constitutional avoidance is a tool for choosing between competing plausible interpretations of a statutory text, resting on the reasonable presumption that Congress did not intend [an] alternative [that could] raise serious constitutional doubts. This canon is a means of giving effect to congressional intent, not of subverting it. In the instant case, the doctrine is particularly compelling. The Supreme Court has long held that the Fourth Amendment bars the Government from obtaining the contents of communication without a showing of probable cause. Because the Government's reading of the Pen/Trap Statute would violate this long-standing principle, the instant application must be denied.

Id. at 335.

4.   Does the difference between contents and DRAS justify the very different protections of the Wiretap Act and the Pen Register statute? Daniel Solove contends that content and non-content addressing information raise equally strong privacy concerns and should be protected under the same statutory scheme:

> The distinction between content and envelope information does not correlate well to the distinction between sensitive and innocuous

information. Envelope information can be quite sensitive; content information can be quite innocuous. Admittedly, in many cases, people do not care very much about maintaining privacy over the identities of their friends and associates. But it is also true that in many cases, the contents of communications are not very revealing. Many e-mails are short messages which do not reveal any deep secrets, and even Kerr would agree that this should not lessen their protection under the law. This is because content information has the potential to be quite sensitive—but this is also the case with envelope information.

Daniel J. Solove, *Reconstructing Electronic Surveillance Law*, 72 Geo. Wash. L. Rev. 1264, 1288 (2004).

Do you agree? Should Congress come up with a new way to distinguish high-privacy communications from low-privacy communications? If so, what distinction would you propose? Should there be two categories, three categories, or more? *See generally* Susan Freiwald, *Online Surveillance: Remembering the Lessons of the Wiretap Act*, 56 Ala. L. Rev. 9, 69–74 (2004).

5.   The Pen Register statute regulates prospective surveillance but not retrospective surveillance. The textual hook for this conclusion is the exclusion found in the definition of "pen register" in 18 U.S.C. § 3127(3). According to the definition, the term "pen register" does not include:

> any device or process used by a provider or customer of a wire or electronic communication service for billing, or recording as an incident to billing, for communications services provided by such provider or any device or process used by a provider or customer of a wire communication service for cost accounting or other like purposes in the ordinary course of its business.

Although this language is not a model of clarity, it has the effect of excluding retrospective surveillance from the scope of the Pen Register statute. If the government seeks records that were already made in the past and are stored by the provider, those records must have been made "in the ordinary course" of the provider's business for "cost accounting or other like purposes."

6.   *Exceptions to the Pen Register statute.* The exceptions to the Pen Register statute appear in 18 U.S.C. § 3121(b):

> The prohibition of subsection (a) does not apply with respect to the use of a pen register or a trap and trace device by a provider of electronic or wire communication service—

> (1)   relating to the operation, maintenance, and testing of a wire or electronic communication service or to the protection of the rights or property of such provider, or to the protection of users of that service from abuse of service or unlawful use of service; or

> (2)   to record the fact that a wire or electronic communication was initiated or completed in order to protect such provider, another

provider furnishing service toward the completion of the wire communication, or a user of that service, from fraudulent, unlawful or abusive use of service; or

(3)   where the consent of the user of that service has been obtained.

These exceptions are best understood in reference to the analogous exceptions of the Wiretap Act. Starting at the bottom, the consent exception in § 3121(b)(3) appears to mirror the Wiretap Act's consent exception in 18 U.S.C. § 2511(2)(c)–(d). Presumably the same standards apply. The consent exception in the Pen Register statute has a particularly important common-sense application: It makes sure that caller ID services are not illegal. *See, e.g.,* Wisconsin Professional Police Ass'n v. Public Service Commission, 555 N.W.2d 179 (Wisc. App. 1996).

The exceptions in § 3121(b)(1)–(2) appear to create an expanded version of the Wiretap Act's provider exception, 18 U.S.C. § 2511(2)(a)(i). The Pen Register statute's version starts with the common "rights or property" language, and then adds protection of users from abuse of service or unlawful service as well as protection of providers from fraudulent, unlawful, or abusive service. No cases explain how far these exceptions extend beyond the provider exception of the Wiretap Act, but it seems likely that courts would give such language the expansive reading the text suggests.

Although the statute is not explicit on this point, monitoring justified under the trespasser exception of the Wiretap Act for content data apparently would fall within 18 U.S.C. §§ 3121(b)(1)–(2) for non-content information. The trespasser exception requires that the trespasser must have engaged in access without authorization, and such access will always be unlawful and an abuse of the computer service under 18 U.S.C. §§ 3121(b)(1)–(2).

7.   United States v. Freeman, 524 F.2d 337 (7th Cir. 1975), also suggests that exceptions to the Pen Register statute should be construed broadly. In *Freeman*, the telephone company was investigating blue box fraud and installed a Hekimian Dialed Number Recorder (DNR) on the suspect telephone line. The DNR was a type of pen register; it registered outgoing calls made on a paper tape, and transcribed the time of a call, the date, and the number called. When the DNR would signal that a fraudulent phone call had been placed, the phone company would connect a wiretapping device that would record the first two minutes of the phone call. The government then used the device to convict the defendant Freeman of wire fraud.

On appeal, Freeman challenged the wiretapping of his phone calls, but the Seventh Circuit held that the wiretapping was in compliance with the provider exception, 18 U.S.C. § 2511(2)(a)(i). Freeman next challenged the use of the DNR under 47 U.S.C. § 605, a predecessor statute to the Wiretap Act that also covered some non-content information. The Seventh Circuit rejected the argument on policy grounds:

An affirmative answer to this question would lead to an anomalous, if not absurd, result. To arrive at such an answer we would have to conclude that the paper taping operation, a lesser intrusion of privacy, compels suppression while the conversation recording, a greater intrusion, does not.

Freeman, 524 F.2d at 341. If the same reasoning applies to the Pen Register statute, its exceptions presumably are at least as broad as analogous exceptions to the Wiretap Act.

8. As explained earlier, the Cybersecurity Act of 2015 creates a legal privilege allowing monitoring on one's own network for a cybersecurity purpose. *See* 6 U.S.C. § 1501 *et seq.* This legal privilege is effectively an exception to the Pen Register statute just as it is effectively an exception to the Wiretap Act.

9. *Problem.* Sam is the system administrator of a computer network at a small college. One day, a student named Kelly contacts him and reports that she suspects that someone has been breaking into her school e-mail account. Kelly believes that her ex-boyfriend Charles may be the perpetrator, and that Charles guessed her password and is reading her mail. Sam agrees to help. The next day, Sam writes a software program that logs whenever anyone accesses Kelly's e-mail account: the software automatically records the time and IP address of the login. He then writes a program to record every IP address assigned to Charles' account. Over the course of the next 48 hours, Sam's program records 9 different logins to Kelly's account. In three of the cases, the IP address of the login matches the IP address used by Charles's account, indicating that Charles has in fact logged into Kelly's account.

Has Sam violated the Pen Register statute? Would he violate the Pen Register statute if he next began monitoring all non-content information sent to or from Charles's account? If he switched to full-content monitoring, would that surveillance violate the Wiretap Act?

10. Does the Pen Register statute permit wide-scale monitoring, or must the monitoring be limited to a single user or account? Imagine the FBI receives an anonymous tip that an ISP subscriber with the last name "Smith" is a narcotics dealer who frequently e-mails his sources in Mexico to arrange for more deliveries. Can the FBI obtain a pen register order requiring the ISP to monitor all of the e-mails sent from all of the accounts owned by customers named Smith, and to collect the e-mail addresses and mail headers (minus the subject lines) for all of those e-mails? Can the FBI obtain a pen register order compelling the ISP to collect the e-mail headers (minus subject lines) for every e-mail sent by a customer named Smith to one of the major ISPs in Mexico? *See* 18 U.S.C. §§ 3122–23.

11. *Intended and inadvertent collection.* When evaluating the legality of any prospective network surveillance, the first question should be whether the surveillance targets the collection of "contents" or "dialing, routing, addressing, or signaling information." If the surveillance targets contents, the Wiretap Act applies and the monitoring requires a Title III order or an applicable exception

from 18 U.S.C. § 2511(2). If not, the Pen Register statute applies and the monitoring requires a Pen/Trap order or an exception from 18 U.S.C. § 3121(b).

What happens if surveillance targets DRAS, but due to technological limitations inadvertently collects contents? The inadvertent collection will not violate the Wiretap Act, as the Wiretap Act prohibits only intentional interception of contents. *See* 18 U.S.C. § 2511(1)(a). *See also* 18 U.S.C. § 3121(c) (requiring that pen register orders be implemented using technologies "reasonably available" to the government that "restrict[ ] the recording or decoding of electronic or other impulses to the dialing, routing, addressing, and signaling information utilized in the processing and transmitting of wire or electronic communications so as not to include the contents of any wire or electronic communications").

D. THE STORED COMMUNICATIONS ACT

The third statutory privacy law is the Stored Communications Act ("SCA"), codified at 18 U.S.C. §§ 2701–11. The SCA regulates the retrospective surveillance of telephone and Internet communications. More specifically, the SCA governs interactions between government investigators and system administrators in the case of stored content and non-content records.

The SCA shares common themes with the Wiretap Act and Pen Register statute, but it is also very different in two important ways. First, the SCA deals with retrospective surveillance instead of prospective surveillance. In other words, the SCA applies when investigators seek information already in a provider's possession rather than communications in transit. Second, the SCA is considerably more limited in its scope. Whereas the Wiretap Act and the Pen Register statute apply broadly to accessing communications in transit, the SCA only regulates records relating to legitimate customers and subscribers of two specific types of providers.

The heart of the SCA is found in § 2702 and § 2703. The former regulates voluntary disclosure and the latter regulates compelled disclosure. The other important sections for our purposes are the delayed notice provisions found in § 2705, the remedies limitation of § 2708, and the definitions of § 2711.

1. THE BASIC STRUCTURE[2]

The SCA offers network account holders a range of statutory privacy rights against access to stored account information held by network service providers. The statute creates a set of Fourth Amendment-like privacy protections by statute, regulating the relationship between government

---

[2] This discussion is adapted from Orin S. Kerr, *A User's Guide to the Stored Communications Act, and A Legislator's Guide to Amending It*, 72 Geo. Wash. L. Rev. 1208, 1212–23 (2004).

investigators and service providers in possession of users' private information. It does this in two ways. First, the statute creates limits on the government's ability to compel providers to disclose information in their possession about their customers and subscribers. Although the Fourth Amendment may require no more than a subpoena to obtain e-mails, the statute confers greater privacy protection. Second, the statute places limits on the ability of ISPs to voluntarily disclose information about their customers and subscribers to the government. Although the private search doctrine of the Fourth Amendment allows private providers to make such disclosures, the SCA imposes limitations on the circumstances in which such a disclosure can occur.

Entities Regulated by the Stored Communications Act

The focal point of the SCA is the set of network service providers regulated by the statute. The statute creates rights held by "customers" and "subscribers" of network service providers in both content and non-content information held by two particular types of providers. To know whether and how the SCA protects the privacy of a particular communication, you must start by classifying the provider to see whether it falls within the scope of the providers regulated by the statute—and if it does, which category of provider applies. If the provider fits within the two categories, the SCA protects the communication; otherwise, only Fourth Amendment protections apply.

The SCA provides privacy protection to communications held by two types of providers. As the 1986 Senate Report on the SCA explains, computer network account holders at that time generally used third-party network service providers in two ways. First, account holders used their accounts to send and receive communications such as e-mail. The use of computer networks to communicate prompted privacy concerns because in the course of sending and retrieving messages, it was common for computers to copy the messages and store them temporarily pending delivery. The copies that these providers of "electronic communication service" created and placed in temporary "electronic storage" in the course of transmission sometimes stayed on a provider's computer for several months.

The second reason account holders used network service providers was to outsource computing tasks. For example, users paid to have remote computers store extra files or process large amounts of data. (This was in the era before spreadsheet programs, so users generally needed to outsource tasks to perform what by today's standards are simple number-crunching jobs.) When users hired such commercial "remote computing services" to perform tasks for them, they would send a copy of their private information to a third-party computing service, which retained the data for storage or processing. Remote computing services raised privacy concerns because the service providers often retained these copies of their customers' files for long periods of time.

The SCA adopts these two distinctions, freezing into the law the understandings of computer network use as of 1986. The text regulates two types of providers: providers of electronic communication service ("ECS") and providers of remote computing service ("RCS"). The statute defines ECS as "any service which provides to users thereof the ability to send or receive wire or electronic communications," and it defines "electronic storage" as "any temporary, intermediate storage of a wire or electronic communication incidental to the electronic transmission thereof," 18 U.S.C. § 2510(17)(A), plus any backup copies of files in such temporary storage. RCS is defined as "the provision to the public of computer storage or processing services by means of an electronic communications system." 18 U.S.C. § 2711(2). An "electronic communications system" is in turn defined as "any wire, radio, electromagnetic, photooptical or photoelectronic facilities for the transmission of electronic communications, and any computer facilities or related electronic equipment for the electronic storage of such communications." 18 U.S.C. § 2510(14).

The narrow scope of the SCA has two important implications. First, there are many problems of Internet privacy that the SCA does not address. The SCA is not a catch-all statute designed to protect the privacy of stored Internet communications; instead it is narrowly tailored to provide a set of Fourth Amendment-like protections for computer networks.

The second implication of the two distinctions adopted by the SCA is that we need to distinguish between providers of ECS, providers of RCS, and providers that provide neither ECS nor RCS. These distinctions are important because, as we will see shortly, the scope of privacy protections hinges on such distinctions. The distinction between providers of ECS and RCS is made somewhat confusing by the fact that most network service providers are multifunctional. They can act as providers of ECS in some contexts, providers of RCS in other contexts, and as neither in some contexts as well.

In light of this, it is essential to recognize the functional nature of the definitions of ECS and RCS. The classifications of ECS and RCS are context sensitive: the key is the provider's role with respect to a particular copy of a particular communication, rather than the provider's status in the abstract. A provider can act as an RCS with respect to some communications, an ECS with respect to other communications, and neither an RCS nor an ECS with respect to other communications.

What does this mean in practice? Some cases are easy. For example, when an e-mail sits unopened on an ISP's server, the ISP is acting as a provider of ECS with respect to that e-mail. On the other hand, if I author a document and send it via ftp to a commercial long-term storage site for safekeeping, the storage site is acting as a provider of RCS with respect to that file. There are closer cases, however, and some of these closer cases are important ones.

In particular, the proper treatment of opened e-mail is currently unclear. The traditional understanding has been that a copy of opened e-mail sitting on a server is protected by the RCS rules, not the ECS rules. The thinking is that when an e-mail customer leaves a copy of an already-accessed e-mail stored on a server, that copy is no longer "incident to transmission" nor a backup copy of a file that is incident to transmission: rather, it is just in remote storage like any other file held by an RCS.

An example can help explain how the rules fit together under this traditional understanding. Imagine that I send an e-mail to my friend Jane who has an account at a commercial Internet provider. When the message first arrives at the provider, the provider acts as a provider of ECS with respect to the e-mail. The e-mail is in "electronic storage" awaiting Jane's retrieval of the message. Once Jane retrieves my e-mail, she can either delete the message from the provider's server or leave the message stored on the provider's server for safekeeping. If Jane chooses to store the e-mail with the provider, the provider now acts as a provider of RCS (and not ECS) with respect to that copy of the e-mail so long as the provider is available to the public. The role of the provider has changed from a transmitter of the e-mail to a storage facility available to the public, from an ECS to an RCS. If the provider is not available to the public, then the provider provides neither ECS nor RCS, and the remotely stored e-mail now is protected only under the Fourth Amendment. If Jane downloads a copy of the e-mail onto her personal computer, the provider acts as neither a provider of ECS nor RCS with respect to the downloaded copy regardless of whether the provider is available to the public. The provider is not holding the downloaded copy either incident to transmission or for storage; in fact, the provider does not hold that copy at all. As a result, only Fourth Amendment privacy protections apply.

Although this is the traditional understanding of how the ECS/RCS distinction applies to e-mail, circuit caselaw has taken a different approach. In Theofel v. Farey-Jones, 359 F.3d 1066 (9th Cir. 2004), the Ninth Circuit concluded that all e-mails held by a server are protected under the ECS rules until "the underlying message has expired in the normal course," regardless of whether the e-mail has been accessed. This appears to be a fact-sensitive test: under *Theofel*, a server acts as a provider of ECS with respect to a message until both the user and the ISP no longer need the e-mail message. The Fourth Circuit has largely agreed with the Ninth Circuit, taking a relatively similar approach. *See, e.g.,* Hately v. Watts, 917 F.3d 770, 791 (4th Cir. 2019) (holding that "a wire or electronic communication is stored for purposes of backup protection if it is a copy or duplicate of the communication stored to prevent, among other things, its destruction," and that "copies of previously delivered and opened emails retained on the server of the host of a web-based email service" are in electronic storage under this test).

The Privacy Protections of the Stored Communications Act

The privacy protections contained in 18 U.S.C. §§ 2702 and 2703 provide the heart of the SCA. Section 2703 provides the rules that the government must follow when it seeks to compel a provider to disclose information. Section 2702 provides the rules that govern whether a provider can disclose information to the government voluntarily.

A. Compelled Disclosure Rules in 18 U.S.C. § 2703

Section 2703 mandates different standards the government must satisfy to compel different types of communications. To compel a provider of ECS to disclose contents of communications in its possession that are in temporary "electronic storage" for 180 days or less, the government must obtain a search warrant. To compel a provider of ECS to disclose contents in electronic storage for greater than 180 days or to compel a provider of RCS to disclose contents, the government has three options. First, the government can obtain a search warrant. Alternatively, investigators can use less process than a warrant, as long as they combine that process with prior notice. Specifically, the government can use either a subpoena or a "specific and articulable facts" court order pursuant to 18 U.S.C. § 2703(d), combined with prior notice to the "subscriber or customer" (which can be delayed in some circumstances). The court order found in § 2703(d), often referred to as a "2703(d)" order or simply a "d" order, is something like a mix between a subpoena and a search warrant. To obtain the order, the government must provide "specific and articulable facts showing that there are reasonable grounds to believe" that the information to be compelled is "relevant and material to an ongoing criminal investigation." If the judge finds that the factual showing has been made, the judge signs the order. The order is then served like an ordinary subpoena; investigators bring or fax the order to the ISP, and the ISP complies by turning over the information to the investigators.

The rules governing compelled disclosure also cover non-content records, such as logs maintained by a network server. The rules are the same for providers of ECS and RCS and give the government several ways to compel non-content records. First, the government can obtain a 2703(d) order to compel such records. Alternatively, the government can obtain a search warrant instead. Investigators can also compel the disclosure of non-content records if they obtain the consent of the customer or subscriber to such disclosure, and in the rare case that involves telemarketing fraud, they can obtain non-content records merely by submitting a formal written request to the provider. Finally, the SCA has special rules for compelling a subset of non-content records that Congress has deemed less private than other records. These records are sometimes known as "basic subscriber information" because they mostly involve information about the subscriber's identity. The government can obtain the basic subscriber information with a mere subpoena according to 18 U.S.C. § 2703(c)(2).

One interesting aspect of § 2703 is that it generally allows the government to obtain greater process when lesser process will do. If a provision of § 2703 allows government agents to compel information with a subpoena, it also allows them to obtain that information with a 2703(d) order; if it allows agents to obtain information with a 2703(d) order, then a search warrant is also acceptable. Why might the government want this option? The main reason is efficiency. Investigators may decide that they need to compel several types of information, some of which can be obtained with lesser process and some of which requires greater process. The "greater includes the lesser" rule in § 2703 allows the government to obtain only one court order—whatever process is greatest—and compel all of the information in one order all at once.

B.   Voluntary Disclosure Rules in 18 U.S.C. § 2702

The rules regulating voluntary disclosure by providers of RCS and ECS appear in 18 U.S.C. § 2702. Importantly, § 2702 imposes restrictions only on providers of ECS and RCS that provide services "to the public." Nonpublic providers can voluntarily disclose information freely without violating the SCA. Among providers to the public, providers are also free to disclose non-content information to nongovernment entities. For example, a company can disclose records about how its customers used its services to a marketing company. In contrast, § 2702(a) generally bans disclosure of contents by public providers, as well as the disclosure of non-content records to any government entities. The statute then provides specific exceptions in which voluntary disclosure is allowed.

For mostly historical reasons that are of little importance today, § 2702 has slightly different exceptions depending on whether the information to be voluntarily disclosed consists of content or non-content information.

Of the eight exceptions in § 2702(b), numbers one through four are common sense exceptions: a provider can divulge contents if it needs to do so in order to deliver the communication (§ 2702(b)(1), (4)), if otherwise authorized by law (§ 2702(b)(2)), or if the person whose rights are at stake consents (§ 2702(b)(3)). The remaining exceptions deal with specific circumstances in which an individual's privacy rights give way to other competing interests. A provider can disclose contents when disclosure is necessary given a dangerous emergency (§ 2702(b)(8)); when the provider inadvertently discovers the evidence and it relates to a crime (§ 2702(b)(7)); when such disclosure is needed to protect the provider, such as from unauthorized use of the network (§ 2702(b)(5)); and when a provider discovers images of child pornography that the provider must disclose to the police by federal law (§ 2702(b)(6)).

The exceptions for the disclosure of non-content records in § 2702(c) are similar, but not quite identical, to those for contents.

Putting the Pieces Together

Although the rules found in § 2702 and § 2703 can seem maddeningly complicated at first, they prove surprisingly straightforward in practice. The rules for compelled disclosure operate like an upside-down pyramid. Because the SCA's rules allow greater process to include the lesser, different levels of process can compel different groups of information. The higher up the pyramid you go, the more information the government can obtain.

At the lowest threshold, only a simple subpoena is needed to compel basic subscriber information. Higher up the pyramid, a 2703(d) order compels all non-content records. A simple subpoena combined with prior notice compels three categories of information: basic subscriber information, plus any opened e-mails or other permanently held files (covered by the RCS rules), plus any contents in temporary "electronic storage" such as unretrieved e-mails in storage for more than 180 days. A 2703(d) order plus prior notice is sufficient to compel all non-content records, plus any opened e-mails or other permanently held files (covered by the RCS rules), plus any contents in temporary "electronic storage" such as unretrieved e-mails in storage for more than 180 days. Put another way, a 2703(d) order plus prior notice compels everything except contents in temporary "electronic storage" 180 days or less. Finally, a search warrant is needed to compel everything stored in an account.

The rules governing voluntary disclosure by providers are even simpler in practice. Nonpublic providers can disclose without restriction. Providers of ECS or RCS to the public ordinarily cannot disclose either content or non-content information. Disclosure is allowed only when an exception applies: in the case of contents, the facts must fit within one of the eight exceptions found in § 2702(b); in the case of non-content records, the facts must fit within one of the six exceptions found in § 2702(c).

This chart summarizes the basic rules of the SCA under both the traditional understanding and *Theofel v. Farey-Jones*. The first two columns on the left-hand side represent the categories of information under both the traditional understanding and *Theofel*. The columns in the center cover the voluntary disclosure rules for those categories, and the columns on the right-hand side cover the compelled disclosure rules.

Traditional Under-standing	Theofel v. Farey-Jones	Voluntary Disclosure Allowed?		Mechanisms to Compel Disclosure	
		Public Provider	Non-Public Provider	Public Provider	Non-Public Provider
Unopened e-mail in storage 180 days or less	"Unexpired" e-mail in storage 180 days or less	No, unless § 2702(b) exception applies [§ 2702(a)(1)]	Yes [§ 2702(a)(1)]	Search warrant [§ 2703(a)]	Search warrant [§ 2703(a)]
Unopened e-mail in storage more than 180 days	"Unexpired" e-mail in storage more than 180 days	No, unless § 2702(b) exception applies [§ 2702(a)(1)]	Yes [§ 2702(a)(1)]	Subpoena with notice; 2703(d) order with notice; or search warrant [§ 2703(a,b)]	Subpoena with notice; 2703(d) order with notice; or search warrant [§ 2703(a,b)]
Opened e-mail, other content files being remotely stored or processed	Files not covered above being remotely stored or processed	No, unless § 2702(b) exception applies [§ 2702(a)(2)]	Yes [§ 2702(a)(2)]	Subpoena with notice; 2703(d) order with notice; or search warrant [§ 2703(b)]	SCA doesn't apply [§ 2711(2)]
Most non-content records	Most non-content records	No, unless § 2702(c) exception applies [§ 2702(a)(3)]	Yes [§ 2702(a)(3)]	2703(d) order or search warrant [§ 2703(c)(1)]	2703(d) order or search warrant [§ 2703(c)(1)]
Basic subscriber information, session logs, IP addresses	Basic subscriber information, session logs, IP addresses	No, unless § 2702(c) exception applies [§ 2702(a)(3)]	Yes [§ 2702(a)(3)]	Subpoena; 2703(d) order; or search warrant [§ 2703(c)(2)]	Subpoena; 2703(d) order; or search warrant [§ 2703(c)(2)]

NOTES AND QUESTIONS

1.　Although the SCA is significantly more complicated than the Wiretap Act and the Pen Register statute, it borrows a number of their terms. The SCA borrows the terms "wire communication," "electronic communication," "provider," "consent," "necessarily incident to the rendition of the service or to the protection of the rights or property of the provider," and "contents" from § 2510 of the Wiretap Act. See 18 U.S.C. § 2711(1). The SCA also borrows the term "court of competent jurisdiction" from § 3127 of the Pen Register statute. See 18 U.S.C. § 2711(3).

2.　The most difficult aspect of the SCA is the scope of the two types of covered providers, providers of electronic communications service (ECS) and remote computing service (RCS). Before you spend time trying to master the difference, keep in mind that the meaning of these terms will matter only in two discrete ways. First, a threshold decision must be made in every SCA case as to whether the provider is a covered provider under the statute. Second, the difference between ECS and RCS becomes important primarily to determine the scope of protection for opened e-mails. The next few notes take a closer look at these two issues.

3.   *Providers not covered by the SCA.* Computer network operators can be exempt from the SCA if they provide neither ECS nor RCS. Consider the facts of In re Jetblue Airways Corp. Privacy Litigation, 379 F. Supp.2d 299 (E.D.N.Y. 2005). A nationwide class of airline customers sued the airline JetBlue under the SCA for disclosing customer data. The airline had disclosed data from the JetBlue Passenger Reservation System computer to a company that had contracted with the government to explore data mining techniques. The plaintiffs claimed that the disclosure of customer data violated the voluntary disclosure provisions of 18 U.S.C. § 2702. The district court correctly held that JetBlue did not violate the SCA because it was not a provider covered by the statute. First, JetBlue did not provide ECS:

> The term "electronic communication service," as defined, refers to a service that provides users with capacity to transmit electronic communications. Although JetBlue operates a website that receives and transmits data to and from its customers, it is undisputed that it is not the provider of the electronic communication service that allows such data to be transmitted over the Internet. Rather, JetBlue is more appropriately characterized as a provider of air travel services and a consumer of electronic communication services. The website that it operates, like a telephone, enables the company to communicate with its customers in the regular course of business. Mere operation of the website, however, does not transform JetBlue into a provider of internet access, just as the use of a telephone to accept telephone reservations does not transform the company into a provider of telephone service. Thus, a company such as JetBlue does not become an "electronic communication service" provider simply because it maintains a website that allows for the transmission of electronic communications between itself and its customers.

> This reading of the statute finds substantial support in the case law. Although the Second Circuit has not yet had occasion to construe the term "electronic communication service," a number of courts in this and other circuits have done so, some in cases factually similar to this case. The weight of this persuasive authority holds that companies that provide traditional products and services over the Internet, as opposed to Internet access itself, are not "electronic communication service" providers within the meaning of the ECPA.

Id. at 307. Next, the court held that JetBlue was not a provider of RCS:

> Plaintiffs have also failed to establish that JetBlue is a remote computing service. Plaintiffs simply make the allegation without

providing any legal or factual support for such a claim. As discussed, the term "remote computing service" is defined in the ECPA as "the provision to the public of computer storage or processing services by means of an electronic communication system." 18 U.S.C. § 2711(2). The statute's legislative history explains that such services exist to provide sophisticated and convenient data processing services to subscribers and customers, such as hospitals and banks, from remote facilities. *See* S. Rep. No. 99–541 (1986), *reprinted in* 1986 U.S.C.C.A.N. 3555, 3564. By supplying the necessary equipment, remote computing services alleviate the need for users of computer technology to process data in-house. Customers or subscribers may enter into time-sharing arrangements with the remote computing service, or data processing may be accomplished by the service provider on the basis of information supplied by the subscriber or customer. Although plaintiffs allege that JetBlue operates a website and computer servers, no facts alleged indicate that JetBlue provides either computer processing services or computer storage to the public. As such, under the plain meaning of the statute, JetBlue is not a remote computing service.

Id. at 310.

4.   A court reached a similar result to that in the *JetBlue* litigation in United States v. Standefer, 2007 WL 2301760 (S.D. Cal. 2007), a case involving subpoenas issued to compel account records from a payment processing service called "e-gold." E-gold is akin to the popular site Paypal: It allows individuals to make online purchases and send payments. In *Standefer*, account records obtained in the investigation revealed evidence of crime. The defendant challenged the evidence collection on the ground that the subpoenas to e-gold violated the Stored Communications Act. The District Court rejected the challenge on the ground that e-gold was not regulated by the Stored Communications Act. First, the court concluded that the site did not provide ECS:

> The Court concludes that e-gold is not a service which *provides* users the ability to send or receive electronic communications, rather e-gold is a service which *utilizes* the ability to send or receive electronic communications to permit the instant transfer of gold ownership between its users. Therefore, the Government was not required by [the SCA] to utilize a warrant to obtain the requested information from e-gold.

Id. at *4. The court next held that e-gold did not provide RCS:

> The Court concludes that e-gold provides neither computer storage nor processing services, as those terms are used in § 2711(2), to the public. A client of e-gold does not outsource tasks, but rather uses e-gold to transfer gold ownership to other users. Neither does an e-gold customer use e-gold to simply store electronic data.

Id. at *5.

5. *The surprisingly difficult case of opened e-mails.* Courts are presently divided on how the ECS/RCS distinction applies to opened e-mails. The source of the difficulty is the complex definition of "electronic storage" in 18 U.S.C. § 2510(17). This definition is critical because contents in "electronic storage" are the only types of contents held by providers of ECS. In other words, only contents in "electronic storage" receive ECS protections. As a result, the meaning of "electronic storage" defines whether particular contents receive ECS protections or RCS protections.

18 U.S.C. § 2510(17) defines "electronic storage" as:

(A) any temporary, intermediate storage of a wire or electronic communication incidental to the electronic transmission thereof; and

(B) any storage of such communication by an electronic communication service for purposes of backup protection of such communication.

Note that this is a counterintuitive definition. It refers only to a particular type of electronic storage rather than all electronic storage. Specifically, § 2510(17)(A) reflects the very specific function of ECS providers: servers may make temporary copies of e-mails in the course of transmission, and § 2510(17)(A) protects those temporary copies made pending transmission of communications. For example, unopened e-mail in a user's in-box is in "electronic storage," as it is awaiting the user's retrieval of the message.

The difficult question is how to interpret the text of the backup provision, § 2510(17)(B). Consider two possibilities. First, the backup provision may refer to backups made by the provider for the provider's purposes. It is common for system administrators to make backup copies of their files in the event of a system malfunction, and § 2510(17)(B) may simply ensure that the copies of e-mails generated as part of the backup process receive the same protections as originals.

An example shows the role of § 2510(17)(B) under this interpretation. Imagine an ISP makes backup copies of its entire server every night, and criminal investigators want a copy of an unopened e-mail in a particular customer's account. A day after the e-mail arrives, the ISP will have two copies of the opened e-mail, not one: it will have both the original copy in the account and the backup copy. Unlike the original, however, the backup copy is not a "temporary" or "intermediate" copy in storage "incidental" to transmission. It is a permanent copy made by the provider in the event of a system malfunction. Without § 2510(17)(B), the backup copy would not receive the same treatment as the original. Under this interpretation, the backup provision of the definition makes clear that the same legal rules govern access to the original and the backup copy.

Alternatively, the backup provision may refer to copies stored by the user for the user's purposes. After reading an e-mail, users often leave the e-mail on the ISP's server. At that point, the e-mail is no longer stored "incidental to the electronic transmission" of the communication. Users may think of their opened e-mails left with their ISP as "backups" of their messages. Under this approach, the purpose of § 2510(17)(B) is to ensure that opened and unopened e-mails receive the same protection. Opening an e-mail takes an e-mail from electronic storage in § 2510(17)(A) to electronic storage in § 2510(17)(B).

The difference between these two interpretations may seem very technical, but it has tremendous practical importance. Although there are no statistics on this question, it seems likely that most e-mail stored with ISPs is opened e-mail. Under the first approach, opened e-mails are no longer covered by the ECS rules because they are not in "electronic storage." Under the second approach, in contrast, opened e-mails are still in "electronic storage."

So which interpretation is correct? Right now, the answer is frustratingly unclear. The Justice Department and several courts have endorsed the first approach. *See, e.g.*, DOJ Search and Seizure Manual (2002); Fraser v. Nationwide Mut. Ins., 135 F. Supp.2d 623 (E.D. Pa. 2001), *aff'd on other grounds*, 352 F.3d 107 (3d. Cir. 2003); In re DoubleClick, Inc. Privacy Litig., 154 F. Supp.2d 497, 511–12 (S.D.N.Y. 2001). *See also* H.R. Rep. No. 99–647, at 64–65 (1986) (suggesting that opened e-mail should be covered by provisions relating to RCS rather than ECS).

In contrast, the Ninth Circuit endorsed the second approach in Theofel v. Farey-Jones, 359 F.3d 1066 (9th Cir. 2004). *Theofel* involved an abusive tactic in a civil discovery dispute. The defendants sent an overly broad subpoena to the plaintiffs' ISP; the subpoena asked for all of the plaintiffs' e-mails. The ISP responded to the subpoena by providing the defendants with all of the e-mails from the plaintiffs' accounts. Compliance with the subpoena presumably violated § 2703, but the plaintiffs did not sue under that statute. Instead, the plaintiffs sued under 18 U.S.C. § 2701, on the theory that issuing the overly broad subpoena had "accessed" the ISP "without authorization."

Surprisingly, Judge Kozinski agreed. Writing for the panel, Judge Kozinski held that the plaintiff's use of the overbroad subpoena to get information was an unauthorized access, the legal equivalent of hacking into the ISP. *See id.* at 1073–74. (Aside: Do you agree with this interpretation?) Notably, however, § 2701 applies only to contents in electronic storage held by providers of ECS. As a result, Judge Kozinski needed to conclude that the e-mails disclosed—most of which, presumably, had been opened and read—were in "electronic storage."

Judge Kozinski held that the e-mails in the accounts were in electronic storage regardless of whether they had been opened. According to Kozinski, the opened e-mails in the accounts were covered by the backup provisions of 18 U.S.C. § 2510(17)(B):

> An obvious purpose for storing a message on an ISP's server after delivery is to provide a second copy of the message in the event that the user needs to download it again—if, for example, the message is accidentally erased from the user's own computer. The ISP copy of

the message functions as a "backup" for the user. Notably, nothing in the Act requires that the backup protection be for the benefit of the ISP rather than the user. Storage under these circumstances thus literally falls within the statutory definition.

The United States, as *amicus curiae*, disputes our interpretation. It first argues that, because subsection (B) refers to "any storage of such communication," it applies only to backup copies of messages that are themselves in temporary, intermediate storage under subsection (A). The text of the statute, however, does not support this reading. Subsection (A) identifies a type of communication ("a wire or electronic communication") and a type of storage ("temporary, intermediate storage . . . incidental to the electronic transmission thereof"). The phrase "such communication" in subsection (B) does not, as a matter of grammar, reference attributes of the type of storage defined in subsection (A). The government's argument would be correct if subsection (B) referred to "a communication in such storage," or if subsection (A) referred to a communication in temporary, intermediate storage rather than temporary, intermediate storage of a communication. However, as the statute is written, "such communication" is nothing more than shorthand for "a wire or electronic communication."

The government's contrary interpretation drains subsection (B) of independent content because virtually any backup of a subsection (A) message will itself qualify as a message in temporary, intermediate storage. The government counters that the statute requires only that the underlying message be temporary, not the backup. But the lifespan of a backup is necessarily tied to that of the underlying message. Where the underlying message has expired in the normal course, any copy is no longer performing any backup function. An ISP that kept permanent copies of temporary messages could not fairly be described as "backing up" those messages.

Id. at 1075–76.

Which interpretation do you think is most consistent with the text of the statute? Which interpretation is better from the standpoint of policy?

6. *Applying the ECS/RCS distinction to Facebook, Twitter, and LinkedIn.* How does the ECS/RCS distinction apply to the following popular social media sites?

A. *Facebook. See* Crispin v. Christian Audigier, Inc., 717 F. Supp.2d 965, 972–73 (C.D.Cal. 2010) (concluding that Facebook either is an ECS or an RCS and is therefore regulated by the Stored Communications Act); Juror Number One v. Superior Court 206 Cal.App.4th 854, 862–63 (Cal. App. 3 Dist. 2012) (considering whether Facebook acts as an ECS or RCS but declining to reach the issue absent better factual development). *See generally* Allen

　　　D. Hankins, Note, *Compelling Disclosure of Facebook Content Under the Stored Communications Act*, 17 Suffolk J. Trial & App. Advoc. 295 (2012).

B.　*Twitter. See* People v. Harris, 949 N.Y.S.2d 590 (N.Y.City Crim.Ct. 2012) (concluding that Twitter acts as both an ECS and RCS).

C.　*LinkedIn. See* Low v. LinkedIn Corp., 2012 WL 2873847 (N.D.Cal. 2012) (holding that LinkedIn is neither an ECS nor an RCS, and thus is not regulated by the Stored Communications Act).

　　　7.　*Access to stored text messages.* Companies that provide text messaging services sometimes store copies of sent text messages that are generated in the course of transmission. If the government seeks copies of the text messages, which legal framework applies? Are the text messages held in electronic storage by providers of ECS, or are they remotely stored files held as a provider of RCS? In Quon v. Arch Wireless Operating Co., 529 F.3d 892 (9th Cir. 2008), the Ninth Circuit concluded that the text messages are contents in electronic storage held by providers of ECS, not remotely stored files held as a provider of RCS:

> We turn to the plain language of the SCA, including its common-sense definitions, to properly categorize Arch Wireless. An ECS is defined as "any service which provides to users thereof the ability to send or receive wire or electronic communications." 18 U.S.C. § 2510(15). On its face, this describes the text-messaging pager services that Arch Wireless provided. Arch Wireless provided a "service" that enabled Quon and the other Appellants to "send or receive . . . electronic communications," i.e., text messages. Contrast that definition with that for an RCS, which "means the provision to the public of computer storage or processing services by means of an electronic communications system." *Id.* § 2711(2). Arch Wireless did not provide to the City "computer storage"; nor did it provide "processing services." By archiving the text messages on its server, Arch Wireless certainly was "storing" the messages. However, Congress contemplated this exact function could be performed by an ECS as well, stating that an ECS would provide (A) temporary storage incidental to the communication; and (B) storage for backup protection. *Id.* § 2510(17).
>
> In the Senate Report [on the SCA], Congress made clear what it meant by "storage and processing of information." It provided the following example of storage: "physicians and hospitals maintain medical files in offsite data banks." Congress appeared to view "storage" as a virtual filing cabinet, which is not the function Arch Wireless contracted to provide here. The Senate Report also provided an example of "processing of information": "businesses of all sizes transmit their records to remote computers to obtain sophisticated

data processing services." In light of the Report's elaboration upon what Congress intended by the term "Remote Computer Services," it is clear that, before the advent of advanced computer processing programs such as Microsoft Excel, businesses had to farm out sophisticated processing to a service that would process the information. Neither of these examples describes the service that Arch Wireless provided to the City.

Id. at 901–02.

On the other hand, the district court in Flagg v. City of Detroit, 252 F.R.D. 346 (E.D. Mich. 2008), reached a different result in a case involving old text messages stored by a provider long after the account had been terminated. In *Flagg*, the City of Detroit had contracted with SkyTel to provide text pagers to a number of the City's employees. Although the contract with the City had terminated four years earlier, SkyTel continued to store thousands of old text messages belonging to the City. Judge Rosen ruled that SkyTel was a provider of RCS rather than ECS with respect to the text messages that SkyTel was continuing to store:

> In light of the SCA's functional, context-specific definitions of an ECS and an RCS, it is not dispositive that SkyTel indisputably did provide an ECS to the City of Detroit in the past, or that it presumably kept text messages in "electronic storage" at times in connection with the ECS that it provided. Rather, the ECS/RCS inquiry in this case turns upon the characterization of the service that SkyTel *presently* provides to the City, pursuant to which the company is being called upon to retrieve text messages from an archive of communications sent and received by City employees in years past using SkyTel text messaging devices. The resolution of this issue, in turn, depends upon whether SkyTel has maintained this archive "for purposes of backup protection," 18 U.S.C. § 2510(17)(B), so that its contents may be deemed to be held in "electronic storage" by an ECS, 18 U.S.C. § 2702(a)(1), or whether this archive is more properly viewed as "computer storage" offered by an RCS, 18 U.S.C. § 2711(2).

> SkyTel is no longer providing, and has long since ceased to provide, a text messaging service to the City of Detroit—the City, by its own admission, discontinued this service in 2004, and the text messaging devices issued by SkyTel are no longer in use. Consequently, any archive of text messages that SkyTel continues to maintain on the City's behalf constitutes the *only* available record of these communications, and cannot possibly serve as a "backup" copy of communications stored elsewhere. The service provided by SkyTel may properly be characterized as a "virtual filing cabinet" of communications sent and received by City employees. The Court finds, therefore, that the archive maintained by SkyTel constitutes "computer storage," and that the company's maintenance of this

archive on behalf of the City is a "remote computing service" as defined under the SCA.

Id. at 362–63.

8. *Applying the SCA to websites with messaging services.* Modern websites often permit users to create accounts that allow users to send and receive messages with other users. The dual functionality of such websites raises a question: Does the SCA treat the messages sent and received like e-mails that are covered by the SCA, or does it treat them like other website records not covered by the SCA?

This issue arose in Casillas v. Cypress Ins. Co., 770 Fed. Appx. 329 (9th Cir. 2019). Casillas had an account at a website operated by HQ Sign-Up Services ("HQSU"). According to Casillas, agents of the Cypress Insurance Company hacked into his account and stole electronic case files that Casillas had stored in his account. Casillas sued Cypress under the civil provision of the SCA, which applies only to unauthorized access to providers of ECS. The district court ruled that the stolen files were being held by HQSU acting as a provider of RCS, not a provider of ECS, and therefore that the civil SCA suit could not proceed. *See* Casillas v. Berkshire Hathaway Homestate Cos., 2017 WL 2813145 (C.D. Cal. 2017).

On appeal, the Ninth Circuit affirmed in an unpublished opinion using a different and broader rationale. According to the Ninth Circuit, the suit could not proceed because HQSU was not configured properly to provide ECS even though it enabled users to send and receive messages:

> It is evident that HQSU does not permit users to communicate directly with each other. The documents and accompanying comments do not travel directly from the sender to the recipient; instead, the recipient of any message would have to *retrieve* it by downloading it from HQSU's server.

> Because Plaintiffs do not allege that any direct communication takes place, the district court correctly determined that Plaintiffs fail to plead that HQSU constitutes an ECS provider. Plaintiffs argue that the district court drew a false dichotomy between an RCS and an ECS when it determined that HQSU can be characterized only as an RCS. This argument lacks merit. An RCS is an off-site provider that processes and stores data, such as physicians and hospitals maintaining medical files in offsite data banks. In other words, an RCS is a virtual filing cabinet.

> Plaintiffs correctly point out that, in some cases, a single entity may be both an ECS and an RCS. But such a duality will exist only when the service provider fulfills both of the provided definitions; separate analyses are required. Here, even if HQSU's website, database, and servers constitute an RCS, the inability to communicate directly with users leaves HQSU outside of the SCA's definition of an ECS.

Id. at 331.

Does this distinction make sense? What is the difference between messaging services that send messages "directly" from sender to recipient and those that require the recipient to "retrieve" the message from the server? Consider a web-based e-mail provider. On one hand, it is a classic example of an ECS provider. On the other hand, users have to log in to their accounts and retrieve their web-based e-mails from the server. Can the Ninth Circuit's reasoning be correct?

2. COMPELLED DISCLOSURE UNDER § 2703

Section 2703 contains the rules that govern compelled disclosure of stored records. Section 2703(a) covers the requirements for compelling contents from a provider of ECS; § 2703(b) addresses requirements for compelling contents from providers of RCS; and § 2703(c) turns to the rules that regulate non-content records.

UNITED STATES V. WEAVER

United States District Court for the Central District of Illinois, 2009.
636 F. Supp.2d 769.

JEANNE E. SCOTT, DISTRICT JUDGE.

This matter comes before the Court on the Government's Motion to Compel Compliance With Subpoena to Produce Documents. For the reasons stated below, this Motion is allowed.

FACTS

In pursuing a child pornography charge against Defendant Justin Weaver, the Government sought to discover the contents of emails it believes Weaver sent or received at a Microsoft/MSN Hotmail account. The Government submitted a trial subpoena for the records to the Clerk of Court on May 15, 2009, and the Clerk issued the subpoena the same day. On May 19, 2009, the Government executed the subpoena by faxing it to Microsoft/MSN (Microsoft), which accepts such service. The subpoena stated that the Government sought to compel production of "the contents of electronic communications (not in 'electronic storage' as defined by 18 U.S.C. § 2510(17))" and specified that the "contents of communications not in 'electronic storage' include the contents of previously opened or sent email." According to the Government, Microsoft produced some of the information requested, but it failed to produce the content of previously accessed, viewed, or downloaded emails that had been stored for fewer than 181 days. The Government now has moved to compel production of the contents of these emails.

Neither Weaver nor Microsoft has responded to the Government's Motion, but Microsoft asked the Government to include a letter with the Government's Motion. Microsoft's associate general counsel wrote this letter to the Government explaining that it objected to the Government's subpoena to the extent that it requested material that the Ninth Circuit Court of Appeals has held requires a warrant. Microsoft asserts that because its headquarters are located within the Ninth Circuit, it must comply with Ninth Circuit precedent. The Government disagrees with Microsoft's position and has asked the Court to compel Microsoft to produce the materials it requested.

ANALYSIS

The issue here is whether a court can compel an Internet Service Provider (ISP), such as Microsoft, to comply with a trial subpoena and produce the contents of a subscriber's opened emails which are less than 181 days old. Based on provisions of the Stored Communications Act and the Wiretap Act, a Court can.

The Stored Communications Act governs the disclosure of electronic communications maintained on computers. It sets forth the methods by which the Government may obtain electronic communications, such as email messages, from electronic communication services and providers of remote computing services. Here, Microsoft acted as both an electronic communication service and a provider of remote computing services.

Under section 2703, governmental entities must use a warrant to obtain certain types of electronic communications, but they can access others using only a trial subpoena. Subsection (a), which sets out the warrant requirement, provides:

> A governmental entity may require the disclosure by a provider of electronic communication service of the contents of a wire or electronic communication, that is in electronic storage in an electronic communications system for one hundred and eighty days or less, only pursuant to a warrant issued using the procedures described in the Federal Rules of Criminal Procedure by a court with jurisdiction over the offense under investigation or equivalent State warrant.

18 U.S.C. § 2703(a). Where an electronic communication "has been in electronic storage in an electronic communications system" for at least 181 days, only a trial subpoena is necessary. *Id.* Further, only a trial subpoena is necessary for:

> any wire or electronic communication that is held or maintained on [a remote computing] service—
>
> (A) on behalf of, and received by means of electronic transmission from (or created by means of computer processing of communications received by means of electronic transmission from) a subscriber or customer of such remote computing service; and

(B) solely for the purpose of providing storage or computer processing services to such subscriber or customer, if the provider is not authorized to access the contents of any such communications for purposes of providing any services other than storage or computer processing.

18 U.S.C. § 2703(b)(2). Thus, for emails less than 181 days old, the question of whether a warrant is necessary turns on whether the emails are "in electronic storage" or are "held or maintained solely for the purpose of providing storage or computer processing services to [the] subscriber or customer." *Compare* 18 U.S.C. § 2703(a) *with* 18 U.S.C. § 2703(b)(2). If the emails the Government requested here are in electronic storage, Microsoft need not produce them without a warrant, but if they are held or maintained solely to provide the customer storage or computer processing services, Microsoft must comply with the Government's subpoena.

This determination turns on the difference between "electronic storage" and "storage." *Compare* 18 U.S.C. § 2703(a) *with* 18 U.S.C. § 2703(b)(2). Under the Stored Communications Act, these similar terms are not the same. The Stored Communications Act refers back to the Wiretap Act for definitions. 18 U.S.C. § 2711. The Wiretap Act does not define "storage," but it defines "electronic storage" as:

(A) any temporary, intermediate storage of a wire or electronic communication incidental to the electronic transmission thereof; and

(B) any storage of such communication by an electronic communication service for purposes of backup protection of such communication. . .

18 U.S.C. § 2510(17). Because the emails here have been opened, they are not in temporary, intermediate storage incidental to electronic transmission. *See Theofel v. Farey-Jones,* 359 F.3d 1066, 1075 (9th Cir. 2004); *In re DoubleClick Inc. Privacy Litig.,* 154 F. Supp.2d 497, 512 (S.D.N.Y. 2001). The question is whether the emails are in storage "for purposes of backup protection," in which case they are in "electronic storage" and protected by the warrant requirement.

The Seventh Circuit has not addressed this issue, but Microsoft relies on a Ninth Circuit case to assert that the requested emails are in storage for backup protection. In *Theofel v. Farey-Jones,* a civil defendant subpoenaed emails held on the ISP of the plaintiffs' employer. The ISP granted the defendant's attorneys access to emails that remained on its server after users received them through their workplace email program. *Id.* at 1075. The Ninth Circuit concluded that this production violated the Stored Communications Act, in part because it found that the emails were stored for backup protection and thus were in electronic storage. According to the Ninth Circuit:

An obvious purpose for storing a message on an ISP's server after delivery is to provide a second copy of the message in the event that the user needs to download it again-if, for example, the message is accidentally erased from the user's own computer. The ISP copy of the message functions as a "backup" for the user. Notably, nothing in the Act requires that the backup protection be for the benefit of the ISP rather than the user. Storage under these circumstances thus literally falls within the statutory definition.

Id. at 1070. The Ninth Circuit held that once a user receives an email, any version on the ISP's server is a copy that is being stored for backup until the user's version "expires in the normal course." *Id.* at 1070.

The Ninth Circuit's reasoning here relies on the assumption that users download emails from an ISP's server to their own computers. That is how many email systems work, but a Hotmail account is "web-based" and "remote." Hotmail users can access their email over the web from any computer, and they do not automatically download their messages to their own computers as non-web-based email service users do. *See* James X. Dempsey, *Digital Search & Seizure: Standards for Government Access to Communications and Associated Data,* 970 PLI/Pat 687, 707 (2009). Instead, if Hotmail users save a message, they generally leave it on the Hotmail server and return to Hotmail via the web to access it on subsequent occasions.

The distinction between web-based email and other email systems makes *Theofel* largely inapplicable here. As the Ninth Circuit acknowledged in *Theofel* itself, "A remote computing service might be the only place a user stores his messages; in that case, the messages are not stored for backup purposes." Users of web-based email systems, such as Hotmail, default to saving their messages only on the remote system. A Hotmail user can opt to connect an email program, such as Microsoft Outlook, to his or her Hotmail account and through it download messages onto a personal computer, but that is not the default method of using Hotmail. Thus, unless a Hotmail user varies from default use, the remote computing service is the only place he or she stores messages, and Microsoft is not storing that user's opened messages for backup purposes. Instead, Microsoft is maintaining the messages "solely for the purpose of providing storage or computer processing services to such subscriber or customer." 18 U.S.C. § 2703(b)(2). In the case of web-based email systems, *Theofel* generally is distinguishable.

Moreover, to the extent that *Theofel* is on-point, the Court finds it unpersuasive. The Ninth Circuit's interpretation of storage for backup protection under the Stored Communication Act cannot be squared with legislative history and other provisions of the Act. In 1986, drafters of the

Stored Communications Act considered what would happen when an email recipient opened an email but then left it on his ISP's server:

> Sometimes the addressee, having requested and received a message, chooses to leave it in storage on the service for re-access at a later time. The Committee intends that, in leaving the message in storage, the addressee should be considered the subscriber or user from whom the system received the communication for storage, and that such communication should continue to be covered by section 2702(a)(2).

H.R.Rep. No. 99–647, at 65 (1986). Section 2702(a)(2) provides that an entity offering the public remote computing service cannot knowingly divulge to any entity the contents of any communication maintained on the service:

> (A) on behalf of, and received by means of electronic transmission from (or created by means of computer processing of communications received by means of electronic transmission from), a subscriber or customer of such service;

> (B) solely for the purpose of providing storage or computer processing services to such subscriber or customer, if the provider is not authorized to access the contents of any such communications for purposes of providing any services other than storage or computer processing.

18 U.S.C. § 2702(a)(2). This is the identical language used to describe electronic communications that the Government can obtain by trial subpoena.

Thus, if the Stored Communications Act drafters intended emails a user leaves on an email service for re-access at a later date to be covered by section 2702(a)(2), they also must have intended them to be covered by the Government's trial subpoena power. Any other reading fails to reconcile these two sections of the statute.

Previously opened emails stored by Microsoft for Hotmail users are not in electronic storage, and the Government can obtain copies of such emails using a trial subpoena. Microsoft must comply with the Government's subpoena here.

NOTES AND QUESTIONS

1. *Compelling non-content records.* The SCA has two sets of rules for compelling non-content records from covered providers. Basic subscriber information listed in 18 U.S.C. § 2703(c)(2) can be compelled with a subpoena. Compelling other non-content records requires a § 2703(d) order. As noted in the *Kennedy* case, the § 2703(d) standard requires "specific and articulable facts showing that there are reasonable grounds to believe" that the

information sought is "relevant and material to an ongoing criminal investigation."

Congress borrowed the "specific and articulable facts" language from Fourth Amendment law, and specifically the temporary stop standard articulated in Terry v. Ohio, 392 U.S. 1, 21 (1968) ("[I]n justifying the particular intrusion the police officer must be able to point to specific and articulable facts which, taken together with rational inferences from those facts, reasonably warrant that intrusion."). Did the government have enough information to make such a showing in *Kennedy*?

2.   *Legislative history.* The two-tiered approach to compelling non-content records was enacted as part of the Communications Assistance for Law Enforcement Act of 1994, Pub. L. No. 103–414 (1994) ("CALEA"). A Senate Report issued during work on S. 2375, a bill introduced on the way to the passage of CALEA, justified the change on the following grounds:

> In the 8 years since the enactment of ECPA, society's patterns of using electronic communications technology have changed dramatically. Millions of people now have electronic mail addresses. Business, nonprofit organizations and political groups conduct their work over the Internet. Individuals maintain a wide range of relationships on-line. Transactional records documenting these activities and associations are generated by service providers. For those who increasingly use these services, this transactional data reveals a great deal about their private lives, all of it compiled in one place.

> Therefore, S. 2375 includes provisions, which FBI Director Freeh supported in his testimony, that add protections to the exercise of the Government's current surveillance authority. Specifically, the bill eliminates the use of subpoenas to obtain E-mail addresses and other similar transactional data from electronic communications service providers. Currently, the Government can obtain transactional logs containing a person's entire on-line profile merely upon presentation of an administrative subpoena issued by an investigator without any judicial intervention. Under S. 2375, a court order would be required.

S. Rep. No. 103–402, at 17–18 (1994).

3.   *Compelling non-content records, stored versus in real-time.* Note that the SCA requires "specific and articulable facts" for the retrospective surveillance of non-content transactional information, but the Pen Register statute only requires a certification of relevance for prospective surveillance of such information. In other words, government investigators can obtain non-content transactional information more easily prospectively than retrospectively. Does this make sense? Should the standards for prospective surveillance be lower than retrospective surveillance?

4.   *Compelling content records.* The SCA's rules for compelling contents are also two-tiered. The top tier, required when the government seeks to

compel contents from an ECS in electronic storage for 180 days or fewer, requires a probable cause search warrant. *See* 18 U.S.C. § 2703(a). The second tier, required when the government seeks to compel contents from an ECS in storage greater than 180 days or when it seeks to compel contents from an RCS, requires either a subpoena with prior notice, a § 2703(d) order with prior notice, or a search warrant. *See* 18 U.S.C. § 2703(b). Of course, what exactly this covers hinges on how you interpret the ECS/RCS distinction, as noted earlier in the discussion of *Theofel.*

5.   *18 U.S.C. § 2703(b) and the Fourth Amendment.* Under Warshak v. United States, 631 F.3d 266 (6th Cir. 2010), reliance on § 2703(b) is likely unconstitutional as applied to a person who has Fourth Amendment rights. Section 2703(b) may allow access to contents with a subpoena or a 2703(d) order if the contents are stored by a provider of ECS for more than 180 days or if the contents are held by an RCS, but such access is likely unconstitutional absent unusual circumstances. In those circumstances, the Fourth Amendment ordinarily requires a warrant.

6.   *When is notice to the customer required?* The SCA only requires "prior notice from the governmental entity to the subscriber or customer" when investigators seek to compel contents of stored communications from covered providers with legal process lesser than a search warrant. *See* 18 U.S.C. § 2703(b)(1)(B). In all other contexts, no notice to the subscriber or customer need be given. Because the Fourth Amendment generally requires a warrant for contents under *Warshak,* notice will be only rarely required.

Further, the "prior notice" provision is subject to the delayed notice provisions of § 2705(a). The delayed notice provisions permit a delay of notice up to 90 days "if there is reason to believe" that notice would trigger an "adverse result," defined as: "(A) endangering the life or physical safety of an individual; (B) flight from prosecution; (C) destruction of or tampering with evidence; (D) intimidation of potential witnesses; or (E) otherwise seriously jeopardizing an investigation or unduly delaying a trial." 18 U.S.C. § 2705(a)(2). The government may also obtain extensions beyond the initial delay period.

Magistrate Judge Stephen Smith has argued that the Stored Communications Act should be amended so that targets ordinarily receive notice before orders are executed and evidence is collected. In the view of Judge Smith, targets should then have a right to challenge the order before it is executed and to appeal any adverse decisions to the court of appeals and perhaps the United States Supreme Court. Although Judge Smith agrees that investigators should be allowed to delay notice in appropriate circumstances, he argues that the default rule should be notice and an opportunity to be heard. *See* Stephen Wm. Smith, *Gagged, Sealed, and Delivered: ECPA's Secret Docket,* 6 Harv. L. & Pol'y Rev. 601 (2012).

Do you agree with Judge Smith? How much notice is enough? How much notice is too much?

7.   *When is notice to the customer permitted? Gag order provisions and their limits.* Although government notice is rarely required under the SCA, many providers will wish to provide notice to their customers. Some providers have a policy of always notifying customers if it is legal to do so. But can they? 18 U.S.C. § 2705(b) states that the government may apply to a court for an order

> commanding a provider of electronic communications service or remote computing service to whom a warrant, subpoena, or court order is directed, for such period as the court deems appropriate, not to notify any other person of the existence of the warrant, subpoena, or court order.

In other words, the government can apply for a gag order forbidding the provider from disclosing the fact that the government obtained a customer's records. The statute requires a court to enter the gag order "if it determines that there is reason to believe that notification of the existence of the warrant, subpoena, or court order" will cause one of the harms listed an adverse result that would justify delayed notice. *See* 18 U.S.C. § 2705(b)(1)–(5).

The gag order provision of § 2705(b) raises two questions. First, how long is an "appropriate" period during which notice can be forbidden? And second, does the provision satisfy the First Amendment?

Judges have disagreed on the statutory question. Several judges have concluded that an "appropriate" period can be any period—including forever— so long as the judge deems that period appropriate. *See* Matter of Search Warrant for [redacted].com, 248 F. Supp.3d 970 (C.D. Cal. 2017) (Mumm, M.J.) (citing cases). On the other hand, one magistrate judge concluded that an "appropriate" period must have some limit. *See* In the Matter of Grand Jury Subpoena for: [Redacted]@yahoo.com, 79 F. Supp.3d 1091, 1093 (N.D. Cal. 2015 (Grewal, M.J.).

Several recent decisions have identified First Amendment difficulties with the gag order provision of § 2705(b). *See, e.g.*, Microsoft Corporation v. United States Department of Justice, 233 F. Supp.3d 887, 906–912 (W.D.Wash. 2017); Matter of Search Warrant for [redacted].com, 2017 WL 1450314 at *7 (citing cases). Several courts have reasoned that § 2705(b) acts as a content-based restriction on speech because it is premised on the harms that a specific message would cause. As such, the restrictions must satisfy strict scrutiny. *See id.* at *7–*9. Left unclear, however, is the remedy. One court has found that a 180 day gag order satisfies strict scrutiny although an indefinite gag would not. *See id.* Another court ruled that indefinite gag orders ordinarily violate the First Amendment but did not establish what time limit might be permissible. *See Matter of Grand Jury Subpoena for: [Redacted]@yahoo.com*, 579 F. Supp.3d at 1094–95.

In response to these uncertainties, the Justice Department introduced a new policy governing § 2705(b) orders in October 2017. *See* U.S. Department of Justice, Policy Regarding Applications for Protective Orders Pursuant to 18

U.S.C. § 2705(b), October 19, 2017, available at https://www.justice.gov/criminal-ccips/page/file/1005791/download. Under the policy, federal prosecutors should only seek a § 2705(b) order "when circumstances require" it based on "an individualized and meaningful assessment." Further, federal prosecutors may only seek to delay notice for up to one year "barring exceptional circumstances." *Id.*

For more on the First Amendment limits of § 2705(b) orders, *see* In re Application of Subpoena 2018R00776, 947 F.3d 148 (3d Cir. 2020) (holding that § 2705(b) orders are content-based restrictions subject to strict scrutiny, but that a one-year § 2705(b) order accompanying grand jury subpoena passes strict scrutiny because it serves the compelling interest of "protecting the secrecy of an investigation" is narrowly tailored, and is the least restrictive means).

8. *Preservation requests.* 18 U.S.C. § 2703(f) permits investigators to notify providers that they plan to seek a court order requiring the disclosure of particular records. Providers must then "take all necessary steps" to preserve those records. 18 U.S.C. § 2703(f)(1). As the Justice Department explains:

> Some providers retain records for months, others for hours, and others not at all. As a practical matter, this means that evidence may be destroyed or lost before law enforcement can obtain the appropriate legal order compelling disclosure. For example, agents may learn of a child pornography case on Day 1, begin work on a search warrant on Day 2, obtain the warrant on Day 5, and then learn that the network service provider deleted the records in the ordinary course of business on Day 3. To minimize this risk, ECPA permits the government to direct providers to "freeze" stored records and communications pursuant to 18 U.S.C. § 2703(f).

Searching and Seizing Computers (2002). Importantly, the authority under § 2703(f) has no prospective effect. Providers must preserve records already generated in the ordinary course of business, but the authority does not permit investigators to request prospective monitoring.

Does a preservation request raise Fourth Amendment issues? Imagine the government issues a request directing a provider to "freeze" the contents of the suspect's e-mail account while the government seeks a warrant. In response, the provider generates a copy of the suspect's e-mail account and holds it for the government. Does that copying amount to a Fourth Amendment seizure of the suspect's e-mails? If it is, consider the constitutional implications if there is very little cause for a particular request or the government delays for months before applying for a warrant. Is that seizure unreasonable under the Fourth Amendment?

9. *A hypothetical.* Assume that an ISP retains the following information relating to an Internet account:

A. name, address, home phone number, and credit card number

B. login records for the last 30 days

    C.　records of IP addresses assigned to that account for 20 days

    D.　e-mail addresses associated with that account

    E.　"buddy list" of other accounts belonging to friends of the subscriber

    F.　opened e-mails received a year ago

    G.　unopened e-mails received a year ago

    H.　opened e-mails received the previous day

    I.　unopened e-mails received the previous day

    J.　copies of all outgoing e-mails for the last year

What legal process must the government use under the SCA to compel the ISP to disclose these records? In which cases does the answer hinge on whether you adopt the Justice Department's or the Ninth Circuit's approach to the ECS/RCS distinction?

    10. *Can attorneys for a criminal defendant obtain § 2703(d) orders in the course of trial preparation?* In United States v. Amawi, 552 F. Supp.2d 679 (N.D. Ohio 2008), the Office of the Federal Public Defender in the Northern District of Ohio sought to obtain such an order. The court rejected the application on the ground that the Office of the Federal Public Defender was not a "government entity":

> 18 U.S.C. § 2703(d) permits disclosure by a provider to a "government entity" upon court order. Defendant claims that, as part of the United States Courts, the Office of the Federal Public Defender is a "government entity" which can seek a court order compelling production of electronic communications.
>
> The government contends, and its contention is well taken, that the Office of the Federal Public Defender is not a "government entity" within the meaning of § 2703. "Government entity" is defined in 18 U.S.C. § 2711(4), as "a department or agency of the United States or any State or political subdivision thereof." The judiciary is not a department or agency of the United States; thus, the judiciary and its components, including the Federal Public Defender, cannot obtain a court order under § 2703(d).

Id. at 680.

    11. *Does § 2703(d) confer discretion on magistrate judges to require warrants?* When investigators seek to collect evidence under 18 U.S.C. § 2703(d), do individual magistrate judges have the discretion to deny the application and instead require the government to seek a warrant based on probable cause? Or does the magistrate judge have to sign the § 2703(d) order if the statutory threshold has been satisfied? 18 U.S.C. § 2703(d) provides, with emphasis added:

> A court order for disclosure under subsection (b) or (c) *may* be issued
> by any court that is a court of competent jurisdiction and shall issue
> only if the governmental entity offers specific and articulable facts
> showing that there are reasonable grounds to believe that the
> contents of a wire or electronic communication, or the records or other
> information sought, are relevant and material to an ongoing criminal
> investigation.

There are two ways to interpret the italicized word "may" in the above
sentence. The more common understanding has been that the word grants
judges the power to issue orders. Courts do not have an inherent power to issue
court orders, and the quoted language above empowers courts to issue
§ 2703(d) orders when the government establishes the necessary cause.
Alternatively, perhaps the word "may" is a grant of power to deny orders rather
than to issue them. On this reading, § 2703(d) gives judges the discretion to
decide whether they will grant or deny applications for § 2703(d) orders when
the government applies for such an order and establishes the necessary cause.

Courts have divided over the proper interpretation. In one case, In re
Application of U.S. for an Order Directing a Provider of Electronic
Communication Service to Disclose Records to Government, 620 F.3d 304 (3d
Cir. 2010), the Third Circuit concluded that magistrates have the discretion to
reject the application and require a warrant:

> We focus first on the language that an order "may be issued" if the
> appropriate standard is met. This is the language of permission,
> rather than mandate. If Congress wished that courts "shall," rather
> than "may," issue § 2703(d) orders whenever the intermediate
> standard is met, Congress could easily have said so. At the very least,
> the use of "may issue" strongly implies court discretion, an
> implication bolstered by the subsequent use of the phrase "only if" in
> the same sentence.

> The Government argues that when the statutory scheme is read as a
> whole, it supports a finding that a magistrate judge does not have
> "arbitrary" discretion to require a warrant. We agree that a
> magistrate judge does not have arbitrary discretion. Indeed, no judge
> in the federal courts has arbitrary discretion to issue an order. Orders
> of a magistrate judge must be supported by reasons that are
> consistent with the standard applicable under the statute at issue.

> Because the statute as presently written gives the MJ the option to
> require a warrant showing probable cause, we are unwilling to
> remove that option although it is an option to be used sparingly
> because Congress also included the option of a § 2703(d) order.

On the other hand, in In re Application of the United States for an Order
Pursuant to 18 U.S.C. 2703(d), 830 F. Supp.2d 114 (E.D.Va. 2011), the District
Court rejected the Third Circuit's interpretation and held that magistrate
judges have no such discretion:

On a grammatical level, the Third Circuit's interpretation incorrectly treats the phrase "may be issued" as if it governs the rest of the first sentence of § 2703(d), when in fact it governs only the first independent clause of the first sentence. 18 U.S.C. § 2703(d). The provision that the order "may be issued" is enabling language that allows the government to seek an order in any court of competent jurisdiction. The next sentence in the paragraph confirms that "may be issued" governs the question of who can issue the order because "and shall issue only if" establishes the appropriate action once the government has satisfied its factual predicate. Moreover, the fact that a state governmental authority "shall not issue" an order when state law forbids it makes clear that the default rule is issuance. When viewed in this way, it is clear that the general rule is that the judicial officer "shall issue" an order that meets the factual burden.

Petitioners argue, as did the Third Circuit, that this does not end the inquiry because the phrase includes the words "only if." The Third Circuit relied on a prior case holding that the phrase "only if" established a necessary but not sufficient condition. The Court agrees that "only if" serves that function here. The fact that "only if" creates a necessary but not sufficient condition, however, does not automatically create a gap in the statute that should be filled with judicial discretion. The Court considers it more likely that the "only if" language in § 2703(d) clarifies that any conditions established by (b) and (c) are cumulative with respect to the standard set forth in paragraph (d). The default rule remains that the judicial officer "shall issue" an order when the government meets its burden.

Id. at 147–48.

Which is the more persuasive reading as a matter of statutory interpretation? And which is a preferable reading as a matter of policy? On the policy question, consider whether it makes sense to give each individual magistrate judge the power to effectively create the law in each case as to what level of cause the judge will require the government to satisfy. Relatedly, consider how magistrate judges in the Third Circuit should interpret the guidance to require a warrant "sparingly," and what reasons to demand a warrant should count as reasons "consistent with the standard applicable under the statute at issue."

On the other hand, if judges must issue a § 2703(d) order when the government establishes specific and articulable facts, what should a judge do if the government applies for a § 2703(d) order but the magistrate judge concludes that the information sought is protected by the Fourth Amendment? Does the judge have the power to deny the application on the ground that the judge fears that the order would be executed in a way that would violate the Fourth Amendment? Note that under the alternative reading, the judge has a ready course of action: The judge can demand a warrant on the grounds that the Fourth Amendment requires one and that § 2703(d) confers the discretion to deny the application based on the lower threshold.

3. VOLUNTARY DISCLOSURE UNDER § 2702

The SCA's rules that regulate voluntary disclosure by providers appear in 18 U.S.C. § 2702. The first important question under § 2702 is whether the provider provides services "to the public." If the provider does not provide services to the public, disclosure is allowed. If the services are provided to the public, the next question is whether voluntary disclosure is allowed pursuant to one of the exceptions found in §§ 2702(b)–(c). The following two cases consider these two issues in turn.

ANDERSEN CONSULTING LLP v. UOP

United States District Court for the Northern District of Illinois, 1998.
991 F. Supp. 1041.

BUCKLO, DISTRICT JUDGE.

Plaintiff, Andersen Consulting LLP, brought an eight count complaint against the defendants, UOP and its counsel, the law firm of Bickel & Brewer. Andersen alleges that the defendants knowingly divulged, or caused to be divulged, the contents of Andersen's e-mail messages in violation of the Electronic Communications Privacy Act, 18 U.S.C. § 2701 *et seq.* For the reasons set forth below, the defendants' motion to dismiss is granted.

UOP hired Andersen to perform a systems integration project in 1992. During the project, Andersen employees had access to and used UOP's internal e-mail system to communicate with each other, with UOP, and with third parties.

Dissatisfied with Andersen's performance, UOP terminated the project in December 1993. Subsequently UOP hired Bickel and Brewer and brought suit in Connecticut state court charging Andersen with breach of contract, negligence, and fraud. Andersen countersued in two different suits for defamation.

While these three cases were pending, UOP and Bickel and Brewer divulged the contents of Andersen's e-mail messages on UOP's e-mail system to the *Wall Street Journal*. The *Journal* published an article on June 19, 1997 titled "E-Mail Trail Could Haunt Consultant in Court." The article excerpted some of Andersen's e-mail messages made during the course of its assignment at UOP. This disclosure of the e-mail messages and their subsequent publication is the basis of this suit.

18 U.S.C. § 2702(a)(1) states that "a person or entity providing an electronic communication service to the public shall not knowingly divulge to any person or entity the contents of a communication while in electronic

storage by that service." Andersen claims that the defendants violated this section by knowingly divulging the contents of its e-mail message to the Wall Street Journal.

To be liable for the disclosure of Andersen's e-mail messages, UOP must fall under the purview of the Act: UOP must provide "electronic communication service to the public." 18 U.S.C. § 2702(a)(1). The statute defines "electronic communication service" as "any service which provides to users thereof the ability to send or receive wire or electronic communications." 18 U.S.C. § 2510(15). The statute does not define "public." The word "public," however, is unambiguous. Public means the "aggregate of the citizens" or "everybody" or "the people at large" or "the community at large." *Black's Law Dictionary* 1227 (6th ed. 1990). Thus, the statute covers any entity that provides electronic communication service (e.g., e-mail) to the community at large.

Andersen attempts to render the phrase "to the public" superfluous by arguing that the statutory language indicates that the term "public" means something other than the community at large. It claims that if Congress wanted public to mean the community at large, it would have used the term "general public." However, the fact that Congress used both "public" and "general public" in the same statute does not lead to the conclusion that Congress intended public to have any other meaning than its commonly understood meaning. *Compare* 18 U.S.C. § 2511(2)(g) (using the term "general public") *with* §§ 2511(2)(a)(i), (3)(a), (3)(b), (4)(c)(ii) (using the term "public").

Andersen argues that the legislative history indicates that a provider of electronic communication services is subject to Section 2702 even if that provider maintains the system primarily for its own use and does not provide services to the general public. This legislative history argument is misguided. A court's starting point to determine the intent of Congress is the language of the statute itself. If the language is clear and unambiguous, the court must give effect to the plain meaning of the statute. Since the meaning of "public" is clear, there is no need to resort to legislative history.

Even if the language was somehow ambiguous, the legislative history does not support Andersen's interpretation. The legislative history indicates that there is a distinction between public and proprietary. In describing "electronic mail," the legislative history stated that "electronic mail systems may be available for public use or may be proprietary, such as systems operated by private companies for internal correspondence." S. Rep. No. 99–541, at 8 (1986), *reprinted in* 1986 U.S.C.C.A.N. 3555, 3562. Thus, Andersen must show that UOP's electronic mail system was available for public use.

In its complaint, Andersen alleges that UOP "is a general partnership which licenses process technologies and supplies catalysts, specialty chemicals, and other products to the petroleum refining, petrochemical, and gas processing industries." Complaint ¶ 3. UOP is not in the business of providing electronic communication services. It does, however, have an e-mail system for internal communication as e-mail is a necessary tool for almost any business today. *See State Wide Photocopy v. Tokai Fin. Servs., Inc.*, 909 F. Supp. 137, 145 (S.D.N.Y. 1995) (finding that defendant was in the business of financing and that the mere use of fax machines and computers, as necessary tools of business, did not make it an electronic communication service provider).

UOP hired Andersen to provide services in connection with the integration of certain computer systems. As part of the project, "UOP provided an electronic communication service for Andersen to use. That electronic communication service could be used, and was used by Andersen and UOP personnel, to electronically communicate with (*i.e.*, send e-mail messages to, and receive e-mail messages from) other Andersen personnel, UOP personnel, third-party vendors and other third-parties both in and outside of Illinois." Complaint ¶ 10.

Based on these allegations, Andersen claims that UOP provides an electronic communication service to the public. However, giving Andersen access to its e-mail system is not equivalent to providing e-mail to the public. Andersen was hired by UOP to do a project and as such, was given access to UOP's e-mail system similar to UOP employees. Andersen was not any member of the community at large, but a hired contractor. Further, the fact that Andersen could communicate to third-parties over the internet and that third-parties could communicate with it did not mean that UOP provided an electronic communication service to the public. UOP's internal e-mail system is separate from the internet. UOP must purchase internet access from an electronic communication service provider like any other consumer; it does not independently provide internet services.

NOTES AND QUESTIONS

1.   *Disclosure of university e-mails to law enforcement.* A pair of recent Third Circuit decisions deals with an interesting twist on voluntarily disclosure. Here's the question: If law enforcement officials go to a university seeking an university employee's e-mails, and the university officials are willing to turn them over if they get some kind of legal process, how does the SCA apply if the law enforcement officials provide invalid legal process before the university turns over the e-mails?

This issue arose in a dispute involving Pennsylvania State University that led to two Third Circuit decisions, Walker v. Coffey, 905 F.3d 138 (3d Cir. 2018) (*Walker I*) and Walker v. Coffey, 956 F.3d 163 (3d Cir. 2020) (*Walker II*). Pennsylvania state law enforcement officials sought e-mails from Penn State about a Penn State employee, Carol Walker, as part of an investigation into crimes believed to have been committed by Walker's husband.

The officials first approached the university and asked the university employees to voluntarily disclose Walker's e-mails under § 2702. The university employees balked, telling the officials that they instead wanted some kind of formal documentation. In response, the officials obtained a blank subpoena form from a local court which they filled out only in part. Much of the subpoena was left blank. The officials then sent the partly blank subpoena to the Penn State General Counsel's Office. The General Counsel's Office was satisfied and disclosed Walker's e-mails to the officials.

When the criminal investigation into Walker was later dropped without charges, Walker sued the officials under (among other things) the SCA. The Third Circuit ruled that the SCA was not violated. In *Walker I*, the court ruled that the disclosure of the e-mails to the officials was voluntary, not compelled:

> Upon receipt of the subpoena, Penn State exercised its independent authority to consent to a search and produced Walker's work emails. Penn State was not merely a private party induced to perform a search; rather, it was a third party with common authority over Walker's emails and the independent ability to consent to a search. As alleged in Walker's complaint, Appellees presented the subpoena to Penn State's Assistant General Counsel. Rather than contest the validity of the subpoena or otherwise limit any search, the Assistant General Counsel instructed an employee in her office to assist with the production of Walker's emails. That decision was within the authority of Penn State—acting through its attorney—as Walker's employer.

Walker I, 905 F.3d at 149–50.

In *Walker II*, the court ruled that the voluntary disclosure of Walker's e-mails made the disclosure lawful because Penn State does not provide services to the public:

> Given that Penn State acted voluntarily, we note that the disclosure of Walker's emails is governed by section 2702 of the SCA, aptly titled "Voluntary disclosure of customer communications or records." Section 2702 requires electronic communication service providers to keep communications confidential unless a court order, warrant, or subpoena is produced. However, these restrictions apply only to providers offering services *"to the public."* 18 U.S.C. § 2702(a)(1) (emphasis added).

> Penn State offers electronic communication services to its employees, not to the community at large. Walker's work emails, therefore, fall outside of the scope of the SCA's protection. Because the Act did not restrict Penn State from voluntarily providing [the officials] with the requested emails from its server, we will affirm the District Court's finding that Walker failed to state a cause of action under the SCA.

Walker II, 956 F.3d at 170–71.

    2.   *Why doesn't the SCA impose restrictions on voluntary disclosure by non-public providers?* Here is some speculation:

> Nonpublic accounts may exist more for the benefit of providers than for the benefit of users. For example, companies often provide e-mail accounts to employees for work-related purposes; the U.S. military often provides accounts to service members for official government business. These nonpublic providers generally have a legitimate interest in controlling and accessing the accounts they provide to users. Plus, their users tend to recognize that the providers will view those provider interests as more important than the privacy interests of users.

> In contrast, an individual who contracts with a commercial ISP available to the public usually does so solely for his own benefit. The account belongs to the user, not the provider. As a result, the user may understandably rely more heavily on the privacy of the commercial account from the public provider rather than another account with a nonpublic provider. Many Internet users have experienced this dynamic. When an e-mail exchange using a work account turns to private matters, it is common for a user to move the discussion to a commercial account. "I don't want my boss to read this," a user might note, "I'll e-mail you from my personal account later." The law recognizes this distinction by drawing a line between accounts held with public and nonpublic providers. In practice, the public/nonpublic line often acts as a proxy for the distinction between a user's private account and one assigned to him by his employer.

> A related explanation for this distinction is that private providers with a relationship to their users may approach their users' privacy differently than would commercial providers available to the public. To a commercial ISP, a particular customer is a source of revenue, no more and no less. In contrast, nonpublic providers may have a long-term, multifaceted relationship with their users, giving nonpublic providers unique incentives to protect the privacy of their users. The law may wish to protect privacy more heavily in the case of public providers because there is less incentive for public providers to protect their users' privacy. Alternatively, the law may take a more hands-off approach with respect to nonpublic providers in recognition of the different relationships that nonpublic providers may have with their users.

Orin S. Kerr, *A User's Guide to the Stored Communications Act, and A Legislator's Guide to Amending It*, 72 Geo. Wash. L. Rev. 1208, 1226–27 (2004).

    Assuming this explanation is right as a descriptive matter, is the argument persuasive as a normative matter? Should § 2702 be amended to restrict disclosures by all providers? If an account exists for the provider's purposes rather than the user's, won't the provider obtain the user's consent to disclosure? Why not set a pro-privacy default and permit providers to contract around it?

3. *Does content moderation eliminate the § 2702 non-disclosure rule?* Social media providers like Facebook and Twitter often engage in content moderation. They may ban a user account, or delete particular files, that violate their terms of service. Imagine a social media company deletes an account or file while exercising its content moderation role, but that the company opts to store for its own purposes a copy of the data that (from the user's perspective) was deleted. Does § 2702 continue to apply to the stored copy? Or is the company no longer acting as either an ECS or an RCS with respect to that data, so that the SCA doesn't apply and the moderated data can now be disclosed? *See* Republic of the Gambia v. Facebook, 2021 WL 4304851 (D.D.C. 2021) (Faruqui, M.J.) (concluding that § 2702 does not apply to provider-deleted accounts because the provider is no longer acting as an ECS or an RCS).

JAYNE V. SPRINT PCS

United States District Court for the Eastern District of California, 2009.
2009 WL 426117.

GREGORY G. HOLLOWS, UNITED STATES MAGISTRATE JUDGE.

Plaintiff, a state prisoner proceeding pro se, seeks relief pursuant to 42 U.S.C. § 1983.

[According to the plaintiff's complaint,] a Miss Shanda Kessler went to the Anderson police to file a restraining order against plaintiff. [According to the complaint, Anderson police] coerced Kessler into saying plaintiff had held her against her will for six hours.

These officers then sent an exigent circumstances request/demand to plaintiff's cell phone provider, saying that plaintiff was wanted for kidnapping and that the cell phone service was to provide plaintiff's cell phone records and GPS location. Plaintiff asserts that this request/demand was made "without a warrant or real cause," and claims that defendant Sprint PCS provided the cell phone records to the Anderson police "based on this false and illegal pretense."

Defendant Sprint identifies itself as a wireless communications company having customers in every state, including California, and acknowledges that plaintiff was one such customer. Further, Sprint accepts as true plaintiff's allegation that Sprint provided plaintiff's cell phone records to defendants upon a demand/request by [the Anderson police] predicated on exigent circumstances.[4] Nor does Sprint, which disclaims any

---

[4] In fact, defendant Sprint expressly affirms that it provided "the records requested in reliance on the certification from Anderson Police that the records were necessary because of an exigent situation involving danger of death or serious physical injury to any person."

knowledge of plaintiff's interaction with law enforcement, in any manner contest plaintiff's version of the facts with regard to the legitimacy of the basis for the defendants' request.

What this defendant does assert, however, is that plaintiff "has alleged precisely the facts that establish by law that Sprint has no liability for the disclosure of his phone records in response to an emergency request from law enforcement." Sprint contends that under the Stored Communications Act at 18 U.S.C. § 2702(c)(4), service providers are permitted to disclose telephone records so long as they have a good faith belief that there is an emergency requiring authorization. Defendant Sprint seeks dismissal from this action with prejudice.

Sprint argues that the SCA, pursuant to 18 U.S.C. § 2702(c)(4), allows service providers to disclose telephone records if the provider has a good faith belief that an emergency exists requiring disclosure.

To his opposition, plaintiff attaches as Exhibit A, an unauthenticated copy of a document entitled "Mandatory Information for Exigent Circumstance Requests," which appears to be a Sprint PCS form, which indicates that the Anderson Police Department sought plaintiff's phone records from Sprint and set forth the alleged exigent circumstances therein. In reply, Sprint does not challenge the accuracy or authenticity of the form.

Under 18 U.S.C. § 2702(c)(4), a provider of an electronic communication service "may divulge a record or other information pertaining to a subscriber to or customer of such service (not including the contents of communications covered by subsection (a)(1) or (a)(2)—":

> to a governmental entity, if the provider, in good faith, believes that an emergency involving danger of death or serious physical injury to any person requires disclosure without delay of information relating to the emergency.

Defendant Sprint, a cell phone provider, identifies itself as a provider of an electronic communication service. Congress passed the Stored Communications Act in 1986 as part of the Electronic Communications Privacy Act. The SCA was enacted because the advent of the Internet presented a host of potential privacy breaches that the Fourth Amendment does not address. Generally, the SCA prevents "providers" of communication services from divulging private communications to certain entities and/or individuals.

From the papers submitted by the United States Attorney, it is clear that the disclosure without a court order by the provider in the instant case was due to the fact that the government was investigating a kidnapping which included a demand for ransom. This is precisely the type of emergency situation which involves immediate danger of death or serious physical injury to a person. A year after the passage of the Patriot Act, Congress, in the Homeland Security Act of 2002, Pub L. 107–296, § 225(h)(1) amended 18 U.S.C. § 2703(e) to provide that:

> No cause of action shall lie in any court against any provider of wire or electronic communication service, its officers, employees, agents, or other specified persons for providing information, facilities, or assistance in accordance with the terms of a court order, warrant, subpoena, *statutory authorization.*

Thus, a provider who discloses records or other information pursuant to the authorization contained in 18 U.S.C. § 2702(c)(4) in emergency circumstances has the same protection from lawsuits as a provider who discloses the records pursuant to a court order.

In his opposition, plaintiff contends that the Anderson police acted in a conspiracy to illegally obtain evidence by misstating the facts on a Sprint PCS form claiming plaintiff was wanted for kidnapping. Plaintiff further challenges the legality of the form such that it could have been sufficient to permit Sprint to divulge his personal information, including call logs, GPS locations, and social security number "without legal oversight or a warrant."

Sprint is correct that plaintiff's allegations regarding any claimed conspiracy by law enforcement is irrelevant to plaintiff's claim against Sprint. To the extent that Sprint's actions came within the provision of 18 U.S.C. § 2702(c)(4), on the face of it, under § 2703(e), Sprint should be dismissed with prejudice as a defendant.

NOTES AND QUESTIONS

1.   Disclosure of customer-related records by public providers is forbidden under § 2702 unless one of the statutory exceptions applies. The exceptions appear in § 2702(b) for contents and § 2702(c) for non-content records. Some of the § 2702 exceptions mirror analogous exceptions in the Wiretap Act. For example, the SCA has a consent exception, *see* § 2702(b)(3) (contents), § 2702(c)(2) (non-content records), and also has a provider exception, *see* § 2702(b)(5) (contents), § 2702(c)(3) (non-content records). Presumably these exceptions have the same meaning in the context of the SCA that they have in the context of the Wiretap Act.

2.   The *Jayne* case applies the emergency exception in § 2702 that is somewhat analogous to the exigent circumstances exception to the Fourth Amendment's warrant requirement. The emergency exception permits disclosure "to a governmental entity, if the provider, in good faith, believes that an emergency involving danger of death or serious physical injury to any person requires disclosure without delay of [communications or information] relating to the emergency." 18 U.S.C. § 2702(b)(8) (contents), § 2702(c)(4) (non-content records).

Do you think Sprint had a good faith belief that an emergency involving danger of death or serious bodily injury required disclosure without delay of Jayne's records? Is Sprint entitled to rely on the representation of law enforcement officers that an emergency exists? In other words, does receipt of the "exigent circumstances request/demand" resolve Sprint of all liability? Or must Sprint inquire as to the basis of the government's belief?

3.   *The NSA Call Records Program.* In 2006, the *USA Today* revealed the existence of a classified program of the National Security Agency (NSA) that involved collecting the customer call records of the largest telephone companies, AT&T, Verizon and BellSouth. *See* Leslie Caulie, *NSA Has Massive Database of Americans' Phone Calls*, USA Today, May 11, 2006. The NSA approached the telephone companies shortly after the September 11, 2001 attacks and asked the companies to disclose their call records to the NSA. According to *USA Today*, "the agency made an urgent pitch: National security is at risk, and we need your help to protect the country from attacks." *Id.* The NSA reportedly told the companies that the call records would be very helpful to track terrorists in the United States and to prevent another terrorist attack. The companies then disclosed many millions of call records to the NSA.

Did the phone companies' disclosures violate § 2702(c)(4)? Was the disclosure lawful on the ground that the phone companies had a good faith belief that an "emergency involving danger of death or serious physical injury to any person required disclosure without delay of information relating to the emergency"?

4.   Section 2702(b)(7) contains an exception for contents that is roughly analogous to the Fourth Amendment's plain view exception. It states that the disclosure of contents is permitted "to a law enforcement agency . . . if the contents (i) were inadvertently obtained by the service provider; and (ii) appear to pertain to the commission of a crime." 18 U.S.C. § 2702(b)(7). This exception permits a system administrator to disclose evidence of crime to law enforcement if he happens to come across such evidence in the course of his usual duties.

5.   *The CSAM reporting requirement, and its allowance in § 2702.* 18 U.S.C. § 2702(b)(6) and § 2702(c)(5) permit reports to the National Center for Missing and Exploited Children mandated by 47 U.S.C. § 13032. 47 U.S.C. § 13032 imposes a reporting requirement on public providers of ECS and RCS for evidence relating to child exploitation and child pornography crimes:

> Whoever, while engaged in providing an electronic communication service or a remote computing service to the public, through a facility or means of interstate or foreign commerce, obtains knowledge of facts or circumstances from which a violation of section 2251, 2251A, 2252, 2252A, 2252B, or 2260 of Title 18, involving child pornography (as defined in section 2256 of that title), or a violation of section 1466A of that title, is apparent, shall, as soon as reasonably possible, make a report of such facts or circumstances to the Cyber Tip Line at the National Center for Missing and Exploited Children, which shall

forward that report to a law enforcement agency or agencies designated by the Attorney General.

47 U.S.C. § 13032(b)(1).

6. *Can the government get around the SCA using intermediaries?* Section 2702 does not prohibit the disclosure of non-content records when the disclosure is to a non-governmental entity. *See* 18 U.S.C. § 2702(a)(3). This provision allows providers to sell non-content user data to marketers, databrokers, and other companies without triggering liability under the SCA. Imagine the government wants to obtain records held by an ECS or RCS, but that it lacks the reasonable suspicion required to compel those records under § 2703(c)(1). Can the government wait until the provider sells or gives away the records to a non-governmental entity that does not provide ECS or RCS, as allowed by § 2702(a)(3), and then subpoena the records from *that* entity?

7. *Who can consent to voluntary disclosure under § 2702?* The voluntary disclosure provisions of § 2702 assign the right to consent to disclosure based on the nature of the service and whether the disclosure involves contents or non-content information. In the case of contents held by an ECS, the right to consent is held by "the originator or an addressee or intended recipient of such communication." In the case of contents held by an RCS, the right to consent is held by the "subscriber." In the case of non-content information, the right to consent is held by "the customer or subscriber." 18 U.S.C. § 2702(b)(3) (contents), § 2702(c)(2) (non-content records).

In some cases, it can be tricky to identify exactly who has the right to consent. Consider Flagg v. City of Detroit, 252 F.R.D. 346 (E.D. Mich. 2008), a civil discovery dispute involving text messages sent between Detroit Mayor Kwame Kilpatrick and his former Chief of Staff Christine Beatty on their city-issued SkyTel pagers. The plaintiff, Flagg, attempted to obtain the messages directly from the City of Detroit, even though the files were stored with the provider, SkyTel. Whether the messages were discoverable from the City ended up hinging on who had the right to control consent to disclose the messages pursuant to § 2702.

The City argued that SkyTel was acting as a provider of ECS. As a result, the City had no control over the messages: the rights to consent were held by Kilpatrick and Beatty as "the originator or an addressee or intended recipient of such communication." Flagg responded that the City had the right to control access to the messages because SkyTel was a provider of RCS, not ECS. As a result, the proper question was not who was the "originator" or "addressee" but rather who was the account "subscriber." Both Flagg and the City agreed that the City was the "subscriber" because it had purchased the pagers and provided them to Kilpatrick and Beatty.

The district court held that given the specific facts of the case, SkyTel was acting as a provider of RCS. The City had the right to consent and to control access to the text messages under § 2702 and the messages were therefore discoverable from the City. *Id.* at 363. The court added that even if SkyTel was acting as a provider of ECS, Kilpatrick and Beatty had likely consented to the disclosure pursuant to workplace monitoring rules in effect at their office. Even if they had the right to control their access to the messages, they had impliedly waived that right and consented to the disclosure. *Id.* at 365–66.

8.   *Drawing the line between voluntary and compelled disclosure.* The SCA presupposes a sharp line between compelled disclosure (covered by § 2703) and voluntary disclosure (covered by § 2702). However, the line can be hazy in practice. For example, a police officer might ask a company if it is interested in disclosing voluntarily; the company might agree only because it feels pressured to do so. Alternatively, a company may want to disclose voluntarily, but may ask for a subpoena to be served so its lawyers have some legal process for their records. Should such cases be analyzed under § 2702, § 2703, or both?

In Freedman v. America Online, 303 F. Supp.2d 121 (D. Conn. 2004), police officers were investigating a threatening e-mail and wanted to know who had sent the e-mail. The officers filled out a state warrant application seeking the identity of the subscriber and faxed it to the provider, AOL, without the warrant being signed by a judge. AOL complied with the warrant form and disclosed the plaintiff's identity. The plaintiff later sued, contending that the use of an unsigned warrant violated § 2703. The officers first argued that they had not violated § 2703 because they had merely requested disclosure, not actually required it. The court disagreed:

> Defendants' argument that they merely requested but did not require AOL to disclose the information is disingenuous and does not absolve them from liability under the ECPA. The ECPA imposes an obligation on governmental entities to follow specific legal processes when seeking such information. 18 U.S.C. § 2703(c). Congress designed such procedures to both (1) protect personal privacy against unwarranted government searches and (2) preserve the legitimate needs of law enforcement. To conclude that Defendants did not act improperly upon merely requesting such information without following the ECPA procedural safeguards ignores the fact that a request accompanied by a court form has substantial resemblance to a compulsory court order. The deficiency would have excused AOL from complying. In what was submitted Young and Bensey clearly intended that AOL supply the information sought. That AOL responded was nothing less than what was intended and cannot be found to be otherwise. To hold that AOL was less than expected, i.e. required to respond, would erode Congress's intended protection in the ECPA and would undermine personal privacy rights. In soliciting the information from AOL, Defendants knew, or should have known, that AOL was requested to violate the ECPA. Even if AOL acted without lawful authority in disclosing the information, this does not absolve Defendants from unlawfully requesting or soliciting AOL's disclosure. Putting the burden and obligation on *both* the government

and ISPs is consistent with Congress's intent to protect personal privacy. Violation by one does not excuse the other.

Id. at 127.

9. *The SCA and civil discovery.* The application of the SCA to civil discovery has become an important question in civil litigation. If *A* sues *B*, and *A* wants to obtain *B*'s e-mails as part of *A*'s discovery, can *A* subpoena *B*'s e-mail provider for the e-mails as part of the civil discovery process? In general, courts have concluded that the SCA blocks such discovery requests. Because the SCA requires a warrant to compel the contents of communications, a mere civil discovery subpoena cannot be used to compel the provider to disclose contents. *See, e.g.*, Thayer v. Chiczewski, 2009 WL 2957317 (N.D.Ill. 2009) (citing cases); Crispin v. Christian Audigier, Inc., 717 F. Supp.2d 965 (C.D.Cal. 2010). Under these cases, *A* must subpoena *B* directly, and *B* must obtain the contents from the provider by accessing his own account and then handing over the contents to *A*.

10. *Court-ordered consent under the Stored Communications Act.* 18 U.S.C. § 2702 permits a provider to disclose if its user consents. Can a court order a user to consent and then order the provider to disclose, all as a way to facilitate access to the user's private communications? This raises two questions. First, if a court orders a party to consent to disclosure of the contents of communications under 18 U.S.C. § 2702, and the party consents only because the court order requires it, is that consent valid for purposes of § 2702? And second, if the consent is valid, can the same court then compel the provider to disclose the contents of the communications without satisfying § 2703?

In Negro v. Superior Court, 179 Cal.Rptr.3d 215 (Cal. App. 2014), the court answered both questions "yes." In civil litigation between Negro and Navalimpianti, Navalimpianti sought copies of e-mails from Negro. Navalimpianti became convinced that Negro was not handing over all of his e-mails, so Navalimpianti served a civil discovery subpoena on Negro's e-mail provider, Google, seeking copies of Negro's e-mails directly from Google. Google declined to comply with the subpoena on the ground that compliance would violate § 2702.

In response, Navalimpianti obtained an order from the trial court ordering Negro to send an e-mail to Google consenting to Google's disclosure of Negro's e-mails to Navalimpianti's counsel. According to Navalimpianti, the trial court's order constituted consent from Negro, taking the disclosure outside the SCA and thus rendering the civil discovery subpoena on Google enforceable. Faced with the threat of discovery sanctions for failure to comply with the trial court's order, Negro sent an e-mail to Google stating that he consented to Google's disclosure of his e-mails.

The California Court of Appeal ruled that Google was required to comply with Navalimpianti's civil discovery subpoena. According to the Court of Appeal, the existence of the trial court order requiring Negro to express his consent did not itself constitute consent. When the order was issued, Negro had not yet consented. On the other hand, when Negro agreed to comply with the order to avoid sanctions, Negro's compliance with the order constituted valid consent under the SCA:

> We emphatically reject Negro's claim that his consent is vitiated by "judicial coercion." Courts in a variety of other settings have compelled parties to consent to a third party's disclosure of material where such consent was a prerequisite to its production.
>
> If "judicial coercion" were enough to vitiate the resulting instrument, these powers would be illusory. We cannot entertain such a dramatic and disruptive departure from existing law without a far more compelling demonstration than Negro has attempted to make.
>
> The simple fact is that Negro was not deprived of volition in this matter. He was presented with a choice between facilitating the discovery sought by Navalimpianti, or risking such sanctions as the [trial] court might elect to impose. He seeks to have the best of both worlds by complying with the court's order while denying that his decision to do so should be given legal effect. We reject this contention and hold that the consent expressly given by him pursuant to court order constituted "lawful consent" under the SCA.

The Court of Appeal next ruled that the SCA did not prohibit enforcement of Navalimpianti's civil discovery subpoena on Google. Google argued that the consent of a user under § 2702 made disclosure permissive, not mandatory. According to Google, § 2702 gives providers the power to decide whether to disclose by stating that providers "may" disclose when a user consents. *See* 18 U.S.C. § 2702(b), § 2702(b)(3). Assuming Negro's consent was valid, Google had decided not to disclose. Google reasoned that Google's decision should end the matter: A civil discovery subpoena could not trump Google's statutorily-provided discretion and force it to disclose.

The California Court of Appeal disagreed and ordered Google to comply with the subpoena. Specifically, the court rejected Google's argument that the word "may" gave Google the power to decide whether to disclose the e-mails:

> This approach simply does not work in the present context, where the "may" in question is juxtaposed not with a "shall"—real or hypothesized—but with an earlier "shall not"—specifically, the Act's declaration that a service provider "shall not" knowingly disclose protected materials. (18 U.S.C. § 2702(a).) The subdivision where "may" appears is framed not as a grant of discretionary power *or* as the imposition of a mandatory duty but as a special *exception* to a general *prohibition*.
>
> In such a context all "may" means is that the actor is excused from the duty, liability, or disability otherwise imposed by the prohibition. Stating that the actor "may" engage in the otherwise proscribed conduct is a natural way—indeed the most natural way—to express such an exception. Thus a traffic law might declare that a driver *shall*

not proceed against a red light, but *may* proceed, under stated conditions, to make a right turn. This means only that when the stated conditions are present, the driver is relieved of the obligation to wait for a green light. It does not exempt the driver from duties arising under other laws, such as not to obstruct traffic, or to get out of the way of emergency vehicles. The use of "may" in such a context can connote that the actor is not *obliged* in all cases to perform the contemplated action; but it has no tendency, by itself, to excuse the actor from obligations or liabilities arising from other sources.

In sum, we find no sound basis for the proposition that the Act empowers service providers to defy civil subpoenas seeking discovery of materials that are excepted from the Act's prohibitions on disclosure. Insofar as the Act permits a given disclosure, it permits a court to compel that disclosure under state law. It follows that when a user has expressly consented to disclosure, the Act does not prevent enforcement of a subpoena seeking materials in conformity with the consent given.

See also Facebook v. Superior Court, 4 Cal.5th 1245, 1282–85 (Cal. 2018) (agreeing with the reasoning of *Negro*); Facebook v. Pepe, 241 A.3d 248 (D.C. 2020) (same).

Do you agree? If Congress had intended to require providers to comply with civil discovery subpoenas whenever a user consented, why didn't Congress make such process one of the authorized means of compelled disclosure under § 2703?

11. *The SCA and access to e-mails after death.* When you die, who will have access to your e-mails? And what if anything does the Stored Communications Act have to say about that? In Ajemian v. Yahoo!, Inc., 84 N.E.3d 766 (Mass. 2017), the siblings of John Ajemian were appointed the personal representatives of his estate by the Probate and Family Court after Ajemian died unexpectedly in an accident. When the siblings sought access to the contents of Ajemian's personal e-mail account, the provider, Yahoo, refused to comply with their request on the ground that § 2702 prohibited the disclosure. According to Yahoo, only John Ajemian could consent to the disclosure of his personal e-mails. Because Ajemian was dead, Yahoo could not release his e-mails to anyone else.

The Massachusetts Supreme Judicial Court disagreed. The court ruled that Yahoo could lawfully disclose Ajemian's e-mails to his siblings because, as their brother's legal representatives, they took over his rights and could lawfully consent on his behalf under the consent exception of 18 U.S.C. § 2702(b)(3):

Personal representatives provide consent lawfully on a decedent's behalf in a variety of circumstances under both Federal and common law. For example, a personal representative may provide consent to the disclosure of a decedent's health information pursuant to the

Health Insurance Portability and Accountability Act (HIPAA). In like manner, a personal representative may provide consent on a decedent's behalf to a government search of a decedent's property.

At common law, a personal representative also may provide consent on a decedent's behalf to the waiver of a number of rights, including the attorney-client, physician-patient, and psychotherapist-patient privilege. Under the Uniform Probate Code, a personal representative may sell a decedent's property; bring claims on the decedent's behalf; and vote the decedent's stocks. Thus, a construction of lawful consent that allows personal representatives to accede to the release of a decedent's stored communications accords with the broad authority of a lawfully appointed personal representative to act on behalf of a decedent.

Finally, had Congress intended lawful consent to mean only actual consent, it could have used language such as "actual consent" or "express consent" rather than "lawful consent." Accordingly, nothing in the language of the "lawful consent" exception evinces a clear congressional intent to preempt State probate and common law allowing personal representatives to provide consent on behalf of a decedent.

Id. at 776–77.

Are you persuaded? Recall that the SCA's consent exception permits disclosure based on "the lawful consent of the originator or an addressee or intended recipient of such communication, or the subscriber in the case of remote computing service." 18 U.S.C. § 2702(b)(3). Is the personal representative of a decedent's estate the "originator," an "addressee," the "intended recipient," or the "subscriber" of his personal e-mail account? More broadly, should personal e-mails be thought of as traditional property that a personal representative can control or as special personal property that belongs only to the account holder?

While you're at it, consider how the Computer Fraud and Abuse Act should apply to access after death. Imagine the personal representative of an estate knows the decedent's password, and she uses the password to access his personal e-mails. Is her access authorized or without authorization under 18 U.S.C. § 1030?

12. *Disclosure for a cybersecurity purpose.* Under the Cybersecurity Act of 2015, any person or party can disclose "for a cybersecurity purpose and consistent with the protection of classified information, share with, or receive from, any other non-Federal entity or the Federal Government a cyber threat indicator or defensive measure." 6 U.S.C. § 1503(c)(1).

Under the 6 U.S.C. § 1501(6), a "cyber threat indicator" is defined as "information that is necessary to describe or identify" any of the following:

(A) malicious reconnaissance, including anomalous patterns of communications that appear to be transmitted for the purpose of gathering technical information related to a cybersecurity threat or security vulnerability;

(B) a method of defeating a security control or exploitation of a security vulnerability;

(C) a security vulnerability, including anomalous activity that appears to indicate the existence of a security vulnerability;

(D) a method of causing a user with legitimate access to an information system or information that is stored on, processed by, or transiting an information system to unwittingly enable the defeat of a security control or exploitation of a security vulnerability;

(E) malicious cyber command and control;

(F) the actual or potential harm caused by an incident, including a description of the information exfiltrated as a result of a particular cybersecurity threat;

(G) any other attribute of a cybersecurity threat, if disclosure of such attribute is not otherwise prohibited by law; or

(H) any combination thereof.

Before the sharing of a "cyber threat indicator" occurs, the data must first be scrubbed of irrelevant personal information. *See* 6 U.S.C. § 1503(d)(2).

Under 6 U.S.C. § 1501(7)(A), a "defensive measure" is defined as "an action, device, procedure, signature, technique, or other measure applied to an information system or information that is stored on, processed by, or transiting an information system that detects, prevents, or mitigates a known or suspected cybersecurity threat or security vulnerability."

13. *The consent exception and public postings.* Imagine a private party issues a subpoena to Facebook directing Facebook to disclose status updates that the user had posted on his Facebook wall. Imagine some of the status updates were configured to be visible to the general public, while other status updates were configured so that they could be viewed only by the person's Facebook friends. Must Facebook comply with the subpoena, or is compliance blocked by the Stored Communications Act?

In Facebook v. Superior Court, 4 Cal.5th 1245 (Cal. 2018), the Supreme Court of California held that the answer depends on the privacy settings of the status update. If the privacy settings are set to public, the court reasoned, then the posting of the contents in a way available to the public amounts to consent to disclosure that is permitted by the implied consent provision of 18 U.S.C. 2702(b)(3). *See id.* at 1274–7. On the other hand, if the posting is restricted, then there is no implied consent. That is true, the court held, even if "a communication was configured by the user to be accessible to a large group of friends or followers." *Id.* at 1281.

Do you agree that a user's privacy settings can create implied consent to disclose communications? If so, what is the relevant timeframe for consent?

Users can change the privacy settings for particular communications at any time. Imagine a user posts a public status update in 2018. Two years later, in 2020, the user is embroiled in litigation and restricts the status update to friends only. Does the 2020 restriction amount to a withdrawal of consent?

14. *Pre-enforcement challenges to SCA warrants.* Imagine you find out that the government has just obtained a search warrant to collect your e-mails but that the provider has not yet turned over anything. What are your legal options? On one hand, you can wait and see what the provider turns over. You can then file a civil lawsuit against the government for violating your rights. And if you are charged, you can file a motion to suppress on Fourth Amendment grounds. But can you challenge the warrant before the provider complies, litigating your rights before the search is executed?

The court answered this question "no" in United States v. Information Associated with Email Account, 449 F. Supp.3d 469 (E.D.Pa. 2020):

> The United States Constitution protects the rights of persons subject to search warrants by imposing ex ante, the deliberate, impartial judgment of a judicial officer between the citizen and the police and by providing, ex post, a right to suppress evidence improperly obtained and a cause of action for damages. Courts thus generally review challenges to search warrants either in a motion to suppress during a criminal case or in an after-the-fact civil rights lawsuit, not in a pre-execution motion to quash. This stands in contrast to subpoenas, which are regularly challenged pre-execution.

> [Petitioner's] rights are adequately protected by mechanisms that would be available to him at trial should the Government indict him. If he has reason to conclude that the warrant was issued without probable cause or that the Government acted in an unconstitutional manner while executing the warrant, he has within his defensive arsenal the option of filing a motion to suppress the evidence.

> Practical concerns support the conclusion that Petitioner cannot challenge the warrant ex ante in this case. Allowing targets of SCA warrants to challenge the warrant could open the floodgates to huge numbers of such challenges, straining judicial resources. Allowing litigation of these types of claims at this point in the proceeding runs a high risk of unduly compounding the proceeding, turning the swift execution of warrants into protracted legal battles that would prevent the Government from timely resolving its investigations.

Id. at 475–76.

E. PROBLEMS

In each of the following problems, consider whether the investigation violated any of the statutory privacy laws or the Fourth Amendment.

PROBLEM ONE

You are a law student at Kennedy University. You find out that someone is using your Gmail e-mail account without your permission and is sending out all sorts of e-mails in your name. You suspect that this "someone" is fellow law student Fred Rowley, your arch enemy, who uses an e-mail account frowley@law.kennedy.edu.

You contact the FBI for help. An FBI agent calls both Gmail and the computer center at Kennedy University asking for their help to catch Fred. Both are eager to help. The contact at Gmail agrees to send the FBI all of the stored e-mails and account records relating to your account, and the system administrator at Kennedy University agrees to do the same with Fred's stored e-mails and account records.

The system administrator at Kennedy University also agrees to monitor Rowley's account prospectively, albeit in a limited way. He writes a program that logs the IP address of every login to Rowley's account and sends the results to the FBI every few days to keep the FBI informed of Rowley's whereabouts.

When all the e-mails and records are in, however, it turns out that Rowley is not the individual who is using your account.

PROBLEM TWO

John Jefferson is a system administrator for an online auction site, www. better-than-ebay.com. One day, Jefferson notices that the server is acting strangely, and he suspects that the site may have been accessed by an intruder. Jefferson pulls up the server logs and quickly sees that yes, a hacker coming in from the IP address 152.163.159.233 had connected to the network a few hours earlier. Jefferson knows that this IP address is controlled by an Internet provider named MindThink, and he concludes that someone using a MindThink account hacked into his network.

Jefferson is terribly worried. He decides that he will try to catch the intruder in the act the next time and watch his every move. Jefferson installs a sniffer on his network and configures it to record all incoming information originating from any IP address belonging to MindThink. Whenever any MindThink user connects to www.better-than-ebay.com, the sniffer will record everything.

Over the course of the next few days, the sniffer collects a tremendous amount of data unrelated to the hacking, including thousands of requests for webpages and hundreds of messages sent to www.better-than-ebay.com by MindThink subscribers who are legitimate users of the auction site. The sniffer also picks up the hacker re-entering the auction site server. The sniffer records the commands that the hacker entered, enabling Jefferson to reconstruct that the hacker broke in to the network, looked around, and then read opened and unopened e-mail of the auction site employees who have work e-mail accounts stored on the auction site server.

Jefferson contacts the FBI, and speaks with FBI Special Agent Mary Markley. Jefferson tells Markley what happened and volunteers to send Markley copies of all of the documents he has collected. Markley agrees and opens a criminal investigation into the computer intrusion incident. Jefferson sends Markley copies of all of the logs, the entire output of the sniffer, and the employee e-mails stored on the server belonging to www.better-than-ebay.com.

PROBLEM THREE

FBI Special Agent Free Louis is undercover in an chatroom run by an adult website. Members of the website can create chatrooms of any title and can then join the chatrooms. They can also send and receive e-mail messages and instant messages among them. Agent Louis uses the screenname "britney14f" and joins the chatroom "helikesthemyoung." An individual in the chat room who uses the screenname "FunTimeinCA" sends an instant message to "britney14f" asking if she "likes to party with older men."

Special Agent Louis suspects that the person who controls "FunTimeinCA" is a pedophile in possession of child pornography. To confirm his suspicions, Louis serves a subpoena on the operators of the website ordering them to disclose a) any information about the name and address of the user associated with the screenname "FunTimeinCA," b) any additional screennames associated with the account, and c) any images of child pornography stored as an attachment in any e-messages sent from or stored in the account associated with "FunTimeinCA."

An employee of the website receives the subpoena and attempts to comply with it. First, he accesses the server and prints out a page containing all of the basic subscriber information listed in 18 U.S.C. § 2703(c)(2) relating to the "FunTimeinCA" account. The page includes the alternative screennames associated with the "FunTimeinCA" account.

The employee then looks through the stored e-mail in the account. The employee finds nine images of what appear to be child pornography. He sends a fax to Special Agent Louis containing the page of basic subscriber information and the nine images.

CHAPTER 7

JURISDICTION

■ ■ ■

Traditional crimes typically occur in a single jurisdiction. Investigators collect evidence locally, and charges are brought under state criminal codes. Computer crimes are different. The borderless Internet makes jurisdictional issues routine. In most computer crime cases, the defendant, intermediaries, and the victim are located in different states— and sometimes in different countries. The Internet is borderless but the law is not, resulting in complex questions of both substantive and procedural law.

This chapter considers the jurisdictional questions that arise frequently in computer crime cases. The first part of the chapter considers the role of federal law. Does the borderless nature of the Internet make all computer crime law federal computer crime law? What are the limits on federal power to regulate computer crimes?

The second part turns to the role of the states in the enforcement of computer crime law. What powers do states have to prohibit interstate computer crimes? How are state authorities governing the collection of digital evidence different from analogous federal authorities? How can state investigators collect digital evidence located beyond state borders?

The third part of the chapter turns to international computer crimes. When is an international computer crime a violation of United States law? Procedurally, what laws govern the collection of evidence outside the United States needed for computer crime prosecutions inside the United States? What laws govern the collection of evidence inside the United States for prosecutions abroad? When can suspects in computer crime cases be extradited to face charges in a different country?

As you read these materials, consider the role of uniformity. The borderless Internet exerts strong pressures toward uniform computer crime laws. Uniform laws simplify both the investigation and prosecution of criminal activity. Is uniformity desirable? What are the alternatives?

A. FEDERAL POWER

This book has focused largely on federal law; the materials in this section will help explain why. Congress has almost limitless power to regulate computer crimes, and statutory jurisdictional hurdles usually are easy to meet. This section considers the limits of federal criminal law in domestic computer crime investigations. It analyzes three questions: First, what constitutional limits exist on the ability of Congress to punish computer crimes in the United States? Second, what evidence is required to establish statutory jurisdictional hooks, such as interstate commerce requirements? Third, what procedural limits exist on how federal investigators can gather digital evidence located in different states?

1. CONSTITUTIONAL LIMITS

Most federal computer crimes have been enacted under the Congressional power "to regulate Commerce . . . among the several States" granted by Article I, Section 8, Clause 3 of the United States Constitution. The Supreme Court has construed the Commerce Clause power very broadly. United States v. Lopez, 514 U.S. 549, 558–59 (1995), explains the three basic types of conduct that can be regulated under the Commerce Clause:

> First, Congress may regulate the use of the channels of interstate commerce. Second, Congress is empowered to regulate and protect the instrumentalities of interstate commerce, or persons or things in interstate commerce, even though the threat may come only from intrastate activities. Finally, Congress's commerce authority includes the power to regulate those activities having a substantial relation to interstate commerce, i.e., those activities that substantially affect interstate commerce.

Federal statutes that regulate the telephone network and the Internet are generally covered by the first and second categories, as interstate communications networks are considered both channels and instrumentalities of interstate commerce. As the Eleventh Circuit emphasized in United States v. Hornaday, 392 F.3d 1306, 1311 (11th Cir. 2004):

> The Internet is an instrumentality of interstate commerce. Congress clearly has the power to regulate the Internet, as it does other instrumentalities and channels of interstate commerce, and to prohibit its use for harmful or immoral purposes regardless of whether those purposes would have a primarily intrastate impact.

Such broad readings of the Commerce Clause give Congress broad and unquestioned authority to regulate interstate computer networks and the Internet. *See also* United States v. Gilbert, 181 F.3d 152 (1st Cir. 1999) (holding that the telephone network is an instrumentality of interstate commerce, even when a specific call in question is intrastate); United States v. Carnes, 309 F.3d 950 (6th Cir. 2002) (upholding the Wiretap Act as a valid regulation of interstate commerce because "telecommunications are both channels and instrumentalities of interstate commerce"); United

States v. Mitra, 405 F.3d 492, 496 (7th Cir. 2005) ("Section 1030 is within the national power as applied to computer-based channel-switching communications systems.").

The harder questions arise in cases that involve stand-alone computers. For example, the child pornography laws prohibit producing or possessing child pornography images within one state when the images are "produced using materials that have been mailed, or shipped or transported" in interstate commerce. 18 U.S.C. § 2252(a)(4)(B), § 2252A(a)(5)(B), and § 2251(a). The law does not require that the images have been transported in interstate commerce, or that they have been distributed or received over the Internet. Rather, it generally prohibits the storage of images on the ground that the materials used to produce the images have themselves been transported in interstate commerce. Is this prohibition within the scope of Congressional power?

UNITED STATES V. JERONIMO-BAUTISTA

United States Court of Appeals for the Tenth Circuit, 2005.
425 F.3d 1266.

SEYMOUR, CIRCUIT JUDGE.

Virgilio Jeronimo-Bautista was indicted, in part, for coercing a minor to engage in sexually explicit conduct "for the purpose of producing visual depictions of such conduct using materials that have been transported in interstate and foreign commerce," in violation of 18 U.S.C. § 2251(a). The district court dismissed the charge, concluding that as applied to Mr. Jeronimo-Bautista, § 2251(a) exceeded Congress's authority under the Commerce Clause. The government appeals, and we reverse.

I

While Mr. Jeronimo-Bautista asserts he is actually innocent, for the purposes of our review * * * we make all factual inferences in favor of the government, assuming it could prove the facts alleged against Mr. Jeronimo-Bautista at a trial. Accordingly, for the purposes of this appeal only, we assume the following facts.

On January 29, 2004, Mr. Jeronimo-Bautista and two other men, while in the company of a thirteen year-old girl, entered a vacant residence in Magna, Utah. At some point the girl became unconscious, possibly after ingesting an intoxicating substance. After she lost consciousness, the three men removed her clothing, sexually assaulted her, and took photographs of their actions. The camera used to take the photographs was not manufactured in the state of Utah.

One of the men took the film to a one-hour photo lab for processing. In the course of developing the film, staff at the lab noticed images that appeared to depict the sexual assault of a minor female. The manager of the lab called the police, who viewed the photographs and then initiated an investigation resulting in the arrest and indictment of Mr. Jeronimo-Bautista. As noted by the district court, it was undisputed that Mr. Jeronimo-Bautista was a citizen of Mexico and resided in the State of Utah. The victim was born in Utah and was not transported across state lines in connection with the acts charged in the indictment. Moreover, the photos were never disseminated, were not stored or transmitted electronically via the Internet, the United States Postal Service, nor by any other method across state lines or internationally.

The indictment charged that Mr. Jeronimo-Bautista, along with the two other men, did knowingly employ, use, persuade, induce, entice, and coerce a minor to engage in sexually explicit conduct for the purpose of producing visual depictions of such conduct, which visual depictions were produced using materials that have been mailed, shipped, and transported in interstate and foreign commerce, and did aid and abet each other therein, thereby violating § 2251(a) (production of child pornography) and 18 U.S.C. § 2 (aiding and abetting). Mr. Jeronimo-Bautista moved to dismiss the indictment on the ground that the district court did not have subject matter jurisdiction over the acts charged against him, contending § 2251(a) violated the Commerce Clause as applied to him. The district court agreed, concluding that Mr. Jeronimo-Bautista's charged activity "was not of a type demonstrated to be substantially connected or related to interstate commerce." This case is now before us on the government's appeal.

II

The United States Constitution grants to Congress the power to regulate Commerce among the several States. U.S. Const. art I, § 8, cl. 3. As relevant here, "Congress's commerce authority includes the power to regulate those activities having a substantial relation to interstate commerce, i.e., those activities that substantially affect interstate commerce." *United States v. Lopez*, 514 U.S. 549, 558–59 (1995). Hence we must determine whether Mr. Jeronimo-Bautista's local production of pornographic images of a child substantially affects interstate commerce.

In addressing Mr. Jeronimo-Bautista's as applied challenge to the statute, the district court noted the four factors delineated by the Supreme Court in *United States v. Morrison*, 529 U.S. 598 (2000), and in *Lopez* for consideration in addressing the constitutionality of a statute based upon Commerce Clause authority. The court accurately described those factors as (1) whether the prohibited activity is commercial or economic in nature; (2) whether the statute's reach was limited by an express jurisdictional element; (3) whether Congress made findings about the effects of the prohibited conduct on interstate commerce; and (4) whether there exists a link between the prohibited conduct and the effect on interstate commerce.

Working its way through the *Lopez/Morrison* factors, the district court first rejected the argument that Mr. Jeronimo-Bautista's activity was economic in nature and, in doing so, rejected the assertion that Mr. Jeronimo-Bautista's intrastate activities could, in the aggregate, affect interstate commerce. Second, the court determined § 2251(a)'s express jurisdictional element failed to place any meaningful restrictions on federal jurisdiction and failed to establish the link between the violation and interstate commerce. Third, the court was not convinced the existence of Congressional findings regarding the child pornography industry was sufficient, by itself, to sustain the constitutionality of Commerce Clause legislation as applied to the facts of this case. Finally, referring back to its determination that Mr. Jeronimo-Bautista's activity could not be deemed economic in nature, the court also rejected the use of an aggregation theory to support the argument that there existed something more than only a tenuous link between Mr. Jeronimo-Bautista's prohibited activity and interstate commerce. The court dismissed the indictment against Mr. Jeronimo-Bautista on the grounds that as applied to the specific facts of his case, § 2251(a) violated the Commerce Clause.

Pending this appeal, the Supreme Court decided *Gonzales v. Raich*, 545 U.S. 1 (2005), in which it rejected an as applied challenge to the Controlled Substances Act (CSA), 21 U.S.C. § 801 *et seq.*, and held that Congress could regulate the purely local production, possession, and use of marijuana for personal medical purposes. As we discuss in more detail below, the Court's reasoning in *Raich*, coupled with the standard four factor *Lopez/Morrison* analysis, supports our conclusion that the district court erred in concluding § 2251(a) violates the Commerce Clause as applied to Mr. Jeronimo-Bautista.

We begin by examining the findings accompanying the comprehensive scheme developed by Congress to eliminate the production, possession, and dissemination of child pornography. When Congress first passed the Protection of Children Against Sexual Exploitation Act of 1977, it noted "that child pornography has become a highly organized, multimillion dollar industry that operates on a nationwide scale and that the sale and distribution of such pornographic materials are carried on to a substantial extent through the mails and other instrumentalities of interstate and foreign commerce." S. Rep. No. 95–438, at 5 (1977), *reprinted in* 1978 U.S.C.C.A.N. 40, 42–43. Findings supporting the 1977 Act also noted that

> since the production, distribution and sale of child pornography is often a clandestine operation, it is extremely difficult to determine its full extent. At present, however, a wide variety of child pornography is available in most areas of the country. Moreover, because of the vast potential profits involved, it would appear that this sordid enterprise is growing at a rapid rate.

Id. at 43.

Amendments to the Act in 1984 eliminated the requirement that the production, receipt, transportation, or distribution of child pornography be for a pecuniary profit. The purpose of this amendment was to eliminate an enforcement gap in the statute: "Many of the individuals who distribute materials covered by the statute do so by gift or exchange without any commercial motive and thus remain outside the coverage of this provision." H.R. Rep. No. 98–536, at 2 (1983), *reprinted in* 1984 U.S.C.C.A.N. 492, 493. Likewise, in 1984, in support of § 2251, Congress echoed its findings supporting the original 1977 legislation, stating in part that "child pornography has developed into a highly organized, multi-million-dollar industry which operates on a nationwide scale." H.R. 3635, 98th Cong. (2nd Sess. 1984).

In 1996, Congress further amended the Act regarding the electronic creation of child pornography. The findings supporting those amendments noted that "the existence of child pornographic images inflames the desires of child molesters, pedophiles, and child pornographers who prey on children, thereby increasing the creation and distribution of child pornography." S. Rep. No. 104–358, at 2 (1996). Congress also stated that "prohibiting the possession and viewing of child pornography will encourage the possessors of such material to rid themselves of or destroy the material, thereby helping to protect the victims of child pornography and to eliminate the market for the sexual exploitative use of children." *Id.* at 3. Finally, in a 1998 amendment to the Act, a jurisdictional element was added to cover child pornography created "using materials that have been mailed, shipped, or transported in interstate or foreign commerce by any means." § 2251(a). This addition reflected Congress's concern about federal law enforcement's current inability to prosecute 'a number of cases where the defendant produced the child pornography but did not intend to transport the images in interstate commerce.

In reviewing this history, we acknowledge that Congress may not have engaged in specific fact finding regarding how the intrastate production of child pornography substantially affects the larger interstate pornography market. But the Supreme Court noted in *Raich*, 545 U.S. at 21, that it has "never required Congress to make particularized findings in order to legislate." Moreover, we agree with our colleagues on the First Circuit that Congress's explicit findings regarding the extensive national market in child pornography and the need to diminish that national market support the contention that prohibiting the production of child pornography at the local level helps to further the Congressional goal.

The decision in *Raich* also supports the conclusion that Mr. Jeronimo-Bautista's production of the images in this case is economic in nature. "Economics refers to the production, distribution, and consumption of commodities." *Raich*, 545 U.S. at 25. The Court held that the Controlled Substances Act "is a statute that regulates the production, distribution, and consumption of commodities for which there is an established, and lucrative, interstate market. Prohibiting the intrastate possession or manufacture of an article of commerce is a rational (and commonly utilized) means of regulating commerce in that product." *Id.* at 26. The same reasoning is applicable to the intrastate production of child pornography. Like the CSA, the child pornography statutes regulate the production, distribution, and consumption of commodities for which there is an established, and lucrative, interstate market. Congress's prohibition against the intrastate possession or manufacture of child pornography is a rational (and commonly utilized) means of regulating commerce in that product.

In holding that a sufficient link existed between the local production and use of marijuana and its effect on interstate commerce, the Court in *Raich* relied extensively on *Wickard v. Filburn*, 317 U.S. 111 (1942). In *Wickard*, the Court upheld the Agriculture Adjustment Act of 1938, 52 Stat. 31, which permitted congressional regulation of a farmer's wholly intrastate production and consumption of wheat on his farm. *Wickard* "establishes that Congress can regulate purely intrastate activity that is not itself 'commercial,' in that it is not produced for sale, if it concludes that failure to regulate that class of activity would undercut the regulation of the interstate market in that commodity." *Raich*, 545 U.S. at 18. The Court noted that

> in *Wickard*, we had no difficulty concluding that Congress had a rational basis for believing that, when viewed in the aggregate, leaving home-consumed wheat outside the regulatory scheme would have a substantial influence on price and market conditions. Here too, Congress had a rational basis for concluding that leaving home-consumed marijuana outside federal control would similarly affect price and market conditions.

Id. at 19. It viewed its task as not to determine whether respondents' activities, taken in the aggregate, substantially affect interstate commerce in fact, but only whether a 'rational basis' exists for so concluding.

Dismissing arguments that regulation of locally cultivated and possessed marijuana was beyond the "outer limits" of Congress's Commerce Clause authority, the Court observed:

> one need not have a degree in economics to understand why a nationwide exemption for the vast quantity of marijuana (or other drugs) locally cultivated for personal use (which presumably would include use by friends, neighbors, and family members) may have a substantial impact on the interstate market for this extraordinarily popular substance. The congressional judgment

that an exemption for such a significant segment of the total market would undermine the orderly enforcement of the entire regulatory scheme is entitled to a strong presumption of validity.

Id. Finally, noting the "findings in the CSA and the undisputed magnitude of the commercial market for marijuana, the decisions in *Wickard v. Filburn* and the later cases endorsing its reasoning," the Court concluded Congress could regulate the "intrastate, noncommercial cultivation, possession and use of marijuana." *Id.* at 32–33.

This reasoning applies to the child pornography statute at issue here. Under the aggregation theory espoused in *Wickard* and in *Raich*, the intrastate production of child pornography could, in the aggregate, have a substantial effect on the interstate market for such materials. In *Raich*, the respondents were "cultivating, for home consumption, a fungible commodity for which there was an established, albeit illegal, interstate market." *Id.* at 18. Child pornography is equally fungible and there is no question an established market exists for its sale and exchange. The Court in *Raich* reasoned that where there is a high demand in the interstate market for a product, the exemption from regulation of materials produced intrastate "tends to frustrate the federal interest in eliminating commercial transactions in the interstate market in their entirety." *Id.* at 19. For the same reasons, § 2251(a) is squarely within Congress's commerce power because production of the commodity meant for home consumption, be it wheat, marijuana, or child pornography has a substantial effect on supply and demand in the national market for the commodity.

Mr. Jeronimo-Bautista is challenging the statute's constitutionality as applied to him. The Court in *Raich* held the plaintiffs' as applied challenges to the CSA failed because the Court had no difficulty concluding that Congress acted rationally in determining that the intrastate, noncommercial, cultivation, possession, and use of marijuana for personal medical uses, whether viewed individually or in the aggregate, did not compel an exemption from the CSA. So too in Mr. Jeronimo-Bautista's case. Congress's decision to deem illegal Mr. Jeronimo-Bautista's local production of child pornography represents a rational determination that such local activities constitute an essential part of the interstate market for child pornography that is well within Congress's power to regulate.

NOTES AND QUESTIONS

1.   Can you distinguish the market in marijuana at issue in *Gonzales v. Raich* from the market for child pornography images at issue in this case?

2.   Federal child pornography laws prohibit producing or possessing child pornography images within one state when the images are "produced using materials that have been mailed, or shipped or transported" in interstate

commerce. 18 U.S.C. § 2252(a)(4)(B), § 2252A(a)(5)(B), and § 2251(a). Is this jurisdictional hook constitutionally required? Under *Gonzales v. Raich*, as interpreted in *Jeronimo-Bautista*, could Congress remove this requirement and simply prohibit possessing images of child pornography?

3.   Is any computer crime beyond the Commerce Clause power? Is any storage device beyond the commerce clause? Can you envision any criminal activity involving any kind of computer or electronic storage devices that cannot be regulated by the federal government?

2.   SUBSTANTIVE STATUTORY LIMITS

As the preceding materials suggest, Congress has virtually plenary authority to punish computer-related activity in the United States. Most statutes do not go this far. Federal computer crime statutes often impose some kind of statutory interstate requirement that the government must satisfy in each prosecution.

UNITED STATES V. KAMMERSELL

United States Court of Appeals for the Tenth Circuit, 1999.
196 F.3d 1137.

PAUL KELLY, JR., CIRCUIT JUDGE.

Defendant-Appellant Matthew Joseph Kammersell entered a conditional guilty plea to a charge of transmitting a threatening communication in interstate commerce, in violation of 18 U.S.C. § 875(c). Upon recommendation of the magistrate judge, the district court rejected Mr. Kammersell's contention that federal jurisdiction did not exist because both he and the recipient of the threat were located in the same state when the transmission occurred. He was sentenced to four months imprisonment, and twenty-four months supervised release. Our jurisdiction arises under 28 U.S.C. § 1291 and we affirm.

Background

The facts in this case are undisputed. On January 16, 1997, Mr. Kammersell, then nineteen years old, logged on to the Internet service provider America OnLine from his home computer in Riverdale, Utah. Mr. Kammersell's girlfriend was employed at AOL's service center in Ogden, Utah. He sent a bomb threat to her computer terminal via instant message, hoping that the threat would enable her to leave work early so they could go on a date.

When he sent the bomb threat, it was automatically transmitted through interstate telephone lines from his computer in Utah to the AOL server in Virginia and then back to Utah to his girlfriend's terminal at the Ogden service center. Every message sent via AOL automatically goes from the state of origin to AOL's main server in Virginia before going on to its final destination. This pattern of transmission is the same whether the communication is an electronic mail message or an instant message.

Mr. Kammersell does not contest that the threat traveled out of Utah to Virginia before returning to Utah. Nor does he contest that his message constituted a sufficient "threat" to trigger § 875(c). His only claim is that the jurisdictional element of § 875(c) cannot be met if based solely on the route of the transmission, where the sender and recipient are both in the same state.

Discussion

The district court's refusal to dismiss the case on jurisdictional grounds was based upon its interpretation of § 875(c), therefore, its conclusion is reviewed de novo. Section 875(c) provides:

> Whoever transmits in interstate or foreign commerce any communication containing any threat to kidnap any person or any threat to injure the person of another, shall be fined under this title or imprisoned not more than five years, or both.

This provision was enacted in 1934, and its last significant amendment was in 1939. At that time, the telegraph was still the primary mode of interstate communication.

Mr. Kammersell argues that the statute must be interpreted in light of the sweeping changes in technology over the past 60 years and with reference to Congressional intent. The government urges the court to adhere to the plain meaning of the statute; because Mr. Kamersell's threat was transmitted from Utah to Virginia to Utah, it was "transmitted in interstate commerce." Because so many local telephone calls and locally-sent Internet messages are routed out of state, under the government's interpretation, federal jurisdiction would exist to cover almost any communication made by telephone or modem, no matter how much it would otherwise appear to be intrastate in nature. Mr. Kammersell argues that such an interpretation will immeasurably broaden federal criminal jurisdiction without any discussion by Congress of the matter, and it would be wrong to view sixty years of Congressional inaction on the statute as clear intent.

This may be a compelling argument that Congress should re-examine the statute, but it cannot remove Mr. Kammersell from the reach of the current statute. A federal court must give effect to the will of Congress, and where its will has been expressed in reasonably plain terms, that language must ordinarily be regarded as conclusive. As long as the statutory scheme is coherent and consistent, there generally is no need for a court to inquire beyond the plain language of the statute. A threat that was unquestionably transmitted over interstate telephone lines falls within the literal scope of the statute and gives rise to federal jurisdiction.

Mr. Kammersell argues that the threat should not be considered as transmitted interstate because only the recipient could have viewed this instant message. An instant message can only be sent if the recipient is online at the time of transmission, whereas an e-mail may be held in a holding center until it is retrieved. According to Mr. Kammersell, this distinction is crucial because it means that no one outside of the State of Utah could have seen the threat. The distinction, even if correct, is immaterial. No requirement exists under § 875(c) that the threat actually be received or seen by anyone out of state. The gravamen of the crime is the threat itself.

The "instant message" distinction does enable Kammersell to distinguish the primary case upon which the Government relies, but in the end this does not help him either. Because this is a case of first impression, both sides must rely on analogies. The Government relies upon *United States v. Kelner*, 534 F.2d 1020 (2d Cir. 1976). There, the defendant was convicted under § 875(c) for threatening to assassinate Yasser Arafat during a television interview that was broadcast over three states. Both the defendant and Arafat were in New York at the time the threat was made. Like Mr. Kammersell, Kelner argued that the nexus of his activity was predominantly local, and that the statute should not be read literally to reach into spheres of primarily local concern. In upholding Kelner's conviction, the court noted:

> However much we might agree as a matter of principle that the congressional reach should not be overextended or that prosecutorial discretion might be exercised more frequently to permit essentially local crimes to be prosecuted locally, we do not feel that Congress is powerless to regulate matters in commerce when the interstate features of the activity represent a relatively small, or in a sense unimportant, portion of the overall criminal scheme. Our problem is not whether the nexus of the activity is "local" or "interstate"; rather, under the standards which we are to apply, so long as the crime involves a necessary interstate element, the statute must be treated as valid.

Id. at 1024. While *Kelner* can be distinguished on the ground that it involved a transmission that was seen by people in more than one state, the Second Circuit's logic remains just as cogent when applied to the current case.

Finally, Mr. Kammersell contends that, based on the spirit of the Supreme Court's decision in *United States v. Lopez*, 514 U.S. 549 (1995), federal jurisdiction is inappropriate in this case. "*Lopez* stands for the proposition that Congress may not limitlessly expand the federal criminal jurisdiction based on the commerce clause," and "after *Lopez* the constitutionality of assertions of federal jurisdiction over what are essentially local crimes must be closely scrutinized." Aplt. Br. at 34. Yet, we cannot overlook plain language in favor of the "spirit" of *Lopez*, particularly given the difference between the deficient statute in *Lopez*, 18 U.S.C. § 922(q)(1)(A), and § 875(c). The deficient statute in *Lopez* did not require an interstate jurisdictional nexus. *See Lopez*, 514 U.S. at 561 (noting that statute does not contain a requirement that would ensure that the firearm possession in question would affect interstate commerce). Because § 875(c) requires the use of a channel of interstate commerce, it is not subject to the same limiting interpretation as *Lopez*.

NOTES AND QUESTIONS

1. *Technology expands the scope of federal criminal law.* The federal interstate threat statute is phrased in general terms. It covers "any communication" transmitted in interstate or foreign commerce. Under *Kammersell*, this means that the scope of the statute depends on the technical details of the network. If AOL configured its networks so that the instant message stayed inside Utah, the federal statute apparently would not apply. But AOL's technical decision to route all IMs through Virginia seems to ensure that all IMs are covered by the federal statute (except those from one person in Virginia to another person in Virginia). Does this make sense? Should the communication's physical path make a difference?

2. *Knowledge of an interstate nexus is not required.* Should it matter whether Matthew Kammersell knew that the instant message he sent traveled out of Utah in the course of delivery? According to one news report, Kammersell was a former employee of AOL. The prosecutor in the case argued that Kammersell presumably knew that his threat traveled to Virginia and back in the course of delivery. *See* Sheila R. McCann, '*Net Threat A Federal Offense?; Prosecutors Argue It Crossed State Lines*, Salt Lake Trib., Oct. 14, 1997, at A1. In other cases, however, the defendant may have no idea that his communication traveled interstate. Should the defendant's awareness of the interstate nexus make a difference?

When a federal criminal statute is based on the Commerce Clause, knowledge of an interstate nexus is not required. *See* United States v. Darby, 37 F.3d 1059, 1067 (4th Cir. 1994). Whether the defendant knew that the communication crossed state lines is irrelevant. *See, e.g.,* United States v. Veliz, 2004 WL 964005 (S.D.N.Y. 2004) (refusing to dismiss an indictment for sending an interstate threat when the defendant in New York called the victim's New York cell phone number and the victim answered the phone when in Florida).

3. *A slow day at the U.S. Attorney's Office?* Assuming Kammersell's conduct fell within the federal threat statute, we are still left wondering why he was prosecuted. The full text of the bomb threat is unknown, as is the reaction of AOL to the threat. One news clip on Kammersell's arrest makes the threat seem fairly innocuous. According to that report, the threat included the following:

> You should really check out those new keyboards, if you know what I mean, . . . We are sick of your censorship and bad service. You can kiss your assess [sic] goodbye.

High-Tech Bomb Scare, Salt Lake Trib., March 8, 1997, at B2.

Following his conviction and sentencing to four months in prison, Kammersell was interviewed by a reporter and had the following comment:

> I do recognize what I did was wrong. I just think this is going too far for a prank. It's like putting me in front of a firing squad for throwing an apple.

Ray Rivera, *Cyber-Prank Earns Prison Term*, Salt Lake Trib., October 16, 1998, at D6.

4.   *The jurisdictional limits of the federal child pornography laws.* In 2007, Congress eliminated the statutory jurisdictional threshold that had existed up to that point in the federal child pornography laws. *See* The Effective Child Pornography Prosecution Act of 2007, Pub. L. No. 110–358. Before 2007, federal law required the government to prove that images of child pornography had been shipped or transported "in interstate or foreign commerce." Courts grappled with how the government could prove that an image crossed state or national lines. *See, e.g.,* United States v. Lewis, 554 F.3d 208 (1st Cir. 2009). The 2007 Act replaced the jurisdictional requirement "in interstate or foreign commerce" with the new requirement "using any means or facility of interstate or foreign commerce or in or affecting interstate or foreign commerce."

The change was a significant one. When Congress uses the phrase "affecting interstate commerce," that is generally understood to express Congress's intent to regulate as far as the Commerce Clause will allow. *See* Russell v. United States, 471 U.S. 858, 859 (1985) (noting that prohibition regulating conduct "affecting interstate or foreign commerce" expresses "an intent by Congress to exercise its full power under the Commerce Clause"); Scarborough v. United States, 431 U.S. 563, 571 (1977) ("Congress is aware of the distinction between legislation limited to activities 'in commerce' and an assertion of its full Commerce Clause power so as to cover all activity substantially affecting interstate commerce.").

In other words, when Congress uses the jurisdictional hook of "affecting interstate commerce," or its close cousin "affecting interstate or foreign commerce," the scope of the jurisdictional hook is defined by constitutional limitations on the Commerce Clause. There is no separate statutory limitation.

After the Effective Child Pornography Prosecution Act of 2007, and considering cases like Gonzales v. Raich, 545 U.S. 1 (2005), and United States v. Jeronimo-Bautista, 425 F.3d 1266 (10th Cir. 2005), are there now *any* jurisdictional limits on the federal child pornography laws?

5.   *Jurisdictional hurdles in Computer Fraud and Abuse Act cases: The changing definition of "protected computer."* The 2007 amendment to the child pornography laws is part of a broader trend. In recent years, Congress has

tended to minimize or even eliminate the interstate jurisdictional requirements in computer crime statutes.

Consider the amendments to the meaning of the term "protected computer" in the Computer Fraud and Abuse Act, 18 U.S.C. § 1030. From 1996 to 2001, the meaning of the term "protected computer" included a computer "which is used in interstate or foreign commerce or communication." In 2001, as part of the USA Patriot Act, Congress expanded that definition. The 2001 version stated that a "protected computer" includes a computer

> which is used in interstate or foreign commerce or communication, *including a computer located outside the United States that is used in a manner that affects interstate or foreign commerce or communication of the United States.*

18 U.S.C. § 1030(e)(2)(B) (2001) (with language added in 2001 in italics). In 2008, § 207 of the Vice President Protection Act expanded this definition to the scope of Congress's commerce power. The 2008 version states that a "protected computer" is a computer

> which is used in *or affecting* interstate or foreign commerce or communication, including a computer located outside the United States that is used in a manner that affects interstate or foreign commerce or communication of the United States.

18 U.S.C. § 1030(e)(2)(B) (2008) (with language added in 2008 in italics). The 2008 language is somewhat awkward, but the use of the phrase "affecting" appears to express Congress's intent to extend the scope of 18 U.S.C. § 1030 to any computer that could be regulated under the Commerce Clause. In other words, a "protected computer" is *any* computer that can be regulated by Congress's power to regulate interstate commerce as a matter of constitutional law.

In 2020, Congress further expanded the definition of "protected computer" as part of the Defending the Integrity of Voting Systems Act, Pub.L. 116–179. This amendment, which added 18 U.S.C. § 1030(e)(2)(C), reflected a concern that some kind of electronic voting machines might not count as "protected computers" under the then-existing statute. To ensure that hacking into any voting machine was covered by the CFAA, Congress added language establishing that the term "protected computer" includes any computer "that. . . is part of a voting system" and that "is used for the management, support, or administration of a Federal election" or else "has moved in or otherwise affects interstate or foreign commerce." 18 U.S.C. § 1030(e)(2)(C).

As a practical matter, are there any computers that are not also protected computers?

6.   *The policy question.* What limits should Congress impose on the scope of federal computer crimes? Should Congress regulate all computer crimes, no matter how local, and then permit the proper division of federal and state power to be drawn as a matter of prosecutorial discretion? Or should Congress

carve out a category of local computer crimes that are beyond the reach of federal law enforcement authorities?

7. *The special maritime and territorial jurisdiction of the United States.* A number of federal crimes regulate conduct within "the special maritime and territorial jurisdiction of the United States." *See, e.g.*, 18 U.S.C. § 2252(a)(3)(A), § 2252(a)(4)(A). This phrase is defined in 18 U.S.C. § 7, and it mostly refers to places owned by the United States government such as United States military bases and federal parks.

The meaning of "special maritime and territorial jurisdiction" has particular importance under the Assimilative Crimes Act, 18 U.S.C. § 13. The Assimilative Crimes Act makes it a federal crime to violate a state criminal law within "the special maritime and territorial jurisdiction of the United States." As the name of the Act suggests, the statute assimilates state law, in effect federalizing the law of the home state. Here is the relevant text:

> Whoever within or upon any of the places now existing or hereafter reserved or acquired as provided in [18 U.S.C. § 7] is guilty of any act or omission which, although not made punishable by any enactment of Congress, would be punishable if committed or omitted within the jurisdiction of the State, Territory, Possession, or District in which such place is situated, by the laws thereof in force at the time of such act or omission, shall be guilty of a like offense and subject to a like punishment.

18 U.S.C. § 13(a).

The Assimilative Crimes Act can be used in computer crime cases when a state's computer crime laws are broader than federal law. For example, if a person on a United States military base commits a computer-related offense that violates state law, the person can be charged in federal court under the federal Assimilated Crimes Act based on the state law violation. *Cf.* United States v. Smith, 47 M.J. 588 (N.M. Ct. Crim. App. 1997) (charging defendant on a military base in North Carolina with violations of the Assimilative Crimes Act for showing another person images of child pornography in violation of North Carolina state law).

3.   PROCEDURAL LIMITS

Procedural limits on the scope of federal power can also impact the investigatory powers of federal agents. This part focuses on two limits. First, what are the territorial limitations inside the United States of federal court orders needed to collect digital evidence? And second, what are the territorial limitations of where federal criminal prosecutions can be brought?

a)   National Versus Local Court Orders

The first procedural limit on the scope of federal power concerns the enforcement of federal orders that cross state or district lines. When federal investigators wish to obtain a court order, must they obtain the order in the district where the evidence is stored? Or can they obtain an order in one state permitting the collection of evidence in another state?

Most federal statutes permit the federal government to obtain legal process in one state or district for evidence in another state or district. Let's consider each form of legal process in turn.

- *Subpoenas.* Federal grand jury subpoenas are nationwide in scope. *See generally* Weinberg v. United States, 126 F.2d 1004, 1008 (2d Cir. 1942) (citing American Lithographic Co. v. Werckmeister, 221 U.S. 603 (1911)). As a result, a federal prosecutor in state *A* can serve a subpoena on an Internet provider in state *B*, and the provider must comply with the out-of-state federal subpoena.

- *Pen register orders and SCA orders.* Court orders obtained under the Pen Register statute and 18 U.S.C. § 2703(d) of the Stored Communications Act also are nationwide in scope. 18 U.S.C. § 3121(a) of the Pen Register statute states that pen/trap orders "authoriz[e] the installation and use of a pen register or trap and trace device anywhere within the United States." Similarly, the text of § 2703(d) provides that "any court that is a court of competent jurisdiction" may issue the order, and 18 U.S.C. § 2711(3) establishes that this includes "any" Federal court "without geographic limitation."

- *SCA search warrants.* Search warrants under the Stored Communications Act are also nationwide in scope. Prior to the passage of the USA Patriot Act in 2001, 18 U.S.C. § 2703(a) required warrants to be obtained in the district where the evidence was located. Section 220 of the USA Patriot Act amended 18 U.S.C. § 2703(a) to specify that search warrants obtained to satisfy that section must be obtained "using the procedures described in the Federal Rules of Criminal Procedure by a court with jurisdiction over the offense." This amendment permits nationwide warrants obtained under 18 U.S.C. § 2703(a). Any court with an open investigation into the offense has "jurisdiction over the offense," and federal courts in those districts should be able to issue § 2703(a) warrants "using the procedures described" in Rule 41. As a result, a federal district court in state *A* can issue a warrant under the SCA for evidence held by an Internet provider in state *B*. *See, e.g.,* In re Search of Yahoo, Inc., 2007 WL 1539971 at *5 (D.Ariz. 2007) ("Congress intended to authorize the federal district court located in the district where the alleged crime occurred to issue out-of-district warrants for the seizure of electronically-stored communications.").

- *Wiretap orders.* Wiretap orders obtained under 18 U.S.C. § 2518 can be obtained in the state where the tap is placed or where the investigators who will review the collected evidence are located. Although the statute only authorizes a district judge to approve "interception within the territorial jurisdiction of the court in which the judge is sitting," 18 U.S.C. § 2518(3), courts have held that an interception also occurs where the recording is first heard and understood by human ears. *See, e.g.,* United States v. Rodriguez, 968 F.2d 130, 136 (2d Cir. 1992). As a result, use of a monitoring device in state *A* that pipes data to officials located in state *B* is an intercept in state *B* for purposes of the statute. The practical implication is that federal agents in state *B* can obtain a Wiretap order in state *B* even though the device is installed in state *A*.

- *Rule 41 search warrants.* Federal search warrants present a somewhat different picture. Search warrants for physical evidence traditionally must be obtained in the district where the physical evidence is located. *See, e.g.,* Fed. R. Crim. Pro. 41(b)(1) (stating that "a magistrate judge with authority in the district—or if none is reasonably available, a judge of a state court of record in the district—has authority to issue a warrant to search for and seize a person or property located within the district").

In 2016, however, Rule 41 was amended to permit federal magistrate judges to authorize remote-access computer searches outside their districts in two circumstances:

a magistrate judge with authority in any district where activities related to a crime may have occurred has authority to issue a warrant to use remote access to search electronic storage media and to seize or copy electronically stored information located within or outside that district if:

(A) the district where the media or information is located has been concealed through technological means; or

(B) in an investigation of a violation of 18 U.S.C. § 1030(a)(5), the media are protected computers that have been damaged without authorization and are located in five or more districts.

Fed. R. Crim. P. 41(b)(6) (effective December 1, 2016).

These amendments respond to two distinct problems. The first amendment, the new Rule 41(b)(6)(A), deals with the use of anonymizing services over the Internet. Services such as Tor effectively hide an Internet user's location from investigators. When investigators wish to search the computer of a user who is accessing the Internet using an anonymizing service, agents may wish to search the computer remotely because it is the only known means of access to the computer.

Under the prior version of Rule 41, however, it was not clear that judges were authorized to issue a warrant in such cases. Rule 41(b)(1) allows magistrate to issue warrants "to search for and seize a person or property located *within the district*." (emphasis added) When an anonymizing service hides the location of the user, however, the district is unknown. Some judges took the view that no warrant could be issued when the location was unknown due to an anonymizing service because there was no assurance that the Internet user's computer would happen to be located inside the magistrate judge's district. *See, e.g.,* In re Warrant to Search a Target Computer at Premises Unknown, 958 F. Supp.2d 753 (S.D. Tex. 2013) (Smith, M.J.). If the warrant was issued and the computer searched ended up being outside the magistrate's district, some judges held that the warrant was null and void and the government had committed an illegal warrantless search because the magistrate judge had no authority to issue a search in that district. *See, e.g.,* United States v. Levin, 2016 WL 2596010 at *10–13 (D. Mass. 2016) (Young, J.).

In response to this difficulty, Rule 41(b)(6)(A) allows "a magistrate judge with authority in any district where activities related to a crime may have occurred" to issue a warrant "to use remote access to search electronic storage media and to seize or copy electronically stored information located within or outside that district" if "the district where the media or information is located has been concealed through technological means." Use of an anonymizing service such as Tor will "conceal" the identity of the district where the computer is located "through technological means," allowing a magistrate judge to issue a warrant to conduct a "remote access" search for information "outside that district" so long as "activities related to [the] crime may have occurred" in the magistrate judge's district and all of the other requirements of Rule 41 and the Fourth Amendment have been met.

The second amendment, Rule 41(b)(6)(B), deals with botnets. Botnets are networks of computers that, unbeknownst to their owners, are infected with malicious software and are secretly controlled by wrongdoers. Botnets can be used to send out spam messages, to send distributed denial of service attacks, or for other reasons. When the government investigates a botnet in an effort to identify and prosecute the wrongdoer, it may want to send communications to the network of infected computers. Perhaps the government will want to query the network to identify how many infected computers are part of the botnet. Or perhaps the government will want to send code to disable the malicious software. Because botnets generally involve computers located around the country or even around the world, communicating with the botnet may "search" computers in every district.

Rule 41(b)(6)(B) allows the government to obtain a single warrant to obtain information from a botnet instead of obtaining warrants for every district in which the infected computers are located. It applies only "in an investigation of a violation of 18 U.S.C. § 1030(a)(5)," the computer damage provision of the CFAA, when the media to be searched "are protected computers that have been damaged without authorization and are located in five or more districts." In those circumstances, a magistrate can issue a single warrant to communicate remotely with the botnet even if the computers to be searched are outside the district. Importantly, however, the rule only applies to where warrants must be obtained. It authorizes the "where" of searches in terms of districts, but it does not say whether warrants to communicate with botnets are required or whether they satisfy the Fourth Amendment when obtained.

The 2016 amendments to Rule 41 were controversial. Critics argued that the rule changes approve mass-scale electronic warrants and that they facilitate forum-shopping in computer search cases. Critics also argued that Congress should enact a new law to regulate remote searches that imposes greater privacy protection than the traditional search warrant standard of Rule 41. Do you agree?

b) Venue for Federal Prosecutions

A second limit on federal power concerns where charges may be brought. In federal criminal law, this concept is known as "venue." Venue has both constitutional and statutory origins. U.S. Const. Art. III, § 2, cl. 3 requires that criminal trials must be held "in the State where the said Crimes shall have been committed." Federal Rule of Criminal Procedure 18 codifies this right by requiring that "the Government must prosecute an offense in a district where the offense was committed."

Importantly, venue in federal criminal law is different from the concept of personal jurisdiction that arises in civil cases. In the context of a civil lawsuit, the Supreme Court has held that notions of due process require "certain minimum contacts with [the forum] such that the maintenance of the suit does not offend traditional notions of fair play and substantial justice." International Shoe Co. v. Washington, 326 U.S. 310, 316 (1945). Venue in criminal cases is different. In criminal law, charges can be brought wherever the crime was committed. Congress has enacted statutes, and courts have created interpretive doctrines, to answer the "place" of where different criminal offenses can be deemed to have occurred.

The venue requirement can raise difficult questions in computer crime cases. Computer crimes routinely cross both district and state lines. When this occurs, where exactly was the computer crime committed?

The following case considers that question. The case began when Daniel Spitler discovered that servers hosting an AT&T website had a security flaw allowing anyone to collect e-mail addresses of iPad owners who had AT&T wireless accounts. With the assistance of the defendant, Andrew Auernheimer, Spitler created an automated computer program that he called the "account slurper" that visited AT&T's website hundreds of thousands of times and collected 114,000 e-mail addresses and serial numbers known as "ICC-IDs." In an effort to bring attention to their hacking skills, Auernheimer contacted Ryan Tate, a reporter at Gawker, to advertise how Spitler and Auernheimer created the program. Auernheimer sent a copy of the e-mail addresses to Tate to prove their acts. Gawker published a story about Spitler and Auernheimer that was picked up by the Drudge Report and became a national news story. Criminal charges followed, leading to this opinion about venue for federal computer crime prosecutions.

UNITED STATES V. AUERNHEIMER

United States Court of Appeals for the Third Circuit, 2014.
748 F.3d 525.

CHAGARES, CIRCUIT JUDGE.

This case calls upon us to determine whether venue for Andrew Auernheimer's prosecution for conspiracy to violate the Computer Fraud and Abuse Act, 18 U.S.C. § 1030, and identity fraud under 18 U.S.C. § 1028(a)(7) was proper in the District of New Jersey. Venue in criminal cases is more than a technicality; it involves matters that touch closely the fair administration of criminal justice and public confidence in it. This is especially true of computer crimes in the era of mass interconnectivity. Because we conclude that venue did not lie in New Jersey, we will reverse the District Court's venue determination and vacate Auernheimer's conviction.

I.

Evidence at trial showed that at all times relevant to this case, Spitler was in San Francisco, California and Auernheimer was in Fayetteville, Arkansas. The servers that they accessed were physically located in Dallas, Texas and Atlanta, Georgia. Although no evidence was presented regarding the location of the *Gawker* reporter, it is undisputed that he was not in New Jersey.

Despite the absence of any apparent connection to New Jersey, a grand jury sitting in Newark returned a two-count superseding indictment charging Auernheimer with conspiracy to violate the CFAA, 18 U.S.C. § 1030(a)(2)(C) and (c)(2)(B)(ii), in violation of 18 U.S.C. § 371 (count one), and fraud in connection with personal information in violation of 18 U.S.C. § 1028(a)(7) (count two, commonly referred to as "identity fraud"). To enhance the potential punishment from a misdemeanor to a felony, the Government alleged that Auernheimer's CFAA violation occurred in furtherance of a violation of New Jersey's computer crime statute, N.J. Stat. Ann. § 2C:20–31(a). *See* 18 U.S.C. § 1030(c)(2)(B)(ii).*

Auernheimer moved to dismiss the superseding indictment shortly after it was returned by the grand jury. In addition to asserting several challenges concerning the CFAA violation, he argued that venue was not proper in the District of New Jersey. The District Court acknowledged that neither he nor Spitler was ever in New Jersey while allegedly committing the crime, and that the servers accessed were not in New Jersey, but denied his motion nonetheless. It held that venue was proper for the CFAA conspiracy charge because Auernheimer's disclosure of the email addresses of about 4,500 New Jersey residents affected them in New Jersey and violated New Jersey law. It further held that because venue was proper for the CFAA count, it was also proper for the identity fraud count because proving the CFAA violation was a necessary predicate to proving the identity fraud violation.

Auernheimer's trial lasted five days and resulted in a guilty verdict on both counts. Initially, both parties requested a jury instruction on venue. Venue is a question for the jury and the court must specifically instruct the jury on venue if (1) the defendant objects to venue prior to or at the close of the prosecution's case-in-chief, (2) there is a genuine issue of material fact with regard to proper venue, and (3) the defendant timely requests a jury instruction.

Although Auernheimer objected to venue and requested an instruction, the District Court held that there was no genuine issue of material fact. It concluded that the Government had established that venue was proper in New Jersey as a matter of law and declined to instruct the jury on venue. After denying Auernheimer's post-trial motions, the District Court sentenced him to forty-one months of imprisonment. Auernheimer timely appealed. Our review of the District Court's legal decision regarding venue is plenary.

II.

Although this appeal raises a number of complex and novel issues that are of great public importance in our increasingly interconnected age, we find it necessary to reach only one that has been fundamental since our country's founding: venue. The proper place of colonial trials was so important to the founding generation that it was listed as a grievance in the Declaration of Independence. *See* The Declaration of Independence para. 21 (U.S. 1776) (objecting to "transporting us beyond seas to be tried for pretended offences"). It was of such concern that the Constitution of the

---

* Editor's Note: Spitler was also charged, but he pled guilty and testified against Auernheimer in exchange for a reduced sentence.

United States twice safeguards the defendant's venue right. Article III requires that "the Trial of all Crimes shall be held in the State where the said Crimes shall have been committed." U.S. Const. art. III, § 2, cl. 3. The Sixth Amendment further provides that "in all criminal prosecutions, the accused shall enjoy the right to a speedy and public trial, by an impartial jury of the State and district wherein the crime shall have been committed." This guarantee is codified in the Federal Rules of Criminal Procedure, which require that "the Government must prosecute an offense in a district where the offense was committed."

Congress may prescribe specific venue requirements for particular crimes. Where it has not, as is the case here, we must determine the crime's *locus delicti*. *See* Black's Law Dictionary 1025 (9th ed. 2009) (defining *locus delicti* as the "place where an offense was committed"). The *locus delicti* must be determined from the nature of the crime alleged and the location of the act or acts constituting it. To perform this inquiry, we must (1) initially identify the conduct constituting the offense and then (2) discern the location of the commission of the criminal acts. Venue should be narrowly construed.

Continuing offenses, such as conspiracy, that are "begun in one district and completed in another, or committed in more than one district, may be inquired of and prosecuted in any district in which such offense was begun, continued, or completed." 18 U.S.C. § 3237(a). In the context of a conspiracy charge, venue can be established wherever a co-conspirator has committed an act in furtherance of the conspiracy. The Government must prove venue by a preponderance of the evidence.

In performing our venue inquiry, we must be careful to separate 'essential conduct elements' from 'circumstance elements.' For example, in *United States v. Cabrales*, 524 U.S. 1, 4 (1998), the Supreme Court considered whether venue for money laundering activities was proper in Missouri. Laundered proceeds were generated by illegal narcotics sales in Missouri, but all acts constituting the money laundering offense took place in Florida. The Court held that venue was improper in Missouri. The Supreme Court, later reflecting on *Cabrales,* observed that the "existence of criminally generated proceeds" was only a "circumstance element" of money laundering. *United States v. Rodriguez-Moreno*, 526 U.S. 275, 280 n.4 (1999). Although it was an element of the crime that the Government had to prove to the jury, it was a 'circumstance element' because it was simply a fact that existed at the time that the defendant performed her laundering acts. Only 'essential conduct elements' can provide the basis for venue; 'circumstance elements' cannot.

A.

Count one charged Auernheimer with conspiracy to violate 18 U.S.C. § 1030(a)(2)(C) and (c)(2)(B)(ii). In the indictment and at trial, the

Government identified the nature of the conduct constituting the offense as the agreement to commit a violation of the CFAA in furtherance of a violation of New Jersey's computer crime statute, N.J. Stat. Ann. § 2C:20–31(a). Venue would be proper in any district where the CFAA violation occurred, or wherever any of the acts in furtherance of the conspiracy took place.

The charged portion of the CFAA provides that "whoever intentionally accesses a computer without authorization or exceeds authorized access, and thereby obtains . . . information from any protected computer shall be punished as provided in subsection (c) of this section." 18 U.S.C. § 1030(a)(2)(C). To be found guilty, the Government must prove that the defendant (1) intentionally (2) accessed without authorization (or exceeded authorized access to) a (3) protected computer and (4) thereby obtained information. The statute's plain language reveals two essential conduct elements: *accessing* without authorization and *obtaining* information.[3]

New Jersey was not the site of either essential conduct element. The evidence at trial demonstrated that the accessed AT&T servers were located in Dallas, Texas, and Atlanta, Georgia. In addition, during the time that the conspiracy began, continued, and ended, Spitler was obtaining information in San Francisco, California, and Auernheimer was assisting him from Fayetteville, Arkansas. No protected computer was accessed and no data was obtained in New Jersey.

This is not the end of our analysis, however, because the Government did not just charge Auernheimer with conspiracy to commit an ordinary violation of the CFAA, but also with conspiring to violate the CFAA in furtherance of a state crime. The Government can increase the statutory maximum punishment for a subsection (a)(2) violation from one year to five years if it proves one of the enhancements contained in § 1030(c)(2)(B). The enhancement relevant here provides for such increased punishment if "the offense was committed in furtherance of any criminal or tortious act in violation of the laws of any State." *Id.* § 1030(c)(2)(B)(ii). Any facts that increase the prescribed range of penalties to which the criminal defendant is exposed' are elements of the crime" that must be proven to the jury beyond a reasonable doubt.[4] This is true even if they are explicitly termed "sentence enhancements" in the statute.

---

[3]   The Department of Justice's own manual on prosecuting computer crimes provides in its section devoted to venue that "it would seem logical that a crime under section 1030(a)(2)(C) is committed where the offender initiates access *and* where the information is obtained." Computer Crime & Intellectual Prop. Section, Dep't of Justice, Prosecuting Computer Crimes 118, *available at* http://www.justice.gov/criminal/cybercrime/docs/ccmanual.pdf.

[4]   Just because the enhancement is an "element" that the Government needed to prove beyond a reasonable doubt does not mean that it was an "essential conduct element" of a § 1030(a)(2)(C) violation within the meaning of *Rodriguez-Moreno* that could establish venue. For the purposes of this opinion, however, we will assume (without deciding) that the enhancement could contain "essential conduct elements."

The New Jersey statute allows for criminal liability "if the person purposely or knowingly and without authorization, or in excess of authorization, accesses any computer or computer system and knowingly or recklessly discloses, or causes to be disclosed any data or personal identifying information." N.J. Stat. Ann. § 2C:20–31(a). Its essential conduct elements are accessing without authorization (or in excess of authorization) and disclosing data or personal identifying information.

Here, none of the essential conduct elements of a violation of the New Jersey statute occurred in New Jersey. As discussed, neither Auernheimer nor Spitler accessed a computer in New Jersey. The disclosure did not occur there either. The sole disclosure of the data obtained was to the *Gawker* reporter. There was no allegation or evidence that the *Gawker* reporter was in New Jersey. Further, there was no evidence that any email addresses of any New Jersey residents were ever disclosed publicly in the *Gawker* article. The alleged violation of the New Jersey statute thus cannot confer venue for count one.

Just as none of the conduct constituting the CFAA violation or its enhancement occurred in New Jersey, none of the overt acts that the Government alleged in the superseding indictment occurred in New Jersey either. The indictment listed four overt acts: writing the account slurper program, deploying the account slurper program against AT&T's servers, emailing victims to inform them of the breach, and disclosing the emails addresses obtained to *Gawker*. The co-conspirators collaborated on the account slurper program from California and Arkansas and deployed it against servers located in Texas and Georgia. The Government offered no evidence whatsoever that any of the victims that Auernheimer emailed were located in New Jersey, or that the *Gawker* reporter to whom the list of email addresses was disclosed was in the Garden State.

Because neither Auernheimer nor his co-conspirator Spitler performed any "essential conduct element" of the underlying CFAA violation or any overt act in furtherance of the conspiracy in New Jersey, venue was improper on count one.

B.

We now turn to count two of the indictment because venue must be analyzed independently for each count. Count two charged Auernheimer with violating 18 U.S.C. § 1028(a)(7), which punishes anyone who "knowingly transfers, possesses, or uses, without lawful authority, a means of identification of another person with the intent to commit, or to aid or abet, or in connection with, any [federal crime, or state or local felony]." The statute's plain language indicates that the statute punishes someone who (1) knowingly (2) transfers, possesses, or uses without lawful authority (3) a means of identification of another person (4) with the intent to commit, or in connection with, any violation of federal law or any state felony.

The two essential conduct elements under § 1028(a)(7) are transfer, possession, or use, and doing so in connection with a federal crime or state felony. Starting with the latter essential conduct element, the Government charged Auernheimer with committing identity fraud "in connection with" the ordinary violation of CFAA § 1030(a)(2)(C). As should be clear by now, no conduct related to the ordinary CFAA violation occurred in New Jersey.

There was also no evidence that Auernheimer's transfer, possession, or use occurred in New Jersey. The Government advances two theories of how he could have satisfied this essential conduct element. First, it contends that he violated § 1028(a)(7) by knowingly using the ICC-IDs of other people's iPads to access AT&T's servers. Venue fails under this theory because there was no allegation or evidence that he used the ICC-IDs in New Jersey. The alleged conspirators used the ICC-IDs in their account slurper program, which was programmed from California and Arkansas, and did not access any computer or obtain any information in New Jersey.

The Government also argues that Auernheimer violated the statute by transferring the list of email addresses that he obtained to *Gawker* with the intent to violate the New Jersey computer crime statute. But there was no allegation in the indictment or evidence at trial that the *Gawker* reporter to whom he transferred the email addresses was in New Jersey— and no essential conduct element of the alleged violation of New Jersey law occurred in New Jersey either.

Because Auernheimer did not commit any essential conduct of the identity fraud charge in New Jersey, venue was also improper on count two.

III.

Undoubtedly there are some instances where the location in which a crime's effects are felt is relevant to determining whether venue is proper. But those cases are reserved for situations in which an essential conduct element is itself defined in terms of its effects.

Sections of the CFAA other than § 1030(a)(2)(C) do speak in terms of their effects. For example, § 1030(a)(5)(B) criminalizes intentionally accessing a computer without authorization and recklessly causing damage. Because that crime is defined in terms of its effects—the damage caused—venue could be proper wherever that occurred.

Congress, however, did not define a violation of § 1030(a)(2)(C) in terms of its effects. The statute simply criminalizes accessing a computer without authorization and obtaining information. It punishes only the actions that the defendant takes to access and obtain. It does not speak in terms of the effects on those whose information is obtained. The crime is complete even if the offender never looks at the information and immediately destroys it, or the victim has no idea that information was ever taken.

Venue issues are animated in part by the danger of allowing the Government to choose its forum free from any external constraints. The ever-increasing ubiquity of the Internet only amplifies this concern. As we progress technologically, we must remain mindful that cybercrimes do not happen in some metaphysical location that justifies disregarding constitutional limits on venue. People and computers still exist in identifiable places in the physical world. When people commit crimes, we have the ability and obligation to ensure that they do not stand to account for those crimes in forums in which they performed no "essential conduct element" of the crimes charged.

For the forgoing reasons, we will reverse the District Court's venue determination and vacate Auernheimer's conviction.

NOTES AND QUESTIONS

1.   *Venue in child pornography cases.* In child pornography cases, venue will generally be proper in any district where the child pornography moved or was present. *See, e.g.,* United States v. Kapordelis, 569 F.3d 1291, 1308 (11th Cir. 2009); United States v. Cameron, 733 F. Supp.2d 177, 181 (D.Me. 2010) ("Under § 3237(a), venue for child pornography prosecution lies in any district from, through, or into which the child pornography moves.").

2.   *Venue created by an undercover agent.* An undercover agent can often create venue: By committing his acts in a particular district, the undercover agent may cause the necessary conduct to occur in that district. In response to concerns that this can let the government bring cases in districts that are particularly tough on defendants, Judge Easterbrook has replied:

> If our reading ... gives prosecutors leeway that could be misused, that would be nothing new. Prosecutors often have wide choice of venue. In drug cases, for example, prosecutors may choose the crime's location by deciding where undercover agents offer to buy or sell drugs from suspects, or from what districts they place phone calls that set up transactions. We have rejected all arguments that use of these options is forbidden—provided only that the activity falls short of entrapment.

United States v. Rodriguez-Rodriguez, 453 F.3d 458, 462 (7th Cir. 2006).

3.   *Venue when a crime is committed from outside the United States.* Computer crimes targeting victims in the United States are often committed from outside the United States. Where can the prosecution be brought? Congress has enacted a special venue provision for such situations:

> The trial of all offenses begun or committed upon the high seas, or elsewhere out of the jurisdiction of any particular State or district, shall be in the district in which the offender, or any one of two or more

joint offenders, is arrested or is first brought; but if such offender or offenders are not so arrested or brought into any district, an indictment or information may be filed in the district of the last known residence of the offender or of any one of two or more joint offenders, or if no such residence is known the indictment or information may be filed in the District of Columbia.

18 U.S.C. § 3238.

4.   For a helpful overview of venue principles in federal criminal cases, *see* Brian Doyle, Venue: A Legal Analysis of Where a Federal Crime May Be Tried (Congressional Research Service 2014).

B. STATE POWER

Congress has virtually plenary power to regulate computer-related crimes, and most federal court orders can be obtained with nationwide effect. State powers are quite different. State officials face considerable substantive and procedural barriers to the successful investigation and prosecution of computer crimes. The materials that follow start with substantive law, and in particular the limits imposed on state efforts to regulate interstate computer crimes imposed by the so-called "dormant" Commerce Clause. The materials then turn to procedural laws, and study the procedural hurdles faced by state computer crime investigators. As you read these materials, keep this question in mind: What role can states play in the enforcement of computer crime laws?

1.   SUBSTANTIVE LIMITS

AMERICAN LIBRARY ASSOCIATION V. PATAKI

United States District Court for the Southern District of New York, 1997.
969 F. Supp. 160.

PRESKA, DISTRICT JUDGE.

The plaintiffs in the present case filed this action challenging New York Penal Law § 235.21(3). Plaintiffs contend that the Act is unconstitutional because it unduly burdens interstate commerce in violation of the Commerce Clause. For the reasons that follow, the motion for a preliminary injunction is granted.

The Act in question amended N.Y. Penal Law § 235.21 by adding a new subdivision. The amendment makes it a crime for an individual:

Knowing the character and content of the communication which, in whole or in part, depicts actual or simulated nudity, sexual conduct or sado-masochistic abuse, and which is harmful to minors, to intentionally use any computer communication system allowing the input, output, examination or transfer, of computer data or computer programs from one computer to another, to initiate or engage in such communication with a person who is a minor.

Violation of the Act is a Class E felony, punishable by one to four years of incarceration. The Act applies to both commercial and non-commercial disseminations of material.

Section 235.20(6) defines "harmful to minors" as:

that quality of any description or representation, in whatever form, of nudity, sexual conduct, sexual excitement, or sado-masochistic abuse, when it:

(a) Considered as a whole, appeals to the prurient interest in sex of minors; and

(b) Is patently offensive to prevailing standards in the adult community as a whole with respect to what is suitable material for minors; and

(c) Considered as a whole, lacks serious literary, artistic, political and scientific value for minors.

N.Y. Penal Law § 235.20(6). The statute provides six defenses to liability. First, Section 235.15(1) provides the following affirmative defense to prosecution under § 235.21(3):

In any prosecution for obscenity, or disseminating indecent material to minors in the second degree in violation of subdivision three of section 235.21 of this article, it is an affirmative defense that the persons to whom the allegedly obscene or indecent material was disseminated, or the audience to an allegedly obscene performance, consisted of persons or institutions having scientific, educational, governmental or other similar justification for possessing, disseminating or viewing the same.

The statute further provides four regular defenses to prosecution:

(a) The defendant made a reasonable effort to ascertain the true age of the minor and was unable to do so as a result of the actions taken by the minor; or

(b) The defendant has taken, in good faith, reasonable, effective and appropriate actions under the circumstances to restrict or prevent access by minors to materials specified in such subdivision, which may involve any appropriate measures to restrict minors from access to such communications, including any method which is feasible under available technology; or

(c) The defendant has restricted access to such materials by requiring use of a verified credit card, debit account, adult access code or adult personal identification number; or

(d) The defendant has in good faith established a mechanism such that the labeling, segregation or other mechanism enables such material to be automatically blocked or screened by software or other capabilities reasonably available to responsible adults wishing to effect such blocking or screening and the defendant has not otherwise solicited minors not subject to such screening or blocking capabilities to access that material or circumvent any such screening or blocking.

N.Y. Penal Law § 235.23(3). And, finally, Section 235.24 provides that no individual shall be held liable:

solely for providing access or connection to or from a facility, system, or network not under that person's control, including transmission, downloading, intermediate storage, access software, or other related capabilities that are incidental to providing such access or connection that do not include the creation of the content of the communication.

N.Y. Penal Law § 235.24.

The borderless world of the Internet raises profound questions concerning the relationship among the several states and the relationship of the federal government to each state, questions that go to the heart of "our federalism."

The unique nature of the Internet highlights the likelihood that a single actor might be subject to haphazard, uncoordinated, and even outright inconsistent regulation by states that the actor never intended to reach and possibly was unaware were being accessed. Typically, states' jurisdictional limits are related to geography; geography, however, is a virtually meaningless construct on the Internet. The menace of inconsistent state regulation invites analysis under the Commerce Clause of the Constitution, because that clause represented the framers' reaction to overreaching by the individual states that might jeopardize the growth of the nation—and in particular, the national infrastructure of communications and trade—as a whole.

The Commerce Clause is more than an affirmative grant of power to Congress. As long ago as 1824, Justice Johnson in his concurring opinion in *Gibbons v. Ogden*, 9 Wheat. 1, 231–32 (1824), recognized that the Commerce Clause has a negative sweep as well. In what commentators have come to term its negative or "dormant" aspect, the Commerce Clause restricts the individual states' interference with the flow of interstate commerce in two ways. The Clause prohibits discrimination aimed directly at interstate commerce, and bars state regulations that, although facially nondiscriminatory, unduly burden interstate commerce. Moreover, courts have long held that state regulation of those aspects of commerce that by their unique nature demand cohesive national treatment is offensive to the Commerce Clause.

Thus, as will be discussed in more detail below, the New York Act is concerned with interstate commerce and contravenes the Commerce Clause for three reasons. First, the Act represents an unconstitutional projection of New York law into conduct that occurs wholly outside New York. Second, the Act is invalid because although protecting children from indecent material is a legitimate and indisputably worthy subject of state legislation, the burdens on interstate commerce resulting from the Act clearly exceed any local benefit derived from it. Finally, the Internet is one of those areas of commerce that must be marked off as a national preserve to protect users from inconsistent legislation that, taken to its most extreme, could paralyze development of the Internet altogether. Thus, the Commerce Clause ordains that only Congress can legislate in this area, subject, of course, to whatever limitations other provisions of the Constitution (such as the First Amendment) may require.

A.   The Act Concerns Interstate Commerce

At oral argument, the defendants advanced the theory that the Act is aimed solely at intrastate conduct. This argument is unsupportable in light of the text of the statute itself, its legislative history, and the reality of Internet communications. The section in question contains no such limitation; it reads:

> A person is guilty of disseminating indecent material to minors in the second degree when:

> Knowing the character and content of the communication which, in whole or in part, depicts actual or simulated nudity, sexual conduct or sado-masochistic abuse, and which is harmful to minors, he intentionally uses any computer communication system allowing the input, output, examination or transfer, of computer data or computer programs from one computer to another, to initiate or engage in such communication with a person who is a minor.

N.Y. Penal Law § 235.21(3). Section 235.20, which contains the definitions applicable to the challenged portion of the Act, does not import any restriction that the criminal communication must take place entirely within the State of New York. By its terms, the Act applies to any communication, intrastate or interstate, that fits within the prohibition and over which New York has the capacity to exercise criminal jurisdiction.

The conclusion that the Act must apply to interstate as well as intrastate communications receives perhaps its strongest support from the nature of the Internet itself. The Internet is wholly insensitive to geographic distinctions. In almost every case, users of the Internet neither know nor care about the physical location of the Internet resources they access. Internet protocols were designed to ignore rather than document geographic location; while computers on the network do have "addresses," they are logical addresses on the network rather than geographic addresses in real space.

Moreover, no aspect of the Internet can feasibly be closed off to users from another state. An internet user who posts a Web page cannot prevent New Yorkers or Oklahomans or Iowans from accessing that page and will not even know from what state visitors to that site hail. Nor can a participant in a chat room prevent other participants from a particular state from joining the conversation. Someone who uses a mail exploder is similarly unaware of the precise contours of the mailing list that will ultimately determine the recipients of his or her message, because users can add or remove their names from a mailing list automatically. Thus, a person could choose a list believed not to include any New Yorkers, but an after-added New Yorker would still receive the message.

The New York Act, therefore, cannot effectively be limited to purely intrastate communications over the Internet because no such communications exist. No user could reliably restrict her communications only to New York recipients. Moreover, no user could avoid liability under the New York Act simply by directing his or her communications elsewhere, given that there is no feasible way to preclude New Yorkers from accessing a Web site, receiving a mail exploder message or a newsgroup posting, or participating in a chat room. Similarly, a user has no way to ensure that an e-mail does not pass through New York even if the ultimate recipient is not located there, or that a message never leaves New York even if both sender and recipient are located there.

The courts have long recognized that railroads, trucks, and highways are themselves "instruments of commerce," because they serve as conduits for the transport of products and services. The Internet is more than a means of communication; it also serves as a conduit for transporting digitized goods, including software, data, music, graphics, and videos which can be downloaded from the provider's site to the Internet user's computer.

The inescapable conclusion is that the Internet represents an instrument of interstate commerce, albeit an innovative one; the novelty of the technology should not obscure the fact that regulation of the Internet impels traditional Commerce Clause considerations. The New York Act is therefore closely concerned with interstate commerce, and scrutiny of the Act under the Commerce Clause is entirely appropriate. As discussed in the following sections, the Act cannot survive such scrutiny, because it places an undue burden on interstate traffic, whether that traffic be in goods, services, or ideas.

B.   New York Has Overreached by Enacting a Law That Seeks to Regulate Conduct Occurring Outside its Borders

The interdiction against direct interference with interstate commerce by state legislative overreaching is apparent in a number of the Supreme Court's decisions. In *Baldwin v. G.A.F. Seelig, Inc.*, 294 U.S. 511, 521 (1935), for example, Justice Cardozo authored an opinion enjoining enforcement of a law that prohibited a dealer from selling within New York milk purchased from the producer in Vermont at less than the minimum price fixed for milk produced in New York. Justice Cardozo sternly admonished, "New York has no power to project its legislation into Vermont by regulating the price to be paid in that state for milk," finding that "such a power, if exerted, would set a barrier to traffic between one state and another as effective as if customs duties, equal to the price differential, had been laid upon the thing transported."

In the present case, a number of witnesses testified to the chill that they felt as a result of the enactment of the New York statute; these witnesses refrained from engaging in particular types of interstate commerce. In particular, I note the testimony of Rudolf Kinsky, an artist with a virtual studio on Art on the Net's Website. Mr. Kinsky testified that he removed several images from his virtual studio because he feared prosecution under the New York Act. As described above, no Web siteholder is able to close his site to New Yorkers. Thus, even if Mr. Kinsky were located in California and wanted to display his work to a prospective purchaser in Oregon, he could not employ his virtual studio to do so without risking prosecution under the New York law.

The nature of the Internet makes it impossible to restrict the effects of the New York Act to conduct occurring within New York. An Internet user may not intend that a message be accessible to New Yorkers, but lacks the ability to prevent New Yorkers from visiting a particular Website or viewing a particular newsgroup posting or receiving a particular mail exploder. Thus, conduct that may be legal in the state in which the user acts can subject the user to prosecution in New York and thus subordinate the user's home state's policy—perhaps favoring freedom of expression over a more protective stance—to New York's local concerns. New York has deliberately imposed its legislation on the Internet and, by doing so, projected its law into other states whose citizens use the Net. This encroachment upon the authority which the Constitution specifically confers upon the federal government and upon the sovereignty of New York's sister states is per se violative of the Commerce Clause.

C.   The Burdens the Act Imposes on Interstate Commerce Exceed Any Local Benefit

Even if the Act were not a per se violation of the Commerce Clause by virtue of its extraterritorial effects, the Act would nonetheless be an invalid indirect regulation of interstate commerce, because the burdens it imposes on interstate commerce are excessive in relation to the local benefits it confers. The Supreme Court set forth the balancing test applicable to indirect regulations of interstate commerce in *Pike v. Bruce Church*, 397 U.S. 137, 142 (1970). *Pike* requires a two-fold inquiry. The first level of examination is directed at the legitimacy of the state's interest. The next, and more difficult, determination weighs the burden on interstate commerce in light of the local benefit derived from the statute.

In the present case, I accept that the protection of children against pedophilia is a quintessentially legitimate state objective—a proposition with which I believe even the plaintiffs have expressed no quarrel. The defendants spent considerable time in their Memorandum and at argument asserting the legitimacy of the state's interest. Even with the fullest recognition that the protection of children from sexual exploitation is an indisputably valid state goal, however, the present statute cannot survive even the lesser scrutiny to which indirect regulations of interstate commerce are subject under the Constitution.

The local benefits likely to result from the New York Act are not overwhelming. The Act can have no effect on communications originating outside the United States. Further, in the present case, New York's prosecution of parties from out of state who have allegedly violated the Act, but whose only contact with New York occurs via the Internet, is beset with practical difficulties, even if New York is able to exercise criminal jurisdiction over such parties. The prospect of New York bounty hunters dragging pedophiles from the other 49 states into New York is not consistent with traditional concepts of comity.

The Act is, of course, not the only law in New York's statute books designed to protect children against sexual exploitation. The State is able to protect children through vigorous enforcement of the existing laws criminalizing obscenity and child pornography. Moreover, plaintiffs do not challenge the sections of the statute that criminalize the sale of obscene materials to children, over the Internet or otherwise, and prohibit adults from luring children into sexual contact by communicating with them via the Internet. *See* N.Y. Penal Law § 235.21(1); N.Y. Penal Law § 235.22(2). The local benefit to be derived from the challenged section of the statute is therefore confined to that narrow class of cases that does not fit within the parameters of any other law. The efficacy of the statute is further limited, as discussed above, to those cases which New York is realistically able to prosecute.

Balanced against the limited local benefits resulting from the Act is an extreme burden on interstate commerce. The New York Act casts its net worldwide; moreover, the chilling effect that it produces is bound to exceed the actual cases that are likely to be prosecuted, as Internet users will steer clear of the Act by significant margin. At oral argument, the State asserted that only a small percentage of Internet communications are "harmful to minors" and would fall within the proscriptions of the statute; therefore, the State argued, the burden on interstate commerce is small. On the record before me, I conclude that the range of Internet communications potentially affected by the Act is far broader than the State suggests. I note that in the past, various communities within the United States have found works including *I Know Why the Caged Bird Sings* by Maya Angelou, *Funhouse* by Dean Koontz, *The Adventures of Huckleberry Finn* by Mark Twain, and *The Color Purple* by Alice Walker to be indecent.

D.   *The Act Unconstitutionally Subjects Interstate Use of the Internet to Inconsistent Regulations*

Finally, a third mode of Commerce Clause analysis further confirms that the plaintiffs are likely to succeed on the merits of their claim that the New York Act is unconstitutional. The courts have long recognized that certain types of commerce demand consistent treatment and are therefore susceptible to regulation only on a national level. The Internet represents one of those areas; effective regulation will require national, and more likely global, cooperation. Regulation by any single state can only result in chaos, because at least some states will likely enact laws subjecting Internet users to conflicting obligations. Without the limitation's imposed by the Commerce Clause, these inconsistent regulatory schemes could paralyze the development of the Internet altogether.

The Internet requires a cohesive national scheme of regulation so that users are reasonably able to determine their obligations. Regulation on a local level, by contrast, will leave users lost in a welter of inconsistent laws, imposed by different states with different priorities. New York is not the only state to enact a law purporting to regulate the content of communications on the Internet. Already Oklahoma and Georgia have enacted laws designed to protect minors from indecent communications over the Internet; as might be expected, the states have selected different methods to accomplish their aims. Georgia has made it a crime to communicate anonymously over the Internet, while Oklahoma, like New York, has prohibited the online transmission of material deemed harmful to minors. *See* Ga. Code Ann. § 16–19–93.1 (1996); Okla. Stat. tit. 21, § 1040.76 (1996).

Moreover, the regulation of communications that may be "harmful to minors" taking place over the Internet poses particular difficulties. New York has defined "harmful to minors" as including:

that quality of any description or representation, in whatever form, of nudity, sexual conduct, sexual excitement, or sado-masochistic abuse, when it:

(a) Considered as a whole, appeals to the prurient interest in sex of minors; and

(b) Is patently offensive to prevailing standards in the adult community as a whole with respect to what is suitable material for minors; and

(c) Considered as a whole, lacks serious literary, artistic, political and scientific value for minors.

N.Y. Penal Law § 235.20(6). Courts have long recognized, however, that there is no single "prevailing community standard" in the United States. Thus, even were all 50 states to enact laws that were verbatim copies of the New York Act, Internet users would still be subject to discordant responsibilities.

As discussed at length above, an Internet user cannot foreclose access to her work from certain states or send differing versions of her communication to different jurisdictions. In this sense, the Internet user is in a worse position than the truck driver or train engineer who can steer around Illinois or Arizona, or change the mudguard or train configuration at the state line; the Internet user has no ability to bypass any particular state. The user must thus comply with the regulation imposed by the state with the most stringent standard or forego Internet communication of the message that might or might not subject her to prosecution.

Further development of the Internet requires that users be able to predict the results of their Internet use with some degree of assurance. Haphazard and uncoordinated state regulation can only frustrate the growth of cyberspace. The need for uniformity in this unique sphere of commerce requires that New York's law be stricken as a violation of the Commerce Clause.

NOTES AND QUESTIONS

1. Other courts have agreed with the approach of the *Pataki* decision, and have enjoined similar statutes enacted in other states. *See, e.g.*, American Booksellers Foundation v. Dean, 342 F.3d 96 (2d Cir. 2003) (enjoining a Vermont law); American Civil Liberties Union v. Johnson, 194 F.3d 1149 (10th Cir. 1999) (enjoining a New Mexico law); PSINet, Inc. v. Chapman, 362 F.3d 227 (4th Cir. 2004) (Virginia statute).

2. *Does the dormant Commerce Clause require exclusively federal regulation of the Internet?* Consider American Booksellers Foundation v. Dean, 342 F.3d 96, 103–04 (2d Cir. 2003), commenting on a Vermont statute similar to the one struck down in *Pataki*:

> Even if a website is never visited by people in Vermont, it is available to them in a way that a beer purchase in New York or Massachusetts is plainly not. Vermont's interest in out-of-state internet activity is thus more significant than a state's interest in the price of out-of-state beer sales. However, internet regulation of the sort at issue here still runs afoul of the dormant Commerce Clause because the Clause protects against inconsistent legislation arising from the projection of one state regulatory regime into the jurisdiction of another State. Thus, at the same time that the internet's geographic reach increases Vermont's interest in regulating out-of-state conduct, it makes state regulation impracticable. We think it likely that the internet will soon be seen as falling within the class of subjects that are protected from State regulation because they imperatively demand a single uniform rule.

For a critical perspective on this "common wisdom," and an argument that the dormant Commerce Clause permits vigorous state regulation of the Internet, see Jack L. Goldsmith & Alan O. Sykes, *The Internet and the Dormant Commerce Clause*, 110 Yale L.J. 785 (2001).

     3.   *Online solicitation distinguished.* In People v. Hsu, 99 Cal.Rptr.2d 184 (Cal. App. 2000), a man in California e-mailed pornographic pictures to a 14-year-old boy in California in an effort to convince the boy to meet him for sexual activities. The defendant was charged with violating California Penal Code § 288.2(b), which prohibits knowingly sending "harmful matter" to a minor with the intent of seducing that minor. A state court rejected the defendant's argument that the statute violated the dormant Commerce Clause:

> Under the *Pike* test, section 288.2, subdivision (b) does not violate the commerce clause. Statutes affecting public safety carry a strong presumption of validity, and the definition and enforcement of criminal laws lie primarily with states. States have a compelling interest in protecting minors from harm generally and certainly from being seduced to engage in sexual activities. Conversely, it is difficult to conceive of any legitimate commerce that would be burdened by penalizing the transmission of harmful sexual material to known minors in order to seduce them. To the extent section 288.2, subdivision (b) may affect interstate commerce, its effect is incidental at best and far outweighed by the state's abiding interest in preventing harm to minors.

Id. at 983–84. The court distinguished *Pataki* as follows, *id.* at 984–85:

> The knowledge and intent elements missing from the New York statute but present in section 288.2, subdivision (b) significantly distinguish the two statutes. The New York statute broadly banned the communication of harmful material to minors via the Internet. The scope of section 288.2, subdivision (b) is much narrower. Only when the material is disseminated to a *known* minor with the *intent* to arouse the prurient interest of the sender and/or minor and with

the *intent* to seduce the minor does the dissemination become a criminal act. The proscription against Internet use for these specifically defined and limited purposes does not burden interstate commerce by subjecting Internet users to inconsistent regulations. As *Pataki* itself observed,* * * New York could realistically prosecute violations of New York Penal Law section 235.22(2), which, like section 288.2, subdivision (b), prohibits adults from luring minors into sexual contact via Internet communication of harmful material, without violating the commerce clause.

When section 288.2, subdivision (b) is harmonized with the entire California penal scheme, it does not effectively regulate activities beyond California. California prosecutes only those criminal acts that occur wholly or partially within the state. Statutes must be construed in the light of the general principle that, ordinarily, a state does not impose punishment for acts done outside its territory. Section 288.2, subdivision (b) makes no reference to place of performance, so courts must assume the Legislature did not intend to regulate conduct taking place outside the state. Given the historical and statutory limitations on California's ability to prosecute, section 288.2, subdivision (b) cannot be enforced beyond what is jurisdictionally allowed. Consequently, such enforcement would not burden interstate commerce.

See also Ex parte Ingram, 533 S.W.3d 887 (Tex. Ct. Crim. App. 2017) (similar).

4. *State anti-spam statutes.* Several states prohibit the distribution of spam, unsolicited commercial e-mail. Most states have upheld such statutes against Commerce Clause challenges. For example, in State v. Heckel, 24 P.3d 404 (Wash. 2001), the Washington Supreme Court upheld a state law that prohibited using false or misleading subject lines in commercial e-mail sent in or to residents of Washington. The Court held that the truthfulness requirement satisfied the *Pike* balancing test, as it protected ISPs and consumers without placing any burden on commerce.

The permissible scope of state anti-spam statutes is also limited by the preemption provision in the federal anti-spam statute, the Controlling the Assault of Non-Solicited Pornography and Marketing (CAN-SPAM) Act of 2003, Pub. L. No. 108–187 (2003). Section 8(b)(1) of the Act states:

This Act supersedes any statute, regulation, or rule of a State or political subdivision of a State that expressly regulates the use of electronic mail to send commercial messages, except to the extent that any such statute, regulation, or rule prohibits falsity or deception in any portion of a commercial electronic mail message or information attached thereto.

15 U.S.C. § 7707(b)(1). For a discussion of how this provision applies to state anti-spam statutes, see Roger Allan Ford, *Preemption of State Spam Laws By The Federal CAN-SPAM Act*, 72 U. Chi. L. Rev. 355, 370–79 (2005).

5. *Pennsylvania's effort to block the availability of CSAM.* In 2002, Pennsylvania enacted the Internet Child Pornography Act, codified at 18 Pa. Cons. Stat. §§ 7621–30, in an effort to block the availability of CSAM over the Internet from Pennsylvania. The statute permits law enforcement officials in Pennsylvania to seek an ex parte court order ordering an ISP located anywhere in the United States to "remove or disable items residing on or accessible through" an ISP's service upon a showing of probable cause that the item constitutes CSAM and is available in Pennsylvania. The apparent thinking behind the statute is that states have no power to block the distribution of out-of-state CSAM, but they may be able to require ISPs to block such information and thus make it unavailable from inside the state. When challenged in court, however, a district court invalidated the Pennsylvania law on dormant Commerce Clause grounds (among other rationales):

> The burdens imposed by the Act are clearly excessive in relation to the local benefits. Defendant claims the Act is justified by reducing the sexual abuse of children. However, as discussed, defendant did not produce any evidence that the Act effectuates this goal. To the contrary, there have been no prosecutions of child pornographers and the evidence shows that individuals interested in obtaining or providing child pornography can evade blocking efforts using a number of different methods.

> Moreover, there is evidence that this Act places a substantial burden on interstate commerce. Defendant argues that the Act only burdens child pornography, which is not a legitimate form of commerce. To the contrary, the evidence demonstrates that implementation of the Act has impacted a number of entities involved in the commerce of the Internet—ISPs, web publishers, and users of the Internet. To comply with the Act, ISPs have used two types of filtering—IP filtering and DNS filtering—to disable access to alleged child pornography. This filtering resulted in the suppression of 376 web sites containing child pornography, certainly a local benefit. However, the filtering used by the ISPs also resulted in the suppression of in excess of 1,190,000 web sites not targeted by defendant and, as demonstrated at trial, a number of these web sites, probably most of them, do not contain child pornography. The overblocking harms web publishers which seek wide distribution for their web sites and Internet users who want access to the broadest range of content possible. For example, as a result of a block implemented by AOL in response to an Informal Notice, Ms. Goldwater, a self employed documentary film maker, was unable to access a web site selling movie posters.

> This Act [also] has the practical effect of exporting Pennsylvania's domestic policies. As an example, a WorldCom witness testified that a customer in Minnesota would not be able to access a web site hosted in Georgia if an IP Address was blocked by a Pennsylvania order. The Act is even more burdensome than the legislation examined in *Pataki*

because Pennsylvania has suppressed speech that was not targeted by the Act. Thus, a Minnesotan would be prevented from accessing a Georgia web site that is not even alleged to contain child pornography.

Center For Democracy & Technology v. Pappert, 337 F. Supp.2d 606, 661–63 (E.D. Pa. 2004). Should the result be the same if the Pennsylvania law only applies to ISPs based in Pennsylvania? Would such a law be effective? For a critique of the Pennsylvania law, see Jonathan Zittrain, *Internet Points of Control*, 44 B.C. L. Rev. 653, 674–88 (2003).

6. *State Internet gambling bans.* In Rousso v. State, 239 P.3d 1084 (Wash. 2010) (en banc), an on-line poker player in Washington brought a pre-enforcement challenge on dormant Commerce Clause grounds to a state gambling prohibition, RCW 9.46.240. The statute punishes "whoever knowingly transmits or receives gambling information by telephone, telegraph, radio, semaphore, the internet, a telecommunications transmission system, or similar means." The Supreme Court of Washington rejected the dormant Commerce Clause challenge. First, the law was not discriminatory, *see id.* at 1088:

> It equally prohibits Internet gambling regardless of whether the person or entity hosting the game is located in Washington, another state, or another country. Neither does RCW 9.46.240 have a direct discriminatory effect on interstate commerce. The statute prohibits Internet gambling evenhandedly, regardless of whether the company running the web site is located in or outside the state of Washington.

Second, the law passed the *Pike* balancing test:

> The State wields police power to protect its citizens' health, welfare, safety, and morals. On account of ties to organized crime, money laundering, gambling addiction, underage gambling, and other societal ills, the regulation of gambling enterprises lies at the heart of the state's police power.
>
> Internet gambling introduces new ways to exacerbate these same threats to health, welfare, safety, and morals. Gambling addicts and underage gamblers have greater accessibility to on-line gambling— able to gamble from their homes immediately and on demand, at any time, on any day, unhindered by in-person regulatory measures. Concerns over ties to organized crime and money laundering are exacerbated where on-line gambling operations are not physically present in-state to be inspected for regulatory compliance. Washington has a legitimate and substantial state interest in addressing the effects of Internet gambling.
>
> RCW 9.46.240 imposes a burden on interstate commerce by walling off the Washington market for Internet gambling from interstate commerce. The extent of this burden is mitigated somewhat. First, the ban does not prevent or hinder Internet gambling businesses from

operating throughout the rest of the world. Second, those businesses can easily exclude Washingtonians. If an individual during registration marks his or her location as the state of Washington, the gambling web site can end the registration there. Nevertheless, preventing Internet gambling businesses from having access to Washington consumers who would otherwise patronize those businesses still has a considerable impact on interstate commerce. This burden on interstate commerce is comparable to the substantial state interest stemming from the State's police power to protect the health, welfare, safety, and morals of its citizens.

Rousso argues regulating Internet gambling is a less restrictive alternative. This falls short of the mark because (1) it is not clear regulation could avoid concerns over Internet gambling as well as a complete ban and (2) it is not clear, even if regulation providing comparable protection is possible, the burden on interstate commerce would be decreased through that regulation.

Internet gambling has its own unique dangers and pitfalls. A regulatory system to monitor and address concerns unique to Internet gambling would take significant time and resources to develop and maintain. Even so, no regulatory system is perfect. Some concerns will not be fully addressed, while loopholes may permit others to slip through the cracks. The legislature decided to avoid the shortcomings and ongoing process of regulation by banning Internet gambling altogether. The legislature could have decided to step out in the rain with an umbrella, but instead it decided to stay home, dry, and without the possibility that its umbrella would break a mile from home. The judiciary has no authority to second-guess that decision, rebalancing public policy concerns to determine whether it would have arrived at a different result.

Id. at 1090–91.

2. PROCEDURAL LIMITS

State investigators confront a number of procedural hurdles to the collection of digital evidence that their federal counterparts do not encounter. Like federal investigators, state officers are bound by the Fourth Amendment and federal privacy laws. Unlike federal investigators, however, state investigators are also bound by four additional limits:

(1) federal privacy laws that expressly regulate the states,

(2) state statutory laws that extend beyond federal statutory laws,

(3) state constitutional protections that extend beyond the federal Fourth Amendment, and

(4) limits on the ability of state subpoena and search warrant authorities to demand evidence out-of-state.

Let's start with the first case, federal privacy laws that expressly regulate the states. Each of the federal statutory privacy laws has special rules that apply to state investigations, and that determine when and how state officials can obtain court orders. For example, the Wiretap Act places significant federal limits on state wiretapping laws. 18 U.S.C. § 2516(2) provides that state investigators can only obtain wiretapping orders "when such interception may provide or has provided evidence of the commission of the offense of murder, kidnapping, gambling, robbery, bribery, extortion, or dealing in narcotic drugs, marihuana or other dangerous drugs, or other crime dangerous to life, limb, or property, and punishable by imprisonment for more than one year." Further, a state investigator can only obtain a wiretapping order if the state legislature has decided to enact a wiretapping statute. If the state has chosen not to pass a wiretapping law, state investigators cannot obtain wiretap orders. *But see* 18 U.S.C. § 2703(d) (explaining when state courts can issue SCA orders); 18 U.S.C. § 3122(a)(2) (permitting state courts to issue pen register orders).

Second, state statutory privacy laws can impose greater restrictions than federal law. Such restrictions are binding only on state investigators: Under the Supremacy Clause, federal officials acting in the course of their official duties are not bound by state statutory privacy laws. However, states may choose to limit state investigators more than federal law requires. States may impose higher thresholds than federal law, or may carve out narrower exceptions. For example, a number of states require the consent of all parties to satisfy the consent exception of state wiretap statutes. If state undercover investigators wish to record telephone calls or Internet communications, state law may require the consent of the monitored parties even if federal law does not. *See generally* Charles H. Kennedy & Peter P. Swire, *State Wiretaps and Electronic Surveillance After September 11*, 54 Hastings L.J. 971, 987–1162 (2003) (summarizing state approaches).

Even if a state enacts statutory surveillance laws that match federal standards, state courts are free to construe state constitutions in ways that impose greater restrictions than those imposed by the Fourth Amendment.

STATE V. REID

Supreme Court of New Jersey, 2008.
945 A.2d 26.

CHIEF JUSTICE RABNER delivered the opinion of the Court.

Modern technology has raised a number of questions that are intertwined in this case: To what extent can private individuals "surf" the "Web" anonymously? Do Internet subscribers have a reasonable expectation of privacy in their identity while accessing Internet websites? And under what circumstances may the State learn the actual identity of Internet users?

In this case, defendant Shirley Reid allegedly logged onto an Internet website from her home computer. The site belonged to a company that supplied material to her employer's business. While on the supplier's website, Reid allegedly changed her employer's password and shipping address to a non-existent address.

Whenever an individual logs onto an Internet website, that user's identity is revealed only in the form of a unique multi-digit number (an "IP address") assigned by the user's Internet Service Provider ("ISP"). A website may collect that number, but only a service provider can translate it into the name of an actual user or subscriber.

Here, the supplier's website captured a ten-digit IP address, and the supplier told Reid's employer what had occurred. The employer, in turn, reported the IP address to local authorities. They issued a deficient municipal subpoena to Comcast, the service provider, and Comcast revealed that the IP address was assigned to Shirley Reid.

Reid is now under indictment for second-degree computer theft. She successfully moved to suppress the subscriber information obtained via the municipal subpoena.

We now hold that citizens have a reasonable expectation of privacy, protected by Article I, Paragraph 7, of the New Jersey Constitution, in the subscriber information they provide to Internet service providers-just as New Jersey citizens have a privacy interest in their bank records stored by banks and telephone billing records kept by phone companies. Law enforcement officials can satisfy that constitutional protection and obtain subscriber information by serving a grand jury subpoena on an ISP without notice to the subscriber.

Because the police used a deficient municipal subpoena to obtain protected subscriber information in this case, defendant's motion to suppress was properly granted. However, records of the protected subscriber information existed independently of the faulty process the police used, and the conduct of the police did not affect that information. As a result, the State may seek to reacquire the subscriber information with a proper grand jury subpoena.

I.

On August 27, 2004, Timothy Wilson, the owner of Jersey Diesel, reported to the Lower Township Police Department that someone had used a computer to change his company's shipping address and password for its suppliers. The shipping address was changed to a non-existent address.

In response to a question by the police, Wilson explained that Shirley Reid, an employee who had been on disability leave, could have made the changes. Reid returned to work on the morning of August 24, had an argument with Wilson about her temporary light duty assignment, and left. According to Wilson, Reid was the only employee who knew the company's computer password and ID.

Wilson learned of the changes through one of his suppliers, Donaldson Company, Inc. Both the password and shipping address for Jersey Diesel had been changed on Donaldson's website on August 24, 2004. According to an information technology specialist at Donaldson, someone accessed their website and used Jersey Diesel's username and password to sign on at 9:57 a.m. The individual changed the password and Jersey Diesel's shipping address and then completed the requests at 10:07 a.m.

Donaldson's website captured the user's IP address, 68.32.145.220, which was registered to Comcast. When Wilson contacted Comcast and asked for subscriber information associated with that address—so that he could identify the person who made the unauthorized changes—Comcast declined to respond without a subpoena.

On September 7, 2004, a subpoena *duces tecum* issued by the Lower Township Municipal Court was served on Comcast. The subpoena sought "any and all information pertaining to IP Address information belonging to IP address: 68.32.145.220, which occurred on 08/24/04 between 8:00 a.m. and 11:00 a.m. EST." The subpoena was captioned "Timothy C. Wilson, Plaintiff, vs. Shirley Reid, Defendant," although no such case was pending.

Comcast responded on September 16, 2004 and identified Reid as the subscriber of the IP address. In addition, Comcast provided the following information: Reid's address, telephone number, type of service provided, IP assignment (dynamic), account number, e-mail address, and method of payment.

An arrest warrant was issued on September 29, 2004, and Reid was arrested ten days later. On February 22, 2005, the Cape May County Grand Jury returned an indictment charging Reid with second-degree computer theft, in violation of *N.J.S.A.* 2C:20–25(b).

Reid moved to suppress the evidence obtained via the municipal court subpoena. On September 22, 2005, the trial court granted Reid's motion. The court identified various flaws with the municipal court subpoena and noted that the procedure followed by the police was "unauthorized in its entirety." The court also concluded that Reid had an expectation of privacy in her Internet subscriber information on file with Comcast. Therefore, the trial court held that the subpoena violated Reid's "right to be free from unreasonable searches and seizures" and was unconstitutional.

II.

We first consider the existence of a New Jersey citizen's privacy interest in Internet subscriber information.

Both the Fourth Amendment to the United States Constitution and Article I, Paragraph 7, of the New Jersey Constitution protect, in nearly identical language, the right of the people to be secure against unreasonable searches and seizures.

Federal case law interpreting the Fourth Amendment has found no expectation of privacy in Internet subscriber information. Those decisions draw on settled federal law that a person has no reasonable expectation of privacy in information exposed to third parties, like a telephone company or bank. *See Smith v. Maryland,* 442 U.S. 735, 742 (1979) (finding no privacy interest in telephone numbers dialed). The logic of those precedents extends to subscriber information revealed to an ISP.

Our inquiry does not end there because despite the congruity of the language, the search and seizure protections in the federal and New Jersey Constitutions are not always coterminous. Indeed, on multiple occasions this Court has held that the New Jersey Constitution affords our citizens greater protection against unreasonable searches and seizures than the Fourth Amendment.

During the past twenty-five years, a series of New Jersey cases has expanded the privacy rights enjoyed by citizens of this state. In 1982, this Court concluded in *State v. Hunt,* 91 N.J. 338, 347 (1982), that telephone toll billing records are "part of the privacy package." In language that resonates today on the subject of computers, the Court observed that the telephone has become an essential instrument in carrying on our personal affairs. Moreover, a list of telephone numbers dialed in the privacy of one's home could reveal the identities of the persons and the places called, and thus reveal the most intimate details of a person's life. Finding that Article I, Paragraph 7, of the New Jersey Constitution provides more protection than federal law affords, this Court concluded that a person "is entitled to assume that the numbers he dials in the privacy of his home will be recorded solely for the telephone company's business purposes. The Court rejected the underpinnings of federal case law by explaining that

> It is unrealistic to say that the cloak of privacy has been shed because the telephone company and some of its employees are aware of this information. This disclosure has been necessitated because of the nature of the instrumentality, but more significantly the disclosure has been made for a limited business purpose and not for release to other persons for other reasons.

More recently, in *State v. McAllister,* 184 N.J. 17, 32–33 (2005), this Court held that the New Jersey Constitution provides bank account holders a reasonable expectation of privacy in their bank records. As in *Hunt*, the Court noted that bank accounts have become an indispensable part of modern commerce for our citizens. Like long distance billing records, bank records reveal a great deal about the personal affairs, opinions, habits, and associations of depositors. The Court also noted that, although bank customers voluntarily provide information to banks, "they do so with the understanding that it will remain confidential." The disclosure is done to facilitate financial transactions, not to enable banks to broadcast the affairs of their customers.

B.

ISP records share much in common with long distance billing information and bank records. All are integrally connected to essential activities of today's society. Indeed, it is hard to overstate how important computers and the Internet have become to everyday, modern life. Citizens routinely access the Web for all manner of daily activities: to gather information, explore ideas, read, study, shop, and more.

Individuals need an ISP address in order to access the Internet. However, when users surf the Web from the privacy of their homes, they have reason to expect that their actions are confidential. Many are unaware that a numerical IP address can be captured by the websites they visit. More sophisticated users understand that that unique string of numbers, standing alone, reveals little if anything to the outside world. Only an Internet service provider can translate an IP address into a user's name.

In addition, while decoded IP addresses do not reveal the content of Internet communications, subscriber information alone can tell a great deal about a person. With a complete listing of IP addresses, one can track a person's Internet usage. "The government can learn the names of stores at which a person shops, the political organizations a person finds interesting, a person's fantasies, her health concerns, and so on." Daniel Solove, *The Future of Internet Surveillance Law*, 72 Geo. Wash. L. Rev. 1264, 1287 (2004). Such information can reveal intimate details about one's personal affairs in the same way disclosure of telephone billing records does. Although the contents of Internet communications may be even more revealing, both types of information implicate privacy interests.

It is well-settled under New Jersey law that disclosure to a third-party provider, as an essential step to obtaining service altogether, does not upend the privacy interest at stake. In the world of the Internet, the nature of the technology requires individuals to obtain an IP address to access the Web. Users make disclosures to ISPs for the limited goal of using that technology and not to promote the release of personal information to others. Under our precedents, users are entitled to expect confidentiality under these circumstances.

One additional point bears mention about the right to privacy in ISP subscriber information: the reasonableness of the privacy interest may change as technology evolves. A *reasonable* expectation of privacy is required to establish a protected privacy interest. Internet users today enjoy relatively complete IP address anonymity when surfing the Web. Given the current state of technology, the dynamic, temporarily assigned, numerical IP address cannot be matched to an individual user without the help of an ISP. Therefore, we accept as reasonable the expectation that one's identity will not be discovered through a string of numbers left behind on a website.

The availability of IP Address Locator Websites has not altered that expectation because they reveal the name and address of service providers but not individual users. Should that reality change over time, the reasonableness of the expectation of privacy in Internet subscriber information might change as well. For example, if one day new software allowed individuals to type IP addresses into a "reverse directory" and identify the name of a user—as is possible with reverse telephone directories—today's ruling might need to be reexamined.

C.

We turn next to the type of protection ISP subscriber information should receive in the face of legitimate investigative needs.

Recent case law informs our discussion. In *McAllister,* this Court concluded that issuance of a grand jury subpoena to obtain bank records, upon a showing of relevance, satisfies the constitutional protection against improper government intrusion. The Court further found that notice to the account holder was not constitutionally required. The same principles apply here.

In *McAllister,* the Court rejected arguments similar to those advanced in this case. In declining to adopt a heightened standard of probable cause to support the issuance of a grand jury subpoena, the Court found guidance in the words of Chief Justice Weintraub, writing in *In re Addonizio,* 53 N.J. 107 (1968). His explanation rings true today:

> A grand jury's power to investigate would be feeble indeed if the grand jury had to know at the outset everything needed to arrest a man or to invade his home. Nor would it serve the public interest to stay a probe until the grand jury reveals what it has or what it seeks. Such disclosures could defeat the inquiry and impede the apprehension of the culprit. This is one of the reasons why the law cloaks the grand jury investigation with secrecy.

More recently, in *State v. Domicz,* 188 N.J. 285, 297 (2006), this Court determined that acquiring electric utility records with a grand jury subpoena was proper under our Constitution. The Court noted that "whatever privacy interest attached" to utility records, obtaining them through the use of a grand jury subpoena satisfies Article I, Paragraph 7, of the State Constitution.

Utility records expose less information about a person's private life than either bank records or subscriber information. But we see no material difference between bank records and ISP subscriber information and decline to treat them differently. They reveal comparably detailed information about one's private affairs and are entitled to comparable protection under our law. In both cases, a grand jury subpoena based on a relevancy standard is sufficient to meet constitutional concerns.

The police in this case used a defective municipal subpoena to obtain Reid's ISP subscriber information from Comcast. We turn now to the consequences that flow from this violation of her rights.

Suppression under the circumstances present here does not mean that the evidence is lost in its entirety. Comcast's records existed independently of the faulty process the police followed. And unlike a confession coerced from a defendant in violation of her constitutional rights, the record does not suggest that police conduct in this case in any way affected the records Comcast kept. As a result, the records can be reliably reproduced and lawfully reacquired through a proper grand jury subpoena.

This outcome is readily apparent if viewed in the context of a motion to quash. Had Comcast sought to quash the municipal court subpoena, the trial court would have granted that relief for the same reasons it gave at the motion to suppress. At that point, nothing would have prevented the police from seeking the subscriber information from Comcast a second time, this time armed with an appropriate grand jury subpoena.

Therefore, the State may attempt to reacquire Comcast's records with a proper grand jury subpoena limited to seeking subscriber information for the IP address in question.

To recap, the trial court properly suppressed the subscriber information obtained, and the State may not proceed with the pending indictment absent proof that the indictment has a sufficient basis without relying on the suppressed evidence. Alternatively, the State may move to dismiss the pending indictment, re-serve a proper grand jury subpoena on Comcast, and seek a new indictment.

NOTES AND QUESTIONS

1. *The New Jersey equivalent of the Fourth Amendment.* The *Reid* court applies the New Jersey Constitution's privacy protections differently than courts apply the federal Fourth Amendment. *Reid* extends state privacy protections broadly, but it then makes a decision as to how much privacy protection is needed. The federal Fourth Amendment is different.

Constitutional protections do not extend as far. Once information is protected, however, it is generally protected by a full warrant requirement.

How might the rationale of *Reid* apply to other kinds of digital evidence? How much authority do the police need to install an Internet pen/trap device? To obtain logs from a service provider? To conduct real time monitoring of Internet accounts? Given the flexible nature of the New Jersey constitution, as applied in *Reid*, do you know the New Jersey rules until New Jersey courts announce them?

2.   *The third-party doctrine in the states.* According to a 2006 article by Stephen Henderson, New Jersey is one of eleven states in which courts have rejected the third-party disclosure principle underlying *Smith v. Maryland* as a matter of state constitutional law. In those eleven states, state investigators must obtain a probable cause search warrant to install a pen register. In contrast, courts in eighteen states either have explicitly adopted *Smith v. Maryland* as a matter of state constitutional law or else have strongly suggested they would do so if the question were directly raised. The remaining states have not addressed the question. *See* Stephen E. Henderson, *Learning From All Fifty States: How to Apply the Fourth Amendment and its State Analogs to Protect Third Party Information From Unreasonable Search*, 55 Cath. U. L. Rev. 373, 395–412 (2006).

3.   *Some states have amended their state constitutions to address privacy in electronic records.* The search and seizure provisions in state constitutions mostly resemble the text of the federal Fourth Amendment. A few states have amended their constitutions, however, to explicitly protect electronic communications and data.

In 2014, Missouri voters approved Amendment 9, an amendment to the Missouri Constitution that added the language in italics below to the preexisting text of Mo. Const. Art. I, § 15:

> The people shall be secure in their persons, papers, homes, effects, *and electronic communications and data*, from unreasonable searches and seizures; and no warrant to search any place, or seize any person or thing, *or access electronic data or communication*, shall issue without describing the place to be searched, or the person or thing to be seized, *or the data or communication to be accessed*, as nearly as may be; nor without probable cause, supported by written oath or affirmation.

What legal effect should this language have? The ballot question on which Missourians actually voted framed the question as follows:

> Shall the Missouri Constitution be amended so that the people shall be secure in their electronic communications and data from unreasonable searches and seizures as they are now likewise secure in their persons, homes, papers and effects?

_____ Yes

_____ No

So framed, voters passed the Amendment by a 3 to 1 vote. *See* https://ballot pedia.org/Missouri_Electronic_Data_Protection,_Amendment_9_(August_ 2014).

The legislative co-sponsor of Amendment 9, Republican state Sen. Rob Schaaf, offered the following perspective on its legal significance:

> Schaaf says that the amendment's specific legal impact will "take time to sort out" in Missouri, but he believes that the court will interpret it along the same lines as it interprets the right to privacy in person, paper, home, and effects. However, he believes that the national attention that the amendment receives will be its biggest impact, as that may inspire other states to follow suit.
>
> "I think other states will look at this vote and they will follow Missouri's lead," Schaaf says.

Becca Stanek, *Missouri Passes Constitutional Amendment to Protect Electronic Privacy*, Time, August 6, 2014.

A Missouri appellate court has interpreted the amendment to have no legal effect because the federal Fourth Amendment already protects electronic communications:

> [Amendment 9] added the express restrictions on issuance of warrants to "access any electronic data or communication" without probable cause supported by written oath or affirmation. So, in this respect, article I, section 15 differs from the Fourth Amendment. However, courts have long already interpreted the Fourth Amendment's protections as covering electronic communications and data in addition to "persons, houses, papers, and effects." *See, e.g., Katz v. United States*, 389 U.S. 347, 353 (1967). Because the Fourth Amendment is already being interpreted to protect electronic communications and data, we conclude that article I, section 15, even as amended, is not currently measurably more restrictive on the government than is the Fourth Amendment.

State ex rel. Koster v. Charter Communications, 461 S.W.3d 851, 858 (Mo. Ct. App. 2015).

Do you think this is a persuasive reading of the state constitutional language? Shouldn't a new constitutional amendment be interpreted to have some kind of effect? On the other hand, what specific effect should it have if even its co-sponsor is not sure what it does? *Cf.* Aaron Hadlow, *It's Probable: Missouri Constitution Article I, Section 15 Requires a Higher Standard to Obtain a Warrant for Real-Time or Prospective CSLI*, 82 Mo. L. Rev. (2017) (arguing pre-*Carpenter* that Amendment 9 should be interpreted to extend state constitutional protection to cell-site location records, which under then-existing law was outside federal Fourth Amendment protection).

More recently, in 2020, Michigan voters approved a similar amendment to the Michigan Constitution by a 89% to 11% vote. *See* https://ballotpedia.org/Michigan_Proposal_2,_Search_Warrant_for_Electronic_Data_Amendment_(2020).

4.   *CalECPA.* In 2015, the California legislature enacted the California Electronic Communications Privacy Act ("CalECPA"), Cal. Penal Code §§ 1546, 1546.1, 1546.2 and 1546.4. CalECPA imposes the most strict limits of any present or past surveillance regime in the United States. The law is binding on California law enforcement but not the federal government or investigators from other states.

CalECPA imposes a warrant requirement on access to all records held by third parties (including contents and metadata) with a relatively narrow exception. The exception, which roughly corresponds to the category of basic subscriber information found in 18 U.S.C. § 2703(c)(2), permits California officials to use a subpoena to obtain the following information:

> the name, street address, telephone number, email address, or similar contact information provided by the subscriber to the provider to establish or maintain an account or communication channel, a subscriber or account number or identifier, the length of service, and the types of services used by a user of or subscriber to a service provider.

CalECPA § 1546(*l*). All other information requires a warrant.

CalECPA also imposes new limits on how warrants can be obtained and how they can be executed. According to the law:

> (1)   The warrant shall describe with particularity the information to be seized by specifying the time periods covered and, as appropriate and reasonable, the target individuals or accounts, the applications or services covered, and the types of information sought.

> (2)   The warrant shall require that any information obtained through the execution of the warrant that is unrelated to the objective of the warrant shall be sealed and not subject to further review, use, or disclosure without a court order. A court shall issue such an order upon a finding that there is probable cause to believe that the information is relevant to an active investigation, or review, use, or disclosure is required by state or federal law.

CalECPA § 1546.1(d). *See, e.g.,* People v. Bell, 2021 WL 363233 (Cal. Ct. App. 2021) (considering a defense challenge to a warrant under CalECPA).

The statute then imposes additional limits on what the government must do if it obtains data through voluntary disclosure:

> If a government entity receives electronic communication information voluntarily provided pursuant to subdivision (f), it shall destroy that information within 90 days unless one or more of the following circumstances apply:

(1) The entity has or obtains the specific consent of the sender or recipient of the electronic communications about which information was disclosed.

(2) The entity obtains a court order authorizing the retention of the information. A court shall issue a retention order upon a finding that the conditions justifying the initial voluntary disclosure persist, in which case the court shall authorize the retention of the information only for so long as those conditions persist, or there is probable cause to believe that the information constitutes evidence that a crime has been committed.

(3) The entity reasonably believes that the information relates to child pornography and the information is retained as part of a multiagency database used in the investigation of child pornography and related crimes.

CalECPA § 1546.1(g).

The law also requires notice to the account holder when information other than basic subscriber information is obtained:

Any government entity that executes a warrant, or obtains electronic information in an emergency pursuant to Section 1546.1, shall serve upon, or deliver to by registered or first-class mail, electronic mail, or other means reasonably calculated to be effective, the identified targets of the warrant or emergency request, a notice that informs the recipient that information about the recipient has been compelled or requested, and states with reasonable specificity the nature of the government investigation under which the information is sought. The notice shall include a copy of the warrant or a written statement setting forth facts giving rise to the emergency. The notice shall be provided contemporaneously with the execution of a warrant, or, in the case of an emergency, within three days after obtaining the electronic information.

CalECPA § 1546.1(d). Any violation of any part of CalECPA can lead to suppression of the evidence. *See id.* § 1546.4. CalECPA also grants automatic statutory standing to challenge CalECPA violations. *See id.* § 1546.4(a).

For a detailed discussion of CalECPA, *see* Susan Freiwald, *At the Privacy Vanguard: California's Electronic Communication Privacy Act (CalECPA)*, 33 Berkeley Tech. L.J. 131 (2018).

5. *State legal process and the Full Faith and Credit clause.* As a general rule, state court orders issued in one state are not enforceable outside the state. For example, a state subpoena or warrant issued in state *A* for evidence in state *B* does not have binding force in state *B*. *See, e.g.*, Ex parte Dillon, 29 S.W.2d 236, 238 (Mo. Ct. App. 1930) (holding that Full Faith and Credit clause does not require states to recognize court orders from other states); National Institute of Justice, Electronic Crime Needs Assessment for State and Local Law Enforcement 25 (2001).

6. *Out-of-state legal process and the Stored Communications Act.* If you are an investigator in one state, and you need digital evidence located in another state, how can you ensure that you can collect the out-of-state evidence? Under the Stored Communications Act, providers can and ordinarily do comply with out-of-state legal process. *See, e.g.,* United States v. Orisakwe, 624 Fed.Appx. 149, 155 (5th Cir. 2015); State v. Rose, 330 P.3d 680, 685–86 (Or.App. 2014). However, compliance with out-of-state legal process is ordinarily optional rather than mandatory.

7. *Opening a home state investigation.* One way for state investigators to collect out-of-state evidence is to persuade law enforcement officials in the other state to open an investigation and obtain court orders locally. Some state law enforcement offices set aside resources to provide this service for investigators in sister states as a matter of comity. The sheriff's office in Loudoun County, Virginia, provided a good example during the heyday of America Online (AOL). In 2000, AOL was by far the most popular service used to access the Internet in the United States. At a time when about half of American adults used the Internet, AOL alone had 23 million customers. State criminal investigators around the country needed investigative help from AOL, which was based only in Loudoun County, Virginia, and had all of its servers there.

To assist state officials around the country, the sheriff's office assigned a Detective, Ron Horak, the task of opening Virginia investigations and obtaining Virginia warrants to serve on AOL. When contacted by state investigators from outside Virginia, Horak would open a local investigation, obtain the local warrant, serve it on AOL, and then forward the information sent to him from AOL to the investigators outside Virginia. *See* Maria Glod, *Loudoun's AOL Detective Finds Clues in E-Mail*, Wash. Post, Aug. 28, 2000, at A1.

If you are a state or local computer crime investigator, can you rely on such arrangements to collect evidence outside your state? What if you need evidence from a small provider in Rhode Island rather than a large provider in Silicon Valley?

8. *The Uniform Act to Secure the Attendance of Witnesses.* Every state except North Dakota has enacted a model law, *The Uniform Act to Secure the Attendance of Witnesses from Without a State in Criminal Proceedings* ("The Uniform Act"). The Uniform Act was first proposed by a law reform group in 1931 to secure out-of-state witnesses to testify in criminal trials. Some courts have held that the law also can be used to enforce out-of-state grand jury subpoenas to compel documents and records.

Under the Act, a court can issue a certificate to a court in another state asserting the need for a "material witness" in a pending case. The second state court receives the certificate, and it then holds a hearing to determine if "the witness is material and necessary" and whether "it will not cause undue hardship to the witness to be compelled to attend and testify in the prosecution or a grand jury investigation in the other state, and that the laws of the state in which the prosecution is pending, or grand jury investigation has commenced or is about to commence, will give to the witness protection from arrest and the service of civil and criminal process." Fla. Stat. Ann. § 942.02(2). If the judge is persuaded that this is the case, the judge can issue a summons requiring the witness to testify in the sister state proceeding.

A majority of state courts have held that the Uniform Act also applies to grand jury subpoenas for documents and other records. *See, e.g.,* Ulloa v. CMI, Inc., 133 So.3d 914, 923 (Fla. 2013) (citing cases). This permits investigative authorities in one state to seek help from a court in another state to enforce the subpoena in the second state. However, the procedure is time-consuming, requires an adversary hearing, and requires the coordination of judges in two states. As the Florida Supreme Court has explained:

> This process requires two courts to work together, with both courts finding that the witness in question is material and necessary. The witness also has an opportunity to be heard, and the sister state can ensure that the witness endures no undue hardship. This process guarantees that both sovereign states are coordinating their efforts, that the witness has the opportunity to be heard by his or her own state court, and that the witness does not need to travel to another state unless his or her own state's court has also determined that he or she is material and necessary to the case.

Id. at 922.

9.   *State laws that require providers to comply with out-of-state legal process.* In response to the perceived inadequacy of relying on voluntary assistance to enforce court orders extraterritorially, a few states have passed laws requiring Internet providers to comply with out-of-state legal process. An example of such a law is Cal. Penal Code § 1524.2. Under this law, ISPs incorporated in California must comply with out-of-state warrants:

> A California corporation that provides electronic communication services or remote computing services to the general public, when served with a warrant issued by another state to produce records that would reveal the identity of the customers using those services, data stored by, or on behalf of, the customer, the customer's usage of those services, the recipient or destination of communications sent to or from those customers, or the content of those communications, shall produce those records as if that warrant had been issued by a California court.

Cal. Penal Code § 1524.2(c). Further, providers that do business in California must comply with California state warrants:

> The following provisions shall apply to any search warrant issued pursuant to this chapter allowing a search for records that are in the actual or constructive possession of a foreign corporation that provides electronic communication services or remote computing services to the general public, where those records would reveal the

identity of the customers using those services, data stored by, or on behalf of, the customer, the customer's usage of those services, the recipient or destination of communications sent to or from those customers, or the content of those communications.

When properly served with a search warrant issued by the California court, a foreign corporation subject to this section shall provide to the applicant, all records sought pursuant to that warrant within five business days of receipt, including those records maintained or located outside this state.

Cal. Penal Code § 1524.2(b)–(b)(1).

10. *Should Congress pass a federal law requiring provider compliance with out-of-state legal process?* A government-funded research report on state and local cybercrime law summarized the problem of extraterritorial evidence collection as follows:

Currently there is no formal legal mechanism to allow for the enforcement of State subpoenas in other States. Cooperation can be achieved when one State attorney general's office voluntarily assists a sister State authority in either serving an out-of-State subpoena or seeking an in-State court order to enforce the out-of-State subpoena. However, the reliability and consistency of this procedure is not uniform, and the ability to secure enforcement of an out-of-State subpoena on a recalcitrant party is questionable at best.

To enhance the authority of State and local law enforcement to investigate cybercrimes that are too small to justify the investment of Federal resources but nevertheless require interstate process, more effective tools are required for enforcing State subpoenas in other jurisdictions. There are at least two possible models for creating these tools. One model is to develop an interstate compact that would establish procedures for signatory States to follow in enforcing out-of-State subpoenas. The Uniform Act to Secure the Attendance of Witnesses from Without a State in Criminal Proceedings is a comparable legal regime that has been adopted in the 50 States, the District of Columbia, Puerto Rico, and the Virgin Islands.

A second model involves a Federal statute empowering the Federal courts to issue "full faith and credit" orders enforcing out-of-State criminal subpoenas. This alternative might avoid the complexities of developing and adopting an interstate agreement, but it could possibly raise federalism concerns. Whichever type of approach is pursued, action is necessary in this area to ensure that victims of Internet crime have an effective recourse to which they can turn for protection and enforcement.

National Institute of Justice, Electronic Crime Needs Assessment for State and Local Law Enforcement 25–26 (2001).

Professor Brenner has discussed one effort to draft a federal statute. Susan W. Brenner, *Need for Reciprocal Enforcement of Warrants and Subpoenas in Cybercrime Cases*, 37 Prosecutor 29, 30 (2003). The National Institute of Justice's Electronic Crime Partnership Initiative prepared the following draft statute:

18 U.S. Code § ___

(a) Full Faith and Credit—Any production order issued that is consistent with subsection (b) of this section by the court of another State (the issuing State) shall be accorded full faith and credit by the court of another State (the enforcing State) and enforced as if it were the order of the enforcing state.

(b) Production Order—A production order issued by a State court is consistent with this subsection if—(1) The order is pursuant to the investigation or prosecution of a crime of the issuing state; (2) The order was issued in accordance with the law of the issuing state; and (3) Such court had jurisdiction over the criminal investigation or prosecution under the law of the issuing state.

(c) "Production Order" means any order, warrant, or subpoena for the production of records, issued by a court of competent jurisdiction.

(d) "Records" includes those items in whatever form created or stored.

Should Congress enact such a statute?

11. *The proper role of states in the investigation of computer crimes.* How important is it for state computer crime investigators to have the legal tools necessary to collect digital evidence nationwide? Is voluntary compliance adequate? Are model state statutes needed? Or is a federal statute the best solution? If a federal solution is needed, should the federal statute focus specifically on network service providers and computer crime cases or should it be more general in scope? Alternatively, is it appropriate in our federal system that state investigators cannot compel evidence nationwide?

C. INTERNATIONAL COMPUTER CRIMES

Computer crimes can cross national boundaries just as easily as they can cross state lines. As a result, investigators routinely face international jurisdictional issues. Investigators might want to prosecute a defendant for committing a computer crime that originated domestically but targeted computers outside its borders, or they might want to punish a crime originating abroad that targets a computer inside the United States. Evidence might need to be collected outside the United States for an otherwise domestic investigation.

Foreign governments face the same questions. Law enforcement officials from other countries may wish to punish computer crimes originating in the United States directed at computers in their home countries, or they may need to collect evidence in the United States to help domestic investigations. The following materials consider the law regulating international computer crime investigations.

1. UNITED STATES SUBSTANTIVE LAW

Do computer crime laws in the United States apply to conduct either originating from outside the United States or targeting computers located outside the United States?

UNITED STATES V. IVANOV

United States District Court for the District of Connecticut, 2001.
175 F. Supp.2d 367.

THOMPSON, DISTRICT JUDGE.

Defendant Aleksey Vladimirovich Ivanov has been indicted, in a superseding indictment, on charges of conspiracy, computer fraud and related activity, extortion and possession of unauthorized access devices. Ivanov has moved to dismiss the indictment on the grounds that the court lacks subject matter jurisdiction. Ivanov argues that because it is alleged that he was physically located in Russia when the offenses were committed, he cannot be charged with violations of United States law. For the reasons set forth below, the defendant's motion is being denied.

I. Background

Online Information Bureau, Inc. ("OIB"), the alleged victim in this case, is a Connecticut corporation based in Vernon, Connecticut. It is an "e-commerce" business which assists retail and Internet merchants by, among other things, hosting their websites and processing their credit card data and other financial transactions. In this capacity, OIB acts as a financial transaction "clearinghouse," by aggregating and assisting in the debiting or crediting of funds against each account for thousands of retail and Internet purchasers and vendors. In doing so, OIB collects and maintains customer credit card information, merchant account numbers, and related financial data from credit card companies and other financial institutions.

The government alleges that Ivanov hacked into OIB's computer system and obtained the key passwords to control OIB's entire network. The government contends that in late January and early February 2000, OIB received from Ivanov a series of unsolicited e-mails indicating that the defendant had obtained the "root" passwords for certain computer systems operated by OIB. A "root" password grants its user access to and control over an entire computer system, including the ability to manipulate, extract, and delete any and all data. Such passwords are generally reserved for use by the system administrator only.

The government claims that Ivanov then threatened OIB with the destruction of its computer systems (including its merchant account database) and demanded approximately $10,000 for his assistance in making those systems secure. It claims, for example, that on February 3, 2000, after his initial solicitations had been rebuffed, Ivanov sent the following e-mail to an employee of OIB:

> [name redacted], now imagine please Somebody hack you network (and not notify you about this), he download Atomic software with more than 300 merchants, transfer money, and after this did 'rm-rf' and after this you company be ruined. I don't want this, and because this I notify you about possible hack in you network, if you want you can hire me and im allways be check security in you network. What you think about this?[1]

The government contends that Ivanov's extortionate communications originated from an e-mail account at Lightrealm.com, an Internet Service Provider based in Kirkland, Washington. It contends that while he was in Russia, Ivanov gained access to the Lightrealm computer network and that he used that system to communicate with OIB, also while he was in Russia. Thus, each e-mail sent by Ivanov was allegedly transmitted from a Lightrealm.com computer in Kirkland, Washington through the Internet to an OIB computer in Vernon, Connecticut, where the e-mail was opened by an OIB employee.

The parties agree that the defendant was physically located in Russia (or one of the other former Soviet Bloc countries) when, it is alleged, he committed the offenses set forth in the superseding indictment.

The superseding indictment comprises eight counts. Count One charges that beginning in or about December 1999, or earlier, the defendant and others conspired to commit the substantive offenses charged in Counts Two through Eight of the indictment, in violation of 18 U.S.C. § 371. Count Two charges that the defendant, knowingly and with intent to defraud, accessed protected computers owned by OIB and by means of this conduct furthered a fraud and obtained something of value, in violation of 18 U.S.C. §§ 2, 1030(a)(4) and 1030(c)(3)(A). Count Three charges that the defendant intentionally accessed protected computers owned by OIB and thereby obtained information, which conduct involved interstate and foreign communications and was engaged in for purposes of financial gain and in furtherance of a criminal act, in violation of 18 U.S.C. §§ 2, 1030(a)(2)(C) and 1030(c)(2)(B).

Count Six charges that the defendant transmitted in interstate and foreign commerce communications containing a threat to cause damage to protected computers owned by OIB, in violation of 18 U.S.C. §§ 1030(a)(7)

---

[1]　An individual with "root access" who inputs the UNIX command "rm-rf" will delete all files on the network server, including all operating system software.

and 1030(c)(3)(A). Count Seven charges that the defendant obstructed, delayed and affected commerce, and attempted to obstruct, delay and affect commerce, by means of extortion by attempting to obtain property from OIB with OIB's consent, inducing such consent by means of threats to damage OIB and its business unless OIB paid the defendant money and hired the defendant as a security consultant, in violation of 18 U.S.C. § 1951(a). Count Eight charges that the defendant, knowingly and with intent to defraud, possessed unauthorized access devices, which conduct affected interstate and foreign commerce, in violation of 18 U.S.C. § 1029(a)(3).

II. Discussion

The defendant and the government agree that when Ivanov allegedly engaged in the conduct charged in the superseding indictment, he was physically present in Russia and using a computer there at all relevant times. Ivanov contends that for this reason, charging him under the Hobbs Act, 18 U.S.C. § 1951, under the Computer Fraud and Abuse Act, 18 U.S.C. § 1030, and under the access device statute, 18 U.S.C. § 1029, would in each case require extraterritorial application of that law and such application is impermissible. The court concludes that it has jurisdiction, first, because the intended and actual detrimental effects of Ivanov's actions in Russia occurred within the United States, and second, because each of the statutes under which Ivanov was charged with a substantive offense was intended by Congress to apply extraterritorially.

A. The Intended and Actual Detrimental Effects of the Charged Offenses Occurred Within the United States

As noted by the court in *United States v. Muench,* 694 F.2d 28 (2d Cir. 1982), the intent to cause effects within the United States makes it reasonable to apply to persons outside United States territory a statute which is not expressly extraterritorial in scope. It has long been a commonplace of criminal liability that a person may be charged in the place where the evil results, though he is beyond the jurisdiction when he starts the train of events of which that evil is the fruit. The Government may punish a defendant in the same manner as if he were present in the jurisdiction when the detrimental effects occurred.

The Supreme Court has quoted with approval the following language from Moore's International Law Digest:

The principle that a man, who outside of a country willfully puts in motion a force to take effect in it, is answerable at the place where the evil is done, is recognized in the criminal jurisprudence of all countries. And the methods which modern invention has furnished for the performance of criminal acts in that manner has made this principle one of constantly growing importance and of increasing frequency of application.

Moreover, the court noted in *Marc Rich & Co. v. United States*, 707 F.2d 663 (2d Cir. 1983) that:

> It is certain that the courts of many countries, even of countries which have given their criminal legislation a strictly territorial character, interpret criminal law in the sense that offences, the authors of which at the moment of commission are in the territory of another State, are nevertheless to be regarded as having been committed in the national territory, if one of the constituent elements of the offence, and more especially its effects, have taken place there.

Id. at 666.

Here, all of the intended and actual detrimental effects of the substantive offenses Ivanov is charged with in the indictment occurred within the United States. In Counts Two and Three, the defendant is charged with accessing OIB's computers. Those computers were located in Vernon, Connecticut. The fact that the computers were accessed by means of a complex process initiated and controlled from a remote location does not alter the fact that the accessing of the computers, i.e. part of the detrimental effect prohibited by the statute, occurred at the place where the computers were physically located, namely OIB's place of business in Vernon, Connecticut.

Count Two charges further that Ivanov obtained something of value when he accessed OIB's computers, that "something of value" being the data obtained from OIB's computers. In order for Ivanov to violate § 1030(a)(4), it was necessary that he do more than merely access OIB's computers and view the data. *See United States v. Czubinski,* 106 F.3d 1069, 1078 (1st Cir. 1997) ("Merely viewing information cannot be deemed the same as obtaining something of value for purposes of this statute. This section should apply to those who steal information through unauthorized access."). The indictment charges that Ivanov did more than merely gain unauthorized access and view the data. Ivanov allegedly obtained root access to the OIB computers located in Vernon, Connecticut. Once Ivanov had root access to the computers, he was able to control the data, e.g., credit card numbers and merchant account numbers, stored in the OIB computers; Ivanov could copy, sell, transfer, alter, or destroy that data. That data is intangible property of OIB. In determining where, in the case of intangibles, possession resides, the measure of control exercised is the deciding factor.

At the point Ivanov gained root access to OIB's computers, he had complete control over that data, and consequently, had possession of it. That data was in OIB's computers. Since Ivanov possessed that data while it was in OIB's computers in Vernon, Connecticut, the court concludes that he obtained it, for purposes of § 1030(a)(4), in Vernon, Connecticut. The fact that Ivanov is charged with obtaining OIB's valuable data by means of a complex process initiated and controlled from a remote location, and that he subsequently moved that data to a computer located in Russia, does not alter the fact that at the point when Ivanov first possessed that data, it was on OIB's computers in Vernon, Connecticut.

Count Three charges further that when he accessed OIB's computers, Ivanov obtained information from protected computers. The analysis as to the location at which Ivanov obtained the information referenced in this count is the same as the analysis as to the location at which he obtained the "something of value" referenced in Count Two. Thus, as to both Counts Two and Three, it is charged that the balance of the detrimental effect prohibited by the pertinent statute, i.e., Ivanov's obtaining something of value or obtaining information, also occurred within the United States.

Count Six charges that Ivanov transmitted a threat to cause damage to protected computers. The detrimental effect prohibited by § 1030(a)(7), namely the receipt by an individual or entity of a threat to cause damage to a protected computer, occurred in Vernon, Connecticut because that is where OIB was located, where it received the threat, and where the protected computers were located. The analysis is the same as to Count Seven, the charge under the Hobbs Act.

Count Eight charges that Ivanov knowingly and with intent to defraud possessed over ten thousand unauthorized access devices, i.e., credit card numbers and merchant account numbers. For the reasons discussed above, although it is charged that Ivanov later transferred this intangible property to Russia, he first possessed it while it was on OIB's computers in Vernon, Connecticut. Had he not possessed it here, he would not have been able to transfer it to his computer in Russia. Thus, the detrimental effect prohibited by the statute occurred within the United States.

Finally, Count One charges that Ivanov and others conspired to commit each of the substantive offenses charged in the indictment. The Second Circuit has stated that "the jurisdictional element should be viewed for purposes of the conspiracy count exactly as we view it for purposes of the substantive offense." *United States v. Blackmon*, 839 F.2d 900, 910 (2d Cir. 1988). Federal jurisdiction over a conspiracy charge is established by proof that the accused planned to commit a substantive offense which, if attainable, would have violated a federal statute, and that at least one overt act has been committed in furtherance of the conspiracy. Here, Ivanov is charged with planning to commit substantive offenses in violation of federal statutes, and it is charged that at least one overt act was committed in furtherance of the conspiracy. As discussed above, the court has jurisdiction over the underlying substantive charges. Therefore, the court has jurisdiction over the conspiracy charge, at a minimum, to the extent it relates to Counts Two, Three, Six, Seven or Eight.

Accordingly, the court concludes that it has subject matter jurisdiction over each of the charges against Ivanov, whether or not the statutes under which the substantive offenses are charged are intended by Congress to apply extraterritorially, because the intended and actual detrimental effects of the substantive offenses Ivanov is charged with in the indictment occurred within the United States.

B.   Intended Extraterritorial Application

The defendant's motion should also be denied because, as to each of the statutes under which the defendant has been indicted for a substantive offense, there is clear evidence that the statute was intended by Congress to apply extraterritorially. This fact is evidenced by both the plain language and the legislative history of each of these statutes.

There is a presumption that Congress intends its acts to apply only within the United States, and not extraterritorially. However, this presumption against extraterritoriality may be overcome by showing clear evidence of congressional intent to apply a statute beyond our borders. Congress has the authority to enforce its laws beyond the territorial boundaries of the United States. Whether Congress has in fact exercised that authority in a particular case is a matter of statutory construction.

The Computer Fraud and Abuse Act was amended in 1996 by Pub. L. No. 104–294, 110 Stat. 3491, 3508. The 1996 amendments made several changes that are relevant to the issue of extraterritoriality, including a change in the definition of "protected computer" so that it included any computer "which is used in interstate *or foreign* commerce or communication." 18 U.S.C. § 1030(e)(2)(B) (emphasis added). The 1996 amendments also added subsections (a)(2)(C) and (a)(7), which explicitly address "interstate or foreign commerce," and subsection (e)(9), which added to the definition of "government entity" the clause "any foreign country, and any state, province, municipality or other political subdivision of a foreign country."

The plain language of the statute, as amended, is clear. Congress intended the CFAA to apply to computers used "in interstate or foreign commerce or communication." The defendant argues that this language is ambiguous. The court disagrees. The Supreme Court has often stated that "a statute ought, upon the whole, to be so construed that, if it can be prevented, no clause, sentence, or word shall be superfluous, void, or insignificant." *Regions Hosp. v. Shalala,* 522 U.S. 448, 467 (1998). In order for the word "foreign" to have meaning, and not be superfluous, it must mean something other than "interstate." In other words, "foreign" in this context must mean international. Thus, Congress has clearly manifested its intent to apply § 1030 to computers used either in interstate or in foreign commerce.

The legislative history of the CFAA supports this reading of the plain language of the statute. The Senate Judiciary Committee issued a report explaining its reasons for adopting the 1996 amendments. S. Rep. No. 357, 104th Congr., 2d Sess. (1996). In that report, the Committee specifically noted its concern that the statute as it existed prior to the 1996 amendments did not cover "computers used in foreign communications or commerce, despite the fact that hackers are often foreign-based." *Id.* at 4. The Committee cited two specific cases in which foreign-based hackers had infiltrated computer systems in the United States, as examples of the kind of situation the amendments were intended to address:

> For example, the 1994 intrusion into the Rome Laboratory at Grifess Air Force Base in New York, was perpetrated by a 16 year-old hacker in the United Kingdom. More recently, in March 1996, the Justice Department tracked down a young Argentinean man who had broken into Harvard University's computers from Buenos Aires and used those computers as a staging ground to hack into many other computer sites, including the Defense Department and NASA.

Id. at 4–5. Congress has the power to apply its statutes extraterritorially, and in the case of 18 U.S.C. § 1030, it has clearly manifested its intention to do so.

NOTES AND QUESTIONS

1. *The policy question.* As a matter of policy, should it be a federal crime for a person located abroad to hack into or damage a computer located in the United States? Why not let officials in the other country handle the case? Is it likely that Russian authorities would prosecute Ivanov for his unauthorized access into United States computers?

2. *The policy question in reverse.* Should it be a federal crime for a person located in the United States to hack into or damage a computer located in a foreign country? Imagine that a person in the United States dislikes the government of China, and he decides to launch a denial-of-service attack against computers owned by the Chinese government located in China. Does the attack violate United States law? As a matter of policy, should it?

3. *The scope of § 1030 and international investigations.* The USA Patriot Act of 2001 amended the definition of "protected computer" in 18 U.S.C. § 1030(e)(2) so that it now explicitly includes computers located outside of the United States. Before the Patriot Act, the term "protected computer" was defined (as in the *Ivanov* case) as including a computer "which is used in interstate or foreign commerce or communication." 18 U.S.C. § 1030(e)(2) (1996). The Patriot Act added the phrase "including a computer located outside the United States that is used in a manner that affects interstate or foreign commerce or communication of the United States." The Justice Department has offered the following explanation for the amendment:

Because of the interdependency and availability of global computer networks, hackers from within the United States are increasingly targeting systems located entirely outside of this country. The statute did not explicitly allow for prosecution of such hackers. In addition, individuals in foreign countries frequently route communications through the United States, even as they hack from one foreign country to another. In such cases, their hope may be that the lack of any U.S. victim would either prevent or discourage U.S. law enforcement agencies from assisting in any foreign investigation or prosecution.

Section 814 of the Act amends the definition of "protected computer" to make clear that this term includes computers outside of the United States so long as they affect "interstate or foreign commerce or communication of the United States." 18 U.S.C. § 1030(e)(2)(B). By clarifying the fact that a domestic offense exists, the United States can now use speedier domestic procedures to join in international hacker investigations. As these crimes often involve investigators and victims in more than one country, fostering international law enforcement cooperation is essential.

In addition, the amendment creates the option, where appropriate, of prosecuting such criminals in the United States. Since the U.S. is urging other countries to ensure that they can vindicate the interests of U.S. victims for computer crimes that originate in their nations, this provision will allow the U.S. to provide reciprocal coverage.

Computer Crime and Intellectual Property Section (CCIPS), Field Guidance on New Authorities that Relate to Computer Crime and Electronic Evidence Enacted in the USA Patriot Act of 2001 (2001).

Note that the Justice Department mostly justifies the expansion of 18 U.S.C. § 1030 based on its impact on international investigations. According to DOJ, "the United States can now use speedier domestic procedures to join in international hacker investigations." When an international computer crime does not violate U.S. law, officials must follow fairly complicated and time-consuming evidence-collecting procedures (described later in this chapter). On the other hand, if an international computer crime violates 18 U.S.C. § 1030, U.S. law enforcement officials can open a *domestic* investigation into the violation. They can then use statutes such as the Electronic Communications Privacy Act to collect digital evidence in the United States and forward their findings on to counterparts abroad. As a result, a change in the substantive law of 18 U.S.C. § 1030 can have important procedural implications for international computer crime cases.

We observed a similar dynamic in the context of state criminal investigations that cross state lines. Recall that if investigators in state *A* need electronic evidence in state *B*, law enforcement officials in state *B* can open an investigation in that state, obtain the evidence, and then send it to officials in state *A*. Opening a second investigation in the jurisdiction where the evidence is located circumvents the hurdle of extraterritorial evidence collection, at least if the officials in the second jurisdiction are willing to help. The Patriot Act's amendment to § 1030(e)(2)(B) permits United States officials to perform the same role for foreign authorities investigating international computer crimes.

Is this a good idea? One commentator has argued that this expansion of 18 U.S.C. § 1030 goes too far:

> Where the affect on U.S. computer networks is slight—to the point of non-existence—the U.S. should not impose its law on the activity.
>
> The new statute requires no threshold of damage or even effect on U.S. computers to trigger U.S. sovereignty. The vast majority of Internet traffic travels through the United States, with more than half of the traffic traveling through Northern Virginia alone. The mere fact that packets relating to the criminal activity travel through the United States should not be enough to trigger U.S. jurisdiction, even though such traffic would "affect" international commerce, albeit infinitesimally.

Mark Rasch, *Ashcroft's Global Internet Power-Grab* (Nov. 25, 2001), http:// www.securityfocus.com/columnists/39. Should Congress change the law back to the 1996 version?

4. *United States law and global computer viruses.* In May 2000, the Internet was hit by an e-mail-based computer virus known as the "I Love You" virus. The virus was sent by Onel A. de Guzman, a 23-year-old computer programmer from the Philippines. Guzman first sent an infected e-mail using an account in the Philippines to various individuals with e-mail accounts in the Philippines. The virus quickly spread outside the Philippines and infected computers all around the world. Businesses around the world (including many in the United States) were forced to shut down in response to the infection.

Did Onel de Guzman violate 18 U.S.C. § 1030? Does the answer depend on whether the definition of "protected computer" is the 1996 definition or the current definition enacted by the Patriot Act? Does the answer depend on de Guzman's *mens rea* with respect to whether the virus would damage computers located in the United States?

5. *Should the United States be the world's police for Internet crime?* Consider Ellen S. Podgor, *International Computer Fraud: A Paradigm for Limiting National Jurisdiction*, 35 U.C. Davis L. Rev. 267, 269–70, 317 (2002):

> Should the United States acquire jurisdiction of all criminal activity when the medium for the crime involves the use of a computer, and the activity has an effect in this country? U.S. law enforcement should tread carefully in imposing its jurisdiction throughout the world. It is one thing to lead the charge in prosecuting international computer fraud crimes; it is another, however, to take charge. Until sufficient international measures are operational, it is important for the United States to remind itself that it is not the world's police, prosecutor and court.

Do you agree? Why is this important?

6.   *The global reach of the Wire Act.* In United States v. Lyons, 740 F.3d 702 (1st Cir. 2014), the First Circuit expressly rejected the defendant's extraterritoriality claim in an Internet gambling prosecution brought under the Wire Act. Lyons and Eremian worked for a sports betting business based in Antigua that did most of its business with customers in the United States. According to the First Circuit, this connection with the United States was sufficient to generate criminal liability under the Wire Act:

> Lyons's and Eremian's convictions were not an improper extraterritorial application of the Wire Act. It is a longstanding principle of American law that legislation of Congress, unless a contrary intent appears, is meant to apply only within the territorial jurisdiction of the United States. The Wire Act expresses such a contrary intent because it explicitly applies to transmissions between the United States and a foreign country. 18 U.S.C. § 1084. The communications giving rise to these convictions had at least one participant inside the United States and therefore fall within the statute's scope.

Id. at 718.

7.   *Punishing conduct outside the United States and the scope of the Foreign Commerce Clause.* The constitutional hook for most federal crimes that punish conduct outside the United States is the Foreign Commerce Clause, which gives Congress the power "[t]o regulate Commerce with foreign Nations." U.S. Const. Art. I, § 8, cl. 3. Under this clause, what limits (if any) are placed on Congress's power to criminally punish conduct outside the United States?

In United States v. Baston, 818 F.3d 651 (11th Cir. 2016), the Eleventh Circuit rejected a Foreign Commerce Clause challenge to 18 U.S.C. § 1596(a)(2), a 2008 law that creates extra-territorial jurisdiction over sex trafficking crimes that occur abroad when the defendant is "present in the United States." Judge William Pryor offered the following commentary about the scope of the Foreign Commerce Clause:

> What little guidance we have from the Supreme Court establishes that the Foreign Commerce Clause provides Congress a broad power. The Supreme Court has described the Foreign Commerce Clause, like the Indian Commerce Clause, as granting Congress a power that is plenary and broad. Also like the Indian Commerce Clause, the Foreign Commerce Clause does not pose the federalism concerns that limit the scope of the Interstate Commerce Clause. Indeed, the Supreme Court has suggested that the power to regulate commerce when exercised in respect of foreign commerce may be broader than when exercised as to interstate commerce. Although the Constitution grants Congress power to regulate commerce 'with foreign Nations' and 'among the several States' in parallel phrases, the Supreme

Court has explained, there is evidence that the Founders intended the scope of the foreign commerce power to be the greater. The Supreme Court has cited James Madison, for example, who described the Foreign Commerce Clause as a "great and essential power" that the Interstate Commerce Clause merely "supplements." The Federalist No. 42, at 283.

Id. at 667–68.

2. STATUTORY PRIVACY LAWS

When a computer crime occurs entirely in the United States, federal investigators must comply with the Fourth Amendment, the Wiretap Act, the Pen Register Statute, and the Stored Communications Act. But what laws govern investigations when the collection of evidence occurs in part or in whole outside the United States? The following materials explore that question. They begin by considering the statutory privacy laws, and they turn next to the Fourth Amendment.

As a general rule, the statutory privacy laws were designed for domestic application. They apply inside the United States and do not regulate outside the United States. This principle is easy to state but sometimes difficult to apply. The Internet is global, and a domestic United States Internet provider might store records or contents on a server outside the United States. If United States investigators seek to compel records or contents stored outside the United States by a U.S.-based Internet provider, can they use domestic legal process?

The Second Circuit's opinion reprinted below considered the extraterritorial scope of the Stored Communications Act as it existed in 2016. Notably, the decision reflects the beginning of a debate rather than the end of one. The Supreme Court subsequently reviewed the Second Circuit's ruling, holding oral argument in February 2018. Congress took action soon after: In March 2018, before the Supreme Court handed down a ruling, Congress enacted the Clarifying Lawful Overseas Use of Data (CLOUD) Act as part of the Consolidated Appropriations Act, Pub.L. 115–141. The Supreme Court dismissed the *Microsoft* case a few weeks later because the CLOUD Act mooted the prior dispute. *See* United States v. Microsoft Corp., 138 S.Ct. 1186 (2018) (per curiam) (concluding that, because the government obtained a warrant under the new CLOUD Act, "no live dispute remains between the parties over the issue with respect to which certiorari was granted").

Although the Second Circuit's decision below is no longer an accurate statement of the law, it still provides a useful introduction to the policy problem and helps illuminate the 2018 statute that Congress enacted to solve it.

MICROSOFT CORPORATION V. UNITED STATES
United States Court of Appeals for the Second Circuit, 2016.
829 F.3d 197.

SUSAN L. CARNEY, CIRCUIT JUDGE.

Microsoft Corporation appeals from orders of the United States District Court for the Southern District of New York denying its motion to quash a warrant issued under § 2703 of the Stored Communications Act, 18 U.S.C. §§ 2701 *et seq.*, and holding Microsoft in contempt of court for refusing to execute the Warrant on the government's behalf. The Warrant directed Microsoft to seize and produce the contents of an e-mail account that it maintains for a customer who uses the company's electronic communications services. A United States magistrate judge (Francis, *M.J.*) issued the Warrant on the government's application, having found probable cause to believe that the account was being used in furtherance of narcotics trafficking. The Warrant was then served on Microsoft at its headquarters in Redmond, Washington.

Microsoft produced its customer's non-content information to the government, as directed. That data was stored in the United States. But Microsoft ascertained that, to comply fully with the Warrant, it would need to access customer content that it stores and maintains in Ireland and to import that data into the United States for delivery to federal authorities. It declined to do so. Instead, it moved to quash the Warrant. The magistrate judge, affirmed by the District Court, denied the motion to quash and, in due course, the District Court held Microsoft in civil contempt for its failure.

Microsoft and the government dispute the nature and reach of the Warrant that the Act authorized and the extent of Microsoft's obligations under the instrument. For its part, Microsoft emphasizes Congress's use in the Act of the term "warrant" to identify the authorized instrument. Warrants traditionally carry territorial limitations: United States law enforcement officers may be directed by a court-issued warrant to seize items at locations in the United States and in United States-controlled areas, *see* Fed. R. Crim. P. 41(b), but their authority generally does not extend further.

The government, on the other hand, characterizes the dispute as merely about "compelled disclosure," regardless of the label appearing on the instrument. It maintains that "similar to a subpoena, an SCA warrant requires the recipient to deliver records, physical objects, and other materials to the government" no matter where those documents are located, so long as they are subject to the recipient's custody or control. It relies on a collection of court rulings construing properly-served subpoenas as imposing that broad obligation to produce without regard to a document's location.

We think that Microsoft has the better of the argument. When, in 1986, Congress passed the Stored Communications Act as part of the broader Electronic Communications Privacy Act, its aim was to protect user privacy in the context of new technology that required a user's interaction with a service provider. Neither explicitly nor implicitly does the statute envision the application of its warrant provisions overseas. Three decades ago, international boundaries were not so routinely crossed as they are today, when service providers rely on worldwide networks of hardware to satisfy users' 21st-century demands for access and speed and their related, evolving expectations of privacy.

Rather, in keeping with the pressing needs of the day, Congress focused on providing basic safeguards for the privacy of domestic users. Accordingly, we think it employed the term "warrant" in the Act to require pre-disclosure scrutiny of the requested search and seizure by a neutral third party, and thereby to afford heightened privacy protection in the United States. It did not abandon the instrument's territorial limitations and other constitutional requirements. The application of the Act that the government proposes—interpreting "warrant" to require a service provider to retrieve material from beyond the borders of the United States—would require us to disregard the presumption against extraterritoriality that the Supreme Court re-stated and emphasized in *Morrison v. National Australia Bank Ltd.*, 561 U.S. 247 (2010), and, just recently, in *RJR Nabisco, Inc. v. European Cmty.*, 136 S.Ct. 2090 (2016). We are not at liberty to do so.

We therefore decide that the District Court lacked authority to enforce the Warrant against Microsoft. Because Microsoft has complied with the Warrant's domestic directives and resisted only its extraterritorial aspects, we reverse the District Court's denial of Microsoft's motion to quash, vacate its finding of civil contempt, and remand the cause with instructions to the District Court to quash the Warrant insofar as it directs Microsoft to collect, import, and produce to the government customer content stored outside the United States.

GERARD E. LYNCH, CIRCUIT JUDGE, concurring in the judgment:

I am in general agreement with the Court's conclusion that, in light of the presumption against extraterritorial application of congressional enactments, the Stored Communications Act ("SCA" or the "Act") should not, on the record made by the government below, be construed to require Microsoft to turn over records of the content of emails stored on servers in Ireland. I write separately to clarify what, in my view, is at stake and not at stake in this case; to explain why I believe that the government's arguments are stronger than the Court's opinion acknowledges; and to emphasize the need for congressional action to revise a badly outdated statute.

I

An undercurrent running through Microsoft's and several of its amici's briefing is the suggestion that this case involves a government threat to individual privacy. I do not believe that that is a fair characterization of the stakes in this dispute. To uphold the warrant here would not undermine basic values of privacy as defined in the Fourth Amendment and in the libertarian traditions of this country.

In this case, the government complied with the most restrictive privacy-protecting requirements of the Act. Those requirements are consistent with the highest level of protection ordinarily required by the Fourth Amendment for the issuance of search warrants: a demonstration by the government to an independent judicial officer that evidence presented on oath justifies the conclusion that there is probable cause to believe that a crime has been committed, and that evidence of such crime can be found in the communications sought by the government.

That point bears significant emphasis. In this case, the government proved to the satisfaction of a judge that a reasonable person would believe that the records sought contained evidence of a crime. That is the showing that the framers of our Bill of Rights believed was sufficient to support the issuance of search warrants. U.S. Const. amend. IV ("[N]o Warrants shall issue, but upon probable cause . . . ."). In other words, in the ordinary domestic law enforcement context, if the government had made an equivalent showing that evidence of a crime could be found in a citizen's home, that showing would permit a judge to authorize law enforcement agents to forcibly enter that home and search every area of the home to locate the evidence in question, and even (if documentary or electronic evidence was sought) to rummage through file cabinets and to seize and examine the hard drives of computers or other electronic devices.

I emphasize these points to clarify that Microsoft's argument is not that the government does not have sufficiently solid information, and sufficiently important interests, to justify invading the privacy of the customer whose emails are sought and acquiring records of the contents of those emails. Microsoft does not ask the Court to create, as a matter of constitutional law, stricter safeguards on the protection of those emails— and the Court does not do so. Rather, the sole issue involved is whether Microsoft can thwart the government's otherwise justified demand for the emails at issue by the simple expedient of choosing—in its own discretion— to store them on a server in another country.

That discretion raises another point about privacy. Under Microsoft's and the Court's interpretation of the SCA, the privacy of Microsoft's customers' emails is dependent not on the traditional constitutional safeguard of private communications—judicial oversight of the government's conduct of criminal investigations—but rather on the business decisions of a private corporation. The contract between Microsoft and its customers does not limit the company's freedom to store its customers' emails wherever it chooses, and if Microsoft chooses, for whatever reasons of profit or cost control, to repatriate the emails at issue here to a server in United States, there will be no obstacle to the government's obtaining them.

As the Court points out, Microsoft does in fact choose to locate the records of anyone who *says* that he or she resides in the United States on domestic servers. It is only *foreign* customers, and those Americans who *say* that they reside abroad, who gain any enhanced protection from the Court's holding. And that protection is not merely enhanced, it is *absolute*: the government can never obtain a warrant that would require Microsoft to turn over those emails, however certain it may be that they contain evidence of criminal activity, and even if that criminal activity is a terrorist plot. Or to be more precise, the customer's privacy in that case is absolute *as against the government*; her privacy is protected against *Microsoft* only to the extent defined by the terms of her (adhesion) contract with the company.

II

The government's characterization of the warrant at issue as domestic, rather than extraterritorial, is thus far from frivolous, and renders this, for me, a very close case to the extent that the presumption against extraterritoriality shapes our interpretation of the statute. One additional potential fact heightens the complexity. We do not know, on this record, whether the customer whose emails were sought by the government is or is not a United States citizen or resident. It is not clear that whether the customer is a United States person or not matters to the rather simplistic "focus" test adopted by the Supreme Court in *Morrison*, although it would have mattered to the more flexible test utilized by the Second Circuit in that case. *See Morrison v. Nat'l Australia Bank Ltd.*, 547 F.3d 167, 171 (2d Cir. 2008).

But it seems to me that it *should* matter. The Supreme Court has rightly pointed out that the presumption against extraterritoriality is more than simply a means for avoiding conflict with foreign laws. *See Morrison*, 561 U.S. at 255, 130 S.Ct. 2869. At the same time, the presumption that Congress legislates with domestic concerns pre-eminent in its collective mind does not fully answer the question what those domestic concerns are in any given case. *See id.* at 266, 130 S.Ct. 2869. Particularly in connection with statutes that provide tools to law enforcement, one imagines that Congress is concerned with balancing liberty interests of various kinds against the need to enforce *domestic* law.

Thus, when Congress authorizes the (American) government to obtain access to certain information, one might imagine that its focus is on balancing the liberty interests of *Americans* (and of other persons residing in the U.S.) against the need to enforce *American* laws. Congress might also reasonably be concerned about the diplomatic consequences of over-extending the reach of American law enforcement officials. This suggests a more complex balancing exercise than identifying a single "focus" of the legislation, the latter approach being better suited to determining whether given *conduct* fitting within the literal words of a prohibition should be characterized as domestic or extraterritorial.

Because Microsoft relies solely on customers' self-reporting in classifying customers by residence, and stores emails (but only for the most part, and only in the interests of efficiency and good customer service) on local servers—and because the government did not include in its warrant application such information, if any, as it had about the target of its investigation—we do not know the nationality of the customer. If he or she is Irish (as for all we know the customer is), the case might present a troubling prospect from an international perspective: the Irish government and the European Union would have a considerable grievance if the United States sought to obtain the emails of an Irish national, stored in Ireland, from an American company which had marketed its services to Irish customers in Ireland.

The case looks rather different, however—at least to me, and I would hope to the people and officials of Ireland and the E.U.—if the American government is demanding from an American company emails of an American citizen resident in the U.S., which are accessible at the push of a button in Redmond, Washington, and which are stored on a server in Ireland only as a result of the American customer's misrepresenting his or her residence, for the purpose of facilitating domestic violations of American law, by exploiting a policy of the American company that exists solely for reasons of convenience and that could be changed, either in general or as applied to the particular customer, at the whim of the American company.

Given that the extraterritoriality inquiry is essentially an effort to capture the congressional will, it seems to me that it would be remarkably formalistic to classify such a demand as an extraterritorial application of what is effectively the subpoena power of an American court.

III

Despite ultimately agreeing with the result in this case, I dwell on the reasons for thinking it close because the policy concerns raised by the government are significant, and require the attention of Congress. I do not urge that Congress write the government's interpretation into the Act. That is a policy judgment on which my own views have no particular persuasive force. My point is simply that the main reason that both the majority and I decide this case against the government is that there is no evidence that Congress has *ever* weighed the costs and benefits of authorizing court orders of the sort at issue in this case. The SCA became law at a time when there was no reason to do so. But there is reason now, and it is up to Congress to decide whether the benefits of permitting subpoena-like orders of the kind issued here outweigh the costs of doing so.

Moreover, while I do not pretend to the expertise necessary to advocate a particular answer to that question, it does seem to me likely that a sensible answer will be more nuanced than the position advanced by either party to this case. As indicated above, I am skeptical of the conclusion that the mere location abroad of the server on which the service provider has chosen to store communications should be controlling, putting those communications beyond the reach of a purely "domestic" statute. That may be the default position to which a court must revert in the absence of guidance from Congress, but it is not likely to constitute the ideal balance of conflicting policy goals.

Nor is it likely that the ideal balance would allow the government free rein to demand communications, wherever located, from any service provider, of whatever nationality, relating to any customer, whatever his or her citizenship or residence, whenever it can establish probable cause to believe that those communications contain evidence of a violation of American criminal law, of whatever degree of seriousness. Courts interpreting statutes that manifestly do not address these issues cannot easily create nuanced rules: the statute either applies extraterritorially or it does not; the particular demand made by the government either should or should not be characterized as extraterritorial.

Our decision today is thus ultimately the application of a default rule of statutory interpretation to a statute that does not provide an explicit answer to the question before us. It does not purport to decide what the answer should be, let alone to impose constitutional limitations on the range of solutions Congress could consider.

Congress need not make an all-or-nothing choice. It is free to decide, for example, to set different rules for access to communications stored abroad depending on the nationality of the subscriber or of the corporate service provider. It could provide for access to such information only on a more demanding showing than probable cause, or only (as with wiretapping) where other means of investigation are inadequate, or only in connection with investigations into extremely serious crimes rather than in every law enforcement context. Or it could adopt other, more creative solutions that go beyond the possibilities evident to federal judges limited by their own experience and by the information provided by litigants in a particular case.

NOTES AND QUESTIONS

1. *Congress resolves the Microsoft issue by enacting the CLOUD Act.* Congress passed a new law in March 2018 to resolve the question in the *Microsoft* case. The new law, the Clarifying Lawful Overseas Use of Data Act (CLOUD) Act, was enacted as part of the Consolidated Appropriations Act of 2018, Pub. L. 115–141. The CLOUD Act requires a provider to disclose contents or records "regardless of whether such communication, record, or other information is located within or outside the United States." 18 U.S.C. § 2713. In that sense, the new statute reflects the government's goal in the *Microsoft* litigation. Providers now cannot refuse to comply with domestic legal process based on the foreign location of stored data.

At the same time, the CLOUD Act gives providers a limited statutory basis on which to challenge domestic legal process that involves a conflict with foreign law. The provider has 14 days to file a motion to quash or modify the legal process on the grounds of a perceived conflict of law. The circumstances in which this challenge can succeed are very narrow, however. Under 18 U.S.C. § 2703(h)(2)(A), a provider can file a challenge to domestic legal process only when the following five conditions are all met:

(1) the domestic legal process is seeking the contents of communications;

(2) the provider reasonably believes that the customer or subscriber is not a United States person;

(3) the provider reasonably believes that the customer or subscriber does not reside in the United States;

(4) the disclosure implicates the law of a foreign government that has been designated a "qualifying foreign government"; and

(5) the provider reasonably believes that the required disclosure would create a material risk that the provider would violate the law of the qualifying foreign government.

The meaning of "qualifying foreign government" is discussed later in this Chapter starting at page 866. It essentially refers to a foreign government with U.S.-like privacy laws that has been pre-approved as having sufficient privacy protection to permit mutual legal compliance.

After hearing a response from the government, the court can modify or quash (that is, annul) legal process under this provision only if the court makes three findings:

(i) the required disclosure would cause the provider to violate the laws of a qualifying foreign government;

(ii) based on the totality of the circumstances, the interests of justice dictate that the legal process should be modified or quashed; and

(iii) the customer or subscriber is not a United States person and does not reside in the United States.

18 U.S.C. § 2703(h)(2)(B).

The "interests of justice" factors are detailed in 18 U.S.C. § 2703(h)(3). Courts should consider, "as appropriate," the following eight factors:

(A) the interests of the United States, including the investigative interests of the governmental entity seeking to require the disclosure;

(B) the interests of the qualifying foreign government in preventing any prohibited disclosure;

(C) the likelihood, extent, and nature of penalties to the provider or any employees of the provider as a result of inconsistent legal requirements imposed on the provider;

(D) the location and nationality of the subscriber or customer whose communications are being sought, if known, and the nature and extent of the subscriber or customer's connection to the United States, or if the legal process has been sought on behalf of a foreign authority pursuant to section 3512, the nature and extent of the subscriber or customer's connection to the foreign authority's country;

(E) the nature and extent of the provider's ties to and presence in the United States;

(F) the importance to the investigation of the information required to be disclosed;

(G) the likelihood of timely and effective access to the information required to be disclosed through means that would cause less serious negative consequences; and

(H) if the legal process has been sought on behalf of a foreign authority pursuant to section 3512, the investigative interests of the foreign authority making the request for assistance.

Note that the basis for challenging domestic legal process under the CLOUD Act is exceedingly narrow. The provider must take the initiative and file the challenge. The disclosure must be unlawful under the law of a government that has been designated a "qualifying foreign government." The interests of justice must favor quashing or modifying the legal process. And the account holder must be a non-U.S. person who does not reside in the United States. If any of these requirements has not been met, the domestic legal process is binding on the provider despite the foreign law implications of the process.

How often is that likely to happen?

2. *The policy question.* As a matter of policy, should the government be allowed to use a traditional search warrant to compel the contents of user files stored outside the United States? Should the answer depend on whether the user is a United States citizen or someone who lives in the United States (on

one hand) or a foreign citizen living abroad (on the other)? If so, how can the government or a provider know who the user is and where he or she lives?

3. *The comparatively easy case of the Wiretap Act.* Although the extraterritorial application of the Stored Communications Act raises complex and difficult questions, the extraterritorial application of the Wiretap Act is fairly simple. The Wiretap Act applies only to interception inside the United States. Any interception of wire or electronic communications outside the United States is not covered by the Act. *See, e.g.*, United States v. Cotroni, 527 F.2d 708, 711 (2d Cir. 1975). As a district court has explained:

> Congress intended Title III to protect the integrity of United States communications systems against unauthorized interceptions taking place in the United States. If Congress had meant to require law enforcement agencies to satisfy Title III for interceptions conducted outside the United States, it would have provided some mechanism by which agents could obtain such approval. Congress did not do so.

United States v. Angulo-Hurtado, 165 F. Supp.2d 1363, 1369 (N.D. Ga. 2001).

4. *The territoriality of the Pen Register statute.* Although courts have not addressed the question, it seems likely that the Pen Register statute has the same territorial limit as the Wiretap Act. The Pen Register statute shares common roots with the Wiretap Act, as well as many statutory terms, so it seems probable that it shares the Wiretap Act's territorial scope.

3. THE FOURTH AMENDMENT ABROAD

Fourth Amendment limits on the acquisition of digital evidence outside the United States are relatively complicated. Existing caselaw remains fairly sparse, but the framework appears to hinge on two key questions: first, who is being monitored, and second, who is doing the monitoring. The next case introduces the framework.

UNITED STATES V. BARONA
United States Court of Appeals for the Ninth Circuit, 1995.
56 F.3d 1087.

WALLACE, CHIEF JUDGE.

Following extensive investigation, including wiretaps in foreign countries, the appellants were indicted and convicted of drug-related crimes.

I

The issues we discuss arose in the context of a criminal prosecution of six individuals for an ongoing conspiracy to distribute cocaine. Mario Ernesto Villabona-Alvarado and Brian Bennett organized and supervised the operation. Cocaine from Colombia entered the United States through a source named "Oscar." The cocaine was then delivered by Maria Barona and Luz Janneth Martinez to Michael McCarver and Michael Harris for further distribution.

Several events led to the identification of this conspiracy and its participants. Between 1985 and 1987, the Drug Enforcement Administration and the Los Angeles Police Department conducted a money-laundering investigation code-named "Operation Pisces." The result of this investigation was the arrest of Leonardo Gomez in Villabona's residence. Then in December 1987, Villabona and Bennett traveled to Copenhagen, Denmark, and registered at the Savoy Hotel. On December 7, 1987, Villabona, his wife (Helle Nielsen), and Bennett traveled to Aalborg, Denmark, to stay with Nielsen's parents. While in Aalborg, Villabona placed calls from the Nielsen residence and from a public telephone. On December 8, 1987, Villabona and Bennett returned to Copenhagen and stayed at the Hotel Sara-Dan. From Copenhagen, Villabona and Bennett flew to Milan, Italy, and registered at the Hilton International Hotel on December 9, 1987. In late March 1988, Villabona returned to Aalborg, Denmark, and again used the same public telephone. In each of these locations, the telephone calls made by Villabona were monitored by the Danish (or in one case, Italian) authorities. Tapes of these wiretaps were played for the jury and were relied on at least in part to convict Villabona, Bennett, Martinez, Barona, Harris, and McCarver.

Between March and November 1988, Bennett asked Stanley McCarns to transport 502 kilograms of cocaine from Los Angeles to Detroit and to return with millions of dollars. Stanley McCarns then arranged for Willie Childress and his cousin, James McCarns, to transport the cocaine. Childress and James McCarns were stopped en route on November 6, 1988, and a Missouri state trooper seized the cocaine. On November 11, 1988, domestic wiretaps commenced on two cellular telephones used by Villabona. These taps also resulted in the interception of several incriminating conversations.

II

The district court ruled on the motion to suppress the Denmark wiretap evidence as follows:

> The Court agrees with the Defense, that other than the Milan Wiretap, that these were wiretaps which were engaged in as a joint venture by the United States and Denmark. The Court finds that the order issued by the Danish Court was lawful and in accordance with their law. The Court finds that the United States authorities reasonably relied upon the representations of the Danish officials with respect to the wiretaps, and therefore they were acting—in the Court's opinion—in good faith.

The question of whether the wiretaps were a joint venture requires the district court to scrutinize the attendant facts. Therefore, we will not disturb such a finding unless it is clearly erroneous. We review de novo, however, the finding that the wiretaps were conducted in accordance with foreign law, *United States v. Peterson,* 812 F.2d 486, 490 (9th Cir. 1987), as well as the question of whether United States agents reasonably relied in good faith upon the foreign officials' representations that the wiretaps were legal under foreign law.

A.

When determining the validity of a foreign wiretap, we start with two general and undisputed propositions. The first is that Title III of the Omnibus Crime Control and Safe Streets Act of 1968, 18 U.S.C. §§ 2510– 21, "has no extraterritorial force." *Peterson,* 812 F.2d at 492. Our analysis, then, is guided only by the applicable principles of constitutional law. The second proposition is that neither our Fourth Amendment nor the judicially created exclusionary rule applies to acts of foreign officials.

Two very limited exceptions apply. One exception, clearly inapplicable here, occurs if the circumstances of the foreign search and seizure are so extreme that they shock the judicial conscience, so that a federal appellate court in the exercise of its supervisory powers can require exclusion of the evidence. This type of exclusion is not based on our Fourth Amendment jurisprudence, but rather on the recognition that we may employ our supervisory powers when absolutely necessary to preserve the integrity of the criminal justice system. The wiretaps at issue cannot be said to shock the conscience. Even when no authorization for a foreign wiretap was secured in violation of the foreign law itself, we have not excluded the evidence under this rationale, nor should we. Here, the foreign courts were involved and purported to authorize the wiretaps. The conduct here, therefore, does not come close to requiring the invocation of this exception.

The second exception to the inapplicability of the exclusionary rule applies when United States agents' participation in the investigation is so substantial that the action is a joint venture between United States and foreign officials. If a joint venture is found to have existed, the law of the foreign country must be consulted at the outset as part of the determination whether or not the search was reasonable. If foreign law was not complied with, the good faith exception to the exclusionary rule becomes part of the analysis. The good faith exception is grounded in the realization that the exclusionary rule does not function as a deterrent in cases in which the law enforcement officers acted on a reasonable belief that their conduct was legal.

It is this exception that the appellants invoke, asking us to conclude (1) that the United States and foreign officials were engaged in a joint venture, (2) that a violation of foreign law occurred making the search unreasonable, and (3) that the United States did not rely in good faith upon the foreign officials' representations that their law was being complied with.

B.

Because this exception is based solely on the Fourth Amendment, the appellants must first show that they are among the class of persons that the Fourth Amendment was meant to protect. In this case, three appellants, Martinez, Barona, and Villabona, are not United States citizens.

The Supreme Court has said, with regard to foreign searches involving aliens with "no voluntary connection" to the United States, that the Fourth Amendment is simply inapplicable. *See United States v. Verdugo-Urquidez,* 494 U.S. 259, 274–75 (1990). *Verdugo* reversed a decision of this circuit in which the panel majority found the Fourth Amendment applicable to a search of a Mexican citizen's Mexicali residence. *See United States v. Verdugo-Urquidez,* 856 F.2d 1214 (9th Cir. 1988), *rev'd,* 494 U.S. 259 (1990). The Supreme Court rejected this court's "global view of the Fourth Amendment's applicability which would plunge us into a sea of uncertainty as to what might be reasonable in the way of searches and seizures conducted abroad." *Verdugo,* 494 U.S. at 274.

Unlike the Due Process Clause of the Fifth Amendment, which protects all "persons," the Fourth Amendment protects only "the People of the United States." *Id.* at 265 (explaining that the term "people" used in the Fourth Amendment was a term of art employed in selected parts of the Constitution to refer to "the People of the United States"). This term "refers to a class of persons who are part of a national community or who have otherwise developed sufficient connection with this country to be considered part of that community." *Id.* The Fourth Amendment therefore protects a much narrower class of individuals than the Fifth Amendment.

Because our constitutional theory is premised in large measure on the conception that our Constitution is a "social contract," *Verdugo-Urquidez,* 856 F.2d at 1231–33, the scope of an alien's rights depends intimately on the extent to which he has chosen to shoulder the burdens that citizens must bear. Not until an alien has assumed the complete range of obligations that we impose on the citizenry may he be considered one of 'the people of the United States' entitled to the full panoply of rights guaranteed by our Constitution.

The term "People of the United States" includes "American citizens at home and abroad" and lawful resident aliens within the borders of the United States "who are victims of actions taken *in the United States* by American officials." *Verdugo-Urquidez,* 856 F.2d at 1234 (Wallace, J., dissenting) (emphasis in original). It is yet to be decided, however, whether a resident alien has undertaken sufficient obligations of citizenship or has otherwise developed sufficient connection with this country to be considered one of "the People of the United States" even when he or she steps outside the territorial borders of the United States.

It is not clear, therefore, that Villabona or the other non-citizen defendants in this case are entitled to receive any Fourth Amendment protection whatsoever. Any entitlement that they may have to invoke the Fourth Amendment in the context of an *extraterritorial* search is by no means clear. We could hold, therefore, that Barona, Martinez, and Villabona have failed to demonstrate that, at the time of the extraterritorial search, they were "People of the United States" entitled to receive the full panoply of rights guaranteed by our Constitution. We choose, however, not to reach the question because even if they were entitled to invoke the Fourth Amendment, their effort would be unsuccessful.

C.

Bennett, Harris, and McCarver are all United States citizens, and thus can invoke the protection of the Fourth Amendment generally. Our cases establishing the exception as to when the Fourth Amendment can be invoked in an extraterritorial search control our analysis.

First, the district court did not clearly err in finding that the four Danish wiretaps at issue were "joint ventures." In *Peterson,* we gave weight to the fact that the DEA "was involved daily in translating and decoding intercepted transmissions as well as advising the foreign authorities of their relevance." 812 F.2d at 490. Similarly here, the American Embassy was interested in the movement of Villabona and Bennett, American agents requested the wiretaps, information obtained was immediately forwarded to them, and throughout the surveillance a Spanish to English interpreter was provided by the United States.

Because there was a joint venture, we must decide whether the search was reasonable. In determining whether the search was reasonable, we must first consult the law of the relevant foreign countries. The relevant provisions of Danish law are: (1) section 191 of the Danish Criminal Code (Code) and (2) sections 780–791 of the Danish Administration of Justice Act (Justice Act).

Justice Act § 781(1) authorizes the intervention of secret communications, including the wiretapping of telephonic communications, if: (1) "weighty reasons" exist to assume messages are being conveyed via the medium in question, (2) the intervention is of decisive importance to the investigation, and (3) the investigation concerns an offense punishable by six or more years or is one of several other specifically enumerated offenses. Under Code § 191(1), the drug offenses at issue here are punishable by six or more years, thus satisfying section 781(1)(3).

In addition to these three requirements under Justice Act § 781(1), Danish law is somewhat more strict when it comes to monitoring conversations by use of a listening device or "bug" rather than by the tapping of telephone lines. Justice Act § 781(4) allows the use of such devices to intercept communications only if the suspected offense involves "danger to the lives or welfare of human beings or considerable social assets." This latter section was relevant to the Danish Court in two of the surveillances because the government sought to use both a listening device and wiretaps. The section is not relevant to us, however, because it appears that no surveillance evidence, other than wiretap evidence, was used at trial. Even if such evidence were admitted, however, section 781(4) was followed.

Justice Act § 783 outlines procedures to acquire a wiretap, section 784 provides for an attorney to be appointed for the target party, and section 788 provides for notification of the wiretap to the target party, unless the court omits or postpones such notification under section 788(4). After carefully reviewing the record, we are satisfied that Danish law was followed.

The first monitoring of communications occurred at the Savoy Hotel, Copenhagen, from December 4 to 7, 1987. The Danish police monitored communications both by tapping the hotel telephone lines, and by installing an electronic listening device in Villabona's room. In accordance with Danish law, the court held a hearing on December 5, 1987, at 10:00 a.m. to determine whether the wiretap and electronic eavesdropping, begun on December 4, 1987, was to be maintained. Justice Act § 783(3) allows police to make the necessary intervention subject to court approval within 24 hours. The Danish court gave its approval based on information that Villabona, Nielsen (who is not a party in this appeal), and Bennett (the occupants of the room) were suspected of violations of Code § 191, that they had transferred large amounts of money to Danish bank accounts, and that within a few days they had spent thousands of dollars on telephone calls. The Danish court concluded: "According to the available information, including, especially the transfers of money and the extent of the telephone bills, definite reasons exist to believe that the said telephone is being used to give information to, or from, a person suspected of violation of Penal Code § 191." These findings satisfied Justice Act §§ 781(1), (3), and the Danish court satisfied Justice Act § 781(2) by determining that the monitoring was of definite importance to the investigation. The targeted parties had been appointed counsel according to Justice Act § 784(1)(1)–(3). The court authorized the monitoring until December 11, 1987.

The second wiretaps were of the Nielsen residence and the public telephone, Aalborg, from December 7 to 9, 1987. On December 7, 1987, the court was notified that Villabona, Bennett, and Nielsen had made plans to travel to Aalborg. The Danish police then requested permission to monitor the telephone at Nielsen's residence in Aalborg, as well as authorization to install an electronic eavesdropping device in any hotel rooms they might move to, and to monitor any telephone calls from any such hotel rooms. The court granted the requested authorization until December 11, 1987.

After investigators observed Villabona making calls from the public telephone in Aalborg, Danish officials requested that the public telephone calls also be monitored. The Aalborg court allowed the monitoring of the public telephone calls until December 11, 1987. Again, the provisions of the Justice Act were followed. On December 18, 1987, the court, in accordance with Justice Act § 788 found that Nielsen and the owner of the public telephone "should not be informed about the phone bugging undertaken, as disclosure would be damaging to the investigation of the case."

The third wiretap involved the Hotel Sara-Dan, Copenhagen, from December 8 to 9, 1987. On December 9, 1987, the Copenhagen Municipal Court was told that on December 8 a tap was placed on a telephone at the Hotel Sara-Dan. Villabona and Bennett had returned from Aalborg to Copenhagen so that they could fly to Milan on December 9, 1987. The court, in accordance with Justice Act § 781, found that "definite reasons" existed to believe that the monitored communications contained information concerning suspected violations of Penal Code § 191, and that the monitoring "must be considered of decisive importance for the investigation." The monitoring stopped on December 9 because Villabona, Bennett, and Nielsen left the hotel. As in the previous episodes, the court waived the "duty to notify" the targets in accordance with Justice Act § 788(4).

The fourth tap involved the Nielsen residence and the public telephone, Aalborg, from March 28 to April 16, 1988. The Aalborg court was informed that Villabona and Nielsen were to return to Aalborg on March 28. Permission to tap the telephone at Nielsen's residence and the public telephone were sought. The Aalborg court found that based on Villabona's and Nielsen's last visit and telephone use, the tap was justified under the Justice Act. The tap was to expire on April 22, 1988, "with the provision that monitoring must be discontinued immediately if the defendants move."

A fifth wiretap occurred in Milan, Italy. On December 9, 1987, Villabona and Bennett arrived in Milan from Copenhagen. The day before, the Danish police notified a United States special agent of this planned trip. He, in turn, telephoned a United States special agent in Milan and requested physical surveillance. The latter agent contacted Major Rabiti of the Guardia Di Finanza and requested a watch on Villabona and Bennett. Rabiti obtained authorization to wiretap their hotel room.

The district court found that this wiretap was not the product of a joint venture between United States and Italian authorities. That a United

States agent told Rabiti about Villabona and Bennett did not create a "joint venture" between the United States and Italy regarding this wiretap. We hold that the district court did not clearly err when it found no joint investigation surrounding the Milan wiretap, and, therefore, that Fourth Amendment principles do not apply. Because the wiretap was conducted by foreign officials without substantial United States involvement, the results are admissible.

In summary, the finding that the Milan wiretap was not a joint venture is not clearly erroneous. The finding that the Danish wiretaps were conducted pursuant to a joint venture is also not clearly erroneous, but Danish law was complied with for each Danish wiretap. None of the evidence from the wiretaps is therefore subject to exclusion under the Fourth Amendment.

REINHARDT, CIRCUIT JUDGE, dissenting.

Here, in a few, short, deceptively simple paragraphs, the majority has taken another substantial step toward the elimination of what was once a firmly established constitutional right—the right of American citizens to be free from unreasonable searches conducted by their own government.

This time, the majority holds that for all practical purposes the Fourth Amendment's protections do not extend beyond our borders, and that the only limitations on searches of Americans abroad are those imposed by foreign governments, *even when our government initiates and participates in the search*. Oddly, the majority reaches this erroneous and unfortunate result by first acknowledging what it must—that the Fourth Amendment *is* applicable to such searches. However, it then strips this important principle of all significance by holding that we must look exclusively to *foreign law* when determining whether the search violates the Fourth Amendment. According to the majority, our government's decision to initiate the search of an American citizen satisfies the requirements of that once powerful Amendment so long as the foreign officials who conduct the search comply with their own laws. Thus, the majority opinion stands for the paradoxical rule that the Fourth Amendment applies to searches of American citizens in which United States agents play a substantial role but that probable cause, the most basic requirement of the Fourth Amendment, does not—except in the unlikely circumstance that the foreign land in which the search is conducted happens to have the identical requirements that our Constitution imposes.

The practical consequences of the majority's opinion can be simply stated. Without the probable cause requirement, the Fourth Amendment is without any real force. Searches of American citizens abroad can be instigated at the will of government agents. Any American traveling outside our nation's boundaries on vacation, business, or just visiting his family, is now fair game for wiretapping, surreptitious searches, and other invasions of privacy *whenever* members of the CIA, the DEA, the FBI, or who knows how many other alphabet law enforcement agencies, so desire.

Put simply, what the majority holds is that the only Fourth Amendment protections United States citizens who travel abroad enjoy vis-a-vis the United States government are those safeguards, if any, afforded by the laws of the foreign nations they visit. Under the majority's holding, the Fourth Amendment's requirements are wholly redundant since they provide nothing more than is already provided by foreign law. In fact, under the majority's rule, the Fourth Amendment provides even less protection than foreign law since, according to the principal case on which the majority relies, the Constitution does not even require foreign officials to comply with their own law; all that is required is that American officials have a good faith belief that they did so. Thus, even though the majority concedes that the Fourth Amendment applies to joint-venture searches like the one before us, it holds that when Americans enter Iraq, Iran, Singapore, Kuwait, China, or other similarly inclined foreign lands, they can be treated by the United States government exactly the way those foreign nations treat their own citizens—at least for Fourth Amendment purposes.

NOTES AND QUESTIONS

1. *The first question: Who is being monitored?* As the *Barona* case explains, the threshold Fourth Amendment question in a case involving extraterritorial evidence collection is the identity of the person subject to surveillance.

The key case is United States v. Verdugo-Urquidez, 494 U.S. 259 (1990), which considered a search of Mexican residences belonging to a suspected drug kingpin who was a citizen of Mexico. The defendant was arrested in Mexico by Mexico authorities, and he was turned over to the United States to face criminal charges in the United States. United States agents arranged a search of the defendant's home as part of a joint operation between United States and Mexico law enforcement agencies. A search of Verdugo-Urquidez's residence in Mexicali, Mexico, uncovered a "tally sheet" that investigators believed reflected quantities of marijuana smuggled into the United States. When charges were filed against Verdugo-Urquidez in the United States, his attorney moved to suppress the tally sheet on the ground that the search of the defendant's Mexicali home violated the Fourth Amendment.

In a majority opinion by Chief Justice Rehnquist, the Supreme Court concluded that the defendant had no Fourth Amendment rights because he lacked sufficient voluntary contacts with the United States to be among "the People" covered by the Fourth Amendment:

> What we know of the history of the drafting of the Fourth Amendment suggests that its purpose was to restrict searches and seizures which might be conducted by the United States in domestic matters. The available historical data show that the purpose of the

Fourth Amendment was to protect the people of the United States against arbitrary action by their own Government; it was never suggested that the provision was intended to restrain the actions of the Federal Government against aliens outside of the United States territory.

We think that the text of the Fourth Amendment, its history, and our cases discussing the application of the Constitution to aliens and extraterritorially require rejection of respondent's claim. At the time of the search, he was a citizen and resident of Mexico with no voluntary attachment to the United States, and the place searched was located in Mexico. Under these circumstances, the Fourth Amendment has no application.

For better or for worse, we live in a world of nation-states in which our Government must be able to function effectively in the company of sovereign nations. Some who violate our laws may live outside our borders under a regime quite different from that which obtains in this country. Situations threatening to important American interests may arise half-way around the globe, situations which in the view of the political branches of our Government require an American response with armed force. If there are to be restrictions on searches and seizures which occur incident to such American action, they must be imposed by the political branches through diplomatic understanding, treaty, or legislation.

Id. at 266, 274–75.

Justice Kennedy provided the fifth vote for the *Verdugo-Urquidez* majority opinion, but he also wrote a concurring opinion suggesting a different approach. Justice Kennedy rejected Chief Justice Rehnquist's focus on the original meaning of "the People," and instead focused on the practical difficulty of applying a warrant requirement overseas:

I cannot place any weight on the reference to "the people" in the Fourth Amendment as a source of restricting its protections. With respect, I submit these words do not detract from its force or its reach. Given the history of our Nation's concern over warrantless and unreasonable searches, explicit recognition of "the right of the people" to Fourth Amendment protection may be interpreted to underscore the importance of the right, rather than to restrict the category of persons who may assert it. The restrictions that the United States must observe with reference to aliens beyond its territory or jurisdiction depend, as a consequence, on general principles of interpretation, not on an inquiry as to who formed the Constitution or a construction that some rights are mentioned as being those of "the people."

The conditions and considerations of this case would make adherence to the Fourth Amendment's warrant requirement impracticable and anomalous. The Constitution does not require United States agents to obtain a warrant when searching the foreign home of a nonresident alien. If the search had occurred in a residence within the United States, I have little doubt that the full protections of the Fourth Amendment would apply. But that is not this case. The absence of local judges or magistrates available to issue warrants, the differing and perhaps unascertainable conceptions of reasonableness and privacy that prevail abroad, and the need to cooperate with foreign officials all indicate that the Fourth Amendment's warrant requirement should not apply in Mexico as it does in this country. For this reason, in addition to the other persuasive justifications stated by the Court, I agree that no violation of the Fourth Amendment has occurred in the case before us.

Id. at 276, 278 (Kennedy, J., concurring). Justice Brennan dissented, joined by Justice Marshall:

The majority ignores the most obvious connection between Verdugo-Urquidez and the United States: he was investigated and is being prosecuted for violations of United States law and may well spend the rest of his life in a United States prison. The "sufficient connection" is supplied not by Verdugo-Urquidez, but by the Government. Respondent is entitled to the protections of the Fourth Amendment because our Government, by investigating him and attempting to hold him accountable under United States criminal laws, has treated him as a member of our community for purposes of enforcing our laws. He has become, quite literally, one of the governed. Fundamental fairness and the ideals underlying our Bill of Rights compel the conclusion that when we impose societal obligations such as the obligation to comply with our criminal laws, on foreign nationals, we in turn are obliged to respect certain correlative rights, among them the Fourth Amendment.

Id. at 283–84 (Brennan, J., dissenting).

Lower courts have divided on whether the controlling opinion in *Verdugo-Urquidez* is the majority opinion or Justice Kennedy's concurring opinion. The issue was briefed for decision by the Supreme Court in Hernandez v. Mesa, 137 S.Ct. 2003 (2017), but the Court issued a narrow opinion that did not resolve it.

2.　　*The second question: Who is doing the monitoring?* Assuming that a defendant has Fourth Amendment rights under *Verdugo-Urquidez*, the next question considers who is doing the monitoring. There are three categories to consider: investigations conducted by foreign governments; joint investigations by U.S. officials and foreign government investigators; and investigations conducted exclusively by U.S. officials. The following notes consider these three categories.

3. *Investigations conducted by foreign governments.* As the *Barona* case indicates, the Fourth Amendment does not apply to investigations by foreign governments. This makes sense: The Fourth Amendment does not regulate conduct by private actors, and officials from foreign governments are the equivalent of private actors from a constitutional standpoint. At the same time, some courts have suggested that there are limits on the admissibility of evidence from searches and seizures by foreign governments. The *Barona* case articulates the standard that has been recited a number of times in the Ninth Circuit: the test is whether the search and seizure by the foreign government "shocks the judicial conscience." If it does, the court can require exclusion of the evidence "in the exercise of its supervisory powers." *But see* United States v. Mount, 757 F.2d 1315, 1320 (D.C. Cir. 1985) (Bork, J., concurring) (arguing that lower courts lack supervisory powers to impose an exclusionary rule for searches by foreign governments).

4. *Joint investigations.* The Fourth Amendment does apply to searches and seizures undertaken as part of a joint investigation by U.S. officials and foreign government investigators. The governing law here is rather murky, as the Supreme Court has never directly addressed the relevant legal standard. In the Ninth Circuit, however, the general Fourth Amendment command is reasonableness; specifically, it is reasonableness measured by reference to the law in the country where the search occurred. If investigators in the United States ask French investigators to wiretap an e-mail account in France, for example, the constitutional reasonableness of the surveillance is measured by reference to French law. This standard requires judges to apply foreign law and determine if the monitoring was legal where it occurred. If it was legal, the thinking goes, it was constitutionally reasonable. *See* United States v. Peterson, 812 F.2d 486, 490 (9th Cir. 1987) (Kennedy, J.).

This standard incorporates a good faith exception. So long as United States officials reasonably rely on representations of foreign officials that searches comply with foreign law, the evidence will not be suppressed. As then-Judge, now-Justice Anthony Kennedy explained in *Peterson*, 812 F.2d at 492:

> The good faith exception is grounded in the realization that the exclusionary rule does not function as a deterrent in cases in which the law enforcement officers acted on a reasonable belief that their conduct was legal. It is true, as appellants note, that *Leon* speaks only in terms of good faith reliance on a facially valid search warrant. That is not dispositive, however. We conclude that the reasoning applies as well to reliance on foreign law enforcement officers' representations that there has been compliance with their own law. American law enforcement officers were not in an advantageous position to judge whether the search was lawful, as would have been the case in a domestic setting. Holding them to a strict liability standard for failings of their foreign associates would be even more incongruous than holding law enforcement officials to a strict liability standard as to the adequacy of domestic warrants. We conclude that

the good faith exception to the exclusionary rule announced in *Leon* applies to the foreign search.

We do not suggest that objectively unreasonable reliance on foreign law officers can cloak the search with immunity from the exclusionary rule. That said, permitting reasonable reliance on representations about foreign law is a rational accommodation to the exigencies of foreign investigations.

5. *Searches and seizures conducted exclusively by the United States government.* The Fourth Amendment also applies to searches abroad conducted exclusively by United States officials. Few cases reveal how the law applies in this situation, as United States officials normally will work with governments abroad in criminal cases. In such instances, the cooperation will trigger the "joint investigation" standards. For the most part, international searches conducted exclusively by the United States abroad will occur in national security cases rather than in criminal cases. The Fourth Amendment issues will be litigated only in the rare event that the national security investigation eventually leads to criminal charges in the United States.

A significant case in which this occurred was In re Terrorist Bombings of U.S. Embassies in East Africa, 552 F.3d 157 (2d Cir. 2008). This case involved surveillance of a United States citizen, Wadih El-Hage, when he was located in Kenya and was operating as part of an Al Qaeda terrorist cell. The United States listened in on El-Hage's telephone calls without a warrant and without cooperating with Kenyan officials. When El-Hage was later brought to the United States and charged with involvement in the bombings of United States Embassies in Africa, he moved to suppress on the ground that the warrantless surveillance had violated his Fourth Amendment rights.

In an opinion by Judge Cabranes, the Second Circuit held that the Warrant Clause of the Fourth Amendment has no application to searches and seizures outside the United States. Thus, searches and seizures outside the United States did not require the United States to obtain a warrant:

First, there is nothing in our history or our precedents suggesting that U.S. officials must first obtain a warrant before conducting an overseas search. El-Hage has pointed to no authority—and we are aware of none—directly supporting the proposition that warrants are necessary for searches conducted abroad by U.S. law enforcement officers or local agents acting in collaboration with them; nor has El-Hage identified any instances in our history where a foreign search was conducted pursuant to an American search warrant. This dearth of authority is not surprising in light of the history of the Fourth Amendment and its Warrant Clause as well as the history of international affairs.

Second, nothing in the history of the foreign relations of the United States would require that U.S. officials obtain warrants from foreign magistrates before conducting searches overseas or, indeed, to suppose that all other states have search and investigation rules akin to our own. The American procedure of issuing search warrants on a showing of probable cause simply does not extend throughout the globe and, pursuant to the Supreme Court's instructions, the Constitution does not condition our government's investigative powers on the practices of foreign legal regimes quite different from that which obtains in this country.

Third, if U.S. judicial officers were to issue search warrants intended to have extraterritorial effect, such warrants would have dubious legal significance, if any, in a foreign nation. A warrant issued by a U.S. court would neither empower a U.S. agent to conduct a search nor would it necessarily compel the intended target to comply. It would be a nullity, or in the words of the Supreme Court, "a dead letter."

Fourth and finally, it is by no means clear that U.S. judicial officers could be authorized to issue warrants for overseas searches, although we need not resolve that issue here.

Id. at 169–71. According to the Second Circuit, the constitutionality of a search or seizure overseas should be governed by a "totality of the circumstances" reasonableness standard, balancing "the degree to which it intrudes upon an individual's privacy" and "the degree to which it is needed for the promotion of legitimate governmental interests." *Id.* at 172.

Are the legal rules that govern foreign searches exclusively by the United States Government consistent with the legal rules that govern foreign searches by joint investigations? Imagine the United States and Belgium cooperate to wiretap a United States citizen located in Belgium. Belgian law requires a warrant to conduct the monitoring, which means that a proper Belgian warrant is needed to satisfy the Fourth Amendment. On the other hand, if the United States decides to ignore the Belgian authorities and wiretap the account on its own, then no warrant needs to be obtained.

Are these rules inconsistent? Note that there is a way to reconcile the two sets of law. If you assume that a Belgian warrant is not actually a "warrant" for Fourth Amendment purposes, then the requirement of obtaining a Belgian warrant in the joint investigation is not formally a warrant requirement. Rather, obtaining the Belgian warrant is necessary only to make the search "reasonable" even though a United States warrant is not necessary.

6.   *The implications of different standards.* In the *Barona* case, Judge Wallace and Judge Reinhardt disagree on the Fourth Amendment framework that should apply to "joint investigations" outside the United States. Judge Wallace measures reasonableness based on compliance with the law where the search occurs, whereas Judge Reinhardt apparently would analyze joint searches outside the United States using the same Fourth Amendment rules that apply inside the United States to searches conducted exclusively by United States investigators.

Which approach makes more sense? Let's break down the possibilities. If the Fourth Amendment and foreign search and seizure law happen to be identical, then it makes no difference which approach is followed. If foreign law is more privacy-protective than the Fourth Amendment, however, Judge Wallace's approach will hold investigators to a higher standard than will Judge Reinhardt's standard. For example, if surveillance law in Freedonia does not have a consent exception, a joint investigation that listens in on a telephone call of a United States citizen vacationing in Freedonia with the other party's consent would violate the Fourth Amendment even if the same surveillance technique would not violate the Fourth Amendment if it occurred inside the United States. On the other hand, if foreign law is less protective than the Fourth Amendment, Judge Wallace's approach will hold investigators to a lower standard than Judge Reinhardt's standard. For example, if surveillance law in Freedonia lets the police obtain a wiretap order based only on reasonable suspicion (that is, without probable cause), a joint investigation that taps a phone in Freedonia would not violate the Fourth Amendment even if the same technique would violate the Fourth Amendment if it occurred inside the United States.

Does it make sense that the Fourth Amendment rights of United States citizens fluctuates based on the domestic law of the country where they are physically present? Does your answer depend on whether foreign law only determines the reasonableness of searches, as compared to compliance with the Fourth Amendment more broadly? The difference may be important. For example, suppose the Freedonia Constitution requires a probable cause search warrant to install a pen register. Does this mean that the warrantless use of a pen register in Freedonia to monitor a United States citizen violates the Fourth Amendment? Or does *Smith v. Maryland* apply to the question of what is a search, with the *Barona* inquiry into foreign law used only to determine whether a search or seizure is reasonable?

Finally, consider how Judge Reinhardt's approach might work (or not work) in practice. If United States investigators must follow the same Fourth Amendment rules abroad that they follow in the United States, they may need to obtain court orders or follow procedures that local law does not have or even flatly forbids. For example, one pillar of Fourth Amendment law is that warrants must be issued by a detached and neutral magistrate. *See* Johnson v. United States, 333 U.S. 10, 13–14 (1948). Foreign judges may not qualify under this standard, as not every country follows the tripartite scheme of separation of powers found in the United States. Does this mean that foreign search warrants may not satisfy the Fourth Amendment, even if they require probable cause and particularity? If so, how can United States investigators collect evidence without violating the Fourth Amendment?

7.　*Foreign law and the exclusionary rule*. In his *Barona* dissent, Judge Reinhardt claims that "under the majority's holding, the Fourth Amendment's requirements are wholly redundant since they provide nothing more than is already provided by foreign law." Is this accurate? Fourth Amendment protection adds something critically important: the remedy of a constitutional exclusionary rule. The exclusionary rule is very rare outside the United States, and where it applies it is optional rather than mandatory. *See* Craig M. Bradley, *The Emerging International Consensus as to Criminal Procedure Rules*, 14 Mich. J. Int'l L. 171, 174 (1993).

4. MUTUAL LEGAL ASSISTANCE

When digital evidence is located abroad, and the United States seeks its use in a domestic criminal case, the evidence typically will be collected by agents of foreign governments under laws that govern mutual legal assistance. These laws regulate both the collection of evidence in the United States by United States officials at the behest of foreign governments and also the collection of evidence outside of the United States by foreign governments at the behest of the United States.

Understanding mutual legal assistance in computer crime cases requires studying three topics. The first topic is the traditional regime of mutual legal assistance treaties and letters rogatory. The second topic is the Council of Europe Cybercrime Convention, and the third topic is the CLOUD Act of 2018. The materials below cover the three topics in that order.

a) Mutual Legal Assistance Treaties and Letters Rogatory

T. MARKUS FUNK—MUTUAL LEGAL ASSISTANCE TREATIES AND LETTERS ROGATORY: A GUIDE FOR JUDGES (2014)

I. Introduction

The investigation of transnational criminal conduct, like the discovery process for transnational civil proceedings, often involves gathering evidence located in foreign countries. However, national sovereignty, international treaties, and international law preclude U.S. law enforcement officials from simply flying to a foreign country to conduct searches, question suspects, obtain documents, and proceed with arresting individuals for trial in the United States. In the absence of a foreign country's agreement to cooperate in a criminal investigation or civil litigation, U.S. prosecutors or civil litigation counsel have limited options. For this reason, transnational cooperation and collaboration is an integral component of contemporary justice systems.

For criminal proceedings, there are two primary means of obtaining evidence: a Mutual Legal Assistance Treaty (MLAT) and a letter rogatory. For civil proceedings, there is only a letter rogatory. Evidence obtained from abroad through these tools may be presented as part of court proceedings, requiring U.S. judges to be familiar with the legal issues implicated by transnational requests for assistance. In addition, judges should be aware that diplomacy, executive agreements, and information exchange through informal communications also play an important role in transnational criminal investigations and civil litigation.

Requests for transnational assistance requiring judicial oversight most commonly involve activities necessary for proceeding with a criminal investigation or prosecution or a transnational civil proceeding, such as serving subpoenas, locating evidence and individuals, and taking testimony. The court's role in reviewing these requests will vary depending upon the applicable treaties and foreign law.

The MLAT is a treaty-based mechanism for seeking foreign law enforcement cooperation and assistance in support of an ongoing criminal investigation or proceeding. The MLAT process, and its benefits, are available only to government officials, typically prosecutors. MLATs do not apply to civil litigants or proceedings. Supervising the execution of incoming MLATs—requests for assistance from foreign jurisdictions—requires direct federal district court oversight and involvement. In contrast, the courts play no part in initiating or processing outgoing MLAT requests. That is the province of the executive branch.

Letters rogatory, in contrast, have a considerably broader reach than MLATs: they can be issued by U.S. federal and state courts as part of criminal, civil, and administrative proceedings, and they can be sent to U.S. federal and state courts by any foreign or international tribunal or "interested person."

Letters rogatory (also known as "letters of request" when presented by a nonparty "interested person") were first used to facilitate cooperation among the courts of the several states of the Union. Today, the letter rogatory process is used internationally and is codified at 28 U.S.C. §§ 1781 and 1782 (the "Judicial Assistance Statute"). Letters rogatory are available to prosecutors, defendants, and civil litigants once formal proceedings have commenced; they typically cannot issue during the *investigative* stage of criminal proceedings. The process for letters rogatory is more time-consuming and unpredictable than that for MLATs. This is in large part because the enforcement of letters rogatory is a matter of comity between courts, rather than treaty-based.

For these reasons, prosecutors typically consider letters rogatory an option of last resort for accessing evidence abroad, to be exercised only when MLATs are not available. In contrast, because MLATs are never available to private parties, defense counsel and civil litigants must rely on letters rogatory to gather evidence located abroad. This disparity in access to evidence may result in delayed proceedings and cause the defense to raise access to justice issues.

Requests from abroad ("incoming requests") for legal assistance are directed to a country's designated "central authority," usually the Department (or Ministry) of Justice. The central authority, in turn, transmits the MLAT or letterrogatory-related communication to the appropriate court or government entity.

When a federal prosecutor appears before a U.S. district court requesting assistance on behalf of a foreign state or provides notice that the U.S. government will seek assistance from a foreign state, the prosecutor acts at the direction of the U.S. Department of Justice's Office of International Affairs (OIA). OIA is the United States' central authority and de facto functional hub for all outgoing and incoming requests for transnational investigation and litigation assistance. Its attorneys process the paperwork for incoming and outgoing requests for assistance, issue guidance, and draft the form motions used by federal prosecutors. If the court has questions or concerns about the request, the judge may address them directly to OIA, typically through the local United States Attorney's Office.

II. *Mutual Legal Assistance Treaties*

MLATs are the principal vehicle through which law enforcement officials make transnational requests for assistance relating to evidence gathering and other law enforcement activities. They are available for use by law enforcement officials involved in criminal investigations and proceedings (or in some civil matters where the case is related to a criminal matter). MLATs are legally binding negotiated commitments. Nonetheless, courts review specific requests for assistance and may deny them if they fail to comply with applicable domestic law or procedure.

- MLATs provide for mutual cooperation between nations in the investigation and prosecution of transnational crime, and they do so through explicitly enumerated categories of law enforcement assistance unique to each treaty. The types of assistance MLATs usually provide for include the following:

- serving judicial or other documents;

- locating or identifying persons or things;

- taking testimony;

- examining objects and sites;

- requesting searches and seizures;

- obtaining documents or electronic evidence;

- identifying, tracing, and freezing or confiscating proceeds or instrumentalities of crime and/or other assets;

- transferring persons in custody for testimonial purposes or to face charges, as in extradition cases;

- freezing assets; and

- any other assistance permitted by the foreign law and specified in the applicable treaty.

Most MLATs also include a catchall provision authorizing the transfer of any evidence not prohibited by the requested nation's law. The United States has bilateral MLATs in force with every European Union member state, many of the Organization of American States member states, and many other countries around the world. An MLAT is negotiated by the U.S. Department of Justice in cooperation with the U.S. Department of State. The Secretary of State formally submits the proposed MLAT, typically together with a report detailing the function and purposes of the MLAT's key provisions, to the President of the United States for transmittal to the U.S. Senate. Following the advice and consent of the Senate, the President signs the treaty and directs the Secretary of State to take the actions necessary for the treaty to enter into force. Once signatory countries have complied with entry-into-force provisions, the MLAT becomes binding under international law.

When a foreign country requests assistance pursuant to an MLAT, the U.S. court must determine whether (1) the terms of the MLAT prescribe practices or procedures for the taking of testimony and production of evidence, (2) the Federal Rules of Procedure and Evidence apply, or (3) the MLAT requires some sort of a hybrid approach. It is also acceptable to follow specified practices and procedures of the requesting country— provided they are consistent with U.S. law, including the rules relating to privilege. MLATs executed in the United States must follow U.S. constitutional requirements, including the protection of Fourth Amendment and Fifth Amendment rights. That said, U.S. legal standards do not apply to the seizure of evidence overseas when the foreign country is conducting the investigation independently and seizes evidence later introduced in a U.S. court, nor does the Sixth Amendment right to counsel attach to civil depositions.

To assist the U.S. court in reviewing an incoming MLAT request, the following information is usually included (or should be made available by the assistant U.S. attorney handling the matter):

Basic information

- the name of the authority conducting the investigation, prosecution, or other proceeding to which the request relates;

- a description of the subject matter and the nature of the investigation, prosecution, or proceeding, including the specific criminal offenses that relate to the matter;

- a description of the evidence, information, or other assistance sought; and

- a statement of the purpose for which the evidence, information, or other assistance is sought.

Assistance-specific details

- information concerning the identity and location of any person from whom evidence is sought;

- information concerning the identity and location of a person to be served, that person's relationship to the proceeding, and the manner in which service is to be made;

- information on the identity and whereabouts of a person to be located;

- a precise description of the place or person to be searched and items to be seized;

- a description of the manner in which any testimony or statement is to be taken and recorded;

- a list of questions to be asked of a witness; and

- a description of any particular procedure to be followed in executing the request.

An MLAT request containing this information provides the district court with a general basis for evaluating the request for assistance. If necessary, the court may ask the assigned prosecutor to provide additional information (typically through OIA).

Although there is a presumption in favor of honoring MLAT requests, the district court must still review the terms of each request, checking that they comply with the terms of the underlying treaty and comport with U.S. law. For example, in *United Kingdom v. United States*, 238 F.3d 1312, 1315 (11th Cir. 2001), appellants awaiting trial in England requested disclosure of law enforcement documents they claimed were requested by British law enforcement officials pursuant to the U.S.-U.K. MLAT. The Eleventh Circuit denied the motion, finding that the underlying U.K. request for evidence did not conform to the specific protocol set forth in the treaty and, accordingly, no valid MLAT request had been made.

U.S. courts will also consider constitutional challenges to a request for legal assistance. Although such cases are rare, a district court may not enforce a subpoena that would offend a constitutional guarantee, such as a subpoena that would result in an egregious violation of human rights.

While the majority of requests for assistance pursuant to an MLAT proceed uneventfully, courts sometimes are called upon to resolve related legal issues, such as dual criminality, defense access to evidence located abroad, delay, and statute of limitations.

Unlike extradition treaties enforced in U.S. courts, MLATs do not require dual criminality—that the offense for which the foreign state seeks assistance also constitutes a crime in the requested state. The utilitarian reason for this deviation from the norm is to facilitate responsiveness. MLATs, after all, are intended to improve law enforcement cooperation between countries, and the United States' law enforcement objectives often depend upon timely assistance from treaty signatories. The United States has committed to responding to requests under MLATs even if the doctrine of dual criminality exists as part of the requesting country's domestic law. This approach establishes a high standard of responsiveness, enabling the United States to urge that foreign authorities respond to our requests for evidence with comparable speed. Most MLATs expressly state that the dual criminality principle does not apply.

Some MLATS, however, are drafted to include limitations that are triggered if the requested assistance requires a court warrant or other compulsion and the underlying offense is not a crime in the requested country. In jurisdictions where domestic law requires dual criminality for international treaties, the MLAT is often drafted to include a nonexclusive list of covered offenses that allow for mutual legal assistance.

The MLAT process was created to facilitate international cooperation in the investigation and prosecution of criminal cases. Each treaty's terms apply only to the contracting nations' parties, and the benefits conferred are available only to the governmental officials of those nations. The first three MLATs signed by the United States—those with Switzerland, Turkey, and the Netherlands—include provisions granting defense counsel permission to access evidence pursuant to an MLAT. Subsequent MLATs do not include comparable provisions.

Thus, access to evidence through an MLAT is restricted to prosecutors, government agencies that investigate criminal conduct, and government agencies that are responsible for matters ancillary to criminal conduct, including civil forfeiture. In fact, the vast majority of MLATs signed by the United States explicitly exclude non-government access to U.S. processes. Criminal defendants, like civil litigants, must use letters rogatory to secure evidence located abroad, a process that is less efficient and less reliable.

III. Letters Rogatory

Letters rogatory are formal requests for judicial assistance made by a court in one country to a court in another country. Once issued, they may be conveyed through diplomatic channels, or they may be sent directly from court to court. Letters rogatory are often used to obtain evidence, such as compelled testimony, that may not be accessible to a foreign criminal or civil litigant without judicial authorization. They are used primarily by non-government litigants who do not have access to the MLAT process. While it has been held that federal courts have inherent power to issue and respond to letters rogatory, such jurisdiction has largely been regulated by congressional legislation.

The letter rogatory process is less formal than pursuing evidence through an MLAT, but its execution can be more time-consuming. Outgoing letters rogatory—requests for assistance with obtaining evidence abroad, made by counsel through the U.S. court—are issued by the U.S. State Department pursuant to 28 U.S.C. § 1781, and provided for under Federal Rules of Civil Procedure 28(b) and 4(f)(2)(B). Section 1781(b), however, also allows for a district court (and, for that matter, a foreign court) to bypass the State Department and transmit the outgoing letter rogatory directly to the foreign tribunal, officer, or agency.

In most cases, foreign courts honor requests issued pursuant to letters rogatory. However, international judicial assistance is discretionary, based upon principles of comity rather than treaty, and is also subject to legal procedures in the requested country. Compliance with a letter rogatory request is left to the discretion of the court or tribunal in the "requested" jurisdiction (that is, the court or tribunal to which the letter rogatory is addressed). For example, if a request for compelled testimony is granted by a foreign court, the taking of that testimony may not necessarily follow procedures similar to those of the United States, such as through depositions.

Because the letter rogatory process is time-consuming and may involve unique issues of foreign procedural law, parties seeking evidence can arrange for local counsel in the foreign country to file the letter rogatory on their behalf, a strategy that may facilitate the process. The U.S. trial proceedings may be impacted by delays flowing from the foregoing procedural and practical hurdles.

Incoming letters rogatory—requests for judicial assistance originating in a foreign or international tribunal—are also covered by 28 U.S.C. §§ 1781 and 1782. OIA receives incoming letters rogatory from foreign or international tribunals and transmits each request to the federal court in the district where the evidence is located or witness resides. After reviewing the request, the district court may order the taking of testimony or production of evidence for use in the foreign proceeding. The evidence is then provided to the requesting foreign party by OIA.

The U.S. court may prescribe the practice and procedure, which may be in whole or part the practice and procedure of the foreign country or the international tribunal, for taking the testimony or statement or producing the document or other thing. Or, if nothing in the request prescribes otherwise, the court may follow the Federal Rules of Civil Procedure. Legal privileges are respected, and privileged testimony cannot be compelled. The process typically takes place ex parte, though a court has the authority to require notification of other parties in the foreign litigation prior to the issuance of an order.

In contrast to MLATs, letters rogatory are not treaty-based; there is no guarantee that the requested country or tribunal will act on a request for assistance, or if it acts, how it will act. When evaluating a defendant's request for letters rogatory to secure evidence located abroad, courts consider the following factors:

- Is the proffered evidence exculpatory?

- Is it cumulative of evidence more readily available in the United States?

- Was the request for evidence made in a timely manner?

If the evidence in question is necessary to ensure a fair trial, obtaining it will most likely warrant the delay inherent in the letter rogatory process.

The letter rogatory process may take as long as a year, presenting courts with case management challenges. Although delays may be mitigated by transmitting a copy of the request through INTERPOL or some other more direct route, even in urgent cases, such requests often take at least a month to execute. To minimize unnecessary delay, the court may choose to review outgoing letters rogatory or inquire of counsel whether steps were taken to ensure as expeditious a response as possible.

IV. *Information Exchange Through Informal Channels*

Although formal MLATs, letters rogatory, and other international conventions are the public face of transnational legal assistance, a significant amount of criminal investigation-related information is exchanged through informal channels: investigator to investigator, prosecutor to prosecutor, defense counsel to local counterpart. Indeed, personal, cooperative law enforcement relationships can be so informal and "off the grid" that law enforcement agencies, courts, and defendants may only learn of them by accident.

Responding to the challenges of transnational law enforcement, the FBI and other U.S. law enforcement agencies have aggressively sought to develop institutional relationships with their foreign counterparts. Teams of U.S. law enforcement officers regularly coordinate with each other and with their foreign counterparts in a task force approach, often working out of offices in U.S. embassies and missions around the world. This "bricks and mortar" outreach enables U.S. law enforcement officials to cultivate professional relationships and more readily access other sources of information in the host countries.

The U.S. Departments of State, Treasury, and Justice institutionalize crossborder cooperation through memoranda of understanding (MOU) structured to improve the handling and sharing of law enforcement information in foreign jurisdictions. Although the benefits of this cooperation are significant, the process has limitations. Courts should be aware that information gathered in the informal manner described in this section may be incomplete and is not always tendered to prosecutors or, through the discovery process, provided to the defense.

NOTES AND QUESTIONS

1.   *Letters rogatory by state officials.* State law enforcement officials can obtain letters rogatory to collect evidence abroad much like federal officials can. *See* Susan W. Brenner & Joseph J. Schwerha IV, *Transnational Evidence Gathering and Local Prosecution of International Cybercrime*, 20 J. Marshall J. Computer & Info. L. 347, 384–85 (2002).

2.   *Letters rogatory by the defense.* After a defendant is charged, counsel for the defendant can obtain letters rogatory for use at trial. The defendant must ask the trial court for the authority to issue the letter, and must satisfy any other legal requirements for the request. *See, e.g.,* United States v. Korogodsky, 4 F. Supp.2d 262 (S.D.N.Y. 1998). *See also* Ellen S. Podgor, Understanding International Criminal Law 89 (2004).

3.   *Mutual Legal Assistance and the Fourth Amendment.* For an example of how MLAT procedures intersect with Fourth Amendment doctrine, consider United States v. Vilar, 2007 WL 1075041 (S.D.N.Y. 2007). Law enforcement in the United States worked closely with authorities in the United Kingdom (U.K.) pursuant to the U.S.-U.K. MLAT to search the London offices of individuals suspected of crimes in the United States. After the search occurred and the evidence was brought to the United States for trial, the defendants moved to suppress the evidence on the ground that the U.K. warrants obtained by U.K. officials in consultation with U.S. officials were defective under the doctrines that regulated warrants in the U.K. Judge Karas treated the U.S.-U.K. investigation as a "joint investigation" for Fourth Amendment purposes, and he then engaged in a long and scholarly analysis of U.K. search and seizure law. He concluded that the investigation followed U.K. law, and that if any errors had occurred, they occurred in good faith. Thus the investigation in the U.K. had not violated the Fourth Amendment, or at the very least no suppression remedy applied.

The *Vilar* case shows how the MLAT process impacts the scope of Fourth Amendment protection. Mutual legal assistance turns the investigation into a "joint investigation" for Fourth amendment purposes, triggering the *Barona* standard and raising the issue of whether the investigators complied with foreign law.

4.   *Uniformity versus diversity and the problem of reciprocity.* In recent years, the United States government has encouraged other countries to synchronize their substantive and procedural computer crime laws to encourage reciprocal legal assistance. Is this inevitable? Is it desirable? Should the entire world adopt a single model approach to computer crime laws, or are

local differences desirable? How much of the substantive criminal law covered in Chapters 2 and 3 is normatively desirable at the global level? How much of the procedural law covered in Chapters 5 and 6 is normatively desirable at the global level?

Is it possible to resolve the tension between the need for uniform laws to enforce computer crime statutes and the need for regional variation based on local preferences? Consider the case of child pornography. Imagine the government of Freedonia decides that it should be legal to possess or distribute images of child pornography in Freedonia, including on servers located in Freedonia that are connected to the Internet. Will such a decision have a significant impact on the enforcement of child pornography laws worldwide? Can an individual simply post images from Freedonia and escape liability (or at least capture)? Does the popularity of Internet gambling sites based in countries like Antigua provide empirical support for the answer?

Alternatively, consider foreign criminal laws prohibiting racist speech, the sale of Nazi memorabilia, or the distribution of virtual child pornography. In the United States, First Amendment protection renders such laws unenforceable. Should the United States be allowed to "opt out" of assisting other countries in their efforts to prosecute violations of these laws? Is there an argument that the United States should be able to opt out of helping foreign governments with investigations that violate the First Amendment, but that Freedonia should not be allowed to opt out of assisting other countries with child pornography prosecutions?

b) The Council of Europe Convention on Cybercrime

The most important effort to synchronize computer crime laws to date is the Council of Europe Convention on Cybercrime. The Convention articulates a set of principles that member states agree to adopt in their domestic law. The United States is not a member of the Council of Europe, but representatives of the United States Department of Justice, State, and Commerce were "observers" and active participants in the negotiating and drafting of the convention. The United States was one of the thirty countries that signed the convention in 2001, and the United States Senate ratified the convention in 2006. Here are the key portions of the text:

COUNCIL OF EUROPE—CONVENTION ON CYBERCRIME
http://conventions.coe.int/Treaty/en/Treaties/Html/185.htm (2001).

Section 1—Substantive criminal law

Article 2—Illegal access

Each Party shall adopt such legislative and other measures as may be necessary to establish as criminal offences under its domestic law, when committed intentionally, the access to the whole or any part of a computer system without right. A Party may require that the offence be committed by infringing security measures, with the intent of obtaining computer data or other dishonest intent, or in relation to a computer system that is connected to another computer system.

Article 3—Illegal interception

Each Party shall adopt such legislative and other measures as may be necessary to establish as criminal offences under its domestic law, when committed intentionally, the interception without right, made by technical means, of non-public transmissions of computer data to, from or within a computer system, including electromagnetic emissions from a computer system carrying such computer data. A Party may require that the offence be committed with dishonest intent, or in relation to a computer system that is connected to another computer system.

Article 4—Data interference

1.   Each Party shall adopt such legislative and other measures as may be necessary to establish as criminal offences under its domestic law, when committed intentionally, the damaging, deletion, deterioration, alteration or suppression of computer data without right.

2.   A Party may reserve the right to require that the conduct described in paragraph 1 result in serious harm.

Article 7—Computer-related forgery

Each Party shall adopt such legislative and other measures as may be necessary to establish as criminal offences under its domestic law, when committed intentionally and without right, the input, alteration, deletion, or suppression of computer data, resulting in inauthentic data with the intent that it be considered or acted upon for legal purposes as if it were authentic, regardless whether or not the data is directly readable and intelligible. A Party may require an intent to defraud, or similar dishonest intent, before criminal liability attaches.

Article 8—Computer-related fraud

Each Party shall adopt such legislative and other measures as may be necessary to establish as criminal offences under its domestic law, when committed intentionally and without right, the causing of a loss of property to another by:

a.   any input, alteration, deletion or suppression of computer data,

b.   any interference with the functioning of a computer system,

with fraudulent or dishonest intent of procuring, without right, an economic benefit for oneself or for another.

Article 9—Offences related to child pornography

Each Party shall adopt such legislative and other measures as may be necessary to establish as criminal offences under its domestic law, when committed intentionally and without right, the following conduct:

a. producing child pornography for the purpose of its distribution through a computer system;

b. offering or making available child pornography through a computer system;

c. distributing or transmitting child pornography through a computer system;

d. procuring child pornography through a computer system for oneself or for another;

e. possessing child pornography in a computer system or on a computer-data storage medium.

Article 10—Offences related to infringements of copyright and related rights

Each Party shall adopt such legislative and other measures as may be necessary to establish as criminal offences under its domestic law the infringement of copyright, as defined under the law of that Party pursuant to the obligations it has undertaken under the Paris Act of 24 July 1971 of the Bern Convention for the Protection of Literary and Artistic Works, the Agreement on Trade-Related Aspects of Intellectual Property Rights and the WIPO Copyright Treaty, with the exception of any moral rights conferred by such Conventions, where such acts are committed wilfully, on a commercial scale and by means of a computer system.

Section 2—Procedural law

Article 14—Scope of procedural provisions

Each Party shall adopt such legislative and other measures as may be necessary to establish the powers and procedures provided for in this Section for the purpose of specific criminal investigations or proceedings.

Article 15—Conditions and safeguards

Each Party shall ensure that the establishment, implementation and application of the powers and procedures provided for in this Section are subject to conditions and safeguards provided for under its domestic law, which shall provide for the adequate protection of human rights and liberties, including rights arising pursuant to obligations it has undertaken under the 1950 Council of Europe Convention for the Protection of Human Rights and Fundamental Freedoms, the 1966 United Nations International Covenant on Civil and Political Rights, and other applicable international human rights instruments, and which shall incorporate the principle of proportionality.

Article 16—Expedited preservation of stored computer data

Each Party shall adopt such legislative and other measures as may be necessary to enable its competent authorities to order or similarly obtain the expeditious preservation of specified computer data, including traffic data, that has been stored by means of a computer system, in particular where there are grounds to believe that the computer data is particularly vulnerable to loss or modification.

Article 18—Production order

1.   Each Party shall adopt such legislative and other measures as may be necessary to empower its competent authorities to order:

a.   a person in its territory to submit specified computer data in that person's possession or control, which is stored in a computer system or a computer-data storage medium; and

b.   a service provider offering its services in the territory of the Party to submit subscriber information relating to such services in that service provider's possession or control;

3.   For the purpose of this article, "subscriber information" means any information, contained in the form of computer data or any other form, that is held by a service provider, relating to subscribers of its services, other than traffic or content data, by which can be established:

a.   the type of the communication service used, the technical provisions taken thereto and the period of service;

b.   the subscriber's identity, postal or geographic address, telephone and other access number, billing and payment information, available on the basis of the service agreement or arrangement;

c.   any other information on the site of the installation of communication equipment available on the basis of the service agreement or arrangement.

Article 19—Search and seizure of stored computer data

1.   Each Party shall adopt such legislative and other measures as may be necessary to empower its competent authorities to search or similarly access:

a.   a computer system or part of it and computer data stored therein; and

b.   computer-data storage medium in which computer data may be stored in its territory.

2.   Each Party shall adopt such legislative and other measures as may be necessary to ensure that where its authorities search or similarly access a specific computer system or part of it, pursuant to paragraph 1(a), and have grounds to believe that the data sought is stored in another computer system or part of it in its territory, and such data is lawfully accessible from or available to the initial system, such authorities shall be able to expeditiously extend the search or similar accessing to the other system.

3.   Each Party shall adopt such legislative and other measures as may be necessary to empower its competent authorities to seize or similarly secure computer data accessed according to paragraphs 1 or 2. These measures shall include the power to:

a.   seize or similarly secure a computer system or part of it or a computer-data storage medium;

b.   make and retain a copy of those computer data;

c.   maintain the integrity of the relevant stored computer data; and

d.   render inaccessible or remove those computer data in the accessed computer system.

Article 20—Real-time collection of traffic data

Each Party shall adopt such legislative and other measures as may be necessary to empower its competent authorities to:

a.   collect or record through application of technical means on the territory of that Party, and

b.   compel a service provider, within its existing technical capability, to:

i.   collect or record through application of technical means on the territory of that Party, or ii. co-operate and assist the competent authorities in the collection or recording of, traffic data, in real-time, associated with specified communications in its territory transmitted by means of a computer system.

Article 21—Interception of content data

Each Party shall adopt such legislative and other measures as may be necessary, in relation to a range of serious offences to be determined by domestic law, to empower its competent authorities to:

a.   collect or record through application of technical means on the territory of that Party, and

b.   compel a service provider, within its existing technical capability, to:

i.   collect or record through application of technical means on the territory of that Party, or ii. co-operate and assist the competent authorities in the collection or recording of, content data, in real-time, of specified communications in its territory transmitted by means of a computer system.

Chapter III—International co-operation

Article 23—General principles relating to international co-operation

The Parties shall co-operate with each other, in accordance with the provisions of this chapter, and through the application of relevant international instruments on international co-operation in criminal matters, arrangements agreed on the basis of uniform or reciprocal legislation, and domestic laws, to the widest extent possible for the purposes of investigations or proceedings concerning criminal offences related to computer systems and data, or for the collection of evidence in electronic form of a criminal offence.

Article 24—Extradition

1.   This article applies to extradition between Parties for the criminal offences established in accordance with Articles 2 through 11 of this Convention, provided that they are punishable under the laws of both Parties concerned by deprivation of liberty for a maximum period of at least one year, or by a more severe penalty.

2.   The criminal offences described in paragraph 1 of this article shall be deemed to be included as extraditable offences in any extradition treaty existing between or among the Parties. The Parties undertake to include such offences as extraditable offences in any extradition treaty to be concluded between or among them.

Article 25—General principles relating to mutual assistance

The Parties shall afford one another mutual assistance to the widest extent possible for the purpose of investigations or proceedings concerning criminal offences related to computer systems and data, or for the collection of evidence in electronic form of a criminal offence.

Article 27—Procedures pertaining to mutual assistance requests in the absence of applicable international agreements

Where there is no mutual assistance treaty or arrangement on the basis of uniform or reciprocal legislation in force between the requesting and requested Parties, the provisions of paragraphs 2 through 9 of this article shall apply. The provisions of this article shall not apply where such treaty, arrangement or legislation exists, unless the Parties concerned agree to apply any or all of the remainder of this article in lieu thereof.

Article 31—Mutual assistance regarding accessing of stored computer data

A Party may request another Party to search or similarly access, seize or similarly secure, and disclose data stored by means of a computer system located within the territory of the requested Party.

Article 32—Trans-border access to stored computer data with consent or where publicly available

A Party may, without the authorisation of another Party:

a. access publicly available (open source) stored computer data, regardless of where the data is located geographically; or

b. access or receive, through a computer system in its territory, stored computer data located in another Party, if the Party obtains the lawful and voluntary consent of the person who has the lawful authority to disclose the data to the Party through that computer system.

Article 33—Mutual assistance regarding the real-time collection of traffic data

1. The Parties shall provide mutual assistance to each other in the real-time collection of traffic data associated with specified communications in their territory transmitted by means of a computer system. Subject to the provisions of paragraph 2, this assistance shall be governed by the conditions and procedures provided for under domestic law.

2. Each Party shall provide such assistance at least with respect to criminal offences for which real-time collection of traffic data would be available in a similar domestic case.

Article 34—Mutual assistance regarding the interception of content data

The Parties shall provide mutual assistance to each other in the real-time collection or recording of content data of specified communications transmitted by means of a computer system to the extent permitted under their applicable treaties and domestic laws.

Article 35—24/7 Network

Each Party shall designate a point of contact available on a twenty-four hour, seven-day-a-week basis, in order to ensure the provision of immediate assistance for the purpose of investigations or proceedings concerning criminal offences related to computer systems and data, or for the collection of evidence in electronic form of a criminal offence. Such assistance shall include facilitating, or, if permitted by its domestic law and practice, directly carrying out the following measures:

a.   the provision of technical advice;

b.   the preservation of data pursuant to Articles 29 and 30;

c.   the collection of evidence, the provision of legal information, and locating of suspects.

NOTES AND QUESTIONS

1.   Are any provisions of the COE convention inconsistent with United States law? Or are the terms of the convention a restatement of the basic elements of United States computer crime law? *See generally* Richard W. Downing, *Shoring up the Weakest Link: What Lawmakers Around the World Need to Consider in Developing Comprehensive Laws to Combat Cybercrime*, 43 Colum. J. Transnat'l L. 705 (2005).

2.   *The additional protocol on "racist and xenophobic" acts.* In 2002, at the request of the French government, the Council of Europe added an additional protocol "concerning the criminalisation of acts of a racist and xenophobic nature committed through computer systems." The protocol requires each country that signs it to criminalize a number of acts, including: distributing racist and xenophobic material to the public through a computer system; sending an Internet threat solely because of a person's race, national origin or religion; insulting a person through a computer communication on the basis of the person's race, national origin or religion; and denying, grossly minimizing, or justifying atrocities or crimes against humanity. *See generally* Christopher D. Van Blarcum, Note, *Internet Hate Speech: The European Framework and the Emerging American Haven*, 62 Wash. & Lee L. Rev. 781, 787–802 (2005).

A number of countries have signed the additional protocol, which acts as a separate agreement in addition to the cybercrime convention. Of course, the United States has not signed the protocol. Government officials have indicated that the United States cannot agree to the protocol because its provisions would violate the First Amendment. *See* Declan McCullagh, *U.S. Won't Support Net "Hate Speech" Ban*, C-Net News, Nov. 15, 2002. As a result, the requirements of the additional protocol have no effect on United States policy.

3.   The COE cybercrime convention has been controversial less for what it does than for what it does not do. Privacy advocates and civil liberties groups note that the convention focuses on law enforcement powers but does not address privacy protections beyond the general statement in Article 15. The convention empowers governments without limiting how they might exercise those new powers. Consider the perspective offered by one group, the Center for Democracy and Technology:

> The treaty is fundamentally imbalanced: it includes very detailed and sweeping powers of computer search and seizure and government surveillance of voice, email and data communications, but no correspondingly detailed standards to protect privacy and limit government use of such powers, despite the fact that privacy is the

#1 concern of Internet users worldwide who see an increase, not a decrease, in the surveillance capabilities of governments brought on by the digital revolution.

While the treaty's express terms do not require companies to modify their equipment or business practices, the treaty must be viewed as part of the ongoing government efforts nationally and internationally to require telephone companies, Internet service providers, web site operators, and computer hardware and software manufacturers to design their systems, their record-keeping procedures and their very business models to guarantee the practical effectiveness of such surveillance authorities.

Comments of the Center for Democracy and Technology on the Council of Europe Draft "Convention on Cyber-crime," *available at* http://www.cdt.org/international/cybercrime/010206cdt.shtml.

Should the COE convention mandate privacy protections as well as law enforcement powers? If so, what should those protections look like? Should the convention require every country to impose a probable cause warrant requirement for wiretapping or government access to stored e-mail? Should the requirements track current United States law, or should they be more (or less) protective? Does an international consensus exist on standards for Internet privacy law? If not, who should decide what the standard will be?

4.　　Another criticism of the COE convention is that its requirements are too general. The convention's broad language requires general categories of legislation instead of specific statutes. Are general categories sufficient to achieve the uniformity that the convention's drafters had in mind? If one country enacts a narrow statute and another enacts a broad one, will the laws be sufficiently uniform to facilitate international evidence collection and extradition? Should the convention itself contain the precise statutory text of the criminal prohibitions and procedural laws that signatories must enact? For such a suggestion, see Shannon Hopkins, *Cybercrime Convention: A Positive Beginning to a Long Road Ahead*, 2 J. High Tech. L. 101, 104–07 (2003).

Imagine COE countries decided to adopt this suggestion. What would the model law look like? Suppose the COE convention were amended so that every country was required to copy United States computer crime law as it exists today in every detail. Would this be a good idea? Is existing United States law an appropriate model?

Of course, it is highly unlikely that the United States could persuade COE member countries to adopt existing United States law as a universal model. Different countries have very different traditions, legal systems, and constitutional requirements. If it were possible to reach an agreement on the specific text for a uniform set of computer crime laws, it seems likely that the language chosen would involve a major re-writing of existing United States law. United States negotiators would have some influence over this process, but would be only one voice among many.

Further, such an agreement would block individual countries from attempting to improve their own computer crime statutes unilaterally. To change United States computer crime law without violating the convention, United States officials would be required to renegotiate the cybercrime convention first. The new language agreed to by the members of the Council of Europe would then be submitted for Senate approval, requiring a vote on the very specific language negotiated abroad. Is this desirable?

Finally, some variation in the law is inevitable because different courts will construe the same language differently. Imagine every country adopted a uniform computer crime law that prohibited "access without authorization," "unreasonable searches and seizures," and "interception of the contents of communications without the consent of a party." What are the chances that the United States Supreme Court, the French Cour de Cassation, and the German Bundesgerichtsh would interpret these phrases in exactly (or even roughly) the same way?

c) Cross-Border Data Requests Under the Cloud Act of 2018

In 2018, Congress created a new legal framework for cross-border data requests with pre-approved foreign governments as part of the Clarifying Lawful Overseas Use of Data Act ("CLOUD") Act. Under the statute, the United States government can determine that a foreign government is a "qualifying foreign government." *See* 18 U.S.C. § 2523 (establishing the process). When a U.S.-based provider receives foreign legal process from a qualifying foreign government, new exceptions to the U.S. surveillance laws permit the provider to comply with the foreign legal process without violating U.S. law.

Importantly, the CLOUD Act does not require the provider to comply with foreign legal process. The legal burden to comply with the foreign legal process comes, if at all, from the law of the foreign government. Instead, the CLOUD Act removes the federal legal prohibition on compliance with the foreign legal process so long as the foreign government has been declared a "qualifying foreign government" under the process provided by 18 U.S.C. § 2523.

In effect, the CLOUD Act supplements mutual legal assistance with a regime of mutual legal facilitation. Instead of the government of Country A helping the government of Country B with Country B's investigation, the government of Country A agrees to get out of the way and let Country B's legal process take effect on the large corporate entities that likely provide Internet service in both countries. And because the agreement is mutual, Country B agrees to get out of the way and let Country A's legal process take effect on those same large corporate entities.

The CLOUD Act achieves this result by adding new exceptions to each of three major federal statutory surveillance laws for conduct in response to foreign legal process. *See, e.g.,* 18 U.S.C. § 2702(b)(9) (new exception to the Stored Communications Act permits disclosure of contents "to a foreign government pursuant to an order from a foreign government that is subject to an executive agreement that the Attorney General has determined and certified to Congress satisfies section 2523"); 18 U.S.C. § 2702(b)(9) (new exception to the Stored Communications Act permits disclosure of non-content records "to a foreign government pursuant to an order from a foreign government that is subject to an executive agreement that the Attorney General has determined and certified to Congress satisfies section 2523"); 18 U.S.C. § 2511(2)(j) (new exception to the Wiretap Act permitting "a provider of electronic communication service to the public or remote computing service to intercept or disclose the contents of a wire or electronic communication in response to an order from a foreign government that is subject to an executive agreement that the Attorney General has determined and certified to Congress satisfies section 2523."); 18 U.S.C. § 3121(a) (new exception to the Pen Register statute permits installation of a pen register and trap and trace device pursuant to "an order from a foreign government that is subject to an executive agreement that the Attorney General has determined and certified to Congress satisfies section 2523.").

The effect of the CLOUD Act is to create an "insider's club" among countries in terms of legal process. When a foreign government is admitted into the club by being designated a "qualifying foreign government," evidence collection using foreign legal process becomes relatively easy. Domestic providers can follow foreign court orders—the foreign equivalent of their Wiretap orders, 2703(a) warrants, and pen/trap orders—just like they follow domestic legal process. And under the reciprocity requirements that are part of being a "qualifying foreign government"—as explained below—domestic legal process can be followed by foreign providers just like they now comply with foreign legal process.

The CLOUD Act's regime for cross-border data requests hinges on designation of a foreign government as a "qualifying foreign government." The procedure for this designation is detailed in 18 U.S.C. § 2523. The procedure is complex, but the basics can be readily understood here. First, the foreign government must enter into an executive agreement with the United States concerning mutual legal assistance that satisfies a long list of statutory requirements. When the executive agreement is made, the Attorney General, with the concurrence of the Secretary of State, submits a written certification to Congress that a foreign government is properly qualifying. Congress then has an opportunity to reject the agreement. If Congress does not act after 180 days, the executive agreement goes into effect and the foreign government is a "qualifying foreign government" for five years.

The terms of the executive agreement are explained in § 2523(b). First, "the domestic law of the foreign government, including the implementation of that law," must afford "robust substantive and procedural protections for privacy and civil liberties in light of the data collection and activities of the foreign government that will be subject to the agreement." § 2523(b)(1). Factors to be considered to determine if the foreign government's laws and practices are adequate include whether the government demonstrates respect for the rule of law and principles of nondiscrimination; whether it adheres to applicable international human rights obligations and commitments or demonstrates respect for international universal human rights; and whether it has sufficient mechanisms to provide accountability and appropriate transparency regarding the collection and use of electronic data. *See id.* at § 2523(b)(1)(B).

The executive agreements must also be mutual. Just as the United States will permit U.S.-based providers to comply with foreign legal process, so must the foreign governments permit their providers to comply with U.S. legal process. *See* § 2523(b)(4)(I) ("[T]he foreign government shall afford reciprocal rights of data access, to include, where applicable, removing restrictions on communications service providers, including providers subject to United States jurisdiction, and thereby allow them to respond to valid legal process sought by a governmental entity (as defined in section 2711) if foreign law would otherwise prohibit communications-service providers from disclosing the data.").

After the Attorney General certifies that a valid executive agreement exists, the Attorney General must submit the certification to Congress. Congress then has 180 days in which to consider the executive agreement. If Congress has not acted in 180 days, the agreement goes into effect. *See* § 2523(d). On the other hand, if Congress enters a joint resolution in the 180-day period disapproving of the executive agreement, then the executive agreement does not go into effect. *See* § 2523(d)(4)(B). Executive agreements are valid for five years and can be renewed for additional five-year periods. If revisions are made to the executive agreements as part of their proposed renewal, the Attorney General must resubmit the revised executive agreement to Congress to give Congress a 90-day window in which to consider the agreement. *See* § 2523(h).

NOTES AND QUESTIONS

1. *The United Kingdom becomes the first "qualifying foreign government" in July 2020.* In October 2019, the Attorney General of the United States and the Home Secretary of the United Kingdom announced that they had signed the first CLOUD Act agreement. *See* U.S. Department of Justice, *U.S. And UK Sign Landmark Cross-Border Data Access Agreement to Combat Criminals and Terrorists Online,* October 3, 2019. Following some delays, the agreement took legal effect on July 8, 2020.

The text of the US/UK agreement is 17 pages long. The agreement includes a number of transparency and civil liberties protections not found in the CLOUD Act itself. First, a designated authority in the issuing country must certify in writing that the order complies with both the agreement and any applicable law.

Second, if a provider in Country A objects to an order served on it from Country B, the provider can file an objection with the government of Country B. If that objection it is not resolved to the satisfaction of the provider, the provider can file its objection before Country A, which then has veto power over whether the provider must comply with Country B's order.

Third, each government must file an annual report on how often the CLOUD Act was used. *See generally* Jennifer Daskal & Peter Swire, *The U.K.-U.S. CLOUD Act Agreement Is Finally Here, Containing New Safeguards*, Lawfare Blog, October 8, 2019, available at https://www.lawfareblog.com/uk-us-cloud-act-agreement-finally-here-containing-new-safeguards.

2.   *Negotiations are ongoing to make Australia the next "qualifying foreign government."* On October 7, 2019, the Attorney General of the United States and the Minister for Home Affairs of Australia announced that the United States and Australia had entered into formal negotiations over the terms of a bilateral agreement between the United States and Australia under the CLOUD Act. *See* https://www.justice.gov/opa/pr/joint-statement-announcing-united-states-and-australian-negotiation-cloud-act-agreement-us.

In March 2020, the Australian government released a bill designed to make Australia compliant with the CLOUD Act and to facilitate a U.S./Australia agreement. As of the time this casebook is going to print, Australia's legislature is still considering the bill. *See* Asha Barbaschow, PJCIS Demands 23 Changes Before Foreign Entities Get Australian Data Under IPO Regime, ZDNet, May 13, 2021.

3.   *The global picture.* The materials in this chapter suggest that the legal issues raised by computer-related crime are not merely questions for the legal system in the United States. Most industrialized countries are facing the same issues, and all are being called on to adjust their domestic regimes of criminal law and criminal procedure in response to the new dynamics of computer crimes.

In light of the materials you have read in this book, do you think governments face a major challenge? Does computer crime require a fundamental rethinking of domestic and international approaches to criminal investigations and prosecutions? Will computer crimes "change everything"? Or do the new crimes simply require a slight tweaking of the old principles, or even no adjustment at all?

Are computers and the Internet the kind of transformative technologies that are likely to have a profound effect on criminal law doctrine? Some legal historians have argued that the invention of the railroad had a profound effect on tort law principles a century ago. Will computers and the Internet have a similar impact on criminal law and procedure in the next century?

5. EXTRADITION

The last jurisdictional topic is the law and process of extradition. Imagine the United States seeks to prosecute a suspect for computer crimes but the suspect is located outside the United States. The United States may ask the country where the suspect is located to surrender that person to the United States to face criminal charges. And the converse is true as well, of course: Another country may seek the surrender of a suspect located in the United States. How does this work?

CONGRESSIONAL RESEARCH SERVICE,
EXTRADITION TO AND FROM THE UNITED STATES:
OVERVIEW OF THE LAW AND CONTEMPORARY
TREATIES (2016)

Introduction

'Extradition' is the formal surrender of a person by a State to another State for prosecution or punishment. Extradition to or from the United States is a creature of treaty. The United States has extradition treaties with over a hundred of the nations of the world, although there are many with which the United States has no extradition treaty.

Whether by practice's failure to follow principle or by the natural evolution of the principle, modern extradition treaties and practices began to emerge in this country and elsewhere by the middle 18th and early 19th centuries.

The first U.S. extradition treaty consisted of a single terse article in Jay's Treaty of 1794 with Great Britain. Since then, the United States has relied almost exclusively upon bilateral agreements as a basis for extradition. However, the United States has entered into several multilateral agreements that may also provide legal authority for extradition. Such agreements take two forms. One form is a multilateral agreement that exclusively concerns extradition. The United States is currently a party to two such agreements: the 1933 Montevideo Convention on Extradition, which apparently has never served as a basis for extradition, and the Extradition Agreement Between the United States and the European Union, which entered into force in February 2010.

The United States is also a party to several multilateral agreements that generally aim to deter and punish transnational criminal activity or serious human rights abuses, including by imposing an obligation upon signatories to prosecute or extradite persons who engage in specified conduct. Although these agreements are not themselves extradition treaties, they often contain provisions stating that specified acts shall be treated as extraditable offenses in any extradition treaty between parties.

Bars to Extradition

Extradition treaties are in the nature of a contract, and by operation of international law, a state party to an extradition treaty is obligated to comply with the request of another state party to that treaty to arrest and deliver a person duly shown to be sought by that state (a) for trial on a charge of having committed a crime covered by the treaty within the jurisdiction of the requesting state, or (b) for punishment after conviction of such a crime and flight from that state, provided that none of the grounds for refusal to extradite set forth in the treaty is applicable.

Subject to a contrary treaty provision, federal law defines the mechanism by which the United States honors its extradition treaty obligations. Although some countries will extradite in the absence of an applicable treaty as a matter of comity, it was long believed that the United States could only grant an extradition request if it could claim coverage under an existing extradition treaty. Dicta in several court cases indicated that this requirement, however, was one of congressional choice rather than constitutional requirement.

No Treaty Crime

Extradition is generally limited to crimes identified in the treaty. Early treaties often recite a list of the specific extraditable crimes.... While many existing U.S. extradition treaties continue to list specific extraditable offenses, the more recent ones feature a dual criminality approach, and simply make all felonies extraditable (subject to other limitations found elsewhere in their various provisions).

Military and Political Offenses

In addition to an explicit list of crimes for which extradition may be granted, most modern extradition treaties also identify various classes of offenses for which extradition may or must be denied. Common among these are provisions excluding purely military and political offenses. The military crimes exception usually refers to those offenses like desertion which have no equivalents in civilian criminal law. The exception is of relatively recent vintage. In the case of treaties that list specific extraditable offenses, the exception is unnecessary since purely military offenses are not listed. The exception became advisable, however, with the advent of treaties that make extraditable any misconduct punishable under the laws of both treaty partners.

Capital Offenses

A number of nations have abolished or abandoned capital punishment as a sentencing alternative. Several of these have preserved the right to deny extradition in capital cases either absolutely or in absence of assurances that the fugitive will not be executed if surrendered. More than a few countries are reluctant to extradite in a capital case even though their extradition treaty with the United States has no such provision, based on opposition to capital punishment or to the methods and procedures associated with execution bolstered by sundry multinational agreements to which the United States is either not a signatory or has signed with pertinent reservations. Additionally, though almost all extradition treaties are silent on this ground, some states may demand assurances that the fugitive will not be sentenced to life in prison, or even that the sentence imposed will not exceed a specified term of years.

Want of Dual Criminality

Dual criminality addresses the reluctance to extradite a fugitive for conduct that the host nation considers innocent. Dual criminality exists when the parties to an extradition treaty each recognize a particular form of misconduct as a punishable offense. Historically, extradition treaties have handled dual criminality in one of three ways: (1) they list extraditable offenses and do not otherwise speak to the issue; (2) they list extraditable offenses and contain a separate provision requiring dual criminality; or (3) they identify as extraditable offenses those offenses condemned by the laws of both nations. Today, under most international agreements a person sought for prosecution or for enforcement of a sentence will not be extradited if the offense with which he is charged or of which he has been convicted is not punishable as a serious crime in both the requesting and requested state.

Although there is a split of authority over whether dual criminality resides in all extradition treaties that do not deny its application, the point is largely academic since it is a common feature of all American extradition treaties. Subject to varying interpretations, the United States favors the view that treaties should be construed to honor an extradition request if possible. Thus, dual criminality does not require that the name by which the crime is described in the two countries shall be same; nor that the scope of the liability shall be coextensive, or, in other respects, the same in the two countries. It is enough if the particular act charged is criminal in both jurisdictions. When a foreign country seeks to extradite a fugitive from the United States, dual criminality may be satisfied by reference to either federal or state law.

U.S. treaty partners do not always construe dual criminality requirements as broadly. In the past, some have been unable to find equivalents for attempt, conspiracy, and crimes with prominent federal jurisdictional elements (e.g., offenses under the Racketeer Influenced and Corrupt Organizations and Continuing Criminal Enterprise statutes). Many modern extradition treaties contain provisions addressing the problem of jurisdictional elements and/or making extraditable an attempt or conspiracy to commit an extraditable offense. Some include special provisions for tax and customs offenses as well.

Procedure for Extradition from the United States

A foreign country usually begins the extradition process with a request submitted to the State Department sometimes including the documentation required by the treaty. When a requesting nation is concerned that the fugitive will take flight before it has time to make a formal request, it may informally ask for extradition and provisional arrest with the assurance that the full complement of necessary documentation will follow. In either case, the Secretary of State, at his discretion, may forward the matter to the Department of Justice to begin the procedure for the arrest of the fugitive to the end that the evidence of criminality may be heard and considered.

Hearing

The precise menu for an extradition hearing is dictated by the applicable extradition treaty, but a common checklist for a hearing conducted in this country would include determinations that

- there exists a valid extradition treaty between the United States and the requesting state;
- the relator is the person sought;
- the offense charged is extraditable;
- the offense charged satisfies the requirement of double criminality;
- there is "probable cause" to believe the relator committed the offense charged;
- the documents required are presented in accordance with United States law, subject to any specific treaty requirements, translated and duly authenticated . . .; and
- other treaty requirements and statutory procedures are followed.

An extradition hearing is not, however, in the nature of a final trial by which the prisoner could be convicted or acquitted of the crime charged against him. Instead, it is essentially a preliminary examination to determine whether a case is made out which will justify the holding of the accused and his surrender to the demanding nation. The judicial officer who conducts an extradition hearing thus performs an assignment in line with his or her accustomed task of determining if there is probable cause to hold a defendant to answer for the commission of an offense.

The purpose of the hearing is in part to determine whether probable cause exists to believe that the individual committed an offense covered by the extradition treaty. The rules of criminal procedure and evidence that would apply at trial have no application at the hearing. Warrants, depositions, and other authenticated documents are admissible as evidence. The individual may offer evidence to contradict or undermine the existence of probable cause, but affirmative defenses that might be available at trial are irrelevant. Hearsay is not only admissible but may be relied upon exclusively; the *Miranda* rule has no application; initiation of extradition may be delayed without regard for the Sixth Amendment right to a speedy trial or the Fifth Amendment right of due process; nor do the Sixth Amendment rights to the assistance of counsel or cross examine witnesses apply. Due process, however, will bar extradition of informants whom the government promised confidentiality and then provided the evidence necessary to establish probable cause for extradition.

Review

If at the conclusion of the extradition hearing, the court concludes there is some obstacle to extradition and refuses to certify the case, the requesting government's recourse to an unfavorable disposition is to bring a new complaint before a different judge or magistrate, a process it may reiterate apparently endlessly. . . .

If the court concludes there is no such obstacle to extradition and certifies to the Secretary of State that the case satisfies the legal requirements for extradition, the fugitive has no right of appeal, but may be entitled to limited review under habeas corpus. . . .

Extradition for Trial or Punishment in the United States

The laws of the country of refuge and the applicable extradition treaty govern extradition back to the United States of a fugitive located overseas. The request for extradition comes from the Department of State whether extradition is sought for trial in federal or state court or for execution of a criminal sentence under federal or state law.

The Justice Department's Office of International Affairs must approve requests for extradition of fugitives from federal charges or convictions and may be asked to review requests from state prosecutors before they are considered by the State Department. Provisions in the United States Attorneys' Manual and the corresponding Justice Department's Criminal Resource Manual sections supplement treaty instructions on the procedures to be followed in order to forward a request to the State Department and thereafter.

The first step is to determine whether the fugitive is extraditable. The Justice Department's checklist for determining extraditability begins with an identification of the country in which the fugitive has taken refuge. If the United States has no extradition treaty with the country of refuge, extradition is not a likely option. When there is a treaty, extradition is an option only if the treaty permits extradition. Common impediments include citizenship, dual criminality, statutes of limitation, and capital punishment issues.

Many treaties permit a country to refuse to extradite its citizens even in the case of dual citizenship. As for dual criminality, whether the crime of conviction or the crime charged is an extraditable offense will depend upon the nature of the crime and where it was committed. If the applicable treaty lists extraditable offenses, the crime must be on the list. If the applicable treaty insists only upon dual criminality, the underlying misconduct must be a crime under the laws of both the United States and the country of refuge.

Where the crime was committed matters; some treaties will permit extradition only if the offense was committed within the geographical confines of the United States. Timing also matters. The speedy trial features of U.S. law require a good faith effort to bring to trial a fugitive who is within the government's reach. Furthermore, the lapse of time or speedy trial component of the applicable extradition treaty may preclude extradition if prosecution would be barred by a statute of limitations in the country of refuge.

Specialty

Under the doctrine of specialty, sometimes called speciality, a person who has been brought within the jurisdiction of the court by virtue of proceedings under an extradition treaty, can only be tried for one of the offences described in that treaty, and for the offence with which he is charged in the proceedings for his extradition, until a reasonable time and opportunity have been given him after his release or trial upon such charge, to return to the country from whose asylum he had been forcibly taken under those proceedings.

The limitation, expressly included in many treaties, is designed to preclude prosecution for different substantive offenses but does not bar prosecution for different or additional counts of the same offense. And some courts have held that an offense whose prosecution would be barred by the doctrine may nevertheless be considered for purposes of the federal sentencing guidelines, or for purposes of criminal forfeiture. At least where an applicable treaty addresses the question, the rule is no bar to prosecution for crimes committed after the individual is extradited.

Alternatives to Extradition

The existence of an extradition treaty does not preclude the United States acquiring personal jurisdiction over a fugitive by other means, unless the treaty expressly provides otherwise.

Foreign Prosecution

A final alternative when extradition for trial in the United States is not available, is trial within the country of refuge. The alternative exists primarily when a U.S. request for extradition has been refused because of the fugitive's nationality and/or when the crime occurred under circumstances that permit prosecution by either country for the same misconduct. The alternative can be cumbersome and expensive and may be contrary to U.S. policy objectives.

NOTES AND QUESTIONS

1.   *Extradition can take several years, and it may not succeed at all.* It is not uncommon for suspects in computer crime cases to spend several years litigating extradition to the United States from a foreign country. In some cases, defendants succeed in blocking extradition entirely. *See, e.g.,* Tim Castle, Britain Blocks Hacker's Extradition to United States, Reuters, October 16, 2012 (reporting on the seven-year legal dispute seeking extradition of alleged hacker Gary McKinnon from the United Kingdom to the U.S., which ended when the UK Home Secretary blocked extradition on the ground that it raised too high a risk that McKinnon would commit suicide).

2.   *The "I Love You" virus and the role of foreign law.* The contractual nature of extradition treaties means that extradition can hinge on the details of criminal law in the country from which extradition is sought. Consider the "I Love You" computer virus distributed in May 2000 by Onel de Guzman, a young man in the Phillipines. The virus quickly spread globally, shutting down businesses around the world and causing billions of dollars of losses. Mr. de Guzman was arrested in Manila and acknowledged his responsibility, but criminal charges in the Phillipines were dropped because prosecutors concluded that his acts were not criminal under then-existing Phillipines criminal law (which at the time did not include a computer crime law). *See* Robert Frank, Philippine Prosecutors Drop Charges in 'Love Bug' Case, The Wall Street Journal, Aug. 22, 2000.

The dropping of charges against de Guzman made extradition to the United States difficult because the extradition treaty between the United States and the Phillipines requires dual criminality. An unverified report in 2003 suggested that the FBI was still seeking ways to extradite de Guzman. *See* Bebot Sison Jr. & Cecille Suerte Felipe, FBI Still Out to Get 'Virus Man', The Phillipine Star, May 4, 2003. But no extradition request was made, and de Guzman was never prosecuted for his conduct by the United States or by any other country. The Phillipines enacted a dedicated computer crime law in June 2000, a month after the "I Love You" virus circulated, but it could not be used against de Guzman under the principle of ex post facto. *See generally* Gilbert C. Sosa, Country Report on Cybercrime: The Phillipines (2009).

3.   *The continuing extradition saga of Kim Dotcom.* Perhaps the most remarkable example of a continuing extradition dispute for a computer crime

defendant is the case against Kim Dotcom and his alleged co-conspirators. From 2005 to 2012, Dotcom operated a Hong-Kong-based business that hosted a series of websites, the best known of which was *megaupload.com*. The website made copyrighted materials available to anyone for free online without permission from copyright owners. At the time, such materials were not widely available from streaming services. Individual users would upload their own copies of copyrighted materials, such as the latest movies and television shows, making them available to the public. *Megaupload.com* became one of the most popular websites on the Internet. Kim Dotcom and his colleagues allegedly made well over $100 million from selling premium subscriptions and advertising on the site.

In 2012, the United States Department of Justice indicted Dotcom and his colleagues for copyright infringement, racketeering, money laundering, and other offenses. Dotcom was living in New Zealand at the time. The United States has been seeking Dotcom's extradition from New Zealand ever since. The legality of Dotcom's extradition under New Zealand law has been exhaustively litigated in the New Zealand court system. Roughly speaking, the initial question was what evidence could be considered in evaluating whether the requirements of extradition had been satisfied. After that litigation was completed, the next question was whether, based on that evidence, the requirements of extradition have been satisfied.

In November 2020, the New Zealand Supreme Court provisionally ruled that Dotcom could be extradited to the United States to face charges. But the Court also gave Dotcom additional rights of appeal to pursue before any final decision was to be made. *See* Kim Dotcom Can Be Extradited to US But Can Also Appeal, BBC.com, November 4, 2020.

In the most recent ruling of the New Zealand Supreme Court before this casebook is going to print, the Court in May 2021 rejected Doctcom's request to enjoin the lower court proceeding evaluating Doctom's rights of appeal based on Dotcom's claim that the lower court judges should recuse themselves. According to the New Zealand Supreme Court, the lower court proceeding should continue, and Dotcom can then argue his recusal claim in the Supreme Court whenever the lower court proceedings may have concluded. *See* Dotcom v. United States and District Court at North Shore, SC 47/2021 [2021], *available at* https://www.courtsofnz.govt.nz/assets/cases/2021/2021-NZSC-36.pdf.

It remains unclear when New Zealand courts might reach a final ruling as to whether Dotcom can be extradited.

4. *Alternatives when a suspect is located in a country without an extradition agreement, Part 1: The waiting game.* When no extradition agreement exists between the United States and a country where a suspect is located, the government might have to wait until the suspect travels to a different country. This issue has arisen with hackers based in Russia, as there is no extradition agreement between the United States and Russia. Further, the Russian government is purported to take an unusual attitude toward local

hackers: "Russian cybercriminals operate with relative impunity inside Russia as long as they do not breach targets in their country. In return for such immunity, cybercriminals are often tapped to work for Russia's intelligence agencies." Nicole Perlroth, Russian Hacker Sentenced to 27 Years in Credit Card Case, New York Times, April 21, 2017.

One tactic has been for United States officials to wait until the hacker is on vacation in a country that has an extradition treaty with the United States. Officials in that country can make the arrest for the United States under their extradition treaty. *See, e.g.,* Russian Hackers Arrested on Vacation in US-Led Operation, Fox News, August 1, 2017. This tactic comes with an important limit, however: Hackers can learn which countries have extradition treaties with the United States, and they can avoid vacationing there.

5. *Alternatives when a suspect is located in a country without an extradition agreement, Part 2: Informal arrangements.* In unusual cases, U.S. officials can reach informal agreements with officials in countries that lack extradition agreements with the United States. Russian hacker Roman Valerevich Seleznev learned this lesson the hard way. Seleznev knew that the United States wanted to prosecute him for computer crimes. Seleznev carefully avoided traveling to any country that had an extradition treaty with the United States. In 2014, Seleznev traveled with his girlfriend to the Republic of Maldives, a small island country in the Indian Ocean. Seleznev thought he was safe from arrest, as the Maldives lacks an extradition treaty with the United States.

But Seleznev had miscalculated. Officials from the Republic of Maldives agreed to arrest Seleznev for the United States even in the absence of a extradition treaty. The officials arrested Seleznev and turned him over to U.S. authorities for prosecution. He is now serving a long prison sentence in the United States. *See* Nicole Perlroth, Russian Hacker Sentenced to 27 Years in Credit Card Case, New York Times, April 21, 2017.

6. *Alternatives when a suspect is located in a country without an extradition agreement, Part 3: Undercover operations.* In the absence of an extradition agreement, U.S. officials also can try to lure a suspect to the United States using an undercover operation. Officials can arrest the suspect after he enters the United States. For example, in United States v. Gorshkov, 2001 WL 1024026 (W.D. Wash. 2001), undercover FBI agents lured a suspected hacker from Russia to the United States. The agents used the pretext that they ran a computer security company, Invita, that was interested in hiring Gorshkov as a computer security consultant. After Gorshkov arrived in the United States, the employees at "Invita" (who were really FBI agents) had him show off his skills for them. Once it became clear that Gorshkov was the suspected hacker, the FBI placed him under arrest.

7. *The role of customary international law.* Given the difficulties and limits of the options above, why can't U.S. officials simply go to the foreign country, arrest a suspect, and bring the suspect back to face prosecution in the U.S.? Under customary international law, officials from one country cannot

exercise law enforcement functions in another country without consent. *See* Restatement (Third) of Foreign Relations Law of the United States § 432(2) (Am. Law Inst. 1987) (recognizing that "a state's law enforcement officers may exercise their functions in the territory of another state only with the consent of the other state").

CHAPTER 8

NATIONAL SECURITY

■ ■ ■

The United States government conducts surveillance to gather information about threats to the United States and the status of foreign governments with the hope that United States government officials can use the information to protect the United States and further its interests in world affairs. National security surveillance plays no role in most computer crime cases, but it can play an essential role in a few particularly important investigations. A great deal of intelligence surveillance involves e-mail and other Internet communications, and individuals subject to intelligence monitoring eventually may be charged criminally. In such cases, digital evidence collected under national security authorities may be essential to the government's case.

The use of digital evidence collected for national security reasons raises three important questions. First, how does the Fourth Amendment apply to the collection of digital evidence for national security purposes? Second, how does the Foreign Intelligence Surveillance Act (FISA) regulate the collection of digital evidence for such purposes? And third, when can digital evidence collected under FISA be admitted in criminal prosecutions?

A. THE FOURTH AMENDMENT

In the decades before Katz v. United States, 389 U.S. 347 (1967), government officials conducted warrantless wiretapping for national security purposes with little or no legal restriction. The Fourth Amendment did not apply to wiretapping under Olmstead v. United States, 277 U.S. 438 (1928). The Communications Act of 1934 prohibited "intercepting" and "disclosing" wire communications, but the Justice Department construed this to prohibit only the combination of wiretapping and publicly disclosing the fruits of the monitoring. Because national security wiretapping did not require public disclosure, government agents could tap telephone and telegraph lines unhindered by statutory or constitutional regulation.

Katz changed the legal picture considerably, although it settled very little. The *Katz* court certainly was aware of the special constitutional questions raised by national security monitoring. However, Justice Stewart's majority opinion expressly declined to take a position on these issues. *See Katz,* 389 U.S. at 358 n.23 ("Whether safeguards other than prior authorization by a magistrate would satisfy the Fourth Amendment in a situation involving the national security is a question not presented by this case."). Justice White's solo concurrence was more explicit, and expressed the following opinion:

> Wiretapping to protect the security of the Nation has been authorized by successive Presidents. The present Administration would apparently save national security cases from restrictions against wiretapping. We should not require the warrant procedure and the magistrate's judgment if the President of the United States or his chief legal officer, the Attorney General, has considered the requirements of national security and authorized electronic surveillance as reasonable.

Id. at 363 (White, J., concurring).

Congress took a hands-off approach to national security surveillance when it passed the Wiretap Act in 1968, a year after *Katz*. In the original version of the Wiretap Act, Congress carved out an exception to the statute for national security monitoring. When the President deemed it necessary to use his constitutional power to conduct national security monitoring, such monitoring was exempt from the statutory prohibition of the Wiretap Act. *See* 18 U.S.C. § 2511(3) (1968). This approach left open the constitutional question of the President's authority to conduct such monitoring in light of the *Katz*-era Fourth Amendment. The following case was the first (and so far, the only) Supreme Court case to help answer this question.

UNITED STATES V. UNITED STATES DISTRICT COURT
Supreme Court of the United States, 1972.
407 U.S. 297.

MR. JUSTICE POWELL delivered the opinion of the Court.

The issue before us is an important one for the people of our country and their Government. It involves the delicate question of the President's power, acting through the Attorney General, to authorize electronic surveillance in internal security matters without prior judicial approval. Successive Presidents for more than one-quarter of a century have authorized such surveillance in varying degrees, without guidance from the Congress or a definitive decision of this Court. This case brings the issue here for the first time. Its resolution is a matter of national concern, requiring sensitivity both to the Government's right to protect itself from unlawful subversion and attack and to the citizen's right to be secure in his privacy against unreasonable Government intrusion.

This case arises from a criminal proceeding in the United States District Court for the Eastern District of Michigan, in which the United

States charged three defendants with conspiracy to destroy Government property in violation of 18 U.S.C. § 371. One of the defendants, Plamondon, was charged with the dynamite bombing of an office of the Central Intelligence Agency in Ann Arbor, Michigan.

During pretrial proceedings, the defendants moved to compel the United States to disclose certain electronic surveillance information and to conduct a hearing to determine whether this information "tainted" the evidence on which the indictment was based or which the Government intended to offer at trial. In response, the Government filed an affidavit of the Attorney General, acknowledging that its agents had overheard conversations in which Plamondon had participated. The affidavit also stated that the Attorney General approved the wiretaps "to gather intelligence information deemed necessary to protect the nation from attempts of domestic organizations to attack and subvert the existing structure of the Government." The logs of the surveillance were filed in a sealed exhibit for *in camera* inspection by the District Court.

On the basis of the Attorney General's affidavit and the sealed exhibit, the Government asserted that the surveillance was lawful, though conducted without prior judicial approval, as a reasonable exercise of the President's power (exercised through the Attorney General) to protect the national security. The District Court held that the surveillance violated the Fourth Amendment, and ordered the Government to make full disclosure to Plamondon of his overheard conversations.

The Government then filed in the Court of Appeals for the Sixth Circuit a petition for a writ of mandamus to set aside the District Court order, which was stayed pending final disposition of the case. After concluding that it had jurisdiction, that court held that the surveillance was unlawful and that the District Court had properly required disclosure of the overheard conversations. We granted certiorari.

I

Title III of the Omnibus Crime Control and Safe Streets Act, 18 U.S.C. §§ 2510–20, authorizes the use of electronic surveillance for classes of crimes carefully specified in 18 U.S.C. § 2516. Such surveillance is subject to prior court order. Section 2518 sets forth the detailed and particularized application necessary to obtain such an order as well as carefully circumscribed conditions for its use. The Act represents a comprehensive attempt by Congress to promote more effective control of crime while protecting the privacy of individual thought and expression. Much of Title III was drawn to meet the constitutional requirements for electronic surveillance enunciated by this Court in Berger v. New York, 388 U.S. 41 (1967), and Katz v. United States, 389 U.S. 347 (1967).

Together with the elaborate surveillance requirements in Title III, there is the following proviso, 18 U.S.C. § 2511(3):

Nothing contained in this chapter or in section 605 of the Communications Act of 1934 shall limit the constitutional power of the President to take such measures as he deems necessary to protect the Nation against actual or potential attack or other hostile acts of a foreign power, to obtain foreign intelligence information deemed essential to the security of the United States, or to protect national security information against foreign intelligence activities. *Nor shall anything contained in this chapter be deemed to limit the constitutional power of the President to take such measures as he deems necessary to protect the United States against the overthrow of the Government by force or other unlawful means, or against any other clear and present danger to the structure or existence of the Government.* The contents of any wire or oral communication intercepted by authority of the President in the exercise of the foregoing powers may be received in evidence in any trial hearing, or other proceeding only where such interception was reasonable, and shall not be otherwise used or disclosed except as is necessary to implement that power. (Emphasis supplied.)

The Government relies on § 2511(3). It argues that "in excepting national security surveillances from the Act's warrant requirement Congress recognized the President's authority to conduct such surveillances without prior judicial approval." Brief for United States 7, 28. The section thus is viewed as a recognition or affirmance of a constitutional authority in the President to conduct warrantless domestic security surveillance such as that involved in this case.

We think the language of § 2511(3), as well as the legislative history of the statute, refutes this interpretation. The relevant language is that: "Nothing contained in this chapter . . . shall limit the constitutional power of the President to take such measures as he deems necessary to protect" against the dangers specified. At most, this is an implicit recognition that the President does have certain powers in the specified areas. Few would doubt this, as the section refers—among other things—to protection "against actual or potential attack or other hostile acts of a foreign power." But so far as the use of the President's electronic surveillance power is concerned, the language is essentially neutral.

Section 2511(3) certainly confers no power, as the language is wholly inappropriate for such a purpose. It merely provides that the Act shall not be interpreted to limit or disturb such power as the President may have under the Constitution. In short, Congress simply left presidential powers where it found them.

Nothing in § 2511(3) was intended to *expand* or to *contract* or to *define* whatever presidential surveillance powers existed in matters affecting the national security. If we could accept the Government's characterization of § 2511(3) as a congressionally prescribed exception to the general requirement of a warrant, it would be necessary to consider the question of whether the surveillance in this case came within the exception and, if so, whether the statutory exception was itself constitutionally valid. But viewing § 2511(3) as a congressional disclaimer and expression of neutrality, we hold that the statute is not the measure of the executive authority asserted in this case. Rather, we must look to the constitutional powers of the President.

II

It is important at the outset to emphasize the limited nature of the question before the Court. This case raises no constitutional challenge to electronic surveillance as specifically authorized by Title III of the Omnibus Crime Control and Safe Streets Act of 1968. Nor is there any question or doubt as to the necessity of obtaining a warrant in the surveillance of crimes unrelated to the national security interest. Katz v. United States, 389 U.S. 347 (1967); Berger v. New York, 388 U.S. 41 (1967). Further, the instant case requires no judgment on the scope of the President's surveillance power with respect to the activities of foreign powers, within or without this country. The Attorney General's affidavit in this case states that the surveillances were "deemed necessary to protect the nation from attempts of *domestic organizations* to attack and subvert the existing structure of Government" (emphasis supplied). There is no evidence of any involvement, directly or indirectly, of a foreign power.[1]

Our present inquiry, though important, is therefore a narrow one. The determination of this question requires the essential Fourth Amendment inquiry into the "reasonableness" of the search and seizure in question, and the way in which that "reasonableness" derives content and meaning through reference to the warrant clause.

We begin the inquiry by noting that the President of the United States has the fundamental duty, under Art. II, § 1, of the Constitution, to "preserve, protect and defend the Constitution of the United States." Implicit in that duty is the power to protect our Government against those who would subvert or overthrow it by unlawful means. In the discharge of this duty, the President—through the Attorney General—may find it necessary to employ electronic surveillance to obtain intelligence

---

[1] Although we attempt no precise definition, we use the term "domestic organization" in this opinion to mean a group or organization (whether formally or informally constituted) composed of citizens of the United States and which has no significant connection with a foreign power, its agents or agencies. No doubt there are cases where it will be difficult to distinguish between "domestic" and "foreign" unlawful activities directed against the Government of the United States where there is collaboration in varying degrees between domestic groups or organizations and agents or agencies of foreign powers. But this is not such a case.

information on the plans of those who plot unlawful acts against the Government. The use of such surveillance in internal security cases has been sanctioned more or less continuously by various Presidents and Attorneys General since July 1946. Herbert Brownell, Attorney General under President Eisenhower, urged the use of electronic surveillance both in internal and international security matters on the grounds that those acting against the Government

> "turn to the telephone to carry on their intrigue. The success of their plans frequently rests upon piecing together shreds of information received from many sources and many nests. The participants in the conspiracy are often dispersed and stationed in various strategic positions in government and industry throughout the country."[11]

Though the Government and respondents debate their seriousness and magnitude, threats and acts of sabotage against the Government exist in sufficient number to justify investigative powers with respect to them. The covertness and complexity of potential unlawful conduct against the Government and the necessary dependency of many conspirators upon the telephone make electronic surveillance an effective investigatory instrument in certain circumstances. The marked acceleration in technological developments and sophistication in their use have resulted in new techniques for the planning, commission, and concealment of criminal activities. It would be contrary to the public interest for Government to deny to itself the prudent and lawful employment of those very techniques which are employed against the Government and its law-abiding citizens.

It has been said that the most basic function of any government is to provide for the security of the individual and of his property. And unless Government safeguards its own capacity to function and to preserve the security of its people, society itself could become so disordered that all rights and liberties would be endangered.

But a recognition of these elementary truths does not make the employment by Government of electronic surveillance a welcome development—even when employed with restraint and under judicial supervision. There is, understandably, a deep-seated uneasiness and apprehension that this capability will be used to intrude upon cherished privacy of law-abiding citizens. We look to the Bill of Rights to safeguard this privacy. Though physical entry of the home is the chief evil against which the wording of the Fourth Amendment is directed, its broader spirit now shields private speech from unreasonable surveillance. Our decision in *Katz* refused to lock the Fourth Amendment into instances of actual physical trespass. Rather, the Amendment governs "not only the seizure of

---

[11] Brownell, The Public Security and Wire Tapping, 39 Cornell L.Q. 195, 202 (1954).

tangible items, but extends as well to the recording of oral statements without any 'technical trespass under local property law.'" *Katz, supra*, 389 U.S. at 353. That decision implicitly recognized that the broad and unsuspected governmental incursions into conversational privacy which electronic surveillance entails necessitate the application of Fourth Amendment safeguards.

National security cases, moreover, often reflect a convergence of First and Fourth Amendment values not present in cases of "ordinary" crime. Though the investigative duty of the executive may be stronger in such cases, so also is there greater jeopardy to constitutionally protected speech. History abundantly documents the tendency of Government—however benevolent and benign its motives—to view with suspicion those who most fervently dispute its policies. Fourth Amendment protections become the more necessary when the targets of official surveillance may be those suspected of unorthodoxy in their political beliefs. The danger to political dissent is acute where the Government attempts to act under so vague a concept as the power to protect "domestic security." Given the difficulty of defining the domestic security interest, the danger of abuse in acting to protect that interest becomes apparent. The price of lawful public dissent must not be a dread of subjection to an unchecked surveillance power. Nor must the fear of unauthorized official eavesdropping deter vigorous citizen dissent and discussion of Government action in private conversation. For private dissent, no less than open public discourse, is essential to our free society.

III

As the Fourth Amendment is not absolute in its terms, our task is to examine and balance the basic values at stake in this case: the duty of Government to protect the domestic security, and the potential danger posed by unreasonable surveillance to individual privacy and free expression. If the legitimate need of Government to safeguard domestic security requires the use of electronic surveillance, the question is whether the needs of citizens for privacy and free expression may not be better protected by requiring a warrant before such surveillance is undertaken. We must also ask whether a warrant requirement would unduly frustrate the efforts of Government to protect itself from acts of subversion and overthrow directed against it.

Over two centuries ago, Lord Mansfield held that common-law principles prohibited warrants that ordered the arrest of unnamed individuals who the *officer* might conclude were guilty of seditious libel. "It is not fit," said Mansfield, "that the receiving or judging of the information should be left to the discretion of the officer. The magistrate ought to judge; and should give certain directions to the officer." Leach v. Three of the King's Messengers, 19 How. St. Tr. 1001, 1027 (1765).

Lord Mansfield's formulation touches the very heart of the Fourth Amendment directive: that, where practical, a governmental search and seizure should represent both the efforts of the officer to gather evidence of wrongful acts and the judgment of the magistrate that the collected evidence is sufficient to justify invasion of a citizen's private premises or conversation. Inherent in the concept of a warrant is its issuance by a "neutral and detached magistrate." The Fourth Amendment does not contemplate the executive officers of Government as neutral and disinterested magistrates. Their duty and responsibility are to enforce the laws, to investigate, and to prosecute. But those charged with this investigative and prosecutorial duty should not be the sole judges of when to utilize constitutionally sensitive means in pursuing their tasks. The historical judgment, which the Fourth Amendment accepts, is that unreviewed executive discretion may yield too readily to pressures to obtain incriminating evidence and overlook potential invasions of privacy and protected speech.

It is true that there have been some exceptions to the warrant requirement. But those exceptions are few in number and carefully delineated; in general, they serve the legitimate needs of law enforcement officers to protect their own well-being and preserve evidence from destruction. Even while carving out those exceptions, the Court has reaffirmed the principle that the police must, whenever practicable, obtain advance judicial approval of searches and seizures through the warrant procedure.

The Government argues that the special circumstances applicable to domestic security surveillances necessitate a further exception to the warrant requirement. It is urged that the requirement of prior judicial review would obstruct the President in the discharge of his constitutional duty to protect domestic security. We are told further that these surveillances are directed primarily to the collecting and maintaining of intelligence with respect to subversive forces, and are not an attempt to gather evidence for specific criminal prosecutions. It is said that this type of surveillance should not be subject to traditional warrant requirements which were established to govern investigation of criminal activity, not ongoing intelligence gathering.

The Government further insists that courts as a practical matter would have neither the knowledge nor the techniques necessary to determine whether there was probable cause to believe that surveillance was necessary to protect national security. These security problems, the Government contends, involve a large number of complex and subtle factors beyond the competence of courts to evaluate.

There is, no doubt, pragmatic force to the Government's position. But we do not think a case has been made for the requested departure from

Fourth Amendment standards. The circumstances described do not justify complete exemption of domestic security surveillance from prior judicial scrutiny. Official surveillance, whether its purpose be criminal investigation or ongoing intelligence gathering, risks infringement of constitutionally protected privacy of speech. Security surveillances are especially sensitive because of the inherent vagueness of the domestic security concept, the necessarily broad and continuing nature of intelligence gathering, and the temptation to utilize such surveillances to oversee political dissent. We recognize, as we have before, the constitutional basis of the President's domestic security role, but we think it must be exercised in a manner compatible with the Fourth Amendment. In this case we hold that this requires an appropriate prior warrant procedure.

We cannot accept the Government's argument that internal security matters are too subtle and complex for judicial evaluation. Courts regularly deal with the most difficult issues of our society. There is no reason to believe that federal judges will be insensitive to or uncomprehending of the issues involved in domestic security cases. Certainly courts can recognize that domestic security surveillance involves different considerations from the surveillance of "ordinary crime." If the threat is too subtle or complex for our senior law enforcement officers to convey its significance to a court, one may question whether there is probable cause for surveillance.

Thus, we conclude that the Government's concerns do not justify departure in this case from the customary Fourth Amendment requirement of judicial approval prior to initiation of a search or surveillance. Although some added burden will be imposed upon the Attorney General, this inconvenience is justified in a free society to protect constitutional values. Nor do we think the Government's domestic surveillance powers will be impaired to any significant degree. A prior warrant establishes presumptive validity of the surveillance and will minimize the burden of justification in post-surveillance judicial review. By no means of least importance will be the reassurance of the public generally that indiscriminate wiretapping and bugging of law-abiding citizens cannot occur.

IV

We emphasize, before concluding this opinion, the scope of our decision. As stated at the outset, this case involves only the domestic aspects of national security. We have not addressed, and express no opinion as to, the issues which may be involved with respect to activities of foreign powers or their agents. Nor does our decision rest on the language of § 2511(3) or any other section of Title III of the Omnibus Crime Control and Safe Streets Act of 1968. That Act does not attempt to define or delineate the powers of the President to meet domestic threats to the national security.

Moreover, we do not hold that the same type of standards and procedures prescribed by Title III are necessarily applicable to this case. We recognize that domestic security surveillance may involve different policy and practical considerations from the surveillance of "ordinary crime." The gathering of security intelligence is often long range and involves the interrelation of various sources and types of information. The exact targets of such surveillance may be more difficult to identify than in surveillance operations against many types of crime specified in Title III. Often, too, the emphasis of domestic intelligence gathering is on the prevention of unlawful activity or the enhancement of the Government's preparedness for some possible future crisis or emergency. Thus, the focus of domestic surveillance may be less precise than that directed against more conventional types of crime.

Given those potential distinctions between Title III criminal surveillances and those involving the domestic security, Congress may wish to consider protective standards for the latter which differ from those already prescribed for specified crimes in Title III. Different standards may be compatible with the Fourth Amendment if they are reasonable both in relation to the legitimate need of Government for intelligence information and the protected rights of our citizens. For the warrant application may vary according to the governmental interest to be enforced and the nature of citizen rights deserving protection. As the Court said in Camara v. Municipal Court, 387 U.S. 523, 534–535 (1967):

> In cases in which the Fourth Amendment requires that a warrant to search be obtained, 'probable cause' is the standard by which a particular decision to search is tested against the constitutional mandate of reasonableness. In determining whether a particular inspection is reasonable—and thus in determining whether there is probable cause to issue a warrant for that inspection—the need for the inspection must be weighed in terms of these reasonable goals of code enforcement.

It may be that Congress, for example, would judge that the application and affidavit showing probable cause need not follow the exact requirements of § 2518 but should allege other circumstances more appropriate to domestic security cases; that the request for prior court authorization could, in sensitive cases, be made to any member of a specially designated court (*e.g.*, the District Court for the District of Columbia or the Court of Appeals for the District of Columbia Circuit); and that the time and reporting requirements need not be so strict as those in § 2518.

The above paragraph does not, of course, attempt to guide the congressional judgment but rather to delineate the present scope of our own opinion. We do not attempt to detail the precise standards for domestic security warrants any more than our decision in *Katz* sought to set the refined requirements for the specified criminal surveillances which now constitute Title III. We do hold, however, that prior judicial approval is required for the type of domestic security surveillance involved in this case and that such approval may be made in accordance with such reasonable standards as the Congress may prescribe.

NOTES AND QUESTIONS

1. *A reasonable warrant requirement.* Justice Powell's opinion is quintessentially pragmatic. Justice Powell views the constitutional question as a balance between government and individual interests in the context of domestic security surveillance cases. The key language appears at the beginning of Part III:

> Our task is to examine and balance the basic values at stake in this case: the duty of Government to protect the domestic security, and the potential danger posed by unreasonable surveillance to individual privacy and free expression. If the legitimate need of Government to safeguard domestic security requires the use of electronic surveillance, the question is whether the needs of citizens for privacy and free expression may not be better protected by requiring a warrant before such surveillance is undertaken. We must also ask whether a warrant requirement would unduly frustrate the efforts of Government to protect itself from acts of subversion and overthrow directed against it.

Justice Powell concludes that the balance favors a warrant requirement: in his view, the requirement would better protect the needs of citizens and would not unduly frustrate the efforts of the government.

At the same time, the warrant requirement Justice Powell has in mind is no ordinary warrant requirement. Part IV of the opinion explains that Congress is free to enact a new type of warrant procedure and a new type of warrant that is tailored to the needs of domestic security investigations. The new procedures simply need to be "reasonable both in relation to the legitimate need of Government for intelligence information and the protected rights of our citizens." Once again, the standard is reasonableness. Putting Part III and Part IV of the opinion together, a warrant is required in domestic security cases because some kind of reasonable warrant requirement would be a reasonable limitation on government surveillance practices.

2. *Domestic security versus foreign intelligence.* Justice Powell's opinion considers legal standards for domestic security surveillance, but it explicitly excludes foreign intelligence surveillance. What's the difference?

Although the opinion does not elaborate extensively on the two categories, it seems that domestic security surveillance refers to the monitoring of threats to the nation from United States citizens operating in the United States, while foreign intelligence surveillance refers to gathering intelligence concerning foreign nations, governments, and their agents. The two categories may not seem intuitive today. The idea that the Nation would face threats to its existence from its own citizenry may seem puzzling, as does the notion that foreign threats are limited to threats from foreign governments and their agents. At the time of the Supreme Court's opinion, however, these two categories seemed more natural. Domestic intelligence referred to monitoring of American citizens who were believed to be communists, fascists, or members of radical groups committed to overthrowing the United States government. Foreign intelligence referred to the monitoring of foreign governments and their agents, such as Soviet spies and employees of foreign embassies.

Today the most important goal of national security monitoring is to identify and disrupt terror attacks planned by groups such as the Al Qaeda network. Does monitoring designed to disrupt such attacks count as foreign intelligence, domestic intelligence, or something else? *See* 50 U.S.C. § 1801(a)(4) (defining "foreign power" to include "a group engaged in international terrorism or activities in preparation therefor").

3.   *Fourth Amendment standards for foreign intelligence surveillance.* The Supreme Court has never addressed whether and when foreign intelligence surveillance requires a search warrant, or what kind of warrant it may require. However, the Court's opinions in related areas narrow the inquiry. For example, a great deal of foreign intelligence surveillance does not trigger Fourth Amendment protections under United States v. Verdugo-Urquidez, 494 U.S. 259 (1990). Under *Verdugo*, foreign nationals located outside the United States normally have no Fourth Amendment rights. *Verdugo* thus permits a great deal of monitoring by United States intelligence authorities abroad.

Second, the border search exception to the Fourth Amendment as interpreted in cases like United States v. Ramsey, 431 U.S. 606 (1977), probably permits intelligence agencies to monitor computer traffic entering and exiting the United States. Finally, in both the domestic and foreign intelligence surveillance context, Fourth Amendment protections exist only to the extent a user has a reasonable expectation of privacy in remote data.

Let's assume that none of these doctrines eliminate Fourth Amendment protection, and that a computer user normally has a reasonable expectation of privacy in the contents of his communications online. According to *United States v. United States District Court*, the government normally must obtain a warrant to monitor that individual's communications if the government is engaging in domestic intelligence surveillance. But does the warrant requirement apply if the government is conducting *foreign* intelligence surveillance?

Two court of appeals cases shed light on this question. United States v. Butenko, 494 F.2d 593 (3d Cir. 1974) (en banc), involved the prosecution of a Soviet national and an American citizen for transmitting defense information to the Soviet Union. The Soviet national, Igor Ivanov, sought disclosure of the fruits of warrantless wiretapping against him on the ground that the monitoring was illegal. In an opinion by Judge Adams, the Third Circuit concluded that the Fourth Amendment did not require a warrant before the government conducted foreign intelligence surveillance:

> Foreign intelligence gathering is a clandestine and highly unstructured activity, and the need for electronic surveillance often cannot be anticipated in advance. Certainly occasions arise when officers, acting under the President's authority, are seeking foreign intelligence information, where exigent circumstances would excuse a warrant. To demand that such officers be so sensitive to the nuances of complex situations that they must interrupt their activities and rush to the nearest available magistrate to seek a warrant would seriously fetter the Executive in the performance of his foreign affairs duties.

Id. at 605. According to the Third Circuit, the Fourth Amendment merely requires that foreign intelligence surveillance be reasonable:

> The government interest here—to acquire the information necessary to exercise an informed judgment in foreign affairs—is surely weighty. Moreover, officers conceivably undertake certain electronic surveillance with no suspicion that a criminal activity may be discovered. Thus, a demand that they show that before engaging in such surveillance they had a reasonable belief that criminal activity would be unearthed would be to ignore the overriding object of the intrusions. Since the primary purpose of these searches is to secure foreign intelligence information, a judge, when reviewing a particular search must, above all, be assured that this was in fact its primary purpose and that the accumulation of evidence of criminal activity was incidental. If the court, for example, finds that members of a domestic political organization were the subjects of wiretaps or that the agents were looking for evidence of criminal conduct unrelated to the foreign affairs needs of a President, then he would undoubtedly hold the surveillances to be illegal and take appropriate measures.

Id. at 606.

The Fourth Circuit reached a similar conclusion in United States v. Truong Dinh Hung, 629 F.2d 908 (4th Cir. 1980). A Vietnamese citizen was convicted of espionage for passing classified diplomatic cables and sensitive strategic plans to the government of the Socialist Republic of Vietnam. The defendant's home telephone was tapped for 268 consecutive days without a warrant, and the evidence was used against him at trial. The defendant challenged the surveillance under the Fourth Amendment, but the Fourth Circuit held that the monitoring was legal:

> The needs of the executive are so compelling in the area of foreign intelligence, unlike the area of domestic security, that a uniform warrant requirement would, following *United States v. United States*

District Court, "unduly frustrate" the President in carrying out his foreign affairs responsibilities. First of all, attempts to counter foreign threats to the national security require the utmost stealth, speed, and secrecy. A warrant requirement would add a procedural hurdle that would reduce the flexibility of executive foreign intelligence initiatives, in some cases delay executive response to foreign intelligence threats, and increase the chance of leaks regarding sensitive executive operations.

More importantly, the executive possesses unparalleled expertise to make the decision whether to conduct foreign intelligence surveillance, whereas the judiciary is largely inexperienced in making the delicate and complex decisions that lie behind foreign intelligence surveillance. The executive branch, containing the State Department, the intelligence agencies, and the military, is constantly aware of the nation's security needs and the magnitude of external threats posed by a panoply of foreign nations and organizations. On the other hand, while the courts possess expertise in making the probable cause determination involved in surveillance of suspected criminals, the courts are unschooled in diplomacy and military affairs, a mastery of which would be essential to passing upon an executive branch request that a foreign intelligence wiretap be authorized. Few, if any, district courts would be truly competent to judge the importance of particular information to the security of the United States or the "probable cause" to demonstrate that the government in fact needs to recover that information from one particular source.

Perhaps most crucially, the executive branch not only has superior expertise in the area of foreign intelligence, it is also constitutionally designated as the pre-eminent authority in foreign affairs. The President and his deputies are charged by the constitution with the conduct of the foreign policy of the United States in times of war and peace. Just as the separation of powers in *United States v. United States District Court* forced the executive to recognize a judicial role when the President conducts domestic security surveillance, so the separation of powers requires us to acknowledge the principal responsibility of the President for foreign affairs and concomitantly for foreign intelligence surveillance.

Id. at 913–14. The Court limited this holding to contexts in which two requirements were met. "First, the government should be relieved of seeking a warrant only when the object of the search or the surveillance is a foreign power, its agent or collaborators." *Id.* at 915. Second, "the executive should be excused from securing a warrant only when the surveillance is conducted primarily for foreign intelligence reasons." *Id.* The court explained:

Once surveillance becomes primarily a criminal investigation, the courts are entirely competent to make the usual probable cause determination, and individual privacy interests come to the fore and government foreign policy concerns recede when the government is primarily attempting to form the basis for a criminal prosecution. We thus reject the government's assertion that, if surveillance is to any degree directed at gathering foreign intelligence, the executive may ignore the warrant requirement of the Fourth Amendment.

Id. In those contexts, warrantless surveillance was permissible so long as it was "reasonable."

4. *The Fourth Amendment and extraterritorial national security searches.* In the case of In re Terrorist Bombings of U.S. Embassies in East Africa, 552 F.3d 157 (2d Cir. 2008), the Second Circuit concluded that the constitutionality of warrantless wiretapping that targeted a U.S. citizen in Kenya should be evaluated under a general reasonableness standard. In that case, the government learned of five phone numbers being used by active members of Al Qaeda. One such number happened to belong to El-Hage, who was an American citizen. His home telephone was monitored without a warrant for about one year. The Second Circuit concluded that the warrantless wiretapping of El-Hage's telephone in Kenya was reasonable and therefore constitutional under the circumstances:

> It cannot be denied that El-Hage suffered, while abroad, a significant invasion of privacy by virtue of the government's year-long surveillance of his telephonic communications. The Supreme Court has recognized that, like a physical search, electronic monitoring intrudes on "the innermost secrets of one's home or office" and that "few threats to liberty exist which are greater than that posed by the use of eavesdropping devices." *Berger v. New York*, 388 U.S. 41, 63 (1967). For its part, the government does not contradict El-Hage's claims that the surveillance was broad and loosely minimized. Instead, the government sets forth a variety of reasons justifying the breadth of the surveillance. These justifications, regardless of their merit, do not lessen the intrusion El-Hage suffered while abroad, and we accord this intrusion substantial weight in our balancing analysis.

> Turning to the government's interest, we encounter again the self-evident need to investigate threats to national security presented by foreign terrorist organizations. When U.S. intelligence learned that five telephone lines were being used by suspected al Qaeda operatives, the need to monitor communications traveling on those lines was paramount, and we are loath to discount—much less disparage—the government's decision to do so.

> Our balancing of these competing, and competing, interests turns on whether the scope of the intrusion here was justified by the government's surveillance needs. We conclude that it was, for at least the following four reasons.

First, complex, wide-ranging, and decentralized organizations, such as al Qaeda, warrant sustained and intense monitoring in order to understand their features and identify their members.

Second, foreign intelligence gathering of the sort considered here must delve into the superficially mundane because it is not always readily apparent what information is relevant.

Third, members of covert terrorist organizations, as with other sophisticated criminal enterprises, often communicate in code, or at least through ambiguous language. Hence, more extensive and careful monitoring of these communications may be necessary.

Fourth, because the monitored conversations were conducted in foreign languages, the task of determining relevance and identifying coded language was further complicated.

Because the surveillance of suspected al Qaeda operatives must be sustained and thorough in order to be effective, we cannot conclude that the scope of the government's electronic surveillance was overbroad. While the intrusion on El-Hage's privacy was great, the need for the government to so intrude was even greater. Accordingly, the electronic surveillance was reasonable under the Fourth Amendment.

Id. at 175–76.

5. *Reasonable warrants under the USA Patriot Act. United States v. United States District Court* establishes that warrants are required for domestic security surveillance, and advises that such warrants must be "reasonable both in relation to the legitimate need of Government for intelligence information and the protected rights of our citizens." What does this mean? What types of warrants can Congress authorize in intelligence cases that will satisfy this test?

This issue arose in In re Sealed Case, 310 F.3d 717 (Foreign Intel. Surv. Ct. Rev. 2002), which considered the constitutionality of amendments to the Foreign Intelligence Surveillance Act (FISA) put in place by the USA Patriot Act of 2001. Before the Patriot Act, FISA conditioned the issuance of national security warrants on the absence of intent to collect evidence for possible criminal prosecution. Specifically, FISA required investigators seeking a national security warrant to establish probable cause that the person monitored was an agent of a foreign power and that "the purpose of the surveillance is to obtain foreign intelligence information."

The Patriot Act changed the standard to permit intelligence officials to share information collected under FISA with criminal investigators. The new standard requires the government to establish probable cause that the person monitored is the agent of a foreign power, and that "a significant purpose" of surveillance is to obtain foreign intelligence information. 50 U.S.C. § 1804(a)(7)(B). It also adds a provision allowing "Federal officers who conduct electronic surveillance to acquire foreign intelligence information" to "consult with Federal law enforcement officers to coordinate efforts to investigate or protect against" attack or other grave hostile acts, sabotage or international terrorism, or clandestine intelligence activities, by foreign powers or their agents. 50 U.S.C. § 1806(k)(1).

The Foreign Intelligence Surveillance Court of Review, a special court of three federal appellate judges, ruled that this statutory framework satisfies the reasonableness standard:

> FISA's general programmatic purpose, to protect the nation against terrorists and espionage threats directed by foreign powers, has from its outset been distinguishable from "ordinary crime control." After the events of September 11, 2001, though, it is hard to imagine greater emergencies facing Americans than those experienced on that date.

> Although the threat to society is not dispositive in determining whether a search or seizure is reasonable, it certainly remains a crucial factor. Our case may well involve the most serious threat our country faces. Even without taking into account the President's inherent constitutional authority to conduct warrantless foreign intelligence surveillance, we think the procedures and government showings required under FISA, if they do not meet the minimum Fourth Amendment warrant standards, certainly come close. We, therefore, believe firmly, applying the balancing test drawn from *United States v. United States District Court*, that FISA as amended is constitutional because the surveillances it authorizes are reasonable.

In re Sealed Case, 310 F.3d at 746.

UNITED STATES V. MOHAMUD

United States Court of Appeals for the Ninth Circuit, 2016.
843 F.3d 420.

OWENS, CIRCUIT JUDGE.

Mohamed Osman Mohamud appeals from his conviction for attempting to detonate a large bomb during the annual Christmas Tree Lighting Ceremony in Pioneer Courthouse Square in downtown Portland, Oregon, in violation of 18 U.S.C. § 2332a(a)(2)(A). We affirm.

Factual Background

In many respects, Mohamud was like any other American teenager. He liked music, the Los Angeles Lakers, and hanging out with his friends. Born in Somalia, he immigrated to the United States at the age of three, and grew up in the Portland area.

But after a December 2008 incident at London's Heathrow Airport, things changed. Believing that airport security racially profiled him,

Mohamud wrote an email in London stating that it is "the evil zionist-crusader lobbyists who control the world," and calling on Allah to send fighters against them. He also created a new email account while in London—truthbespoken@googlemail.com. That email account would play a significant role in the prosecution's case.

In 2009, Mohamud began communicating over the Internet with Samir Khan, a United States citizen then living in North Carolina. Khan published *Jihad Recollections*, an online magazine aimed at English-speaking al-Qaeda supporters. From February to August 2009, Mohamud and Khan exchanged roughly 150 emails, with Mohamud using his truthbespoken email account. Topics included Islamic law and advice about personal relationships. They also outlined Mohamud's support for Osama bin Laden.

Mohamud also struck up a relationship with Amro Al-Ali, a Saudi citizen who Mohamud met at a Portland mosque and who subsequently left the United States. On August 31, 2009, Al-Ali sent information to Mohamud at his truthbespoken email account about an Islamic school in Yemen. That same day, Mohamud called his father to say that he was leaving the country. His father begged him to stay in the United States, but Mohamud told him it was too late—he had his passport, visa, and ticket ready to go. When his parents confirmed that his passport was missing, they feared that Mohamud might return to Somalia, his place of birth. And when they could not reach Mohamud, they called the FBI and asked an agent to stop their son from leaving the country.

Eventually, Mohamud's mother got in touch with her son, scolded him, and brought him home. Mohamud did not actually have a visa or plane ticket, and he returned his passport to his parents. A few days later, Mohamud's father called the FBI agent back and told him that Mohamud had agreed to finish college and would not leave the country until he graduated. He also explained that his son had wanted to go to Yemen to study Arabic and Islam. Mohamud's father forwarded the FBI an email from his son about a school in Yemen, which allowed the FBI to identify Mohamud as the user of the truthbespoken email account.

In September 2009, Mohamud began studying engineering at Oregon State University in Corvallis, where he had a "typical" college experience: he had a roommate, made friends, and attended parties (where he drank alcohol and used marijuana). His activities and religious principles often clashed, and in November 2009 he sought advice from a Muslim website on the difficulties of living a pious life on a college campus.

After the urgent August 31, 2009 call from Mohamud's father, the FBI opened an investigation into Mohamud. Agents conducted physical and electronic surveillance of Mohamud, but did not identify any overtly dangerous communications.

[Undercover FBI agents communicated with Mohamud and learned of his plans to set off a bomb. Mohamud's e-mail communications with a foreign national located abroad were collected pursuant to § 702 of the Foreign Intelligence Surveillance Act. Mohamud was arrested and convicted, and his legal challenge on appeal included the following Fourth Amendment claim challenging the collection of his e-mail communications with the foreign national.]

Legal Background

In 1978, Congress enacted FISA to authorize and regulate certain governmental electronic surveillance of communications for foreign intelligence purposes. To do so, the government must obtain a FISA warrant from the FISC. The FISA Court of Review assesses any denials by the FISC of applications for electronic surveillance. Thirty years later, Congress enacted § 702 as part of the FISA Amendments Act of 2008.

Section 702 supplements pre-existing FISA authority by creating a new framework under which the Government may seek the FISC's authorization of certain foreign intelligence surveillance targeting the communications of non-U.S. persons located abroad. Unlike traditional FISA surveillance, § 702 does not require the Government to demonstrate probable cause that the target of the electronic surveillance is a foreign power or agent of a foreign power. And, unlike traditional FISA, § 702 does not require the Government to specify the nature and location of each of the particular facilities or places at which the electronic surveillance will occur. Instead, § 702 mandates that the government obtain the FISC's approval of 'targeting' procedures, 'minimization' procedures, and a governmental certification regarding proposed surveillance.

No Fourth Amendment Violation

Although § 702 potentially raises complex statutory and constitutional issues, this case does not. As explained below, the initial collection of Mohamud's email communications did not involve so-called "upstreaming" or targeting of Mohamud under § 702, more controversial methods of collecting information. It also did not involve the retention and querying of incidentally collected communications. All this case involved was the targeting of a foreign national under § 702, through which Mohamud's email communications were incidentally collected. Confined to the particular facts of this case, we hold that the § 702 acquisition of Mohamud's email communications did not violate the Fourth Amendment.

At our request post-argument, the government declassified certain facts about Mohamud's surveillance. Through the monitoring of a foreign national's email account, the United States government learned that Mohamud was in contact with that foreign national, who was located overseas. This contact—a limited number of emails between Mohamud and the foreign national—was used to obtain a FISA warrant to surveil

Mohamud and his activities. None of these emails was introduced at trial. We permitted the parties to file supplemental briefs to address the facts offered in the post-argument disclosure.

No Warrant Required to Intercept Overseas Foreign
National's Communications or to Intercept U.S.
Person's Communications Incidentally

As a threshold matter, the Fourth Amendment does not apply to searches and seizures by the United States against a non-resident alien in a foreign country. Thus, the government's monitoring of the overseas foreign national's email fell outside the Fourth Amendment.

Mohamud argues that under United States v. Verdugo-Urquidez, 494 U.S. 259, 274–75 (1990), the location of the search matters, and that here, the searches took place in the United States. Indeed, the government acknowledges that collection from service providers under Section 702 takes place within the United States. Yet, as one court put it, "what matters here is the location of the *target*," and not where the government literally obtained the electronic data. *United States v. Hasbajrami*, No. 11-CR-623, 2016 WL 1029500, at *9 n.15 (E.D.N.Y. Mar. 8, 2016).

Consistent with *Verdugo-Urquidez* and our precedent, we hold that this particular type of non-upstream collection—where a search was not directed at a U.S. person's communications, though some were incidentally swept up in it—does not require a warrant, because the search was targeted at a non-U.S. person with no Fourth Amendment right.

The FISA Review Court in *In re Directives Pursuant to Section 105B of FISA*, 551 F.3d 1004, 1015 (FISA Ct. Rev. 2008), similarly applied this principle, holding that "incidental collections occurring as a result of constitutionally permissible acquisitions do not render those acquisitions unlawful."

Mohamud and Amici urge us not to apply this "incidental overhear" approach. First, Amici contend that surveillance of U.S. persons' communications under § 702 is not "incidental" because the monitoring of communications between foreign targets and U.S. persons was specifically contemplated and to some degree desired. We agree that such communications were anticipated. As the Privacy and Civil Liberties Oversight Board found with respect to PRISM collection, the collection of communications to and from a target inevitably returns communications in which non-targets are on the other end, some of whom will be U.S. persons. Such 'incidental' collection of communications is not accidental, nor is it inadvertent. The fact that the government knew some U.S. persons' communications would be swept up during foreign intelligence gathering does not make such collection any more unlawful in this context than in the Title III or traditional FISA context.

Mohamud and Amici also contend that the "sheer amount of 'incidental' collection" separates § 702 from prior cases where courts have found such collection permissible. We agree with the district court's observation that the most troubling aspect of this "incidental" collection is not whether such collection was anticipated, but rather its volume, which is vast, not *de minimis*. This quantity distinguishes § 702 collection from Title III and traditional FISA interceptions. However, the mere fact that more communications are being collected incidentally does not make it unconstitutional to apply the same approach to § 702 collection, though it does increase the importance of minimization procedures once the communications are collected.

For these reasons, and because the target of the surveillance was a non-U.S. person located outside of the United States at the time of the surveillance, the government was not required to obtain a search warrant to collect Mohamud's email communications with the overseas foreign national as an incident to its lawful search of the foreign national's email.

Collection of Mohamud's Emails was Reasonable

Assuming that Mohamud had a Fourth Amendment right in the incidentally collected communications, the search at issue was reasonable under the Fourth Amendment. Even if a warrant is not required, a search is not beyond Fourth Amendment scrutiny; for it must be reasonable in its scope and manner of execution. In deciding reasonableness, we examine the totality of the circumstances and weigh the promotion of legitimate governmental interests against the degree to which the search intrudes upon an individual's privacy. We agree with the district court that under these circumstances, the search was reasonable under the Fourth Amendment.

i.   Government Interest

The Government's interest in combating terrorism is an urgent objective of the highest order. Neither Mohamud nor Amici challenge this. Instead, they argue that (1) the statutory definition of "foreign intelligence information" in § 702 is overbroad because it is not confined to national security information but also includes "the conduct of foreign affairs"; and (2) even if national security justifies the initial acquisition, it is unreasonable to then retain and later search U.S. persons' § 702-acquired communications without a warrant.

The declassified facts foreclose both arguments. First, as the district court observed, the discovery in this case all concerned protecting the country from a terrorist threat and did not stray into the broader category of the conduct of foreign affairs. Thus, we need not determine whether the collection of foreign affairs communications is reasonable. Similarly, the second argument is also outside the scope of our review, as no such retention and querying is at issue in this case.

ii. Mohamud's Privacy Interest

The parties agree that Mohamud had some expectation of privacy in his electronic communications, but disagree as to the strength of his interest. The government argues that U.S. persons have a limited expectation of privacy when communicating electronically with non-U.S. persons located outside the United States because of the Fourth Amendment's "third-party" doctrine—that a person's privacy interest is diminished where he or she reveals information to a third party, even in confidence. Mohamud contends that the voluntary disclosure of information to third parties does not reduce the expectation of privacy. The district court determined that under the third-party doctrine, Mohamud had a reduced expectation of privacy in his communications to third parties. We agree.

With respect to a U.S. person's privacy interest, we treat emails as letters. Accordingly, until electronic communications reach the recipient, they retain the same level of privacy interest as if they were still in the home. But as with letters, a person's reasonable expectation of privacy may be diminished in transmissions over the Internet or e-mail that have already arrived at the recipient.

It is true that prior case law contemplates a diminished expectation of privacy due to the risk that the recipient will reveal the communication, not that the government will be monitoring the communication unbeknownst to the third party. While these cases do not address the question of government interception, the communications at issue here had been sent to a third party, which reduces Mohamud's privacy interest at least somewhat, if perhaps not as much as if the foreign national had turned them over to the government voluntarily.

Thus, Mohamud's interest in the privacy of his communications received by the overseas foreign national is diminished.

iii. Privacy Protecting Measures

An important component of the reasonableness inquiry is whether the FISC-approved targeting and minimization measures sufficiently protect the privacy interests of U.S. persons. Targeting and minimization procedures govern, respectively, who may be targeted for surveillance and how intercepted communications are to be retained and disseminated.

In brief, targeting procedures must be "reasonably designed" to "ensure that any acquisition authorized under [the certification] is limited to targeting persons reasonably believed to be located outside the United States" and to "prevent the intentional acquisition of any communication as to which the sender and all intended recipients are known at the time of the acquisition to be located in the United States." 50 U.S.C. § 1881a(d)(1). Among other requirements, minimization procedures must be "reasonably designed" "to minimize the acquisition and retention, and prohibit the dissemination, of nonpublicly available information concerning unconsenting United States persons consistent with the need of the United States to obtain, produce, and disseminate foreign intelligence information." 50 U.S.C. §§ 1801(h)(1), 1881a(e)(1).

After evaluating the protections detailed in § 702 and the classified minimization procedures, the district court concluded that as applied to Mohamud, § 702 is reasonable under the Fourth Amendment. Based on our review of the classified record, we agree that the applicable targeting and minimization procedures, which were followed in practice, sufficiently protected Mohamud's privacy interest.

Under the totality of the circumstances, we conclude that the applied targeting and minimization procedures adequately protected Mohamud's diminished privacy interest, in light of the government's compelling interest in national security.

In sum, even assuming Mohamud had a Fourth Amendment right in the incidentally collected communications, the search was reasonable. Thus, we hold that the application of § 702 did not violate the Fourth Amendment under the particular facts of this case.

NOTES AND QUESTIONS

1. The Ninth Circuit concludes in *Mohamud* that the warrant requirement does not apply when the government's surveillance is targeting a person with no Fourth Amendment rights. Is that persuasive? Mohamud was a United States citizen residing inside the United States, and his e-mails were collected from inside the United States. Why should it matter whether the government's collection of Mohamud's e-mail resulted from "targeting" Mohamud or a foreign national abroad? Either way, isn't it the same e-mail?

2. The Ninth Circuit concludes that the warrantless surveillance in *Mohamud* was reasonable in part because Mohamud had "a limited expectation of privacy . . . because of the Fourth Amendment's third-party doctrine." Notably, however, the third-party doctrine does not limit expectations of privacy: Where it applies, the third-party doctrine entirely eliminates expectations of privacy. Given that the Ninth Circuit seems to acknowledge that individuals have a reasonable expectation of privacy in the contents of their e-mails, how can that be "limited" by the third-party doctrine that would defeat that expectation?

3. Although *Mohamud* arose in the context of a national security investigation, much of its reasoning appears applicable to a criminal case. How should a court apply the Fourth Amendment to a criminal investigation in which a United States citizen was e-mailing with a foreign national abroad? Should the result be the same, or should a court construe *Mohamud* as only a national security case?

B. THE FOREIGN INTELLIGENCE
SURVEILLANCE ACT

United States v. United States District Court pointed to the need for statutory regulation of national security surveillance. That need became particularly clear in the mid 1970s during hearings into intelligence collection abuses held by the United States Senate Select Committee to Study Governmental Operations with Respect to Intelligence Activities, presided over by Senator Frank Church. The so-called "Church Committee" published 14 reports in 1975 and 1976 detailing the intelligence practices of several government agencies, and the reports led to calls for a new statute to regulate intelligence surveillance. *See generally* Peter P. Swire, *The System of Foreign Intelligence Surveillance Law*, 72 Geo. Wash. L. Rev. 1306, 1315–20 (2004).

Congress responded by enacting the Foreign Intelligence Surveillance Act (FISA), Pub. L. 95–511 (1978). FISA replaced the reservation clause of 18 U.S.C. § 2511(3) (1968), and imposed direct regulation of Executive Branch intelligence activities. *See* 18 U.S.C. § 2511(2)(f). Under FISA, if the government seeks evidence of domestic security violations, it must follow the usual criminal law authorities. If the President wishes to conduct foreign intelligence surveillance, the President must comply with the requirements of the FISA statute, which acts as a cousin of the criminal-law statutory privacy laws covered in Chapter 6.

FISA requires the Executive Branch to apply for and obtain court orders to conduct foreign intelligence surveillance from the Foreign Intelligence Surveillance Court. Eleven United States District Court judges are appointed to the court by the Chief Justice of the United States. *See* 50 U.S.C. § 1803. When the government needs a FISA order signed, it submits an application to one of the eleven judges assigned to the Court.

FISA's Equivalent of the Wiretap Act

The FISA equivalent of the Wiretap Act is codified at 50 U.S.C. §§ 1801–11. In lieu of regulating the interception of contents of wire and electronic communications, FISA regulates engaging in "electronic surveillance." "Electronic surveillance" is defined in a fairly complicated way by 50 U.S.C. § 1801(f):

> (1) the acquisition by an electronic, mechanical, or other surveillance device of the contents of any wire or radio communication sent by or intended to be received by a particular, known United States person who is in the United States, if the contents are acquired by intentionally targeting that United States person, under circumstances in which a person has a reasonable expectation of privacy and a warrant would be required for law enforcement purposes;

(2) the acquisition by an electronic, mechanical, or other surveillance device of the contents of any wire communication to or from a person in the United States, without the consent of any party thereto, if such acquisition occurs in the United States, but does not include the acquisition of those communications of computer trespassers that would be permissible under section 2511(2)(i) of Title 18;

(3) the intentional acquisition by an electronic, mechanical, or other surveillance device of the contents of any radio communication, under circumstances in which a person has a reasonable expectation of privacy and a warrant would be required for law enforcement purposes, and if both the sender and all intended recipients are located within the United States; or

(4) the installation or use of an electronic, mechanical, or other surveillance device in the United States for monitoring to acquire information, other than from a wire or radio communication, under circumstances in which a person has a reasonable expectation of privacy and a warrant would be required for law enforcement purposes.

It is important to note that FISA's version of the Wiretap Act contains definitions that differ from the same terms used in the Wiretap Act. For example, "contents" are defined more broadly in FISA than in the Wiretap Act. According to 50 U.S.C. § 1801(n), "contents" as used in FISA "includes any information concerning the identity of the parties to such communication or the existence, substance, purport, or meaning of that communication." Similarly, "wire communication" in FISA does not mean a call containing the human voice, but rather means "any communication while it is being carried by a wire, cable, or other like connection furnished or operated by any person engaged as a common carrier in providing or operating such facilities for the transmission of interstate or foreign communications." *Id.* § 1801(*l*). FISA also occasionally hinges rules on whether the subject of monitoring is a "United States person," which essentially means a United States citizen or permanent resident alien. *See id.* § 1801(i).

FISA prohibits intentionally conducting electronic surveillance "except as authorized by statute," *id.* § 1809(a)(1), and provides a statutory authority for obtaining FISA wiretap orders. *See* 50 U.S.C. § 1804. The government's application to the FISC must be personally reviewed by the Attorney General, and must include the following, *id.* § 1804(a):

(1) the identity of the Federal officer making the application;

(2) the authority conferred on the Attorney General by the President of the United States and the approval of the Attorney General to make the application;

(3) the identity, if known, or a description of the target of the electronic surveillance;

(4) a statement of the facts and circumstances relied upon by the applicant to justify his belief that—

(A) the target of the electronic surveillance is a foreign power or an agent of a foreign power; and

(B) each of the facilities or places at which the electronic surveillance is directed is being used, or is about to be used, by a foreign power or an agent of a foreign power;

(5) a statement of the proposed minimization procedures;

(6) a detailed description of the nature of the information sought and the type of communications or activities to be subjected to the surveillance;

(7) a certification or certifications by the Assistant to the President for National Security Affairs or an executive branch official or officials designated by the President from among those executive officers employed in the area of national security or defense and appointed by the President with the advice and consent of the Senate—

(A) that the certifying official deems the information sought to be foreign intelligence information;

(B) that a significant purpose of the surveillance is to obtain foreign intelligence information;

(C) that such information cannot reasonably be obtained by normal investigative techniques;

(D) that designates the type of foreign intelligence information being sought according to the categories described in section 1801 (e) of this title; and

(E) including a statement of the basis for the certification that—(i) the information sought is the type of foreign intelligence information designated; and (ii) such information cannot reasonably be obtained by normal investigative techniques;

(8) a statement of the means by which the surveillance will be effected and a statement whether physical entry is required to effect the surveillance;

(9) a statement of the facts concerning all previous applications that have been made to any judge under this subchapter involving any of the persons, facilities, or places specified in the application, and the action taken on each previous application;

(10) a statement of the period of time for which the electronic surveillance is required to be maintained, and if the nature of the intelligence gathering is such that the approval of the use of electronic surveillance under this subchapter should not automatically terminate when the described type of information has first been obtained, a description of facts supporting the belief that additional information of the same type will be obtained thereafter; and

(11) whenever more than one electronic, mechanical or other surveillance device is to be used with respect to a particular proposed electronic surveillance, the coverage of the devices involved and what minimization procedures apply to information acquired by each device.

The reviewing judge must then issue the order if the statutory requirements are met and "there is probable cause to believe that . . . the target of the electronic surveillance is a foreign power or an agent of a foreign power," provided that "no United States person may be considered a foreign power or an agent of a foreign power solely upon the basis of activities protected by the first amendment to the Constitution of the United States." 50 U.S.C. § 1805(a)(3).

FISA's Equivalent of the Pen Register Statute

The FISA equivalent of the Pen Register statute is codified at 50 U.S.C. §§ 1841–46. Pen registers and trap and trace devices are defined under FISA using the definitions in the Pen Register statute. *See* 50 U.S.C. § 1841(2). FISA states that a pen/trap order can be obtained if investigators submit:

a certification by the applicant that the information likely to be obtained is foreign intelligence information not concerning a United States person or is relevant to an ongoing investigation to protect against international terrorism or clandestine intelligence activities, provided that such investigation of a United States person is not conducted solely upon the basis of activities protected by the first amendment to the Constitution.

50 U.S.C. § 1842(c)(2).

FISA's Equivalent of the Stored Communications Act

FISA's equivalent of the Stored Communications Act is found among several different statutes. When FBI investigators seek to compel non-content information from ISPs for intelligence cases, they use 18 U.S.C. § 2709. Section 2709 is a "National Security Letter" provision in the SCA itself. The National Security Letter provision in § 2709 is something like an administrative subpoena authority, as it does not require an order signed by a judge or issued by a court. Instead, high-ranking FBI officials can request information from ISPs via written letters. According to § 2709, a "wire or electronic communication service provider shall comply with a request for subscriber information and toll billing records information, or electronic communication transactional records in its custody or possession" made by appropriate authorities within the FBI. 18 U.S.C. § 2709(a). The records sought must be "relevant to an authorized investigation to protect against international terrorism or clandestine intelligence activities, provided that such an investigation of a United States person is not conducted solely on the basis of activities protected by the first amendment to the Constitution of the United States." *Id.* § 2709(b).

Intelligence investigators normally compel the contents of communications held by ISPs using the authorities in 50 U.S.C. §§ 1821–29. These provisions regulate "physical searches," defined as "any physical intrusion within the United States into premises or property (including examination of the interior of property by technical means) that is intended to result in a seizure, reproduction, inspection, or alteration of information, material, or property, under circumstances in which a person has a reasonable expectation of privacy and a warrant would be required for law enforcement purposes." 50 U.S.C. § 1821(5). Although the scope of this authority is somewhat unclear in the case of Internet investigations, it seems that intelligence investigators generally have interpreted this provision as the required statutory framework that applies to the compelled disclosure of contents of communications from ISPs. The statute requires the government to establish probable cause that:

(A) the target of the physical search is a foreign power or an agent of a foreign power, except that no United States person may be considered an agent of a foreign power solely upon the basis of activities protected by the first amendment to the Constitution of the United States; and

(B) the premises or property to be searched is owned, used, possessed by, or is in transit to or from an agent of a foreign power or a foreign power.

50 U.S.C. § 1824(a)(3). In the case of Internet communications, the "premises or property" presumably would be the account and its contents rather than the physical ISP.

Intelligence investigators also can compel information from ISPs using Section 215 orders. *See* 50 U.S.C. §§ 1861–62. Section 215 orders are the national security equivalent of grand jury subpoenas, and are so-named because the authority was expanded under Section 215 of the USA Patriot Act. The Section 215 authority has been the subject of particular controversy in recent years. In 2013, disclosures by former NSA contractor Edward Snowden revealed that the government was using the Section 215 authority in bulk to obtain the telephone records of millions of Americans at once. This led to the passage of the USA Freedom Act, Pub. L. No. 114–23 (2015), which cuts back on the authority of the government to obtain bulk records under Section 215 and adds in other kinds of civil liberties protections.

Voluntary disclosure by ISPs in national security cases is governed by 18 U.S.C. § 2702, just as in criminal investigations. Note that the emergency disclosure provisions in § 2702 are phrased in general terms: they permit disclosure to "a governmental entity," not just to law enforcement officials. 18 U.S.C. §§ 2702(b)(8), 2702(c)(4).

NOTES AND QUESTIONS

1.   How do the surveillance standards for foreign intelligence investigations compare to the standards for criminal investigations? Are they lower? Higher? Or are they just different? Consider the Foreign Intelligence Surveillance Court of Review's comparison of the wiretapping authorities in Title III and FISA:

> With limited exceptions not at issue here, both Title III and FISA require prior judicial scrutiny of an application for an order authorizing electronic surveillance.

> The statutes differ to some extent in their probable cause showings. Title III allows a court to enter an ex parte order authorizing electronic surveillance if it determines on the basis of the facts submitted in the government's application that there is probable cause for belief that an individual is committing, has committed, or is about to commit a specified predicate offense. FISA by contrast requires a showing of probable cause that the target is a foreign power or an agent of a foreign power. FISA applies only to certain carefully delineated, and particularly serious, foreign threats to national security.

> Turning then to the first of the particularity requirements, while Title III requires probable cause to believe that particular communications concerning the specified crime will be obtained through the interception, FISA instead requires an official to designate the type of foreign intelligence information being sought, and to certify that the information sought is foreign intelligence information. When the target is a U.S. person, the FISA judge reviews the certification for clear error, but this standard of review is not, of course, comparable to a probable cause finding by the judge. Nevertheless, FISA provides additional protections to ensure that only pertinent information is sought. The certification must be made by a national security officer—typically the FBI Director—and must be approved by the Attorney General or the Attorney General's Deputy. Congress recognized that this certification would assure

written accountability within the Executive Branch and provide an internal check on Executive Branch arbitrariness.

With respect to the second element of particularity, although Title III generally requires probable cause to believe that the facilities subject to surveillance are being used or are about to be used in connection with the commission of a crime or are leased to, listed in the name of, or used by the individual committing the crime, FISA requires probable cause to believe that each of the facilities or places at which the surveillance is directed is being used, or is about to be used, by a foreign power or agent. In cases where the targeted facilities are not leased to, listed in the name of, or used by the individual committing the crime, Title III requires the government to show a nexus between the facilities and communications regarding the criminal offense. The government does not have to show, however, anything about the target of the surveillance; it is enough that "an individual"—not necessarily the target—is committing a crime. On the other hand, FISA requires probable cause to believe the target is an agent of a foreign power (that is, the individual committing a foreign intelligence crime) who uses or is about to use the targeted facility. Simply put, FISA requires less of a nexus between the facility and the pertinent communications than Title III, but more of a nexus between the target and the pertinent communications.

Both statutes have a "necessity" provision, which requires the court to find that the information sought is not available through normal investigative procedures. Although the court's clearly erroneous review under FISA is more limited than under Title III, this greater deference must be viewed in light of FISA's additional requirement that the certification of necessity come from an upper level Executive Branch official. The statutes also have duration provisions; Title III orders may last up to 30 days, while FISA orders may last up to 90 days for U.S. persons. This difference is based on the nature of national security surveillance, which is often long range and involves the interrelation of various sources and types of information.

Moreover, the longer surveillance period is balanced by continuing FISA court oversight of minimization procedures during that period. And where Title III requires minimization of what is acquired, as we have discussed, for U.S. persons, FISA requires minimization of what is acquired, retained, and disseminated. The FISA court notes, however, that in practice FISA surveillance devices are normally left on continuously, and the minimization occurs in the process of indexing and logging the pertinent communications. The reasonableness of this approach depends on the facts and circumstances of each case. Less minimization in the acquisition stage may well be justified to the extent the intercepted communications are ambiguous in nature or apparently involve guarded or coded language, or the investigation is focusing on what is thought to be a widespread conspiracy where more extensive surveillance may be justified in an attempt to determine the precise scope of the enterprise. Given the targets of FISA surveillance, it will often be the case that intercepted communications will be in code or a foreign language for which there is no contemporaneously available translator, and the activities of foreign agents will involve multiple actors and complex plots.

Based on the foregoing, it should be evident that while Title III contains some protections that are not in FISA, in many significant respects the two statutes are equivalent, and in some, FISA contains additional protections.

In re Sealed Case, 310 F.3d 717, 738–41 (Foreign Intel. Surv. Ct. of Rev. 2002). Do you agree? How do the standards compare when investigators seek to install a pen register or to compel content or non-content information stored with Internet providers?

Some commentators argue that FISA standards are considerably lower than ECPA standards used in criminal investigations, and have expressed concern that criminal investigators may use the lower standards under FISA to conduct investigations with far fewer checks and balances than exist in the criminal law context. They argue that criminal investigators can use FISA authorities to conduct surveillance even in cases where the investigators do not have a *bona fide* purpose to collect foreign intelligence information. The ACLU has offered the following perspective:

> Under [FISA as modified by] the Patriot Act, the FBI can secretly conduct a physical search or wiretap on American citizens to obtain evidence of crime without proving probable cause, as the Fourth Amendment explicitly requires.
>
> A 1978 law called the Foreign Intelligence Surveillance Act created an exception to the Fourth Amendment's requirement for probable cause when the purpose of a wiretap or search was to gather foreign intelligence. The rationale was that since the search was not conducted for the purpose of gathering evidence to put someone on trial, the standards could be loosened. In a stark demonstration of why it can be dangerous to create exceptions to fundamental rights, however, the Patriot Act expanded this once-narrow exception to cover wiretaps and searches that *do* collect evidence for regular domestic criminal cases. FISA previously allowed searches only if the primary purpose was to gather foreign intelligence. But the Patriot Act changes the law to allow searches when "a significant purpose" is intelligence. That lets the government circumvent the Constitution's probable cause requirement even when its main goal is ordinary law enforcement.

Surveillance Under the USA PATRIOT Act (Apr. 3, 2003).

Is the ACLU's description accurate? How likely is it that criminal investigators will obtain court orders under FISA instead of obtaining orders under the Wiretap Act, the Pen Register statute, and the Stored Communications Act?

2. *Surveillance of individuals reasonably believed to be outside the United States.* The United States intelligence agencies may wish to monitor individuals believed to be outside the United States who are believed to be agents of foreign powers. The statutory rules that regulate such monitoring depend on the target's relationship to the United States and where the monitoring will occur. If the person is a United States citizen or permanent U.S. resident believed to be an agent of a foreign power, and the U.S. Government is seeking foreign intelligence information, the Executive branch must obtain a warrant based on "probable cause to believe that the target is (i) a person reasonably believed to be located outside the United States; and (ii) a foreign power, an agent of a foreign power, or an officer or employee of a foreign power;" 50 U.S.C. § 1881b(c)(1)(B). If that person is not a U.S. citizen or permanent U.S. resident, and the monitoring is occurring from monitoring sites located outside the United States, then the monitoring is not regulated by FISA.

On the other hand, many communications of non-citizens and non-residents located outside the United States are routed through the United States in the course of transmission. The United States government may wish to monitor those communications. The FISA Amendments Act of 2008, Pub. L. 110–261, analyzed earlier in the *Mohamud* case, creates a procedure for such monitoring. As explained in 50 U.S.C. § 1881a(a), "the Attorney General and the Director of National Intelligence may authorize jointly, for a period of up to 1 year from the effective date of the authorization, the targeting of persons reasonably believed to be located outside the United States to acquire foreign intelligence information."

A certification is then filed before the Foreign Intelligence Surveillance Court as to the nature of the monitoring, as well as to the fact that the planned monitoring will comply with statutory requirements. The FISC then evaluates the certification to determine if it complies with the law, and in particular whether "the procedures are reasonably designed to ensure that an acquisition authorized under subsection (a) is limited to targeting persons reasonably believed to be located outside the United States . . . and prevent the intentional acquisition of any communication as to which the sender and all intended recipients are known at the time of the acquisition to be located in the United States." 50 U.S.C. § 1881a(i)(2)(B).

C. USE OF FISA EVIDENCE IN CRIMINAL CASES

Evidence collected under FISA can be used in criminal cases subject to the Fourth Amendment's exclusionary rule and the procedures and statutory suppression remedies found in 50 U.S.C. § 1806 (electronic surveillance), § 1825 (physical searches), and § 1845 (pen/trap). The procedures are designed to permit judicial review without the disclosure of sensitive national security information.

The statutory procedures are essentially the same under the different authorities. The government must first notify the court and the defendant that it seeks to use evidence either collected under FISA or derived from such evidence. *See* 50 U.S.C. § 1806(c). The defendant can then file a motion to suppress electronic surveillance or its fruits on the ground that (1) the information was unlawfully acquired; or (2) the surveillance was not made in conformity with an order of authorization or approval. *See id.* § 1806(e). Next, the Attorney General ordinarily will file an affidavit under oath taking the position that disclosure of how the evidence was obtained or an adversary hearing addressing that question would harm the national security of the United States. *See id.* § 1806(f). If such an application is filed, the district court must:

> review in camera and ex parte the application, order, and such other materials relating to the surveillance as may be necessary to determine whether the surveillance of the aggrieved person was lawfully authorized and conducted. In making this determination, the court may disclose to the aggrieved person, under appropriate security procedures and protective orders, portions of the application, order, or other materials relating to the surveillance only where such disclosure is necessary to make an accurate determination of the legality of the surveillance.

Id. If the court concludes that disclosure of materials relating to the surveillance is not necessary for the court to make an accurate determination of the legality of the surveillance, the court will not disclose the materials to the defendant. Instead, the court will make the determination in chambers without an adversary hearing.

UNITED STATES V. SQUILLACOTE
United States Court of Appeals for the Fourth Circuit, 2000.
221 F.3d 542.

TRAXLER, CIRCUIT JUDGE.

Appellants Theresa Squillacote and her husband Kurt Stand appeal from their convictions on various espionage-related charges. We affirm.

I.

Viewed in the light most favorable to the government, the evidence presented at trial established the following. Kurt Stand's parents fled to the United States from Germany during Hitler's reign. After the war, his family maintained contact with friends in the German Democratic Republic ("East Germany"). When Stand was approximately 18, his father introduced him to Lothar Ziemer, an officer with the Ministerium fur

Staatssicherheit ("MfS"), East Germany's intelligence agency. The "HVA" was the foreign intelligence arm of the MfS, and Ziemer was in charge of Section 3 of the HVA's Department XI. The "primary mission" of Department XI was the operational reconnaissance of North America. Its purpose was to "acquire data of significance to the German Democratic Republic that could not be acquired by legal means." In the early 1970s, Stand began working for Ziemer as an HVA agent.

Stand's HVA activities consisted primarily of recruiting other agents. In 1976, Stand invited James Michael Clark, a college friend, to travel with him to Germany. Stand introduced Clark to an HVA operative, who introduced him to Ziemer. Ziemer invited Clark to join his organization, which he described as performing intelligence work on behalf of East Germany and other socialist countries, as well as "liberation movements" in Asia, Latin America, and Africa. Clark agreed. Sometime between 1979 and 1981, Stand brought his wife Theresa Squillacote into the fold, and she too became what Ziemer described as an "informal collaborator." At some point, Squillacote's relationship with Ziemer became more than professional, and they had an affair that lasted until 1996.

The HVA devoted substantial resources to the training of Stand, Squillacote, and Clark. They traveled to many countries, including East Germany and Mexico, to meet with their "handlers." They received training on detecting and avoiding surveillance, receiving and decoding messages sent by shortwave radio from Cuba, mailing and receiving packages through the use of "accommodation" addresses, using codewords and phrases, using a miniature camera to photograph documents, and removing classified markings from documents. HVA records indicate that the three conspirators were together paid more than $40,000 between 1985 and 1989, primarily as reimbursement for travel expenses.

As part of his "operational plan" devised with Ziemer, Clark moved to Washington, D.C., and obtained a master's degree in Russian. For a time Clark worked for a private company in a position that required him to obtain a security clearance. He later obtained a position with the United States Army, in its environmental law division, which also required a security clearance. Clark had friends who worked for the State Department, and through them he obtained numerous classified documents that he turned over to the HVA.

Squillacote and Stand also moved to Washington, D.C., and she went to law school at the HVA's suggestion. Squillacote first followed in her father's footsteps by becoming an attorney for the National Labor Relations Board. When she realized that she had taken a career path that was not "in the best direction," she began trying to move her professional work more in line with the commitments that she had made. To that end, Squillacote used her father's connections to obtain an unprecedented temporary detail from the NLRB to the House Armed Services Committee. In 1991, Squillacote obtained a permanent job as an attorney in the Department of Defense, eventually becoming the Director of Legislative Affairs in the Office of the Undersecretary of Defense (Acquisition Reform), a position that required a security clearance and provided access to valuable information. During her tenure with the federal government, Squillacote applied for numerous government jobs, including positions with the Central Intelligence Agency, the National Security Agency, United States Army, Navy, and Air Force, and the Departments of State, Commerce, Energy, and Treasury. Apparently it was not until she began working for the Department of Defense that Squillacote gained access to the kind of information sought by her handlers. However, by that time, East Germany had collapsed.

After the fall of the Berlin Wall, Ziemer began working with the KGB, the Soviet Union's intelligence agency. Ziemer maintained his relationships with Stand, Squillacote, and Clark during this time, and they, too, became involved with the KGB. Stand, Squillacote, and Clark each traveled overseas to meet with Ziemer during the period after the collapse of East Germany. Ziemer instructed the conspirators to purchase Casio digital diaries with interchangeable memory cards. The conspirators, Ziemer, and their KGB contacts communicated with each other by exchanging memory cards.

In April 1992, Ziemer and another former HVA official were arrested and ultimately convicted for their post-unification intelligence activities with the KGB. Stand, Squillacote, and Clark became understandably concerned about their personal safety after Ziemer's arrest. They knew that "western services" were looking for two men and one woman operating out of Washington, D.C., and that the western services were aware of code names they had used. However, they believed that Ziemer and other former HVA officials would not compromise their identities. When Ziemer was released from prison in September 1992, Stand, Squillacote, and Clark re-established a system of communication with him, one purpose of which was to keep everyone informed about any threats to their safety.

From the beginning of their involvement with the HVA, Stand, Squillacote, and Clark operated independently of each other and generally were unaware of the others' activities. After Ziemer's arrest in 1992, however, the three began talking in detail about their activities and precautions needed to maintain their security. They began discussing the possibility of future intelligence work, perhaps for Vietnam or Cuba. Squillacote also talked to Clark about her interest in South Africa's Communist Party.

In 1994, Squillacote, as part of her search for "another connection," went to Amsterdam to speak to David Truong, whom she had met in college. Truong, who had been convicted of espionage on behalf of North Vietnam, was intrigued, but took no further action.

In 1995, Squillacote went to great lengths to obtain a post office box under the name of "Lisa Martin." In June 1995, Squillacote, as Lisa Martin, sent a letter to Ronnie Kasrils, the Deputy Defense Minister of South Africa. Kasrils was a Communist party official, and had received training in East Germany, the Soviet Union, and Cuba. The letter, which took Squillacote months to write, was primarily devoted to Squillacote's explanation for the collapse of socialism that began with the fall of the Berlin Wall, and her views on how the communist movement should proceed in the future. The letter was an attempt by Squillacote to make a connection with Kasrils, whom Squillacote hoped would "read between the lines." Stand and Clark were aware of the letter, but Clark apparently doubted its effectiveness.

In February 1996, Squillacote received a Christmas card from Kasrils addressed to L. Martin. In the card, Kasrils thanked "Lisa" for "the best letter" he had received in 1995. Stand and Squillacote were thrilled they received the note, and they began to think that perhaps a connection could be made. In September 1996, Squillacote found another letter from Kasrils in her Lisa Martin post office box. The letter stated that "you may have the interest and vision to assist in our struggle," and invited Squillacote to a meeting in New York City with a representative of "our special components."

Squillacote and Stand, however, were unaware that, for many years, they had been the subjects of an intense FBI investigation. As part of its investigation, the FBI in January 1996 obtained authorization to conduct clandestine electronic surveillance, which included the monitoring of all conversations in the Appellants' home, as well as calls made to and from their home and Squillacote's office. Through its investigation, the FBI had learned of Squillacote's letter to Kasrils and the Appellants' response to the February 1996 note from Kasrils. The September 1996 Kasrils letter in fact was written by the FBI as part of a "false flag" operation intended to uncover information about the prior espionage activities of Stand, Squillacote, and Clark.

When designing the false flag operation, the FBI's Behavioral Analysis Program Team prepared a report to examine the personality of Squillacote, and based on this examination, to provide suggestions that could be used to obtain evidence regarding the subject's espionage activity. The report (the "BAP report") was based on information the FBI had learned during its extensive investigation and surveillance of the Appellants.

The BAP report traced Squillacote's family background, including the suicide of her older sister and her mother's history of depression. The report stated that Squillacote was suffering from depression and listed the anti-depressant medications she was taking. The primary focus of the BAP report, however, was Squillacote's emotional makeup and how to tailor the approach to her emotional characteristics. The BAP report also made very specific recommendations about how the false flag operation should be designed:

> The following scenario has been developed upon an analysis of the subject's personality, and includes suggestions designed to exploit her narcissistic and histrionic characteristics. It is believed that Squillacote will be susceptible to an approach through her mail drop based on her recent rejection by her long-term German handler, and her thrill at receiving a Christmas card from the South African official.

J.A. 2064.

The false flag letter received by Squillacote in September 1996 served its intended purpose. Unaware of any FBI involvement, Squillacote and Stand were thrilled about the letter, and Squillacote began enthusiastically making plans for a trip to New York City to meet the South African emissary.

In October 1996, Squillacote met with an undercover FBI agent posing as a South African intelligence officer. She had face-to-face meetings with the agent a total of four times, including one meeting where she brought Stand and her two children. Several letters were also exchanged, including a letter that Squillacote wrote at the request of the undercover agent describing her previous activities with Ziemer. In these meetings and letters, Squillacote expressed her enthusiasm for her new South African connection and her hope for a productive collaboration.

Throughout her association with the undercover agent, Squillacote discussed the possibility of bringing Ziemer and other former East German contacts into the operation. In December 1996, she contacted Ziemer to see if he was interested in the operation. According to Squillacote, Ziemer's response was "yes, yes, yes, yes, yes!"

At the second meeting with the undercover agent on January 5, 1997, Squillacote presented the agent with four classified documents she had obtained from the Department of Defense. Although the agent had never requested any documents or classified information from Squillacote, she explained that one day when she and her secretary were alone in her office, she decided to "score what she could score."

Squillacote and Stand were convicted of conspiracy to transmit information relating to the national defense, *see* 18 U.S.C. § 794(a) and (c); attempted transmission of national defense information, *see* 18 U.S.C. § 794(a); and obtaining national defense information, *see* 18 U.S.C. § 793(b).

II.

The government conducted 550 consecutive days of clandestine surveillance of the Appellants, surveillance that was authorized under the Foreign Intelligence Surveillance Act of 1978, 50 U.S.C. § 1801–1811. FISA was enacted to put to rest a troubling constitutional issue regarding the President's "inherent power to conduct warrantless electronic surveillance in order to gather foreign intelligence in the interests of national security," *ACLU Found. of Southern California v. Barr*, 952 F.2d 457, 460 (D.C. Cir. 1991), a question that had not been definitively answered by the Supreme Court. FISA thus created a secure framework by which the Executive Branch may conduct legitimate electronic surveillance for foreign intelligence purposes within the context of this Nation's commitment to privacy and individual rights.

Prior to trial, the Appellants sought to suppress the fruits of the FISA surveillance. They attacked the validity of the surveillance on several grounds, all of which were rejected by the district court. On appeal, however, the Appellants press only one FISA-related issue: They contend that the surveillance was improper because there was no probable cause to believe that Squillacote or Stand were agents of a foreign power. We disagree.

Under FISA, an agent of a foreign power is any person who "knowingly engages in clandestine intelligence gathering activities for or on behalf of a foreign power, which activities involve or may involve a violation of the criminal statutes of the United States." 50 U.S.C. § 1801(b)(2)(A). One who knowingly aids and abets another engaging in such clandestine intelligence activities, or one who knowingly conspires with another to engage in the clandestine intelligence activities, is also considered an agent of a foreign power. *See* 50 U.S.C. § 1801(b)(2)(D). A "United States person" may not be determined to be an agent of a foreign power "solely upon the basis of activities protected by the first amendment to the Constitution of the United States." 50 U.S.C. § 1805(a)(3)(A).

FISA provides that the district court must review *in camera* and *ex parte* the FISA application and other materials necessary to rule upon a defendant's suppression motion "if the Attorney General files an affidavit under oath that disclosure or an adversary hearing would harm the national security of the United States." 50 U.S.C. § 1806(f). Because the Attorney General filed such an affidavit in this case, the district court reviewed the applications and other materials *in camera*, and the documents were not disclosed to counsel for the Appellants. *See* 50 U.S.C. § 1806(f) (The district court "may disclose to the aggrieved person, under appropriate security procedures and protective orders, portions of the application, order, or other materials relating to the surveillance only where such disclosure is necessary to make an accurate determination of the legality of the surveillance.").

After reviewing the applications, the district court concluded that each of the more than 20 FISA applications established probable cause to believe that the Appellants were agents of a foreign power. We have reviewed de novo the relevant materials, and likewise conclude that each FISA application established probable cause to believe that Squillacote and Stand were agents of a foreign power at the time the applications were granted, notwithstanding the fact that East Germany was no longer in existence when the applications were granted. *See* 50 U.S.C. § 1801(a) (defining "foreign power"); 50 U.S.C. § 1801(b) (defining "agent of a foreign power"). We are also satisfied that the Appellants were not targeted solely because of any protected First Amendment activities in which they may have engaged. Given the sensitive nature of the information upon which we have relied in making this determination and the Attorney General's conclusion that disclosure of the underlying information would harm the national security, it would be improper to elaborate further.

NOTES AND QUESTIONS

1. The FISA Court issued more than 20 orders permitting 550 days of consecutive monitoring. On one hand, the facts described in the opinion clearly indicate that the appellants were agents of a foreign power at some point. On the other hand, the opinion does not tell us enough to establish probable cause that the appellants were agents of a foreign power each time the orders were granted. As a result, the opinion does not establish that the evidence used against the appellants was collected using properly obtained FISA orders. Instead, the court recites public facts and the relevant legal standard, and then announces that the court is satisfied that the legal standards were met and that "it would be improper to elaborate further."

Is this a satisfying resolution of the appellants' case? Are you confident that the court was correct? On the other hand, what are the alternatives? If the basis for the court's conclusion involves national security secrets, disclosing that basis would disclose the secret. Are there alternatives to this approach that can better balance interests in judicial review with interests in secrecy? Or is this the best that can be done?

2. *The Classified Information Procedures Act.* Shortly after the passage of FISA, Congress enacted the Classified Information Procedures Act (CIPA), Pub. L. 96–456 (1980), codified at 18 U.S.C. app. §§ 1–16. CIPA regulates the discovery and use of classified information in criminal trials. The statute authorizes judges to control the disclosure of classified information using *ex parte, in camera* proceedings. Under CIPA, the presiding judge serves a gatekeeping function, hearing all claims concerning the discovery of and disclosure of classified information pre-trial. The gatekeeping serves a number of functions, including limiting a defendant's ability to avoid prosecution by

threatening to disclose secrets if prosecuted (a practice known as "greymail"). *See generally* Saul M. Pilchen & Benjamin B. Klubes, *Using the Classified Information Procedures Act in Criminal Cases: A Primer for Defense Counsel,* 31 Am. Crim. L. Rev. 191 (1994).

The requirements of CIPA arose in United States v. Scarfo, 180 F. Supp.2d 572 (D.N.J. 2001), a case involving a Key Logger System (KLS) installed on a mob boss's computer to collect his passphrase and decrypt his seized files. When Scarfo sought discovery of the details of the KLS to argue his motion to suppress, the United States objected on the ground that the workings of the KLS were classified. Judge Politan resolved the discovery dispute under CIPA as follows:

> In light of the government's grave concern over the national security implications such a revelation might raise, the Court permitted the United States to submit any additional evidence which would provide particular and specific reasons how and why disclosure of the KLS would jeopardize both ongoing and future domestic criminal investigations and national security interests.

> The United States responded by filing a request for modification of this Court's August 7, 2001, Letter Opinion and Order so as to comply with the procedures set forth in the Classified Information Procedures Act, Title 18, United States Code, Appendix III, § 1 et seq. ("CIPA"). Defendant Scarfo objected to the government's request, alleging that the United States did not make a sufficient showing that the information concerning the KLS had been properly classified.

> In response to Scarfo's objection, the United States submitted the affidavit of Neil J. Gallagher, Assistant Director, Federal Bureau of Investigation, dated September 6, 2001. In his affidavit, Mr. Gallagher stated that the characteristics and/or functional components of the KLS were previously classified and marked "SECRET" at or around November 1997.

> The Court heard oral argument on September 7, 2001, to explore whether the government may invoke CIPA and, specifically, whether the government had classified the KLS. Although the defense conceded that the KLS was classified for purposes of CIPA, the Court reserved on that question and ordered the government to provide written submissions to the Court. The government then filed an *ex parte, in camera* motion for the Court's inspection of the classified material.

> On September 26, 2001, the Court held an *in camera, ex parte hearing* with several high-ranking officials from the United States Attorney General's office and the F.B.I. Because of the sensitive nature of the material presented, all CIPA regulations were followed and only those persons with top-secret clearance were permitted to attend.

Pursuant to CIPA's regulations, the United States presented the Court with detailed and top-secret, classified information regarding the KLS, including how it operates in connection with a modem. The government also demonstrated to the Court how the KLS affects national security.

After reviewing the classified material, I issued a Protective Order pursuant [to] CIPA on October 2, 2001, wherein I found that the government could properly invoke CIPA and that the government made a sufficient showing to warrant the issuance of an order protecting against disclosure of the classified information. The October 2, 2001, Protective Order also directed that the government's proposed unclassified summary of information relating to the KLS under Section 4 of CIPA would be sufficient to allow the defense to effectively argue the motion to suppress. Accordingly, the Protective Order permitted the government to provide Scarfo with the unclassified summary statement in lieu of the classified information regarding the KLS. Pursuant to Section 6(d) of CIPA, the Court also sealed the transcript of the September 26th ex parte, in camera hearing and the government's supporting Affidavits. The government filed with the Court and served on Scarfo the unclassified summary on October 5, 2001, in the form of an October 4, 2001, Affidavit of Randall S. Murch, Supervisory Special Agent of the Federal Bureau of Investigation, Laboratory Division (the "Murch Affidavit").

Pursuant to CIPA, the United States requested a hearing in order to block the disclosure of supposedly classified information concerning the KLS technique. The Court held an *in camera, ex parte* hearing on September 26, 2001, to assess the classified nature of the KLS and the sufficiency of the unclassified summary proposed by the government. Prior to the September 26th *in camera, ex parte* hearing, and as expressed during the September 7th hearing, the Court was not satisfied that the KLS was properly classified as defined by CIPA. Nor was the Court at the time content with the United States' conclusory and generalized expressions of concern that revelation of the KLS would compromise the national security of the United States.

However, as a result of the September 26th *in camera, ex parte hearing*, the Court is now satisfied that the KLS was in fact classified as defined by CIPA. The Court also concludes that under Section 4 and 6(c) of CIPA the government met its burden in showing that the information sought by the Defendants constitutes classified information touching upon national security concerns as defined in CIPA. Moreover, it is the opinion of the Court that as a result of the September 26th hearing, the government presented to the Court's satisfaction proof that disclosure of the classified KLS information would cause identifiable damage to the national security of the

United States. The Court is precluded from discussing this information in detail since it remains classified.

Further, upon comparing the specific classified information sought and the government's proposed unclassified summary, the Court finds that the United States met its burden in showing that the summary in the form of the Murch Affidavit would provide Scarfo with substantially the same ability to make his defense as would disclosure of the specific classified information regarding the KLS technique. The Murch Affidavit explains, to a reasonable and sufficient degree of specificity without disclosing the highly sensitive and classified information, the operating features of the KLS. The Murch Affidavit is more than sufficient and has provided ample information for the Defendants to litigate this motion. Therefore, no further discovery with regard to the KLS technique is necessary.

Id. at 575–76, 580–81. For more on CIPA, see Richard P. Salgado, Note, *Government Secrets, Fair Trials, and the Classified Information Procedures Act*, 98 Yale L.J. 427 (1988); Brian Z. Tamanaha, *A Critical Review of the Classified Information Procedures Act*, 13 Am. J. Crim. L. 277 (1986).

3.   *Information warfare.* If the law of intelligence surveillance is the national security analog of criminal procedure, the law of information warfare is the national security analog of computer misuse law. United States government networks can come under attack by agents of foreign governments engaging in "information warfare." Such attacks raise a number of questions. For example, when should a computer intrusion be treated as an act of war instead of as a simple criminal act? What rights do United States government officials have to launch counterattacks to defend the United States? *See, e.g.,* Richard W. Aldrich, *How Do You Know You Are at War in the Information Age?*, 22 Hous. J. Int'l L. 223, 224–26 (2000): Michael N. Schmitt, *Computer Network Attack and the Use of Force in International Law: Thoughts on a Normative Framework*, 37 Colum. J. Transnat'l L. 885 (1999); Eric Talbot Jensen, *Computer Attacks on Critical National Infrastructure: A Use of Force Invoking the Right of Self-Defense*, 38 Stan. J. Int'l L. 207 (2002). *Cf.* 18 U.S.C. § 1030(f) ("This section does not prohibit any lawfully authorized investigative, protective, or intelligence activity of a law enforcement agency of the United States, a State, or a political subdivision of a State, or of an intelligence agency of the United States.").

INDEX

References are to Pages
